Routledge Handbook of Applied Communication Research

The *Routledge Handbook of Applied Communication Research* provides a state-of-the-art review of communication scholarship that addresses real-world concerns, issues, and problems. This comprehensive examination of applied communication research—including its foundations, research methods employed, significant issues confronted, important contexts in which such research has been conducted, and overviews of some exemplary programs of applied communication research—shows how such research has and can make a difference in the world and in people's lives.

The sections and chapters in this handbook:

- explain what constitutes applied communication scholarship, encompassing a wide range of approaches and clarifying relationships among theoretical perspectives, methodological procedures, and applied practices;
- demonstrate the breadth and depth of applied communication scholarship;
- review and synthesize literature about applied communication areas and topics in coherent, innovative, and pedagogically sound ways; and
- set agendas for future applied communication scholarship.

Unique to this volume are chapters presenting exemplary programs of applied communication research that demonstrate the principles and practices of such scholarship, written by the scholars who conducted the programs.

As an impressive benchmark in the ongoing growth and development of communication scholarship, editors Lawrence R. Frey and Kenneth N. Cissna provide an exceptional resource that will help new and experienced scholars alike to understand, appreciate, and conduct high-quality communication research that can positively affect people's lives.

Lawrence R. Frey (PhD, University of Kansas, 1979) is a professor in the Department of Communication at the University of Colorado at Boulder, where he teaches undergraduate and graduate courses on applied communication, quantitative and qualitative research methods, and group interaction. His applied communication scholarship focuses on communication activism, social justice, community studies, and health communication. He is the author or editor of 15 books, three special journal issues, and more than 65 journal articles and book chapters, and is the recipient of 14 awards for scholarship, including the 2000 Gerald M. Phillips Award for Distinguished Applied Communication Scholarship from the National Communication Association.

Kenneth N. Cissna (PhD, University of Denver, 1975) is a professor and chair of the Department of Communication at the University of South Florida, where he teaches undergraduate and graduate courses in interpersonal communication, group communication, and dialogue theory and practice. He has published scores of scholarly book chapters and journal articles, and five books. He served as editor of the *Journal of Applied Communication Research* and of the *Southern Communication Journal*, and is past president of both the Florida Communication Association and the Southern States Communication Association (SSCA). His awards include SSCA's 2007 T. Earle Johnson—Edwin Paget Distinguished Service Award and the National Communication Association's 2008 Gerald M. Phillips Award for Distinguished Applied Communication Scholarship.

Routledge Handbook of Applied Communication Research

Edited by
Lawrence R. Frey
Kenneth N. Cissna

Routledge
Taylor & Francis Group

NEW YORK AND LONDON

First published 2009
by Routledge
270 Madison Ave., New York, NY 10016

Simultaneously published in the UK
by Routledge
2 Park Square, Milton Park, Abingdon, Oxon OX14 4RN

Routledge is an imprint of the Taylor & Francis Group, an informa business

© 2009 Taylor & Francis

Typeset in Sabon by EvS Communication Networx, Inc.
Printed and bound in the United States of America on acid-free paper by Sheridan Books, Inc.

Library of Congress Cataloging in Publication Data
Routledge handbook of applied communication research /
edited by Lawrence R. Frey & Kenneth N. Cissna.
p. cm.
1. Communication—Research. 2. Communication—Research--Methodology.
I. Frey, Lawrence R. II. Cissna, Kenneth N. III. Title: Handbook of applied
communication research. IV. Title: Applied communication research.
P91.3.R68 2009
302.207'2—dc22
2008047304

ISBN10: 0-8058-4983-1 (hbk)
ISBN10: 0-8058-4984-X (pbk)
ISBN10: 0-203-87164-2 (ebk)

ISBN13: 978-0-8058-4983-7 (hbk)
ISBN13: 978-0-8058-4984-4 (pbk)
ISBN13: 978-0-203-87164-5 (ebk)

Contents

List of Figures and Tables

Figures

Tables

Editors

Lawrence R. Frey (PhD, University of Kansas, 1979) is a professor in the Department of Communication at the University of Colorado at Boulder, where he teaches undergraduate and graduate courses on applied communication, quantitative and qualitative research methods, and group interaction. His applied communication scholarship focuses on communication activism, social justice, community studies, and health communication. He is the author or editor of 15 books, three special journal issues, and more than 65 journal articles and book chapters, and is the recipient of 14 awards for scholarship, including the 2000 Gerald M. Phillips Award for Distinguished Applied Communication Scholarship from the National Communication Association (NCA). His most recent book, *Communication Activism* (2 Vols., coedited with Kevin M. Carragee), received the 2008 Outstanding Edited Scholarly Book Award from NCA's Applied Communication Division. Other awards include the 2000, 2003, 2004, and 2007 Ernest Bormann Research Award from NCA's Group Communication Division, a 1999 Special Recognition Award from NCA's Applied Communication Division for an edited special issue of the *Journal of Applied Communication Research* on "Communication and Social Justice Research," and a 1998 National Jesuit Book Award for his coauthored text (with Mara B. Adelman), *The Fragile Community: Living Together With AIDS*. He is a past president of the Central States Communication Association and a recipient of the Outstanding Young Teacher Award from that organization, as well as a recipient of the Master Teacher Award from the Communication and Instruction Interest Group of the Western States Communication Association.

Kenneth N. Cissna (PhD, University of Denver, 1975) is a professor and chair of the Department of Communication at the University of South Florida, where he teaches undergraduate and graduate courses in interpersonal communication, group communication, and dialogue theory and practice. He has published scores of scholarly book chapters and journal articles, and five books, including *Applied Communication in the 21st Century*, which received the 1995 Outstanding Book Award from the Applied Communication Division of the National Communication Association (NCA); *Moments of Meeting: Buber, Rogers, and the Potential for Public Dialogue* (with Rob Anderson); and *Dialogue: Theorizing Difference in Communication Studies* (with Rob Anderson and Leslie A. Baxter). He served as editor of the *Journal of Applied Communication Research* and of the *Southern Communication Journal*, and is past president of both the Florida Communication Association and the Southern States Communication Association (SSCA). His awards include SSCA's 2007 T. Earle Johnson—Edwin Paget Distinguished Service Award and NCA's 2008 Gerald M. Phillips Award for Distinguished Applied Communication Scholarship.

Contributors

Patricia Amason (PhD, Purdue University, 1993) is an associate professor and associate chair of the Department of Communication at the University of Arkansas, where she teaches courses in interpersonal, health, small group communication, and communication theory. Her research focuses on the provision of social support in interpersonal relationships, communication skills training and development, and quality of work–life issues. She has published in *Journal of Applied Communication Research*, *Communication Studies*, *Communication Yearbook*, *Health Communication*, *Journal of Family Communication*, *Sex Roles: A Journal of Research*, and *Southern Communication Journal*. Currently, she is exploring the communicative behaviors enacted by health-care providers as members of cancer patients' social support networks, and serves as president of the Southern States Communication Association.

Dawna I. Ballard (PhD, University of California, Santa Barbara, 2002) is an associate professor in the Department of Communication Studies at The University of Texas at Austin. Her research examines organizational temporality, with particular attention to ways in which time shapes and is shaped by a range of communication processes. Her published research appears in outlets such as *Communication Monographs*, *Communication Research*, *Communication Yearbook*, *Management Communication Quarterly*, and *Small Group Research*, as well as in several interdisciplinary edited volumes, including *Time and Memory*, *Workplace Temporalities*, and *Time in Organizational Research*.

J. Kevin Barge (PhD, University of Kansas, 1985) is a professor in the Department of Communication at Texas A&M University, where he teaches courses in organizational communication, leadership, and dialogue. His major research interests center on developing a communication perspective to management and leadership, and studying ways communication can be structured to initiate and sustain large-scale organizational change. His work has been published in the *Journal of Applied Communication Research*, *Academy of Management Review*, *Communication Monographs*, *Management Communication Quarterly*, and *OD Practitioner: Journal of the Organization Development Network*. His consultancy work focuses on developing frameworks that promote dialogic and appreciative forms of communication to manage conflict and foster constructive change.

Benjamin R. Bates (PhD, University of Georgia, 2003) is an assistant professor in the School of Communication Studies at Ohio University. As displayed in more than 40 peer-reviewed articles and book chapters, most of his research addresses rhetoric as enacted in the public understanding of complex policy formation. Most recently, he and his research partners have begun investigating how rhetorical principles can be used to improve communication campaigns to promote clean indoor air legislation and to encourage wildfire prevention by landowners.

Ellen W. Bonaguro (PhD, Ohio University, 1986) is an associate professor in the Department of Communication and director of the Academic Advising and Retention Center at Western Kentucky University. She teaches undergraduate and graduate courses in organizational communication, interpersonal communication, and research methods, and has developed minors in health communication at three universities. She has presented and published numerous studies on health communication campaigns, provider–client communication, and targeting health-promotion messages in *Health Education* and *Journal of Health Communication*, and in several edited books—most recently, *Beyond These Walls: Readings in Health Communication*. She presented a paper on communication as palliative care for older people with cancer at the 2005 International Conference on Aging at the Mei Ho Institute of Technology in Pingtong, Taiwan, and has consulted in the health communication field for many years, including for a health project in Belize in 2007.

Patrice M. Buzzanell (PhD, Purdue University, 1987) is a professor and the W. Charles and Ann Redding Faculty Fellow in the Department of Communication at Purdue University. Her area of specialization is organizational communication, with her research centering on career, leadership, and work–life issues. She has edited the books *Rethinking Organizational and Managerial Communication from Feminist Perspectives*, *Gender in Applied Communication Contexts* (with Helen Sterk and Lynn H. Turner), and *Distinctive Qualities in Communication Research* (in press, with Donal Carbaugh). She has published numerous articles in journals, including the *Journal of Applied Communication Research*, as well as chapters in handbooks, such as *The Sage Handbook on Gender and Communication*. She has served as editor of *Management Communication Quarterly*; Research Board member for the National Communication Association; president of the Organization for the Study of Communication, Language and Gender; and editorial board member for numerous journals and handbooks. Currently, she is president of the International Communication Association and of the Council of Communication Associations, and faculty advisor of the Anita Borg Institute for Women and Technology (ABIWT) team in Purdue's Engineering Projects in Community Service (EPICS) program, where she works with students to design software and hardware to attract girls aged 9 to 11 to technology and careers in science, technology, engineering, and math. She has received numerous awards for research, teaching, mentoring, and service.

Marcia J. Clinkscales (PhD, University of Denver, 1975) is a faculty member in the School of Business at the University of Connecticut. She is founder and principal consultant of The Montgomery Clinkscales Group, a consulting firm that specializes in organizational development, leadership development, executive and management communication, and organizational restructuring and change. She has over 20 years of experience as an organizational consultant in the nonprofit, government, and private sectors, focusing on creating common ground via communication processes and working to foster healthier systems and healthier people. She is coauthor of the book *Understanding Organization through Culture and Structure: Relational and Other Lessons from the African-American Organization* (with Anne Maydan Nicotera and Felicia Walker).

Celeste M. Condit (PhD, University of Iowa, 1982) is a Distinguished Research Professor in the Department of Speech Communication at the University of Georgia. She has published (with coauthors and coeditors) five books focusing on rhetorical processes and public communication about race and equality, reproductive rights, women's health, rhetorical theory, and the social meanings of the genetic revolution; over 70 scholarly articles, chapters, and book reviews; and has coedited two academic journals. Condit has received grant funding from the federal government for over 10 years to understand and improve public communication about genetics. She is a research project leader in the Southern Center for Communication, Health & Poverty, and works with local agencies to reduce persistent poverty. She has been named a Distinguished Scholar by the National Communication Association.

Jennifer R. Considine (PhD, Texas A&M University, 2006) is an assistant professor in the Department of Communication at The University of Wisconsin Oshkosh. Her research examines the role of spirituality and emotion in organizations, with journal articles published in *Communication Studies*, *Health Communication*, *Journal on Excellence in College Teaching*, and *Management Communication Quarterly*.

Robert T. Craig (PhD, Michigan State University, 1976) is a professor in the Department of Communication at the University of Colorado at Boulder. He is a past president of the International Communication Association and was founding editor of the journal *Communication Theory*. His publications have addressed a range of topics in communication theory and philosophy, discourse studies, and argumentation. His current research investigates and analyzes conceptual assumptions in both ordinary practical discourse and theoretical discourse about various aspects of communication.

Ann L. Darling (PhD, University of Washington, 1987) is an associate professor and chair of the Department of Communication at The University of Utah, where she teaches courses in communication education and instructional communication. Her work on graduate student socialization and teaching assistant training has been published in journals that include *Communication Education*, *Journal of Thought*, and *Teaching and Teacher Education*. In 1987, her work on communication and teacher socialization (with Ann Q. Staton) received the National Research Award from the Association of Teacher Educators. She now is turning her attention to questions regarding public discourse about education and communication education as an act of social justice.

Gerardine DeSanctis (PhD, Texas Tech University, 1982) was the Thomas F. Keller Professor of Business Administration in the Fuqua School of Business at Duke University, and previously taught at the University of Minnesota. Her interests were in the general areas of computer-mediated work and management of information technology. Most of her research examined the impacts of electronic communication systems on teams and organizations. She also studied the evolution of online learning communities and e-communication overload. She served as senior editor of the journals *Organization Science* and *MIS Quarterly*, associate editor for *MIS Quarterly*, and on the advisory board for *Information Systems Research*. She coauthored the book *Organizational Design: A Step-by-Step Approach* (with Richard M. Burton and Børge Obel), and coedited two books: *Shaping Organization Form: Communication, Connection, and Community* (with Janet Fulk) and *Information Technology and the Future Enterprise: New Models for Managers* (with Gary W. Dickson). Dr. DeSanctis passed away in August 2005.

Laura K. Dorsey (PhD, Howard University, 2000) is an associate professor in the Department of Communication at Morgan State University. Her areas of teaching and research expertise include organizational communication, small group communication, interpersonal communication, racial/ethnic relations, leadership development, unconscious group processes, and internalized oppression within predominantly African-descended groups. Her research has been published in the *Electronic Journal of Communication* and the *Florida Communication Journal*, as well as in edited collections. She has over a decade of experience in organizational consultation and training, both nationally and internationally, and she is a certified Tavistock trainer/consultant.

William F. Eadie (PhD, Purdue University, 1974) is a professor in the School of Journalism and Media Studies at San Diego State University. His research interests focus on the history of communication and on the evolving structure of the communication discipline. He was an early advocate for applied communication research and served as the first editor of the *Journal of Applied Communication Research* after the National Communication Association (NCA) became its publisher. He previously served as associate director of NCA, where his responsibilities focused on projects to develop the quality of research in the communication discipline and to promote communication research to media sources, government agencies, and the general public. He currently serves as editor of *21st Century Communication: A Reference Handbook*, a comprehensive two-volume set of essays on aspects of the communication discipline, written for undergraduates. He is a recipient of NCA's Golden Anniversary Award for an outstanding scholarly article and the Samuel L. Becker Distinguished Service Award for contributions to NCA and to the communication discipline.

Kristen Campbell Eichhorn (PhD, University of Miami, 2003) is an assistant professor in the Department of Communication Studies at the State University of New York at Oswego, where she teaches research methods, communication theory, and interpersonal communication. She also has taught a wide variety of other courses, including organizational communication, nonverbal communication, persuasion, and business and professional communication. Her primary area of research is interpersonal communication in organizational, instructional, and health settings. Her research has been published in a variety of journals, including *College Student Journal*, *Communication Research Reports*, *International Journal of Leadership Studies*, *Journal of Computer-Mediated Communication*, and *Public Relations Review*, and she is the coauthor of the book *Interpersonal Communication: Building Rewarding Relationships* (with Candice Thomas-Maddox and Melissa Bekelja Wanzer).

Eric M. Eisenberg (PhD, Michigan State University, 1982) is a professor in the Department of Communication and interim dean of the College of Arts and Sciences at the University of South Florida. He previously directed the master's program in applied communication at Temple University before moving to the University of Southern California. He twice received the Outstanding Research Publication Award from the Organizational Communication Division of the National Communication Association, as well as the Burlington Foundation award for excellence in teaching. Eisenberg is the author of over 70 articles, chapters, and books on organizational communication and communication theory. His best-selling textbook, *Organizational Communication: Balancing Creativity and Constraint* (currently in its 5th edition, with H. L. Goodall, Jr. and Angela Tretheway), received the Textbook and Academic Authors Association's Texty Award for the best textbook of the year. He is a communication consultant to prominent organizations in the public, private, and nonprofit sectors, and he has worked closely with executives and employees from organizations across a wide variety of industries, including Hughes Aircraft, State Farm, Orange County Government (Florida), Lutheran Ministries, Starwood Hotels and Resorts, Time Customer Service, and the Baystate Health System.

Laura L. Ellingson (PhD, University of South Florida, 2001) is an associate professor in the Department of Communication and the Women's and Gender Studies Program at Santa Clara University. Her research focuses on feminist qualitative methodology, gender studies, and communication in health-care organizations, including interdisciplinary communication, teamwork, and patient–provider communication. She is the author of the books *Communicating in the Clinic: Negotiating Frontstage and Backstage Teamwork* and *Engaging Crystallization in Qualitative Research: An Introduction*, and has published articles in *Health Communication*, *Journal of Social and Personal Relationships*, *Qualitative Health Research*, and other journals. Currently, she is conducting an ethnography of a dialysis clinic and a qualitative study of communication between aunts and their nieces/nephews.

Beth Eschenfelder (PhD, University of South Florida, 2007) is an assistant professor in the Department of Communication at The University of Tampa. Her scholarly interests are in interorganizational relationships between and among nonprofits, governments, and communities (including businesses, neighborhoods, and citizen groups), and the communicative practices these entities utilize to foster strong partnerships. Prior to returning to the university setting, Eschenfelder worked in nonprofit management and served in numerous community leadership positions that involved bringing diverse publics together to address pressing community problems, including business district redevelopment, neighborhood–social service zoning, park revitalization, and homelessness.

María Elena Figueroa (PhD, Johns Hopkins University, 1997) is an assistant scientist in the Department of Health, Behavior and Society, director of the Global Program on Water and Hygiene, and research director at the Center for Communication Programs in the Johns Hopkins University Bloomberg School of Public Health. Her research interests include communication for social and behavior change in developing countries, measurement of outcomes from community-based health interventions, and the role of household traits on health behavior. Her current research focuses on the psychosocial and socioecological determinants of health behavior related to HIV and AIDS, hygiene, and the environment. Her work on applied communication for health and development extends to several countries, including Bolivia, Cambodia, Ecuador, Ghana, Guatemala, Haiti, Honduras, Indonesia, Mexico, Mozambique, Nicaragua, Pakistan, Peru, and Zambia, and has been published in the journals *International Family Planning Perspectives*, *International Journal for Quality in Health Care*, and *International Quarterly of Community Health Education*.

Eileen S. Gilchrist (PhD, University of Oklahoma, 2009) is an assistant professor in the Department of Communication and Journalism at the University of Wyoming. Her research interests include communication competence, social support, and relational maintenance strategies across selected health, family, and organizational contexts, focusing primarily on elderly populations. She has published three book chapters and journal articles in *Communication Monographs* and *Journal of Social and Personal Relationships*, and has received two top-paper awards.

Martha Womack Haun (PhD, University of Illinois at Urbana-Champaign, 1971) is associate professor and director of graduate studies in the Jack J. Valenti School of Communication at the University of Houston, where she teaches relational communication, communication theory, health communication, and effective meeting management. She is the cofounder and director of the University of Houston's Center for Health and Crisis Communication. She has published textbooks on public speaking, communication theory, and crisis communication, and more than two dozen journal articles on meeting management and communication processes. She was named University Educator of the Year in 1999 by the Texas Speech Communication Association (TSCA), and served as editor of the *TSCA Journal* for 17 years and of the international *Parliamentary Journal* for 7 years. She has been involved in volunteer and chaplaincy services for over 20 years at M. D. Anderson Hospital and Cancer Center in Houston. She is past national president and past executive director of Phi Beta National Professional Fraternity for the Creative and Performing Arts, and past chair of the Commission on American Parliamentary Practice.

Michael L. Hecht (PhD, University of Illinois at Urbana-Champaign, 1976) is a Distinguished Professor in the Department of Communication Arts and Sciences at The Pennsylvania State University, where he teaches courses in interpersonal communication. His National Institute on Drug Abuse-funded Drug Resistance Strategies (DRS) project (1989–present) was among the first to study the social processes of adolescent drug offers, including an examination of the role of ethnicity and acculturation in these processes. The DRS project developed a successful, multicultural, school-based intervention for middle school students that was selected as an evidence-based program by the U.S. government's Substance Abuse and Mental Health Services Administration, and he currently is studying adaptation processes in bringing this curriculum to rural schools. His recent book, *Adolescent Relationships and Drug Use* (with Michelle A. Miller-Day, Janet Alberts, Melanie R. Trost, and Robert L. Krizek), summarizes some of this work. The videotapes produced for this project have won numerous international and national awards, including a series of 2000 regional Emmy Awards for student productions. His books include *Redefining Culture: Perspectives across the Disciplines* (with John R. Baldwin, Sandra L. Faulkner, and Sheryl L. Lindsley) and two books on culture and identity (*African American Communication: Exploring Identity and Culture*, with Ronald L. Jackson and Sidney A. Ribeau, and the edited collection *Communicating Prejudice*). He has received many awards, including the National Communication Association's Gerald M. Philips Award for Distinguished Applied Communication Scholarship.

Mark Hickson, III (PhD, Southern Illinois University, 1971) is a professor in the Department of Communication Studies at the University of Alabama at Birmingham, where he teaches applied communication research and qualitative research methods. He has published more than 100 journal articles and 13 books. He was the founding publisher and editor of the *Journal of Applied Communications Research*; has served on the editorial boards of *Communication Education*, *Communication Research Reports*, and *Quarterly Journal of Speech*; and is the current editor of *Qualitative Research Reports in Communication*. His recent applied communication research has been in the area of legal communication.

Lynda Lee Kaid (PhD, Southern Illinois University, 1974) is a professor in the Department of Telecommunication in the College of Journalism and Communications at the University of Florida. She previously served as the director of the Political Communication Center and supervised the Political Commercial Archive at The University of Oklahoma. Her research specialties include political advertising and news coverage of political events. A Fulbright Scholar, she has done work on political television in several European countries. She is the author or editor of more than 25 books, including the *Encyclopedia of Political Communi-*

cation, Political Advertising in Western Democracies: Parties & Candidates on Television (both with Christina Holtz-Bacha), *Handbook of Political Communication Research,* and *Videostyle in Presidential Campaigns: Style and Content of Televised Political Advertising* (with Anne Johnston). She has written over 150 journal articles and book chapters, and has presented numerous conference papers on various aspects of political communication. She has received nearly $2 million in external grant funds for her research efforts, including support from the Federal Election Assistance Commission, U.S. Department of Commerce, U.S. Department of Education, National Endowment for the Humanities, and the National Science Foundation.

D. Lawrence Kincaid (PhD, Michigan State University, 1972) is an associate scientist in the Department of Health, Behavior and Society in the Johns Hopkins University Bloomberg School of Public Health, where he conducts evaluation of health communication programs in the Center for Communication Programs and teaches health communication and evaluation research. He is the author or editor of four books, and his work has been published in the journals *Communication Research, Communication Theory, Journal of Health Communication,* and *Social Science & Medicine,* as well as in edited books. His recent research includes evaluation of the impact of communication programs for HIV and AIDS prevention in South Africa; evaluation of television dramas for health promotion in South Africa, Vietnam, and Bangladesh; promotion of household water treatment in Pakistan and Honduras; and the role of bounded normative influence on health behavior change.

Laura Bochenek Klein (MA, Bowling Green State University, 1993) is associate director of professional communications in the Center for Student Professional Development and a lecturer in the Program for Communication Excellence at Rice University, and has served as a postgraduate research assistant for the Center for Health and Crisis Communication at the University of Houston. She has more than 15 years of organizational communication experience, including developing and executing communication strategies, internal communications, marketing and brand management, and community relations for the corporate and nonprofit health-care sectors. She has been featured in the business periodical *Strategic Communication Management* for driving best practices throughout organizations.

Gary L. Kreps (PhD, University of Southern California, 1979) is a professor and chair of the Department of Communication at George Mason University, where he holds the Steve and Eileen Mandell Endowed Chair in Health Communication, serves as the founding director of the Center for Health and Risk Communication, and is a member of the governing board for the Center for Social Science Research. He teaches courses in health communication and communication research methods. He has published more than 40 books and 225 articles and monographs concerning health and risk communication, health promotion, cancer prevention and control, e-Health, and organizational communication, with a particular focus on the role of communication in reducing health disparities and improving quality of care. He has edited special issues of a number of scholarly journals, including, currently, *Communication Education* and *Social Marketing Quarterly.* He has received research funding from several private foundations and agencies of the federal government, and has received many awards for distinguished scholarship. He edits two book series for Hampton Press (on "Health Communication" and "Communication and Social Organization") and advises federal and international government agencies on health communication research and policy.

Liz Leckie (MS, University of Utah, 1999) is a doctoral candidate in the Department of Communication at The University of Utah, where she also is the assistant dean for undergraduate affairs in the College of Humanities, coordinating academic advising and undergraduate services for that college. Her research interests include undergraduate student socialization in higher education, social justice pedagogy and practices in educational contexts, and communication education. She has taught courses in both communication and composition. Her current research includes exploring communicative practices of students as related to power, race, and privilege in the college classroom.

Daisy R. Lemus (PhD, University of California, Santa Barbara, 2006) is an assistant professor in the Department of Communication Studies at California State University, Northridge, where she teaches courses in organizational communication, communication research methodology, group communication, communication and technology, and communication theory. Her current research explores communication processes during retirement planning. Her interests in organizational communication extend to the areas of group communication and technology, organizational change, and the use of mixed methods in organizational communication research. Her work has been published in *Communication Yearbook*, *Human Communication Research*, and *Journal of Communication*.

Leah A. Lievrouw (PhD, University of Southern California, 1986) is a professor in the Department of Information Studies at the University of California, Los Angeles. Her research and writing interests focus on the relationship between media and information technologies and social change, particularly the role of technologies in social differentiation and oppositional social and cultural movements, and intellectual freedom in pervasively mediated social settings. She is the author of more than 40 journal and proceedings articles, book chapters, and other works related to new media and information society issues. She is coeditor of *The Handbook of New Media* and the forthcoming *Sage Benchmarks in Communication: New Media* (both with Sonia Livingstone), and former coeditor of the journal *New Media & Society*. Her current projects include the books *Media and Meaning: Understanding Communication, Technology, and Society* and *Alternative and Activist New Media*.

Mitchell S. McKinney (PhD, University of Kansas, 1996) is an associate professor in the Department of Communication at the University of Missouri, where he teaches courses in political communication and rhetorical theory and criticism. His research on presidential debates, political campaigns, media and politics, and presidential rhetoric has been published in leading communication, journalism, and political science journals, including *American Behavioral Scientist*, *Communication Monographs*, *Communication Studies*, *Journal of Communication*, and *Journalism Studies*. He has combined practical political experience with his training as a political communication scholar, having served as a staff member in the U.S. Senate and at the White House. He served as a consultant to C-SPAN and to the Commission on Presidential Debates, advising the Commission on how U.S. presidential debates might be structured better to educate voters.

Rebecca J. Meisenbach (PhD, Purdue University, 2004) is an assistant professor in the Department of Communication at the University of Missouri. Her research focuses on intersections of identity, ethics, and rhetoric, with particular attention to nonprofit and gendered organizing. Currently, she is studying the negotiation of occupational identities among fund-raisers. Her work has appeared in *Communication Monographs*, *Commu-*

nication Yearbook, *International Journal of Strategic Communication*, and *Management Communication Quarterly*.

Katherine I. Miller (PhD, University of Southern California, 1985) is a professor in the Department of Communication at Texas A&M University, where she teaches courses in organizational communication, health communication, and communication theory. Her research centers on issues of emotion and identity in the workplace, and the experiences of human service workers and family caregivers. Her work has been published in journals that include *Journal of Applied Communication Research*, *Communication Monographs*, *Health Communication*, and *Management Communication Quarterly*. She is the author of two textbooks: *Organizational Communication: Approaches and Processes* and *Communication Theories: Perspectives, Processes, and Contexts*.

Michelle Miller-Day (PhD, Arizona State University, 1995) is an associate professor in the Department of Communication Arts and Sciences at The Pennsylvania State University, where she teaches qualitative research methods, family communication, and interpersonal communication. Her current research interests include how interpersonal and family communication affect health and well-being. Her work has been published in journals that include *Journal of Applied Communication Research*, *Health Communication*, *Journal of Social and Personal Relationships*, and *Qualitative Inquiry*. Her books—such as *Adolescent Relationships and Drug Use* (with Janet Alberts, Michael L. Hecht, Melanie R. Trost, and Robert L. Krizek); *Communication among Grandmothers, Mothers, and Adult Daughters: A Qualitative Study of Women across Three Generations*; and *Communication and Intimacy in Older Adulthood* (with Jon F. Nussbaum and Carla Fisher)—focus on health topics and communication within close personal relationships. She works on community-based action research efforts outside of the academy and takes student groups to the island of St. Martin/St. Maarten in the Caribbean to promote cultural exchange and conduct ethnographic inquiry.

Julien C. Mirivel (PhD, University of Colorado at Boulder, 2005) is an assistant professor in the Department of Speech Communication at the University of Arkansas at Little Rock, where he teaches courses in interpersonal communication, communication theory, and ethics. Using discourse analysis and ethnography, he studies face-to-face interaction in institutional settings, focusing especially on communicative events that are controversial, culturally dilemmatic, or ethically questionable. His current work explores videotaped encounters between plastic surgeons and patients who seek cosmetic surgery to alter their bodily appearance. His work has been published in the journals *Discourse & Communication*, *Health Communication*, and *Research on Language and Social Interaction*, and in the forthcoming edited volume *Multimodality and Human Activity: Research on Behavior, Action, and Communication*.

Karen K. Myers (PhD, Arizona State University, 2005) is an assistant professor in the Department of Communication at the University of California, Santa Barbara. Her research focuses on organizational socialization and assimilation, with an emphasis on workgroup development and maintenance in high-reliability organizations. Her recent work examines vocational anticipatory socialization of girls and young women, and how socialization influences selection of educational and career paths. Her work has appeared in journals such as *Journal of Applied Communication Research*, *Communication Monographs*, *Human Communication Research*, and *Management Communication Quarterly*.

Anne Maydan Nicotera (PhD, Ohio University, 1990) is an associate professor in the Department of Communication at George Mason University, where she teaches courses in organizational and interpersonal communication. Her research is grounded in a constitutive perspective and focuses on culture and conflict, diversity, race and gender, and aggressive communication, with a particular interest in health-care organizations. Her research is published in five books; numerous national journals, including *Communication Theory, Health Communication, Human Communication Research*, and *Management Communication Quarterly*; and in several edited collections. Her current research includes examining structurational divergence as experienced by nurses in a hospital setting and the unique organizational structure and form of hospitals.

Marnel N. Niles (PhD, Howard University, 2007) is an assistant professor in the Department of Communication at California State University, Fresno, where she teaches courses in small group and organizational communication. Her research interests include group friendship, gender and communication, organizational culture, and group decision making, and her work has been published in the *Journal of the Alliance of Black School Educators*. She works actively with Black Students United and the Black Faculty and Staff Association on her campus.

Julie M. Novak (PhD, North Dakota State University, 2006) is an assistant professor in the Department of Communication at Wayne State University, where she teaches and conducts research in the areas of health, risk, organizational, and applied communication. Her research interests include democratic communicative practices in organizations within high-risk environments. Her work has been published in the *Journal of Applied Communication Research, Communication Research Reports, Journal of International Communication* and *Journal of Organizational Change Management*. Her transdisciplinary research privileges researching in teams and draws from her nutrition education and nonprofit, health, and intercultural/international experiences.

Jon F. Nussbaum (PhD, Purdue University, 1981) is a professor in the Department of Communication Arts and Sciences and the Department of Human Development and Family Studies at The Pennsylvania State University. He has served as president of the International Communication Association and as editor of the *Journal of Communication*. He was awarded a Fulbright Research Fellowship in the United Kingdom and recently was named a Fellow of the International Communication Association and within the Adult Development and Aging Division of the American Psychological Association. He has a well-established publication record (10 books and over 70 refereed journal articles and book chapters) studying communicative behaviors and patterns across the life span, including research on family, friendship, and professional relationships with well and frail older adults.

Jennifer E. Ohs (PhD, The Pennsylvania State University, 2008) is an assistant professor in the Department of Communication at Saint Louis University. Her primary line of research examines personal social networks involved in making decisions about health care at the end of the life span. Her investigations focus on interactions in various communicative contexts, including the organizational, religious/spiritual, and familial. In addition to her work on health-related decision making, her research has examined issues of ageism in communication, family communication and decision making, and ethics and professionalism in health care. Her work has appeared in the *Journal of Divorce and Remarriage* and *Journal of Social Issues*.

John Parrish-Sprowl (PhD, Bowling Green State University, 1983) is a professor of communication studies and codirector of the Global Health Communication Center (GHCC) in the School of Liberal Arts at Indiana University-Purdue University Indianapolis. He also is an adjunct professor of informatics and a member of both the University College and the Russian and Eastern Europe Institute faculties of Indiana University. He is known for his international applied communication research and project consultancies, focusing on issues of economic development, education, and health. He has lectured, conducted research, and consulted with universities, businesses, and nongovernmental organizations in a number of countries, including Belarus, France, Ghana, Indonesia, Kenya, Macedonia, Poland, Russia, and Thailand. Currently, he is contributing to the Community Health Engagement Program of the Clinical Translational Sciences Institute of Indiana and collaborating with the World Health Organization to work with Ministries of Health in developing countries to create better health communication to improve health-care access and indices.

Kimberly Pearce (MA, San Jose State University, 1984) has been teaching at De Anza College for over 20 years. In addition to full-time teaching, she is a cofounder of two organizations, the Public Dialogue Consortium and Pearce Associates, working with clients to create better patterns of communication in private and public settings. Pearce's commitments as a practitioner and researcher involve the connections among Buberian dialogue, adult transformational learning, interpersonal neuroscience, and the coordinated management of meaning (CMM) theory as leverages for creating more inclusive and reflexive ways of being and acting in a globalized, postmodern world. She has authored a handbook on facilitating dialogic communication, as well as articles on dialogue and CMM. Her work as a practitioner includes a number of projects in the United States, as well as in Argentina, Brazil, Colombia, Denmark, England, France, Greece, and Ireland.

W. Barnett Pearce (PhD, Ohio University, 1969) is a professor emeritus in the School of Human & Organization Development at Fielding Graduate University. He has served on the faculties of The University of North Dakota, University of Kentucky, University of Massachusetts at Amherst, and Loyola University Chicago, in the position of department chair at the latter two institutions. Improving the quality of communication has been his driving professional commitment, first taking the form of developing a conceptual understanding of communication, known as "the coordinated management of meaning" (CMM), and, more recently, integrating scholarship with the practice of designing and facilitating communication, particularly in public meetings about community issues. He is a member of the core faculty at Fielding of the Dialogue, Deliberation & Public Engagement graduate certificate program, and a founder of the Transforming Communication Project. As a practitioner, he has worked on six continents through the nonprofit Public Dialogue Consortium and the for-profit Pearce Associates. He has published nine books, including *Moral Conflict: When Social Worlds Collide* (with Stephen Littlejohn), *Interpersonal Communication: Making Social Worlds*, and *Communication and the Human Condition*. His most recent publications include the book *Making Social Worlds: A Communication Perspective* and the article "Toward a New Repertoire of Communication Skills for Leaders and Managers," published in *Quality Management Forum*.

Valerie Pedrami (BA, University of Houston, 2008) is a multilingual graduate from the Jack J. Valenti School of Communication at the University of Houston. She has experience with various public relations firms.

Marshall Scott Poole (PhD, University of Wisconsin-Madison, 1980) is David and Margaret Romano Professorial Scholar, professor of communication, and senior research scientist at the National Center for Supercomputing Applications at the University of Illinois at Urbana-Champaign. Previously, he taught at the University of Minnesota and Texas A&M University. His research interests include group and organizational communication, information systems, collaboration technologies, organizational innovation, and theory construction. He is the author of over 100 journal articles and book chapters, and has coauthored or edited 10 books, including *Communication and Group Decision Making* (two editions, with Randy Y. Hirokawa), *Theories of Small Groups: Interdisciplinary Perspectives* (with Andrea B. Hollingshead), *Organizational Change and Innovation Processes: Theory and Methods for Research* (with Andrew H. Van de Ven, Kevin Dooley, and Michael E. Holmes), and *The Handbook of Organizational Change and Innovation* (with Van de Ven). He has been named a Fellow of the International Communication Association and a Distinguished Scholar of the National Communication Association, and he received the Steven Chaffee Career Productivity Award from the International Communication Association.

Jim L. Query, Jr. (PhD, Ohio University, 1990) is a professor and director of the Institute for Health and Environmental Communication at James Madison University, where he teaches courses in health communication, research methods, and group communication. He has been president of the Alzheimer's Association of Tulsa, editor of *Communication Studies*, and a member of 14 editorial boards and 13 Scientific Review Boards for the National Institutes of Health and the Centers for Disease Control and Prevention. His primary research interests include the expression of social support across a variety of life situations (e.g., retirement, returning to higher education, and job stress) and chronic health conditions (e.g., Alzheimer's, cancer, diabetes, HIV, and AIDS), with a particular focus on Hispanics/Latino/as and African Americans, as well as physician–patient interaction and e-Health. His scholarship appears in journals that include *Journal of Applied Communication Research*, *Communication Studies*, *Health Communication*, and *Journal of Health Communication*, and in several books, including *Applied Health Communication*, *The Handbook of Communication and Cancer Care*, *The Handbook of Group Communication Theory and Research*, and *Qualitative Research: Applications in Organizational Life* (both editions).

Robyn Remke (PhD, Purdue University, 2006) is an assistant professor in the Department of Intercultural Communication and Management at the Copenhagen Business School. Motivated by questions of social injustice, her research uses a critical–feminist lens to examine ways in which organizational members respond to and resist irrationality in public service organizations. In addition, she studies alternative forms of workplace organizational structures and gendered identity in the workplace. Remke has published journal articles in *Communication Studies* and *Communication Monographs*, and is a coauthor of chapters that appear in the forthcoming books *What's Wrong with Leadership? How Leaders Fail by Treating Dissent as a Threat and What Can Be Done about It* and *The Destructive Side of Organizational Communication*.

Anthony J. Roberto (PhD, Michigan State University, 1995) is an associate professor in the Hugh Downs School of Human Communication at Arizona State University. His primary research and teaching interests are in the areas of social influence and health communication, and he has received numerous research and teaching awards. His research has been published in the *Journal of Applied Communication Research*, *Communication Research*, *Health Communication*, *Human Communication Research*, *Journal of Com-*

munication, and *Journal of Health Communication*. He is lead author of *Influence in Action: A Student Handbook* (with Gary Meyer), and five lessons he created have been published in *Communication Teacher*.

Matthew W. Seeger (PhD, Indiana University, 1982) is a professor and chair of the Department of Communication at Wayne State University. His work on applied communication and crisis management has appeared in the *Journal of Applied Communication Research*, *Communication Research Reports*, *Communication Studies*, *Communication Yearbook*, *Encyclopedia of Public Relations*, *Journal of Health Communication*, *Journal of Organizational Change Management*, *Handbook of Public Relations*, and *Southern Communication Journal*, among others. His work on communication ethics has been published in the *Free Speech Yearbook*, *Journal of Business Communication*, *Journal of Business Ethics*, and *Management Communication Quarterly*, as well as in several edited books. His books include *Crisis Communication and the Public Health*, *Effective Crisis Communication: Moving from Crisis to Opportunity*, *Communication and Organizational Crisis* (all with Timothy L. Sellnow and Robert R. Ulmer), and *Ethics and Organizational Communication*.

David R. Seibold (PhD, Michigan State University, 1975) is a professor in the Department of Communication (College of Letters and Science) and director of the Graduate Program in Management Practice (College of Engineering) at the University of California, Santa Barbara. He teaches courses on micro- and macro-organizational communication, small group communication, interviewing, and managing innovation and change. He has published more than 100 articles and chapters on communication and organizational change, temporality, small group decision making, interpersonal influence, structuration, and theory–practice relationships, works that have appeared in journals and books in communication, psychology, management, and health. A former editor of the *Journal of Applied Communication Research*, he has served on the editorial boards of 13 journals headed by 24 editors. He has engaged in research and service with more than 75 government, health, service, and business organizations during the past 30 years, and is a recipient of the National Communication Association's (NCA) Gerald M. Phillips Award for Distinguished Applied Communication Scholarship. He recently was named an NCA Distinguished Scholar for a lifetime of scholarly achievement.

Timothy L. Sellnow (PhD, Wayne State University, 1987) is a professor in the Department of Communication at the University of Kentucky, where he teaches courses in communication theory and crisis/risk communication. His research focuses on communication strategies for managing risk and responding to crisis. He has worked with the Department of Homeland Security and the U.S. Department of Agriculture to develop prevention programs and rapid response strategies for bioterrorism, and with the Centers for Disease Control and Prevention to develop crisis communication planning and training strategies for pandemic influenza. He recently served as editor of the *Journal of Applied Communication Research*.

Thomas J. Socha (PhD, University of Iowa, 1988) is ODU University Professor and an associate professor of Communication in the Department of Communication & Theatre Arts at Old Dominion University, where he teaches courses in family, children's, interpersonal, and group communication, as well as communication research methods. He has published two books and numerous articles and chapters on parent–child communication, children's communication, family communication, group communication, communication education, and the newly emerging topic of positive communication. He

was the founding editor of the *Journal of Family Communication*, received the Bernard J. Brommel Award from the National Communication Association (NCA) for outstanding research and service in family communication, and is on the National Advisory Board for the revision of the Praxis II exam in Speech Communication (Educational Testing Service, Princeton, NJ). Currently, he is coediting (with Glen Stamp) a book titled *Parents & Children Communicating with Society: Managing Relationships Outside of Home*, coauthoring a book (with Julie Yingling) on children's communication in families, continuing to teach courses in family communication at NCA's Summer Faculty Development Institute, and serving as vice-president of the Southern States Communication Association.

Shawn Spano (PhD, Indiana University, 1988) is a professor in the Department of Communication Studies at San José State University and a senior consultant with the Public Dialogue Consortium. He conducts community-based, action research projects and teaches courses in dialogic communication theory and practice, primarily in public and organizational settings. He is the author of the book *Public Dialogue and Participatory Democracy: The Cupertino Community Project*, and has published articles in the *Basic Communication Course Annual*, *Human Systems*, *Political Communication*, and *Southern Communication Journal*, among other outlets. He does communication consulting, facilitation, and training workshops for a variety of government, education, and nonprofit organizations, including multiyear projects with two municipalities in the San Francisco Bay Area.

Helen Sterk (PhD, University of Iowa, 1986) is a professor and chair of the Department of Communication Arts and Sciences at Calvin College, where she held the William Spoelhof Teacher Scholar Chair. She has written widely on rhetoric, feminism, gender, and popular culture, including the books *Gender in Applied Communication Contexts* (with Patrice M. Buzzanell and Lynn H. Turner), *Who's Having This Baby? Perspectives on Birthing* (with Krista Ratcliffe, Carla H. Hay, Alice B. Kehoe, and Leona VandeVusse), *Differences that Make a Difference: Examining the Assumptions in Gender Research* (with Turner), and *Constructing and Reconstructing Gender: The Links Among Communication, Language, and Gender* (with Linda A. M. Perry & Turner), as well as in journals and edited collections. Her work has been recognized with awards for outstanding scholarship. She edited the *Journal of Communication and Religion* and currently serves on three editorial boards. She also served as president of the Organization for the Study of Communication, Language and Gender, and of the Religious Communication Association. She also was chapter president for the American Association of University Professors (AAUP) and a member of the state executive board for the AAUP (Michigan).

SunWolf (PhD, University of California, Santa Barbara, 1998; JD, University of Denver College of Law, 1976) is an associate professor in the Department of Communication (teaching relationships, group dynamics, conflict, and social persuasion) and a visiting professor at the School of Law at Santa Clara University. She serves on the editorial boards of the *Journal of Applied Communication Research*, *Review of Communication*, and *Small Group Research*. She is the originator of decisional regret theory, which explains how people reduce anxiety about anticipated choice–regret with counterfactual what-if stories. Her books include *Peer Groups: Expanding Our Study of Small Group Communication* and *Practical Jury Dynamics2: From One Juror's Trial Perceptions to the Group's Decision-Making Processes*. Her scholarship has appeared in *Journal of Applied Communication Research*, *Communication Monographs*, *Communication*

Studies, Howard Journal of Communications, Journal of Language and Social Psychology, Journal of Moral Education, and *Small Group Research*, as well as in a number of edited books. Her newest book describes the biocognitive processes of individual moral thinking or religious beliefs during group decision making. She was the recipient of Santa Clara University's 2008 Research Award for most outstanding research during the last 5 years that made a substantial contribution to the field.

John C. Tedesco (PhD, University of Oklahoma, 1996) is an associate professor and director of graduate studies in the Department of Communication at Virginia Tech University, where he teaches courses in research methods, political communication, and public relations. His articles on political communication and public relations are published in *Argumentation & Advocacy, Communication Studies, Harvard International Journal of Press/Politics, Journal of Advertising, Journal of Broadcasting & Electronic Media*, and *Journalism Studies*. He is research coordinator (along with Lynda Lee Kaid and Mitchell S. McKinney) of UVote, a national election research team that studies young adults' political efficacy and engagement.

Karen Tracy (PhD, University of Wisconsin, 1981) is a professor in the Department of Communication at the University of Colorado at Boulder, where she teaches courses on discourse analysis, language and identities, and the practices and problems of meetings. Her recent research, focusing on the practices of school board meetings, has appeared in the *Journal of Applied Communication Research, Communication Theory*, and *Discourse & Communication*. She coedited (with James P. McDaniel and Bruce E. Gronbeck) the volume *The Prettier Doll: Rhetoric, Discourse, and Ordinary Democracy*, and is in the final stage of preparing a book, titled *Challenges of Ordinary Democracy: Discourse, Community, and Reasonable Hostility at a Local School Board*.

Lynn H. Turner (PhD, Northwestern University, 1989) is a professor in the Department of Communication Studies at Marquette University, where she teaches both undergraduate and graduate courses. Her research areas include interpersonal, gendered, and family communication. She has published over 10 books, as well as many articles and book chapters. Her books include *From the Margins to the Center: Contemporary Women and Political Communication* (with Patricia A. Sullivan; recipient of the 1997 Best Book Award from the Organization for the Study of Communication, Language and Gender [OSCLG]); *Gender in Applied Communication Contexts* (with Patrice M. Buzzanell and Helen Sterk); and *Introducing Communication Theory: Analysis and Application, Perspectives on Family Communication*, and *The Family Communication Sourcebook* (all with Richard West). Her articles have appeared in the *Journal of Applied Communication Research, Journal of Family Communication, Management Communication Quarterly, Western Journal of Communication*, and *Women and Language*. She was the recipient of the Marquette University College of Communication Outstanding Research Award in 1999 and 2007. She has held a number of service positions, including director of graduate studies for the College of Communication at Marquette, president of OSCLG and of the Central States Communication Association, and currently is second vice president of the National Communication Association.

Robert R. Ulmer (PhD, Wayne State University, 1998) is a professor and chair of the Department of Speech Communication at the University of Arkansas at Little Rock, where he teaches courses in organizational and crisis communication. He recently coauthored (with Timothy L. Sellnow and Matthew M. Seeger) the book *Effective Crisis Com-*

munication: Moving from Crisis to Opportunity, which uses organizational renewal as a framework to help organizations prepare for and respond better to crises. He has worked with many state and national organizations, including the Centers for Disease Control and Prevention, and the U.S. Department of Homeland Security, on issues of risk and crisis communication.

Melinda R. Weathers (MA, University of Houston, 2008) is a doctoral student in the Department of Communication at George Mason University, where she teaches interpersonal communication courses. She also has taught or assisted in public speaking, communication theory, and technical communications courses. Her current research explores communication competence, social support, perceived coping, and religious coping among Hispanic family members caring for loved ones with Alzheimer's disease. She has presented papers at numerous conferences and conventions.

Kim Witte (PhD, University of California, 1991) is a retired (and now adjunct) professor in the Department of Communication at Michigan State University (MSU), where she conducted health communication research in a variety of domestic and international locations. She has been chair of the health communication divisions of the International Communication Association and the National Communication Association (NCA). She sits on several editorial boards; served as an expert consultant to the National Libraries of Medicine, Centers for Disease Control & Prevention (CDC), National Institute of Occupational Safety and Health (NIOSH), and other organizations; and has received funding from, among others, CDC, NIOSH, and the American Cancer Society. She is the lead author (with Gary Meyer and Dennis Martell) of *Effective Health Risk Messages: A Step-by-Step Guide*, which received the 2001 Distinguished Book Award from NCA's Applied Communication Division. Her work has appeared in numerous journals and has received over a dozen "top paper" conference awards and the Distinguished Article Award from NCA's Applied Communication Division. In 1997, she received MSU's "Teacher–Scholar Award" for excellence in research and undergraduate education, and, in 2000, was named the Lewis Donohew Outstanding Scholar in Health Communication. Currently, she sits on the United Nations World Health Organization's Global Polio Eradication research committee.

Kevin B. Wright (PhD, University of Oklahoma, 1999) is an associate professor in the Department of Communication at The University of Oklahoma, where he teaches courses in health communication, computer-mediated communication, interpersonal communication, and quantitative research methods. He has published a number of articles dealing with social support and health outcomes, and with provider–patient interaction in journals that include the *Journal of Applied Communication Research*, *Health Communication*, *Journal of Communication*, and *Journal of Social and Personal Relationships*. His current research focuses on social support and health outcomes among people coping with illness and people dealing with everyday stress in both computer-mediated and face-to-face contexts.

Introduction

Kenneth N. Cissna
University of South Florida

Lawrence R. Frey
University of Colorado at Boulder

People today are confronted by myriad problems that include how to create and sustain high-quality interpersonal relationships; raise and educate children in healthy families and schools; structure work environments to make people's experiences both meaningful and productive; cope with and help others to face significant illnesses; prevent ageism, racism, sexism, and other forms of discrimination; and talk together constructively in local, national, and international settings to make effective collective decisions about important, controversial, and often deeply contested issues facing communities, countries, and, indeed, the world. For these and the many other important issues facing people, communication is absolutely crucial, making those who study communication central to creating better social worlds.

Communication scholars, teachers, and practitioners have always been concerned with understanding and managing significant real-world issues and problems, starting with the goal of making people better public speakers. In the last half century, the study of communication expanded to include many areas and topics that were unknown to the founders of the field—interpersonal and family communication, group and organizational communication, health and aging communication, and communication media and technology, to name only a few. Some communication scholars focus on theoretical issues related to these areas and topics, whereas others approach them from a more practical perspective, seeking to develop knowledge that both advances the discipline and, hopefully, improves some aspect of people's lives. The study of real-world communication concerns, issues, and problems is known as *applied communication research.*

As documented in the first two chapters of this handbook, over the course of the past 40 years or so, applied communication research has become institutionalized in the communication discipline as a highly respected field of study, with a journal devoted explicitly to this scholarship, the *Journal of Applied Communication Research* (*JACR*), applied communication divisions and interest groups in professional communication associations, and awards given for the highest quality applied communication scholarship. Furthermore, the notion that communication scholarship should seek to understand and do something about real-world communication concerns, issues, and problems cuts across the communication discipline. Neuman, Davidson, Joo, Park, and Williams (2008), for instance, recently reported "seven deadly sins" and corresponding "virtues" of communication research from a study of reviews written about manuscripts submitted for publication in the *Journal of Communication.* Among the virtues they identified was *normative connection,* "the evaluation of the *potential relevance* of the reported research to social, culture, or political values and *matters of real-world public concern*" (p. 224, italics added). As another example, Nakayama's (2008) "Editor's Statement" in the inaugural issue of the National Communication Association's (NCA) latest journal, the *Journal of International and Intercultural Communication,* indicates that communication scholarship should "not simply present facts or discuss issues" but "engage contemporary situations" and "intervene to solve problems" (p. 2). As a final example, *Communication Monographs* published a special forum on "Can We Enhance People's Lives?" (Hample, 2008a). In his introduction to the forum, Hample (2008b) identified the "primary goal of research in communication" as being to "help people have better lives" (p. 319). Significantly, none of these journals, and especially not the *Journal of Communication* or *Communication Monographs*, has been known as particularly "applied" journals. Moreover, applied scholarship now is regularly published in virtually every communication journal. Thus, even in mainstream communication journals not known for applied communication scholarship, relevance to real-world concerns, issues, and problems has become part of the expectation for what constitutes high-quality communication scholarship.

Given the institutionalization of applied communication as a distinct field of study within the communication discipline, coupled with the accepted centrality of applied research to the study of virtually all aspects of communication, it is time to take stock of that scholarship by exploring where it has been and where it needs to go. This handbook attempts to accomplish that goal.

At the outset of this project, each of us was approached by a different publisher who thought such a handbook desirable and timely, asking us to serve as its editor. We soon learned about each other's project, talked together, and decided to consolidate our efforts to produce a single handbook that addressed this important form of scholarship. We are grateful to Linda Bathgate and others at Routledge, Taylor and Francis for their support of this handbook.

The next step we took was to form an editorial board of distinguished scholars and to seek their guidance. We started with lists that included current members and past officers of NCA's Applied Communication Division, editors and editorial board members of *JACR*, recipients of NCA's Gerald M. Phillips Award for Distinguished Applied Communication Scholarship, scholars who published frequently in *JACR*, and others who were known by us for the high quality of their applied communication scholarship. Initially, we had well over 100 names; eventually, we selected the 19 people listed at the beginning of this handbook as board members. We want to thank the board members and the additional listed reviewers who contributed their time and energy to this project.

After selecting and consulting with the board, we issued a broad public call for chapter proposals, as well as approached some distinguished applied communication scholars about submitting proposals. We wanted the flexibility both to issue that call so that we might be surprised by people or topics we might not have previously considered, and to solicit chapters from experts whose work we felt confident about or to represent areas that were not forthcoming in response to the open call. We received 43 proposals, which we organized topically and had reviewed by editorial board members. Nearly a third of those proposals eventually were accepted, some in modified form. In the end, of the 23 chapters commissioned for this handbook, in addition to the two chapters coauthored by the editors, 13 chapters were submitted in response to the call and 10 chapters were invited. Along the way, one proposer of a chapter was unable to produce it and was dropped from the volume, authors of two chapters withdrew and others graciously and ably stepped into their places, and two chapters were consolidated into one. Several authors took on additional coauthors as their projects progressed through the stringent review process. We want to thank the authors for their excellent chapters; their receptivity to feedback provided by editorial board members, reviewers, and us; and for putting up with our seemingly endless editing of their chapters.

The result of these processes is a handbook that provides a resource for those who are interested in studying how communication potentially can have important effects on people's lives. More specifically, this handbook (1) conceptualizes and delineates what constitutes applied communication scholarship in ways that encompass the range and diversity of perspectives and clarify relationships among theoretical perspectives, methodological procedures, and applied practices; (2) demonstrates the breadth and depth of applied communication scholarship; (3) reviews and synthesizes literature in and about various applied communication areas and topics in coherent, innovative, and pedagogically sound ways; and (4) sets agendas for future applied communication scholarship.

Organization of the Handbook

Organizing any field of study, especially one as diverse as applied communication research, is no easy matter; whatever organizational scheme we might employ would capture only part of the complexity of applied communication scholarship. The sections (and chapters) of this handbook emerged from an interplay among the exchange of ideas between the two editors based on our years of experience conducting applied communication research and contributing to conversations about that scholarship; consulting with editorial board members and processing their responses to our initial ideas; and receiving and evaluating, with editorial board members, proposed chapters submitted in response to the open call. The interaction of those processes resulted in dividing this handbook into five sections.

The first section of the handbook begins with three chapters that explore *foundations* of applied communication research, including the development of applied communication research, deep divides and great debates that have characterized applied communication scholarship, and the nature and contributions of practical theory to that scholarship. The second section considers a variety of *research methods* that scholars employ to conduct applied communication research: quantitative methods, rhetorical methods, ethnography, and discourse analysis. The chapters in the third section explore five significant, but understudied *issues* that cut across virtually all applied communication scholarship, regardless of the research methods utilized or the contexts explored: gender, race, technology, globalization, and ethics. The fourth and largest section summarizes the literature in major *contexts* in which applied communication research has been conducted, ranging from family communication and organizational communication to health, helping, aging, political, educational, and development communication. The fifth and final section, unique to handbooks in our experience, features four *exemplary programs* of applied communication research, written by the principals who conducted those programs, that demonstrate principles and practices of high-quality applied communication scholarship: programs about helping youth to resist drugs, using group decision support systems to help members of decision-making interact more effectively, constructing effective fear appeal health messages, and engaging productively in public dialogue about difficult issues. The chapters in each of these sections are explained below.

Part I: Foundations of Applied Communication Research

In chapter 1, Kenneth N. Cissna, William F. Eadie, and Mark Hickson, III provide an historical account of the development of applied communication scholarship. Cissna et al. start by exploring some significant political issues that influenced the creation and development of the formal academic discipline of communication, including moving beyond a concern with pedagogy to generate research-based knowledge to manage social problems. That applied research focus, as the authors explain, "burst" onto the scene at the 1968 New Orleans Conference on Research and Instructional Development, reflecting, in large measure, salient social and political issues that dominated the national landscape during the 1960s, with the conference resulting in numerous recommendations for conducting socially relevant communication research. Cissna et al. trace in detail some significant actions that occurred after that conference, including the creation of *JACR* and the formation of applied communication divisions in the national and some regional communication associations. The authors show how those and other actions resulted in the institutionalization of applied research in the communication discipline.

Chapter 2, by Lawrence R. Frey and SunWolf, complements Cissna et al.'s chapter by offering an intellectual history of great debates about some deep divides that have characterized the development of applied communication scholarship. Specifically, the authors examine discourse about four significant issues associated with the institutionalization of applied communication scholarship: (1) the shift from applied communication and organizational communication consulting to applied communication research; (2) the deconstruction of the basic–applied research divide to link communication theory and application; (3) the use of a wide range of methodologies to produce both rigorous and relevant applied communication scholarship; and (4) most recently, the recognition and negotiation of the chasm between observational and intervention-oriented (especially social justice activist) applied communication scholarship.

Chapter 3, by J. Kevin Barge and Robert T. Craig, explores the integrated relationship between theory and application in applied communication scholarship that was introduced in the previous chapter. After explaining how the role of theory has evolved in applied communication scholarship, the authors focus on "practical theory" as an alternative to traditional social-scientific theory. They trace the development of this concept and explicate various approaches to practical theory, including distinguishing among practical theory as mapping, engaged reflection, and transformative practice, and describing how each approach has been employed in applied communication research. Barge and Craig conclude the chapter by summarizing findings from their review of the theory–practice relationship and the process of practical theorizing, and by examining important issues associated with the future use of practical theory in applied communication scholarship.

Part II: Methods of Applied Communication Research

Chapter 4, by Jim L. Query, Jr., Kevin B. Wright, Patricia Amason, Kristen Campbell Eichhorn, Melinda R. Weathers, Martha Womack Haun, Eileen S. Gilchrist, Laura Bochenek Klein, and Valerie Pedrami, begins the examination of applied communication research methods by exploring quantitative methods. The authors first situate the current use of quantitative methods in applied communication scholarship by distinguishing a traditional positivistic perspective from the postpositivistic perspective that typically now is employed. They then examine five quantitative methods commonly used in applied communication research—survey research, experimental research, content analysis, interaction analysis, and meta-analysis—explaining their strengths and limitations, and providing examples of their use. Their content analysis of recent quantitative applied communication research studies sheds additional light on the use of those methods, leading to suggestions for increasing the quality of such research in the future.

In chapter 5, Celeste M. Condit and Benjamin R. Bates explain the use of rhetorical methods in applied communication scholarship. They first identify three binaries that influence the extent to which rhetorical studies are applied: (1) critical studies (examining discourse to discover how it works) as distinct from construction-oriented studies (seeking effective means for presenting one's case), (2) general studies compared to those that focus on the immediate or particular, and (3) whether the audience for the work is academics or change agents. Condit and Bates then describe key assumptions of applied rhetorical criticism, offer three exemplars of such scholarship that illustrate different combinations of critical and construction-oriented approaches directed toward academic and broader audiences, and explain four prominent theoretical approaches used in applied rhetorical studies: metaphoric analysis, narrative studies, fantasy theme analysis, and ideological critique. They conclude the chapter by offering suggestions for making rhetorical studies, especially construction-oriented studies, more applied, and by identifying important benefits of applied research for rhetorical studies.

Chapter 6, by Laura L. Ellingson, examines how ethnography is employed in applied communication research. Ellingson first explains ethnography, including its definition, goals (ideological, practical, and theoretical), and history. She then identifies, based on a review of ethnographic applied communication scholarship published from 1990 to 2005, four broad topic areas that have been studied ethnographically: health communication, organizational communication, community group communication, and communication education. She subsequently examines specific practices associated with collecting ethnographic data (e.g., field roles, field notes, and other types of data), analyzing those data (e.g., grounded theory and member checks), and writing ethnographic reports (e.g., use of first-person voice and thick description). Ellingson concludes the chapter by discussing some lessons learned about conducting ethnography from extant applied communication research and by offering suggestions for future applied communication ethnographies.

Karen Tracy and Julien C. Mirivel, in chapter 7, conclude the discussion of research methods by examining discourse analysis (DA), the close study of interaction. Although DA has been used in only a small number of applied communication studies, Tracy and Mirivel show how this method is useful for studying problems in the social world. They start by describing DA, including how it is studied in other disciplines (e.g., linguistics and psychology); explicating four basic activities involved in conducting DA in the communication field (audiotaping or videotaping interaction, making transcripts of the taped discourse, holding data sessions, and developing scholarly arguments); and differentiating DA from ethnographic methods, rhetorical criticism, and quantitative coding of interaction. They then reflect on how DA fits with the goal of applied communication research of understanding problems of the social world but demonstrates difficulty linking to the community of applied communication scholars. Tracy and Mirivel then discuss examples of practically useful DA research in three applied sites: health contexts, workplace interaction, and community governance meetings. They conclude the chapter by describing how a modified DA research practice that they call "focused reflection" could become a useful intervention in communication training and teaching venues.

Part III: Issues in Applied Communication Research

Chapter 8, by Patrice M. Buzzanell, Rebecca J. Meisenbach, Robyn Remke, Helen Sterk, and Lynn H. Turner, explores the positioning of gender in applied communication research through a feminist lens. That lens highlights not only the need for applied communication researchers to be more sensitive to gender by including sex as a demographic variable of study but especially the need to uncover inequitable power relations based on biological sex and psychological gender, and to suggest more equitable, emancipatory, and empowering ways of communicating. Buzzanell et al. illustrate this need by describing feminist research developments in four applied communication contexts—family life, educational institutions, organizations, and health care—starting with investigations of gender differences and then broadening their review with studies on gendered interaction, organizing processes, and societal ramifications. They conclude the chapter by showing how taking the feminist turn to studying gender in applied communication scholarship necessitates being concerned with public policy creation and implementation, and by focusing on two cases (the feminization of poverty and workplace policies) that display the interrelationships of gender and the four applied contexts covered in the chapter.

Chapter 9, by Anne Maydan Nicotera, Marcia J. Clinkscales, Laura K. Dorsey, and Marnel N. Niles, examines the concept of race in applied communication scholarship. The authors start by explaining race as a social–political construction, a position that resonates with a communication perspective but that has not been sufficiently acknowledged, implicitly or explicitly, by applied communication scholars. They then review and critique the small body of applied communication scholarship that examines race, identifying four primary problematic issues of race (identity, racism, discrimination, and diversity) and two fallacies (race is biological and race is culture) in that research. Nicotera et al. subsequently advance an original model, grounded in a social constructionist understanding, that explicates relationships among culture, ethnicity, class, and race; ties those concepts to the four problematic issues of race that are evidenced in applied communication scholarship; and promotes a research agenda about those issues that subverts erroneous assumptions about and provides a more holistic understanding of race.

In chapter 10, Leah A. Lievrouw examines the implications of new communication technologies, and the social changes they have created, for applied communication research. She begins by providing an overview of how communication technologies have been conceptualized and studied in the communication discipline over time, contrasting the traditional mass media instrumental perspective with the more recent constitutive view of technology and communication as "mediation." Lievrouw then reviews applied communication studies drawn from four contexts (organizational, health, political, and instructional communication) where the relationship between communication technology and communicative action has been extensively studied. She concludes the chapter by returning to the concept of mediation, showing how it offers an important way forward for applied communication research by approaching technology not as a set of tools for accomplishing particular applied ends (what she calls "technology *in* applied communication research") but as enabling and constituting communication, meaning, and culture, and as continuously recreated and made meaningful in practice (what she calls "technology *as* communication and applied communication research").

Chapter 11, by John Parrish-Sprowl, discusses the significance of globalization—the ever-increasing interconnectedness of the world's population that is fundamentally changing how people live, regardless of where they reside—for applied communication scholarship. Parrish-Sprowl first offers an historical overview of globalization, showing that although globalization processes (e.g., movement across the planet) have been occurring for a long time, current processes are qualitatively different from those of previous eras. He then examines how communication changes and is changed by globalization processes, changes that should be studied by internationalizing applied communication research. Parrish-Sprowl argues that applied communication scholars need to study international populations, concern themselves with issues that are important worldwide, conduct applied projects in places other than the United States, and take into account the global context when studying U.S. domestic issues. He concludes the chapter by reviewing applied communication research within the context of globalization and proposing agendas for such scholarship with respect to seven significant topics: (1) information technology and computer-mediated communication, (2) health communication, (3) transborder conflict, (4) civil societies, (5) public relations and advertising, (6) international commerce, and (7) intercultural communication.

Chapter 12, by Matthew W. Seeger, Timothy L. Sellnow, Robert R. Ulmer, and Julie

M. Novak, concludes this section of the handbook by focusing on the role of ethics in applied communication scholarship, summarizing and critiquing the literature on applied communication ethics and exploring ethical issues, orientations, and value premises of such scholarship. Seeger et al. first provide an overview of the applied ethics movement, situating this revolutionary trend within the general study of ethics and tracing its modern roots to societal concerns expressed during the 1960s (e.g., the civil rights movement). They then examine the relationship between (applied) communication and ethics, and consider some general ethical goals (do no harm, effect positive outcomes, and promote social justice), procedures (e.g., institutional review of research), and challenges confronting (applied communication) researchers (use of deception, potential exploitation of children, and research conducted in developing countries). They then examine how these and other ethical issues arise and have been addressed by scholars conducting applied research about health communication, organizational communication, and media. Seeger et al. conclude the chapter by discussing salient value premises within applied communication scholarship, including social justice, empowerment, and voice, as well as free speech and access to information, and by posing a research agenda for applied communication ethics.

Part IV: Contexts of Applied Communication Research

Thomas J. Socha begins this section of the handbook, in chapter 13, by exploring applied research that has been conducted on family communication. He first reviews the types of "problems" that applied researchers have focused on pertaining to family communication or the role of family communication in remedying problems that confront family members, their relationships inside and outside the family, and family units. His critical review of the applied family communication literature, including important problems that have not received sufficient attention, leads Socha to offer an alternative framework for applied family communication research, based on positive psychology and systems theory, which directs attention away from the dominant paradigm of fixing problems after they occur toward prevention, empowerment, and other positive processes and outcomes. He concludes the chapter with an extended example of how positive applied family communication scholarship might profitably focus on the creation of hope in families and their members.

Chapter 14, by David R. Seibold, Daisy R. Lemus, Dawna I. Ballard, and Karen K. Myers, examines applied research about organizational communication. To narrow the focus of this vast literature, Seibold et al. review applied research that has been conducted and pose questions and directions for future research about four organizational communication areas that have long traditions: (1) organizational socialization/assimilation, (2) organizational culture, (3) diffusion of organizational innovations, and (4) communication and planned organizational change. They conclude the chapter by addressing three approaches to the relationship between theory and practice (parallel, intersecting, and integrated) articulated in these research areas, and by discussing the emergence of a new form of applied organizational communication scholarship—engaged research.

Chapter 15, by Eric M. Eisenberg and Beth Eschenfelder, complements the previous chapter by exploring applied communication research about nonprofit organizations. After explaining the broadening of organizational communication research from a primary focus on for-profit organizations with a managerial bias to studying nonprofit organizations, governments, nongovernmental organizations (NGOs), and communities, they provide background on the complex environment in which nonprofit organizations operate, and how they are similar to and different from other organizations. Through a comprehensive review of the literature, Eisenberg and Eschenfelder identify three critical communication challenges to successfully managing nonprofit organizations: (1) partnering, (2) clarifying mission and identity, and (3) fostering employee involvement and identification. They conclude the chapter by suggesting directions for future applied communication research on nonprofit organizations.

Chapter 16, by Gary L. Kreps and Ellen W. Bonaguro, focuses on applied research conducted about health communication. They first provide an overview of health communication inquiry, explaining the powerful role that communication plays in health and describing the distinct but related areas of applied communication research on health care and health promotion. Kreps and Bonaguro then explore the breadth and depth of applied health communication scholarship as reflected in the multiple levels of interaction investigated; the numerous, diverse communication channels covered; the many health-care settings studied; and the variety of methodologies that researchers employ. They subsequently discuss the contributions of health communication research to promoting public health. Kreps and Bonaguro conclude the chapter by examining two contemporary directions for applied health communication research—studying the dissemination of health information via new communication technologies and designing and evaluating sophisticated communication campaigns to influence people's health beliefs, attitudes, values, and behaviors—and by discussing the future of such inquiry.

Chapter 17, by Katherine I. Miller and Jennifer R. Considine, extends the previous chapter by considering the role of communication in the helping professions—those providing human and social services (such as nursing, counseling, and social work). The authors begin by exploring the foundations of the helping professions, examining their historical development and moral bases, as well as people's motivations for entering them and how they are socialized into those professions. They then consider the role of communication in establishing interpersonal relationships between providers and clients in those professions, looking at two models of care, as well as research about the communication choices encountered in the helping relationship and the effects of those choices on providers and recipients. Miller and Considine subsequently situate the interpersonal relationship between care providers and recipients in the group, organizational, and institutional (specifically, managed care) contexts in which helping professionals work and communicate. They end the chapter by posing directions for future applied communication research about the helping professions.

In chapter 18, Jon F. Nussbaum and Jennifer E. Ohs explicate applied research related to communication and aging. They begin by pointing out that researchers typically focus on problems associated with aging, and although Nussbaum and Ohs consider that research, their review also explores applied communication research that seeks to describe, explain, and enhance the normal, everyday experience of aging. They first explain some normal changes in communication faculties that occur as people age. They then review applied communication research conducted in two important contexts for aging adults: (1) health communication (exploring provider–older patient interactions; issues of dependency and control among older patients, physicians, and third parties in the medical encounter; and socialization of elderly residents in long-term care settings), and (2) interpersonal interactions (specifically, with friends and family). Nussbaum and Ohs close the chapter by offering recommendations for future applied communication research on aging.

Chapter 19, by Lynda Lee Kaid, Mitchell S. McKinney, and John C. Tedesco, explores what applied research reveals about the political communication processes that inform a democracy. Specifically, they focus on five political communication research areas where applications and interventions occur most frequently: (1) political speaking, (2) political campaign debates (both presidential and nonpresidential, as well as media coverage of debates and the effects of debate formats on candidates' messages), (3) political advertising (including negative political advertising, the communication channels employed in political advertising, and the effects of political advertising on people's knowledge of and attitudes toward candidates and on their voting behavior), (4) political news (including media gatekeeping, news bias, news media content research, agenda-setting and agenda-building, and news media framing), and (5) political uses of new technologies (including how the Internet relates to campaign communication content and effects, e-Government initiatives, political activism, the public sphere, and voter uses and gratifications). Kaid et al. conclude the chapter by identifying some significant challenges that face future research conducted by applied political communication scholars.

Chapter 20, by Ann L. Darling and Liz Leckie, discusses applied communication research in educational contexts. They start by explaining their twin assumptions: that education is a fundamental tool of democracy and that participation in educational institutions is a communicative accomplishment. They then distinguish between communication education research and instructional communication research, and offer a third, more recent alternative—the scholarship of teaching and learning (SoTL). After defining applied communication in an educational context, and articulating their concern with education that promotes social justice, Darling and Leckie review research studies from the three perspectives of communication education, instructional communication, and SoTL that relate to three propositions: (1) teaching is an applied communication process; (2) classrooms, including service-learning classes that place students in local communities, are an applied communication context; and (3) schools are communities created by and through applied communication, with schools embedded within communities and functioning as communities. Darling and Leckie conclude the chapter by discussing directions for future applied communication research in educational contexts, especially research that promotes social justice, and by considering problems associated with conducting such research.

D. Lawrence Kincaid and María Elena Figueroa conclude this section of the handbook in chapter 21 by considering applied research related to development communication. They first distinguish two approaches to development communication—one focused on media campaigns designed to change individual behavior and the other about communication for participatory development within local communities—and explain their choice to emphasize the role of dialogue, group communication, and social networks within communication for participatory development. They then identify eight issues related to communication for participatory development that emerged from their review of the literature, and present a conceptualization and model of participatory development communication that addresses those issues, as well as other controversial issues that hinder progress in the field. As Kincaid and Figueroa explain the model, its various components, and its relationship to social change, they review relevant literature and discuss how the model can be used by practitioners to design and implement development programs, and by applied communication scholars to conduct research on those programs. They conclude the chapter by discussing significant unanswered questions related to their theoretical model and its application that should guide future applied development communication research and practice.

Part V: Exemplary Programs of Applied Communication Research

Chapter 22 describes the Drug Resistance Strategies project, Michael L. Hecht and Michelle Miller-Day's interdisciplinary, multimethodological, funded program of research that seeks to reduce the use and abuse of drugs by youth. The authors begin by explaining how this applied intervention-oriented communication research program is based on narrative theory (to explicate youths' experiences of drugs, drug use, and drug offers) and communication competence theory (to understand drug offer–resistance interactions as culturally, relationally, and skills-based phenomena). They then offer an account of the program's history, walking through their initial project in the late 1980s in Mesa, Arizona, that focused on how drugs are offered to adolescents of high school and college age, and what drug-resistance strategies are used. That work provided a descriptive base for understanding the social processes of drug offers and served as a pilot test of a narrative approach to intervention. They subsequently expanded the program to examine the role of ethnicity and gender in adolescent drug use, focusing on younger, middle school youth. In the third stage of the project, they developed, implemented, and evaluated an interdisciplinary, culturally grounded, participatory, middle school curriculum, called *keepin' it REAL*, that promoted antidrug norms and taught resistance and other social skills. The current fourth stage explores the role of developmental processes, examining age, risk and resiliency factors, and cultural factors on the success of the intervention, using a longitudinal 5-year design. Hecht and Miller-Day conclude the chapter by explaining the theoretical, methodological, and practical significance of this exemplary applied communication research program.

Chapter 23, by Marshall Scott Poole and the late Gerardine DeSanctis, describes their 20-year applied communication research program on the use of group decision support systems (GDSSs), a computer-based technology that structures communication to facilitate problem solving, decision making, conflict management, and related activities in task groups. They first explain the foundations of this research program, including the core research questions posed (with the fundamental problem pursued being why technology often fails to provide the expected benefits to group decision making), their development of a theoretical framework (adaptive structuration theory) to illuminate those questions, their research team and research plan, and the Software Aided Meeting Management (SAMM) GDSS laboratory they constructed at the University of Minnesota. Their initial studies, as they explain, were conducted in that lab and focused on GDSS effects (especially on group decision making) and processes associated with using GDSSs. Later, they conducted field studies in various organizations, detailing their work with the Internal Revenue Service and Texaco. Poole and DeSanctis conclude the chapter by discussing the contributions of this research to practice, significant factors that contributed to its success, challenges and difficulties they experienced, and lessons they learned from this applied communication research program.

In chapter 24, Kim Witte and Anthony J. Roberto describe their approach to constructing persuasive health campaigns based on appropriate use of fear appeals. They first explain the extended parallel process model (EPPM) of persuasion developed by Witte, which considers the effects of four variables—perceived susceptibility and perceived severity, constituting perceived threat; and response-efficacy and self-efficacy, constituting perceived efficacy, the degree of viable action that can be taken against a threat—on whether people engage in fear control (e.g., threat denial) or danger control (behavior change). After providing a brief history of EPPM research since its initiation in the early 1990s, they describe the design, implementation, and evaluation of two of their applied communication research projects that were explicitly guided by the EPPM. One project focused on preventing the growing rate of HIV and AIDS in the East-African country of Ethiopia, using *Journey of Life*, an entertainment–educational radio serial that highlighted the dangers of these diseases and encouraged family planning. The second project sought to reduce unintentional firearm-related injuries and deaths in Michigan by persuading gun owners, through a variety of communication means, especially a radio public service announcement, to store and handle guns safely, including securing and using a free gun trigger-lock that was offered to listeners. Witte and Roberto conclude the chapter by providing several recommendations to applied communication researchers and practitioners, particularly those interested in using the EPPM, that emerged from these projects, including the importance of (1) using previous theory and research; (2) targeting messages based on appraisals of audiences' susceptibility, severity, response-efficacy, and self-efficacy; (3) measuring both fear and danger control; (4) conducting formative, process, and outcome evaluations; and (5) employing multiple research methods.

Chapter 25 concludes this section and the handbook by featuring the work of Kimberly Pearce, Shawn Spano, and W. Barnett Pearce, founding members of the Public Dialogue Consortium (PDC), a nonprofit organization committed to facilitating dialogue among community members about issues that are difficult to discuss. They begin by describing the development of the PDC and a number of its public dialogue projects in the United States and in Indonesia, explaining in some detail their work in San Carlos, California, from 1999 through 2001. They then explain the contributions of their work to applied communication scholarship, conceptualizing it with respect to three levels, any one of which can have priority in any particular situation, although the others always are at least in the background: service delivery, theory development, and research and evaluation. Pearce et al. subsequently describe the way the PDC works, which includes taking a communication approach, focusing on the form of communication, and using concepts from the coordinated management of meaning theory to understand communication processes and to develop their model of public dialogue. They conclude the chapter by describing a number of paradoxes and tensions they have experienced, and lessons they have learned about civic engagement, public dialogue, and applied communication research, as they pursue their dream of helping to create better social worlds.

Conclusion

Applied communication research—the systematic investigation of real-world concerns, issues, and problems to help people better manage them—is a significant form of scholarship that contributes both intellectually to the communication discipline and pragmatically to society by helping people live better lives. Such research undoubtedly will be even more essential in the future, given the fast-changing world of the 21st century.

This handbook, we hope, helps both experienced scholars and those just starting out to understand and appreciate more fully this form of scholarship—its foundations, research methods employed, significant issues confronted, important contexts in which such research has been conducted, and how its principles and practices have been employed in some exemplary programs of applied communication scholarship. Working together on this handbook over the last several years and with the chapter authors, editorial board members, and reviewers has reinforced our view of the value, virtues, and vitality of applied communication scholarship. We hope that this handbook has the same effect on others who want to know how communication research has and can make a difference in the world, and, most important, we hope that it will lead to even better applied communication research in the future.

References

Hample, D. (Ed.). (2008a). Can we enhance people's lives? [Special forum]. *Communication Monographs, 75,* 319–350.

Hample, D. (2008b). Introduction: How can communication theory and research improve people's lives? *Communication Monographs, 75,* 319.

Nakayama, T. (2008). Editor's statement: On (not) feeling rebellious. *Journal of International and Intercultural Communication, 1,* 1–2.

Neuman, W. R., Davison, R., Joo, S.-H., Park, Y. J., & Williams, A. E. (2008). The seven deadly sins of communication research. *Journal of Communication, 58,* 220–237.

Part I

Foundations of Applied Communication Research

1 The Development of Applied Communication Research

Kenneth N. Cissna
University of South Florida

William F. Eadie
San Diego State University

Mark Hickson, III
University of Alabama at Birmingham

Applied communication research is a concept that emanated from the "speech" tradition in the communication discipline. Scholars working from the "journalism" tradition saw no need for such a concept because they assumed that all of their research necessarily had "applied" value. On the speech side of communication, the idea of doing "applied" research was a revolutionary one, a reaction in revolutionary times to what some saw as a hidebound conflict over control of the theoretical and methodological heart of the discipline. Indeed, the idea of "applied" took many forms and became a covering term for a number of research and professional agendas.

In this chapter, we trace the development of the concept of applied communication research primarily from a political and institutional standpoint. As this handbook illustrates, the terms *applied communication* and *applied communication research* have come to describe a number of strands of scholarship and to serve a variety of purposes. Any attempt to trace more fully the historical development and emergence of all of the various strands of scholarship; to provide details about the contents of the *Journal of Applied Communication Research* and other applied publications; to identify all significant applied communication scholars, teachers, and practitioners; to discuss the applied communication units of the various professional communication associations; or to compare various courses or curricula in applied communication, although undoubtedly worthy projects, is beyond the scope of—and the space allotted to—our chapter. Instead, this essay is informed not only by our research into the development of applied communication but also by our unique involvement in that process over more than 3 decades, including, especially, our perspectives as the first three primary editors of the *Journal of Applied Communication Research* (Hickson, 1973–1980; Cissna, 1981–1986; Eadie, 1990–1992).

We begin by delving into the evolution of the communication discipline to understand how the concept of "applied communication research" became a natural solution for a number of political tensions. Consequently, we start by reviewing how a group of teachers and scholars came to form the discipline, describe the struggles that early writers faced in defining the discipline and its scholarship, and show how the concept of research that could be called "applied" burst into consciousness in 1968. We continue by showing how the early development of the *Journal of Applied Communications Research* (*JACR*) capitalized on a newly found enthusiasm for doing socially relevant work, how the Applied Communication Section of the National Communication Association (NCA) aided the acceptance of the word *applied*, and how the purchase of *JACR* by NCA set the stage for "applied communication research" to mature.

Issues Influencing the Development of Applied Communication Research

Since the founding of the communication discipline, the field has coped frequently and repeatedly with four interrelated issues. These issues set a political agenda for the development of the communication discipline.

The first issue concerns the discipline's search for respectability within the academy. Like many other "new" disciplines,[1] communication scholars struggled for respectability in both academic and public circles. In fact, the need to establish a separate academic unit in communication was driven largely by a desire to develop respectability within the university as teachers rather than as scholars. Founding a distinctive discipline was seen as a means by which communication scholars could gain some importance and not be dominated by former colleagues, mostly in English departments.

The second issue was the desire to build a research-based body of knowledge about communication. The belief that communication is both an important activity and a significant area of study has roots in the earliest philosophical writings of a variety of cultures. Attempts to describe what constitutes effective communication and the impact of such communication have survived from early writings as cultural knowledge, and basic courses in public speaking still rely to a great extent on teaching that received cultural knowledge rather than on a body of contemporary knowledge built from systematic research. Many successful attempts have been made to validate that cultural knowledge, however, and from those attempts, new knowledge and theory have been generated. Efforts to move beyond those basic principles to produce sophisticated understandings of message production and effects, the social and cultural generation of meaning, and the impact of communication technology have led to a growing body of specific knowledge. The extent to which this knowledge is distinguished from knowledge claims made by other disciplines sometimes is uncertain, however, and difficulty in making those distinctions has kept communication scholars from achieving the recognition that scholars from other disciplines have received.

The third issue involves the need to generate knowledge that contributes to solving social problems. Although communication scholarship has always exhibited a rather practical bent, often it has been directed more toward improving pedagogy than toward solving social problems. Furthermore, the scholarship of the field can be criticized as somewhat parochial, being created primarily for one's colleagues and students. In recent years, however, applied communication research efforts have been directed specifically toward the solution of social problems.

The fourth issue concerns the need to insure that the public is aware of and uses communication-based knowledge. Communication professors have succeeded in convincing their university colleagues that communication skills are essential to effective citizenship and to success in everyday life. As a consequence, some form of communication study is required of many, if not most, university students in North America. The rising popularity of communication as an academic major in the United States also has produced a pool of graduates who have begun to make their mark on corporate and societal institutions. As more and more students have become exposed to communication principles, often via engaging, highly effective teaching, the communication discipline is starting to be seen as an ordinary part of university education, and communication students increasingly are looked on as having the ability to contribute to organizational and societal life from unique perspectives. Still, to date, the discipline has produced no scholar whose work instantly comes to mind when educated people think of the study of communication. We have, however, a cadre of commentators who appear on the national scene as critics and analysts of various communication events, and these scholar–teachers have made the public, policy makers, and scholars from other disciplines aware of the insights that communication research can provide in understanding and managing problematic situations.

Although communication has been understood from its earliest academic roots as a "practical discipline" (see Craig, 1989; see also Barge & Craig, this volume), academics in communication needed to be convinced that research, other than investigations into how to improve instruction, was necessary. In the earliest statement about the need for research in communication, James A. Winans (1915) wrote:

> I hold that by the scholarship which is the product of research the standing of our work in the academic world will be improved. It will make us orthodox. Research is the standard way into the sheepfold.
>
> We have lacked scholarship. We complain of prejudice and unjust discrimination, and we have grounds; but we had best face the truth. In the long run men pass for what they are. We have lacked scientific foundation for our special work. (p. 17)

Winans had to work hard to gain acceptance for his point of view. The result of his efforts was that many members of the communication discipline came to view research and theory building as necessary evils for academic respectability. Eventually, however, efforts to promote research within the discipline were successful enough that by the middle of the 20th century, a small body of theory began to emerge. Efforts to build theory and conduct research were spurred on by successes in researching communication disorders and in a burgeoning interest in media effects and propaganda. Interest in the study of communication (e.g., persuasion, group dynamics, and interpersonal relations) by scholars in other disciplines also began to influence the culture of the field. Eventually, the development of a more rigorous research culture in the field, along with a growing consciousness of the necessity for social relevance, birthed the notion that communication research could concern "applied" matters without threatening the discipline's potential standing in the academy.

In the sections that follow, we outline how a research culture developed in the communication field, how discussions and conflicts eventually led to a call for socially responsible research, how the field reacted to that call, and how the term *applied* was used both to start a journal with a particular agenda and to label a unit in the field's largest disciplinary society that had another agenda.

The Struggle for Disciplinary Identity and the (Sudden) Emergence of Applied Communication Research

We now take for granted that communication is a discipline whose scholarly understanding necessarily leads to application. That idea, however, has been axiomatic for a relatively brief period, fewer than 40 of the nearly 100 years since the establishment of a formal discipline of communication. Indeed, the founding of the discipline was driven primarily by a perceived need to separate from the field of English and to be seen as different from the discredited elocution movement (Gray, 1964). To gather information on how the idea of "applied communication research" emerged, we consulted the archives of the field's journals, newsletters, and convention programs in an effort to gauge the concerns of the field's leaders over time. We found that the concept responded at least as much to political disputes within the discipline as it did to scholarly ones.

It is entirely possible that parochial concerns, such as regional rivalries and jockeying for prestige within the academy, were as responsible as anything else for the formation in

1914 of the National Association of Academic Teachers of Public Speaking (NAATPS), the first name of the organization now known as NCA. James M. O'Neill, the first president of NAATPS, recalled in 1928 that the idea of a separate organization first was proposed in 1913 among a rump group of public speaking teachers who met following the conclusion of the National Council of Teachers of English (NCTE) conference, itself a new organization founded only 2 years earlier in 1911. The group decided to mail a questionnaire to more than 100 members of the NCTE section for teachers of public speaking, with the results indicating wide support for a new organization (O'Neill, 1928). The sticking point was whether the new organization should be independent of or affiliated with NCTE, with the vote split about equally for each choice. After the NCTE section met again in 1914 without reaching a decision, 17 members of the section decided that they would break away and form their own organization (Cohen, 1994).

The founding group was interesting in at least three ways. First, its membership was entirely from colleges and universities, although the NCTE section contained a large number of high school teachers. Second, these 17 members hailed heavily from the Midwestern United States and overwhelmingly represented large state, often land-grant universities, such as the universities of Illinois, Iowa, Minnesota, and Wisconsin. Third, the organization they formed was not the first organization devoted to public speaking. A separate organization, the Eastern Public Speaking Conference, was founded in 1910 at the initiative of Paul Pearson of Swarthmore College, and its first conference included members from many of the highly selective, private universities in the Mid-Atlantic states. Although this organization expanded to include national participation, convention attendance came primarily from the Northeast, including from such Ivy League institutions as Columbia, Cornell, Harvard, the University of Pennsylvania, and Yale. Winans of Cornell and Irvah L. Winter of Harvard, 2 of the 17 founders of NAATPS, also were among the founding members of the Eastern conference, but once NAATPS became established, the Eastern conference lost some of its appeal. Eventually, public speaking as a field of study disappeared at most of the institutions that had formed the Eastern Public Speaking Conference (Cohen, 1994), and the organization took on a regional identity as the Eastern Speech Association, now called the Eastern Communication Association (ECA).

The new national association needed members, so it opened its doors as widely as the founders felt was comfortable. It welcomed not only those who taught public speaking at any level of education but also those academics who developed students' or clients' vocal abilities; those who worked to correct speech disorders, such as stuttering; and those who taught dramatic performance.

A year after voting to establish the association, the group launched a journal, the *Quarterly Journal of Public Speaking*. In its initial issue, Winans (1915) published his frank assessment of the new field, a section of which was quoted previously. Winans found the new discipline to be lacking an intellectual core, and he called for research, which he contended was needed to provide some empirical basis regarding the superiority of particular teaching practices and to resolve philosophical differences. Although Winans's call led to the establishment of a Research Committee, whose work continued well into the 1950s, progress was slow. The *Quarterly Journal of Public Speaking* functioned for many years more like a newsletter than what we now think of as a scholarly journal. It published position statements on the discipline, often ones originally delivered as speeches at the association's annual meeting, and included quite a few contributions describing the structure of individual courses or curricula. The popular "News and Notes" column, with which contemporary readers of *Spectra* (NCA's newsletter) are familiar, was published originally in this journal. Aside from an occasional attempt at building theory (most notably by Charles H. Woolbert [e.g., 1917] of the University of Illinois), the closest the journal came in its early years to publishing what contemporary scholars call "research" was in the area of speech correction, primarily on stuttering.

This trend continued for many years, even after the association began publication in 1934 of *Speech Monographs* as an outlet for longer, more serious pieces of scholarship, as initially that journal was dominated by scholarship in what then was called "speech science." Although this speech-science work could be termed "applied" in the sense that its results could be translated into clinical practice, its authors were at least equally concerned with developing theories of how the vocal mechanism worked and of the psychological and physical barriers that must be overcome to eliminate stuttering. Hence, the concept of "research" was slow in taking hold in the new discipline, whose members thought of themselves primarily as "teachers" rather than as "scholars." If research itself was a problem, distinguishing "applied research" was superfluous.

Despite their differences, the founders of the new discipline had one overriding concern: to devise the best possible methods for teaching people to be effective public speakers. They assumed that people used this ability to make positive differences in their lives and in the lives of those around them, but that assumption, for the most part, was unstated and never tested. The term *public speaking* proved to be awkward as a name for a national organization, and, consequently, members of the association soon settled on *speech* as a covering term for their concerns. By 1918, the association changed its name to the National Association of Teachers of Speech (NATS), a name that persisted until 1946, and renamed its journal as the *Quarterly Journal of Speech*, which is still its name today.

In a 1922 speech at the NATS annual convention and subsequently published in 1923, Woolbert attempted to define the discipline of speech. He distinguished between speech as an activity and speech as a discipline. He described the activity of speech as any face-to-face communication; thus, Woolbert defined the *discipline of speech* as "the study and practice of such data as speech the activity as helps the student and the practitioner to adjust himself to his environment and to be useful to his fellows" (p. 2). Woolbert (p. 3) characterized the domain of the discipline as including the study of (1) speaking and all forms of talk, including the rhetoric underlying speech; (2) oral reading and performance of the words of others; (3) production of sound through the vocal mechanism; and (4) speech science, a "body of significant and useful facts and principles" drawn primarily from the other three areas of the discipline and contributing to their development. The primary goal of this work, according to Woolbert, was to advance teaching. No one quarreled seriously with Woolbert's definition of the discipline for many years.

Almost half a century later, in 1968, the idea that communication research should be focused on socially relevant concerns burst on the scene. The "burst" came in the form of an invited paper that one of the "Young Turks" of the field, Gary L. Cronkhite, presented to the New Orleans Conference on Research and Instructional Development, which was published in Kibler and Barker's (1969) book-length report of that conference. The New Orleans Conference was highly influential, as it essentially recommended a major revision of Woolbert's (1923) definition of the discipline and constituted a turning point in the development of the field. The conference advocated changing the covering term of the field from the then 60-year-old *speech* to *speech-communication*,[2] which led to renaming the national association from the Speech Association of America (SAA) to the Speech Communication Association (SCA). Titling his paper "Out of the Ivory Palaces: A Proposal for Useful Research in Communication and Decision," Cronkhite (1969) argued that communication scholars must do more to make the results of their research public and to assure that research addresses the "real communicative problems of a real society" (p. 115). Not only was the conference influential in the field but Cronkhite's essay also was influential within the conference, as the following 7 of the conference's 27 recommendations dealt with social relevance:

RECOMMENDATION 9: The conferees encourage colleagues to accept the view that the central concern of the speech-communication area is with spoken symbolic interaction and is thus socially relevant.

RECOMMENDATION 10: The conference participants encourage speech-communication scholars to design and execute research dealing with the speech-communication dimensions of current social problems.

RECOMMENDATION 11: The conferees encourage speech-communication scholars to make every effort to apply the findings of their research to the solution of contemporary individual and social problems.

RECOMMENDATION 12: The conferees encourage scholars in the speech-communication area and where appropriate the Speech Association of America, to pursue representation of their positions at all levels of government.

RECOMMENDATION 13: The conferees encourage scholars in the speech-communication area to recognize their continuing obligation to expose what they consider to be instances of unethical communication.

RECOMMENDATION 14: The conferees vigorously encourage speech-communication scholars to include a broader cultural, geographical, and racial representation in our professional associations.

RECOMMENDATION 15: The conferees encourage speech-communication scholars to make a continuing effort to communicate pertinent content and research findings to the general public through appropriate channels. Such efforts should be accorded the respect and appreciation of the profession. (Kibler & Barker, 1969, pp. 24–27)

These recommendations provided a mandate for the discipline: Some (particularly 12, 14, and 15) quickly became part of the ongoing agenda for the national association, whereas others (9, 10, and 11) took longer to develop, and one (13) only recently has become a significant concern of the association's leadership.

Cronkhite's (1969) essay may have provided the catalyst for action, but some of its ingredients had been bubbling for quite some time prior to 1968. The earliest indicator probably was the formation of the National Society for the Study of Communication (NSSC). As Weaver (1977) recounted the story, Elwood Murray, a leading social-scientific scholar, contacted James McBurney, President of SAA, and asked him to arrange a time during the 1949 convention when a group of social scientists could discuss the formation of a group that would affiliate with SAA. That meeting led the next year to the formation of NSSC as a separate organization. NSSC was intended to be interdisciplinary and focused on producing social-scientific results that could be used outside of the laboratory. Many of the founding members were affiliated with industrial and governmental organizations. Over time, the influence of the nonacademics faded, and, perhaps not coincidentally, in 1968, NSSC revised its focus somewhat and renamed itself the International Communication Association (ICA).

Other trends also were important. In 1953, the Eastern Speech Association undertook the first of many efforts to popularize speech and communication research. The association founded a publication called *Today's Speech*, which was intended to be a general interest magazine; later, that magazine took on an exclusively scholarly mission and eventually became *Communication Quarterly*. In addition, SAA began publishing *Speech Teacher* (later *Communication Education*), with Ewbanks's (1952) essay in the inaugural issue calling for scholars to do socially relevant research. Furthermore, growing interest in intercultural communication, particularly in Black rhetoric and speech patterns (see Buck, 1968; Burgess, 1968; Gregg & McCormack, 1968; Nash, 1967; Smith, 1966), probably also contributed to the readiness of the discipline's members to react positively to Cronkhite's (1969) call.

The reaction to the recommendations of the New Orleans Conference and to Cronkhite's (1969) essay urging the field toward greater social relevance was swift. At the 1968 SAA summer conference, a Committee on Social Responsibility in the Discipline was formed. This committee had several foci, including providing a forum for those who believed that SAA was not welcoming to people of color, in general, and African Americans, in particular. Evidence suggests that such contentions were correct: Jack Daniel (1995), an African-American member of the committee, recalled cowering in his hotel room at the 1968 SAA annual meeting after he and his wife were awakened by a group shouting racial epithets outside his door.

In addition, the next year, SAA's summer conference, held in Chicago, was titled the "Conference on Social Engagement" (Roever, 1969), and drew 250 people, a large attendance for a summer gathering. Lyndrey Niles, of Federal City College, argued for the discipline spending more time studying the present rather than doing so much historical work. Thomas Pace, of Southern Illinois University, took the position that those teaching speech should undertake in situ research in their communities, escaping both the dingy library basements and half-acre computer centers, a direct slap at the battle for theoretical and methodological dominance in the field that was raging between the more traditional rhetoricians and the generally younger quantitative social scientists. Perhaps the fact that the conference was held in Chicago, home of the uproarious 1968 Democratic National Convention the previous year, encouraged participants to press for change. The conference, as a whole, was devoted to encouraging members of the association to engage actively in their communities, and such engagement itself provided fodder for a type of research suited to the times. The conference report was mimeographed and made available to the members of the organization, but little else was heard of the conference.

Still, the winds of change in the communication field were blowing at gale force from 1968 to 1970. SAA wrote a new constitution and changed its name to the Speech Communication Association (SCA), the Committee on Social Responsibility spawned the Black Caucus, and intercultural communication became a theme of the 1970 annual meeting under First Vice President William Howell.

Changes were afoot in the country as well. The civil rights movement was in full swing, anti-Vietnam War protests had become significant, and the women's liberation and gay liberation movements were underway. Clearly, an underlying change in societal values occurred in rather short order, with many students and faculty on college and university campuses fervently engaged in the quest for relevance. For many, relevance meant that what students were learning should have some pragmatic application in contexts outside the university, whether personal or professional.

Others in the field, however, counseled a more measured approach to change, including Marie Hochmuth Nichols in her 1969 presidential address to the SAA convention, which she provocatively titled "The Tyranny of Relevance." Blankenship (2001) reported that a number of SAA members, including more than one former president, attended the speech in order to walk out of it in protest. Thus, the excitement about a call to conduct socially relevant research amidst a time of change became the backdrop for founding the first publication of the communication field that used the word *applied* in its title.

The Institutionalization of Applied Communication Research

In 1971, Mark Hickson, III completed his doctoral dissertation at Southern Illinois University, codirected by Thomas Pace, who was one of the key participants in the 1969 SAA summer conference. Hickson's dissertation employed participant observation to analyze a community action agency. Two weeks after graduation, Hickson was conscripted into the U.S. Army, where he was assigned to desk duty at the Pentagon. Concerned with maintaining his viability as a university professor during his military service, he submitted several papers to conventions and journals during that first year. Although a number of his submissions were accepted for presentation at conventions, the journal submissions were another story. As with many young professors (privates, too), he became frustrated with the process.

Hickson met Don Stacks while both were working at the Pentagon, and they worked together on various military publications, eventually becoming frequent research collaborators. Both had relatively practical approaches to the communication discipline and were members of the Metropolitan Washington Speech Communication Association, where they interacted with Niles, Patti Gillespie, Kathleen Hall Jamieson, Andrew and Darlyn Wolvin, Jerry Hendrix, Joanne Yamauchi, and others, including Ray Falcione, who was very interested in the emerging area of organizational communication.

Hickson attended the 1972 ICA convention in Atlanta, where he participated in a multiple-day event designed to begin construction of the first communication audit program, which sought to provide organizations with reliable data about their internal communication that could be compared with other organizations. This program attracted so many participants that the paper presentations had to be abbreviated to allow time for them all. At the conclusion of those sessions, Gerald Goldhaber (see 1993), from the State University of New York at Buffalo, assumed responsibility for continuing the audit project, with Howard Greenbaum, who was at Motor Parts Industries, as the cochair. For Hickson, the audit project confirmed that the communication discipline had social relevance and could provide information that could be meaningful outside the halls of academia.

For some months, Hickson and Stacks discussed the absence of publication outlets within the communication field for ethnographic and participant–observational studies and for applied research, and the possibility of creating a new journal to fill this gap. They had access to an MT/ST (magnetic tape/Selectric typewriter), which allowed them to edit on the machine and set type without utilizing a printer. Through this low-budget approach, they thought they could produce a journal that sold for $4.00 per year for two issues. Besides, they reasoned, not entirely tongue-in-cheek, if they owned it, they could publish in it.[3] Within a year, while both still worked at the Pentagon, Hickson and Stacks founded the *Journal of Applied Communications Research*.

Although they had some initial funding, subscriptions were necessary to keep the journal afloat; consequently, they began soliciting manuscripts, editorial board members, and subscriptions, utilizing Hickson's personal contacts, as well as SCA's *Spectra* and ICA's *Newsletter*. Initially, they were more successful in securing library subscriptions than individual subscribers, with hundreds of libraries purchasing the journal. Occasionally, they sent copies gratis to libraries, hoping that after a library had three issues on hand, it would continue with a subscription, and sometimes that worked. After the third issue,

Winter–Spring 1974, both Hickson and Stacks left the Army: Stacks went on to complete his doctoral work; Hickson returned to Mississippi State University where he had taught for a year prior to serving in the Army. Although Stacks continued to be involved in supporting the journal, he no longer contributed physically to typing the pages, and most of the responsibility fell to Hickson as editor. Initially, Mississippi State University provided facilities for the journal through the campus newspaper office, and after 2 years, the Office of Graduate Studies and Research contributed some monetary support.

JACR, however, was not the only applied project underway in the evolving communication field. Hickson and Greenbaum cochaired the organizational communication abstracts project, the purpose of which was to create a single place where all of the information on organizational communication from various disciplines could be found in one index. Although contemporary studies of organizational communication were not concerned typically with social problems, the "field-study" nature of much of that research led a number of communication scholars to assume that organizational communication research inherently was "applied." The organizational communication abstract project began with a volume by Greenbaum and Falcione (1975) and was published annually through the auspices of the American Business Communication Association and the ICA, and, later, Sage Publications, until it was discontinued after the 1985 volume. During that period, the index moved from an 87-page paperback to a hardback text of 384 pages.

The area of organizational communication developed largely along two lines. One line was founded at Michigan State University and concerned the analysis of communication structures in organizations (e.g., Rogers & Farace, 1975; Rudolph, 1973). The other approach focused on interpersonal relationships within organizations and resulted from the work of Charles Redding at Purdue University. Redding had been one of the founders of ICA, and he had ties to several of its nonacademic founders. In those days, ICA was the only professional association in communication with a division devoted to organizational communication research; SCA's interest group structure included a unit titled "Business and Professional Speaking." The ICA communication audit project was perhaps the last large-scale effort by that organization to promote close cooperation between academics and nonacademics. The project generated considerable enthusiasm initially, and a certification process was created to train ICA members as auditors. The audit process proved to be comprehensive but more costly and time-consuming than most organizations were willing to tolerate. As a result, it attracted little corporate support and operated on a limited budget, provided primarily by ICA's Organizational Communication Division (Goldhaber, 1993). Once the division and ICA Board of Directors decided to abandon the project in 1978, all of the procedures and measures became public property, with individual researchers being allowed to use them freely, as long as the ICA name was not invoked.

From the outset, however, Hickson and Stacks thought that *JACR* could not and should not be limited to organizational communication. They believed that articles for the journal should (1) address significant social issues and (2) utilize data (or *capta*, that which is taken from experience) collected in an environment other than the university. In fact, in *JACR*'s first issue, only one article concerned organizational communication; the others dealt with political communication (Gonchar & Hahn, 1973) and documentary broadcasting (Flannery, 1973), along with Hickson's (1973) opening essay. As the journal developed, it focused attention on context to analyze the unique qualities of the types of places where communication occurred, with, for example, early articles on health communication (Ayres, Brand, & Faules, 1973), marketing (King, 1974), marital communication (Feldman & Jorgensen, 1974), intercultural communication (Peterson, 1975), and child rearing (Blumenfeld, 1976). The approaches used in these articles varied from fieldwork and participant observation to theoretical to criticism to experimental. In 1975, Hickson published what became the first of many special issues, symposia, and forums in *JACR*, with a brief symposium on organizational communication, featuring short contributions by Greenbaum, Falcione, and Goldhaber that originally were presented at the 1975 ECA convention.

Situated research also was showing up occasionally in other journals, due primarily to a few communication scholars' interests in qualitative methods, in general, and ethnography, in particular. Gerry Philipsen's (1975) article, "Speaking 'Like a Man' in Teamsterville," elaborated on human interaction within a specific subculture (a blue-collar, low-income neighborhood on the south side of Chicago) and was the precursor to much of the ethnographic work that was undertaken later by a wide range of scholars, including Dwight Conquergood (e.g., 1988, 1991a, 1991b, 1992, 1994, 1995), whose theoretical, methodological, and ethnographic scholarship transformed performance studies and contributed to critical ethnographic and social justice orientations to applied communication as well (see also Ellingson, this volume; Frey & SunWolf, this volume). Similarly, Robert Nofsinger's (1975) article, "The Demand Ticket: A Conversational Device for Getting the Floor," led the way for the use of various methodological approaches to the study of conversation/discourse, which also later influenced applied communication research (see Tracy & Mirivel, this volume).

The idea of applied communication was making itself manifest in the professional communication associations as well, although initially, at least, for different reasons than was the case in the scholarly journals. In the mid-1970s, SCA revised its interest group structure to include divisions (units, such as Rhetorical and Communication Theory, that represented major areas of study); commissions (units, such as Freedom of Expression, that represented secondary or emerging areas of study); sections (units, such as the Community College Section, that represented members by their institutional affiliations); and caucuses (units, such as the Black Caucus, that provided institutional homes for the concerns and political agendas of "underrepresented" groups within SCA). Through the efforts of Jane Work, a Vice President of the National Association of Manufacturers (and wife of SCA's Executive Secretary William Work) and Darrell Piersol, an executive with International Business Machines (IBM), the sections included one titled "Applied Communication." From the beginning, that section had something of a multiple identity: Although it was intended to provide a home for nonacademic members of SCA, it also functioned as a place for academics who were interested in consulting and as an outlet for presenting applied communication research.[4]

This dual, multiple identity of the Applied Communication Section (APCOM) was reflected at the 1977 SCA convention in Washington, DC, the first to include programs sponsored by the new section. The section sponsored only two programs that year: a business meeting for interested individuals and a scholarly panel titled "Applied Communication: Four Meta Papers," featuring scholars Redding, John Wiemann and David Schuelke, Larry Browning, and Michael Burgoon presenting position papers about their conceptions of applied communication research. Described as the "debut" program for the new section and chaired by Lillian Davis of IBM, the abstract of the panel published in the convention program indicated that the panel was "designed to establish the perspective and goals for future programs on this topic" (Speech Communication Association, 1977, p. 56).

The first official "directory" of participants in the Applied Communication Section was published in the first issue of the *APCOM Newsletter*, which followed the 1977 convention.[5] APCOM's "Mission Statement" described its purposes as "to provide a forum for the discussion, study, and analysis of issues pertaining to the application of communication principles to communication problems in government/business/industrial organizations" (Applied Communication Section, n.d.). In addition, the newsletter sought to provide opportunities for academics and communication specialists in those organizations to talk and work together.

Early leaders of the section included Davis, who served as the first chairperson of that section, and Jane Work, who served as the second chairperson. These two nonacademics were followed in the position of section chair by Browning, a University of Texas organizational communication scholar who also was an active organizational consultant, and by Andrew Wolvin, University of Maryland, a listening scholar who had significant interests in training. To some degree, the new unit did provide a home for nonacademics, as the first group of APCOM participants included members affiliated with, among others, Blue Cross-Blue Shield, the U.S. Air Force, Caterpillar Tractor Company, the Salvation Army, and the National 4-H Council.

The 1978 SCA convention saw nine programs sponsored by APCOM, including a business meeting and a "continental breakfast and idea exchange" on applied communication, as well as panels on program evaluation and intervention strategies, supervisory communication (with equal representation of practitioners and academics), communication and learning in business, the role of the applied communication consultant, the physician–patient relationship as a model for organizational consulting, and one on communication problems in academia, cosponsored with the Association for Communication Administration. The most memorable, and controversial, program concerned "Certifying the Communication Specialist." Chaired by William Eadie, the program involved short presentations by several academics, followed by responses from several practitioners. The most notable presentation came from Davis, one of the respondent–practitioners, who told the large crowd in no uncertain terms that SCA should not become involved in certifying practitioners. After that program, the issue was dropped and has not been considered seriously since then.

The regional communication associations also were beginning to demonstrate an interest in the idea of "applied communication." The Eastern Speech Association created a section in 1976 with Gerald Phillips (Pennsylvania State University) as its first chairperson (for whom NCA later named its award for distinguished applied communication scholarship) and Donna Sacket of Prudential Life Insurance as vice chairperson (Wolvin, n.d.). In 1979, the Southern Speech Communication Association (SSCA) had its first programs on applied communication—a panel chaired by Hickson and cosponsored by the Communication Theory and Speech Education divisions on "Communication Applications," and another program consisting of five papers on "Applied Communication Research" sponsored by association Vice President Carl Kell. Two years later, the Communication Theory Division, again, sponsored an applied communication panel, titled "Applied Communication Research, 1981," also chaired by Hickson. (Interestingly, the call for papers for that SSCA program appeared in the November 1979 issue of *JACR;* p. 134.) In 1982, an Applied Communication Caucus was listed as a sponsor of panels, and in 1985, the Applied Communication Division was founded officially, with Deborah Weider-Hatfield as its first chair and Karl Krayer as vice chair. Neither of the other regional communication associations, Western or Central, ever formed an applied unit, although both now house applied work within other interest groups.

By 1980, SCA's Applied Communication Section had grown to 478 members (Faules, Kline, Parrella, Work, & Rudolph, 1981), and *JACR* had been published for 7 years. In 1980, Hickson ran a brief advertisement in SCA's *Spectra*, titled "Journal for Sale," hoping that someone would relieve him of the responsibility of producing the journal and assuring that the journal continued. The advertisement caught the attention of several communication faculty members at the University of South Florida (USF).

The Development of the Journal and the Section

The Department of Communication at USF had a regionally known and respected master's program. Its faculty included John Sisco (department chair), Jon Keith Jensen, David Carter, and Kenneth Cissna (who had joined the department in 1979). The faculty believed that publishing a journal, even a small and fledgling one, might improve the department and publicize its efforts, and the journal's focus on applied communication seemed consistent with the department's emphases. Thinking back on those times, Carter wrote that acquiring the journal was "one of many means of enhancing the quality and recognition of our programs" and served to "establish a voice in the application of communication theories to 'real-world' issues of the day" (personal communication, December 9, 2004). Consequently, arrangements were made for USF to purchase *JACR* from Hickson, assuming the journal's name, ownership of the copyright on the first eight volumes, and physical possession of the back issues, which the department at USF hoped might be sold. Jensen became its first editor, with Cissna serving as coeditor, a term that presumably provided some undefined status. Michael Lewis was named book review editor; Nancy Newell Taylor served as business manager; and Carter, Sisco, and Bryan Burgess of USF's General Counsel's office completed the Publication Board. They dropped the "s" that Hickson had given to the word *communication* in the journal title, and, no doubt going unnoticed by many, slightly renamed it the *Journal of Applied Communication Research*, the name that has continued to the present.

Under Jensen's direction, the team set about promoting the journal and producing its first issue under USF ownership. Jensen described his conception of applied communication and the journal this way:

> To many, the phrase "applied communication" denotes the use of principles, procedures, methods, or techniques, in non-university settings. Hearing the phrase "applied communication," some think of their consulting work, others of training people in specific skills, and others recall that study they read that didn't occur on a campus, didn't fit the formulas for an experiment, but made good sense and was interesting.
>
> Of course, all of these may be applied communication; for any individual, any one may be. But as we begin our ambitious task of publishing a journal titled "Applied Communication Research," we feel, as an editorial board, and I feel, as editor, a need to understand how each and all of the meanings we have for "Applied Communication" can coexist and all contribute to our understanding of what it means to "communicate."[6]

Although Hickson (1973) envisioned a journal of situation-specific, microlevel studies that used participant–observation methods, and was aimed at achieving social relevance, the focus shifted slightly at USF. The "Notice to Contributors" for the issues published at USF included this statement of publication policy: "The *Journal of Applied Communication Research* publishes articles focusing on questions and problems regarding pragmatic social phenomena addressed through the analysis of human communication." Furthermore, it stated, "It is the intent of the Publication Board that the articles not be characterized by any particular context, methodology, epistemology, or conclusions."

Having shaped the first USF issue of *JACR*, Jensen died unexpectedly the evening of July 8, 1981, without seeing the page proofs of that issue, which were waiting in his department mailbox to review the next day. Cissna became editor and Carter coeditor, but the focus of the journal remained unchanged and the same policy statement continued to appear.

The journal continued to face many of the same issues it experienced during Hickson's ownership and editorship, including that the range of submissions was not nearly as broad as the conceptualization of applied communication research offered by the editor. The next year, Cissna used an "Editor's Note" to explain his conception of applied communication research and to elaborate on the policy statement developed by Jensen and the initial Publication Board of the journal. Applied communication research, Cissna (1982b) wrote, "contributes to knowledge by answering a real, pragmatic, social question or by solving a real, pragmatic, social problem…through the analysis of human communication" (pp. iii–iv). Thus, applied communication was not considered to be isomorphic with organizational communication, although some applied communication is conducted in organizations and some organizational communication scholarship is applied. Applied communication research, Cissna maintained, did not require researchers to adopt or eschew any particular research methods, or to use or avoid using quantitative designs and statistical analysis.

Shortly thereafter, in an effort to enhance the stature of the journal, Cissna (1984) published acceptance and rejection statistics for the 4 years that USF had published *JACR*, showing that only 16% of unsolicited manuscripts had been published. Although this figure was down considerably from the early years of *JACR*, nearly half the published articles were "thematic" or "invited," categories with higher rates of acceptance. Equally important, the number of unsolicited manuscripts submitted had more than doubled from 17.5 during Hickson's ownership to more than 40 per year.

During the years that USF owned *JACR*, a number of important statements about applied communication research were published in outlets other than that journal. A series of "Research Editorials" appeared in *Spectra* under the direction of SCA's Research Board and its chair, Roderick Hart of the University of Texas. Many of those editorials addressed issues related to applied communication research, including "Researchers as Brethren" by Phillips (1981, p. 2), in which he asserted that "pure research is nothing more than the preliminary phases of applied research," and Ronald Gordon's (1982) take on "practical theory" (see Barge & Craig, this volume). The most provocative of the essays, by Donald Ellis (1982), called applied communication "The Shame of Speech Communication" for being "an intellectual whorehouse" that was "narrow, theoretically vacuous, without a research base, and, just as an aside, morally degenerate and politically naïve" (p. 1). This essay caused quite a stir and even occasioned another research editorial in response contesting it (Hugenberg & Robinson, 1982), as well as a number of letters to the editor. Perhaps the most significant of the editorials, though, in terms of its long-term impact, was Eadie's (1982, p. 1) essay, in which he made "The Case for Applied Communication Research," arguing that "applied communication…represents a kind of research" rather than, as with SCA's Applied Communication Section, merely a place of employment. Eadie had been emboldened to write his essay because of the success of Browning's term as chair of APCOM, where research rather than consulting practice had been the focus of the convention programming, as well as because of the connection that Cissna had begun to forge between APCOM and *JACR* (see below). That same year, SCA's Legislative Council voted to establish an Organizational Communication Division, which helped to mark further the distinction between applied and organizational communication research (see also Frey & SunWolf, this volume).

These years also saw important articles about applied communication research published in other scholarly journals in the field. Hickson (1983) proposed, in an article published in the *Southern Speech Communication Journal* (*SSCJ*), making ethnomethodology and participant observation the primary methods for applied communication research. Gerald Miller and Michael Sunnafrank (1984) argued for theoretically grounded applied communication research in the *Quarterly Journal of Speech*. Dan O'Hair (1988) edited a thematic issue of *SSCJ* on "Relational Communication in Applied Contexts." In addition, book-length works concerning applied communication began to appear, including John Cragan and Donald Shield's (1981) *Applied Communication Research: A Dramatistic Approach* and an applied communication book series under the editorship of Teresa Thompson published by Lawrence Erlbaum Associates (e.g., Nussbaum, 1989; Ray & Donohew, 1990), which included what might now be looked upon as the first effort at producing a "handbook" of applied communication, although it was not called that then (O'Hair & Kreps, 1990). In addition, during the late 1980s, other journals with applied bents were developed by commercial publishers, including Erlbaum's *Health Communication* under the editorship of Thompson and Sage's *Management Communication Quarterly*, coedited by JoAnne Yates, Christine Kelly, and Paul Feingold.

The USF group continued to be concerned with having enough manuscripts of sufficient quality to fill the journal. One of the strategies that Cissna and his colleagues used to assure that they could publish the journal, which continued to be a semiannual publication of approximately 80 pages, even as they developed an acceptance rate that was comparable to the major national communication journals, was to publish issues that addressed particular themes, with articles derived from sources other than the unsolicited manuscripts sent to the editor. One useful source of manuscripts involved collaboration between *JACR* and SCA's Applied Communication Section. From 1981 to 1983, APCOM issued a special call for convention papers on a particular theme, with the best work being considered for publication in *JACR*. The first symposium, on "Conversation in Interviews," appeared in the Fall 1981 issue, featuring three articles (Adams, 1981; Ragan & Hopper, 1981; Watson & Ragsdale, 1981) and a brief response (Meyer, 1981). A second APCOM-related symposium on "Ethics in Communication Consulting" appeared in the Fall 1982 issue, with articles by Browning (1982) and Teresa Harrison (1982). The final, jointly produced symposium, "Strategies for Planned Change" (Cissna, 1983), became a full issue featuring five articles, as well as a set of related book reviews and a review of journals that published work on the topic. Cissna also published two other thematic issues or symposia, including one on "The Application of Communication Theory to Communication Practice" (Cissna, 1982a), which featured articles by seven noted theoreticians of human communication, including Ernest Bormann, Frank Dance, B. Aubrey Fisher, Stephen Littlejohn, and Lee Thayer, and another thematic issue guest-edited by David Smith (1985) of USF that included five articles on doctor–patient communication. The tradition of special issues, symposia, and forums, prominent during USF's ownership, continued to serve *JACR* well in future years.

After 5 years as editor, Cissna stepped down, and his colleague, D. Thomas Porter, assumed the editor position. Porter continued the policies and practices of the previous USF editors, although his term was a brief one. He published only three issues, after which most of the issues were thematic and edited by a USF faculty member: Smith (1988) edited a second issue on "Values in Health Communication"; Arthur Bochner (1989) produced an issue on "Applying Communication Theory to Family Practice"; Lynne Webb (1990), of the University of Florida, served as guest editor for an issue on "Communication and Aging"; and Carol Jablonski (1990) edited an issue on "Organizational Rhetoric." The one issue from this period that contained unsolicited manuscripts was described as the product of the "Board of Directors," a group that then included Bochner, Burgess, Cissna, Navita Cummings James, Loyd Pettegrew, Smith, and Marsha Vanderford.

The most significant development in the late 1980s, however, was an interest on the part of SCA in producing an applied communication publication. Although informal discussions began as early as 1985, in 1987, SCA's Administrative Committee, under the guidance of James Chesebro, Chair of SCA's Publications Board, began exploring a number of options for an applied publication, ranging from a slick magazine format similar to *Psychology Today* to a traditional scholarly journal much like SCA's existing journals (Chesebro, 1987; Chesebro & Shields, 1988). Those who were involved agreed that an SCA-sponsored applied publication should be part of its "outreach strategy" to the general public and that readability was a significant feature. In letters written to Chesebro by Bochner (March 12, 1987), Cissna (March 12, 1987), and Porter (February 27, 1987), Board of Directors of *JACR* at USF made clear that it supported having SCA assume ownership and control of the journal, thinking that it was in the best interests of the journal and of the emerging field of applied communication, and certainly not wanting SCA to develop a competing applied communication journal. Eventually, SCA decided to purchase *JACR* from USF, issuing its call for a new editor in February 1989.

To mark the transfer of *JACR* from USF to SCA (as well as to inaugurate the new doctoral program in communication at USF), Robert Avery, Chair of SCA's Publications Board, and Bochner, Chair of USF's Communication Department, explored holding a conference on applied communication in Tampa. Cissna was designated as conference director and the "Applied Communication in the 21st Century: Tampa Conference on Applied Communication" occurred in March 1991. All of the major conference papers, along with most of the replies to those papers, a series of postconference reflections, and appendices that documented the conference (naming the conference participants, explaining the conference design, and listing the recommendations of the conference) were subsequently published in book form (Cissna, 1995).

Eadie was chosen as the first editor of *JACR* published under the auspices of SCA. Eadie (1990) established three criteria for applied communication research: That the research (1) "thoroughly explores a specific communication problem or situation, or its results are immediately applicable to specific communication problems or situations"; (2) "reveals significant and substantive information about the situation being explored"; and (3) "is securely based in theory but its purpose is not immediate theory building" (p. 2). Eadie's first issue, which appeared in the summer of 1991, invited leading scholars to address the agenda of applied communication research and included articles by renowned organizational theorists Karl Weick (with Browning, 1991) and James March (1991), as well as articles by communication scholars Browning and Leonard Hawes (1991), Timothy Plax (1991), and Gary Kreps, Lawrence Frey, and O'Hair (1991). *JACR* flourished as an SCA journal, becoming a quarterly publication, with 96 pages per issue, although the number of pages has varied since then. Under Eadie's editorship, it took its outreach mission seriously, and, in addition to a section for "research reports," included two new sections "applications" (review essays on how research findings could be applied) and "commentaries." At the urging of James Gaudino, SCA's Executive Director, Eadie worked with Science Press, the printing house for SCA's journals, to design a more reader-friendly format, one that included pictures of the authors, a 4-color cover and 2-color printing, and wide margins containing pull-quotes.

Eadie favored publishing a wide range of scholarship and discouraged proposals for thematic issues. However, his editorial board's response to the treatment of both Anita Hill and Clarence Thomas during Thomas's confirmation hearings for a seat on the U.S. Supreme Court convinced Eadie that *JACR* could be used for activism purposes, if pursued in a scholarly manner. Consequently, he accepted a proposal by Julia Wood, a member of his editorial board, to publish a symposium on sexual harassment. Wood's proposal was groundbreaking, as she wanted both to expose and analyze sexual harassment episodes that had occurred within the communication discipline. Eadie put out a call for such stories and received 37 of them, mostly from women, but a few from men (including one by an individual who had been accused of sexual harassment). The stories were turned over anonymously to Bryan Taylor and Charles Conrad (1992) and Mary Strine (1992), who wrote "microlevel" and "macrolevel" assessments, respectively, of them. The stories referenced by those scholars in their assessments were printed in the journal, guest-edited by Wood (1992), so that readers could view the "data" from which these scholars were working. That special issue concluded by acknowledging those individuals who wished to be recognized as having contributed stories, some of whom were referred to in the analyses.

Eadie (1993) reported that many people continued to misunderstand applied communication to mean organizational communication, despite over 20 years of efforts by editors Hickson, Cissna, and himself, as well as others (e.g., O'Hair & Kreps, 1990) to suggest otherwise. Although the journal received and published its share of studies of organizations, Eadie also published studies on instruction (in educational, corporate, and public settings); health, environmental, and risk communication; political communication; intergroup communication; media; new communication technologies; and the treatment of communication apprehension. He even received a submission to *JACR*, which was published during the next editor's term, that included as a coauthor a man who was homeless (Schmitz, Rogers, Phillips, & Paschal, 1995). The published research included articles utilizing a range of quantitative, qualitative, and rhetorical methods.

In the end, although very successful, the format of the new *JACR* also was very expensive; Eadie exhausted his page allotment well before his final issue, and SCA's Publications Board decided to switch to a style that made *JACR* conform to the other NCA journals. The "Applications" section was dropped after Eadie's editorship concluded, along with pictures of the authors, wide margins, and pull-quotes, and commentaries became less frequent. Rather than something new and innovative, *JACR* subsequently became much like the other NCA journals because both the high number of submissions and their quality required that the pages of *JACR* should be devoted to publishing as much as possible of the best available applied communication scholarship.

Wood was named the second SCA editor of *JACR*. She reported that selecting her as editor, as with Eadie's selection as SCA's first *JACR* editor, "conveyed the message that *JACR* was about more than organizational communication" (personal communication, December 4, 2004), as neither of them were known as organizational communication scholars (interestingly, nor were Hickson or Cissna). To avoid any inference that organizational communication somehow was a defining feature of applied communication or of the journal, Wood solicited a special issue on applied family communication guest-edited by Gail Whitchurch and Webb (1995).

Not until the third SCA editor, David Seibold, did SCA select a scholar who significantly identified with organizational communication. Compared with his predecessors, Seibold's conception of applied communication research favored somewhat more "theory-driven socially relevant research" from authors who were "committed to advancing scholarship" (personal communication, December 16, 2004). As Seibold (2000) wrote later, whatever differences there might have been between his conception and those of his predecessors were less matters of boundaries than of emphases. He also attempted, not as successfully as he wished, to encourage submission of reports of large-scale, often grant-supported, research projects (personal communication, December 16, 2004). Seibold also commissioned several special issues, including two especially significant ones that suggested alternative metaphors and directions for applied communication scholarship. Frey (1998), following up on a brief symposium in *Communication Studies* 2 years earlier (see Frey, Pearce, Pollack, Artz, & Murphy, 1996), in a full issue of the journal, presented the case for putting applied communication research to the service of social justice and included five exemplar studies that promoted social justice, as well as a response essay by Barnett Pearce (1998; see also Frey & SunWolf, this volume; Seeger, Sellnow, Ulmer, & Novak, this volume). Sandra Petronio (1999) served as guest editor for an issue on translating scholarship into practice, and Ellen Edwards and Howard Giles (1998) produced an issue of the journal on intergenerational communication.

Of the next four editors, O'Hair, Joann Keyton, Timothy Sellnow, and, currently, Laura Stafford, Keyton is most identified with organizational communication. O'Hair attempted to encourage more policy-making research, but, like Seibold, was somewhat disappointed with his success in attracting such submissions (personal communication, December 6, 2004). O'Hair also commissioned, in 2000, a special forum on defining communication scholarship, which included contributions from several previous editors of *JACR* (Cissna, 2000; Eadie, 2000; Seibold, 2000; and Wood, 2000), as well as contributions from Keyton (2000; who became the next editor) and from Frey (2000). During her editorship, Keyton implemented, to good effect, a requirement (that continues today) that all work published in *JACR* include a section on how the results could be applied. These editors also continued the practice of devoting journal space to special issues, with O'Hair publishing special issues or forums on communication and managed care (K. Miller, 2001) and on funded research (Buller & Slater, 2002); Keyton having issues devoted to irrationality in organizations (Tretheway & Ashcraft, 2004) and Institutional Review Boards (Kramer & Dougherty, 2005), and Sellnow publishing a special issue on the 2005 Atlantic hurricane season (Gouran & Seeger, 2007); a special section on "Best Practices in Risk and Crisis Communication" (Venette, 2006), and a special forum titled "Toward Purposeful and Practical Models of Engaged Scholarship" (Barge, Simpson, & Shockley-Zalabak, 2008), as well as a series of commentaries on translating research into practice (see Petronio, 2007). Stafford has planned a special issue on health and healing from a narrative perspective, as well as one on communication and distance, and a joint forum between *JACR* and *Communication Monographs*, in which four scholars (Celeste Condit, Lawrence Frey, Mary Lee Hummert, and Matthew Seeger) answer the question, "Has communication research made a difference?" and readers respond to those essays. Stafford also has initiated a feature, called "In Point of Practice," wherein an established scholar synthesizes his or her program of research and offers practical applications, and she published the first autoethnography to appear in *JACR* (Tillman, 2009).

After SCA's acquisition of *JACR*, the association also initiated an applied communication book series under the editorship of Kreps. The series was short-lived, but published one film (Adelman & Schultz, 1992) and nine books. In 1994, it became apparent to the SCA leadership that this publication venture was bigger and more expensive than it had anticipated. Although the SCA book series was terminated, Kreps started two new applied communication book series with Hampton Press, which had copublished the earlier volumes, one on "Health Communication" and the other on "Communication as a Social Organization," both of which continue to the present. Other applied communication books also appeared, including Cragan and Shields (1995) and textbooks by Buddenbaum and Novak (2001) and Harris (1993).

In 1995, SCA's Applied Communication Section successfully petitioned SCA's Legislative Council to become a division, a move that changed its identity in the SCA structure formally from a unit for individuals who shared having nonacademic employers to a unit whose content represented a substantive part of the discipline. Simultaneously, the Legislative Council approved the establishment of a Training and Development Commission, a move that effectively removed the concerns of training and development practitioners from being a major focus of APCOM. As a division, APCOM instituted awards for an outstanding article and book, as well as awards that honored top convention papers. In 1994, a year before APCOM formally became a division, SCA inaugurated the annual Gerald M. Phillips Award for Distinguished Applied Communication Scholarship, which was an association-wide award that honored a body of applied communication research. Given first to the University of Iowa's Samuel Becker, subsequent recipients, in chronological order, include Everett Rogers, Donald Cushman, Patricia Hayes Andrews, Kreps, Seibold, Frey, Michael Hecht, Eileen Berlin Ray, Harold L. Goodall, Jr., Brent D. Ruben, Philip Palmgreen, Lawrence Rosenfeld, Wood, and Cissna. Since its inception, APCOM's outstanding article award has been given to three articles on social issues in communication in organizations, three articles on social influence processes (one in a health setting and two in group settings), and one article each on risk communication, crisis communication, and communication and social justice.

Conclusion

In 1997, the Speech Communication Association changed its name to the National Communication Association. The series of events that began in 1968 with a recommendation to change the association's name to include the word *communication*, along with recommendations for the discipline's scholars to engage in socially relevant research, came full circle with the elimination of the word *speech* from the association's name at a time coincident with the maturation of the concept of applied communication research. That concept now is situated comfortably within the lexicon of communication scholars, even as applied communication scholars continue to contest its precise meaning (see Frey & SunWolf, this volume). Members of the communication discipline now accept having a strong applied dimension to the field's scholarship, and articles published in *JACR* are respected for their quality and recognized for the scope of their contributions to the field. In fact, recent analyses of communication journals indicated that *JACR* had moved up from 42nd of the 44 journals ranked in 2003 to 27th of 42 journals ranked in 2004 (Zarefsky, 2005) and to 20th in 2007 (Taylor & Francis Group, 2008).

Although prompted most immediately by the dramatic events of the 1960s both from within the communication field and outside it, the transformation of the field to one that accepts applied communication scholarship was rooted in older concerns, ones that the field has faced throughout its history: achieving academic respectability, developing a research-based body of knowledge, contributing to solving social problems, and informing the public of the potential uses of communication knowledge.[7] It is likely that these themes will recur as the field of communication continues to develop in the 21st century, with applied communication research as a robust contributor to its scholarly dialogue.

Notes

1. We acknowledge that the roots of the communication discipline are ancient and that some type of study of communication has been part of formal education from its earliest recorded times. We begin our story, however, at the time when U.S. universities were separating faculties into distinct academic "disciplines," and from this standpoint, communication is a relatively new field of study.
2. The conferees wrestled with what to call the discipline other than speech. Some advocated changing the name to "communication," but such a change was disputed by claims that the

"speech" tradition would be lost in doing so. Conferees compromised on "speech-communication," but the hyphen between the words was dropped quickly by most users, including those in the Speech Association of America, in favor of the compound noun speech communication.

3. During the 8 years that Hickson served as editor of *JACR*, he coauthored one article in the journal (in addition to a brief, lead essay in the inaugural issue), and Stacks authored another.

4. The new interest group structure did not include a unit devoted to the study of organizational communication; consequently, scholars interested in that topic were drawn to the Applied Communication Section as a possible home for their work within SCA.

5. The early editions of the *APCOM Newsletter* were neither dated nor numbered, although we have been able to reconstruct the dates and order by examining the texts of the issues. Cissna was given copies of several early newsletters, as well as the mission statement, by Andrew Wolvin.

6. These two paragraphs, handwritten on a single page of a legal pad, were among Jensen's papers that were found in his office after his death.

7. NCA recently launched a new effort to connect the scholarship of the field to the general public with *Communication Currents*, a free, online, Web-based "ezine," under the editorship of Keyton and tailored to a public audience (see http://www.communicationcurrents.com). Now in its fourth year, whether this e-zine will result in the communication field becoming better known and respected by the general public is yet to be determined.

References

Adams, K. L. (1981). Question/answer adjacency pairs in a performance appraisal interview. *Journal of Applied Communication Research, 9*, 72–84.

Adelman, M. B. (Producer), & Schultz, P. (Director). (1992). *The pilgrim must embark: Living in community* [Motion picture]. Chicago: Terra Nova Films.

Applied Communication Section—Speech Communication Association. (n.d.). *Mission statement*.

Ayres, H. J., Brand, V. R., & Faules, D. F. (1973). An assessment of the flow of communication in nursing teams. *Journal of Applied Communications Research, 1*, 75–90.

Barge, J. K., Simpson, J. L., & Shockley-Zalabeck, P. (Eds.). (2008). Toward purposeful and practical models of engaged scholarship [Special forum]. *Journal of Applied Communication Research, 36*, 243–297.

Blankenship, J. (2001). *Marie Hochmuth Nichols: President of the National Communication Association, 1969*. Retrieved May 20, 2005, from http://www.natcom.org/nca/Template2.asp?bid=1212

Blumenfeld, E. R. (1976). Childrearing literature as an object of content analysis. *Journal of Applied Communications Research, 4*, 75–88.

Bochner, A. P. (Ed.). (1989). Applying communication theory to family process [Special issue]. *Journal of Applied Communication Research, 17*(1–2).

Browning, L. D. (1982). The ethics of intervention: A communication consultant's apology. *Journal of Applied Communication Research, 10*, 101–116.

Browning, L. D., & Hawes, L. C. (1991). Style, process, surface, context: Consulting as postmodern art. *Journal of Applied Communication Research, 19*, 32–54.

Buck, J. F. (1968). The effects of Negro and White dialectal variations upon attitudes of college students. *Speech Monographs, 35*, 181–186.

Buddenbaum, J. M., & Novak, K. B. (2001). *Applied communication research*. Ames: Iowa State University Press.

Buller, D. B., & Slater, M. D. (Eds.). (2002). Funded research [Special forum]. *Journal of Applied Communication Research, 30*, 314–417.

Burgess, P. G. (1968). The rhetoric of Black power: A moral demand? *Quarterly Journal of Speech, 54*, 122–133.

Chesebro, J. (1987, March 23). *Chesebro to SCA Administrative Committee.* Unpublished memorandum.

Chesebro, J. W., & Shields, D. C. (1988, September). *Action item.* Unpublished memorandum to Speech Communication Association Administrative Committee.

Cissna, K. N. (Ed.). (1982a). Application of communication theory to communication practice [Special issue]. *Journal of Applied Communication Research, 10*(1).

Cissna, K. N. (1982b). Editor's note: What is applied communication research? *Journal of Applied Communication Research, 10,* iii–v.

Cissna, K. N. (Ed.). (1983). Communication strategies for planned change [Special issue]. *Journal of Applied Communication Research, 11*(1).

Cissna, K. N. (1984). Editor's note. *Journal of Applied Communication Research, 12,* iii–iv.

Cissna, K. N. (Ed.). (1995). *Applied communication in the 21st century.* Mahwah, NJ: Erlbaum.

Cissna, K. N. (2000). Applied communication research in the 21st century. *Journal of Applied Communication Research, 28,* 169–173.

Cohen, H. (1994). *The history of speech communication: The emergence of a discipline, 1914–1945.* Annandale, VA: Speech Communication Association.

Conquergood, D. (1988). Health theatre in a Hmong refugee camp: Performance, communication, and culture. *TDR: Journal of Performance Studies, 32,* 174–208.

Conquergood, D. (1991a). "For the nation!" How street gangs problematize patriotism. In R. Troester & C. Kelley (Eds.), *Peacemaking through communication* (pp. 8–21). Annandale, VA: Speech Communication Association.

Conquergood, D. (1991b). Rethinking ethnography: Towards a critical cultural politics. *Communication Monographs, 58,* 179–194.

Conquergood, D. (1992). Life in Big Red: Struggles and accommodations in a Chicago polyethnic tenement. In L. Lamphere (Ed.,), *Structuring diversity: Ethnographic perspectives on the new immigration* (pp. 95–144). Chicago: University of Chicago Press.

Conquergood, D. (1994). Homeboys and hoods: Gang communication and cultural space. In L. R. Frey (Ed.), *Group communication in context: Studies of natural groups* (pp. 23–55). Hillsdale, NJ: Erlbaum.

Conquergood, D. (1995). Between rigor and relevance: Rethinking applied communication. In K. N. Cissna (Ed.), *Applied communication in the 21st century* (pp. 79–96). Mahwah, NJ: Erlbaum.

Cragan, J. F., & Shields, D. C. (1981). *Applied communication research: A dramatistic approach.* Prospect Heights, IL: Waveland Press.

Cragan, J. F., & Shields, D. C. (1995). *Symbolic theories in applied communication research: Bormann, Burke, and Fisher.* Cresskill, NJ: Hampton Press.

Craig, R. T. (1989). Communication as a practical discipline. In B. Dervin, L. Grossberg, B. J. O'Keefe, & E. Wartella (Eds.), *Rethinking communication: Vol. 1. Paradigm issues* (pp. 97–122). Newbury Park, CA: Sage.

Cronkhite, G. L. (1969). Out of the ivory palaces: A proposal for useful research in communication and decision. In R. J. Kibler & L. L. Barker (Eds.), *Conceptual frontiers in speech-communication: Report of the New Orleans Conference on Research and Instructional Development* (pp. 113–135). New York: Speech Association of America.

Daniel, J. L. (1995). *Changing the players and the game: A personal account of the Speech Communication Association Black Caucus origins.* Annandale, VA: Speech Communication Association.

Eadie, W. F. (1982, November). The case for applied communication research. *Spectra, 18,* 1, 4.

Eadie, W. F. (1990, November). Being applied: Communication research comes of age [Special issue]. *Journal of Applied Communication Research,* 1–6.

Eadie, W. F. (1993). Editorial. *Journal of Applied Communication Research, 21,* v–vi.

Eadie, W. F. (2000). Changing boundaries, changing expectations, changing results. *Journal of Applied Communication Research, 28,* 174–177.

Edwards, H., & Giles, H. (Eds.). (1998). Applied research in language and intergenerational communication [Special issue]. *Journal of Applied Communication Research, 26*(1).

Ellis, D. (1982, March). The shame of speech communication. *Spectra, 18*, 1–2.

Ewbanks, H. L. (1952). Teaching speech for human relations. *Speech Teacher, 1*, 9–13.

Faules, D., Kline, J., Parrella, G., Work, J., & Rudolph, E. (1981, November). *Just what is the Applied Communication Section anyway?* Paper presented at the meeting of the Speech Communication Association, Los Angeles, CA.

Feldman, R. A., & Jorgensen, D. D. (1974). Communication and marital conflict. *Journal of Applied Communications Research, 2*, 53–66.

Flannery, G. V. (1973). Applied communications in broadcasting: Documenting the documentary. *Journal of Applied Communications Research, 1*, 49–59.

Frey, L. R. (Ed.). (1998). Communication and social justice research [Special issue]. *Journal of Applied Communication Research, 26*(2).

Frey, L. R. (2000). To be applied or not to be applied, that isn't even the question; but wherefore art thou, applied communication researcher? Reclaiming applied communication research and redefining the role of the researcher. *Journal of Applied Communication Research, 28*, 178–182.

Frey, L. R., Pearce, W. B., Pollock, M. A., Artz, L., Murphy, B. A. O. (1996). Looking for justice in all the wrong places: On a communication approach to social justice. *Communication Studies, 47*, 110–127.

Goldhaber, G. M. (1993). *Organizational communication* (6th ed.). Madison, WI: Brown & Benchmark.

Gonchar, R. M., & Hahn, D. F. (1973). Richard Nixon and presidential mythology. *Journal of Applied Communications Research, 1*, 25–48.

Gordon, R. (1982, October). Practical theory. *Spectra, 18*, 1–2.

Gouran, D. S., & Seeger, M. W. (2007). The 2005 Atlantic hurricane season [Special issue]. *Journal of Applied Communication Research, 35*(1).

Gray, G. W. (1964). The founding of the Speech Association of America: Happy birthday. *Quarterly Journal of Speech, 50*, 342–345.

Greenbaum, H. H., & Falcione, R. L. (1975). *Organizational communication abstracts 1974.* Urbana, IL & Austin, TX: American Business Communication Association & International Communication Association.

Gregg, R. B., & McCormack, A. J. (1968). "Whitey" goes to the ghetto: A personal chronicle of a communication experience with Black youths. *Today's Speech, 16*(3), 25–30.

Harris, T. E. (1993). *Applied organizational communication: Perspectives, principles, and pragmatics.* Hillsdale, NJ: Erlbaum.

Harrison, T. M. (1982). Toward an ethical framework for communication consulting. *Journal of Applied Communication Research, 10*, 87–100.

Hickson, M., III (1971). *A systems analysis of the communication adaptation in a community action agency.* Unpublished doctoral dissertation, Southern Illinois University, Carbondale.

Hickson, M., III (1973). Applied communications research: A beginning point for social relevance. *Journal of Applied Communications Research, 1*, 1–5.

Hickson, M., III (Ed.). (1975). Organizational communication—1975 [Special symposium]. *Journal of Applied Communications Research, 3*, 103–116.

Hickson, M., III (1983). Ethnomethodology: The promise of applied communication research? *Southern Speech Communication Journal, 48*, 182–195.

Hugenberg, L. W., & Robinson, D. J. (1982, June). Response to Don Ellis' essay: "The Shame of Speech Communication." *Spectra, 18*, 1–2.

Jablonski, C. (Ed.). (1990). Organizational rhetoric [Special issue]. *Journal of Applied Communication Research, 18*(2).

Keyton, J. (2000). Applied communication research should be practical. *Journal of Applied Communication Research, 28*, 166–168.

Kibler, R. J., & Barker, L. L. (Eds.). (1969). *Conceptual frontiers in speech communication: Report of the New Orleans Conference on Research and Instructional Development.* New York: Speech Association of America.

King, A. S. (1974). The eye in advertising. *Journal of Applied Communications Research, 2,* 1–12.

Kramer, M. W., & Dougherty, D. S. (Eds.). (2005). Communication research and institutional review boards [Special issue]. *Journal of Applied Communication Research, 33*(3).

Kreps, G. L., Frey, L. R., & O'Hair, D. (1991). Applied communication research: Scholarship that can make a difference. *Journal of Applied Communication Research, 19,* 71–87.

March, J. G. (1991). Organizational consultants and organizational research. *Journal of Applied Communication Research, 19,* 20–31.

Meyer, J. L. (1981). Response to "Conversation in interviews." *Journal of Applied Communication Research, 9,* 104–108.

Miller, G. R., & Sunnafrank, M. J. (1984). Theoretical dimensions of applied communication research. *Quarterly Journal of Speech, 70,* 255–263.

Miller, K. (Ed.). (2001). Communication in the age of managed care [Special issue]. *Journal of Applied Communication Research, 29*(2).

Nash, R. L. (1967). Teaching speech improvement to the disadvantaged. *Speech Teacher, 16,* 69–73.

Nofsinger, R. E., Jr. (1975). The demand ticket: A conversational device for getting the floor. *Speech Monographs, 42,* 1–9.

Nussbaum, J. F. (Ed.). (1989). *Life-span communication: Normative processes.* Hillsdale, NJ: Erlbaum.

O'Hair, D. (1988). Relational communication in applied communication: Current status and future directions. *Southern Speech Communication Journal, 52,* 317–330.

O'Hair, D. (Ed.). (2000). Defining applied communication scholarship [Special forum]. *Journal of Applied Communication Research, 28,* 164–191.

O'Hair, D., & Kreps, G. L. (Eds.). (1990). *Applied communication theory and research.* Hillsdale, NJ: Erlbaum.

O'Neill, J. M. (1928). After thirteen years. *Quarterly Journal of Speech, 14,* 242–253.

Pearce, W. B. (1998). On putting social justice in the discipline of communication and putting enriched concepts of communication in social justice research and practice. *Journal of Applied Communication Research, 26,* 272–278.

Peterson, J. P. (1975). The teacher as learner: A year with the Choctaws. *Journal of Applied Communications Research, 3,* 1–7.

Petronio, S. (Ed.). (1999). Translating scholarship into practice [Special issue]. *Journal of Applied Communication Research, 27*(2).

Petronio, S. (2007). *JACR* commentaries on translating research into practice. *Journal of Applied Communication Research, 35,* 215–217.

Phillips, G. M. (1981, September). Researchers as brethren. *Spectra, 17,* 2.

Philipsen, G. (1975). Speaking "like a man" in Teamsterville: Culture patterns of role enactment in an urban neighborhood. *Quarterly Journal of Speech, 61,* 13–22.

Plax, T. G. (1991). Understanding applied communication inquiry: Researcher as organizational consultant. *Journal of Applied Communication Research, 19,* 55–70.

Ragan, S. L., & Hopper, R. (1981). Alignment talk in the job interview. *Journal of Applied Communication Research, 9,* 85–103.

Ray, E. B., & Donohew, L. (1990). *Communication and health: Systems and applications.* Hillsdale, NJ: Erlbaum.

Roever, J. E. (1969, October). 250 attend conference. *Spectra, 5,* 4.

Rogers, L. E., & Farace, R. V. (1975). Analysis of relational communication in dyads: New measurement procedures. *Human Communication Research, 1,* 222–239.

Rudolph, E. E. (1973). Informal human communication systems in a large organization. *Journal of Applied Communications Research, 1,* 7–23.

Schmitz, J., Rogers, E. M., Phillips, K., & Paschal, D. (1995). The Public Electronic Network (PEN) and the homeless in Santa Monica. *Journal of Applied Communication Research, 23,* 26–43.

Seibold, D. R. (2000). Applied communication scholarship: Less a matter of boundaries than of emphases. *Journal of Applied Communication Research, 28,* 183–187.

Smith, D. H. (1966). Teaching speech to the culturally disadvantaged. *Speech Teacher, 15,* 140–144.

Smith, D. H. (Ed.). (1985). Doctor–patient communication [Special issue]. *Journal of Applied Communication Research,* 13(2).

Smith, D. H. (Ed.). (1988). Values in health communication [Special issue]. *Journal of Applied Communication Research,* 16(1).

Speech Communication Association. (1977). *Convention program: 63rd annual meeting.* Annandale, VA: Author.

Strine, M. S. (1992). Understanding "how things work": Sexual harassment and academic culture. *Journal of Applied Communication Research, 20,* 391–400.

Taylor & Francis Group. (2008). *Communication titles.* Retrieved May 14, 2008, from http://www.tandf.co.uk/journals/journals.asp?subcategory=SS220000

Taylor, B., & Conrad, C. (1992). Narratives of sexual harassment: Organizational dimensions. *Journal of Applied Communication Research, 20,* 401–418.

Tillman, L. M. (2009). Body and bulimia revisited: Reflections on "A Secret Life." *Journal of Applied Communication Research, 37, 98*–112.

Tretheway, A., & Ashcraft, K. L. (Eds.). (2004). Organized irrationality? Coping with paradox, contradiction, and irony in organizational communication [Special issue]. *Journal of Applied Communication Research,* 32(2).

Venette, S. J. (Ed.). (2006). Best practices in risk and crisis communication [Special section]. *Journal of Applied Communication Research, 34,* 229–262.

Watson, K. W., & Ragsdale, J. D. (1981). Linguistic indices of truthful and deceptive responses to employment interview questions. *Journal of Applied Communication Research, 9,* 59–71.

Weaver, C. H. (1977). A history of the International Communication Association. In B. D. Ruben (Ed.), *Communication yearbook* (Vol. 1, pp. 607–618). New Brunswick, NJ: Transaction Books.

Webb, L. (Ed.). (1990). Communication and aging [Special issue]. *Journal of Applied Communication Research,* 18(2).

Weick, K. E., & Browning, L. D. (1991). Fixing with the voice: A research agenda for applied communication. *Journal of Applied Communication Research, 19,* 1–19.

Whitchurch, G. G., & Webb, L. M. (Eds.). (1995). Applied communication research in families [Special issue]. *Journal of Applied Communication Research,* 23(4).

Winans, J. A. (1915). The need for research. *Quarterly Journal of Public Speaking, 1,* 17–23.

Wolvin, A. (n.d.). Forms applied communication section. *Applied Communication Section Newsletter, 1,* 4.

Wood, J. T. (Ed.). (1992). "Telling our stories": Sexual harassment in the communication discipline [Special section]. *Journal of Applied Communication Research, 20,* 349–418.

Wood, J. T. (2000). Applied communication research: Unbounded and for good reason. *Journal of Applied Communication Research, 28,* 188–191.

Woolbert, C. H. (1917). Conviction and persuasion: The consequences of theory. *Quarterly Journal of Speech, 3,* 249–264.

Woolbert, C. H. (1923). The teaching of speech as an academic discipline. *Quarterly Journal of Speech Education, 9,* 1–18.

Zarefsky, D. (2005, December). Publications board studies ISI data base and "impact factor" analysis. *Spectra, 41,* 1, 6.

2 Across Applied Divides
Great Debates of Applied Communication Scholarship

Lawrence R. Frey
University of Colorado at Boulder

SunWolf
Santa Clara University

> Applied research sets out to contribute to knowledge by answering a real, pragmatic, social question or by solving a real pragmatic, social problem. Applied *communication* research involves such a question or problem of human communication or examines human communication in order to provide an answer or solution to the question or problem. The intent or goal of the inquiry (as manifest in the research report itself) is the hallmark of applied communication research. Applied communication research involves the development of knowledge regarding a real human communication problem or question. (Cissna, 1982, p. iv)

Applied communication scholarship, as this handbook demonstrates, is a well-respected intellectual pursuit that spans (and even pervades) every area of the communication discipline, as attested to, for instance, by the use of the word *applied* in the titles of recent books on such diverse topics as communication studies (Bollinger, 2005), nonverbal communication (Riggio & Feldman, 2005), interpersonal communication (Buzzanell, Sterk, & Turner, 2004; Dailey & Le Poire, 2006; Motley, 2008), organizational communication and public relations (Fine & Schwandt, 2008; Harris & Nelson, 2008; Lamb & McKee, 2005; Oliver, 2004; Veech, 2002), health communication (e.g., Wright & Moore, 2007), intercultural communication (Sharifian & Palmer 2007), performance studies and theater (Nicholson, 2005; Prentki & Preston, 2008), media studies (Rosenberry & Vicker, 2008, Zettl, 2008), and even communication research methods (Buddenbaum & Novak, 2001). Cissna, Eadie, and Hickson's (this volume) historical overview documented how this form of scholarship became institutionalized in the communication discipline. The institutionalization of applied communication scholarship, however, did not come without costs; many great debates, heated arguments, and growing pains occurred along the way, as well as, more recently, nuanced issues and concerns that emerged once the legitimacy of this research had been established.

This chapter provides an intellectual history of some great debates about deep divides characterizing the development of applied communication scholarship. These developmental growing pains include moving from applied communication and organizational communication consulting to applied communication research; deconstructing the basic–applied research dichotomy to link communication theory and application; employing the wide range of available methodologies to produce both rigorous and relevant applied communication scholarship; and, most recently, recognizing the continuum of, but also the chasm between, observational and intervention-oriented applied communication scholarship (see Figure 2.1).

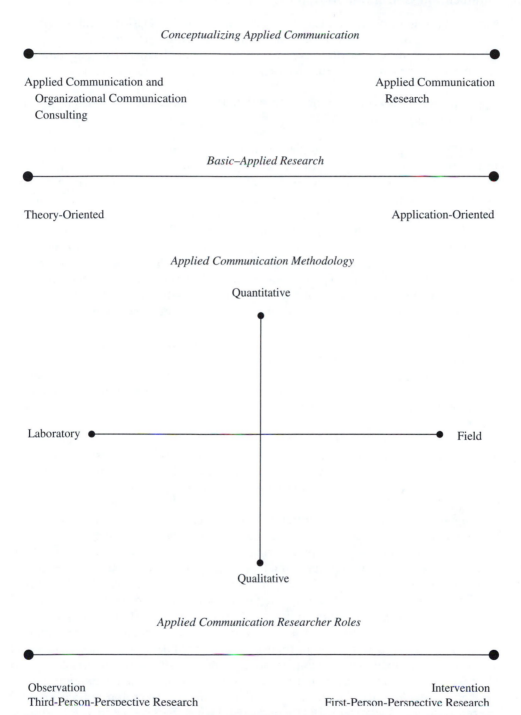

Figure 2.1 Prominent debates and divides in applied communication scholarship.

Across the Great Divide: From Applied Communication and Organizational Communication Consulting to Applied Communication Research

> Most programs in organizational communication, public relations, and advertising are narrow, theoretically vacuous, without a research base, and, just as an aside, morally degenerate and politically naive.... These professional arms of speech communication do a disservice to the true goal of scholarly inquiry. (Ellis, 1982, pp. 1, 2)

> Applied research is crucial to the professional and intellectual development of communication. (Ellis, 1991, p. 122)

Although Ellis's (1982) statement was directed toward professional communication education programs and related outreach efforts (i.e., organizational communication consulting), it was widely interpreted (including by Ellis, 1991) as an indictment of applied communication scholarship that generated fierce counter-responses (see, e.g., Eadie, 1982; Hugenberg & Robinson, 1982). Ellis's (1982) objection to professionally oriented communication programs and activities certainly was contestable, for historically, the "practical discipline" (Craig, 1989, 1995) of communication (dating back at least to antiquity and rhetoric's "original concern with applicability and application"; Weick & Browning, 1991, p. 16) emerged from seeking solutions to practical issues related to communication, such as teaching people to become better speakers in everyday interactions and the public sphere, and to engage in effective communicative practices for democratic group decision making.

More important, however, Ellis (1982) conflated "applied communication" with "applied communication scholarship." Ellis's inability to draw this distinction was understandable given, at the time, that (1) applied research was a relatively new concept in the communication discipline, (2) newly created applied communication graduate education programs were not informed by a research orientation, and (3) consulting and organizational communication (more generally) had been conflated with applied communication scholarship.

First, as the historical overview by Cissna et al. (this volume) made clear, despite the initial focus of communication scholars and educators on applied matters, it took a relatively long time to apply the concept of "applied" to communication *research*—most notably, at the 1968 New Orleans Conference on Research and Instructional Development (Kibler & Barker, 1969), followed shortly thereafter in 1973 by the creation of the *Journal of Applied Communication Research* (*JACR*). Given communication scholars' tendency to emulate the more established social sciences, primarily psychology (Frey, Botan, & Kreps, 2000), it is somewhat surprising that applied communication research did not emerge sooner. After all, the concept had a long history in the social sciences (Hickson, 1973), with, according to the U.S. Library of Congress, the first book on "applied psychology" written in 1833 (Braddock) and the first book on "applied sociology" published in 1883 (Ward); the *Journal of Applied Psychology* appearing in 1917 (see Hall, Baird, & Giessler's foreword and Giessler's article on defining applied psychology in the inaugural issue); Allen's (1927) description of journalism as an "applied social science"; the Social Science Research Council's sponsorship, starting in the late 1920s, of projects connected to public issues, such as the creation of the U.S. Social Security system (Calhoun, 2008); and probably most famous, Lazarsfeld's "administrative" (market and mass communication) research (e.g., Lazarsfeld, 1941) conducted during the 1930s and 1940s to solve clients' specific problems, including his creation in 1944 of the Bureau of Applied Social Research at Columbia University (see, e.g., Barton, 1982; Delia, 1987).

This orientation toward research that produced useful knowledge, however, changed after World War II, with "pure" knowledge or "knowledge for knowledge's sake" taking precedence over applied research, largely because U.S. government financial support shifted from emphasizing practical applications of research knowledge (e.g., the 1887 Hatch Act and 1914 Smith-Lever Act) to privileging basic scientific research (Bylerly & Pielke, 1995; England, 1982; McCall & Groack, 2007), with the social sciences soon emulating that orientation. It took until the late 1960s—perhaps most famously, G. A. Miller's (1969) call in his presidential address at the American Psychological Association convention "to give psychology away" to practitioners, policy makers, and the general public to improve the human condition—for psychology and other social sciences (including communication) to reclaim the concept and significance of applied research (see also Hilgard, 1971).

Second, McCroskey (1979), an early proponent of an applied communication graduate education that represented a "shift from a single-minded emphasis on research and theory generation to one which recognizes the importance of both knowledge generation and the application of that knowledge," argued that this pedagogical approach was most appropriate for "non-research-oriented students" (pp. 353, 356). These non-research-oriented (and non-theory-oriented; see Powers & Love, 1999) applied communication graduate students were to be taught by "high quality practicing communication professionals, people at the top levels of their respective professions" (Steinfatt, 1997, p. 131), to produce, according to Powers and Love's (1999) survey of applied mass communication master's programs, "practitioners with enhanced career potential in the work place" (p. 105; see also Davis & Krapels, 1999). As applied communication scholarship developed, however, applied communication graduate programs—such as those at the University of South Alabama (Stacks & Chalfa, 1981) and Indiana University-Purdue University Indianapolis (Schrader, Mills, & Dick, 2001)—started to emphasize research (and theory) as integral to application (Plax, 1991).

Third, initial conceptions often conflated applied research with consulting. DeMartini (1982), in sociology, and Levy-Leboyer (1988), in psychology, for instance, referred to applied research as "client-centered efforts." In a seminal essay on applied communication scholarship, G. R. Miller and Sunnafrank (1984) contended that "applied research is undertaken after an area of social concern to a sponsoring agency has been identified" (p. 257). Although they were talking about sponsorship of applied communication research by grant-funding agencies, such as the National Science Foundation, most scholars (and practitioners) during the 1980s and 1990s viewed for-profit organizations as the primary sponsor of such research and, consequently, framed applied communication scholarship as a form of, or arising from, communication consulting (e.g., Browning & Hawes, 1991; Cragan & Shields, 1995, 1999; DeWine, 1987; Jarboe, 1992; Lange, 1984; March, 1991; O'Hair, Kreps, & Frey, 1990; Skopec, 1992; Stewart, 1983; Weick & Browning, 1991), with Plax (1991) advancing a "consultancy model for conducting applied communication inquiry" (p. 60).[1] Undoubtedly because of the perceived connection between consulting and applied communication research, relatively early issues of *JACR* featured articles about consulting (e.g., Browning, 1982; Harrison, 1982; Lange, 1984; Stewart, 1983). Indeed, in summarizing the essays in a special issue on "The Agenda for Applied Communication" (Eadie, 1991a) that began the publication of *JACR* by the National Communication Association (NCA), Eadie (1991b), the editor, pointed out that "a common theme running through the essays was the relationship between research and application, mainly through consulting" (p. v). The relationship between applied communication scholarship and consulting was so taken for granted that DeWine (1987) and Kreps, Frey, and O'Hair (1991) identified it as a major misconception about applied communication research (see also Phillips, 1992).

A related misconception that Kreps et al. (1991) identified, stemming, in part, from its conflation with consulting, was viewing applied communication research as being synonymous with "organizational communication research and...concerned exclusively with organizational issues" (p. 78). March (1991, p. 22), for instance, contended that applied communication research "involves gathering systematic data about organizations or speculating about them in a systematic way," and Browning and Hawes (1991) noted that the common image of the applied communication researcher was "an intervener coming into an organization to *alter* its communication" (p. 47). Undoubtedly because of the assumed connection between applied communication research and the organizational context, much of the early work published in *JACR* focused on (for-profit) organizational communication (e.g., Beaver & Jandt, 1973; Falcione, 1974; Rudolph, 1973; Stacks, 1974). Applied communication research, however, as this handbook shows (see especially the fourth section on applied communication research contexts), was then and still is conducted in a wide variety of contexts and addresses many communication issues other than those relevant to organizational settings. Moreover, not all organizational communication research (or research conducted in any other context) necessarily is applied; some of that research addresses philosophical, conceptual, or theoretical issues (Cissna, 1982; Kreps et al., 1991; Seibold, Lemus, Ballard, & Myers, this volume).

As scholars worked through these issues, they moved away from viewing applied communication as nonresearch oriented or research related to organizational communication consulting to conceiving of applied communication *research* that spanned the communication discipline. Although some scholars continued to perceive such research as client centered (e.g., Buddenbaum & Novak, 2001), the great divide between applied communication scholarship and applied communication and organizational communication consulting had been crossed. Crossing that divide explains, in part, Ellis's (1991) epiphany, less than 10 years after his inflammatory statement, about the importance of applied research to the communication discipline. Applied communication scholarship, however, faced an even larger challenge—linking theory and application to deconstruct the supposed divide between basic and applied communication research.

Across the Great Divide: Linking Theory and Application in Applied Communication Research

There is nothing so practical as a good theory. (Lewin, 1951, p. 169)

There is nothing so theoretical as a good application. (Levy-Leboyer, 1988, p. 785)

There is an old saying that there are two types of people: those who divide people into two types or those who do not. Of course, carving out any new discipline, field, area, or approach—in this case, applied communication scholarship—requires simultaneously defining the referent and distinguishing it from related terms—in this case, other forms of scholarship.

Although scholarship can be categorized in various ways,[2] probably the most popular way across the social sciences (Johnson, 1991; O'Hair, 1988) has been to distinguish applied research from basic (pure or "fundamental") research. In essence, *basic research* tests theories (or, more accurately, propositions derived from theories) to advance disciplinary knowledge, whereas *applied research* seeks knowledge to address real-world practical problems.[3]

Distinguishing theory-oriented and practical-oriented research offered an initial way to carve out a niche for applied communication scholarship. It did not take long to realize, however, that drawing a hard distinction between theory and application, and treating basic and applied research as parallel types of scholarship ("practice *and* theory," as Seibold et al., this volume, labeled it, p. 345), was detrimental to those conducting applied communication research. Conquergood (1995) noted that whenever a binary opposition is proposed, "one term is privileged by virtue of its domination over the other term" (p. 80). Not surprisingly, given the emphasis across academic disciplines on generating knowledge for the sake of knowledge, theory-oriented research was privileged over application-oriented research and, consequently, basic researchers were viewed quite differently from applied researchers. As G. R. Miller and Sunnafrank (1984) put it:

> The bright, shiny connotations of the term "pure research" conjure images of persons of unquestioned ability and impeccable ethics pursuing essential theoretical work. Theirs is the seeking after knowledge for its own sake. They are the truly important scholars and their labors culminate in truly significant work.
>
> The images associated with "applied research" are tawdry by comparison. Here are the users and abusers of the substantive knowledge and methods of inquiry produced by the scholarly community. Theirs is the seeking after knowledge and information for self-enhancement: at worst, they are snake oil salesmen who distort and twist knowledge for personal gain; at best, they are naïve scholarly drones who dirty their hands with dull, theoretically trivial labor. (p. 255)

In such a dichotomized world, applied research becomes "prostituted science" (Conquergood, p. 81) conducted by "have-gun-will-travel social science mercenaries" (Sanjek, 1987, p. 168; see also Ellis, 1991; Goodall, 1995; Yep, 2008).[4]

One response to privileging basic over applied communication research was to suggest that it should be the other way around. Phillips (1981) articulated this position when he asserted that "most hard scientists recognize that pure research is nothing more than the preliminary phases of applied research" (p. 2). Other communication scholars did not necessarily argue for the superiority of applied over basic research but pointed out that, ultimately, theory and research must affect application. Thayer (1982, p. 22), for instance, asked the question, "What is a theory *for*?" and answered that it "has to be relevant to some human or social problem" (see also Seibold, 1995), and Craig (1995) argued that "all research in a practical discipline [such as communication] is ultimately pursued not for its own sake but for the sake of practice" (p. 151).

Most applied communication scholars, however, tried to "put Humpty Dumpty back together again" by weaving together theory and application. Most of those attempts assumed the legitimacy of and, thereby, reified the two forms of basic and applied scholarship, but argued for their inherent interdependence. Eadie (1982), for instance, claimed that although

> theoretical and applied communication research have different ends, the two can serve each other. The results of theoretical research can guide the applied researcher toward deciding both what variables to observe and what relationships are likely to exist among those variables. The applied researcher's results can be useful to the theoretical researcher in providing evidence for the replicability of theoretical findings, as well as furnishing negative cases that allow the theorist to revise, to strengthen, and often to add to the power of the theory. (p. 4)

Moving beyond seeing theory and application as separate endeavors that can inform one another, Kreps et al. (1991) categorized studies with regard to their emphasis on theoretical and practical issues. A study that places low emphasis both on theory and practice constitutes poor research; a study emphasizing theory but not practice constitutes the stereotypical view of basic research; and a study that emphasizes application but not theory represents the stereotypical view of applied research. Although there are many studies in-between, Kreps et al. argued that a study demonstrating high concern both for theory and practice

> defies the stereotypes of basic and applied research suggested by the traditional definitional dichotomy, and illustrates what we claim is the best approach to applied communication research, a study that is grounded in theory and designed to solve a practical problem. (p. 75)[5]

Infusing applied studies with theory ("theory *into* practice/theory *from* practice"; Seibold et al., this volume, p. 345) became part and parcel of conducting high-quality applied communication scholarship. G. R. Miller and Sunnafrank (1984, p. 262) claimed that "a concern for developing and testing communication theory is an indispensable dimension of applied communication research"; O'Hair et al. (1990, p. 13) asserted that "applied researchers need to be guided by theory. Underlying all good research is a theoretical position"; and in a special forum of *JACR* on "Defining Applied Communication Scholarship" (O'Hair, 2000a), O'Hair (2000b) concluded that "at least basic communication theorists are making a difference in the lives of applied scholars. I know that I cannot conduct my applied research without them" (p. 165).

The importance of using theory to guide applied communication scholarship became institutionalized in *JACR* when Porter (1986), the editor, explained that "the cornerstone of *JACR's* mission is to provide an outlet for scholars who test communication theory in the crucible of applied communication settings" (p. 67). The emphasis on theory continued when Eadie (1990) became editor and articulated three criteria for publishing articles in that journal: In addition to exploring a specific communication problem or situation (called the "constitutive criterion") and revealing significant and substantive information about that problem or situation (the "significance criterion"), the third criterion (the "focus criterion") was that "the research is securely based in theory," although "its purpose is not immediate theory building" (p. 4).

Frequently, however, applied communication scholarship privileged theory over application (see Barge & Craig, this volume). Keyton (2000), for instance, after reviewing manuscripts submitted to the Applied Communication Division for presentation at the 1998 NCA convention, noted that "too frequently, authors gave an overabundant focus to theory. Theories would be articulated and reviewed, and then the applied problem would appear as an incidental test of the theory" (p. 167; see also similar comments Keyton, 2005, made about manuscripts submitted during her editorship of *JACR*). Even Seibold (2000), probably the most theoretically oriented editor of *JACR*, remarked that

> given my own strong commitment to pursuing theoretically driven applied communication research, I may have overemphasized theory at times during my editorship of *JACR*. This was especially evident when some authors struggled to specify the "implications for practice" associated with their findings. (p. 184)

This emphasis on theory still characterized *JACR's* editorial policy in 2009, with the word "theory" (italicized for emphasis) occurring more than any other descriptive term:

The Journal of Applied Communication Research publishes original scholarship that addresses or challenges the relation between *theory* and practice in understanding communication in applied contexts. All *theoretical* and methodological approaches are welcome, as are all contextual areas. Original research studies should apply existing *theory* and research to practical situations, problems, and practices; should illuminate how embodied activities inform and reform existing *theory*; or should contribute to *theory* development. Research articles should offer critical summaries of *theory* or research and demonstrate ways in which the critiques can be used to explain, improve, or understand communication practices or process in a specific context. (Stafford, 2009, n.p.)

Although theory still may be overemphasized in research published in *JACR*, scholars have recognized the limitations of and deconstructed the theory–application divide (e.g., G. R. Miller, 1995). As Wood (1995) explained:

Applied communication research is practicing theory and theorizing practice. I am not contending merely that a dynamic dialectic of theory and practice should characterize applied scholarship, but that it necessarily does.... Theory is practice or, if you prefer, theoria is praxis. (pp. 157, 162)

This view of applied communication scholarship represents full integration of theory and practice ("theory *with* practice/practice *with* theory"; Seibold et al., this volume, p. 345). Emerging from this integrated view is the notion of "practical theory" (see Barge & Craig, this volume). Moreover, deconstructing the theory–application divide undoubtedly had a significant impact on the methodologies employed in applied communication scholarship and the recognition that both rigor and relevance could characterize such research.

Across the Great Divide: Practicing Rigor and Relevance in Applied Communication Research

In our view, social scientists are faced with a fundamental choice that hinges on a dilemma of rigor or relevance. If social scientists tilt toward the rigor of normal science that currently dominates departments of social science in American universities, they risk becoming irrelevant to practitioners' demands for usable knowledge. If they tilt toward the relevance of...research, they risk falling short of prevailing disciplinary standards of rigor.... The challenge is to define and meet standards of *appropriate* rigor without sacrificing relevance. (Argyris & Schön, 1991, p. 85)

Debates about methodological procedures for conducting applied communication research and the methodological sophistication of such research accompanied the distinction drawn between basic and applied research, and the desire to infuse applied communication research with theory. These methodological debates about applied communication scholarship reflected, in part, larger debates that characterized the 1970s, and continued for some time, about theories and methods employed to study communication phenomena, in general (e.g., Benson & Pearce, 1977; Cronkhite & Liska, 1977; Fisher, 1978). As Frey (1996, pp. 25, 22, 26) noted in reviewing group communication research conducted during the "decade of discontent" (1970s) that followed the "grand old days" (1945–1970) where such research flourished, scholars experienced an "epistemic crisis" that led them to question taken-for-granted theoretical and methodological practices.

Given that applied communication research emerged during the time of those debates and was viewed by some scholars as the "black sheep" or "Rodney Dangerfield" ("I don't get no respect") of communication research, it was especially affected by those debates.

Although a number of methodological issues were debated at that time, two interrelated issues were especially relevant to applied communication scholarship: (1) laboratory versus field research, and (2) quantitative versus qualitative methods. With regard to the site for research, in line with privileging basic research in the social sciences, social-scientific communication scholars had adopted the "gold standard" of conducting (quantitative, experimental) research under controlled conditions in a laboratory. A number of scholars, however, questioned the external validity (or "generalizability") of the findings from such research because of the artificiality of the laboratory and what researchers often asked people to do in it. Applied communication scholars, in particular, threw this accepted practice into relief because of their desire to study communication in the natural contexts in which it occurred. G. R. Miller and Sunnafrank (1984), for instance, argued that a

> major practical concession of much communication research concerns the contrived nature of many research situations. For instance, research participants are frequently asked to role play situations of theoretical interest to the researcher, or to observe and to assess hypothetical communication transactions.... The best antidote consists of studies conducted in research settings closely approximating the actual communication environment of interest. (p. 260)

Cusella and Thompson (1995) were even more adamant, insisting that applied communication research "must be conducted in the field, where the interplay between context and process is an ever present empirical concern" (p. 182; see also Whitchurch, 2001).

The assumption that applied research should be conducted in the field was so prevalent (e.g., it was the definition employed in the first issue of *JACR* edited by Hickson, 1973) that Kreps et al. (1991) identified it as another major misconception of applied communication scholarship. The corresponding supposition that all field research was applied also was challenged, with Cissna (1982, p. iii) pointing out that "research conducted in field settings is often not applied research," and Kreps et al. explaining that "basic research studies are often conducted in field settings to enhance the ecological validity of propositions derived from theory" (pp. 75–76). Moreover, scholars maintained that applied communication research could be conducted in the laboratory. In identifying problematic characteristics commonly associated with applied communication scholarship, Cissna (1982), as editor of *JACR*, explained that

> the assertion sometimes is made that applied communication research is conducted in the field (or in *situ*) rather than in laboratories, and hence uses "real people" rather than college students as subjects. Although this is often the case, and usually is desirable, it is not necessarily so. Applied communication research can be conducted in laboratory situations and can use students as subjects. (p iii; see also Whitchurch & Webb, 1995)

Cardy (1991a), arguing against what he perceived to be a knee-jerk reaction, claimed, in the context of studying organizational communication, that "laboratory studies can have great applied value even though they are extremely artificial" (p. 112). To Cardy (1991a), only the internal validity of laboratory research was important and its external validity was irrelevant, for its applied value lay in testing theories and models. Steinfatt (1991a) agreed that external validity was not important to applied organizational communication laboratory research, but argued that studying students rather than organizational employees and ignoring the significant contextual factors that affect employees was problematic precisely because such procedures called into question the internal validity of laboratory research (see the subsequent exchange between Cardy, 1991b, and Steinfatt, 1991b).

Closely related to the debate about conducting (applied) communication research in the laboratory versus the field was the debate about the merits of quantitative versus qualitative methods. Like their counterparts in the other social sciences, social-scientific communication scholars privileged methods that produced quantitative data (primarily experiments and surveys). Many applied communication researchers also relied on quantitative methods—most notably, the survey method. Indeed, as Query et al. (this volume) documented in their review of quantitative methods in applied communication scholarship, the survey method was used most often in articles published in *JACR* from 1973 to 1989. Because of its extensive use, Kreps et al. (1991) pointed out that another misconception of applied communication scholarship was that "applied researchers depend exclusively upon the survey research method" (p. 77).

Employing quantitative methods in applied communication research probably was due to graduate school training. Indeed, textbooks from psychology and sociology (e.g., Babbie, 1975; Kerlinger, 1973; Selltiz, Wrightsman, & Cook, 1976) used to teach research methods in communication graduate programs and early communication research methods textbooks (e.g., Bowers & Courtright, 1984; Emmert & Brooks, 1970; M. J. Smith, 1982; Tucker, Weaver, & Berryman-Fink, 1981; Wimmer & Dominick, 1983) emphasized quantitative methods.[6]

However, once qualitative methods, which had a long history in other social sciences, started to influence the study of communication,[7] applied communication researchers were quick to argue for and adopt them. In articles published in early issues of *JACR*, Fish and Dorris (1975) explained how phenomenology could inform applied communication research, Shuter (1975) pointed to the promise of participant–observation research, Lanigan (1976) showed how speech act theory could stimulate research, Gonchar and Hahn (1978) argued for critical methodologies, Deetz (1981) explicated metaphor analysis, and Hickson (1983) championed ethnomethodogy in applied communication scholarship. Cragan and Shields (1981) also published a book promoting a dramatistic approach to applied communication scholarship. The value of qualitative methods also was highlighted by scholars studying communication in natural settings that were considered most conducive for applied research, such as families (Riggs, 1979), organizations (e.g., Browning, 1978) and the media (e.g., Gelles, 1974).

Qualitative methods became so associated with applied communication scholarship that Cissna (1982) identified it as another perceived problematic characteristic, stating:

> I have read or heard that applied research utilizes participant observation, non-quantitative, and phenomenological models of inquiry. While some applied communication studies are of these types, these qualitative studies are not necessarily (by their method alone) applied research, and research of these types is often not applied. (pp. ii–iv)

Perhaps because of the emphasis placed on studying communication in natural settings using qualitative methods, applied communication research was viewed by some scholars as being less rigorous than quantitative, laboratory communication research. Kreps et al. (1991, p. 71) noted that applied communication research "has long suffered from an unfortunate and inaccurate disciplinary stigma of appearing to lack scholarly rigor and merit," and Pettegrew (1988, p. 331) sought to "inject more rigor into our field's use of the term 'applied research,'" because the quality of most applied research, according to

Becker (1995), "has been terrible" (p. 100). DeWine (1987), however, questioned the view that applied communication research was "less rigorous" or "is only done by those who can't do 'real' research" (pp. 3, 4). As DeWine explained, "There is nothing that inherently separates 'pure' research from applied research in terms of the rigor of the method" (p. 3; see also Frey, O'Hair, & Kreps, 1990). Moreover, social-scientific scholars who conducted rigorous quantitative laboratory research simultaneously were questioning the relevance of their research. Hirsh-Pasek and Golinkoff (2007) recently concluded about such research: "Ironically, as our methodological skills improved, relevance went out the window" (p. 185).

Over time, scholars demonstrated how various methods (many of which are documented in the second section of this volume) could be employed to achieve both rigor and relevance in field- and laboratory-based applied communication research. Indeed, today, no one debates the use of quantitative and qualitative methods to study (applied) communication phenomena, whether applied communication research can or should be conducted in the natural setting or the laboratory, the supposed divide between research rigor and relevance, or the quality of applied communication scholarship. As Wood (2000) concluded:

> A primary reason for the change in many communication scholars' views of applied communication research is the indisputable quality of much published applied work. The scholarship done under the name of applied communication research has established its validity and value both in and beyond the ivory tower. (p. 191)

Across the Great Divide: From Observation to Intervention

> We should start from the premise that, in research, "to put into practice" [the dictionary definition of "applied"] applies to *researchers....* Accordingly, *applied communication scholarship* might be defined as "the study of researchers putting their communication knowledge and skills into practice." Hence, applied communication scholarship involves scholars bringing their communication resources to bear to make a difference in people's lives. (Frey, 2000, p. 179)

Although the debates described above resulted in the legitimation and institutionalization of applied research in the communication discipline, with applied communication scholars no longer having to justify their research, the debates did not cease but, instead, turned inward to confront issues raised by those who conduct such scholarship. Perhaps the greatest of those divides has been between applied communication scholars who *observe* how people manage pragmatic communication issues and those who *intervene* to facilitate change, engaging, in the most extreme case, in communication activism to promote social justice.

At the minimal definitional end of the applied communication scholarship continuum, researchers observe people confronting pragmatic communication issues to describe, interpret, explain, and, in some cases, critique what occurs for the purpose of enlightening other scholars. Although many communication scholars engage in these practices, applied communication scholars include in their written reports recommendations for practitioners or people affected by the communication issue to influence subsequent practice. Indeed, the editorial policy of *JACR* now requires that "all manuscripts must include a separate section detailing the intended or potential practical applications of findings, critique, or commentary" (Stafford, 2009, n.p.). First recommended by Eadie (2000), Keyton (2005) started this "Practical Applications" section when she edited the journal to demonstrate that "communication scholars can draw meaningful conclusions and make meaningful contributions to how people practice communication" (p. 289). Including such applications, according to this flagship journal, by definition, makes the scholarship applied.

Although providing practical applications of communication research studies should be relatively easy, as Keyton (2005) noted toward the end of her editorship:

> Some authors remarked on the difficulty of moving from theoretical platforms to practical ones. Others struggled with *what should be done* versus *what can be done* in a particular communication setting. Such difficulty suggests that we are more comfortable working in idealized forms, and are perhaps less knowledgeable about contexts than we should be. For *JACR*, I believe, we must find a way to bridge from theory to practice. (p. 289)

Despite these difficulties, the majority of applied communication research, especially articles published in *JACR*, is of this type.

To illustrate the observational end of the observational–intervention continuum using a recent example, consider K. I. Miller and Koesten's (2008) study of the emerging role of emotion in the workplace—in this case, among professional financial planners—which revealed that

> there is a great deal of emotion experienced in the financial planning profession and that relationships and communication with clients may indeed be more central to the work of financial planners than portfolio reports and changes in estate tax laws. (p. 23)

After explaining insights gained about how financial planners' emotions and communication relate to burnout and job satisfaction, and after discussing the findings in light of theory and research, the authors offered, in the practical applications section, ideas for training financial planners (and other service providers) that stressed understanding relationships and providing them with skills in relational development. K. I. Miller and Koesten, thus, observed people confronting important pragmatic issues (burnout and job satisfaction) related to communication (of information and emotion), addressed the traditional scholarship requirement of situating their findings within relevant theory and research, and met the minimal applied communication scholarship requirement established by *JACR* of offering recommendations for practice. Their research, however, did not constitute (or study) an intervention with financial planners, nor did they enact any of their recommendations for training financial planners. Indeed, there is no indication in the article that the findings from the study even were shared with participants.[8]

The approach to applied communication scholarship that relies on observations and recommendations without intervening in some way is what Frey and Carragee (2007b) called "third-person-perspective research" (p. 6). This research approach may be derived from the traditional privileging of theory over application in the academy, with the word *theory* coming from the Greek words *theoria* ("contemplation"), *theorein* ("look at"), *theoros* ("spectator"), and *thea* ("a view"; Online Etymology Dictionary, 2006). Hence, from such a perspective, scholars are supposed to be, and most likely were trained to be, spectators whose work is best done by looking at and contemplating what occurs without trying to affect it.

Almost from the beginning of applied communication scholarship, however, some scholars questioned this observational-spectator model that now culminates in offering recommendations for others to enact. Cissna (1982), for instance, argued that "applied communication is not sufficiently characterized by a particular kind of discussion and conclusions" (p. iv). As Cissna (1982) explained:

> Some have argued that applied communication research contains discussion and conclusions sections which orient the reader toward the policy implications (broadly construed) of the research which has been undertaken, regardless of any of its other characteristics. The practical orientation of the discussion and conclusions is *necessary but not sufficient* to describe applied communication research. (p. iv)

Johnson (1991) went even further, questioning, in the context of organizational communication, whether observing and offering recommendations constitutes applied communication research:

> That a study is conducted in an organizational setting, is grounded in the research literature, provides logically and empirically valid explanations and predictions, and offers some practical implications of these findings in the discussion section does not make the study "applied." Applied communication research centers on solving existing and real problems.... Research that is strictly descriptive, explanatory, and/ or predictive is not applied communication research because it does not meet the criterion of control. (pp. 341–342)

A stronger position about applied communication scholarship than observing and offering recommendations, which developed, in part, because it never is clear whether practitioners and the public can physically obtain or understand studies published in scholarly journals, even applied articles,[9] is that of *translational scholarship*, advanced by Petronio (1999, 2002, 2007a), in which applied communication researchers "take the knowledge discovered through research or theory and interpret it for everyday use" (Petronio, 1999, p. 88). Petronio (2007a) identified five pathways for translating research knowledge into practice: (1) selecting societal problems most likely to benefit from translational research, (2) assessing the fit between audience needs and research applications, (3) redesigning research to accomplish translation (which was considered the most pressing need), (4) converting research findings into practices that benefit people, and (5) developing delivery systems to bring translational knowledge to those who most need it.

Some applied communication scholars have framed their research (often post hoc) as translational scholarship (e.g., Giles, 2008; Hecht & Miller-Day, 2007; Miller-Day, 2008; Parrott, 2008; Petronio, 2007b). Delivery systems also are being developed to bring translational knowledge to those who most need it. Keyton (2005) noted applied communication scholars' inability "to talk more directly with public audiences about what we do and how our research can help identify communication problems and provide viable options" (p. 290; see also Avery & Eadie, 1993; Eadie, 1995; Goodall, 2004). In response, NCA created the online Web magazine ("ezine") *Communication Currents* (http://www.communicationcurrents.com/) to translate communication journal articles into "a form understandable and usable for broad audiences, including communication experts working with lay audiences, instructors and students, the press, and other interested members of the public" (National Communication Association, 2008, ¶1). Recent articles in that magazine include "Communicating with In-laws: Reframing and Accepting Change" (Prentice, 2008b; based on Prentice, 2008a), "The Role of E-mail in Parent–Teacher Communication" (Thompson, 2008b; based on Thompson, 2008a), and "Fighting the Prison–Industrial Complex with Communication Activism" (Hartnett, 2007a; based on PCARE, 2007).

Communication scholars also have written (1) articles in practitioner journals, sometimes with practitioners, such as Adelman, Frey, and Budz (1994) on creating community in long-term care facilities, based on their longitudinal applied research program on communication and community at a residential facility for people with AIDS (see, e.g., Adelman & Frey, 1997); (2) books for practitioners, such as Sunwolf's (2004, 2005, 2006b) translation of her research and other scholarship on jury communication tools and strategies for attorneys; and (3) books for the general public, such as Jamieson (2000) on political communication campaigns and Jackson and Jamieson (2007), founders of the Web site FactCheck.org, on distinguishing factual information from disinformation. Communication scholars also have produced video documentaries (e.g., Adelman & Schultz, 1991; Conquergood & Siegel, 1990; McHale, Wylie, & Huck, 2002, 2005). In fact, Freimuth (1995) argued that "to have an impact on public policy and social change, communication research must be disseminated in nontraditional ways" (p. 43).

Translational scholarship counters the notion that disseminating research is not a priority for scholars and, in fact, can be detrimental to them (e.g., for tenure and promotion; see the essays in Welch-Ross & Fasig, 2007). However, some translational research may be based on the questionable assumption (see McCall & Groark, 2007; Ruben, 2005) that simply making research accessible results in "useable knowledge" (Argyris, 1995, p.1). Instead, some scholars argue passionately, such as the quotation from Frey (2000) at the beginning of this section, that applied communication scholars should conduct research about their interventions with relevant audiences to manage or solve communication problems and to promote needed social change.[10] Such intervention-oriented research is what Frey and Carragee (2007b, p. 6) called "first-person-perspective research" and represents the other definitional end of the applied communication scholarship continuum.

Some early applied communication scholars did engage in intervention (or facilitation) research. Perry (1973), for instance, conducted survey research about public sentiment in Bromley, Ohio about a proposed tax levy and, based on the findings, suggested communication strategies to overcome resistance to the levy that were enacted by a group of concerned citizens, with voters subsequently approving the levy. Peterson (1975) discussed his teaching of a basic communication course in a program providing college coursework and on-the-job-training for Choctaw Indian students in Philadelphia, Mississippi. Burke, Becker, Arbogast, and Naughton (1987) reported on their theoretically based intervention program to reduce adolescents' tobacco use. Conquergood (1988) described his collaborative creation of a grassroots theater troupe in a Hmong refugee camp in Thailand that performed skits using proverbs, stories, and songs to promote hygiene and sanitation practices.[11]

Although these studies were the exception to the observational research (including studies about interventions conducted by other people; e.g., Hunt & Ebeling, 1983; Lannamann, 1989; Pohl & Freimuth, 1983; Schwarz-Gehrke, 1983) that, until recently, dominated applied communication scholarship, over time, more applied communication scholars have engaged in intervention research. The interventions range from facilitating group interaction to promoting public dialogue to conducting media campaigns (Table 2.1 lists some interventions employed and an example of their use by applied communication scholars; see other studies in Frey, 1995, 2006b; Frey & Carragee, 2007a; the exemplary applied communication scholarship programs featured in this volume by Hecht & Miller-Day; Pearce, Spano, & Pearce; Poole & DeSanctis; Witte & Roberto). Although these interventions differed in important ways (e.g., short-term versus long-term or microlevel versus macrolevel interventions), in all cases, researchers intervened to address important communication issues, facilitated communicative practices, and studied the processes or effects of their interventions (e.g., conducted evaluation research).

One important reason for the growth of intervention-oriented applied communication research is the amount of grant funding now available for it. The widespread recognition

Table 2.1 Interventions/Facilitations Employed by Applied Communication Researchers

Brochures: Created by S. W. Smith et al. (2008) to increase agricultural workers' intentions to use on-the-job hearing protection

Collaborative Conversations (a courtroom-based method of lawyer–potential-juror dialogue): Developed by Sunwolf (2007) to facilitate discussions of the death penalty with citizens ("death talk") and to teach attorneys how to embrace jurors' opinions with which they disagree and to initiate collaborative talk with them about how to solve trial tasks

Collaborative Learning (a group-based method that integrates systems thinking, conflict management, and adult learning): Used by Walker, Daniels, and Cheng (2006) to work through conflict between stakeholder groups about environmental issues

Communication Assessment Instruments: Orbe (2007) created an instrument to assess the civil rights health of communities, employed it in three communities in Michigan, and facilitated conversations about the results and strategic planning

Communication Consulting: Crabtree and Ford (2007) consulted with a sexual assault recovery center, engaging in media relations, promotion, fund-raising, training, and other activities

Communication Skills Training: Seibold, Kudsi, and Rude (1993) provided presentational skill training to members of manufacturing, service, production, and research organizations

Debates: Hartnett (1998) had students in his prison class restage the Lincoln–Douglas debates about slavery, adding the Black abolitionist David Walker, to see how the tropes of racism carried through to today

Dialogue Forums: Facilitated by Murphy (1995) to increase awareness, identify issues, promote constructive dialogue, and propose solutions to gender issues in an international professional service firm concerned about the lack of women in its upper management

Emergent Consensus Program: Employed by Palmer (2007) to build consensus in a progressive activist antiglobalization group as it planned for and took part in an international trade summit protest

Empathic Attunement (designed for the initial meeting of small, zero-history training groups of professional helpers, in place of traditional icebreaker activities, to develop empathy for clients): Created by Sunwolf (2006a) to help defense attorneys empathize with and develop new case strategies for their indigent incarcerated defendants

Feedback Techniques: Keyton (1995) used SYMLOG (System for the Multiple Level Observation of Groups; a quantitative observational scheme that can help a group to reflect on its interaction) to ease tensions within a functional work group comprised of physicians, medical residents, and nursing staff

Focus Groups: Employed by Zorn, Roper, Broadfoot, and Weaver (2006) to increase participants' confidence and motivation to participate in public dialogues about controversial topics (in this case, human biotechnology)

Group Decision Support Systems (GDSSs; electronic meeting systems that combine communication and computer technologies with group decision support technologies): Used by Poole, DeSanctis, Kirsch, and Jackson (1995) to build teams involved in a quality enhancement effort at a large service organization (see also Poole & DeSanctis, this volume)

Inoculation Treatments: Employed by Compton and Pfau (2008) to combat university plagiarism by protecting students' attitudes against pro-plagiarism justification arguments

Interactive Management (IM; a computer-assisted methodology to help group members identify relationships among ideas and impose order on complex issues): Used by Broome (2006) to manage conflict and build peace between Greeks and Turks on Cyprus

Kinetic Exercises (physical movement): Employed by Kawakami (2006) to promote group formation and development with diverse (e.g., ethnic) groups

Media Literacy: Cooks and Scharrer (2007) taught sixth graders, their teachers, and their families about media and interpersonal violence, and conflict resolution strategies

Media Campaigns: Engaged in by Ryan, Caragee, and Schwerner (1998) to influence policy formation and public attitudes concerning workplace reproductive rights that resulted in a positive U.S. Supreme Court decision

Metaphoric Illumination: Used by Gribas and Sims (2006) to reveal differences among team members in their understanding of the word "team" and to move the group forward

Newspapers: Novek and Sanford (2007) produced a newspaper at a state prison for women that examined, for instance, the harshness of prison life

Performance/Theatre: Harter, Sharma, Pant, Singhal, and Sharma (2007) facilitated participatory theatre workshops and performances in India that protested the practice of dowry

Table 2.1 Continued

Political Communication: Hartnett (2007b) facilitated teach-ins, political art, marches, vigils, rallies, and other political communication activities to protest the Iraq War

Public Service Announcements (PSA): Roberto, Meyer, Johnson, Atkin, and Smith (2002) created a radio PSA focusing on the danger to children from an unlocked and loaded gun that was aired in a Michigan county (see also Witte & Roberto, this volume)

Service Learning: Used by Crabtree (1998) to engage in participatory development communication projects directed toward social justice in El Salvador and Nicaragua

Support Groups: Albeck, Adwan, and Bar-On (2006) brought together descendants of Holocaust survivors and descendents of Nazi perpetrators to share their family narratives

Web Resources: Scheerhorn, Warisse, and McNeilis (1995) created an Internet bulletin board to promote communication among families affected by hemophilia

Workshops: Shapiro and Guttman (2007) offered a 2-day psycho-communicative-educational workshop for couples experiencing transition to parenthood

Video/DVD Documentaries: McHale (2007) made a documentary that helped to free an innocent man on death row in Missouri

of the role of communication in managing significant societal issues has led to increased large-scale grants, especially from philanthropic foundations, for applied communication research about socially responsible intervention programs (Dearing & Larson, 2002; Slater, 2002).

Intervention-oriented research constitutes what has been called "engaged scholarship" (Applegate, 2002; Barge, Simpson, & Shockley-Zalabak, 2008; Cheney, Wilhelmsson, & Zorn, 2002; Van de Ven, 2007). Although generally welcomed by scholars, Seibold (2000) claimed that restricting applied communication scholarship to first-person-perspective research, as Frey (2000) argued, is too limiting. In fact, in some contexts, researchers' intervention may be undesirable. Whitchurch and Webb (1995), for instance, argued that "applied family communication must address implications for practice with families while not conducting the actual interventions.... The appropriate role for applied family research is to *inform* practice, rather than *be* therapy per se" (p. 244).

Scholarship, however, can be engaged in another, more deeply ideological, sense, as Conquergood (1995) explained:

> The choice is no longer between pure and applied research. Instead, we must choose between research that is "engaged" or "complicit." By engaged I mean a clear-eyed, self-critical awareness that research does not proceed in epistemological purity or moral innocence. There is no immaculate perception. Engaged individuals take responsibility for how the knowledge that they produce is used instead of hiding behind pretenses and protestations of innocence.... As engaged intellectuals we understand that we are entangled within world systems of oppression and exploitation.... Our choice is to stand alongside or against domination, but not outside, above, or beyond it. (p. 85)

From such a perspective, significant differences exist not only between observational and intervention applied communication research but also between intervention research that potentially maintains systems of domination and that which challenges oppression.

Responding to Conquergood's (1995) ideological challenge, Frey, Pearce, Pollock, Artz, and Murphy (1996) articulated a *communication and social justice* approach to applied communication scholarship that involves "engagement with and advocacy for those in our society who are economically, socially, politically, and/or culturally underresourced" (p. 110; see also Frey, 1998b, 2006a; Pearce, 1998; Pollock, Artz, Frey, Pearce,

& Murphy, 1966). As Frey, Pearce et al. noted, "A concern with social justice from a communication perspective...identifies and foregrounds the grammars that oppress or underwrite relationships of domination and then reconstructs those grammars" (p. 112). Frey (1998a) subsequently edited a special issue of *JACR* on "Communication and Social Justice Research" that featured "empirically grounded case studies that demonstrated ways in which applied communication researchers have made a difference in the lives of those who are disadvantaged by prevalent social structures" (Frey, 1998b, p. 158).

One important component of the communication and social justice approach is the adoption of an activist orientation. As Frey, Pearce et al. (1996) explained:

> It is not enough merely to demonstrate or bemoan the fact that some people lack the minimal necessities of life, that others are used regularly against their will and against the interests by others for their pleasure or profit, and that some are defined as "outside" the economic, political, or social system because of race, creed, lifestyle, or medical condition.... A social justice sensibility entails a moral imperative to *act* as effectively as we can to do something about sustained inequalities. To continue to pursue justice, it is perhaps necessary that we who act be personally ethical, but that is not sufficient. Our actions must engage and transform social structure. (p. 111)

Expanding on this orientation, Frey and Carragee (2007a, 2007b) recently articulated, and showcased research studies of, a *communication activism* approach to scholarship that involves researchers engaging in direct vigorous action to promote social justice (see also the activist approaches advanced by Broome, Carey, De La Garza, Martin, & Morris, 2005; Yep, 2008; Zoller, 2005).[12]

Although a number of scholars have pursued social justice and communication activism scholarship (e.g., Artz, 2000; Jones & Bodtker, 1998; Leets, 2001; Palmeri, 1996; Pestana & Swartz, 2008; Sorrells & Nakagawa, 2008; Swan, 2002; the essays in Swartz, 2006), many issues still need to be worked out about this approach (regarding ethical issues, see Seeger, Sellnow, Ulmer, & Novak, this volume). For instance, Sunwolf (2007) used the example of national workshops she conducts with lawyers who defend those facing the death penalty to discuss differences between *local activism*, where researchers are privy to the outcomes of their activism, and *itinerate activism*, conducted with people not from researchers' local communities and with the outcomes perhaps never being known to researchers.

Important concerns also have been raised about this approach by communication scholars who support and work conscientiously for social justice. Wood (1996), for instance, pointing to specific communication scholarship (some of which emerged from the decades-old feminist research tradition), took exception to Frey, Pearce et al.'s (1996) claim that "little research by communication scholars had focused on social justice and that work of this sort is not highly regarded in our discipline" (p. 128; although see the rejoinder by Pollock et al., 1996). Makau (1996, p. 140) argued for an "invitational approach to communication practice and pedagogy" rather than what she called the "adversarial model" implicit in Frey, Pearce et al. (cf. Frey's, 2006a, criticism of the invitational approach to social change). Finally, Olson and Olson (2003) contended that the litmus test of "usable knowledge" in the approach of Frey, Pearce, et al. unduly restricted acceptable social justice communication research to "short-term case studies aimed at immediately measurable outcomes produced by the researcher him- or herself, qualities that do not necessarily match the complex nature of problems of social in(justice)" (p. 438). Hence, although communication activism for social justice is a significant form of applied communication scholarship, it is not without controversy and debate.

Conclusion

Applied communication scholarship has come a long way in the past few decades, scaling many heights and traversing many valleys as scholars engaged in great debates and confronted deep divides. These controversies and contestations included (1) establishing applied communication as a research endeavor, (2) linking theory and application, (3) using the wide range of methodologies to produce rigorous and relevant research, and (4) confronting the chasm between observation-oriented and intervention-oriented (and especially social justice activist) applied communication scholarship. Thus, as is the case for any developing field of study, applied communication research has addressed issues related to "finding identity, contesting foci, debating an agenda, [and] elaborating methods" (Seibold, 2008, p. 189). In confronting these issues, like Odysseus in Greek mythology, who maneuvered between Scylla and Charybdis, the two sea monsters situated on the opposite sides of the narrow Strait of Messina, applied communication scholars have navigated some treacherous waters. What emerged from that process is a well-respected form of scholarship that, as Seibold (2000) maintained, may have started as an extension of the communication field but increasingly has become a reflection of the purpose, potential, and promise of communication research to make an important difference in the world. Although debates about this scholarship undoubtedly will continue, the legitimacy, quality, and value of applied communication scholarship is no longer debatable.

Notes

1. Although (grant) funding always has been an important impetus for applied (communication) research, its impact never has been adequately appreciated or addressed. Some scholars undoubtedly became advocates for applied communication research as they evolved from nonfunded, laboratory-based basic researchers focused primarily on theoretical questions to funded, field-oriented applied researchers interested in practical problems (with theoretical implications), such as G. R. Miller's shift from laboratory research on persuasion and attitude change to applied research on videotaped courtroom testimony. With the exception of consulting, the significance of funding for applied communication research, including its enabling and constraining effects, however, has been virtually ignored; indeed, in contrast to the many articles in *JACR* about consulting, not a single article about funding appeared in that journal until a 2002 special forum on it (Buller & Slater, 2002). One reason for this omission may be that, with some exceptions, prominent figures who have shaped applied communication scholarship do not have a history of sustained, continuous, peer-reviewed, externally funded, (often) large-scale grant research from government agencies or philanthropic foundations. Moreover, those who have a record of very fine, fully funded applied communication research (for some specific people and projects, see the essays in Buller & Slater, 2002) typically have not served in leadership roles in the field (e.g., as *JACR* editor), contributed to debates about this scholarship, or necessarily published their work in *JACR* (and there is no list of publications resulting from such funding). This difference in funded applied communication research experience, especially in the current university climate promoting research funding, suggests another divide that has not (yet) been bridged. As Rogers (2002) maintained, "One can think of two categories of communication scholars: Those who conduct funded research versus those who do not" (p. 342).
2. Boyer (1990), for instance, proposed four forms of scholarship: discovery, integration, application, and teaching. The *scholarship of application* is designed to answer the question, "How can knowledge be responsibly applied to consequential problems?" (Boyer, p. 21).
3. Other terms used to differentiate these two forms of scholarship include (corresponding to basic and applied, respectively) *discipline* and *policy* (Coleman, cited in Lazarsfeld & Reitz, 1975; with Craig, 1995, using the term *disciplinary*), and *conclusion oriented* and *decision oriented* (Tukey, 1960).

4. It should be noted that basic communication researchers routinely have been criticized (by themselves and others) for borrowing theories whole cloth or deriving their theories from other social sciences (see, e.g., Slater, 2002).

5. Stokes (1999) articulated a similar 2 × 2 matrix for categorizing scientific research using "quests for fundamental understanding" and "consideration of use" to identify the four categories of (a) explanation of the particular (low on both), (b) pure basic research (high on understanding, low on use), (c) pure applied research (low on understanding, high on use), and (d) use-inspired basic research (high on both).

6. Although some research methods textbooks in communication included qualitative methods, their coverage paled in comparison to quantitative methods and occurred after quantitative methods had been explained, thereby framing those methods through that lens.

7. Qualitative methods were employed in some early speech disorder research published in communication journals (e.g., Brown & Oliver, 1939; Steer, 1935) but virtually disappeared from communication journals until the 1970s.

8. K. I. Miller and Koesten may have engaged in these activities but not reported them, although *JACR* welcomes such information, unlike some journals in which applied communication scholarship is published that may ask authors to remove such information to discuss in more detail the development of theory (Cissna, 2000).

9. Krayer (1988) pointed out that

> the camps for deciding who has the responsibility for applied results are…divided. One view could be that academicians write for academicians and if laypeople cannot understand an article, they are at fault for not having the education or background to do so. Another view is that providing practical-based advice concerning how to use certain findings is as an inherent a part of a journal article as the method or results section or providing information about how the results affect theory or add to the body of knowledge. (p. 341)

10. Petronio (1999, p. 89) identified *"interventions, training, distribution, and instruction"* as potential ways to convert research findings into practices that benefit people, but she was suggesting translational activities that occurred after applied communication research had been conducted rather than being the initial basis for such research.

11. Other applied communication scholars may have conducted interventions as part of community service but did not write about them for scholarly publication.

12. The notion of activist scholarship resonates in other disciplines (e.g., G. L. Anderson & Herr, 2007; Hale, 2008; Lempert, 2001; Woodhouse, Hess, Breyman, & Martin, 2002), and there is a listserv for it (https://lists.riseup.net/www/info/activistscholarship).

References

Adelman, M. B., & Frey, L. R. (1997). *The fragile community: Living together with AIDS*. Mahwah, NJ: Erlbaum.

Adelman, M. B., Frey, L. R., & Budz, T. (1994). Keeping the community spirit alive. *Journal of Long-Term Care Administration, 22*(2), 4–7.

Adelman, M. B. (Producer), & Schultz, P. (Director). (1991). *The pilgrim must embark: Living in community* [Motion picture]. Chicago: Terra Nova Films.

Albeck, J. H., Adwan, S., & Bar-On, D. (2006). Working through intergenerational conflicts by sharing personal stories in dialogue groups. In L. R. Frey (Ed.), *Facilitating group communication: Innovations and applications with natural groups: Vol. 1. Facilitating group creation, conflict, and conversation* (pp. 155–181). Cresskill, NJ: Hampton Press.

Allen, E. W. (1927). Journalism as applied social science. *Journalism Bulletin, 4,* 1–7.

Anderson, G. L., & Herr, K. G. (Eds.). (2007). *Encyclopedia of activism and social justice.* Thousand Oaks, CA: Sage.

Applegate, J. L. (2002). Skating to where the puck will be: Engaged research as a funding activity. *Journal of Applied Communication Research, 30,* 402–410.

Argyris, C. (1995). Knowledge when used in practice tests theory: The case of applied communication research. In K. N. Cissna (Ed.), *Applied communication in the 21st century* (pp. 1–19). Mahwah, NJ: Erlbaum.

Argyris, C., & Schön, D. A. (1991). Participatory action research and action science compared: A commentary. In W. F. Whyte (Ed.), *Participatory action research* (pp. 85–98). Newbury Park, CA: Sage.

Artz, L. (2001). Critical ethnography for communication studies: Dialogue and social justice in service-learning. *Southern Communication Journal, 66,* 239–250.

Avery, R. K., & Eadie, W. F. (1993). Making a difference in the real world. *Journal of Communication, 43*(3), 174–179.

Babbie, E. R. (1975). *The practice of social research.* Belmont, CA: Wadsworth.

Barge, J. K., Simpson, J. L., & Shockley-Zalabeck, P. (Eds.). (2008). Toward purposeful and practical models of engaged scholarship [Special forum]. *Journal of Applied Communication Research, 36,* 243–297.

Barton, A. (1982). Paul Lazarsfeld and the invention of the University Institute for Applied Social Research. In B. Holzner & J. Nehnevajsa (Eds.), *Organizing for social research* (pp. 17–83). Cambridge, MA: Schenkman.

Beaver, C. D., & Jandt, F. E. (1973). A pilot study on alienation and anxiety during a rumored plant closing. *Journal of Applied Communications Research, 1,* 105–114.

Becker, S. L. (1995). Response to Conquergood: Don Quixotes in the academy—Are we tilting at windmills? In K. N. Cissna (Ed.), *Applied communication in the 21st century* (pp. 97–104). Mahwah, NJ: Erlbaum.

Benson, T., & Pearce, W. B. (Eds.). (1977). Alternative theoretical bases for the study of human communication: A symposium [Special issue]. *Communication Quarterly, 25*(1).

Bollinger, D. M. (Ed.). (2005). *Introduction to communication studies: An applied research perspective.* Dubuque, IA: Kendall/Hunt.

Bowers, J. W., & Courtright, J. A. (1984). *Communication research methods.* Glenview, IL: Scott, Foresman.

Boyer, E. L. (1990). *Scholarship reconsidered: Priorities of the professoriate.* Princeton, NJ: Carnegie Foundation for the Advancement of Teaching.

Braddock, A. P. (1833). *Applied psychology for advertisers.* London: Butterworth.

Broome, B. J. (2006). The role of facilitation in protracted conflict situations: Promoting citizen peace-building efforts in Cyprus. In L. R. Frey (Ed.), *Facilitating group communication: Innovations and applications with natural groups: Vol. 1. Facilitating group creation, conflict, and conversation* (pp. 125–154). Cresskill, NJ: Hampton Press.

Broome, B. J., Carey, C., De la Garza, S. A., Martin, J., & Morris, R. (2005). In the thick of things: A dialogue about the activist turn in intercultural communication. In W. J. Starosta & G.-M. Chen (Eds.), *Taking stock in intercultural communication: Where to now?* (pp. 145–175). Washington, DC: National Communication Association.

Brown, S. F., & Oliver, D. (1939). A qualitative study of the organic speech mechanism abnormalities associated with cleft palate. *Speech Monographs, 6,* 127–146.

Browning, L. D. (1978). A grounded organizational communication theory derived from qualitative data. *Communication Monographs, 45,* 93–109.

Browning, L. D. (1982). The ethics of intervention: A communication consultant's apology. *Journal of Applied Communication Research, 10,* 101–116.

Browning, L. D., & Hawes, L. C. (1991). Style, process, surface, context: Consulting as postmodern art. *Journal of Applied Communication Research, 19,* 32–54.

Buddenbaum, J. M., & Novak, K. B. (2001). *Applied communication research.* Ames: Iowa State University Press.

Buller, D. B., & Slater, M. D. (Eds.). (2002). Funded research [Special forum]. *Journal of Applied Communication Research, 30,* 314–417.

Burke, J. A., Becker, S. L., Arbogast, R. A., & Naughton, M. J. (1987). Problems and prospects of applied research: The development of an adolescent smoking prevention program. *Journal of Applied Communication Research, 15,* 1–18.

Buzzanell, P. M., Sterk, H., & Turner, L. H. (Eds.). (2004). *Gender in applied communication contexts*. Thousand Oaks, CA: Sage.

Byerly, R., Jr., & Pielke, R. A., Jr. (1995). The changing ecology of United States science. *Science, 269*, 1531–1532.

Calhoun, C. (2008). Foreword. In C. R. Hale (Ed.), *Engaging contradictions: Theory, politics, and methods of activist scholarship* (pp. xiii–xxvi). Berkeley: University of California Press.

Cardy, R. L. (1991a). The applied value of laboratory research. *Management Communication Quarterly, 5*, 111–119.

Cardy, R. L. (1991b). Contextual variables in laboratory and field research: Theoretical importance versus theoretical meaningfulness. *Management Communication Quarterly, 5*, 240–246.

Cheney, G., Wilhelmsson, M., & Zorn, T., Jr. (2002). 10 strategies for engaged scholarship. *Management Communication Quarterly, 16*, 92–100.

Cissna, K. N. (1982). Editor's note: What is applied communication research? *Journal of Applied Communication Research, 10*, iii–v.

Cissna, K. N. (2000). Applied communication research in the 21st century. *Journal of Applied Communication Research, 28*, 169–173.

Compton, J., & Pfau, M. (2008). Inoculating against pro-plagiarism justifications: Rational and affective strategies. *Journal of Applied Communication Research, 36*, 98–119.

Conquergood, D. (1988). Health theatre in a Hmong refugee camp: Performance, communication, and culture. *TDR: Journal of Performance Studies, 32*, 174–208.

Conquergood, D. (1995). Between rigor and relevance: Rethinking applied communication. In K. N. Cissna (Ed.), *Applied communication in the 21st century* (pp. 79–96). Mahwah, NJ: Erlbaum.

Conquergood, D. (Producer), & Siegel, T. (Producer & Director). (1990). *The heart broken in half* [Motion picture]. Chicago: Siegel Productions.

Cooks, L., & Scharrer, E. (2007). Learning and change in the media literacy and violence prevention project. In L. R. Frey & K. M. Carragee (Eds.), *Communication activism: Vol. 2. Media and performance activism* (pp. 129–154). Cresskill, NJ: Hampton Press.

Crabtree, R. D. (1998). Mutual empowerment in cross-cultural participatory development and service learning: Lessons in communication and social justice from projects in El Salvador and Nicaragua. *Journal of Applied Communication Research, 26*, 182–209.

Crabtree, R. D., & Ford, L. A. (2007). Community activist and communication consultant: Managing the dialectics of outsider-within status at a sexual assault recovery services center. In L. R. Frey & K. M. Carragee (Eds.), *Communication activism: Vol. 1. Communicating for social change* (pp. 249–285). Cresskill, NJ: Hampton Press.

Cragan, J. F., & Shields, D. C. (1981). *Applied communication research: A dramatistic approach*. Prospect Heights IL: Waveland Press.

Cragan, J. F., & Shields, D. C. (1995). *Symbolic theories in applied communication research: Bormann, Burke, and Fisher*. Cresskill, NJ: Hampton Press.

Cragan, J. F., & Shields, D. C. (1999). Translating scholarship into practice: Communication studies reflecting the value of theory-based research to everyday life. *Journal of Applied Communication Research, 27*, 92–106.

Craig, R. T. (1989). Communication as a practical discipline. In B. Dervin, L. Grossberg, B. J. O'Keefe, & E. Wartella (Eds.), *Rethinking communication: Vol. 1. Paradigm issues* (pp. 97–122). Newbury Park, CA: Sage.

Craig, R. T. (1995). Applied communication research in a practical discipline. In K. N. Cissna (Ed.), *Applied communication in the 21st century* (pp. 147–155). Mahwah, NJ: Erlbaum.

Cronkhite, G., & Liska, J. (Eds.). (1997). What criteria should be used to judge the admissibility of evidence to support theoretical propositions regarding communication research? [Special symposium]. *Western Journal of Speech Communication, 41*(1).

Cusella, L. P., & Thompson, T. L. (1995). A bridge to be crossed: Levels of social control in future applied communication theory and research. In K. N. Cissna (Ed.), *Applied communication in the 21st century* (pp. 181–192). Mahwah, NJ: Erlbaum.

Dailey, R. M., & Le Poire, B. A. (Eds.). (2006). *Applied interpersonal communication matters: Family, health, & community relations*. New York: Peter Lang.

Davis, B. D., & Krapels, R. H. (1999). Applied communication consulting. *Business Communication Quarterly, 62*(3), 96–100.

Dearing, J. W., & Larson, R. S. (2002). Private foundation funding of applied communication research. *Journal of Applied Communication Research, 30,* 358–368.

Deetz, S. A. (1981). Metaphor analysis of social reality in organizations. *Journal of Applied Communication Research, 9,* 1–15.

Delia, J. G. (1987). Communication research: A history. In C. R. Berger & S. H. Chaffee (Eds.), *Handbook of communication science* (pp. 20–98). Newbury Park, CA: Sage.

DeMartini, J. R. (1982). Basic and applied sociological work: Divergence, convergence, or peaceful coexistence? *Journal of Applied Behavioral Science, 18,* 204–215.

DeWine, S. (1987, May). *"Myth busting" for applied communication research.* Paper presented at the meeting of the Eastern Communication Association, Syracuse, NY.

Eadie, W. F. (1982, November). The case for applied communication research. *Spectra, 18,* 1, 4.

Eadie, W. F. (1990). Being applied: Communication research comes of age [Special issue]. *Journal of Applied Communication Research,* 1–6.

Eadie, W. F. (Ed.). (1991a). The agenda for applied communication research [Special issue]. *Journal of Applied Communication Research, 19*(1–2).

Eadie, W. F. (1991b). Editor's introduction. *Journal of Applied Communication Research, 19,* v–vi.

Eadie, W. F. (1995). Making a difference: The status and challenges of applied communication research. In K. N. Cissna (Ed.), *Applied communication in the 21st century* (pp. 169–180). Mahwah, NJ: Erlbaum.

Eadie, W. F. (2000). Changing boundaries, changing expectations, changing results. *Journal of Applied Communication Research, 28,* 174–177.

Ellis, D. G. (1982, March). The shame of speech communication. *Spectra, 18,* 1–2.

Ellis, D. G. (1991). The oneness of opposites: Applied communication and theory. *Journal of Applied Communication Research, 19,* 116–122.

Emmert, P., & Brooks, W. D. (1970). *Methods of research in communication.* New York: Houghton Mifflin.

England, M. (1982). *A patron for pure science: The National Science Foundation's formative years, 1945–1947.* Washington, DC: National Science Foundation.

Falcione, R. L. (1974). Communication climate and satisfaction with immediate supervision. *Journal of Applied Communications Research, 2,* 13–20.

Fine, E., & Schwandt, B. (2008). *Applied communication in organizational and international contexts.* St. Ingert, Germany: Röhrig Universitätsverlag.

Fish, S. L., & Dorris, J. M. (1975). Phenomenology and communication research. *Journal of Applied Communications Research, 3,* 9–26.

Fisher, W. R. (Ed.). (1978). What criteria should be used to judge the admissibility of evidence to support theoretical propositions regarding communication research? [Special symposium continued]. *Western Journal of Speech Communication, 42*(1).

Freimuth, V. S. (1995). Response to Seibold: Applied health communication research. In K. N. Cissna (Ed.), *Applied communication in the 21st century* (pp. 39–45). Mahwah, NJ: Erlbaum.

Frey, L. R. (Ed.). (1995). *Innovations in group facilitation: Applications in natural settings.* Cresskill, NJ: Hampton Press.

Frey, L. R. (1996). Remembering and "re-membering": A history of theory and research on communication and group decision making. In R. Y. Hirokawa & M. S. Poole (Eds.), *Communication and group decision making* (2nd ed., pp. 19–51). Thousand Oaks, CA: Sage.

Frey, L. R. (Ed.). (1998a). Communication and social justice research [Special issue]. *Journal of Applied Communication Research, 26*(2).

Frey, L. R. (1998b). Communication and social justice research: Truth, justice, and the applied communication way. *Journal of Applied Communication Research, 26,* 155–164.

Frey, L. R. (2000). To be applied or not to be applied, that isn't even the question; but wherefore art thou, applied communication researcher? Reclaiming applied communication research and redefining the role of the researcher. *Journal of Applied Communication Research, 28,* 178–182.

Frey, L. R. (2006a). Across the great divides: From nonpartisan criticism to partisan criticism to applied communication activism for promoting social change and social justice. In O. Swartz (Ed.), *Social justice, partisan criticism, and communication scholarship: Diverse perspectives on social change* (pp. 35–51). Mahwah, NJ: Erlbaum.

Frey, L. R. (Ed.). (2006b). *Facilitating group communication in context: Innovations and applications with natural groups* (2 Vols.). Cresskill, NJ: Hampton Press.

Frey, L. R., Botan, C. H., & Kreps, G. L. (2000). *Investigating communication: An introduction to research methods* (2nd ed.). Needham Heights, MA: Allyn & Bacon.

Frey, L. R., & Carragee, K. M. (Eds.). (2007a). *Communication activism* (2 Vols.). Cresskill, NJ: Hampton Press.

Frey, L. R., & Carragee, K. M. (2007b). Introduction: Communication activism as engaged scholarship. In L. R. Frey & K. M. Carragee (Eds.), *Communication activism* (2 Vols., pp. 1–64). Cresskill, NJ: Hampton Press.

Frey, L. R., O'Hair, D., & Kreps, G. L. (1990). Applied communication methodology. In D. O'Hair & G. L. Kreps (Eds.), *Applied communication theory and research* (pp. 23–56). Hillsdale, NJ: Erlbaum.

Frey, L. R., Pearce, W. B., Pollock, M. A., Artz, L., & Murphy, B. A. O. (1996). Looking for justice in all the wrong places: On a communication approach to social justice. *Communication Studies, 47,* 110–127.

Geissler, L. R. (1917). What is applied psychology? *Journal of Applied Psychology, 1,* 46–60.

Gelles, R. J. (1974). The television news interview: A field study. *Journal of Applied Communications Research, 2,* 31–44.

Giles, H. (2008). Accommodating translational research. *Journal of Applied Communication Research, 36,* 121–127.

Gonchar, R. M., & Hahn, D. F. (1978). Political rhetoric: A reconsideration of critical methodologies. *Journal of Applied Communications Research, 6,* 55–63.

Goodall, H. L., Jr. (1995). Response to Miller: Sexing his text for plurals. In K. N. Cissna (Ed.), *Applied communication in the 21st century* (pp. 57–77). Mahwah, NJ: Erlbaum.

Goodall, H. L., Jr. (2004). Narrative ethnography as applied communication research. *Journal of Applied Communication Research, 32,* 185–194.

Gribas, J., & Sims, J. (2006). Metaphoric illumination and symbolic ambiguity: Applying the team metaphor for perceptual reorientation. In L. R. Frey (Ed.), *Facilitating group communication in context: Innovations and applications with natural groups: Vol. 2. Facilitating group task and team communication* (pp. 177–201). Cresskill, NJ: Hampton Press.

Hale, C. R. (Ed.). (2008). *Engaging contradictions: Theory, politics, and methods of activist research.* Berkeley: University of California Press.

Hall, S. G., Baird, J. W., & Geissler, L. R. (1917). Foreword. *Journal of Applied Psychology, 1,* 5–7.

Harris, T. E., & Nelson, M. D. (2008). *Applied organizational communication: Theory and practice in a global environment* (3rd ed.). New York: Erlbaum.

Harrison, T. M. (1982). Toward an ethical framework for communication consulting. *Journal of Applied Communication Research, 10,* 87–100.

Harter, L., Sharma, D., Pant, S., Singhal, A., & Sharma, Y. (2007). Catalyzing social reform through participatory folk performances in rural India. In L. R. Frey & K. M. Carragee (Eds.), *Communication activism: Vol. 2. Media and performance activism* (pp. 285–314). Cresskill, NJ: Hampton Press.

Hartnett, S. (1998). Lincoln and Douglas meet the abolitionist David Walker as prisoners debate slavery: Empowering education, applied communication, and social justice. *Journal of Applied Communication Research, 26,* 232–253.

Hartnett, S. J. (2007a, December). Fighting the prison–industrial complex with communication activism. *Communication Currents, 2*(6). Retrieved May 20, 2008, from http://www.communicationcurrents.com/index.asp?sid=1&issuepage=65&False

Hartnett, S. J. (2007b). "You are fit for something better": Communicating hope in antiwar activism. In L. R. Frey & K. M. Carragee (Eds.), *Communication activism: Vol. 1. Communication for social change* (pp. 195–246). Cresskill, NJ: Hampton Press.

Hawes, L. C. (1978). The reflexivity of communication research. *Western Journal of Speech Communication, 42*, 12–20.

Hecht, M. L., & Miller-Day, M. (2007). The drug resistance strategies project as translational research. *Journal of Applied Communication Research, 35*, 343–349.

Hickson, M., III (1973). Applied communications research: A beginning point for social relevance. *Journal of Applied Communications Research, 1*, 1–5.

Hickson, M., III (1983). Ethnomethodology: The promise of applied communication research? *Southern Speech Communication Journal, 48*, 182–195.

Hilgard, E. R. (1971). Toward a responsible social science. *Journal of Applied Social Psychology, 1*, 1–6.

Hirsh-Pasek, K., & Golinkoff, R. (2007). From the lab to the living room: Stories that talk the talk and walk the walk. In M. K. Welch-Ross & L. G. Fasig (Eds.), *Handbook on communicating and disseminating behavioral science* (pp. 185–202). Thousand Oaks, CA: Sage.

Hugenberg, L. W., & Robinson, D. J. (1982, June). Response to Don Ellis' essay: "The Shame of Speech Communication." *Spectra, 18*, 1–2.

Hunt, G. T., & Ebeling, R. E. (1983). The impact of a communication intervention on work-unit productivity and employee satisfaction. *Journal of Applied Communication Research, 11*, 57–68.

Jackson, B., & Jamieson, K. H. (2007). *UnSpun: Finding facts in a world of disinformation*. New York: Random House.

Jamieson, K. H. (2000). *Everything you think you know about politics...and why you're wrong*. New York: Basic Books.

Jarboe, S. (1992). They do it for the money (?): A response to G. M. Phillips. *Journal of Applied Communication Research, 20*, 225–233.

Johnson, J. (1991). Some critical attributes of applied communication research. *Journal of Applied Communication Research, 19*, 340–346.

Jones, T. S., & Bodtker, A. (1998). A dialectical analysis of a social justice process: International collaboration in South Africa. *Journal of Applied Communication Research, 26*, 357–373.

Kawakami, H. (2006). Kinetic facilitation techniques for diverse groups. In L. R. Frey (Ed.), *Facilitating group communication: Innovations and applications with natural groups: Vol. 1. Facilitating group creation, conflict, and conversation* (pp. 93–121). Cresskill, NJ: Hampton Press.

Kerlinger, F. N. (1973). *Foundations of behavioral research* (2nd ed.). New York: Holt, Rinehart & Winston.

Keyton, J. (1995). Using SYMLOG as a self-analytical group facilitation technique. In L. R. Frey (Ed.), *Innovations in group facilitation: Applications in natural settings* (pp. 119–147). Cresskill, NJ: Hampton Press.

Keyton, J. (2000). Applied communication research should be practical. *Journal of Applied Communication Research, 28*, 166–168.

Keyton, J. (2005). Letter from the editor. *Journal of Applied Communication Research, 33*, 285–293.

Kibler, R. J., & Barker, L. L. (Eds.). (1969). *Conceptual frontiers in speech communication: Report of the New Orleans Conference on Research and Instructional Development*. New York: Speech Association of America.

Krayer, K. J. (1988). Wither applied interpersonal communication research: A practical perspective for practicing practitioners. *Southern Speech Communication Journal, 53*, 339–343.

Kreps, G. L., Frey, L. R., & O'Hair, D. (1991). Conceptualizing applied communication research: Scholarship that can make a difference. *Journal of Applied Communication Research, 19*, 71–87.

Lamb, L. F., & McKee, K. B. (2005). *Applied public relations: Cases in stakeholder management*. Mahwah, NJ: Erlbaum.

Lange, J. I. (1984). Seeking client resistance: Rhetorical strategy in communication consulting. *Journal of Applied Communication Research, 12*, 50–62.

Lanigan, R. L. (1976). The speech act theory of interpersonal communication: Stimulus for research. *Journal of Applied Communications Research, 4*, 98–101.

Lannamann, J. W. (1989). Communication theory applied to relational change: A case study in Milan systemic family therapy. *Journal of Applied Communication Research, 17,* 71–91.

Lazarsfeld, P. F. (1941). Remarks on administrative and critical communications research. *Studies in Philosophy and Social Science, 9,* 2–16.

Lazarsfeld, P. F., & Reitz, J. G. (with Pasanella, A. K.). (1975). *An introduction to applied sociology.* New York: Elsevier.

Leets, L. (2001). Interrupting the cycle of moral exclusion: A communication contribution to social justice research. *Journal of Applied Social Psychology, 31,* 1859–1891.

Lempert, R. O. (2001). Activist scholarship. *Law & Society Review, 35,* 23–32.

Levy-Leboyer, C. (1988). Successes and failure in applying psychology. *American Psychologist, 43,* 779–785.

Lewin, K. (1951). *Field theory in social science: Selected theoretical papers* (D. Cartwright, Ed.). New York: Harper & Row.

Makau, J. M. (1996). Notes on communication education and social justice. *Communication Studies, 47,* 131–141.

March, J. G. (1991). Organizational consultants and organizational research. *Journal of Applied Communication Research, 19,* 20–31.

McCall, R. B., & Groark, C. J. (2007). A perspective on the history and future of disseminating behavioral and social science. In M. K. Welch-Ross & L. G. Fasig (Eds.), *Handbook on communicating and disseminating behavioral sciences* (pp. 15–32). Thousand Oaks, CA: Sage.

McCroskey, J. C. (1979). Applied graduate education: An alternative for the future. *Communication Education, 28,* 353–358.

McHale, J. P. (2007). Unreasonable doubt: Using video documentary to promote justice. In L. R. Frey & K. M. Carragee (Eds.), *Communication activism: Vol. 2. Media and performance activism* (pp. 195–222). Cresskill, NJ: Hampton Press.

McHale, J. P. (Producer/Director), Wylie, R. (Producer/Editor), & Huck D. (Producer/Assistant Editor). (2002). *Unreasonable doubt: The Joe Amrine case* [Motion picture]. (Available from John P. McHale, School of Communication, Illinois State University, 453 Fell Hall, Normal, IL 61761-4480)

McHale, J. P. (Producer/Director), Wylie, R. (Producer/Editor), & Huck, D. (Producer/Assistant Editor). (2005). *Picture this: A fight to save Joe Amrine* [Motion picture]. (Available from John P. McHale, School of Communication, Illinois State University, 453 Fell Hall, Normal, IL 61761-4480)

Miller, G. A. (1969). Psychology as a means of promoting human welfare. *American Psychologist, 24,* 1063–1075.

Miller, G. R. (1995). "I think my schizophrenia is better today," said the communication research unanimously: Some thoughts on the dysfunctional dichotomy between pure and applied communication research. In K. N. Cissna (Ed.), *Applied communication in the 21st century* (pp. 47–55). Mahwah, NJ: Erlbaum.

Miller, G. R., & Berger, C. R. (1978). On keeping the faith in matters scientific. *Western Journal of Speech Communication, 42,* 44–57.

Miller, G. R., & Sunnafrank, M. J. (1984). Theoretical dimensions of applied communication research. *Quarterly Journal of Speech, 70,* 255–263.

Miller, K. I., & Koesten, J. (2008). Financial feeling: An investigation of emotion and communication in the workplace. *Journal of Applied Communication Research, 36,* 8–32.

Miller-Day, M. (2008). Translational performances: Toward, relevant, engaging, and empowering social science. *Forum: Qualitative Social Research, 9*(2), Article 54. Retrieved June 22, 2008, from http://www.qualitative-research.net/index.php/fqs/article/view/402/872

Motley, M. T. (Ed.). (2008). *Studies in applied interpersonal communication.* Thousand Oaks, CA: Sage.

Murphy, B. O. (1995). Promoting dialogue in culturally diverse workplace environments. In L. R. Frey (Ed.), *Innovations in group facilitation: Applications in natural settings* (pp. 77–93). Cresskill, NJ: Hampton Press.

National Communication Association. (2008). *About communication currents.* Retrieved May 20, 2008, from http://www.communicationcurrents.com/index.asp?sid=1&issuepage=14

Nicholson, H. (2005). *Applied drama: The gift of theatre*. New York: Palgrave Macmillan.

Novek, E., & Sanford, R. (2007). At the checkpoint: Journalistic practices, researcher reflexivity, and dialectical dilemmas in a women's prison. In L. R. Frey & K. M. Carragee (Eds.), *Communication activism: Vol. 2. Media and performance activism* (pp. 67–95). Cresskill, NJ: Hampton Press.

O'Hair, D. (1988). Relational communication in applied contexts: Current status and future directions. *Southern Speech Communication Journal, 53*, 317–330.

O'Hair, D. (Ed.). (2000a). Defining applied communication scholarship [Special forum]. *Journal of Applied Communication Research, 28*, 164–191.

O'Hair, D. (2000b). Editor's introduction to the forum on defining applied communication scholarship. *Journal of Applied Communication Research, 28*, 164–165.

O'Hair, D., Kreps, G. L., & Frey, L. R. (1990). Conceptual issues. In D. O'Hair & G. L. Kreps (Eds.), *Applied communication theory and research* (pp. 3–22). Hillsdale, NJ: Erlbaum.

Oliver, S. (Ed.). (2004). *A handbook of corporate communication and strategic public relations: Pure and applied*. New York: Routledge.

Olson, K. M., & Olson, C. D. (2003). Problems of exclusionary research criteria: The case against the "usable knowledge" litmus test for social justice communication research. *Communication Studies, 54*, 438–450.

Online Etymology Dictionary. (2006). *Theory*. Retrieved May 15, 2006, from http://www.etymonline.com/index.php?term=theory

Orbe, M. P. (2007). Assessing the civil rights health of communities: Engaged scholarship through dialogue. In L. R. Frey & K. M. Carragee (Eds.), *Communication activism: Vol. 1. Communication for social change* (pp. 133–156). Cresskill, NJ: Hampton Press.

Palmer, D. L. (2007). Facilitating consensus in an antiglobalization affinity group. In L. R. Frey & K. M. Carragee (Eds.), *Communication activism: Vol. 1. Communication for social change* (pp. 325–353). Cresskill, NJ: Hampton Press.

Palmeri, A. J. (1996). Fostering social justice in an electronic age: The teacher as public intellectual. *Journal of Communication Inquiry, 20*(1), 3–17.

Parrott, R. (2008). A multiple discourse approach to health communication: Translational research and ethical practice. *Journal of Applied Communication Research, 36*, 1–7.

PCARE. (2007). Fighting the prison–industrial complex: A call to communication and cultural studies scholars to change the world. *Communication and Critical/Cultural Studies, 4*, 402–420.

Pearce, W. B. (1998). On putting social justice in the discipline of communication and putting enriched concepts of communication in social justice research and practice. *Journal of Applied Communication Research, 26*, 272–278.

Perry, B. L. (1973). Winning an election: A communication case study. *Journal of Applied Communications Research, 2*, 61–71.

Pestana, C., & Swartz, O. (2008). Communication, social justice, and creative democracy. In O. Swartz (Ed.), *Transformative communication studies: Culture, hierarchy, and the human condition* (pp. 91–114). Leicester, UK: Troubador.

Peterson, J. P. (1975). The teacher as learner: A year with the Choctaws. *Journal of Applied Communications Research, 3*, 1–7.

Petronio, S. (1999). "Translating scholarship into practice": An alternative metaphor. *Journal of Applied Communication Research, 27*, 87–91.

Petronio, S. (2002). The new world and scholarship translation practices: Necessary changes in defining evidence. *Western Journal of Communication, 66*, 507–512.

Petronio, S. (2007a). JACR commentaries on translating research into practice: Introduction. *Journal of Applied Communication Research, 35*, 215–217.

Petronio, S. (2007b). Translational research endeavors and the practices of communication privacy management. *Journal of Applied Communication Research, 35*, 218–222.

Pettegrew, L. S. (1988). The importance of context in applied communication research. *Southern Speech Communication Journal, 53*, 331–338.

Phillips, G. M. (1981, September). Researchers as brethren. *Spectra, 15*, 2.

Phillips, G. M. (1992). They do it for the money. *Journal of Applied Communication Research, 20*, 219–224.

Plax, T. G. (1991). Understanding applied communication inquiry: Researcher as organizational consultant. *Journal of Applied Communication Research, 19,* 55–70.

Pohl, S. N., & Freimuth, V. S. (1983). Foods for health: Involving organizations in planned change. *Journal of Applied Communication Research, 11,* 17–27.

Pollock, M. A., Artz, L., Frey, L. R., Pearce, W. B., & Murphy, B. A. O. (1996). Navigating between Scylla and Charybdis: Continuing the dialogue on communication and social justice. *Communication Studies, 47,* 142–151.

Poole, M. S., DeSanctis, G., Kirsch, L., & Jackson, M. (1995). Group decision support systems as facilitators of quality team efforts. In L. R. Frey (Ed.), *Innovations in group facilitation: Applications in natural settings* (pp. 299–321). Cresskill, NJ: Hampton Press.

Porter, D. T. (1986). The challenge of applied communication research and the *Journal of Applied Communication Research. Journal of Applied Communication Research, 14,* 67–68.

Powers, W. G., & Love, D. E. (1999). Traditional and applied graduate education: Special challenges. *Journal of the Association for Communication Administration, 28,* 104–109.

Prentice, C. M. (2008a). The assimilation of in-laws: The impact of newcomers on the communication routines of families. *Journal of Applied Communication Research, 36,* 74–97.

Prentice, C. M. (2008b, February). Communicating with in-laws: Reframing and accepting change. *Communication Currents, 3*(1). Retrieved May 20, 2008, from http://www.communicationcurrents.com/index.asp?sid=1&issuepage=76&False

Prentki, T., & Preston, S. (Eds.). (2008). *The applied theatre reader.* New York: Routledge.

Riggio, R., & Feldman, R. S. (Eds.). (2005). *Applications of nonverbal communication.* Mahwah, NJ: Erlbaum.

Riggs, C. J. (1979). Thee and they: A natural look at some effects of long-term interaction on individual perception and behavior. *Journal of Applied Communications Research, 7,* 35–44.

Roberto, A. J., Meyer, G., Johnson, A. J., Atkin, C. K., & Smith, P. K. (2002). Promoting gun trigger-lock use: Insights and implications from a radio-based health communication intervention. *Journal of Applied Communication Research, 30,* 210–230.

Rogers, E. M. (2002). Funding international communication research. *Journal of Applied Communication Research, 30,* 341–349.

Rosenberry, J., & Vicker, L. A. (2008). *Applied mass communication theory: A guide for media practitioners.* Boston: Allyn & Bacon Pearson.

Ruben, B. D. (2005). Linking communication scholarship and professional practices in colleges and universities. *Journal of Applied Communication Research, 33,* 294–304.

Rudolph, E. E. (1973). Informal human communication systems in a large organization. *Journal of Applied Communications Research, 1,* 7–23.

Ryan, C., Carragee, K. M., & Schwerner, C. (1998). Media, movements, and the quest for social justice. *Journal of Applied Communication Research, 26,* 165–181.

Sanjek, R. (1987). Anthropological work at a Gray Panther health clinic: Academic, applied, and advocacy goals. In L. Mullings (Ed.), *Cities of the United States: Studies in urban anthropology* (pp. 148–175). New York: Columbia University Press.

Scheerhorn, D., Warisse, J., & McNeilis, K. (1995). Computer-based telecommunication among an illness-related community: Design, delivery, early use, and the functions of HIGHnet. *Health Communication, 7,* 301–325.

Schrader, S. M., Mills, K. W., & Dick, R. (2001). Unique characteristics of a graduate program in applied communication. *Journal of the Association for Communication Administration, 30,* 71–82.

Schwarz-Gehrke, C. (1983). Communication and agricultural development: The case of the medfly program in México. *Journal of Applied Communication Research, 11,* 45–56.

Seibold, D. R. (1995). *Theoria* and *praxis*: Means and ends in applied communication research. In K. N. Cissna (Ed.), *Applied communication in the 21st century* (pp. 23–45). Mahwah, NJ: Erlbaum.

Seibold, D. R. (2000). Applied communication scholarship: Less a matter of boundaries than of emphases. *Journal of Applied Communication Research, 28,* 183–187.

Seibold, D. R. (2008). Applied communication research. In W. Donsbach (Ed.), *The international encyclopedia of communication* (Vol. 1., pp. 189–194). Malden, MA: Wiley-Blackwell.

Seibold, D. R., Kudsi, S., & Rude, M. (1993). Does communication training make a difference? Evidence for the effectiveness of a presentation skills program. *Journal of Applied Communication Research, 21,* 111–131.

Selltiz, C., Wrightsman, L. S., & Cook, S. W. (with Balch, G. I., Hofstetter, R., & Bickman, L.). (1976). *Research methods in social relations* (3rd ed.). New York: Holt, Rinehart & Winston.

Shapiro, A. F., & Gottman, J. M. (2007). Effects on marriage of a psycho-communicative-educational intervention with couples undergoing the transition to parenthood, evaluation at 1-year post intervention. *Journal of Family Communication, 5,* 1–24.

Sharifian, F., & Palmer, G. B. (Eds.). (2007). *Applied cultural linguistics: Implications for second language and intercultural communication.* Philadelphia: John Benjamins.

Shuter, R. (1975). The promise of participant observation research. *Journal of Applied Communications Research, 3*(2), 1–7.

Skopec, E. W. (1992). To the editor: An advisory board member responds. *Journal of Applied Communication Research, 20,* 116–118.

Slater, M. D. (2002). Communication research on a broader stage: An introduction to the special forum on funded research in communication. *Journal of Applied Communication Research, 30,* 315–320.

Smith, M. J. (1982). *Contemporary communication research methods.* Belmont, CA: Wadsworth.

Smith, S. W., Rosenman, K. D., Kotowski, M. R., Glazer, E., McFeters, C., Keesecker, N. M., et al. (2008). Using the EPPM to create and evaluate the effectiveness of brochures to increase the use of hearing protection in farmers and landscape workers. *Journal of Applied Communication Research, 36,* 200–218.

Sorrells, K., & Nakagawa, G. (2008). Intercultural communication praxis and the struggle for social responsibility and social justice. In O. Swartz (Ed.), *Transformative communication studies: Culture, hierarchy, and the human condition* (pp. 17–43). Leicester, UK: Troubador.

Stacks, D. W. (1974). Organizational communication: A survey of publications. *Journal of Applied Communications Research, 2,* 67–74.

Stacks, D. W., & Chalfa, J. J., Jr. (1981). The undergraduate research team: An applied approach to communication education. *Communication Education, 30,* 180–183.

Stafford, L. (2009). Editorial policy. *Journal of Applied Communication Research, 27*(1), n.p.

Steer, M. D. (1935). A qualitative study of breathing in young stutterers. *Speech Monographs, 2,* 152–154.

Steinfatt, T. M. (1991a). External validity, internal validity, and organizational reality: A response to Robert L. Cardy. *Management Communication Quarterly, 5,* 120–125.

Steinfatt, T. M. (1991b). Internal validity and the problem of context: A response to Robert L. Cardy. *Management Communication Quarterly, 5,* 247–255.

Steinfatt, T. M. (1997). Predicting trends in graduate communication education. *Communication Education, 46,* 128–133.

Stewart, J. (1983). Reconsidering communication consulting. *Journal of Applied Communication Research, 11,* 153–167.

Stokes, D. (1999). *Pasteur's quadrant: Basic science and technological innovation.* Washington, DC: Brookings Institute.

Sunwolf. (2004). *Practical jury dynamics: From one juror's trial perceptions to the group's decision-making process.* Charlottesville, VA: LexisNexus.

Sunwolf. (2005). *Jury thinking.* Charlottesville, VA: LexisNexus.

Sunwolf. (2006a). Empathic attunement facilitation: Stimulating immediate task engagement in zero-history training groups of professional helpers. In L. R. Frey (Ed.), *Facilitating group communication in context: Innovations with natural groups: Vol. 1. Facilitating group creation, conflict, and conversation* (pp. 63–92). Cresskill, NJ: Hampton Press.

Sunwolf. (2006b). *Juror competency juror compassion.* Charlottesville, VA: LexisNexus.

Sunwolf. (2007). Creating collaborative courtroom conversations about the death penalty between attorneys and jurors. In L. R. Frey & K. M. Carragee (Eds.), *Communication activism: Vol. 1. Communicating for social change* (pp. 287–323). Cresskill, NJ: Hampton Press.

Swan, S. (2002). Rhetoric, service, and social justice. *Written Communication, 19,* 76–108.

Swartz, O. (Ed.). (2006). *Social justice and communication scholarship.* Mahwah, NJ: Erlbaum.

Thayer, L. (1982). What would a theory of communication be *for? Journal of Applied Communication Research, 10,* 21–28.

Thompson, B. (2008a). Characteristics of parent–teacher e-mail communication. *Communication Education, 57,* 201–223.

Thompson, B. (2008b, April). The role of e-mail in parent–teacher communication. *Communication Currents, 3*(2). Retrieved May 20, 2008, from http://www.communicationcurrents.com/index.asp?sid=1&issuepage=88&False

Tucker, R. K., Weaver, R. L., II, & Berryman-Fink, C. (1981). *Research in speech communication.* Englewood Cliffs, NJ: Prentice-Hall.

Tukey, J. W. (1960). Conclusions vs. decisions. *Technometrics, 2,* 423–433.

Van de Ven, A. H. (2007). *Engaged scholarship: A guide for organizational and social research.* New York: Oxford University Press.

Veech, A. M. (2002). *Managerial communication strategies: An applied casebook.* Upper Saddle River, NJ: Prentice-Hall.

Walker, G. B., Daniels, S. E., & Cheng, A. S. (2006). Facilitating dialogue and deliberation in environmental conflict: The use of groups in collaborative learning. In L. R. Frey (Ed.), *Facilitating group communication in context: Innovations with natural groups: Vol. 1. Facilitating group creation, conflict, and conversation* (pp. 205–238). Cresskill, NJ: Hampton Press.

Ward, L. F. (1883). *Dynamic sociology: Or applied social science, as based upon statistical sociology and the less complex sciences* (2 Vols.). New York: D. Appleton.

Weick, K. E., & Browning, L. D. (1991). Fixing with the voice: A research agenda for applied communication. *Journal of Applied Communication Research, 19,* 32–54.

Welch-Ross, M. K., & Fasig, L. G. (Eds.). (2007). *Handbook of communicating and disseminating behavioral sciences.* Thousand Oaks, CA: Sage.

Whitchurch, G. G. (2001). Stayin' applied. *Journal of Family Communication, 1,* 9–13.

Whitchurch, G. G., & Webb, L. M. (1995). Applied family communication research: Casting light upon the demon. *Journal of Applied Communication Research, 23,* 239–246.

Wimmer, R. D., & Dominick, J. R. (1983). *Mass media research: An introduction.* Belmont, CA: Wadsworth.

Wood, J. T. (1995) Theorizing practice, practicing theory. In K. N. Cissna (Ed.), *Applied communication in the 21st century* (pp. 181–192). Mahwah, NJ: Erlbaum.

Wood, J. T. (1996). Social justice: Alive and well in the field of communication. *Communication Studies, 47,* 128–134.

Wood, J. T. (2000). Applied communication research: Unbounded and for good reason. *Journal of Applied Communication Research, 28,* 188–191.

Woodhouse, E., Hess, D., Breyman, S., & Martin, B. (2002). Science studies and activism. *Social Studies of Science, 32,* 297–319.

Wright, K., & Moore, S. D. (Eds.). (2008). *Applied health communication.* Cresskill, NJ: Hampton Press.

Yep, G. A. (2008). The dialectics of intervention: Toward a reconceptualization of the theory/activism divide in communication scholarship and beyond. In O. Swartz (Ed.), *Transformative communication studies: Culture, hierarchy and the human condition* (pp. 191–207). Leicester, UK: Troubador.

Zettl, H. (2008). *Sight, sound, motion: Applied media aesthetics.* Belmont, CA: Thomson/Wadsworth.

Zoller, H. M. (2005). Health activism: Communication theory and action for social change. *Communication Theory, 15,* 341–364.

Zorn, T. E., Roper, J., Broadfoot, K., & Weaver, C. K. (2006). Focus groups as sites of influential interaction: Building communicative self-efficacy and effecting attitudinal change in discussing controversial topics. *Journal of Applied Communication Research, 34,* 115–140.

3 Practical Theory in Applied Communication Scholarship

J. Kevin Barge
Texas A&M University

Robert T. Craig
University of Colorado at Boulder

The relationship between theory and practice is viewed as an important feature of applied communication research. Grounded in Lewin's (1951, p. 169) notion that there is "nothing so practical as a good theory," applied communication scholars have been encouraged over the last 25 years to address practical problems in ways that simultaneously test or develop theoretically informed interventions and contribute to theory building. Accompanying this growing emphasis on the role of theory in applied communication research, however, has been the questioning of traditional concepts of social-scientific theory. Social-scientific theories traditionally have been designed to provide generalizable, empirically testable explanations that enable prediction and control of phenomena. Although many applied researchers still subscribe to this traditional ideal of theory, others have proposed various new forms of theory or theorizing practices intended to be more "useful" or "practical" than traditional theory; however, no consensus has emerged on how to make theories of communication more practical. This chapter traces the development of the idea of "practical theory" and shows how recent work on practical theory offers several alternative ways for applied communication scholars and practitioners to simultaneously address practical problems and build useful theory.

Practical theory is explicitly designed to address practical problems and generate new possibilities for action. Although there is a growing consensus among many communication scholars that "theory should improve the lives of people and have applicability for enhancing their capacities for action" (Barge, 2001b, p. 6), views about what counts as practical theory vary greatly among different approaches to practical theory. Practical theory, thus, is not a unitary concept with a singular fixed meaning; rather, what it means to do practical theorizing and the concepts and methods one employs in the process of being a practical theorist vary according to the approach one takes.

We open this chapter by tracing the evolution of views on the role of theory in applied communication research, showing both the growing role of theory in applied research and the emergence of practical theory as an alternative to traditional models of social-scientific theory. We then turn to the ways that practical theory has been practiced by applied communication scholars. Using Barge's (2001b) distinctions among practical theory as mapping, engaged reflection, and transformative practice, we examine the concepts, assumptions, and methods of each approach as they are evidenced in the theory and research conducted by applied communication scholars. Although our review reveals that theory already is widely used for practical purposes in applied communication research, the contribution of explicit practical theory approaches, as we show, is to provide conceptual models and exemplary lines of work that can be used to articulate, critique, and further advance already existing practical tendencies in the use of theory by applied communication scholars. We conclude the chapter with a consideration of issues affecting the future development of practical theory in applied communication scholarship.

Evolving Views on Theory in Applied Communication Research

As context for the emergence of practical theory, we review explicit statements about theory by prominent applied communication scholars over the last 3 decades (see also Frey & SunWolf, this volume). An examination of several *Journal of Applied Communication Research* (*JACR*) editorial policy statements over the years gives a clear sense of evolving views on the role of theory in such research. Editorial statements in the 1970s (Hickson, 1973) and 1980s (Cissna, 1982b) contained no references at all to theory. As of 1990, however, when the Speech Communication Association (SCA, now the National Communication Association; NCA) started publishing this journal (see Cissna, Eadie, & Hickson, this volume), *JACR*'s editorial policy included the criterion that applied communication research "is securely based in theory but its purpose is not immediate theory building" (Eadie, 1990, p. 2). A 2004 policy statement asked, as the first of four editorial criteria for publishing research studies in *JACR*, "Is the research securely based in theory? Does the study build from or lead to theory?" (Keyton, 2004, p. 1). Finally, at the time of this writing, *JACR*'s policy states:

> The *Journal of Applied Communication Research* publishes original scholarship that addresses or challenges the relation between theory and practice in understanding communication in applied contexts.... Original research studies should apply existing theory and research to practical solutions, problems, and practices; should illuminate how embodied activities inform and reform existing theory or should contribute to theory development. (Stafford, 2009, n.p.)

Obviously, the role of theory in applied communication scholarship has expanded significantly over time and the debate that produced this evolution of *JACR* editorial policies is worth a closer look.

Calls for more attention to theory in applied communication research clearly were rising by the early 1980s. A series of research editorials in SCA's newsletter, *Spectra*, attacked what were perceived to be intellectually shallow applied concerns as being "The Shame of Speech Communication" (Ellis, 1982), defended the traditional distinction between applied and theoretical scholarship but noted that the former "is always informed by theory" (Eadie, 1982, p. 4), and advocated a turn to practical theory in the tradition of Lewin (Gordon, 1982). The first issue of *JACR* under Kenneth N. Cissna's editorship contained a seven-article symposium on "Application of Communication Theory to Communication Practice" (Cissna, 1982a), in which prominent communication theorists suggested how their theories could be practically applied. Most of the suggested applications were rather sketchy, but Bormann (1982) reported an extensive program of applied communication research based on his symbolic convergence theory (e.g., Cragan & Shields, 1981). Although one could infer from Bormann's article that this applied research program may have contributed to the development of symbolic convergence theory, neither his nor any of the other symposium articles explicitly mentioned the possibility that applied communication research could not only use theory but also elaborate theory.

G. R. Miller and Sunnafrank (1984) argued influentially that "applied research, when properly conceived and conducted, can contribute to the development and understanding of communication theory," and that such theoretically oriented applied research was beneficial "both in its practical and social value to the sponsor and its intellectual interest to the scholarly community" (p. 255). Using G. R. Miller's program of research on videotaped trial testimony (e.g., G. R. Miller & Fontes, 1979) as an exemplar, G. R. Miller and Sunnafrank advocated research that tested social-scientific theory and, at the same time, addressed applied issues of concern to the research sponsor.

Eadie (1990, p. 5), although agreeing that "theory-building research can be done in applied settings," maintained that theory building per se should not be a necessary criterion for applied communication research. Ellis (1991), however, in Eadie's (1991) inaugural special issue of *JACR* on "The Agenda for Applied Communication Research," argued that *JACR*'s new editorial policy about theory-based applied research actually was consistent with G. R. Miller and Sunnafrank's (1984) position. In that same special issue, Weick and Browning (1991, citing Thomas & Tymon, 1982) presented five characteristics of "useful ideas" (descriptive relevance, focus on outcomes, operational validity, nonobviousness, and timeliness) that could be regarded as criteria for employing theory in applied communication scholarship. Kreps, Frey, and O'Hair (1991, p. 80, citing Snizek & Furhman, 1980; see also O'Hair, Kreps, & Frey, 1990) argued that applied communication research should be guided by theory that is "practically relevant" rather than "academically elegant," and that such research can test the predictive validity of theory. In various ways, these scholars suggested that applied communication research should test the usefulness of theoretical ideas, which themselves should be explicitly designed to be useful in practice—a central goal of practical theory.

The role of theory—as seen from remarkably diverse epistemological perspectives—also was a prominent theme of the 1991 Tampa Conference on Applied Communication, a key moment in the institutionalization of applied communication research (Cissna, 1995b; see also Cissna et al., this volume). Recommendation 8 (of 21 recommendations formally adopted by the conference) stated that "applied communication researchers, like all scholars, should strive to develop and refine theory so that insights gained are useful in situations beyond the specific ones studied" (Cissna, 1995a, p. 197). Most chapters in the text that Cissna (1995b) edited from that conference spoke directly to the role of theory in applied communication research. G. R. Miller (1995) defended the position argued earlier by G. R. Miller and Sunnafrank (1984), and Seibold (1995), although basically agreeing with G. R. Miller's concept of theory, argued for the value of a broader range of theory-applying, as well as theory-building, applied communication research. Other contributors offered radical alternatives for applied research, challenging the traditional concept of explanatory scientific theory that had dominated the communication field and had been applied whole cloth to applied communication scholarship. Argyris (1995) distinguished between knowledge that merely is *applicable* (relevant) and knowledge that actually is *usable* (by describing a sequence of actions that leads to specified consequences), and advocated an approach to applied communication research based on theories of practice, such as action-science models, rather than traditional social-scientific theories based on a hypothetico-deductive model. In Conquergood's (1995, p. 85) view, applied communication researchers should be "engaged intellectuals" who use theory for purposes of critical reflection and ideological critique. Craig (1995) and Wood (1995) also argued, in different ways, that theory should be understood and employed as a form of critical reflection on communicative practices. Although only Craig (1995) explicitly used the term *practical theory*, each of these essays expressed impulses that converged toward one or another of the approaches to practical theory that we examine in the following sections.

Three special issues or sections of *JACR* published between 1998 and 2000 (Frey, 1998a; O'Hair, 2000a; Petronio, 1999a) reflected the growing influence of practical theory as a concept in applied communication scholarship, although these works did not use that term explicitly. Introducing a special issue on "Communication and Social Justice Research," Frey (1998b), citing several of the essays in Cissna (1995b) and related writings, claimed that most communication scholars no longer recognized a categorical distinction between theory and application. Moreover, as Frey, Pearce, Pollock, Artz, and

Murphy (1996) previously had noted, applied communication scholarship from a social justice perspective requires that "the very form of theory envisioned as guiding research must shift" (p. 115, see also Frey & SunWolf, this volume). Proposing yet another way of merging theory and practice in her introduction to a special issue on "Translating Scholarship into Practice," Petronio (1999b) defined *translation* as "using the 'science of interpretation' to translate theoretical orientations and research findings into usable information in the everyday world" at the same time that scholars "preserve the integrity of the research and theory" (pp. 87, 88). Finally, introducing a special forum in which several prominent scholars offered definitions of applied communication scholarship, O'Hair (2000b, pp. 164–165) found one of three "harmonious themes" running through the forum to be "the recursive nature of theory and practice—one informs and improves the other," but he questioned how practice actually had informed theory.

Our review of the evolving role of theory in applied communication scholarship over the last 3 decades warrants several conclusions. First, although the role of theory has expanded steadily and a consensus has emerged that applied communication research should be grounded in theory, the diversity of epistemological approaches to grounding applied research in theory has increased apace. Second, a growing consensus exists that applied communication research can contribute to theory development, although there is continuing disagreement as to how and how much it should do so. Third, discussions of theory increasingly have emphasized the need for some distinct type of "usable" or "practical" theory in applied research, but "practical theory" per se has not yet become a common term for describing the work done by applied communication researchers. Many applied communication scholars, thus, seem to be groping implicitly toward some type of practical theory, but without the guidance of an explicit model or set of principles. A barrier to articulating an explicit model is that the implicit impulses toward practical theory seem to be pushing in several different directions, leading to the need to distinguish different approaches to practical theory. Consequently, we turn to three approaches to practical theorizing.

The Practice of Practical Theorizing: Three Approaches

A special issue of the journal *Communication Theory* on "Practical Theory," edited by Barge (2001a), provided a welcome opportunity to crystallize and reflect on some creative alternatives that have emerged in the theory and practice of applied communication scholarship. It quickly became apparent to Barge, as the editor, that practical theory meant different things to the scholars who submitted essays to the special issue. Some submitters adopted a more Lewinian position that viewed practical theory as a high-quality description of (1) the problems, puzzles, dilemmas, or challenges constituting a practice; (2) the particular communicative strategies, moves, and structures that manage those problems; and (3) the consequences of performing particular communicative strategies. By offering high-quality descriptions using a variety of scientific, interpretive, and critical modes of inquiry, these submitters developed theories that have practical implications for solving important problems and addressing salient issues. Other submitters grounded their work in Craig's (1989) view of practical theory as a normative reconstruction of practice. Still other submitters based their approach in Cronen's (1995, 2001) articulation of practical theory as a tool for informing a grammar of practice that facilitates joining with the grammars of others to explore their unique patterns of situated action. Hence, although every submitter was concerned with articulating the theory–practice relationship from a practical theory perspective, they did so in different ways.

To make sense of the variety of studies submitted for that special issue, Barge (2001b) distinguished three broad approaches to practical theory that took different perspectives to the theory–practice relationship: (1) mapping, (2) engaged reflection, and (3) transformative practice. First, *practical theory as mapping* begins by creating a high-quality map of reality through scientific, interpretive, or critical methods that subsequently can be used to inform practice. The idea that the maps of reality created by scholars can inform practice is present in Lewin's (1951) oft-quoted dictum that "there is nothing so practical as a good theory" (p. 169; see also Gordon, 1982), as well as G. R. Miller and Sunnafrank's (1984) merger of theoretical and applied research, and Petronio's (1999b) translation concept. Each of these theorists embraced a mapping approach to the development of practical theory.

Second, *practical theory as engaged reflection* explicitly addresses the reflexive relationship between theory and practice—how each can inform the other—and, therefore, reflects an integration of practical and theoretical discourses. From this perspective, theory emerges from a systematic reflection on communicative practice in terms of the kinds of problems, dilemmas, and sites that people engage in the conduct of their lives and how they manage them. Conquergood (1995), Craig (1995), Frey et al. (1996), and Wood (1995) all expressed impulses that converge toward the idea of engaged reflection.

Third, *practical theory as transformative practice* emphasizes "the immediate transformation of the practice and the abilities of both the members of a community and the practical theorist" (Barge, 2001b, p. 9). Practical theory from this perspective is viewed as a useful resource for theorists and practitioners to help them make sense of situations and take action that is intended to improve those situations. Developed by Shotter (1984) and Cronen (1995, 2001), among other scholars, this approach is less clearly represented than the other two approaches in the literature reviewed to this point, although it resonates in certain ways with the various impulses toward direct and immediate intervention in practical situations expressed by scholars such as Hickson (1973), Argyris (1995), and Frey et al. (1996).

Our contention is that these three approaches, although by no means exhausting all possibilities or encompassing all existing views, offer a useful framework for reflecting on the goals of practical theory in applied communication scholarship and provide clear alternatives to facilitate the creative and systematic development of practical theory in the future. The following sections examine these three approaches, and variations within each, in more detail, summarizing their main concepts and methods, reviewing illustrative applied communication studies (based on a search of 5 recent years of *JACR*), and identifying and assessing assumptions and issues of each approach.

Practical Theorizing as Mapping

This approach toward practical theory highlights the importance of theory in creating a map of the communicative territory of people's experience and identifying the important landmarks and pathways that distinguish that landscape. Within this broad approach, different perspectives toward viewing practical theory as mapping have emerged in applied communication scholarship. Specifically, a scientific approach based on traditional hypothetico-deductive models of social-scientific theory can be distinguished from interpretive and critical approaches that have embraced social constructionist assumptions.

Scientific Approach to Mapping

Some applied communication scholarship aspires to a scientific ideal in theory building. Anderson and Baym (2004) referred to such scholarship as "foundational/empirical" because it emphasizes a *foundational epistemology* that views knowledge as the correspondence between the mental images that people have of a phenomenon and an independent, stable material reality, and privileges *empiricism*, the systematic observational experience of human communication. Scientific theory reflects the assumptions and values typically associated with theory in the natural sciences, in that "the archetypal character of theory is ... axiomatic and causal; its method, objective, and metric, its arguments generalized and syllogistic deductions that make claims about prediction and control of a stable, determined, and material reality" (Anderson & Baym, 1995, p. 593). In this view, high-quality scientific theory typically is evaluated according to the criteria of explanation, prediction, control, and heuristic value.

There are several implications that flow from this view of theory for the theory–practice relationship. First, theorizing is viewed as a distinct activity from practice; it is a context-independent activity that generates generalizable explanations of human behavior. Applied communication scholarship, however, typically focuses on a problem or issue involving practice (e.g., Cissna, 2000; Keyton, 2000); the term *practice* in that context refers to different types of communicative conduct, such as sexual harassment, supervisor communication, and emotion management, or to communication in various institutional scenes, such as health-care teams, public meetings, and classrooms (Craig & Tracy, 1995). Practices are situated in time and space in a way that theory is not; a particular theory, therefore, can be applied to a specific communication problem or issue and its fit with the material reality of that problem or issue assessed.

In the case of applied communication scholarship, a wide variety of scientific theories have been used to explore communication problems and issues, such as Witte's (1992, 1994) extended parallel processing model (EPPM; Morman, 2000; Slater, Karan, Rouner, & Walthers, 2002; see also Witte & Roberto, this volume), Petronio's (1991) communication boundary management theory (Golish & Caughlin, 2002), Burgoon's (1995; Burgoon & Hale, 1988) nonverbal expectancy violation theory (McPherson, Kearney, & Plax, 2003), Sunnafrank's (1986) predicted outcome value theory (Bippus, Kearney, Plax, & Brooks, 2003), and inoculation theory (Compton & Pfau, 2004). In each of these studies, a particular communication problem or issue was identified and a relevant causal theory was selected as a way to engage the problem and determine how it might best be addressed. For example, Morman (2000) focused on how persuasive messages can be structured to motivate men to perform testicular self-examinations on a regular basis. Using the EPPM, Morman's experimental study found that high-threat/high-efficacy messages motivated men to perform testicular self-exams to a larger degree than did high-threat/low-efficacy messages.

Second, from the perspective of practical theory as mapping, theory building is viewed as a more important activity than practical application. In her discussion of scholarship as translation, Petronio (1999b) suggested that theory and application are distinct activities:

> Through translation, we are able to preserve the integrity of the research and theory because it bridges knowledge production with knowledge utilization. Translating means that we take the knowledge discovered through research or theory and interpret it for everyday use. Translators develop pathways for converting research knowledge into practice. (p. 88)

The metaphor of translation, thus, privileges theory over application, because application or knowledge utilization is not possible without the knowledge initially generated by theory.

A cursory examination of discussion sections of applied communication research articles within the foundational/empirical tradition emphasizes the importance of theory over practice. Although it is rare for the practical implications of theory and research not to be explicitly stated in applied communication scholarship, typically, a discussion of the theoretical implications of the research initially is offered followed by an examination of the practical implications. Carson and Cupach (2000), for instance, began the discussion section of their article (which received the 2001 Distinguished Article Award from NCA's Applied Communication Division), by highlighting how their study of workplace reproaches validates the importance of using perceived face threat to explain relational outcomes, such as interactional fairness, anger, and communication competence, in theories of facework. This discussion of theory was followed by some implications of the research study for managers, which included recommendations such as using facework strategies during face-threatening situations. As another example, Feeley (2000) initially suggested in the discussion section of the article that, based on his study of communication and employee turnover, the erosion model needs reconceptualization and then followed up with a series of practical suggestions for managers who wish to retain employees, such as integrating employees into the social network of the organization as soon as possible. The sequencing of these topics within the discussion sections of these *JACR* articles strongly suggests that theory and theory development are more important than applications, because they are the foundation on which applications may be built.

The scholarship of translation also emphasizes a unidirectional flow of communication from theorists and researchers to practitioners once a research study has been completed. The scholarship of translation focuses on ways that knowledge can be brought to an audience that preserves the nuance and integrity of the theory and research but also connects with particular communities of practice. The issue becomes how scholars can transmit information in ways that are most beneficial for the target population or populations (Petronio, 1999b). Activities such as interventions, training, and instructional programs (see Frey & SunWolf, this volume) can be designed once a study has been conducted, as the practical implications of research become possible only after its completion.

Third, as previously stated, scientific theory is evaluated according to a correspondence criterion that emphasizes the importance of there being a clear correspondence between the mental images of the phenomena created in theories and the material world. This criterion leads theorists to employ the language of validation when assessing theory. Consider the following phrases (with italics added) from foundational/empirical applied communication scholarship:

- "These findings *validate* POV theory." (Bippus et al., 2003, p. 260)
- "These effects are *consistent with the EPPM-based proposition*." (Slater et al., 2002, p. 45)
- "The findings demonstrated that variation in perceptions of intergroup contact is related to perceptions of experiences of outgroup variability in the *predicted* fashion." (Soliz & Harwood, 2003, p. 337)

The italicized phrases highlight that good theory should be validated by data that are consistent with the predictions offered by the deduced hypotheses. When data do not comport with a priori predictions, the theory often needs to be revised to reflect more accurately the material reality. For example, Feeley (2000) revised his erosion model of employee turnover and Eastman, Schwartz, and Cai (2005) revised their general salience model of the impact of on-air promotions on televised movie ratings in light of the data they obtained.

Interpretive and Critical Approaches to Mapping

Interpretive and critical approaches to theory building entail mapping problems, puzzles, dilemmas, or challenges constituting a practice; describing particular communicative strategies, moves, and structures to manage those problems; articulating consequences of performing particular communicative strategies; and (in critically oriented studies) critiquing existing practices and sometimes proposing alternative practices to promote positive social change. Like a scientific approach to mapping, interpretive and critical approaches also view theory as a resource that can be used to analyze and make sense of data. As a result, such theoretical perspectives embrace reflexivity, adopting a social constructionist epistemology that acknowledges knowledge production as a social accomplishment that occurs through language (Alvesson & Sköldberg, 2000; Anderson & Baym, 2004). This approach to mapping entails three important ideas.

First, theory is a reflexive resource for describing and critiquing practice. A theory becomes a lens or prism through which to view, analyze, and critique a practice, and it is selected because it enables the theorist to consider questions that have not been addressed in previous research (Huspek, 2000). For example, Baxter, Braithwaite, Golish, and Olsen (2002) used dialectical theory to illuminate complex contradictions in support groups and to suggest useful communicative strategies for managing these contradictions; Dougherty and Smythe's (2004, p. 312) study of sexual harassment used "sense making as a theoretical lens"; and Harter's (2004) study of cooperatives highlighted "the dialectic of independence and solidarity [as] a revealing prism through which to make sense of how members enact cooperative life" (p. 99).

A theoretical analysis and description of a practice is not the same as developing a theory of that practice, although the results from the inquiry are reflexively turned back on the preexisting theory to rethink and reconceptualize it. For instance, applied communication research based on interpretive mapping has led to a rethinking of Jablin's (1987) socialization model (Gibson & Papa, 2000), role development theory and strategic ambiguity (K. Miller, Joseph, & Apker, 2000), Weick's (1995) sense-making theory (Murphy, 2001), and dialectical theory (Baxter et al., 2002; Medved et al., 2001). This form of theorizing does not diminish the importance of theoretically reflecting on or conceptualizing a practice but the theoretical description of the practice does not itself constitute a theory.

Second, theorizing a practice is viewed as a distinct activity from intervention. Similar to scientific mapping, intervention is something that typically happens after, not during, the research act. For example, Baxter et al. (2002) clearly separated theorizing dialectical tensions that women experience when their husbands suffer from adult dementia from conducting intervention activities, concluding their essay by translating their findings into a suggested intervention activity where support groups for these women could make dialectical tensions a focus for discussion. One possible exception is Sherblom, Keränen, and Withers's (2002) use of structuration theory to study tensions that game wardens face during an organizational transition. They collected data as part of a larger consultation process with game wardens and developed specific training to aid them during an organizational transition. However, it is unclear whether the analysis presented in their research report actually was used during the consultation to inform training of the game wardens.

Given the reflexive nature of interpretive and critical mapping approaches, it is surprising that relevant research reports do not indicate how participants were influenced by the research process. In the studies we examined, member checks typically were conducted to verify theorists' analyses, especially if a particular organization or organizational unit served as the research site (e.g., Ellingson, 2003; Harter & Krone, 2001; Morgan & Krone, 2001; Ruud, 2000). These member checks involved the researchers conducting individual interviews or focus groups to have participants reflect on the researchers' findings. Although we suspect that these conversations directly influenced participants' understanding of the research and their subsequent activity in that site, there were no explicit references in these reports regarding whether and how participants subsequently used this knowledge.

Third, practical theory from this perspective is judged according to its heuristic value. When practical theory is conceived as a lens or prism for viewing a practice, the primary issue is whether this particular lens provides a useful way of viewing the phenomenon. One way this issue is determined is when practical theorists employ a particular theory because it opens up a set of questions that previously have not been addressed. For example, Dougherty (2001) used feminist standpoint theory to gain new insights about male and female perspectives on sexual harassment, and Zoller (2003) employed critical theory to examine the material implications of ideological discourse associated with occupational health and safety. A second way to determine the usefulness of a particular theoretical lens is when the theoretical description of a practice generates new insights regarding key ideas and concepts of the theory and their potential use (see, e.g., Lucas & Buzzanell, 2004; Martin, 2004). Both approaches emphasize the heuristic aspects of theory construction.

Practical Theory as Engaged Reflection

A second broad approach to practical theorizing works to sustain a productive reflexivity between theory and practice such that each informs the other. From this perspective, theory emerges out of a systematic reflection on communication problems and practices and, in that sense, is grounded in practice. Theories also potentially contribute to the ongoing social construction of the practices they conceptualize insofar as they actually are incorporated into practical discourse among ordinary members of communities of practice as ways of understanding, guiding, and critiquing their practices. The metaphors of "maps" and "lens" used by scientific and interpretive and critical practical theorists become problematic for theory from this perspective, because the theoretical "map" not only describes but also potentially shapes the territory, and the theoretical "lens" is scrutinized and shaped from the standpoint of the scene in which it is used to observe. Applied communication research has a necessary role in this process of engaged reflection, not only as a means by which practical theory can be tested in use but also as a means by which communication problems and practices can be conceptualized and, thereby, contribute to the construction of practical theory.

Two distinct approaches to practical theory as engaged reflection have been explicitly formulated and currently contribute to applied communication research: grounded practical theory and design theory. Each is introduced along with applied research examples.

Grounded Practical Theory

Grounded practical theory (GPT; Craig & Tracy, 1995) was developed within a general framework of communication studies as a "practical discipline." Craig (1983) began this line of inquiry into what he called *practical theory* (theory adapted to values and concerns intrinsic to social practices other than those of pure science) and *practical discipline* (an academic discipline with rigorous methods for developing practical theory). These concepts subsequently were elaborated with regard to the role of various social-scientific methods (Craig, 1984), how the discipline as a whole can be designed to cultivate communication as a practical art (Craig, 1989), the role of applied communication research (Craig, 1995), the underlying process of practical reflection (Craig, 2001), and how meta-discourse (practical discourse about discourse) mediates the dialectic of theory and practice (Craig, 1996, 1999a, 1999b, 2006).

GPT incorporates some elements of traditional grounded theory methodology (Glaser & Strauss, 1967), but with the goal of constructing practical theory rather than traditional social-scientific theory. The GPT method moves back and forth between interpretive empirical studies of particular communicative practices and an evolving normative model or "rational reconstruction" that conceptualizes values and principles (or "situated ideals") already partly implicit in those practices. Studies of practices can be conducted through various ethnographic (see Ellingson, this volume) and discourse-analytic methods (see Tracy and Mirivel, this volume). Especially useful is action-implicative discourse analysis (AIDA), a method explicitly oriented toward creating GPT (K. Tracy, 1995, 2005).

When creating GPT, practices can be rationally reconstructed at three interrelated levels of description:

* *Problem level*: dilemmas that are commonly experienced.
* *Technical level*: communication strategies available for managing problems.
* *Philosophical level*: reasoned principles, grounded in the situated ideals of ordinary participants, that can inform reflective thinking and discourse about problems and strategies. (Craig & Tracy, 1995)

Existing theories of communication, regardless of whether they were intentionally constructed according to this model, also can be grounded in practice by assessing their usefulness as resources for engaged reflection on problems, strategies, and principles in applied situations.

Examples of applied communication research taking an explicitly GPT approach include studies of practical dilemmas in conducting academic colloquia (K. Tracy, 1997a) and classroom discussions (Craig & Tracy, 2005; Muller, 2002), interaction problems between callers and call-takers at a 911 emergency service (K. Tracy, 1997b; K. Tracy & Tracy, 1998), constructing community in a women's safe house (Ashcraft, 2001), negotiations between the Federal Bureau of Investigation and David Koresh during the 1993 Waco siege (Agne & Tracy, 2001), and managing conflict in a local school board (Craig & Tracy, 2005; K. Tracy & Ashcraft, 2001; K. Tracy & Muller, 2001).

We expand on a few of these examples to illustrate some different options when constructing GPT. K. Tracy and Ashcraft's (2001) study of disputes over the wording of a school district's diversity goals illustrates inductive theory building at the technical, problem, and philosophical levels. Their discourse analysis of school board meetings identified three strategies for framing wording changes in a proposed policy, and found that each frame sometimes was challenged. The group's struggles over wording reflected members' efforts to manage a dilemma between crafting a policy that was committed to clear values but divisive versus a policy that was ambiguous but more widely acceptable. On the philosophical level, K. Tracy and Ashcraft (p. 312) argued in the conclusion to the article that framing a value conflict as "a mere wording difference" can be a good way for a group to engage in value-based conflict and keep the group together.

A study of a women's safe house by Ashcraft (2001) shows how GPT can be pursued through ethnographic methods. A key problem faced by nonbureaucratic organizations grounded in feminist principles, such as safe houses, is "a persistent pull between the ideals of feminist empowerment ideology and the practical demands of organizing" (Ashcraft, p. 81). Ashcraft's ethnographic analysis identified strategies used by safe-house members attempting to implement the organization's formal communication principles, revealed tensions and problematic assumptions within those principles, and proposed a normative model of empowering community.

K. Tracy and Muller's (2001) study of how school boards formulate problems illustrates the reflexive grounding of existing theories by engaging critically both with a group's practices and with the theories themselves. Theories of argumentation, rhetorical fact construction, and moral conflict each led to a different diagnosis of the school board's communication problems. After showing how each theory illuminated certain group practices, but fell short in some ways, the authors concluded with reflections on the importance of a group's choices about how to formulate its problems and on issues that need to be addressed by a practical theory of problem formulation.

Finally, Craig and Tracy's (2005) study of pragmatic uses of "the issue" in classroom group discussions and school board meetings illustrates how a comparison of two applied situations can contribute to GPT. In student classroom discussions, references to "the issue" generally were used to raise and clarify points of controversy in ways compatible with normative argumentation theory, whereas participants in school board meetings actively avoided framing problems as controversial issues. The authors argued that the comparison suggested normative criteria for selecting an argument or problem-solving frame for conducting a group discussion.

Although GPT has not yet been widely used as an explicit theoretical approach in applied communication scholarship, it is not uncommon for applied researchers to propose theoretical conceptualizations of practices that are discovered empirically in actual use. Williams and Olaniran (2002), in an analysis of how organizations respond to a public controversy involving race, identified a previously untheorized strategy of "limited apology" (p. 310). Similarly, Seeger and Ulmer (2002) conceptualized an alternative rhetorical approach to crisis communication. S. J. Tracy (2004), in an ethnographic study that applied theories of dialectics, dilemmas, and pragmatic paradoxes to the interpretation of organizational tensions, proposed a grounded theoretical model that conceptualized alternative strategies for framing such tensions. Lucas and Buzzanell (2004), studying occupational narratives of blue-collar workers, found discursive practices that could be theorized to provide alternatives to white-collar conceptions of career and success. The central contribution of these studies was to conceptualize one or more communication techniques that had been used implicitly in practice and to assess those practices in terms of a theoretically informed interpretation of the problematic situation. Although these studies that proposed grounded theoretical conceptualizations of practice did not explicitly use a GPT methodology, they are broadly consistent with GPT and, in the future, might be usefully pursued in that framework.

Design Theory

A second approach to practical theory as engaged reflection conducts communication research as a disciplined design enterprise that, at once, is both theoretical and applied (see Aakhus & Jackson, 2005; Jackson, 1998). As Aakhus and Jackson (2005, p. 413) noted, "design is a natural fact about communication," observable in the behavior of ordinary communicators, as well as experts, such as in their study of facilitators and developers of new group communication technologies (see Poole & DeSanctis, this volume). Aakhus and Jackson argued that designs for communication always involve "hypotheses about how things work," but "professional communities that practice communication design can be unreflective about the communicative theory underpinning the knowledge of their craft" (pp. 413, 416). Design theory, consequently, as Aakhus and Jackson explained, puts the design process on a theoretical basis:

> The body of theory built up in a design enterprise is a body of interactional puzzles and the solutions designed to solve these puzzles. It is also built up through the development of the concepts and rationales used in judging what counts as a problem to be solved, what counts as an appropriate solution, and the justificatory link between problem and solution. In this sense, design expertise constitutes a practical theory about communication and interaction (Craig & Tracy, 1995). The activity in design enterprise, however, never moves far from the actual creation of useable procedures for communication. (p. 417)

Design theory, like GPT, generates both empirical descriptions and ideal normative models of communication. However, unlike the empirically grounded "situated ideals" of GPT, design theory pursues the creation of new designs for bringing communicative practices into closer alignment with ideal norms. Although we regard it as form of engaged reflection, design theory also has some resemblance to practical theory as transformative practice (discussed below) in that it is intended to be used by communication practitioners for the purpose of direct intervention into specific situations to transform communicative practices.

Applied communication research utilizing a design approach has included work on the design of Web-based instructional support protocols (Jackson, 1998; Jackson & Madison, 1999; Jackson & Wolski, 2001), discourse for policy controversy (Aakhus, 1999), tools to facilitate reflective dialogue in group meetings (Aakhus, 2001), and techniques of third-party mediation (Jacobs, Jackson, Hallmark, Hall, & Stearns, 1987). Harrison and Morrill (2004) used normative pragmatics and social–contextual approaches to identify normative ideals of dispute-resolution processes as a basis for "critical analysis of communication systems and protocols for the purposes of reengineering features to help achieve an ideal system" (p. 322). Also worth mentioning is work by Kaufer and Butler (1996) on rhetoric as a design art, and Goodwin's (2002) line of design work in argumentation theory, both of which have shown important pedagogical applications.

Aakhus (2001), in a study of the professional beliefs of group decision support system facilitators, presented an interesting hybrid of the GPT and design theory approaches. Based on individual interview and focus group data, Aakhus reconstructed and critiqued what, in GPT terms, was the situated ideal of group facilitation: a philosophy of process management based on the assumption that content and process can be clearly separated. Arguing that this philosophy encounters several problems and contradictions, including a failure to understand communication as a constitutive process, Aakhus recommended that facilitators should adopt an alternative philosophy based in a design stance that emphasizes communicative expertise. The study illustrates that the GPT and design theory approaches to engaged reflection, although different in some ways, are not fundamentally incompatible.

Practical Theory as Transformative Practice

Practical theory also may be viewed as a transformative practice that simultaneously emphasizes the elaboration of the abilities of practical theorists and research participants. Cronen's (1995, 2001; Cronen & Chetro-Szivos, 2001) view of practical theory best reflects this approach. Grounded in a pragmatic–systemic approach toward inquiry, Cronen (2001) argued that:

> A practical theory informs a grammar of practice that facilitates joining with the grammars of others to explore their unique patterns of situated action. The proximal reason for joining is the cocreation of new affordances and constraints for creative participation in the instrumental and consummatory dimensions of experience. (p. 26)

To understand how this perspective toward practical theory approaches the practice–theory relationship, we explore the implications of this definition, highlight a research exemplar that adopts this approach, and reflect on ways that such an approach may be evaluated.

The Implications of Transformative Practice

Several implications flow from this definition of practical theory. First, practical theory informs a "grammar" of practice, a notion drawn from Wittgenstein's (1953) ideas concerning "meaning-as-use" and "language games" as a grammar of practice reflected in the rules for meaning and action that people use in situated moments of conversation. Articulating a grammar of practice focuses attention on rules that people use to inform their practice and how the rules-in-use obligate, permit, or prohibit ways of making sense and acting into situations. For example, scholars who adopt a quantitative approach to study communication and other social sciences (see Query et al., this volume) use rules to make choices about what statistical tests are appropriate given the unique intersection of their theoretical presuppositions and hypotheses, the way they operationalized the variables studied, the type of data collected, and the particular characteristics of the research participant population. Similarly, family therapists make situated choices about questions to ask during sessions with clients. In both examples, a practical theory helps to inform the abilities of practitioners to act within an emerging situation.

Practical theories are explicitly heuristic in that they offer a set of guides in the form of models, concepts, principles, and practices that people use to make sense of and respond to situations. For those who view practical theory as mapping, these guides are used to describe reality. Even for those practical theorists who engage in interpretive and critical mapping, and recognize the fleeting and partial character of their depictions, models, concepts, and principles still are used to render a coherent mapping of the meaning of a communicative practice. The key difference between viewing practical theory as a form of mapping and transformative practice is that the models, concepts, and principles become instrumentalities or tools for furthering inquiry within the domain of transformative practice.

Second, practical theorists explicitly engage and address the interests of research participants. K. A. Pearce and Pearce (2001) argued that practical theorists are concerned with "helping participants in the projects they engage.... This implies engagement with, not just observations of, participants in our projects" (p. 109). This stance requires practical theorists to pay close attention to the unique, situated patterns of experience that participants cocreate, and to find ways to create new affordances and constraints for action. Practical theory as transformative practice embraces a participatory action research model, where there is shared ownership of the research projects by researchers and research participants, a joint analysis of social problems, and an orientation to action (Kemmis & McTaggart, 2000). This stance, therefore, emphasizes the importance of collaborative learning during the process of practical theorizing.

K. A. Pearce and Pearce (2001) suggested that this process of joint learning involves developing the abilities to answer two questions: "What's going on here?" and "What should I do?" (p. 109). More specifically, the questions are "What are the patterns of meaning and action that people create in their everyday practices that inform their way of living together?" and "In light of those patterns, how do they inform what I do next?" The first question emphasizes learning with others about how to expand one's vocabulary to make sense of situations; the second question involves learning how to elaborate one's vocabulary of action. This learning occurs at two levels: In conversation with research participants, practical theorists enlarge their ability and vocabulary to describe situations and take actions; furthermore, as a result of the collaborative learning process with practical theorists and among other research participants, research participants enlarge their abilities to make sense of situations and act.

Third, practical theorists arrange conversations among other practical theorists, practitioners, and research participants (K. A. Pearce & Pearce, 2001). Research occurs at the nexus of several conversations, including the larger scholarly community in which one participates, which involves Institutional Review Boards (see Seeger, Sellnow, Ulmer, & Novak this volume), journal editorial boards, and the like, as well as a network of practitioners who share an interest in the domain of study and the research participants themselves (Hardy, Phillips, & Clegg, 2001). The decision that scholars must make is what conversations to privilege over others in the research process. Practical theorists focusing on transformative practice emphasize conversations with the research participants in their projects and with other practitioners and scholars within a particular area of study. A failure to keep in conversation with research participants inhibits the ability of practical theorists to respond to participants' needs; a failure to talk to other practitioners and scholars within a particular domain lessens the likelihood of creating theory that addresses important issues and concerns within a given community of practice.

Highlighting Research Exemplars

Our review of five volumes of *JACR* found only one exemplar of applied communication scholarship that closely matched this view of practical theory: Meares, Oetzel, Torres, Derkacs, and Ginossar's (2004) use of muted group theory as a frame for exploring employee mistreatment and employee voice within an organizational setting. These scholars employed muted group theory to inform their inquiry, subsequently shared their research results with employees, and engaged them in discussion about future directions for the organization in light of their findings. The findings also were used to elaborate muted group theory by articulating the role of paradox in employee mistreatment. Meares et al.'s study, however, represents one isolated instance of practical theorizing as transformative practice. Grounding our understanding of practical theorizing as transformative practice is aided by examining a program of research rather than an isolated study. To that end, we examine how W. B. Pearce and Cronen's (1980; Cronen, 1991, 1994; W. B. Pearce, 1989, 1994; see also Barge, 2004) coordinated management of meaning theory (CMM) has been used to promote public participation and dialogue processes as a case study of practical theory as transformative practice.

In the mid-1990s, a group of communication scholars and practitioners formed the Public Dialogue Consortium (PDC), which focused on developing public participation and dialogue processes to enhance democratic engagement within communities (see K. Pearce, Spano, & Pearce, this volume). The PDC's Cupertino Project is its best-known work. This multiyear public communication project in Cupertino, California, was designed to "create communication structures and processes that would allow residents and city officials to work together to identify concerns, articulate visions, and develop action plans that enhance, strengthen, and build community" (Spano, 2001, p. xiv). The members of the PDC were guided by a social constructionist theoretical perspective that included CMM and they employed an eclectic set of interventionist practices. The PDC's use of CMM reflects practical theory as transformative practice in several ways.

First, CMM provided a set of powerful descriptive–diagnostic tools that informed the PDC's grammar of practice. The PDC's ability to explore how persons-in-conversation coordinated their actions and the types of consequences that were produced relied on a variety of CMM concepts and models, such as constitutive and regulative rules (W. B. Pearce & Cronen, 1980), the hierarchy of meaning (W. B. Pearce, 1994), forms of communication (W. B. Pearce, 1989), and the serpentine model of communication (W. B. Pearce, 1994).

Second, the descriptive–diagnostic tools associated with CMM and their grammar of practice evolved during the Cupertino Project. For example, the PDC's engagement with Cupertino led its members to reconsider important CMM concepts, such as "episode," when they moved to the larger public context. As W. B. Pearce and Pearce (2000) explained:

> CMM researchers and theorists have usually thought of them [episodes] as relatively short, uninterrupted patterns of interaction in face-to-face interaction, such as the phases of mediation or therapy sessions. The Cupertino Project required us to think on a very different scale, both in terms of the temporal extension and number of people and groups involved. (p. 414)

Rethinking the concept of episode led to the development of a three-level public dialogue process model that broadened episode to include: (1) *strategic process design*—the overarching plan or roadmap for a sequence of events intended to lead to particular outcomes; (2) *event design*—a series of activities that occur within a given event; and (3) *communication facilitation skills*—how facilitators respond to event participants, which includes conventional practices, such as keeping time and reframing comments (Spano, 2006).

Third, the abilities of research participants to work with one another were elaborated through their participation in the project. Their abilities grew as they appreciated new ways of making sense of their situation and taking action based on that new way of sense making. Consider the comment by a citizen who participated in a town-hall meeting (see Kaid, McKinney, & Tedesco, this volume) about the issue of cultural richness. At that meeting, six high school students who had participated in an intergenerational interview project about Cupertino's future presented the information the project had generated. After hearing about the project and its findings, one citizen responded by saying, "Some of the best ideas I heard tonight came from the six kids that were sitting up here and who went out into the field and talked to people" (Spano, 2001, p. 107). This learning led to citizens organizing themselves and creating new community initiatives that addressed these ideas. For example, a group called the "Citizens of Cupertino Cross-Cultural Consortium" emerged out of a training and team-building program, and subsequently designed a series of culturally based activities.

Fourth, the PDC emphasized keeping a number of simultaneous conversations going. PDC members kept in close contact with the public dialogue participants and continually adjusted their discussion strategies depending on participants' emerging needs. Moreover, throughout the process, conversations between PDC members and other theorists were maintained in the form of convention papers, book chapters, and journal articles, and by inviting scholars to offer feedback on the process. Conversations with other practitioners were generated by PDC members conducting workshops at professional meetings and publishing essays in practitioner-based journals.

Practical theory from a transformative perspective can be used both prospectively and retrospectively. It can be used prospectively in the sense that it provides a set of resources for theorists and practitioners to employ as they think through and anticipate the type of intervention activities they wish to develop during inquiry. For example, in the Cupertino

Project, the expanded notion of episode proved to be a useful concept when PDC members began to design training activities. This new view of episode became a valuable resource for PDC members as they reflected on how they wanted to position themselves later in the process. Practical theory also can be used retrospectively in the sense that it provides a set of tools for making sense of unfolding interaction. For example, CMM tools, such as the hierarchy of meaning and coordination, became important when PDC members reflected on the information that was generated from the intervention activities to create an account of why particular consequences came into being and others did not. The continued use of a practical theory's descriptive–diagnostic tools within various situations and sustained reflection on their use generate new concepts, ideas, methods, and techniques that can be employed both prospectively and retrospectively.

Assessing Practical Theory as Transformative Practice

Given its grounding in the interests of participants and the importance of generating new opportunities for meaning making and action, the primary criterion for assessing practical theory is a pragmatic one. Simply put, practical theory is judged by whether it informed patterns of practice that made life better (Cronen, 1995). To make life better, a practical theory must construct coherent descriptions of situations that implicate lines of action in the form of interventions to improve the situation (Cronen, 2001). From this perspective, descriptions of situations are not themselves a theory but are the findings that emerge from a process of inquiry. The findings then serve as important data for whether the pattern of practice informed by the theory facilitated making the situation better and whether the concepts, methods, and tools associated with the practical theory are useful.

The Prospect for Practical Theory in Applied Communication Research

Several findings emerge from our review of the theory–practice relationship and the process of practical theorizing. First, applied communication scholars are concerned with connecting theory to practice. Whether theory is used to develop predictive models for the design of communicative events to achieve planned outcomes, conceptualize practice, interpret and understand practical situations, or to reform current practices, applied communication scholars emphasize the importance of theory in their research. Second, Barge's (2001a) characterization of the three approaches to practical theory reveals how applied communication scholars have viewed the theory–practice relationship, as examples of each approach were present in the discourse of applied communication scholarship. Third, applied communication scholars tend to adopt a view of practical theory that is rooted in the metaphors of mapping and lens rather than viewing practical theory as a form of reflective engagement or transformative practice. Our examination of *JACR* found numerous examples of practical theory as either scientific or interpretive/critical mapping, but relatively few examples of practical theory as reflective engagement or transformative practice.

Through our analyses, we have attempted to enlarge the vocabulary regarding what it means to engage in practical theorizing and to become practical theorists. By articulating various alternatives that scholars may engage in as they do practical theory, we hope to have provided a resource that facilitates making informed choices. Our belief is that the term *practical theory* has multiple meanings and that the particular meaning a scholar ascribes to it depends on his or her epistemological and ontological assumptions. Thus, we want to avoid fixing the meaning of practical theory by associating it with a particular set of assumptions. For example, W. B. Pearce (1993) suggested that practical theorists are guided by a temperament that is rooted in curiosity conducted about a pluralistic social world that is best known by taking a participant position. From his perspective, theorists who view the world as monistic and conduct research to search for certainty are not engaged in practical theory.

Our point is that what practical theory means depends on the tradition of practice in which a scholar locates him or herself. For example, the work of health communication scholars using theories such as the EPPM (see Witte & Roberto, this volume) represents a scientific mapping approach, which emphasizes a unitary view of the world and a quest for certainty, and, as such, is not viewed as practical theory, according to W. B. Pearce's (1993) theoretical commitments. However, such scholars hardly are passive observers of communication phenomena; they are passionately involved researchers, trying to make a better world by improving, for example, the effectiveness of public health campaigns. Their research is driven by curiosity and openness to whatever they can learn that will be useful, and they are actively involved in conversations with practitioners (e.g., public health professionals) to learn about health-related problems and needs that they can address in their research; indeed, their research often is conducted in conjunction with actual health campaigns. However, they (1) assume that causal patterns can be found, (2) use quantitative hypothesis-testing methods to verify knowledge claims against competing causal explanations, and (3) understand theories (models of underlying causal patterns) to be logically independent from their application in practice. They are practical theorists in the tradition of Lewin (1951), but they approach the theory–practice relationship differently than scholars in the engaged reflection or transformative practice traditions, given their philosophical assumptions.

Given that practical theory can take on different meanings and be employed in different ways, applied communication scholars need to make conscious choices about how they position themselves in relation to the theory–practice relationship. Although we offered a tripartite system for distinguishing approaches to practical theory, theorizing a given practice and conducting a particular research study is not as simple as determining which of the three approaches to adopt. We offered these three approaches as ideal types, but recognize that in the course of doing theory and research, practical theorists may blur the boundaries among approaches and develop a blended approach for a specific research project. The task for practical theorists is how to manage the tension between the epistemological and ontological assumptions they adopt and the specific research problems and sites they engage.

To manage this tension, it is important for applied communication scholars to ask the question, "What contribution or difference do I want my scholarship to make?" This question highlights several important related questions that applied communication scholars need to consider when doing practical theory. First, does the research project emphasize more of a theoretical or practical contribution? As Cronen (2001) observed, "Practical theory does not require that everyone be a practitioner and theorist in equal degree. In any kind of work, various people will emphasize some aspects more than others, and practical theory is no exception" (p. 29). Practical theorists are concerned about the theory–practice relationship, but what position they take on this continuum varies as a function of their specific research project. There will be times when a scholar conducts research primarily to develop theory or to change an existing practice, but an emphasis on either theory or practice does not preclude a concern with the other. Although a single research project may focus on one end of the continuum, the long-term commitment of practical theorists is to keep theory and practice in a constructive tension.

Second, who needs to be involved in the research conversation to make this contribution a reality? The choice point for practical theorists is which conversations need to be emphasized—those with other theorists, practitioners, or research participants. For example, if a practical theorist wants to create a causal map of a practice, the primary conversational partners are other theorists, with practitioner conversations occupying a secondary position. Moreover, those conversations with practitioners would focus on whether they find the map useful for creating intervention activities and how the theoretical findings subsequently can be applied, rather than conversations about the validity of the theory. In contrast, the transformative practice approach emphasizes developing theory in the process of conversation with practitioners and research participants, and simultaneously maintaining ongoing conversations with other theorists to share insights gained from the research project.

Third, when do I want my scholarship to make a difference? One response to this question is to say that the scholarship will make a difference in people's lives after a particular research project has been completed or a program of research is sufficiently developed. This is the position of those individuals who adhere to the notion of the scholarship of translation, as the theoretical knowledge gained from empirical research studies will be translated to practitioners or the public in the form of academic textbooks, training, and development programs (Petronio, 1999a; see also Frey & SunWolf, this volume). Once practical theorists have sufficient confidence in their research findings, they can enter the public conversation about how their work may make a difference in areas such as public policy, community development, and other intervention activities. Engaged reflection also allows for a temporal gap between practical theory construction and application, taking "a broader view that extends the theory–practice loop into the wider society and over a longer span of time" and envisioning that practical theories "may, in the long run, find a niche in the 'ecology' or 'marketplace' of ideas and thereby may influence [practice]" (Craig & Tracy, 1995, p. 268). The result is that the theory and research may not directly and immediately contribute to improving the lives of research participants but may, at some later date, influence them, as the knowledge generated from the theory and research becomes part of the larger public discourse on a particular topic.

A second response to this question is that researchers may decide that it is important to find ways to structure their theory and research to improve research participants' lives, in addition to subsequently becoming part of the larger public discourse on a particular activity. This position suggests that practical theorists take more of an action research or collaborative learning approach (e.g., Costello, 2003; Reason & Bradbury, 2007; Stringer, 2007) and directly feed back the results of their inquiry to research participants so that participants can make wise choices of what to do next. These two answers are not mutually exclusive but practical theorists need to consider when they want their scholarship to make a difference and in what form.

Conclusion

Engaging in practical theory is important work that can positively influence people's lives and improve the quality of practice. Given applied communication scholars' commitment to addressing substantive, real-world problems, practical theory is an important part of making a difference in social worlds. By elaborating in this chapter the vocabulary of what it means to do practical theory and become practical theorists, we hope that applied communication scholars will make more informed choices about their position regarding the theory–practice relationship, the types of differences they wish to make in improving practice, and when they wish to make them.

References

Aakhus, M. (1999). Science court: A case study in designing discourse to manage policy controversy. *Knowledge, Technology, & Policy, 12*(2), 20–37.

Aakhus, M. (2001). Technocratic and design stances toward communication expertise: How GDSS facilitators understand their work. *Journal of Applied Communication Research, 29*, 341–371.

Aakhus, M., & Jackson, S. (2005). Technology, interaction, and design. In K. L. Fitch & R. E. Sanders (Eds.), *Handbook of language and social interaction* (pp. 411–435). Mahwah, NJ: Erlbaum.

Agne, R. R., & Tracy, K. (2001). "Bible babble": Naming the interactional trouble at Waco. *Discourse Studies, 3*, 269–294.

Alvesson, M., & Sköldberg, K. (2000). *Reflexive methodology: New vistas for qualitative research.* Thousand Oaks, CA: Sage.

Anderson, J. A., & Baym, G. (2004). Philosophies and philosophic issues in communication, 1995–2004. *Communication Theory, 54*, 589–615.

Argyris, C. (1995). Knowledge when used in practice tests theory: The case of applied communication research. In K. N. Cissna (Ed.), *Applied communication in the 21st century* (pp. 1–19). Mahwah, NJ: Erlbaum.

Ashcraft, K. L. (2001). Feminist organizing and the construction of "alternative" community. In G. J. Shepherd & E. W. Rothenbuhler (Eds.), *Communication and community* (pp. 79–110). Mahwah, NJ: Erlbaum.

Barge, J. K. (Ed.). (2001a). Practical theory [Special issue]. *Communication Theory, 11*(1).

Barge, J. K. (2001b). Practical theory as mapping, engaged reflection, and transformative practice. *Communication Theory, 11*, 5–13.

Barge, J. K. (2004). Articulating CMM as a practical theory. *Human Systems: The Journal of Systemic Consultation & Management, 15*, 13–32.

Baxter, L. A., Braithwaite, D. O., Golish, T. D., & Olson, L. (2002). Contradiction of interaction for wives of elderly husbands with adult dementia. *Journal of Applied Communication Research, 30*, 1–26.

Bippus, A. M., Kearney, P., Plax, T. G., & Brooks, C. F. (2003). Teacher access and mentoring abilities: Predicting the outcome value of extra class communication. *Journal of Applied Communication Research, 31*, 260–275.

Bormann, E. G. (1982). The symbolic convergence theory of communication: Applications and implications for teachers and consultants. *Journal of Applied Communication Research, 10*, 50–61.

Burgoon, J. K. (1995). Cross-cultural and intercultural applications of expectancy violations theory. In R. L. Wiseman (Ed.), *Intercultural communication theory* (pp. 194–214). Thousand Oaks, CA: Sage.

Burgoon, J. K., & Hale, J. L. (1988). Nonverbal expectancy violations: Model elaboration and application to immediacy behaviors. *Communication Monographs, 55*, 58–79.

Carson, C. L., & Cupach, W. R. (2000). Facing corrections in the workplace: The influence of perceivd face threat on the consequences of managerial reproaches. *Journal of Applied Communication Research, 28*, 215–234.

Cissna, K. N. (Ed.). (1982a). Application of communication theory to communication practice [Special issue]. *Journal of Applied Communication Research, 10*(1).

Cissna, K. N. (1982b). Editor's note: What is applied communication research? *Journal of Applied Communication Research, 10*, iii–v.

Cissna, K. N. (1995a). Appendix A: Recommendations formally adopted by the Tampa Conference on Applied Communication. In K. N. Cissna (Ed.), *Applied communication in the 21st century* (pp. 195–199). Mahwah, NJ: Erlbaum.

Cissna, K. N. (Ed.). (1995b). *Applied communication in the 21st century.* Mahwah, NJ: Erlbaum.

Cissna, K. N. (2000). Applied communication research in the 21st century. *Journal of Applied Communication Research, 28,* 169–173.

Compton, J. A., & Pfau, M. (2004). Use of inoculation to foster resistance to credit card marketing targeting college students. *Journal of Applied Communication Research, 32,* 343–364.

Conquergood, D. (1995). Between rigor and relevance: Rethinking applied communication. In K. N. Cissna (Ed.), *Applied communication in the 21st century* (pp. 79–96). Mahwah, NJ: Erlbaum.

Costello, P. J. M. (2003). *Action research.* New York: Continuum.

Cragan, J. F., & Shields, D. C. (1981). *Applied communication research: A dramatistic approach.* Prospect Heights, IL: Waveland Press.

Craig, R. T. (1983). Galilean rhetoric and practical theory. *Communication Monographs, 50,* 395–412.

Craig, R. T. (1984). Practical criticism of the art of conversation: A methodological critique. *Communication Quarterly, 32,* 178–187.

Craig, R. T. (1989). Communication as a practical discipline. In B. Dervin, L. Grossberg, B. J. O'Keefe, & E. Wartella (Eds.), *Rethinking communication: Vol. 1. Paradigm issues* (pp. 97–122). Newbury Park, CA: Sage.

Craig, R. T. (1995). Applied communication research in a practical discipline. In K. N. Cissna (Ed.), *Applied communication in the 21st century* (pp. 147–155). Mahwah, NJ: Erlbaum.

Craig, R. T. (1996). Practical–theoretical argumentation. *Argumentation, 10,* 461–474.

Craig, R. T. (1999a). Communication theory as a field. *Communication Theory, 9,* 119–161.

Craig, R. T. (1999b). Metadiscourse, theory, and practice. *Research on Language and Social Interaction, 32,* 21–29.

Craig, R. T. (2001). Dewey and Gadamer on practical reflection: Toward a methodology for the practical disciplines. In D. K. Perry (Ed.), *American pragmatism and communication research* (pp. 131–148). Mahwah, NJ: Erlbaum.

Craig, R. T. (2006). Communication as a practice. In G. J. Shepherd, J. St. John, & T. Striphas (Eds.), *Communication as...: Perspectives on theory* (pp. 38–47). Thousand Oaks, CA: Sage.

Craig, R. T., & Tracy, K. (1995). Grounded practical theory: The case of intellectual discussion. *Communication Theory, 5,* 248–272.

Craig, R. T., & Tracy, K. (2005). "The issue" in argumentation practice and theory. In F. H. van Eemeren & P. Houtlosser (Eds.), *Argumentation in practice* (pp. 11–28). Philadelphia: John Benjamins.

Cronen, V. E. (1991). Coordinated management of meaning theory and postenlightenment ethics. In K. J. Greenberg (Ed.), *Conversations on communication ethics* (pp. 21–54). Norwood, NJ: Ablex.

Cronen, V. E. (1994). Coordinated management of meaning: Practical theory for the complexities and contradictions of everyday life. In J. Siegfried (Ed.), *The status of common sense in psychology* (pp. 183–207). Norwood, NJ: Ablex.

Cronen, V. E. (1995). Practical theory and the tasks ahead for social approaches to communication. In W. Leeds-Hurwitz (Ed.), *Social approaches to communication* (pp. 217–242). New York: Guilford Press.

Cronen, V. E. (2001). Practical theory, practical art, and the pragmatic–systemic account of inquiry. *Communication Theory, 11,* 14–35.

Cronen, V. E., & Chetro-Szivos, J. (2001). A naturalistic view of inquiry. In D. Perry (Ed.), *American pragmatism and communication research* (pp. 27–66). Mahwah, NJ: Erlbaum.

Dougherty, D. S. (2001). Sexual harassment as [dys]functional process: A feminist standpoint analysis. *Journal of Applied Communication Research, 29,* 372–402.

Dougherty, D. S., & Smythe, M. J. (2004). Sensemaking, organizational culture, and sexual harassment. *Journal of Applied Communication Research, 32,* 293–317.

Eadie, W. F. (1982, November). The case for applied communication research. *Spectra, 18,* 1, 4.

Eadie, W. F. (1990). Being applied: Communication research comes of age [Special issue]. *Journal of Applied Communication Research,* 1–6.

Eadie, W. F. (Ed.). (1991). The agenda for applied communication research [Special issue]. *Journal of Applied Communication Research, 19*(1–2).

Eastman, S. T., Schwartz, N. C., & Cai, X. (2005). Promoting movies on television. *Journal of Applied Communication Research, 33,* 139–158.

Ellingson, L. L. (2003). Interdisciplinary health care teamwork in the clinic backstage. *Journal of Applied Communication Research, 31,* 93–117.

Ellis, D. G. (1982, March). The shame of speech communication. *Spectra, 18,* 1–2.

Ellis, D. G. (1991). The oneness of opposites: Applied communication and theory. *Journal of Applied Communication Research, 19,* 116–122.

Feeley, T. H. (2000). Testing a communication network model of employee turnover based on centrality. *Journal of Applied Communication Research, 28,* 262–277.

Frey, L. R. (Ed.). (1998a). Communication and social justice research [Special issue]. *Journal of Applied Communication Research, 26*(2).

Frey, L. R. (1998b). Communication and social justice research: Truth, justice, and the applied communication way. *Journal of Applied Communication Research, 26,* 155–164.

Frey, L. R., Pearce, W. B., Pollock, M. A., Artz, L., & Murphy, B. A. O. (1996). Looking for justice in all the wrong places: On a communication approach to social justice. *Communication Studies, 47,* 110–127.

Gibson, M. K., & Papa, M. J. (2000). The mud, the blood, and the beer guys: Organizational osmosis in blue-collar work groups. *Journal of Applied Communication Research, 28,* 68–88.

Glaser, B. G., & Strauss, A. L. (1967). *The discovery of grounded theory: Strategies for qualitative research.* Chicago: Aldine.

Golist, D. D., & Caughlin, J. P. (2002). "I'd rather not talk about it": Adolescents' and young adults' use of topic avoidance in stepfamilies. *Journal of Applied Communication Research, 30,* 78–106.

Goodwin, J. (2002). Designing issues. In F. H. van Eemeren & P. Houtlosser (Eds.), *Dialectic and rhetoric: The warp and woof of argumentation analysis* (pp. 81–96). Boston: Kluwer Academic.

Gordon, R. (1982, October). Practical theory. *Spectra, 18,* 1–2.

Hardy, C., Phillips, N., & Clegg, S. (2001). Reflexivity in organization and management theory: A study of the production of the research "subject." *Human Relations, 54,* 531–560.

Harrison, T. R., & Morrill, C. (2004). Ombuds processes and disputant reconciliation. *Journal of Applied Communication Research, 32,* 318–342.

Harter, L. M. (2004). Masculinity(s), the agrarian frontier myth, and cooperative ways of organizing: Contradictions and tensions in the experience and enactment of democracy. *Journal of Applied Communication Research, 32,* 89–118.

Harter, L. M., & Krone, K. J. (2001). The boundary-spanning role of a cooperative support organization: Managing the paradox of stability and change in non-traditional organizations. *Journal of Applied Communication Research, 29,* 248–277.

Hickson, M., III (1973). Applied communication research: A beginning point for social relevance. *Journal of Applied Communications Research, 1,* 1–5.

Huspek, M. (2000). Oppositional codes: The case of the penitentiary of New Mexico riot. *Journal of Applied Communication Research, 28,* 144–163.

Jablin, F. M. (1987). Organizational entry, assimilation, and exit. In F. M. Jablin, L. L. Putnam, K. H. Roberts, & L. W. Porter (Eds.), *Handbook of organizational communication: An interdisciplinary perspective* (pp. 679–740). Newbury Park, CA: Sage.

Jackson, S. (1998). Argument by design. *Argumentation, 12,* 183–198.

Jackson, S., & Madison, C. (1999). Instruction by design: Technology in the discourse of teaching and learning. In A. L. Vangelisti, J. A. Daly, & G. W. Friedrich (Eds.), *Teaching communication: Theory, research, and methods* (2nd ed., pp. 393–408). Mahwah, NJ: Erlbaum.

Jackson, S., & Wolski, S. (2001). Identification of and adaptation to students' preinstructional beliefs in introductory research methods: Contributions of interactive Web technology. *Communication Education, 50,* 189–205.

Jacobs, S., Jackson, S., Hallmark, J., Hall, B., & Stearns, S. A. (1987). Ideal argument in the real world: Making do in mediation. In J. W. Wenzel (Ed.), *Argument and critical practices: Proceedings of the Fifth SCA/AFA Conference on Argumentation* (pp. 291–298). Annandale, VA: Speech Communication Association.

Kaufer, D. S., & Butler, B. S. (1996). *Rhetoric and the arts of design*. Mahwah, NJ: Erlbaum.

Kemmis, S., & McTaggart, R. (2000). Participatory action research. In N. K. Denzin & Y. S. Lincoln (Eds.), *Handbook of qualitative research* (2nd ed., pp. 567–606). Thousand Oaks, CA: Sage.

Keyton, J. (2000). Applied communication research should be practical. *Journal of Applied Communication Research, 28*, 166–168.

Keyton, J. (2004). Letter from the editor. *Journal of Applied Communication Research, 32*, 1–3.

Kreps, G. L., Frey, L. R., & O'Hair, D. (1991). Applied communication research: Scholarship that can make a difference. *Journal of Applied Communication Research, 19*, 71–87.

Lewin, K. (1951). *Field theory in social science: Selected theoretical papers* (D. Cartwright, Ed.). New York: Harper & Row.

Lucas, K., & Buzzanell, P. M. (2004). Blue-collar work, career, and success: Occupational narratives of *Sisu*. *Journal of Applied Communication Research, 32*, 273–292.

Martin, D. M. (2004). Humor in middle management: Women negotiating the paradoxes of organizational life. *Journal of Applied Communication Research, 32*, 147–170.

McPherson, M. B., Kearney, P., & Plax, T. G. (2003). The dark side of instruction: Teacher anger as classroom norm violations. *Journal of Applied Communication Research, 31*, 76–90.

Meares, M. M., Oetzel, J. G., Torres, A., Derkacs, D., & Ginossar, T. (2004). Employee mistreatment and muted voices in the culturally diverse workplace. *Journal of Applied Communication Research, 32*, 4–27.

Medved, C. E., Morrison, K., Dearing, J. W., Larson, R. S., Cline, G., & Brummans, B. H. J. M. (2001). Tensions in community health improvement initiatives: Communication and collaboration in a managed care environment. *Journal of Applied Communication Research, 29*, 137–152.

Miller, G. R. (1995). "I think my schizophrenia is better today," said the communication researcher unanimously: Some thoughts on the dysfunctional dichotomy between pure and applied communication research. In K. N. Cissna (Ed.), *Applied communication in the 21st century* (pp. 47–55). Mahwah, NJ: Erlbaum.

Miller, G. R., & Fontes, N. E. (1979). *Videotape on trial: A view from the jury box*. Beverly Hills, CA: Sage.

Miller, G. R., & Sunnafrank, M. J. (1984). Theoretical dimensions of applied communication research. *Quarterly Journal of Speech, 70*, 255–263.

Miller, K., Joseph, L., & Apker, J. (2000). Strategic ambiguity in the role development process. *Journal of Applied Communication Research, 28*, 193–214.

Morgan, J. M., & Krone, K. J. (2001). Bending the rules of "professional" display: Emotional improvisation in caregiver performances. *Journal of Applied Communication Research, 29*, 317–341.

Morman, M. T. (2000). The influence of fear appeals, message design, and masculinity on men's motivation to perform the testicular self-exam. *Journal of Applied Communication Research, 28*, 91–116.

Muller, H. L. (2002). *Navigating the dilemmas in collegiate classroom discussion*. Unpublished doctoral dissertation, University of Colorado at Boulder.

Murphy, A. G. (2001). The flight attendant dilemma: An analysis of communication and sensemaking during in-flight emergencies. *Journal of Applied Communication Research, 29*, 30–53.

O'Hair, D. (Ed.). (2000a). Defining applied communication scholarship [Special forum]. *Journal of Applied Communication Research, 28*, 164–191.

O'Hair, D. (2000b). Editor's introduction to the forum on defining applied communication scholarship. *Journal of Applied Communication Research, 28*, 164–165.

O'Hair, D., Kreps, G. L., & Frey, L. R. (1990). Conceptual issues. In D. O'Hair & G. L. Kreps (Eds.), *Applied communication theory and research* (pp. 3–22). Hillsdale, NJ: Erlbaum.

Pearce, K. A., & Pearce, W. B. (2001). The Public Dialogue Consortium's school-wide dialogue process: A communication approach to develop citizenship skills and enhance school climate. *Communication Theory, 11*, 105–123.

Pearce, W. B. (1989). *Communication and the human condition*. Carbondale: Southern Illinois University Press.

Pearce, W. B. (1993). Achieving dialogue with "the Other" in the postmodern world. In P. Gaunt (Ed.), *Beyond agendas: New directions in communication research* (pp. 59–74). Westport, CT: Greenwood Press.

Pearce, W. B. (1994). *Interpersonal communication: Making social worlds.* New York: Harper Collins.

Pearce, W. B., & Cronen, V. E. (1980). *Communication, action, and meaning: The creation of social realities.* New York: Praeger.

Pearce, W. B., & Pearce, K. A. (2000). Extending the theory of the coordinated management of meaning (CMM) through a community dialogue process. *Communication Theory, 10,* 405–424.

Petronio, S. (1991). Communication boundary management: A theoretical model of managing disclosure of private information between marital couples. *Communication Theory, 1,* 311–335.

Petronio, S. (Ed.). (1999a). Translating scholarship into practice [Special issue]. *Journal of Applied Communication Research,* 27(2).

Petronio, S. (1999b). "Translating scholarship into practice": An alternative metaphor. *Journal of Applied Communication Research, 27,* 87–91.

Reason, P., & Bradbury, H. (Eds.). (2006). *Handbook of action research* (2nd ed.). Thousand Oaks, CA: Sage.

Ruud, G. (2000). The symphony: Organizational discourse and the symbolic tensions between artistic and business ideologies. *Journal of Applied Communication Research, 28,* 117–143.

Seeger, M. W., & Ulmer, R. R. (2002). A post–crisis discourse of renewal: The cases of Malden Mills and Cole Hardwoods. *Journal of Applied Communication Research, 30,* 126–142.

Seibold, D. R. (1995). *Theoria* and *praxis*: Means and ends in applied communication research. In K. N. Cissna (Ed.), *Applied communication in the 21st century* (pp. 23–45). Mahwah, NJ: Erlbaum.

Sherblom, J. C., Keränen, L., & Withers, L. A. (2002). Tradition, tension, and transformation: A structuration analysis of a game warden service in transition. *Journal of Applied Communication Research, 30,* 143–162.

Shotter, J. (1984). *Social accountability and selfhood.* New York: Blackwell.

Slater, M. D., Karan, D. N., Rouner, D., & Walters, D. (2002). Effects of threatening visuals and announcer differences on responses to televised alcohol. *Journal of Applied Communication Research, 30,* 27–49.

Snizek, W. E., & Fuhrman, E. R. (1980). The role of theory in applied behavioral science research. *Journal of Applied Behavioral Science, 16,* 93–103.

Soliz, J., & Harwood, J. (2003). Perceptions of communication in a family relationship and the reduction of intergroup prejudice. *Journal of Applied Communication Research, 31,* 320–345.

Spano, S. (2001). *Public dialogue and participatory democracy: The Cupertino community project.* Cresskill, NJ: Hampton Press.

Spano, S. (2006). Theory, practice, and public dialogue: A case study in facilitating community transformation. In L. R. Frey (Ed.), *Facilitating group communication in context: Innovations and applications with natural groups: Vol. 1. Facilitating group creation, conflict, and conversation* (pp. 271–298). Cresskill, NJ: Hampton Press.

Stafford, L. (2009). Editorial policy. *Journal of Applied Communication Research,* 37(1), n.p.

Stringer, E. T. (2007). *Action research* (3rd ed.). Thousand Oaks, CA: Sage.

Sunnafrank, M. (1986). Predicted outcome value during initial interactions: A reformulation of uncertainty reduction theory. *Human Communication Research, 13,* 3–33.

Thomas, K. W., & Tymon, W. G., Jr. (1982). Necessary properties of relevant research: Lessons from recent criticisms of the organizational sciences. *Academy of Management Review, 7,* 345–352.

Tracy, K. (1995). Action-implicative discourse analysis. *Journal of Language and Social Psychology, 14,* 195–215.

Tracy, K. (1997a). *Colloquium: Dilemmas of academic discourse.* Norwood, NJ: Ablex.

Tracy, K. (1997b). Interactional trouble in emergency service requests: A problem of frames. *Research on Language and Social Interaction, 30,* 315–343.

Tracy, K. (2005). Reconstructing communicative practices: Action-implicative discourse analysis. In K. L. Fitch & R. E. Sanders (Eds.), *Handbook of language and social interaction* (pp. 301–319). Mahwah, NJ: Erlbaum.

Tracy, K., & Ashcraft, C. (2001). Crafting policies about controversial values: How wording disputes manage a group dilemma. *Journal of Applied Communication Research, 29,* 297–316.

Tracy, K., & Muller, H. (2001). Diagnosing a school board's interactional trouble: Theorizing problem formulating. *Communication Theory, 11,* 84–104.

Tracy, K., & Tracy, S. J. (1998). Rudeness at 911: Reconceptualizing face and face attack. *Human Communication Research, 25,* 225–251.

Tracy, S. J. (2004). Dialectic, contradiction, or double bind? Analyzing and theorizing employee reactions to organizational tension. *Journal of Applied Communication Research, 32,* 119–146.

Weick, K. E. (1995). *Sensemaking in organizations.* Thousand Oaks, CA: Sage.

Weick, K. E., & Browning, L. D. (1991). Fixing with the voice: A research agenda for applied communication. *Journal of Applied Communication Research, 19,* 1–19.

Williams, D. E., & Olaniran, B. A. (2002). Crisis communication in racial issues. *Journal of Applied Communication Research, 30,* 293–313.

Witte, K. (1992). Putting the fear back into fear appeals: The extended parallel process model. *Communication Monographs, 59,* 329–349.

Witte, K. (1994). Fear control and danger control: A test of the extended parallel process model (EPPM). *Communication Monographs, 61,* 113–134.

Wittgenstein, L. (1953). *Philosophical investigations* (G. E. M. Anscombe, Trans.). New York: Macmillan.

Wood, J. T. (1995). Theorizing practice, practicing theory. In K. N. Cissna (Ed.), *Applied communication in the 21st century* (pp. 157–167). Mahwah, NJ: Erlbaum.

Zoller, H. M. (2003). Health on the line: Identity and disciplinary control in employee occupational health and safety discourse. *Journal of Applied Communication Research, 31,* 118–139.

Part II

Methods of Applied Communication Research

4 Using Quantitative Methods to Conduct Applied Communication Research

Jim L. Query, Jr.
James Madison University

Kevin B. Wright
The University of Oklahoma

Patricia Amason
University of Arkansas

Kristen Campbell Eichhorn
State University of New York at Oswego

Melinda R. Weathers
George Mason University

Martha Womack Haun
University of Houston

Eileen S. Gilchrist
University of Wyoming

Laura Bochenek Klein
Rice University

Valerie Pedrami
University of Houston

Over the last couple of centuries, quantitative methods have dominated both the natural and social sciences. Such methods became part of the methodological canon because they enable investigators to measure variables and test for relationships between and among variables that are consistent with theoretical predictions. More specifically, *quantitative methods* allow researchers to assign meaningful numerical values to variables and then to analyze those values using descriptive and inferential statistics to describe the data, infer population characteristics from sample attributes, and discover significant differences between groups/conditions and relationships between variables.

Applied communication research as part of the social sciences has a brief, yet rich history of tackling pressing social issues through the use of quantitative methods. Indeed, ever since the challenge issued to communication scholars at the New Orleans Conference on Research and Instructional Development to conduct rigorous investigations about vexing social conditions (see Cissna, Eadie, & Hickson, this volume; Kibler & Barker, 1969), as even a cursory review of the literature reveals, applied communication scholars have employed a variety of quantitative methods to address important issues.

This chapter explores the nature and use of quantitative methods in applied communication scholarship. First, we contextualize the current use of quantitative methods in applied communication scholarship by distinguishing a traditional positivistic perspective from a postpositivistic perspective. We then examine five common quantitative methods—survey research, experimental research, content analysis, interaction analysis, and meta-analysis—employed in applied communication research, illustrating their use in early studies published in the *Journal of Applied Communication Research* (*JACR*) between 1973 and 1989 (before the National Communication Association [NCA] assumed ownership of the journal; see Cissna et al., this volume). We then report the results of a content analysis of quantitative studies published between 1990 and 2006 in five communication journals that regularly feature applied communication scholarship to understand the current use of such methods. We conclude the chapter with suggestions for using quantitative methods in future applied communication research.

Positivistic Versus Postpositivistic Perspectives on Quantitative Methods

Traditionally, quantitative methods have been associated with *positivism*, a philosophy proposed by Compte (1865/1986) that offered an alternative to metaphysics (which focuses on principles of reality transcending those of any particular science) by privileging the use of the scientific method to gather, through experimentation, observable empirical evidence of the natural world to test hypotheses derived from theory. From a traditional positivistic perspective, there is a single, objective reality that can be discovered by an unbiased researcher (who is independent from the phenomenon being investigated) using deductive logic and the scientific method. The result of this process is the discovery of universal Truths (with a capital "T").

Over time, and especially after World War II, positivism (and its more stringent form of logical positivism) came under significant attack from philosophers, especially from those subscribing to the *naturalistic paradigm*, who argued that there are multiple, intersubjective realities that can be studied only by value-laden researchers who are interdependent with the phenomena being investigated, and that are best studied using qualitative methods. In response, Popper (1959) and others offered the *postpositivism* perspective to address some of the criticisms leveled against positivism but still preserve many of its basic assumptions (for other discussions of this history, see, e.g., Guba & Lincoln, 1994; Lincoln & Guba, 1985).

Similar to positivists, postpositivists believe that there is an external reality that can be apprehended by researchers. However, postpositivists adopt what is called "critical realism" (Guba, 1990, p. 20), the belief that humans cannot grasp all of the natural forces in the world due to their sensory limitations, which is especially true in the study of human beings (such as in communication research). Moreover, postpositivists do not believe in a single, objective reality, and they acknowledge the interdependent relationship between the knower and the known. G. Morgan (1983b), for instance, argued that social scientists' interaction with the targets of their investigation is colored by various lenses, or frames of reference, such that what subsequently is observed and discovered is a product of that interaction. Tashakkori and Teddlie (1998) noted that research is influenced, to some degree, by investigators' values (e.g., what and why they study something), which are influenced by researchers' cultural experiences and worldviews. Researchers also are influenced by their theoretical underpinnings, with theory "determining method; it indicates what data are appropriate and places limits on how these data may be obtained" (Poole & McPhee, 1985, pp. 100–101). In addition, investigators cannot neatly or completely divorce themselves from their humanity, thereby jettisoning the traditional positivistic ideal of pure objectivity and opting, instead, for a "reasonable closeness" (Guba, 1990, p. 21) of neutrality. The result of these assumptions, as G. Morgan (1983a) explained, is "to see science as being concerned with the realization of potentialities—of possible knowledges" (p. 13). Subsequently,

> the practice of social research can proceed most effectively if we replace the view that science involves a quest for certain knowledge that can be evaluated in an unambiguous way, with the view that it involves modes of human engagement on which we can and should converse to improve our understanding and practice. (G. Morgan, 1983a, p. 18)

Hence, whereas the goal of positivists was to uncover Truths, postpositivists seek to find the most accurate answers possible, or to "get it right as best they can."

To try to "get it right," postpositivists value *triangulation*, the use of multiple, inherently error-filled methods to study phenomena of interest, for any single method can help only partly to understand a phenomenon. Consequently, the use of multiple or mixed methods, what Cook (1985) called "critical multiplism," has supplanted the positivistic notion that one methodology in particular (i.e., experimentation) is superior to all others. As Guba (1990) concluded, "If human sensory and intellective mechanisms cannot be relied upon, it is essential that the 'findings' of an inquiry be based on as many sources— of data, investigators, theories, and methods—as possible" (p. 21).

The understanding and use of quantitative methods in social-scientific research, thus, has experienced significant change over time. It is within this shift from a positivistic to a postpositivistic perspective that we examine the nature and use of quantitative methods in applied communication scholarship.

Quantitative Methodologies in Applied Communication Research

In this section, we provide a brief description of five common quantitative methodologies employed in applied communication research—survey research, experimental research, content analysis, interaction analysis, and meta-analysis—and consider their relative strengths and limitations. To illustrate the prevalence of these methods and how they have been used historically to conduct applied communication research, we provide examples from studies published in a variety of communication journals, including *JACR*.

Survey Research

Survey research seeks to ascertain the beliefs, attitudes, values, or behaviors of a population of interest from a sample of respondents selected from that population. To accomplish that goal, survey researchers typically select a sample from the population of interest and ask respondents, via a questionnaire or an interview, questions designed to measure the variables of interest. The results obtained from the sample then are generalized back to the parent population.

Babbie (1999) traced the genesis of survey research back to the census-taking procedures used to collect taxes during the Roman Empire. Survey procedures have been used ever since that time, with Babbie reporting that one of the largest survey administrations was a questionnaire administered by Marx in 1880 to approximately 25,000 workers. However, survey procedures came of age in the 20th century, primarily because of their use in applied settings, such as public opinion, market, and evaluation research. In particular, George Gallup created a "scientific" approach to polling during the 1930s (Hogan, 1997) that has been refined into what now is an artful science.

Building on these rich, applied traditions, scholars from many disciplines employ the survey method to conduct research. Indeed, Babbie (1999) concluded that survey research is the "most frequently used mode of observation in the social sciences" (p. 234). Communication research is no exception, with scholars noting that it is the method used most often in published communication research (Anderson, 1987, 1996; Potter, Cooper, & Dupagne, 1993).

In survey research and other quantitative methods, the variables of interest are measured in as precise a manner as possible, preferably using interval or ratio scales in which there are equal distances between the points on the scale, as those scales allow the data obtained to be analyzed using advanced statistical procedures. Numerous strategies also are available to demonstrate the reliability (consistency) and validity (accuracy) of the scaled instruments employed.

Once a case can be made for reliable and valid measurement procedures, survey researchers identify target populations (or segments of populations) that exhibit characteristics (e.g., demographic, psychological, and behavioral variables) they want to measure. In applied communication research, these variables are associated typically with some practical issue affecting the population of interest that has been identified by prior theory or research. Researchers then select a sample of individuals using *probability sampling procedures* (in which every member of the population of interest has an equal chance of being selected) or *nonprobability sampling procedures* (in which population members do not have an equal chance of being selected), based on the feasibility of these procedures for the particular research situation (e.g., whether a population list exists) and given the available resources (e.g., time and money).

The data collected from survey research and other quantitative methods typically are analyzed using statistical computer software packages, such as the Statistical Package for the Social Sciences (SPSS), to identify patterns in the data. In survey research, these procedures involve inferential statistics, called *estimation*, designed to infer population characteristics from sample attributes, which is appropriate when researchers have selected probability samples. One of the most important goals of survey research, therefore, is trying to obtain a representative sample that facilitates generalizations about the population of interest. Assuming that such sampling practices are employed, in conjunction with a sufficient sample size and effective procedures (e.g., appropriate readability of a questionnaire), the data obtained demonstrate normality (e.g., they are distributed in a bell-shaped curve) and, subsequently, can be generalized to the population of interest. However, survey researchers often rely on nonprobability samples for a variety of reasons (e.g., lack of a complete population list, such as those who watch a particular television show). Indeed, the vast majority of scholarly survey studies employ nonprobability samples, and applied communication research is no exception.

Survey research and other quantitative methods (especially experiments) also employ inferential statistics to assess statistical relationships (correlations, typically in the form of shared variance) between the variables studied. Correlation is one of three prerequisites for establishing causation between variables (along with the independent variable preceding the dependent variable in time and ruling out alternative explanations for observed changes in the dependent variable). Hence, survey research can establish relationships between variables but does not indicate whether they are causal relationships (see the discussion of experimental research below).

Survey research also demonstrates other potential limitations, such as most often relying on self-reports (although others' reports often can be obtained) and being susceptible to the adverse impact of social desirability, with participants responding to questions in ways designed to please others (including the researcher) or to follow acceptable social norms. Another potential concern is that members of a target population may not be very familiar or comfortable with the format of a survey procedure (e.g., many elderly individuals are not comfortable with some instruments that initially were developed from studying college student samples). A final concern is that survey research can impose, to some extent, investigator priorities and values on matters that may not be as germane to the population being studied. Survey procedures also typically compel respondents to use numerical values to indicate their beliefs, attitudes, values, and practices rather than obtaining their native language terms.

In applied communication research, survey procedures allow researchers to gain insight into communicative behaviors that may reveal potential solutions to practical problems or issues within the setting and/or population of interest. Indeed, an examination of early applied communication research published in *JACR*, from 1973 to 1989, reveals that survey research was the most prominent method employed. These studies largely avoided the typical college student samples that were (and still are) studied by many other communication researchers and focused, instead, on other people, often in organizational settings. For example, Rudolph (1973) used a questionnaire to identify informal communication patterns within a large organization, discovering a number of illuminating findings, including that informal information within the organization was 80% accurate and that it was disseminated through downward and horizontal channels rather than through upward channels. Although Rudolph did not discuss whether this information was shared with stakeholders of this organization—which helps to identify a plan of action to ameliorate a problem or to provide empirical support for communication and other behavior patterns within the context that may inform decisions at a later date—the results have a number of implications for understanding patterns of informal communication within similar types of organizations. Similarly, Falcione (1974), using a questionnaire to study employees' perceptions of their immediate supervisor's credibility in a large Midwestern U.S. industrial organization, showed that a number of supervisor communicative behaviors predicted supervisors' perceived credibility, including soliciting subordinates' views on safety issues and upcoming organizational decisions, and being aware of and responsive to subordinates' feelings. These findings have implications for understanding and influencing information exchange in organizations and employee satisfaction and turnover.

In later issues of *JACR* during that time period, researchers continued to employ the survey method to study traditional industrial organizations, but they also branched into other applied contexts, such as health-care and family settings. For example, Morse and Piland (1981) studied the communication competencies required in physician–nurse, nurse–nurse, and nurse–patient relationships, identifying differences in communication skills required for these various relationships, as well as constraints on the communication patterns in those dyads based on social norms associated with the respective relationships. DiBerardinis, Barwind, and Wilmot (1981) surveyed nursing home residents to understand the relationship between interpersonal network involvement and perceived life satisfaction/need accommodations, discovering that residents who were more interpersonally involved with their social networks had higher life satisfaction scores and felt that their needs were being met more than people who were less involved. In the field of family communication, Warren and Neer (1986) used the survey method to examine how families talk about sex issues, finding that a family's sex communication orientation was predictive of children's open discussion about sex with their parents and with their dating partners.

More recent applied communication survey research, conducted from 1990 to 2006, continued to use the survey method to study health communication topics, including large-scale, community-based surveys of people's health perceptions and practices (e.g., Egbert & Parrott, 2001; Trost, Langan, & Kellar-Guenther, 1999). However, survey research during this time period also examined new applied topics and contexts, including customer satisfaction (Ford, 2001), community involvement (Rothenbuhler, 1991), and communication anxiety and signing efficacy among deaf individuals (Booth-Butterfield & Booth-Butterfield, 1994).

Survey research, thus, is an important quantitative methodology that applied communication researchers have employed extensively to explore communicative behaviors, with the overarching goal of understanding practical problems and issues across a variety of applied settings (e.g., organizational, health-care, and family contexts). Once those problems and issues are documented and understood more fully, potential solutions can be developed to address them.

Experimental Research

Whereas survey research uncovers statistical correlations between variables, *experimental research* is conducted to discover *causal relationships* between variables. In their most basic form, experiments involve randomly assigning participants either to a treatment group (or various treatment and comparison groups) in which at least one independent variable is manipulated by the researcher or to a no-treatment (or control) group that does not receive the exposure, and then measuring and comparing the effects of that exposure on the dependent variable(s). Moreover, attempts are made to control for extraneous variables to rule out competing explanations for differential changes noted in the dependent variable(s) between the treatment and no-treatment conditions. If a high degree of control has been exercised, any observed changes in the dependent variable(s) can be attributed directly to the causal effects of the manipulation of the independent variable(s).

One of the most important characteristics of experimental research is *random assignment* of participants to treatment and comparison/control conditions (also called *randomization*), such that participants have an equal chance of being assigned to each condition. Randomization is the best procedure for minimizing the most important threat to claiming that the manipulation of the independent variable(s) caused changes in the dependent variable(s): That participants in the different experimental conditions did not start off equivalent with regard to the dependent variable(s) and other variables (e.g., intelligence or communication competence) that might affect observed changes in the dependent variable(s). Random assignment is the best guarantee that all of the other variables (many of which may not be known) that might influence the results are evenly distributed across the experimental conditions. Hence, the overarching goal of random assignment is to create equivalent groups prior to the administration of the manipulation of the independent variable(s).

Another key characteristic of experimental research is whether the independent variable(s) is manipulated or observed by researchers. When researchers manipulate the independent variable(s), a high degree of control has been exercised over participants' exposure to those modifications. In contrast, when researchers observe someone else manipulating an independent variable (e.g., a health communication campaign conducted by a government agency) or treat something that occurs naturally as an independent variable manipulation (e.g., studying the effects of a hurricane on community mobilization), researchers have less control over participants' exposure to the independent variable(s).

When participants have been randomly assigned to experimental conditions and researchers manipulate the independent variable(s), researchers have conducted a *full experiment* that has a high degree of control. However, when random assignment is not possible, which often is the case when conducting experiments in natural environments (e.g., it usually is not possible to randomly assign patients to physicians or subordinates to supervisors), regardless of whether the independent variable(s) were manipulated or observed, researchers can conduct only a *quasi-experiment* that has a moderate amount of control and limits the claim of a causal connection between the independent and dependent variables. In such cases, researchers rely on *pretests* (measurements taken before the experimental manipulation) to try to rule out initial differences between the participants in the experimental conditions, although only those differences that were assessed can be ruled out. If there is no random assignment to experimental conditions, regardless of whether the independent variable(s) were manipulated or observed, and no attempt is made to assess initial differences between participants in the experimental conditions, researchers have conducted a *preexperiment* or what some call a *nonexperiment* (for more information about experimental procedures and types of experiments, see the classic works by D. T. Campbell & Stanley, 1963; Cook & Campbell, 1979).

Experiments have a relatively long history of applied use, especially in the natural sciences, with early experiments often addressing problems such as randomly assigning various types of soil, water conditions, and fertilizer to assess their impact on crop growth (Snedecor & Cochran, 1956). Experiments also are the standard method employed in medical research, with the "double-blind experiment" (in which neither the participants nor the researchers know who belongs to the treatment and control/comparison groups) being the "gold standard" of such research.

Because of the amount of control that is desired, researchers most often conduct experiments in a laboratory. However, applied researchers were instrumental in moving experiments from the laboratory to the field (see, e.g., Frey & SunWolf, this volume; Poole & DeSanctis, this volume). In doing so, researchers encountered many challenges, including not being able to assign participants randomly to experimental conditions and not being able to manipulate the independent variable(s), as well as ethical concerns raised about control group members not receiving the potential research benefits, leading to the use of comparison groups that receive some form of the independent variable or variables (see Seeger, Sellnow, Ulmer, & Novak, this volume).

Perhaps these problems explain why early studies published in *JACR* show that although applied communication researchers began using experimental designs in the mid- to late 1970s, relatively few experiments were conducted during that period. Moreover, the experiments conducted relied on student samples rather than participants in other settings. For example, Beatty and Springhorn (1977) used an experimental design to examine message discrepancy and attitude change among a sample of undergraduate students. Although the title of the article claimed that these variables were examined in a field setting, the researchers relied on students' responses to a relevant, simulated university issue (a tuition raise). Beatty and Springhorn, however, did involve several campus entities (e.g., the campus newspaper) to create the appearance of a legitimate tuition raise to strengthen the ecological validity of the procedures (i.e., how well they reflect what occurs in the natural environment, which is one factor, along with sampling and replication, affecting the external validity of research findings). In other experiments conducted during that time period, M. M. Cohen and Saine (1977) studied the influence of profanity and sex on impression formation among a small sample of undergraduate students; Infante, Rancer, Pierce, and Osborne (1980) examined the relationship between physical attractiveness and first-name likeability of journalists on impression formation among undergraduates; and Blau (1986) assessed the influence of source competence on workers' satisfaction with supervisors, although the "workers" actually were undergraduate business majors.

Although the findings from these and other studies have implications for communication issues across a variety of applied contexts (e.g., university–student relations, journalist credibility ratings, and organizational employee satisfaction), the majority of these studies appear to have been motivated by theoretical concerns rather than particular social problems or issues per se, as is characteristic of applied communication research (e.g., Cissna, 2000; Keyton, 2000). The experimental designs used in these studies, however, did allow researchers to examine the effects of the independent variables studied and simultaneously control for the influence of extraneous variables. Moreover, even early on, several researchers were cognizant of the need to strengthen the ecological validity of experimental research (despite the use of college student samples) to increase the generalizability of the findings to natural settings.

Later experimental studies published in *JACR*, in the mid- to late-1980s, focused on a wider range of issues than did previous studies, although many researchers continued to study student samples. For instance, Wadsworth et al. (1987) created six 60-second political advertisements to study the effects of female candidates running for political office who used masculine versus feminine communication strategies on students' perceptions of candidate image and effectiveness, with the results revealing that more masculine communication strategies were associated with greater perceived effectiveness. The experimental design, thus, compared the effectiveness of different types of campaign strategies, information that has practical value in making decisions about which strategies to use in a campaign advertisement prior to spending considerable money on production costs.

There were at least two examples of field experiments conducted during this time period. Hunt and Ebeling (1983), using a pretest–posttest design, demonstrated that a 10-week program designed to communicate both job-specific and general information increased the satisfaction of assembly line workers and work-unit productivity in a large health-care industrial plant. Rosenfeld and Fowler (1983) compared face-to-face communication and telephone communication (and a combination of the two) on unemployment insurance workers' abilities to share and discuss information in administrative appeals. Employing a randomized factorial block design, the administrative hearing officer's travel was supplanted by a split phone-hearing condition. In the first experimental condition, participants chose the location from which to make the call connecting them to a phone conference; in the second condition, participants went to a designated office meeting with the administrative hearing officer to make the conference call. Although the results indicated that there were few differences between these modes of communication for the seven hypotheses tested, three significant differences emerged. First, employees in the designated office condition reported that they shared more information with the hearing officer than did those in the office telephone condition. Second, participants stated that they were better able to stay abreast of the information when using the in-person method compared to the split phone or office phone conditions. Third, participants felt better understood by the hearing officer when using the split phone option than the office telephone. It was not clear, however, whether these findings were shared with the stakeholders of that organization or whether any changes in that organization were enacted.

Experimental designs also were frequently employed in applied communication research from 1990 to 2006. As might be expected because of their use in medical research, experiments were employed most often in health communication research, including an increase over earlier time periods in using relatively sophisticated, community-based intervention designs (e.g., Parrott & Duggan, 1999; Roberto, Meyer, Johnson, Atkin, & Smith, 2002; Stephenson et al., 1999; see also the exemplary applied communication research programs described in this volume by Hecht & Miller-Day; Poole & DeSanctis; Witte & Roberto). However, the majority of applied experimental studies continued to employ undergraduate student samples. Morman (2000), for instance, used an experimental design to assess the efficacy of testicular cancer health-education materials, with the sample comprised primarily of Caucasian undergraduate students, with only one respondent having a family member who had experienced testicular cancer. However, in the absence of sampling participants at higher risk levels (e.g., those who had a family history of the disease or males in this age group with a testicular cancer diagnosis), the subsequent findings were somewhat limited. Lee and Guerrero (2001) also conducted an experiment with students that employed a simulated sexual harassment video vignette created by the researchers, even though the focus was on sexual harassment among coworkers.

Although studying student samples in the laboratory certainly enables researchers to exercise a high degree of control and, thereby, increases the internal validity of the findings (the extent to which findings are accurate for the participants studied), doing so can lead to lower levels of external validity than conducting field experiments with the actual populations that applied communication researchers often want to study (e.g., organizational employees). Such studies, however, can provide a springboard for subsequent research with populations most likely to be affected by the social problem or issue of interest.

Experiments, thus, are employed in applied communication research to ascertain the causal effects of independent variables on dependent variables. Understanding those causal relationships potentially enables them to be controlled by researchers, practitioners, and those most affected by them in the natural setting.

Content Analysis

Content analysis involves "the systematic, objective, quantitative analysis of message characteristics" (Neuendorf, 2002, p. 1) embedded in texts (see also classic texts by Berelson, 1952; Holsti, 1969; Krippendorf, 2004). Originally, content analysis was developed as a method for analyzing the message characteristics of mediated and public texts, with its applied use traced back to World War II, when the Allies analyzed how the music played on German radio stations (compared to music played in other occupied territories) indicated troop concentrations in Europe, and to the formulas (e.g., Flesch's, 1949, reading ease formula) that newspaper editors employed to make sure that the content of news stories was readable at a relatively low educational level (see, e.g., Frey, Botan, & Kreps, 2000; Wimmer & Dominick, 1994). Early content analysis by scholars included Speed's (1893) study of how leading New York newspapers had decreased coverage of religious, scientific, and literary issues in favor of gossip, sports, and scandals; Mathews's (1910) investigation of the amount of space that newspapers devoted to "demoralizing," "unwholesome," and "trivial" rather than "worthwhile" news items; and McDiarmid's (1937) analysis of symbols (e.g., national identity and historical reference) in 30 U.S. presidential inaugural addresses. Today, content analysis (which includes both quantitative and qualitative forms) is one of the most widely employed methodologies in the study of media, as well as in other areas of the communication discipline, including applied communication research (Neuendorf, 2002).

Quantitative content analysis essentially involves analyzing types of messages embedded in an appropriately selected set of texts by having coders use a category scheme developed a priori to first identify discrete units and then to code those units into discrete categories. Hence, content analysis is a "systematic, replicable technique for compressing many words of text into fewer content categories based on explicit rules of coding" (Stemler, 2001, p. 1).

Content analysts start by identifying the messages of interest, typically chosen on the basis of theory and previous research, as well as, in applied communication research, their pragmatic significance (e.g., sexist messages). Researchers then select an appropriate set of texts in which to analyze those messages (e.g., sexist messages represented in particular newspapers, magazines, books, television shows, or Internet sites). In cases where the number of texts is small, content analysts might be able to study the entire population (called a *census*), but in most cases, like survey researchers, they select a sample of texts and then generalize the results from that sample to the population (called a "universe" for a set of texts). Content analysts, thus, use probability sampling whenever possible to ensure that the results from the sample of texts selected can be generalized to its parent universe. In cases where it might not be possible to use probability sampling, content analysts rely on nonprobability samples, but then must be careful generalizing the results from the sample to the universe.

Once a set of texts has been selected, they are coded by at least two trained coders who are unfamiliar with the research questions or hypotheses being studied. Coders first identify each unit of analysis in the texts (e.g., every sexist message) and then code those units into categories that are equivalent, mutually exclusive, and exhaustive. There also are some computer programs (e.g., Diction 5.0, NUD*IST, and HyperRESEARCH) that can be used to code texts. Coders must demonstrate high reliability, which involves both stability (with coders placing units into the same categories each successive try) and reproducibility (where additional coders can use the same categories to group the data; see Stemler, 2001). Intercoder reliability is calculated using statistical procedures, such as Scott's (1955) *pi*, Spearman's *rho*, and Pearson's *r* for pairs of coders, or J. Cohen's (1960) *kappa* or Krippendorf's *alpha* when using more than two coders. A Program for Reliability Assessment with Multiple Coders (PRAM) also is available to compute intercoder reliability for Excel files (see http://www.geocities.com/skymegsoftware/pram.html). Once units and categories have been coded in a reliable manner, the data can be analyzed using appropriate descriptive and inferential statistics.

Content analysis demonstrates at least two strengths as a quantitative research methodology. First, it is a relatively unobtrusive technique because researchers study texts that already have been produced rather than interact with research participants (such as in survey and experimental research). Second, content analysis can handle large volumes of data, especially when computer coding systems are employed. For instance, Wang and Gantz (2007) examined health content contained in 1,863 local television news stories that aired on four English-language channels and one Spanish-language channel in seven U.S. markets during a composite week in 2000. However, significant challenges associated with using content analysis include the difficulties of precisely defining the unit of analysis, obtaining a representative sample, and training coders to achieve the high reliability needed to obtain useful data (e.g., Schonbom, 1976).

In contrast to survey and experimental methods, relatively few early applied communication studies employed content analysis; most used qualitative approaches to textual analysis (primarily rhetorical criticism; see Condit & Bates, this volume). Schonborn (1976) published one of the only studies in *JACR* during that time period, content analyzing episodes of violence from a sample of early 1970s television programs, and Shyles and Ross (1984) content analyzed the inducements offered and demands made of potential volunteers in Army recruitment brochures. Schonberg's study was relatively sophisticated, considering the time period, examining a number of variables, including frequency of violence, realism of the violence depicted, weapons used, and the role of law enforcement officers in violent episodes. Other early applied communication researchers, however, did not discuss the procedures used to classify units of analysis or whether coders actually were used, such as Bryski (1978), who examined the type of evidence used by each candidate during the first 1976 Ford–Carter U.S. presidential debate, procedures that are crucial to be clear about if future applied communication scholars are to build on past literature.

More recently, applied communication scholars have employed content analysis to examine significant messages across a variety of contexts. For example, Cahudhi and Wang (2007) content analyzed the Web sites of the top 100 information technology companies to ascertain whether they communicated corporate social responsibility; Campo and Mastin (2007) content analyzed three mainstream and three African-American women's magazines published between 1984 and 2000 for differences in how those magazines placed the burden on individuals for being overweight and obese; Daniels and Loggins (2007) examined four local television stations' coverage of severe weather; Feeley and Vincent (2007) and S. W. Morgan, Harrison, Chewning, Davis, and DiCorcia (2007) used the method to discern how organ donation is represented in newspaper articles and entertainment television in the United States, respectively; and Edy and Meirick (2007) employed content analysis to examine network television nightly news during late October 2001 about the events of September 11, 2001, and concurrently surveyed 328 Tennesseans to gauge their degree of support for the war in Afghanistan. These examples demonstrate the utility of content analysis for conducting applied communication scholarship, both as a separate methodology and in conjunction with the other quantitative methods discussed in this chapter and the qualitative and rhetorical methods discussed in this section of the handbook.

Interaction Analysis

The study of interactions between people employs both quantitative procedures, called *interaction analysis*, and qualitative procedures, called *conversation analysis* or *discourse analysis* (see Tracy & Mirivel, this volume). Cappella (1990) and Heritage (1989) identified the goal of interaction analysis as capturing empirically the sequencing of messages and their related functions within focal conversations by employing a priori categories, and Frey et al. (2000) noted that interaction analysis may focus on linguistic features, content, purposes, and strategies, as well as how those features influence relational outcomes. Interaction analysis essentially mirrors quantitative content analysis in how it is conducted, except that it is directed toward dyadic and group conversations rather than public or mediated texts. Hence, like content analysts, interaction analysts decide what interactions to study, obtain an appropriate sample of interaction (deciding whether that interaction, for instance, needs to be real/natural or can be hypothetical, as well as how to record the interaction, such as via audiotaping, videotaping, iPoding, or observational notes taken by researchers), and then have coders analyze the interaction using a priori developed coding schemes. Consequently, many of the same strengths, limitations, and challenges characterizing content analysis also apply to interaction analysis.

Only a few studies employed interaction analysis during the early years of *JACR*. Examples include Watson and Ragsdale's (1981) study of linguistic indices of truthful and deceptive responses to employment interview questions, which used an early computerized program to analyze the interactions, and Garvin and Kennedy's (1986) study of confirmation and disconfirmation in conversations between physicians and nurses. More recently, interaction analysis has been used primarily in applied health communication studies to examine conversational features between physicians and patients. For example, Pittam and Gallois's (2000) interaction analysis of how heterosexual Australians use language to distance themselves from individuals who are HIV positive revealed that the farther away people with HIV or AIDS were viewed from one's in-group, the more the language surrounding talk about HIV or AIDS shifted from personal responsibility to intergroup negative stereotypes. Other examples of interaction analyses of health-related communication include Heritage and Robinson's (2006) observation and coding of 302 physician–patient visits, which found that general inquiry questions initiated by physicians elicited more than one symptom from patients, that older patients took longer than younger patients to present their medical problem, and that physicians residing in a large urban practice were more likely to use confirmatory-type questions than physicians residing in a rural practice. Roter and Larson (2001) also employed interaction analysis to examine dominant, passive, and egalitarian interactions in provider–patient relationships. More recently, Harrington, Norling, Witte, Taylor, and Andrews (2007) audiotaped and coded "sick child" office visits following an intervention that involved communication skills training for both pediatricians and parents.

Researchers also have used interaction analysis in political communication scholarship. Doerfel and Marsh (2003), for instance, employed semantic network analysis of the 1992 presidential debates engaged in by Bush, Clinton, and Perot to determine (using a computerized program) word frequencies and patterns of similarity among those candidates. More recently, Ellis and Maoz (2007) used a conversational argument scheme to code online arguments between Israeli Jews and Palestinians, with binomial statistical tests of the codes conducted to assess whether arguments were reciprocated.

Applied communication scholars, thus, employ interaction analysis to examine the nature and effects of messages in dyadic and group conversations that are focused on significant problems and issues (e.g., health concerns). The use of interaction analysis in applied communication research has increased over the years, which could be a result of greater training of researchers in this method, the somewhat unobtrusive nature of this type of inquiry in many situations, and the increased number of software programs to aid in the analysis of quantitative interaction data.

Meta-Analysis

Meta-analysis is a statistical procedure that summarizes the results of several quantitative research studies conducted on the same topic (Kerlinger & Lee, 2000) to determine whether there are consistent patterns across the findings. As Rosenthal (1991) explained:

> Meta-analytic reviews go beyond the traditional reviews [of the literature] in the degree to which they are more systematic, more explicit, more exhaustive, and more quantitative. Because of these features, meta-analytic reviews are more likely to lead to summary statements of greater thoroughness, greater precision, and greater intersubjectivity or objectivity. (p. 17)

The first meta-analysis, although it was not called that at the time, was performed by Pearson (1904) to overcome the problem of low statistical power in studies conducted with small samples that had documented a correlation between injection of the smallpox vaccine and survival rates. The first published use of the term *meta-analysis* was by Glass (1976) in an analysis of educational research, followed by Smith and Glass's (1977) study of approximately 400 research articles on the effectiveness of various methods of psychotherapeutic treatment, with Glass, McGaw, and Smith (1981) soon thereafter writing the first book about the technique.

Conducting a meta-analysis involves researchers first identifying quantitative studies conducted on the same topic and then using statistical procedures to compare the results obtained in those studies. Most typically, average effect sizes are computed to indicate whether the effects obtained across the studies conducted are "small," "medium," or "large" (J. Cohen, 1992). Two problems, however, can occur in the reporting and interpreting of effect sizes. First, because journals typically publish only studies that find significant effects, a "file drawer effect" can occur in which studies that showed "no effects" are placed into researchers' file drawers and never seen again. Hence, meta-analysis may overestimate the effects demonstrated by studies, because only those in which significant effects were discovered were included in the analysis. Second, effect sizes frequently have been misreported, perhaps because computer statistical programs vary in how they calculate and label them, leading to misinterpretation of data (Levine & Hullet, 2002). Given that the results of meta-analyses may be used to make policy decisions, reporting accurate effect sizes is critical (Hullet & Levine, 2003). Conversion formulas are available for researchers interested in calculating effect sizes from information reported in the research article (e.g., Hullet & Levine, 2003), although doing so assumes such information has been reported fully and properly. As the number of communication scholars who use meta-analysis increases, it may be possible to reach consensus on effective ways to manage this measurement issue and to encourage more uniformity in software developers' creation of meta-analytical programs; in the meantime, caution should be exercised when interpreting such results. Finally, similar to other data-analytic methods, sample size and its representativeness play integral roles in ascertaining the efficacy and explanatory power of findings discovered using this approach.

Although Noar (2006) contended that relatively few applied communication researchers have employed meta-analysis, applied communication scholars have used it recently to synthesize research on lie detection training (Frank & Feeley, 2003); family communication patterns (Schrodt, Witt, & Messersmith, 2008); the impact of celebrity announcements about health conditions, such as positive HIV status (Casey et al., 2003); mediated health communication campaign effects on behavior change (Snyder et al., 2004); whether sexual offenders possess fewer social skills than nonoffenders (Emmers-Sommer et al., 2004); media influence on body image (Holmstrom, 2004); the relationship between safer sexual communication and condom use (Noar, Carlyle, & Cole, 2006); the perceived versus actual effectiveness of persuasive messages, with implications offered for formative campaign research (Dillard, Weber, & Vail, 2007); the relative persuasiveness of gain-framed and loss-framed messages for encouraging disease-prevention behaviors (O'Keefe & Jensen, 2007, 2008); the presentation of sexual and violent content on prime-time television (Hetsroni, 2007a, 2007b); and the effects of messages in the home and in school on dropping out of high school (Strom & Boster, 2007). Scholars also have used meta-analysis to compare research designs, with Ayers et al. (1993), for instance, comparing the effect sizes obtained in their experimental studies of communication apprehension to those reported in studies that relied on self-reported data.

Meta-analysis, thus, is a relatively new quantitative method being employed in contemporary applied communication research. Given its recent emergence, coupled with a somewhat small pool of quantitative applied communication studies that consistently have focused on the same topic or problem, as the body of applied communication scholarship continues to grow, it is likely that researchers will use this quantitative method more often to determine patterns (e.g., effects) among studies focused on the same issues and problems.

Content Analysis of Quantitative Methods Used in Applied Communication Research, 1990–2006

To obtain a more detailed understanding and appreciation of the use of quantitative methods in applied communication scholarship in recent years, we conducted a content analysis of applied communication studies published from 1990 to 2006.[1] In total, we analyzed 704 quantitative applied studies published during that time in five communication journals that were chosen because of the relatively high number of applied communication studies that regularly appear in them: *JACR* (129 studies), *Communication Quarterly* (137 studies), *Communication Research Reports* (195 studies), *Health Communication* (156 studies), and *Journal of Health Communication* (87 studies).[2]

The most frequent method used in this sample of applied communication research studies was the survey method (474 articles), followed by experiments (129), content analysis (68), interaction analysis (29), and meta-analysis (4).[3] (Eighty-eight studies included a qualitative component along with the primary quantitative method employed.) Table 4.1 reports the use of these quantitative methods in the five journals selected; Table 4.2 reports the use of these methods with respect to the applied communication topic studied, indicating, for instance, that the survey method was used most often to conduct health communication and communication education research.

The frequency of using these quantitative research methods is similar to the selected review of *JACR* articles published from 1973 to 1989, except that meta-analysis was not employed in the earlier period and emerged in the literature during the 1990s. The relative frequency of use of these methods may be due to pragmatic issues (such as ease of administration and the amount of participant completion time required).

In addition to the frequency of particular quantitative methods employed in applied communication research and their association with various research topics, the follow-

Table 4.1 Frequency of Applied Quantitative Methods within the Sample of Communication Journals

Journal	Survey	Experiment	Content Analysis	Interaction Analysis	Meta-Analysis
Journal of Applied Communication Research	91	36	15	2	1
Communication Quarterly	90	23	11	10	
Communication Research Reports	138	28	14	7	
Health Communication	123	16	7	5	2
Journal of Health Communication	57	16	7	2	

Table 4.2 Frequency of Quantitative Methods by Applied Communication Topic

Topic	Survey	Experiment	Content Analysis	Interaction Analysis	Meta-Analysis
Health Communication	253	46	27	8	2
Communication Education	83	20	4	5	
Organizational Communication	56	16	6	7	1
Political Communication	2	7	8	1	
Family Communication	50	4	2	1	
Aging and Communication	9	5	4	2	
Other	46	21	5	4	

ing sections examine some key issues related to the use of quantitative research methods, including sampling procedures, reliability and validity, and effect size for meta-analyses.

Sampling Procedures (Types and Sizes) in Applied Communication Studies from 1990 to 2006

The overwhelming majority of applied communication studies used nonprobability samples (*n* = 644) rather than probability samples (*n* = 60). Probability sampling types included simple random, stratified, and cluster samples (e.g., Roberto et al., 2002), with convenience and snowball/network the most frequent types of nonprobability samples (e.g., McPherson, Kearney, & Plax, 2003; Wright, 2002). It seems reasonable to suggest that the use of nonprobability samples is due largely to access and resource constraints of conducting applied communication research in natural settings. However, given the limited ability to generalize findings from nonprobability samples to their population, applied communication researchers benefit from increasing the number of probability samples studied whenever possible.

Regarding observed sample sizes, the median for all studies in the literature sampled was 201 participants (e.g., Ogata Jones, Denham, & Springston, 2006). This summary statistic must be interpreted cautiously, however, as externally funded projects typically have larger sample sizes than nonfunded research (e.g., Palmgreen, Lorch, Stephenson, Hoyle, & Donohew, 2007), although there are at least two notable, recent exceptions (Becker & O'Hair, 2007; Leets & Sunwolf, 2004), and research about highly traumatized populations may be much lower in size than many other populations (e.g., S. W. Campbell & Kelley, 2006).

Reliability and Validity Issues in Applied Communication Studies from 1990 to 2006

In terms of instrument reliability estimates, Cronbach's alpha was reported in 399 articles and was the most frequent measure employed. Three studies used a test–retest approach to assess instrument reliability, and one study employed the split-half method. Eighty-six studies reported using various intercoder reliability measures, such as Scott's *pi* and Cohen's *kappa*. Hence, the majority of the studies assessed the internal consistency of measures and reported adequate reliability coefficients (.70 or greater for Cronbach's alpha). The majority of the studies using coders also reported sufficient intercoder reliabilities (e.g., .80 or higher).

An overwhelming majority of the studies in the sample, however, did not provide a detailed discussion of validity issues related to the measurement instruments employed. Only 35 articles referenced construct validity, 22 articles mentioned content validity, and 11 articles discussed criterion-related validity. Part of this lack of coverage of validity is due to the widespread use of established instruments to measure key variables. It may be useful, however, to distinguish between "established" measures that have been employed only in a limited, "one-shot" study and those that have been used and refined in numerous studies. It, thus, is important for applied communication researchers to be concerned with, and provide some information about, the validity of the measurement instruments and other procedures they employ. The majority of the articles in which new measures were developed provided adequate information about validity, but in some cases, the argument for the validity of those measures was weakened by low factor loadings for factor analyses, cross-loadings, and relatively few tests of criterion-related validity (e.g., R. G. Campbell & Babrow, 2004; Dickson-Markman & Shern, 1990; Unger, Cruz, Schuster, Flora, & Johnson, 2001; Waldeck, Kearney, & Plax, 2001).

Effect Size Findings for Meta-analyses in Applied Communication Studies from 1990 to 2006

Although applied communication scholars are using meta-analysis with more frequency to summarize moderately sized bodies of research, they oftentimes do not report effect sizes. Indeed, relatively few studies reported effect sizes for statistically significant relationships among variables. When they were reported, 119 articles used *r*-squared, 53 *eta*-squared, 7 *omega*-squared, and 1 employed *epsilon*-squared. Applied communication scholars, thus, should be more attuned to providing this key piece of information when reporting the results of a meta-analysis.

Toward Furthering the Momentum of Applied Communication Research

Although applied communication researchers have come a long way in using quantitative methods, we offer several suggestions to increase the quality of such research. In particular, we discuss the importance of employing mixed methods and reinforcing the imperative to translate applied communication research for the focal communities studied.

Employing Mixed Methods in Applied Communication Research

As noted toward the beginning of this chapter, postpositivists appreciate the dual nature of reality that only partially can be apprehended using quantitative or qualitative methods, for any data-collection method demonstrates relative strengths and limitations. Rather than privileging one method over another, it is essential to ensure that the nature of the investigation—its research questions and/or hypotheses, both of which should be undergirded by communication theory—plays a fundamental role in the selection of the method employed. It also is essential to contemplate the "assumptive bases, typical practices, and emerging challenges" (Miller, 2001, p. 138) of both quantitative and qualitative methods.

We are especially heartened by the number of mixed-methods designs employed in applied communication research (88 studies published between 1990 and 2007) and fully expect that number to increase significantly in the coming years because such multifaceted designs are better positioned than is a monolithic methodological approach (Tashakkori & Teddlie, 1998; Teddlie & Tashakkori, 2003) to address the complex problems and issues that confront applied communication scholars. Innovative practices also have emerged to "quantitize" narrative data (Tashakkori & Teddlie, 1998). For example, in Sandelowski, Harris, and Holditch-Davis's (1991) study of infertile couples transitioning to parenthood, narrative interview data were gathered first and coded using a grounded theory approach to discover themes that explained couples seeking amniocentesis and those declining the procedure. Fisher's exact probability test then was employed on the data to reveal a nonsignificant relationship between OBGYN encouragement and a decision to undergo the procedure. A line of research by Query and associates (see Bible & Query, 2007; Cutsinger & Query, 2007; O'Brien, 2006; Query & Kreps, 1993; Query & Wright, 2003) provides additional examples of using mixed methods in applied communication scholarship, with narrative data obtained from a wide range of populations about pressing social issues through the use of the critical incident technique (Flanagan, 1954), data that then are coded in a grounded theory manner, with the emerging themes analyzed using post hoc chi-square tests. Qualitative data also can be translated into quantitative form in a process referred to as "qualitizing" (Sandelowski, 2003). For instance, cluster analysis (a quantitative technique for grouping objects of a similar type into respective categories) can be used initially to create distinct participant groups based on participants' responses to multiple data-gathering instruments, with a grounded theory approach then used "to validate that mutually distinctive groups have been identified and to explicate further the features of the individual members of these groups that make them more like each other than members of the other groups identified" (Sandelowski, 2003, p. 327).

Another impetus propelling the use of mixed methods in applied communication research is the pursuit of external funding from governmental organizations (e.g., the Centers for Disease Control and Prevention [CDC], National Institutes of Health [NIH], and National Science Foundation [NSF]) and nonprofit health-driven organizations and foundations (e.g., Alzheimer's Association, Kaiser Family Foundation, and Robert Wood Johnson Foundation). Heritage and Robinson's (2006) longitudinal, multimethodological study, described earlier, for instance, was funded by the NIH. Continuing its long-standing tradition as a leader in the communication discipline, a University of Kentucky team (Palmgreen et al., 2007) secured a large grant from the National Institute of Drug Abuse to conduct a longitudinal, multimethodological study that investigated substance abuse patterns among preteens and adolescents drawn from two Midwestern states using a 4-year independent and interrupted time series design. Their study focused on four variable classes (demographic variables, risk factors, protective factors, and substance abuse) and involved sample sizes of over 4,000 participants. Their findings contrasted with a nationwide representative survey of parents and youth that showed the targeted marijuana initiative campaign had little impact or positive effects on participants' attitudes, resistance strategies, and use of marijuana. As another example, aided by a grant from the Robert Wood Johnson Foundation, researchers at George Mason University, with communication scholar Gary Kreps as the principal investigator, are training bilingual hospital employees to become interpreters across several ethnic groups to facilitate communication between health-care providers and patients with little or no English-speaking skills.

To compete effectively for external funding, scholars have to embark on an incremental approach spanning some years of preparation, as well as network across related disciplines to become part of interdisciplinary teams proposing longitudinal, mixed-method research. Kreps and colleagues (Kreps, 2003; Kreps, Query, & Bonaguro, 2008; Kreps, Vishwanath, & Harris, 2002) also encouraged scholars to adopt a "big-science" orientation by becoming familiar with funding agencies, developing interdisciplinary networks and research teams, and actively pursuing external funding (see also Kreps & Bonaguro, this volume). Moreover, as Query and Weathers (2005) noted, to increase the chances of receiving external funding, pluralistic research methods and designs are paramount and often viewed by Scientific Review Board (SRB) members as normative and expected. Although these recommendations are quite sound, they are best enacted over time, especially by junior faculty members.

To crystallize those research opportunities, applied communication scholars should be open to building and testing theory by using both qualitative and quantitative methods (Query & Weathers, 2005). A good example is Peterson's (2002) Group Dynamics Q-Sort (GDQ), a 100-item instrument designed to study group interaction that combines qualitative and quantitative procedures. As Peterson observed:

> The GDQ also addresses concern for increased external validity by being compatible with longitudinal research of groups and drawing on a variety of data sources that historically have been available to qualitative researchers and of limited use to quantitative study (e.g., academic historical case studies, popular press accounts of group dynamics, and participant observation). The q-sort method, therefore,

addresses some of the weakness of both qualitative and quantitative (e.g., experimental) methods. It allows for theory testing and detailed group description across numerous (bona fide) groups with a standardized data language. (p. 80)

Translating Applied Communication Research for Communities Studied

In addition to using mixed methods to conduct applied communication research, translation of the findings for focal communities should be viewed as a fundamental component of applied communication research (Cragan & Shields, 1999; Petronio, 1999, 2002, 2007; see also Frey & SunWolf, this volume). If communities are to be positively affected by applied communication research, the research findings, of course, must be shared with those communities.

One exemplar of such applied communication research is the systematic, longitudinal, mixed-methodological, award-winning applied research about communicative practices associated with creating and sustaining community among residents and staff of Bonaventure House, a residential facility for people living with AIDS (e.g., Adelman & Frey, 1997; Frey, Adelman, Flint, & Query, 2000; Frey, Adelman, & Query 1996; Frey, Query, Flint, & Adelman, 1998). As these scholars demonstrated, it is not enough merely to answer research questions and confirm hypotheses quantitatively; investigators also need to honor the lived experiences of those they are privileged to study to provide life-altering narrative accounts of effective communicative practices (Bible & Query, 2007; O'Brien, 2006; Query & Wright, 2003; Siriko, Query, Wright, & Yamasaki, 2005) and to give back the research results to the communities affected (e.g., through reports written for residence administrators and through a video documentary made by Adelman and Schultz, 1991, that was shown on the Public Broadcasting System), as well as help those communities to facilitate needed changes (e.g., through training new staff members and helping administrators to make specific changes in the residence). Thus, although it is theoretically beneficial to demonstrate statistically significant differences between conditions/groups and relationships between variables, it is equally important to hear, through qualitative methods, participants' voices; to share the results of applied research with those studied; and to document benefits gained from the research conducted, with the understanding that it may take some time before those benefits are recognized.

To enhance the attainment of theoretical and pragmatic payoffs, one strategy that has shown some success in securing external funding of research is the creation of community advisory boards from the outset of a study to its conclusion and follow-up (e.g., Quinn, 2004). Although they are time and labor intensive, advisory boards comprised of interdisciplinary scholars, key stakeholders, opinion leaders, and community members concerned about a particular social issue should guide applied communication inquiry whenever possible, especially because such boards facilitate the dissemination of research findings back to the communities studied and potentially affected.

Conclusion

Nearly 40 years ago, the communication discipline was challenged to conduct theory-based research addressing pressing social issues. In 1991, the "Applied Communication in the 21st Century: Tampa Conference on Applied Communication" (Cissna, 1995a; Cissna et al., this volume) reinforced that imperative, with scholars arguing that applied communication investigators must demonstrate both the scientific rigor and relevance of their work to enhance the likelihood of achieving desirable practical outcomes (see Frey & SunWolf, this volume). Numerous researchers have accepted that challenge and used one or more of the quantitative methods discussed in this chapter. As applied communication scholarship moves forward, it is imperative to capitalize on the inroads that have been made with regard to refining the quantitative methods employed. Applied communication inquiry has matured to where theoretically grounded designs, using quantitative methods, are commonplace among researchers who study pressing social problems and how those problems might be lessened. Furthermore, translation of research findings to focal communities should be viewed as a fundamental component of applied communication research. Many contextual, theoretical, and methodological challenges undoubtedly will continue to confront applied communication scholars who employ quantitative methods. The extent to which these challenges are managed, in large measure, will determine the quality of quantitative (and qualitative) applied communication scholarship in the decades ahead.

Notes

1. A similar approach was employed by Beck et al. (2004) to assess the frequency of health research, topics, methodological approaches, and theoretical frameworks appearing in communication journals.
2. This time frame is comparable to similar reviews (e.g., Allen, Gotcher, & Siebert, 1993; Beck et al., 2004; Greenbaum & Query, 1999), coincided with NCA taking ownership of *JACR*, and enabled an analysis of articles published across different editors of the same journal. Although there are many other journals that feature applied communication research articles, these five journals provide a fairly representative cross-section of the common types of applied studies conducted within the communication discipline. Following Seibold's (1995) view of applied communication scholarship, articles were selected when communication theories and quantitative or qualitative methodologies were used in applied settings or to achieve applied outcomes, and when the focus was on issues of social relevance (Cissna, 1995b). Thus, the articles selected are scientifically rigorous and conducted using field research that builds on and extends basic communication research tenets, with a particular focus on how various aspects of communication play a role in addressing pressing social issues.
3. As the review of meta-analysis revealed, a number of studies published in 2007 employed this method but were not included in this content analysis of the literature.

References

Adelman, M. B., & Frey, L. R. (1997). *The fragile community: Living together with AIDS*. Mahwah, NJ: Erlbaum.

Adelman, M. B. (Producer), & Schultz, P. (Director). (1991). *The pilgrim must embark: Living in community* [Motion picture]. Chicago: Terra Nova Films.

Allen, M. W., Gotcher, A. J. M., & Siebert, J. H. (1993). A decade of organizational communication research: Journal articles 1980–1991. In S. A. Deetz (Ed.), *Communication yearbook* (Vol. 16, pp. 252–330). Newbury Park, CA: Sage.

Anderson, J. A. (1987). *Communication research: Issues and methods*. New York: McGraw-Hill.

Anderson, J. A. (1996). *Communication theory: Epistemological foundations*. New York: Guilford Press.

Ayers, J., Ayers, F. E., Baker, A. L., Colby, N., DeBlasi, C., Dimke, D., et al. (1993). Two empirical tests of a videotape designed to reduce public speaking anxiety. *Journal of Applied Communication Research, 21*, 132–147.

Babbie, E. (1999). *The basics of social research*. Belmont, CA: Wadsworth.

Beatty, M., & Springhorn, R. G. (1977). The immediate and sustained effects of message discrepancy on attitude change in a field setting. *Journal of Applied Communications Research, 5*, 9–14.

Beck, C. S., Benitez, J. L., Edwards, A., Olson, A., Pai, A., & Torres, M. B. (2004). Enacting "health communication": The field of health communication as constructed through publication in scholarly journals. *Health Communication, 16*, 475–492.

Becker, J. A. H., & O'Hair, H. D. (2007). Machiavellians' motives in organizational citizenship behavior. *Journal of Applied Communication Research, 35,* 246–267.

Berelson, B. (1952). *Content analysis in communication research.* Glencoe, IL: Free Press.

Bible, S., & Query, J. L., Jr. (2007, March). *Assessing the role of communication competence and social support between cancer patients transitioning to survivor roles and their oncologists.* Paper presented at the meeting of the Central States Communication Association, Minneapolis, MN.

Blau, G. J. (1986). The effect of source competence on worker attitudes. *Journal of Applied Communication Research, 14,* 20–36.

Booth-Butterfield, M., & Booth-Butterfield, S. (1994). Communication anxiety and signing effectiveness: Testing an interference model among deaf communicators. *Journal of Applied Communication Research, 22,* 273–286.

Bryski, B. G. (1978). An analysis of evidence in the first Ford/Carter debate. *Journal of Applied Communications Research, 6,* 19–30.

Cahudhri, V., & Wang, J. (2007). Communicating corporate social responsibility on the Internet: A case study of the top 100 information technology companies in India. *Management Communication Quarterly, 21,* 232–247.

Campbell, D. T., & Stanley, J. C. (1963). *Experimental and quasi-experimental designs for research.* Chicago: Rand McNally.

Campbell, R. G., & Babrow, A. S. (2004). The role of empathy in responses to persuasive risk communication: Overcoming resistance to HIV prevention messages. *Health Communication, 16,* 159–182.

Campbell, S. W., & Kelley, M. J. (2006). Mobile phone use in AA networks: An exploratory study. *Journal of Applied Communication Research, 34,* 191–208.

Campo, S., & Mastin, T. (2007). Placing the burden on the individual: Overweight and obesity in African American and mainstream women's magazines. *Health Communication, 22,* 229–240.

Cappella, J. N. (1990). The method of proof by example in interaction analysis. *Communication Monographs, 57,* 236–242.

Casey, M. K., Allen, M., Emmers-Sommers, T., Sahlstein, E., Degooyer, D., Winters, A., et al. (2003). When a celebrity contracts a disease: The example of Earvin "Magic" Johnson's announcement that he was HIV positive. *Journal of Health Communication, 8,* 249–265.

Cissna, K. N. (Ed.). (1995a). *Applied communication in the 21st century.* Mahwah, NJ: Erlbaum.

Cissna, K. N. (1995b). Introduction. In K. N. Cessna (Ed.), *Applied communication in the 21st century* (pp. ix–xiv). Mahwah, NJ: Erlbaum.

Cissna, K. N. (2000). Applied communication research in the 21st century. *Journal of Applied Communication Research, 28,* 169–173.

Cohen, J. (1960). A coefficient of agreement for nominal scales. *Educational and Psychological Measurement, 20,* 37–46.

Cohen, J. (1992). A power primer. *Psychological Bulletin, 112,* 155–159.

Cohen, M. M., & Saine, T. J. (1977). The role of profanity and sex variables in interpersonal impression formation. *Journal of Applied Communications Research, 5,* 45–51.

Compte, A. (1986). *A general view of positivism* (J. H. Bridges, Trans.). London: Trübner. (Original work published 1865)

Cook, T. D. (1985). Postpositivist critical multiplism. In R. L. Shotland & M. M. Mark (Eds.), *Social science and social policy* (pp. 21–62). Beverly Hills, CA: Sage.

Cook, T. D., & Campbell, D. T. (1979). *Quasi-experimentation: Design & analysis issues for field settings.* Boston: Houghton Mifflin.

Cragan, J. F., & Shields, D. C. (1999). Translating scholarship into practice: Communication studies reflecting the value of theory-based research to everyday life. *Journal of Applied Communication Research, 27,* 92–106.

Cutsinger, K. D., & Query, J. L., Jr. (2007, March). *Engaging health educators and clients: A multi-methodological approach informing organizational practices.* Paper presented at the meeting of the Central States Communication Association, Minneapolis, MN.

Daniels, G. L., & Loggins, G. M. (2007). Conceptualizing continuous coverage: A strategic model for wall-to-wall local television weather broadcasts. *Journal of Applied Communication Research, 35,* 48–66.

DiBerardinis, J., Barwind, J. A., & Wilmot, W. W. (1981). Interpersonal networks and quality of life of nursing home residents. *Journal of Applied Communication Research, 9,* 120–130.

Dickson-Markman, F., & Shern, D. L. (1990). Social support and health in the elderly. *Journal of Applied Communication Research, 18,* 49–63.

Dillard, J. P., Weber, K. M., & Vail, R. G. (2007). The relationship between the perceived and actual effectiveness of persuasive messages: A meta-analysis with implications for formative campaign research. *Journal of Communication, 57,* 613–631.

Doerfel, M. L., & Marsh, P. S. (2003). Candidate–issue positioning in the context of presidential debates. *Journal of Applied Communication Research, 31,* 212–237.

Edy, J. A., & Meirick, P. C. (2007). Wanted, dead or alive: Media frames, frame adoption, and support for the war in Afghanistan. *Journal of Communication, 57,* 119–141.

Egbert, N., & Parrott, R. (2001). Self-efficacy and rural women's performance of breast and cervical cancer detection practices. *Journal of Health Communication, 6,* 219–233.

Ellis, D. G., & Maoz, I. (2007). Online argument between Israeli Jews and Palestinians. *Human Communication Research, 33,* 291–309.

Emmers-Sommer, T. M., Allen, M., Bourhis, J., Sahlstein, E., Laskowski, K., Falato, W. L., et al. (2004). A meta-analysis of the relationship between social skills and sexual offenders. *Communication Reports, 17,* 1–10.

Falcione, R. L. (1974). Communication climate and satisfaction with immediate supervision. *Journal of Applied Communications Research, 2,* 13–20.

Feeley, T. H., & Vincent, D., III (2007). How organ donation is represented in newspaper articles in the United States. *Health Communication, 21,* 125–131.

Flanagan, J. C. (1954). The critical incident technique. *Psychological Bulletin, 51,* 327–358.

Flesch, R. (1949). *The art of readable writing.* New York: Collier.

Ford, W. S. Z. (2001). Customer expectations for interactions with service providers: Relationship versus encounter. *Journal of Applied Communication Research, 29,* 1–29.

Frank, M. G., & Feeley, T. H. (2003). To catch a liar: Challenges for research in lie detection training. *Journal of Applied Communication Research, 31,* 58–75.

Frey, L. R., Adelman, M. B., Flint, L. J., & Query, J. L., Jr. (2000). Weaving meanings together in an AIDS residence: Communicative practices, perceived health outcomes, and the symbolic construction of community. *Journal of Health Communication, 5,* 53–72.

Frey, L. R., Adelman, M. B., & Query, J. L., Jr. (1996). Symbolic practices in the social construction of health in an AIDS residence. *Journal of Health Psychology, 1,* 383–397.

Frey, L. R., Botan, C. H., Friedman, P. G., & Kreps, G. L. (1992). *Interpreting communication research: A case study approach.* Englewood Cliffs, NJ: Prentice Hall.

Frey, L. R., Botan, C. H., & Kreps, G. L. (2000). *Investigating communication: An introduction to research methods* (2nd ed.). Needham Heights, MA: Allyn & Bacon.

Frey, L. R., Query, J. L., Jr., Flint, L. J., & Adelman, M. B. (1998). Living together with AIDS: Communication and social support processes in a residential facility. In V. J. Derlega & A. P. Barbee (Eds.), *HIV infection and social interaction* (pp. 129–146). Thousand Oaks, CA: Sage.

Garvin, B. J., & Kennedy, C. W. (1986). Confirmation and disconfirmation in nurse/physician communication. *Journal of Applied Communication Research, 14,* 1–18.

Glass, G. V. (1976). Primary, secondary, and meta-analysis of research. *Educational Research, 10,* 3–8.

Glass, G. V., McGaw, B., & Smith, M. L. (1981). *Meta-analysis in social research.* Beverly Hills, CA: Sage.

Greenbaum, H. H., & Query, J. L., Jr. (1999). Communication in organizational work groups: A review and analysis of natural work group studies. In L. R. Frey (Ed.), D. S. Gouran & M. S. Poole (Assoc. Eds.,) *The handbook of group communication theory and research* (pp. 539–564). Thousand Oaks, CA: Sage.

Guba, E. G. (1990). The alternative paradigm dialog. In E. G. Guba (Ed.), *The paradigm dialog* (pp. 17–27). Newbury Park, CA: Sage.

Guba, E. G., & Lincoln, Y. S. (1994). Competing paradigms in qualitative research. In N. K. Denzin & Y. S. Lincoln (Eds.), *Handbook of qualitative research* (pp. 105–117). Thousand Oaks, CA: Sage.

Harrington, N. G., Norling, G. R., Witte, F. M., Taylor, J., & Andrews, E. (2007). The effects of communication skills training on pediatricians' and parents' communication during "sick child" visits. *Health Communication, 21,* 105–114.

Heritage, J. (1989). Current developments in conversation analysis. In D. Roger & P. Bull (Eds.), *Conversation: An interdisciplinary perspective* (pp. 21–47). Philadelphia: Multilingual Matters.

Heritage, J., & Robinson, J. D. (2006). The structure of patients' presenting concerns: Physicians' opening questions. *Health Communication, 19,* 89–102.

Hetsroni, A. (2007a). Three decades of sexual content on prime-time network programming: A longitudinal meta-analytic review. *Journal of Communication, 57,* 318–348.

Hetsroni, A. (2007b). Four decades of violent content on prime-time network programming: A longitudinal meta-analytic review. *Journal of Communication, 57,* 759–784.

Hogan, J. M. (1997). George Gallup and the rhetoric of scientific discovery. *Communication Monographs, 64,* 161–179.

Holmstrom, A. J. (2004). The effects of the media on body image: A meta-analysis. *Journal of Broadcasting & Electronic Media, 48,* 196–217.

Holsti, O. R. (1969). *Content analysis for the social sciences and humanities.* Reading, MA: Addison-Wesley.

Hullet, C. R., & Levine, T. R. (2003). The overestimation of effect sizes from F values in meta-analysis: The cause and solution. *Communication Monographs, 70,* 52–67.

Hunt, G. T., & Eberling, R. E. (1983). The impact of a communication intervention on work-unit productivity and employee satisfaction. *Journal of Applied Communication Research, 11,* 57–68.

Infante, D. A., Rancer, A. S., Pierce, L. L., & Osborne, W. J. (1980). Effects of physical attractiveness and likeableness of first name on impressions formed of journalists. *Journal of Applied Communications Research, 8,* 1–9.

Kerlinger, F. N., & Lee, H. B. (2000). *Foundations of behavioral research* (4th ed.). Fort Worth, TX: Harcourt College.

Keyton, J. (2000). Applied communication research should be practical. *Journal of Applied Communication Research, 28,* 166–168.

Kibler, R. J., & Barker, L. L. (Eds.). (1969). *Conceptual frontiers in speech communication: Report of the New Orleans Conference on Research and Instructional Development.* New York: Speech Association of America.

Kreps, G. L. (2003). Opportunities for health communication scholarship to shape public health policy and practice: Examples from the National Cancer Institute. In T. Thompson, R. Parrott, K. Miller, & A. Dorsey, (Eds.), *The handbook of health communication* (pp. 609–624), Mahwah, NJ: Erlbaum.

Kreps, G. L., Query, J. L., & Bonaguro, E. W. (2008). The interdisciplinary study of health communication and its relationship to communication science. In L. C. Lederman (Ed.), *Beyond these walls: Readings in health communication,* (pp. 3–14). New York: Oxford University Press.

Kreps, G. L., Viswanath, K., & Harris, L. M. (2002). Advancing communication as a science: Opportunities from the federal sector. *Journal of Applied Communication Research, 30,* 369–381.

Krippendorff, K. (2004). *Content analysis: An introduction to its methodology* (2nd ed.). Thousand Oaks, CA: Sage.

Lee, J. W., & Guerrero, L. K. (2001). Types of touch in cross-sex relationships between coworkers: Perceptions of relational and emotional messages, inappropriateness, and sexual harassment. *Journal of Applied Communication Research, 29,* 197–220.

Leets, L., & Sunwolf. (2004). Being left out: Rejecting outsiders and communicating group boundaries in childhood and adolescent peer groups. *Journal of Applied Communication Research, 32*, 195–223.

Levine, T. R., & Hullet, C. R. (2002). Eta-squared, partial eta-squared, and misreporting of effect size in communication research. *Human Communication Research, 28*, 612–625.

Lincoln, Y. S., & Guba, E. G. (1985). *Naturalistic inquiry.* Beverly Hills, CA: Sage.

Matthews, B. C. (1910). A study of a New York daily. *Independent, 68*, 82–86.

McDiarmid, J. (1937). Presidential inaugural addresses: A study in verbal symbols. *Public Opinion Quarterly, 1*, 79–82.

McPherson, M. B., Kearney, P., & Plax, T. G. (2003). The dark side of instruction: Teacher anger as classroom norm violations. *Journal of Applied Communication Research, 31*, 76–90.

Miller, K. (2001). Quantitative research methods. In F. M. Jablin & L. L. Putnam (Eds.), *The new handbook of organizational communication: Advances in theory, research, and methods* (pp. 137–160). Thousand Oaks, CA: Sage.

Morgan, G. (1983a). Research as engagement: A personal view. In G. Morgan (Ed.), *Beyond method: Strategies for social research* (pp. 11–18). Beverly Hills, CA: Sage.

Morgan, G. (1983b). Toward a more reflective social science. In G. Morgan (Ed.), *Beyond method: Strategies for social research* (pp. 368–376). Beverly Hills, CA: Sage.

Morgan, S. E., Harrison, T. R., Chewning, L., Davis, L., & DiCorcia, M. (2007). Entertainment (mis)education: The framing of organ donation in entertainment television. *Health Communication, 22*, 143–151.

Morman, M. T. (2000). The influence of fear appeals, message design, and masculinity on men's motivation to perform the testicular self-exam. *Journal of Applied Communication Research, 28*, 91–116.

Morse, B. W., & Piland, R. N. (1981). An assessment of communication competencies needed by intermediate-level health care providers: A study of nurse–patient, nurse–doctor, nurse–nurse communication relationships. *Journal of Applied Communication Research, 9*, 30–41.

Neuendorf, K. A. (2002). *The content analysis guidebook.* Thousand Oaks, CA: Sage.

Noar, S. M. (2006). In pursuit of cumulative knowledge in health communication: The role of meta-analysis. *Health Communication, 20*, 169–175.

Noar, S. M., Carlyle, K., & Cole, C. (2006). Why communication is crucial: Meta-analysis of the relationship between safer sexual communication and condom use. *Journal of Health Communication, 11*, 365–390.

O'Brien, C. J. (2006). *Self-reported communication skills, social support, coping, and openness to disclose among abused women.* Unpublished master's thesis, University of Houston, TX.

Ogata Jones, K., Denham, B., & Springston, J. K. (2006). Effects of mass and interpersonal communication on breast cancer screening: Advancing agenda-setting theory in health contexts. *Journal of Applied Communication Research, 34*, 94–113.

O'Keefe, D. J., & Jensen, J. D. (2007). The relative persuasiveness of gain-framed and loss-framed messages for encouraging disease prevention behaviors: A meta-analytic review. *Journal of Health Communication, 12*, 623–644.

O'Keefe, D. J., & Jensen, J. D. (2008). Do loss-framed persuasive messages engender greater message processing than do gain-framed messages? A meta-analytic review. *Communication Studies, 59*, 51–67.

Palmgreen, P., Lorch, E. P., Stephenson, M. T., Hoyle, R. H., & Donohew, L. (2007). Effects of the Office of National Drug Control Policy's marijuana initiative campaign on high-sensation-seeking adolescents. *American Journal of Public Health, 97*, 1644–1649.

Parrott, R., & Duggan, A. (1999). Using coaches as role models of sun protection for youth: Georgia's "Got Youth Covered" project. *Journal of Applied Communication Research, 27*, 107–119.

Pearson K. (1904). Report on certain enteric fever inoculation statistics. *British Medical Journal, 3*, 1243–1246.

Peterson, R. S. (2002). The group dynamics Q-sort in group communication research. In L. R. Frey (Ed.), *New directions in group communication* (pp. 79–96). Thousand Oaks, CA: Sage.

Petronio, S. (1999). "Translating scholarship into practice": An alternative metaphor. *Journal of Applied Communication Research, 27,* 87–91.

Petronio, S. (2002). The new world and scholarship translation practices: Necessary changes in defining evidence. *Western Journal of Communication, 66,* 507–512.

Petronio, S. (2007). *JACR* commentaries on translating research into practice: Introduction. *Journal of Applied Communication Research, 35,* 215–217.

Pittam, J., & Gallois, C. (2000). Malevolence, stigma, and social distance: Maximizing intergroup differences in HIV/AIDS discourse. *Journal of Applied Communication Research, 28,* 24–43.

Poole, M. S., & McPhee, R. D. (1985). Methodology in interpersonal communication research. In M. L. Knapp & G. R. Miller (Eds.), *Handbook of interpersonal communication* (pp. 100–170). Beverly Hills, CA: Sage.

Popper, K. R. (1959). *The logic of scientific discovery.* New York: Basic Books.

Potter, W. J., Cooper, R., & Dupagne, M. (1993). The three paradigms of mass media research in mainstream communication journals. *Communication Theory, 3,* 317–335.

Query, J. L., Jr., & Kreps, G. L. (1993). Using the critical incident method to evaluate and enhance organizational effectiveness. In S. L. Herndon & G. L. Kreps (Eds.), *Qualitative research: Applications in organizational communication* (pp. 63–77). Cresskill, NJ: Hampton Press.

Query, J. L., Jr., & Weathers, M. R. (2005, October). *Health-related issues affecting accountability in families.* Paper presented at the meeting of the Texas Speech Communication Association, Galveston, TX.

Query, J. L., Jr., & Wright, K. (2003). Assessing communication competence in an online study: Toward informing subsequent interventions among older caregivers with cancer, their lay caregivers, and peers. *Health Communication, 15,* 203–218.

Quinn, S. C. (2004). Ethics in public health research: Protecting human subjects: The role of community advisory boards. *American Journal of Public Health, 94,* 918–922.

Roberto, A. J., Meyer, G., Johnson, A. J., Atkin, C. K., & Smith, P. K. (2002). Promoting gun trigger-lock use: Insights and implications from a radio-based health communication intervention. *Journal of Applied Communication Research, 30,* 210–230.

Rosenfeld, L. B., & Fowler, G. D. (1983). Media effects on information sharing: A field experiment. *Journal of Applied Communication Research, 11,* 136–152.

Rosenthal, R. (1991). *Meta-analytic procedures for social research* (Rev. ed.). Newbury Park, CA: Sage.

Roter, D. L., & Larson, S. (2001). The relationship between residents' and attending physicians' communication during primary care visits: An illustrative use of the Roter interaction analysis system. *Health Communication, 13,* 33–48.

Rothenbuhler, E. W. (1991). The process of community involvement. *Communication Monographs, 58,* 63–78.

Rudolph, E. E. (1973). Informal human communication systems in a large organization. *Journal of Applied Communications Research, 1,* 7–23.

Sandelowski, M. (2003). Tables or tableaux? The challenges of writing and reading mixed method studies. In A. Tashakkori & C. Teddlie (Eds.), *Handbook of mixed methods in social & behavioral research* (pp. 321–350). Thousand Oaks, CA: Sage.

Sandelowski, M., Harris, B. G., & Holditch-Davis, D. (1991). Amniocentesis in the context of infertility. *Health Care for Women International, 12,* 167–178.

Schonborn, K. (1976). Violence on television: Some cross-time and cross-cultural comparisons. *Journal of Applied Communications Research, 4,* 65–74.

Schrodt, P., Witt, P. L., & Messersmith, A. S. (2008). A meta-analytic review of family communication patterns and their associations with information processing, behavioral, and psychosocial outcomes. *Communication Monographs, 75,* 248–269.

Scott, W. A. (1955). Reliability of content analysis: The case of nominal scale coding. *Public Opinion Quarterly, 19,* 321–325.

Seibold, D. R. (1995). *Theoria* and *praxis*: Means and ends in applied communication research. In K. N. Cissna (Ed.), *Applied communication in the 21st century* (pp. 23–38). Mahwah, NJ: Erlbaum.

Shyles, L., & Ross, M. (1984). Recruitment rhetoric in brochures advertising the all volunteer force. *Journal of Applied Communication Research, 12,* 34–49.

Siriko, T. L., Query, J. L., Jr., Wright, K. B., & Yamasaki, J. (2005, November). *Exploring communication competence, social support, and perceived coping in lay caregivers for patients with Alzheimer's disease.* Paper presented at the meeting of the National Communication Association, Boston, MA.

Smith, M. L., & Glass, G. V. (1977). Meta-analysis of psychotherapy outcome studies. *American Psychologist, 32,* 752–760.

Snedecor, G. W., & Cochran, W. G. (1956). *Statistical methods applied to experiments in agriculture and biology* (5th ed.). Ames: Iowa State University Press.

Snyder, L. B., Hamilton, M. A., Mitchell, E. W., Kiwanuka-Tondo, J., Fleming-Milici, F., & Proctor, D. (2004). A meta-analysis of the effect of mediated health communication campaigns on behavior change in the United States. *Journal of Health Communication, 9,* 71–96.

Speed, G. J. (1893). Do newspapers now give the news? *Forum, 15,* 705–711.

Stemler, S. (2001). An overview of content analysis. *Practical Assessment, Research & Evaluation, 7*(17). Retrieved September 14, 2007, from http://pareonline.net/getvn.asp?v=7&n=17

Stephenson, M. T., Palmgreen, P., Hoyle, R. H., Donohew, L., Lorch, E. P., & Colon, S. E. (1999). Short-term effects on an anti-marijuana media campaign targeting high sensation-seeking adolescents. *Journal of Applied Communication Research, 27,* 175–195.

Strom, R. E., & Boster, F. J. (2007). Dropping out of high school: A meta-analysis of the effect of messages in the home and in school. *Communication Education, 56,* 433–452.

Tashakkori, A., & Teddlie, C. (1998). *Mixed methodology: Combining qualitative and quantitative approaches.* Thousand Oaks, CA: Sage.

Teddlie, C., & Tashakkori, A. (2003). Major issues and controversies in the use of mixed methods in the social and behavioral sciences. In A. Tashakkori & C. Teddlie (Eds.), *Handbook of mixed methods in social & behavioral research* (pp. 3–50). Thousand Oaks, CA: Sage.

Trost, M. R., Langan, E. J., & Kellar-Guenter, Y. (1999). Not everyone listens when you "just say no": Drug resistance in relational context. *Journal of Applied Communication Research, 27,* 120–138.

Unger, J. B., Cruz, T. B., Schuster, D., Flora, J. A., & Johnson, C. A. (2001). Measuring exposure to pro- and anti-tobacco marketing among adolescents: Intercorrelations among measures and associations with smoking status. *Journal of Health Communication, 6,* 11–29.

Wadsworth, A. J., Patterson, P., Kaid, L. L., Cullers, G., Malcomb, D., & Lamirand, L. (1987). "Masculine" versus "feminine" strategies in political ads: Implications for female candidates. *Journal of Applied Communication Research, 15,* 77–94.

Waldeck, J. H., Kearney, P., & Plax, T. G. (2001). Teacher e-mail message strategies and students' willingness to communicate online. *Journal of Applied Communication Research, 29,* 54–71.

Wang, Z., & Gantz, W. (2007). Health content in local television news. *Health Communication, 21,* 213–222.

Warren, C., & Neer, M. (1986). Family sex communication orientation. *Journal of Applied Communication Research, 14,* 86–107.

Watson, K. W., & Ragsdale, J. D. (1981). Linguistic indices of truthful and deceptive responses to employment interview questions. *Journal of Applied Communication Research, 9,* 59–61.

Wimmer, R. D., & Dominick, R. L. (1994). *Mass media research: An introduction* (4th ed.). Belmont, CA: Wadsworth.

Wright, K. (2002). Social support within an on-line cancer community: An assessment of emotional support, perceptions of advantages and disadvantages, and motives for using the community from a communication perspective. *Journal of Applied Communication Research, 3,* 195–209.

5 Rhetorical Methods of Applied Communication Scholarship

Celeste M. Condit
University of Georgia

Benjamin R. Bates
Ohio University

In about 330 BCE, Aristotle (1991) defined *rhetoric* as "an ability, in each [particular] case, to see the available means of persuasion" (Bk. 1, ch. 1.1). Rhetoric, thus, originally was conceived as a practical art, a pragmatic counterpart to philosophy. Rhetorical studies usually were written to be applied to the business of participating in democratic life, which included substantial speech making, at least by the class of persons for whom rhetorical treatises were written. The most important topic for Aristotle was the inventional resources available to a speaker, but he also focused on the generic characteristics and standard topics of speaking situations, and the role of ethos and pathos in persuasion. Stylistic issues were common subjects for rhetoricians, and issues of arrangement and delivery have become more or less important at different historical periods.

Aristotle's view of rhetoric was "speaker centered" and for centuries, Aristotle's followers interpreted the formation of rhetorical principles as aimed at those who sought to compose messages. By the end of the 20th century, however, that focus had shifted to an "audience-centered" perspective (at least within the research tradition in communication departments). Instead of formulating principles to assist speakers, applications of rhetorical theory increasingly were envisioned from an audience's perspective, with the study of rhetoric often focused on assisting audiences to resist the persuasive messages of the powerful.

Several factors probably contributed to this shift, including the expansion of human populations and the media, the broader reach of higher education, and the professional interests and perspectives of academic elites. Whatever the causes may have been, this domination of rhetorical criticism over the older practice of what one might call "rhetorical construction" influences the focus of this chapter. As a summary of prevailing practices in the research literature, this chapter must primarily address rhetorical criticism. However, we begin by situating criticism and constructionism within the concept of "applied research," and we close with recommendations to encourage additional constructionist efforts. In between, we describe the basic assumptions that shape rhetorical methods and four particular approaches to applied rhetorical criticism: metaphoric analysis, narrative studies, fantasy theme analysis, and ideological critique.

Binaries and Categories of Applied Rhetorical Studies

Three binaries shape the distinction between "more and less" applied rhetorical studies. The first is the distinction between criticism and construction. *Critical studies* examine discourse to discover how it works. Criticism need not be hostile but most contemporary criticism is biased toward showing that a particular discourse is undesirable in some way. This tenor puts criticism at odds with *construction-oriented studies*, which seek effective means for presenting one's case. Although the construction orientation to rhetorical studies is the common core of the public speaking course, it rarely appears elsewhere in the curriculum, and rhetoricians rarely publish on this subject.

The second binary demarcating more from less applied rhetorical studies is the immediate or particular versus the general. Some studies address a particular case, at a narrowly defined moment. For example, Dow (1996) examined television programs about women during the political rise of feminism from 1970 up to the writing of her book. Other studies address a topic across a broader expanse of time, such as Darsey's (1997) exploration of prophetic forms of address across history. Applied work usually is perceived as requiring a narrow focus, but studies of more general topics that focus, at least in part, on the present also may have applied qualities.

The third distinction regards the audience of an academician's discourse. That audience may consist of academics and students, or what we call "change agents"—people and institutions that have a relatively direct and immediate ability to influence outcomes related to a particular issue. Discourse addressed to other academics and students potentially reshapes the world in the long run. Academics influence other academics and, together, they influence students, and students may learn from prescriptions generated by rhetorical methods and apply what they have rehearsed to issues they face throughout their life (Hart, 1993; Sproule, 1990). However, these applications are diffuse; although academics are members of the public, they are a teeny fraction of the public and are not sufficiently organized to influence public processes directly. Given sensibilities about what constitutes "applied" work, such work usually is perceived to require a nonacademic audience. However, given the disjunction in outlets for public and academic discourses, applied work in rhetorical studies also may appear in academic journals.

Given these three sets of binaries, and their complications, the published studies that appear as lowest in their applied qualities are critical studies that focus on general issues and address academic or student audiences. Such studies occasionally might be undertaken solely to "understand" the world. However, because most contemporary rhetorical theories suggest that people's understanding of the world entails attitudes toward things in the world, and that such attitudes further entail actions, even critical efforts that seek only understanding have implications for shaping the world. Thus, as Black (1965) suggested, "If the critic has a motive for understanding—and he [she] usually does—that motive is to enhance the quality of human life" (p. 9). To this extent, all rhetorical studies are applied, at least to some degree. However, studies that focus on the construction of messages about particular topics and address audiences of change agents more closely fit the general notion of "applied communication research" (Cissna, 1995) and, more specifically, intervention-oriented applied communication research (see Frey & SunWolf, this volume).

Although there are eight combinations of these binaries (see Figure 5.1), the four types targeted to academic audiences are more visible than the four types targeted to change agents, and critical studies are far more common than construction-oriented studies. At the "least applied" end of the continuum are critical studies of general phenomena that appear exclusively in academic outlets (e.g., Campbell & Jamieson, 1976). These studies provide general tools for enhanced critical perception of major groups of discourse to enable academics to better resist rhetorical appeals, in general, and perhaps to assist students to resist these pulls as well. The second category consists of critical studies of particular phenomena intended to increase resistance to the particular content of particular discourses by academics and students, and, perhaps, the broader community (e.g., DeLuca & Demo, 2000).

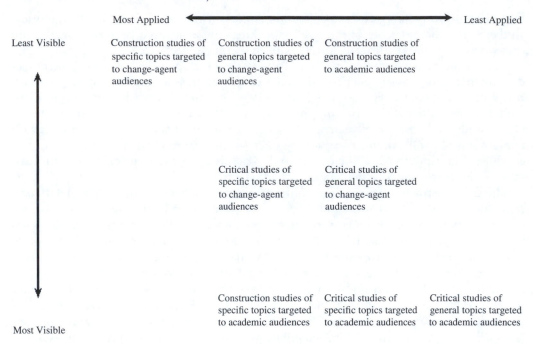

Figure 5.1 A continuum of more to less applied and most to least visible rhetorical studies.

Construction-oriented rhetorical studies are far less common in academic publications. Some critics would deny the distinction between critical and constructive discourse, and argue that all critical discourses are constructive. Others would argue that constructive discourse is presence making and, therefore undesirable. Assuming some difference between criticism and constructivism, and assuming the desirability of constructive discourse, it nonetheless is understandable that academic publications rarely urge academics to take specific actions, except actions pertaining specifically to academic practices, because constructive discourse that appears in academic venues might well be indistinguishable from constructive discourse that appears in nonacademic venues. Such discourse threatens the legitimacy of academic discourses as worthy of special funding and support. Such exhortations also might not be a particularly good use of space and energy because the academic audience is small and not organized to promote specific social change. The closest group of construction-oriented rhetorical studies published for an academic audience consists of theories explicitly intended for use in message construction within a particular context, such as an apologia (see pp. 111–112 below). Such theories are intended to be applied by students or by consultants, and, obviously, are more likely to be general than particular.

It is more difficult to assess the four categories of rhetorical work presented to change agents, because such applied efforts are not conveniently gathered in academic journals. Nonetheless, there probably are few instances of either critical or constructive discourses focusing on only general concepts addressed to change agents. Exceptions may be media interviews of rhetoricians asking for explanations of inaugurals or presidential debates, and the few books about political processes that have managed to reach a public audience (e.g., Jamieson, 2000). Such general commentary perhaps is rare or rarely successful because the U.S. public is uninterested in general concepts and because the nature of change processes calls forth more particular responses. However, with regard to particular and immediate topics, both critical and constructive rhetorical efforts addressed to change agents may prosper.

Rhetorical critiques of particular and immediate discourses addressed to change agents perhaps are best exemplified by Campbell's (1972) critiques of public speeches broadcast over radio station KPFK in Los Angeles in the late 1960s. She used rhetorical criticism to encourage the public audience to resist speeches such as President Richard Nixon's "Vietnamization" address. In more recent critical efforts, Stephen Hartnett, a rhetorician, has facilitated public dialogues about the death penalty in an interactive art space (a death row cell) and organized social protest against the war on Iraq (Hartnett, 2007).

The use of rhetorical studies to construct discourse probably is more common than the sharing of critical works with change agents. Many rhetoricians undoubtedly write letters to newspapers and speak to organizations, such as Rotary International or Kiwanis International, in favor of particular actions, and other rhetoricians use their training to consult. When producing messages, rhetoricians inevitably draw on their rhetorical training. However, less common is scholarship about such activities. For example, Condit heard many stories about Michael Calvin McGee's efforts to promote Michael Osborn's campaign for public office. Both of these rhetoricians drew on rhetorical theories to construct messages during the campaign, but neither of them wrote analyses of this effort. A welcome exception to academic silence about applied rhetorical construction is the case study by Esrock, Hart, and Leichty (2007) describing their efforts to promote an increase in the Kentucky tobacco excise tax. This academic report, of course, is about their use of rhetorical principles to construct discourse for a change-agent audience rather than discourse aimed at the change agents per se. However, more academic discourse about such efforts might legitimate and improve such applications.

Given the paucity of treatments of constructive efforts and efforts to address non-academic audiences, the remainder of this chapter necessarily focuses on critical efforts by academics, most of which are at the lower half of the "applied" continuum. We first describe key assumptions of rhetorical criticism that feed into its applied character and then explain four types of critical efforts.

Assumptions of Applied Rhetorical Criticism

Rhetorical criticism might be defined as the study of ways in which symbolic components of particular discourse shape or constitute beliefs, attitudes, and actions. Four guiding assumptions of rhetorical criticism are crucial to it functioning as an applied communication research method: (1) rhetorical criticism examines texts; (2) rhetorical criticism is guided, but should not be controlled, by theory; (3) rhetorical criticism engages in evaluation; and (4) the goal of rhetorical criticism is to produce change in the world.

Rhetorical Criticism Examines Texts

By *text*, we do not mean only a single speech, television show, or other statement but, rather, the broader understanding of any cultural product that can serve as the object of critical analysis. Although "great speeches" can serve as texts for analysis, Wrage (1947, p. 451) is correct that "exclusive devotion to monumental works is hopelessly inadequate as a way of discovering and assessing those ideas which find expression in the marketplace," because the force of ideas is found when those ideas are expressed in common discourse, in addition to the statements of monumental speakers. A focus on a monumental work alone neglects some of the critic's important scholarly and practical responsibilities—namely, the substantive origins of discourse, its injection into an actual content, and the results linked to the deployment of the work (Baskerville, 1977). Rather than viewing texts as externally existent singularities, a more useful perspective is that texts are the result of multiple discursive fragments brought together by the critic (McGee, 1990). By clumping fragments together with respect to similarities perceived by the critic, patterns in discourse can be described as expressions of ideas that have permeated a culture. These fragments then can be used to reconstruct the ideational environment in which the apparently finished discourse emerged. The critic can proceed to describe the "solid intellectual residue" left by ideas as they are "integrated with, refracted by, modified by, and substituted for one another in the process of rhetorical formation" (Wrage, 1947, p. 451).

Rhetorical Criticism is Guided, but Should Not Be Controlled, by Theory

To describe this intellectual residue, the critic should be guided by rhetorical theory. Although there are many theoretical concepts in rhetoric, there are few rigid methodologies of rhetorical criticism. Many critics are likely to agree with Lucas (1981) that critics should "reject the application of predetermined formulas, which are most likely to produce scholarship which is dull, mechanical, unimaginative, and commonplace" (p. 16). Rather than adopt methods, rhetorical critics first adopt a critical posture and then choose critical referents for their analyses. Having received formal training in rhetorical theories, the critic selects the critical referents that best help to understand a given text. As Baird and Thonssen (1947) claimed, a good critic "will wisely refuse to succumb to the rigidities of any formula" in performing analysis; instead, the good critic will "define clearly his [or her] critical referents but will exercise reasonable independence and flexibility in the application of his [or her] norms" (p. 136). As such, concepts help to perform criticism but should not predetermine the analysis performed.

Rhetorical Criticism Engages in Evaluation

In addition to using theoretical concepts to explain a text, the rhetorical critic evaluates discourse. R. L. Scott and Brock (1972) said that rhetorical criticism employs artistic/ aesthetic, effects/pragmatic, and ethical/truth standards to evaluate rhetorical acts. Using these criteria, the critic is most "likely to enter the arena of social influence" (R. L. Scott & Brock, p. 405), by understanding how messages become meaningful to participants in a rhetorical situation. Wichelns (1925) argued that the rhetorical critic must foreground pragmatic standards to understand the "persuasive purpose" that a rhetor enacts in "a concrete situation" (pp. 207, 208). Similarly, Rosenfield (1968) claimed that "the critic's objective is to explicate that [terminal] condition" of the rhetorical event "and the communication factors which contribute to retard the transaction" (p. 62; for an opposing view, see Whitson & Poulakos, 1993). Although the critic is concerned with a rhetorical act's structure, style, evidence, and the like, an account of how a rhetor used these elements for persuasion is only half of the critic's task.

Beyond pragmatic standards, Hochmuth (1955) urged the critic to employ ethical standards. As Hochmuth put it, the critic must "be ready to alert a people, to warn what devices of exploitation are being exercised, by which skillful manipulations of motives men [and women] are being directed to or dissuaded from courses of action" (p. 17). When the critic evaluates rhetoric with an eye for its effectiveness and its ethicality, rhetorical criticism—an act that "lies at the boundary of politics" (Wichelns, 1925, p. 215)—can cross into politics proper.

The Goal of Rhetorical Criticism is to Produce Change in the World

As a critic pronounces judgments about rhetorical acts, rhetorical criticism crosses into the realm of politics. Bitzer (1968) claimed that "rhetoric as a discipline is justified insofar as it provided principles, concepts, and procedures by which we effect valuable changes in reality" (p. 66). These changes occur at two levels: the conceptual and social. At the conceptual level, rhetorical criticism produces change by shaping ways audiences view later rhetorical acts. Because many rhetorical situations are recurrent, the analysis of the response to one situation can alter people's judgment of other responses to similar situations. More concretely, R. L. Scott and Brock (1972, p. 7) claimed that "criticism is a potent social force" because, although academic critics typically are more cautious than their counterparts, both "usually embrace vigorously the possibility of the persuasive impact of their acts" for the larger public. When a critic pronounces a rhetorical act effective, he or she attempts to influence others to see that rhetorical act as successful and to take action accordingly. Similarly, if a critic determines that a rhetorical actor has employed unethical means, the intent is to dissuade audience members from adopting the speaker's advocacy. This type of criticism, Wander (1983) insisted, "carries us to the point of recognizing good reasons and engaging in right action" and, thus, assists "the efforts of real people to create a better world" (p. 18).

Exemplars of Applied Rhetorical Criticism

Although most rhetorical studies are applied communication research in that they employ theory to construct or critique communicative acts about important issues, some rhetorical applications more directly bring rhetorical tools "to bear to make a difference in people's lives" (Frey, 2000, p. 179; see also Eadie, 2000). To illustrate various ways in which rhetorical studies may be applied, we offer examples from three categories of applied rhetorical studies. The first case, William Benoit's work on image restoration discourse, exemplifies applied research that is construction oriented, providing prescriptions for constructing discourse but directed at an academic audience. The second case, George Cheney's studies of workplace democracy, exemplifies work that uses critical approaches to expand academic and student audiences' understanding of discursive possibilities. The third case, the Health and Heritage Team's work on public understanding of the relationship between race and genetics, illustrates a construction-oriented approach for intervening in processes of institutional and expert formation of discourse.

Benoit's Studies of Image Restoration Strategies

Benoit uses rhetorical criticism to analyze the defenses offered by communicators accused of wrongdoing. In his research on image restoration, Benoit demonstrates how rhetorical criticism can aid understanding of communicative acts in concrete situations and, thereby, the formulation of specific recommendations for addressing similar situations in the future.

Benoit (1995a) studies image restoration discourse "because blame occurs throughout human society and...the felt need to cleanse one's reputation with discourse occurs throughout our lives" (p. 5). As a genre, image repair discourse is an extension of Ware and Linkugel's (1973) theory of apologia and Burke's (1970) theory of purification. Although Benoit (1995a) drew much of his theoretical inspiration from these sources, he held that these accounts were merely *descriptive*. To make image restoration scholarship more useful and applied, Benoit emphasized the *prescriptive* possibilities of rhetorical analysis. That is, if rhetorical critics indicate which image restoration strategies work and why, they can supply, through education or consultancy, useful information to rhetors attempting to account for a discrediting action by naming the options available, as well as by offering examples where these options succeeded or failed.

In theorizing image repair discourse, Benoit (1995a, 1997b) identified five major strategies and 14 specific types of image repair that rhetors use. These strategies have been used by numerous individuals in widely varying situations, including attempts by Kenneth Starr (Benoit & McHale, 1999) and Tonya Harding (Benoit & Hanczor, 1994) to prove their sense of fair play, and defenses offered by Clarence Thomas (Benoit & Nill, 1998) and Hugh Grant (Benoit, 1997a) of their sexual propriety. Moreover, although apologia is considered primarily as a defense employed by an individual, Benoit expanded the theory of image repair to organizational communication, including studies of defenses given by Tylenol (Benoit & Lindsey, 1987) and Dow Corning (Brinson & Benoit, 1996) regarding the safety of their products, and responses by Sears (Benoit, 1995b) and AT&T (Benoit & Brinson, 1994) to charges of corporate malfeasance.

Through these case studies, Benoit has drawn general conclusions about the efficacy of image repair strategies, using the standard methodological assumptions and practices of rhetorical scholars. In several studies, Benoit has supplemented close examination of the components of the discourse and the context with the testimony of persons who created or received the discourse, poll data, and comparisons of discourse and other behavior before and after exposure to a text. Using these methods, Benoit consistently has found that apologies, concessions, and corrective actions are the most effective and audience-appropriate strategies for image restoration (Benoit, 1995a; Benoit & Drew, 1997), whereas bolstering, minimization, provocation, and simple denial are the least effective and least likely to be seen as appropriate. Through analysis of specific cases and interpretation of patterns across these cases, Benoit has illustrated how genre theory can have a pragmatic impact. Specifically, Benoit's use of rhetorical criticism helps to understand communicative acts in particular situations and to offer recommendations for rhetors who face similar situations in the future.

Cheney's Analysis of Rhetorical Identification in Organizations

Whereas Benoit's analyses generate prescriptions to be used in constructive discourse secondhand, Cheney's research on workplace democracy illustrates critical assessment directed at expanding academic/student critique. Cheney realizes that organizations are corporate units that take on identities separate from those of their constituents. Because organizations engage in communication to advance their interests, Cheney (1991) asserted that "organizations are rhetorical and rhetoric is organizational" (p. 9). For instance, to recruit and socialize members, organizations attempt to create a shared identity among members so that they identify their interests with those of the organization.

Cheney (1983a, 1983b, 1995, 1999) has spent substantial time studying the Mondragón cooperative in Spain, a worker-based, interlocking network of businesses formulated on the principles of ownership and governance by the workers. Cheney applied Burke's (1969) concept of "rhetorical identification" to explore ways in which concepts, such as "social solidarity," shape identities within that organization. By understanding how organizations preserve organizational interests without violating members' other corporate identities, Stohl and Cheney (2001) found that apparent contradictions in identities actually can strengthen organizations when organizations select interests that are consubstantial with individual members' interests and deselect interests that drive members to withdraw (see also C. R. Scott, Corman, & Cheney, 1998). The most acute tension experienced by workers may be that between their identities as citizens and as employees. Stohl and Cheney found that as organizations increasingly use the language of a "democratic workplace," organizations experience additional tensions between their desire for efficient, productive workers and a workplace with a high degree of worker agency. By examining these moments of tension and understanding how identifications are fostered or discouraged, feasible strategies for adapting to future tensions can be articulated. For example, by outlining patterns of identificatory practices at Mondragón, Cheney (1999) noted instances where workplace democracy has been interpreted simultaneously as increased demands on workers, a disguise for increased control and surveillance, and as allowing employees to determine their work conditions. By examining the efficacy of each interpretation, Cheney indicated how Mondragón could serve as a model of the potential impacts of different discursive choices. Throughout Cheney's work on corporate identification, he illustrates ways in which Burke's theories open possibilities for rethinking worker and consumer roles to encourage a more democratic workplace. His emphasis on using such work to maintain critical thinking about rhetorical processes is illustrated by the way in which Cheney (1997) closed one of his essays on the Mondragón cooperative, with the last sentence reading, "It's time to reflect carefully on what our organizations are doing for us and to us" (p. 70).

The Health and Heritage Team's Efforts to Reshape Genetic Medicine

Benoit's and Cheney's use of rhetorical criticism has urged communication scholars to revise theories and critical perspectives to make them more helpful in concrete situations. That work, however, is shaped by the commitments that these scholars have made to communication as an independent field. The Health and Heritage Project, in contrast, is directed largely at change agents outside the communication field. Specifically, the Health and Heritage Team, of which we are members, has sought to use research to reform labeling practices and discriminatory assumptions in developing race-based medicine. To do so, this team has combined rhetorical analyses of discourse about race and genetics with focus group and survey studies revealing lay understandings of race and genetics, and the impact of messages about genetics.

Our team addressed some of the findings from this research program to academic audiences through communication journals (e.g., Condit, 2000; Condit, Bates et al., 2002; Condit, Condit, & Achter, 2001; Ramsey, Achter, & Condit, 2001). Nevertheless, because our target audience has been researchers developing, disseminating, and employing new technologies, we have reached these audiences by publishing in their journals—both journals in the broader field of science (e.g., Condit, 1999a; Condit, Parrott, & Harris, 2002) and in mainline medical and genetics journals read by physicians and geneticists (e.g., Condit, 2001, 2004c; Condit, Achter, Lauer, & Sefcovic, 2002; Parrott et al., 2005; Sankar et al., 2004)—and by presenting at their academic conferences (Condit, 2003b, 2004b). We also have presented work from this project in venues beyond academic outlets, including discussions with museum curators and presentations at events sponsored by the National Institutes of Health and at seminars designed to help the press report more effectively about genetics (e.g., Condit, 2002, 2003a, 2004a).

Throughout these investigations, we consistently employ two rhetorical concepts: rhetorical formations and audiences. The way in which we use these concepts, however, illustrates the stark difference between rhetorical criticism for humanist understanding and rhetorical criticism as intervention-oriented applied communication research. If engagement with change-agent audiences outside one's academic field is taken seriously, one's approach needs to be tailored to that audience's assumptions. We believe that the academic journals and conferences where new technical medical practices are being debated is the best site for intervention. Because this audience is accustomed to research based on experimental procedures, we triangulate rhetorical criticism with social-sci-entific methods to use a language and structure that is familiar to the medical-genetics audience but framed within a program shaped by the perspectives of rhetorical studies (the fullest explanation is in Condit, 1999b). Had we presented arguments only using the language and procedures of rhetorical studies, the audience likely would have regarded it as "merely" speculative work. Publication would have been unlikely and essays that were published would not be convincing to most target readers. The choice to use the language and structure of science, thus, is a rhetorical device to persuade a particular audience.

The commitment to audience adaptation may make rhetorical criticism as applied communication research more likely to persuade audiences that can affect real change. In this particular case, we believe that our interventions won a few battles but they were insufficient to influence the larger "war." At one conference, for example, a presentation by Condit (2003b) was well received, and the top prize among the posters was awarded to a poster that supported our social claims about genetic evidence. Participants explicitly linked the selection of that award-winning poster to the influence of Condit's talk. The development of race-based medicine, nonetheless, goes forward because of the economic returns it offers. From a rhetorical perspective, however, the goal of a good rhetor is to discover and employ the available means of persuasion, regardless of whether those means ultimately prove effective. Indeed, from a rhetorical perspective, a single instance of discourse, or even a program of discourse, is unlikely to change measurably the flow of social discourse, and certainly not in the short term. Performing good rhetoric is done as an act of conscience, with hope for good outcomes, not with a sense of scientific certainty about one's ability to produce predictable effects.

Theoretical Approaches to Rhetorically Informed Applied Communication Research

The research exemplars of Benoit, Cheney, and the Health and Heritage Team illustrate different combinations of critical and construction-oriented approaches, directed toward academic and broader audiences. These three examples represent only a small sampling of the theoretical tools available to rhetorical scholars for conducting applied work. There are over 2000 years of theoretical development in rhetoric, providing a smorgasbord of rhetorical concepts. It is not possible to summarize the full range of theories available; instead, we select four theoretical strains that have been prominent among applied work in rhetorical studies: metaphoric analysis, narrative criticism, fantasy theme analysis, and ideological critique. Although many researchers who employ these theories do not consider themselves to be rhetorical critics, these techniques have their origins in theories written by Aristotle (metaphor), Quintilian (*narratio*), Bormann (1982; fantasy theme analysis), and a host of ideological critics of discourse. The lack of distinct boundaries for rhetorical criticism does not seem to us to be particularly problematic, given the emphasis in applied studies on changing the world rather than maintaining academic traditions.

Metaphoric Analysis

Metaphoric analysis presumes that terms can be employed to refer to two unlike objects, events, or concepts to suggest a similarity. In a metaphor, the vehicle ("the 'figure' of the speech") is different from the tenor ("the principal subject") for a reason; it produces new associations that encourage the auditor to understand the tenor in a new way (Richards,

1936, p. 95). If Lakoff and Johnson (1980) are correct that metaphors are constitutive of reality, understanding the entailments of these metaphors can help us to understand how social reality is created. On a more practical level, once this process is understood, different metaphors can be employed to help people construct alternative realities.

Enumerating and categorizing the metaphors employed can provide insight into the operational code of a group or organization; these enduring metaphorical patterns, in turn, can be used to assess the group or organizational members, and to lay the groundwork for future action (Coffman, 1992; Gibbs & Franks, 2002; Gorden & Nevins, 1987; Yerby, 1989). Beyond describing which metaphors are commonly used, researchers identify alternative metaphors to offer opportunities for enacting positive changes (e.g., Gribas & Sims, 2006). Metaphoric analyses have found that when management personnel view an organization as a culture (Nicotera & Cushman, 1992), a protean beast (Shockley-Zalabak, 2002), or as being in chaos (Sellnow, Seeger, & Ulmer, 2002), employees' thoughts and actions often become literalized as enactments of management's preferred metaphors. Furthermore, as Koch and Deetz (1981) argued, identifying metaphors allows critics to perform hermeneutic readings of organizational documents to show how these metaphors become unquestioned guides to action. By grounding advocacy in reaction to the linguistic micropolitics of organizations, these metaphorical analyses identify political opportunities within constraining systems for practical action.

Despite many calls to investigate the efficacy of using metaphors to enact change, relatively few studies have done so. Most work showing how metaphoric analysis contributes to change is speculative (e.g., Burrell, Buzzanell, & McMillan, 1992; David & Graham, 1997; Rawlins, 1989). However, Czarniawska-Joerges and Joerges's (1988) study of Swedish organizations showed how changing metaphors can change everyday practices. They found that when an oil company replaced mechanical with agricultural metaphors, members began to think that management was attempting to provide the best conditions for their growth and development (e.g., as a gardener does with plants). Workplace satisfaction and increases in productivity, subsequently, were associated with this metaphor change. Czarniawska-Joerges and Joerges concluded that metaphors have an instrumental use in altering perceptions of reality, but that this power is limited by the need for a metaphor acceptable to both the speaker and auditor. Hence, although metaphoric analysis can identify opportunities for intervention, simply using a new metaphor is not a panacea. This form of applied communication research, thus, demonstrates how rhetoric may alter reality.

Narrative Criticism

A second strain of rhetorical criticism widely used in applied communication research is narrative criticism. There are many different uses of narrative approaches; here, we focus on two uses. Fisher (1985) held that texts are persuasive because they tell stories that foreground "good reasons" accepted by auditors or they fail to be persuasive because the good reasons foregrounded or the methods of foregrounding are improper. According to Fisher, the critic's task is to discern the good reasons offered in a story and to evaluate them for narrative probability and fidelity. Judging *narrative probability* involves determining whether "a story coheres or 'hangs together'"; judging *narrative fidelity* involves assessing the "'truth qualities' of the story" and considering the story's "soundness of reasoning and the value of its values" (Fisher, pp. 349–350). When a rhetorical act is evaluated in these ways, the critic can determine "whether or not one *should* adhere to the stories one is encouraged to endorse or to accept as the basis for decisions and actions" (Fisher, p. 348).

Fisher's (1985) call to examine the external legitimation of narratives has been taken seriously by applied communication researchers to examine how persuasive such messages are to their target audience (e.g., Kelly & Zak, 1999; Kenny, 2002; Stutts & Barker, 1999). Several researchers have examined the use of narratives to socialize and monitor organizational members, especially with regard to how narrative consistency manages norms and limits change (e.g., Adelman & Frey, 1997; Brown, 1990; Vanderford, Stein, Sheeler, & Skochelak, 2001). Other critics have focused on how individuals in power positions reconstruct narratives to ensure that they retain narrative consistency (e.g., Anderson & Geist-Martin, 2003; Conrad & Millay, 2001; Eggly, 2002). These analyses indicate that narrative consistency is a technique that identifies opportunities for advocacy by highlighting where a story is beginning to disintegrate and offering new ways to integrate that story.

Although narrative consistency is a powerful resource, a coherent story may not have suasory impact on a community if it lacks narrative fidelity. When a narrative "rings true" for its auditors, the narrative's value structure reinforces the values of a community (Smart, 1999). Unfortunately, this closure can authorize antisocial behavior. In studies of tobacco use (DeSantis, 2002), excessive drinking (Workman, 2001), and domestic violence (Stamp & Sabourin, 1995), researchers found that when a smoker, alcoholic, or abusive male told his story to other members of that population, the story was read as having fidelity and allowed both the storyteller and auditors to justify these behaviors. Although narrative analysis can identify barriers to change, the act of sharing narratives can restrict change by enhancing the fidelity of socially destructive narratives. Despite this danger, critics also have found the reinforcing properties of narrative fidelity useful for advocating prosocial change. For instance, Clair, Chapman, and Kunkel (1996) Taylor and Conrad (1992), and Wood (1992) found that as sexual harassment narratives were told, women perceived fidelity between these narratives and their experiences. As such, these stories became a teaching tool that allowed women to identify sexual harassment and served as a normative declaration against such behavior. In the conclusion to these studies, each of these narrative analyses became pedagogical acts and authorized collective storytelling to seek change.

Fantasy Theme Analysis

Bormann's (1972) fantasy theme analysis examines narratives using a different conceptual apparatus than that of narrative analysis. Whereas Fisher (1985) emphasized narrative consistency and fidelity, Bormann (1972) focused on stories that "chain out" among group members. Bormann (1972) called such stories *rhetorical fantasies*, and suggested that they "cast there-and-then events in narrative frames and provide a structured, understandable, and meaningful interpretation of what happened" (p. 134). These rhetorical fantasies, however, have little power until they are shared through a process called *fantasy theme chaining*, which is identified when consistent patterns are found of "similar dramatizing material such as wordplay, narratives, figures of speech and analogies [having] cropped up in a variety of messages in different contexts" (Bormann, Kroll, Watters, & McFarland, 1984, p. 289). Because these elements, in a successful fantasy theme analysis, become articulated as consistent and convergent, Bormann renamed his method "symbolic convergence theory." Both labels currently are in use, reflecting, to some extent, a divergence in methodological techniques.

Fantasy theme analyses represent a hybrid methodology, with early studies using methods of close textual analysis and later investigations employing a Q-sort methodology (for an overview, see Bormann et al., 1984). In the Q-sort approach, dramas are identified in texts that articulate possible stock fantasy types for a community using traditional close textual analysis. Members of the community then are asked to sort the components of these dramas according to their fidelity to their experience, and researchers determine which elements emerge as most salient for different forms of social consciousness. This method has been used successfully with many populations, including lawyers (McFarland, 1985), public relations personnel (Palenchar & Heath, 2002), hog farmers (Cragan & Shields, 1992), teachers (Putnam, van Hoeven, & Bullis, 1991), and students (Stone, 2002). In each case, understanding the narratives shared through fantasy themes allowed the researchers to make recommendations for improving communication.

Ideological Critique

As explained by Grossberg (1979), rhetorical criticism centered on ideological critique has four characteristics: it (1) examines concrete phenomena in addition to abstract ideas, (2) examines these phenomena in relation to other phenomena, (3) holds that these relations are those of contradiction that produce identities, and (4) holds that these identities are related to the experience of human reality through shared discourse. Many ideological critics are concerned that, in the analysis of rhetoric, relationships that exist outside of the texts immediately under examination are forgotten or ignored too often. Wander (1983) argued that criticism bound only to a text without awareness of historical, social, and institutional forces impinging on that text is ineffective as advocacy because it fails to account for psychological and material factors that are not wholly captured by speech. Rather than passing over these forces, ideological critics hold that the analysis of these social structures is essential for politically powerful rhetorical criticism (e.g., Jandt, 1980).

Because ideological criticism is concerned with the intersection of assumptions, language, and ideology, it often is performed under the auspices of Marxian, Foucaultian, feminist (see Buzzanell, Meisenbach, Remke, Sterk, & Turner, this volume), race (see Nicotera, Clinkscales, Dorsey, & Niles, this volume), or ethnically based theories. Although these theories may clash in their different manifestations, all are useful because they allow different approaches to the same problematic. As Mumby (1993, p. 21) put it, because these theories are concerned with how some groups "struggle to fix and institutionalize the dominance of certain groups and meaning structures over others," they help critics to reflect on "the complex system of discursive and nondiscursive practices" that make up human relations. Moreover, ideological criticism itself is a political act. Rushing and Frentz (1991, p. 385) explained that practicing ideological criticism "is to perform a morally significant act of fighting oppression by unmasking the rhetorical strategies that maintain it" because exposure of contradictions of a dominant order makes it possible to act against oppression. This desire for rhetorical criticism to oppose dominant ideologies is widely shared, but it also might be desirable for ideological criticism to transcend oppositional stances and account for ways that ideologies emerge through multiple relations among people, as well as the particular modes by which ideologies are expressed (Condit, 1994; Fiske, 1986). By presenting unresolved contradictions of an ideology, a critic encourages auditors to choose whether to accept the ideology by relying on the structural coherencies that resolve most contradictions or to struggle against the ideology by focusing on the places where the structure fails to do so.

Ideological critics who emphasize dominant ideology often dispute the possibility of social change. Some of these critics indicate that social change is nearly impossible, as the interactions among, for instance, gender relations and capitalism (Clair & Thompson, 1996), science and education (Schiebel, 1996), and technology and expertise (Coogan,

2002) allow normative assumptions to sediment in such a way that oppression becomes multifaceted and enduring. Examinations of ideologies of health (Easland, 1994), law (Goodwin, 1996), art (David, 1999), education (Artz, 1998), work (Ralston & Kirkwood, 1995), and research (Williams & Coupland, 1998) indicate that although ideological norms come into conflict with other ideological forces (e.g., liberalism, social justice, or equality), the opportunities opened when the structure becomes momentarily destabilized are foreclosed when consistency is presumed and made operant.

Critics focused on places where dominant ideologies come into conflict explicitly argue that, when two ideologies collide, whichever ideology is better able to mobilize discursive and nondiscursive resources will override the influence of the other. Brenton (1993) and Sherblom, Keränen, and Withers (2002), for instance, each found that when two powerful ideological forces conflicted, resolution occurred when one force displaced the other and made it no longer relevant to the issue under dispute. Applied communication researchers often outline conflicts between capitalist values and other social values, such as democracy (Harter & Krone, 2001), sex roles (Buzzanell & Glodzwig, 1991; Kirby & Krone, 2002), health and safety (Gillespie, 2001; Zoller, 2003), and tradition (Boyd, 2000; Jones & Bodtker, 1998).

The resolutions offered by many applied communication researchers adopting ideological approaches often are reformist. Nevertheless, the obligation of applied communication researchers to work toward practical solutions makes accommodation an attractive strategy. The fundamental question for ideological critique in applied communication research is not "How can the structure be overthrown?" but, as Pearce (1998) asked, "What research might we do if we focused on communication per se as well as marginalization, stigmatization, and being underresourced?" (p. 278; see also Frey & SunWolf, this volume). The first type of research involves analysis of communication that deconstructs ideological forces that "promote and maintain inequality and injustice" (Frey, Pearce, Pollock, Artz, & Murphy, 1996, p. 123). The second type of applied ideological criticism offers mediations or moderations that ameliorate the effects of oppressive ideologies, in which critics seek to "identify the grammars that oppress or underwrite relationships of domination and bring their communication resources to bear to reconstruct those grammars in more socially just ways" (Frey, 1998, p. 157). Practical projects, such as using teledemocratic computer networks as a compromise between values of full democracy and norms of efficiency (O'Sullivan, 1995), and facilitating debates within prisons to negotiate the need for control and the desire to hear the voice of prisoners (Hartnett, 1998), are not perfect. Nevertheless, given that these researchers found a clash of ideologies and then instigated a small change that allowed for a more socially just resolution, they used ideological criticism to authorize progressive change.

Making Rhetorical Studies More Applied

We have identified key assumptions of applied rhetorical studies and categorized these studies based on their audience, whether the approach is critical or construction oriented, and the generality or particularity of the objects of study. We illustrated three of these categories with descriptions of extended research programs, and described four theoretical approaches to conducting applied rhetorical research. This overview makes it evident that existing applications of rhetorical methods are more commonly found, or at least more visible, at the critical/academic/general end of the spectrum than at the end of the spectrum where particular constructed messages are targeted to change agents. In light of that distribution, it seems appropriate to consider suggestions for making rhetorical studies more applied.

To enable more rhetorical work, we suggest that rhetorical critics be prepared to speak to audiences other than rhetorical critics. In the standard mode of rhetorical criticism, critics speak primarily to other scholars, most of whom are familiar with a complex grid of shared vocabularies and agreed-on knowledge bases. Nominally, our collective goal is to make a better world, but we enact this goal in two ways. First, we may increase people's knowledge of rhetorical processes so that they can attend to messages in more informed and critical ways. Our primary conduit for this enactment is through teaching and scholarship, because that is the way knowledge is shared within the academic community. In the second mode, however, we may seek to address an immediate problem. In this mode, we want people to understand rhetorical processes immediately, so that they act to shape the outcomes of the problem. In such cases, rhetorical critics address an audience that is not comprised primarily of other scholars or students. Scholars, therefore, cannot presume that their audience will share a rhetorical vocabulary or assumptions about communication. This difference in premises means that scholars should learn the assumptions and vocabulary of the audience to be addressed and insert the audience's vocabulary in carefully selected and well-explained places. In our work on medical genetics, for example, to speak to an audience of medical geneticists, we had to learn their scientific terms, understand their applications, and determine assumptions within that community. Had we approached this community with the presumption that only rhetorical vocabularies are valuable, it is unlikely that this work would be read by the audience we were addressing.

In addition to learning the assumptions and vocabularies of target audiences, rhetorical critics should be prepared to adopt their audiences' rhetorical forms. This requirement means that critics need to focus their efforts on producing research products designed for a specific suasory end, not on retaining fidelity to a set of particular means for conducting rhetorical criticism. For example, in an article published in the journal *Clinical Genetics*, Condit, Parrott, Bates, Bevan, and Achter (2004) enacted this requirement. Based on our understanding of the history of racist rhetoric, we believed that messages that linked race and genetics increased levels of racism in the general population. To persuade scientists, we adopted their rhetorical forms, for if we had presented the argument through traditional rhetorical analysis, scientists likely would have seen the argument as theoretical speculation at best and polemical assertion at worst. Therefore, we designed a "message impact study" that used rhetorical concepts—namely, that messages targeted to inform people about a particular idea have suasory effects that legitimate other social structures—a principle recognized by everyone from conservative theorist Weaver (1970) to leftist theorist Foucault (2001). However, these concepts were delivered in the rhetorical form of an experiment, with the random assignment to conditions and manipulation of variables under controlled conditions demanded in medical studies (see Query et al., this volume). This approach was necessary if we were to be accepted as a legitimate voice within that community. In addition, this acquired legitimacy allowed us to publish the findings in a medical genetics journal. As such, our methodological choices made it more likely that our target audience read the study, as few physicians or geneticists read communication journals.

A final modification that rhetorical critics may wish to make is to be ready to speak to "lay" audiences. Most rhetorical acts are addressed to audiences other than rhetorical critics; for instance, political speeches are addressed to voters and health messages are directed to physicians and consumers. Rhetorical critics, however, too often do not take these audiences into account as helpful interpreters of messages; instead, they perform their work without reference to an audience of actual nonacademic people. We do not believe that professional rhetoricians are the only ones capable of interpreting and judging messages, even highly technical messages. Therefore, instead of presuming that laypeople were not able to process messages about genomics and race, we set out to explore how they processed those messages (e.g., Bates & Harris, 2004; Bates, Lynch, Bevan, & Condit, 2005; Bevan et al., 2003; Condit, Templeton, Bates, Bevan, & Harris 2003). To do this, we conducted focus groups in which people were given messages about race and asked to process those messages. Again, out of sensitivity to our audience of medical geneticists, we used quantitative procedures to analyze and discuss the content of those focus group discussions. These choices allowed us to engage with actual readers of messages, who opened up unexpected areas of discussion and contributed a broader interpretative frame that more closely corresponded to the views of public audiences. Hence, if rhetorical criticism is to have greater public utility, rhetorical critics need to consult more often with that public to see how messages actually are perceived and used.

As we noted in the first section of this chapter, rhetorical criticism as a practice is highly visible in communication journals. In contrast, construction-oriented rhetorical efforts are far less visible. Although some rhetorical scholars are engaging in construction-oriented efforts, we encourage others interested in conducting applied work to report more frequently in journals regarding their rhetorical construction-oriented products because such reports build a background of experience and might increase the legitimacy of such efforts. There are several barriers, however, to the development of such a scholarly genre. To publish that type of an article, the scholars involved must expose their political commitments (and even their rhetorical skill levels) to the scrutiny of colleagues. In addition, in the absence of generic specifications, such articles seem perilously close to academic bragging. We do not today have a well-thought-out genre for such articles. Although such articles can focus on the topoi of "what works to make applied rhetorical construction effective," it is not immediately clear what topoi will be most immediately helpful to others seeking to engage in applied rhetorical efforts. There also is the risk that such efforts might kill the goose from which they draw their theoretical golden eggs. Given the passion for social justice shared by some applied communication scholars (see Frey & Sun-Wolf, this volume), legitimating applied construction-oriented efforts rather than strictly theoretical and critical efforts for rhetorical scholars might limit the flow of theory construction and deep critical analysis on which good applied communication scholarship depends. There undoubtedly are other constraints that must be addressed as well. At this point, our hope is to begin a discussion about the desirability and means for increasing applied rhetorical construction-oriented work.

Benefits of Applied Research for Rhetorical Studies

Using rhetorical criticism in applied communication research can make important contributions to identifying opportunities for social change and intervening in practical situations. Rhetorical criticism, thus, has significant potential for enhancing applied communication research. Although the benefits of using rhetorical criticism as applied communication research named by Pettegrew (1988) emphasized the persuasive stylistic frames employed in rhetorical criticism, its theoretical, philosophical, and analytic concepts also can benefit applied communication research. Even as rhetorical criticism provides applied communication research with additional possibilities for analysis, the emphasis in the latter on providing solutions to particular situations supplies rhetorical critics with three helpful impulses: a multimethodological orientation, a concretization of research values, and a reemphasis on Isocratean purposes of rhetoric.

First, applied communication research has highlighted the value of multimethodological approaches to communication analysis. The use of rhetorical criticism in applied communication research has made clear the utility of even further expansion. Compiling diverse textual fragments through experiments, surveys, individual and group interviews, bibliometrics, and participant observation (see Ellingson, this volume), and combining these fragments with monumental texts in close textual analysis, allows for a greater selection of the contextual reality in which rhetorical acts occur. The use of several methods of data collection under the aegis of a critical referent derived from the rhetorical tradition can greatly expand and enrich the analysis. In addition, techniques common in applied communication research that authorize audience studies and participants' contributions to research can enhance the critical qualities of rhetorical criticism and check the monologic impulse that is so common in rhetorical criticism. Limiting the monologic impulse is necessary to preserve the emphasis in rhetoric on the audience and the notion that communication always takes place within a community. Moreover, including alternative voices increases the probability that recommendations critics offer for social change will be acceptable possibilities to readers.

Second, in addition to making multimethodological approaches more relevant to criticism, the values of practical action foregrounded in applied communication research enrich the long-standing interest of rhetorical criticism in practical wisdom. The need for applied communication research to make a difference in people's life leads rhetorical criticism to be more explicit about its aims and criteria. If rhetorical criticism seeks to judge the value of a text, applied communication research demands that the standards employed in rhetorical criticism be defined clearly and operationalized effectively. This demand increases the likelihood that research findings will be relevant to future situations, because parallel factors in the new situation can be clearly identified and divergent factors can be taken into account. Applied communication research also has helped to concretize the policy actions encouraged by rhetorical criticism. Thus, applied communication research can help rhetorical critics to offer particular solutions to concrete problems.

Finally, the focus in applied communication research on the study of communication for intervention (see Frey & SunWolf, this volume), as well as insight, may help to encourage the Isocratean impulse in rhetoric. Rhetoricians have made much of Isocrates's (1929b) claim that "there is no institution devised by man [or woman] which the power of speech has not helped us to establish" (p. 327). Rhetorical critics have justified their studies by positing rhetoric as essential to the formation of human communities. Isocrates, however, urged more than reflection; the study of rhetoric was supposed to *improve* communities. Isocrates (1929a) attacked thinkers who "pretend to have knowledge of the future but are incapable either of saying anything pertinent or of giving any counsel regarding the present" (p. 167). To more fully implement Isocrates's vision, rhetorical critics may want to enact applied communication research more regularly with a particular emphasis on giving pertinent counsel about present situations and future actions. This call to make rhetorical criticism most useful to communities may be the most important contribution that applied communication research has made to the rhetorical tradition.

Conclusion

Human beings innately are rhetorical beings. It is not surprising, therefore, that studies of the rhetorical facets of our being are thousands of years old. The accumulated wisdom from such studies has been applied to shape human societies, institutions, and relationships uncountable times. In this sense, applied rhetorical studies are pervasive. Within the confines of scholarly publication, however, some categories of applied rhetorical studies are more visible than others. Specifically, rhetorical criticism has become the dominant practice, with critical studies having a limited scope of operation, as they are shared primarily with other rhetoricians and students rather than with the public at large or with particular external groups. That stance is unfortunate, for there are a plethora of well-developed theories and methods available for conducting applied rhetorical work, and it may well be time for rhetorical scholars to consider expanding the audiences for criticism and reporting construction-oriented rhetorical efforts. Rhetorical studies were founded as an applied art, and the future health of the field may well be tied to the diversity and richness of its applications.

References

Adelman, M. B., & Frey, L. R. (1997). *The fragile community: Living together with AIDS*. Mahwah, NJ: Erlbaum.

Anderson, J. O., & Geist-Martin, P. (2003). Narratives and healing: Exploring one family's stories of cancer survivorship. *Health Communication, 15*, 133–143.

Aristotle. (1991). *On rhetoric: A theory of civic discourse* (G. A. Kennedy, Trans.). New York: Oxford University Press.

Artz, L. (1998). African-Americans and higher education: An exigence in need of applied communication. *Journal of Applied Communication Research, 26*, 210–231.

Baird, A. C., & Thonssen, L. (1947). Methodology in the criticism of public address. *Quarterly Journal of Speech, 33*, 134–138.

Baskerville, B. (1977). Must we all be "rhetorical critics"? *Quarterly Journal of Speech, 63*, 107–116.

Bates, B. R., & Harris, T. M. (2004). The Tuskegee study of untreated syphilis and public perceptions of biomedical research: A focus group study. *Journal of the National Medical Association, 96*, 1051–1064.

Bates, B. R., Lynch, J. A., Bevan, J. L., & Condit, C. M. (2005). Warranted concerns, warranted outlooks: A focus group study of public understandings of genetics research. *Social Science & Medicine, 60*, 331–344.

Benoit, W. L. (1995a). *Accounts, excuses, and apologies: A theory of image restoration strategies*. Albany: State University of New York Press.

Benoit, W. L. (1995b). Sears' repair of its auto service image: Image restoration discourse in the corporate sector. *Communication Studies, 46*, 89–105.

Benoit, W. L. (1997a). Hugh Grant's image restoration discourse: An actor apologizes. *Communication Quarterly, 45*, 251–267.

Benoit, W. L. (1997b). Image repair discourse and crisis communication. *Public Relations Review, 23*, 177–186.

Benoit, W. L., & Brinson, S. L. (1994). AT&T: "Apologies are not enough." *Communication Quarterly, 42*, 75–88.

Benoit, W. L., & Drew, S. (1997). Appropriateness and effectiveness of image repair strategies. *Communication Reports, 10*, 153–163.

Benoit, W. L., & Hanczor, R. S. (1994). The Tonya Harding controversy: An analysis of image restoration strategies. *Communication Quarterly, 42*, 416–433.

Benoit, W. L., & Lindsey, J. J. (1987). Argument strategies: Antidote to Tylenol's poisoned image. *Journal of the American Forensic Association, 23*, 136–146.

Benoit, W. L., & McHale, J. P. (1999). Kenneth Starr's image repair discourse viewed in *20/20*. *Communication Quarterly, 47*, 265–280.

Benoit, W. L., & Nill, D. M. (1998). A critical analysis of Judge Clarence Thomas's statement before the Senate Judiciary Committee. *Communication Studies, 49*, 179–195.

Bevan, J. L., Lynch, J. A., Dubriwny, T. N., Harris, T. M., Achter, P. J., Reeder, A. L., et al (2003). Informed lay preferences for delivery of racially varied pharmacogenomics. *Genetics in Medicine, 5*, 393–399.

Bitzer, L. F. (1969). The rhetorical situation. *Philosophy & Rhetoric, 1*, 1–14.

Black, E. (1965). *Rhetorical criticism: A study in method*. New York: Macmillan.

Bormann, E. G. (1972). Fantasy and rhetorical vision: The rhetorical criticism of social reality. *Quarterly Journal of Speech, 58,* 396–407.

Bormann, E. G. (1982). A fantasy theme analysis of the television coverage of the hostage release and the Reagan inaugural. *Quarterly Journal of Speech, 68,* 133–145.

Bormann, E. G., Kroll, B. W., Watters, K., & McFarland, D. (1984). Rhetorical visions of committed voters: Fantasy theme analysis of a large sample survey. *Critical Studies in Mass Communication, 1,* 287–310.

Boyd, J. (2000). Selling home: Corporate stadium names and the destruction of commemoration. *Journal of Applied Communication Research, 28,* 330–346.

Brenton, A. L. (1993). Demystifying the magic of language: A critical linguistic case analysis of legitimation of authority. *Journal of Applied Communication Research, 21,* 227–244.

Brinson, S. L., & Benoit, W. L. (1996). Attempting to restore a public image: Dow Corning and the breast implant crisis. *Communication Quarterly, 44,* 29–41.

Brown, M. H. (1990). "Reading" an organization's culture: An examination of stories in nursing homes. *Journal of Applied Communication Research, 18,* 64–75.

Burke, K. (1969). *A rhetoric of motives.* Berkeley: University of California Press.

Burke, K. (1970). *The rhetoric of religion: Studies in logology.* Berkeley: University of California Press.

Burrell, N. A., Buzzanell, P. M., & McMillan, J. J. (1992). Feminine tensions in conflict situations as revealed by metaphoric analysis. *Management Communication Quarterly, 6,* 115–149.

Buzzanell, P. M., & Goldzwig, S. R. (1991). Linear and nonlinear career models: Metaphors, paradigms, and ideologies. *Management Communication Quarterly, 4,* 466–505.

Campbell, K. K. (1972). *Critiques of contemporary rhetoric.* Belmont, CA: Wadsworth.

Campbell, K. K., & Jamieson, K. H. (1976). *Form and genre: Shaping rhetorical action.* Falls Church, VA: Speech Communication Association.

Cheney, G. (1983a). On the various and changing meanings of organizational membership: A field study of organizational identification. *Communication Monographs, 50,* 342–362.

Cheney, G. (1983b). The rhetoric of identification and the study of organizational communication. *Quarterly Journal of Speech, 69,* 143–158.

Cheney, G. (1991). *Rhetoric in an organizational society: Managing multiple identities.* Columbia: University of South Carolina Press.

Cheney, G. (1995). Democracy in the workplace: Theory and practice from the perspective of communication. *Journal of Applied Communication Research, 23,* 167–200.

Cheney, G. (1997). The many meanings of "solidarity": The negotiation of values in the Mondragón worker-cooperative complex under pressure. In B. D. Sypher (Ed.), *Case studies in organizational communication 2: Perspectives on contemporary work life* (pp. 68–83). New York: Guilford Press.

Cheney, G. (1999). *Values at work: Employee participation meets market pressure at Mondragón.* Ithaca, NY: Cornell University Press.

Cissna, K. N. (1995). Appendix A: Recommendations formally adopted by the Tampa Conference on Applied Communication. In K. N. Cissna (Ed.), *Applied communication in the 21st century* (pp. 195–199). Mahwah, NJ: Erlbaum.

Clair, R. P., Chapman, P. A., & Kunkel, A. W. (1996). Narrative approaches to raising consciousness about sexual harassment: From research to pedagogy and back again. *Journal of Applied Communication Research, 24,* 241–259.

Clair, R. P., & Thompson, K. (1996). Pay discrimination as a discursive and material practice: A case concerning extended housework. *Journal of Applied Communication Research, 24,* 1–20.

Coffman, S. L. (1992). Staff problem with geriatric care in two types of health care organizations. *Journal of Applied Communication Research, 20,* 292–307.

Condit, C. M. (1994). Hegemony in a mass-mediated society: Concordance about reproductive technologies. *Critical Studies in Mass Communication, 11,* 205–230.

Condit, C. M. (1999a). How the public understands genetics: Non-deterministic and non-discriminatory interpretations of the "blueprint" metaphor. *Public Understanding of Science, 8,* 169–180.

Condit, C. M. (1999b). *Meanings of the gene: Public debates about human heredity*. Madison: University of Wisconsin Press.

Condit, C. M. (2000). Women's reproductive choices and the genetic model of medicine. In M. M. Lay, L. J. Gurak, C. Gravon, & C. Myntti (Eds.), *Body talk: Rhetoric, technology, reproduction* (pp. 125–141). Madison: University of Wisconsin Press.

Condit, C. M. (2001). What is "public opinion" about genetics? *Nature Reviews: Genetics, 2,* 811–815.

Condit, C. M. (2002, October). *Communicating about race and genetics with the public* [Press briefing]. Boston: Whitehead Institute.

Condit, C. M. (2003a, February). *Lay understandings of race and genetics*. Speech presented to the Human Variation Consortium, National Institutes of Health, Bethesda, MD.

Condit, C. M. (2003b, November). *Impact of messages about race and genetics on racism*. Speech presented to the meeting on International Single Nucleotide Polymorphism and Complex Genome Analysis, Washington. DC.

Condit, C. M. (2004a, March). *Reporting of human genetic variation research to the public*. Speech presented at the National Human Genome Research Institute's "Roundtable on Race," Bethesda, MD.

Condit, C. M. (2004b, October). *How lay people respond to messages about race, health, and genetics*. Speech presented to the meeting of the American Society for Human Genetics, Toronto, Canada.

Condit, C. M. (2004c). Science reporting to the public: Does the message get twisted? *Canadian Medical Association Journal, 170,* 1415–1416.

Condit, C. M., Achter, P. J., Lauer, I., & Sefcovic, E. (2002). The changing meanings of "mutation": A contextualized study of public discourse. *Human Mutation, 19,* 69–75.

Condit, C. M., Bates, B. R., Galloway, R., Brown Givens, S. B., Haynie, C. K., Jordan, J. W., et al. (2002). Recipes or blueprints for our genes? How contexts selectively activate the multiple meanings of metaphors. *Quarterly Journal of Speech, 88,* 303–325.

Condit, C. M., Condit, D. M., & Achter, P. J. (2001). Human equality, affirmative action, and genetic models of human variation. *Rhetoric & Public Affairs, 4,* 85–108.

Condit, C. M., Parrott, R. L., Bates, B. R., Bevan, J. L., & Achter, P. J. (2004). Exploration of the impact of messages about genes and race on lay attitudes. *Clinical Genetics, 66,* 402–408.

Condit, C. M., Parrott, R., & Harris, T. M. (2002). Lay understandings of the relationship between race and genetics: Development of a collectivized knowledge through shared discourse. *Public Understanding of Science, 11,* 373–387.

Condit, C., Templeton, A., Bates, B. R., Bevan, J. L., & Harris, T. M. (2003). An exploration of attitudinal barriers to delivery of race-targeted pharmacogenomics among informed lay persons. *Genetics in Medicine, 5,* 385–392.

Conrad, C., & Millay, B. (2001). Confronting free market romanticism: Health care reform in the least likely place. *Journal of Applied Communication Research, 29,* 153–170.

Coogan, D. (2002). Public rhetoric and public safety at the Chicago Transit Authority: Three approaches to accident analysis. *Journal of Business and Technical Communication, 16,* 277–305.

Cragan, J. F., & Shields, D. C. (1992). The use of symbolic convergence theory in corporate strategic planning: A case study. *Journal of Applied Communication Research, 20,* 199–218.

Czarniawska-Joerges, B., & Joerges, B. (1988). How to control things with words: Organizational talk and control. *Management Communication Quarterly, 2,* 170–193.

Darsey, J. (1997). *The prophetic tradition and radical rhetoric in America*. New York: New York University Press.

David, C. (1999). Elitism in the stories of US art museums: The power of a master narrative. *Journal of Business and Technical Communication, 13,* 318–335.

David, C., & Graham, M. B. (1997). Conflicting values: Team management portrayed in epic metaphors. *Journal of Business and Technical Communication, 11,* 24–48.

DeLuca, K. M., & Demo, A. T. (2000). Imaging nature: Watkins, Yosemite, and the birth of environmentalism. *Critical Studies in Media Communication, 17,* 241–260.

DeSantis, A. D. (2002). Smoke screen: An ethnographic study of a cigar shop's collective rationalization. *Health Communication, 14,* 167–198.

Dow, B. J. (1996). *Prime-time feminism: Television, media culture, and the women's movement since 1970.* Philadelphia: University of Pennsylvania Press.

Eadie, W. (2000). Changing boundaries, changing expectations, changing results. *Journal of Applied Communication Research, 28,* 174–177.

Easland, L. S. (1994). Habermas, emancipation, and relationship change: An exploration of recovery processes as a model for social transformation. *Journal of Applied Communication Research, 22,* 162–176.

Eggly, S. (2002). Physician–patient co-construction of illness narratives in the medical interview. *Health Communication, 14,* 339–360.

Esrock, S. L., Hart, J. L., & Leichty, G. (2007). Smoking out the opposition: The rhetoric of reaction and the Kentucky cigarette excise tax campaign. In L. R. Frey & K. M. Carragee (Eds.), *Communication activism: Vol. 1. Communication for social change* (pp. 385–410). Cresskill, NJ: Hampton Press.

Fisher, W. R. (1985). The narrative paradigm: An elaboration. *Communication Monographs, 52,* 347–367.

Fiske, J. (1986). Television: Polysemy and popularity. *Critical Studies in Mass Communication, 3,* 391–408.

Foucault, M. (2001). *Fearless speech* (J. Pearson, Ed.). Los Angeles: Semiotext(e).

Frey, L. R. (1998). Communication and social justice research: Truth, justice, and the applied communication way. *Journal of Applied Communication Research, 26,* 155–164.

Frey, L. R. (2000). To be applied or not to be applied, that isn't the question; but wherefore art thou, applied communication research? Reclaiming applied communication research and redefining the role of the researcher. *Journal of Applied Communication Research, 28,* 178–182.

Frey, L. R., Pearce, W. B., Pollock, M. A., Artz, L., & Murphy, B. A. O. (1996). Looking for justice in all the wrong places: On a communication approach to social justice. *Communication Studies, 47,* 110–127.

Gribas, J., & Sims, J. (2006). Metaphoric illumination and symbolic ambiguity: Applying the team metaphor for perceptual reorientation. In L. R. Frey (Ed.), *Facilitating group communication in context: Innovations and applications with natural groups: Vol. 2: Facilitating group task and team communication* (pp. 177–201). Cresskill, NJ: Hampton Press.

Gibbs, R. W., & Franks, H. (2002). Embodied metaphor in women's narratives about their experiences with cancer. *Health Communication, 14,* 139–165.

Gillespie, S. R. (2001). The politics of breathing: Asthmatic Medicaid patients under managed care. *Journal of Applied Communication Research, 29,* 97–116.

Goodwin, J. T. (1996). "Cover your tracks": A case study of genre, rhetoric, and ideology in two psycholegal reports. *Journal of Business and Technical Communication, 10,* 167–186.

Gorden, I. G., & Nevins, R. J. (1987). The language and rhetoric of quality: Made in the USA. *Journal of Applied Communication Research, 15,* 19–34.

Grossberg, L. (1979). Marxist dialectics and rhetorical criticism. *Quarterly Journal of Speech, 65,* 235–249.

Hart, R. P. (1993). Why communication? Why education? Toward a politics of teaching. *Communication Education, 42,* 97–105.

Harter, L. M., & Krone, K. J. (2001). The boundary-spanning role of a cooperative support organization: Managing the paradox of stability and change in non-traditional organizations. *Journal of Applied Communication Research, 29,* 248–277.

Hartnett, S. (1998). Lincoln and Douglas meet the abolitionist David Walker as prisoners debate slavery: Empowering education, applied communication, and social justice. *Journal of Applied Communication Research, 26,* 232–253.

Hartnett, S. J. (2007). "You are fit for something better": Communicating hope in antiwar activism. In L. R. Frey & K. M. Carragee (Eds.), *Communication activism: Vol. 1. Communication for social change* (pp. 195–246). Cresskill, NJ: Hampton Press.

Hochmuth, M. (1955). The criticism of rhetoric. In M. Hochmuth (Ed.), *A history and criticism of American public address* (Vol. 3., pp. 1–23). New York: Longmans, Green.

Isocrates. (1929a). Against the sophists. In G. Norlin (Trans.), *Isocrates II* (pp. 160–177). Cambridge MA: Harvard University Press.

Isocrates. (1929b). Antidosis. In G. Norlin (Trans.), *Isocrates II* (pp. 181–365). Cambridge, MA: Harvard University Press.

Jamieson, K. H. (2000). *Everything you think you know about politics…and why you're wrong*. New York: Basic Books

Jandt, F. E. (1980). Gay liberation as ideological conflict. *Journal of Applied Communication Research, 8*, 128–138.

Jones, T. S., & Bodtker, A. (1998). A dialectical analysis of a social justice process: International collaboration in South Africa. *Journal of Applied Communication Research, 26*, 357–373.

Kelly, C., & Zak, M. (1999). Narrativity and professional communication: Folktales and community meaning. *Journal of Business and Technical Communication, 13*, 297–317.

Kenny, R. W. (2002). The death of loving: Maternal identity as moral constraint in a narrative testimonial advocating physician assisted suicide. *Health Communication, 14*, 243–270.

Kirby, E. L., & Krone, K. J. (2002), "The policy exists but you can't really use it": Communication and the structuration of work–family politics. *Journal of Applied Communication Research, 30*, 50–77.

Koch, S., & Deetz, S. (1981). Metaphor analysis of social reality in organizations. *Journal of Applied Communication Research, 9*, 1–15.

Lakoff, G., & Johnson, M. (1980). *Metaphors we live by*. Chicago: University of Chicago Press.

Lucas, S. E. (1981). The schism in rhetorical scholarship. *Quarterly Journal of Speech, 67*, 1–20.

McFarland, D. D. (1985). Self-images of law professors: Rethinking the schism in legal education. *Journal of Legal Education, 35*, 232–260.

McGee, M. C. (1990). Text, context, and the fragmentation of contemporary culture. *Western Journal of Communication, 54*, 274–289.

Mumby, D. K. (1993). Critical organizational communication studies: The next 10 years. *Communication Monographs, 60*, 18–25.

Nicotera, A. M., & Cushman, D. P. (1992). Organizational ethics: A within-organization view. *Journal of Applied Communication Research, 20*, 437–462.

O'Sullivan, P. B. (1995). Computer networks and political participation: Santa Monica's teledemocracy project. *Journal of Applied Communication Research, 23*, 93–107.

Palenchar, M. J., & Heath, R. L. (2002). Another part of the risk communication model: Analysis of communication processes and message content. *Journal of Public Relations Research, 14*, 127–158.

Parrott, R. L., Silk, K. J., Dillow, M. R., Krieger, M. A., Harris, T. M., & Condit, C. M. (2005). Development and validation of tools to assess genetic discrimination and genetically based racism. *Journal of the National Medical Association, 97*, 980–991.

Pearce, W. B. (1998). On putting social justice in the discipline of communication and putting enriched concepts of communication in social justice research and practice. *Journal of Applied Communication Research, 26*, 172–178.

Pettegrew, L. S. (1988). The importance of context in applied communication research. *Southern Communication Journal, 53*, 331–338.

Putnam, L. L., Van Hoeven, S. A., & Bullis, C. A. (1991). The role of rituals and fantasy themes in teachers' bargaining. *Western Journal of Speech Communication, 55*, 85–103.

Ralston, S. M., & Kirkwood, W. G. (1995). Overcoming managerial bias in employment interviewing. *Journal of Applied Communication Research, 23*, 75–92.

Ramsey, E. M., Achter, P. J., & Condit, C. M. (2001). Genetics, race, and crime: An audience study exploring *The Bell Curve* and book reviews. *Critical Studies in Media Communication, 18*, 1–22.

Rawlins, W. K. (1989). Metaphorical views of interaction in families of origin and future families. *Journal of Applied Communication Research, 17*, 52–70.

Richards, I. A. (1936). *The philosophy of rhetoric*. New York: Oxford University Press.

Rosenfield, L. W. (1968). The anatomy of critical discourse. *Speech Monographs, 35,* 50–69.

Rushing, J. H., & Frentz, T. S. (1991). Integrating ideology and archetype in rhetorical criticism. *Quarterly Journal of Speech, 77,* 385–406.

Sankar, P., Cho, M. K., Condit, C. M., Hunt, L. M., Koenig, B., Marshall, P., et al. (2004). Genetic research and health disparities. *Journal of the American Medical Association, 291,* 2985–2989.

Scott, C. R., Corman, S. R., & Cheney, G. (1998). Development of a structurational model of identification in the organization. *Communication Theory, 8,* 298–336.

Scott, R. L., & Brock, B. L. (1972). *Methods of rhetorical criticism: A twentieth-century perspective.* New York: Harper & Row.

Sellnow, T. L., Seeger, M. W., & Ulmer, R. R. (2002). Chaos theory, information needs, and natural disasters. *Journal of Applied Communication Research, 30,* 269–292.

Sherblom, J. C., Keränen, L., & Withers, L. A. (2000). Tradition, tension, and transformation: A structuration analysis of a game warden service in transition. *Journal of Applied Communication Research, 30,* 143–162.

Shockley-Zalabak, P. (2002). Protean places: Teams across time and space. *Journal of Applied Communication Research, 30,* 231–250.

Smart, G. (1999). Storytelling in a central bank: The role of narrative in the creation and use of specialized economic knowledge. *Journal of Business and Technical Communication, 13,* 249–273.

Sproule, J. M. (1990). Organizational rhetoric and the rational-democratic society. *Journal of Applied Communication Research, 18,* 129–140.

Stamp, G. H., & Sabourin, T. C. (1995). Accounting for violence: An analysis of male spousal abuse narratives. *Journal of Applied Communication Research, 23,* 284–307.

Stohl, C., & Cheney, G. (2001). Participatory processes/paradoxical practices: Communication and the dilemmas of organizational democracy. *Management Communication Quarterly, 14,* 349–407.

Stone, J. F. (2002). Using symbolic convergence theory to discern and segment motives for enrolling in professional master's degree programs. *Communication Quarterly, 50,* 227–243.

Stutts, N. B., & Barker, R. T. (1999). The use of narrative paradigm theory in assessing audience value conflict in image advertising. *Management Communication Quarterly, 13,* 209–244.

Taylor, B., & Conrad, C. (1992). Narratives of sexual harassment: Organizational dimensions. *Journal of Applied Communication Research, 20,* 401–418.

Vanderford, M. L., Stein, T., Sheeler, R., & Skochelak, S. (2001). Communication challenges for experienced clinicians: Topics for an advanced communication curriculum. *Health Communication, 13,* 261–284.

Wander, P. (1983). The ideological turn in modern criticism. *Central States Speech Journal, 34,* 1–18.

Ware, B. L., & Linkugel, W. A. (1973). They spoke in defense of themselves. *Quarterly Journal of Speech, 59,* 273–283.

Weaver, R. M. (1970). *Language is sermonic: Richard M. Weaver on the nature of rhetoric* (R. L. Johannesen, R. Strickland, & R. T. Eubanks, Eds.). Baton Rouge: Louisiana State University Press.

Whitson, S., & Poulakos, S. (1993). Nietzsche and the aesthetics of rhetoric. *Quarterly Journal of Speech, 79,* 131–145.

Wichelns, H. A. (1925). The literary criticism of oratory. In A. M. Drummond (Ed.), *Studies in rhetoric and public speaking in honor of James Albert Winans, by pupils and colleagues* (pp. 181–126). New York: Century.

Williams, A., & Coupland, N. (1998). Epilogue: The socio-political framing of communication and aging research. *Journal of Applied Communication Research, 26,* 139–154.

Wood, J. T. (1992). Telling our stories: Narratives as a basis for theorizing sexual harassment. *Journal of Applied Communication Research, 20,* 349–362.

Workman, T. A. (2001). Finding the meanings of college drinking: An analysis of fraternity drinking stories. *Journal of Health Communication, 13,* 427–447.

Wrage, E. J. (1947). Public address: A study in social and intellectual history. *Quarterly Journal of Speech, 33,* 451–457.

Yerby, J. (1989). A conceptual framework for analyzing family metaphors. *Journal of Applied Communication Research, 17,* 42–51.

Zoller, H. M. (2003). Health on the line: Identity and disciplinary control in employee occupational health and safety discourse. *Journal of Applied Communication Research, 31,* 118–139.

6 Ethnography in Applied Communication Research

Laura L. Ellingson
Santa Clara University

"Nothing is stranger than this business of humans observing other humans in order to write about them," claimed anthropologist Behar (1996, p. 5) in her discussion of ethnography. Anyone who has conducted ethnography (especially participant observation) can attest to how strange it feels, particularly at first, to set oneself apart as an observer and turn a discerning eye to the taken-for-granted processes of a particular social setting. Strange though the endeavor may seem at times, ethnography has proven enormously useful to applied communication researchers for exploring, participating in, and documenting the rich details of daily life as they unfold (Gans, 1999).

Ethnography, broadly defined, "refers to a social scientific description of a people and the cultural basis of their peoplehood" (Vidich & Lyman, 2000, p. 40). Berg (2001) added that "ethnography is primarily a process that attempts to describe and interpret social expressions between people and groups" (p. 134). The validity of ethnography is grounded in the claim that a researcher has *been there*—wherever "there" might be (Lindlof & Taylor, 2002). Being there and writing about what one sees, hears, feels, smells, and tastes there constitute the essence of conducting ethnography. Applied communication ethnographers seek to *be there* in various sites for the purpose of learning about and assisting in the development, change, or improvement of that site or other related sites. Thus, this chapter explores how and for what purposes applied communication researchers do ethnography—as participant observers in the field, as data producers and analysts, and as writers.

To provide an overview of the use of ethnography in applied communication research, I collected articles and chapters published over the 15-year period from 1990 to 2005. Using online search engines, articles in communication journals that used the terms *ethnography* and *applied communication* first were found. I then conducted a more general search using the term *ethnography*, selecting only those articles that focused on applied communication. Finally, I searched through the *Journal of Applied Communication Research* (*JACR*) and several edited collections of applied communication research, selecting articles or chapters that used ethnography as their method. In total, 41 articles and book chapters were gathered, forming a rich and varied collection that reflects the breadth of ethnographic inquiry in contemporary applied communication scholarship and forms the foundation for my commentary.

In this chapter, I first explore definitions of ethnography, the goals of this research, and the history of the method, including an overview of applied communication topics addressed using ethnography. I then examine common practices for data gathering, data analysis, and writing subsumed under the umbrella of ethnography. The final section discusses what we have learned about ethnography through its use in applied communication research and offers some suggestions for applied communication ethnographers.

Definitions of Ethnography in Applied Communication Research

Ethnography is a broad methodology that encompasses many practices, approaches, and philosophies. The methodology is difficult to define, and no consensus exists within communities of ethnographers on its ideal definition or description (Atkinson, Coffey, Delamont, Lofland, & Lofland, 2001; Potter, 1996). The method assumes a *naturalistic paradigm* (see Lincoln & Guba, 1985), meaning that it involves studying groups of people in their natural contexts (Frey, Botan, & Kreps, 2000). Ethnography requires being present in the space being studied, for the ability to make claims is grounded in researchers' direct observation of that space (e.g., Lindlof & Taylor, 2002). Field notes and subsequent reports of ethnographic work should convey "thick description" of the culture studied, including as many specific details as possible (Geertz, 1973). Many ethnographers and methodology textbooks also highlight that ethnography embraces the dual perspectives of (1) *emic*, research participants' perspective; and (2) *etic*, an outsider or more detached perspective (Potter, 1996).

Communication ethnographers focus directly on symbolic processes within the settings they study (Lindlof & Taylor, 2002). The emphasis on communication departs from the focus of sociologists and anthropologists on social structures, kinship configurations, and other aspects of cultural systems. Communication scholars also examine structures, but they study how structures are constituted by communication among members of a culture. Potter (1996) suggested that ethnography can be divided into two basic orientations: (1) *macroethnography* (also called *holistic* or *general ethnography*), in which researchers seek to explain the workings and worldview of a culture; and (2) *microethnography*, which focuses more narrowly on particular behaviors or symbols within a cultural group.

In practice, definitions of ethnography vary considerably among applied communication researchers. Some authors offered no definition or explanation of what they meant by ethnography or participant observation (e.g., Amason, Allen, & Holmes, 1999; Meyer, 2004; Novek, 1995; Zoller, 2003). Other scholars offered no formal definition, but did provide insights into their understanding of the method, such as Adelman and Frey's (1994) explanation of participant observation as part of the naturalistic paradigm they adopted. Other applied communication scholars defined their method explicitly; for example, Gillespie (2001) drew on Denzin's (1997, p. xi) definition of ethnography as "that form of inquiry and writing that produces descriptions and accounts about the ways of life of the writer and those written about," and DeSantis (2002) invoked Trujillo's (1992, p. 352) process-oriented definition that "ethnographic methods require researchers to immerse themselves in the field for an extended period of time in order to gain a detailed understanding of how members interpret their culture."

Some researchers describe their work as subsumed within a particular type of ethnography. For example, *critical ethnography* critiques cultural groups, norms, power structures, and institutions; often is based on neo-Marxist, feminist, queer, postcolonial, or other philosophical perspectives; and seeks to promote social change (e.g., Conquergood, 1991; Foley & Valenzuela, 2005; Madison, 2005; Thomas, 1993). Conquergood (1994, p. 24) noted in his critical ethnography of the communication of street gangs that he was "committed to ethnographic research methods that are intensely participative and critically engaged," and Ashcraft (1999) claimed that her ethnography "reflect[s] a critical, participatory bent. A critical approach seeks knowledge of social action in the service of social change" (p. 249). Several researchers labeled their projects as *feminist ethnographies*, a subtype of critical ethnography, such as Meyer and O'Hara (2004), who cited Lengel (1998) and DeVault (1999) as the bases for their definition: "Feminist ethnography challenges theoretical, methodological, epistemological, and political assumptions that undergird traditional (patriarchal, elitist, capitalist, colonialist) ethnography and offers an alternative form of inquiry that examines power relations of self and other in a self-reflexive manner" (p. 7). Scrutinizing the (mis)use of power and its accommodation or resistance is appropriate, even necessary to applied communication research that seeks to make a positive difference in the world.

The long tradition of *ethnography of speaking* (also called *ethnography of communication*; Saville-Troike, 1989) also was evidenced in this sample. Boone (2003) explained that her ethnographic study of the use of a call–response speech pattern in the classroom "involves describing speaking practices as situated within, and constitutive of, particular speech communities and cultures" (p. 217). Boone posited that the focus on natural contexts of speaking is the ideal way to capture speaking patterns for analysis (see also Braithwaite, 1997).

Clearly, applied communication researchers use a wide variety of ethnographic approaches, all of which potentially are useful. Ethnographers determine their individual approach—which often blends elements of one or more types of ethnography—depending on political, philosophical, methodological, and practical commitments.

Stated Goals of Applied Communication Ethnography

Attaining a deep understanding and producing a rich description of a culture are the traditional goals of ethnography (e.g., Van Maanen, 1988). Applied communication researchers clearly embrace this fundamental goal in the work examined. In addition, three other types of goals emerged: ideological/political, pragmatic, and theoretical. In practice, applied communication research goals tend to overlap, producing pragmatic suggestions to evoke political change, for example, or producing deep understanding of a group that offers significant theoretical insights.

Understanding and Description

Ethnographers translate the details of one culture for an audience usually unfamiliar with that culture. Some applied communication scholars argue that ethnographic research has higher ecological validity for explaining communication than does experimental laboratory research (see Query et al., this volume) because studying existing groups provides insights into natural contexts (Frey, O'Hair, & Kreps, 1990). Morgan and Krone (2001), for instance, stated that their goal in conducting an organizational ethnography was to, as Van Maanen (1979) articulated, "uncover and explicate the ways in which people in particular settings come to understand, account for, take action, and otherwise manage their day-to-day situation" (p. 540). This deep understanding of daily life is uniquely accessible through ethnography, because of the prolonged interaction of the researcher with the group studied. Having stated their goals as uncovering and explicating these detailed processes, Morgan and Krone then provided rich details of the interactions they witnessed, such as the following instance of atypical emotional "improvisation":

> The patient, a prominent businessman, became increasingly agitated the longer he waited for the doctor to come visit him. He had finished his test hours earlier.... When the doctor finally arrived, the patient was irate, and...shouted, "If I ran my business the way you ran yours, I would be out of business!" The doctor was visibly stunned by the patient's display. (p. 328)

Providing such concrete and specific details strengthens applied communication ethnographers' credibility. All of the studies reflected this goal and provided good details, with some studies offering more than other studies. Exemplars of particularly rich descriptions include Conquergood (1994) and Elwood, Dayton, and Richard (1995).

Ideological/Political Goals

The second type of goal of applied communication ethnography is ideological or political, which involves a researcher uncovering and ideologically problematizing the "taken-for-grantedness" of a cultural group (Gergen, 1994) through the use of critical ethnography. This goal often involves attention to the overt and hidden ways in which power operates to privilege some people and oppress others. Although many studies do not explicitly state the goal of ideological or political change, Conquergood (1995) argued that the goal of applied communication research always is political, potentially revolutionary, and never neutral:

> We must choose between research that is "engaged" or "complicit." By engaged I mean clear-eyed, self-critical awareness that research does not proceed in epistemological purity or moral innocence: There is no immaculate perception.... The scholarly commitment of the engaged intellectual is to praxis.... By praxis I mean a combination of analytical rigor, participatory practice, critical reflection, and political struggle. (p. 85)

For Conquergood (1995), it is impossible for researchers to remain uninvolved; to refuse to advocate or assist is to be complicit with existing power relations, not to remain impartial (see also Frey & SunWolf, this volume).

Conquergood's (1994) study of youth gangs in Chicago is an outstanding example of applied communication research that strives to promote social justice. As he wrote in the conclusion to that study:

> My research calls for a radical reorientation of the many gang-intervention programs that deploy fear appeals and shame tactics aimed at scaring street youth out of gangs.... The work of communication needs to be redirected toward rallying and awakening communities and public policymakers to a sense of social justice and responsibility to these youngsters and their families. (p. 55)

Conquergood (1994), thus, sought to alter public views of gang members and, thereby, to alter social policy.

Goodwin (2002) sought to debunk stereotypes of women's and girls' talk as always reflecting feminine norms of inclusion and equality, with men's and boys' communication viewed as competitive and aggressive. Her political goal was to provide a complex understanding of how female talk is manifested rather than a reaffirmation of oppressive gender stereotypes. She documented differences *among* females rather than emphasized only those differences *between* females and males. Similarly, Warren (2001) studied the performance of Whiteness within university classrooms to make performances of racial identity evident to those whose interests are served by ignoring or denying the realities of racism and White privilege. As Warren explained, chinking the armor of denial and complacency is political work:

The generative power of performativity—the potential of locating race in its own process of reiteration—offers us the possibility of interrupting the discursive process of racial formation, as well as the naturalization and sedimentation of those racial categories. The ability to see how race gets accomplished in everyday life might just present the possibility of constituting race differently. (p. 105)

Warren advocated attention to the possibilities of reimagining race and, thereby, challenging racism (see also Nicotera, Clinkscales, Dorsey, & Niles, this volume). For many applied communication ethnographers, political goals are expressed through concrete recommendations for altering oppressive practices within the group studied or within similar groups, as well as recommendations for enacting progressive social policy and creating positive change in communities (e.g., Harter, Berquist, Titsworth, Novak, & Brokaw, 2005).

Practical Goals

Ultimately, practical implications of research are what make applied communication *applied*. Frey (2000) argued that applied communication research should seek to assist participants in bringing about change in their collective communicative practices. Intervention from this perspective involves "researchers putting their communication knowledge and skills into practice...to make a difference in people's lives" (Frey, 2000, p. 179; see also Frey & SunWolf, this volume). To assist in improving the particular setting under study, researchers must attain in-depth knowledge of the workings of the group. As Frey et al. (1990) explained, "Most applied research occurs in the field because researchers study how a specific problem within a particular setting can be solved" (p. 37).

Other scholars take a broader approach, suggesting that applied research should have as its goal the production of pragmatic strategies for use in specific contexts, but not necessarily for the group with whom the study was conducted (e.g., Eadie, 2000; Keyton, 2000; Seibold, 2000; Wood, 2000). I also urge researchers not to dismiss the microlevel activism accomplished through a researcher's embodied presence that calls attention to everyday patterns of communication within a setting. Not all activism is large in scale but all forms of activism can contribute to social change.

Some scholars state their practical goals upfront. Ashcraft (2000, p. 378) claimed that her purpose was to assist in "the development of practical, empowering, gender-conscious alternatives to traditional organizational relationships," and then generated strategies for how organizations can foster more empowering work relations. In a study of cigar smoking, DeSantis (2002, p. 169) stated that his purpose was "to explain why such efforts from loved ones, the media, and the medical establishment are unsuccessful at persuading these men to stop smoking"; he then developed strategies for prevention agencies to reach cigar smokers. S. J. Tracy (2002, p. 137) explicitly stated that her purpose was "to improve our understanding of problems and difficulties associated with the 911 call-taking encounter," and then provided specific way to improve emergency communicative practices between employees and callers in 911 call centers. Elwood et al. (1995) pointed out the shortcomings in public health campaigns targeting illegal drug users and argued for both the effectiveness of outreach programs and the utility of ethnography for studying such programs. Finally, Braithwaite (1997) and Boone (2003) elaborated on ways in which instructors can be reflexive about the cultural specificity of their pedagogy and accommodate students' expressions of their diverse cultural speaking traditions, reflecting these scholars' goals of improving classroom experiences for both instructors and students.

Theoretical Goals

The final type of goal in applied communication ethnography is theoretical. Theoretical goals often involve generation of grounded theories, inductive typologies, or new concepts, or seek to extend existing theories or perspectives (see Barge & Craig, this volume). The primary goal of applied communication research is not immediate theory building but theory still may be instrumental to its accomplishment or be generated as one result of a study (Eadie, 2000). Given that ethnography usually is conceptualized as inductive rather than deductive—that is, seeking rich description and generating deep understanding rather than testing preconceived propositions—the role of theory in the beginning, middle, and end of ethnographic research can vary considerably.

Many applied communication ethnographers cited no specific theories in their research reports (e.g., Amason et al., 1999; Elwood et al., 1995; English-Lueck, Darrah, & Saveri, 2002; Novek, 1995), although they provided detailed reviews of literature that grounded the inquiry. For example, Apker (2001) provided an overview of research on sense making and role development in organizations in her study of nurses' role in managed care systems; Meyer (2004) reviewed the meanings of feminist pedagogy, values, practices, opportunities, and tensions in her study of a classroom; and Martin (2004) focused her ethnographic study of women managers on humor, situating it within the literature on organizational paradox.

When theory was used to frame ethnographic applied communication research, it generally served to ground the research questions posed rather than to generate hypotheses to test. Moreover, much of the theoretical work invoked may be thought of more properly as providing a philosophical framework or as establishing a metatheoretical perspective for the inquiry rather than as invoking a theory per se. Theoretical perspectives of power and knowledge were common in the sample studied; for instance, Foucault's (1971, 1979, 1980) work on disciplinary power and resistance was employed by several researchers (e.g., Edley, 2000; Gillespie, 2001; Zoller, 2003), and Croft (1999) drew on Fiske's (1993) theory of imperializing and localizing power. Feminist theories of the gendered nature of power and resistance (see Buzzanell, Meisenbach, Remke, Sterk, & Turner, this volume) also were common and included the feminist case against bureaucracy (Ferguson, 1984), feminist standpoint theory (Harding, 1991), subaltern counterpublics (Fraser 1990–1991), and strategic essentializing (Spivak, 1988). Performance theory also commonly was used, drawing on Goffman's (1959) dramaturgical theory, Butler's (1990) theory of the performative nature of gendered (and other) identities, and other relevant theories (e.g., Morgan & Krone, 2001; Murphy, 2001; S. J. Tracy, 2002; Warren, 2001). Other theories used to frame applied communication research included symbolic convergence theory (Lesch, 1994), play theory (Brooks & Bowker, 2002), dialectical theory (Adelman & Frey, 1997; Alemán, 2001), structuration theory (Howard & Geist, 1995), and peer cluster theory (DeSantis, 2002).

Some studies in this sample sought to extend existing theory or models. Miller (1995), in her study of a family of four generations of women who had attempted suicide, extended the "basic suicidal syndrome outlined by Breed (1972)" with a model of communication that described the "intersubjective experience of the mother–daughter relationship and the perpetuation of the suicidal tradition" (pp. 264, 268). Similarly, in my research on a health-care team (Ellingson, 2003), I extended the bona fide group perspective (Putnam & Stohl, 1990) by proposing the concept of "embedded teamwork"—work done in dyads and triads of team members outside of team meetings. Lammers and Krikorian (1997) earlier articulated the role of organizational context in bona fide groups in their study of communication on surgical teams. Finally, S. J. Tracy (2004) extended theoretical perspectives on framing by developing a model of framing techniques for organizational tensions that suggests employees commonly frame tensions as simple contradictions, complementary dialectics, or pragmatic paradoxes.

Theoretical perspectives, thus, form a starting point that aids applied communication ethnographers in focusing and grounding their inquiry. Given these definitions and goals, I now contextualize the current state of ethnography within the broader history of the methodology.

History of Ethnography

Ethnography has its roots in 17th- to 19th-century conquerors describing natives in colonial outposts, reports that were intended to establish the uncivilized nature of indigenous groups by providing detailed descriptions of those groups' religious, cultural, family, and daily life practices. Anthropologists eventually professionalized ethnography, developing an evolutionary perspective of cultural development (Vidich & Lyman, 2000). Bronislaw Malinowski generally is regarded as having established modern norms and standards of ethnographic fieldwork (Conquergood, 1991). By the late 1920s, ethnography was being conducted by sociologists (many of the Chicago School) and by anthropologists in urban and immigrant enclaves, as well as in small towns, in the United States—meaning that the ethnographic gaze no longer was restricted to exotic locales (Atkinson et al., 2001). Whyte (1943) coined the term *participant observation* in his classic study of young men's street culture. In the post-World War II 20th century, the 1960s in particular, anthropologists and sociologists became critical of the idea of "the primitive" versus "the civilized" world. The 1970s saw the beginnings of postmodernist challenges to positivism with its emphasis on scientific objectivity (e.g., Clifford & Marcus, 1986; see also Query et al., this volume), and feminists have been instrumental in deconstructing patriarchal biases of ethnography (e.g., Reinharz, 1992).

Denzin and Lincoln (2005) summarized the development of qualitative methods (principally, ethnography) as comprising eight overlapping historical periods: (1) traditional period of positivist, scientific ethnography (1900–1950); (2) modernist phase that celebrated rigorous, systematic qualitative analysis (1950–1970); (3) time of blurred genres, in which diverse approaches to collecting and analyzing data were recognized and valued (1970–1986); (4) crisis of representation, which eschewed classic research norms and embraced reflexivity (1986–1990); (5) postmodern, a period of experimental ethnographies that tried to make sense of the crises of the previous period (1990–1995); (6) postexperimental inquiry, which saw an explosion of outlets for publishing experimental ethnography (1995–2000); (7) methodologically contested present that was/is a time of tension and conflict within the qualitative field (2000–2004); and (8) the future, which is now (2005–). This map of ethnographic development is a useful heuristic that concisely identifies historical trends, ideological shifts, and developments in practice. However, Atkinson et al. (2001) cautioned ethnographers to remember that progress is not linear and the past was not homogenous. At any point in time, there always have been diverse ethnographic practices; for instance, not all current ethnographers are postmodern or experimental in their representations, nor were all past ethnographies representative of a single approach (such as the Chicago school). We, thus, should be careful not to misrepresent or "glos[s] over the historical persistence of tensions and differences" (Atkinson et al., p. 3).

The current state of ethnography in communication, sociology, anthropology, and other social sciences is hotly contested and increasingly critical in nature. Conquergood (1991) suggested four fundamental themes that intersect in critical ethnography and critiques of ethnography: (1) the return of the body as the site of knowledge production; (2) boundaries, borderlands, and "zones of contest" (p. 184) among and within cultures as the focus of engagement rather than an assumed-unified culture; (3) the rise of the performance paradigm of interpreting culture (i.e., viewing life as performed on a daily basis); and (4) rhetorical reflexivity about the writing processes involved in fieldwork and analysis. Likewise, Denzin and Lincoln (2000) suggested that ethnographers currently are "concerned with moral discourse...[and ask] that the social sciences and the humanities become sites for critical conversations about democracy, race, gender, class, nation-states, globalization, freedom, and community" (p. 3).

Current Use of Ethnography in Applied Communication Research

Applied communication researchers have employed ethnography to address a wide range of topics. The central purpose of such research is producing rich descriptions of communication in specific contexts, with the goal of understanding communicative practices and making recommendations for improving them. Most of the ethnographies in this sample addressed nonprofit and community organizations, with topics falling into four broad areas: health communication, organizational communication, community groups, and education.

Applied communication ethnographers have investigated many aspects of health communication. In one study, Gillespie (2001) explored the experiences of Medicaid patients receiving asthma treatment in managed care organizations, finding that administrative and medical procedures further disenfranchised patients as they sought assistance. Other health communication studies focused on creating and sustaining community in a residential facility for people with AIDS (Adelman & Frey, 1994, 1997), professional role development among nurses (Apker, 2001), collective rationalization of health risks by cigar smokers (DeSantis, 2002), backstage communication among members of a geriatric health-care team (Ellingson, 2003), efficacy of outreach for HIV prevention among illegal drug users (Elwood et al., 1995), communication on surgical teams (Lammers & Krikorian, 1997), mother–daughter communication in families where women have attempted suicide (Miller, 1995), professionalism and emotional expression by health-care professionals (Morgan & Krone, 2001), construction of narrative knowledge among caregivers (Morgan-Witte, 2005), nature and role of shared ideology in Alcoholics Anonymous groups (Wright, 1997), and employee occupational health and safety discourse in a manufacturing plant (Zoller, 2003).

Organizational communication topics also were common in applied communication ethnographies. Murphy's (2001) ethnography of sense making and strategic communication choices of flight attendants during in-flight emergencies provides an excellent exemplar. Murphy explored the feminization of the flight-attendant role, the social construction of masculine power of pilots, how this organizational context contributes to communication difficulties during nonroutine incidents, and how airline management could improve training and coordination of flight crews. Other studies of communication in work settings explored stress and social support in a multicultural workplace (Amason et al., 1999); maternity leave and leadership in an organization (Ashcraft, 1999); a feminist organization's efforts to empower members through personalizing work relations (Ashcraft, 2000); communicative practices on self-directed work teams (Barker, Melville, & Pacanowsky, 1993); communication codes used by university faculty and administration (Baxter, 1993); discourses of "play at work" in a new-media forecast research firm (Brooks & Bowker, 2002); the influence of environment on communication in fast-food restaurants (Eaves & Leathers, 1991); gender stereotypes and strategic essentialism in a woman-owned business (Edley, 2000); cultural construction of trust among technology workers in global, high-technology communities (English-Lueck et al., 2002); management of uncertainty among employees of a company undergoing a merger (Howard & Geist, 1995); use of humor by women managers to negotiate organizational paradoxes (Martin, 2004); tension between artistic and business ideologies in a symphony orchestra (Ruud, 2000); emotion management among firefighters (Scott & Myers, 2005); "bitching" communication among corporate secretaries (Sotirin & Gottfried, 1999); question asking and facework by 911 call-takers (S. J. Tracy, 2002); correctional officers' strategies for negotiating organizational tensions (S. J. Tracy, 2004); and emotional labor among 911 call-takers (S. J. Tracy & Tracy, 1998).

Communication within community groups forms the third cluster of ethnographic applied communication studies (for a recent review of research on communication and community, see underwood & Frey, 2008). These studies focused on topics such as complaining among residents of a retirement community (Alemán, 2001), intracommunal communicative practices among gang members (Conquergood, 1994), identity and storytelling in a group home for men with mental retardation (Croft, 1999), social invisibility of homeless youth (Harter et al., 2005), performance of counternarratives of disability among artists in a sheltered workshop for people with developmental disabilities (Harter, Scott, Novak, Leeman, & Morris, 2006), group roles within a community theater group (Kramer, 2002), consciousness-sustaining communication in a coven (Lesch, 1994), and the discursive interface between members of a women's music festival and a university as they shared space (Meyer & O'Hara, 2004). Of particular interest is Goodwin's (2002) study of power asymmetry among members of a core group of ethnically diverse female elementary school students, which found—contrary to prevailing belief that girls are more inclusive and equitable than are boys—that girls used deliberate communication strategies to exclude or marginalize other girls.

The final topic category was the education setting, with ethnographies exploring marginalized people, practices, and points of view within classrooms (see also Darling & Leckie, this volume). Topics included the pedagogical and cultural impact of the African-American "call–response" form of communication in Black college classrooms (Boone, 2003), communicative practices intended to foster a sense of Navajo culture and identity in a Navajo community college (Braithwaite, 1997), opportunities and challenges of using feminist pedagogy in a feminist organizational communication course (Meyer, 2004), strategic communication among African-American youth at an inner-city high school (Novek, 1995), and performance of racial identity and reification of Whiteness in a classroom (Warren, 2001). These scholars sought to disrupt dominant discourses that privilege some racial, gender, and class groups at others' expense by providing insights and strategies for reflecting on and altering teaching and learning practices.

Practices of Applied Communication Ethnography

A large variety of practices fall under the umbrella of ethnography. Ethnography often involves, for instance, observation/fieldwork, formal and informal interviewing, analysis of documents, interaction with participants, functioning in a job or role particular to the research site, writing field notes, keeping a field journal, coding data, constructing narratives, member checking, and conducting interventions (e.g., Atkinson et al., 2001). Much of what is involved in conducting applied communication ethnography is not reported in publications, probably due to space constraints, particularly because qualitative research requires as much thick description as possible as evidence (Ellis & Ellingson, 2000; Lindlof & Taylor, 2002). Description of these practices (or lack thereof) has implications for understanding ethnographic applied communication scholarship. In exploring current norms for reporting methodological practices, there was significant variation in terminology, format for describing practices, length of explanation, and selection of details. Such variation is unsurprising because lack of standardization in reporting methods and findings characterizes qualitative methods, in general (Potter, 1996). Although good reasons exist for diverse practices, the underlying assumption that readers share a common understanding of ethnographic practices that needs little explanation is an unfortunate vestige of positivist research writing conventions that are more tightly defined, regulated, and rule bound, and that are not warranted by the current range of research approaches being utilized. I divide this overview of practices reported in this sample of applied communication research into the categories of data gathering, data analysis, and writing issues.

Data Gathering

Lindlof and Taylor (2002) defined *participant observation* as "the professional craft of experiencing and recording events in social settings" (p. 134). As Atkinson et al. (2001) explained, participant observation requires a presence in the field: "Whatever the range of data collection techniques...ethnographic research remains firmly rooted in the first-hand exploration of research settings. It is this sense of social exploration and protracted investigation that gives ethnography its abiding and continuing character" (p. 5). Participant observation involves adopting a role in the field, producing field notes, and collecting other types of data.

Field Roles

Ethnographers adopt a wide variety of roles. Gold's (1958) classic typology identified four master roles in fieldwork: (1) *complete observer* (a researcher does not interact with a group and members do not know they are being observed), (2) *observer-as-participant* (a researcher behaves as much like a "real" member of a group as possible but members are aware of being observed), (3) *participant-as-observer* (a researcher acts in a limited capacity as a group member and interviews members), and (4) *complete participant* (a researcher fully joins a group, with members not knowing that they are being observed). These are ideal types only; in practice, ethnographers adopt more nuanced identities with respect to the people studied (e.g., Ellingson, 1998) and may enact various roles over time (e.g., Howard & Geist, 1995). Ethnography is an embodied practice that involves not just watching but paying attention to all of one's senses (Conquergood, 1991; see also Murphy, 2001). Moreover, the researcher's body (e.g., gender, race, and age) has meanings to those being studied and should be a major consideration when researchers reflect on how those being observed relate to them (Coffey, 1999).

The applied communication ethnographers in this sample described many different ways of relating to those they studied. Morgan and Krone (2001, p. 324), for instance, tried to be "as silent as possible" by positioning themselves at the "periphery of a given scene," as they observed communication among busy medical professionals carrying out patient procedures. Kramer (2002) auditioned for a community theatre production; after winning the role, he asked participants for permission to study the group. Meyer and O'Hara (2004) were "festigoers" and also volunteered to work at the women's music festival explored in their study. Zoller (2003) initially was a consultant at the factory whose health and safety discourse formed the basis for her study; she explained how she separated from that role to become a researcher. In a different type of role, I explained

(Ellingson, 2003) that I am a cancer survivor and considered how the lasting physical and emotional effects of that disease affected my communication with the geriatric oncology team members and their patients that I studied. Croft (1999) offered an insightful discussion of how she functioned within a group home for men with mental retardation, particularly in how her availability to listen and her freedom from having to reinforce rules enabled her to be an appreciative audience for residents' narratives. With great specificity, Edley (2000) listed tasks she performed at an interior design firm she studied:

> I worked alongside the designers, office workers, owners, and warehouse workers. I answered telephones, filed forms, wrote advertising copy, helped with inventory, waited on customers, sat in on staff meetings and client meetings, assisted designers in selecting wallpaper and fabric samples for presentations to clients, and accompanied the designers to clients' homes. (p. 283)

Scott and Myers (2005) similarly explained that during fieldwork at a fire station, they "assisted with station chores, observed training sessions, prepared and shared meals, and accompanied the firefighters on fire and emergency medical service (EMS) calls" (p. 72). Elwood et al. (1995) characterized each of themselves as ethnographers and the outreach workers they observed in descriptions ranging from one to seven paragraphs in length that offered rich detail about these individuals' communication styles and ways of relating to the drug users who were the outreach workers' clientele.

Although residing with the group being studied was atypical, there were examples of ethnographers who did so. Conquergood (1994), for instance, lived for several years in a tenement building in the Chicago neighborhood where he studied gangs. Similarly, Novek's (1995) study of African-American youth involved her living in the community for 6 years, conducting research and teaching journalism at the community's high school, teaching in a weekend education program and at a community recreation center, and serving as a literacy tutor.

All of the researchers in this sample fell somewhere between participant-as-observer and observer-as-participant, and all (eventually) were known as researchers to the groups they studied. For many, this openness facilitated the "informal interviews" they conducted, which involved asking questions about the meaning of people's practices and discussing research-related topics with them as they worked or performed tasks (e.g., Amason et al., 1999; Edley, 2000; Sotirin & Gottfried, 1999). At the same time, these interviews reinforced the ethnographers' outsider identity, as they asked questions about practices that likely were taken for granted by group/cultural members.

Field Notes

Perhaps the most characteristic element of ethnography is the production of *field notes*, firsthand accounts of ethnographers' participant observation. Field notes should be rich with details and thick description of experiences (Geertz, 1973). Ideally, researchers should record data reflecting all the senses: taste, smell, touch, and hearing, as well as sight (Berg, 2001). Field notes also may include reflections, questions, and musings that arise as researchers compose notes. Richardson (2000), drawing on classic work by Glaser and Strauss (1967), provided a useful typology of field notes: observation notes, methodological notes, theoretical notes, and personal notes. In addition, she suggested that researchers keep a separate journal in which they record their feelings about the work, a practice with a long tradition in anthropology.

Applied communication ethnographers varied in the amount and type of detail they provided about field notes. Boone (2003) gave the most detailed explanation of events she recorded in her field notes of classroom observations "that included descriptions of the setting and activities, the sequence of events, descriptions of the participants and their verbal and nonverbal behaviors, descriptions of how the participants interacted with one another, and other personal interpretations and observations" (p. 218). Most scholars, however, did not elaborate on what was in their field notes and reported only quantities produced. Commonly reported details included number of hours of observation, number of pages of field notes, and frequency and length of observation sessions. At one end of the continuum, English-Lueck et al. (2002, p. 93) stated that they used "traditional anthropological tools such as in-depth interviews and participant observation," but cited no methodological texts or ethnographic exemplars as models for their practices. A bit more specifically, Adelman and Frey (1994) reported that they did participant observation but offered no estimate of how many hours they observed, nor the volume of their field notes (see also Barker et al., 1993; Eaves & Leathers, 1991). A few researchers characterized their field notes as "extensive" (e.g., Baxter, 1993; Brooks & Bowker, 2002). Reported length of observation also varied tremendously. For example, at the briefer end of the continuum, Lesch (1994) observed and taped three 2.5-hour meetings, whereas Boone (2003) observed one summer session of a public speaking class and provided the exact dates of May 27 to June 25 for her period of observation. Morgan and Krone (2001) stated that they conducted 2 months of observations, 4 times per week, for 2 to 4 hours per session. In the middle of the range, Kramer (2002) reported that, acting in a theatrical production, he engaged in 75 hours of observation and generated 68 pages of field notes, and S. J. Tracy (2002) reported 100 hours of participant observation and 200 pages of field notes.

At the lengthy end of the continuum, Ashcraft (2000) reported conducting 230 hours of participant observation, plus an additional 50 hours of observing meetings, and generated more than 700 pages of detailed field notes. Martin (2004) stated that, in total, she produced over 950 pages of field notes, meeting transcripts, and interview transcripts (although these were not categorized by type of data). Like Conquergood (1994), Goodwin (2002), who conducted participant observation in a middle school for 3 years, at lunch and in classrooms, focusing on a core group of ethnically diverse girls, and English-Lueck et al. (2002), who conducted a 10-year project in four global, high-technology communities, reported that their studies relied on extensive periods of observation but did not offer details such as those described above. Field notes as data remain at the center of ethnographic inquiry, but no consensus exists as to the necessary or ideal quantity, or the degree of detail in which field notes can or should be described in published work.

Other Types of Data

In addition to field notes, the vast majority of applied communication ethnographies involved gathering other types of data. After field notes, the most common form of data was audio-recorded, transcribed interviews with participants following observation of them. These interviews differed from the fleeting opportunistic interviews conducted informally during observations and were designed to elicit participants' perspectives on the meanings of their communicative and cultural practices. For example, Ashcraft (1999) interviewed 21 company members at the office furniture company she studied, and Howard and Geist (1995) interviewed 19 employees of the utility company they studied.

Analysis of documents generated by or pertaining to the group under investigation also was common. Murphy (2001), for instance, conducted archival research at airline headquarters, analyzing newspaper stories, magazine articles, and old flight-attendant manuals. Braithwaite (1997) examined documents produced by a community college that explained Navajo philosophy, culture, and traditions, and how those traditions were incorporated into courses. Similarly, Sotirin and Gottfried (1999, p. 65) examined documents "on secretarial protocols and company procedures" pertaining to secretaries whose "bitching" communication they studied, and S. J. Tracy and Tracy (1998) examined 911 call-center materials, including training manuals, year-end public reports, and internal memos.

Other ethnographers recorded and transcribed naturally occurring interactions among participants, such as staff meetings at a zoo (Martin, 2004); interactions among patients, patients' companions, and geriatric team members (Ellingson, 2003); coven meetings (Lesch, 1994); and residents' narratives in a group home (Croft, 1999). Ruud (2000) distributed a "brief" questionnaire to the board of directors and musicians asking about communication concerns of symphony orchestra members, and Amason et al. (1999) administered a quantitative questionnaire to employees following observation and interviews with them. Finally, Miller (1995) asked each of her participants to keep a journal of thoughts and reflections on their emotions and family dynamics.

Methods of Data Analysis

In addition to the variety of data gathered by ethnographic applied communication researchers, varying methods of data analysis were employed. Again, some researchers in this sample were much more specific about their data-analytic procedures than were others. Some gave no explanation of data-analytic procedures; they simply described their involvement in a particular setting and then proceeded directly to their findings (e.g., Barker et al., 1993; Brooks & Bowker, 2002; Meyer, 2004; Novek, 1995).

Other ethnographers clearly identified an analytical step between data gathering and presenting results. Many ethnographers analyzed data using grounded theory procedures as delineated by Glaser and Straus (1967; see also Bryant & Charmaz, 2007; Charmaz, 2000, 2006; Corbin & Strauss, 2008); exemplars included S. J. Tracy and Tracy (1998), Miller (1995), Zoller (2003), and Wright (1997), who provided an unusually detailed explanation of the method in his article. Other researchers conducted analyses that were similar to grounded theory in the sense of being inductive and discerning patterns, but did not follow precisely the exact guidelines. Deriving themes was one way of describing inductive analysis; for instance, Apker (2001, p. 121) "reviewed [data] for emergent themes," and Gillespie (2001) employed Owen's (1984) criteria for themes (repetition, recurrence, and forcefulness) to determine which ideas were representative in the data (see also Meyer & O'Hara, 2004). *Patterns* was another term invoked to describe inductive analyses: Morgan and Krone (2001, p. 325) analyzed data for "patterns of performances," and Baxter (1993, p. 315) noted that she "searched for emergent patterns" in her data. Braithwaite (1997) also looked for themes and patterns, and added that he "stopped collecting data when I identified recurring patterns of interaction...when I stopped seeing something 'new'...when my informants did not tell me anything I had not heard before" (p. 223). Ruud (2000) described his inductive data analysis using Geertz's (1973) process of searching for symbols, significant clusters of symbols, and contradictions among symbols. Still other ethnographers specified methods of analysis that were uniquely suited to their projects and were not found elsewhere in this sample: conversational analysis (Goodwin, 2002), fantasy theme analysis (Bormann 1972, cited in Lesch, 1994), "grounded practical theory" (Craig & Tracy, 1995, cited in Ashcraft, 2000; see Barge & Craig, this volume); and action-implicative discourse analysis (K. Tracy, 1995, cited in S. J. Tracy, 2002; see Barge & Craig, this volume, Tracy & Mirivel, this volume).

Use of grounded theory and other inductive procedures often is compatible with other analytical perspectives. For example, Zoller (2003) stated that she drew "upon Fairclough's (1995) conception of critical discourse analysis as the attempt to understand the role of ideological discursive formations in naturalizing ideologies and transforming them into common sense" (p. 124); this reflected Zoller's choice of Foucault's (1971, 1979, 1980) theories on power and discourse to frame her study of contradictions in workplace health and safety discourses (see also K. Tracy & Mirivel, this volume). In a similar manner, Meyer and O'Hara (2004, p. 9) used standpoint theory as "another analytic lens" and "identified discursive and counterdiscursive moves" to address their research questions, which focused on discourse and subaltern counterpublics.

A final aspect of data analysis reported by several ethnographers in this sample was *recalcitrance*, or inviting feedback from selected participants to consider their responses to researchers' preliminary findings (Tompkins, 1994). Kramer (2002), for instance, invited two theater group members and two outsiders to read and comment on the initial draft of his manuscript. Alemán (2001) conducted "member checks" intended to clarify her understanding of participants' perspectives, particularly with regard to comparing management and employee points of view. Morgan and Krone (2001) held an informal meeting with five participants for feedback that was integrated into their data analysis. Novek (1995) showed her student participants a draft of her ethnography and quoted the following from their responses:

> Kahn wrote, "This is an excellent paper. It covers all points on how young black youth survive and strive in [West Urbania]. You excellently used phrases that showed pain in some of the students, as well as their happiness." He felt I had used the word "some" too often to describe situations experienced by only "a few" students, however. (p. 184)

Inviting participants' voices into the data-analysis process and providing space for divergent views in research reports, as Novek did, is a common practice among feminist and other critical theory scholars (Reinharz, 1992).

Writing Strategies

The ethnographies in this sample were written using postpositivist academic writing conventions, following standard research report format (i.e., the American Psychological Association's guidelines that specify introduction, literature review, methods, results, discussion, and conclusion as the sections of research articles), and utilizing existing theories, concepts, and research to justify and contextualize their inquiry. Far more similarities than differences in writing style emerged within the sample. Two common elements of writing included first-person voice and inclusion of (some) thick description as support for claims made.

The vast majority of authors wrote in the first person, rhetorically taking responsibility for their actions and claims, a common postpositivist practice that departs from the passive voice characteristic of positivist research. For example, Gillespie (2001, p. 106) noted, "In my official position at the Center, then, I worked within a cognitive anthropological framework," and Lesch (1994) stated that "I observed, audiotaped, and took notes during each 2 1/2-hour meeting" (p. 61; see also Adelman & Frey, 1994, 1997; Alemán, 2001; Meyer, 2004; Miller, 1995; Warren, 2001; Zoller, 2003). Far fewer authors wrote in the third person and, in each case, the article was written by multiple authors who served in different roles during the study, making the use of "I" or "we" difficult and potentially confusing. For example, Morgan and Krone (2001) explained that "the first author originally looked for…" and that "patterns of performance were identified" (p. 325; see also Amason et al., 1999; Brooks & Bowker, 2002; English-Lueck et al., 2002). First-person voice appears normative and certainly is consistent with current trends in qualitative social science (Ellis & Ellingson, 2000).

The other characteristic aspect of the writing style involves incorporating thick description in the form of short excerpts from field notes, reconstructed dialogue, and summaries of interactions witnessed; in most cases, ethnographers included some lengthier, indented block quotes that were interspersed with a larger number of brief quotes or paraphrases that were woven into the analysis (e.g., Ashcraft, 2000; Gillespie, 2001; Martin, 2004; Meyer & O'Hara, 2004. Other ethnographers engaged in variations on this manner of presenting evidence to support their claims. English-Lueck et al. (2002) and Goodwin (2002) included extended examples transcribed from interview tapes, and I (Ellingson, 2003) offered a narrative account of an interaction at the beginning of the findings and referred back to the lines of that narrative throughout the analysis. Miller (1995) succinctly summed up the conundrum of wanting to provide rich details but not having sufficient (journal) space within which to fit them when she introduced her findings with a disclaimer: "Due to space considerations, these categories are briefly described omitting fully descriptive detail" (p. 253). Although sufficient details were included in each of the articles, we can safely assume that many more were omitted.

Further economizing on space was accomplished through being as concise as possible throughout the report. DeSantis's (2002) account stood out as an exception to this rule with his opening narrative of a fellow cigar smoker's funeral and humorous references to old television shows to introduce the cigar shop: "The interior design, to use the term very loosely, can best be thought of as a cross between Sanford and Son's living room and Floyd's Mayberry barber shop…. As one wife observed, 'the room is done in tasteless testosterone'" (p. 168). Elwood et al. (1995) also devoted space to the lexicon of African-American communities on the South Side of Houston that were the focus of their study on HIV prevention, when they wrote, "There, anyone who's anyone knows Ms. Phyllis…. But Phyllis isn't the Diva of the South Side simply because people know her. She also is 'all that.'… She reminds people to use condoms when they're doing the wild thing" (pp. 265–266). Elwood et al. did not just quote participants' words; they incorporated some of the participants' style into the prose. They also used contractions and second-person voice (e.g., "If you interrupt her…"), strategies that typically are not used in formal academic writing but are effective in illuminating participants' worlds. Harter et al. (2006) went even further by including in their article two photographs of artwork produced by adults with developmental disabilities in the workshop they studied. Such evocative details take up space, but they enhance the richness of the accounts significantly (see Adelman & Frey, 1997).

The dearth of richly evocative accounts of lived experiences in most communication research reports underlies Goodall's (2004) call for applied communication researchers to engage in autoethnography and write personal narratives. *Autoethnography* is a type of ethnography that shifts the focus from a group to a researcher's lived experiences as the object of study and often generates narrative or other artistic representations as findings (Ellis, 2004). Goodall posited that personal narratives are "ways of explaining things" that connect research on important issues with individuals' "actual telling of a life story," and that "this form of reporting is a new embodiment of applied communication research" (p. 187). Goodall's position that such tales constitute applied research is not widely shared, at least as reflected in venues that publish applied communication research. Although such alternative, or creative-analytic, representations have become more widely accepted (e.g., fiction stories, poetry, and performance art; see Richardson, 2000), space has not been allotted to them in "mainstream" journals, such as *JACR* (see Tillman, 2009), nor in most edited collections of applied communication research, such as Buzzanell, Sterk, and Turner's (2004) book, *Gender in Applied Communication Contexts*. Some applied researchers publish autoethnographic, narrative, or confessional accounts of ethnography separately from conventional analyses (e.g., Adelman & Frey, 2001; Ellingson, 1998) or mix autoethnography and grounded theory analysis in a book-length ethnography (Ellingson, 2005).

Lessons Learned About Ethnography in Applied Communication Scholarship

This chapter has described how ethnography has been employed in applied communication research. In this section, I reflect on what we have learned about ethnography as a methodology through the studies explored here, with particular attention to ethnographers' descriptions of difficulties encountered and stated limitations of their studies. Although a discussion of research limitations generally is expected in published monographs (and obligatory in some journals) as a qualifier for claims made on the basis of one's data, this brief segment of articles, along with discussions of methods and sometimes conclusions, also functions as a site for the negotiation of methodological legitimacy. That is, by examining the professed limitations of ethnographic methods and findings, we can explore ways in which applied communication topics, goals, and implications illuminate the practices of ethnography.

Some of the published ethnographic research reviewed did not directly address any limitations (e.g., Gillespie, 2001; Meyer & O'Hara, 2004; Morgan & Krone, 2001; Murphy, 2001; S. J. Tracy, 2004). This absence is notable in light of the fading but persistent legacy of quantitative research conventions employed in communication journals. Although qualitative methods now are widely embraced, many reviewers and editors support traditional writing norms that require at least a nod toward identifying limitations of a study. For qualitative research, this nod often included eschewing claims of generalizability based on the limited number of sites or participants studied; some applied communication authors went so far as to argue for limitations that were so significant "as to deny the validity of the theory or method. In essence, authors argued successfully against their own research project" (Keyton, 2000, p. 167). On a positive note, it appears that the time for being overly defensive about the value and utility of qualitative findings largely has passed. Still, some authors in this sample did address methodological limitations that provide insights into the use of ethnography in applied communication scholarship.

To begin, the traditional qualitative lament of the lack of generalizability of findings was evident in this sample, as reflected in Kramer's (2002) statement that the "transferability [of his findings] to other settings is speculative" (p. 168). This acknowledgment is grounded in the fact that ethnographic studies usually are confined to an in-depth exploration of a single site (e.g., Lindolf & Taylor, 2002). Given the specificities of the particular group studied, variation across groups is to be expected and has to be accounted for in applying findings. For most studies, this fact went unstated, indicating that it was understood and did not require repeating. In one case, Lammers and Krikorian (1997) indicated that it was difficult to gain access to multiple hospitals for observation but that doing so was imperative because "to draw reliable and valid conclusions, the cooperation of a single facility…is insufficient" (p. 28).

As another limitation, Alemán (2001) noted the problem of field notes (rather than recordings) as data:

Most instances of complaining were reconstructed in my fieldnotes from observed conversations. While I recognize the limitations of these reconstructed acts and episodes, complaining events were fleeting and ephemeral, often captured in the hallways and elevators making audio recording difficult. (p. 95)

The necessity of reconstructing events is inherent to ethnography because the method requires simultaneous observation, sense making, and note taking (that is, recording of data), but this issue was raised only by a few authors.

Other limitations concerned points of view reflected or excluded from the ethnography and awareness that ethnographers often differ in important ways from their participants, which may limit their ability to understand participants' perspectives. Amason et al. (1999) noted that they were Anglo, whereas many of the people they studied were Hispanic, and Zoller (2003, p. 136) explained that her "study was limited to the often-silenced voices of employees" and suggested that further research should incorporate other voices (e.g., management). Novek (1995) stated the limitations of her perspective but also advocated for its value:

The observations...offered here are a limited effort to describe what the author saw, heard, and experienced.... They illuminate the strategic communication behaviors of specific adolescents in a specific time and place, described to the best of one observer's ability. Still the descriptions, whatever their limitations, had real resonance for some participants. (p. 184)

A few authors expressed critical awareness of the difficulties of writing their accounts. One issue that authors raised was power, for ethnographic writing inescapably is political and cannot produce a neutral account; as Van Maanen (1988) explained, "ethnographies are politically mediated, since the power of one group to represent another is always involved" (pp. 4–5). Warren (2001) said that he sought to "take the cautions about ethnographic objectivity...seriously [that] argue that ethnography is always already an interpretive process—that any view of culture, my own included, stems from a source with a particular history and ideological point of view" (p. 106).

Similarly, Meyer (2004) acknowledged her viewpoint in her ethnography of teaching using feminist pedagogy: "Like all ethnographies, the tale I tell is not some incontestable truth, but, to a certain degree, a fiction (Van Maanen, 1988) written from my perspective—which is...unique, yet partial, partisan, and problematic" (Eisenberg & Goodall, 1997, p. 199).

In a somewhat different vein, Adelman and Frey (1994) noted the limitations of language and writing conventions for expressing the painful events they witnessed during fieldwork:

The discussions of dialectical tensions, communication practices, and metaphors... fall short in conveying the personal struggle to live and die within [an AIDS residence]. How can we convey the depth of feeling while watching a sick resident risk his survival to go outside in the bitter cold of a Chicago winter to release a balloon for a fellow resident who has died? (p. 20)

Adelman and Frey (1994, 1997) also suggested that ethnographic accounts must capture participants' perspectives and that the research process and reporting methods should privilege participant' voices (see also Novek, 1995).

Given the often close relationship in ethnography between researchers and those they study, ethical dilemmas inevitably arise at all stages of research that may limit researchers' ability to represent those individuals (e.g., Berg, 2001; Lindlof & Taylor, 2002). Overt discussion of ethics in these reports, however, was rare. One example is Conquergood (1994), who stated in a footnote that as he studied gangs and their secret credos, he confronted "ethical dilemmas, conundrums, and predicaments. I must negotiate continuously that delicate boundary between respect and sensitivity to my field consultants, and the need to write the fullest, most complex ethnographic account of their communication practices that my data support" (p. 28). Zoller (2003, p. 124) also discussed the issue of employee confidentiality, but she raised this less as an ethical issue and more as a way to assert the validity of her interview data: "I have confidence in the interview texts," she explained, after noting that she reassured participants of confidentiality for both individual employees and the corporation. Similarly, Edley (2000) argued that the employees she studied felt free to express complaints against the owners of the firm because she assured them that their comments were confidential.

Suggestions for Applied Communication Ethnographers

Having reviewed the existing state(s) of ethnography in applied communication research, I now offer some suggestions for ethnographers. I advocate that published applied communication ethnographies should consistently provide (1) clarification of key methodological terms, (2) more complete and accurate roadmaps of their work processes, (3) recommendations for practitioners beyond the academy, and (4) support for wider variation in the length of journal articles.

A great deal of ambiguity and inconsistency exists regarding the specific ethnographic practices reported (and omitted) by applied communication ethnographers, and, consequently, greater clarity is needed. Potter (1996) pointed out that inconsistency in the use of key terms is characteristic of ethnography and qualitative research, in general. Like Potter, I eschew calls for uniformity and, instead, promote methodological diversity. However, the lack of standardization of practice and language should not encourage ethnographers to ignore the implications of this diversity, as was the case in many of these ethnographies. Authors should define key terms that they invoke (e.g., ethnography and inductive analysis), either by citing a relevant methodological treatise or by providing more precise details of their procedures. This level of detail is particularly important in explaining how data were analyzed, as readers deserve to know how researchers get from field notes to finished product. Ethnographers need not be defensive about their choices but they should be more complete in documenting those choices. This suggestion may add length to a manuscript, which is a problem given that publication space often is in short supply, but given ethnographers' goal of providing thick description, citing a text or definition could be done succinctly.

Second, applied communication ethnographers need to acknowledge, if only briefly, the messiness, imperfections, and mistakes that inevitably are part of the actual process of conducting such research. If our exemplars are to be useful to those who are heading into the field or trying to make sense of what they experienced there, we must include more of the underbelly of ethnography. As Van Maanen (1988) explained:

> Accident and happenstance shapes fieldworkers' studies as much as planning or foresight; numbing routine as much as living theatre; impulse as much as rational choice; mistaken judgments as much as accurate ones. This may not be the way fieldwork is reported, but it is the way it is done. (p. 2)

Most certainly, ethnography is not reported this way in applied communication research. Ethnographers—myself included—want to publish the most credible and persuasive version of our stories when our goal is to influence policy, practice, or theory. Hence, ethnographers tend to sanitize their accounts, omitting missteps as irrelevant, tangential, or overly personal; historically, such confessional tales were kept separate from authoritative accounts of research (Van Maanen, 1988). Granted it is risky to combine confessions of embarrassing moments (see Ellingson, 2005, for a scene in which I engaged in a heated debate about the Virgin Mary and feminism with the oncologist I was observing, with disastrous results) with passionate calls for social, political, and professional change based on one's findings; not everyone will forgive such truthfulness, let alone see it as enhancing a researcher's credibility through realism. However, when we pretend that research processes are linear and smooth, we provide inaccurate and deceptively simplistic maps for those who read our work for guidance. I am not suggesting that we humiliate ourselves by detailing every imperfection but that we note in methodology sections (some) roadblocks encountered, opportunities seized or missed, ethical dilemmas faced, and mistakes made.

I also urge applied communication ethnographers to make explicit and specific their recommendations for practitioners in the area in which they conduct their ethnographies. Since Keyton's editorship, all articles published in *JACR* must include, in a separate section, concrete suggestions for professionals/practitioners (see Frey & SunWolf, this volume). Articles and chapters sampled here that were published elsewhere (or earlier in *JACR*'s history) often lacked such specific applications to real-world contexts. In every article sampled, significant theoretical or conceptual insights were provided that implied possibilities for application; in all cases, such insights should be articulated in pragmatic form (see also Barge & Craig, this volume). After all, communication research cannot claim to be applied if the findings from it cannot be translated into useful practices (Frey, 2000).

Finally, let us remember that journal publication guidelines are neither natural nor inevitable but are socially constructed and, hence, changeable. Despite resource limitations, we should advocate for the merits of accepting—at least occasionally—longer ethnographic accounts in journals that publish applied communication research. I am not naïve about the challenges of journal editing, and I have the highest respect for those who perform that vital service. However, ethnographic thick descriptions often look rather thin by the time they are shrunk into standard article length. In addition to flexibility on article length, perhaps Web technology could be used, enabling authors to print links to further illustrative examples or to longer electronic versions of articles. Of course, ethnographers need to make the best possible use of additional space through strategic writing choices.

Conclusion

Ethnography is alive and well in applied communication research. Although significant variety exists in how ethnography is defined and practiced, common threads weave through the applied communication research that employs this method. The strength of ethnography is its attunement to the smallest mundane details of day-to-day life. Given that applied communication researchers seek to understand and enhance the daily life of individuals, groups, and organizations, ethnography has and will continue to contribute significantly to applied communication scholarship.

References

Adelman, M. B., & Frey, L. R. (1994). The pilgrim must embark: Creating and sustaining community in a residential facility for people with AIDS. In L. R. Frey (Ed.), *Group communication in context: Studies of natural groups* (pp. 3–22). Hillsdale, NJ: Erlbaum.

Adelman, M. B., & Frey, L. R. (1997). *The fragile community: Living together with AIDS.* Mahwah, NJ: Erlbaum.

Adelman, M. B., & Frey, L. R. (2001). Untold tales from the field: Living the autoethnographic life in an AIDS residence. In S. L. Herndon & G. L. Kreps (Eds.), *Qualitative research: Applications in organizational life* (pp. 205–226). Cresskill, NJ: Hampton Press.

Alemán, M. W. (2001). Complaining among the elderly: Examining multiple dialectical oppositions to independence in a retirement community. *Western Journal of Communication, 65,* 89–112.

Amason, P., Allen, M. W., & Holmes, S. A. (1999). Social support and acculturative stress in the multicultural workplace. *Journal of Applied Communication Research, 27,* 310–334.

Apker, J. (2001). Role development in the managed care era: A case of hospital-based nursing. *Journal of Applied Communication Research, 29,* 117–136.

Ashcraft, K. L. (1999). Managing maternity leave: A qualitative analysis of temporary executive succession. *Administrative Science Quarterly, 44,* 240–280.

Ashcraft, K. L. (2000). Empowering "professional" relationships: Organizational communication meets feminist practice. *Management Communication Quarterly, 13,* 347–392.

Atkinson, P., Coffey, A., Delamont, S., Lofland, J., & Lofland, L. (2001). Editorial introduction. In P. Atkinson, A. Coffey, S. Delamont, J. Lofland, & L. Lofland (Eds.), *Handbook of ethnography* (pp. 1–7). Thousand Oaks, CA: Sage.

Barker, J. R., Melville, C. W., & Pacanowsky, M. E. (1993). Self-directed teams at XEL: Changes in communication practices during a program of cultural transformation. *Journal of Applied Communication Research, 21,* 297–312.

Baxter, L. A. (1993). "Talking things through" and "putting it in writing": Two codes of communication in an academic institution. *Journal of Applied Communication Research, 21,* 313–326.

Behar, R. (1996). *The vulnerable observer: Anthropology that breaks your heart.* Boston: Beacon Press.

Berg, B. L. (2001). *Qualitative research methods for the social sciences* (4th ed.). Boston: Allyn & Bacon.

Boone, P. R. (2003). When the "amen corner" comes to class: An examination of the pedagogical and cultural impact of call–response communication in the Black college classroom. *Communication Education, 52,* 212–229.

Bormann, E. (1972). Fantasy and rhetorical vision: The rhetorical criticism of social reality. *Quarterly Journal of Speech, 58,* 396–407.

Braithwaite, C. A. (1997). Sa'ah naaghái bik'eh hózhóón: An ethnography of Navajo educational communication practices. *Communication Education, 46,* 219–233.

Breed, W. (1972). Five components of a basic suicide syndrome. *Life-Threatening Behavior, 3,* 3–18.

Brooks, L. J., & Bowker, G. (2002). Playing at work: Understanding the future of work practices at the institute for the future. *Information, Communication and Society, 5,* 109–136.

Bryant, A., & Charmaz, K. (Eds.). (2007). *The Sage handbook of grounded theory.* Thousand Oaks, CA: Sage.

Butler, J. (1990). Performative acts and gender constitution: An essay in phenomenology and feminist theory. In S.-E. Case (Ed.), *Performing feminisms: Feminist critical theory and theatre* (pp. 270–282). Baltimore: Johns Hopkins University Press.

Buzzanell, P. M., Sterk, H., & Turner, L. H. (Eds.). (2004). *Gender in applied communication contexts.* Thousand Oaks, CA: Sage.

Charmaz, K. (2000). Grounded theory: Objectivist and constructivist methods. In N. K. Denzin & Y. S. Lincoln (Eds.), *Handbook of qualitative research* (2nd ed., pp. 509–535). Thousand Oaks, CA: Sage.

Charmaz, K. (2006). *Constructing grounded theory.* Thousand Oaks, CA: Sage.

Clifford, J., & Marcus, G. E. (Eds.). (1985). *Writing culture: The poetics and politics of ethnography*. Berkeley: University of California Press.

Coffey, A. (1999). *The ethnographic self: Fieldwork and the representation of identity*. Thousand Oaks, CA: Sage.

Conquergood, D. (1991). Rethinking ethnography: Towards a critical cultural politics. *Communication Monographs, 58,* 179–194.

Conquergood, D. (1994). Homeboys and hoods: Gang communication and cultural space. In L. R. Frey (Ed.), *Group communication in context: Studies of natural groups* (pp. 23–55). Hillsdale, NJ: Erlbaum.

Conquergood, D. (1995). Between rigor and relevance: Rethinking applied communication. In K. N. Cissna (Ed.), *Applied communication in the 21st century* (pp. 79–96). Mahwah, NJ: Erlbaum.

Corbin, J., & Strauss, A. L. (2008). *Basics of qualitative research: Grounded theory procedures and techniques* (3rd ed.). Thousand Oaks, CA: Sage.

Craig, R. T., & Tracy, K. (1995). Grounded practical theory: The case of intellectual discussion. *Communication Theory, 3,* 248–272.

Croft, S. E. (1999). Creating locales through storytelling: An ethnography of a group home for men with mental retardation. *Western Journal of Communication, 63,* 329–347.

Denzin, N. K. (1997). *Interpretive ethnography: Ethnographic practices for the 21st century.* Thousand Oaks, CA: Sage.

Denzin, N. K., & Lincoln, Y. S. (2000). Introduction: The discipline and practice of qualitative research. In N. K. Denzin & Y. S. Lincoln (Eds.), *Handbook of qualitative research* (2nd ed., pp. 1–28). Thousand Oaks, CA: Sage.

Denzin, N. K., & Lincoln, Y. S. (2005). Introduction: The discipline and practice of qualitative research. In N. K. Denzin & Y. S. Lincoln (Eds.), *The Sage handbook of qualitative research* (3rd ed., pp. 1–32). Thousand Oaks, CA: Sage.

DeSantis, A. D. (2002). Smoke screen: An ethnographic study of a cigar shop's collective rationalization. *Health Communication, 14,* 167–198.

DeVault, M. L. (1999). *Liberating method: Feminism and social research.* Philadelphia: Temple University Press.

Eadie, W. F. (2000). Changing boundaries, changing expectations, changing results. *Journal of Applied Communication Research, 28,* 174–177.

Eaves, M. H., & Leathers, D. G. (1991). Context as communication: McDonald's vs. Burger King. *Journal of Applied Communication Research, 19,* 263–289.

Edley, P. P. (2000). Discursive essentializing in a woman-owned business: Gender stereotypes and strategic subordination. *Management Communication Quarterly, 14,* 271–306.

Eisenberg, E. M., & Goodall, H. L., Jr. (1997). *Organizational communication: Balancing creativity and constraint* (2nd ed.). New York: St. Martin's Press.

Ellingson, L. L. (1998). "Then you know how I feel": Empathy, identification, and reflexivity in fieldwork. *Qualitative Inquiry, 4,* 492–514.

Ellingson, L. L. (2003). Interdisciplinary health care teamwork in the clinic backstage. *Journal of Applied Communication Research, 31,* 93–117.

Ellingson, L. L. (2005). *Communicating in the clinic: Negotiating frontstage and backstage teamwork.* Cresskill, NJ: Hampton Press.

Ellis, C. (2004). *The ethnographic I: A methodological novel about autoethnography.* Walnut Creek, CA: AltaMira.

Ellis, C., & Ellingson, L. L. (2000). Qualitative methods. In E. F. Borgatta & R. J. V. Montgomery (Eds.), *Encyclopedia of sociology* (2nd ed., Vol. 4., pp. 2287–2296). New York: Macmillan.

Elwood, W. N., Dayton, C. A., & Richard, A. J. (1995). Ethnography and illegal drug users: The efficacy of outreach as HIV prevention. *Communication Studies, 46,* 261–275.

English-Lueck, J. A., Darrah, C. N., & Saveri, A. (2002). Trusting strangers: Work relationships in four high-tech communities. *Information, Communication and Society, 5,* 90–108.

Fairclough, N. (1995). *Critical discourse analysis: The critical study of language.* New York: Longman.

Ferguson, K. E. (1984). *The feminist case against bureaucracy.* Philadelphia: Temple University Press.

Fiske, J. (1993). *Power plays, power works.* New York: Verso.

Foley, D., & Valenzuela, A. (2005). Critical ethnography: The politics of collaboration. In N. K. Denzin & Y. S. Lincoln (Eds.), *The Sage handbook of qualitative research* (3rd ed., pp. 217–234). Thousand Oaks, CA: Sage.

Foucault, M. (1971). *The order of things: An archaeology of the human sciences.* New York: Pantheon Books.

Foucault, M. (1979). *Discipline and punish: The birth of the prison* (A. Sheridan, Trans.). New York: Vintage Books.

Foucault, M. (1980). *Power/knowledge: Selected interviews and other writings, 1972–1977* (C. Gordon, Ed.; C. Gordon, L. Marshall, J. Mepham, & K. Soper, Trans.). New York: Pantheon Books.

Fraser, N. (1990–1991). Rethinking the public sphere: A contribution to the critique of actually existing democracy. *Social Text, 25/26,* 178–182.

Frey, L. R. (2000). To be applied or not to be applied: That isn't even the question; but wherefore art thou, applied communication researcher? Reclaiming applied communication research and redefining the role of the researcher. *Journal of Applied Communication Research, 28,* 178–182.

Frey, L. R., Botan, C. H., & Kreps, G. L. (2000). *Investigating communication: An introduction to research methods* (2nd ed.). Needham Heights, MA: Allyn & Bacon.

Frey, L. R., O'Hair, D., & Kreps, G. L. (1990). Applied communication methodology. In D. O'Hair & G. L. Kreps (Eds.), *Applied communication theory and research* (pp. 23–56). Hillsdale, NJ: Erlbaum.

Gans, H. J. (1999). Participant observation in the era of "ethnography." *Journal of Contemporary Ethnography, 28,* 540–548.

Geertz, C. (1973). *The interpretation of cultures: Selected essays.* New York: Basic Books.

Gergen, K. J. (1994). *Realities and relationships: Soundings in social construction.* Cambridge, MA: Harvard University Press.

Gillespie, S. R. (2001). The politics of breathing: Asthmatic Medicaid patients under managed care. *Journal of Applied Communication Research, 29,* 97–116.

Glaser, B. G., & Strauss, A. L. (1967). *The discovery of grounded theory: Strategies for qualitative research.* Chicago: Aldine.

Goffman, E. (1959). *The presentation of self in everyday life.* Garden City, NY: Doubleday.

Gold, R. L. (1958). Roles in sociological field observations. *Social Forces, 36,* 217–223.

Goodall, H. L., Jr. (2004). Narrative ethnography as applied communication research. *Journal of Applied Communication Research, 32,* 185–194.

Goodwin, M. H. (2002). Building power asymmetries in girls' interaction. *Discourse & Society, 13,* 715–130.

Harding, S. (1991). *Whose science? Whose knowledge? Thinking from women's lives.* Ithaca, NY: Cornell University Press.

Harter, L. M., Berquist, C., Titsworth, B. S., Novak, D., & Brokaw, T. (2005). The structuring of invisibility among the hidden homeless: The politics of space, stigma, and identity construction. *Journal of Applied Communication, 33,* 305–327.

Harter, L. M., Scott, J. A., Novak, D. R., Leeman, M., & Morris, J. F. (2006). Freedom through flight: Performing a counter-narrative of disability. *Journal of Applied Communication, 34,* 3–29.

Howard, L. A., & Geist, P. (1995). Ideological positioning in organizational change: The dialectic of control in a merging organization. *Communication Monographs, 62,* 110–131.

Keyton, J. (2000). Applied communication research should be practical. *Journal of Applied Communication Research, 28,* 166–168.

Kramer, M. W. (2002). Communication in a community theater group: Managing multiple group roles. *Communication Studies, 53,* 151–170.

Lammers, J. C., & Krikorian, D. H. (1997). Theoretical extension and operationalization of the bona fide group construct with an application to surgical teams. *Journal of Applied Communication Research, 25,* 17–38.

Lengel, L. B. (1998). Researching the "other," transforming ourselves: Methodological considerations of feminist ethnography. *Journal of Communication Inquiry, 22,* 229–250.

Lesch, C. L. (1994). Observing theory in practice: Sustaining consciousness in a coven. In L. R. Frey (Ed.), *Group communication in context: Studies of natural groups* (pp. 57–82). Hillsdale, NJ: Erlbaum.

Lincoln, Y. S., & Guba, E. G. (1985). *Naturalistic inquiry.* Beverly Hills, CA: Sage.

Lindolf, T. R., & Taylor, B. C. (2002). *Qualitative communication research methods* (2nd ed.). Thousand Oaks, CA: Sage.

Madison, D. S. (2005). *Critical ethnography: Method, ethics, and performance.* Thousand Oaks, CA: Sage.

Martin, D. M. (2004). Humor in middle management women negotiating the paradoxes of organizational life. *Journal of Applied Communication Research, 32,* 147–170.

Meyer, M. (2004). From transgression to transformation: Negotiating the opportunities and tensions of engaged pedagogy in the feminist organizational communication classroom. In P. M. Buzzanell, H. Sterk, & L. H. Turner (Eds.), *Gender in applied communication contexts* (pp. 195–213). Thousand Oaks, CA: Sage.

Meyer, M., & O'Hara, L. S. (2004). When they know who we are: The National Women's Music Festival comes to Ball State University. In P. M. Buzzanell, H. Sterk, & L. H. Turner (Eds.), *Gender in applied communication contexts* (pp. 3–23). Thousand Oaks, CA: Sage.

Miller, M. (1995). An intergenerational case study of suicidal tradition and mother–daughter communication. *Journal of Applied Communication Research, 23,* 247–270.

Morgan, J. M., & Krone, K. J. (2001). Bending the rules of "professional" display: Emotional improvisation in caregiver performance. *Journal of Applied Communication Research, 29,* 317–340.

Morgan-Witte, J. M. (2005). Narrative knowledge development among caregivers: Stories from the nurse's station. In L. M. Harter, P. M. Japp, & C. S. Beck (Eds.), *Narratives, health, and healing: Communication theory, research, and practice* (pp. 217–236). Mahwah, NJ: Erlbaum.

Murphy, A. G. (2001). The fight attendant dilemma: An analysis of communication and sensemaking during in-flight emergencies. *Journal of Applied Communication Research, 29,* 30–53.

Novek, E. M. (1995). West Urbania: An ethnographic study of communication practices in inner-city youth culture. *Communication Studies, 46,* 169–186.

Owen, W. F. (1984). Interpretive themes in relational communication. *Quarterly Journal of Speech, 70,* 274–287.

Potter, W. J. (1996). *An analysis of thinking and research about qualitative methods.* Mahwah, NJ: Erlbaum.

Putnam, L. L., & Stohl, C. (1990). Bona fide groups: A reconceptualization of groups in context. *Communication Studies, 41,* 248–265.

Reinharz, S. (1992). *Feminist methods in social research.* New York: Oxford University Press.

Richardson, L. (2000). Writing: A method of inquiry. In N. K. Denzin & Y. S. Lincoln (Eds.), *Handbook of qualitative research* (2nd ed., pp. 923–943). Thousand Oaks, CA: Sage.

Ruud, G. (2000). The symphony: Organizational discourse and the symbolic tensions between artistic and business ideology. *Journal of Applied Communication Research, 28,* 117–143.

Saville-Troike, M. (1989). *The ethnography of communication: An introduction* (2nd ed.). New York: Basil Blackwell.

Scott, C., & Myers, K. K. (2005). The socialization of emotion: Learning emotion management at the fire station. *Journal of Applied Communication Research, 33,* 67–92.

Seibold, D. R. (2000). Applied communication scholarship: Less a matter of boundaries than of emphases. *Journal of Applied Communication Research, 28,* 183–187.

Sotirin, P., & Gottfried, H. (1999). The ambivalent dynamics of secretarial "bitching": Control, resistance, and the construction of identity. *Organization, 6,* 57–80.

Spivak, G. C. (1988). Can the subaltern speak? In C. Nelson & L. Grossberg (Eds.), *Marxism and the interpretation of culture* (pp. 271–313). Urbana: University of Illinois Press.

Thomas, J. (1993). *Doing critical ethnography*. Newbury Park, CA: Sage.

Tillman, L. M. (2009). Speaking into silences: Autoethnography, communication, and applied research. *Journal of Applied Communication Research, 37,* 94–97.

Tompkins, P. K. (1994). Principles of rigor for assessing evidence in "qualitative" communication research. *Western Journal of Communication, 58,* 44–50.

Tracy, K. (1995). Action-implicative discourse analysis. *Journal of Language and Social Psychology, 14,* 195–215.

Tracy, S. J. (2002). When questioning turns to face threat: An interactional sensitivity in 911 call-taking. *Western Journal of Communication, 66,* 129–157.

Tracy, S. J. (2004). Dialectic, contradiction, or double bind? Analyzing and theorizing employee reactions to organizational tension. *Journal of Applied Communication Research, 2,* 119–146.

Tracy, S. J., & Tracy, K. (1998). Emotion labor at 911: A case study and theoretical critique. *Journal of Applied Communication Research, 26,* 390–411.

Trujillo, N. (1992). Interpreting (the work and the talk of) baseball: Perspectives on ballpark culture. *Western Journal of Communication, 56,* 350–371.

underwood, e. d., & Frey, L. R. (2008). Communication and community: Clarifying the connection across the communication community. In C. S. Beck (Ed.), *Communication yearbook* (Vol. 31, pp. 370–418). New York: Erlbaum.

Van Maanen, J. (1979). The fact of fiction in organizational ethnography. *Administrative Science Quarterly, 24,* 535–550.

Van Maanen, J. (1988). *Tales of the field: On writing ethnography*. Chicago: University of Chicago Press.

Vidich, A. J., & Lyman, S. M. (2000). Qualitative methods: Their history in sociology and anthropology. In N. K. Denzin & Y. S. Lincoln (Eds.), *Handbook of qualitative research* (2nd ed., pp. 37–84). Thousand Oaks, CA: Sage.

Warren, J. T. (2001). Doing whiteness: On the performative dimensions of race in the classroom. *Communication Education, 50,* 91–108.

Whyte, W. F. (1943). *Street corner society: The social structure of an Italian slum*. Chicago: University of Chicago Press.

Wood, J. T. (2000). Applied communication research: Unbounded and for good reason. *Journal of Applied Communication Research, 28,* 188–191.

Wright, K. (1997). Shared ideology in Alcoholics Anonymous: A grounded theory approach. *Journal of Health Communication, 2,* 83–99.

Zoller, H. M. (2003). Health on the line: Identity and disciplinary control in employee occupational health and safety discourse. *Journal of Applied Communication Research, 31,* 118–139.

7 Discourse Analysis
The Practice and Practical Value of Taping, Transcribing, and Analyzing Talk

Karen Tracy
University of Colorado at Boulder

Julien C. Mirivel
University of Arkansas at Little Rock

Sacks (1992) noted that "from close looking at the world you can find things that we couldn't, by imagination, assert were there" (p. 420). Over the past 30 years, scholars in communication, sociology, linguistics, anthropology, education, and psychology have looked closely at communication between people as they interact. *Discourse analysis* (DA) is the umbrella term that has emerged for this multidisciplinary set of theoretical–methodological approaches. At its simplest, DA involves recording interaction; transcribing the tape; repeated study of the tape; formulating claims about the conversational moves, structures, and strategies demonstrated in the interaction; and then building an argument with transcript excerpts that are analyzed.

Many strands of DA could be considered applied communication research because they begin with problems of the social world. "Applied communication research," however, is not a label that discourse analysts use to describe their work. In the last decade, for instance, only a few DA studies (Pittam & Gallois, 2000; Sachweh, 1998; K. Tracy, 2007; K. Tracy & Ashcraft, 2001) have appeared in the *Journal of Applied Communication Research* (*JACR*).

In this chapter, we show why looking closely at talk and its surrounding context is a valuable method for communication scholars who want to conduct research that is practically implicative. We first describe DA, with particular attention to features that differentiate it from three methodological neighbors. We then reflect on various meanings of applied communication research to consider why DA research is applied, but why discourse analysts rarely think of their research that way. In the next section, we review DA studies in three applied sites: health contexts, workplace interaction, and community meetings. We conclude the chapter by describing how "focused reflection," the name we give to a modified DA research practice, could become a broadly useful training and teaching intervention.

The Character of Discourse Analysis

In 1985, the first handbook of discourse analysis appeared (van Dijk). If one looks at that volume, as well as subsequent texts devoted entirely to DA (Schiffrin, Tannen, & Hamilton, 2001; van Dijk, 1997a, 1997b; Wetherell, Taylor, & Yates, 2001) or where DA is an important component of a larger enterprise (Fitch & Sanders, 2005), it is not surprising that first-time visitors become confused about DA's identity, for there is incredible diversity in such work.

DA is a multidisciplinary endeavor that is performed differently across academic fields. In linguistics, for instance (e.g., Stubbs, 1983), the size of language units and the topical focus of analysis define the nature of DA work. Studying units of language larger than a single sentence or studying pragmatic uses of language rather than the syntactic, semantic, or phonological structures are key features that distinguish discourse analysts from other linguists. For linguists, the intellectual divide is between those who analyze discourse and those who focus on sentences. Schiffrin (1994), for instance, argued that DA is a topic and *not* a method. From this perspective, quantitative interaction coding studies, ethnographic observations of conversations, and analyses of textual data all count as DA. This is not the case in other fields.

In psychology, sociology, and communication—other social-scientific disciplines in which DA work is particularly visible—it is the interest in language phenomena generally, as well as the way these phenomena are studied, that distinguish discourse analysts from their disciplinary colleagues. Because few scholars in these disciplines focus on sentence-length or smaller units, the issue that animates linguistics is not relevant in these other fields. In traditional psychology, cognitive phenomena, often treated as internal and individual, are the focus of attention, but in discursive psychology, a strand of DA, the focus is on how cognitive matters are discursively realized. In addition, and quite important, discursive psychologists record small numbers of people talking with each other as they engage in activities in the world, rather than bringing large numbers of people into a laboratory where they are assigned particular tasks to perform (e.g., D. Edwards & Potter, 1992; Wood & Kroger, 2000).

In sociology, where the focus is on studying causes of social problems, questionnaires, quantitative coding, interviews, and participant observation are the traditional methods employed. Although discourse analysts in sociology do share the broad concern of their disciplinary colleagues, their preferred method for studying these same issues is markedly different (Silverman, 2004, 2006). To complicate matters, DA, in many quarters, is used as an umbrella term that subsumes conversation analysis (CA; e.g., Cameron, 2001; K. Tracy, 2001), a method of studying talk-in-interaction that emerged in sociology. In other quarters, however, DA is treated as a methodological option different from CA (see the essays in Fitch & Sanders, 2005). Such complexities surrounding the meaning of DA are an inevitable part of ideas and practices that are useful in diverse scholarly corners.

Given that many of the DA handbooks that have appeared in recent years are multidisciplinary, albeit tilted toward the discipline of the editor(s), it should be apparent why delimiting DA is not a straightforward task. Discussions of the complexities surrounding definition tied to the multidisciplinary footing of discourse studies can be found elsewhere (K. Tracy & Haspel, 2004). In this chapter, we focus on describing DA and contrasting it with three methodological neighbors in the communication field.[1]

In addition to confusion surrounding the term *discourse analysis*, another complexity deserves mention. Recently, "discourse" also has become a focal interest in organizational communication study (Fairhurst & Putnam, 2004; Grant, Hardy, Oswick, & Putnam, 2004; Putnam & Fairhurst, 2001), reflecting the discursive turn that has taken place in many disciplines. In this burgeoning area, DA has become the term used to describe the analyses that organizational scholars do. Sometimes the "discourse analysis" is straightforwardly an instance of DA as we describe it here (e.g., Castor, 2004; Cooren, 2003). At other times, however, it is not. That an analysis of discourse is not always a DA is the case because two meanings of the term *discourse* circulate among scholarly communities.

Discourse, as we use the term in this chapter, refers to actual instances of talk (or written texts). A second meaning for discourse, informed by Foucault (1972), refers to long-standing systems of ideas—what we think of as reigning ideologies, or complex social practices, as are cued by referring to the "discourses" of medicine or capitalism. This second meaning for discourse directs attention to the "powerful forces that reside beyond the text" (Fairhurst & Cooren, 2004, p. 132). Such analyses of discourse often are not interested in how language is used in social settings—the focus of the first meaning. Instead, Foucault-linked analyses of institutional discourse expose broad patterns of meaning—ways of thinking about the social world. Moreover, these studies employ a wide variety of interpretive methods, ones we think are more aptly labeled as, for instance, rhetorical criticism (e.g., Cheney, Christensen, Conrad, & Lair, 2004; Condit & Bates, this volume) or narrative analysis (Gabriel, 1998).

Conley and O'Barr (1998) distinguished these two meanings for discourse by labeling the first as "micro-discourse" and the second as "macro-discourse"; Gee (1999) called the two types "little d" and "big D" discourse. Some strands of DA link these two domains of discourse, as can be seen in critical discourse analyses (e.g., Fairclough, 2003; Fairclough & Wodak, 1997) that show how particulars of language use relate to taken-for-granted power structures and patterns. Other organizational studies address big-D discourse issues but give limited attention to language use in social settings (e.g., Ashcraft, 2005). In a handbook of organizational discourse, Alvesson (2004) argued that the term *discourse* has become a "catch-all," "covering too much and revealing too little" (p. 327). He suggested limiting the meaning of that term to studies of language use in social settings and excluding those studies that investigate ways of thinking about the social world and characterize broad social practices. We do not dispute the value of analyzing macro- or big-D discourses but unless a study analyzes segments of talk or written texts to explicate language use in social settings, we are not treating it as using *the method* of DA.

The Basics of Discourse Analysis

DA in the communication discipline involves four main activities. The first activity is to audio- or videotape human interaction, which might occur on the telephone (e.g., Beach, 2001), radio (e.g., Katriel, 2004), or television (e.g., Clayman, 1995); in a business meeting (e.g., Mirivel & Tracy, 2005), classroom (e.g., Craig & Sanusi, 1999), or support group (Hsieh, 2004); or among family and friends at home (e.g., Blum-Kulka, 1997). Typically, the interaction that is taped occurs naturally in a social or institutional site. By *naturally occurring*, we mean that it has not been brought into existence through the efforts of a researcher, as is the case with interviews. Whether discourse analysts should study only naturally occurring interaction is, in fact, controversial (e.g., Speer, 2002; ten Have, 2002). Suffice it to say that discourse analysts who study researcher-generated interviews (e.g., Pittam & Gallois, 2000; Wooffitt, 1992) ask different questions of the interview materials, analyze them differently, and, in the writing-up process, orient to the possibility that their selection of materials might be challenged by other discourse analysts.

The second activity in DA is to make a transcript of selected segments of the taped interaction. Creating a transcript is fundamental to doing DA and, consequently, a large number of transcription systems have been developed (J. A. Edwards & Lampert, 1993). However, by and large, communication researchers draw on the Jeffersonian transcription system that was developed in CA. This transcription notation represents words as they were pronounced (e.g., gonna and yep), includes hearable nonspeech sounds (e.g., uh and mhm), and captures repetition and restarts (I wa- we wanted to say). The system also uses symbols to capture features of vocal quality, such as loud and quiet speech, breathiness, laughed speech, stressing or prolonging of a syllable, and pause placement and length. Finally, CA transcription attends to utterance timing in that the exact places where speakers overlapped or spoke simultaneously are represented. Table 7.1 provides an overview of key transcription symbols (for more detailed explanations of these symbols, see Atkinson & Heritage, 1999; Hutchby & Wooffitt, 1998; ten Have, 1999).

Table 7.1 The Basic Conversation Analysis Transcription Symbols

.	(period) Falling intonation
?	(question mark) Rising intonation
,	(comma) Continuing intonation
-	(hyphen) Marks an abrupt cutoff
::	(colon[s]) Prolonging of sound
ne<u>ver</u>	(underlining) Stressed syllable or word
WORD	(all caps) Loud speech
°word°	(degree symbols) Quiet speech
>word<	(more than & less than) Quicker speech
<word>	(less than & more than) Slowed speech
hh	(series of hs) Aspiration or laughter
.hh	(hs preceded by dot) Inhalation
[ ]	(brackets) Simultaneous or overlapping speech
=	(equals sign) Contiguous utterances
(2.4)	(number in parentheses) Length of a silence
(.)	(period in parentheses) Micro-pause, 2/10 second or less
( )	(empty parentheses) Non-transcribable segment of talk
(word)	(word or phrase in parentheses) Transcriptionist doubt
((gazing toward the ceiling))	(double parentheses) Description of non-speech activity

Although DA research is an interpretive rather than a positivistic enterprise, it regards accuracy of representing the communicative world that is to be analyzed as an important first step. In comparing transcripts from four experienced CA transcribers, Roberts and Robinson (2004) found high reliability for many features (e.g., semantics, overlap, and sound stretch) and a reasonably high level for constructed indices, such as is accomplished by treating speech emphasis as a matter of increasing loudness, stressing a sound, or prolonging a syllable.

Although most communication scholars use some version of the Jeffersonian system, it is common to see markedly simplified versions of the system in use. K. Tracy (2005), for instance, gave limited attention to prosody and utterance timing, defending her decisions by arguing for (1) the value of focusing on features of talk that people can reflect about and change, and (2) the advantage of looking at larger stretches of interaction less precisely rather than at smaller segments transcribed in more detail. Clearly, choices about what to include in transcribing are theoretical decisions (Ochs, 1979). One cannot capture everything that goes on; hence, what to include in a transcript is a choice guided by a researcher's aims and assumptions.

Whereas some discourse analysts use a simplified CA transcription system, others use an enhanced version. A strand of DA work, often referred to as *microethnography* (Streeck & Mehus, 2005), studies social meanings and practices in interactive sites in which talk interfaces with visible activities such as gaze, gestures, and features of the material surround. DA scholars in this tradition have developed innovative ways to transcribe these additional features that affect interaction (e.g., Bavelas, Coats, & Johnson, 2002; Beach, 2002; LeBaron & Jones, 2002).

A third activity in DA research, often referred to as having a "data session," is for a small group of people to repeatedly listen to or view a tape of an interaction accompanied by a transcript, which is followed by group analysis. The discussion that occurs during a data session is diverse and partly dependent on the intellectual traditions out of which the members come. If most group members are conversation analysts, a commitment to keeping analysis focused on what participants themselves are orienting to (Schegloff, 1997) is likely. If, however, a data session includes scholars more steeped in critical, rhetorical, or ethnographically linked discourse traditions, the discussion is likely to be more free-wheeling (i.e., open to reflections, reactions, and interpretive insights). A shared belief across the many strands of DA is that data sessions help participants to become skilled analysts. By repeatedly looking/listening and then trying out arguments on equally obser-vant others, scholars can construct more insightful and persuasive analyses of discourse strategies, conversational structures, or communicative practices.

What types of contextual information should be brought to analyses of talk is a con-tested issue among discourse analysts. Anchoring one side of the controversy is the posi-tion that analyses should not go beyond what participants in their talk are orienting to. Other DA scholars regard it as legitimate to bring contextual information to analy-ses, including participants' membership categories (e.g., institutional roles), information gained from institutional documents or interviews with participants who possess relevant experiences or expertise, and historical or ethnographic knowledge of the interactional site. Entire books (Duranti & Goodwin, 1992), special journal issues (K. Tracy, 1998), and extended colloquia (Billig, 1999a, 1999b; Schegloff, 1998, 1999a, 1999b; Wetherell, 1998) have addressed this debate.

The final activity in DA work is to develop a scholarly argument. In this last stage, subtle observations and analytic points, some of which emerged in data sessions, are brought into a larger frame. Reflecting on what has been observed in the discourse, in light of relevant literatures, a claim is developed. Writing also is a crucial part of doing DA. Analysis and writing are soul mates; one does DA through writing up an analysis of excerpts of discourse.

How Discourse Analysis Differs From Methodological Neighbors

DA is best understood by contrasting it with the methods with which it has the most in common. DA's closest methodological neighbors are (1) ethnographic methods (see Ellingson, this volume); (2) rhetorical criticism (see Condit & Bates, this volume), and (3) quantitative coding of interaction (see Query et al., this volume).

As a term, *ethnographic methods*, also frequently labeled "qualitative" or "fieldwork methods," references a range of approaches that draw on participant observation, inter-views, and analysis of written documents. Included among ethnographic approaches are traditional ethnographies that study distinct speech communities, as seen, for instance, in Fitch's (1998, 1999) studies of middle-class Colombians and Carbaugh's (1996) studies of Blackfeet Indians and middle-class Americans (for a review of ethnography of commu-nication, see Philipsen & Coutu, 2005). Also included are organizational ethnographies that unpack features of communication in workplaces, such as agrarian cooperative coun-cils (Harter, 2004) and automobile manufacturing (Zoller, 2003), or that examine issues important to the conduct of work, such as emotion labor (S. J. Tracy, 2004). Another strand of ethnographic methods is studies using in-depth interviews, in which a purpo-sive sample of a category of people are interviewed, as seen in Baxter, Hirokawa, Lowe, Nathan, and Pearce's (2004) interviews with women about drinking and pregnancy, or Braithwaite and Eckstein's (2003) interviews with persons with disabilities about how they manage and respond to offers of help.

Like ethnographic methods, DA begins in the everyday world of participants. How-ever, how the two families of methods differ is a complex question, because the differences between DA and ethnographic methods depend on which theoretical–methodological option is selected as a comparison point. Among ethnographers of communication, for instance, in addition to participant observation and informant interviews, the analysis of recorded discourse has become an equally important way to study culture. What distinguishes discourse analysts from ethnographers of communication is the research focus. DA seeks to understand problems in discursive practices and to explicate interaction structures and strategies, whereas ethnographers of communication study how communicative practices operate within cultural systems. Just as ethnographers of communication increasingly use discourse methods, so too are some discourse analysts using ethnographic methods. Holmes and Stubbe's (2003) study of politeness practices in workplaces and K. Tracy's (1997) analysis of academic colloquia are two examples of DA studies that use participant observation and in-depth interviews as supplemental methods.

Differences between organizational ethnographies and DA studies are nicely displayed in two studies of the same emergency communication center. In the organizational ethnography by S. J. Tracy and Tracy (1998), the research focus was on the types of emotional labor practices that 911 call-takers used; field notes taken during participant observation and interviews were the key data. In the DA study by K. Tracy and Tracy (1998), the focus was on understanding moments of face attack in 911 telephone calls. For this study, two transcribed calls that included raised voices and anger cues were the main focus, and the analysis described how citizens and 911 call-takers were rude and attacked each other's face. Thus, DA studies of institutional talk and organizational ethnographies differ in terms of the theoretical literatures on which they typically draw, their likely research questions, and whether field notes or transcribed talk are the primary data.

Discourse analysts also study interviews that occur in a range of institutions, such as focus groups run by market researchers (Puchta & Potter, 2004), medical interviews (Robinson, 1998, 2003), or job interviews (Scheuer, 2001). When DA scholars study interviews, though, the objective is to explain what interviewers and interviewees are doing through their talk. As such, discourse analysts differ as to whether they see *research interviews* as reasonable sources of informant data, and for important reasons, approach interview data with caution.

A first reason to be cautious is skepticism that what interviewees say in response to a direct question actually mirrors what they believe or do. People do not necessarily know how they actually communicate, and, if they do know, there are self-presentational reasons why they might say something different than what observation of their actions reveals. Second, interviews are communicative events whose unfolding is shaped by the conversational procedures that affect all instances of talk, with answers to questions taking their meaning from the larger conversational context. The upshot of these points is that interviews cannot be thought of as straightforward events in which participants simply convey "information" about their experiences and worlds. Third, and related, there is a strong sense that the meaning of an answer is deeply dependent on how an interview question was formulated and what other talk preceded it. The common writing practice of taking respondents' comments out of their interview question context is seen as insensitive to this connection.

Discourse analysts who use research interviews as a source of data agree with their DA colleagues that these are problems that must be given attention and monitored in any study. They disagree, however, that the problems warrant avoiding interview data entirely. There are communicative issues that occur so rarely or are so sensitive that they can be learned about only from informants. In addition, how people talk about an event to an interviewer can be a topic of interest in its own right. As long as analysts keep in mind that what they have in research interviews is a product of the joint conversation and is "talk about X" rather than "X" itself, they can build persuasive and interesting analyses, as seen in recent DA studies, such as Buttny's (2004) study of race talk, Condor's

(2000) analysis of how British speakers display themselves as not being prejudiced when talking about Britain, and Weltman's (2003) study of politicians' justifications for getting into their particular political party.

A second methodological neighbor of DA is rhetorical criticism. DA shares with rhetorical criticism a focus on and fascination with language and particulars of texts. Both methods study texts in the complexities of the contexts in which they occur, but they differ on three grounds. First, DA grew within the social-scientific tradition of the field and looks to sociology, linguistics, anthropology, and psychology as its cognate disciplines; in contrast, rhetorical criticism is grounded in the humanistic tradition and takes philosophy, political theory, and literary studies as cognate disciplines (K. Tracy, 2007b). Second, rhetorical criticism typically focuses on culturally significant texts (e.g., speeches by political figures), whereas DA focuses on mundane institutional and intimate talk. Clearly, this difference is not absolute (e.g., Hauser, 1998, 1999). Third, DA scholars in communication largely study interaction that requires taping and transcribing rather than focusing on written texts (e.g., letters to the editor) or oral ones available in public written transcripts, often without their oral base (e.g., the performed speech or a tape of the meeting). The subtle differences between these two neighboring methods are visible in an edited volume that analyzes 14 speeches of a contentious school board meeting as its focus (K. Tracy, McDaniel, & Gronbeck, 2007).

The third methodological neighbor of DA is quantitative coding of interaction (interaction analysis). Although DA and interaction analysis previously were methodological competitors, they now are finding some common ground. Prior to the 1990s, studies using Bales's (1950) interaction process analysis system or Rogers and Farace's (1975) relational coding system, for instance, applied the theoretically developed codes to segments of interaction and then reported the distribution of categories. DA does not begin with theoretical categories but, instead, works inductively, studying talk in particular situations to identify what are the socially meaningful units. If one sees DA as the first step, and interaction analysis as a valuable, but not mandatory, second step, the two methods function as friends.

Clayman and Heritage (2002), for instance, studied the question-and-answer exchanges in a small set of press conferences held by U.S. presidents Dwight Eisenhower and Ronald Reagan. Using DA, they identified which discourse features contributed to questions being adversarial or deferential. Then, using their feature analysis, which they developed inductively through close study of the exchanges, they formulated question categories and applied them to a sample of the press conferences. By coding and counting the different forms of questions, after showing the reliability of the categories, Clayman and Heritage evidenced that across time, presidential press conferences in the United States have become markedly less deferential. DA and interaction analysis, then, are easily distinguishable methods, but they can be complementary companions. DA enables researchers to identify interactional differences that make a difference; interaction analysis enables researchers to assess whether a pattern exists in important categories of talk. Studies that pair DA with interaction analysis, either within a single study or across several studies, have become especially prevalent in health-care contexts (e.g., Robinson & Nussbaum, 2004; Stivers, Mangione-Smith, Elliott, McDonald, & Heritage, 2003).

Why Discourse Analysis Is and Is Not Applied

A trademark of DA scholarship is researchers' direct involvement in sites of social interaction. Like ethnographers, discourse analysts move outside the walls of academic institutions, carrying audio- or video-recorders to interactional sites of interest and recording "live" pieces of the world that make up participants' social and institutional lives. In considering practices such as police interrogations (e.g., LeBaron & Streeck, 1997), HIV counseling sessions (e.g., Silverman, 1997), group meetings in organizations (e.g., Boden, 1994; K. Tracy & Naughton, 2000), therapy sessions (e.g., Duff Wrobbel, 2003), medical education (Koschmann & LeBaron, 2002; Pomerantz, 2003), or cosmetic surgery encounters (Mirivel, 2008), discourse analysts display a collective engagement in what, by any definition, are applied communication issues.

Defining applied communication research, and calling for more of it, has been a frequent activity during the last 15 years. The first issue of *JACR* that appeared under the aegis of the National Communication Association (NCA) articulated an agenda for such research (Eadie, 1991), with additional proposals coming later (Cissna, 1995; Frey, 1998; O'Hair, 2000). Admittedly, applied communication research is an enterprise that stretches well beyond the boundaries of *JACR*, as this handbook illustrates, but given difficulties in locating exact boundaries, *JACR* provides a reasonable sample of studies warranting the label "applied communication research." Using *JACR* as a touchstone, then, three frames for conceptualizing this type of research are apparent: applied communication research (1) seeks to understand problems of the social world, (2) links to the community of applied communication researchers, or (3) commits to directly solving problems. DA research, as explained below, fits the first frame, but has only a small overlap with the other two frames.

Frame 1: Understanding Problems of the Social World

As a field, communication is a practical discipline, with research connected to the activities and problems of the everyday world (e.g., Craig, 1989; Keyton, 2000; G. R. Miller, 1995; Seibold, 2000). However, even if most communication research has a practical component, there is variation in how developed the practical piece of any communication study actually will be. Craig (1995) suggested that communication research is best conceptualized on a continuum, anchored on one end by studies that begin with the world and its problems (the applied end) and, on the other, by studies that focus on disciplinary puzzles. Most actual studies are hybrids, attending to both theory and practice (Seibold, 1995) and pursuing some degree of rigor and relevance (Conquergood, 1995). As Craig (1995) put it, "Applied and disciplinary research differ, then, not dichotomously, but along a continuum" (p. 152; see also Frey & SunWolf, this volume).

DA research begins in the social world. In taping, transcribing, and analyzing moments of interaction that involve people doing things that matter to them, it is applied in its basic impulse. In seeking to understand how meanings are made and how practical actions and activities are accomplished in actual communicative sites, DA studies may focus on what makes interactions go smoothly or how they go awry. Studies of problematic interactional sites have focused on better understanding the tensions and sensitivities in communicative activities such as advising college students (Erickson & Shultz, 1982), counseling new parents (Heritage & Sefi, 1992), training therapists (Morris & Chenail, 1995), or talking to distressed citizens in 911 calls (K. Tracy & Agne, 2002; Whalen & Zimmerman, 2005). When applied communication research is conceptualized as beginning with problems in the world, DA research is very much "applied."

Frame 2: Linking to the Applied Communication Research Community

A second way to conceptualize applied communication research is to think of it as a particular community of scholars, asking such questions as, "What topics of research are the foci of studies published in *JACR*?" and "What theoretical concepts and literatures are most visible?" The range of *JACR* articles is diverse, but there are certain literatures and research traditions that dominate the journal's pages. Organizational communication research is one of those traditions. Beginning with the articles in the early 1990s that linked applied work to organizational consulting (e.g., March, 1991; Plax, 1991; see also Frey & SunWolf, this volume) to the more recent feminist–critical studies (e.g., Harter, 2004; Martin, 2004; see also Buzzanell, Meisenbach, Remke, Sterk, & Turner, this volume), articles that draw on organizational communication theories to study various sites have been a mainstay (see Eisenberg & Eschenfelder, this volume; Seibold, Lemus, Ballard, & Myers, this volume). Similarly, issues about college-level teaching have been a long-standing concern (e.g., Barge & Loges, 2003; see Darling & Leckie, this volume), as have been questions related to health settings (e.g., Morgan & Miller, 2002; see also Kreps & Bonagura, this volume; K. Miller & Considine, this volume). As we show in the next section, DA researchers have attended to some of the topical areas that are the foci of applied communication research, but they only occasionally orient to the community of applied communication researchers.

By and large, DA research appears in other communication journals (e.g., *Journal of Communication*), multidisciplinary journals committed to DA research (e.g., *Research on Language and Social Interaction*), or journals focused on settings whose scope is broader than communication, such as those that address scholars and practitioners in health-care (e.g., *Social Science & Medicine* and *Family Practice*) or organizational contexts (e.g., *Management Communication Quarterly*). To the degree that applied communication research refers to a community of scholars who orient to each other's scholarly claims and the journal that bears its name, DA is not a method often used by the applied communication research community.

Frame 3: Focusing on Practical Applications

A final way that applied communication research is conceptualized is as research that has practical applications. *JACR*'s editorial policy, for instance, requires all manuscripts to "include a separate section detailing the intended or potential practical applications of findings, critique, or commentary" (Stafford, 2009, n.p.). Although DA research frequently has practical implications (see below), discourse analysts are reluctant to spell out applications directly. In large measure, their reluctance to detail practical applications is grounded in the DA stance toward the world. Discourse analysts see suitable actions as deeply dependent on particulars of prior talk and the interactional context in which discursive action is performed. As a research genre, studies that offer practical applications may gloss scene and talk particulars, treating identification of the occasions in which specific suggestions are to be applied as a small issue. For discourse analysts, making the types of generalizing moves that most application requires, therefore, is problematic.

Although giving advice and detailing practical applications are activities to which there is resistance, much DA research is practically useful. In providing a grounded, detailed understanding of a situation or problematic scene, DA work is helpful. By describing communicative practices and their observed interactional and relational consequences, as well as noticing, naming, and linking actions that go unnoticed in socially important situations, DA research enables professionals and other situation participants to develop strategies for responding to complex problems. In addition, *critical discourse analysis*, a strand of DA to which the journal *Discourse & Society* is devoted, explores how language and discourse processes normalize inequality and perpetuate injustices of many types. In exposing how communicative practices that claim fairness and neutrality actually privilege particular parties, critical discourse analysis lays the groundwork for social change. However, because offering practical application sits uneasily with a view that communication is situated action, DA research rarely makes explicit behavioral suggestions. Yet, in enabling participants to reflect more wisely about situations they face, DA research inherently is useful. Consider three research areas in which this claim is particularly true.

Examples of Practically Useful Discourse-Analytic Research

Health Settings

DA research about physician–patient communication has thrived since the early 1980s (e.g., Atkinson & Heath, 1981; Fisher & Todd, 1983; Heath, 1986; West, 1984; for reviews of this work, see Beck et al., 2004; Maynard, 2003). Here, we highlight two lines of DA research that focus on communicative problems in the health-care context.

A first example is Stiver's (2002, 2005a, 2005b) analyses of pediatric encounters during acute-care visits. A problem that has been documented in several studies (Mangione-Smith, Stivers, Elliott, McDonald, & Heritage, 2003; Stivers et al., 2003) is that children are prescribed antibiotics that they do not need. This practice is not inconsequential, as across time, overprescribing leads to antibiotic treatments becoming less effective. In conjunction, studies have shown "a strong association between physicians' perceptions of patient–parent pressure for antibiotic treatment and inappropriate prescribing of antibiotics" (Stivers, 2002, p. 200). By looking closely at how parents present their child's medical problems to physicians, Stivers discovered two conversational methods that parents use, which she labeled as "symptoms only" and "candidate diagnosis." In the first approach, parents (usually mothers) present symptoms of the medical problems by describing what their child is experiencing. In the second approach, parents both provide a description of the symptoms and formulate a diagnosis. Excerpts 1 and 2 (which have been simplified) illustrate each of these approaches, respectively.

Excerpt 1: "Symptoms-Only" (Stivers, 2002, p. 305)

```
 1 DOC:    And so do- what's been bothering her
 2          (0.4)
 3 MOM:    uhm she's had a cough and stuffing- stuffy nose,
 4          and then yesterday in the afternoon she started to get
 5          really goopy eye[s and every=
 6 DOC:                    [Mm hm,
 7 MOM:    =few minutes [she was [(having the)
 8 DOC:                 [.hh      [Okay so she ha- so then when
 9          she woke [up this morning were her eyes =
10 MOM:             [(      )
11 DOC:    =all stuck shut,
```

Excerpt 2: "Symptoms + Candidate Diagnosis" (Stivers, 2002b, p. 309)

```
 1 DOC:    .hh so how long has she been sick
 2          (1.2)
 3 MOM:    just (.) I came down with it last Wednesday, so she
 4          probably had it (0.2)
 5 DOC:    uh huh
```

```
 6  MOM:    (like) over- four days
 7           (1.0)
 8  MOM:    and she's been complaining of headaches.
 9           (.)
10  MOM:    so I was thinking she had like uh sinus in[fection=
11  DOC:                                              [.hhh
12  MOM:    =or something.=
```

The subtle differences in the ways that the mothers initially present and formulate their child's medical problem in these two excerpts have consequences. The first conversational method forecasts an interactional project (Robinson, 2003) that "allows" physicians first to diagnose patients and subsequently to provide a medical recommendation that fits the evidence gathered through a physical examination. The second conversational method, one that occurs more frequently in situations in which physicians report "feeling pressured," requires physicians to respond to parents' proposed diagnoses, either confirming or disconfirming them. When parents do not mitigate their candidate diagnosis, physicians feel pressured to prescribe antibiotics. Clearly, physicians do not necessarily succumb to discursive pressure but this way of formulating a child's problem does increase the likelihood that they will prescribe antibiotics.

Stivers's (2002) work, which offered a more detailed analysis than is possible here, exemplifies how fine-grained discourse differences contribute to understanding a problem that is important to medical professionals. In fact, her analyses have found interest beyond communication and discourse scholars; she and her colleagues have published in a variety of medical journals (e.g., *Journal of Family Practice* and *Pediatrics*), and her work has been featured and made publicly available to the medical community in the form of Web sites, such as on those for the Rand Child Policy Project and the Agency for Healthcare Research and Quality.[2]

A second example of DA research that addresses applied objectives is Maynard's (1991, 1992, 1997, 2003) work on how physicians deliver bad news to their patients. For medical professionals, delivering bad news to patients clearly is a challenge (Platt, 1995); telling parents that their child is "retarded" or revealing to a patient that he or she is HIV positive are emotionally charged moments for recipients and uncomfortable ones for health-care providers. By investigating how bad news is conveyed in naturally occurring interaction, Maynard (2003) exposed how those interactions are structurally and sequentially organized, leading him to propose how medical practitioners might deliver such news to patients more effectively.

In the final chapter of his book, for instance, Maynard (2003) spoke to the issue of how physicians should disclose bad news. In line with a DA position, Maynard asked professionals to "pay attention to the particularities of interaction when engaged in delivering news" (p. 247). Because physicians may see "bad news delivery" as routine institutional work, Maynard asked practitioners to keep in mind that receiving such news is "a crisis for recipients" (p. 247). Maynard (2003, pp. 247–248) noted that "there is no sure-fire method of delivery for the professional that guarantees 'success' across the board" but that physicians can prepare for delivering bad news by reflecting about what it means for a moment to be a crisis *for* the recipient. Reflecting about the meaning of the situation from the recipient's perspective, he suggested, leads professionals to *adequately* prepare themselves and the environment in which the news is to be delivered, interactionally *forecast* the bad news through audible and visible cues (which he detailed in his book), and *elicit the patient's perspective* prior to engaging in a bad news delivery sequence.

In addition to these examples, many other health-linked problems have been the focus of DA research. To mention a few, DA scholars have examined how: (1) medical professionals give advice to laypersons about mothering (Heritage & Lindström, 1998) or assist clients in initiating safer sex practices with long-term romantic partners (Mattson & Roberts, 2001), (2) risks and uncertainties are addressed in genetic counseling (Candlin & Candlin, 2002), (3) interviewing skills are taught to novice dieticians (Tapsell, 2000), (4) family members manage a mother's malignant cancer (Beach 2001, 2002), and (5) preceptors both educate medical students and keep their identities intact in front of patients (Pomerantz, 2003; Pomerantz, Fehr, & Ende, 1997).

Workplace Interaction

Discourse analysts also have studied interaction in a variety of institutional settings, including archaeological excavations (Goodwin, 2000), police and Federal Bureau of Investigation (FBI) interrogations (Agne, 2003; Agne & Tracy, 2001; Komter, 2003), phone conversations between citizens and emergency call takers (e.g., Baker, Emmison, & Firth, 2005; K. Tracy & Andersen, 1999), and in airline traffic telecommunication control centers (Hindmarsh & Heath, 2000). Medical, justice, and educational institutions have been the mainstay sites for DA research, but interaction in business and government settings increasingly is garnering attention (e.g., Clark, Drew, & Pinch, 2003; Milburn, Kenefick, & Lambert, 2006; Sarangi & Roberts, 1999). Until very recently, DA studies of institutional interaction operated as a tradition relatively distinct from most research on organizational communication, but in the last few years, this divide is crumbling (Fairhurst & Putnam, 2004; Putnam & Fairhurst, 2001). As noted earlier, not all studies of organizational discourse use DA, but some do (for two more examples, see Anderson, 2004; Cooren, 2006).

One especially impressive study of *workplace interaction*—the term we use for the study of business talk—is the Wellington Language in the Workplace Project. Working from 2,000+ hours of audiotaped interactions of 400+ participants (e.g., managers and workers with disabilities) in different New Zealand workplaces (e.g., factories, large corporations, and small businesses), Holmes and her colleagues (Holmes, 2003; Holmes, Marra, & Burns, 2001; Holmes & Stubbe, 2003; Holmes, Stubbe, & Vine, 1999) have sought to "identify characteristics of effective communication...causes of miscommunication, and to disseminate the results of the analysis to the benefit of workplace practitioners" (Holmes & Stubbe, 2003, p. 12). How professionals manage their working relationships in fleeting conversational moments, they argued, is crucial to workplace effectiveness. "Small-talk" conversations, for instance, are a major way that coworkers negotiate organizational status, enact collegiality, and create solidarity. In such conversations, politeness strategies and the use of humor (Holmes, 2000), often treated as trivial talk, make a difference. Take the following excerpt as an illustration:

Excerpt 3: Small Talk (Holmes, 2003, p. 67)

Context: Small talk between three workers in a plant nursery at the start of the day.

Des is the manager. Tom is a worker with an intellectual disability. Ros is the plant nursery worker who works alongside Tom. (All names are pseudonyms.)

```
1 Des:    Be a nice day when it all warms up a bit though
2 Ros:    Yeah (2.4) okay
3 Des:    So you haven't done anything all week (1.7) eh you
```

4		haven't done anything exciting (2.6) talk to any girls
5	Tom:	No
6	Des:	Oh that's all right then
7	Ros:	((laughs))
8	Des:	You don't want to talk to girls they're more they're
9		trouble Tom (1.2) they get you into trouble (1.6) look
10		at me (2.7) I would have been rich and good looking if I
11		hadn't had girls now I'm just good looking (1.6) see ya
12		Tom
13	Tom:	((no response))

Of note in this excerpt is Tom's lack of conversational participation in moments that call on him to join in. Des "does" small talk by inviting conversation about the weather (Drew & Chilton, 2000) and inquiring about Tom's life outside of the workplace in a fashion that implicates a shared laugh. Tom, however, fails to respond to Des's inquiries; he does not react to Des's inquiries in lines 3 to 4 and provides a minimal response in line 5. Conversational engagement, we could say, is noticeably absent. By not chit-chatting and joking with his coworkers, Tom contributes to a working environment that lacks relational connections. As Greespan and Shoultz (1981) noted, "It is an inability to interact effectively with other people, rather than an inability to operate machines or perform job tasks that often causes many mentally retarded adults to get fired from competitive jobs" (p. 23).

The analyses of conversations in the workplace by Holmes and colleagues suggest that workers with intellectual disabilities benefit from education to "acquire basic socio-linguistic and pragmatic skills as preparation for genuine workplace interaction" (Holmes, 2003, p. 79). Besides drawing out implications for workers who are disabled, scholars in the Language in the Workplace Project have applied their insights to the professionals they study. For instance, they have held regular feedback sessions in the organizations they studied, playing segments of interaction to employees and managers, and framing for participants what they noticed. In contrast to teaching prepackaged courses, the most common training procedure (Holmes & Stubbe, 2003, p. 173), these DA researchers cultivate communication praxis by developing professionals' "observational and analytical skills" and offering them a discursive space to reflect about the complexities of communicative action (Jones & Stubbe, 2004).

Community Governance Meetings

Our final example of DA research that pursues applied ends are the community-level studies by K. Tracy and colleagues that focus on interaction problems at school board meetings. Using *action-implicative discourse analysis* (K. Tracy, 1995, 2005), a DA method informed by grounded practical theory (see Barge & Craig, this volume; Craig & Tracy, 1995), K. Tracy and colleagues seek to identify the communication problems that different categories of participants face (i.e., elected officials, citizens in the community, teachers, and other staff), conversational moves that reveal those problems, discursive strategies that participants use to manage them,[3] and the situated ideals of good conduct that frame evaluation of communicative action in these settings.

Problems examined in this body of work include: (1) naming of communicative troubles that are experienced in meetings and how different names point blame (and the need for change) toward particular parties (K. Tracy & Muller, 2001), (2) advantages and disadvantages for citizens in framing the concern they bring to public participation in board meetings as "an issue" versus "a problem" (Craig & Tracy, 2005), (3) taking a position about appropriate ways to talk about race and communicative conduct (Haspel & Tracy, 2007), and (4) institutional stances toward gays and lesbians (K. Tracy & Ashcraft, 2001). Other studies have examined the conversational strategies that board members use to influence the group when they are in a minority position (K. Tracy & Standerfer, 2003), partially deflect (and partially accept) criticism when a serious crisis has arisen (K. Tracy, 2007), or to criticize other members' communicative conduct and minimize the likelihood that they will be countercharged with the same type of communicative impropriety (K. Tracy, 1999). Because the significance of DA studies is found in the particulars, we conclude this section by illustrating one of these analyses.

Participants in school board meetings and other community groups frequently treat "democracy" as a communicative ideal whose meaning is transparent to all. Sometimes explicitly, but often implicitly, democracy is invoked to critique other participants' actions. In a study of three conflict-rich public meetings, K. Tracy and Craig (2005) showed how democracy and communication terms were linked to criticize others and defend the self. The analysis of the various uses of these terms made visible three sets of contrary beliefs that reveal an ideological complexity that is characteristic of school board meetings.

A first set of contrary beliefs concerned the role of elected officials: Were they responsible for representing their constituency or expected to exercise their judgment? These contrary definitions, recognized in democratic theorizing (Schudson, 1998), regularly surfaced in criticisms directed toward officials. A second set of contrary beliefs concerned unitary and adversary notions of democracy (Mansbridge, 1980), with school board meetings talked about as both a place where a community of people sharing a common interest work together to solve problems and bring about their vision (a unitary view), and, often in the same meeting, as a site of competing interests where people should advocate passionately for what they believe and a vote should determine the outcome (the adversary view). The third set of contrary beliefs revolved around how to think about rules in democratically committed groups. In meeting talk, rules and procedures were treated both as agreed-on social arrangements that facilitated fairness and as instruments that blocked justice. Excerpt 4, a comment from a board member holding a minority position, illustrates the first function; Excerpt 5 illustrates the second function.

Excerpt 4: Board Member (Kingdom) in Minority Position, 8/8/96–Line 725

As of this week, I was really uh extremely discouraged that our hiring processes have once again been compromised, uh instead of processes where we've had a committee set up and we've had a procedure that we can all count on I feel like we have not followed those. There's been examples in intimidation, there's been board interference, we've undermined our hiring processes, and we've had individuals then consequently who are afraid of losing their job if they don't comply with the dictates of this board. As a board member it's my responsibility to share this concern with the public. Our fair and democratic processes, I feel are being compromised by certain individuals. Our 25,000 students in this- in this district will suffer because we haven't hired the most qualified and best candidates for jobs. If a candidate does not make it as a finalist that person needs to ask was it a fair and respectful process?

Excerpt 5: Board Member Shoemaker Statement, 12/12/96 Minutes

School board members pledge not to reveal any information presented or discussed in executive session, under penalty of censure.... My decision to reveal this information is a most difficult one, but I believe that my highest duty as an elected official is to tell the citizens of this community the truth to which they are entitled. Believing that the actions taken at the executive session were unethical and in violation of BVSD policy, I cannot in good faith adhere to the confidentiality rules in this particular case.

Whereas the first statement aligns democracy with following rules and its failure with a variety of negatively weighted communicative actions (e.g., "intimidation," "interference," "undermining of decisions," and "lack of fair and respectful process"), the second statement positions rule violation, at least "in this particular case," as related to the "highest duty" of an elected official to tell the truth at moments of "unethical" action. These contradictory beliefs about democracy, K. Tracy and Craig (2005) argued, evidence the need to reframe the meaning of inconsistency in ideals. Rather than treating competing beliefs about democracy as choice points for theoretical reflection—having to be one or the other—contradictory themes about democracy are conceptualized as resources—argumentative tools for difficult deliberative moments. There are, then, two truths about democracy and rules: Rules matter because they are essential to democratic action, yet, at times, rules get in the way of what democracy seeks to promote. Citizens' comments recognize these competing truths, seeking to persuade others in their community group which diagnosis is warranted in that particular moment.

To summarize, in community meetings, workplace conversations, and medical encounters, DA research reflects on important social problems. As a method, DA describes interactional sequences, speech acts, and linguistic–argumentative designs, and, in many studies, reveals how these features link to valued and disvalued institutional and relational consequences.

Discourse Analysis as Intervention: Focused Reflection

In this chapter, we explained why taping, transcribing, and analyzing talk—that is, DA—deserves to be mastered and used regularly by communication scholars who are committed to doing practically useful research. By examining in detail the discursive practices that constitute people's social and institutional lives, and attending to those practices that are both problematic and unproblematic, DA is a useful tool for communication scholars with applied commitments.

Sometimes DA research is criticized for being "just," "merely," or "only" descriptive. There are multiple reasons why this is an inappropriate criticism; the one we highlight here is the assumption that describing is an activity of limited value (e.g., Frey & SunWolf, this volume). As we argued earlier, description of interactional problems, conversational moves, structures, and strategies makes possible thoughtful reflection and provides the starting point for defensible and effective situated action. To close this chapter, we turn our attention to a different meaning of applied, suggesting how a modification of DA, which we label "focused reflection," could become a useful tool in a variety of communication training and teaching venues.

Focused reflection is a training practice that adapts the logic of data sessions for a category of institutional actors (e.g., mediators, 911 call takers, and physicians) to help them communicate more effectively. More generally, focused reflection is a teaching practice than can be used to help students, whether in classrooms or in job and professional training workshops, to understand how valued interpersonal and professional qualities (e.g., being open-minded, fair, and respectful) are accomplished through the particulars of talk. Similar to data sessions, focused reflection begins with listening/viewing of tapes accompanied by transcripts of selected interactional moments. Focused reflection can occur in small groups, or it can be done in one-on-one consulting. It may involve listening/viewing taped interaction in which members of the group are the parties whose interaction has been taped, or it could involve unknown others who perform the communication activity that a focused reflection session is seeking to improve.

Watching videotaped interaction is a common practice in teaching and training settings; college students learning how to give a speech, medical students practicing how to interview patients, and beginning teachers improving their teaching are examples. Focused reflection extends this practice in a key way. By providing participants with transcripts of interaction, after teaching them how to look at them, focused reflection enables participants to connect talk with valued and disvalued interactional identities, and with attitudinal stances. As its name suggests, it focuses participants' reflections by supplying a record of the actual wording choices that speakers used.

Focused reflection requires a teacher/consultant to do three activities. The first task is to select relevant interactional moments and to prepare transcripts for viewing or listening. Segments of interaction should feature tasks that are problematic for practitioners and that prompt discussion about communicative ideals that are espoused, the tensions among them, and good and poor ways to discursively enact them. To set the stage, the teacher/trainer helps participants to articulate their ideals about communication to then identify any constraints they perceive themselves facing in the task/situation that is the object of the focused reflection.

A second activity is to teach participants how to interpret transcripts. Typically, transcripts are presented in a simpler form than what discourse researchers use, but they include the nonfluencies and repairs that are part of everyday talk. When people have little experience with transcripts, they tend to fixate on the "uhs," "ums," and frequent repairs that are part of ordinary speaking. Much as discourse analysts come to use repairs and other perturbations to develop claims about interactional difficulty, a focused reflection session teaches participants how to understand the functions of these discourse tokens. In particular, it teaches them to interpret these tokens as a sign of people experiencing situational difficulties rather than as evidence of poor communication.

The final task in a focused reflection session is to lead a discussion about the selected interactional moments. In doing so, the teacher/consultant guides the discussion toward two main issues: (1) assessments (and reasons for them) about how well the taped individual(s) or group accomplished the multiple aims held for the focal activity; and (2) what particular discursive actions, pointed to in the transcripts, enacted or endangered the situation's ideals and constraints.

In a study of cosmetic plastic surgeons, for instance, Mirivel (2006) analyzed an encounter with a patient that a surgeon described as "difficult" (see also Mirivel, 2007). Prior to viewing the videotape and looking at the transcript, questions were posed about the surgeon's aims during initial consultations. The surgeon espoused the following: "When I meet with patients for the first time, basically one of my goals is to ascertain their expectations, find out what they want to achieve, and find out if what they want to achieve is realistic" (Mirivel, 2006, p. 136). The surgeon added that patients sought a surgeon "who is going to be honest with them, and is going to be compassionate, that's going to be empathetic, and who will identify with them" (Mirivel, 2006, p. 238). These comments reflected what this surgeon, and presumably many surgeons, thought *ought* to happen communicatively during initial encounters with patients. Of note, this surgeon's beliefs about what was good communication in opening moments existed alongside another belief about the importance of not letting such encounters take too much time. Plastic surgery is a business and a certain number of consultations are needed if it is to remain viable. With the ideals and the time constraints framing the surgeon's meeting with the patient, the problematic moment and its transcript were examined, with the central goal of unpacking how and why the encounter was difficult.

Prior to examining the interactional data and the accompanying transcript, the surgeon attributed the difficulties to the patient's poor communicative performance. From the surgeon's perspective, the patient, Marilyn (a pseudonym), "was really non-descript about what she wanted done" and "was a terrible historian" (Mirivel, 2006, pp. 197, 205). His initial comments, thus, blamed Marilyn for the communication problems the two of them encountered. However, as the focused reflection session progressed, the surgeon's interactional challenges, rather than the "patient as problem," became the frame. For instance, rather than labeling the patient as being "non-descript," the interactional trouble was reframed in terms of the surgeon's needed tact to *avoid speaking for patients* in collecting information about what surgical procedures they were seeking. The collaborative analysis also helped the surgeon to identify a series of missed conversational opportunities—discursive actions that lacked empathy or interruptions that took over the patient's conversational floor—that, if performed differently, could have assisted Marilyn to communicate better, and, thereby, smooth the overall unfolding of interaction. In analyzing the encounter a bit like a discourse analyst, the surgeon developed an appreciation of his communicative actions as contributing to the direction of the encounter.

In essence, then, focused reflection helps participants to connect abstract ideals, such as respect, empathy, and honesty, with specifics of talk. Focused reflection sessions help students and practitioners to understand how desired ideals can be accomplished or endangered in the particulars of expression. It assists them in building concrete understandings of effective and problematic interactional moves, and in reflecting thoughtfully about what tradeoffs among ideals are reasonable. By giving people a chance to observe and talk about the communication challenges they routinely face, and by focusing on specific instances that allow for connecting interaction particulars with communicative ideals, focused reflection offers a way to apply DA to improve communication teaching and enhance workplace and professional training.

Conclusion

This chapter has argued that taping, transcribing, and analyzing talk is a scholarly practice that is valuable for conducting applied communication research. Implicit in this claim is that describing the social–communicative world in its discursive details can help laypersons and professionals to make wiser, more reflective choices about how to act or interpret others' actions. Foucault once wrote that "people know what they do; they frequently know why they do what they do; but what they don't know is what what they do does" (cited in Dreyfus & Rabinow, 1982, p. 187). Discourse-analytic work, we believe, could change this situation by teaching people that communicative behaviors serve specific functions that carry important relational, institutional, and cultural consequences.

Notes

1. We specify the field of communication because DA studies in linguistics are equally likely to focus on analyses of written texts.
2. Visit the project's Web site (http://www.vuw.ac.nz/lals/lwp/workplace-culture.aspx) to see how DA work can reach both academic and professional communities.
3. The difference between conversational "moves" and "strategies" is a subtle one. *Moves* make visible the presence of interactional trouble; the occurrence of moves reflects the existence of a problem. *Strategies*, in contrast, are discursive actions interpretable as responses to an interactional problem, an in-the-moment solution.

References

Agne, R. R. (2003). *Negotiation discourse: The FBI and David Koresh at Waco.* Unpublished doctoral dissertation, University of Colorado at Boulder.

Agne, R. R., & Tracy, K. (2001). "Bible babble": Naming the interactional trouble at Waco. *Discourse Studies, 3,* 269–294.

Alvesson, M. (2004). Organizational culture and discourse. In D. Grant, C. Hardy, C. Oswick, & L. L. Putnam (Eds.), *The Sage handbook of organizational discourse* (pp. 317–335). Thousand Oaks, CA: Sage.

Anderson, D. L. (2004). The textualizing functions of writing for organizational change. *Journal of Business and Technical Communication, 18,* 141–164.

Ashcraft, K. L. (2005). Resistance through consent? Occupational identity, organizational form, and the maintenance of masculinity among commercial airline pilots. *Management Communication Quarterly, 19,* 67–90.

Atkinson, P., & Heath, C. (Eds.). (1981). *Medical work: Realities and routines.* Aldershot, UK: Gower.

Atkinson, J. M., & Heritage, J. (1999). Jefferson's transcript notation. In A. Jaworski & N. Coupland (Eds.), *The discourse reader* (pp. 158–166). New York: Routledge.

Baker, C. D., Emmison, M., & Firth, A. (Eds.). (2005). *Calling for help: Language and social interaction in telephone helplines.* Philadelphia: John Benjamins.

Bales, R. F. (1950). A set of categories for the analysis of small group interaction. *American Sociological Review, 15,* 257–263.

Barge, J. K., & Loges, W. E. (2003). Parent, student, and teacher perceptions of parental involvement. *Journal of Applied Communication Research, 31,* 140–163.

Bavelas, J. B., Coats, L., & Johnson, T. (2002). Listener responses as a collaborative process: The role of gaze. *Journal of Communication, 52,* 566–580.

Baxter, L. A., Hirokowa, R., Lowe, J. B., Nathan, P., & Pearce, L. (2004). Dialogic voices in talk about drinking and pregnancy. *Journal of Applied Communication Research, 32,* 224–248.

Beach, W. A. (2001). Stability and ambiguity: Managing uncertain moments when updating news about mom's cancer. *Text, 21,* 221–250.

Beach, W. A. (2002). Between dad and son: Initiating, delivering, and assimilating bad cancer news. *Health Communication, 14,* 271–298.

Beck, C. S., Benitez, J. L., Edwards, A., Olson, A., Pai, A., & Torres, M. B. (2004). Enacting "health communication": The field of health communication as constructed through publication in scholarly journals. *Health Communication, 16,* 475–492.

Billig, M. (1999a). Conversation analysis and the claims of naiveté. *Discourse & Society, 10,* 572–576.

Billig, M. (1999b). Whose terms? Whose ordinariness? Rhetoric and ideology in conversation analysis. *Discourse & Society, 10,* 543–558.

Blum-Kulka, S. (1997). *Dinner talk: Cultural patterns of sociability and socialization in family discourse.* Mahwah, NJ: Erlbaum.

Boden, D. (1994). *The business of talk: Organizations in action.* Cambridge, MA: Polity Press.

Braithwaite, D. O., & Eckstein, N. J. (2003). How people with disabilities communicatively manage assistance: Helping as instrumental social support. *Journal of Applied Communication Research, 31,* 1–26.

Buttny, R. (2004). *Talking problems: Studies of discursive construction.* Albany: State University of New York Press.

Cameron, D. (2001). *Working with spoken discourse.* Thousand Oaks, CA: Sage.

Candlin, C. N., & Candlin, S. (2002). Discourse, expertise, and the management of risk in health care settings. *Research on Language and Social Interaction, 35,* 115–137.

Carbaugh, D. (1996). *Situating selves: The communication of social identities in American scenes.* Albany: State University of NewYork Press.

Castor, T. R. (2004). Constructing social reality in organizational decision making: Account vocabularies in a diversity discussion. *Management Communication Quarterly, 18,* 479–508.

Cheney, G., Christensen, L. T., Conrad, C., & Lair, D. J. (2004). Corporate rhetoric as organizational discourse. In D. Grant, C. Hardy, C. Oswick, & L. L. Putnam (Eds.), *The Sage handbook of organizational discourse* (pp. 79–103). Thousand Oaks, CA: Sage.

Cissna, K., N. (Ed.). (1995). *Applied communication in the 21st century.* Mahwah, NJ: Erlbaum.

Clark, C., Drew, P., & Pinch, T. (1994). Managing customer "objections" during real-life sales negotiation. *Discourse & Society, 5,* 437–462.

Clayman, S. E. (1995). Defining moments, presidential debates, and the dynamics of quotability. *Journal of Communication, 45*(3), 118–146.

Clayman, S., & Heritage, J. (2002). Questioning presidents: Journalistic deference and adversarialness in the press conferences of U.S. Presidents Eisenhower and Reagan. *Journal of Communication, 52,* 749–775.

Condor, S. (2000). Pride and prejudice: Identity management in English people's talk about "this country." *Discourse & Society, 11,* 175–205.

Conley, J. M., & O'Barr, W. M. (1998). *Just words: Law, language, and power.* Chicago: University of Chicago Press.

Conquergood, D. (1995). Between rigor and relevance: Rethinking applied communication. In K. N. Cissna (Ed.), *Applied communication in the 21st century* (pp. 79–96). Mahwah, NJ: Erlbaum.

Cooren, F. (2003). The communicative achievement of collective minding: Analysis of board meeting excerpts. *Management Communication Quarterly, 17,* 517–557.

Cooren, F. (Ed.). (2006). *Interacting and organizing: Analysis of a management meeting.* Mahwah, NJ: Erlbaum.

Craig, R. T. (1989). Communication as a practical discipline. In B. Dervin, L. Grossberg, B. J. O'Keefe, & E. Wartella (Eds.), *Rethinking communication: Vol. 1. Paradigm issues* (pp. 97–122). Newbury Park CA: Sage.

Craig, R. T. (1995). Applied communication research in a practical discipline. In K. N. Cissna (Ed.), *Applied communication in the 21st century* (pp. 147–156). Mahwah, NJ: Erlbaum.

Craig, R. T., & Sanusi, E. (1999). "I'm just saying": Discourse markers of standpoint continuity. In F. H. van Eemeren, R. Grootendorst, J. A. Blair, & C. Willard (Eds.), *Proceedings of the Fourth International Conference of the International Society for the Study of Argumentation* (pp. 103–108). Amsterdam: SicSat.

Craig, R. T., & Tracy, K. (1995). Grounded practical theory: The case of intellectual discussion. *Communication Theory, 5,* 248–272.

Craig, R. T., & Tracy, K. (2005). "The issue" in argumentation practice and theory. In F. H. van Eemeren & P. Houtlosser (Eds.), *Argumentation in practice* (pp. 11–28). Philadelphia: John Benjamins.

Drew, P., & Chilton, K. (2000). Calling just to keep in touch: Regular and habitualised telephone calls as an environment for small talk. In J. Coupland (Ed.), *Small talk* (pp. 137–162). New York: Longman.

Dreyfus, H. L., & Rabinow, P. (1982). *Michel Foucault: Beyond structuralism and hermeneutics.* Chicago: University of Chicago Press.

Duff Wrobbel, E. (2003). The interactional construction of self-revelation: Creating an "aha" moment. In P. J. Glenn, C. D. LeBaron, & J. Mandelbaum (Eds.), *Studies in language and social interaction: In honor of Robert Hopper* (pp. 353–362). Mahwah, NJ: Erlbaum.

Duranti, A., & Goodwin, C. (Eds.). (1992). *Rethinking context: Language as an interactive phenomenon.* New York: Cambridge University Press.

Eadie, W. F. (Ed.). (1991). The agenda for applied communication research [Special issue]. *Journal of Applied Communication Research, 19*(1–2).

Edwards, D., & Potter, J. (1992). *Discursive psychology.* Newbury Park, CA: Sage.

Edwards, J. A., & Lampert, M. D. (Eds.). (1993). *Talking data: Transcription and coding in discourse research.* Hillsdale, NJ: Erlbaum.

Erickson, F., & Shultz, J. (1982). *The counselor as gatekeeper: Social interaction in interviews.* New York: Academic Press.

Fairclough, N. (2003). *Analysing discourse: Textual analysis for social research*. New York: Routledge.

Fairclough, N., & Wodak, R. (1997). Critical discourse analysis. In T. A. van Dijk (Ed.), *Discourse as social interaction* (pp. 258–284). Thousand Oaks, CA: Sage.

Fairhurst, G. T., & Cooren, F. (2004). Organizational language in use: Interaction analysis, conversation analysis, and speech act schematics. In D. Grant, C. Hardy, C. Oswick, & L. L. Putnam (Eds.), *The Sage handbook of organizational discourse* (pp. 131–152). Thousand Oaks, CA: Sage.

Fairhurst, G. T., & Putnam, L. (2004). Organizations as discursive constructions. *Communication Theory, 14*, 5–26.

Fisher, S., & Todd, A. D. (Eds.). (1983). *The social organization of doctor–patient communication*. Washington, DC: Center for Applied Linguistics.

Fitch, K. L. (1998). Text and context: A problematic distinction for ethnography. *Research on Language and Social Interaction, 31*, 91–107.

Fitch, K. L. (1999). Pillow talk? *Research on Language and Social Interaction, 32*, 41–50.

Fitch, K. L., & Sanders, R. E. (Eds.). (2005). *Handbook of language and social interaction*. Mahwah, NJ: Erlbaum.

Foucault, M. (1972). *The archaeology of knowledge* (A. M. Sheridan Smith, Trans.). New York: Pantheon Books.

Frey, L. R. (Ed.). (1998). Communication and social justice research [Special issue]. *Journal of Applied Communication Research, 26*(2).

Gabriel, Y. (1998). Same old story or changing stories? Folklore, modern, and postmodern mutations. In D. Grant, T. Keenoy, & C. Oswick (Eds.), *Discourse and organization* (pp. 84–103). Thousand Oaks, CA: Sage.

Gee, J. P. (1999). *An introduction to discourse analysis: Theory and method*. New York: Routledge.

Goodwin, C. (2000). Action and embodiment within situated human interaction. *Journal of Pragmatics, 32*, 1489–1522.

Grant, D., Hardy, C., Oswick, C., & Putnam, L. L. (2004). Introduction: Organizational discourse: Exploring the field. In D. Grant, C. Hardy, C. Oswick, & L. L. Putnam (Eds.), *The Sage handbook of organizational discourse* (pp. 1–36). Thousand Oaks, CA: Sage.

Greespan, S., & Shoultz, B. (1981). Why mentally retarded adults lose their jobs: Social competence as a factor in work adjustment. *Applied Research in Mental Retardation, 2*, 23–38.

Harter, L. (2004). Masculinity(s), the agrarian frontier myth, and cooperative ways of organizing: Contradictions and tensions in the experience and enactment of democracy. *Journal of Applied Communication Research, 32*, 89–118.

Haspel, K., & Tracy, K. (2007). Marking and shifting lines in the sand: Discursive moves of ordinary democracy. In K. Tracy, J. P. McDaniel, & B. E. Gronbeck (Eds.), *The prettier doll: Rhetoric, discourse, and ordinary democracy* (pp. 142–175). Tuscaloosa: University of Alabama Press.

Hauser, G. A. (1998). Vernacular dialogue and the rhetoricality of public opinion. *Communication Monographs, 65*, 83–107.

Hauser, G. A. (1999). *Vernacular voices: The rhetoric of publics and public spheres*. Columbia: University of South Carolina Press.

Heath, C. (1986). *Body movement and speech in medical interaction*. New York: Cambridge University Press.

Heritage, J., & Lindström, A. (1998). Motherhood, medicine, and morality: Scenes from a medical encounter. *Research on Language and Social Interaction, 31*, 397–438.

Heritage, J., & Sefi, S. (1992). Dilemmas of advice: Aspects of the delivery and reception of advice in interactions between health visitors and first-time mothers. In P. Drew & J. Heritage (Eds.), *Talk at work: Interaction in institutional settings* (pp. 359–417). New York: Cambridge University Press.

Hindmarsh, J., & Heath, C. (2000). Embodied reference: A study of deixis in workplace interaction. *Journal of Pragmatics, 32*, 1855–1878.

Holmes, J. (2000). Politeness, power, and provocation: How humour functions in the workplace. *Discourse Studies, 2,* 159–185.

Holmes, J. (2003). Small talk at work: Potential problems for workers with an intellectual disability. *Research on Language and Social Interaction, 36,* 65–84.

Holmes, J., Marra, M., & Burns, L. (2001) Women's humour in the workplace: A quantitative analysis. *Australian Journal of Communication, 28,* 83–108.

Holmes, J., & Stubbe, M. (2003). *Power and politeness in the workplace: A sociolinguistic analysis of talk at work.* London: Longman.

Holmes, J., Stubbe, M., & Vine, B. (1999). Constructing professional identity: "Doing power" in policy units. In C. Sarangi & C. Roberts (Eds.), *Talk, work, and institutional order: Discourse in medical, mediation, and management settings* (pp. 351–385). New York: Mouton de Gruyter.

Hsieh, E. (2004). Stories in action and the dialogic management of identities: Storytelling in transplant support group meetings. *Research on Language and Social Interaction, 37,* 39–70.

Hutchby, I., & Wooffitt, R. (1998). *Conversation analysis: Principles, practices, and applications.* Malden, MA: Polity Press.

Jones, D., & Stubbe, M. (2004). Communication and the reflective practitioner: A shared perspective from sociolinguistics and organisational communication. *International Journal of Applied Linguistics, 14,* 185–211.

Katriel, T. (2004). *Dialogic moments: From soul talks to talk radio in Israeli culture.* Detroit, MI: Wayne State University Press.

Keyton, J. (2000). Applied communication research should be practical. *Journal of Applied Communication Research, 28,* 166–169.

Komter, M. (2003). The interactional dynamics of eliciting a confession in a Dutch police interrogation. *Research on Language and Social Interaction, 36,* 433–470.

Koschmann, T., & LeBaron, C. D. (2002). Learner articulation as interactional achievement: Studying the conversation of gesture. *Cognition and Instruction, 20,* 249–282.

LeBaron, C. D., & Jones, S. E. (2002). Closing up closings: Showing the relevance of the social and material surround to the completion of interaction. *Journal of Communication, 52,* 542–565.

LeBaron, C., & Streeck, J. (1997). Built space and the interactional framing of experience during a murder interrogation. *Human Studies, 20,* 1–25.

Mangione-Smith, R., Stivers, T., Elliott, M. N., McDonald, L., & Heritage, J. (2003). Online commentary during the physical examination: A communication tool for avoiding inappropriate antibiotic prescribing? *Social Science & Medicine, 56,* 313–320.

Mansbridge, J. J. (1980). *Beyond adversary democracy.* New York: Basic Books.

March, J. G. (1991). Organizational consultants and organizational research. *Journal of Applied Communication Research, 19,* 20–31.

Martin, D. M. (2004). Humor in middle management: Women negotiating the paradoxes of organizational life. *Journal of Applied Communication Research, 32,* 147–170.

Mattson, M., & Roberts, F. (2001). Overcoming truth telling as an obstacle to initiating safer sex: Clients and health practitioners planning deception during HIV test counseling. *Health Communication, 13,* 343–362.

Maynard, D. W. (1991). Bearing bad news in clinical settings. In B. Dervin (Ed.), *Progress in communication sciences* (Vol. 10, pp. 143–172). Norwood, NJ: Ablex.

Maynard, D. W. (1992). On clinicians co-implicating recipients' perspective in the delivery of diagnostic news. In P. Drew & J. Heritage (Eds.), *Talk at work: Interaction in institutional settings* (pp. 331–358). New York: Cambridge University Press.

Maynard, D. W. (1997). The news delivery sequence: Bad news and good news in conversational interaction. *Research on Language and Social Interaction, 30,* 93–130.

Maynard, D. W. (2003). *Bad news, good news: Conversational order in everyday talk and clinical settings.* Chicago: University of Chicago Press.

Milburn, T., Kenefick, J. V., & Lambert, A. (2006). Facilitating communication during a board of directors' retreat: Enacting change at a family center. In L. R. Frey (Ed.), *Facilitating group communication in context: Innovations and applications with natural groups: Vol. 2. Facilitating group task and team communication* (pp. 63–88). Cresskill, NJ: Hampton Press.

Miller, G. R. (1995). "I think my schizophrenia is better today," said the communication researcher unanimously: Some thoughts on the dysfunctional dichotomy between pure and applied communication research. In K. N. Cissna (Ed.), *Applied communication in the 21st century* (pp. 47–55). Mahwah, NJ: Erlbaum.

Mirivel, J. C. (2006). *Getting "nipped and tucked" through talk: A communication take on cosmetic surgery*. Unpublished doctoral dissertation, University of Colorado at Boulder.

Mirivel, J. C. (2007). Managing poor surgical candidacy: Communication problems for plastic surgeons. *Discourse & Society, 1*, 309–336.

Mirivel, J. C. (2008). The physical examination in cosmetic surgery: Communication strategies to promote the desirability of surgery. *Health Communication, 23*, 153–170.

Mirivel, J. C., & Tracy, K. (2005). Premeeting talk: An organizationally crucial form of talk. *Research on Language and Social Interaction, 38*, 1–34.

Morgan, S. E., & Miller, J. K. (2002). Beyond the organ donor card: The effect of knowledge, attitudes, and values on willingness to communicate about organ donation to family members. *Health Communication, 14*, 121–134.

Morris, G. H., & Chenail, R. J. (1995). *The talk of the clinic: Explorations in the analysis of medical and therapeutic discourse*. Hillsdale, NJ: Erlbaum.

Ochs, E. (1979). Transcription as theory. In E. Ochs & B. B. Schieffelin (Eds.), *Developmental pragmatics* (pp. 43–72). New York: Academic Press.

O'Hair, D. (Ed.). (2000). Defining applied communication scholarship [Special forum]. *Journal of Applied Communication Research, 28*(2), 164–191.

Philipsen, G., & Coutu, L. M. (2005). The ethnography of speaking. In K. L. Fitch & R. E. Sanders (Eds.), *Handbook of language and social interaction* (pp. 355–380). Mahwah, NJ: Erlbaum.

Pittam, J., & Gallois, C. (2000). Malevolence, stigma, and social distance: Maximizing intergroup differences in HIV/AIDS discourse. *Journal of Applied Communication Research, 28*, 24–43.

Platt, F. W. (1995). *Conversation repair: Case studies in doctor–patient communication*. Boston: Little, Brown.

Plax, T. G. (1991). Understanding applied communication inquiry: Researcher as organizational consultant. *Journal of Applied Communication Research, 19*, 55–70.

Pomerantz, A. M. (2003). Modeling as a teaching strategy in clinical training: When does it work? In. P. J. Glenn, C. D. LeBaron, & J. Mandelbaum (Eds.), *Studies in language and social interaction: In honor of Robert Hopper* (pp. 381–392). Mahwah, NJ: Erlbaum.

Pomerantz, A., Fehr, B. J., & Ende, J. (1997). When supervising physicians see patients: Strategies used in difficult situations. *Human Communication Research, 23*, 589–615.

Puchta, C., & Potter, J. (2004). *Focus group practice*. Thousand Oaks, CA: Sage.

Putnam, L. L., & Fairhurst, G. T. (2001). Discourse analysis in organizations: Issues and concerns. In F. M. Jablin & L. L. Putnam (Eds.), *The new handbook of organizational communication: Advances in theory, research, and methods* (pp. 78–136). Thousand Oaks, CA: Sage.

Roberts, F., & Robinson, J. D. (2004). Interobserver agreement on first-stage conversation analytic transcription. *Human Communication Research, 30*, 376–410.

Robinson, J. D. (1998). Getting down to business: Talk, gaze, and body orientation during openings of doctor–patient consultations. *Human Communication Research, 25*, 97–123.

Robinson, J. D. (2003). An interactional structure of medical activities during acute visits and its implications for patients' participation. *Health Communication, 15*, 27–57.

Robinson, J. D., & Nussbaum, J. F. (2004). Grounding research and medical education about religion in actual physician–patient interaction: Church attendance, social support, and older adults. *Health Communication, 16*, 63–85.

Rogers, L. E., & Farace, R. V. (1975). Relational communication analysis: New measurement procedures. *Human Communication Research, 1*, 222–239.

Sachweh, S. (1998). Granny darling's nappies: Secondary babytalk in German nursing homes for the aged. *Journal of Applied Communication Research, 26*, 52–65.

Sacks, H. (1992). *Lectures on conversation* (Vol. 2, G. Jefferson, Ed.). Cambridge, MA: Blackwell.

Sarangi, C., & Roberts, C. (Ed.). (1999). *Talk, work, and institutional order: Discourse in medical, mediation, and management settings.* New York: Mouton de Gruyter.

Schegloff, E. A. (1997). Whose text? Whose context? *Discourse & Society, 8,* 165–187.

Schegloff, E. A. (1998). Positioning and interpretative repertoires: Conversation analysis and post-structuralism in dialogue—Reply to Wetherell. *Discourse & Society, 9,* 413–416.

Schegloff, E. A. (1999a). "Schegloff's texts" as "Billig's data": A critical reply. *Discourse & Society, 10,* 558–572.

Schegloff, E. A. (1999b). Naivete vs. sophistication or discipline vs. self-indulgence: A rejoinder to Billig. *Discourse & Society, 10,* 577–582.

Scheuer, J. (2001). Recontextualization and communicative styles in job interviews. *Discourse Studies, 3,* 223–248.

Schiffrin, D. (1994). *Approaches to discourse.* Cambridge, MA: Blackwell.

Schiffrin, D., Tannen, D., & Hamilton, H. (Eds.). (2001). *The handbook of discourse analysis.* Malden, MA: Blackwell.

Schudson, M. (1998). *The good citizen: A history of American civic life.* New York: Martin Kessler Books.

Seibold, D. R. (1995). *Theoria* and *praxis*: Means and ends in applied communication research. In K. N. Cissna (Ed.), *Applied communication in the 21st century* (pp. 23–38). Mahwah, NJ: Erlbaum.

Seibold, D. R. (2000). Applied communication scholarship: Less a matter of boundaries than of emphases. *Journal of Applied Communication Research, 28,* 183–188.

Silverman, D. (1997). *Qualitative research: Theory, method and practice.* Thousand Oaks, CA: Sage.

Silverman, D. (2004). *Qualitative research: Theory, method and practice* (2nd ed.). Thousand Oaks, CA: Sage.

Silverman, D. (2006). *Interpreting qualitative data: Methods for analysing talk, text and interaction* (3rd ed.). Thousand Oaks, CA: Sage.

Speer, S. A. (2002). "Natural" and "contrived" data: A sustainable distinction? *Discourse Studies, 4,* 511–525.

Stafford, L. (2009). Editorial policy. *Journal of Applied Communication Research, 37*(1), n.p.

Stivers, T. (2002). Presenting the problem in pediatric encounters: "Symptoms only" versus "candidate diagnosis" presentations. *Health Communication, 14,* 299–338.

Stivers, T. (2005a). Non-antibiotic treatment recommendations: Delivery formats and implications for parent resistance. *Social Science & Medicine, 60,* 949–964.

Stivers, T. (2005b). Parent resistance to physicians' treatment recommendations: One resource for initiating a negotiation of the treatment decision. *Health Communication, 18,* 41–74.

Stivers, T., Mangione-Smith, R., Elliott, M. N., McDonald, L., & Heritage, J. (2003). Why do physicians think parents expect antibiotics? What parents report vs. what physicians believe. *Journal of Family Practice, 52,* 140–148.

Streeck, J., & Mehus, S. (2005). Microethnography: The study of practices. In K. L. Fitch & R. E. Sanders (Eds.), *Handbook of language and social interaction* (pp. 381–404). Mahwah, NJ: Erlbaum.

Stubbs, M. (1983). *Discourse analysis: The sociolinguistic analysis of natural language.* Chicago: University of Chicago Press.

Tapsell, L. (2000). Using applied conversation analysis to teach novice dietitians history taking skills. *Human Studies, 23,* 281–307.

ten Have, P. (1999). *Doing conversation analysis: A practical guide.* Thousand Oaks, CA: Sage.

ten Have, P. (2002). Ontology or methodology? Comments on Speers's "natural" and "contrived" data: A sustainable distinction. *Discourse Studies, 4,* 527–530.

Tracy, K. (1995). Action-implicative discourse analysis. *Journal of Language and Social Psychology, 14,* 195–215.

Tracy, K. (1997). *Colloquium: Dilemmas of academic discourse.* Norwood, NJ: Ablex.

Tracy, K. (1998). Analyzing context: Framing the discussion. *Research on Language and Social Interaction, 31,* 1–28.

Tracy, K. (1999). The usefulness of platitudes in arguments about conduct. In F. H. van Eemeren, R. Grootendorst, J. A. Blair, & C. A. Willard (Eds.), *Proceedings of the Fourth International Conference of the International Society for the Study of Argumentation* (pp. 799–803). Amsterdam: SicSat.

Tracy, K. (2001). Discourse analysis in communication. In D. Schiffrin, D. Tannen, & H. Hamilton (Eds.), *Handbook of discourse analysis* (pp. 725–749). Malden, MA: Blackwell.

Tracy, K. (2005). Reconstructing communicative practices: Action-implicative discourse analysis. In K. L. Fitch & R. E. Sanders (Eds.), *Handbook of language and social interaction* (pp. 301–319). Mahwah, NJ: Erlbaum.

Tracy, K. (2007a). The discourse of crisis in public meetings: Case study of a school board's multimillion dollar error. *Journal of Applied Communication Research, 35,* 418–441.

Tracy, K. (2007b). Introduction: A moment of ordinary democracy. In K. Tracy, J. P. McDaniel, & B. E. Gronbeck (Eds.), *The prettier doll: Rhetoric, discourse, and ordinary democracy* (pp. 3–21). Tuscaloosa: University of Alabama Press.

Tracy, K., & Agne, R. R. (2002). "I just need to ask somebody some questions": Sensitivities in domestic dispute calls. In J. Cottrell (Ed.), *Language in the legal process* (pp. 75–89). New York: Palgrave.

Tracy, K., & Anderson, D. L. (1999). Relational positioning strategies in calls to the police: A dilemma. *Discourse Studies, 1,* 201–226.

Tracy, K., & Ashcraft, C. (2001). Crafting policies about controversial values: How wording disputes manage a group dilemma. *Journal of Applied Communication Research, 29,* 297–316.

Tracy, K., & Craig, R. T. (2005, November). *Invoking democracy: A powerful discourse strategy in public meetings.* Paper presented at the meeting of the National Communication Association, Boston, MA.

Tracy, K., & Haspel, K. (2004). Language and social interaction: Its institutional identity, intellectual landscape, and discipline-shifting agenda. *Journal of Communication, 54,* 788–816.

Tracy, K., McDaniel, J. P., & Gronbeck, B. E. (Eds.). (2007). *The prettier doll: Rhetoric, discourse, and ordinary democracy.* Tuscaloosa: University of Alabama Press.

Tracy, K., & Muller, H. (2001). Diagnosing a school board's interactional trouble: Theorizing problem formulating. *Communication Theory, 11,* 84–104.

Tracy, K., & Naughton, J. M. (2000). Institutional identity-work: A better lens. In J. Coupland (Ed.), *Small talk* (pp. 62–83). New York: Longman.

Tracy, K., & Standerfer, C. (2003). Selecting a school superintendent: Sensitivities in group deliberation. In L. R Frey (Ed.), *Group communication in context: Studies of bona fide groups* (2nd ed., pp. 109–134). Mahwah, NJ: Erlbaum.

Tracy, K., & Tracy, S. J. (1998). Rudeness at 911: Reconceptualizing face and face-attack. *Human Communication Research, 25,* 225–251.

Tracy, S. J. (2004). Dialectic, contradiction, or double bind: Analyzing and theorizing employee reactions to organizational tension. *Journal of Applied Communication Research, 32,* 119–146.

Tracy, S. J., & Tracy, K. (1998). Emotion labor at 911: A case study and theoretical critique. *Journal of Applied Communication Research, 26,* 390–411.

van Dijk, T. A. (1985). (Ed.). *Handbook of discourse analysis* (4 vols.). London: Academic Press.

van Dijk, T. A. (Ed.). (1997a). *Discourse as social interaction: A multidisciplinary introduction.* Thousand Oaks, CA: Sage.

van Dijk, T. A. (Ed.). (1997b). *Discourse as structure and process: A multidisciplinary introduction.* Thousand Oaks, CA: Sage.

Weltman, D. (2003). The pragmatics of peremptory assertion: An ideological analysis of the use of the word "just" in local politicians' denials of politics. *Discourse & Society, 14,* 349–373.

West, C. (1984). *Routine complications: Troubles with talk between doctors and patients.* Bloomington: Indiana University Press.

Wetherell, M. (1998). Positioning and interpretative repertoires: Conversation analysis and poststructuralism in dialogue. *Discourse & Society, 9,* 387–412.

Wetherell, M., Taylor, S., & Yates, S. J. (2001). *Discourse as data: A guide for analysis*. Thousand Oaks, CA: Sage.

Whalen, J., & Zimmerman, D. H. (2005). Working a call: Multiparty management of calls for help. In C. D. Baker, M. Emmison, & A. Firth (Eds.), *Calling for help: Language and social interaction in telephone helplines* (pp. 309–345). Philadelphia: John Benjamins.

Wood, L. A., & Kroger, R. O. (2000). *Doing discourse analysis: Methods for studying action in talk and text*. Thousand Oaks, CA: Sage.

Wooffitt, R. (1992). *Telling tales of the unexpected: The organization of factual discourse*. Savage, MD: Barnes & Noble Books.

Zoller, H. M. (2003). Health on the line: Identity and disciplinary control in employee occupational health and safety discourse. *Journal of Applied Communication Research, 31*, 118–139.

Part III

Issues in Applied Communication Research

8 Positioning Gender as Fundamental in Applied Communication Research

Taking a Feminist Turn

Patrice M. Buzzanell
Purdue University

Rebecca J. Meisenbach
University of Missouri

Robyn Remke
Copenhagen Business School

Helen Sterk
Calvin College

Lynn H. Turner
Marquette University

Applied communication researchers seek to make a difference in the world by focusing on critical features of communication grounded in everyday discourse and practices. Wood (2000) noted that applied communication research creates a distinctive "posture toward the goals of scholarly inquiry, an inclination to ask particularly pragmatic questions about how communication does, might, and should operate in a range of settings and how communication practices in sundry settings inform theory" (p. 189). Feminist research takes this pragmatic posture a step further by requiring attention to the ongoing tensions between reinforcement of dominant societal expectations and personal agency. When gender is seen as an organizing principle for everyday interactions as influenced by institutional and societal structures, and when researchers advocate for equitable participation of women and men in communication venues, applied communication scholarship and practice takes a feminist turn.

A feminist perspective also challenges the biology-is-destiny approach, from its simplest form in sex-difference research to more complex understanding of gendered processes and practices. In this feminist turn, scholars question how cultural reifications of difference, particularly those assumed to be caused by biology, influence people's understandings of self and other (Turner & Sterk, 1994). For scholars in the field of communication, feminist research has grown and expanded in all contexts since initial publications over 30 years ago. As Dow and Condit (2005) noted, much of contemporary feminist communication research cuts across traditional contexts in ways that emphasize sex-difference research, analyses of gender ideology and practices that perpetuate gender injustice, and construction of feminist theoretical frameworks. As such, feminist scholarship responds to challenges, such as appropriate ways to deal with ethical concerns and develop systems that promote diversity, that people face and will continue to face in a global society (E. Jones, Watson, Gardner, & Gallois, 2004).

In this chapter, we attend to the processes by which gender politicizes communication across applied communication contexts. The research we highlight is not just "gender sensitive" in terms of including sex as a demographic variable but is overtly feminist with respect to uncovering inequitable power relations based on biological sex and psychological gender, and suggesting alternative, more equitable, ways of communicating. Feminist applied communication research not only highlights how communication enacts gender but also how communication can contest and change gender roles and relations, leading to a fuller life for all participants. As such, this research flows from an emancipatory agenda.

In a publication sponsored by the National Communication Association, Poole and Walther (2002) argued that the communication field should work toward enhancing a "vigorous, self-renewing democracy," the "health and well-being of all," organizational and institutional change to "enable our society to prosper in the emerging global economy," and people's abilities to enjoy "meaningful lives and...fulfilling relationships" (p. 4). Taking our cue from that agenda, we propose a feminist agenda for applied communication research whose aim is to (1) promote full, empowered participation of all people in communication that dispels gender hierarchies; (2) define well-being as equitable access to material and symbolic resources, as well as voice in the distribution of those resources; (3) suggest alternatives to normative, gendered communication processes across contexts; and (4) promote fulfilling human relationships that honor women and men as full human beings.

We begin by describing feminist research developments in four applied communication contexts: family life, educational institutions, organizations, and health care. Although there are many other contexts that we could have included in this chapter, we selected these four for several reasons. Not only do these contexts represent key applied areas that span a person's life but they also progress from an individual's "first group" (i.e., family) to more macrosettings in which contexts overlap (e.g., health communication is shaped by and shapes organizational and interpersonal communication, as well as instruction in health education). More important, we included contexts that have been institutionalized in our field as some of the earliest settings in which communication was studied (i.e., instructional and organizational communication), as well as some newer areas that have grown out of and cut across intradisciplinary areas (i.e., family and health communication), and that show great promise in terms of interventions, policy making, and policy implementation.

Within each of these four contexts, we review recent published research and, in particular, discuss the impact of historical, social, economic, and cultural forces on the lives of people in the United States, as well as around the globe. We draw the sections together by questioning the differences that this research should make for individuals, groups, organizations, and communities. We use the United States as one example of how applied communication research affects and should affect public policy. As a result, we integrate research on applied communication contexts in a section on politicizing gender, which focuses on how this research makes a difference in U.S. public policies and beyond. In our conclusion, we reaffirm feminist commitments to put scholarship into practice and to develop applied communication research programs around human needs, particularly those of women. This chapter, thus, provides a comprehensive, yet concise, feminist view of gender in applied communication research.

Overview of Gendered Communication within Applied Contexts

In this section, we describe some traditional and emerging developments in gendered communication research. In each subsection, we begin with investigations of sex differences and then broaden the review with studies on gendered interaction, organizing processes, and societal ramifications. As mentioned, we focus attention on four applied communication contexts: (1) empowering family, (2) constructing pedagogy, (3) organizing gender, and (4) gendering health.

Empowering Family

The family forms a key context for learning and enacting gender. As Galvin (2004) observed, "Gender is embedded in all family interactions as a thread or theme, implicit or explicit" (p. 311). Gender literally is talked into being through family encounters, ranging from stereotyped admonitions (e.g. "Boys don't cry" and "Girls don't like math") to discussions about task allocation and a wide range of other everyday conversations. However, according to Wood (2006), any approach to understanding the relationship between family and gender presupposes a definition of family, but defining family is not a simple or innocent undertaking; it involves ideology and "depends on the particularities of specific cultures that exist in specific historical moments" (p. 198). These considerations make defining family a site of struggle (Coontz, 1999).

We continue this struggle, in large part, because of the importance of family in shaping individuals' personalities and enduring communication patterns. The family has been called "the first group" (Socha, 1999) because members of a family-of-origin typically constitute the first and longest lasting set of connections of a person's life (see Socha, this volume). As Bochner (1976) observed, families are characterized by a state of structural permanence that makes them, unlike any other group, significant socializing agents.

Despite the acknowledgment of the family's critical importance, our understanding of what constitutes a family is not universal. By some counts, there are over 200 definitions for family (Jorgenson, 1994). To contend with this conceptual confusion and to avoid excluding any type of family, Turner and West (2006) argued for an inclusive definition, asserting that any group whose members call themselves a "family" is one. Fitzpatrick and Ritchie (1993) also circumvented the definitional problem by focusing on metaphors about family that underscore researchers' approaches to the study of family communication—metaphors that include a private miniculture, a resource-exchange system, and a set of relationships.

It is possible to review the literature focused on gender in the family context using the metaphors discussed by Fitzpatrick and Ritchie (1993). The metaphor of a private culture privileges family narratives, storytelling processes, and other meaning-making practices (Wood, 1998). Langellier and Peterson (2004) maintained that the processes of constructing stories and the narratives themselves actually define family, asserting that "family is a human communication practice—as much a way of 'doing things with words' as it is a set of ties and sentiments" (p. 33). Narayan (1997) also argued that family storytelling embodies a feminist tension, noting that daughters and mothers often recount the same stories in different terms, which reflects their different approaches to issues affecting women.

Langellier and Peterson (2004) pointed out the importance of focusing on how storytelling tasks, such as ordering narrative events, construct gender in the family culture. They contrasted a mother–daughter interaction with a father–son interaction in two families. Although both pairs came from comparable families in the same geographic locale, the interactions in these families proceeded differently, in part, because of gendered processes. Langellier and Peterson observed that the female pair told their story through conarrating, capturing a sense of playfulness and establishing alliances across generations. In the father–son interaction, "the son serves as a host who announces and showcases his father's stories" (Langellier & Peterson, p. 92). The son's contributions supported the father's story and persona; the son did not further develop the story in the same way the daughter did for her mother. The two storytelling patterns emerged out of the strategic demands of the situation, and Langellier and Peterson concluded that family provides a context for gender performance, a process that is "strategic and multiply contextualized" (p. 93).

In viewing family as a resource-exchange system, Fitzpatrick and Ritchie (1993) focused on family members' provision of resources to one another. In family interactions, gendered notions of resources surface in multiple, layered ways. According to Jurik (1998), many women work at home to reconcile or balance the competing demands of career and family, a movement that Jurik called a "gendered phenomenon" (p. 8). Buzzanell and Turner (2003) observed balance in other ways, finding that, in White, middle-class U.S. families where a male wage earner had lost his job, a main function of the family's communication was to reinstitute traditional masculinities, which was accomplished through complex message transactions allowing family members to maintain viewing these men as firmly ensconced in the world of work, despite having lost their jobs. Specifically, Buzzanell and Turner asserted that men created this construction themselves, but because their masculinities were fragile, they required family members' active collaboration to sustain their perception. One result of this collaboration was to situate men's stories of career, work, and other activities as primary in the family and to reify men's place in the public space.

Finally, considering family as a set of relationships means that a cluster of overlapping relationships (e.g., mother–daughter, mother–son, husband–wife, brother–brother, aunt–niece, and grandmother–grandson) taken together constitutes family (Fitzpatrick & Ritchie, 1993). Examining the family through a relational lens has been common in the communication literature. In their reviews of family communication literature, Fitzpatrick and Badzinski (1985) and Vangelisti (1993) noted that few studies examine communication in the whole family; instead, most use this relationship metaphor to examine some specific family dyad. Although scholars have critiqued this metaphor as underrepresenting family, it continues to be a dominant approach, with mother–daughter relationships being the dyad studied most in the literature on family (Penington & Turner, 2004).

Some researchers, however, have established connections between and among family dyads in complex ways. Woodward (1999) called female intergenerational relationships in the family the "motherline," by which she meant the three-generational line from grandmother to adult daughter/mother to daughter/granddaughter. Edelman (1999) touched on the motherline's continuity and differentiation as she watched her daughter play: "She is a child and I am her mother; she is me and I am my mother; she is my mother and I am my grandmother" (p. 254).

In addition, researchers have examined gender differences in the family context. For example, Fitness and Duffield (2004) reviewed gender differences in marital emotion communication, noting that women generally are better than men at both encoding and decoding emotions. In discussing family influences on health, D. J. Jones, Beach, and Jackson's (2004) literature review noted gender differences in responses to conflict, leading them to conclude that women are more likely than men to suffer adverse health effects as a result of family conflict.

Although all of this research is important, most of it does not provide a specifically feminist approach to examining family and family communication. This turn is needed to interrogate some of the taken-for-granted aspects of families and to more fully illuminate family communicative practices. As Cassidy (2001) commented, entrenched gendered notions permeate the family context and frame U.S. homes as the site of women's labor and influence (see also Bem, 1993; Sullivan & Turner, 1996; Tronto, 1993), in contrast to the public sphere, where men exert influence.

This gendered bifurcation has been problematized in the literature examining the relationship between work and family (e.g., Garlick, Dixon, & Allen, 1992; Jorgenson, 2000; Nippert-Eng, 1996). As Edley (2004) noted, "At work, individuals are located predominantly in the public realm of business and economics but do not shed private roles of parent, significant other, sibling, child, and friend" (p. 257). However, Kanter (1977) found that corporate America requires its workers to forget about loyalties to anyone or anything in their private lives, and J. Martin (1990; see also Buzzanell & Liu, 2006) argued that this requirement creates suppressed gender conflicts in the workplace, as home-related concerns are ignored.

Wood (2006) noted that training a feminist lens on family prompts scholars to ask different questions than previously posed, such as how fathers reconcile careers and parenting, why a father's home chores are called "helping out," and why sex discrimination is accepted in task assignments at home but not in the workplace. As Wood (2006) pointed out, these are merely some of the questions that taking a feminist turn prompts us to ask. By pursuing such questions, we would discover a wealth of information that addressed policy and other applied issues with reference to family.

However, no matter what lens is used to conceptualize family, the enactment of gender is an inescapable fact of family life. Gendering, through communication, is embedded in the fabric of family encounters, and family encounters reflect gendered assumptions endemic to the family, as well as those superimposed from the general culture. It is impossible to speak of family, therefore, without acknowledging gender, and it is impossible to speak of gender without acknowledging that the context of family animates gender in specific, significant ways. Taking a feminist turn, consequently, demands that applied communication scholars examine this relationship in a more critical manner to empower both women and men.

Constructing Pedagogy

Ever since the American Association of University Women's (AAUW; 1992) pioneering work on the chilly climate for women in the classroom, the impact of gender on the applied communication of teaching has been a key topic. After the family group, school acts as a "second group," serving as a crucial training ground for relational learning, in general (e.g., T. H. Allen & Plax, 2002), and gender relations, in particular. Whether the particular context is elementary, middle, or high school, or college/university, what constitutes gender-sensitive pedagogy has been a site of struggle for the past decade.

Early scholarship on gender and education focused on differences between the sexes, such as girls' seemingly lesser abilities in math and science and boys' higher standardized test scores, and how such differences turned into disadvantages for females, such as less access to higher level courses and less ability to get into highly selective colleges (Bunch & Pollack, 1983). Publication of the book *Women's Ways of Knowing: The Development of Self, Voice, and Mind* in 1986 by Belenkey, Clincy, Goldberger, and Tarule heightened the realization that gender makes a difference in learning styles more than for learning outcomes and led to more responsive teaching, with teachers implementing techniques such as group learning for girls and encouraging girls to take math and science courses. Very soon, public attention focused on girls' schooling, with books, such as Sadker and Sadker's (1995) *Failing at Fairness: How America's Schools Cheat Girls*, appearing, helping teachers to develop communication strategies that encouraged young women to speak up in class. Soon, a sophisticated scholarship on feminist pedagogy flourished, incorporating feminist content and developing distinctive feminist theories of teaching that highlighted issues of authority, power, class, and race.

When attention focused on feminist teaching content and practices, key characteristics of applied communication immediately emerged. Feminist analyses, such as these conducted by the AAUW, showed how: (1) girls and women routinely received less attention in class than did boys and men; (2) topics especially germane to women and girls were given short shrift; (3) girls and women were directed away from math, science, and computers; and (4) role modeling within education reflected the dominant cultural gender hierarchy, with women overrepresented as teachers in elementary schools and under-represented in colleges/universities and as administrators at all levels. Without greater equity in the areas mentioned in the AAUW reports, girls and women are assured a lower quality education as compared to men. Education as a particular type of communication is markedly pragmatic and contextual; its communication choices have direct effects.

Women's studies, as a stand-alone department and as a subarea within communication (and other) departments, has become a mainstay of most college campuses. From a time when that area of scholarship needed advocacy (Culley & Portuges, 1985) to now, progress has been made in terms of theory, research, and courses about women's history, and about ways in which gender affects communicative processes (Meyer, 2004). Textbooks and scholarly texts support the study of women's rhetoric (e.g., Campbell, 1989; K. A. Foss, Foss, & Griffin, 1999; S. K. Foss & Griffin, 1995; Ritchie & Ronald, 2001) and how gender operates in communication (e.g., Buzzanell, Sterk, & Turner, 2004; Ivy & Backlund, 2008; Jaasma, 2004; Pearson, West, & Turner, 1995; Wood, 2007).

More germane to pedagogy as an applied communication endeavor, feminism has transformed ways of teaching through encouraging teachers to enact key feminist principles. One such principle is to *reduce hierarchy* in the classroom by engaging students in interactive learning. This principle begins with recognizing that the position of teacher itself imposes authority relations between teachers and students (e.g., Ropers-Huilman, 1999). Recognition often leads to a conscious leveling of hierarchy through engaging in interactive pedagogies (e.g., Maher & Thompson Tetreault, 2001; Robertson, 1994; Shue & Beck, 2001), whose goal echoes another key feminist principle—*empowerment*, which emerges when students engage with faculty in a mutual quest for knowledge (Bell, 1997; Cohee et al., 1998; Cooks & Sun, 2002; Falk-Rafael, 2004; Fraiman, 1997; Luke, 1996, West, 2004). Indeed, students and faculty are encouraged to *interrogate the concept of authority* itself to intervene actively in traditional power dynamics and produce more democratic attitudes toward teaching (Maher, 1999).

Feminist theory, however, has been challenged to recognize its inherent biases, particularly the bias in favor of White, middle- to upper class experience (e.g., Culley & Potuges, 1985; hooks, 1994, Johnson & Bhatt, 2003). As a counter to that bias, scholars encourage teachers to pull in students' lived experience through exploring their life metaphors (Buzzanell, 2004), engaging in service projects that are directly related to their lives (Meyer, 2004; Novek, 1999), and studying and discussing women's embodiment as a means toward self- and cultural awareness (Russ, 2004). By far, the strongest marker of feminism in pedagogy is a critical stance against the status quo of asymmetrical gender relations, a stance that motivates feminist principles and styles of teaching discussed above (Cooks & Sun, 2002; Crabtree & Sapp, 2003; Safarik, 2002). Critical pedagogies, collaborative learning, and service learning all contribute to the erosion of hierarchies, highlighting race and class as influential in gender relations, showing concern for empowerment of relatively powerless people, and privileging experience (see Darling & Leckie, this volume).

In effect, the feminist premise that asymmetrical power relations are not healthy is based on a core belief in the values of mutuality and respect. As S. K. Foss and Griffin (1995) argued, communicative practices that grow organically from respecting the authentic, authoritative identity of all people enact *invitation*, which encourages interactants to enter into communication and other action because they desire it, not because they are forced to do so. This idea of invitation infuses feminist pedagogical practices, including reduction of hierarchy, practices of empowerment, and interrogation of the concept of authority.

Feminist perspectives also opened the door to considering how traditional educational communicative practices have disadvantaged men and boys, as well as women and girls. The American Association of University Women (1999) published an update to the earlier work cited, showing that although girls had caught up in almost every educational category, boys had fallen behind girls in literacy—the ability to read and write in a wide variety of genres. Research shows that feminist principles of invitation, listening, and understanding embody lived experience and also meet boys' and men's needs in educational settings (e.g., Gurian & Smithson, 2000; Silverstein & Rashbaum, 1994).

In sum, the aim of feminist approaches to applied communication study in the area of pedagogy is, first, to increase awareness of gender hierarchies as key problematic social structures. This awareness, in turn, undermines those structures and empowers students to enter actively into communication, seeing their experiences as valid sources of thought, and speaking and listening for themselves, with increased empathy for others. Research in the applied communication of pedagogy should continue to analyze and evaluate how gender hierarchies affect girls/women and boys/men in school settings, encourage the use of transformative teaching styles, and suggest new areas of content related to gender, to help people empower themselves to live a full life.

Organizing Gender

All of the communicative contexts we discuss are "organizational" on some level, in the sense that families, educational settings, and health organizations can be studied as organizing processes and outcomes. However, this section focuses specifically on exploring ways that gender, discourse, and organizational contexts intersect, shift, and conflict. Ashcraft and Mumby (2004) posited that organizing is inherently and necessarily gendered, arguing that studies of organizations and organizing, therefore, are incomplete without serious consideration of gender.

Until recently, most applied organizational research addressing gender did so either from a sex-difference perspective, in which researchers assumed or focused on how gender is related to different communicative behaviors, styles, and patterns, or by emphasizing communication associated with the integration of women in the workplace (Fairhurst, 1986). Early research examined gender differences in management and leadership styles, and included women's contributions to organizing processes that previously had been neglected (e.g., Calás & Smircich, 1992; Eagly & Johannesen-Schmidt, 2001; Eagly & Johnson, 1990). Such research suggested that women in the workplace indicate preferences for affiliative communication strategies (Baker, 1991; Lucas & Lovaglia, 1998); indirect negotiation strategies, such as suggesting and withdrawing (Sagrestano, 1992); and participative, democratic styles (Eagly & Johnson, 1990). However, in a study of 302 managers and employees from 11 companies, Gayle (1991) found no significant differences between the conflict management styles of women and men. More recently, Lizzio, Wilson, Gilchrist, and Gallois (2003) found that male and female managers both rated a feminine style of delivering negative feedback in the workplace higher than a masculine style. They described a feminine style as including concern about the context of the feedback, affirming the subordinate prior to offering criticism, and taking into account her or his reaction. This research offers conflicting findings and relatively unproblematized notions of sex and gender outcomes.

Employment interviewing research also has emphasized consequences over processes, with empirical investigations analyzing the roles and outcomes of same- and cross-sex applicant–recruiter dyads (e.g., Chapman & Rowe, 2001; Graves & Powell, 1995, 1996). For example, Graves and Powell (1996) found that female interviewers evaluated female candidates more favorably than male candidates. Buttner and McEnally (1996) found that males were more likely than females to receive job offers by using assertive tactics in an interview, whereas females were more likely than males to receive offers if they used rational, unemotional approaches, suggesting that gender influences the interview styles that applicants can use successfully. Despite its popularity, however, a sex-difference approach renders inconclusive, and sometimes conflicting, findings (Buzzanell & Meisenbach, 2006; Conrad, 1991).

Such contradictions in empirical research findings create problems, as an outcome perspective regarding the influence of gender has difficulty accounting for individuals who deviate from typical patterns. Furthermore, Ashcraft and Mumby (2004, p. 7) pointed out that outcome studies "suffer from a general lack of context," an untenable situation for applied research. Buzzanell and Meisenbach (2006) critiqued existing studies of the intersections of gender and employment interviewing, specifically calling for studies that go beyond the outcome perspective on gender and organizing. Buzzanell and Meisenbach (p. 22) argued that "analyses of employment interviewing as gendered performances embedded within specific contexts" still are missing from the literature. Thus, outcome studies not only fail to predict the behaviors of males and females within or across contexts but they also overlook cyclical and structural relations among gender, discourse, and organizational contexts.

Moving beyond an outcome focus, Ashcraft and Mumby (2004), in their articulation of a feminist communicology of organizing, highlighted three other ways to understand relations among gender, communication, and organizing that address these concerns. Their first alternative frame focuses on ways in which individual discourse of microlevel talk organizes gender and gendered identities; their second frame stresses ways in which middle-level organizational discourses, such as formal published job descriptions, engender and are gendered by organizations and organizing; and their third frame directs researchers' attention to ways in which societal discourses engender organizations. Thus, their lenses expand understanding of gender in organizational contexts from consideration of the gendered nature of microlevel individual discourses, through midlevel organizational discourses, to societal discourse–gender intersections. We believe that gendered applied communication scholarship should explore all of these levels.

Feminist researchers already have begun addressing many of these intersections. Collinson and Collinson (1989) argued that the surface-level desexualization of the workplace has only masked the deeply seated masculine nature of organizations, and other scholars have offered evidence for this claim. For example, Ashcraft and Pacanowsky (1996) considered how middle-level discourses engender and are engendered by organizing processes when they argued that standard organizational practices are couched in traditional masculine frameworks that become "normal." Hylmö's (2004) consideration of gendered telecommuting experiences offered an example of an organization reproducing patriarchal systems of meaning in new forms of organizing, with telecommuting at that organization articulated as "another way to enact and embrace masculine rationality and efficiency without question" (p. 68). Her work goes beyond a sex-difference perspective to consider how telecommuting easily reproduces gendered identities and norms, offering an example of gendered research that considers how discourse both engenders and is engendered by organizations and organizing.

Recent gendered and feminist research in organizational communication focuses on a variety of applied issues, such as workplace sexuality and harassment policies from these mid- and macrolevel perspectives. Early definitions of sexual harassment, for example, articulated it as unwelcome, nonreciprocated "male behavior that asserts a woman's sex role over her function as a worker" (Farley, 1978, p. 14), but understanding of harassment has expanded to include women harassing men and harassment within same-sex dyads. The wide range of possible harassment now is a frequent topic of gender-related communication research in organizational contexts (e.g., Clair, 1998; Dougherty, 2001; Jansma, 2000; Taylor & Conrad, 1992; Townsley & Geist, 2000).

Buzzanell (2004) reviewed existing theoretical frameworks for describing and predicting sexual harassment before outlining how poststructuralist and standpoint perspectives stemming from a feminist ethical approach can enrich understanding of harassment and direct different courses of action for multiple stakeholders in harassment processes. Buzzanell maintained that it is the *struggle* to enact equity in everyday life that differentiates feminist from other ethical stances. A feminist ethical approach stresses an iterative and highly contextualized sense-making process (i.e., an ongoing construction of pivotal and mundane events arranged in various ways at different times to make sense to the different storytellers) that evolves over time and place as particular events, people, and details emerge into the foreground of competing versions. This vision of ethics is one in which the embodied, daily struggle of redefining and reframing discourse focuses on the ironies, paradoxes, and contradictions in "doing ethics" (Haney, 1994), and sets standards for what an equitable workplace community looks like (see also the discussion of ethics in applied communication scholarship by Seeger, Sellnow, Ulmer, & Novak, this volume). Some implications for this vision are that training sessions should devote time to participants' construction of highly contextualized accounts that incorporate their reactions to real cases. These sessions should take place in small, informal groups where discussion is prominent.

Just as sexual harassment research has moved beyond an assumption that women are always its victims, other applied feminist organizational research recently has moved in the direction of studying gender as being broader than only a woman's issue. The past decade has seen an emergence of applied scholarship regarding the social construction of masculinities in the workplace (e.g., Cheng, 1996; Collinson, 1992; Collinson & Hearn, 1996; Knights & McCabe, 2001). Furthermore, feminist communication researchers have called for "a more nuanced understanding of what constitutes diversity in organizations" (Meyer & O'Hara, 2004, p. 3; see also B. J. Allen, 1995; Fine, 1996; Nicotera, Clinkscales, Dorsey, & Niles, this volume). For example, Meyer and O'Hara (2004) used a feminist lens to investigate how the subaltern counterpublic of the National Women's Music Festival and the festival's host (Ball State University), as a dominant public, contributed to and resisted various power-laden identity constructions and discourses. Ashcraft and Kedrowicz's (2002) study highlighted how existing models of empowerment used even in a nonprofit feminist organization limit participation and emancipation of diverse members. These areas of exploration have begun the project of seriously advancing feminist consideration of gender in applied communication research. These studies, however, have tended to take a descriptive approach to these issues, describing problems of sexual harassment, feminist organizing groups, and the like, but offering few solutions to the problems revealed. Just as the broader field of organizational studies has grown from descriptive and interpretive studies into critical research that offers emancipating options, so should applied feminist organizational research move toward a focus on solutions.

Gendering Health

According to the International Communication Association's (2009) Health Communication Division, *health communication* is concerned with "the role of communication theory, research and practice in health promotion and health care. Areas of research include provider–patient interaction, social support networks, health information systems, medical ethics, and health policy and promotion" (¶ 1–2; see also Kreps & Bonaguro, this volume; Thompson, Dorsey, Miller, & Parrott, 2003). Using this definition as a springboard, we use the phrase *gendering health* to foreground the active processes by which health is gendered continuously from the microlevel of individual, dyadic, and group concerns to the macrolevel of health policies at the national and global levels, as well as the ways in which the health-care context evokes gender in particular ways.

Health communication research often looks at one sex group or comparisons between the sexes in terms of diseases, treatments, information acquisition and use, and related issues. The focus on one sex group only makes sense insofar as particular illnesses tend to strike primarily members of that group rather than the other. Hence, research on breast cancer, menopause, and other relevant health concerns focuses on how women deal with these issues in terms of physical changes, perceptions of their physical attractiveness, drug use or treatment protocols, support from others, and effects of communication about these health phenomena on overall quality of life (e.g., Ellingson, 2004; Parrott & Condit, 1996a; Quintanilla, Cano, & Ivy, 2004; Sotirin, 2004). For instance, aging breasts or mastectomies may prompt questions about one's femininity given societal constructions of ideal breast appearances and functions (Sotirin, 2004). Feminist research has highlighted the importance of situating women's experiences, such as menopause, within the context of particular women's lives, so that the diversity of their perceptions, biological or physiological changes, treatment choices, and relational changes with significant others can be addressed (Quintanilla et al., 2004).

Comparisons between women and men also have become a staple of health communication research. Through studies exploring gender, culture, and illness, researchers have found that depression manifests itself differently in males and females over the course of their lifetimes and relationships (Uebelacker, Courtnage, & Whisman, 2003). Different antecedent conditions, treatments, and consequences for depression, as well as other health concerns, provide insight into ways in which communication about and surrounding health can be changed to enhance treatment and preventative measures for women (and men). For instance, promotion of community support, whether face-to-face or online, seems important for women because it fits feminine values and approaches that emphasize connection, personal knowledge, and relationships as the heart of personal development (e.g., Goldberger, Tarule, Clinchy, & Belenky, 1996). Thus, it comes as no surprise that social and community network involvement are essential for women's well-being (e.g., when women live in violent relationships; see Klein, 2004), and that a more personalized approach by health-care providers to medical procedures, such as gynecological exams, are preferred by many women (Brann & Mattson, 2004).

Besides looking at health concerns for one sex group or at differences between women and men, health communication researchers also note how specific interactions within health-care contexts are gendered in ways that sustain traditional power imbalances (Kreps, 2004). As an example of power imbalances, physicians attend to female patients' concerns less carefully and seriously than they do to male patients' concerns (Gabbard-Alley, 1995). Health issues, such as menstruation, birthing, menopause, and some forms of cancers or other diseases found predominantly in women, lack sufficient research attention (E. Martin, 2001; Quintanilla et al., 2004). Even when women's needs are the center of attention, health communication and examination techniques may not meet the interests and voiced concerns of many women who desire high-quality caring relationships with their health-care providers and who want to participate fully in decisions regarding their care (Brann & Mattson, 2004).

Moreover, interactions in health-care settings, such as those between providers and patients, may maintain specific notions of gender rather than enlarge gender conceptualizations. Arrington (2000), for instance, found that masculinities may be tightly defined or circumscribed insofar as physicians often try to deemphasize or change the topic when men discuss sexuality following prostate cancer treatment. Arrington found that physicians did not ask about sexual functioning, in general, or sexual problems, specifically, during prostate cancer support group discussions because they feared embarrassing elderly patients, but such omissions perpetuate embarrassment, often leading men to be ashamed to initiate talk about sexuality. However, members did talk frequently about sexuality when psychologists led the support groups. Thus, unless challenged, cultural assumptions about gender identity, sexuality, and discourses appropriate for public or private contexts may hinder development of effective and satisfying health care.

Taking a broader look at gender, health research and funding possibilities have been gendered in ways that reflect sex inequity (Kreps, 2004; Parrott & Condit, 1996b) and that neglect alternative ways of conceiving health communication. In many health communication studies, a biomedical model that is associated with Western medical practices and assumes expert knowledge of providers about patients' bodies and relies on technology is privileged over low-technology, alternative medical approaches, and nonexpert or presumably unreliable knowledge of patients (Ellingson, 2004; Sterk, Hay, Kehoe, Ratcliffe, & Vande Vusse, 2002; Vanderford, Jenks, & Sharf, 1997). Women, children, and members of disenfranchised groups across the globe are underrepresented in studies that position the male and Western culture as normative standards (Dutta-Bergman, 2004; Wear, 1997).

Social-scientific studies that examine the effectiveness of message transmission between health-care providers and actual or potential patients, whether at the dyadic, team, organizational, or public health levels, also traditionally have received greater attention than narrative explorations of people's understandings of treatment, wellness–illness, and life changes (Ellingson, 2005; Geist-Martin, Ray, & Sharf, 2003; Harter, Japp, & Beck, 2005). In distinct contrast to traditional health communication studies, Ellingson (2005) analyzed gender using a multimethodological approach and with varied gender lenses. These lenses included her positionality as a woman and former person with cancer within gendered (masculine) spaces, the role of physician as vested with masculine power despite physician sex, gendered communication patterns among oncology clinic members and patients, gendered disciplinary hierarchies in multidisciplinary oncology teams, and the medical establishment as a sexist institution. Ellingson found, for instance, that although health-care teams usually intended to promote egalitarian interactions between themselves and patients, they maintained professional hierarchies more than they subverted them. She concluded that hierarchy constrained backstage communication at an oncology center to such an extent that informal information and impression sharing primarily occurred among same-status team members and reinforced gendered meanings of teamwork; oncologists' demands were privileged routinely over those of others; team information was funneled through oncologists who felt no obligations to report their findings to other team members in the clinic; and patterns of naming themselves, using titles, and referring to other team members' interventions as "assisting oncologists" reinforced physicians' expertise and devalued the contributions of other team members.

In short, health communication research takes a feminist turn when it explores ways in which members of each sex separately and together understand and gain access to information, treatment, relationships with health-care providers, and preventative measures that they consider to be appropriate, empowering, and of high quality. A feminist approach to health communication not only embraces females' concerns and ways in which males and females treat and are treated differently by health-care providers but also examines the very nature of health communication research and policy. As such, there continues to be great need to advocate for communication discovery and engagement that incorporate feminist praxis and social justice interventions (e.g., Frey, 2006; see also Frey & SunWolf, this volume). Such research studies and practices combine health issues with gendered, cultural, economic, and public policy issues to create change in both everyday micropractices and macropractices, such as health program design and implementations that can benefit the Santalis in India (Dutta-Bergman, 2004), the construction of community hygiene features (Papa, Singhal, & Papa, 2006), and health campaigns in remote areas of the world (Sypher, McKinley, Ventsam, & Valdeavellano., 2002).

Politicizing Gender

The logical conclusion of taking gender seriously in applied communication contexts is a concern for policy. Researchers need to transcend contextual boundaries, exploring common issues regarding gender and the well-being of diverse groups. Positioning gender in applied contexts takes a feminist turn to advocacy because of the commitment of feminism to praxis. Although applied gender communication research has failed to account fully for public policy implications on bodies, families, educational institutions, organizations, communities, and societies, in this section, we discuss important issues and consequences of the politics of gender in applied communication scholarship.

As relevant as communication is to public policy research, relatively little applied communication research directly responds to or is informed by public policy. One could ask, then, why communication researchers should be interested in public policy. Our response lies in the nature and functions of communication. Specifically, communication never exists in a vacuum; it becomes meaningful only when understood within a context. Public policy is part of the communicative context; it colors the communication of all those involved. Moreover, applied communication is important because public policy fails when it does not respond to a communicative accounting of its implications. Thus, a feminist applied communication lens provides insight and critique that not only are unique to public policy research but also are essential to the development and implementation of public policy programs that affect the everyday lives of the community members those public policies claim to help.

What follows are two cases of policy that display the interrelationships of the four applied contexts and gender. Although most of this research either originates in or investigates public policy issues in North America, and particularly that of the United States, a growing body of literature explores international public policy issues that originate from varied and diverse cultures that are outside the scope of this chapter. Here, we aim our gendered lens toward the feminization of (1) poverty and (2) workplace policy.

The feminization of poverty, and policies that stem from this construction, raise issues in family, heath, organizational, and instructional contexts. Whether accurate or not, most people assume that the average poor person in the United States is the stereotypical urban "welfare queen" who has several children, each with a different father, an abusive boyfriend, a drug problem, and no job prospects (Zucchino, 1997). The gendered face of poverty is neither an insignificant detail nor an arbitrary construction. Indeed, the reaction to this image helps to shape and define poverty policy (Asen, 2002; Schram,

2000). The strategic rhetorical construction of the welfare queen—the poor woman with children—as lazy, abusive, defiant, and dependent demands an equally rigid response in the form of policy that addresses her abuse, laziness, defiance, and dependence (Schram, 2000). Like the policies that are created to aid women and children, "the welfare queen is a textual spectacle and a spectral text" (Schram, 2000, p. 55), and when understood as a communicative and gendered text, the political implications and realities of welfare policies become more apparent. Preferred texts function to disadvantage less preferred texts, meaning that already marginalized texts and those who embody the real face of poverty are reduced to two-dimensional stereotypes with superficial needs, which enable policy makers to reduce assistance to surface-level responses that inadequately meet legitimate needs (Asen, 2002).

As evidence of the implications of applied research, a number of scholars have challenged the otherwise much-acclaimed success of the Clinton-era welfare reform: the Personal Responsibility and Work Opportunity Reconciliation Act of 1996 (Asen, 2002; Friedlander & Hamilton, 1996; Greenberg, 1999; Schram, 2000; Seccombe, Walters, & James, 1999). Motivated by decreasing welfare enrollment, many research firms and government agencies praised the welfare reform, but these scholars argued that "success" is not necessarily demonstrated by job employment or decreased welfare enrollment levels. Because the experience of life off welfare rarely is the datum used to determine success or failure of the social program, "successful" programs actually may position women in situations that are more dangerous than when they were on welfare. For example, some women, particularly women with children, may have to return to abusive home situations (an abusive partner, parent, or grandparent) because their allotted time of welfare support (2 years in most states) expired. With little or no government help, these women must rely on others, even if they are abusive, to meet their basic needs. Communicatively accounting for the applied implications of public policy reform is the one method for accurately determining policy value.

A second growing area of public policy in the United States and globally that touches on issues of health, family, and organizational life is work and family management with respect to family leave. In the United States, the passage of the Family and Medical Leave Act of 1993 (FMLA) guaranteed many workers 6 (now 12) weeks of unpaid leave to care for a newborn or adopted child, and for an ill child, partner, or parent, and was heralded as a landmark law that was going to radically change the way men and women work outside the home. However, many parents, especially fathers and women lacking the financial resources to afford unpaid leaves, do not use the FMLA (Kirby, Golden, Medved, Jorgenson, & Buzzanell, 2003; Kirby & Krone, 2002). Leave policy enactment is an instance where progressive policy exists but it neither adequately considers nor understands workers' needs and U.S. work culture (Grant, Hatcher, & Patel, 2005). Although work–family management issues cannot be reduced to simple cause-and-effect equations, communicative approaches to work and family issues indicate that workers need more than guaranteed unpaid leave. People also need to work in organizational cultures that expect members to take family leave; that is, to prioritize family over work-related issues at particular times in their lives (Buzzanell & Liu, 2005; Kirby & Krone, 2002). Ideally, this prioritization means that organizations would make it possible for members to provide care by paying employees during the leave and that those members are encouraged, rather than discouraged, from using such policies. Leave discourse and its implications are examples of where applied communication scholarship comments directly on public policy and its appropriateness and effectiveness, and a feminist lens is particularly helpful in understanding the gendered expectations that shape, and are shaped by, such policy.

The communication research on welfare reform and the FMLA increases our understanding of those affected by these policies. This research also has clear applications to future policy developments. As society changes, new problems and issues develop that require revisions of existing policy. Applied communication research can and, indeed, should inspire creative approaches to both theorizing and implementing policy creation and revision. The reform of existing federal immigration laws and the restriction of women's reproductive and health rights are two emerging policy areas in which feminist applied communication research is highly relevant. At the time of this writing, no revised immigration laws have been passed. However, highly charged public debates over issues of terrorism, illegal workers, low-paying labor, and the welfare system increasingly are becoming galvanized (Campo-Flores, 2006). Set within the context of an economy dependent on both the work of illegal and migrant workers who work for far less than the federal minimum wage and are responsible for much of the agricultural and service work performed in the United States, and on social services, such as public education and health care, that are stretched beyond their budgetary allocations, the U.S. federal government must now respond to growing public concern for homeland safety, especially border security. As evidenced by the diverse reforms proposed by politicians, scholars, and activists from all sides, policy that adequately addresses these problems and meets the relevant needs is hard to come by (Lochhead, 2006). Feminist applied communication research—with its simultaneous focus on both the public and private spheres of society, the heard and unheard subgroups within U.S. culture, and the macro- and microlevels of communication—is uniquely qualified to interpret the current social–political situation and to analyze the lived experience of those affected by newly implemented policies.

Similarly, applied communication research, particularly when conducted with a feminist lens, is especially important for the study of recent advances and legal decisions in women's reproductive rights and health care. In the United States and elsewhere, government policy affects women and their health in a number of ways: access to abortion and the "morning after pill" and other forms of contraception (Kaufman, 2006; Richwine, 2006); research funding for women's diseases (e.g., cervical and uterine cancer; Society for Women's Health Research, 2008); creating and monitoring sexual health education programs for youth ("Sex Education in America," 2004); and establishing and enforcing sexual assault protocols for police, paramedics, and emergency room nurses and physicians.

It has proven challenging in the contemporary political climate to create comprehensive and effective laws, although applied communication research can and often does inform and help to develop legislative policy. Complicating the development of feminist legislation is the issue of *needs interpretation*—the struggle over who and how needs are defined for certain populations (Ferguson, 1984; Fraser, 1989). The U.S. Congress, entrusted with the responsibility to create laws that meet the needs of its citizens and constituents, can be rendered ineffective because of the highly politicized nature of needs interpretation. Bills targeting the very issues mentioned above often are defeated because of conflicting earmarks (e.g., a pro-life Congressional member who supports a bill to increase federal spending for female cancer research may vote against it because of a passage that supports guaranteed access to contraception).

Alternatively, some bills never are debated and voted on, and are left "dead" because the bill was not passed before a new Congress was called into session. In fact, bill introduction (and not necessarily passage), itself, has become politicized, with several members of Congress proposing identical bills, knowing that the bills never would be passed, just to have their names associated with the represented cause or issue (e.g., the bill, H.R. 819: The Prevention First Act, was introduced but never passed in the four previous Congresses and currently is listed under several different bills and names, including

H.R. 2523: Unintended Pregnancy Reduction Act and H.R. 464: The Compassionate Assistance for Rape Emergencies Act of 2007).

The politicization of needs interpretation affects women, men, and children all over the world. Beyond U.S. borders, millions of women still suffer from rape and sexual assault as part of ongoing genocides and civil wars, genital mutilation, and forced participation in sex trafficking. Epidemic and ongoing poverty combined with dangerous social mores and sexual norms in Africa and parts of Asia that permit men to demand unprotected sex from their wife/wives and other women continue to place women and, consequently, children at risk for sexually transmitted diseases, such as HIV and AIDS (Gupta, 2005).

In response to these tragedies, U.S. foreign policy directly affects women who suffer these and similar traumas. However, not all policies are enacted as they were intended. For example, the 2001 reinstatement of the Mexico City policy, also known as the Global Gag Rule (revoked in the opening days of the Obama administration), a U.S. policy that prohibited public health-care workers from discussing abortion options with patients, severally limited women's access to health-care in very poor areas (Population Action International, 2004). Because women usually are the primary caregivers within family structures and often responsible for the gathering and cooking of meals, the health of the wife/mother has a large impact on the entire family and community (clearly demonstrated by the epidemic of children left orphaned by AIDS in Africa and Asia).

As these few cases demonstrate, political decisions directly affect the personal lives of both women *and* men. Given the gravity of these issues, applied communication research is needed to assess the fairness, utility, and changes in these policies. Thus, we urge applied communication scholars to further explore public policy issues from a feminist communication perspective. Being able to speak to these issues, frame and reframe political discussions, and assist with the concrete implementation of policy change must be part of our understanding of what it means to conduct applied communication research.

Conclusion

Positioning gender as fundamental in applied communication scholarship means not only that gender operates as a lens from which theory and research within and across particular applied communication contexts can be enriched productively and pragmatically but also that such scholarship takes as its raison d'être the challenge to put scholarship into practice. For feminist applied communication researchers, this charge insists on scholarship that influences public policy creation and implementation. At its most basic level, this charge requires that applied communication scholars must engage in "translation" of research for various audiences, so that it is usable in the everyday world, as translation "bridges knowledge production with knowledge utilization" (Petronio, 1999, p. 88; see also Frey & SunWolf, this volume).

Taking our cue from Petronio (1999), we urge applied communication researchers to (1) better incorporate solutions to everyday social problems that take into consideration the gendered, hierarchical culture in which people live and that influences each applied communication context; (2) reflect on ways in which scholarship translations can be brought to different audiences who, in turn, shape further scholarship; and (3) work *with* diverse communities to create accessible translations (e.g., through interventions, training, distribution, and instruction) and context-specific practical theory (see Barge & Craig, this volume). In short, we view applied communication scholars as active agents of change through the conduct of inquiry and the dissemination of results and advocacy plans. The important part of this chapter is not simply our report that gender has been researched in multiple ways but, rather, our call to reexamine the goals for feminist applied communication researchers. We hope, therefore, to see an expansion of our field's focus on practical problems embedded within taken-for-granted gendered power relations in diverse applied communication contexts.

References

Allen, B. J. (1995). "Diversity" and organizational communication. *Journal of Applied Communication Research, 23,* 143–155.

Allen, T. H., & Plax, T. G. (2002). Exploring consequences of group communication in the classroom: Unraveling relational learning. In L. R. Frey (Ed.), *New directions in group communication* (pp. 219–234). Thousand Oaks, CA: Sage.

American Association of University Women. (1992). *How schools shortchange girls: The AAUW report: A study of major findings on girls and education.* Washington, DC: National Education Association.

American Association of University Women. (1999). *Gender gaps: Where schools still fail our children.* New York: Marlowe.

Arrington, M. I. (2000). Thinking inside the box: On identity, sexuality, prostate cancer, and social support. *Journal of Aging and Identity, 5,* 151–158.

Asen, R. (2002). *Visions of poverty: Welfare policy and political imagination.* East Lansing: Michigan State University Press.

Ashcraft, K. L., & Kedrowicz, A. (2002). Self-direction or social support? Non-profit empowerment and the tacit employment contract of organizational communication studies. *Communication Monographs, 69,* 88–110.

Ashcraft, K. L., & Mumby, D. K. (2004). *Reworking gender: A feminist communicology of organization.* Thousand Oaks, CA: Sage.

Ashcraft, K. L., & Pacanowsky, M. E. (1996). "A woman's worst enemy": Reflections on a narrative of organizational life and female identity. *Journal of Applied Communication Research, 24,* 217–239.

Baker, M. A. (1991). Gender and verbal communication in professional settings: A review of research. *Management Communication Quarterly, 5,* 36–63.

Belenky, M. F., Clinchy, B. M., Goldberger, N. R., & Tarule, J. M. (1986). *Women's ways of knowing: The development of self, voice, and mind.* New York: Basic Books.

Bell, E. (1997). Listen up. You have to: Voices from "Women and Communication." *Western Journal of Communication, 61,* 89–100.

Bem, S. L. (1993). *The lenses of gender: Transforming the debate on sexual inequality.* New Haven, CT: Yale University Press.

Bochner, A. P. (1976). Conceptual frontiers in the study of families: An introduction to the literature. *Human Communication Research, 2,* 381–397.

Brann, M., & Mattson, M. (2004). Reframing communication during gynecological exams: A feminist virtue ethic of care perspective. In P. M. Buzzanell, H. Sterk, & L. H. Turner (Eds.), *Gender in applied communication contexts* (pp. 147–168). Thousand Oaks, CA: Sage.

Bunch, C., & Pollack, S. (Eds.). (1983). *Learning our way: Essays in feminist education.* Trumansburg, NY: Crossing Press.

Buttner, E. H., & McEnally, M. (1996). The interactive effect of influence tactic, applicant gender, and type of job on hiring recommendations. *Sex Roles, 34,* 581–591.

Buzzanell, P. M. (2004). Metaphor in the classroom: Reframing traditional and alternative uses of language for feminist transformation. In P. M. Buzzanell, H. Sterk, & L. H. Turner (Eds.), *Gender in applied communication contexts* (pp. 195–214). Thousand Oaks, CA: Sage.

Buzzanell, P. M., & Liu, M. (2005). Struggling with maternity leave policies and practices: A poststructuralist feminist analysis of gendered organizing. *Journal of Applied Communication Research, 33,* 1–25.

Buzzanell, P. M., & Liu, M. (2006). *It's "give and take": Maternity leave as a conflict management process.* Unpublished manuscript.

Buzzanell, P. M., & Meisenbach, R. M. (2006). The gendered nature of employment interviewing processes: Framing approaches for future research and practice. In M. Barrett & M. J. Davidson (Eds.), *Gender and communication at work* (pp. 19–37). Burlington, VT: Ashgate.

Buzzanell, P. M., Sterk, H., & Turner, L. H. (Eds.). (2004). *Gender in applied communication contexts*. Thousand Oaks, CA: Sage.

Buzzanell, P. M., & Turner, L. H. (2003). Emotion work revealed by job loss discourse: Backgrounding-foregrounding of feelings, construction of normalcy, and (re)instituting of traditional masculinities. *Journal of Applied Communication Research, 31*, 27–57.

Calás, M. B., & Smircich, L. (1992). Re-writing gender into organizational theorizing: Directions from feminist perspectives. In M. Reed & M. Hughes (Eds.), *Rethinking organization: New directions in organization theory and analysis* (pp. 227–253). Newbury Park, CA: Sage.

Campo-Flores, A. (2006, April 10). America's divide. *Newsweek*, pp. 28–38.

Campbell, K. K. (1989). *Man cannot speak for her: Vol. 1. A critical study of early feminist rhetoric*. New York: Greenwood Press.

Cassidy, M. F. (2001). Cyberspace meets domestic space: Personal computers, women's work, and the gendered territories of the family home. *Critical Studies in Media Communication, 18*, 44–65.

Chapman, D. S., & Rowe, P. M. (2001). The impact of videoconference technology, interview structure, and interviewer gender on interviewer evaluations in the employment interview: A field experiment. *Journal of Occupational and Organizational Psychology, 74*, 279–298.

Cheng, C. (Ed.). (1996). *Masculinities in organizations*. Thousand Oaks, CA: Sage.

Clair, R. P. (1998). *Organizing silence: A world of possibilities*. Albany: State University of New York Press.

Cohee, G. E., Daumer, E., Kemp, T. D., Krebs, P. M., Lafky, S. A., & Runzo, S. (Eds.). (1998). *The feminist teacher anthology: Pedagogies and classroom strategies*. New York: Teacher's College Press.

Collinson, D. L. (1992). *Managing the shopfloor: Subjectivity, masculinity, and workplace culture*. New York: Walter de Gruyter.

Collinson, D. L., & Collinson, M. (1989). Sexuality in the workplace: The domination of men's sexuality. In J. Hearn, D. L. Sheppard, P. Tancred-Sheriff, & G. Burrell (Eds.), *The sexuality of organization* (pp. 91–109). Newbury Park, CA: Sage.

Collinson, D. L., & Hearn, J. (Eds.). (1996). *Men as managers, managers as men: Critical perspectives on men, masculinities, and managements*. Thousand Oaks, CA: Sage.

Conrad, C. (1991). Communication in conflict: Style-strategy relationships. *Communication Monographs, 58*, 135–155.

Cooks, L., & Sun, C. (2002). Constructing gender pedagogies: Desire and resistance in the "alternative" classroom. *Communication Education, 51*, 293–310.

Coontz, S. (1999). Introduction. In S. Coontz (Ed.; with M. Parson & G. Raley), *American families: A multicultural reader* (pp. ix–xxxiii). New York: Routledge.

Crabtree, R. D., & Sapp, D. A. (2003). Theoretical, political, and pedagogical challenges in the feminist classroom: Our struggles to walk the walk. *College Teaching, 51*, 131–140.

Culley, M., & Portuges, C. (1985). *Gendered subjects: The dynamics of feminist teaching*. Boston: Routledge & Kegan Paul.

Dougherty, D. S. (2001). Sexual harassment as [dys]functional process: A feminist standpoint analysis. *Journal of Applied Communication Research, 29*, 372–402.

Dow, B. J., & Condit, C. M. (2005). The state of the art in feminist scholarship in communication. *Journal of Communication, 55*, 448–478.

Dutta-Bergman, M. (2004). The unheard voices of Santalis: Communicating about health from the margins of India. *Communication Theory, 14*, 237–263.

Eagly, A. H., & Johannesen-Schmidt, M. C. (2001). The leadership styles of women and men. *Journal of Social Issues, 57*, 781–797.

Eagly, A. H., & Johnson, B. T. (1990). Gender and leadership style: A meta-analysis. *Psychological Bulletin, 18*, 233–256.

Edelman, H. (1999). *Mother of my mother: The intricate bond between generations*. New York: Dial Press.

Edley, P. P. (2004) Entrepreneurial mothers' balance of work and family. In P. M. Buzzanell, H. Sterk, & L. H. Turner (Eds.), *Gender in applied communication contexts* (pp. 255–273). Thousand Oaks, CA: Sage.

Ellingson, L. L. (2004). Making meaning of chronic illness, disability, and complementary medicine. In P. M. Buzzanell, H. Sterk, & L. H. Turner (Eds.), *Gender in applied communication contexts* (pp. 79–98). Thousand Oaks, CA: Sage.

Ellingson, L. L. (2005). *Communicating in the clinic: Negotiating frontstage and backstage teamwork*. Cresskill, NJ: Hampton Press.

Fairhurst, G. T. (1986). Male–female communication on the job: Literature review and commentary. In M. L. McLaughlin (Ed.), *Communication yearbook* (Vol. 9, pp. 83–116). Beverly Hills, CA: Sage.

Falk-Rafael, A. R. (2004). The effectiveness of feminist pedagogy in empowering a community of learners. *Journal of Nursing Education, 43,* 107–115.

Family and Medical Leave Act, 5 U.S.C. § 630 (1993).

Farley, L. (1978). *Sexual shakedown: The sexual harassment of women on the job.* New York: McGraw-Hill.

Ferguson, K. E. (1984). *The feminist case against bureaucracy.* Philadelphia: Temple University Press.

Fine, M. G. (1996). Cultural diversity in the workplace: The state of the field. *Journal of Business Communication, 33,* 485–502.

Fitness, J., & Duffield, J. (2004). Emotion and communication in families. In A. L. Vangelisti (Ed.), *Handbook of family communication* (pp. 473–494). Mahwah, NJ: Erlbaum.

Fitzpatrick, M. A., & Badzinski, D. M. (1985). All in the family: Interpersonal communication in kin relationships. In M. L. Knapp & G. R. Miller (Eds.), *Handbook of interpersonal communication* (pp. 687–736). Beverly Hills, CA: Sage.

Fitzpatrick, M. A., & Ritchie, L. D. (1993). Communication theory and the family. In P. G. Boss, W. J. Doherty, R. LaRossa, W. R. Schumm, & S. K. Steinmetz (Eds.), *Sourcebook of family theories and methods: A contextual approach* (pp. 565–589). New York: Plenum Press.

Foss, K. A., Foss, S. K., & Griffin, C. L. (1999). *Feminist rhetorical theories.* Thousand Oaks, CA: Sage.

Foss, S. K., & Griffin, C. L. (1995). Beyond persuasion: A proposal for invitational rhetoric. *Communication Monographs, 62,* 2–18.

Fraiman, S. (1997). "Diversity" in adversity: The retreat from affirmative action. *NWSA Journal, 9*(1), 39–43.

Fraser, N. (1989). *Unruly practices: Power, discourse, and gender in contemporary social theory.* Minneapolis: University of Minnesota Press.

Frey, L. R. (2006). Across the great divides: From nonpartisan criticism to partisan criticism to applied communication activism for promoting social change and social justice. In O. Swartz (Ed.), *Social justice and communication scholarship* (pp. 35–51). Mahwah, NJ: Erlbaum.

Friedlander, D., & Hamilton, G. (1996). The impact of a continuous participation obligation in a welfare employment program. *Journal of Human Resources, 31,* 734–756.

Gabbard-Alley, A. S. (1995). Health communication and gender: A review and critique. *Health Communication, 7,* 35–54.

Galvin, K. M. (2004). Commentary: The pastiche of gender and family communication. In P. M. Buzzanell, H. Sterk, & L. H. Turner (Eds.), *Gender in applied communication contexts* (pp. 311–316). Thousand Oaks, CA: Sage.

Garlick, B., Dixon, S., & Allen, P. (Eds.). (1992). *Stereotypes of women in power: Historical perspectives and revisionist views.* New York: Greenwood Press.

Gayle, B. (1991). Sex equity in workplace conflict management. *Journal of Applied Communication Research, 19,* 152–169.

Geist-Martin, P., Ray, E. B., & Sharf, B. F. (2003). *Communicating health: Personal, cultural, and political complexities.* Belmont, CA: Wadsworth/Thompson Learning.

Goldberger, N. R., Tarule, J. M., Clinchy, B. M. & Belenky, M. F. (Eds.). (1996). *Knowledge, difference, and power: Essays inspired by* Women's Ways of Knowing. New York: Basic Books.

Grant, J., Hatcher, T., & Patel, N. (2005). *Expecting better: A state-by-state analysis of parental leave programs.* Washington, DC: National Partnership for Women & Families. Retrieved May 31, 2006, from http://www.nationalpartnership.org/portals/p3/library/PaidLeave/ParentalLeaveReportMay05.pdf

Graves, L. M., & Powell, G. N. (1995). The effect of sex similarity on recruiters' evaluations of actual applicants: A test of the similarity–attraction paradigm. *Personnel Psychology, 48,* 85–98.

Graves, L. M., & Powell, G. N. (1996). Sex similarity, quality of the employment interview and recruiters' evaluation of actual applicants. *Journal of Occupational and Organizational Psychology, 69,* 243–261.

Greenberg, M. (1999). Welfare restructuring and work-poor family policy: The new context. In J. F. Handler & L. White (Eds.), *Hard labor: Women and work in the post–welfare era* (pp. 24–47). Armonk, NY: M. E. Sharpe.

Gupta, G. R. (2005, April 13). *Testimony on women and HIV/AIDS: Presented to Committee on International Relations U.S. House of Representatives.* Retrieved June 1, 2006, from http://www.icrw.org/docs/Speeches/05.04.13%20Testimony%20on%20Women%20and%20Aids.pdf

Gurian, M., & Smithson, I. (2000). *A fine young man: What parents, mentors, and educators can do to shape adolescent boys into exceptional men.* Los Angeles: Jeremy P. Tarcher/Putnam.

Haney, E. H. (1994). What is feminist ethics? A proposal for continuing discussion. In L. K. Daly (Ed.), *Feminist theological ethics: A reader* (pp. 3–12). Louisville, KY: Westminster John Knox Press.

Harter, L. M., Japp, P. M., & Beck, C. S. (2005). Vital problematics of narrative theorizing about health and healing. In L. M. Harter, P. M. Japp, & C. S. Beck (Eds.), *Narratives, health, and healing: Communication theory, research, and practice* (pp. 7–29). Mahwah, NJ: Erlbaum.

hooks, b. (1994). *Teaching to transgress: Education as the practice of freedom.* New York: Routledge.

Hylmö, A. (2004). Women, men, and changing organizations: An organizational culture examination of gendered experiences of telecommuting. In P. M. Buzzanell, H. Sterk, & L. H. Turner (Eds.), *Gender in applied communication contexts* (pp. 47–68). Thousand Oaks, CA: Sage.

International Communication Association. (2009). *Divisions.* Retrieved August 25, 2004, from http://www.icahdq.org/divisions/index.html#DIVISION8

Ivy, D. K., & Backlund, P. (2008). *GenderSpeak: Personal effectiveness in gender communication* (4th ed.). Boston: Pearson/Allyn and Bacon.

Jaasma, M. A. (2004). Aggression in interethnic encounters: Reports by female and male youth in an ethnically diverse school district. In P. M. Buzzanell, H. Sterk, & L. H. Turner (Eds.), *Gender in applied communication contexts* (pp. 231–246). Thousand Oaks, CA: Sage.

Jansma, L. L. (2000). Sexual harassment research: Integration, reformulation, and implications for mitigation efforts. In M. E. Roloff (Ed.), *Communication yearbook* (Vol. 23, pp. 163–225). Thousand Oaks, CA: Sage.

Johnson, J. R., & Bhatt, A. J. (2003). Gendered and racialized identities and alliances in the classroom: Formations in/of resistive space. *Communication Education, 52,* 230–244.

Jones, D. J., Beach, S. R. H., & Jackson, H. (2004). Family influences on health: A framework to organize research and guide intervention. In A. L. Vangelisti (Ed.), *Handbook of family communication* (pp. 647–672). Mahwah, NJ: Erlbaum.

Jones, E., Watson, B., Gardner, J., & Gallois, C. (2004). Organizational communication: Challenges for the new century. *Journal of Communication, 54,* 722–750.

Jorgenson, J. (1994). Situated address and the social construction of "in-law" relationships. *Southern Communication Journal, 59,* 196–204.

Jorgenson, J. (2000). Interpreting the intersections of work and family: Frame conflicts in women's work. *Electronic Journal of Communication, 10*(3–4). Retrieved August 25, 2004, from http://www.cios.org/getfile/JORGEN_V10n3400

Jurik, N. C. (1998). Getting away and getting by: The experiences of self-employed homeworkers. *Work and Occupations, 25,* 7–35.

Kanter, R. M. (1977). *Men and women of the corporation.* New York: Basic Books.

Kaufman, M. (2004, June 18). Staff scientists reject FDA's Plan B reasoning. *Washington Post,* p. A02. Retrieved May 23, 2006, from http://www.washingtonpost.com/wp-dyn/articles/A50466-2004Jun17.html

Kirby, E. L., Golden, A. G., Medved, C. E., Jorgenson, J., & Buzzanell, P. M. (2003). An organizational communication challenge to the discourse of work and family research: From problematics to empowerment. In P. J. Kalbfleisch (Ed.), *Communication yearbook* (Vol. 27, pp. 1–44). Mahwah, NJ: Erlbaum.

Kirby, E. L., & Krone, K. J. (2002). "The policy exists but you can't really use it": Communication and the structuration of work–family policies. *Journal of Applied Communication Research, 30,* 50–77.

Klein, R. (2004). Sickening relationships: Gender-based violence, women's health, and the role of informal third parties. *Journal of Social and Personal Relationships, 21,* 149–165.

Knights, D., & McCabe, D. (2001). "A different world": Shifting masculinities in the transition to call centres. *Organization, 8,* 619–646.

Kreps, G. L. (2004). Commentary: Communication and women's health. In P. M. Buzzanell, H. Sterk, & L. H. Turner (Eds.), *Gender in applied communication contexts* (pp. 169–175). Thousand Oaks, CA: Sage.

Langellier, K. M., & Peterson, E. E. (2004). *Storytelling in daily life: Performing narrative.* Philadelphia: Temple University Press.

Lizzio, A., Wilson, K. L., Gilchrist, J., & Gallois, C. (2003). The role of gender in the construction and evaluation of feedback effectiveness. *Management Communication Quarterly, 16,* 341–379.

Lochhead, C. (2006, May 24). The immigration debate: Capitol Hill standoff: Senate moves toward passing a bill that conservatives in House oppose over "amnesty" provisions. *San Francisco Chronicle,* p. A-1. Retrieved May 29, 2006, from http://www.sfgate.com/cgi-bin/article.cgi?file=/c/a/2006/05/24/MNGLAJ15VV1.DTL

Lucas, J. W., & Lovaglia, M. J. (1998). Leadership, status, gender, group size, and emotion in face-to-face groups. *Sociological Perspectives, 41,* 617–637.

Luke, C. (1996). Feminist pedagogy theory: Reflections on power and authority. *Educational Theory, 46,* 283–302.

Maher, F. A. (1999). Progressive education and feminist pedagogies: Issues in gender, power, and authority. *Teachers College Record, 101,* 35–59.

Maher, F. A., & Thompson Tetreault, M. K. (2001). *The feminist classroom: Dynamics of gender, race, and privilege.* New York: Rowman & Littlefield.

Martin, E. (2001). *The woman in the body: A cultural analysis of reproduction.* Boston: Beacon Press.

Martin, J. (1990). Deconstructing organizational taboos: The suppression of gender conflict in organizations. *Organization Science, 1,* 339–357.

Meyer, M. (2004). From transgression to transformation: Negotiating the opportunities and tensions of engaged pedagogy in the feminist organizational communication classroom. In P. M. Buzzanell, H. Sterk, & L. H. Turner (Eds.), *Gender in applied communication contexts* (pp. 195–214). Thousand Oaks, CA: Sage.

Meyer, M., & O'Hara, L. S. (2004). When they know who we are: The National Women's Music Festival comes to Ball State University. In P. M. Buzzanell, H. Sterk, & L. H. Turner (Eds.), *Gender in applied communication contexts* (pp. 3–23). Thousand Oaks, CA: Sage.

Narayan, U. (1997). *Dislocating cultures: Identities, traditions, and Third-World feminism.* New York: Routledge.

Nippert-Eng, C. E. (1996). *Home and work: Negotiating boundaries through everyday life.* Chicago: University of Chicago Press.

Novek, E. M. (1999). Service-learning is a feminist issue: Transforming communication pedagogy. *Women's Studies in Communication, 22,* 230–240.

Papa, M. J., Singhal, A., & Papa, W. H. (2006). *Organizing for social change: A dialectic journey of theory and praxis.* Thousand Oaks, CA: Sage.

Parrott, R. L., & Condit, C. M. (Eds.). (1996a). *Evaluating women's health messages: A resource book*. Thousand Oaks, CA: Sage.

Parrott, R. L., & Condit, C. M. (1996b). Introduction: Priorities and agendas in communicating about women's reproductive health. In R. L. Parrott & C. M. Condit (Eds.), *Evaluating women's health messages: A resource book* (pp. 1–11). Thousand Oaks, CA: Sage.

Pearson, J. C., West, R. L., & Turner, L. H. (1995). *Gender and communication* (3rd ed.). Madison, WI: Brown & Benchmark.

Penington, B. A., & Turner, L. H. (2004). Playground or training ground? The function of talk in African American and European American mother–adolescent daughter dyads. In P. M. Buzzanell, H. Sterk, & L. H. Turner (Eds.), *Gender in applied communication contexts* (pp. 275–294). Thousand Oaks, CA: Sage.

Petronio, S. (1999). "Translating scholarship into practice": An alternative metaphor. *Journal of Applied Communication Research, 27*, 87–91.

Poole, M. S., & Walther, J. B. (2002). *Communication: Ubiquitous, complex, consequential*. Washington, DC: National Communication Association. Retrieved September 28, 2004, from http://www.natcom.org/research/monograph.pdf

Population Action International. (2004, June). *What you need to know about the Global Gag Rule and U.S. HIV/AIDS assistance: An unofficial guide*. Washington, DC: Author. Retrieved February 3, 2009, from http://www.populationaction.org/publications/reports/Global_Gag_Rule_Gag_Rule_and_US_HIV_AIDS_Assistance/The_Global_Gag_Rule_Gag_Rule_and_US_HIV_AIDS_Assistance.pdf

Quintanilla, K., Cano, N. F., & Ivy, D. K. (2004). The defining of menopause. In P. M. Buzzanell, H. Sterk, & L. H. Turner (Eds.), *Gender in applied communication contexts* (pp. 99–121). Thousand Oaks, CA: Sage.

Richwine, L. (2006, May 25). *Top FDA staff say left out of contraceptive ruling*. Retrieved February 3, 2009, from http://www.commondreams.org/headlines06/0525-04.htm

Ritchie, J., & Ronald, K. (2001) *Available means: An anthology of women's rhetoric(s)*. Pittsburgh, PA: University of Pittsburgh Press.

Robertson, L. (1994). Feminist teacher education: Applying feminist pedagogies to the preparation of new teachers. *Feminist Teacher, 8*, 11–15.

Ropers-Huilman, B. (1999). Scholarship on the other side: Power and caring in feminist education. *NWSA Journal, 11*(1), 118-135.

Russ, T. L. (2004). Body shape(ing) discourse: Bakhtinian intertextuality as a tool for studying discourse and relationships. In P. M. Buzzanell, H. Sterk, & L. H. Turner (Eds.), *Gender in applied communication contexts* (pp. 215–230). Thousand Oaks, CA: Sage.

Sadker, M., & Sadker, D. (1995). *Failing at fairness: How America's schools cheat girls*. New York: Scribner.

Safarik, L. (2002). Theorizing feminist transformation in higher education. *Teachers College Record, 104*, 1718–1759.

Sagrestano, L. M. (1992). Power strategies in interpersonal relationships: The effects of expertise and gender. *Psychology of Women Quarterly, 16*, 481–495.

Schram, S. F. (2000). *After welfare: The culture of postindustrial social policy*. New York: New York University Press.

Seccombe, K., Walters, K. B., & James, D. (1999). "Welfare mothers" welcome reform, urge compassion. *Family Relations, 48*, 197–206.

Sex Education in America: General public/parents survey. (2004, January). National Public Radio/Kaiser Family Foundation/Kennedy School of Government. Retrieved February 3, 2009, from http://www.kff.org/newsmedia/upload/Sex-Education-in-America-General-Public-Parents-Survey-Toplines.pdf

Shue, L. L., & Beck, C. S. (2001). Stepping out of bounds: Performing feminist pedagogy within a dance community. *Communication Education, 50*, 125–143.

Silverstein, O., & Rashbaum, B. (1994). *The courage to raise good men*. New York: Viking Press.

Socha, T. J. (1999). Communication in family units: Studying the first "group." In L. R. Frey (Ed.),

D. S. Gouran & M. S. Poole (Assoc. Eds.), *The handbook of group communication theory and research* (pp. 475–492). Thousand Oaks, CA: Sage.

Society for Women's Health Research. (2008, March 5). *Issue: Federal funding for women's health research.* Retrieved February 3, 2009, from http://www.womenshealthresearch.org/site/PageServer?pagename=policy_issues_funding

Sotirin, P. (2004). Consuming breasts: Our breasts, our selves. In P. M. Buzzanell, H. Sterk, & L. H. Turner (Eds.), *Gender in applied communication contexts* (pp. 123–145). Thousand Oaks, CA: Sage.

Sterk, H., Hay, C., Kehoe, A., Ratcliffe, K., & Vande Vusse, L. (2002). *Who's having this baby? Perspectives on birthing.* East Lansing: Michigan State University Press.

Sullivan, P. A., & Turner, L. H. (1996). *From the margins to the center: Contemporary women and political communication.* Westport, CT: Praeger.

Sypher, B. D., McKinley, M., Ventsam, S., & Valdeavellano, E. E. (2002). Fostering reproductive health through entertainment–education in the Peruvian Amazon: The social construction of Bienvenida Salud! *Communication Theory, 12,* 192–205.

Taylor, B., & Conrad, C. (1992). Narratives of sexual harassment: Organizational dimensions. *Journal of Applied Communication Research, 20,* 401–418.

Thompson, T. L., Dorsey, A., Miller, K. I., & Parrott, R. (Eds.). (2003). *Handbook of health communication.* Mahwah, NJ: Erlbaum.

Townsley, N. C., & Geist, P. (2000). The discursive enactment of hegemony: Sexual harassment and academic organizing. *Western Journal of Communication, 64,* 190–217.

Tronto, J. C. (1993). *Moral boundaries: A political argument for an ethic of care.* New York: Routledge.

Turner, L. H., & Sterk, H. M. (Eds.). (1994). *Differences that make a difference: Examining the assumptions in gender research.* Westport, CT: Bergin & Garvey.

Turner, L. H., & West, R. (2006). *Perspectives on family communication* (3rd ed.). Boston: McGraw-Hill.

Uebelacker, L. A., Courtnage, E. S., & Whisman, M. A. (2003). Correlates of depression and marital dissatisfaction: Perceptions of marital communication style. *Journal of Social and Personal Relationships, 20,* 757–769.

Vanderford, M. L., Jenks, E. B., & Sharf, B. F. (1997). Exploring patients' experiences as a primary source of meaning. *Health Communication, 9,* 13–26.

Vangelisti, A. L. (1993). Communication in the family: The influence of time, relational prototypes, and irrationality. *Communication Monographs, 60,* 42–54.

Wear, D. (1997). *Privilege in the medical academy: A feminist examines gender, race, and power.* New York: Teachers College Press.

West, R. (2004). Commentary: Feminist classrooms. In P. M. Buzzanell, H. Sterk, & L. H. Turner (Eds.), *Gender in applied communication contexts* (pp. 247–252). Thousand Oaks, CA: Sage.

Wood, J. T. (1998). Celebrating diversity in the communication field. *Communication Studies, 49,* 172–178.

Wood, J. T. (2000). Applied communication research: Unbounded and for good reasons. *Journal of Applied Communication Research, 28,* 188–191.

Wood, J. T. (2006). Critical feminist theories: A provocative perspective on families. In D. O. Braithwaite & L. A. Baxter (Eds.), *Engaging theories in family communication: Multiple perspectives* (pp. 197–212). Thousand Oaks, CA: Sage.

Wood, J. T. (2007). *Gendered lives: Communication, gender and culture* (7th ed.). Belmont, CA: Thompson/Wadsworth.

Woodward, K. (1999). Inventing generational models: Psychoanalysis, feminism, literature. In K. Woodward (Ed.), *Figuring age: Women, bodies, generations* (pp. 149–168). Bloomington: Indiana University Press.

Zucchino, D. (1997). *The myth of the welfare queen.* New York: Touchstone Books.

9 Race as Political Identity
Problematic Issues for Applied Communication Research

Anne Maydan Nicotera
George Mason University

Marcia J. Clinkscales
University of Connecticut

Laura K. Dorsey
Morgan State University

Marnel N. Niles
California State University, Fresno

We sit on the cusp of an historic period in American history—the administration of our nation's first non-White president. As it was throughout the Obama primary and presidential election campaigns, race is a continual undercurrent in U.S. society. In Philadelphia, on March 18, 2008, in the wake of furor surrounding the racial commentary and sermons of his outspoken and controversial pastor, the Reverend Jeremiah Wright, Barack Obama gave a stirring speech on race, entitled "A More Perfect Union." In that speech, Obama (2008) addressed ways in which race had been an issue in his campaign, saying:

> At various stages in the campaign, some commentators have deemed me either "too black" or "not black enough." We saw racial tensions bubble to the surface during the week before the South Carolina primary. The press has scoured every exit poll for the latest evidence of racial polarization, not just in terms of white and black, but black and brown as well. (p. 2)

Obama went on to say that the United States cannot afford to ignore issues of race but must face them without the simplifying stereotypes that amplify negatives and distort reality. Obama (p. 3) framed these issues as "a part of our union that we have yet to perfect," and called on U.S. citizens to face these issues squarely rather than retreating. He traced several pressing contemporary problems to America's history of racial injustice. In so doing, he validated both "Black anger" and "White resentment" in a way that vilified neither. He pointed out that our past inability to face these issues has distracted us from pressing issues that affect everyone, and that to heal and unify, we must understand and face our racial history. Obama explained that

> the anger [of Black Americans] is real; it is powerful; and to simply wish it away, to condemn it without understanding its roots, only serves to widen the chasm of misunderstanding that exists between the races.... Just as black anger often proved counterproductive, so have these white resentments distracted attention from the

real culprits of the middle class squeeze—a corporate culture rife with inside dealing, questionable accounting practices, and short-term greed; a Washington dominated by lobbyists and special interests; economic policies that favor the few over
the many. And yet, to wish away the resentments of white Americans, to label them
as misguided or even racist, without recognizing they are grounded in legitimate
concerns—this too widens the racial divide, and blocks the path to understanding.
This is where we are right now. It's a racial stalemate we've been stuck in for years....
But I have asserted a firm conviction—a conviction rooted in my faith in God and
my faith in the American people—that working together we can move beyond some
of our old racial wounds, and that in fact we have no choice if we are to continue on
the path of a more perfect union. (pp. 4, 5)

Obama (2008) mentioned several significant events (e.g., the O. J. Simpson trial and
Hurricane Katrina) that have focused national attention on race. Such occasional events
and acts of violence, such as the Rodney King beating and the James Byrd slaying, bring
thorny problems of race to the surface of everyday conversation and public commentary,
but the furor soon recedes to the discursive background, where it simmers, ready to erupt.
Daily newspapers routinely report local eruptions: crimes that are racially motivated (e.g.,
Rucker & Wan, 2006), the racial "achievement gap" in public education (Strauss, 2006),
and racist remarks made by politicians whose attempts to repair the damage done to
their careers only offend even more people (e.g., Shear, 2006). Obama's election has been
accompanied by an unprecedented sense of racial unity, but it also has elicited racially
motivated hatred. In the pre- and post-election period, Barack Obama received more
death threats than any other president-elect in American history (Washington, 2008).
Cross-burnings, hangings in effigy, shouts of "assassinate Obama" (some from children
as young as 7 years old), boxes of human feces left at the door of a home with an Obama
sign displayed, and threats and attacks against Obama supporters—all stemming from
rage at the election of a Black president (Pardington, 2008; Washington, 2008). According to Washington (2008), specific incidents include:

- Four North Carolina State University students admitted writing anti-Obama comments in a tunnel designated for free speech expression, including one that said: "Let's
  shoot that (N-word) in the head."
- At Standish, Maine, a sign inside the Oak Hill General Store read: "Osama Obama
  Shotgun Pool." Customers could sign up to bet $1 on a date when Obama would be
  killed. "Stabbing, shooting, roadside bombs, they all count," the sign said. At the bottom of the marker board was written "Let's hope someone wins."
- Racist graffiti was found in places including New York's Long Island, where two dozen
  cars were spray-painted; Kilgore, Texas, where the local high school and skate park
  were defaced; and the Los Angeles area, where swastikas, racial slurs and "Go Back
  To Africa" were spray painted on sidewalks, houses and cars.
- Second- and third-grade students on a school bus in Rexburg, Idaho, chanted "assassinate Obama," a district official said.
- University of Alabama [communication] professor Marsha L. Houston said a poster
  of the Obama family was ripped off her office door. A replacement poster was defaced
  with a death threat and a racial slur. "It seems the election brought the racist rats out
  of the woodwork," Houston said.
- Black figures were hanged by nooses from trees on Mount Desert Island, Maine, the
  Bangor Daily News reported. The president of Baylor University in Waco, Texas said
  a rope found hanging from a campus tree was apparently an abandoned swing and
  not a noose.

- Crosses were burned in yards of Obama supporters in Hardwick, N.J., and Apolacan Township, Pa.
- A black teenager in New York City said he was attacked with a bat on election night by four white men who shouted 'Obama.'
- In the Pittsburgh suburb of Forest Hills, a black man said he found a note with a racial slur on his car windshield, saying "now that you voted for Obama, just watch out for your house." (¶ 18–26)

Despite these events, Obama's election has been heralded as the country's entry into "post-racial" America. President Obama has commented at length on the social meaning of his racial identity as a potential harbinger of racial unity and national transformation (Fletcher, 2009). To understand this shift in language and thinking, and to facilitate progress toward transformation and unity, we need to understand race and racially motivated hatred. Racially motivated hatred and associated problems cannot be attributable to "race" itself, because "race" is neither a material "thing" nor a fixed idea. Rather, these problems are attributable to the ways we, as citizens and scholars, think (and fail to think) about race. Moreover, this explanation begs the question of what applied communication scholars can do about the ways in which we think about race.

This chapter organizes theoretical and empirical literature into a general conceptual framework that provides an agenda for the study of race in applied communication scholarship. We first establish a foundation from which to understand race as a social–political construction. We then review and critique a small body of applied communication literature that examines race. The selection of that literature was inherently problematic, but we found ourselves in good company, for as Hall (1980) claimed, "attempts to deal with the question of 'race' directly or to analyze those social formations where race is a salient feature constitute, by now, a formidable, immense, and varied literature, which is impossible to summarize at all adequately" (p. 305). There is much written about race, but determining what constitutes "communication" and "applied" research was daunting. Literature is included that supports a theoretic construction of race as an interactive phenomenon or that focuses on practical problems related to race. Some of the most fruitful work on race in the field of communication is rhetorical, but a full review of that literature is beyond the scope and outside the focus of this chapter.[1] Finally, we provide a model to organize the literature, ground it in a social constructionist understanding of race, and offer a framework to guide the study of race in applied communication scholarship.

Race as Socially Constructed

Race is a major source of domination (Nkomo, 1992), but "the poverty of our racial attention span" (Ashcraft & Allen, 2003, p. 32) is pervasive in the field of communication. In response, we promote herein a view of society and communication as raced. Theorists across social disciplines broadly agree that "race" is a social or cultural construct. As Haney Lopez (2000) explained, "Race must be viewed as a social construction. That is, human interaction rather than natural differentiation must be seen as the source and continued basis for racial categorization" (p. 168). Furthermore, "the effort must be made to understand race as an unstable and decentered complex of social meanings constantly being transformed by political struggle" (Omi & Winant, 1994, p. 55). Race is a repeatedly regenerated ideological construct: Interaction reifies race, creating and re-creating race as a set of categories that structure interaction (Miles, 1982, 1989). For example, race signifies and symbolizes social conflicts "by referring to different types of human bodies"; the selection of physical human features for the purpose of racial signification is "necessarily a social and historical process" (Omi & Winant, 1994, p. 55).

Haney Lopez (2000) argued that "race is not determined by a single gene or gene cluster.... The data compiled by various scientists demonstrate, contrary to popular opinion, that intra-group differences exceed inter-group differences" (p. 166). Evolutionary biologist Lewontin's (1972) comprehensive global study of genetic diversity within and between ethnic populations and races concluded that racial classification has "virtually no genetic or taxonomic significance" (p. 397). Biologically, individual human variation is immense, and most of that variation is not culturally attributed to "race" (Lewontin). Biologists and geneticists can identify patterns of genetic mutation and adaptation in human populations, but the differences are small and linked mostly to geography (Jorde & Wooding, 2004).

The physical characteristics used to categorize human beings into "races," of course, are determined genetically. Socially, it is agreed that if a person has particular characteristics, he or she belongs to a particular racial group, but that does not make those characteristics useful for genetic taxonomic purposes. The enormous genetic variation that exists within populations labeled as "races" precludes such genetic categorization. Simply stated, racial categorization of social groups is based on physical features of appearance, not vice versa. In fact, geneticists do not equate "race" with biology. For such things as identifying and treating disease, and susceptibility to disease, individual genetic makeup is a far more useful application of genetic science than is racial categorization (Tishkoff & Kidd, 2004). Disease is associated with groups due to common genetic history, some of which also gets labeled "race," but susceptibility to disease for certain human populations is not determined by "race." For example, all Black people do not get sickle cell disease, and all people who get sickle cell disease are not Black. Disease, therefore, is not a racial marker. Biological and genetic factors certainly contribute to diseases, but that does not mean that they define a racial group. Geneticists explicitly define "race" as a social category (Royal & Dunston, 2004), and that should be our most compelling reason to follow suit.

Although geneticists reject the construct of "race" as a useful taxonomy for categorizing human beings, the idea of race is not going away any time soon. Certain characteristics of human appearance (e.g., skin hue, eye shape, and hair texture) tend to be used as racial markers, but not other visible variations between human populations (e.g., height and ear size). The fact that racial categorization is not defensible by biological or genetic evidence is less important than the implications of this fact for the cultural meanings imposed on these categorizations. In fact, because it is based on phenotypical difference,

> racism discovers what other ideologies have to construct: an apparently "natural" and universal basis in nature itself. Yet, despite this apparent grounding in biological difference, outside history, racism, when it appears, has an effect on other ideological formations within the same society, and its development promotes a transformation of the whole ideological field in which it becomes operative. It can, in this way, harness other ideological discourses to itself—for example it articulates securely with the us/them structure of corporate class consciousness. (Hall, 1980, p. 342)

Race, thus, is a classed phenomenon, but in the field of communication, few scholars outside of rhetoric work to theorize that notion.

The term *race* entered the English language in the 16th century to denote lineage, but it was "during the 18th century, with the scientific assertion of the existence of biologically constituted races, [that] the term 'race' came to mean discrete categories of human beings, based on phenotypical differences, and *ranked with psychological and social capacities* [italics added]" (Torres & Ngin, 1995, p. 57). This explicit ranking in the racial taxonomy reveals the deliberate notion of superiority/inferiority in the political agenda behind the "science." These racial designations (Caucasoid, Negroid, and Mongoloid), the fundamental basis for our contemporary category system, were created by 18th-century European scientists for the overt purpose of class oppression.[2]

In the 19th century, the "scientific" discipline of "ethnology" sought to discover biological criteria by which to define race. DuBois (1940) documented how "race dogma" taught at Harvard University, under the guise of "science," sought empirical evidence of White superiority. Of course, one of the primary aims of ethnology was to provide a biological basis for the continued enslavement of African Americans. A narrative based on the "science" of ethnology published in the *Southern Quarterly Review* in 1851 designated "savagism...and its natural result bondage" as the "native state" or "being" of the "Negro," and "further that he enjoys more pleasure in a savage state, or in bondage, than in civilized freedom" (Browne, 2000, p. 271). Ethnology failed to find scientific criteria to define racial categories by which to privilege some over others. In fact, 19th-century African-American scholars easily refuted the historical arguments of ethnologists (Browne, 2000). Still, although social scientists, geneticists, and biologists reject the notion of race as biological, "few in society seem prepared to relinquish fully their subscription to notions of biological race" (Haney Lopez, 2000, p. 167). We are culturally taught that race is biology, but it is not. Haney Lopez (2000) defined "race" as

> a vast group of people loosely bound together by historically contingent, socially significant elements of their morphology and/or ancestry.... Race must be understood as a sui generic social phenomenon in which contested systems of meaning serve as the connections between physical features, faces, and personal characteristics. In other words, social meanings connect our faces to our souls. Race is neither an essence nor an illusion, but rather an ongoing contradictory, self-reinforcing, plastic process subject to the macro forces of social and political struggle and the micro effects of daily decisions.... The referents of terms like Black and White are social groups, not genetically distinct branches of humankind. (p. 165)[3]

Haney Lopez (2000), writing from a legal standpoint, developed a theory of racial fabrication that provides the basis for the conceptual framework we build here. This theory goes beyond the idea of "racial formation" used by others (e.g., Omi & Winant, 1994) to emphasize social construction and expose "race" as a plastic and inconstant construct. As Haney Lopez argued:

> First, humans rather than abstract social forces produce races. Second, as human constructs, races constitute an integral part of a whole social fabric that includes gender and class relations. Third, the meaning-systems surrounding race change quickly rather than slowly. Finally, races are constructed relationally, against one another, rather than in isolation. Fabrication implies the workings of human hands, and suggests the possible intention to deceive. (p. 168)

The theory of racial fabrication is an excellent foundation for communication scholarship, for the processes emphasized by Haney Lopez are the very stuff of communication theory: interaction, social context, shared meaning, and relationship. We emphasize further that the social fabrication of race is a discursive hegemonic process that upholds the societal political structure of unearned White privilege (van Dijk, 1987, 1993a, 1993b).[4] Given this understanding of "race," we now examine how race has been treated in applied communication research.

The Treatment of Race in Applied Communication Scholarship

Problems associated with race are ripe for analysis by applied communication scholars, but most scholars have not adequately dealt with the construct of race itself. Furthermore, there has been no systematic delineation of the complex practical problems engendered by the complexity of race. We organize the literature to create a systematic set of arenas under the umbrella concept of "applied communication and race." Having introduced the idea that race is a cultural–political construct, it is important to construct through this lens a typology of distinct ways in which race is treated in applied communication research. We find it far more useful to categorize the relevant literature based on the practical problems addressed, rather than on contexts, because what defines applied communication research is its focus on practical problems. From an examination of the literature, we identified four primary arenas of problematic issues of race examined by applied communication scholars: identity, racism, discrimination, and diversity. These arenas, of course, overlap; many studies address more than one arena, and, therefore, could have been categorized differently, but the category scheme serves as a useful organizing framework.

Prior to reviewing that literature, we discuss our understanding of each area, which later translates directly to a theoretic model we propose as a framework to guide the applied communication study of race. Most, but not all, applied communication scholars acknowledge neither implicitly nor explicitly the social construction of race as a fabrication. Consequently, race is not generally understood as a meaning system that is humanly produced, interactively created and woven into the social fabric, along with gender and class, constructed and reconstructed interactively to change the meanings ascribed to it, and constructed relationally among racial groups with one defined against another.

Problematic Issues of Identity

Race often is treated by communication scholars as operating in isolation from other social-identity factors and relevant only in discussions of cultural differences (Ashcraft & Allen, 2003). Under this logic, difference is treated at a surface level, cultural identities are essentialized, and Whiteness becomes "an invisible, homogenous standard" (Ashcraft & Allen, 2003, p. 15). The communication literature on identity shows no consistent use of the terms *race*, *ethnicity*, and *culture*, resulting in confusion and an inability to articulate that which we purport to understand (Jackson & Garner, 1998). We add that a prevalent reduction of "race" to "Black-White" in that literature further obfuscates the issues. The applied communication literature is no exception, for most often, racial categories are imposed, implicitly essentialized as identity, and explicitly treated as a primary identifying factor leading to presumed similarities within and differences between groups. Applied communication scholars only rarely acknowledge that racial identity is culturally wrought. In fact, most of that research treats identity as synonymous with racial classification, typically selected by participants from among a set of labels imposed by researchers, which is true of many studies in the other three categories as well.

The studies reviewed here are divided into two basic types: those that essentialize race as identity and those few that explicitly examine identity (which we consider to be exemplars for a fruitful understanding of problematic issues of identity). To understand the first type of studies, consider the multitude of racial category labels generated over time. Although the 18th-century European three-category scheme has expanded, some labels have changed, and some labels have developed associated subcategories, the category system remains essentially the same. We have known Americans of African descent as *Negroes*, *Colored*, *Blacks*, *Afro-Americans*, and now *African Americans*. Similarly, those who were once *Mongoloid* became *Oriental*, but there now are several categories of *Asian*. A category was added for *Indians*, who became *American Indians* and then *Native Americans*. A cross-racial ethnic designation was created for *Hispanics*, some of whom are known as *Chicano/a*, but all of whom may soon become best known as *Latino/a*. It is interesting to note that the original term *Caucasian* still is used inter-changeably with *White*, and as evidence of its inherent implication of superiority, the term still is free of the degrading connotations attached to *Negro* or *Mongoloid*. Belying the political nature of these terms (Niven & Zilber, 2000), they often are hotly debated and sometimes overtly rejected by those who would be identified by such a label (e.g., Sigelman, Tuch, & Martin, 2005).

The presumption of racial classification based on skin color as integral to identity has become so uncritically accepted that the labels are applied without recognition that the entirety of their meaning is *culturally/politically assigned*, a point West (1993) made in his seminal work, *Race Matters*, when he suggested that the identity construct of "black-ness" has no meaning outside of a cultural system of race-conscious people and practices. Currently, the term *persons of color*, used for all non-Whites, seems, on the surface, to be inclusive, but it serves to establish "White" as the standard and to reify skin hue as a "natural" basis for human social categorization, just as the term *minority* serves to reify dominance by a majority.

Individuals assigned to the same racial group are assumed to identify more readily with one another than with members of other racial groups (e.g., Chambers et al., 1998; Dutton, Singer, & Devlin, 1998). Moreover, the link between race and identity is essentialis-tically assumed in most applied communication research. It is assumed, for instance, that racial grouping is an appropriate and effective way to examine, for example, the effects of health communication campaigns (e.g., Alcalay & Bell, 1996; Bates, Poirot, Harris, Condit, & Achter, 2004), patterns of medical information seeking (e.g., Matthews, Sell-ergren, Manfredi, & Williams, 2002), consumer use of and response to entertainment media (e.g., Oliver, 1996), and patterns of mentoring relationships (e.g., Kalbfleisch & Davies, 1991). Studies of such intergroup "race" differences abound, but the deep cul-tural, political, and historical meanings of racial identity usually go unrecognized. War-ren (2001), thus, argued that there is need for a more "performative reading of racial identity—where the presence of race does not get reduced to a reading of an essentialized raced body, nor is the body divorced from racial identity, creating a false separation" (p. 92). In a similar vein, Berard (2005) found that politically salient categories, such as racial group, are not always relevant in particular contexts, stating:

> Even when they are, their relevance cannot properly be understood without an appre-ciation for the multiplicity and diversity of identities which become relevant in par-ticular contexts and courses of action…. Identity can be respecified more widely and more finely by situating identity within natural language use and social interaction. (p. 1)

Simply put, culture, community, and self-identifications are more salient than color (apparent racial category), which, when it is meaningful, is just one part of social group-ing. Hence, when researchers implicitly assume that racial group category is an important and primary identifying factor warranting generalization, and assessed by forced-choice racial group identification, they ignore numerous factors (e.g., personal background fac-tors, current political climate, education, income, and regional culture and history) that create enormous variance within "racial groups." The extent to which these factors are ignored leads to misplaced and inaccurate conclusions about "race." This tendency is not an indictment of the social-scientific approach per se but, rather, an observation that, with regard to race, such science has not been carefully executed (Davis, Nakayama, & Martin, 2000; Martin & Davis, 2000; Stephan & Stephan, 2000).

Appiah (2002) offered an excellent example of examining phenotypical racial group not as an essentializing category but as an identity factor, examining the links between strength of ethnic identity and response to Web-based media. Appiah found that Blacks with strong ethnic identities spent more time looking at Web sites targeted toward Blacks and responded more favorably toward those sites, whereas Blacks with weak ethnic identities showed no difference in the amount of time looking at a Black or White-targeted Web site, and did not favor one over the other. This racial categorization, however, is a deeply political issue, for to be an "authentic" Black or a Black who "keeps it real" means to identify with certain market forces that are designed specifically for Blacks (Coleman, 2003). Coleman (2003) defined "keeping it real" as remaining true to one's "historical, cultural, and…racial roots," and referred to this term as an "identity politics position [that] relies on an illusionary racial prism, co-mingling essentialist, biological race categories with constructionist cultural claims" (p. 59). Jackson and Heckman (2002) noted that "identity negotiation is already intricate; race complicates the discursive equation and invokes polarity, skin color politics, normativity, and perhaps most of all, liability" (p. 435). As Coleman (2003) explained:

> Naming that which is linked to the Black experience as "Black" serves as an identity politics maneuver where claiming an identity—what it means and how it is produced in the social discourse—particularly an oppressed or marginalized identity, becomes a point of political departure in which the group is mobilized to celebrate the uniqueness and contributory nature of that identity. (p. 56)

Jackson (1999) powerfully documented ways in which African-American and European-American college students communicatively negotiate racial identity. He argued for a conceptualization of race that is both biological and sociological, basing the biological component on the phenological differences that mark racial groups. Themes of identity for European Americans included social adjustment or no concern at all, whereas themes for African Americans included a complex set of factors related to causes and effects of cultural identity negotiation, the necessity of a defined cultural identity, and the importance of African-American identity and distinctiveness (for more detailed treatment, see Jackson, 2006; the special journal issues edited by Jackson, 2001, 2002, and by Jackson & Hendrix, 2003).

Several scholars have illustrated how racially based constructions of identity are a primary force defining things such as the classroom experience (Johnson & Bhatt, 2003), the workplace (Hegde & DiCicco-Bloom, 2002; Parker, 2002), and interracial personal relationships (Diggs & Clark, 2002; Foeman & Nance, 2002). In these contexts, race, gender, culture, and class intersect to make identity at once a deeply personal and deeply political process (Macinlay, 2003). Together, these studies powerfully demonstrate the fluid, relational, personal, and political nature of racial identity; the complex constitution of identity and meaning negotiation; and the operation of the frameworks of race, class, and gender. Indeed, race, class, and gender are "key intersectional dimensions" (Avant-Mier & Hasian, 2002, p. 393) that influence the formation of identities. Race, thus, is an "organizing principle" (Avant-Mier & Hasian, 2002, p. 393) that structures interactions (Parker, 2002; for more in-depth treatment of these issues, see Parker, 2001, 2003, 2005).

Perhaps the most careful treatment of race can be found in Bell and Nkomo's (2001) study of Black and White professional women's experiences, which explored ways in which class, race, and gender intersect to exert profound influence on the development of professional identity. The researchers' understanding of race is embedded in culture, which is embedded in history, leading them to explore participants' formative life and professional experiences, and culminating in a work that is insightful for understanding issues faced by Black and White women in professional contexts.

Problematic Issues of Racism

Many applied communication scholars focus on racism. To frame our critique of this literature, we follow Omi and Winant's (1994) conceptualization of *racism* as practices that create and reproduce "structures of domination based on essentialist categories of race" (p. 71). From this perspective, divisional societal power structures (e.g., government institutions, educational systems, and employment arenas) mutually create and sustain racism, with access to these structures and their privileges determined, in part, by the political imposition of racial categories. The contemporary cultural meaning of race, thus, is rooted in a history of racism (for a thought-provoking essay about the difficulties and political posturing that occur in defining racism, see Barker, 1981).

Representing a growing body of scholars across disciplines (e.g., Coleman, 2002; Domke, McCoy, & Torres, 1999; Gandy & Baron, 1998; Hurwitz & Peffley, 1997; Kinder & Sanders, 1996; Mendelberg, 2001; Pan & Kosicki, 1996; Peffley, Shields, & Williams, 1996; Sniderman & Piazza, 1993; Valentino, 1999) who are examining ways in which public opinion regarding race is systematically framed by communication in the public sphere, Domke (2001) conducted an experiment in which participants were given newspaper articles that framed political policy issues with or without racial cues. Domke found that "the presence or absence of racial cues in political discourse, by priming participants to focus on some considerations and relationships and not others, influences the nature of the associations among individuals' racial perceptions, political ideology, and issue evaluations" (p. 788). Domke also was sensitive to issues of class, but only on a surface level, noting that his sample, although racially diverse, represented an educated, middle-income segment of society. Although Domke essentialized race and ethnicity, and did not attend theoretically to the notion of class, he brought much-needed attention to linkages among public communication, politics, race, society, and racism.

Richardson (2005) also examined the impact of media framing, but with an overt assumption of race as socially constructed. In a study of White, non-Hispanic participants, frames (diversity, remedial action, both, or neither) were embedded in editorials supporting an affirmative action case in higher education. Although frame variation had no effect on feelings toward affirmative action, the diversity frame was linked to more positive perceptions of Blacks.

Other scholars have examined popular entertainment media as a significant site of public communication on race (e.g., B. Cooper, 1998; Entman, 1990; González & González, 2002; Gray, 2001; Harris & Donmoyer, 2000; Meyers, 2004; Prosise & Johnson, 2004; Rockler, 2002; Tan, 2000). Although these studies attend to cultural and political meanings that perpetuate racism, they do not treat racial identity as socially constructed and tend to essentialize racial groups.

Research on racism in the educational system also tends to utilize essentialistic categorization (e.g., Cooks, 2003; Harris, 2003; Johnson & Bhatt, 2003; Mackinlay, 2003), sometimes paying no attention to racial categories beyond Black–White (e.g., Artz, 1998; E. Cooper & Allen, 1998; Priest, 2000). Except for Patton's (2004) thoughtful consideration of political-hegemonic structures and Jackson and Heckman's (2002) discussion of racism on a college campus, "racism" is not generally acknowledged as a social construction. Patton (p. 61) differentiated between three types of racism—overt, denied, and inferential: "overt racisms refers to those actions that we can point to and say, 'that's racist'"; denial of racism "is the belief that racism does not exist or that only a few 'bad people' practice racist behavior"; and inferential racism, which is the most dangerous form of racism, in that it is not overt and, thus, harder to identify because it involves ways in which racist assumptions and practices, usually unknowingly, rest on invisible taken-for-granted presumptions of what seems to be a natural order. As Patton explained about inferential racism:

> These "isms" are often entrenched in higher education through policy and the inad-vertent actions of administrators, faculty, staff, and students.... Hegemonic civility is so ingrained that it shows up everywhere, even in semi-private journal entries crafted to be read by a visibly non-White professor. (p. 62)

Jackson and Heckman's (2002) treatment of hate crimes on college campuses reveals the connection between overt and inferential racism. As Jackson and Heckman explained, racial hate crimes "almost seem endemic to academic institutions, where freedom of expression is celebrated and incivility is often mildly penalized" (p. 435). Moreover, Jack-son and Heckman argued:

> Within an episode where racism is communicated, the dialectical exchange between interactants is immediately engaged by the instrumentation of race—its corporeal visibility, instinctive historical gaze, profound modernist obsession, and significatory political meaning.... Instantaneously it calls White identities into question for two reasons: first, because racism is a power-laden activity meant to sustain privilege, and second, the logic of race equates White identities with White privilege. (p. 425)

In perhaps the most practically applied study of racism, Williams and Olaniran (2002) powerfully documented a 1998 incident in which Hampton University's head basketball coach, her husband, and an assistant coach were falsely accused of running a scam at a Wal-Mart store in Lubbock, Texas, during a visit for a game against Texas Tech Uni-versity. The scam was reported to the Lubbock city police, who detained these three people for several hours. The victim identified one of the coaches as the con-artist, but security tapes clearly exonerated them. The accused individuals were released, but their game was cancelled, and the coach later filed an unsuccessful civil rights lawsuit against the city of Lubbock, claiming that the arrests were racially motivated. Williams and Olaniran concluded that Lubbock's official response—a limited apology and an attack on the accuser—was successful, but risky. This analysis, however, would have profited from a view of race as a social construction. Because the basic assumption of what race means—culturally and politically—was not established by the researchers, any recom-mendations for change could only be given at a surface level. The potential for using this and other such incidents as "teachable moments" about racism and its political bases goes unfulfilled without a treatment of race and racism as socially fabricated.

Problematic Issues of Discrimination

Discrimination is directly related to racism, but their levels of abstraction distinguish them: Studies about racism focus at the level of racist belief systems and may or may not consider their practical implications, whereas studies about discrimination focus specifi-cally on mistreatment, particularly denial of privilege or opportunity, and implicitly or explicitly presume that such treatment is the result of an underlying racist ideology. As done previously, we first frame our discussion of applied communication scholarship with our understanding of "discrimination."

Individuals often experience their race through the construct of systemic mistreatment—as a target or perpetrator of that mistreatment, or as an observer. Race discrimination has become so culturally ingrained that race-discrimination lawsuits are common, with firmly established bureaucratic structures to process them. According to data compiled by the U.S. Equal Employment Opportunity Commission's (EEOC; 2005) national database, since 1992, the number of charge receipts filed and resolved under Title VII alleging race-based discrimination has remained steady—typically, about 28,000 cases annually; in that same time period, the monetary awards of these cases doubled, not including monetary awards gained through litigation. For many, the term *race* most powerfully has meaning when it is associated with illegal acts of "discrimination" (for a critical history of affirmative action and the politics of racism in the United States, see Marable, 1995).

Although communication researchers have examined the relationship between discrimination and gender (e.g., Buzzanell, 1995; Clair & Thompson, 1996; Hutton, 2005; see also Buzzanell, Meisenbach, Remke, Sterk, & Turner, this volume), few have looked at the relationship between discrimination and race. Becker, Lauf, and Lowrey (1999) noted that among journalism and mass communication graduates, race and ethnicity are associated with lower employment levels; indeed, in every year from 1990 to 1997, being Black "was negatively associated with getting a job offer in the field of journalism and mass communication" (p. 640). Hispanics in the United States also report experiencing racial discrimination to a significant degree (Becker et al.), most commonly in work and school contexts, followed by public contexts, with young, affluent White men being the most likely to practice discrimination (Korzenny & Schiff, 1987). According to Pride (1999):

> Explanations for racial inequality in the United States vary considerably and have varied over time. For example, some have attributed inequalities to attributes of Black people themselves, while others have seen African Americans as victims of White discrimination or oppression, past or present. (p. 149)

Race, thus, can be viewed through the effects of racial discrimination. Because these effects often are negative, race often is conceptualized negatively; hence, the meaning of the term *discrimination* gives cultural meaning to the term *race*.

This literature shows two important things. First, precious little applied communication research deeply examines racism or racial discrimination. Second, with just a few notable exceptions, that research is grounded in a limited understanding of race. An understanding of race as a humanly produced meaning system rooted in class oppression potentially leads to promising solutions to problematic issues of racism and racial discrimination.

Problematic Issues of Diversity

Finally, we categorize the remaining research to be reviewed as focusing on diversity. As done previously, a critique of this literature is framed by our approach to the concept of "diversity."

The term *diversity* has become a part of the linguistic mainstream, with applied communication scholars and the general public alike generally thinking of diversity in terms of "representation." Federally mandated EEOC policies to have a population of employees who are "representative" of societal racial demographics have fostered the notion that if there are "representative numbers" of "representative races," diversity is achieved. Similarly, applied communication scholars often treat "diversity" as little more than an offshoot of "discrimination," in that conceptualizations of diversity usually go no further than group representation and tolerance of that representation by the "dominant culture." In our view, representation simply is a way of experiencing opportunity: One has to be present to be involved, and if members of a particular group are not present, then opportunities are denied to them.

Overall, the tone of the applied communication literature is that diversity is inherently difficult. As Allen (1995) noted:

> Differences in employees' racial-ethnic backgrounds can affect formal and informal organizational communication processes: stereotypes and expectations based upon others' race-ethnicity may impede effective interaction; and differences in value systems and cultural norms may influence attitudes, expectations, perceptions, and language behaviors. (p. 148)

Many communication scholars similarly assume that diversity is defined by racial categories (e.g., Carrell, 1997; Gross, Craft, Cameron, & Antecol, 2002; Halualani, Chitgopekar, Morrison & Dodge, 2004; Mellinger, 2003). A number of studies examine diversity management, intercultural interaction of racial groups, and managerial responses to diversity issues, belying an implicit assumption that cultural misunderstanding at the individual level is the root cause of interracial disharmony. These scholars define diversity in numeric terms, with race defined through traditional categories of ethnic group membership, thus treating diversity as racial representation and tolerance (e.g., Amason, Allen, & Holmes, 1999; Brinson & Benoit, 1999; Kossek & Zonia, 1994). Some research using this approach also includes other factors, such as gender, age, education, and sexual orientation, as categories of "difference" (e.g., Meares, Oetzel, Torres, Dekarcs, & Ginossar, 2004).

Although they implicitly define diversity as the numeric mixture of racial groups, several applied communication studies enrich our understanding with a focus on the viewpoint of the "minority" group. Foeman and Pressley (1987), for instance, identified interpersonal skills that African Americans bring to organizations as including forthrightness, ethical awareness, a "highly engaging style" of communication, group identification, and a "unique use of language" (pp. 299, 300). These "Black styles" (Foeman & Pressley, 1987, p. 297), linked to cultural patterns, were distinguished from skills that Whites bring to organizations. Martin, Moore, Hecht, and Larkey (2001, p. 5) examined how African Americans negotiated "interracial communication in daily organizational life," finding a number of conversational strategies, including friendliness and avoidance. They also found that accommodation strategies were employed in both interpersonal and intergroup communication, but in intergroup communication, only divergent strategies were used. Orbe (1994) examined African-American males' communication using a phenomenological approach and found six emergent themes: (1) the importance of communicating with other African Americans, (2) learning how to interact with non-African Americans, (3) "playing the part" when communicating with non-African Americans, (4) keeping a safe distance from non-African Americans, (5) testing the sincerity of non-African Americans, and (6) an intense social responsibility. In another study, Orbe and Warren (2000) examined perceptions of intercultural conflict by race and gender. The European-American female focus group defined "interracial conflict" in terms of gender, whereas the African-American female focus groups defined it in terms of race. The diverse groups (by gender and race, also including three Latinos, an Asian, and a Native American) defined such conflict primarily in terms of race, but then discussed other issues as well. The European-American male group attributed such conflict to personal differences, whereas the African-American male group attributed it to race and personal differences. Orbe and Warren concluded that differences in "perceptions of conflict can be understood within the different standpoints of racialized/gendered groups" (p. 55). Although all of this research might be criticized for essentialism in racial grouping designations, such criticism is misplaced, for those studies focused specifically on the sociopolitical viewpoint that stems from being so grouped societally.

Orbe's (1995, 1998a, 1998b) research employing cocultural theory based on standpoint analysis promotes a promising approach to diversity through a focus on culture and cultural designations of a person's place in society rather than on color. Warren (2001) argued that "scholars who focus on the body as a racial representation—a physical text that people will read and interpret—many times fail to account for how that body comes to have meaning in the first place" (p. 91). Although T. H. Cox (1993, p. 6) defined "cultural diversity" rather simplistically as "the representation, in one social system, of people with distinctly different group affiliations of cultural significance," he did focus on interaction and the potentially positive contributions of culturally different ways of thinking and acting. Studies that take this more theoretically complex approach result in rich outcomes that reveal the positive potential of the diversity experience. For example, Teboul (1999), after studying the socialization of different ethnicities/races in the workplace, called for research on cultural traits, immigration status, and language proficiency as explanations for newcomers' organizational adaptation. Similarly, Buzzanell (1999) found that "non-dominant members" may not receive fair treatment when "routine employment interview practices restrict the introduction of information needed by both parties to be comfortable with each other and to achieve desirable goals" (p. 149). Buzzanell went beyond the inclusion of race/ethnicity to focus on other cultural attributes that can account for difference, including class, religion, sexual orientation, and gender. She recommended that human resource managers and communication specialists reconsider their selection of interviewers and trainers, consider more fully how interpersonal styles are discussed and evaluated, and develop flexibility in evaluations to prevent cultural misunderstandings. Jackson and Crawley (2003) applied this same thinking to the classroom of the Black professor with White students, stating:

> The reality is that universities are culturally diverse, although the faculty and curriculum do not always reflect that. The classroom can be transformed by sensitivity to cultural difference and differing levels of cultural consciousness. Although race has been socially constructed to mean negative difference, it is refreshing to know that even those negative experiences can be positive once we get beyond premature and prejudiced attitudes about the race and gender of Black male professors. (p. 47)

Although not about race per se, Cheney and Barnett's (2005) collection of international and multicultural organizational communication case studies touched on several issues that are germane here. Cheney and Barnett framed their discussion of multiculturalism with a treatment of cultural diversity that was overtly sensitive to issues of power and resistance, signifying a fruitful trend toward more theoretically rich understandings of diversity. In that edited volume, Hafen (2005) critically examined cultural diversity training, with particular attention to racial issues, and dealt directly with institutional structures that create and sustain systemic racism, "the everyday assumptions and interactions that seem 'natural' but that can create a climate of exclusion and/or pressured assimilation" (p. 13) In so doing, Hafen illustrated the interconnectedness of race, identity, political power structures, racism, discrimination, and diversity. In another chapter, Munshi (2005) looked specifically at the mechanism of control in the concept of "managing diversity," compellingly revealing ways in which that metaphor has led to practices that discursively reify a "norm" that excludes racial "others" (read: non-White). She illustrated how "diversity management" is neocolonially practiced as "managing the other," grounding her understanding of diversity management in a rich critical treatment of organizational power structures. Munshi concluded with a call for "polycentric multiculturalism," a multidimensional approach to diversity that is interactively based and breaks down "the historical asymmetries in the configuration of power and culture and managerial hierarchies" (p. 66). Finally, Houston and McPhail (2005) addressed diversity and dialogue in a study of the organizational coherence of the Million Man March, advocating a self-organizing systems approach to diversity and claiming that "a variety of diverse interactions causes a 'creative destruction' of individual inputs and thereby generates a coherent unity. This process of creative destruction emphasizes underlying, nonlinear processes that rely on diversity to produce a self-organized unity" (p. 141). They argued for a reframing of organizations as fluid interactive processes rather than as discrete entities containing linear communication. Their analysis of identity and coherence demonstrated in the march revealed the potential for self-reflection to improve race relations. In particular, the ways in which they linked identity, and the transformation of identity, to race and diversity represented a promising direction for applied communication research of these issues.

Applied communication research on diversity, therefore, is most fruitful when it overcomes the implicit presumption that representation creates a level playing field. Work that does not equate diversity, even implicitly, with a numerically representative mixture of racial groups opens the way for a cultural approach that examines interaction. Furthermore, work that presumes a deeply divisive political power structure inherent in racial category systems begins to reveal that a level playing field is relevant only to the extent that the players are expected to play by the same set of rules.

An Organizing Model for the Applied Communication Study of Race

The literature reviewed in this chapter perpetuates two important fallacies that have plagued applied communication research efforts. Earlier, we explained the first fallacy, that *race is biological*, a problem eloquently summarized by critical race theorists who elucidate the social construction of race: There is a tacit assumption that everyone knows what race is, and in that assumption, we fall prey to the biological fallacy. The second fallacy is that *race is culture*. We elaborate on this issue below as we present a fundamental conceptualization of culture, ethnicity, class, and race.

The Fallacy of Race as Culture

Jackson and Garner (1998) contended that "culture must be defined as something different than, but categorically inclusive of, ethnicity and race" (p. 51). Although both ethnicity and race are related to nationality, race is more obliquely related and, more important, the political frames of these two concepts are different. Ethnicity is marked by shared ancestral origins (Hecht, Jackson, & Ribeau, 2003), such as nationality or tribal membership, language, and religious traditions, and it is linked to a geographical origin (Hall, 1989). Although ethnicity is the primary basis on which race is constructed, we must consider class, which means we must confront political and economic power.

The examination of ethnic culture is inherently flawed if detached from historical and material contexts (Miles, 1982). Class division between ethnic groups is a primary political base for the ongoing racial fabrication process (Haney Lopez, 2000). Class oppression and the history of colonialism frame the processes by which culturally distinct group memberships (ethnicities) continually are socially fabricated as "races." As DuBois (1940) maintained, "The economic foundation of the modern world was based on the recognition and preservation of so-called racial distinctions" (p. 103). Critical race theory (e.g., Darder, 1995; Delgado & Stefancic, 2000; Essed & Goldberg, 2002; Gates, 1997a, 1997b) convincingly argues that race is socially constructed as a means by which class structure, and its associated class oppression, can be maintained. West's (1993, p. xv) description of him being passed over by nine taxicabs in Upper Manhattan only to stand by as a tenth stopped for a "kind, well-dressed, smiling female fellow citizen of European descent," succinctly illustrates this point. This "fellow citizen" commented to West (1993, p. xv), "This is really ridiculous, is it not?" but she did not offer him the taxi, even though, obviously, he was there first. Political constructions and the social construction of race, thus, make possible the privileging of some ethnicities over others. Earlier, we emphasized the explicit ranking of the races by psychological and social capacities in 18th-century European science, which formed the basis of the category system in use today. "Race," as we know it today, was born of the societal political power system. Hence, we must establish the conceptual distinctions and connections among several concepts: culture, ethnicity, race, and class.

Conceptualizing Culture, Ethnicity, and Race

In the extant applied communication research, race has been erroneously and tacitly assumed by many scholars to be synonymous with culture and with ethnicity. We contend that culture underlies norms, mores, values, beliefs, customs, rituals, ceremonies, morals, attitudes, practices, and other such concepts used by scholars in a variety of social disciplines to define culture. Such constructs are but manifestations of culture (Nicotera & Clinkscales, 2003). Following Chen and Starosta (1998), Nicotera and Clinkscales (2003) defined *culture* as "a negotiated set of shared symbolic systems that guide individuals' behaviors and incline them to function as a group" (p. 26). This definition avoids essentializing culture, ethnicity, or nationality by identifying a shared pool of symbolic systems from which persons draw individually and collectively. Culture is the very way that individuals apprehend the world (through their learned symbolic systems). As Chen and Starosta explained:

> We are programmed by our culture to do what we do and to be what we are. In other words, culture is the software of the human mind that provides an operating environment for human behaviors. Although individual behaviors may be varied, all members within the same operating environment share important characteristics of the culture. (p. 25)

Hence, people of different ethnicities and races may or may not be of different cultures, just as people with a common racial grouping may or may not be of the same culture. Culture develops as a shared symbolic meaning system rooted in repeated interactions of a group (manifesting in norms, values, etc.).

By this definition, the early development of different cultures arising from shared collective experiences precedes the development of ethnicity as a way of tracing people's origin and identities, which, in turn, precedes "race" as a sociopolitical category system.

However, once constructions of race appear, they contribute to the ongoing development of culture because they produce yet another set of particular shared meanings by which the world is understood. *Political constructions of race, thus, become embedded in cultural symbolic meaning systems.* Race is not synonymous with culture; it is culturally created through the political class system and, then self-reflexively, embedded in culture as a set of political meanings.

In sum, a person's ethnicity is traced ancestrally to a group that originally shared a symbolic meaning system (culture) and geographic location, regardless of whether the individual continues to share that symbolic meaning system in the present (Hall, 1989). Race is a fabricated (Haney Lopez, 2000) class system based on ethnic origin. Social groups of common racial identity then further engender the development of culture as these groups create meaning systems based on both ethnic origins and racial politics. Thus, ethnicity, race, and culture are not synonymous, nor are the relationships among them linear.

The Importance of Class

The relationships among culture, ethnicity, and race can be understood most fruitfully through a consideration of class. Here, we explicitly equate *class* with a political power system by which elite groups create, enforce, and maintain hegemonic political structures. Hence, class cannot be fully understood without reference to political power structures (van Dijk, 1987, 1993a, 1993b). Figures 9.1 and 9.2 represent our understanding of race. The figures use the term *culture/s* to depict both "culture" as a social process and the simultaneous existence of differing "cultures." As members of groups interact primarily among themselves, cultures emerge. When members of these different cultures interact with members of other groups, social identity is traced to the home culture through the social construct of ethnicity (see Hall, 1989). Figure 9.1, thus, shows ethnicity as a form of social identity growing from culture, with the term *ethnicity/ies* depicting both "ethnicity" as a social process of identity construction and the simultaneous existence of differing "ethnicities" as social identities.

Simultaneously, out of cultures grow class systems, which we conceptualize as inherently hegemonic political–economic systems. Social hierarchy, economic and political power, unearned privilege, and oppression are reflexively part of culture itself (van Dijk, 1987, 1993a, 1993b). As Figure 9.1 shows, culture and class mutually define one another, with the politically and economically hegemonic class system actually being part of culture. As with culture and ethnicity, the term *political–economic hegemony/ies* depicts both the social process of class construction and the simultaneous existence of differing class hierarchies that comprise the political power system.[5] Figure 9.2 shows the development of currently held notions of race in 18th-century Europe, when the social

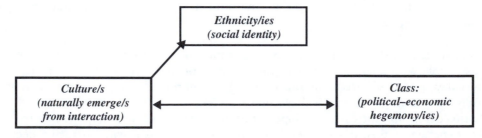

Figure 9.1 Ethnicity and class growing out of culture.

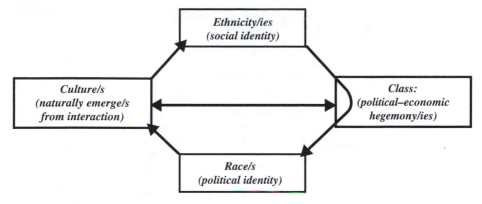

Figure 9.1 The social construction of race.

construction of ethnic identity was filtered through class to create a hierarchical racial taxonomy. As described previously, "race," as it now is socially employed, was invented as a social categorization system by which ethnicity could be used as a source of class oppression (O. C. Cox, 1959).[6] Hence, consistent with Hall's (1989) conceptualization of ethnicity as social identity and Haney Lopez's (2000) theory of racial fabrication as a political process, we conceptualize race as *a political identity process*. Ethnicity is construed by the class system as race, which then becomes part of the cultural system itself—a cultural reality that is taught as a naturalized presumption of social order. This conceptualization of race as a form of political identity, closely linked to class and political hegemony, "expand[s] our approaches beyond the ethnicity-based paradigm that has implicitly dominated much of our research" (Nkomo, 1992, p. 507). Following O. C. Cox (1959) and Montagu (1997), race is embedded in and intertwined with class, with class being a political cultural construction.

Problematic Issues of Race: Organizing Applied Communication Research

Problematic issues of race represented in the applied communication literature, as stated previously, can be categorized into four basic arenas: identity, racism, discrimination, and diversity. Given the conceptual framework of race as a sociopolitical cultural construction (seen in Figures 9.1 and 9.2), we posit, based on the literature reviewed, a set of relationships among these problematic issues of race (see Figure 9.3).

Identity is placed in the center as the means by which ethnicity and race intersect. Each person's self-identity in terms of race stems from and informs his or her cultural, social, political, ethnic, and racial identities. This view accounts for the dual identity of African Americans identified by DuBois (1903/1993) as problematic and commented on by many others. The model also allows for each individual's cultural and political identities to be experienced differently depending on one's position in society. Hecht et al. (2003) provided a thorough treatment of these issues, offering evidence, for example, that political and social identity are separate dimensions for African Americans but a single dimension for European Americans.

In the model, *racism* stems directly from race because the modern construction of "race" was politically motivated (Allahar, 1993; Bracken, 1973; Goldberg, 1993; McPhail, 2002; Nakayama & Martin, 1999; West, 1982)—racism being defined as class oppression based on ethnicity. A thick, double-headed arrow between *class* and *racism* illustrates our explicit conceptual connection between these constructs. DuBois (1940)

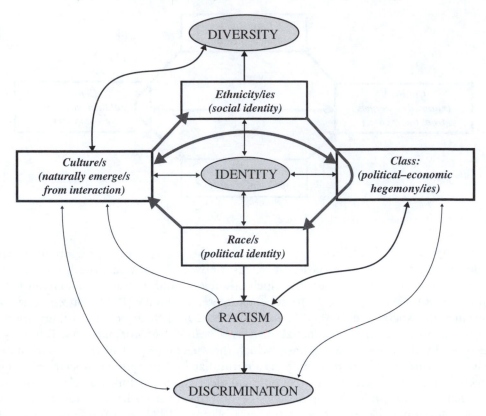

Figure 9.3 Problematic issues of race.

pointed out that "the income-bearing value of race prejudice was the cause and not the result of theories of race inferiority" (p. 129). Racism functions to protect the economic interests of the political and economic elites (Boggs, 1970).[7] *Discrimination*, then, is the result of racism. Racism represents here a belief system of the inherent inferiority of a racial group; discrimination is the denial of opportunity that stems from that belief system. Finally, *diversity*, as we define it and advocate its study, is an outgrowth of ethnicity (social identity), but it cannot be divorced from the totality of cultural experience, and, consequently, a thick, double-headed arrow is drawn between culture and diversity. In this way, diversity can be defined as more than mere representation, which we view as a subset of discrimination. Diversity as related to race becomes a context of intercultural interaction among persons who draw on varied sets of cultural meaning systems that are rooted in the entirety of cultural experience, to include the cultural experience(s) of class, racism, and discrimination. Diversity, of course, does not grow solely out of ethnicity but because our focus is on race, its placement in the model emphasizes cultural differences stemming from ethnicity and from experiences related to ethnicity. The thickness of the double-headed arrow depicts the explicitness of this connection in our conceptualization.

The four problematic issues examined in this chapter—identity, racism, discrimination, and diversity—are mutually influential with culture (illustrated with thinner double-headed arrows) because culture is conceptualized as interactive. Identity also is mutually influential with class (itself a cultural construction), which has a direct influence on both racism and discrimination, which, in turn, reflexively provide the political system with entrenchments of class-based systems of oppression on which structures of dominance are further developed.

Domke's (2001) study is an elegant illustration of these reflexive relationships, as it showed that among his sample of educated middle-class individuals:

> Racial cues in the political environment activate, in tandem, perceptions of specific racial minorities and one's political ideology, and in turn, the dual activation of these constructs prompts individuals to become more ideologically distinct in race-related issue evaluations.… For many individuals, racial and ethnic stereotypes become both cognitively embedded, as scholars have documented (e.g., Devine, 1989; Marín, 1984), and politically enmeshed. (pp. 789–790)

Domke revealed the social process of the creation of symbolic meaning systems, cognitive schema that result from these meaning systems, political communicative process by which social identity (ethnicity) becomes political identity (race), and ways in which the resulting racist assumptions reflect back into the political system.

Hence, as Allen (2004) argued:

> Race is an artificial construction of social identity based upon an ideology of white supremacy, a belief in a racial hierarchy that places whiteness in the superior position. Various power sources have used communication to construct categories of race to reinforce and reproduce this ideology. (p. 92)

The "ideology of White supremacy" is part and parcel of our notion of "class as political hegemony," and the elite (i.e., politically powerful) groups' communicative construction of race to "reinforce and reproduce this ideology" is reflected in the double-headed arrows between class and race, between class and racism, and between class and discrimination. Our contention that constructions of race have become culturally ingrained and, thus, part of all societal members' cultural experience, echoes Allen's (2004) contention that persons of all races communicatively "envision and enact alternative perspectives on race" (p. 92). Allen's observation of changes in racial designations over time further illustrates our point that once "race" is constructed, it becomes part of culture. Finally, just as race is born of the political class system, it reflexively politicizes and becomes politicized, driving class-based conflict even deeper.

Figure 9.4 completes the model by adding the construct "EEOC interventions" to acknowledge the cultural embeddedness of antidiscrimination law (Title VII), which has become central to the cultural experience of race in the United States. EEOC intervention is culturally driven—a legal solution to a cultural problem, embedded in the U.S. cultural system of legislative and judicial intervention. EEOC intervention, as a construct, however, also influences culture—again revealed by and revealing the interactive nature of culture. The EEOC system of intervention via lawsuit is the entrenched U.S. cultural understanding of how to best manage discrimination. The dashed lines in the diagram depict a reversing influence: EEOC intervention can neither eliminate nor prevent discrimination; it merely attempts to reverse its effects on a case-by-case basis.

In contrast, diversity has tremendous potential to subvert class oppression, dilute racism, and prevent discrimination. We conceive of diversity as more than an externally mandated or politically pressured shift in personnel demographics. A more promising definition of diversity begins with an interactive context in which individuals draw on multiple cultural meaning systems. Whereas "representation" is demographic, "diversity" is cultural. Cultural does not mean "ethnic" or "nationality" but the totality of

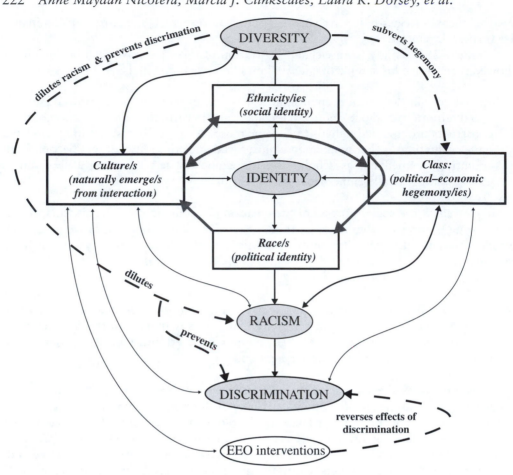

Figure 9.4 Organizing model for research of problematic issues of race.

cultural experience—the cultural meaning systems that arise from the experience of raced, gendered, and classed identities. "Cultural diversity" takes into account the totality of cultural experience, not merely sets of values and norms conflated with ethnicity. To fully understand cultural diversity in this way is to come to terms with ways in which individuals of varying ethnic, raced, gendered, and political identities come to the table with unique individual and group cultural experiences, in addition to the ethnically based cultural meaning systems by which they apprehend the world. A "cultural self" is constructed from these cultural experiences, which include class oppression (or elitism), raced (and gendered) political experiences that deny or bestow privilege, racist ideology (from any angle), and discriminatory practices (whether as perpetrator, target, or observer).

Consistent with the most fruitful treatments of diversity seen in the literature, we believe that the conceptualization of diversity as interaction across salient cultural differences is most ripe for expansion by applied communication scholarship. As thinking about diversity shifts from the numerical status of color counts to something more holistic and organic, we move toward an understanding of diversity as a culture-building phenomenon. When culture building is considered, the focus is less on numbers and more on individuals as "cultural selves." The *cultural self* includes values, traditions, beliefs, and attitudes rooted in culture as traditionally understood, but it also includes individual and group *cultural experiences* that stem from political meanings attached to social categories, such as ethnicity and race (as well as gender, sexual orientation, physical ability, occupation, ad infinitum).

Applications of the Model

It is our hope that applied communication research on race can make use of our model to not only avoid but also to subvert the erroneous implicit assumptions that generally pervade academic and educational discourse (van Dijk, 1993 a, 1993b). We hope that as applied communication scholars address the issues of racial identity, racism, discrimination, and diversity, they do so with a careful and holistic consideration of their conceptual intersections, as recommended below.

Racial Identity

Applied communication scholars and practitioners should strive to treat race not as a separate and singular social identity factor but as intricately tied to culture, class, and sociopolitical forces. The tendency to conflate race with culture and essentialize race as ethnic group membership should be replaced with a richer and, thus, more accurate treatment of race as a politically structured interactive phenomenon. Interpretive and critical scholars are best poised to explore the process of racial social construction, but this does not preclude the potential contributions of the social-scientific approach. Indeed, Stephan and Stephan (2000) argued that the individual and societal importance of racial categories creates for social scientists an "obligation to understand these classification systems and the effects of their usage" (p. 545).

The most important implication of our model is that it illustrates why racial issues in communication are not reducible to intergroup "cultural difference" but are deeply embedded in systems of social and political power, and need to be treated as such. As stated previously, culture, community, and self-identifications are more salient than racial category, which is only one part of social grouping and only sometimes meaningful. Hence, researchers should take great care to avoid implicitly assuming that racial group category is an important and primary identifying factor warranting generalization. Sampling by forced-choice racial group is easy and convenient—and method-driven. Race, in all its complexity, first must be explicitly and theoretically established as a salient factor for the social process of interest; then, it should be treated not as a classification variable unto itself but as one small part of a complex set of factors comprising identity and community that allows us to identify theoretically meaningful social or cultural groups warranting generalization. Once meaningful groups are identified, there must be (1) explicitly defined populations to which we might generalize, (2) a compellingly argued and theoretically based rationale for the purpose of doing so, (3) systematic sampling of those populations, and (4) reliable and valid measurement (Davis et al., 2000; Martin & Davis, 2000; Stephan & Stephan, 2000).

Racism and Discrimination

Applied communication scholarship is not exempt from depictions of the presumptive Whiteness that characterizes the field of communication (Nakayama & Martin, 1999). Our understandings and treatments of race are rooted in generations of elite academic discourse that renders "other" ways of being and thinking invisible. Once the implicit ranking in the racial taxonomy is made apparent, racism is laid bare as the fundamental historical purpose and outcome of that categorization. Applied communication scholars examining race, therefore, have an obligation to acknowledge ways in which their treatments of "race" unintentionally perpetuate the implicit political purposes of the category systems currently in use. Racism has been defined in this chapter as class oppression based on ethnicity, as a belief system based on the inherent superiority of some racial groups over others, and as practices that create and reproduce "structures of domination based on essentialist categories of race" (Omi & Winant, 1994, p. 71). One of the most immediate applications of our model in applied communication research, consequently, is the explicit recognition of the inseparable natures of contemporary racial category systems, racism, and discrimination, the latter of which is defined as the denial of opportunity that stems from racist belief systems. Thus, racism and discrimination must be treated as political and systemic discursive issues, and not blamed on the unfortunate opinions, biases, misunderstandings, and acts of individuals or rooted in uneven demographics, even as they are seen as manifesting there. This approach necessitates a direct confrontation with class—an issue that applied communication scholars thus far largely have ignored or, at best, treated merely as income level. Applied communication research has much to offer by documenting and explicating discriminatory practices, and the racist beliefs that underlie them, and proffering solutions to these problems based on a deep understanding of those practices and beliefs rooted in history and political constructions.

Diversity

Applied communication scholars might benefit from an approach to diversity that focuses on interactive processes and our construct of the cultural self. This approach advances understanding of diversity to include, but also to move beyond, blending, appreciating, and understanding differences (and commonalities). This shift may lead to ways of achieving true multiculturalism rather than "management of the other" (Munshi, 2005), maximizing the power of a diverse society. This potential is possible because this conceptualization embeds people not only in cultural groups but also in political social structures. In this way, this approach links diversity and societal contexts, which has heretofore been missing. The locus of diversity issues is removed from individual action and placed in a broader context of social, historical, and political constructions that influence the development of cultural selves and the performance of those selves in interaction.

When culturally different persons interact with an understanding of the cultural basis for the totality of their differences and come to appreciate their different cultural experiences (or at least understand that the basis for these experiences is, indeed, cultural), productive diversity might be achieved. Furthermore, when the cultural–political bases of racial categorization are laid bare, and the ensuing systems of class oppression revealed, individuals of all races begin to be freed from the political notion of the inherent superiority of one race over others. This deconstruction of the "naturalization" of race subverts hegemony and weakens it as a basis for racism and discrimination. As Wilson (1999) contended, "Neither biology nor racism's hegemony can determine a person's soul if a person understands and engages the surrounding discourse" (p. 211).

We advocate, in short, an approach to diversity that is *embedded in* an understanding of societal power structures, not shielded from it (Ashcraft & Allen, 2003). Anything less results in a strategy (whether scholarly, corporate, or civic) that maximizes the potential of diversity as damage control because anything less can focus only on avoiding the negative impact of "poorly managed" diversity. Our conceptualization of diversity, thus, is humanistic. When diversity among individuals is understood through the concept of the cultural self and, consequently, is seen as rooted in culturally constructed identities grounded in cultural structures related to (but not definable by) surface-level characteristics (e.g., race, ethnicity, and gender), more fruitful applications can result (as exemplified by Cheney & Barnett's, 2005, text).

Conclusion

The most basic implication from this set of ideas is the deep need for awareness and consciousness raising among applied communication scholars. The challenge is whether applied communication research, pedagogy (see Darling & Leckie, this volume), and other practices can provide the type of education that lays bare the politically constructed nature of race and "denaturalizes" racial hierarchies in social discourse. We do not pretend that this modest idea can produce research that eliminates the effects of centuries of class oppression. We do suggest, however, that problematic issues of race can be examined by applied communication scholars thoughtfully via a careful consideration of the ways in which these problematic issues are conceptually related. We have offered in this chapter a theoretic construction on which to base such consideration.

Authors' Note

Deep appreciation is expressed to Dr. Georgia M. Dunston (Chair, Department of Microbiology, and Founding and Current Director of molecular genetics at the National Human Genome Center, Howard University) for her support, encouragement, and invaluable instruction on matters of human genetics and race.

Notes

1. Most notable are Biagi and Kern-Foxworth's (1997) examination of popular culture, Hasian and Delgado's (1998) racialized critical rhetorical theory, Browne's (2000) analysis of the 19th-century race debate, and McPhail's (2002) review of rhetoric and race.
2. West (1982) and Goldberg (1993) traced this sociopolitical history, Allahar (1993) and Nakayama and Martin (1999) argued that the history of contemporary racial categories is inherently oppressive, and McPhail (2002, p. 75) pointed out that "social negation based on skin color is a relatively new phenomenon" (for an insightful essay that questions this widely accepted historical account, see Stoler, 1997).
3. Wilson (1999) linked Haney Lopez's construction of race to DuBois (1903/1993), interpreting his book, *Souls of Black Folk*, as a response to 19th-century biological determinism.
4. Guha (1987) questioned the relationship between dominance and hegemony.
5. Handlin (1957) argued that racism should be treated as its own ideology, not just as one form of class oppression; for a critique of such Marxist accounts of racism, see San Juan (1989).
6. Wetherell and Potter (1992) traced the language of race as a historical–political process "legitimizing" exploitation.
7. Essed (1991) defined racism as politically based power perpetuated in interaction as entrenched White domination. van Dijk (1993a, 1993b) traced racism in elite political, academic, educational, and media discourses to show its perpetuation in social and political systems, produced and reproduced in discursive forms such that it is naturalized and manifests as racism. In previous work, van Dijk (1987) examined the interpersonal enactment of racism, revealing how microlevel communicative practices reproduce ethnic prejudice stemming from and reinforcing a hegemonic political system.

References

Alcalay, R., & Bell, R. A. (1996). Ethnicity and health knowledge gaps: Impact of the California *Wellness Guide* on poor African American, Hispanic, and non-Hispanic women. *Health Communication, 8,* 303–329.

Allahar, A. L. (1993). When Black first became worth less. *International Journal of Comparative Sociology, 34,* 39–55.

Allen, B. J. (1995). "Diversity" and organizational communication. *Journal of Applied Communication Research, 23,* 143–155.

Allen, B. J. (2004). *Difference matters: Communicating social identity.* Long Grove, IL: Waveland Press.

Amason, P., Allen, M. W., & Holmes, S. A. (1999). Social support and acculturative stress in the multicultural workplace. *Journal of Applied Communication Research, 27,* 310–334.

Appiah, O. (2002). Effects of ethnic identification on Web browsers' attitudes toward and navigational patterns on race-targeted sites. *Communication Research, 31,* 312–337.

Artz, L. (1998). African-Americans and higher education: An exigence in need of applied communication. *Journal of Applied Communication Research, 26,* 210–231.

Ashcraft, K. L., & Allen, B. J. (2003). The racial foundation of organizational communication. *Communication Theory, 13,* 5–38.

Avant-Mier, R., & Hasian, M., Jr. (2002). In search of the power of Whiteness: A genealogical exploration of negotiated racial identities in America's ethnic past. *Communication Quarterly, 50,* 391–409.

Barker, M. (1981). *The new racism: Conservatives and the ideology of the tribe.* Frederick, MD: Aletheia Books.

Bates, B. R., Poirot, K., Harris, T. M., Condit, C. M., & Achter, P. J. (2004). Evaluating direct-to-consumer marketing of race-based pharmacogenomics: A focus group study of public understandings of applied genomic medication. *Journal of Health Communication, 9,* 541–559.

Becker, L. B., Lauf, E., & Lowrey, W. (1999). Differential employment rates in the journalism and mass communication labor force based on gender, race, and ethnicity: Exploring the impact of affirmative action. *Journalism & Mass Communication Quarterly, 76,* 631–645.

Bell, E. L. J. E., & Nkomo, S. M. (2001). *Our separate ways: Black and White women and the struggle for professional identity.* Boston: Harvard Business School Press.

Berard, T. J. (2005). On multiple identities and educational contexts: Remarks on the study of inequalities and discrimination. *Journal of Language, Identity, and Education, 4,* 67–77.

Biagi, S., & Kern-Foxworth, M. (1997). *Facing difference: Race, gender, and mass media.* Thousand Oaks, CA: Pine Forge Press.

Boggs, J. (1970). *Racism and the class struggle: Further pages from a Black worker's notebook.* New York: Monthly Review Press.

Bracken, H. M. (1973). Essence, accident, and race. *Hermathena, 116,* 81–96.

Brinson, S. L., & Benoit, W. L. (1999). The tarnished star: Restoring Texaco's damaged public image. *Management Communication Quarterly, 12,* 483–510.

Browne, S. H. (2000). Counter-science: African American historians and the critique of ethnology in nineteenth-century America. *Western Journal of Communication, 64,* 268–284.

Buzzanell, P. M. (1995). Reframing the glass ceiling as a socially constructed process: Implications for understanding and change. *Communication Monographs, 62,* 327–354.

Buzzanell, P. M. (1999). Tensions and burdens in employment interviewing processes: Perspectives of non-dominant group applicants. *Journal of Business Communication, 36,* 134–162.

Carrell, L. H. (1997). Diversity in the communication curriculum: Impact on student empathy. *Communication Education, 46,* 234–245.

Chambers, J. W., Jr., Kambon, K., & Birdsong, B. D., Brown, J., Dixon, P., & Brinson, L. (1998). Afrocentric cultural identity and the stress experience of African American college students. *Journal of Black Psychology, 24,* 368–396.

Chen, G.-M., & Starosta, W. J. (1998). *Foundations of intercultural communication.* Boston: Allyn & Bacon.

Cheney, G., & Barnett, G. A. (Eds.). (2005). *International and multicultural organizational communication.* Cresskill, NJ: Hampton Press.

Clair, R. P., & Thompson, K. (1996). Pay discrimination as a discursive and material practice: A case concerning extended housework. *Journal of Applied Communication Research, 24,* 1–20.

Coleman, R. R. M. (2002). Prospects for locating racial democracy in media: The NAACP network television boycott. *Qualitative Research Reports in Communication, 3*, 25 31.

Coleman, R. R. M. (2003). Elmo is Black! Black popular communication and the marking and marketing of Black identity. *Popular Communication, 1*, 51–64.

Cooks, L. (2003). Pedagogy, performance, and positionality: Teaching about Whiteness in interracial communication. *Communication Education, 52*, 245–257.

Cooper, B. (1998). "The White–Black fault line": Relevancy of race and racism in spectators' experiences of Spike Lee's *Do the Right Thing. Howard Journal of Communications, 9*, 205–228.

Cooper, E., & Allen, M. (1998). A meta-analytic examination of the impact of student race on classroom interaction. *Communication Research Reports, 15*, 151–161.

Cox, O. C. (1959). *Caste, class, & race: A study in social dynamics.* New York: Monthly Review Press.

Cox, T. H., Jr. (1993). *Cultural diversity in organizations: Theory, research, and practice.* San Francisco: Berrett-Koehler.

Darder, A. (Ed.). (1995). *Culture and difference: Critical perspectives on the bicultural experience in the United States.* Westport, CT: Bergin & Garvey.

Davis, O. I., Nakayama, T. K., & Martin, J. N. (2000). Current and future directions in ethnicity and methodology. *International Journal of Intercultural Relations, 24*, 525–539.

Delgado, R., & Stefancic, J. (Eds.). (2000). *Critical race theory: The cutting edge* (2nd ed.). Philadelphia: Temple University Press.

Devine, P. G. (1989). Stereotypes and prejudice: Their automatic and controlled components. *Journal of Personality and Social Psychology, 56*, 5–18.

Diggs, R. D., & Clark, K. D. (2002). *It's a struggle but worth it*: Identifying and managing identities in an interracial friendship. *Communication Quarterly, 50*, 368–390.

Domke, D. (2001). Racial cues and political ideology: An examination of associative priming. *Communication Research, 28*, 772–801.

Domke, D., McCoy, K., & Torres, M. (1999). News media, racial perceptions, and political cognition. *Communication Research, 26*, 570–607.

DuBois, W. E .B. (1940). *Dusk of dawn: An essay toward an autobiography of a race concept.* New York: Harcourt, Brace.

DuBois, W. E. B. (1993). *The souls of Black folk.* New York: Knopf. (Original work published 1903)

Dutton, S. E., Singer, J. A., & Devlin, A. S. (1998). Racial identity of children in integrated, predominantly White, and Black schools. *Journal of Social Psychology, 138*, 41–53.

Entman, R. M. (1990). Modern racism and the images of Blacks in local television news. *Critical Studies in Mass Communication, 7*, 332–345.

Essed, P. (1991). *Understanding everyday racism: An interdisciplinary theory.* Newbury Park, CA: Sage.

Essed, P., & Goldberg, D. T. (Eds.). (2002). *Race critical theories: Text and context.* Malden, MA: Blackwell.

Fletcher, M. A. (2009, January 19). President-elect sees his race as an opportunity. *Washington Post,* pp. A1, 6. Retrieved January 22, 2009, from http://www.washingtonpost.com/wp-dyn/content/article/2009/01/18/AR2009011802547.html?hpid=topnews

Foeman, A. K., & Nance, T. (2002). Building new cultures, reframing old images: Success strategies of interracial couples. *Howard Journal of Communications, 13*, 237–249.

Foeman, A. K., & Pressley, G. (1987). Ethnic culture and corporate culture: Using Black styles in organizations. *Communication Quarterly, 35*, 293–307.

Gandy, O. H., Jr., & Baron, J. (1998). Inequality: It's all in the way you look at it. *Communication Research, 25*, 505–527.

Gates, E. N. (Ed.). (1997a). *The concept of "race" in natural and social science.* New York: Garland.

Gates, E. N. (Ed.). (1997b). *Cultural and literary critiques of the concepts of "race."* New York: Garland.

Goldberg, D. T. (1993). *Racist culture: Philosophy and the politics of meaning.* Cambridge, MA: Blackwell.

González, A., & González, J. (2002). The color problem in Sillyville: Negotiating White identity in one popular "kid-vid." *Communication Quarterly, 50,* 410–421.

Gray, H. (2001). Desiring the network and network desire. *Critical Studies in Media Communication, 18,* 103–108.

Gross, R., Craft, S., Cameron, G. T., & Antecol, M. (2002). Diversity efforts at the *Los Angeles Times*: Are journalists and the community on the same page? *Mass Communication & Society, 5,* 263–277.

Guha, R. (1987). *Dominance without hegemony: History and power in colonial India.* Cambridge, MA: Harvard University Press.

Hafen, S. (2005). Cultural diversity training: A critical (ironic) cartography of advocacy and oppositional silences. In G. Cheney & G. A. Barnett (Eds.), *International and multicultural organizational communication* (pp. 3–43). Cresskill, NJ: Hampton Press.

Hall, S. (1980). Race, articulation, and societies structured in dominance. In UNESCO (Ed.), *Sociological theories: Race and colonialism* (pp. 305–345). Paris: United Nations Educational, Scientific, and Cultural Organization.

Hall, S. (1989). Ethnicity: Identity and difference. *Radical America, 23*(4), 9–20.

Halualani, T. R., Chitgopekar, A. S., Morrison, J. H. T. A., & Dodge, P. S.-W. (2004). Diverse in name only? Intercultural interaction at a multicultural university. *Journal of Communication, 54,* 270–286.

Handlin, O. (1957). *Race and nationality in American life.* Boston: Little, Brown.

Haney Lopez, I. F. (2000). The social construction of race. In R. Delgado & J. Stefancic (Eds.), *Critical race theory: The cutting edge* (2nd ed., pp. 163–175). Philadelphia: Temple University Press.

Harris, T. M. (2003). Impacting student perceptions of and attitudes toward race in the interracial communication course. *Communication Education, 52,* 311–317.

Harris, T. M., & Donmoyer, D. (2000). Is art imitating life? Communicating gender and racial identity in *Imitation of Life. Women's Studies in Communication, 23,* 91–109.

Hasian, M., Jr., & Delgado, F. (1998). The trials and tribulations of racialized critical rhetorical theory: Understanding the rhetorical ambiguities of Proposition 187. *Communication Theory, 8,* 245–270.

Hecht, M. L., Jackson, R. L., II, & Ribeau, S. A. (2003). *African American communication: Exploring identity and culture* (2nd ed.). Mahwah, NJ: Erlbaum.

Hegde, R. S., & DiCicco-Bloom, B. (2002). Working identities: South Asian nurses and transnational negotiations of race and gender. *Qualitative Research Reports in Communication, 3,* 90–95.

Houston, R., & McPhail, M. L. (2005). One million initial conditions: At-one-ment as organizational coherence. In G. Cheney & G. A. Barnett (Eds.), *International and multicultural organizational communication* (pp. 125–144). Cresskill, NJ: Hampton Press.

Hurwitz, J., & Peffley, M. (1997). Public perceptions of race and crime: The role of racial stereotypes. *American Journal of Political Science, 41,* 375–401.

Hutton, J. G. (2005). The myth of salary discrimination in public relations. *Public Relations Review, 31,* 73–83.

Jackson, R. L., II. (1999). *The negotiation of cultural identity: Perceptions of European Americans and African Americans.* Westport, CT: Praeger.

Jackson, R. L., II. (Ed.). (2001). Negotiating race, culture & identity in rural communities [Special issue]. *Journal of Rural Community Psychology, E4*(1).

Jackson, R. L., II (Ed.). (2002). Identity negotiation: An exploration of racial, cultural and gendered identities [Special issue]. *Communication Quarterly, 50*(3/4).

Jackson, R. L., II (2006). *Scripting the Black masculine body: Identity, discourse, and racial politics in popular media.* Albany: State University of New York Press.

Jackson, R. L., II, & Crawley, R. L. (2003). White student confessions about a Black male professor: A cultural contracts theory approach to intimate conversations about race and worldview. *Journal of Men's Studies, 12,* 25–52.

Jackson, R. L., II, & Garner, T. (1998). Tracing the evolution of "race," "ethnicity," and "culture" in communication studies. *Howard Journal of Communications, 9,* 47–56.

Jackson, R. L., II, & Heckman, S. M. (2002). Perceptions of White identity and White liability: An analysis of White student responses to a college campus racial hate crime. *Journal of Communication, 52,* 434–450.

Jackson, R. L., II, & Hendrix, K. G. (Eds.). (2003). Racial, cultural, and gendered identities in educational contexts: Communication perspectives on identity negotiation [Special issue]. *Communication Education, 52*(3/4).

Johnson, J. R., & Bhatt, A. J. (2003). Gendered and racialized identities and alliances in the classroom: Formations in/of resistive space. *Communication Education, 52,* 230–244.

Jorde, L. B., & Wooding, S. P. (2004). Genetic variation, classification and "race." *Nature Genetics, 36*(11 Suppl.), S28–S33.

Kalbfleisch, P. J., & Davies, A. B. (1991). Minorities and mentoring: Managing the multicultural institution. *Communication Education, 40,* 266–271.

Kinder, D. R., & Sanders, L. M. (1996). *Divided by color: Racial politics and democratic ideals.* Chicago: University of Chicago Press.

Korzenny, F., & Schiff, E. N. (1987). Hispanic perceptions of communication discrimination. *Hispanic Journal of Behavioral Science, 9,* 33–48.

Kossek, E. E., & Zonia, S. C. (1994). The effects of race and ethnicity on perceptions of human resource policies in climate regarding diversity. *Journal of Business and Technical Communication, 8,* 319–334.

Lewontin, R. C. (1972). The apportionment of human diversity. *Evolutionary Biology, 6,* 381–398.

Mackinlay, E. (2003). Performing race, culture, and gender in an indigenous Australian women's music and dance classroom. *Communication Education, 52,* 258–272.

Marable, M. (1995). *Beyond Black and White: Transforming African-American politics.* New York: Verso.

Marín, G. (1984). Stereotyping Hispanics: The differential effect of research method, label, and degree of contact. *International Journal of Intercultural Relations, 8,* 17–27.

Martin, J. N., & Davis, O. I. (Eds.). (2000). Ethnicity and methodology [Special issue]. *International Journal of Intercultural Relations, 24*(5).

Martin, J. N., Moore, S., Hecht, M. L., & Larkey, L. K. (2001). An African American perspective on conversational improvement strategies. *Howard Journal of Communications, 12,* 1–27.

Matthews, A. K., Sellergren, S. A., Manfredi, C., & Williams, M. (2002). Factors influencing medical information seeking among African American cancer patients. *Journal of Health Communication, 7,* 205–219.

McPhail, M. L. (2002). *The rhetoric of racism revisited: Reparations or separation?* Lanham, MD: Rowman & Littlefield.

Meares, M. M., Oetzel, J. G., Torres, A., Derkacs, D., & Ginossar, T. (2004). Employee mistreatment and muted voices in the culturally diverse workplace. *Journal of Applied Communication Research, 32,* 4–27.

Mellinger, G. (2003). Counting color: Ambivalence and contradiction in the American Society of Newspaper Editors' discourse of diversity. *Journal of Communication Inquiry, 27,* 129–151.

Mendelberg, T. (2001). *The race card: Campaign strategy, implicit messages, and the norm of equality.* Princeton, NJ: Princeton University Press.

Meyers, M. (2004). African American women and violence: Gender, race, and class in the news. *Critical Studies in Media Communication, 21,* 95–118.

Miles, R. (1982). *Racism and migrant labour.* Boston: Routledge & Kegan Paul.

Miles, R. (1989). *Racism.* New York: Routledge.

Montagu, A. (1997). *Man's most dangerous myth: The fallacy of race* (6th ed.). Walnut Creek, CA: AltaMira Press.

Munshi, D. (2005). Through the subject's eye: Situating the other in discourses of diversity. In G. Cheney & G. A. Barnett (Eds.), *International and multicultural organizational communication* (pp. 45–70). Cresskill, NJ: Hampton Press.

Nakayama, T. K., & Martin, J. N. (1999). *Whiteness: The communication of social identity.* Thousand Oaks, CA: Sage.

Nicotera, A. M., & Clinkscales, M. J. (with Walker, F. R.). (2003). *Understanding organizations through culture and structure: Relational and other lessons from the African-American organization.* Mahwah, NJ: Erlbaum.

Niven, D., & Zilber, J. (2000). Elite use of racial labels: Ideology and preference for African American or Black. *Howard Journal of Communications, 11,* 267–277.

Nkomo, S. M. (1992). The emperor has no clothes: Rewriting "race in organizations." *Academy of Management Review, 17,* 487–513.

Obama, B. (2008, March 18). Barack Obama's speech on race. *The New York Times.* Retrieved January 5, 2009, from http://www.nytimes.com/2008/03/18/us/politics/18text-obama.html

Oliver, M. B. (1996). Influences of authoritarianism and portrayals of race on Caucasian viewers' responses to reality-based crime dramas. *Communication Reports, 9,* 141–150.

Omi, M. & Winant, H. (1994). *Racial formation in the United States: From the 1960s to the 1990s* (2nd ed.). New York: Routledge.

Orbe, M. P. (1994). "Remember, it's always Whites' ball": Descriptions of African American male communication. *Communication Quarterly, 42,* 287–300.

Orbe, M. P. (1995). African American communication research: Toward a deeper understanding of interethnic communication. *Western Journal of Communication, 59,* 61–78.

Orbe, M. P. (1998a). An outsider within perspective to organizational communication: Explicating communicative practices of co-cultural group members. *Management Communication Quarterly, 12,* 230–279.

Orbe, M. P. (1998b). *Constructing co-cultural theory: An explication of culture, power, and communication.* Thousand Oaks, CA: Sage.

Orbe, M. P., & Warren, K. T. (2000). Different standpoints, different realties: Race, gender, and perceptions of intercultural conflict. *Qualitative Research Reports in Communication, 1,* 51–57.

Pan, Z., & Kosicki, G. M. (1997). Priming and media impact on the evaluation of the president's performance. *Communication Research, 24,* 3–30.

Parker, P. S. (2001). African American women executives' leadership communication within dominant-culture organizations: (Re)conceptualizing notions of collaboration and instrumentality. *Management Communication Quarterly, 15,* 42–82.

Parker, P. S. (2002). Negotiating identity in raced and gendered workplace interactions: The use of strategic communication by African American women senior executives within dominant culture organizations. *Communication Quarterly, 50,* 251–268.

Parker, P. S. (2003). Control, resistance, and empowerment in raced, gendered, and classed work contexts: The case of African American women. In P. J. Kalbfleisch (Ed.), *Communication yearbook* (Vol. 27, pp. 257–291). Mahwah, NJ: Erlbaum.

Parker. P. S. (2005). *Race, gender, and leadership: Re-envisioning organizational leadership from the perspectives of African American women executives.* Mahwah, NJ: Erlbaum.

Pardington, S. (2008, September 24). Effigy of Obama alarms George Fox campus. *Oregonian.* Retrieved January 5, 2009, from http://www.oregonlive.com/news/index.ssf/2008/09/racial_incident_rattles_george.html

Patton, T. O. (2004). In the guise of civility: The complicitous maintenance of inferential forms of sexism and racism in higher education. *Women's Studies in Communication, 27,* 60–87.

Peffley, M., Shields, T., & Williams, B. (1996). The intersection of race and crime in television news stories: An experimental study. *Political Communication, 13,* 309–327.

Pride, R. A. (1999). Redefining the problem of racial inequality. *Political Communication, 16,* 147–167.

Priest, P. J. (2000). Theory into practice: Integrating race and gender issues into the basic media writing course. *Journal of Broadcasting & Electronic Media, 44,* 521–528.

Prosise, T. O., & Johnson, A. (2004). Law enforcement and crime on *Cops* and *World's Wildest Police Videos*: Anecdotal form and the justification of racial profiling. *Western Journal of Communication, 68,* 72–91.

Richardson, J. D. (2005). Switching social identities: The influence of editorial framing on reader attitudes toward affirmative action and African Americans. *Communication Research, 34,* 503–528.

Rockler, N. R. (2002). Race, Whiteness, "lightness," and relevance: African American and European American interpretations of *Jump Start* and *The Boondocks*. *Critical Studies in Media Communication, 19,* 398–418.

Royal, C. D. M., & Dunston, G. M. (2004). Changing the paradigm from "race" to human genome variation. *Nature Genetics, 36*(11 Suppl.), S5–S7.

Rucker, P. & Wan, W. (2006, September 27). Hate crimes wake Charles's sleeping giant: Rash of race-based incidents stems from anger over shift in demographics, some residents say. *Washington Post*, p. B01.

San Juan, E., Jr. (1989). Problems in the Marxist project of theorizing race. *Rethinking Marxism, 2,* 58–80.

Shear, M. D. (2006, September 29). Now, even Allen's apologies are getting him in trouble: Sons of Confederate Veterans is the most recent group offended by senator's comments. *Washington Post*, p. B01.

Sigelman, L., Tuch, S. A., & Martin, J. K. (2005). What's in a name? Preference for "Black" versus "African American" among Americans of African descent. *Public Opinion Quarterly, 69,* 429–438.

Sniderman, P. M., & Piazza, T. (1993). *The scar of race*. Cambridge, MA: Belknap Press of Harvard University Press.

Stephan, C. W., & Stephan, W. G. (2000). The measurement of racial and ethnic identity. *International Journal of Intercultural Relations, 24,* 541–552.

Stoler, A. L. (1997). Racial histories and their regimes of truth. *Political Power and Social Theory, 11,* 183–206.

Strauss, V. (2006, September 22). Report calls for improvement in K-8 science education. *Washington Post*, p. A09.

Tan, A. (2000). Television use, stereotypes of African Americans and opinions on affirmative action: An affective model of policy reasoning. *Communication Monographs, 67,* 362–371.

Teboul, JC. B. (1999). Racial/ethnic "encounter" in the workplace: Uncertainty, information-seeking, and learning patterns among racial/ethnic majority and minority new hires. *Howard Journal of Communications, 10,* 97–121.

Tishkoff, S. A., & Kidd, K. K. (2004). Implications of biogeography of human populations for "race" and medicine. *Nature Genetics, 36*(11 Suppl.), S21–S27.

Torres, R. D., & Ngin, C. (1995). Racialized boundaries, class relations, and cultural politics: The Asian-American and Latino experience. In A. Darder (Ed.), *Culture and difference: Critical perspectives on the bicultural experience in the United States* (pp. 55–69). Westport, CT: Bergin & Garvey.

U.S. Equal Employment Opportunity Commission. (2005). *Race-based charges FY 1992–FY 2005*. Retrieved April 22, 2005, from http://www.eeoc.gov/stats/race.html

Valentino, N. A. (1999). Crime news and the priming of racial attitudes during evaluations of the president. *Public Opinion Quarterly, 63,* 293–320.

van Dijk, T. A. (1987). *Communicating racism: Ethnic prejudice in thought and talk*. Newbury Park, CA: Sage.

van Dijk, T. A. (1993a). Denying racism: Elite discourse and racism. In K. Wrench & J. Solomos (Eds.), *Race and migration in Western Europe* (pp. 179–193). Oxford, UK: Berg.

van Dijk, T. A. (1993b). *Elite discourse and racism*. Newbury Park, CA: Sage.

Warren, J. T. (2001). Doing Whiteness: On the performative dimensions of race in the classroom. *Communication Education, 50,* 91–108.

Washington, J. (2008, November 16). Obama election spurs race crimes around country. *USA Today*. Retrieved January 5, 2009, from http://www.usatoday.com/news/nation/2008-11-15-2960000388_x.htm

West, C. (1982). *Prophesy deliverance! An Afro-American revolutionary Christianity*. Philadelphia: Westminster Press.

West, C. (1993). *Race matters*. Boston: Beacon Press.

Wetherell, M., & Potter, J. (1992). *Mapping the language of racism: Discourse and the legitimation of exploitation*. New York: Columbia University Press.

Williams, D. E., & Olaniran, B. A. (2002). Crisis communication in racial issues. *Journal of Applied Communication Research, 30*, 293–313.

Wilson, K. H. (1999). Towards a discursive theory of racial identity: *The Souls of Black Folk* as a response to nineteenth-century biological determinism. *Western Journal of Communication, 63*, 193–215.

10 Technology in/as Applied Communication Research

Leah A. Lievrouw
University of California, Los Angeles

Communication technologies are a pervasive presence in contemporary society. A complex, convergent landscape of conventional media, telecommunications, and computing affords, shapes, and supports (and is itself shaped by) the whole spectrum of human communicative action and understanding. Today's technologies are not merely channels that "deliver" messages or content, in the traditional production–consumption sense of mass media; they also constitute milieux for sociality, blending the familiar routines and conventions of conversation and small group interaction, the reach and connectivity of global networks, and the sensibilities of local communities and larger cultures. The social changes associated with new technologies in the last few decades have encouraged scholars in many disciplines, including communication, to rethink distinctions between content and form, message and medium, structure and action, and cause and effect; they vividly illustrate Latour's (1991) maxim that "technology is society made durable" (p. 103).

As these familiar theoretical and practical distinctions elide, there are important implications for applied communication research. In the first section of this chapter, I present a brief overview of the ways that communication technologies have been conceptualized and studied in the communication discipline over time, beginning with the separation of communication channels and processes that emerged with mass media research and carried over into early studies of new information and communication technologies (ICTs), through more recent frameworks that consider process and channel, interpersonal and mass, and communicative action and technology as inseparable aspects of communication and culture. This latter view frames technology and communication as *mediation* (e.g., Altheide & Snow, 1988; Fornäs, 2002; Gumpert & Cathcart, 1990; Silverstone, 1999, 2005) and redefines communication technologies as both resources for and manifestations of communication, meaning, and culture. I outline several main characteristics of mediation and contrast them with the "mass" perspective in communication research.

In the second section, I discuss selected studies drawn from four social contexts of particular interest to applied communication research where new media and ICTs have been widely adopted and studied (organizational communication, health communication, political communication, and instructional communication), to show how the uses and understanding of communication technologies have evolved in each context. In the final section, I return to the concept of mediation, and argue that because it considers technology and practice as inseparable, mutually determining aspects of communication, it suggests a compelling way forward for applied communication research and for the communication discipline more broadly. Rather than approaching technology instrumentally, as a set of tools for achieving some other "purely" communicative or pragmatic end (a view that might be called "technology *in* communication and applied communication research"), technology can be understood as both enabling and constituting communication, meaning, and culture, and as continuously reinscribed and re-created in practice (what we might call "technology *as* communication and applied communication research").

Of course, the basic insight that systems/structures are both the means and the ends of social action is not new. Giddens's (1984) theory of structuration, for example, posited that social structure provides the "rules and resources" for action, and that structure continually is reconstituted in action. Weick (1979) also argued that communication constitutes organization. A similar point can be made about the relationship between communication and technology across applied communication contexts. If, as Silverstone (2005) observed, mediation is the defining condition of contemporary experience, manifested in technological systems and social relationships alike, frameworks that situate technology *as* communication are better suited to the study of communication (including applied communication research) in an era no longer dominated by "mass" notions of society and communication than are those frameworks that view technology solely as a tool or channel—that is, technology *in* communication.

Defining Communication Technology: From Mass Media to Mediation

What is communication technology? If *communication* has been a notoriously elusive concept for communication scholars to define, they have had little trouble distinguishing between the phenomenon itself and the devices and methods that people use to do it. Throughout most of the discipline's history, communication technology has been defined instrumentally, as a means to an end rather than as a constitutive element of communication per se.

Of course, humans have used technological tools to interact and express themselves since the days of cave paintings, bone carvings, and pictographs (Crowley & Heyer, 2007; Williams, 1981). However, with the introduction of moveable type and print in the 15th century—innovations often characterized as the first mass-production technology—and, to an even greater extent, with electrical technologies in the late-19th and early 20th centuries, scholars began to consider communication technologies as objects of study in their own right. The industrial scale of the technologies, their capital-intensive and large-scale infrastructures, the volume of material being produced and distributed, the size of the audiences they could reach, and, crucially, the influence these systems seemed to have on everything from individuals' attitudes and behavior to popular culture and fashion to large-scale political and social movements, seemed both new and provocative (Graham, 2000). Between the 1930s and 1950s—the height of the age of *mass* production and consumption, *mass* society, *mass* man, and so on—sociologists, critics, psychologists, political scientists, historians, and engineers launched the study of the social, psychological, and cultural effects of mass media and mass communication on individuals, audiences, and societies (E. M. Rogers, 1994).

From this perspective, *channel* became a key variable in communication research, distinct from content and process, particularly in the wake of the "communication theory" model of signal transmission proposed by Shannon and Weaver (1949) and adapted by Berlo (1960) into the "sender–message–channel–receiver" (SMCR) formulation as a "scientific" model of human communication.[1] Channel effects were seen largely as a function of scale: Complex, expensive "big media" (such as newspapers and radio), to use Schramm's (1977) phrase, might be expected to have commensurately powerful and widespread effects on audiences or society at large; "little media" (such as newsletters and slide projection) were more limited in scope and effect.

Indeed, the concept of channel became so ingrained among communication scholars that by the 1980s, E. M. Rogers (1986) could describe the discipline itself (at least in the United States) as a

> dichotomy [divided] on the basis of channels: interpersonal channels, which involve a face-to-face exchange between two or more individuals, and *mass media channels*, all those means of transmitting messages such as radio, television, newspapers, and so on, which enable a source of one or a few individuals to reach an audience of many. This classification is mainly on the basis of the size of the audience. (p. 3)

This emphasis on channels encouraged researchers to define communication technologies primarily on the basis of their technical features, particularly channel capacity. From the cultural fixity and standardization embodied in mechanically printed texts (Eisenstein, 1979) to the "separation of communication from transportation" achieved by the telegraph (Carey, 1989, p. 203) to the reproduction of sounds and images via photography, motion pictures, sound recording, and electronic media (Williams, 1981), communication scholars attributed the significance and influence of media technologies mainly to their role as "extensions of man" (McLuhan, 2003) across time and space.

With the introduction of newer ICTs in the late 1970s and 1980s, communication scholars' attention shifted to the convergence of older media technologies with computing and telecommunications. However, definitions of communication technology remained fixed on technical features and channel capacity. The technologies might be new, but their basic role as tools was not: Whereas mass communication researchers had investigated the *effects* of mass media on audiences, early new media researchers studied the *impacts* of new technologies on organizations and society (Webster, 2002). Rice and Associates (1984) and E. M. Rogers (1986), for example, contrasted the two-way transmission capabilities of new media channels with the one-way transmission of mass media. Durlak (1987) proposed that communication technologies would be perceived as more or less interactive depending on their interface or system features. Later, after the introduction of Internet Web browsers and graphical interfaces, Reeves and Nass (1996) argued that the formal qualities of computer interfaces affect users' cognitive processing of online media content, encouraging users to anthropomorphize computers and other new media devices.

By the late 1980s, however, many researchers and scholars had become dissatisfied with this conventional approach to communication technology, especially the technological determinism implicit in both media effects research and studies of the "impacts" of new technologies. Coincident with the broader shift already underway in the communication field away from large-scale quantitative studies toward a focus on local practices, everyday life, subjectivity, interaction, and meaning (e.g., Gerbner, 1983), these scholars sought to understand communication technologies as embedded within complex, diverse cultural landscapes of artifacts, meanings, and practices, and to reframe people's engagement with technologies as something more than audience membership, reception, or consumption. In an early book on new media technologies, for example, E. M. Rogers (1986) defined communication technology as "the hardware equipment, organizational structures, *and social values* by which individuals collect, process, and exchange information with other individuals" (p. 2). Beniger (1986) also observed that "the nineteenth century revolution in information technology was predicated on, if not directly caused by, social changes associated with earlier innovations" (p. 10).

Beginning in the 1970s, some communication scholars had begun to explore concepts drawn from political economy, cultural studies, critical theory, and science and technology studies (STS), particularly the critique of technological determinism advanced within STS during the period. This critique catalyzed a wave of historical and sociological studies of technology in the 1980s and 1990s across a wide range of disciplines and fields, including communication. The *sociotechnical* approach of STS holds that material aspects of technology must be studied in conjunction with their social, temporal, political, economic, and cultural contexts; indeed, from this perspective, the technical features of technologies may matter less than how they are actually used and the meanings that people attribute to them (MacKenzie & Wajcman, 1999). Concepts from STS, such as *interpretive flexibility, trajectories, reverse salients, mutual shaping, boundary objects*, and especially the *social construction of technology*, found numerous adherents among communication technology researchers and scholars in the 1990s, particularly those investigating the uses of communication technologies in organizations (Fulk, 1993; Jackson, Poole, & Kuhn, 2002; see also Boczkowski & Lievrouw, 2008).

Over the last decade, this reflexive, contextual, and critical approach has been widely adopted among communication technology researchers. As the French media historian Flichy (1995) noted, "The history of an invention is that of a series of technological and social developments, together with interactions between the two spheres. A new communications system is only established at the end of a long process in which each stage warrants attention" (p. 2). The deterministic language of effects and impacts largely has been superseded by more relational, subjective, and meaning-driven frameworks and concepts, such as interactivity, identity formation and self-presentation, and the creation and maintenance of community. The rejection of technological determinism, and a relatively strong form of social constructionism, has become the prevailing perspective in recent new media studies (Lievrouw & Livingstone, 2006a). Definitions of new communication technologies now recognize that their material aspects are fully and inextricably entwined with their cultural, social, historical, economic, and political contexts. For example, Lievrouw and Livingstone (2006b) proposed a definition of *new media* that comprises information and communication technologies, and their associated social contexts, including *artifacts or devices* used to mediate, communicate, or convey information; *activities and practices* in which people engage to communicate or share information; and *social arrangements or organizational forms* that develop around the artifacts/devices and activities/practices.

Perhaps what is most significant about the shift toward these more socially contextualized views is that scholars have had to rethink people's relationships with and understandings of media and communication technology. Consequently, recent media scholarship has moved away from theories of mass communication and mass society, and the preoccupation with technical systems, features, and effects. Mediated content and interaction now are seen as socially and culturally diversified and selective, as well as mass produced and consumed. Some forms of communication are highly individualized, some are collective, and some are mixed modes; in many situations, no longer is it easy (or necessarily meaningful) to separate producers and consumers, senders and receivers, or content and channel. Socially embedded communication technologies can be seen as "doubly material": They are both the tangible means of communicative expression and culture, and tangible cultural expressions in themselves.[2] They are form and content, means and ends, and the action and structure of communication and culture. In a real sense, they fulfill McLuhan's (1967/2003) insight that "the medium is the message" (p. 19).

Given this shift in perspective, a number of scholars have begun to characterize people's engagement with ICTs and new media as *mediation*, in both the technical sense and in terms of interpersonal participation or intervention (Fornäs, 2002; Silverstone, 1999, 2005). Communication scholars first turned to the mediation idea in the 1980s as a conceptual bridge between interpersonal and mass communication (e.g., Altheide & Snow, 1988; Anderson & Meyer, 1988; Gumpert & Cathcart, 1986, 1990; Meyer, 1988). Many had criticized the interpersonal–mass divide in the communication discipline, particularly as new communication technologies diffused into everyday life, work, and leisure (e.g., Kreps, 2001; Lievrouw & Finn, 1990; Reardon & Rogers, 1988; E. M. Rogers, 1999; Rubin & Rubin, 1985).

A full review of the literature related to the mediation perspective is outside the scope of this chapter. However, a few points serve to summarize how the mediation perspective differs from the mass communication perspective as a way to think about people's engagement with communication technologies and media (see Table 10.1).

First, mass communication ordinarily is conceived and represented as a linear, cumulative transmission process, as in the classic SMCR formulation. This conception, in fact, is a metaphor for the transportation of goods over geographic distance, and has dominated mass communication studies historically (e.g., Carey, 1989). Mediation, however, is better understood as *recombinant* and *reflexive*, the result of the continuous interplay of technology development, use, and breakdown; communicative action; social circumstances; and shared meaning. Mediation is "a more or less continuous activity of engagement and disengagement with meanings which have their source or their focus in...texts, but which extend through, and are measured against, experience" (Silverstone, 1999, p. 13). Thus, mediation is closer to relational or meaning-based definitions of communication, such as the convergence model proposed by E. M. Rogers and Kincaid (1981; see also Kincaid & Figueroa, this volume), or Carey's (1989) ritual view, where communication "is directed not toward the extension of messages in space but toward the maintenance of society in time; not the act of imparting information but the representation of shared beliefs" (p. 18). Mediation enables, supports, facilitates, and constrains communicative action and representation; it is not merely the insertion of technology into an otherwise "pure" or unmediated human communication process.

Second, the study of mass communication, given its roots in industrial-era notions of work and society, often is predicated on hierarchies as the natural and archetypal form of social and technological organization. The mass distribution of messages, content, and meaning largely has been conceived as a one-way, one (or few)-to-many flow or cascade from the top to bottom or center to periphery of social systems. However, mediation assumes that in addition to hierarchical structures, society and technology today can be seen as a *network of networks* (Castells, 2001)—flexible, reorganizing, interrelated, point-to-point technological and social webs that can take on the forms or relations that are best suited to the purposes at hand. As Lievrouw and Livingstone (2006b) explained:

Table 10.1 Mass Communication and Mediation Perspectives on Communication Technology

	Mass Communication	*Mediation*
Communication Processes	Linear, cumulative	Recombinant, reflexive
Social/Technological Structures	Hierarchical, centralized: top-down, few-to-many, stable	Networks: N-way, point-to-point, flexible, reorganizing
Distribution and Access	Scarce, costly, limited	Ubiquitous, pervasive
Grounding for Meaning	Production and reception	Emergent from interaction, relations

The term "network" denotes a broad, multiplex interconnection in which many points or "nodes" (persons, groups, machines, collections of information, organizations) are embedded. Links among nodes may be created or abandoned on an as-needed basis at any location in the system, and any node can be either a sender or a receiver of messages—or both. (p. 24)

Third, mass communication studies have assumed that the distribution of, and access to, media technologies, sources, and content are scarce, capital- and resource-intensive, and valuable. In traditional workplace, classroom, and household settings dominated by mass media, technologies, and content are physically fixed, limited in quantity, and typically shared. The mediation perspective, on the other hand, assumes their *ubiquity*, in the sense that technologies "affect everyone in the societies where they are employed" (Lievrouw & Livingstone, 2006b, p. 25), even if not everyone uses or has access to them to the same extent. Silverstone (1999) suggested the sense of ubiquity associated with mediation: "It is difficult, probably impossible, for us...to step out of media culture, our media culture. In this we are like linguists trying to analyze their own language" (p. 13).

Fourth, mass communication studies tend to emphasize the production and consumption/reception of mass-produced content, especially in their focus on media effects. The mediation perspective, in contrast, emphasizes the *interactivity* among people and resources afforded by networked technologies, social structures, information sources, and personal relationships. Fornäs (2002) noted that "our communication society is based on mediations between texts and people, in that people pass and meet each other through texts, just as texts pass and encounter each other through people" (p. 104). Moreover, as Silverstone (1999) pointed out:

The circulation of meaning, which is mediation, is more than a two-step flow.... Meanings circulate in primary and secondary texts, through endless intertextualities, in parody and pastiche, in constant replay, and in the interminable discourses [in which we] act and interact, urgently seeking to make sense of the world. (p. 13)

Communication Technology and Applied Communication Research: Four Contexts

To understand the scope and significance of these shifts in perspective regarding communication and technology, from "mass" to mediation, I turn to four social contexts of particular interest to applied communication researchers where the relationship between communication technology and communicative action has been extensively studied: organizational, health, political, and instructional communication. Individually, each of these contexts has generated a substantial body of research, as shown in the separate chapters in this volume devoted to them; consequently, none of them can be reviewed comprehensively in the space provided here. However, by highlighting a few studies in each area, I hope to illustrate the extent to which the uses and understanding of communication technologies have evolved in the communication discipline, including applied communication research. The chapter closes with a discussion of the implications of the shift toward mediation for future research and scholarship.

Technology and Organizational Communication

Organizational communication is a good place to begin any discussion of communication technology studies, for it was one of the first areas within the communication discipline where scholars recognized the enormous social and relational implications of ICTs and new media (Culnan & Markus, 1987; Fulk & Steinfield, 1990; Jackson et al., 2002; Poole & DeSanctis, this volume; Seibold, Lemus, Ballard, & Myers, this volume; Taylor, Flanagin, Cheney, & Seibold, 2001). The uses of ICTs in organizations was one of the first major research fronts in communication technology studies, mainly because large private- and public-sector organizations often were the first entities that could afford to adopt and use the new technologies, including audio- and videoconferencing, computer-mediated communication (CMC) and collaboration systems, and enhanced telecommunications services.

Broadly speaking, studies of communication technologies in organizations have focused on two main phenomena: organizational structure and organizational communication processes. In the first line of work, many early studies of ICTs in organizations addressed their structural consequences (e.g., Hiltz & Turoff, 1993; Johansen, Vallee, & Spangler, 1979; Kling & Scacchi, 1982). Investigators were particularly interested in the effects of ICTs on superior–subordinate relations, information flow within established structures, and the implementation of (or resistance to) structural change (e.g., Markus & Robey, 1988; Orlikowski & Robey, 1991). In this stream of research, social network analysis and systems theory have been widely employed to investigate structures and relationships within and across organizational boundaries (e.g., Monge & Contractor, 2003).

Over time, the emphasis in research on communication technologies and organizing has shifted toward a view of technological systems, organizational structure, and action as mutually determining. For example, Scott Poole and his associates have advanced *adaptive structuration theory* (AST) to account for the role of communication technologies in organizations (see Poole & DeSanctis, this volume). Based on Giddens's (1984) structuration theory, and influenced by concepts from STS, AST contends that the interplay among ICTs, people, and organizational structures allows people in organizations to construct their own definitions and uses of technology (DeSanctis & Poole, 1994; Poole & DeSanctis, 1990).

Researchers also have examined the influence of ICTs on organizational communication processes. Many early studies in this line of work took a fairly straightforward approach that emphasized channels, comparing the technical capacities and features of new systems with face-to-face interaction for various work situations, message types, or decision-making tasks (e.g., Culnan & Markus, 1987; Daft & Lengel, 1986; Rice & Love, 1987). These studies concentrated on the use of e-mail and computer conferencing, and were often designed as laboratory studies (Rice, 1992). This research suggested, for example, that computer messaging (i.e., e-mail) is similar to telegraphy and probably best suited to simple, unambiguous, task-related messages. CMC also can give users control over information flow, reach more people at one time than is possible via other channels, provide information simultaneously to remote and local workers, and increase the involvement of both groups (Eveland & Bikson, 1988). CMC also allows users to increase their range of contacts and form relationships with others who share their interests but with whom they otherwise are unacquainted (Constant, Sproull, & Kiesler, 1996).

One of the most fully articulated channel-based theories in this line of work is media richness theory (Daft & Lengel, 1986; Daft, Lengel, & Trevino, 1987). Media richness theory hypothesizes that some systems are more suitable for certain types of communication than others, depending on their *bandwidth* (the capacity to carry information). High-bandwidth or *rich* channels (such as full-motion video with audio) are said to be like face-to-face interaction and, thus, better suited to carry messages that are uncertain, equivocal, or ambiguous, such as those involved in bargaining or negotiation. In contrast, *lean* channels with less bandwidth (such as text on a screen, as in e-mail) are better for simple, clear, and unambiguous messages, such as delivering task-related directions. The theory predicts that effective communicators will match the channel they choose with the degree of richness required for a particular message. Rice (1993) later refined this theory to propose the concept of *media appropriateness*.

System- or channel-centered theories, such as media richness theory, were later criticized for failing to capture the complexity of real interaction (Culnan & Markus, 1987; Rudy, 1996). Over time, investigators have placed less emphasis on the channels per se and more on organizational culture, context, and the social construction of technologies (e.g., Fulk, 1993; Jackson et al., 2002). Other studies have emphasized social and interaction processes, including group and organizational dynamics, norms, constraints, and conflict (Aakhus, 2001; Franz & Jin, 1995; Fulk & Steinfield, 1990; Lea, 1992), as well as interpretive and critical perspectives, and ethnographic methods (Taylor et al., 2001).

Technology and Health Communication

Generally speaking, the study of health communication—another key arena for applied communication research—has followed two main paths: (1) interpersonal and group communication (including provider–patient interaction,[3] small group social support processes, and issues related to organizing), and (2) the design of large-scale campaigns that use media (principally, mass media technologies) to deliver authoritative health information to relevant audiences (Kreps, 2001; Kreps & Bonaguro, this volume; Ray & Donohew, 1990). Neuhauser and Kreps (2003) described these two approaches as "the provision of health-care delivery and the promotion of public health…disseminating messages from experts to the public in the hope of motivating the public to change specific behaviors" (p. 8). As this description suggests, the relationships involved often are asymmetrical: Providers and the health-care organizations and institutions they represent typically are cast in the role of expert knowledge resources, whereas patients, families, and the lay public are cast as less informed than these professionals, more in need of education and behavioral change, or otherwise lacking some knowledge or motivation that providers can supply (the ethical implications of this situation are discussed in Guttman, 1997).

Kreps (2001) also noted the parallel between the competing domains of communication in health-care provision and in public health promotion and the historical interpersonal–mass communication divide within the larger communication discipline. The campaign domain has tended to attract mass media effects researchers with interests in medicine and health, whereas the health-care delivery side has engaged interpersonal, group, and organizational communication specialists with health-related interests (Kreps). Some media campaigns have been remarkably effective in raising public awareness of health problems, such as breast cancer, smoking risks, HIV, AIDS, heart disease, and high blood pressure (excellent case studies are collected in Rice & Atkin, 2000; see also Witte & Roberto, this volume).

However, few media-driven campaigns by themselves have produced major changes in individual or collective behavior or health outcomes. Neuhauser and Kreps (2003) observed that "unfortunately, many of our health communication efforts have not succeeded" and wondered "why are our scientifically sound messages not more effective in engaging people to change behavior?" (pp. 8–9). Among health communication researchers, a common rule of thumb has been that interpersonal approaches are far more effective than mass media messages for changing individual behavior, but do not scale to produce population-wide change (Cline & Haynes, 2001; Kreps, 2001). As a result, some well-funded campaigns have employed a combination of broad-based media messages and interpersonal contact and local follow up, bringing together specialists in media research and interpersonal and group communication, such as the Stanford Heart Disease Prevention Program, conducted from the 1970s to the early 1990s (Flora, 2001; Fortmann & Varady, 2000), and the National Cholesterol Education Program, underway since 1985 (Cleeman & Lenfant, 1998).

As in so many other social contexts, new media and communication technologies have had important consequences for health communication; they have blurred familiar lines between interpersonal and mass communication, as well as communication in health-care delivery and public health promotion (see Kreps & Bonaguro, this volume). Beginning in the early 1990s, the rapid growth of the World Wide Web and the introduction of Web browsers made a much wider range of information more accessible to more people than ever before. Web users have discovered a new universe of health-information resources online and new opportunities to seek and share what they learn with others.

Studies by the Pew Internet & American Life Project have documented how rapidly Americans have turned to the Internet for health-care information and support, a phenomenon some researchers are calling "e-Health" (see Kreps & Bonaguro, this volume). Roughly 80% of adult Internet users (113 million in 2006, approximately half of the adult U.S. population) regularly search online for health information, a percentage that has been consistent since 2002 (Fox, 2006; Madden & Fox, 2006). Those who are ill and their caregivers use e-mail and chat rooms to connect with others with similar health problems and to share their experiences, advice, information, and research findings. Pharmaceutical and equipment companies sponsor some of these groups as part of their marketing efforts. In the last few years, there have been significant increases in the proportion of the U.S. population seeking information online about particular physicians or hospitals, or about experimental treatments or new medicines (Fox, 2006). In this evolving context, it has become increasingly difficult to separate interpersonal interaction, constantly updated online information resources, and broad-based media campaigns. Excerpts from e-mail and journal articles get posted to blogs; online support groups discuss and criticize the latest scientific findings. Patients and families seek therapies and advice, enroll in experimental research protocols, and compare the records and reputations of different institutions and providers wherever they are located (Fox, 2006; see also Street, Gold, & Manning, 1997; White & Dorman, 2001; Wright & Bell, 2003).

Today, people's familiarity with online medical information resources, and their growing tendency to bring that information into their consultations with health-care professionals, has begun to alter the relationship between providers, patients, families, and the public. This new engagement with communication technology and its consequences for interaction, are reflected in a growing number of health communication studies (Rice & Katz, 2001; Street et al., 1997). In a review of research on seeking health information online, Cline and Haynes (2001) suggested some of the potential consequences of the power shift associated with new patterns of information access:

> Providers [may be] unprepared to deal with the magnitude of available information.... Providers may be stressed by added responsibilities for information seeking and clarification.... Conflicts between provider and client may be likely as consumers locate information that leads them to challenge, question, or "second-guess" providers, indicating diminished trust in their physicians. (p. 675)

Researchers with the Pew Internet & American Life project have confirmed this scenario; survey respondents reported that when they bring information from outside sources to the office visit, "they are met with mixed reviews from doctors" (Fox & Fallows,

2003, p. 15). Some physicians ignore or dismiss what patients learn on their own as unreliable or unprofessional, sometimes as a way to regain control of the clinical interaction process; others encourage patient learning and exploration, and take on more of an information gatekeeper role, helping patients and families to interpret and evaluate the information they find.

Power relations between providers and patients is not the only aspect of health communication that has been affected by the use of new communication technologies. Another topic is the use of new media technologies in health support groups, especially online, but also via mobile telephony (e.g., S. W. Campbell & Kelley, 2006; Street et al., 1997; Sullivan, 2003; White & Dorman, 2001; Wright, 1999, 2002; Wright & Bell, 2003). A number of techniques also have been proposed for evaluating the quality of online health information and its potential for generating behavior change (Cline & Haynes, 2001; Cummins et al., 2003; Evers et al., 2003).

It seems clear that the use of new media technologies is reshaping health communication at both the interpersonal level and in the wider culture. Indeed, these two spheres of health communication are more interwoven today than was possible when mass media and individual providers supplied virtually all of people's health information. The interpersonal and the cultural continually inform and redirect each other, shaping the content and channels of health communication alike. The linear, directed messages of classic health-information campaigns have given way to a more recombinant, reflexive mode of creation, circulation, and use of health-information resources online. Providers and institutions no longer can assume that they control the flow or direction of information, from reliable, authoritative sources to the larger public; instead, such information is filtered through interpersonal advice networks online and off-line. Medical controversies or research debates previously confined to the pages of specialized journals now circulate in the news and entertainment media and online. Many resources that were once scarce— too arcane, expensive, or remote for laypeople to understand or retrieve—now are readily and broadly accessible. The significance and meaning of health information no longer is established by professionals and institutions, and then delivered to ready and receptive patients or audiences; increasingly, professionals and institutions are being called on to interpret, justify, explain, or defend the information they present, and to use communication technologies effectively to interact and engage with the patients and communities that they serve.

Technology and Political Communication

Another familiar context for applied communication research is political communication, where research traditionally has centered on analyzing the design and effectiveness of advertising and public relations campaigns advocating particular positions, issues, or candidates, on one hand, and news/popular press coverage of those positions, issues, and candidates, on the other (see Kaid, McKinney, & Tedesco, this volume). In both cases, the objective is to assess the influence of such "purposeful communication about politics" (McNair, 2003, p. 4) on broad-based public opinion, political participation, or political choices, particularly voting.

Political communication is one of the oldest specialties in the communication discipline, and has been linked closely with mass media research since the days of Harold Lasswell's studies of propaganda during World War II, which led to his famous definition of communication as *who* says *what*, to *whom* via *what channels*, with *what effect?* (Lasswell, 1948). As a consequence, even today, "the theoretical diversity of political communication displays certain common themes, such as a lasting concern with effects"

(E. M. Rogers, 2004, p. 3). Drawing on studies of rhetoric and persuasion, public opinion research and polling, journalism, speech and press law, and political science, political communication researchers have long considered mass media organizations (especially print and broadcast news and advertising) to be archetypal players and gatekeepers in setting political agendas and shaping public understanding of political issues and debates (Kaid, 2004; McNair, 2003). News organizations and political groups (e.g., political parties, movements, and community groups) alike traditionally have been organized as hierarchies intended to create and maintain control over the consistent presentation of campaign messages, issues, and candidates. Mass media have been seen as the ideal tool in this context, because they afford both centralized control and wide, consistent distribution of content.

McNair (2003, p. 4) justified the central focus on media campaigns and coverage, and the exclusion of interpersonal interaction and group/community communication (e.g., in the context of local government), because interpersonal and group processes are largely "hidden from the analyst"—that is, they are not recorded and distributed through conventional media channels. As a result, until recently, most political communication research, including that conducted by applied communication researchers, has tended to frame communication technologies mainly in terms of their relative effectiveness as carriers of political messages, such as in studies of ways that voters perceive and evaluate political advertising (McKinnon & Kaid, 1999), interests behind news coverage of controversies (Violanti, 1996), or how political candidates position themselves relative to others in televised debates (Doerfel & Marsh, 2003).

One important exception was a research project that examined the implementation of the Public Electronic Network (PEN), a public computer-messaging network available to anyone living or working in the city of Santa Monica, California, and that linked them directly with city officials (Dutton & Guthrie, 1991; O'Sullivan, 1995). Researchers found that PEN encouraged citizen queries and interaction, as well as prompt, personal responses and action from government officials. However, perhaps the most surprising finding was that PEN was adopted quickly and used by many in the community who were assumed to be unfamiliar or uncomfortable with computers and computer messaging, including women and homeless people who sought information about public services and employment opportunities online (Collins-Jarvis, 1993; Schmitz, Rogers, Phillips, & Paschal, 1995).

The PEN studies were significant on several counts. The project expanded the landscape of political communication research beyond the effects of mass media campaigns and news coverage on voters to include mediated interpersonal and group processes, and the role of new media technologies in grassroots political engagement and organizing at the community/local government level. In this respect, the PEN studies were an important predecessor to contemporary studies of e-Government (Layne & Lee, 2001; Moon, 2002). Vis-à-vis new media and communication technology research, the PEN studies constituted something of an intellectual bridge between the concepts of "information utilities" and "wired cities" advanced by technologists and urban planners in the 1970s and 1980s (Dutton, Blumler, & Kraemer, 1987; Light, 2003) and the online citizen movements and community networks that emerged in cities around the world in the 1990s with the introduction the Web and browsers (Tambini, 1999; Tsagarousianou, Tambini, & Bryan, 1998).

The rapid growth and use of new media technologies, especially the Internet, since the 1990s has begun to transform political communication, from e-Government and the mobilization of community groups to political campaigning and the shaping of public opinion. A Harris poll conducted in April 2005 showed that 44% of U.S. Internet users read political blogs ("Two-Fifths of Americans Online," 2005). Another study found that political blogs attracted nearly three times as many visits as any other category (comScore Networks, 2005). Statistics reported by the marketing firm ClickZ indicate that blog traffic spikes with major political news stories (McGann, 2004). In 2006, a study by the Pew Internet & American Life Project found that 53% of adult Internet users surveyed had sought political news and information online (Horrigan, 2006), up from 22% in 2002 (Raine, Cornfield, & Horrigan, 2005). The increase actually is more substantial than these figures indicate, because the proportion of U.S. adults using the Internet rose dramatically in the same period (Madden, 2006).

The relative low cost and potential global reach of new technologies also have fostered a recent renaissance of alternative and oppositional political commentary, engagement, and activism online (e.g., Lievrouw, 2006, 2007). Citizens, activists, and interest groups of both the left and right have adapted communication technologies to new forms of political engagement and advocacy (e.g., Atton, 2005; Chadwick & Howard, 2008; Dartnell, 2006; McCaughey & Ayers, 2003; Pickerill, 2003; Reber & Kim, 2006; Thomas, 2002; van de Donk, Loader, Nixon, & Rucht, 2004).

Despite this dramatic growth in online political information seeking, communication, and activism, however, observers continue to be divided about the significance of new media technologies for political communication. In their analysis of the implications of new media and the Internet for democracy, Jenkins and Thorburn (2003) listed several innovative uses of Web-based information in campaigns introduced in the 2000 U.S. national elections, but also cautioned that more profound changes in democratic participation and "informed citizenship" are likely to take much longer than many technology advocates predict. R. Rogers (2004) was less hesitant, arguing that the use of Web-based information resources, metrics, and indicators already has detached traditional, consensus-based methods of issue debate and deliberation in European nations from their strictly bounded geographic bases, a process he called "de-territorialization" (p. 59).

On the whole, it seems clear that political communication is undergoing a variety of changes in response to new communication technologies. Rainie et al. (2005) pointed out that 2004 "was a breakout year for the role of the Internet in politics" (p. 2). As Cornfield (2005) noted:

> The internet has become an essential medium of American politics…because it can be used in multiple ways. Part deliberative town square, part raucous debating society, part research library, part instant news source, and part political comedy club, the internet connects voters to a wealth of content and commentary about politics. (p. 1)

The variety of metaphors in this quote suggests the extent to which political communication already has moved beyond the assumptions and conventions of the "mass." The rapid proliferation of online information and interaction genres (blogs, mobs, social network sites, etc.) have complicated the efforts of political campaigns to control the distribution and reception of their messages, as demonstrated by the unsuccessful 2006 campaigns of Senator George Allen (R-Virginia) and U.S. Representative and Senate candidate Harold E. Ford, Jr. (D-Tennessee). The discipline and structure of hierarchical campaign organizations have been challenged by grassroots counterorganizing using meet-ups and social network software. Reliance on expensive and relatively scarce media outlets, although still critical for generating awareness and interest among general audiences, cannot target more engaged and activist voters as effectively as can specialized Web-based sources. Polling and other basic forms of feedback still are essential, but voters and constituents are demanding more frequent and direct access to candidates and campaigns, posing questions and critiquing campaign messages and claims.

Technology and Instructional Communication

The use of communication technology in education is as old as pedagogy itself: demonstration props and models; pens and paper; chalkboards, maps, and books; rulers and scales; film and slides; video and calculators; and laptops and Wikipedia all have been enlisted at one time or another to enrich instruction. In U.S. education today, at every level from preschool to higher and continuing education, communication technologies are a routine part of teaching and learning.

However, as in the contexts of health care and politics, in instructional communication research,[4] technology has been viewed as a more or less ancillary tool, secondary to the more basic, or "real," interactional processes of teaching and learning, when it has been considered at all. For example, a recent historical overview of "the scholarship of teaching and learning" within the communication discipline makes no reference to the role of media or communication technologies in instruction (McCroskey, Richmond, & McCroskey, 2002). In a comprehensive review of 186 studies of instructional and developmental communication published in communication journals between 1990 and 1999, Waldeck, Kearney, and Plax (2001) found that just 19 studies investigated the uses or perceptions of technology—usually television—in pedagogy. (In comparison, 27 studies dealt with the effects of mass media on children.) Even in studies where communication technology or media have been taken into account, the great majority have been concerned primarily with the effects of media content or teacher communicative behavior via technological channels (Henrickson, 1996; Waldeck, Kearney, & Plax, 2000). Technology rarely is considered as a fully integrated aspect of instruction for teachers and students alike, even though ICTs have become an essential part of schooling over the last 2 decades. This omission has prompted some scholars to call for more attention to the question of technology in instruction (Nussbaum & Friedrich, 2005; Waldeck et al., 2001).

Instructional communication researchers may find a model in studies of distance education, especially in higher education—one area of educational research where communication technologies have taken center stage in recent years. Although distance education has a long history (from "first-generation" correspondence courses offered through postal mail to "second-generation" telecourses using broadcasting and telephone links to today's "third-generation" multimedia instruction; Rumble, 2001), it has undergone an unprecedented burst of growth over the last decade in parallel with the rapid growth of the Internet.

According to data compiled by the U.S. Department of Education's National Center for Educational Statistics (NCES; "The Condition of Education," 2006), the percentage of all U.S. 2- and 4-year institutions of higher education offering distance education courses rose from 33% in 1995 to 62% in 2004–2005 (Greene & Meek, 1998; Lewis, Snow, Farris, & Levin, 1999; Tabs, 2003). The predominant technologies used by the institutions surveyed by the NCES are the Internet (mainly in asynchronous applications, such as Web sites or discussion boards) and one- and two-way video, often with two-way audio links.

It is unsurprising that so many institutions have moved so quickly to use new media to extend their reach. Colleges and universities played a central role in the development of most contemporary ICTs, and have decades of experience using older technologies, such as broadcasting and film, in undergraduate, graduate, extension, and professional education. Even schools with relatively little distance or extension education experience have undertaken new initiatives, on the assumption that distance education is a relatively low-cost way to reach new students and generate additional revenue, particularly among public institutions that are experiencing declining government support.

However, the expense of designing, supporting, and maintaining distance education courses and programs, and the associated technological infrastructure, is substantial. Most analysts agree that mediated learning is more expensive to develop and offer than face-to-face instruction in almost every respect (e.g., development and teaching time, technology expense, institutional overhead and administration, increased faculty work-load, evaluation procedures, and course "shelf life" and updating; Rumble, 2001). The picture is further complicated by an extensive body of research indicating that student learning is no better using mediated instruction than more basic face-to-face instruction (e.g., Clark, 1983; Russell, 2001). In fact, cost appears to be an important factor for institutions that have chosen not to offer distance education opportunities, which comprised 42% of all U.S. higher education institutions in 1995 and 31% in 2000–2001 (National Center for Educational Statistics, 2006).

Despite the costs, institutions are likely to continue investing in distance education and the communication technologies to support it, not least because of increasing student demand for courses and degrees that fit their schedules, do not require physical attendance, provide greater access to learning materials online, and permit interaction with instructors at students' convenience. Certainly, "live" lectures and seminars—classic forms of instruction that employ linear styles of presentation and reception of content; hierarchical forms of student–teacher relations, course organization, and management; and are limited in availability—still are alive and well in higher education. Increasingly, however, they are being complemented by extensive digital libraries and information services that link students and faculty to diverse networks of print and digital resources far beyond those owned by the home campus. Course-management systems, real-time conferencing and chat facilities, podcasting and virtual classrooms and libraries (such as those recently established in SecondLife by a number of prestigious U.S. universities), online testing and feedback, and a range of other technologically mediated materials and services have altered the processes of teaching and learning. Virtually all of the typical student's interactions or encounters with administrative services, such as admissions, enrollment, financial transactions, and grading, now are conducted via the Internet. Higher education in the United States and other affluent countries today is intensely mediated—pedagogy and technology are inseparable parts of the experience.

Implications of Technology in/as Applied Communication Research

Earlier in this chapter, I outlined two perspectives on communication technology that have developed within the communication discipline over time. I suggested that the instrumental focus on channels and effects that characterized classical mass communication research (and which, in many ways, demarcated media research from speech and interpersonal communication studies) contrasts with the *mediation* perspective that has evolved among analysts of new media and communication technology (the main points are summarized in Table 10.1). Mediation considers communicative action, cultural context, and material resources (especially technology) not as independent phenomena but as inextricable, codetermining aspects of sociality, interaction, expression, and meaning.

A general implication of this dichotomy is that the instrumentalist view suggests that practices, tools, and technologies exist, in a sense, *within* the setting in question (e.g., patient history databases within primary care medicine, computer-supported cooperative work within bureaucratic organizations, televised debates or Web-based fund-raising within political campaigns, or distance education courses within higher education). In essence, social contexts are treated as "containers" for events, actions, or resources. This is a familiar duality in social science: action within structure, content within form, micro within macro. In the study of communication, this idea has been manifested in conduit and transmission metaphors extending back from recent descriptions of media technologies and information systems (e.g., Day, 2000; Sawhney, 1996) to the classic SMCR model of communication to studies that cast writing and even language itself as containers for meaning (Goody, 1981; Reddy, 1993). This perspective, thus, situates technology *in* communication, and communication within social context.

From the mediation perspective, however, social contexts are not merely stages or containers for events, practices, and resources. Rather, social and technological action and structure comprise whole environments that are continuously enacted, inscribed, broken down, recreated, and made meaningful by people in the course of everyday life and interaction. To use Callon's (1986) term, communication and context can be thought of as an *ensemble* that involves technologies, practices, and social arrangements together. Put differently, the mediation perspective resituates technology *as* communication, and communication as inseparable from social context.

The pragmatic orientation of applied communication research aligns with the technology-in-communication perspective, as such research often regards not only technology per se but also communication itself as instrumental, and emphasizes the "utility of the [research] work for ameliorating communication-related problems" (Seibold, 2000, p. 184). The mission of applied communication research, thus, is to employ effective communication techniques to solve problems or achieve goals in particular social contexts, to "make a difference" (Kreps, Frey, & O'Hair, 1991). Similar to action research in other disciplines (e.g., Lather, 1986; Wildavsky, 1987), some applied communication scholars have advocated a stance of praxis, in which research constitutes intervention in problematic or unjust situations, as well as scholarly investigation (Eadie, 1994; Frey, 2000; Frey, Pearce, Pollock, Artz, & Murphy, 1996; Seibold, 1995; see also Frey & SunWolf, this volume). The focus on utility, intervention, and problem solving all seem to place communication and communication technology as tools or resources to be deployed as needed within particular settings.

However, as the preceding discussion suggests, in applied communication research, as in the communication discipline at large, the steady integration of communication technologies into ever more aspects of everyday life, work, and leisure has prompted analysts to reframe their research questions, reconceptualize empirical studies, and develop new theories (at least implicitly), in light of the blurring boundaries between communication processes and media technologies. I suggest two particular implications of these shifts for applied communication research.

The first implication is that by adopting the mediation perspective, applied communication researchers may be better positioned to develop robust theories that are generalizable *across* social settings rather than specific to one setting or another. For example, adaptive structuration theory (AST), mentioned earlier in this chapter, considers structure and action, and communication processes and technologies, to be mutually determining. Although AST originally was developed to explain the uses of group decision support systems in formal business organizations, it clearly is applicable to many other forms of mediated social organization and interaction beyond the workplace. Similarly, online social support groups, the focus of so much recent interest among health communication researchers, may serve as useful models for understanding mediated small group processes more broadly, in contexts ranging from new social movements and political mobilization to scientific or artistic collaborations to the evolution of national, linguistic, or cultural diasporic communities around the globe.

A second implication is the potential empirical and theoretical value of adopting a network view of the multilayered communication relationships among people, systems, and social formations in social settings. For example, the distinction between interpersonal and group processes and that of media campaigns in health communication, and the difficulty of crossing this "micro–macro" divide, both analytically and practically, might be resolved by thinking about communication in terms of network relations and dynamics. Rather than categorizing communication processes according to whether they are technologically mediated or not, or how many people are involved, some researchers already have begun to look at the junctures and articulations between people's personal networks and how they access, use, and share health information and ideas via the media, popular culture, and the Internet. Communication researchers today understand that there is no single formula or "magic bullet" that ensures effective communication; a variety of elements must be taken into account to understand the whole experience of expression, influence, persuasion, and action. The network approach, as a tool for observing and analyzing complex social systems and action, is already widely used in organizational communication studies and is a promising way ahead in other arenas of applied communication research as well.

Conclusion

It may be useful to keep in mind the multiple meanings of the word *mediation* itself. It is an important concept for the study of communication, not only because it relates to the means or channels of expression but also because it suggests processes of moderation, negotiation, or bringing together. Both aspects are necessary conditions for communication and shared meaning. The shift from seeing technology-in-communication to seeing technology-as-communication, and the mediation perspective, more generally, finally may bridge (indeed, mediate) some of the discipline's divides, and perhaps even serve as a new point of departure for applied communication scholarship in this new century.

Notes

1. SMCR still is reproduced in many introductory textbooks as a foundational theory of communication, despite numerous critics' objections that it is better suited to its original application in telephone systems than to the study of human communication (e.g., R. Campbell, Martin, & Fabos, 2006; Straubhaar & LaRose, 2006).
2. My use of the term *double materiality* to characterize communication technologies differs slightly from that of Brügger (2002). In a critique of James Slevin's (2000) book, *The Internet and Society*, Brügger argued that the material aspect of the Internet encompasses both the physical objects built into the system and the "immaterial materiality" of the energy used to represent symbols in the form of data, software, or representations. My definition, like Brügger's, contends that the two elements in question exist in a dialectical relationship; however, I focus on both systems and content as material artifacts rather than on system elements alone. My conception also differs in emphasis from "double articulation" as elaborated by Silverstone (1994; Silverstone & Haddon, 1996), which distinguishes between media as technological objects and as textual representations, but frames both as mechanisms of consumption, particularly in domestic settings (see also Livingstone, 2007).
3. Over time, the language used to describe participants in health communication frequently has shifted. What once routinely was characterized as the "doctor–patient" relationship more recently has become the "provider–patient" relationship (to recognize that physicians are not

the only professionals involved), "provider–consumer," or "provider–client" relationship (to avoid reducing those seeking care to the single, medicalized, and often-stigmatized "patient" role). All of these formulations are problematic in some way. "Consumer" suggests active participation (Cline, 2003; Street, 2003), but also frames health care as a market relationship characterized by rational choice. *Client* seems more neutral, but the term also suggests that the seeker of services sets the terms of the relationship, or acts as the provider's employer, which certainly is not the case in third-party payer systems. Moreover, all of the terms depict communication as a dyadic, interpersonal interchange, although most health communication contexts are far more complex and involve more than two people (Eggly et al., 2006). I use a mix of all these terms (as do several of the other writers cited here) to suggest the complexity of players and roles.

4. The present discussion is limited to *instructional communication*—the study and application of communication techniques across diverse instructional settings and pedagogies. It is distinct from the closely allied specialties of developmental communication and communication education (McCroskey et al., 2002; Nussbaum & Friedrich, 2005; Waldeck, Kearney, & Plax, 2001; see also Darling & Leckie, this volume).

References

Aakhus, M. (2001). Technocratic and design stances toward communication expertise: How GDSS facilitators understand their work. *Journal of Applied Communication Research, 29,* 341–371.

Altheide, D. L., & Snow, R. P. (1988). Toward a theory of mediation. In J. A. Anderson (Ed.), *Communication yearbook* (Vol. 11, pp. 194–223). Newbury Park, CA: Sage.

Anderson, J. A., & Meyer, T. P. (1988) *Mediated communication: A social action perspective.* Newbury Park, CA: Sage.

Atton, C. (2005). *An alternative Internet: Radical media, politics and creativity.* Edinburgh, UK: Edinburgh University Press.

Beniger, J. R. (1986). *The control revolution: Technological and economic origins of the information society.* Cambridge, MA: Harvard University Press.

Berlo, D. K. (1960). *The process of communication: An introduction to theory and practice.* New York: Holt, Rinehart & Winston.

Boczkowski, P., & Lievrouw, L. A. (2008). Bridging STS and communication studies: Scholarship on media and information technologies. In E. J. Hackett, O. Amsterdamska, M. Lynch, & J. Wajcman (Eds.), *New handbook of science and technology studies* (pp. 951–977). Cambridge, MA: MIT Press.

Brügger, N. (2002, March). Does the materiality of the Internet matter? In N. Brügger & H. Bødker (Eds.), *The Internet and society? Questioning answers and answering questions* (pp. 13–22). Aarhus, Denmark: Institute of Information and Media Studies, Centre for Internet Research, Aarhus Universitet. Retrieved January 15, 2007, from http://www.cfi.au.dk/publikationer/cfi/005_brugger_boedker

Callon, M. (1986). The sociology of an actor–network: The case of the electric vehicle. In M. Callon, J. Law, & A. Rip (Eds.), *Mapping the dynamics of science and technology: Sociology of science in the real world* (pp. 19–34). Basingstoke, UK: Macmillan.

Campbell, R., Martin, C. R., & Fabos, B. (2006). *Media & culture: An introduction to mass communication* (5th ed.). Boston: Bedford/St. Martin's Press.

Campbell, S. W., & Kelley, M. J. (2006). Mobile phone use in Alcoholics Anonymous networks: An exploratory study. *Journal of Applied Communication Research, 34,* 191–208.

Carey, J. W. (Ed.). (1989). *Communication as culture: Essays on media and society.* Boston: Unwin Hyman.

Castells, M. (2001). *The Internet galaxy: Reflections on the Internet, business, and society.* New York: Oxford University Press.

Chadwick, A., & Howard, P. N. (Eds.). (2008). *Routledge handbook of Internet politics.* New York: Routledge.

Clark, R. E. (1983). Reconsidering research on learning from media. *Review of Educational Research, 53,* 445–459.

Cleeman, J. I., & Lenfant, C. (1998). The National Cholesterol Education Program: Progress and prospects. *Journal of the American Medical Association, 280,* 2099–2104.

Cline, R. J. W. (2003). At the intersection of micro and macro: Opportunities and challenges for physician–patient communication research. *Patient Education and Counseling, 50,* 13–16.

Cline, R. J. W., & Haynes, K. M. (2001). Consumer health information seeking on the Internet: The state of the art. *Health Education Research, 16,* 671–692.

Collins-Jarvis, L. A. (1993). Gender representation in an electronic city hall: Female adoption of Santa Monica's PEN system. *Journal of Broadcasting & Electronic Media, 37,* 49–65.

comScore Networks. (2005, August). *Behaviors of the blogosphere: Understanding the scale, composition and activities of Weblog audiences.* Retrieved February 1, 2007, from http://www.comScore.com/blogreport/comScoreBlogReport.pdf

Constant, D., Sproull, L., & Kiesler, S. (1996). The kindness of strangers: The usefulness of electronic weak ties for technical advice. *Organization Science, 7,* 119–135.

Cornfield, M. (2005). *The Internet and campaign 2004: A look back at the campaigners.* Retrieved January 15, 2007, from http://www.pewinternet.org/PPF/r/151/report_display.asp

Crowley, D., & Heyer, P. (Eds.). (2007). *Communication in history: Technology, culture, society* (5th ed.). Boston: Pearson Allyn & Bacon.

Culnan, M. J., & Markus, M. L. (1987). Information technologies. In F. M. Jablin, L. L. Putnam, K. H. Roberts, & L. W. Porter (Eds.), *Handbook of organizational communication: An interdisciplinary perspective* (pp. 420–443). Newbury Park, CA: Sage.

Cummins, C. O., Prochaska, J. O., Driskell, M.-M., Evers, K. E., Wright, J. A., Prochaska, J. M., et al. (2003). Development of review criteria to evaluate health behavior change Websites. *Journal of Health Psychology, 8,* 55–62.

Daft, R. L., & Lengel, R. H. (1986). Organizational information requirements, media richness, and structural determinants. *Management Science, 32,* 554–571.

Daft, R. L., Lengel, R. H., & Trevino, L. K. (1987). Message equivocality, media selection, and manager performance: Implications for information systems. *MIS Quarterly, 11,* 355–366.

Dartnell, M. Y. (2006). *Insurgency online: Web activism and global conflict.* Toronto, Canada: University of Toronto Press.

Day, R. E. (2000). The "conduit metaphor" and the nature and politics of information studies. *Journal of the American Society for Information Science, 51,* 805–811.

DeSanctis, G., & Poole, M. S. (1994). Capturing the complexity in advanced technology use: Adaptive structuration theory. *Organization Science, 5,* 121–147.

Doerfel, M. L., & Marsh, P. S. (2003). Candidate–issue positioning in the context of presidential debates. *Journal of Applied Communication Research, 31,* 189–211.

Durlak, J. T. (1987). A typology for interactive media. In M. L. McLaughlin (Ed.), *Communication yearbook* (Vol. 10, pp. 743–756). Newbury Park, CA: Sage.

Dutton, W. H., Blumler, J. G., & Kraemer, K. L. (Eds.). (1987). *Wired cities: Shaping the future of communications.* Boston: G. K. Hall.

Dutton, W. H., & Guthrie, K. (1991). An ecology of games: The political construction of Santa Monica's Public Electronic Network. *Informatization and the Public Sector, 1*(4), 1–24.

Eadie, W. F. (1994). On having an agenda. *Journal of Applied Communication Research, 22,* 81–85.

Eggly, S., Penner, L., Albrecht, T. L., Cline, R. J. W., Foster, T., Naughton, M., et al. (2006). Discussing bad news in the outpatient oncology clinic: Rethinking current communication guidelines. *Journal of Clinical Oncology, 24,* 716–719.

Eisenstein, E. L. (1979). *The printing press as an agent of change: Communications and cultural transformations in early modern Europe.* New York: Cambridge University Press.

Eveland, J. D., & Bikson, T. K. (1988). Work group structures and computer support: A field experiment. *ACM Transactions on Office Information Systems, 6,* 354–379.

Evers, K. E., Prochaska, J. M., Prochaska, J. O., Driskell, M. M., Cummins, C. O., & Velicer, W. F. (2003). Strengths and weaknesses of health behavior change programs on the Internet. *Journal of Health Psychology, 8,* 63–70.

Flichy, P. (1995). *Dynamics of human communication*. London: Sage.

Flora, J. A. (2001). The Stanford community studies: Campaigns to prevent cardiovascular disease. In R. E. Rice & C. K. Atkin (Eds.), *Public communication campaigns* (3rd ed., pp. 139–213). Thousand Oaks, CA: Sage.

Fornäs, J. (2002). Passages across thresholds into the borderlands of mediation. *Convergence International Journal of Research into New Media Technologies, 8*(4), 89–106.

Fortmann, S. P., & Varady, A. N. (2000). Effects of a community-wide health education program on cardiovascular disease morbidity and mortality: The Stanford Five-City Project. *American Journal of Epidemiology, 152,* 316–323.

Fox, S. (2006, October 29). *Online health search 2006: Most Internet users start at a search engine when looking for health information online. Very few check the source and date of the information they find.* Pew Internet & American Life Project. Retrieved January 15, 2007, from http://www.pewinternet.org/pdfs/PIP_Online_Health_2006.pdf

Fox, S., & Fallows, D. (2003, July 14). *Internet health resources: Health searches and email have become more commonplace, but there is room for improvement in searches and overall Internet access.* Pew Internet & American Life Project. Retrieved February 15, 2007 from http://www.pewinternet.org/pdfs/PIP_Health_Report_July_2003.pdf

Franz, C. R., & Jin, K. G. (1995). The structure of group conflict in a collaborative work group during information systems development. *Journal of Applied Communication Research, 23,* 108–127.

Frey, L. R. (2000). To be applied or not to be applied, that isn't even the question; but wherefore art thou, applied communication researcher? Reclaiming applied communication research and redefining the role of the researcher. *Journal of Applied Communication Research, 28,* 178–182.

Frey, L. R., Pearce, W. B., Pollock, M. A., Artz, L., & Murphy, B. A. O. (1996). Looking for justice in all the wrong places: On a communication approach to social justice. *Communication Studies, 47,* 110–127.

Fulk, J. (1993). Social construction of communication technology. *Academy of Management Journal, 36,* 921–950.

Fulk, J., & Steinfeld, C. (Eds.). (1990). *Organizations and communication technology*. Newbury Park, CA: Sage.

Gerbner, G. (Ed.). (1983). Ferment in the field: Communications scholars address critical issues and research tasks of the discipline [Special issue], *Journal of Communication, 33*(3).

Giddens, A. (1984). *The constitution of society: Outline of the theory of structuration*. Berkeley: University of California Press.

Goody, J. (1981). Alphabets and writing. In R. Williams (Ed.), *Contact: Human communication and its history* (pp. 105–126). New York: Thames & Hudson.

Graham, M. (2000). The threshold of the information age: Radio, television, and motion pictures mobilize the nation. In A. D. Chandler, Jr. & J. W. Cortada (Eds.), *A nation transformed by information: How information has shaped the United States from Colonial times to the present* (pp. 137–175). New York: Oxford University Press.

Greene, B., & Meek, A. (1998, February 10). *Issue brief: Distance education in higher education institutions: Incidence, audiences, and plans to expand.* Washington, DC: U.S. Department of Education, National Center for Education Statistics. Retrieved February 15, 2007, from http://nces.ed.gov/pubsearch/pubsinfo.asp?pubid=98132

Gumpert, G., & Cathcart, R. (1986). *Inter/media: Interpersonal communication in a media world* (3rd ed.). London: Oxford University Press.

Gumpert, G., & Cathcart, R. (1990). A theory of mediation. In B. D. Ruben & L. A. Lievrouw (Eds.), *Mediation, information, and communication: Vol. 3. Information and behavior* (pp. 21–36). New Brunswick, NJ: Transaction.

Guttman, N. (1997). Ethical dilemmas in health campaigns. *Health Communication, 9,* 155–190.

Henricksen, L. (1996). Naive theories of buying and selling: Implications for teaching critical-viewing skills. *Journal of Applied Communication Research, 24,* 93–109.

Hiltz, S. R., & Turoff, M. (1993). *The network nation: Human communication via computer* (Rev. ed.). Cambridge, MA: MIT Press.

Horrigan, J. B. (2006, August). *Data memo: Politics online.* Pew Internet & American Life Project. Retrieved January 15, 2007, from http://www.pewinternet.org/pdfs/PIP_Politics%20Aug06_Memo.pdf

Jackson, M. H., Poole, M. S., & Kuhn, T. (2002). The social construction of technology in studies of the workplace. In L. A. Lievrouw & S. Livingstone (Eds.), *The handbook of new media* (pp. 236–253). Thousand Oaks, CA: Sage.

Jenkins, H., & Thorburn, D. (2003). Introduction: The digital revolution, the informed citizen, and the culture of democracy. In H. Jenkins & D. Thorburn (Eds.), & B. Seawell (Assoc. Ed.), *Democracy and new media* (pp. 1–17). Cambridge, MA: MIT Press.

Johansen, R., Vallee, J., & Spangler, K. (1979). *Electronic meetings: Technical alternatives and social choice.* Reading, MA: Addison-Wesley.

Kaid, L. L. (Ed.). (2004). *Handbook of political communication research.* Mahwah, NJ: Erlbaum.

Kling, R., & Scacchi, W. (1982). The web of computing: Computer technology as social organization. In M. Yovits (Ed.), *Advances in computers* (Vol. 21, pp. 1–90). New York Academic Press.

Kreps, G. L. (2001). The evolution and advancement of health communication inquiry. In W. B. Gudykunst (Ed.), *Communication yearbook* (Vol. 24, pp. 231–253). Thousand Oaks, CA: Sage.

Kreps, G. L., Frey, L. R., & O'Hair, D. (1991). Applied communication research: Scholarship that can make a difference. *Journal of Applied Communication Research, 19,* 71–87.

Lasswell, H. D. (1948). The structure and function of communication in society. In L. Bryson (Ed.), *The communication of ideas: A series of addresses* (pp. 37–51). New York: Institute for Religious and Social Studies.

Lather, P. (1986). Research as praxis. *Harvard Educational Review, 56,* 257–277.

Latour, B. (1991). Technology is society made durable. In J. Law (Ed.), *A sociology of monsters: Essays on power, technology and domination* (pp. 103–131). New York: Routledge.

Layne, K., & Lee, J. (2001). Developing the fully functional E-government: A four stage model. *Government Information Quarterly, 18,* 122–136.

Lea, M. (Ed.). (1992). *Contexts of computer-mediated communication.* New York: Harvester Wheatsheaf.

Lewis, L., Snow, K., Farris, E., & Levin, D. (1999, December). *Distance education at postsecondary education institutions, 1997–98.* Washington, DC: U.S. Department of Education, National Center for Education Statistics. Retrieved February 15, 2007, from http://nces.ed.gov/pubs2000/2000013.pdf

Lievrouw, L. A. (2006). Oppositional and activist new media: Remediation, reconfiguration, participation. In G. Jacucci, F. Kensing, I. Wagner, & J. Blomberg (Eds.), *Proceedings of the Participatory Design Conference, PDC 2006: Expanding boundaries in design* (pp. 115–124). Palo Alto, CA: Computer Professionals for Social Responsibility and Association for Computing Machinery.

Lievrouw, L. A. (2007). Oppositional new media, ownership, and access: From consumption to reconfiguration and remediation. In R. E. Rice (Ed.), *Media ownership: Research and regulation* (pp. 391-416). Cresskill, NJ: Hampton Press.

Lievrouw, L. A., & Finn, T. A. (1990). Identifying the common dimensions of communication: The communication systems model. In B. D. Ruben & L. A. Lievrouw (Eds.), *Mediation, information and communication: Vol. 3. Information and behavior* (pp. 37–65). New Brunswick, NJ: Transaction.

Lievrouw, L. A., & Livingstone, S. (2006a). Introduction to the updated student edition. In L. A. Lievrouw & S. Livingstone (Eds.), *The handbook of new media* (Updated student ed., pp. 1–14). Thousand Oaks, CA: Sage.

Lievrouw, L. A., & Livingstone, S. (2006b). Introduction to the first edition. In L. A. Lievrouw &

S. Livingstone (Eds.), *The handbook of new media* (Updated student ed., pp. 15–32). Thousand Oaks, CA: Sage.

Light, J. S. (2003). *From warfare to welfare: Defense intellectuals and urban problems in Cold War America*. Baltimore: Johns Hopkins University Press.

Livingstone, S. (2007). On the material and the symbolic: Silverstone's double articulation of research traditions in new media studies. *New Media & Society, 9*, 16–24.

MacKenzie, E., & Wajcman, J. (Eds.). (1999). *The social shaping of technology*. Philadelphia: Open University Press.

Madden, M. (2006, April). *Data memo: Internet penetration and impact*. Pew Internet & American Life Project. Retrieved January 15, 2007, from http://www.pewinternet.org/pdfs/PIP_Internet_Impact.pdf

Madden, M., & Fox, S. (2006, May 2). *Finding answers online in sickness and in health*. Pew Internet & American Life Project Report. Retrieved January 15, 2007, from http://www.pewinternet.org/pdfs/PIP_Health_Decisions_2006.pdf

Markus, M. L., & Robey, D. (1991). Information technology and organizational change: Causal structure in theory and research. *Management Science, 34*, 583–598.

McCaughey, M., & Ayers, M. D. (Eds.). (2003). *Cyberactivism: Online activism in theory and practice*. New York: Routledge.

McCroskey, L. L., Richmond, V. P., & McCroskey, J. C. (2002). The scholarship of teaching and learning: Contributions from the discipline of communication. *Communication Education, 51*, 383–391.

McGann, R. (2004, November 22). *The blogosphere by the numbers: Traffic patterns*. The ClickZ Network. Retrieved February 15, 2007, from http://www.clickz.com/showPage.html?page=3438891

McKinnon, L. M., & Kaid, L. L. (1999). Exposing negative campaigning or enhancing advertising effects: An experimental study of adwatch effects on voters' evaluations of candidates and their ads. *Journal of Applied Communication Research, 27*, 217–236.

McLuhan, M. (2003). *Understanding media: The extensions of man* (Critical ed., W. T. Gordon, Ed.). Corte Madera, CA: Gingko Press. (Original work published 1964)

McNair, B. (2003). *An introduction to political communication* (3rd ed.). New York: Routledge.

Meyer, T. P. (1988). On mediated communication theory: The rise of format. In J. A. Anderson (Ed.), *Communication yearbook* (Vol. 11, pp. 224–229). Newbury Park, CA: Sage.

Monge, P. R., & Contractor, N. S. (2003). *Theories of communication networks*. New York: Oxford University Press.

Moon, M. J. (2002). The evolution of e-government among municipalities: Rhetoric or reality? *Public Administration Review, 62*, 424–433.

National Center for Educational Statistics. (2006). *The condition of education 2006: Section 5: Contexts of postsecondary education*. Washington, DC: Author. Retrieved January 15, 2007, from http://nces.ed.gov/pubs2006/2006071_5.pdf

Neuhauser, L., & Kreps, G. L. (2003). Rethinking communication in the e-health era. *Journal of Health Psychology, 8*, 7–24.

Nussbaum, J. F., & Friedrich, G. (2005). Instructional/developmental communication: Current theory, research, and future trends. *Journal of Communication, 55*, 578–593.

Orlikowski, W. J., & Robey, D. (1991). Information technology and the structuring of organizations. *Information Systems Research, 2*, 143–169.

O'Sullivan, P. B. (1995). Computer networks and political participation: Santa Monica's tele-democracy project. *Journal of Applied Communication Research, 23*, 93–107.

Pickerill, J. (2003). *Cyberprotest: Environmental activism online*. New York: Manchester University Press.

Poole, M. S., & DeSanctis, G. (1990). Understanding the use of group decision support systems: The theory of adaptive structuration. In C. Steinfield & J. Fulk (Eds.), *Organizations and communication technology* (pp. 175–195). Newbury Park, CA: Sage.

Rainie, L., Cornfield, M., & Horrigan, J. (2005, March 6). *The Internet and campaign 2004: The Internet was a key force in politics last year as 75 million Americans used it to get news, discuss candidates in emails, and participate directly in the political process*. Pew Internet &

American Life Project. Retrieved January 15, 2007, from http://www.pewinternet.org/pdfs/PIP_2004_Campaign.pdf

Ray, E. B., & Donohew, L. (Eds.). (1990). *Communication and health: Systems and applications.* Hillsdale, NJ: Erlbaum.

Reardon, K. K., & Rogers, E. M. (1988). Interpersonal versus mass media communication: A false dichotomy. *Human Communication Research, 15,* 284–303.

Reber, B. H., & Kim, J. K. (2006). How activist groups use Websites in media relations: Evaluating online press rooms. *Journal of Public Relations Research, 18,* 313–333.

Reddy, M. J. (1993). The conduit metaphor: A case of frame conflict in our language about language. In A. Ortony (Ed.), *Metaphor and thought* (2nd ed., pp. 284–324). New York: Cambridge University Press.

Reeves, B., & Nass, C. (1996). *The media equation: How people treat computers, television, and new media like real people and places.* New York: Cambridge University Press.

Rice, R. E. (1992). Contexts of research on organizational computer-mediated communication: A recursive review. In M. Lea (Ed.), *Contexts of computer-mediated communication* (pp. 113–144). New York: Harvester Wheatsheaf.

Rice, R. E. (1993). Media appropriateness: Using social presence theory to compare traditional and new organizational media. *Human Communication Research, 19,* 451–484.

Rice, R. E., & Associates. (1984). *The new media: Communication, research, and technology.* Beverly Hills, CA: Sage.

Rice, R. E., & Atkin, C. K. (2000). *Public communication campaigns* (3rd ed.). Thousand Oaks, CA: Sage.

Rice, R. E., & Katz, J. E. (Eds.). (2001). *The Internet and health communication: Experiences and expectations.* Thousand Oaks, CA: Sage.

Rice, R. E., & Love, G. (1987). Electronic emotion: Socioemotional content in a computer-mediated communication network. *Communication Research, 14,* 85–108.

Rogers, E. M. (1986). *Communication technology: The new media in society.* New York: Free Press.

Rogers, E. M. (1992). Communication campaigns to change health-related lifestyles. *Hygie, 11*(Suppl.2), 29–35.

Rogers, E. M. (1994). *A history of communication study: A biographical approach.* New York: Free Press.

Rogers, E. M. (1999). Anatomy of the two subdisciplines of communication study. *Human Communication Research, 25,* 618–631.

Rogers, E. M. (2004). Theoretical diversity in political communication. In L. L. Kaid (Ed.), *Handbook of political communication research* (pp. 3–16). Mahwah, NJ: Erlbaum.

Rogers, E. M., & Kincaid, D. L. (1981). *Communication networks: Toward a new paradigm for research.* New York: Free Press.

Rogers, R. (2004). *Information politics on the Web.* Cambridge, MA: MIT Press.

Rubin, A. M., & Rubin, R. C. (1985). Interface of personal and mediated communication: A research agenda. *Critical Studies in Mass Communication, 2,* 36–53.

Rudy, I. (1996). A critical review of research on electronic mail. *British Journal of Information Systems, 4,* 198–213.

Rumble, G. (2001). The costs and costing of networked learning. *Journal of Asynchronous Learning Networks, 5*(2), 75–96.

Russell, T. L. (2001). *The no significant difference phenomenon* (5th ed.). Littleton, CO: International Distance Education Certification Center.

Sawhney, H. (1996). Information superhighway: Metaphors as midwives. *Media, Culture & Society, 18,* 291–314.

Schmitz, J., Rogers, E. M., Phillips, K., & Paschal, D. (1995). The Public Electronic Network (PEN) and the homeless in Santa Monica. *Journal of Applied Communication Research, 23,* 26–43.

Schramm, W. (1977). *Big media, little media: Tools and technologies for instruction.* Beverly Hills, CA: Sage.

Seibold, D. (1995). *Theoria* and *praxis*: Means and ends in applied communication research. In

K. N. Cissna (Ed.), *Applied communication in the 21st century* (pp. 23–38). Mahwah, NJ: Erlbaum.

Seibold, D. (2000). Applied communication scholarship: Less a matter of boundaries than of emphases. *Journal of Applied Communication Research, 28,* 183–187.

Shannon, C. E., & Weaver, W. (1949). *The mathematical theory of communication.* Urbana: University of Illinois Press.

Silverstone, R. (1994). *Television and everyday life.* New York: Routledge.

Silverstone, R. (1999). *Why study the media?* Thousand Oaks, CA: Sage.

Silverstone, R. (2005). The sociology of mediation and communication. In C. Calhoun, C. Rojek, & B. S. Turner (Eds.), *The Sage handbook of sociology* (pp. 188–207). Thousand Oaks, CA: Sage.

Silverstone, R., & Haddon, L. (1996). Design and domestication of information and communication technologies: Technical change and everyday life. In R. Mansell & R. Silverstone (Eds.), *Communication by design: The politics of information and communication technologies* (pp. 44–74). New York: Oxford University Press.

Slevin, J. (2000). *The Internet and society.* Malden, MA: Polity Press.

Straubhaar, J., & LaRose, R. (2006). *Media now: Understanding media, culture, and technology* (5th ed.). Belmont, CA: Thomson/Wadsworth.

Street, R. L., Jr. (2003). Mediated consumer–provider communication in cancer care: The empowering potential of new technologies. *Patient Education and Counseling, 50,* 99–104.

Street, R. L., Jr., Gold, W. R., & Manning, T. (Eds.). (1997). *Health promotion and interactive technology: Theoretical applications and future directions.* Mahwah, NJ: Erlbaum.

Sullivan, C. F. (2003). Gendered cybersupport: A thematic analysis of two online cancer support groups. *Journal of Health Psychology, 8,* 83–103.

Tabs, E. D. (2003, July). *Distance education at degree-granting postsecondary institutions: 2000–2001.* Washington, DC: U.S. Department of Education, National Center for Education Statistics. Retrieved March 12, 2007, from http://nces.ed.gov/pubs2003/2003017.pdf

Tambini, D. (1999). New media and democracy: The civic networking movement. *New Media & Society, 1,* 305–329.

Taylor, J. R., Flanagin, A. J., Cheney, G., & Seibold, D. R. (2001). Organizational communication research: Key moments, central concerns, and future challenges. In W. B. Gudykunst (Ed.), *Communication yearbook* (Vol. 24, pp. 98–137). Thousand Oaks, CA: Sage.

Thomas, D. (2002). *Hacker culture.* Minneapolis: University of Minnesota Press.

Tsagarousianou, R., Tambini, D., & Bryan, C. (Eds.). (1998). *Cyberdemocracy: Technology, cities, and civic networks.* New York: Routledge.

Two-fifths of Americans online have read political blogs. (2005, April 13). *Wall Street Journal Online.* Retrieved March 12, 2007, from http://users1.wsj.com/lmda/do/checkLogin?mg=wsj-users1&url=http%3A%2F%2Fonline.wsj.com%2Farticle%2FSB111332546086804781.html%3Fpublicf%3Dyes

van de Donk, W., Loader, B. D., Nixon, P. G., & Rucht, D. (Eds.). (2004). *Cyberprotest: New media, citizens, and social movements.* New York: Routledge.

Violanti, M. T. (1996). Hooked on expectations: An analysis of influence and relationships in the Tailhook reports. *Journal of Applied Communication Research, 24,* 67–82.

Waldeck, J. H., Kearney, P., & Plax, T. G. (2000). Teacher e-mail strategies and students' willingness to communicate online. *Journal of Applied Communication Research, 29,* 54–70.

Waldeck, J. H., Kearney, P., & Plax T. G. (2001). Instructional and developmental communication theory and research in the 1990s: Extending the agenda for the 21st century. In W. B. Gudykunst (Ed.), *Communication yearbook* (Vol. 24, pp. 206–229). Thousand Oaks, CA: Sage.

Webster, F. (2002). *Theories of the information society* (2nd ed.). New York: Routledge.

Weick, K. E. (1979). *The social psychology of organizing* (2nd ed.). Reading, MA: Addison-Wesley.

White, M., & Dorman, S. M. (2001). Receiving social support online: Implications for health education. *Health Education Research, 16,* 693–707.

Wildavsky, A. (1987). *Speaking truth to power: The art and craft of policy analysis* (2nd ed.). New Brunswick, NJ: Transaction Books.

Williams, R. (Ed.). (1981). *Contact: Human communication and its history.* New York: Thames & Hudson.

Wright, K. B. (1999). Computer-mediated support groups: An examination of relationships among social support, perceived stress, and coping strategies. *Communication Quarterly, 47,* 402–414.

Wright, K. B. (2002). Social support within an on-line cancer community: An assessment of emotional support, perceptions of advantages and disadvantages, and motives for using the community from a communication perspective. *Journal of Applied Communication Research, 30,* 195–209.

Wright, K. B., & Bell, S. B. (2003). Health-related support groups on the Internet. *Journal of Health Psychology, 8,* 39–54.

11 Managing a World of Problems

The Implications of Globalization for Applied Communication Research

John Parrish-Sprowl

Indiana University-Purdue University Indianapolis

The linkage between macrolevel and microlevel communication systems has been the subject of investigation in most areas of applied communication scholarship, including groups (e.g., Frey, 2003), organizations (e.g., C. Stohl, 2005), and communities (e.g., Dearing, 2003; Ford & Yep, 2003). As the number of studies in each area grows, the importance of the global interconnectedness in human communication increasingly becomes clearer. Thus, although applied communication research has been conducted around the world for several decades, especially with respect to development (see Kincaid & Figueroa, this volume), the need for applied research reflective of global systems never has been more acute than it is today. This need is due, in part, to the growing realization that what happens in the daily lives of people in places such as Bangalore, India very much affects the lives of people in places such as Lincoln, Nebraska and Fort Wayne, Indiana. As people from differing cultures and nations engage each other with greater regularity, many experience greater economic, social, and political opportunities. At the same time, new tensions emerge between nations and many people feel a sense of unease or loss due to the influence of those who used to be more distant and with whom they had less contact. In recognition of the systemic connection of people, regardless of national boundaries, Williams (2002), echoing Barber's (1995) argument in his book *Jihad vs. McWorld*, noted in the introduction to a special issue of *Communication Studies* devoted to globalization that "the dialectical relationship between 'globalism' and 'localism' is perhaps the defining dialectic of international and intercultural dynamics at the beginning of the new millennium" (p. 1).

This chapter focuses on the importance of conducting applied communication research in response to the rapid changes that grow out of this defining dialectical tension between globalism and localism, generally considered a key feature of globalization. Specifically, I explore the role that applied communication research can play in facilitating the management of a number of issues related to the growing use of information technology and computer-mediated communication, global health concerns (such as HIV and flu pandemics), trans-border conflicts, global issues in public relations and advertising, international commerce, and the increasing volume of intercultural communication. Although development communication is an important area of applied research with a long history, it is the focus of another chapter in this volume and, hence, a discussion of that body of work largely is excluded here.

Globalization

Globalization, a term coined in the 1980s to capture the phenomenon of the growing interconnectedness of the world's population, has developed a broader meaning and usage over the ensuing decades. For some, such as Toynbee (2000), globalization can be considered a synonym for the "Americanization" of global culture. In defining globalization that way, Toynbee evoked the metaphor of a giant strawberry milkshake covering the globe with what might be considered the worst of Western culture—mostly, U.S. consumer values and practices seeping into every crevice of humanity. However, many scholars view globalization as something more than the spread of U.S. culture across the world; they see it as an increasing interconnectedness between all people that is changing, in fundamental ways, through mutual and reflexive influence, how everyone lives, regardless of where they reside. Thus, although Western culture, in general, and U.S. culture, in particular, are major influences around the world, it also is the case that people and events elsewhere are shaping the West. Such influence occurs not only through catastrophic events, such as September 11, 2001, but also through more mundane influences as well. For example, although the United States historically has been a net food exporter, it has shifted to a net importer in the last few years because of an increasing appetite for various "ethnic" foods and year-round fresh produce.

Although Hutton and Giddens (2000b, p. vii) noted that "every generation believes it is living through great change," the increasing interrelatedness among the world's population is not itself a new trend; globalization, in fact, "is a relatively new term used to describe a very old process" (What is Globalization?" n.d., ¶ 1). From the beginning of human existence on Earth, people constantly have spread across the planet, creating and strengthening relationships that span the globe. However, many scholars argue that the current processes of globalization are qualitatively different in a number of important ways from those of previous eras (e.g., Charan, 2006; Hutton & Giddens, 2000a; Prestowitz, 2005; Sachs, 2005).

To contrast globalization in the current age with that of previous eras, Prestowitz (2006) and Sachs (2005), among many authors, suggested that globalization can be understood as unfolding in three waves. The first wave, capped by the Industrial Revolution, occurred in the centuries leading up to World War I. According to Sachs, technology, trade, and communications had developed to such a degree during the Industrial Revolution that many people felt a sense of inevitability about the order of things that is not dissimilar to many voices heard today. As Sachs noted:

> This was the first era of globalization, an era of global trade, an era of global communications over telegraph lines, an era of mass production and industrialization—in short, what would seem to be an era of inevitable progress. And it was globalization under European domination. It was viewed as not only economically unstoppable, but also the natural order of things. This imagined natural order gave rise to the infamous "white man's burden," the right and obligation of European-descended whites to rule the lives of others around the world which they blithely did with a contradictory mix of naiveté, compassion, and brutality. (p. 43)

However, with the ending of World War I, this period effectively was laid to rest.

The second era of globalization, defined as the period from the beginning of World War I to the end of the 20th century, largely was one of globalization disintegration that occurred between the world wars, and led to the rebuilding of a global system from 1947 on. This wave of globalization was marked by political and economic isolationism and fragmentation (Prestowitz, 2006; Sachs, 2005). Such fragmentation was especially evident in the post-World War II era, when nations were considered to be of the First, Second, or Third World, depending on the political and economic zone in which they were situated. With the end of the Cold War (the demise of the Second World) and an increasing realization that the nonaligned nations were failing to prosper (the Third World), most nations decided to participate in the global system of the First World. This participation resulted in greater movement of people and trade among nations that had, for several decades, been politically at odds with, and economically isolated from, one another. These changes set the stage for the third wave of globalization, which was not simply a return to the steady march of interconnectedness that characterized the first wave but, instead, a new form of globalization that was viewed as transformative in nature.

Friedman (2005) labeled the current wave "Globalization 3.0" and likened the transformation to a flattening of the world, suggesting 10 key processes that drive the third wave: the fall of the Berlin Wall, work-flow software, open-sourcing, outsourcing, offshoring, supply chaining, in-sourcing, in-forming, the wireless revolution, and Netscape going public. Charan (2006), with a more narrow focus on business, stated that "this seismic shift began roughly 10 years ago, brought about by three forces: mobility of talent, mobility of capital, and mobility of knowledge, thanks largely to the Internet" (p. 47). Giddens and Hutton (2000, p. 1) noted four key areas of change that led them to conclude that "something very new is happening in the world": (1) the development of global communication systems, particularly the internet; (2) the shift away from an industrial-based economy; (3) the collapse of the Soviet structure; and (4) the impact of current globalization trends on everyday life. Giddens and Hutton argued that "if one puts together these four sets of influences, the level of global transformation they signal is nothing short of spectacular" (p. 2).

Communication and Globalization

It is in the transformative aspects of these global changes that we find the greatest significance of international applied communication research. Specifically, we need to understand how communication changes and is changed by the processes of globalization. Major changes in both communication and transportation technology enable people to connect with each other, either electronically or in person, with both greater speed and ease than ever before. These technologies afford people the ability to meet and work with a greater number of people at a faster pace, altering the manner in which relationships—economic, social, or those in conflict—are developed and maintained. In other words, the third wave of globalization is transformative because it is predicated on a fundamentally different communication system than previously, one that is rapid, both virtual and face-to-face, and global, with an almost infinite capacity to connect people whether they want to be connected or not. C. Stohl (2005), summarizing the connection between the key processes underlying this transformation and communication, identified six processes that are embedded in virtually all theories of globalization:

1. The dramatic increase in economic interdependence worldwide
2. The intensification and deepening of material, political, and cultural exchanges
3. The global and rapid diffusion of ideas and knowledge enabled through new information technologies
4. The compression of time and space
5. The disembedding of events and institutions, which permits new realignment and restructuring of social interaction across time and space
6. Increases in global consciousness through processes of reflexivity. (p. 247)

C. Stohl observed that "communication is central to all six dynamic processes, providing many pathways for communication scholars to contribute to the understanding of organizing and globalization" (p. 248).

One path for research is a focus on the overall processes of globalization. Although some people see unparalleled opportunities in the changes brought about by globalization, others see a need to reexamine how people and nation states engage each other politically, economically, and culturally (Best, 2005; Bruner, 2002; Faux & Mishel, 2000; Hochschild, 2000; Ingram, 2002). Many scholars, political leaders, and social advocates find that globalization has not treated all people equally, and certainly not fairly. Faux and Mishel (2000) reported that "in the spring of 1999, World Bank President James Wolfensohn observed of global financial markets: 'At the level of the people, the system isn't working'" (p. 93). As Faux and Mishel noted:

> Today, from unemployed rioters in Jakarta, to strikers in Michigan, from sullen unpaid miners in Russia, to out of work skinheads in East Germany, one can see signs of building resentment against a globalization that leaves a large number of people behind. (pp. 95–96)

These trends continue and have resulted in protests involving thousands of people at the World Trade Organization (WTO) meetings. Studies such as those by DeLuca and Peeples (2002) and Kahn and Kellner (2004) illustrate how media can be used both to understand and facilitate protests related to the policies and practices of globally focused governments and businesses. DeLuca and Peeples's study examined how media were used in the Seattle WTO protest, concluding that the concept of a "public screen" should be added to the notion of a "public sphere" to reference the role of media coverage of public protest and to understand more fully the impact of such demonstrations. Kahn and Kellner (2004), studying the use of Internet activism by members of social movements, found that media influence the development of globalization (or, as some suggest, antiglobalization; see, e.g., Palmer, 2007; Van Aelst & Walgrave, 2002).

A second path for research is the development of communication theory on globalization. Undoubtedly, communication scholars, along with other scholars, should develop theoretical understandings that illuminate globalization processes, and applied communication scholarship should play a vital and dynamic role in that process. As noted above, C. Stohl (2005) provided a perspective that serves as a beginning frame of reference for the development of scholarship focused on the role of communication in creating, shaping, and sustaining the third wave of globalization.

Seibold (1995) posited two roles for applied communication research, the first of which is testing theory in applied settings to illuminate the relationship between theory and practice. From this perspective, as communication scholars create theories related to globalization processes, applied research testing those theories plays an important role in theory development. Such research not only advances the scholarly enterprise; it also assists practitioners in understanding how communication theory may serve as a useful guide to improving the human condition. For example, Parrish-Sprowl's (2003) study of a group forming an organization in the nascent stages of the Polish transformation to a market economy both contributes to the development of a body of research that employs the bona fide group perspective (Putnam & Stohl, 1990, 1996; C. Stohl & Putnam, 1994, 2003) and increases our understanding of how Poland developed as a postsocialist nation.

The second category of applied communication scholarship described by Seibold (1995) is research conducted specifically to achieve applied ends. Globalization presents a number of challenges that either are a new form of an old problem or a new issue that has developed as a function of the transformation from the second to the third wave. One example of the first type of challenge is the movement, beyond offshoring low-skill factory work, to include highly skilled computer engineering positions that previously were thought to be secure. This issue raises several questions, such as, given the global movement of work, how labor organizations should appeal to potential members in various countries or how organizations can socialize members in a world where jobs are highly ephemeral and still motivate employees.

An example of the second challenge is the difficulties associated with creating a sustainable local economy in the context of greatly expanded global competition for nearly everything (Charan, 2006; Friedman, 2005; Prestowitz, 2005 Sachs, 2005). A number of communication questions emerge from this issue. For instance, a growing area of interest in many places is applied communication research about what constitutes intercultural communication training needs in different locales as organizations seek markets beyond their borders. In addition, the question arises of how culture affects the persuasion processes inherent in advertising and public relations, given differing cultural and political backgrounds across the globe. Thus, applied communication research should reflect the dynamics of globalizing processes, regardless of the locus of the situation or issues studied.

Internationalizing Applied Communication Research

Internationalizing applied communication scholarship does not imply a loss of focus on domestic issues, no matter the country in which the research takes place, but, rather, recognition of the relationship between the local and the global, and the concomitant need to situate research in a larger framework. Internationalizing applied communication research in these ways has at least three important implications.

First, applied communication research should reflect the greater connectedness of people across nations and cultures that has arisen from the processes of globalization. One way of moving in this direction is to focus on international populations in applied research related to theory development and testing. Many theories in communication, as well as in other disciplines, are based on research conducted within a single country. For instance, Petronio and Kovach (1997), recognizing the need to move beyond a theory's country of origin, tested communication privacy theory (which was developed and tested only in the United States) by studying residents of Scottish nursing homes. Because the high privacy needs of Scots provided a unique environment to test communication privacy management theory (Petronio, 1991), this research study examined the utility of this theory across cultures. In another example mentioned previously, Parrish-Sprowl (2003) examined the relationship between a group and its relevant contexts in Poland, in part, because the setting provided an opportunity to study the macro–micro relationship of groups and societies from the bona fide group perspective. Never before in history had such a large-scale, multination, economic transformation been attempted, and the difficulties faced in each nation that was undergoing the myriad of changes associated with the movement to a market economy contained some commonalities, along with unique features arising from local political and economic contexts. Parrish-Sprowl's (2003) study provided not only a different cultural context for testing the bona fide group perspective (which previously had been studied only with U.S. groups) but also explored an aspect of change that was international in scope. In using international populations, such applied studies provide an implicit recognition of connectedness in communication theory as it develops.

Crabtree's (1998) applied communication scholarship illustrates an alternative example of incorporating connectedness, by drawing together research literatures that developed substantially independent of one another to study projects conducted in various nations. Specifically, she intertwined work on development communication, cross-cultural adjustment, and service learning to explain applied communication projects that she and her students conducted in El Salvador and Nicaragua. Her study illustrated how concepts such as social justice and practices such as service learning (see Darling & Leckie, this volume) can serve people both directly and indirectly, across national and cultural boundaries, and acknowledged important issues arising from the local context, due to the participatory action research design that Crabtree employed. At the same time, some investigations, such as Götzenbrucker's (2004) case study of computer-supported social networks in a mobile phone company, most likely located in Europe, can illustrate concepts and their application without explicitly indicating the specific cultural context of the study. In this case, the use of e-mail by work teams to establish and maintain social networks in a corporate setting was assessed. This study, thus, focused on connecting people by electronic communication—a medium not bound by geographical borders and ethnic cultures. By conducting research that theoretically implicitly and explicitly recognizes international connectedness, applied communication research promotes better understanding of the processes of globalization.

The second implication of internationalizing applied communication scholarship is that even research focused on specific domestic issues should take into account the global context in which those issues are situated. Although the disciplinary study of communication is spreading across the globe, the largest national concentration of departments and scholars still is in the United States, making domestic research in this country a useful example to illustrate the point. Researchers, when analyzing communicative practices in natural settings, benefit from an international agenda because of both direct and indirect implications of events occurring elsewhere for domestic issues and practices. War, outsourcing, business competition, and population mobility, for instance, outside of North America all directly affect citizens in the United States. Poverty, HIV, malaria, and political unrest in other countries, to name just a few examples, indirectly influence U.S. citizens' lives, no matter where these problems exist. Although economic developments in a small country, such as Poland, may not seem relevant to people in the United States, those developments, nonetheless, are influenced when Polish computer programmers supplant those in the United States or when profits from a General Motors (GM) or Volvo (Ford) plant built near Krakow, Poland affect stock prices on the New York Stock Exchange. Informed by an increased understanding of communicative practices in countries other than the United States, applied scholars can offer greater insight into U.S. domestic issues.

A more specific example illustrates the global implications for communication practice. The significant cuts in the number of employees in North America by the big three U.S. auto companies are well known. In particular, even as GM's market share in North America shrinks and that of Toyota grows, in China, the opposite is happening, largely because the labor costs there are more equal, as both companies pay lower benefits and neither company has large pension obligations. Moreover, although the big three auto companies have been dramatically reducing the number of employees, European and Asian auto manufacturers have been hiring to staff their U.S. auto plants. As a consequence, the number of auto-manufacturing employees has remained fairly constant in the United States, albeit with a different employer mix. Given this situation, a communication consultant advising either GM or United Auto Workers negotiators must offer advice in a different way than if the competitive situation was more domestic than global. Scholars not only need to consider management–labor negotiations with respect to globalization; when applied researchers assess training programs, organizational structures, and other communication issues for businesses and nongovernmental organizations (NGOs), they also may want to consider both practices from the perspective of other nations and the role of increased international communication between organizational members.

Third, because the local and global become intertwined, some issues are important on a world scale and should be of concern to everyone, even if those issues manifest themselves unevenly across the planet. For example, practicing safe sex to prevent the spread of HIV and AIDS is a global issue, even though, in some places, the number of people infected at present is low and the number of people infected by these diseases is disproportionately located in Sub-Saharan Africa (see Witte & Roberto, this volume). To manage HIV and AIDS effectively, these diseases must be contained everywhere possible, making it a universal problem for everyone, even for those who are not now directly affected. The management of global issues related to the economy, health, environment, and conflict, among many others, thus, merit attention from applied communication scholars. Applied communication studies focused on such global issues, however, often are either few in numbers or absent altogether.

Some recent journal articles and books focused on applied communication research have noted the need to fill the void in our knowledge of global issues. For example, Ellis and Maoz (2002), in their research on trans-border conflict between Israeli Jews and Palestinians, stated that "very little research...examines cross-cultural argument interactions between cultures engaged in extreme macro-political conflict" (p. 181). M. Stohl and Stohl (2005) offered a similar observation in their study of global regimes, stating that "the study of international regimes has been a central area of research in international relations for the last 20 years but virtually ignored in the communication literature" (p. 445). With a few exceptions, applied communication research focused on global issues (aside from development communication), has yet to go global in its reach. Even in a volume covering gender in applied communication contexts, the international dimension essentially was absent (Buzzanell, Sterk, & Turner, 2004; see also Buzzanell, Meisenback, Remke, Sterk, and Turner, this volume). This lack of attention is unfortunate, for there is no deficit of international issues and problems for which applied communication research can have a positive and substantial impact, both in improving the specific situation and increasing our understanding of the relationship between international and local contexts.

Because the third wave of globalization began to unfold in the 1990s and has continued to accelerate into the 21st century, the literature reviewed here generally is from 1995 forward. The applied international research conducted in that time frame, thus far, provides a beginning, but much more need and opportunity remain to be fulfilled. Leaving development communication aside (often treated as the use of mass communication to achieve economic development aims; see Kincaid & Figueroa, this volume), the focus here is on those broad areas that are not necessarily confined to national boundaries. These areas of research are divided into seven broad topics: (1) information technology and computer-mediated communication, (2) improving health communication, (3) trans-border conflict, (4) civil societies, (5) public relations and advertising, (6) international commerce, and (7) general intercultural issues. Each of these areas constitutes an important type of research within the context of globalization.

Information Technology and Computer-Mediated Communication

Perhaps the fastest growing area, in terms of the number of applied studies, is that of information technology (IT) and computer-mediated communication (CMC) research (e.g., Abdulla, 2007; Anderson, Fogelgren-Pedersen, & Varshney, 2003; Bouwman, 2003; Dimitrova & Beilock, 2005; Dimitrova & Connolly-Ahern, 2007; Götzenbrucker, 2004; Gulyás, 1998; Heaton & Taylor, 2002; Manger, Wicklund, & Eikeland, 2003; Masoodian, 2001; Mohammed, 2004; Rasanen & Kouvo, 2007; Valo, 2003; see also Lievrouw, this volume). These studies range from the implementation of information systems to the development of relationships in various CMC cultural contexts. Given the importance of the Internet and IT in the globalization process, it is not surprising that this area has received substantial attention.

Studies such as those by Anderson et al. (2003) and Götzenbrucker (2004) focus on the role that connectivity through CMC plays in both the structure of organizations and relationships among coworkers in a virtual context as communication crosses geographical and national boundaries. Such studies contribute to a body of literature that allows for comparison of CMC usage within one culture to that which occurs within another. More important, as Anderson et al. observed, new communication technologies facilitate business process reengineering and, thereby, reshape organizational communication as it has been studied for the past few decades. Both individuals and organizations alike benefit from greater understanding of how CMC works within, in contrast to, and across cultures as we move forward towards even greater interconnectivity. Because so much interconnectivity occurs in mediated environments, applied communication research in this area is critical for understanding globalization processes.

Adding to this knowledge are studies such as that by Masoodian (2001), which provide a starting point for examining the intersection of virtual and physical culture in CMC work environments. Recognizing that task-based methodologies for computer software design are not conducive to the development of virtual communities created by people with little or no computing technology, Masoodian offered an alternative design that facilitates the development of such communities. Creating ease of use for people interested in connecting via the Internet facilitates the growth of connections between people who otherwise might never meet, virtually or face-to-face. This research, however, needs to be paired with studies of intercultural communication to further unlock the complexities of CMC and international relationships. One example of a study that begins this process is that of Manger et al. (2003), which utilized samples from across three countries to compare interpersonal skills employed in a face-to-face context to those used in a mediated environment. Such research focuses not only on specific organizations but also sheds light on skills needed to achieve professional communication competence in a CMC-oriented international organization. As the number and importance of both face-to-face and CMC cross-national/cultural interactions grow, studies such as this should increase in number as well.

Health Communication

A decade ago, Freimuth (1995) observed that few applied health communication studies had been conducted. Since that time, a number of applied studies of health communication have occurred (see Kreps & Bonaguro, this volume), but the number of international studies still is small relative to the need for such work. Moreover, those studies that have been conducted in countries other than the United States—such as those on breast cancer (Jones, 2004; Sun, Zhang, Tsoh, Wong-Kim, & Chow, 2007), condom usage (Katz, 2006), diabetes (Andersson, Bjäräs, Tillgren, & Östenson, 2007), family planning (Boulay & Valente, 2005), health information (Underwood, Serlemitsos, & Macwangi, 2007), HIV and AIDS (Brotn, Ueno, Smith, Austin, & Bickman, 2007; Dong, Chang, & Chen, 2008; Farr, Witte, Jarato [sic; Jerato], & Menard, 2005; Lombardo & Léger, 2007; A. N. Miller, Fellows, & Kizito, 2007; A. N. Miller et al., 2008; Porto, 2007; Witte, Cameron, Lapinski, & Nzyuko, 1998; Witte, Girma, & Girgre, 2002–2003; see also Roberto & Witte, this volume), medication advertising (Dens, Eagle, & De Pelsmacker, 2008), obesity (Eagle, Bulmer, & De Bruin, 2004), reproductive health (Valente & Saba, 1998), and tobacco smoking (Brugge et al., 2002; Chang, 2005; Goodall & Appiah, 2008; Guttman & Peleg, 2003)—frequently are published in the United States, perhaps limiting access to such research in other locales. Given the scope of the problems related to public health, along with their human and political importance, the need for such research is compelling; consequently, this is an area where applied communication scholarship can fulfill a serious need and, hence, more applied communication scholars need to respond.

Diseases such as malaria, tuberculosis, and AIDS kill millions of people each year. These diseases not only exact a heavy human toll in unnecessary pain and suffering but also play a role in perpetuating a culture of poverty in places such as Sub-Saharan Africa. Although much work has been done in health communication to develop more effective approaches to health care (see Kreps & Bonanguro, this volume), the continual spread of serious health problems suggests that much more needs to be done. In addition, when health communication research is conducted, the important step must be taken to incorporate the findings into the practices of health professionals. Studies such as that by Hoffman-Goetz, Friedman, and Clarke (2005), which examined HIV and AIDS coverage in aboriginal newspapers in Canada, offer important insights into how people process information related to disease. However, although the study provided valuable insight for the development of health campaigns in Canada, the authors did not indicate whether such knowledge actually is being used in campaign design. Applied communication research, thus, is needed to assist public health officials to engage in more effective dissemination of health information to promote the requisite behavioral changes necessary to enhance community and individual health (for an exemplar of such work, see Witte & Roberto, this volume).

As Dearing (2003) noted when discussing the gap between health research and practice, through necessity, communication professionals have moved ahead with health communication programs and training, such as the Communication for Behavioral Impact (COMBI) Program of the World Health Organization. COMBI, as Parks and Lloyd (2004) pointed out, "incorporates the lessons learnt from five decades of public health communication and draws substantially from the experience of private sector consumer communication" (p. v). This communication program has achieved notable success in reducing incidents of diseases, such as lymphatic filariasis and dengue fever, in a number of countries, including Malaysia and India. However, even the creators of this program believe that it could be improved through research about the conduct of COMBI campaigns.

Trans-Border Conflict

The study of conflict interaction has long been of interest to communication scholars. However, despite all of the research conducted about international conflict, little has changed in the world. As Nye (2000) noted:

> Some things about international politics have remained the same over the ages. Thucydides's account of Sparta and Athens fighting the Peloponnesian War 2500 years ago reveals eerie resemblances to the Arab–Israeli conflict after 1947. The world at the end of the twentieth century is a strange cocktail of continuity and change. Some aspects of international politics have not changed since Thucydides. There is a certain logic of hostility, a dilemma about security that goes with interstate politics. Alliances, balance of power, and choice in policy between war and compromise have remained similar over the millennia. (p. 2)

Given the importance of studying conflict, it is surprising that so little applied communication scholarship has focused on trans-border conflict (Ellis & Maoz, 2002), especially given the events of September 11, 2001.

In their studies of interactions between Israeli Jews and Palestinians, Maoz and Ellis (2001, 2006; Ellis & Maoz, 2002, 2007; Maoz, 2000a, 2000b, 2000c, 2002) offer a notable exception that brings a communication perspective to one of the most critical trans-border conflicts in the world. In providing a thoughtful analysis of Israeli Jews–Palestinian interaction patterns, along with helping to facilitate and evaluate structured group interaction between members of these two populations, they demonstrate the potential value of applied communication research by illustrating how theory testing can be done in applied settings, which, in turn, can assist practitioners' work (see also related work by Albeck, Adwan, & Bar-On, 2006; Bar-On, 2000). Certainly, the conflicts between Israel and its neighbors are an important ongoing set of interactions with global ramifications.

Green (2004) provided another example of applied communication research about trans-border conflict. Focusing on the 2002 bombings in Bali, Indonesia, Green examined Australian perspectives on borders with respect to what many people living there consider to be their 9/11. The bombings in Bali were aimed at hotels that normally contain a number of Australians because Bali is a major tourist destination for people from that country. The timing of the bombings proved to be no exception, with a number of Australians killed in the blasts. Thus, in a sense, Australia was attacked, even though no bombs were planted on Australian soil. Green examined the Australian response to the bombings and the attending perceptions of borders that frame Australians' attitudes about the attack. Given the borderless nature of the "war on terror," this study gives a sense of how people might respond in a nationalistic way to attack, even when it is not on their soil. Not only should more studies be done with respect to the conflict related to global terrorism but studies also need to focus on hot spots in more local or regional conflicts as well, such as in Sudan or the Kashmir region of India and Pakistan, both of which have a relationship to how more global conflicts unfold.

Perhaps the best exemplar of applied communication research in an international context related to trans-border conflict is the work conducted in Cyprus by Broome (2003, 2004a, 2004b, 2006; Broome & Murray, 2002). For a decade, Broome has worked to build a peaceful and cooperative island community by bringing together Greek and Turkish Cypriots to create a collective vision for peace. By conducting communal training sessions (at first separately with these populations because they could not gain permission to work together until 3 months into the process), Broome facilitated a process of sharing that has enabled members of these two groups at odds with each other to develop a shared vision of peace. His work illustrates well the interplay of theory and application in relationship building, training, mediation, and negotiation in an effort to promote peace. Although Broome cautioned against using the results of his studies as a template for conflict management in other conflicts around the world, such as the one between Arabs and Israeli Jews, his studies constitute high-quality applied communication research that can improve global conflict management.

Applied communication scholars, however, can do much more to contribute to greater conflict management. As Pearce (1989) and others have pointed out, communication scholarship in the past few decades has produced a broad and deep understanding of the dialogic properties of conflict communicative practices. Works such as Littlejohn and Domenici (2001) and Domenici and Littlejohn (2006), which have been used in various local situations (in the United States and Uganda, for example), can be extended to trans-border conflicts. In particular, extending the theory of facework in the management of communication conflict can facilitate better human relations in a number of contexts. Geographical areas such as Iraq, Israel-Palestine, the Balkans, and Sudan, among many others, deserve attention by applied communication scholars, both to manage conflict in those specific areas and to increase people's capacity to manage conflict, in general.

Civil Societies

Trent and Friedenberg (2000), in the epilogue of their book on political communication, posed the question: "Can a nation, even a county, be adequately, much less skillfully, governed by officials and advisors whose skills reflect the demands of successful political campaigning" (p. 372). U.S. taxpayers spend a considerable sum of money each year to spread democracy around the world, supporting initiatives related to the promotion of democratic government, free and fair elections, and equal opportunity for women, as well as the reduction of ethnic discrimination. Given the role of the United States in nation building, such issues are of particular concern, both to those in the United States, because much is being done in their name, and to those outside of it, due to the potential involvement of Americans in any number of regions and nations. Through both military action and peaceful means, the United States has invested itself in the development of democratic societies across postsocialist Europe, the Middle East, and Central Asia. Political communication (e.g., legislative discussion and debate, public policy hearings, and political campaigns; see Kaid, McKinney, & Tedesco, this volume) is at the heart of developing a civic discourse that sustains a democratic government. Although Trent and Friedenberg most likely posed their question with respect to the United States, it is in our collective best interest that such questions be explored in areas where the United States is involved in developing national institutions.

Our understanding of nation building, however, should not be limited to those projects in which the United States is involved. Lengel (2000, p. 3), in her edited book, predicated her work, in part, on the argument advanced by Kluver and Powers (1999) that "civil society is formed discursively." Although most of the work in Lengel's book is not applied per se, it does create the foundation for applied research that assists in understanding how to build democratic governments and societies that embrace fair and equal opportunities to participate by all. The events of 9/11 are a graphic reminder that the development of a civil society anywhere in the world is not a local or regional problem alone; it is a global one whose breadth and depth is complex. The growing interconnectedness brought on by the processes of globalization offers an imperative to create a rich understanding of the consequences of nation building for all countries, regardless of whether a given nation is directly involved in the process. Applied communication research that offers insight into creating constructive global civic discourse that deepens our collective understanding of nation-building activities in various contexts, thus, is an important need.

Providing a beginning to such research, a small number of applied studies cover a range of issues related to civic discourse in a number of countries, including those dealing with political leaders (Frankel, 1991), ethnic issues (Steyn, 2004), the postsocialist transition in Europe (Ognianova & Scott, 1997), presentations of history (Oteiza, 2003), and gender (Rodriguez, 2001). At the core of all of these issues is the need to understand how to communicate in ways that help governments to be responsive to the needs of their polity and, in turn, to create a polity with the experience and sophistication necessary to govern those who lead. Globalization, thus, creates a practical need for everyone to understand the political discourse of other nations because it is quite likely that their country will become engaged with another country, with understanding of each other needed to create functional civil societies.

Key to understanding effective civic discourse in democratic nations is to illuminate political discourse in nations where citizens have little opportunity to participate in the governing process. Research related to political discourse in undemocratic countries, therefore, enhances our general understanding of those countries and illuminates possible policy alternatives in a given nation's relationship with those countries. Applied research, consequently, should illuminate how communication works, regardless of the desirability of the outcome. For example, countries such as North Korea, Iran, and Syria are problematic for the United States, in part, because so many voters in the United States, as well as a number of people in the U.S. government, need a better understanding of the political discourse of those nations. If civil society is formed discursively, we learn as much from studying how not to create a desirable society as we do from understanding how to achieve one.

Advertising and Public Relations

Advertising and public relations, almost by definition, offer rich opportunities for internationalizing applied communication research. Although both areas have grown steadily worldwide over the past few decades, the volume of advertisements and public relations campaigns exploded with the decline of socialism. With some exceptions, countries from the former Soviet bloc went from virtually no advertising and public relations to having huge industries in just a decade. However, even with all of the accumulated wisdom of decades in the business, multinational advertising firms still frequently managed to stumble when entering these markets, often due to a lack of cultural understanding with respect to the new markets they were entering (e.g., Winter, Carveth, & Parrish-Sprowl, 1994). Without taking culture into account, businesses run the risk of alienating their markets in the process of trying to develop them (Carveth & Parrish-Sprowl, 1998). Public relations and advertising professionals in Poland, for example, recognized the value of applied communication research for helping their economic transformation and, in 1997, invited communication scholars from the United States to address a national meeting in Krakow on good practices (Face '97). This conference was significant in linking applied communication scholars focused on the development of advertising and public relations in the Polish cultural context. Such international linkages are an example of positive globalization processes and provide important opportunities to share applied communication scholarship.

Although the issues facing those in public relations and advertising often are the same in all nations, the cultural context offers a sometimes large and nuanced set of unique features that affect these communication processes. Thus, when Ihlen (2002) studied crisis management in the case of Mercedes Benz in Scandinavia, the issue of how to respond (standing one's ground versus admitting an error) could happen anywhere, but the nature of the response required acknowledging the cultural context. Specifically, Ihlen examined the crisis spurred by pictures published in a Swedish motor magazine of the overturn of a Mercedes A-Class car during a standard maneuver in a Nordic motor test, called the "elk test" or the "moose test." Without some sense of the importance of such a test in Nordic nations, one might fail to grasp the importance of this crisis for the manufacturer. The same can be said for the studies of advertising and public relations in Australia (Jones, 2004); Bulgaria (Braun, 2007); China, including Hong Kong (Chan & Chan, 2005; Lee, 2004; Lock, 2003; Paek & Pan, 2004; Wu & Chan, 2007); Egypt (Keenan & Yeni, 2003); Israel (Avraham & First, 2003); Japan (Kawashima, 2006); Korea (Paek, 2005; Park, Lee, & Song, 2005); Mexico (Beltran, 2007); New Zealand (Eagle, Bulmer, & De Bruin, 2004); the Soviet Union (Tolstikova, 2007); Taiwan (Chang, 2005, Yang, 2004); Thailand (Punyapiroje & Morrison, 2007); Trinidad and Tobago (McFarlane-Alvarez, 2007); and the United Kingdom (Dee, 2007); as well as research about public service announcements in Belgium (Hatfield, Hinck, & Birkholt, 2007) and Finland (Lowe & Alm, 1997). Research that examines and seeks to improve advertising and public relations in foreign contexts not only illuminates issues and practices in those countries but also offers insights that can serve the multicultural population of the United States as well.

With respect to issues related to globalization and nation building, Taylor (2000) offered an interesting perspective on the engagement of public relations strategies in the process. Examining the neighborliness campaign designed to help bridge multicultural issues in Malaysia, Taylor analyzed the Malaysian government's program to improve relationships between those of differing ethnic backgrounds who suddenly found themselves living in proximity due to rapid urbanization. The program began with a focus on safety and expanded to encourage cooperation within neighborhoods. Taylor suggested that a public relations approach based on a relational perspective could strengthen nations with a multicultural heritage. Given the number of multicultural nations grappling with ethnic issues, such work is valuable. As research in development communication (see Kincaid & Figueroa, this volume), along with Taylor's study suggests, the use of public relations and advertising to achieve the aims of social justice and democracy holds great promise (Moemeka, 2000). Such studies demonstrate that applied communication scholarship on public relations and advertising can offer thoughtful contributions in the international context by illuminating issues of common concern to scholars and practitioners alike.

International Commerce

As businesses and other organizations become more globally interconnected, the communication issues they confront grow in both number and complexity. However, as C. Stohl (2005) noted, "It wasn't until the mid-1990s that the terms 'globalizing' and 'globalization' were found in the organizational communication literature" (p. 227). Even with calls from C. Stohl and others (e.g., Wiseman & Shuter, 1994), little has been written about organizations in international contexts (some recent examples include Diamond & Whitehouse, 2007; Dickson, Hargie, & Wilson, 2008; Maneerat, Hale, & Singhal, 2005; McCann & Giles, 2007; Wodak, 2007), especially research that is applied in focus. For instance, two recent textbooks on organizational communication by Conrad and Poole (2005) and K. Miller (2009) addressed globalization, and although both texts discussed a number of issues that applied communication research could help to illuminate, the chapters were notable for the absence of citing such research.

One example of an important issue for both business leaders and workers around the world is that of outsourcing (where businesses hire people from other companies, often in other countries, to do work that displaces employees in the home country), which currently is a $50 billion industry and is projected to continue to grow (McCue, 2005). Although McCue (2005) noted that outsourcing is beneficial to companies in some cases, it has not produced the level of economic benefits anticipated. McCue reported that a study conducted by Gartner, an information and technology research and advisory firm, stated, in part:

> Poor communication between the onsite and offshore project teams as well as between management and employees is also picked out by Gartner as a critical failure factor.
> "Effective communications are critical in offshore outsourcing projects. The reason many offshore deals fail is because of the propagation of misinformation and confusion due to inadequate communications among the project team and its contacts, as well as within the general employee population, executive ranks and local community," the report said. (¶ 8–9)

Globalization, in many ways, is embodied in the practice of outsourcing, with work shifted around the world, altering relationships between workers, companies, and nations. Outsourcing is part of the reason that authors, such as Friedman (2005), see a changing global economic structure on the horizon, one that is based less on national interest and more on the efficient conduct of business. Organizations will focus on their survival regardless of where they must operate to compete. Effectively, this means a shifting of economic power away from the West and toward India and China. Even now, however, businesses in both of those countries are looking to outsource work to become more competitive. Thus, because outsourcing is a major global factor that is likely to grow, applied communication research that illuminates its benefits and drawbacks, along with the ways and means of this practice, proves useful.

The practices, if not the study, of organizational communication have a history of global migration, such as the development of total quality management (TQM) in Japan and its importation to the United States (for an overview of this importation process, see Parrish-Sprowl, 2000). In 1997, I began to consult with a U.S. company that essentially had four major competitors in its North American market. Within 5 years, the number of competitors grew to over 70, with most of those businesses coming from other countries. Given that increased competition creates more pressure in the effort to succeed, organizations turn to various organizational communication systems and practices to survive and thrive. Although greater competitive pressure has been the case for businesses in the United States, it is a global issue. For instance, when the postsocialist nations joined the world market economy, the ways and means of organizing needed to change rapidly. In socialist times, the primary goal of organizations was full employment, not efficient production, but such practices could not survive in a market-driven economy. Applied communication research can reveal key issues and processes that facilitate the changes necessary to be successful in a competitive postsocialist economy (Parrish-Sprowl, 1994). For example, Parrish-Sprowl (2003) studied the strategic development of an organization in Poland as the principal participants attempted to develop an effective organization reflective of the new realities of the postsocialist market. As another example, Ziberi (2006) extended the work of Meares, Oetzel, Torres, Derkacs, and Ginossar (2004), which focused on employee mistreatment, into organizations in Macedonia. As the processes of globalization accelerate the interconnectedness of world business, the need for such research will grow as well.

The United States and Western European nations gave millions in aid to postsocialist countries to assist them in the transformation to a market economy. In the early 1990s, my university received a multimillion dollar grant from the U.S. Agency for International Development (USAID) to assist Poland in its transformation. Initially, the U.S. government did not include communication as part of this project; only after the Poles insisted that it be included was it added to the grant. The absence of international applied communication scholarship, thus, leads the communication discipline to be marginalized, even by the U.S. government. In my experience as a consultant to several businesses and organizations in postsocialist Europe, executives and leaders there have favorable views of communication theory, research, and practice once they are exposed to them. The communication issues involved in international commerce, therefore, need a much higher research priority from applied communication scholars.

Intercultural Communication

Many studies of the connections between people across national boundaries that may be considered applied examine various aspects of intercultural communication. Much of that work, by scholars such as Gudykunst (2001, 2003) and Ting-Toomey (1999), has application in its implications, even if the work is not applied in its focus. Hence, although Gudykunst engaged in extensive testing of anxiety/uncertainty management theory and Ting-Toomey developed face-negotiation theory, much of their research was concerned with how people might engage more productively in intercultural communication. Given the effects of globalization on the increasing amount of international interchange, through both business and leisure activities, intercultural communication skills become fundamental to communication competence (e.g., Baraldi, 2006; Miczo & Welter, 2006; Quingwen, Day, & Callaco, 2008; Starke-Meyerring, Duin, & Palvetzian, 2007; Ting-Toomey, 2007).

One place where the issue of international exchange is particularly salient is in higher education, perhaps the most highly regarded sector of the United States around the world. Each year, thousands of students from virtually every country in the world arrive in the United States to enroll in a university. One consequence of the high quality of U.S. universities is emulation by universities throughout the world. Over the past few years, I (with various colleagues in each location) have been involved in initiatives at several universities in Belarus, Indonesia, Macedonia, Poland, and Russia that are designed to improve pedagogy, curriculum, and assessment of students and faculty. Communication education research, thus, is an important area of applied scholarship (see Darling & Leckie, this volume) that should be extended to the international arena. Educational quality is a global issue because universities operate in an increasingly international context; therefore, communication educational practices across the world benefit from greater study.

Of special importance are the concerns and practices related to multicultural education and service learning, both of which applied communication scholars have much to offer in their implementation and assessment. For instance, in 2004, I attended a conference focused on multicultural education that was held in Jakarta, Indonesia. As a nation with a broad array of cultures, Indonesia needs to improve its multicultural pedagogy. The papers presented at that conference demonstrated that much needs to be done, and that communication education research can play a vital role in enhancing the quality of education across that nation. For example, as Husodo (2004), the keynote speaker for the conference, noted:

> However, similarly to other developing countries..., the enlarging of opportunity to get elementary education is not able to significantly improve the human quality, either in work productivity, moral maturity, personal power and national discipline. It is due to the fact that the learning process experienced by educational participants tends to stress...hearing, recording and memorizing process and not...the teaching [and] learning process that can improve intellectual and vocational ability, strengthening personality and character. (p. 6)

Communication, as a discipline, has a rich tradition in the development of active learning that connects both intellectual material and presentational skills in ways that offer the type of pedagogy called for at the conference held in Indonesia. Service learning also can play a vital role in developing a more responsive education that connects learning to building better communities (see the essays in Droge & Murphy, 1999; see also Darling & Leckie, this volume). Service learning provides an excellent vehicle for applied communication research and, at the same time, offers a pedagogy that enhances both students' education and the communities with which those students collaborate.

Another area of intercultural research with an applied dimension is that of *contrastive rhetoric* (generally, the study of linguistic practices across cultures), including studies such as that conducted by Shi (2004), which focused on issues of writing in a second language (see also the essays in Sharifian & Palmer, 2007). Although Americans primarily operate in the privileged language of English, many others learn English as a second language out of necessity due to globalization. Multilingualism requires a tremendous set of communication abilities, even with the difficulties associated with performance in a second language. In turn, those who practice monolingualism miss the insights into culture that a second language provides, both by not having that second language and by not fully appreciating the difficulties associated with functioning in a second language. Communication issues that arise around multiple language usage in multinational organizations are particularly ripe for applied communication research.

Finally, some studies, such as the one by Valo (1998) that details the development of communication degree programs in Finland, offer insight into the spread of the communication discipline beyond the United States. The international development of the communication discipline is important to the development of applied communication research, for as the number of communication scholars and practitioners grows, so does the size of the disciplinary contribution to theory, research, and practice. The study of communication has begun to grow in postsocialist Europe and across Asia since the collapse of the Soviet Union. Much of the published work in those countries still lacks an applied dimension, although that focus slowly is increasing. The proceedings of the two Russian Communication Association conferences held in 2002 and 2004 contain applied communication research, mostly authored by U.S. scholars, as does an anthology edited by Leontovich and Parrish-Sprowl (2006), published in Russia, which includes the work of both U.S. and Russian communication scholars. International disciplinary growth, by its very nature, infuses an intercultural perspective into communication as a discipline and, more specifically, into applied communication research.

Conclusion

With the increasing recognition that globalization is capable of changing virtually every human activity, applied communication research can improve our understanding of how such change occurs and assist in developing practices that reflect new ways of communicating. Given that societies have become embedded in global realities, so must communication research, in general, and applied communication research, in particular. In any given year, the advancement of the discipline may be indexed by reading the collection of journals sponsored by communication associations, such as the National Communication Association (NCA) and the International Communication Association. In turn, the advance of applied communication research may be indexed, in part, by reading the *Journal of Applied Communication Research* and attending convention panels sponsored by NCA's Applied Communication Division. These applied research outlets offer scholarship that has much to contribute to our understanding of communicative practices associated with globalization trends.

Given the number and importance of the issues that arise from globalization, internationalizing applied communication research offers both a wealth of opportunities for communication scholars and the possibilities of growing appreciation of the value of applied communication research to scholars and practitioners working outside of the discipline. To connect with these opportunities and possibilities, in addition to conducting studies about globalization and its interconnected international environments, applied communication scholars should consider attending more conferences outside of their country or region; teach both short and long term in other countries; offer consulting, training, and development services internationally; and apply for grants that provide technical assistance on other continents. Such actions create connections with scholars from other places and provide opportunities to practice applied communication research elsewhere. Contributions of this nature can help to manage problems, apply and build theory, and connect the communication discipline with critical contemporary world issues. In the final analysis, internationalizing applied communication research not only is necessary but also inevitable.

References

Abdulla, R. (2007). Islam, jihad, and terrorism in post-9/11 Arabic discussion boards. *Journal of Computer-Mediated Communication, 12*(3), Article 15. Retrieved July 12, 2008, from http://jcmc.indiana.edu/vol12/issue3/abdulla.html

Albeck, J. H., Adwan, S., & Bar-On, D. (2006). Working through intergenerational conflicts by sharing personal stories in dialogue groups. In L. R. Frey (Ed.), *Facilitating group communication in context: Innovations and applications with natural groups: Vol. 1. Facilitating group creation, conflict, and communication* (pp. 125–181). Cresskill, NJ: Hampton Press.

Anderson, K. V., Fogelgren-Pedersen, A., & Varshney, U. (2003). Mobile organizing using information technology (MOBIT). *Information, Communication & Society, 6,* 211–228.

Andersson, C. M., Bjäräs, G., Tillgren, P., & Östenson, C. G. (2007). Local media monitoring in process evaluation: Experiences from the Stockholm diabetes prevention programme. *Journal of Health Communication, 12,* 269–284.

Avraham, E., & First, A. (2003). "I buy American": The American image as reflected in Israeli advertising. *Journal of Communication, 53,* 282–299.

Baraldi, C. (2006). New forms of intercultural communication in a globalized world. *Gazette, 68,* 53–69.

Barber, B. R. (1995). *Jihad vs. McWorld.* New York: Times Books.

Bar-On, D. (Ed.; with Kutz, S., & Wegner, D.). (2000). *Bridging the gap: Storytelling as a way to work through political and collective hostilities* (F. Moldenhauer, Trans.). Hamburg, Germany: Körber-Stiftung.

Beltran, U. (2007). The combined effect of advertising and news coverage in the Mexican presidential campaign of 2000. *Political Communication, 24,* 37–63.

Best, K. (2005). Rethinking the globalization movement: Toward a cultural theory of contemporary democracy and communication. *Communication and Critical/Cultural Studies, 2,* 214–237.

Boulay, M., & Valente, T. W. (2005). The selection of family planning discussion partners in Nepal. *Journal of Health Communication, 10,* 519–536.

Bouwman, H. (2003). Communication in the information society: ICT and the (in)visibility of communication science in the low countries. *Communications, 28,* 61–87.

Braun, S. L. (2007). The effects of the political environment on public relations in Bulgaria. *Journal of Public Relations Research, 19,* 199–228.

Broome, B. J. (2003). Responding to the challenges of third-party facilitation: Reflections of a scholar–practitioner in the Cyprus conflict. *Journal of Intergroup Relations, 29*(4), 24–43.

Broome, B. J. (2004a). Building a shared future across the divide: Identity and conflict in Cyprus. In M. Fong & R. Chuang (Eds.), *Communicating ethnic and cultural identity* (pp. 275–294). Lanham, MD: Rowman & Littlefield.

Broome, B. J. (2004b). Reaching across the dividing line: Building a collective vision for peace in Cyprus. *Journal of Peace Research, 41,* 191–209.

Broome, B. J. (2006). Facilitating group communication in protracted conflict situations: Promoting citizen peace-building efforts in Cyprus. In L. R. Frey (Ed.), *Facilitating group communication in context: Innovations and applications with natural groups: Vol. 1. Facilitating group creation, conflict, and communication* (pp. 125–154). Cresskill, NJ: Hampton Press.

Broome, B. J., & Murray, J. S. (2002). Improving third-party decisions at choice points: A Cyprus case study. *Negotiation Journal, 18,* 75–98.

Brotn, T. N., Ueno, K., Smith, C. L., Austin, N. S., & Bickman, L. (2007). The construction of HIV/AIDS in Indian newspapers: A frame analysis. *Health Communication, 21,* 257–266.

Brugge, D., Dejong, W., Hyde, J., Le, Q., Shui, C.-S., Wong, A., et al. (2002). Development of targeted message concepts for recent Asian immigrants about secondhand smoke. *Journal of Health Communication, 7,* 25–37.

Bruner, M. L. (2002). Global constitutionalism and the arguments over free trade. *Communication Studies, 53,* 25–39.

Buzzanell, P. M., Sterk, H., & Turner, L. H. (Eds.). (2004). *Gender in applied communication contexts.* Thousand Oaks, CA: Sage.

Carveth, R. A., & Parrish-Sprowl, J. (1998). Communication and culture: The missing element in the analysis of international competitive advantage. *Polish/American Journal of Communication and Market Studies, 1,* 47–68.

Chan, K., & Chan, F. (2005). Information content of television advertising in China: An update. *Asian Journal of Communication, 15,* 1–15.

Chang, C. (2005). Personal values, advertising, and smoking motivation in Taiwanese adolescents. *Journal of Health Communication, 10,* 621–634.

Charan, R. (2006, July 31). Why it's a small world after all. *Business Week,* 9.

Conrad, C., & Poole, M. S. (2005). *Strategic organizational communication: In a global economy* (6th ed.). Belmont, CA: Thomson/Wadsworth.

Crabtree, R. (1998). Mutual empowerment in cross-cultural participatory development and service learning: Lessons in communication and social justice from projects in El Salvador and Nicaragua. *Journal of Applied Communication Research, 26,* 182–209.

Dearing, J. W. (2003). The state of the art and the state of the science of community organizing. In T. L. Thompson, A. M. Dorsey, K. I. Miller, & R. Parrott (Eds.), *Handbook of health communication* (pp. 207–220). Mahwah, NJ: Erlbaum.

Dee, A.-C. (2007). Regulating against offence: Lessons from the field of UK advertising. *Media, Culture & Society, 29,* 1036–1048.

DeLuca, K. M., & Peeples, J. (2002). From public sphere to public screen: Democracy, activism, and the "violence" of Seattle. *Critical Studies in Media Communication, 19,* 125–151.

Dens, N., Eagle, L. C., & De Pelsmacker, P. (2008). Attitudes and self-reported behavior of patients, doctors, and pharmacists in New Zealand and Belgium toward direct-to-consumer advertising of medication. *Health Communication, 23,* 45–61.

Diamond, C., & Whitehouse, G. (2007). Gender, computing, and the organization of working time: Public/private comparisons in the Australian context. *Information, Communication & Society, 10,* 320–337.

Dickson, D., Hargie, O., & Wilson, N. (2008). Communication, relationships, and religious difference in the Northern Ireland workplace: A study of private and public sector organizations. *Journal of Applied Communication Research, 36,* 128–160.

Dimitrova, D. V., & Beilock, R. (2005). Where freedom matters: Internet adoption among the former socialist countries. *Gazette, 67,* 173–187.

Dimitrova, D. V., & Connolly-Ahern, C. (2007). A tale of two wars: Framing analysis of online news sites in coalition countries and the Arab world during the Iraq war. *Howard Journal of Communications, 18,* 153–168.

Domenici, K., & Littlejohn, S. W. (2006). *Facework: Bridging theory and practice.* Thousand Oaks, CA: Sage.

Dong, D., Chang, T.-K., & Chen, D. (2008). Reporting AIDS and the invisible victims in China: Official knowledge as news in the *People's Daily,* 1986–2002. *Journal of Health Communication, 13,* 357–374.

Droge, D., & Murphy, B. O. (Eds.). (1999). *Voices of strong democracy: Concepts and models for service-learning in communication studies.* Washington, DC: American Association for Higher Education.

Eagle, L., Bulmer, S., & De Bruin, A. (2004). Exploring the link between obesity and advertising in New Zealand. *Journal of Marketing Communications, 10,* 49–67.

Ellis, D. G., & Maoz, I. (2002). Cross-cultural argument interactions between Israeli-Jews and Palestinians. *Journal of Applied Communication Research, 30,* 181–194.

Ellis, D. G., & Maoz, I. (2007). Online argument between Israeli Jews and Palestinians. *Human Communication Research, 33,* 291–309.

Face '97. (1997). Retrieved August 21, 2006, from http://www.gfmp.com.pl/www_face1997.xml

Farr, C. Witte, K., Jarato [sic; Jerato], K., & Menard, T. (2005). The effectiveness of media use in health education: Evaluation of an HIV/AIDS television campaign in Ethiopia. *Journal of Health Communication, 10,* 225–236.

Faux, J., & Mishel, L. (2000). Inequality and the global economy. In W. Hutton & A. Giddens (Eds.), *Global capitalism* (pp. 93–111). New York: New Press.

Ford, L. A., & Yep, G. A. (2003). Working along the margins: Developing community-based strategies for communicating about health with marginalized groups. In T. L. Thompson, A. M. Dorsey, K. I. Miller, & R. Parrott (Eds.), *Handbook of health communication* (pp. 241–262). Mahwah, NJ: Erlbaum.

Frankel, N. (1991). Conversations in Istanbul: An interview with Bulent Ecevit. *Political Communication and Persuasion, 8,* 63–78.

Freimuth, V. S. (1995). Response to Seibold: Applied health communication research. In K. N. Cissna (Ed.), *Applied communication in the 21st century* (pp. 23–38). Mahwah, NJ: Erlbaum.

Frey, L. R. (Ed.). (2003). *Group communication in context: Studies of bona fide groups* (2nd ed.). Mahwah, NJ: Erlbaum.

Friedman, T. L. (2005). *The world is flat: A brief history of the twenty-first century.* New York: Farrar, Straus & Giroux.

Giddens, A., & Hutton, W. (2000). Anthony Giddens and Will Hutton in conversation. In W. Hutton & A. Giddens (Eds.), *Global capitalism* (pp. 1–51). New York: New Press.

Goodall, C., & Appiah, O. (2008). Adolescents' perceptions of Canadian cigarette package warning labels: Investigating the effects of message framing. *Health Communication, 23,* 117–127.

Götzenbrucker, G. (2004). Social.networks@work: Case studies into the importance of computer-supported social networks in a mobile phone company. *Communications, 29,* 467–494.

Green, L. (2004). Bordering on the inconceivable: The Pacific solution, the migration zone, and "Australia's 9/11." *Australian Journal of Communication, 31,* 19–36.

Gudykunst, W. B. (2001). *Asian American ethnicity and communication.* Thousand Oaks, CA: Sage.

Gudykunst, W. B. (Ed.). (2003). *Cross-cultural and intercultural communication.* Thousand Oaks, CA: Sage.

Gulyás, Á. (1998). In the slow lane on the information superhighway: Hungary and the information revolution. *Convergence: The International Journal of Research into New Media Technologies, 4*(2), 76–92.

Guttman, N., & Peleg, H. (2003). Public preferences for an attribution to government or to medical research versus unattributed messages in cigarette warning labels in Israel. *Health Communication, 15,* 1–25.

Hatfield, K. L., Hinck, A., & Birkholt, M. J. (2007). Seeing the visual in argumentation: A rhetorical analysis of UNICEF Belgium's SMURF public service announcement. *Argumentation & Advocacy, 43,* 144–151.

Heaton, L., & Taylor, J. R. (2002). Knowledge management and professional work: A communication perspective on the knowledge-based organization. *Management Communication Quarterly, 16,* 210–236.

Hochschild, A. R. (2000). Global care chains and emotional surplus value. In W. Hutton & A. Giddens (Eds.), *Global capitalism* (pp. 130–146). New York: New Press.

Hoffman-Goetz, L., Friedman, D. B., & Clarke, J. N. (2005). HIV/AIDS risk factors as portrayed in mass media targeting First Nations, Métis, and Inuit peoples of Canada. *Journal of Health Communication, 10,* 145–162.

Husodo, S. H. (2004, September). *To build the national self-reliance is a need for Indonesia.* Paper presented at the International Seminar on Multicultural Education, Jakarta, Indonesia.

Hutton, W., & Giddens, A. (Eds.). (2000a). *Global capitalism.* New York: New Press.

Hutton, W., & Giddens, A. (2000b). Preface. In W. Hutton & A. Giddens (Eds.), *Global capitalism* (pp. vii–xi). New York: New Press.

Ihlen, Ø. (2002). Defending the Mercedes A-Class: Combining and changing crisis-response strategies. *Journal of Public Relations Research, 14,* 185–206.

Ingram, J. (2002). Hegemony and globalism: Kenneth Burke and paradoxes of representation. *Communication Studies, 53*, 4–24.

Jones, S. C. (2004). Coverage of breast cancer in the Australian print media—Does advertising and editorial coverage reflect correct social marketing messages? *Journal of Health Communication, 9*, 309–325.

Kahn, R., & Kellner, D. (2004). New media and Internet activism: From the "Battle of Seattle" to blogging. *New Media & Society, 6*, 87–95.

Katz, I. (2006). Explaining the increase in condom use among South African young females. *Journal of Health Communication, 11*, 737–754.

Kawashima, N. (2006). Advertising agencies, media and consumer market: The changing quality of TV advertising in Japan. *Media, Culture & Society, 28*, 393–410.

Keenan, K. L., & Yeni, S. (2003). Ramadan advertising in Egypt: A content analysis with elaboration on select items. *Journal of Media and Religion, 2*, 109–117.

Kluver, R., & Powers, J. H. (Eds.). (1999). *Civic discourse, civil society, and Chinese communities*. Stamford, CT: Ablex.

Lee, B. K. (2004). Corporate image examined in a Chinese-based context: A study of a young educated public in Hong Kong. *Journal of Public Relations Research, 16*, 1–34.

Lengel, L. (2000). Introduction: Culture and technology in the new Europe. In L. Lengel (Ed.), *Culture and technology in the new Europe: Civic discourse in transformation of post-communist nations* (pp. 1–20). Stamford, CT: Ablex.

Leontovich, O., & Parrish-Sprowl, J. (Eds.). (2006). *Communication studies: A modern anthology*. Volgograd, Russia: Peremena.

Littlejohn, S. W., & Domenici, K. (2001). *Engaging communication in conflict: Systemic practice*. Thousand Oaks, CA: Sage.

Lock, G. (2003). Being international, local, and Chinese: Advertisements on the Hong Kong mass transit railway. *Visual Communication, 2*, 195–214.

Lombardo, A. P., & Léger, Y. A. (2007). Thinking about "think again" in Canada: Assessing a social marketing HIV/AIDS prevention campaign. *Journal of Health Communication, 12*, 377–398.

Lowe, G. F., & Alm, A. (1997). Public service broadcasting as cultural industry: Value transformation in the Finnish market-place. *European Journal of Communication, 12*, 169–191.

Maneerat, N., Hale, C., & Singhal, A. (2005). The glue that binds employees to an organization: A study of organizational identification in two Thai organizations. *Asian Journal of Communication, 15*, 188–214.

Manger, T., Wicklund, R. A., & Eikeland, O.-J. (2003). Speed communication and solving social problems. *Communications, 28*, 323–337.

Maoz, I. (2000a). An experiment in peace: Reconciliation and workshops of Jewish-Israeli and Palestinian youth. *Journal of Peace Research, 34*, 399–419.

Maoz, I. (2000b). Multiple conflicts and competing agendas: A framework for conceptualizing structured encounters between groups in conflict—The case of a coexistence project of Jews and Palestinians in Israel. *Peace and Conflict: Journal of Peace Psychology, 6*, 135–156.

Maoz, I. (2000c). Power relations in intergroup encounters: A case study of Jewish–Arab encounters in Israel. *International Journal of Intercultural Relations, 24*, 259–277.

Maoz, I. (2002). Conceptual mapping and evaluation of peace education programs: The case of education for coexistence through intergroup encounters between Jews and Arabs in Israel. In G. Salomon & B. Nevo (Eds.), *Peace education: The concept, principles, and practices around the world* (pp. 259–271). Cresskill, NJ: Hampton Press.

Maoz, I., & Ellis, D. G. (2001). Going to ground: Argument between Israeli-Jews and Palestinians. *Research on Language and Social Interaction, 4*, 399–419.

Maoz, I., & Ellis, D. G. (2006). Facilitating groups in severe conflict: The case of transformational dialogue between Israeli-Jews and Palestinians. In L. R. Frey (Ed.), *Facilitating group communication in context: Innovations and applications with natural groups: Vol. 1. Facilitating group creation, conflict, and communication* (pp. 183–203). Cresskill, NJ: Hampton Press.

Masoodian, M. (2001). Information-centred design: A methodology for designing virtual meeting DESIGN environments. *Information, Communication & Society, 4*, 247–260.

McCann, R. M., & Giles, H. (2007). Age-differentiated communication in organizations: Perspectives from Thailand and the United States. *Communication Research Reports, 24*, 1–12.

McCue, A. (2005, June 22). Outsourcing flops blamed on tunnel vision. *ZDNet News*. Retrieved July 7, 2005, from http://news.zdnet.com/2100-9589_22-5757832.html

McFarlane-Alvarez, S. L. (2007). Trinidad and Tobago television advertising as third space: Hybridity as resistance in the Caribbean mediascape. *Howard Journal of Communications, 18*, 39–55.

Meares, M. M., Oetzel, J. G., Torres, A., Derkacs, D., & Ginossar, T. (2004). Employee mistreatment and muted voices in the culturally diverse workplace. *Journal of Applied Communication Research, 32*, 4–27.

Miczo, N., & Welter, R. E. (2006). Aggressive and affiliative humor: Relationships to aspects of intercultural communication. *Journal of Intercultural Communication Research, 35*, 61–77.

Miller, A. N., Fellows, K. L., & Kizito, M. N. (2007). The impact of onset controllability on stigmatization and supportive communication goals toward persons with HIV versus lung cancer: A comparison between Kenyan and U.S. participants. *Health Communication, 22*, 207–220.

Miller, A. N., Mutungi, M., Facchini, E., Barasa, B., Ondieki, W., & Warria, C. (2008). An outcome assessment of an ABC-based HIV peer education intervention among Kenyan university students. *Journal of Health Communication, 13*, 245–356.

Miller, K. (2009). *Organizational communication: Approaches and processes* (5th ed.). Belmont, CA: Wadsworth Cengage Learning.

Moemeka, A. A. (Ed.). (2000). *Development communication in action: Building understanding and creating participation*. Lanham, MD: University Press of America.

Mohammed, S. N. (2004). Self-presentation of small developing countries on the World Wide Web: A study of official Websites. *New Media & Society, 6*, 469–486.

Nye, J. S., Jr. (2000). *Understanding international conflicts: An introduction to theory and history* (3rd ed.). New York: Longman.

Ognianova, E., & Scott, B. (1997). Milton's paradox: The market-place of ideas in post-communist Bulgaria. *European Journal of Communication, 12*, 369–390.

Oteiza, T. (2003). How contemporary history is presented in Chilean middle school textbooks. *Discourse & Society, 14*, 639–660.

Paek, H.-J. (2005). Understanding celebrity endorsers in cross-cultural contexts: A content analysis of South Korean and US newspaper advertising. *Asian Journal of Communication, 15*, 133–153.

Paek, H.-J., & Pan, Z. (2004). Spreading global consumerism: Effects of mass media and advertising on consumerist values in China. *Mass Communication and Society, 7*, 491–515.

Palmer, D. (2007). Facilitating consensus in an antiglobalization affinity group. In L. R. Frey & K. N. Carragee (Eds.). *Communication activism: Vol. 1. Communicating for social change* (pp. 325–353). Cresskill, NJ: Hampton Press.

Park, H. S., Lee, H. E., & Song, J. A. (2005). "I am sorry to send you SPAM": Cross-cultural differences in use of apologies in email advertising in Korea and the U.S. *Human Communication Research, 31*, 365–398.

Parks, W., & Lloyd, L. (2004). *Planning social mobilization and communication for dengue fever prevention and control: A step-by-step guide*. Geneva, Switzerland: World Health Organization.

Parrish-Sprowl, J. (1994). Organizational issues in Poland's economic transformation: A communication perspective. In A. Malkiewicz, J. Parrish-Sprowl, & J. Waszkiewicz (Eds.), *Komunikacja spoleczna w procesach transformacyjnych* [*Social communication in the transformation process*] (pp. 77–83). Wroclaw, Poland: Instytutu Nauk Ekonomiczno-spolecznych Politechniki Wroclawskiej.

Parrish-Sprowl, J. (2000). Organizational communication: Linking key processes to effective development. In A. Moemeka (Ed.), *Development communication in action: Building understanding and creating participation* (pp. 179–202). New York: University Press of America.

Parrish-Sprowl, J. (2003). Indexing the Polish transformation: The case of Eco-S from a bona fide group perspective. In L. R. Frey (Ed.), *Group communication in context: Studies of bona fide groups* (2nd ed., pp. 291–308). Mahwah, NJ: Erlbaum.

Pearce, W. B. (1989). *Communication and the human condition*. Carbondale: Southern Illinois University Press.

Petronio, S. (1991). Communication privacy management: A theoretical model of managing disclosure of private information between marital couples. *Communication Theory, 1,* 311–335.

Petronio, S., & Kovach, S. (1997). Managing privacy boundaries: Health providers' perceptions of resident care in Scottish nursing homes. *Journal of Applied Communication Research, 25,* 115–131.

Porto, M. P. (2007). Fighting AIDS among adolescent women: Effects of a public communication campaign in Brazil. *Journal of Health Communication, 12,* 121–132.

Prestowitz, C. (2005). *Three billion new capitalists: The great shift of wealth and power to the East*. New York: Basic Books.

Punyapiroje, C., & Morrison, M. A. (2007). Behind the smile: Reading cultural values in Thai advertising. *Asian Journal of Communication, 17,* 318–336.

Putnam, L. L., & Stohl, C. (1990). Bona fide groups: A reconceptualization of groups in context. *Communication Studies, 41,* 248–265.

Putnam, L. L., & Stohl, C. (1996). Bona fide groups: An alternative perspective for communication and small group decision making. In R. Y. Hirokawa & M. S. Poole (Eds.), *Communication and group decision making* (2nd ed., pp. 147–178). Thousand Oaks, CA: Sage.

Quingwen, D., Day, K. D., & Callaco, C. M. (2008). Overcoming ethnocentrism through developing intercultural communication sensitivity and multiculturalism. *Human Communication, 11,* 27–38.

Rasanen, P., & Kouvo, A. (2007). Linked or divided by the Web? Internet use and sociability in four European countries. *Information, Communication & Society, 10,* 219–241.

Rodriguez, C. (2001). Shattering butterflies and Amazons: Symbolic constructions of women in Colombian development discourse. *Communication Theory, 11,* 472–494.

Sachs, J. D. (2005). *The end of poverty: Economic possibilities for our times*. New York: Penguin Press.

Seibold, D. R. (1995). *Theoria* and *praxis*: Means and ends in applied communication research. In K. N. Cissna (Ed.), *Applied communication in the 21st century* (pp. 23–38). Mahwah, NJ: Erlbaum.

Sharifian, F., & Palmer, G. B. (Eds.). (2007). *Applied cultural linguistics: Implications for second language learning and intercultural communication*. Philadelphia: John Benjamins.

Shi, L. (2004). Textual borrowing in second-language writing. *Written Communication, 21,* 171–200.

Starke-Meyerring, D., Duin, A.-H., & Palvetzian, T. (2007). Global partnerships: Technical communication programs in the context of globalization. *Technical Communication Quarterly, 16,* 139–174.

Steyn, M. E. (2004). Rehabilitating a Whiteness disgraced: Afrikaner White talk in post-apartheid South Africa. *Communication Quarterly, 52,* 143–169.

Stohl, C. (2005). Globalization theory. In S. May & D. K. Mumby (Eds.), *Engaging organizational communication theory and research: Multiple perspectives* (pp. 223–262). Thousand Oaks, CA: Sage.

Stohl, C., & Putnam, L. L. (1994). Group communication in context: Implications for the study of bona fide groups. In L. R. Frey (Ed.), *Group communication in context: Studies of natural groups* (pp. 284–292). Hillsdale, NJ: Erlbaum.

Stohl, C., & Putnam, L. L. (2003). Communication in bona fide groups: A retrospective and prospective account. In L. R. Frey (Ed.), *Group communication in context: Studies of bona fide groups* (2nd ed., pp. 399–414). Mahwah, NJ: Erlbaum.

Stohl, M., & Stohl, C. (2005). Human rights, nation states, and NGOs: Structural holes and the emergence of global regimes. *Communication Monographs, 72,* 442–467.

Sun, A., Zhang, J., Tsoh, J., Wong-Kim, E., & Chow, E. (2007). The effectiveness in utilizing

Chinese media to promote breast health among Chinese women. *Journal of Health Communication, 12,* 157–172.

Taylor, M. (2000). Toward a public relations approach to nation building. *Journal of Public Relations Research, 12,* 179–210.

Ting-Toomey, S. (1999). *Communicating across cultures.* New York: Guilford Press.

Ting-Toomey, S. (2007). Intercultural conflict training: Theory–practice approaches and research challenges. *Journal of Intercultural Communication Research, 36,* 255–271.

Tolstikova, N. (2007). Early Soviet advertising: "We have to extract all the stinking bourgeois elements." *Journalism History, 33,* 42–50.

Toynbee, P. (2000). Who's afraid of global culture? In W. Hutton & A. Giddens (Eds.), *Global capitalism* (pp. 191–212). New York: New Press.

Trent, J. S., & Friedenberg, R. V. (2000). *Political campaign communication: Principles and practices* (4th ed.). Westport, CT: Praeger.

Underwood, C., Serlemitsos, E., & Macwangi, M. (2007). Health communication in multilingual contexts: A study of reading preferences, practices, and proficiencies among literate adults in Zambia. *Journal of Health Communication, 12,* 317–338.

Valente, T. W., & Saba, W. P. (1998). Mass media and interpersonal influence in a reproductive health communication campaign in Bolivia. *Communication Research, 25,* 96–124.

Valo, M. (1998). Speech communication the Finnish way: Fifteen years of university degrees of speech communication in Jyvaskyla, Finland. *Communication Education, 47,* 286–291.

Valo, M. (2003). Workmates, friends or more? Perceived effects of computer-mediatedness on interpersonal relationships. *Electronic Journal of Communication, 13*(1), Article 1. Retrieved February 7, 2006, from http://www.cios.org/www/ejc/v13n1.htm

Van Aelst, P., & Walgrave, S. (2002). New media, new movements? The role of the Internet in shaping the "anti-globalization" movement. *Information, Communication & Society, 5,* 465–483.

Vaughan, L., & Zhang, Y. (2007). Equal representation by search engines? A comparison of Web-sites across countries and domains. *Journal of Computer-Mediated Communication, 12*(3), Article 7. Retrieved July 12, 2008, from http://jcmc.indiana.edu/vol12/issue3/vaughan.html

What is globalization? (n.d.). *YaleGlobal Online.* Retrieved August 31, 2006, from http://yaleglobal.yale.edu/about/

Williams, D. C. (2002). Introduction: Communication perspectives on relationships between globalism and localism. *Communication Studies, 53,* 1–3.

Winter, M., Carveth, R. A., & Parrish-Sprowl, J. (1994). Communicating capitalism: The challenge of Eastern Europe. *Arizona Communication Association Journal, 20,* 68–91.

Wiseman, R., & Shuter, R. (Eds.). (1994). *International and intercultural communication annual: Vol. 18. Communicating in multicultural organizations.* Thousand Oaks, CA: Sage.

Witte, K., Cameron, K. A., Lapinski, M. K., & Nzyuko, S. (1998). Evaluating HIV/AIDS prevention programs according to theory: A field project along the Trans-Africa highway in Kenya. *Journal of Health Communication, 4,* 345–363.

Witte, K., Girma, B., & Girgre, A. (2002–2003). Addressing the underlying mechanisms to HIV/AIDS preventive behaviors in Ethiopia. *International Quarterly of Community Health Education, 21,* 163–176.

Wodak, R. (2007). Discourses in European Union organizations: Aspects, of access, participation, and exclusion. *Text & Talk, 27,* 655–680.

Wu, D. D., & Chan, K. (2007). Multilingual mix in Hong Kong advertising, pre- and post-1997. *Asian Journal of Communication, 17,* 301–317.

Yang, K. C. C. (2004). A comparison of attitudes towards Internet advertising among lifestyle segments in Taiwan. *Journal of Marketing Communications, 10,* 195–212.

Ziberi, L. (2006). *The role of culture in employee perceptions of mistreatment in the workplace.* Unpublished master's thesis, Indiana University, Indianapolis.

12 Applied Communication Ethics
A Summary and Critique of the Research Literature

Matthew W. Seeger
Wayne State University

Timothy L. Sellnow
University of Kentucky

Robert R. Ulmer
University of Arkansas at Little Rock

Julie M. Novak
Wayne State University

Communication scholars, particularly those interested in applied issues, have been slow to embrace research questions related to ethics. Since 1982, for example, only seven articles with an explicit focus on ethics have been published in the *Journal of Applied Communication Research* (*JACR*). In addition, although a 1998 special issue of *JACR* on "Communication and Social Justice Research" (Frey, 1998a) proposed social justice as a value premise for applied communication scholarship, it is not clear that many applied communication scholars have adopted this premise. There is, however, a general recognition that communication plays an instrumental role as both an area around which ethical questions arise and as a process necessary for constituting ethical climates, policies, and practices (Conrad, 1993). The neglect of ethical questions and issues can be attributed to several factors, such as the complexity of moral questions, lack of clarity regarding ethical standards, and traditional emphasis on "amoral" approaches and methods in many applied communication contexts (Redding, 1996). In addition, applied communication typically prioritizes goal-directed strategies and outcomes rather than value-based processes. Underlying these explanations, though, is the fact that examining communication ethics as they are applied in real life is difficult.

The purpose of this chapter is to summarize and critique scholarship in the emerging field of applied communication ethics. Our goal is not simply to summarize the existing literature on communication ethics but to identify those efforts that are distinct in their applied communication orientation. In so doing, we highlight ethical issues and orientations that applied communication scholars are likely to face, and we examine the emerging value premises of applied communication scholarship. We also seek to situate ethical issues and questions more centrally within the larger area of applied communication and to outline research issues and a research agenda. To meet these goals, we first provide an overview of the applied ethics movement. We then identify and review principal research traditions that address ethics within applied communication, including health communication, organizational communication, and media. We next explore several traditions in applied communication research that highlight value premises, including social justice, empowerment, and voice, as well as free speech and access to information.

We conclude this chapter by outlining a proposed research agenda for this important area of inquiry.

Ethics and Applied Ethics

Ethics is a rich field spanning a wide range of disciplines and critical traditions.[1] In general, *ethics* involves the search for fundamental standards of human conduct grounded in various value perspectives and moral traditions. Most often, ethics draws on values, normative systems, and philosophical and religious frameworks to make judgments of good and bad, right and wrong, and acceptable and unacceptable behavior. Thus, most ethical theories privilege specific value premises or perspectives over others. For example, Rawls (1999) emphasized justice as fairness through the treatment of individuals as essentially equal, without prior knowledge of their background or position. Habermas's (1984) social ethic emphasizes the emancipation of the individual, with his theory of universal pragmatics exploring ways in which individuals construct mutual understanding through communicative means. Feminist ethicists, such as Gilligan (1982) and Noddings (1984), developed an ethic of care that privileges relationships over rule-based notions of justice. Deontological perspectives, such as Kant's categorical imperative, emphasize rule-based approaches to ethics. Virtue ethics, initially developed by Aristotle, argue that ethics represent a predisposition to act in a morally compelling way. Virtues, such as honesty, integrity, and responsibility usually are described as internal, character-based tendencies that produce ethical behavior. Recent efforts in ethics and philosophy, however, have turned to the more day-to-day problems of good human conduct to develop theories of applied ethics.[2]

Some observers point to the activism of the 1960s, including the civil rights movement, environmentalism, and the Vietnam War protests, for the germination of applied ethics (e.g., Ozwawa, 2004), in which the public undertook value-driven efforts to right perceived wrongs. The applied ethics movement also is grounded in a larger recognition that philosophy and moral reasoning have not always focused on ethical dilemmas as they are manifest in the real world (Böhme, 2001). Applied ethics is a revolutionary trend in the larger study of ethics. At least two dozen practical and applied ethics centers focusing on a wide array of professional contexts (e.g., the Hastings Center, founded in 1969, to examine practical issues of bioethics) have been established in the last 2 decades. These approaches to the complexities of morality in organizational and professional life largely are interdisciplinary and designed to address specific ethical problems and dilemmas (Association for Practical and Professional Ethics, 2003).

Singer (1986), one of the founders of the modern applied ethics movement, focused on practical issues associated with bioethics. Singer noted that "applied ethics" concerns morality in "practical issues—like the treatment of ethnic minorities, equality for women, the use of animals for food and research, the preservation of the natural environment, abortion, euthanasia, and the obligation of the wealthy to help the poor" (p. 1). Applied ethicists soon recognized that many ethical dilemmas relate to practical issues in professional fields, such as business, law, medicine, computer science, engineering, accounting, and environmental studies. Communication, as a discipline, has been part of this larger applied, practical ethics movement.

Scholars in the applied and professional communication fields have begun to address issues of ethics in a variety of ways. Some, as mentioned previously, have argued for an explicit emphasis on social justice (see Frey & SunWolf, this volume). Journalism and other media scholars and practitioners have a long tradition of addressing ethical questions. A number of professional associations, such as the International Association of

Business Communicators, Society of Professional Journalists, and Public Relations Society of America, have developed codes of professional conduct. The National Communication Association's (1999) "Credo for Ethical Communication" is one manifestation of this trend. These codes indicate a growing recognition of the need for ethical standards and discourse within applied communication areas.

Applied ethics, as an area of inquiry and practice, focuses on issues of ethical decision making and problem solving in professional and organizational communities (Rosenthal & Shehadi, 1988; Singer, 1986; Winkler & Coombs, 1993). Typically, the focus of applied ethics is on identifying norms, standards, guidelines, and processes of professional and organizational practices, and methods for promoting ethical decision making (Böhme, 2001). For example, the role of professional codes of conduct in promoting discussion, informing decision making, and resolving practical ethical problems is central to applied ethics (Schwartz, 2001; Stevens, 1994). Professional standards not only help to ensure that ethics are addressed but also elevate the status and effectiveness of various professions. The applied ethics movement also is grounded in a larger recognition that to be relevant to the ethical choices that individuals face on a day-to-day basis, models and standards must accommodate an understanding of organizational and professional life, and adopt a pragmatic stance regarding the issues and dilemmas encountered.

In addition, an emphasis on professional and community standards allows applied ethics to avoid some of the less productive features of the "universal ethics" debate (Singer, 1986). *Universal ethics* involves the search for generalized standards and often is contrasted to *situational ethics*, or *moral relativism*, which seek to accommodate the unique features of a specific context (Harman & Thomson, 1996). Although most ethicists argue that a universal ethic is both desirable and morally appealing, such views break down in the opposition of various ethical theories and competing cultural and social values (Levy, 2002). *Practical ethics*, instead, focuses on the more parochial contexts of specific professional and organizational communities where narrower parameters can be drawn and agreed-on value traditions identified. Any applied ethic, however, still may be subject to criticism from more universal moralities, a criticism that flows, in part, from variability in the definition of applied ethics.

Communication Perspectives on Applied Ethics

Communication scholars historically have studied ethics from theoretical perspectives, including the study of philosophies of moral action. The goal of theoretical ethics has been to describe general and abstract moral principles for understanding how moral reasoning might function. In contrast, applied ethics, as described earlier, focuses on day-to-day ethical problems and moral dilemmas in work and professional contexts. Communication researchers, for example, frequently study the meanings, interpretations, and management of ethical issues in organizational settings to enlighten and assist individuals and organizations in acting ethically to achieve organizational goals. Equally important, and a focus of this section, are the ethical challenges encountered by researchers engaged in applied communication scholarship.

As noted earlier, an applied orientation to communication ethics includes a variety of issues and questions associated with real-world communication choices and behaviors, and their relationships to accepted values, standards, and norms (see Christians, Rotzoll, & Fackler, 1991; Jaksa & Pritchard, 1988, 1996; Johannesen, 2002; Seeger, 1997). Moreover, the emphasis placed on communication outcomes, strategies, and solutions to problems enhances the ethical significance of applied communication. Applied communication ethics, like the larger domain of applied ethics, focuses on the practical dimensions of ethical reasoning, choice, and behavior, primarily in professional and organizational contexts. This focus includes recognition of the ubiquitous nature of ethical issues concerning communication in professional and public life, the complexity of those issues, and the larger traditions, standards, and generally accepted norms that guide participants' behavior.

The ethical dimensions of human communication are ubiquitous. Johannesen (2002) noted that ethical questions arise whenever one's choices or behaviors have the potential to influence others. Given these parameters, almost all human communication is pregnant with ethical significance, although some aspects clearly have greater moral weight than others (Seeger, 2003). All aspects of the communication process—including messages, languages, channels, senders, and receivers—have the potential to influence others (see, e.g., the essays in Arneson, 2007). Moreover, ethical issues associated with communication never are entirely resolved in some final, unequivocal way but frequently must be revisited and reconsidered.

Applied ethics in communication contexts also acknowledges the inherent complexity in these questions and addresses the intrinsic conflict between alternative value positions. In many communication contexts, these values are associated with the various and diverse audiences participating in the process. The competing value perspective, for example, suggests that for any ethical question, multiple value stances vie with one another for supremacy (Seeger, 1997). For example, in health communication contexts (see Kreps & Bonaguro, this volume), the values of honesty and support often compete as a physician weighs being brutally honest against responding to a patient supportively. A physician may need to bluntly discuss a terminal prognosis to convey the futility of further treatment, yet at the same time, deliver the information in a caring manner. The wants of the patient, values of family members, policies of the hospital, and the larger political, religious, and legal contexts of decision making regarding life further complicate choices in that context. Such competition may create a moral dilemma where different values suggest alternative choices. An applied orientation to communication ethics acknowledges these complexities and suggests two approaches for addressing them.

First, communicators must be sensitive to the ethical implications of their communicative choices. Applied ethics seeks to inculcate sensitivity to value questions and ethical issues. Jaksa and Pritchard (1988) described this sensitivity as the "stimulation of the moral imagination" (p. 5). Part of this sensitivity involves recognition of the ethical dimensions of decisions so that they may be fully considered in the decision process. The goal of applied ethics is to make questions of values and ethics more prominent in efforts to use communication to address problems and create specific outcomes.

Second, communication is viewed as the process whereby decision makers sort through various value positions and determine which should take prominence in a given context. Argument, debate, discussion, and consensual decision making, for example, all have a role to play in sorting through conflicting values (Conrad, 1993; Seeger, 1997). Standards and values that encourage participation, voice, and free exchange of information help to ensure that relevant values are represented (Gorden, Infante, Wilson, & Clarke, 1984; Nielsen, 1974). Organizational democracy, for instance, concerns "principles and practices designed to engage and represent (in the multiple sense of the term) as many relevant individuals and groups as possible in the formulation, execution, and modification of work-related activities" (Cheney et al., 1998, p. 39). Through this diverse engagement, a wide variety of values are considered in relation to one another (see, e.g., Chency, 2008). In this way, communication is a target or field of ethical decision making and a critical part of the ethical reasoning process.

Like other applied ethics disciplines, applied communication ethics draws on institutional, professional, and disciplinary traditions, values, and standards in making ethical judgments. In communication, a rich set of these traditions has developed. Journalistic standards of truthfulness, honesty, balance, First Amendment guarantees of free speech, laws and regulations regarding transparency and openness in public communication, and dialogue, as well as the general recognition of communication and information rights, are important influences on applied communication ethics (Conrad, 1993; Johannesen, 2002; Nielsen, 1974; Seeger, 1997). Recently, social justice also has emerged as a compelling value tradition for applied communication research (Frey, Pearce, Pollock, Artz, & Murphy, 1996; Pearce, 1998; see also Frey & SunWolf, this volume). In addition to these disciplinary traditions, important ethical issues surround the research process itself.

Applied communication researchers only recently have begun to consider and question the ethical choices, practices, and outcomes in the research process (Swartz, 1997). This critique has been driven by a realization that applied communication research includes significant ethical issues that often are ignored in strategy and outcome-driven investigations. Some scholars contend that applied ethics in communication research encompass more than ethical considerations in the arena of study and more than the minimum institutional review process for research involving human participants (discussed below). The research process upon inception involves ethical choices, challenges, and constraints (Gadamer, 1975), as researchers decide what to study, how to engage participants (e.g., as respondents or as coresearchers), which method(s) to employ, and how, when, and where to report results (Frey, 1998b; Frey et al., 1996; Oliver, 2003). These considerations take place within situated, historical contexts, political environments, and value domains (Gagnon, 1992; Swartz, 1997). The research process and product(s) never are politically neutral acts, as researchers inherently privilege certain values, practices, and institutions (Frey, 1998b; Frey & Carragee, 2007; Frey et al., 1996). Therefore, if communication scholars hope to conduct ethical applied research, they must begin by scrutinizing research processes themselves (e.g., Varallo, Ray, & Ellis, 1998). Conquergood (1995) contended that praxis is "fundamentally about placement, about taking a stand, marking (not masking) the self, positioning one's research ethically, politically, as well as conceptually" (p. 86). Such placement also applies to the purposes and methods that guide the research process, and the outcomes and consequences that result from research.

Three common ethical goals for research—"do no harm," "effect positive outcomes," and "promote social justice"—provide a useful context for reviewing and problematizing applied ethics in communication research. When employing the ethical goal of *do no harm*, research purports to avoid harm as a consequence of the research process or outcome, or to balance any potential for harm with anticipated benefits. To demonstrate this commitment, researchers, in coordination with Institutional Review Boards (IRBs), review research proposals to ensure that the anticipated benefits outweigh the risks involved and that participants voluntarily provide their informed consent (e.g., Sieber, 1992).

When employing the ethical goal of *effect positive outcomes*, scholars develop and conduct research that not only purports to do no harm but also intends to promote positive outcomes. These positive outcomes generally pertain to greater efficiency and effectiveness, such as when improvements within organizational communication processes help institutions to better meet the needs of employees, customers, and communities.

The third goal of *promote social justice* often requires a transformative orientation. Rather than conducting research for the primary or exclusive purpose of further understanding the topic and testing or building theory, an equally important goal is to promote social justice. Transformational changes occur as a product of the research process or as outcomes of the research conclusions, when, for example, participants function as researchers, and vice versa, or when changes occur in organizational access to voice and decision making.

These three ethical goals suggest two perspectives for the research process and resulting outcomes: One perspective accepts the context under study and attempts to produce either no harm or some incremental, positive changes; the second perspective champions the disempowered and underempowered, and seeks to transform society through research. IRBs require scholars to employ the first perspective to obtain approval for research, whereas the responsibility to incorporate and propose strategies consistent with the second perspective primarily lies with researchers, not with the institution approving the research. In some cases, however, IRBs, following federal guidelines, encourage researchers to include more underrepresented participants.

The horrific applied research conducted on human participants in Nazi Germany and the negligent treatment of research participants by U.S. researchers in the infamous Tuskegee syphilis experiment (e.g., Harter, Stephens, & Japp, 2000; Solomon, 1985) inspired the formation of protocols for ethical research. As mandated by the National Research Act, Public Law 93-348, an IRB (or Human Subjects Committee) reviews all institutionally based research proposals prior to initiation to ensure that the research plan has considered ethical dimensions and sufficiently protects the legal and ethical rights of human participants (e.g., Sieber, 1992). The IRB process is the most important regulatory guarantee for ensuring the application of at least minimal ethical standards in any institutionally sponsored research, including applied communication research. As such, IRBs now stand as the first level of protection against abusive research practices (Ashcraft & Byers, 2004).

IRBs are charged with two primary tasks that are consistent among all genres of research on human participants. First, IRBs are responsible for considering the potential benefits in relation to the risks to research participants. If the potential benefits do not outweigh the risks, there is no ethical justification for the research. This consideration, however, often is complicated by the fact that benefits and risks may be poorly understood and do not necessarily accrue to the same groups. Risks most often are associated with individuals, whereas benefits usually apply to larger groups. Second, IRBs oversee the *informed consent process*, which involves making all potential participants aware of the potential risks and benefits of any research project (Department of Health and Human Services, National Institutes of Health Office for Protection from Research Risks, 2001). The informed consent process ensures that people receive the necessary information to assess whether there is good reason for their participation and that the choice to participate is made freely and without coercion.

Currently, three of the most pressing difficulties with informed consent involve the use of deception (Wendler, Emanuel, & Lie, 2004), potential exploitation of children, and research in developing countries using less than worldwide standards for best practice (e.g., Kopelman & Murphy, 2004; Sharav, 2004; Wendler et al., 2004). Deception commonly is used in research on human participants in two ways. First, participants may be deceived if the true intent of research is withheld. Second, participants may be deceived into thinking they will receive a treatment when, in fact, they will receive a placebo (Wendler & Miller, 2004). Because informed consent requires a clear explanation of the research objectives, potential benefits, and reasons for participant selection, studies employing deception may violate these basic ethical principles. Currently, the American Psychological Association's (APA; 2002) "Ethical Principles of Psychologists and Code of Conduct" allows deception only when it is justified by the study's prospective value, alternative procedures are not feasible, and the research does not expect to cause physical pain or emotional distress. Furthermore, the APA requires that deception be explained to participants as early as is feasible.

Informed consent is problematized further when it involves powerless groups, such as prisoners and children, where the ability to freely give informed consent is reduced. Federal regulations require that children who serve as research participants must first receive consent from a legally authorized representative (e.g., their parents), followed by the children giving their assent. Several scholars have noted that despite these require- ments, children are vulnerable to manipulation by their guardians and by profit-seeking researchers (e.g., Kopelman & Murphy, 2004; Sharav, 2004). Koppelman and Murphy (2004), consequently, called for more research to resolve the "growing tension between federal regulations and the courts over how to protect children from harm while advanc- ing pediatric knowledge" (p. 1788).

An additional controversy concerns the development and testing of medical treatments in countries with poorly developed health-care systems and few safeguards for research. Wendler et al. (2004, p. 927) posited four conditions to foster ethical research by foreign scholars in developing countries. First, there must be a scientific necessity to "use less than the worldwide best methods to answer a scientific question." Second, "answering the scientific question posed by the trial will help address an important health need of the host community." Third, the trial must have potential to "produce a fair level of benefit for the host community." Finally, research participants must be assured they will not be "prospectively worse off than they would be in the absence of the trial."

Beyond adhering to the provisions of IRBs, scholars also have embraced research goals concerning fundamental social and political change. In the *JACR* special issue edited by Frey (1998a), contributors shared their varied theoretical perspectives and methodologi- cal choices (e.g., action research, participatory research, and feminist research) made in conducting social justice communication research. Varallo et al. (1998), for instance, examined the interviews they conducted with adult incest survivors as a possible trans- formative process, suggesting that the "research interview process itself needs to mirror, or do justice to, the desired effect(s), such as positive change for participants, if it is to serve the purposes of social justice" (p. 266). As another example, Adelman and Frey (1994, 1997) initiated a longitudinal study in an AIDS residential facility that combined action research and participatory methods after volunteering at the residence and being invited to conduct a study in collaboration with administrators and residents.

Applied communication ethics, then, are grounded in the three goals of do no harm, effect positive outcomes, and promote social justice. The primary process of insuring minimum adherence to the first two goals is the IRB review. Some investigators, how- ever, agree in principle with IRB goals but simultaneously point to bureaucratic ironies, tensions, and interferences within the review process (see, e.g., Dougherty & Kramer, 2005; Marshall, 2003; Pritchard, 2002). The IRB process, they suggest, is needlessly bureaucratic, indiscriminate in understanding various research methods, overarching and sometimes arbitrary in oversight, and infringes on academic freedom. Communica- tion scholars, acculturated in values of free speech and the free flow of information, may feel particularly oppressed by the IRB process.[3]

Due to the significant role of the IRB in applied communication research, Kramer and Dougherty (2005) invited essays and narratives of researchers' experiences with IRBs for a *JACR* special issue on "Communication Research and Institutional Review Boards." Contributors identified disturbing ironies in IRB processes, such as emphasizing the pro- tection of the university over that of research participants, shaping scholarship rather than simply supporting it, providing research oversight without answering to any similar oversight, and adding to rather than diminishing the potential risk to research participants. Hamilton (2005) reviewed the development and operation of IRBs, highlighting the often-inappropriate application of a medical research model to social-scientific research when conducting reviews. Nonetheless, the IRB review process is well established as an important institutional check on research ethics, although it is not a panacea and dramatic cases of research abuse continue (Philips, 2000).

Domains of Applied Communication Ethics

As noted earlier, ethical issues arise in all communication contexts. Here, we focus on three domains where applied communication ethics are manifest and that have robust traditions: health communication, organizational communication, and media. These domains illustrate the types of ethical issues that arise and ways they have been addressed in applied communication research.

Health Communication

Medical and public health contexts abound with complex ethical issues for communication researchers and practitioners. Four propositions, delineated by Guttman (2003), highlight the ethical underpinnings in health communication interactions, environments, interventions, and campaigns: (1) Health communication entails purposeful efforts to influence people's health; (2) throughout health communication and related initiatives, from conception to implementation to assessment, researchers/practitioners make decisions that contain inherent, embedded ethical considerations; (3) implicit and secondary ethical issues often create unintended impacts and consequences; and (4) ethical considerations have practical and moral significance.

Researchers and practitioners grapple with ethical decisions regarding which health issues to address; which individuals and populations to target; which methodologies to employ and how to employ them effectively; how to define effective targeting and tailoring of interventions, and by whom; and how to define success and by whom (e.g., Ratzan, 1994). By choosing to address certain health issues, other issues invariably receive less focus and fewer resources. Although targeting and tailoring messages appears to meet ethical obligations to promote equity and comprehensibility, concerns about exclusion and bias surface. Similarly, the effectiveness of communication approaches and intervention strategies depends on perspectives and definitions of "success." Persuasive strategies may influence health behaviors and affect change, but they concurrently may co-opt, appropriate, and confront cultural values. Such strategies also may affect individuals' feelings of blame, shame, culpability, and responsibility, which, in turn, may implicitly affect social stigmas, disparity, and gaps between social groups, and societal hyper-valuing of health.

Ratzan, Payne, and Bishop (1996), in a comprehensive review of the health communication field, identified two major challenges: (1) using ethical means to communicate health information and (2) engaging in ethical decision making. Recent issues of *Health Communication* and the *Journal of Health Communication* highlight additional ethical challenges: issues of informed consent with vulnerable populations, such as adults who have Alzheimer's; control of the meaning and practice of informed consent (Olufowote, 2008); communication models, intercultural communication, and medical interpreting (Dysart-Gale, 2005; J. L. Johnson et al., 2004; Simon, Zyzanski, Durran, Jimenez, & Kodish, 2006); questions of access and accuracy of health information (Williams & Sellnow, 1998); patient rights (Ford, Odallo, & Chorlton, 2003); privacy issues and regulations (Brann & Mattson, 2004; Petronio, 2002); marketing and advertising (Cline & Young,

2004); social/corporate responsibility, managed care, international health responses, and human rights (Ford et al., 2003); entertainment–education (Singhal & Rogers, 2001); and health-promotion campaigns (Dutta-Bergman, 2005; Mattson & Roberts, 2001). In addition, health literacy skills and accompanying ethical issues increasingly are important as new technologies (e.g., online resources, interactive media, computer support systems, and Web-site technology for the design of community) add to the available media for information dissemination (Cline & Haynes, 2001; Finnegan et al., 2001; Lieberman, 2001).

Two of the most discussed areas of applied health communication ethics involve bioethics and public health (Bracci, 2001, 2002; Callahan & Jennings, 2002; Guttman & Ressler, 2001; MacQueen & Buehler, 2004; Sharf, 1999; Thomas, Sage, Dillenberg, & Guillory, 2002). Bioethics focuses on competing values that are inherent to issues such as "organ transplants, genetics, reproductive biology, and resource allocation" (Callahan & Jennings, 2002, p. 170). Attention also has focused on how medical institutions deliberate issues relating to the values of human life and health (Bracci, 2001, 2002). End-of-life issues, for instance (e.g., Barton, 2007) have become increasingly complex with the advent of new life-extending technology. What is of particular importance to communication researchers is how participants with disparate values can manage these deliberations and the attendant discourse (regarding end-of life, see, e.g., Foster, 2006; Keränen, 2007; Planalp & Trost, 2008; Young & Rodriguez, 2006). As Bracci (2002) explained, "Bio-ethics is built on conflict, and seeks resolution of issues through justification, not consensus, since these disparate voices have failed to locate shared first principles to adjudicate their differences" (p. 153).

Much of the bioethics debate is grounded in the conflict over scarce resources. This justificatory process associated with allocations inherently is communicative and illustrates the process nature of communication in applying ethics. Moreover, clear communication of the advantages and disadvantages of a particular bioethical approach requires informed consent. The communication process of informed consent, therefore, is one of the most critical issues associated with bioethics research. We view informed consent similarly to Sharf (1999), who described it as a process of shared interpersonal meaning between researchers and the persons being studied regarding the risks of participating in a study. For this reason, informed consent fundamentally is a communication process.

Sharf (1999) proposed a research agenda for addressing communication issues in bioethics, arguing that communication researchers should bring their

> expertise to such problem areas as (a) informed consent (a concept most often treated as a legal or moral requirement rather than as a matter of interpersonal creation of shared meaning); (b) breaking bad news to patients and their families; (c) generating discussions of such difficult topics as people's life values and advanced directives in preparation for a time when, as a patient, a person may not be able to speak in his or her own behalf, or termination of treatment in the face of apparent futility; (d) negotiating critical differences of opinion and intent between practitioners and patients (individuals who disagree with doctors' recommendations are often treated as noncompliant, incompetent, or even hateful patients); (e) striving for understanding in the face of dissimilar cultural beliefs, practices, and communicative styles; and (f) persuasively approaching family members for organ donation from a newly deceased loved one. (pp. 197–198)

A second fundamental issue in health communication ethics concerns the free flow of information regarding critical public health issues. MacQueen and Buehler (2004), for example, argued that "defining the boundary between public health research and practice remains a critical challenge within the evolving field of public health ethics" (p. 928). Key to this issue is how health organizations can communicate effectively and in a timely way to the public about established and emerging public health risks. A principal focus of applied health communication is effectively disseminating information and persuading the public to engage in healthy behavior (see Kreps & Bonaguro, this volume).

Although research on health promotion is extensive, little of this work focuses explicitly on ethical issues, with a few notable exceptions (Ford et al., 2003; Guttman & Ressler, 2001; Williams & Sellnow, 1998). Guttman and Ressler (2001), for example, developed an extensive list of practice-oriented questions that can be used to deliberate about issues of personal responsibility in health campaigns, such as avoidance of blaming, labeling, and stigmatizing; facilitation of personal autonomy; and respect for different value perspectives. In addition, they identified ethical precepts and social values that may be reinforced in health messages, and described specific appeals to responsibility. This work views ethical issues as strategies that may improve the effectiveness of health messages. Similarly, Ford et al. (2003) identified a human rights perspective as an underlying value in HIV and AIDS campaigns in Africa. They drew on the human rights approach employed by the United Nations Children's Fund to advocate for a communication-based approach that invites an audience into a dialogue and interaction that enhances empowerment and shared decision making. Most important, they advocated for more flexible, audience-centered communication strategies that acknowledge multiple perspectives and diverse needs (see the discussion of such strategies in the context of development by Kincaid & Figueroa, this volume). Williams and Sellnow's (1998) investigation was similarly grounded in questions regarding the flow of information. They studied the changing criteria for administering mammograms, and concluded that the National Cancer Institute's shifting standards created a chilling effect on health-care policy discourse.

Two problems with these research approaches are evident, however. First, they advocate for behaviors using value appeals when the resources necessary to support those behaviors may not be available, with one result being the stigmatization of a group as unethical or immoral. Second, they tend to privilege a narrow set of values, such as access to information, as the only ethical issues inherent to these contexts.

The public health community also has worked to develop consensus on general values of open and honest communication with the public. As MacQueen and Buehler (2003) explained:

> In January 2002, the National Center for HIV, STD, and TB Prevention (NCHSTP) at the Centers for Disease Control and Prevention (CDC) convened a 2-day workshop to examine a series of questions in public health ethics, drawing on case studies from NCHSTP projects and the expertise of a diverse group of invited participants. (p. 928)

The goal was to examine a variety of cases and develop "national discussions concerning the ethical conduct of public health practice" (MacQueen & Buehler, 2003, p. 928). From these discussions, standards can be developed regarding the free flow of information about health risks and prevention, and even informed consent regarding medical issues and procedures.

Uniform standards are particularly important because of the complexities associated with ethics in public health communication. For instance, HIV, tuberculosis, sexually transmitted diseases, and other infectious diseases often are complicated by "stigma, poverty, and discrimination [that] are interwoven with the conditions that affect both the transmission and the outcome of these infections" (MacQueen & Buehler, 2003, p. 929). Thus, ethical issues in health communication also are associated with larger values of social justice, including access to treatment, equality, and empowerment. As with other efforts to articulate applied ethics, the American Public Health Association adopted a code of ethics that features issues pertaining to communication, such as collecting input from community members regarding efficacy of public health programs, including the public in making decisions, and communicating in an expeditious manner regarding public health issues (Thomas et al., 2002).

The applied orientation to health communication ethics primarily consists of developing a fuller understanding of ethical issues and processes in decisions concerning bioethics and health-promotion campaigns. At the time of this writing, this research focuses on developing ethical standards that concern open and honest information exchange about risk and about health issues between health officials and the public, and that clarify the larger value domains of health communication. Similarly, efforts have been made to employ communication to improve health decision making and to represent various competing values in important biomedical questions, such as the use of technology to extend life. Open and honest communication leading to empowerment and informed choice generally has been privileged over other value perspectives in health communication, such as mutual responsibility and care, which actually may be undermined by an exclusive focus on individual responsibility and empowerment.

Organizational Communication

Due to the ongoing ethical challenges that organizations and the people working with or within them face, an elaborate body of scholarship has developed. This includes an extensive body of research and commentary in business ethics encompassing issues such as corporate social responsibility, employee rights, management and leader ethics, environmental exploitation, multinational ethics, executive compensation, ethics codes, and conflict of interest, among many others. Among the primary issues of communication ethics that applied scholars have explored in organizations are privacy and voice (Botan, 1996; Gorden et al., 1984); free speech (Seeger, 1986); honesty, deception, social influence, persuasion, and coercion (Redding, 1996; Seeger & Ulmer, 2003); diversity (Mattson & Buzzanell, 1999); whistleblowing (Near & Miceli, 1986); change, power, domination, authority, and control (Mumby, 1988); organizational democracy (Cheney et al., 1998; Deetz, 1992); discourse and dialogue (Jovanovic & Wood, 2006; Meisenbach, 2006); leadership (C. E. Johnson, 2005; Simms & Brinkman, 2002); legitimacy and corporate social responsibility (Boyd, 2000; Daugherty, 2001; May & Zorn, 2003); recruitment and socialization (Pribble, 1990); ethical climate (Victor & Cullen, 1988; Waters & Bird, 1987); and public relations (Curtin & Boynton, 2001). Case studies of ethical perspectives and practices associated with organizational communication also have been offered (e.g., May, 2006). In addition, scholars have engaged in more general critiques of organizational communication ethics (e.g., Conrad, 1993; Redding, 1986; Seeger, 1997, 2003). Moreover, Cheney and Christensen (2001) argued that the external organizational communication designed to create and maintain organizational identity includes ethical and moral dimensions of:

(1) the posited character or integrity of the source of the message, (2) the defensibility of a particular message, (3) the legitimacy of a pattern or campaign of messages, (4) the practical impact of a messages or the cumulative effect of a series of message, (5) the openness of the structure of communication between an organization and its

publics/audiences, (6) the articulation/representation of genuine public interests, and (7) the question of shared responsibility. (pp. 258–259)

Others working from critical approaches to organizational communication have emphasized equity, empowerment, diversity, and institutional democracy (e.g., Cheney, 1999; Deetz, 1992; Mattson & Buzzanell, 1999; Mumby, 1988, 1996; Mumby & Putnam, 1992). Clearly, organizational communication includes a wide range of profound ethical issues.

Many current paradigms of organizational inquiry, including cultural, interpretive, and critical approaches, emphasize ethics and values (Putnam, 1982; Putnam & Fairhurst, 2001). Nicotera and Cushman (1992) argued that an organization's culture creates a unique value system for making ethical assessments, and Mattson and Buzzanell (1999) applied feminist critical perspectives to judge organizational ethics.

Ethical principles are applied in organizational communication contexts through three general approaches, either individually or as part of an integrated ethics program: (1) ethical codes of conduct; (2) ethics training; and (3) strategies to create more accessible, open, and responsive structures and procedures. First and most common approach is ethical codes in their various iterations (Schwartz, 2001, 2002; Stevens, 1994). Schwartz (2002) reported that over 90% of large corporations have a code of ethics, ranging from general statements of values and goals, usually described as "aspirational codes," to highly specific legalistic prescriptions for employee conduct, often characterized as "legalistic codes" (Frankel, 1989). These codes serve a variety of functions, including reducing legal liability, clarifying ethical issues and responsibilities, enhancing an organization's reputation, and encouraging members' ethical conduct. Such codes now are a standard part of corporate life, although it is not clear how broadly they are communicated and disseminated or how they are used by employees. Several studies have supported the view that codes are at least somewhat effective in promoting organizational ethics (McCabe, Trevino, & Butterfield, 1996; Pierce & Henry, 1996).

Codes and general standards of ethical conduct also have been described for communication consulting. Browning (1982), for example, drew on counter-rational theory and the APA's statement on ethics to explore the ethics of communication consulting. Harrison (1982) approached communication consulting from a rhetorical standpoint, emphasizing participatory and dialogic perspectives as ethical standards. Montgomery, Wiseman, and DeCaro (2001) proposed a wide-ranging code of ethical conduct for consultants that addressed issues such as competency, community service, conflict of interest, confidentiality, and privacy.

A second approach to applying communication ethics in organizations is ethics programs (Seeger, 1997), which include promotions and communication regarding specific types of ethical conduct, sponsored training in ethical decision making, ethics audits and surveys, and the use of ethical codes, as well as related programs and promotions regarding ethics. Training often is a response to specific accusations of organizational or employee wrongdoing. In 2006, for example, military commanders ordered training in core values following accusations that U.S. troops in Iraq had killed civilians. Many organizations also actively promote employees' involvement in social and community causes, including volunteering for projects such as Habitat for Humanity, tutoring in inner-city schools, or helping with recycling programs, to encourage and publicize an image of "good corporate citizenship." These examples of social responsibility acknowledge that organizations have obligations to the larger society (Buchholz, 1990). Good corporate citizenship often is publicized and featured in corporate annual reports, and may represent what Boyd (2000) described as "actional legitimacy." Chief executive officers' speeches often include references to corporate values and missions as a way of enhancing their organization's positive reputation and promoting its ethical conduct (Waters & Bird, 1987). Codes of conduct and corporate value and mission statements often are posted in prominent locations in organizations and on their Web sites, and new employees may be trained in the code of ethics and mission statements as part of larger corporate socialization efforts (Pribble, 1990). In some cases, major decisions are vetted through the organization's code of ethics. However, although codes are an indication that an organization has at least considered ethics, one problem is that ethical codes and programs actually may mask unethical conduct (Seeger & Ulmer, 2003).

Finally, issues of organizational democracy, participation, voice, dissent, and whistle-blowing can broadly be classified as efforts to create more open and ethical organizations characterized by less restricted flows of information and more equality of participation and influence (Cheney et al., 1998; Kassing, 1997; Near & Miceli, 1986). These efforts are supported by values of openness, pluralistic dialogues, and reductions in hierarchical domination (Deetz, 1992). In addition, efforts to create more diverse workplaces on the basis of ethnicity, race (see Nicotera, Clinkscales, Dorsey, & Niles, this volume), gender (see Buzzanell, Meisenbach, Remke, Sterk, & Turner, this volume), and sexual orientation, among other characteristics, serve to expand the range of ideas and perspectives (e.g., Buzzanell, 1994; Mattson & Buzzanell, 1999). These pluralistic dialogues can be expected to create freer flows of information, enhanced decision making, and broader employee participation. Moreover, as Conrad (1993) noted:

> It is through discourse that individuals develop their own views of morality; through discourse that organizations develop and inculcate core values and ethical codes; and through discourse that incongruities within individual and organizational value-sets are managed and contradictions between the value sets of different persons are negotiated. (p. 2)

Application of communication ethics regarding openness, democracy, and pluralism sometimes requires a change in management philosophy and in specific organizational structures and procedures. These changes may include open meetings between managers and employees, ombudspersons who facilitate the free flow of communication between various levels of organizations, and hardcopy and virtual suggestion boxes. Some stakeholder models of organizational communication ethics go so far as to include a variety of external audiences and constituencies in these pluralistic conversations. Scholars advocating these approaches, however, generally have failed to grapple with the fundamental values conflicts and tensions between organizations as hierarchies of domination and as democratic and inclusive systems.

Stewart (2001) summarized work on applied organizational communication ethics with four major conclusions:

1. Our theories of applied ethics must reach beyond the individual level and posit ethical principles for organizations as well as for individuals.
2. Ethics and organizational effectiveness are inextricably linked.
3. Codes of ethics are not just a means of regulating employee and other professionals' behavior, they also provide an important means of facilitating communication with employees and clients.
4. Thinking about ethical issues in organizations must be multidimensional to examine not only the rational dimension of decision making but also the emotional and spiritual. (p. 3)

These core conclusions have helped to unify the study of applied communication ethics in organizational contexts. Issues of organizational and corporate ethics, however, remain diverse because they concern the entire range of organizational stakeholders, structures, industries, technologies, markets, and locations. Some of the most complex questions concern the intersection between the values and ethics of individual managers and other organizational members and the larger institutional values and culture. Although efforts have been made to apply ethical standards to organizational and institutional contexts, these efforts largely are in their infancy. Moreover, codes, ethics programs, and efforts to build more inclusive dialogues often come into direct conflict with the profit motive that dominates so much of modern corporate life. Finally, it is not clear that codes of ethics, ethical climates, or ethical leadership necessarily translate into more ethical organizational communication.

Media

The media have a long tradition of addressing a wide range of ethical issues, such as the standards and values inherent to journalism, including First Amendment protections for free speech and a free press (Elliott, 1986; Entman, 1989), standards regarding truthfulness and accuracy (P. Patterson & Wilkins, 2001), general norms for appropriateness (Lauzen, 2005), ethics and international media (Rao & Lee, 2005), ethics and new technology (Tompkins, 2003), moral development of journalists (Coleman & Wilkins, 2002), and issues of diversity (Biagi & Kern-Foxworth, 1997; Zeldes & Fico, 2005). In addition, issues of privacy, plagiarism, equal access, media ownership, advertising, sex and violence, deception, conflict of interest, and libel have been raised in general critiques of media ethics (Belsey & Chadwick, 1992; Christians et al. 1991; Day, 2000; Gordan & Kittross, 1990; Meyer, 1987).

Given their social impact, the media carry particular moral significance. Journalistic ethics, for example, promote truthful and accurate reporting, in part, because inaccuracy can create widespread harm (Meyer, 1987). The reporting of the Florida results for the 2000 U.S. president, for instance, created widespread confusion and disruption of political institutions. Journalists also are unique in facilitating the free flow of information necessary for a democracy to function (Seigel, 2002). In addition, important standards have developed about the appropriateness of media reporting, including how violence, gender, representation of various groups, diversity, age, and sexuality are portrayed (Christians et al., 2001). Finally, ethical issues in the media are associated with commercialism, including advertising, promotion of consumerism, and the exportation of media culture (Kerr, 2003).

Journalists often face specific ethical dilemmas associated with conflicts between standards for accuracy, truthfulness, and objectivity and other values and standards that are manifest in specific news stories or with larger social values. Covering stories about rape, for example, may create conflict between values regarding truthfulness and privacy (Lake, 1991). A news story regarding violence often comes into conflict with norms regarding appropriateness of graphic coverage (Parsons & Smith, 1988). Reporting of beheadings in Iraq, for instance, raised critical questions regarding whether graphic images should be used to accurately portray a news story. Journalists may be forced to confront conflicts between "objectivity" in news coverage and concerns for the human dignity of individuals involved in the tragedies, as many did in reporting on the AIDS crisis (Childers, 1988). In addition, questions involving conflict of interest arise in the media business, most often around ownership or advertiser interests. Finally, journalists often choose a standard of balance in seeking to manage these dilemmas by weighing the need to cover a story accurately and completely against subject- and audience-based values and sensibilities (M. Johnson & Babcock, 1999).

As with applied ethics in medical and organizational contexts, media organizations have relied primarily on professional training and codes of ethics to promote ethical conduct. Codes of journalistic ethics have existed since at least the early 1900s and were associated with the emergence of journalism as a profession (Boeyink, 1998; Gordan & Kittross, 1999). Codes now are associated with nearly all professional communication or media associations, including advertising, public relations, marketing, television and radio broadcasting (including children's, educational, public, and religious), and, of course, journalism. The American Society of Newspaper Editors (2002) developed its first formal code of conduct in the form of "Canons of Journalism" in 1922 (renamed "Statement of Principles" in 1975). The Society of Professional Journalists (2004) has an elaborate ethical code, adopted in 1996, that is based on four principles: (1) seek truth and report it, (2) minimize harm, (3) act independently, and (4) be accountable. Ethics programs and ombudspersons also are common in many newsrooms. Dramatic cases, such as Jayson Blair plagiarizing and fabricating stories at *The New York Times* (Hindman, 2005; M. J. Patterson & Urbanski, 2006), reiterate the need for journalists to be vigilant in attending to ethics. Many news organizations have developed codes of ethics, which regularly are revised and updated to reflect changes in media practices and social norms, as well as in response to specific ethical lapses (e.g., *The New York Times* undertook a major revision of its ethics code following the Blair scandal). In addition, professional organizations, such as the American Society of Newspaper Editors, frequently survey their members about ethical issues.

Journalism also has addressed many of these ethical dilemmas through extensive training and education. The Poynter Institute, for instance, maintains an extensive set of educational resources for professional, working journalists (http://www.poynter.org/). Among other things, Poynter hosts ethics workshops and training (e.g., on diversity in the profession) and an on-call group is available to provide counseling on ethical issues. The Society of Professional Journalists offers similar resources. In addition, most university degree programs in journalism require ethics as part of the curriculum (Christians, 2008; Hanson, 2002; Whitehouse & McPherson, 2002).

Problems in applying ethics to the media are diverse, complex, and characterized by competing values. For example, as the media have become more widely available and more homogenized, competing value positions have emerged. The U.S. Supreme Court's use of a "contemporary community standard" to determine whether materials are obscene was one effort to address these competing values. Similar tensions have emerged as the media have become more international (Overbeck, 2008) and as globalization increases (Rao & Lee, 2005; Ward, 2005; Wasserman, 2006; Wasserman & Rao, 2008; see also Parrish-Sprowl, this volume). Developing countries often accuse U.S. mainstream media of a type of imperialism by exporting U.S. values. The controversy over competing values is a major source of conflict, as broadcasters claim expansive First Amendment rights to air a wide range of content, whereas community members and interest groups argue that much of that content is objectionable based on specific value positions. Another source of complexity concerns media organizations as businesses. Although the media serve a variety of public interest functions, some of which are constitutionally protected, most media organizations are profit-driven enterprises, and, consequently, competition between profit and public interests dominates many questions of applied media ethics. One place where public values have come into conflict with profit motives is in media convergence (e.g., Lawson-Borders, 2005; Sparks, Young, & Darnell, 2006).

In general, the problems of applied ethics in the media are extensive. Media organizations and professional groups have been active in monitoring ethics issues, educating journalists, and offering resources, such as ethics ombudspersons, ethicists on call, and ethics codes. The competition of values and the profit-making nature of the media suggest that applied ethical issues are unlikely to be resolved anytime soon. Moreover, several efforts have been undertaken at community levels to create more access to the media, efforts that have been enhanced by new communication technologies (see Lievrouw, this volume). In addition, the community or public journalism movement has grown as a response to a belief that traditional journalism is disconnected from community needs and values (e.g., Anderson, Dardenne, & Killenberg, 1994; Glasser, 1999). Community or public journalism involves aligning journalistic practices more closely with community interests and needs by engaging the public in the process of news gathering and reporting. Two efforts to engage media ethics described in the literature are Gerbner's cultural environmental movement and the Media Research and Action Project.

George Gerbner, a prominent scholar of media violence and the primary force behind cultivation theory, founded the cultural environmental movement (CEM), which was modeled after the 1960s to 1970s environmental movement and addresses the decay in the cultural environment associated with the media. The cultural environmental movement, according to Gerbner (1999), is founded on three truths:

1. That all persons are endowed with the right to live in a cultural environment that is respectful of their humanity and supportive of their potential.
2. That all children are endowed with the right to grow up in a cultural environment that fosters responsibility, trust, and community rather than force, fear, and violence.
3. That when the cultural environment becomes destructive of these ends, it becomes necessary to alter it. (p. 351)

The CEM currently exists as a loose association of independent groups and affiliated organizations that has been active in lobbying, education, and research efforts throughout the world. What is most interesting about CEM from an applied communication ethics perspective is Gerbner's (1999, p. 348) conclusion that traditional "research is not enough" and that a new, active approach to answering questions about the media is required. This same recognition helped to launch the initial applied ethics movement in the 1960s.

The Media Research and Action Project (MRAP) is a programmatic effort to create social movement dynamics around efforts to "broaden the discourse in the mainstream media" (Ryan, Carragee, & Schwerner, 1998, p. 166; see also Ryan, Carragee, & Meinhofer, 2001). Founded in 1986 at Boston College, MRAP is a joint effort involving scholars in sociology, political science, education, history, and communication to provide media training and consultancy to community, labor, and nonprofit organizations, giving these organizations the tools to shape media coverage and, thereby, influence the media's agenda and provide more voice to social issues. MRAP has been described as an example of promoting the social justice values of applied communication research (Frey, 1998b).

The efforts to take applied approaches to media ethics are robust and well developed. Many of these approaches are grounded in a larger ethic of social justice, as well as traditional journalistic values of democracy, diversity of voice, and free access to information. In these cases, the values largely complement each other. The impact of these efforts, however, is less clear. The effort to create and maintain a set of ethical guidelines for journalists also is well developed, but the efficacy of these efforts is poorly documented. Despite robust efforts to educate journalists in ethics and to create and maintain codes of ethics, dramatic cases of unethical conduct continue to emerge.

Value Dimensions of Applied Communication Research

Applied communication research is a comparatively new field that has generated more than its share of criticism. As the field has matured, applied scholars have begun to explore underlying ideological values. This discussion, initiated by Frey et al. (1996), tends to center on social justice as a primary ethical frame (see Frey & SunWolf, this volume). In addition, the larger value tradition of communication scholarship on empowerment and voice, and on free speech and access to information, inform applied communication scholarship. Although applied communication scholars appear reluctant to define precisely what they mean by social justice, the concept clearly is grounded in issues of justice, equality, and empowerment. Frey et al. (1996) suggested that a "social justice sensibility" underlying communication inquiry "(a) foregrounds ethical concerns, (b) commits to structural analysis of ethical problems, (c) adopts an activist's orientation, and (d) seeks identification with others" (p. 111). Conquergood (1995) described "engaged" applied communication research as requiring scholars to recognize that they are "entangled within world systems of oppression and exploitation" (p. 85). Wood (1996) also described work in diversity, gender, empowerment, and sexual harassment within the larger frame of social justice. The evolving notion of social justice in applied communication research is most associated with Rawls's (1999) concept of justice as equality. In Rawlsian justice, every individual should have equal access to basic rights, liberties, and opportunities. Social justice as the attainment of human rights, most often referring to a universal set of rights and status that accrue to individuals based solely on their humanity, and the fulfillment of the social contract is evident in applied communication research.

In the 1998 *JACR* special issue on communication and social justice, five research reports focused primarily on programs of social change. The people who were studied were engaged not only as research participants but also as partners in the process of change. In addition to the Varallo et al. (1998) and the MRAP project described earlier (Ryan et al., 1998), articles focused on serving learning and cross-cultural communication (Crabtree, 1998), improved race relations (Artz, 1998), and empowering education of prisoners (Hartnett, 1998). These studies addressed the consequences or outcomes of the applied communication research, as each project was concerned with achieving good consequences as a research outcome, including attaining fairness and equality. This interest in positive outcomes and good consequences occurs in addition to more traditional research concerns, such as methodological rigor and theory building (Frey & Carragee, 2007).

In addition, these and the other applied communication research projects described foreground a specific set of value orientations, among which are empowerment and voice, free speech, and access to information. Empowerment and voice are reflected in much of applied communication work in organizational settings, as well as in investigations framed from a social justice orientation. Empowerment and voice entail offering skills, tools, and opportunities to disenfranchised or powerless groups and individuals so that they can participate and express themselves more effectively and challenge dominant power structures. These values and goals are closely associated with specific processes and methods of communication. Free speech and access to information constitute a well-established value orientation in communication scholarship and are related to voice and empowerment. Access to information is a form of empowerment; moreover, it facilitates critical evaluation and effective decision making. Free speech and access to information often are framed as rights and, like empowerment, are associated with specific processes and structures of communication. Informed consent and the First Amendment role of the media both follow this larger value tradition.

A Research Agenda for Applied Communication Ethics

Although much work has been done in communication ethics, this work is disjointed and isolated by general contexts of communication and by specific issues, such as health-care privacy, organizational codes of ethics, or access to information through media. Moreover, applied communication scholars are only beginning to identify shared ethical issues (e.g., privacy issues) that cut across these contexts. One immediate goal is to connect those areas of inquiry that share an ethical orientation to applied communication scholarship.

Articulating a larger research agenda for applied communication ethics is complicated by the complexity and range of ethical issues and by the lack of consensus regarding what values and standards should be prominent in various contexts. One outcome of the trend toward greater diversity, inclusion, and voice in professional and organizational contexts has been a greater diversity of values, which has made the resulting conversations both more inclusive and complex. There is not always clear consensus, for example, as to what constitutes a good or ethical consequence. In addition, ethics, values, and standards are sensitive areas for investigation that sometimes carry powerful stigmas and sanctions. Many research participants, organizations, and investigators may not be willing to openly discuss these issues. Researchers often must rely on the artifacts of ethics, including decisions, justifications, and documentation of formal values, such as codes of ethics and content-analytical (see Query et al., this volume) or critical methods. Some investigations have employed survey data to assess how members of particular professional communities perceive ethics. Fewer investigations, however, have gone beyond descriptive, critical, or exploratory approaches. These difficulties continue to provide fruitful areas for the study of applied communication ethics.

Another area for future research concerns an expanded understanding of the ethical traditions and standards that are germane to various forms and contexts of applied communication. This understanding includes the value traditions of empowerment and voice, free speech and access to information, and the social justice orientation. All three domains of communication described here include issues of free speech and access to information as important values, but questions remain about how applied communication research can further these values.

In addition, within most applied and professional contexts of communication, core values compete with one another in fundamental ways—one of the defining complexities of applied ethics. Few efforts have been made to understand how these conflicts are managed through communication processes, such as ethics codes. In fact, beyond investigations of whistleblowing, little is known about how individuals use communication to resolve issues of ethics in their professional/organizational life. This represents another significant deficiency in the current understanding of ethics and applied communication scholarship.

Concerns also surround the proposition that social justice should be a guiding ethic in applied communication. This orientation, however, first needs to be clarified more specifically with regard to how applied communication research can promote social justice. Applied communication scholarship, for example, is well positioned to help develop information sources and communication systems that nontraditional groups can use to empower themselves. In addition, applied communication in the form of social influence has the potential to address social wrongs.

Another area of inquiry concerns how applied communication research and other practices can lead to good or ethical consequences. The studies we reviewed suggest at least two modes. First, research results or outcomes can inform or lead to empowerment of communities and audiences in ethically appealing ways. For instance, an investigation into the effectiveness of health communication can result in better understanding of how to reach disempowered groups with health messages, meaning that research results may help indirectly to produce an ethically appealing outcome. Second, the research project itself can be directly structured around ethically appealing questions and issues, which is a departure from more traditional approaches to research and where a social justice orientation most often comes into play. Some of the studies reviewed here, for instance, involved communication programs that were designed to create positive social change, and the researchers then investigated the effectiveness of those efforts. Other scholars have adopted an explicit advocacy stance within their research, targeted toward some larger issues that they see as unethical or unjust.

In addition, scholars should focus on applied communicative practices that lead to negative consequences. Some observers have gone as far as suggesting that applied scholars focus explicitly on the structural impediments to ethical conduct (Stewart, 2001). Thus, investigation of unethical communication and the factors that foster such communication can further this research agenda. Some studies, for example, have investigated the role of culture and ethical behavior (Waters & Bird, 1987); other studies have suggested that an equivocal context may create unethical communicative practices (Seeger & Ulmer, 2003). Moral development also has been examined as a factor in unethical professional communication (Coleman & Wilkins, 2002).

An additional area for research involves expanding the ethical standards for applied communication research. Beyond the provisions of IRBs and considerations of social justice, what research methods and procedures are most appropriate for achieving ethical applied communication research? Do some methods and procedures, for instance, better promote voice and empowerment?

Some of the studies examined here treated people as coresearchers by involving them in the design of projects and shifting ownership of the data to them. Are there other ways in which research projects can be constructed so that research participants are treated in ethically appealing ways? One of the clearest needs for ethical orientations to applied communication research concerns the research process itself. As described earlier, many of the IRB provisions, such as informed consent, essentially are communication phenomena. Scholars interested in applied communication ethics, therefore, should turn their attention to the informed consent process to examine questions of efficacy, clarify how informed consent functions with intercultural audiences or with audiences that have a limited capacity to understand research, and investigate forms of persuasion that influence an informed consent decision (Sharf, 1999).

A final issue concerns how fully the applied communication field should focus on questions of good consequences. Should all applied communication scholars consider ethical issues, beyond the IRB review, in undertaking research? To what degree do applied scholars have a moral obligation to seek good consequences beyond acquiring new knowledge? For example, are practical applications of research leading to desirable outcomes an essential component of ethical applied communication scholarship? Should the reporting of anticipated ethical consequences be part of a published applied communication report? What are the most appropriate ways to stimulate the moral imagination of applied communication scholars? How can conversations about the ethical consequences of applied communication be encouraged? We noted earlier that an emphasis on outcomes, strategies, and solutions enhances the ethical significance faced by applied communication scholars. Given this stance, questions of value and ethics should be central to all aspects of applied communication inquiry.

Conclusion

We began this review by noting that communication scholars, particularly those interested in applied issues, have been slow to embrace research questions related to ethics. Existing research is diverse and poorly integrated around larger themes of communication ethics. Although important value traditions have been established in the larger communication field, these have not always been carried forward in applied communication research (e.g., there are few examples of applied communication research with a social justice orientation). Moreover, many scholars and journal editors may not view such research as meeting established standards for rigorous scholarship. This scarcity of research exists despite almost universal agreement that ethics are central to communication processes and practices, and that applied communication research carries a particularly salient moral obligation. Although the lack of research is problematic, it also suggests opportunities for applied communication scholars. An applied orientation to issues of communication ethics not only has the potential to fill significant gaps in understanding how communication helps to solve problems and create desirable outcomes but, ultimately, also will elevate the moral standards of applied communication theory, research, and practice.

Notes

1. Even a cursory review of ethics and philosophy is beyond the scope of this chapter. This description, however, presents a very small sample of some major themes in ethics.
2. The distinction between theoretical and applied ethics is a matter of emphasis. In some ways, all ethicists are interested in applied issues because they are concerned with judgments of human behavior. The applied ethics orientation, as described here, emphasizes more limited and parochial contexts for ethics rather than develops broad theories that have universal or near-universal application.
3. A journalism colleague of one of us was told by an IRB member that he must receive IRB approval for every story he wrote and have all sources provide written informed consent before they could be quoted. When confronted with a copy of the First Amendment, the IRB representative backed down.

References

Adelman, M. B., & Frey, L. R. (1994). The pilgrim must embark: Creating and sustaining community in a residential facility for people with AIDS. In L. R. Frey (Ed.), *Group communication in context: Studies of natural groups* (pp. 3–22). Hillsdale, NJ: Erlbaum.

Adelman, M. B., & Frey, L. R. (1997). *The fragile community: Living together with AIDS.* Mahwah, NJ: Erlbaum.

American Psychological Association. (2002). *Ethical principles of psychologists and code of conduct.* Retrieved November 25, 2005, from http://www.apa.org/ethics/code2002.html

American Society of Newspaper Editors. (2002, August 28). *ASNE statement of principles.* Retrieved September 5, 2004, from http://www.asne.org/index.cfm?id=888

Anderson, R., Dardenne, R., & Killenberg, G. M. (1994). *The conversation of journalism: Communication, community, and news.* Westport, CT: Praeger.

Arneson, P. (Ed.). (2007). *Exploring communication ethics: Interviews with influential scholars in the field.* New York: Peter Lang.

Artz, L. (1998). African Americans and higher education: An exigence in need of applied communication. *Journal of Applied Communication Research, 26,* 210–231.

Ashcraft, A. S., & Byers, J. F. (2004). The role of institutional review boards. *Critical Care Nurse, 24*(3), 12.

Association for Practical and Professional Ethics. (2003). *Why an association for practical and professional ethics?* Retrieved October 20, 2003, from http://www.indiana.edu/~appe/aims. html

Barton, E. (2007). Situating end-of-life decision making in a hybrid ethical frame. *Communication & Medicine, 4,* 131–140.

Belsey, A., & Chadwick, R. (Eds.). (1992). *Ethical issues in journalism and the media.* New York: Routledge.

Biagi, S., & Kern-Foxworth, M. (1997). *Facing difference: Race, gender, and mass media.* Thousand Oaks, CA: Pine Forge Press.

Boeyink, D. E. (1998). Codes and culture at *The Courier-Journal:* Complexity in ethical decision making. *Journal of Mass Media Ethics, 13,* 165–182.

Böhme, G. (2001). *Ethics in context: The art of dealing with serious questions* (E. Jephcott, Trans.). Malden, MA: Blackwell.

Botan, C. (1996). Communication work and electronic surveillance: A model for predicting panoptic effects. *Communication Monographs, 63,* 293–313.

Boyd, J. (2000). Actional legitimacy: No crisis necessary. *Journal of Public Relations Research, 12,* 341–353.

Bracci, S. L. (2001). Managing health care in Oregon: The search for a civic bioethics. *Journal of Applied Communication Research, 29,* 171–194.

Bracci, S. L. (2002). Bioethics: A "new" prudence for an emergent paradigm? *Argumentation and Advocacy, 38,* 151–168.

Brann, M., & Mattson, M. (2004). Toward a typology of confidentiality breaches in health care communication: An ethic of care analysis of provider practices and patient perceptions. *Health Communication, 16,* 229–251.

Browning, L. D. (1982). The ethics of intervention: A communication consultant's apology. *Journal of Applied Communications Research, 10,* 101–116.

Buchholz, R. A. (1990). The evolution of corporate responsibility. In P. Masden & J. M. Shafritz (Eds.), *Essentials of business ethics* (pp. 298–311). New York: Meridian.

Buzzanell, P. M. (1994). Gaining a voice: Feminist organizational communication theorizing. *Management Communication Quarterly, 7,* 339–383.

Callahan, D., & Jennings, B. (2002). Ethics and public health: Forging a strong relationship. *American Journal of Public Health, 92,* 169–176.

Cheney, G. (1999). *Values at work: Employee participation meets market pressure at Mondragón.* Ithaca, NY: Cornell University Press.

Cheney, G. (2008). Encountering the ethics of engaged scholarship. *Journal of Applied Communication Research, 36,* 281–288.

Cheney, G., & Christensen, L. T. (2001). Organizational identity: Linkages between internal and external communication. In F. M. Jablin & L. L. Putnam (Eds.), *The new handbook of organizational communication: Advances in theory, research, and methods* (pp. 231–269). Thousand Oaks, CA: Sage.

Cheney, G., Straub, J., Speirs-Glebe, L., Stohl, C., deGooyer, D., Whalen, S., et al. (1998). Democracy, participation, and communication at work: A multidisciplinary review. In M. E. Roloff (Ed.), *Communication yearbook* (Vol. 21, pp. 35–91). Thousand Oaks, CA: Sage.

Childers, D. (1988). Medical practices in AIDS coverage and a model for ethical reporting on AIDS victims. *Journal of Mass Media Ethics, 3*(2), 60–65.

Christians, C. G. (2008). Media ethics in education. *Journalism and Communication Monographs, 9,* 179–221.

Christians, C. G., Rotzoll, K. B., & Fackler, M. (1991). *Media ethics: Cases and moral reasoning* (3rd ed.). New York: Longman.

Cline, R. J., & Haynes, K. M. (2001). Consumer health information seeking on the Internet: The state of the art. *Health Education Research, 16,* 671–692.

Cline, R. J. W., & Young, H. N. (2004). Marketing drugs, marketing health care relationships: A content analysis of visual cues in direct-to-consumer prescription drug advertising. *Health Communication, 16,* 131–157.

Coleman, R., & Wilkins, L. (2002). Searching for the ethical journalist: An exploratory study of the moral development of news workers. *Journal of Mass Media Ethics, 17,* 209–225.

Conquergood, D. (1995). Between rigor and relevance: Rethinking applied communication. In K. N. Cissna (Ed.), *Applied communication in the 21st century* (pp. 97–104). Mahwah, NJ: Erlbaum.

Conrad, C. (1993). Introduction: The ethical nexus. In C. Conrad (Ed.), *The ethical nexus* (pp. 1–4). Norwood, NJ: Ablex.

Crabtree, R. D. (1998). Mutual empowerment in cross-cultural participatory development and service learning: Lessons in communication and social justice from projects in El Salvador and Nicaragua. *Journal of Applied Communication Research, 26,* 182–209.

Curtin, P. A., & Boynton, L. A. (2001). Ethics in public relations: Theory and practice. In R. L. Heath (Ed.), *Handbook of public relations* (pp. 411–422). Thousand Oaks, CA: Sage.

Daugherty, E. L. (2001) Public relations and social responsibility. In R. L. Heath (Ed.), *Handbook of public relations* (pp. 389–402). Thousand Oaks, CA: Sage.

Day, L. A. (2000). *Ethics in media communications: Cases and controversies* (3rd ed.). Belmont, CA: Wadsworth.

Deetz, S. A. (1992). *Democracy in an age of corporate colonization: Developments in communication and the politics of everyday life.* Albany: State University of New York Press.

Department of Health and Human Services, National Institutes of Health Office for Protection from Research Risks. (2001). *Title 45 Code of Federal Regulations.* Washington, DC: Author.

Dougherty, D. S., & Kramer, M. W. (2005). Special issue introduction: A rationale for scholarly examination of institutional review boards: A case study. *Journal of Applied Communication Research, 33,* 183–188.

Dutta-Bergman, M. J. (2005). Theory and practice in health communication campaigns: A critical interrogation. *Health Communication, 18,* 103–122.

Dysart-Gale, D. (2005) Communication models, professionalization, and the work of medical interpreters. *Health Communication, 17,* 91–103.

Elliott, D. (Ed.). (1986). *Responsible journalism.* Beverly Hills, CA: Sage.

Entman, R. M. (1989). *Democracy without citizens: Media and the decay of American politics.* New York: Oxford University Press.

Finnegan, J. R., Jr., Alexander, D., Rightmyer, J., Estabrook, B., Gloe, B., Voss, M., et al. (2001). Using the Web to assist communities in public health campaign planning: A case study of the REACT project. In R. E. Rice & J. E. Katz (Eds.), *The Internet and health communication: Experiences and expectations* (pp. 147–166). Thousand Oaks, CA: Sage.

Ford, N., Odallo, D., & Chorlton, R. (2003). Communication from a human rights perspective: Responding to the HIV/AIDS pandemic in Eastern and Southern Africa: A working paper for use in HIV and AIDS programmes. *Journal of Health Communication, 8,* 599–612.

Foster, E. (2006). *Communicating at the end of life: Finding magic in the mundane.* Mahwah, NJ: Erlbaum.

Frankel, M. S. (1989). Professional codes: Why, how, and with what input? *Journal of Business Ethics, 8,* 109–115.

Frey, L. R. (Ed.). (1998a). Communication and social justice research [Special issue]. *Journal of Applied Communication Research, 26*(2).

Frey, L. R. (1998b). Communication and social justice research: Truth, justice, and the applied communication way. *Journal of Applied Communication Research, 26,* 155–164.

Frey, L. R., & Carragee, K. M. (2007). Introduction: Communication activism as engaged scholarship. In L. R. Frey & K. M. Carragee (Eds.), *Communication activism* (2 Vols., pp. 1–64). Cresskill, NJ: Hampton Press.

Frey, L. R., Pearce, W. B., Pollock, M. A., Artz, L., & Murphy, B. A. O. (1996). Looking for justice in all the wrong places: On a communication approach to social justice. *Communication Studies, 46,* 110–127.

Gadamer, H.-G. (1975). *Truth and method* (G. Barden & J. Cumming, Trans. & Eds.). New York: Seabury Press.

Gagnon, J. H. (1992). Epidemics and researchers: AIDS and the practice of social studies. In G. Herdt & S. Lindenbaum (Eds.), *The time of AIDS: Social analysis, theory, and method* (pp. 27–40). Newbury Park, CA: Sage.

Gerbner, G. (1999). Why the cultural environmental movement? In R. M. Baird, W. E. Loges, & S. E. Rosenbaum (Eds.), *The media & morality* (pp. 344–353). Amherst, NY: Prometheus Books.

Gilligan, C. (1982). *In a different voice: Psychological theory and women's development*. Cambridge, MA: Harvard University Press.

Glasser, T. L. (Ed.). (1999). *The idea of public journalism*. New York: Guilford Press.

Gordan, A. D., & Kittross, J. M. (1999). *Controversies in media ethics* (2nd ed.). New York: Longman.

Gorden, W. I., Infante, D. A., Wilson, L., & Clarke, C. (1984). Rationale and development of an employee rights scale. In H. Ewbank (Ed.), *Free speech yearbook* (Vol. 23, pp. 66–79). Annandale, VA: Speech Communication Association.

Guttman, N. (2003). Ethics in health communication interventions. In T. L. Thompson, A. M. Dorsey, K. I. Miller, & R. Parrott (Eds.), *Handbook of health communication* (pp. 651–679). Mahwah, NJ: Erlbaum.

Guttman, N., & Ressler, W. H. (2001). On being responsible: Ethical issues in appeals to personal responsibility in health campaigns. *Journal of Health Communication, 6,* 117–136.

Habermas, J. (1984). *The theory of communicative action: Reason and the rationalization of society* (T. A. McCarthy, Trans.). Boston: Beacon Press.

Hamilton, A. (2005). The development and operation of IRBs: Medical regulations and social science. *Journal of Applied Communication Research, 33,* 189–203.

Hanson, G. (2002). Learning journalism ethics: The classroom versus the real world. *Journal of Mass Media Ethics, 17,* 235–247.

Harman, G., & Thomson, J. J. (1996). *Moral relativism and moral objectivity*. Cambridge, MA: Blackwell.

Harrison, T. M. (1982). Toward an ethical framework for communication consulting. *Journal of Applied Communications Research, 10,* 87–100.

Harter, L. M., Stephens, R. J., & Japp, P. M. (2000). President Clinton's apology for the Tuskegee syphilis experiment: A narrative of remembrance, redefinition, and reconciliation. *Howard Journal of Communications, 11,* 19–34.

Hartnett, S. (1998). Lincoln and Douglas meet the abolitionist David Walker as prisoners debate slavery: Empowering education, applied communication, and social justice. *Journal of Applied Communication Research, 26,* 232–253.

Hindman, E. B. (2005). Jayson Blair, *The New York Times*, and paradigm repair. *Journal of Communication, 55,* 225–241.

Jaksa, J. A., & Pritchard, M. S. (1988). *Communication ethics: Methods of analysis*. Belmont, CA: Wadsworth.

Jaksa, J. A., & Pritchard, M. S. (Eds.). (1996). *Responsible communication: Ethical issues in business, industry, and the professions*. Cresskill, NJ: Hampton Press.

Johannesen, R. L. (2002). *Ethics in human communication* (5th ed.). Prospect Heights, IL: Waveland Press.

Johnson, C. E. (2005). *Meeting the ethical challenges of leadership: Casting light or shadow* (2nd ed.). Thousand Oaks, CA: Sage.

Johnson, J. L., Bootorff, J. L., Browne, A. J., Grewal, S., Hilton, B. A., & Clarke, H. (2004). Othering and being othered in the context of health care services. *Health Communication, 16,* 253–271.

Johnson, M., & Babcock, W. A. (1999). Toward a moral approach to Megan's law. *Journal of Mass Media Ethics, 14,* 133–146.

Jovanovic, S., & Wood, R. V. (2006). Communication ethics and ethical culture: A study of the ethics initiative in Denver city government. *Journal of Applied Communication Research, 34,* 386–405.

Kassing, J. W. (1997). Articulating, antagonizing, and displacing: A model of employee dissent. *Communication Studies, 48,* 311–332.

Keränen, L. (2007). "Cause someday we all die": Rhetoric, agency, and the case of the "patient" preferences worksheet. *Quarterly Journal of Speech*, 93, 179–210.

Kerr, R. L. (2003). Is what's good for General Motors good for the First Amendment? Corporate media concentration's "dagger at the throat" of the press clause. In J. Harper & T. Yantek (Eds.), *Media, profit, and politics: Competing priorities in an open society* (pp. 174–196). Kent, OH: Kent State University Press.

Kopelman, L. M., & Murphy, T. F. (2004). Ethical concerns about federal approval of risky pediatric studies. *Pediatrics*, 113, 1783–1789.

Kramer, M. W., & Dougherty, R. W. (Eds.). (2005). Communication research and institutional review boards [Special issue]. *Journal of Applied Communication Research*, 33(3).

Lake, J. B. (1991). Of crime and consequence: Should newspapers report rape complainants' names? *Journal of Mass Media Ethics*, 6, 106–119.

Lauzen, M. M. (2005). Recognition and respect revisited: Portrayals of age and gender in prime-time television. *Mass Communication & Society*, 8, 241–256.

Lawson-Borders, G. (2005). *Media organizations and convergence: Case studies of media convergence pioneers*. Mahwah, NJ: Erlbaum.

Levy, N. (2002). *Moral relativism: A short introduction*. Oxford, UK: Oneworld.

Lieberman, D. A. (2001). Using interactive media in communication campaigns for children and adolescents. In R. E. Rice & C. K. Atkin (Eds.), *Public communication campaigns* (3rd ed., pp. 373–388). Thousand Oaks, CA: Sage.

MacQueen, K. M., & Buehler, J. W. (2004). Ethics, practice, and research in public health. *American Journal of Public Health*, 94, 928–931.

Marshall, P. A. (2003). Human subjects protections, institutional review boards, and cultural anthropological research. *Anthropological Quarterly*, 76, 269–285.

Mattson, M., & Buzzanell, P. M. (1999). Traditional and feminist organizational communication ethical analyses of messages and issues surrounding an actual job loss. *Journal of Applied Communication Research*, 27, 49–72.

Mattson, M., & Roberts, F. (2001). Overcoming truth telling as an obstacle to initiating safer sex: Clients and health practitioners planning deception during HIV test counseling. *Health Communication*, 13, 343–362.

May, S. (Ed.). (2006). *Case studies in organizational communication: Ethical perspectives and practices*. Thousand Oaks, CA: Sage.

May, S. K., & Zorn, T. E. (Eds.). (2003). Communication and corporate social responsibility [Special forum]. *Management Communication Quarterly*, 16, 595–632.

McCabe, D. L., Trevino, L. K., & Butterfield, K. D. (1996). The influence of collegiate and corporate codes of conduct on ethics-related behavior in the workplace. *Business Ethics Quarterly*, 6, 461–476.

Meisenbach, R. J. (2006). Habermas's discourse ethics and principle of universalization as a moral framework for organizational communication. *Management Communication Quarterly*, 20, 39–62.

Meyer, P. (1987). *Ethical journalism: A guide for students, practitioners, and consumers*. New York: Longman.

Montgomery, D., Wiseman, D. W., & DeCaro, P. (2001). Toward a code of ethics for organizational communication professionals: A working proposal. *American Communication Journal*, 5(1). Retrieved June 15, 2005, from http://www.acjournal.org/holdings/vol5/iss1/special/montgomery.htm

Mumby, D. K. (1988). *Communication and power in organizations: Discourse, ideology, and domination*. Norwood, NJ: Ablex.

Mumby, D. K. (1996). Feminism, postmodernism, and organizational communication studied: A critical reading. *Management Communication Quarterly*, 9, 259–295.

Mumby, D. K., & Putnam. L. L. (1992). The politics of emotion: A feminist reading of bounded rationality. *Academy of Management Review*, 17, 465–486.

National Communication Association. (1999). *NCA credo for ethical communication*. Retrieved September 1, 2004, from http://www.natcom.org/policies/External/EthicalComm.htm

Near, J. P., & Miceli, M. P. (1986). Retaliation against whistleblowing: Predictors and effects. *Journal of Applied Psychology, 71,* 137–145.

Nicotera, A, M., & Cushman, D. P. (1992). Organizational ethics: A within-organization view. *Journal of Applied Communication Research, 20,* 437–462.

Nielsen, T. R. (1974). *Ethics of speech communication* (2nd ed.). Indianapolis, IN: Bobbs-Merrill.

Noddings, N. (1984). *Caring: A feminine approach to ethics & moral education.* Berkeley: University of California Press.

Oliver, P. (2003). *The student's guide to research ethics.* Philadelphia: Open University Press.

Olufowote, J. O. (2008). A structurational analysis of informed consent to treatment: Social evolution, contradiction, and reproductions in medical practice. *Health Communication, 23,* 292–303.

Overbeck, W. (2008). *Major principles of media law* (2009 ed.). Belmont, CA: Wadsworth.

Ozwawa, T. (2004). *What is applied ethics? The activities of the Centre for Applied Ethics of University of British Columbia.* Retrieved August 10, 2004, from http://www.kochi-u.ac.jp/~ozawa/what-text.html

Parsons, P. R., & Smith, W. E. (1988). Budd Dwyer: A case in newsroom decision making. *Journal of Mass Media Ethics, 3,* 84–94.

Patterson, M. J., & Urbanski, S. (2006). What Jayson Blair and Janet Cooke say about the press and the erosion of public trust. *Journalism Studies, 7,* 828–850.

Patterson, P., & Wilkins, L. (Eds.). (2001). *Media ethics: Issues & cases* (4th ed.). Boston: McGraw-Hill.

Pearce, W. B. (1998). On putting social justice in the discipline of communication and putting enriched concepts of communication in social justice research and practice. *Journal of Applied Communication Research, 26,* 272–278.

Petronio, S. (2002). *Boundaries of privacy: Dialectics of disclosure.* Albany: State University of New York Press.

Philips, D. F. (2000). IRBs search for answers and support during a time of institutional change. *Journal of the American Medical Association, 283,* 729–733.

Pierce, M. A., & Henry, J. W. (1996). Computer ethics: The role of personal, informal, and formal codes. *Journal of Business Ethics, 15,* 425–437.

Planalp, S., & Trost, M. R. (2008). Communication issues at the end of life: Reports from hospice volunteers. *Health Communication, 23,* 222–233.

Pribble, P. T. (1990). Making an ethical commitment: A rhetorical case study of organizational socialization. *Communication Quarterly, 38,* 255–267.

Pritchard, I. A. (2002). Travelers and trolls: Practitioner research and institutional review boards. *Educational Researcher, 31*(2), 3–13.

Putnam, L. L. (1982). Paradigms for organizational communication research: An overview and synthesis. *Western Journal of Speech Communication, 46,* 192–206.

Putnam, L. L., & Fairhurst, G. T. (2001). Discourse analysis in organizations: Issues and concerns. In F. M. Jablin & L. L. Putnam (Eds.), *The new handbook of organizational communication: Advances in theory, research, and methods* (pp. 78–136). Thousand Oaks, CA: Sage.

Rao, S., & Lee, A. T. (2005). Globalizing media ethics? An assessment of universal ethics among international political journalists. *Journal of Mass Media Ethics, 20,* 99–120.

Ratzan, S. C. (1994). Editor's introduction: Communication—The key to a healthier tomorrow. *American Behavioral Scientist, 38,* 202–207.

Ratzan, S. G., Payne, J. G., & Bishop, C. (1996). The status and scope of health communication. *Journal of Health Communication, 1,* 25–41.

Rawls, J. (1999). *A theory of justice* (Rev. ed.). Cambridge, MA: Belknap Press.

Redding, C. (1996). Ethics and the study of organizational communication: When will we wake up? In J. A. Jaksa & M. S. Pritchard (Eds.), *Responsible communication: Ethical issues in business, industry, and the professions* (pp. 17–40). Cresskill, NJ: Hampton Press.

Rosenthal, D. M., & Shehadi, F. (Eds.). (1988). *Applied ethics and ethical theory.* Salt Lake City: University of Utah Press.

Ryan, C., Carragee, K. M., & Meinhofer, W. (2001). Theory into practice: Framing, the news media, and collective action. *Journal of Broadcasting and Electronic Media, 45,* 175–182.

Ryan, C., Carragee, K. M., & Schwerner, C. (1998). Media, movements and the search for social justice. *Journal of Applied Communication Research, 26,* 165–181.

Schwartz, M. (2001). The nature and relationship between corporate codes of ethics and behaviour. *Journal of Business Ethics, 31,* 247–262.

Schwartz, M. (2002). A code of ethics for corporate code of ethics. *Journal of Business Ethics, 41,* 27–43.

Seeger, M. W. (1986). Institutional affiliation and free speech. In S. Smith (Ed.), *Free speech yearbook* (Vol. 25, pp. 11–21). Annandale, VA: Speech Communication Association.

Seeger, M. W. (1997). *Ethics and organizational communication.* Cresskill, NJ: Hampton Press.

Seeger, M. W. (2003). Organizational communication ethics: Directions for critical inquiry and application. In D. Tourish & O. Hargie (Eds.), *Key issues in organizational communication* (pp. 220–234). New York: Routledge.

Seeger, M. W., & Ulmer, R. R. (2003). Explaining Enron: Communication and responsible leadership. *Management Communication Quarterly, 17,* 58–84.

Seigel, P. (2002). *Communication law in America.* Boston: Allyn & Bacon.

Sharav, V. H. (2004). Conflicts of interest in biomedical research harm children with and without disabilities. *Journal of Disability Policy Studies, 15,* 50–59.

Sharf, B. (1999). The present and future of health communication scholarship: Overlooked opportunities. *Health Communication, 11,* 195–200.

Sieber, J. E. (1992). *Planning ethically responsible research: A guide for students and internal review boards.* Newbury Park, CA: Sage.

Simms, R. R., & Brinkman, J. (2002). Leaders as moral role models: The case of John Gutfreund at Salomon Brothers. *Journal of Business Ethics, 35,* 327–339.

Simon, C. M., Zyzanski, S. J., Durran, E., Jimenez, X., & Kodish, E. D. (2006). Interpreter accuracy and informed consent among Spanish-speaking families with cancer. *Journal of Health Communication, 11,* 509–522.

Singer, P. (Ed.). (1986). *Applied ethics.* New York: Oxford University Press.

Singhal, A., & Rogers, E. M. (2001). The entertainment–education strategy in communication campaigns. In R. E. Rice & C. K. Atkin (Eds.), *Public communication campaigns* (3rd ed., pp. 343–356). Thousand Oaks, CA: Sage.

Society of Professional Journalists. (2004). *Code of ethics.* Retrieved August 22, 2004, from http://www.spj.org/ethics_code.asp

Solomon, M. (1985). The rhetoric of dehumanization: An analysis of medical reports of the Tuskegee syphilis project. *Western Journal of Speech Communication, 49,* 233–247.

Sparks, R., Young, M. L., & Darnell, S. (2006). Convergence, corporate restructuring, and Canadian online news, 2000–2003. *Canadian Journal of Communication, 31,* 391–423.

Stevens, B. (1994). An analysis of corporate ethical code studies: "Where do we go from here?" *Journal of Business Ethics, 13,* 63–69.

Stewart, L. P. (2001). The importance of addressing issues of applied ethics for communication scholars and consultants. *American Communication Journal, 5*(1). Retrieved August 22, 2004, from http://www.acjournal.org/holdings/vol5/iss1/special/stewart.htm

Swartz, O. (1997). *Conducting socially responsible research: Critical theory, neo-pragmatism, and rhetorical inquiry.* Thousand Oaks, CA: Sage.

Thomas, J. C., Sage, M., Dillenberg, J., & Guillory, V. J. (2002). A code of ethics for public health. *American Journal of Public Health, 92,* 1057–1059.

Tompkins, P. S. (2003). Truth, trust, and telepresence. *Journal of Mass Media Ethics, 18,* 194–212.

Varallo, S. M., Ray, E. B., & Ellis, B. H. (1998). Speaking of incest: The research interview as social justice. *Journal of Applied Communication Research, 26,* 254–271.

Victor, B., & Cullen, J. B. (1988). The organizational basis of ethical work climates. *Administrative Science Quarterly, 33,* 101–125.

Ward, S. J. A. (2005). Philosophical foundations for global journalism ethics. *Journal of Mass Media Ethics, 20,* 3–21.

Wasserman, H. (2006). Globalized values and postcolonial responses: South African perspectives on normative media ethics. *Gazette, 68,* 71–91.

Wasserman, H., & Rao, S. (2008). The glocalization of journalism ethics. *Journalism, 9,* 163–181.

Waters, J. A., & Bird, F. (1987). The moral dimensions of organizational culture. *Journal of Business Ethics, 6,* 15–22.

Wendler, D., Emanuel, E. J., & Lie, R. K. (2004). The standard of care debate: Can research in developing countries be both ethical and responsive to those countries' health needs? *American Journal of Public Health, 94,* 923–928.

Wendler, D., & Miller, F. G. (2004). Deception in the pursuit of science. *Archives of Internal Medicine, 164,* 597–600.

Whitehouse, U., & McPherson, J. B. (2002). Media ethics textbook case studies need new actors and new issues. *Journal of Mass Media Ethics, 17,* 226–234.

Williams, S. L., & Sellnow, T. L. (1998). Chilling effect and significant choice: A case study of the National Cancer Institute and the screening mammography guideline controversy. In M. W. Seeger (Ed.), *Free speech yearbook* (Vol. 36, pp. 118–133). Washington, DC: National Communication Association.

Winkler, E. R., & Coombs, J. R. (Eds.). (1993). *Applied ethics: A reader.* Cambridge, MA: Blackwell.

Wood, J. T. (1996). Social justice research: Alive and well in the communication field. *Communication Studies, 47,* 128–134.

Young, A. J., & Rodriguez, K. L. (2006). The role of narrative in discussing end-of-life care: Eliciting values and goals from text, context, and subtext. *Health Communication, 19,* 49–59.

Zeldes, G. A., & Fico, F. (2005). Race and gender: An analysis of sources and reporters in the networks' coverage of the 2000 presidential campaign. *Mass Communication & Society, 8,* 373–385.

Part IV

Contexts of Applied Communication Research

13 Family as Agency of Potential

Toward a Positive Ontology of Applied Family Communication Theory and Research

Thomas J. Socha
Old Dominion University

"Families" and "family relationships," however defined, are foundational communication contexts. In families and family relationships, many communication firsts occur: first nonverbal messages, verbal messages, relational communication episodes, group communication episodes, exposure to mediated communication, and other communicative practices. Beyond initial experiences, the influence of families and family relationships on a person's communication stretches across the entire life span. Among family members, we experience many of life's most uplifting, validating, and human moments: celebrations of births, holidays, and anniversaries; episodes of deep connection; moments of triumph; and many more. Conversely, family members also weather together some of life's most depressing, damaging, and inhuman moments: abuse (physical and emotional), crime, death, illness, mistreatment, poverty, unemployment, and many others, some at the hands of fellow family members. For better or worse, family and family relationships are relational epicenters of daily and long-term human experience.

From the first publications about family communication, pioneering scholars recognized the potential of communication as a force for good and for ill, and, therefore, firmly rooted family communication scholarship in applied, as well as theoretical, soil. Bochner's (1976) landmark review of the literature—the first family communication article published in a communication journal—cited many marital and family therapists, including Jackson (1965), Satir (1967), and Watzlawick, Beavin, and Jackson (1967), all of whom recognized the significance of communication to the psychological well-being of family members. A few years later, Galvin and Brommel's (1982), *Family Communication: Cohesion and Change* (the communication discipline's first textbook on that topic), embedded the roots of family communication even deeper in applied soil. As Galvin and Brommel explained:

> Within these pages we will present a framework for examining communication within families. By the end of the text you should be able to *apply* this model to an unknown family and eventually understand that family as a communication system. We also hope that you will *apply* what you learn to your own family or to the family you eventually form, in order to *improve* communication among family members. (p. 2; italics added)

In the time since those early publications, family communication researchers have continued to labor on three interrelated fronts, advancing: (1) theoretical understanding of communication in families and family relationships, (2) applied understanding of the role of communication in managing problems in families and family relationships, and (3) family communication education. Stamp's (2004) recent review and analysis of the family communication literature, resulting in a grounded theory model of family life, also reinforced the centrality of communication in the many sides of everyday family life.

Scores of theoretical and applied family communication studies continue to appear in journals in the communication field and beyond. In 2000, the *Journal of Family Communication* began publishing theoretical and applied research studies about family communication, as well as commentaries written by prominent practitioners and scholars from allied fields, including, for example, a commentary about the need for parental mediation of children's home television viewing written by the late "Mister Rogers" (Rogers, 2001).

Along with journal articles, many scholarly books written or edited by communication researchers have showcased theoretical and applied work on marital communication (e.g., Fitzpatrick, 1988), parent–child communication (e.g., Socha & Stamp, 1995), communication in family units and family relationships (e.g., Fitzpatrick & Vangelisti, 1995), and family communication and ethnic culture (Socha & Diggs, 1999a). The ever-widening scope of this work was highlighted in the *Handbook of Family Communication* (Vangelisti, 2004) and in *The Family Communication Sourcebook* (Turner & West, 2006a).

Alongside the scholarly literature, at least nine other textbooks, some in multiple editions, have emerged since Galvin and Brommel's (1982) first edition (Arliss, 1993; Arnold, 2008; Beebe & Masterson, 1986; Galvin, Bylund, & Brommel, 2008; Le Poire, 2006; Noller & Fitzpatrick, 1993; Pearson, 1989; Turner & West, 2006b; Yerby, Buerkel-Rothfuss, & Bochner, 1995), and more undoubtedly are on the horizon. Today, these textbooks rely more on information gleaned from communication publications and far less on research from allied fields, as previously was the case. Moreover, as is true in many areas of the communication field, these textbooks represent a primary vehicle for dissemination of findings obtained from family communication research (applied and theoretical) to the public (i.e., college students).

This chapter takes stock of the potential of applied family communication as a force for promoting positive family life by critically reviewing past work and offering a scaffold on which future work might be built. Specifically, I provide a critical review of applied scholarship that seeks to understand the role of communication in managing family problems or problematic relationships between and among family members, family relationships, family units or groups, and families and societal institutions (such as government, education, and medicine). Based on this review, and drawing on recent work from the emerging area of positive psychology (e.g., Csikszentmihalyi & Csikszentmihalyi, 2006; Lopez, 2009; Seligman & Csikszentmihalyi, 2000; Seligman, Steen, Park, & Peterson, 2005; Snyder, 2000; Snyder & Lopez, 2005, 2007) that turns away from fixing problems after they occur toward prevention, empowerment, and other positive processes and outcomes, I argue that applied family communication research needs to widen its ontological assumptions beyond "a preoccupation...with repairing the worst things in life to also building the best qualities in life" (Seligman, 2002, p. 3). Specifically, scholars should develop a positive, applied approach that focuses on the role of communication in the development of family potentialities by investigating family communication and positive subjective experiences, positive personal traits, and positive relational and group qualities, in addition to the role of family communication in managing (and preventing) problems. I conclude the chapter with recommendations for this type of future research.

A Review of Applied Family Communication Literature

Literature reviews serve as scaffolds on which future research studies stand. This section seeks to widen and extend the scaffold for future scholarship by reviewing studies of "applied" family communication in the contexts of family relationships, family units, and family members interfacing with individuals, relationships, groups, and organizations outside of family units. The Communication Institute for Online Scholarship (CIOS; http://www.cios.org) and the *Communication & Mass Media Complete* (CMMC) databases (through July 2008), as well as published books and textbooks within the family communication field, serve as the primary corpus on which the review is based.

In reviewing the literature, I encountered two preliminary challenges. First, the label "applied" typically is not used to title or subtitle family communication articles. Thus, a broad search strategy using general identifiers, such as "family," was undertaken to generate a corpus of studies from which applied studies could be identified. Second, classifying a given family communication study as applied is not straightforward, as theoretical and applied threads often intertwine or reside side-by-side. Drawing on previous writings in applied communication (e.g., G. R. Miller & Sunnafrank, 1984; Whitchurch & Webb, 1995), I decided to include and examine only those studies that focused primarily on "problems" pertaining to family communication, or to the role of family communication in remedying problems that confront family members, family relationships, family units, or family members interfacing with outside individuals, relationships, and units. This choice represents a conservative framing of applied research, possibly leaving out some salient studies, but it did yield a preliminary list of studies that address issues of the scope of applied family communication research.

As lists were generated and combed to identify potential applied family communication studies, a third challenge emerged concerning how to best organize the numerous studies that focused on a wide variety of problems. This challenge frames the remainder of the chapter and serves as a stimulus for the construction of a positive approach for future applied family communication research studies.

Applied Family Communication and Solving Problems

Given that the traditional focus of applied research on family communication has been on the role of communication in managing real-world, everyday problems in family units (Whitchurch, 2001), an initial research question asked: What types of problems have applied family communication scholars studied? To answer this question, studies of family communication that focused on a problem where communication somehow played a role (e.g., as a significant cause of a problem or as a means to manage a problem) were identified and then sorted using the common label that authors gave to the problem in their studies. This preliminary list of problems addressed in previous applied family communication studies and their accompanying references helped to map the scope of applied family communication inquiry and to estimate the extent of attention given to particular problems.

The preliminary list of problems and accompanying citations is organized alphabetically by problem (see Table 13.1). When many citations were identified for a given problem, such as for divorce or children's television viewing in the home, a select list of citations is included to sketch a representative picture of what has been published thus far in communication journals about each problem.

First, the problems listed in Table 13.1 highlight a familiar pattern: "Families" clearly are open systems that are interconnected to society, such that most of the applied family communication problems also can be found outside families, and some of these problems, such as violence and aggression, can be found across many societal groups and institutions. Moreover, although some problems, such as managing divorce and its aftermath, may originate primarily inside family systems, how families manage these problems affects other societal groups and institutions, such as schools and law enforcement. Reciprocally,

Table 13.1 Problems Examined in a Sample of Applied Family Communication Studies

Problem	Applied Family Communication Studies
Abuse	Clair & Kunkel (1998); Eckstein (2004); Ford, Ray, & Ellis (1999); Givens (1978); Petronio, Flores, & Hecht (1997); Sabourin (1995); Wilson (1999, 2006); Wilson, Hayes, Bylund, Rack, & Herman (2006); Wilson, Morgan, Hayes, Bylund, & Herman (2004)
Adoption	Suter (2008); Wahl, McBride, & Schrodt (2005)
Alcohol and Other Drugs	Austin & Chen (2003); Booth-Butterfield & Sidelinger (1998); Buckley & Ambler (1980); Grant, Rosenfeld, & Cissna (2004); Menees (1997); Tilson, McBride, & Brouwer (2005)
Aging	Fox (1999); Holladay (2002); Pecchioni & Croghan (2002) (see also Nussbaum & Ohs, this volume)
Bereavement/ Grieving	Bosticco & Thompson (2005); Hastings (2001); Hastings, Musambira, & Hoover (2007); Toller (2005)
Caregiving	Bergen, Kirby, & McBride (2007); Bethea, Travis, & Pecchioni (2000); Golden (2007); K. I. Miller, Shoemaker, Willyard, & Addison (2008); Polk (2005)
Children's Empowerment	Chartier & Chartier (1975); Jablin (1998); Koesten, Miller, & Hummert (2002)
Consumer Issues/ Finances	Buckingham (2007); Buijzen & Valkenburg (2008); R. Edwards, Allen, & Hayhoe (2007); Ganong & Coleman (1986); Moore & Moschis (1981)
Conflict	Comstock (1994); Doucet & Aseltine (2003); Dumalo & Botta (2000); Flannery, Montemayor, Eberly, & Torquati (1993); Fujioka & Austin (2002); Koerner & Fitzpatrick (2002); Orrego & Rodriguez (2001); Sheaman & Dumlao, 2008; Zhang (2007)
Divorce and Postdivorce	T. D. Afifi & Keith (2004); T. D. Afifi, McManus, Hutchinson, & Baker (2007); Cushman & Cahn (1986); Donahue, Burrell, & Allen (1993); Gottman, Levenson, & Woodin (2001); Graham (1997); Hayashi & Strickland (1998); Jones (1992); Masheter & Harris (1986); Newcomb (1986); Thomas, Booth-Butterfield, & Booth-Butterfield (1995)
Eating Disorders and Obesity	Botta & Dumlao (2002); Bruss et al. (2005); Miller-Day & Marks (2006); Prescott & Le Poire (2002); Vandebosch & Van Cleemput (2007)
Family Planning	Boulay, Storey, & Sood (2002); Boulay & Valente (2005); Durham (2008); Durham & Braithwaite, 2009; Hindlin et al. (1994); Murphy (2004); Valente, Poppe, & Merritt (1996)
Illness	J. A. Anderson & Geist-Martin (2003); Arrington (2005); Beach (2002); Leslie, Stein, & Rotheram-Borus (2002); Parrott & Lemieux (2003); Pecchioni & Sparks (2007); Unger, Jacobs, & Cannon (1996); Whaley (1999)
In-Law Relationships	Kory & Morr (2003); Prentice (2008)
Interfaith Marriages	Hughes & Dickson (2005)
Long-Distance Relationships	Holladay & Sepike (2007)
Mental Health	Schrodt & Afifi (2007); Schrodt & Ledbetter (2007); Schrodt, Ledbetter, & Ohrt (2007)
New Media	Cho & Cheon (2005); Eastin, Greenberg, & Hofschire (2006); Ling (2007); Livingstone & Helsper (2007); Mesch (2006); Wartella & Robb (2007)

Table 13.1 Continued

Problem	Applied Family Communication Studies
Organ Donation	W. A. Afifi et al. (2006); Morgan & Miller (2002); Smith, Kopfman, Lindsey, Yoo, & Morrison (2004); Smith, Lindsey, Kopfman, Yoo, & Morrison (2008); Vincent (2006)
Political Socialization	Austin & Pinkleton (2001); Connell (1972); Dennis (1986); Meadowcroft (1986); Niemi, Ross, & Alexander (1978); Tims (1986); van Zoonen et al. (2007)
Secrets	T. D. Afifi & Olson (2005); T. D. Afifi, Olson, & Armstrong (2005); Caughlin et al. (2000); Vangelisti, Caughlin, & Timmerman (2001)
Sex and Birth Control	Heisler (2005); C. Warren (1992); C. Warren & Neer (1986)
Sexual Predators	Olson, Daggs, Ellevold, & Rogers (2007)
Sports Participation/ Violence	Kassing & Barber (2007); Kremer-Sadlik & Kim (2007); Turman (2007)
Stepfamilies	T. D. Afifi (2003); T. D. Afifi & Keith (2004); T. D. Afifi & Schrodt (2003); Braithwaite & Baxter (2006); Braithwaite, Olson, Golish, Soukup, & Turman (2001); Braithwaite, Toller, Daas, Durham, & Jones (2008); A. P. Edwards & Shepherd (2007) Golish (2003); Gordon (2003); Schrodt et al. (2007); Soliz (2007)
Suicide	M. Miller (1995); M. Miller & Day (2002)
Support	Burleson & Kunkel (2002); Christian (2005); Egbert, Koch, Coeling, & Ayers (2006); Fitzpatrick, Marshall, Leutwiler, & Kromar (1996); Leach & Braithwaite (1996); Parrott & Lemieux (2003); Yelsma & Marrow (2003)
Television Viewing	Busselle (2003); Holloway & Green (2008); Jennings & Walker, 2009; Nathanson (1999); Nathanson, Wilson, McGee, & Sebastian (2002); Scantlin & Jordan (2006); R. Warren (2001); Weiss & Wilson (1998)
Violence and Aggression	Lloyd & Emery (2000); Martin & Anderson (1997); Rancer, Baukus, & Amato (1986); Sabourin & Stamp (1995); Slater (2003)
Work	Buzzanell et al. (2006); Buzzanell, Waymer, Tagle, & Liu (2007); Golden (2002); Kirby (2006); Krcmar & Vieira (2005); Krouse & Afifi (2007); Langellier & Peterson (2006); Medved (2004); Medved et al. (2006); Parrott & Lemieux (2003); Petronio (2006); Ritchie (1997)

how groups and societal institutions outside of families handle divorce, postdivorce, and stepfamily problems also affects what goes on in the home. The permeable boundaries of family life, thus, make society's problems the problems of families (and visa versa), and suggest that interventions seeking to manage societal problems should include the family (for a discussion about neglecting families in developing interventions to confront the problem of racism, see Socha & Diggs, 1999b).

Second, the list of problems highlights the elastic boundaries that currently frame applied family communication studies; potentially, there is no limit to the types of problems available for exploration in the context of communication among family members. This is good news for applied family communication researchers in that there never will be a shortage of problems to investigate but this list also highlights the need to create better and more grounded understandings of applied family communication, as, for example, families may not experience problems one at a time or in isolation from other problems. Research studies that focus on a single problem, close up, are necessary, of course, but studies that examine connections between and among problems also are needed. For example, physical child abuse (both long and short term) may, at times, co-occur with other problems, including alcoholism, drug use, and financial problems, to name but a few.

Third, the problems focused on also differ in salience among families, as well as various stakeholders (e.g., schools and societal agencies). Some problems pose high potential risks to multiple family resources (e.g., teen pregnancy can have significant effects on economic, educational, and relational resources for some families), whereas other problems may pose lower risks to fewer family resources (e.g., children watching a few minutes of an "adult" television program containing a few curse words). Problems that potentially are high risk (e.g., addiction, bankruptcy, extramarital affairs, illness, and lawsuits), or families that are experiencing many problems simultaneously (of high or low risk), raise stress in the family system, strain interaction among family members, and may deplete resources (e.g., communicative and economic) that potentially need to be augmented (e.g., from extended family, friendships, and professionals). Given that the scope of problems that families confront is wide, a better understanding of the commonalities that cut across problems, in general, as well as features unique to some problems, in particular, is needed to begin to build and test models of intervention and education that might help families to manage or avoid these problems.

Fourth, the problems that applied family communication researchers have chosen to study are driven, in part, by the agenda of individual researchers and, in part, by the agenda of government and nongovernment funding agencies. In contrast, collective efforts in other fields have resulted in awarding large-scale grants to professional associations to advance research. For example, the American Medical Association (AMA), in cooperation with the U.S. federal government, studied excessive television viewing as a contributing factor to U.S. children's increasing obesity. This contributing factor led the AMA and other organizations to develop and promote an annual national campaign: "TV Turn-off Week" (see Dennison, Russo, Burdick, & Jenkins, 2004). Although data concerning the effectiveness of this intervention at trimming obesity trends are not known, a week without television is not likely to harm children and potentially can lead to other benefits, such as increased studying. Unlike the AMA and other professional associations, such as the American Psychological Association, professional communication associations have not sponsored or collaborated with other professional associations in setting or coordinating research agendas that involve large-scale studies, or in developing intervention programs. Because many problems listed in Table 13.1 are "large" (e.g., abuse, divorce, and violence), coordination of research and intervention efforts by professional communication associations could help to prioritize problems for large-scale studies, assist in raising resources for research, and guide the development and testing of communication interventions (see Frey & SunWolf, this volume).

Fifth, because this review is limited to communication journals, the list of problems in Table 13.1 necessarily is preliminary and incomplete, as there are many outlets for applied family communication research outside the communication field. For example, the well-known, programmatic work of psychology scholar John Gottman on marital processes (including communication) and predicting divorce (e.g., Gottman, 1994) is widely cited in family communication studies and textbooks, but with a few exceptions, appears mostly in publications outside the communication field. Furthermore, Gottman's research has led to the development of interventions in the form of mass-marketed books, counselor education programs, and a Web site (e.g., Gottman, 1995; Gottman & Declaire, 2002; Gottman & Silver, 2000; for information about counselor training and couple resources, see The Gottman Institute's Web site—http://www.gottman.com), as well as a psycho-communicative-educational intervention with couples undergoing the transition to parenthood, with a study about it published in the *Journal of Family Communication* (Shapiro & Gottman, 2007).

For some problems, such as eating disorders, applied family communication researchers are joining established programs of research conducted in allied fields. For example, nutritionists (e.g., Larson, 1991; McNamar & Loveman, 1990) linked the problem of eating disorders, in part, to problematic interactions in family systems. Subsequently, communication researchers Botta and Dumlao (2002) and Prescott and Le Poire (2002) shed additional light on the problem in their research. In particular, Prescott and Le Poire, using Le Poire's theory of inconsistent nurturing as control, offered preliminary evidence that an inconsistent, chaotic pattern of communicating parental nurturance might create conditions ripe for later eating disorder development in adolescents.

It also is apparent, however, that many problems have yet to appear much, if at all, on the radar screen of applied family communication researchers. For example, a current problem concerns parental violence directed toward players, coaches, officials, and even other parents at youth sporting events, with 84% of more than 3,300 parents, coaches, youth sports administrators, and youth surveyed saying they have witnessed parents acting violently (e.g., shouting, berating, and using abusive language; "Violence in Youth Sports," n.d.), yet only one study has examined something related to that topic (Kassing & Barber, 2007). Only two other studies (of the hundreds of entries in the databases employed for this chapter that included "sport" or "sports" in the journal article title) dealt with family communication: Kremer-Sadlik and Kim's (2007) study of children's socialization to values through family interaction during sports activities, and Turman's (2007) study of parental influence to encourage young athletes' continued sport participation; although there is relevant scholarship in other disciplines (e.g., Kidman, McKenzie, & McKenzie, 1999). This problem poses potentially significant risks (e.g., physical health and legal) not only to parents (especially those who coach youth) but also to the children who witness parents' antisocial behaviors. The problem is of sufficient significance and scope to prompt government involvement; for example, the provincial government of British Columbia, attempting to respond to increased reports of incidents of parent–coach violence at youth sporting events, requires parents as a condition of children's participation to "sign behavioral contracts to control violence and prevent confrontations that lead to screaming matches and fighting [at youth sporting events]" (Macedo, n.d., ¶ 2).

Another serious problem yet to be studied by applied family communication researchers pertains to children's firearm injuries at home. A search using keywords of *gun(s)*, *firearm(s)*, and related terms yielded only one study that pertained to families, the applied communication study by Roberto, Meyer, Johnson, Atkin, and Smith (2002) about the effectiveness of a public service announcement radio broadcast in Michigan to parents about the danger to children from an unlocked and loaded gun (see also Witte & Roberto, this volume). The lack of such studies is unfortunate, as a report compiled by the nonprofit organization Common Sense about Kids and Guns (n.d.), using data from the National Center for Injury Prevention and Control (2003) database, noted that between 3,000 and 4,000 children's deaths (accidents, homicides, and suicides) are attributed to mishandled or unsecured firearms in the home. Furthermore, other disciplines have responded to this problem; calling firearm injuries to children an "epidemic," the American Academy of Pediatrics (2000), along with the American Psychological Association (2004), developed brochures and Web sites directed to pediatricians and parents, advising them how to talk to children about firearms violence.

Sixth, with a few exceptions, it is difficult (and, in my opinion, premature) to determine the extent of research progress made regarding any particular problem listed in Table 13.1.

One reason pertains to how "progress" is to be defined. If by progress, we mean how close we are to solving the problems listed via family communication education and other interventions, we have a very long way to go. However, if we mean how close we are to better understanding some of the elements or conditions that might inform or lead to promising interventions, we are a bit further along with respect to some problems, as many of the clusters of studies do point out promising antecedents for future inquiry that also might inform the development of interventions. For example, on the assumption that it is desirable for marriages to last (assuming they are good), progress has been made in identifying and testing particular marital communication patterns that increase the chances of divorce (e.g., Gottman's work cited earlier), and considerable progress has been made in documenting the benefits of parental monitoring of children's home television viewing on diminishing its negative effects on children (for an overview, see Van Evra, 2004; for a review of specific benefits of family mediation, see Buerkel-Rothfuss & Buerkel, 2001).

Progress also might be defined by studies that draw attention to significant problems where applied family communication clearly plays a major role. For example, M. Miller (2001) and M. Miller and Day (2002) conducted research on parent–child communication regarding the problem of teen suicidality (tendency toward suicide). These two studies provided preliminary evidence suggesting a correlation between recollections of parents' frequent negative messages (e.g., verbal aggression and attacks on children's self-image) and some children's psychological propensity to consider taking their life. However, because this research is in its early stages, it is far too early to assess its progress, and given the small number of studies, it also is premature to develop and test interventions, although it is important that this work continue, especially because this a unique situation where messages literally can be a matter of life or death.

Although all of the studies cited in Table 13.1 are suggestive of features that might be used to develop educational and intervention programs, they suffer from a few common ailments that limit their potential. First, the small, nonrandom samples that typically are used create external validity problems; clearly, large, national representative samples are needed. To develop effective interventions, including educational materials, it is important, of course, to be sure that the advice fits the population to which it is offered. Without representative samples on which to base advice, extreme caution is de rigueur. Second, these studies await replication. If we are to be confident that education and other interventions are to be effective, testing of multiple populations is needed. Third, applied family communication is a relative newcomer in applied social-scientific fields and, as such, many of its studies necessarily are descriptive (e.g., most rely on correlational analysis), exploratory, and intended to generate theory rather than test theory. These studies typically do not offer advice but, instead, close with cautionary and tentative speculation about ways in which future findings might be applied.

In light of these six points, rather than charting the details of these emerging and evolving lines of inquiry, it is more useful to devote the remaining space to an examination of a particular assumption that underscores applied family communication theory and research, in general. I then use this discussion to suggest that a wider foundation for applied family communication research is needed—specifically, a move toward a positive, integrative model that might better support future applied family communication research.

Toward a Positive Approach to Applied Family Communication

I suspect that most family communication researchers who seek to have others apply their work (not all may be interested in such application) hope that their work might somehow help families to manage life "better." That is, they hope that their applied family communication research, in general, might lead to education and other interventions that help families to improve the quality of their communication (individual, relational, family/group, and family/network), especially as related to solving the many problems they confront, or, in more general terms, to use communication more effectively to manage family life.

Discussion and debate in clinical psychology, however, suggest that framing applied research in terms of "solving problems" and "improvement" actually focuses attention and energies negatively and too narrowly on repairing, fixing, and healing, rather than focusing positively on empowering. According to Seligman (2002), then writing about the emerging field of positive psychology, the focus of past research is too narrow and should include:

> well-being, satisfaction; flow, joy, sensual pleasures, and happiness; constructive cognitions about the future—optimism, hope, and faith. At the individual level, it is about positive personal traits—the capacity for love and vocation, courage, interpersonal skill, aesthetic sensibility, perseverance, forgiveness, originality, future-mindedness, high talent, and wisdom. At the group level, it is about civic virtues and the institutions that move individuals to better citizenship: responsibility, nurturance, altruism, civility, moderation, tolerance, and work ethic. (p. 3)

Positive psychology, thus, challenges the prevailing ontological assumptions of traditional clinical psychology—a negative, disease-based model of "healing"—and, instead, argues for a positive reframing that features "prevention" and "positive therapy." The *Handbook of Positive Psychology* (Snyder & Lopez, 2005), *Oxford Handbook of Methods in Positive Psychology* (Ong & van Dulmen, 2007), and *Handbook of Hope: Theory, Measures, and Applications* (Snyder, 2000), among other texts, are recent examples that report on this approach.

From the vantage point of positive psychology, reviewing the problems and research cited in Table 13.1 shows that past applied family communication research seems to have taken a path similar to that of traditional clinical psychology. This path began with the negative assumption that communication in families is, in some way, deficient and that it is up to family communication scholars to generate research that can inform the development of interventions (e.g., courses, textbooks, and campaigns) designed to help families overcome their communication deficiencies. Instead, following the lead of positive psychologists, it is more useful for family communication scholars to focus on the role of communication and the development of positive qualities (e.g., creativity, hope, and love) that characterize creative, artful, and successful families, and also work to develop preventative measures.

Reframing applied family communication in positive ontological terms has important theoretical and practical implications for family communication. First, a positive reframing opens up new and potentially theoretically useful ways to reconceptualize families and applied family communication. For example, McGeer (2004), a philosopher, mentioned "family" in an essay about the role of societal agencies in creating conditions that facilitate or inhibit development of what she called "good hope." Expanding McGeer's framing further, I see "families" as "agencies of potential" that create conditions for the development of many kinds of potentialities or capacities (e.g., artistic, athletic, economic, educational, psychological, social, and spiritual) on multiple levels (i.e., among family members, family relationships, family units, family networks, and family interfacing with society).

A reframing of families as agencies of potential leads to a redefining of applied family communication as a symbolic process of facilitating or inhibiting potential. There are several advantages to this reframing; in particular, it offers a new starting point for applied family communication research, moving it away from studies of the role of communication in managing "problems" toward studies of the role of communication in creating or destroying conditions necessary to facilitate potential. Instead of studies that examine the communication of "dysfunctional" families relative to communication of "functional" families, and then proposing interventions to turn dysfunctional into functional families, positive family communication researchers would examine the role of family communication in creating or destroying conditions that facilitate versus inhibit development of family potentialities and capacities, and then propose communication interventions designed to augment family resources and refine family processes to facilitate the development of those potentialities and capacities. Such a reframing widens the scaffold for future research by adding a positive focus and concentrating on the role of communication in the development of potentialities and capacities—a communication strengths approach. Below, I consider further what a positive model of applied family communication might look like, first by examining critically the types of inputs studied in past family communication research, and second, by discussing an important positive family quality—hope—and the role that family communication plays in its development.

Toward the Study of Positive Family Communication Inputs and Processes

From its start, family communication studies conceptualized families as systems. All family communication textbooks introduce students to systems theory and frame their foundational discussions of family and family communication in the language of that theory. However, the scholarship in the field has emphasized the communication of individual family members and family dyads, isolated from family units/groups (Socha, 1999), rather than the communication of family units and family networks.

In the basic systems model as applied to families, various types of inputs (e.g., facts and opinions) are processed (e.g., family decision-making practices) into outputs (e.g., family decisions and family member satisfaction). Applied family communication research studies have examined a variety of inputs common to many families, although those studies have tended to focus on family inputs that are relatively unchangeable (e.g., sex of family members, attachment patterns, health conditions, and couple types), rather than inputs that can change as a function of education or other interventions, such as the development of individuals' communication skills. K. L. Anderson, Umberson, and Elliott (2004), for instance, suggested that increasing the individual communication skills of family members can prevent abuse in families.

Researchers also have examined a wide variety of family outputs, although here, too, they often conceptualize family outputs dichotomously—such as functional–dysfunctional, abusive–non-abusive, and violent–nonviolent—rather than as scaled or on a continuum. In a critique of family conflict research, for example, Sillars, Canary, and Tafoya (2004) aptly pointed out the limits of using dichotomies such as productive–unproductive to conceptualize conflict strategies and distressed–non-distressed to conceptualize outputs. Sillars et al. urged researchers, instead, to examine the "range of conflict styles and communication patterns found among families who could be considered '*adequately* [italics added] functioning'" (p. 433). Their critique is useful insofar that it moves us toward ranges, but in light of positive psychology, conceptualizing family output as "adequately functioning," sets the bar rather low. That is, although most families probably do not object to being labeled as "nonviolent" or as "competent," some families might aspire to be more than competent. Although this is an empirical question that requires study, some families might augment positive family inputs (e.g., increasing the family's capacity for compassion, creativity, empathy, forgiveness, hope, laughter, self-esteem, and spirituality), refine and improve positive family communication processes (e.g., moving beyond competent toward caring and elegant), and set higher standards for family outputs (e.g., moving beyond family "satisfaction" toward altruism, integrity, joyfulness, nurturance, peacefulness, and pride).

Thus, in light of positive psychology and McGeer's (2004) notion of family as an agent of potential, applied family communication scholars might best focus their attention and energy in two areas: (1) understanding the role that family communication plays in augmenting positive family inputs (e.g., increasing families' compassion, creativity, hope, and laughter) and (2) understanding the role of family communication processes in creating conditions that facilitate the development of family potential, or how families use communication to create conditions that are optimal for their growth and development (e.g., for a reframing of the concept of "discipline" from this perspective, see Socha, 2006).

If such a shift is taken seriously, studies would focus less on the role of communication in solving family problems and more on the role of family communication in creating conditions that might prevent family problems, as well as on the role of family communication in building positive resources to draw on when problems do arise. To illustrate what a shift to positive applied family communication research might entail, I close this chapter with an extended example, drawn from Snyder's (2000) theory of hope.

Hope

Snyder (2000) argued that hope is an essential aspect of psychological wellness and theorized that hope involves three elements: goals, pathways thoughts, and agency thoughts. *Goals* are end states that individuals perceive, desire, or hope for; *pathways thoughts* are the many ways that individuals imagine themselves reaching a desired goal; and *agency thoughts* are those that "reflect one's appraisal of the capability to persevere in the goal journey" (Snyder, 2000, p. 10). Pathways thoughts are linked, for example, to problem solving and creativity, and agency thoughts are linked to self-efficacy and self-esteem. "Hopeful thinking" is a combination of pathways thinking (individuals imagining ways to reach their desired goals) plus agency thinking (individuals believing that they have what it takes to reach their goals and that they are worthy of reaching those goals). Snyder and colleagues developed and validated scales to measure individual differences in hope for adults (Snyder, Harris et al., 1991) and for children (Snyder, et al., 1997). These scales have been used to study the role of hope in a variety of contexts, problems, and populations, including depression, eating disorders, ethnic cultural relations, surviving breast cancer and AIDS, and with athletes (see Snyder, 2000).

This research shows that individuals differ in their ability to hope (ranging from high hope to low hope) and that differences in hope can be explained, in part, by social processes. For example, Rodriguez-Hanley and Snyder (2000) outlined conditions under which children's capacity to hope can be damaged by abuse and neglect, or lost due to a parent's death or lack of consistent family structure. Snyder (2000) suggested, generally, that communication is a significant process in the facilitation or diminution of hope. For example, families that share their creative insights about new ways of thinking about obstacles they face can increase their capacity for pathways thinking, and families that share messages intended to increase their members' self-worth and encourage a "can-do" spirit can increase their individual and collective capacity for agentic thinking. Thus, according to Snyder's hope theory, families that communicate in ways that increase pathways thinking (ability to understand obstacles and develop pathways to manage those obstacles) and agentic thinking (feelings of efficacy and worth) are likely to increase family hope—a positive psychological condition necessary for optimal growth.

In the context of hope theory, an initial task for applied communication researchers is to examine how families use messages to create conditions favorable for the development of hope as they confront specific obstacles pertaining to the many sides of family life (e.g., finances and wellness–illness). First, in what ways do families use messages to facilitate or inhibit pathways thinking? In the context of family finances, for example, in what ways do families use communication to create more effective ways of managing their money or to create obstacles to better money management? Parents who tell their children, "We are poor—get used to it," for instance, may limit pathways to thinking about family finances, as opposed to parents who promote shared pathways thinking by asking their children, "We need to make every penny count, so how can we work together to make what we have go farther and increase what we have?"

Second, in what ways are families using communication to facilitate or inhibit agentic thinking? Satir (1967, 1972, 1988) and other family therapists established that family members' positive sense of self-worth is an essential element of healthy people and families, and showed that how family members communicate with each other can increase or diminish their self-worth. Continuing the example of family finances, parents who tell their children, "Don't even bother to apply for that scholarship; folks like us have no chance," limit agentic thinking, as opposed to parents who say, "Your odds of getting that scholarship only go up by submitting a well-written application, and you can do it."

How families use messages to create or diminish conditions favorable for high hope, in general, and as they confront particular obstacles is one example of a larger positive applied family communication research agenda. Indeed, families do confront many significant problems, but by refocusing attention on prevention and creating conditions that are favorable to coping, such as high hope, we refocus attention on a changeable factor where applied family communication can make a difference in the quality of family life.

Conclusion

The potential of applied family communication as a force for promoting positive changes for families and society is great. From the studies identified in this review that explore many serious obstacles that families confront, it is clear that applied family communication researchers care about aiding families. I have suggested that reframing applied family communication studies in more positive terms, and refocusing applied family communication studies on the development of family potential, offers a wider and more coherent scaffold on which to build future applied family communication research. Thus, rather than continuing to study the ever-present weeds of family life, family communication researchers should pay attention to the conditions under which both flowers and weeds thrive.

Author's Note

I thank Rachel Cole (Old Dominion University graduate student in English) for her library assistance and contributions in developing the list of family problems.

References

Afifi, T. D. (2003). Feeling caught in stepfamilies: Managing boundary turbulence through appropriate communication privacy rules. *Journal of Social and Personal Relationships, 20,* 729–755.

Afifi, T. D., & Keith, S. (2004). A risk and resiliency model of ambiguous loss in postdivorce step-families. *Journal of Family Communication, 4,* 65–98.

Afifi, T. D., McManus, T., Hutchinson, S., & Baker, B. (2007). Inappropriate parental divorce disclosures, the factors that prompt them, and their impact on parents' and adolescents' well-being. *Communication Monographs, 74,* 78–102.

Afifi, T. D., & Olson, L. (2005). The chilling effect in families and the pressure to conceal secrets. *Communication Monographs, 72,* 192–216.

Afifi, T. D., Olson, L. N., & Armstrong, C. (2005). The chilling effect and family secrets: The role of self protection, other protection, and communication efficacy. *Human Communication Research, 31,* 564–598.

Afifi, T. D., & Schrodt, P. (2003).Uncertainty and avoidance of the state of one's family in step-families, postdivorce single-parent families, and first-marriage families. *Human Communication Research, 29,* 516–532.

Afifi, W. A., Morgan, S. E., Stephenson, M. T., Morse, C., Harris, T., Reichert, T., et al. (2006). Examining the decision to talk with family about organ donation: Applying the theory of motivated information management. *Communication Monographs, 73,* 188–215.

American Academy of Pediatrics. (2004). *Violence prevention in the home.* Retrieved August 29, 2004, from http://www.medem.com/search/article_display.cfm?path=n:&mstr=/ZZZIH-NJ2R7C.html&soc=AAP&srch_typ=NAV_SERCH

American Psychological Association. (2004). *Raising children to resist violence: What you can do.* Retrieved August 29, 2004, from http://www.apahelpcenter.org/articles/article.php?id=15

Anderson, J. A., & Geist-Martin. P. (2003). Narratives and healing: Exploring one family's stories of cancer survivorship. *Health Communication, 15,* 133–144.

Anderson, K. L., Umberson, D., & Elliott, S. (2004). Violence and abuse in families. In A. L. Vangelisti (Ed.), *Handbook of family communication* (pp. 629–645). Mahwah, NJ: Erlbaum.

Arliss, L. P. (1993). *Contemporary family communication: Messages and meanings.* New York: St. Martin's Press.

Arnold, L. B. (2008). *Family communication: Theory and research.* Boston: Allyn & Bacon.

Arrington, M. I. (2005). "She's right behind me all the way": An analysis of prostate cancer narratives and changes in family relationships. *Journal of Family Communication, 5,* 141–162.

Austin, E. W., & Chen, Y. J. (2003). The relationship of parental reinforcement of media messages to college students' alcohol-related behaviors. *Journal of Health Communication, 8,* 157–169.

Austin, E. W., & Pinkleton, B. E. (2001). The role of parental mediation in the political socialization process. *Journal of Broadcasting & Electronic Media, 45,* 221–240.

Beach, W. A. (2002). Between dad and son: Initiating, delivering, and assimilating bad cancer news. *Health Communication, 14,* 271–298.

Beebe, S. A., & Masterson, J. T. (1986). *Family talk: Interpersonal communication in the family.* New York: Random House.

Bergen, K. M., Kirby, E., & McBride, M. C. (2007). "How do you get two houses cleaned?" Accomplishing family caregiving in commuter marriages. *Journal of Family Communication, 7,* 287–307.

Bethea, L. S., Travis, S. S., & Pecchioni, L. (2000). Family caregivers' use of humor in conveying information about caring for dependent older adults. *Health Communication, 12,* 361–376.

Bochner, A. P. (1976). Conceptual frontiers in the study of communication in families: An introduction to the literature. *Human Communication Research, 2,* 381–387.

Booth-Butterfield, M., & Sidelinger, R. (1998). The influence of family communication on the college-age child: Openness, attitudes and actions about sex and alcohol. *Communication Quarterly, 46,* 295–308.

Bosticco, C., & Thompson, T. (2005). The role of communication and story telling in the family grieving system. *Journal of Family Communication, 5*, 255–278.

Botta, R. A., & Dumlao, R. (2002). How do conflict and communication patterns between fathers and daughters contribute to or offset eating disorders? *Health Communication, 14*, 199–219.

Boulay, M., Storey, J. D., & Sood, S. (2002). Indirect exposure to a family planning mass media campaign in Nepal. *Journal of Health Communication, 7*, 379–400.

Boulay, M., & Valente, T. W. (2005). The selection of family planning discussion partners in Nepal. *Journal of Health Communication, 10*, 519–536.

Braithwaite, D. O., & Baxter, L. A. (2006). "You're my parent but you're not": Dialectical tensions in stepchildren's perceptions about communicating with the nonresidential parent. *Journal of Applied Communication Research, 34*, 30–48.

Braithwaite, D. O., Olson, L. N., Golish, T. D., Soukup, C., & Turman, P. (2001). "Becoming a family": Developmental processes represented in blended family discourse. *Human Communication Research, 29*, 221–247.

Braithwaite, D. O., Toller, P. W., Daas, K. L., Durham, W. T., & Jones, A. C. (2008). Centered but not caught in the middle: Stepchildren's perceptions of dialectical contradictions in the communication of co-parents. *Journal of Applied Communication, 36*, 33–55.

Bruss, M. B., Morris, J. R., Dannison, L. L., Orbe, M. P., Quitugua, J. A., & Palacios, R. T. (2005). Food, culture, and family: Exploring the coordinated management of meaning regarding childhood obesity. *Health Communication, 18*, 155–176.

Buckingham, D. (2007). Selling childhood? Children and consumer culture. *Journal of Children and Media, 1*, 15–24.

Buckley, J. E., & Ambler, R. S. (1980). Where high school students go for information about alcohol. *Journal of Applied Communications Research, 8*, 55–68.

Buerkel-Rothfuss, N. L., & Buerkel, R. A. (2001). Family mediation. In J. Bryant & J. A. Bryant (Eds.), *Television and the American family* (2nd ed., pp. 355–376). Mahwah, NJ: Erlbaum.

Buijzen, M., & Valkenburg, P. M. (2008). Observing purchase-related parent–child communication in retail environments: A developmental and socialization perspective. *Human Communication Research, 34*, 50–69.

Burleson, B. R., & Kunkel, A. (2002). Parental and peer contributions to the emotional support skills of the child: From whom do children learn to express support? *Journal of Family Communication, 2*, 79–97.

Busselle, R. W. (2003). Television exposure, parents' precautionary warnings, and young adults' perceptions of crime. *Communication Research, 30*, 530–556.

Buzzanell, P. M., Meisenbach, R., Remke, R., Liu, M., Bowers, V., & Conn, C. (2005). The *good working* mother: Managerial women's sense making and feelings about work–family issues. *Communication Studies, 56*, 261–286.

Buzzanell, P. M., Waymer, D., Tagle, M. P., & Liu, M. (2007). Different transitions into working motherhood: Discourses of Asian, Hispanic, and African American women. *Journal of Family Communication, 7*, 195–220.

Caughlin, J. P., Golish, T. D., Olson, L. N., Sargent, J. E., Cook, J. S., & Petronio, S. (2000). Intrafamily secrets in various family configurations: A communication boundary management perspective. *Communication Monographs, 51*, 116–134.

Chartier, J., & Chartier, M. (1975). Perceived parental communication and self-esteem: An exploratory study. *Western Speech, 39*, 26–31.

Cho, C. H., & Cheon, H. J. (2005). Children's exposure to negative Internet conflict: Effects of family context. *Journal of Broadcasting & Electronic Media, 49*, 488–509.

Christian, A. (2005). Contesting the myth of the "wicked stepmother": A narrative analysis of an online stepfamily support group. *Western Journal of Communication, 69*, 27–48.

Clair, R. P., & Kunkel, A.W. (1998). "Unrealistic realities": Child abuse and the aesthetic resolution. *Communication Monographs, 65*, 24–46.

Common Sense about Kids and Guns. (n.d.). *National firearms deaths* [Table]. Retrieved September 10, 2004, from http://www.kidsandguns.org/study/states_deaths.asp?National

Comstock, J. (1994). Parent–adolescent conflict: A developmental approach. *Western Journal of Communication, 58,* 263–282.

Connell, R. W. (1972). Political socialization and the American family: The evidence re-examined. *Public Opinion Quarterly, 36,* 323–333.

Cushman, D. P., & Cahn, D. D. (1986). A study of communicative realignment between parents and children following the parents' decision to seek a divorce. *Communication Research Reports, 3,* 80–85.

Csikszentmihalyi, M., & Csikszentmihalyi, I. S. (Eds.). (2006). *Life worth living: Contributions to positive psychology.* New York: Oxford University Press.

Dennis, J. (1986). Pre-adult learning of political independence: Media and family effects. *Communication Research, 13,* 401–433.

Dennison, B. A., Russo, T. J., Burdick, P. A., & Jenkins, P. L. (2004). An intervention to reduce television viewing of preschool children. *Archives of Pediatrics and Adolescent Medicine, 158,* 170–176.

Donahue, W. A., Burrell, N., & Allen, M. (1993). Models of divorce mediation. In B. Dervin & U. Hariharan (Eds.), *Progress in communication sciences* (Vol. 11, pp. 101–118). Westport, CT: Greenwood Press.

Doucet, J., & Aseltine, R. H., Jr. (2003). Childhood family adversity and the quality of marital relationships in young adulthood. *Journal of Social and Personal Relationships, 20,* 818–842.

Dumalo, R., & Botta, R. A. (2000). Family communication patterns and the conflict styles young adults use with their fathers. *Communication Quarterly, 48,* 174–189.

Durham, W., & Braithwaite, D. O. (2009). Communication privacy management within the family planning trajectories of voluntarily child-free couples. *Journal of Family Communication, 9,* 43–65.

Durham W. T. (2008). The rules-based process of revealing/concealing the family planning decisions of voluntarily child-free couples: A communication privacy management perspective. *Communication Studies, 59,* 132–147.

Eastin, M. S., Greenberg, B. S., & Hofschire, L. (2006). Parenting the Internet . *Journal of Communication, 56,* 486–504.

Eckstein, N. J. (2004). Emergent issues in families experiencing adolescent-to-parent abuse. *Western Journal of Communication, 68,* 365–388.

Edwards, A. P., & Shepherd, G. J. (2007). An investigation of the relationship between implicit personal theories of communication and community behavior. *Communication Studies, 58,* 359–376.

Edwards, R., Allen, M. W., & Hayhoe, R. (2007). Financial attitudes and family communication about students' finances: The role of sex differences. *Communication Reports, 20,* 90–100.

Egbert, N., Koch, L., Coeling, H., & Ayers, D. (2006). The role of social support in the family and community integration of right-hemisphere stroke survivors. *Health Communication, 20,* 45–56.

Fitzpatrick, M. A. (1988). *Between husbands and wives: Communication in marriage.* Newbury Park, CA: Sage .

Fitzpatrick, M. A., Marshall, L. J., Leutwiler, T. J., & Kromar, M. (1996). The effect of family communication environments on children's social behavior during middle childhood. *Communication Research, 23,* 379–406.

Fitzpatrick, M. A., & Vangelisti, A. L. (Eds.). (1995). *Explaining family interactions.* Thousand Oaks, CA: Sage.

Flannery, D. J., Montemayor, R., Eberly, M., & Torquati, J. (1993). Unraveling the ties that bind: Affective expression and perceived conflict in parent–adolescent interactions. *Journal of Social and Personal Relationships, 10,* 495–509.

Floyd, K., & Morr, M. C. (2003). Human affection exchange: VII. Affectionate communication in the sibling/spouse/sibling-in-law triad. *Communication Quarterly, 51,* 247–261.

Ford, L. A., Ray, E. B., & Ellis, B. H. (1999). Translating scholarship on intrafamilial sexual abuse: The utility of a dialectical perspective for adult survivors. *Journal of Applied Communication Research, 27,* 139–157.

Fox, S. A. (1999). Communication in families with an aging parent: A review of literature and agenda for future research. In M. E. Roloff (Ed.), *Communication yearbook* (Vol. 22, pp. 377–429). Thousand Oaks, CA: Sage.

Fujioka, Y., & Austin, E. W. (2002). The relationship of family communication patterns to parental mediation styles. *Communication Research, 29*, 642–665.

Galvin, K. M., & Brommel, B. J. (1982). *Family communication: Cohesion and change*. Glenview, IL: Scott, Foresman.

Galvin, K. M., Bylund, C. L., & Brommel, B. J. (2008). *Family communication: Cohesion and change* (7th ed.). Boston: Pearson Allyn & Bacon.

Ganong, L. H., & Coleman, M. (1998). An exploratory study of grandparents' and stepgrandparents' financial obligations to grandchildren and stepgrandchildren. *Journal of Social and Personal Relationships, 15*, 39–58.

Givens, D. B. (1978). Contrasting nonverbal styles in mother–child interaction: Examples from a study of child abuse. *Semiotica, 24*, 33–47.

Golden, A. G. (2002). Speaking of work and family: Spousal collaboration on defining role-identities and developing shared meanings. *Southern Communication Journal, 67*, 122–141.

Golden, A. G. (2007). Fathers' frames for childrearing: Evidence toward a "masculine concept of caregiving." *Journal of Family Communication, 7*, 265–286.

Golish, T. D. (2003). Stepfamily communication strengths: Understanding the ties that bind. *Human Communication Research, 29*, 41–80.

Gordon, C. (2003). Aligning as a team: Forms of conjoined participation in (stepfamily) interaction. *Research on Language and Social Interaction, 36*, 395–431.

Gottman, J. M. (1994). *What predicts divorce? The relationship between marital processes and marital outcomes*. Hillsdale, NJ: Erlbaum.

Gottman, J. M., & Declaire, J. (2002). *The relationship cure: A five-step guide for building better connections with family, friends, and lovers*. New York: Crown.

Gottman, J., Levenson, R., & Woodin, E. (2001). Facial expressions during marital conflict. *Journal of Family Communication, 1*, 37–57.

Gottman, J. M. (with Silver, N.). (1995). *Why marriages succeed or fail: What you can learn from the breakthrough research to make your marriage last*. New York: Simon & Schuster.

Gottman, J. M., & Silver, N. (2000). *The seven principles for making marriage work*. New York: Crown.

Graham, E. E. (1997). Turning points and commitment in post-divorce relationships. *Communication Monographs, 64*, 350–368.

Grant, C. H., Rosenfeld, L. B., & Cissna, K. N. (2004). The effects of family-of-origin alcohol abuse on the self-perceived communication competence of the children. *Communication Research Reports, 21*, 47–59.

Hastings, S. O. (2001). Self-disclosure and identity management by bereaved parents. *Communication Studies, 51*, 352–371.

Hastings, S. O., Musambira, G. W., & Hoover, J. D. (2007). Community as a key to healing after the death of a child. *Communication & Medicine, 4*, 153–163.

Hayashi, G. M., & Strickland, B. R. (1998). Long-term effects of parental divorce on love relationships: Divorce as attachment disruption. *Journal of Social and Personal Relationships, 15*, 23–38.

Heisler, J. M. (2005). Family communication and sex: Parents and college-aged offspring recall discussion topics, satisfaction, and parental involvement. *Journal of Family Communication, 5*, 295–312.

Hindlin, M. J., Kincaid, D. L., Kumah, O. M., Morgan, W., Kim, Y. M., & Ofori, J. K. (1994). Gender differences in media exposure and action during a family planning campaign in Ghana. *Health Communication, 6*, 117–158.

Holladay, S. J. (2002). "Have fun while you can," You're only as young only as you feel," and "Don't ever get old!" An examination of memorable messages about aging. *Journal of Communication, 52*, 681–697.

Holladay, S. J., & Sepike, H. L. (2007). Communication between grandparents and grandchildren in geographically separated relationships. *Communication Studies, 58,* 281–298.

Holloway, D., & Green, L. (2008). Room to view: Family television use in the Australian context. *Television and New Media, 9,* 47–61.

Hughes, P. C., & Dickson, F. C. (2005). Communication, marital satisfaction, and religious orientation in interfaith marriages. *Journal of Family Communication, 5,* 25–42.

Jablin, F. (1998). Learning about leadership and followership: Communication during childhood and adolescence: What messages are we sending? *Australian Journal of Communication, 25,* 81–96.

Jackson, D. (1965). The study of family. *Family Process, 4,* 1–20.

Jennings, N. A., & Walker, B. J. (2009). Experiential mediation: Making meaningful differences with the "other parent." *Journal of Family Communication, 9,* 3–27.

Jones, D. C. (1992). Parental divorce, family conflict and friendship networks. *Journal of Social and Personal Relationships, 9,* 219–235.

Kassing, J. W., & Barber, A. M. (2007). "Being a good sport": An investigation of sportsmanship messages provided by youth soccer parents, officials, and coaches. *Human Communication, 10,* 61–68.

Kidman, L., McKenzie, A., & McKenzie, B. (1999). The nature and target of parents' comments during youth sport competition. *Journal of Sport Behavior, 22,* 54–68.

Kirby, E. L. (2006). "Helping you make room in your life for your needs": When organizations appropriate family roles. *Communication Monographs, 73,* 468–473.

Koerner, A. F., & Fitzpatrick, M. A. (2002). You never leave your family in a fight: The impact of family of origin on conflict behavior in romantic relationships. *Communication Studies, 53,* 234–251.

Koesten, J., Miller, K. I., & Hummert, M. L. (2002). Family communication, self-efficacy, and White female adolescents' risk behavior. *Journal of Family Communication, 2,* 7–27.

Krcmar, M., & Vieira, E. T., Jr. (2005). Imitating life, imitating television: The effects of family and television models on children's moral reasoning. *Communication Research, 32,* 267–294.

Kremer-Sadlik, T., & Kim, J. L. (2007). Lessons from sports: Children's socialization to values through family interaction during sports activities *Discourse & Society, 18,* 35–52.

Krouse, S. S., & Afifi, T. D. (2007). Family-to-work spillover stress: Coping communicatively in the workplace. *Journal of Family Communication, 7,* 85–122.

Langellier, K. M., & Peterson, E. E. (2006). "Somebody's got to pick eggs": Family storytelling about work. *Communication Monographs, 73,* 468–473.

Larson, B. J. (1991). Relationship of family communication patterns to eating disorder inventory scores in adolescent girls. *Journal of the American Dietetic Association, 91,* 1065–1067.

Leach, M. S., & Braithwaite, D. O. (1996). A binding tie: Supportive communication of family kinkeepers. *Human Communication Research, 24,* 200–216.

Le Poire, B. A. (2006). *Family communication: Nurturing and control in a changing world.* Thousand Oaks, CA: Sage.

Leslie, M. B., Stein, J. A., & Rotheram-Borus, M. J. (2002). The impact of coping strategies, personal relationships, and emotional distress on health-related outcomes of parents living with HIV or AIDS. *Journal of Social and Personal Relationships, 19,* 45–66.

Ling, R. (2007). Children, youth, and mobile communication. *Journal of Children and Media, 1,* 60–67.

Livingstone, S., & Helsper, E. (2007). Gradations in digital inclusion: Children, young people and the digital divide. *New Media & Society, 9,* 671–696.

Lloyd, S. A., & Emery, B. C. (2000). The context and dynamics of intimate aggression against women. *Journal of Social and Personal Relationships, 17,* 503–521.

Lopez, S. J. (2009). *The encyclopedia of positive psychology.* Malden, MA: Blackwell.

Macedo, R. (n.d.). *Parents may have to sign contracts to control bad behaviour at kids' games.* Retrieved August 29, 2004, from http://www.cariboo.bc.ca/news/PastOct20/HPvlce.html

Martin, M. M., & Anderson, C. M. (1997). Aggressive communication traits: How similar are young adults and their parents in argumentativeness, assertiveness, and verbal aggressiveness? *Western Journal of Communication, 61,* 299–314.

Masheter, C., & Harris, L. M. (1986). From divorce to friendship: A study of dialectic relationship development. *Journal of Social and Personal Relationships, 3,* 177–189.

McGeer, V. (2004). The art of good hope. *Annals of the American Academy of Political and Social Science, 592,* 100–127.

McNamar, K., & Loveman, C. (1990). Differences in family functioning among bulimics, repeat dieters, and nondieters. *Journal of Clinical Psychology, 46,* 518–523.

Meadowcroft, J. M. (1986). Family communication patterns and political development: The child's role. *Communication Research, 13,* 603–624.

Medved, C. E. (2004). The everyday accomplishment of work and family: Exploring practical actions in daily routines. *Communication Studies, 55,* 128–145.

Medved, C. E., Brogan, S. M., McClanahan, A. M., Morris, J. F., & Shepherd, G. J. (2006). Family and work socializing communication: Messages, gender, and ideological implications. *Journal of Family Communication, 6,* 161–180.

Menees, M. M. (1997). The role of coping, social support, and family communication in explaining the self-esteem of children of alcoholics. *Communication Research, 10,* 9–19.

Mesch, G. S. (2006). Family relations and the Internet: Exploring a family boundaries approach. *Journal of Family Communication, 6,* 119–138.

Miller, G. R., & Sunnafrank, M. J. (1984). Theoretical dimensions of applied communication research. *Quarterly Journal of Speech, 70,* 255–263.

Miller, K. I., Shoemaker, M. M., Willyard, J., & Addison, P. (2008). Providing care for elderly parents: A structurational approach to family caregiving identity. *Journal of Family Communication, 8,* 19–43.

Miller, M. (1995). An intergenerational case study of suicidal tradition and mother–daughter communication. *Journal of Applied Communication Research, 23,* 247–271.

Miller, M., & Day, L. E. (2002). Family communication, maternal and paternal expectations, and college students' suicidality. *Journal of Family Communication, 2,* 167–184.

Miller-Day, M., & Marks, J. D. (2006). Perceptions of parental communication orientation, perfectionism, and disordered eating behaviors of sons and daughters. *Health Communication, 19,* 153–164.

Moore, R. L., & Moschis, G. P. (1981). The role of family communication in consumer learning. *Journal of Communication, 31*(4), 42–51.

Morgan, S. E., & Miller, J. K. (2002). Beyond the organ donor card: The effect of knowledge, attitudes, and values on willingness to communicate about organ donation to family members. *Health Communication, 14,* 121–134.

Murphy, E. (2004). Diffusion of innovations: Family planning in developing countries. *Journal of Health Communication, 9,* 124–130.

Nathanson, A. I. (1999). Identifying and explaining the relationship between parental monitoring and children's aggression. *Communication Research, 26,* 124–143.

Nathanson, A. I., Wilson, B. J., McGee, J., & Sebastian, M. (2002). Counteracting the effects of female stereotypes on television via active mediation. *Journal of Communication, 52,* 922–937.

National Center for Injury Prevention and Control. (2003). *WISQARS injury mortality reports, 1999–2002* [Database]. Retrieved September 10, 2004, from http://webapp.cdc.gov/sasweb/ncipc/mortrate10_fy.html

Newcomb, M. D. (1986). Cohabitation, marriage, and divorce among adolescents and young adults. *Journal of Social and Personal Relationships, 3,* 473–494.

Niemi, R. G., Ross, R. D., & Alexander, J. (1978). The similarity of political values of parents and college-age youths. *Public Opinion Quarterly, 42,* 503–520.

Noller, P., & Fitzpatrick, M .A. (1993). *Communication in family relationships.* Englewood Cliffs, NJ: Prentice-Hall.

Olson, L. N., Daggs, J. L., Ellevold, B. L., & Rogers, T. K. K. (2007). Entrapping the innocent:

Toward a theory of child sexual predators' luring communication. *Communication Theory, 17,* 231–251.

Ong, A. D., & van Dulmen, M. H. M. (2007). *Oxford handbook of methods in positive psychology.* New York: Oxford University Press.

Orrego, V. O., & Rodriguez, J. (2001). Family communication patterns and college adjustment: The effects of communication and conflictual independence on college students. *Journal of Family Communication, 1,* 175–189.

Parrott, R., & Lemieux, R. (2003). When the worlds of work and wellness collide: The role of familial support on skin cancer control. *Journal of Family Communication, 3,* 95–105.

Pearson, J. C. (1989). *Communication in the family: Seeking satisfaction in changing times.* New York: Harper & Row.

Pecchioni, L. L., & Croghan, J. M. (2002). Young adults' stereotypes of older adults with their grandparents as targets. *Journal of Communication, 52,* 715–730.

Pecchioni, L. L., & Sparks, L. (2007). Health information sources of individuals with cancer and their family members. *Health Communication, 21,* 143–152.

Petronio, S. (2006). Impact of medical mistakes: Navigating work–family boundaries for physicians and their families. *Communication Monographs, 73,* 462–467.

Petronio, S., Flores, L. A., & Hecht, M. L. (1997). Locating the voice of logic: Disclosure discourse of sexual abuse. *Western Journal of Communication, 61,* 101–113.

Polk, D. M. (2005). Communication and family caregiving for Alzheimer's dementia: Linking attributions and problematic integration. *Health Communication, 18,* 257–274.

Prentice, C. M. (2008). The assimilation of in-laws: The impact of newcomers on the communication routines of families. *Journal of Applied Communication Research, 36,* 74–97.

Prescott, M. E., & Le Poire, B. A. (2002). Eating disorders and mother–daughter communication: A test of inconsistent nurturing as control theory. *Journal of Family Communication, 2,* 59–78.

Rancer, A. S., Baukus, R. A., & Amato, P. A. (1986). Argumentativeness, verbal aggressiveness, and marital satisfaction. *Communication Research Reports, 3,* 28–32.

Ritchie, L. D. (1997). Parents' workplace experiences and family communication patterns. *Communication Research, 24,* 175–187.

Roberto, A. J., Meyer, G., Johnson, A. J., Atkin, C. K., & Smith, P. K. (2002). Promoting gun trigger-lock use: Insights and implications from a radio-based health communication intervention. *Journal of Applied Communication Research, 30,* 210–230.

Rodriguez-Hanley, A., & Snyder, C. R. (2000). The demise of hope: On losing positive thinking. In C. R. Snyder (Ed.), *Handbook of hope: Theory, measures, and applications* (pp. 39–54). San Diego, CA: Academic Press.

Rogers, F. (2001). A point of view: Family communication, television and *Mister Rogers' Neighborhood. Journal of Family Communication, 1,* 71–73.

Sabourin, T. C. (1995). The role of negative reciprocity in spouse abuse: A relational control analysis. *Journal of Applied Communication Research, 23,* 271–283.

Sabourin, T. C., & Stamp, G. H. (1995). Communication and the experience of dialectical tensions in family life: An examination of abusive and nonabusive families. *Communication Monographs, 62,* 213–242.

Satir, V. (1967). *Conjoint family therapy: A guide to theory and technique* (Rev. ed.). Palo Alto, CA: Science and Behavior Books.

Satir, V. (1972). *Peoplemaking.* Palo Alto, CA: Science and Behavior Books.

Satir, V. (1988). *The new peoplemaking.* Mountain View, CA: Science and Behavior Books.

Scantlin, R. M., & Jordan, A. B. (2006). Families' experiences with the V-chip: An exploratory study. *Journal of Family Communication, 6,* 139–159.

Schrodt, P., & Afifi, T. D. (2007). Communication processes that predict young adults' feelings of being caught and their associations with mental health and family satisfaction. *Communication Monographs, 74,* 200–228.

Schrodt, P., Braithwaite, D. O., Soliz, J., Tye-Williams, S., Miller, A., Normand, E. L., et al.

(2007). An examination of everyday talk in stepfamily systems. *Western Journal of Communication, 71*, 216–234.

Schrodt, P., & Ledbetter, A. M. (2007). Communication processes that mediate family communication patterns and mental well-being: A mean and covariance structures analysis of young adults from divorced and nondivorced families. *Human Communication Research, 33*, 330–356.

Schrodt, P., Ledbetter, A. M., & Ohrt, J. K. (2007). Parental confirmation and affection as mediators of family communication patterns and children's mental well-being. *Journal of Family Communication, 7*, 23–46.

Seligman, M. E. P. (2002). Positive psychology, positive prevention, and positive therapy. In C. R. Snyder & S. J. Lopez (Eds.), *Handbook of positive psychology* (pp. 3–9). New York: Oxford University Press.

Seligman, M. E. P., & Csikszentmihalyi, M. (2000). Positive psychology. *American Psychologist, 55*, 5–14.

Seligman, M. E. P., Steen, T. A., Park, N., & Peterson, C. (2005). Positive psychology progress: Empirical validation of interventions. *American Psychologist, 60*, 410–421.

Shapiro, A. F., & Gottman, J. M. (2007). Effects on marriage of a psycho-communicative-educational intervention with couples undergoing the transition to parenthood, evaluation at 1-year post intervention. *Journal of Family Communication, 5*, 1–24.

Shearman, S. M., & Dumlao, R. (2008). A cross-cultural comparison of family communication patterns and conflict between young adults and parents. *Journal of Family Communication, 8*, 186–211.

Sillars, A., Canary, D. J., & Tafoya, M. (2004). Communication, conflict, and the quality of family relationships. In A. L. Vangelisti (Ed.), *Handbook of family communication* (pp. 413–446). Mahwah, NJ: Erlbaum.

Slater, M. D. (2003). Alienation, aggression, and sensation seeking as predictors of adolescent use of violent film, computer, and Website content. *Journal of Communication, 53*, 105–121.

Smith, S. W., Kopfman, J. E., Lindsey, L. L. M., Yoo, J., & Morrison, K. (2004). Encouraging family discussion on the decision to donate organs: The role of the willingness to communication scale. *Health Communication, 16*, 333–246.

Smith, S. W., Lindsey, L. L. M., Kopfman, J. E., Yoo, J., & Morrison, K. (2008). Predictors of engaging in family discussion about organ donation and getting organ donor cards witnessed. *Health Communication, 23*, 142–152.

Snyder, C. R. (Ed.). (2000). *Handbook of hope: Theory, measures, and applications.* San Diego, CA: Academic Press.

Snyder, C. R., Harris, C., Anderson, J. R., Holleran, S. A., Irving, L. M., Sigmon, S. T., et al. (1991). The will and the ways: Development of an individual-difference measure of hope. *Journal of Personality and Social Psychology, 60*, 570–585.

Snyder, C. R., Hoza, B., Pelham, W. E., Rappoff, M., Ware, L., Danovsky, M., et al. (1997). The development and validation of the children's hope scale. *Journal of Pediatric Psychology, 22*, 399–421.

Snyder, C. R., & Lopez, S. J. (Eds.). (2005). *Handbook of positive psychology.* New York: Oxford University Press.

Snyder, C. R., & Lopez, S. J. (Eds.). (2007). *Positive psychology: The scientific and practical explorations of human strengths.* Thousand Oaks, CA: Sage.

Socha, T. J. (1999). Communication and family units: Studying the first "group." In L. R. Frey (Ed.), D. S. Gouran, & M. S. Poole (Assoc. Eds.), *The handbook of small group communication theory and research* (pp. 475–492). Thousand Oaks, CA: Sage.

Socha, T. J. (2006). Orchestrating and directing domestic potential through communication: Towards a positive reframing of discipline. In L. H. Turner & R. West (Eds.), *The family communication sourcebook* (pp. 219–236). Thousand Oaks, CA: Sage.

Socha, T. J., & Diggs, R. C. (Eds.). (1999a). *Communication, race, and family: Exploring communication in Black, White, and biracial families.* Mahwah, NJ: Erlbaum.

Socha, T. J., & Diggs, R. C. (1999b). At the crossroads of communication, race, and family: Towards understanding Black, White, and biracial family communication. In T. J. Socha & R.

C. Diggs (Eds.), *Communication, race, and family: Exploring communication in Black, White, and biracial families* (pp. 1–24). Mahwah, NJ: Erlbaum.

Socha, T. J., & Stamp, G. H. (Eds.). (1995). *Parents, children, and communication: Frontiers of theory and research.* Mahwah, NJ: Erlbaum.

Soliz, J. (2007). Communicative predictors of a shared family identity: Comparison of grandchildren's perceptions of family-of-origin grandparents and stepgrandparents. *Journal of Family Communication, 7,* 177–194.

Stamp, G. H. (2004). Theories of family relationships and a family relationships theoretical model. In A. L. Vangelisti (Ed.), *Handbook of family communication* (pp. 1–30). Mahwah, NJ: Erlbaum.

Suter, E. A. (2008). Discursive negotiation of family identity: A study of U.S. families with adopted children from China. *Journal of Family Communication, 8,* 126–147.

Thomas, C. E., Booth-Butterfield, M., & Booth-Butterfield, S. (1995). Perceptions of deception, divorce disclosures, and communication satisfaction with parents. *Western Journal of Communication, 59,* 228–245.

Tilson, E. C., McBride, C. M., & Brouwer, R. N. (2005). Formative development of an intervention to stop family tobacco use: The parents and children talking (PACT) intervention. *Journal of Health Communication, 10,* 491–508.

Tims, A. R. (1986). Family political communication and social values. *Communication Research, 13,* 5–17.

Toller, P. W. (2005). Negotiation of dialectical contradictions by parents who have experienced the death of a child. *Journal of Applied Communication Research, 33,* 46–67.

Turman, P. D. (2007). Parental sport involvement: Parental influence to encourage young athlete continued sport participation. *Journal of Family Communication, 7,* 151–175.

Turner, L. H., & West, R. (Eds.). (2006a). *The family communication sourcebook.* Thousand Oaks, CA: Sage.

Turner, L. H., & West, R. (2006b). *Perspectives on family communication* (3rd ed.). Boston: McGraw-Hill.

Unger, D. G., Jacobs, S. B., & Cannon, C. (1996). Social support and marital satisfaction among couples coping with chronic constructive [sic] airway disease. *Journal of Social and Personal Relationships, 13,* 123–142.

Valente, T. W., Poppe, P. R., & Merritt, A. P. (1996). Mass-media-generated interpersonal communication as sources of information about family planning. *Journal of Health Communication, 1,* 247–266.

Vandebosch, H., & Van Cleemput, K. (2007). Television viewing and obesity among pre-school children: The role of parents. *Communications, 32,* 417–446.

Van Evra, J. (2004). *Television and child development* (3rd ed.). Mahwah, NJ: Erlbaum.

Vangelisti, A. L. (Ed.). (2004). *Handbook of family communication.* Mahwah, NJ: Erlbaum.

Vangelisti, A. L., Caughlin, J. P., & Timmerman, L. (2001). Criteria for revealing family secrets. *Communication Monographs, 68,* 1–27.

van Zoonen, L., Muller, F., Alinejad, D., Dekker, M., Duits, L., Vis van Romondt, P., et al. (2007). Dr. Phil meets the candidates: How family life and personal experience produce political discussions. *Critical Studies in Media Communication, 24,* 322–338.

Vincent, D. E. (2006). Exploring college students' family discussions about organ and tissue donation. *Communication Research Reports, 23,* 299–308.

Violence in youth sports. (n.d.). Retrieved July 14, 2008, from http://shatteredpeace.com/violence_in_youth_sports.htm

Warren, C. (1992). Perspectives on international sex practices and American family sex communication relevant to teenage sexual behavior in the United States. *Health Communication, 4,* 121–136.

Wahl, S. T., McBride, M. C., & Schrodt, P. (2005). Becoming "point and click" parents: A case study of communication and online adoption. *Journal of Family Communication, 5,* 279–294.

Warren, C., & Neer, M. (1986). Family sex communication orientation. *Journal of Applied Communication Research, 14,* 86–107.

Warren, R. (2001). In words and deeds: Parental involvement and mediation of children's television viewing. *Journal of Family Communication, 1*, 211–231.

Wartella, E., & Robb, M. (2007). Young children, new media. *Journal of Children and Media, 1*, 35–44.

Watzlawick, P., Beavin, J. H., & Jackson, D. D. (1967). *Pragmatics of human communication: A study of interactional patterns, pathologies, and paradoxes.* New York: W. W. Norton.

Weiss, A. J., & Wilson, B. J. (1998). Children's cognitive and emotional responses to the portrayal of negative emotions in family-formatted situation comedies. *Human Communication Research, 24*, 584–609.

Whaley, B. B. (1999). Explaining illness to children: Advancing theory and research by determining message content. *Health Communication, 11*, 185–193.

Whitchurch, G. G. (2001). Stayin' applied. *Journal of Family Communication, 1*, 9–13.

Whitchurch, G. G., & Webb, L. M. (1995). Applied family communication research: Casting light upon the demon. *Journal of Applied Communication Research, 23*, 239–246.

Wilson, S. R. (1999). Child physical abuse: The relevance of language and social interaction research. *Research on Language and Social Interaction, 32*, 173–184.

Wilson, S. R. (2006). First- and second-order changes in a community's response to a child abuse fatality. *Communication Monographs, 73*, 481–487.

Wilson, S. R., Hayes, J., Bylund, C., Rack, J. J., & Herman, A. P. (2006). Mothers' trait verbal aggressiveness and child abuse potential. *Journal of Family Communication, 6*, 279–296.

Wilson, S. R., Morgan, W. M., Hayes, J., Bylund, C., & Herman, A. (2004). Mothers' child abuse potential as a predictor of material and child behaviors during play-time interactions. *Communication Monographs, 71*, 395–421.

Yerby, J., Buerkel-Rothfuss, N., & Bochner, A. P. (1995). *Understanding family communication* (2nd ed.). Scottsdale, AZ: Gorsuch Scarisbrick.

Yelsma, P., & Marrow, S. (2003). An examination of couples' difficulties with emotional expressiveness and their marital satisfaction. *Journal of Family Communication, 3*, 41–62.

Zhang, Q. (2007). Family communication patterns and conflict styles in Chinese parent–child relationships. *Communication Quarterly, 55*, 113–128.

14 Organizational Communication and Applied Communication Research

Parallels, Intersections, Integration, and Engagement

David R. Seibold
University of California, Santa Barbara

Daisy R. Lemus
California State University, Northridge

Dawna I. Ballard
The University of Texas at Austin

Karen K. Myers
University of California, Santa Barbara

At least since the mid-20th century, most members of Western societies have earned a living doing jobs that are *in* organizations in those countries; today, most of those citizens earn a living by doing jobs that either are *in* or associated *with* organizations (Bridges, 1995). Organizations, thus, are significant for persons' lives and livelihoods, and, consequently, organizational communication scholars undertake the description, understanding, and critique of communicative practices in organizational life—especially the complex issues involved in contemporary organizations and organizing. Those researchers are concerned not only with internal organizational communication processes but also with interorganizational interactions, as well as organizations and discourses in social institutions and globally. The organizational communication area, therefore, is rich with opportunities for applied scholarship.

Communication researchers have studied numerous areas of organizational life to answer theoretically interesting questions that have obvious relevance for illuminating significant social issues, improving practices, or redressing societal problems—the aims of applied research (Seibold, 2008). Applied organizational communication scholarship has included analyses of voice and workplace democracy (Cheney, 1995; Stohl & Cheney, 2001), employee participation structures (K. I. Miller & Monge, 1987; Seibold & Shea, 2001), matters of difference in gender and race (B. J. Allen, 2005; Ashcraft, 2005; see also Buzzanell, Meisenbach, Remke, Sterk, & Turner, this volume; Nicotera, Clinkscales, Dorsey, & Niles, this volume), promoting dialogue (Murphy, 1995; Pearce & Pearce, 2001), emotion management at work (Waldron, 2000); compassionate workplace communication (K. I. Miller, 2007), conflict and dispute resolution (Volkema, Bergmann, & Farquhar, 1997), crisis management (Downing, 2007), workplace surveillance (M. W. Allen, Walker, Coopman, & Hart, 2007) and bullying (Tracy, Lutgen-Sandvik, & Alberts, 2006), improving group/team processes (Broome, 1995; Seibold, 1995), conducting job interviews (Jablin & Miler, 1990), leadership (Barge, 1994a; 1994b; Fairhurst, 1993b, 2007; Fairhurst, Rogers, & Sarr, 1987; Fairhurst & Sarr, 1996; Parker, 2001), managerial effectiveness (Barge, 2004; Clampitt, 2009) and supervisory communication with subordinates (Wagoner & Waldron, 1999), organizational work–family policies (Buzzanell & Meina, 2005; Kirby & Krone, 2002), organizational citizenship (Becker & O'Hair, 2007), organizational irrationality (Ashcraft & Trethewey, 2004), customer-service interactions (W. S. Z. Ford & Etienne, 1994), and organizational communication training programs (Seibold, Kudsi, & Rude, 1993).

These merely are a few of the myriad of topics studied by applied organizational communication scholars (for additional foci, see Harris & Nelson, 2008). Furthermore, applied research on organizational communication is authored by scholars with wide interests and broad identification in communication, and it is not always written by, or for, members of "organizational communication divisions" in the field's scholarly societies. Similarly, applied organizational communication research has informed and been informed by theories from across the field of communication. Integrating theory and practice, in which problems do not fit specific functional units in the field nor the theories that cross them, requires a broadening of perspective rather than a narrowing of approach (Seibold, 2005).

For these reasons, it is challenging to settle on which areas of applied organizational communication research to review in detail. Many of the areas identified above (and others, such as teams in organizations, feedback and motivation, temporality, and organizational knowledge) certainly are candidates. However, for several reasons, we focus on four areas: organizational socialization/assimilation, organizational culture, diffusion of organizational innovations, and communication and planned organizational change. First, these areas have a long history, multimethodological foundations, programmatic research, and a critical mass of replicated findings that is not true of most of the other organizational communication research areas mentioned. Second, communication is especially significant for each area. Third, research in each of these areas has been conducted by communication scholars and others outside the field, reflecting a breadth of theoretical perspectives. Fourth, because these areas of scholarship are different from each other, there is much to learn from them. However, they also overlap as foci of both research and practice (e.g., socialization and culture, culture and planned change, and planned change and innovation diffusion), and collectively, they cross micro- to macrolevels of analysis. Hence, they are not as disparate or separate as many of the applied organizational communication research areas listed previously. Fifth, research in each of the areas is similar in terms of the organizations studied: U.S. entities, in the main, with probable generalization to Western organizations (for studies of organizational communication in other cultures, see Parrish-Sprowl, this volume)—but rarely global ones—including both for-profit and nonprofit organizations (regarding applied communication research on nonprofit organizations, see Eisenberg & Eschenfelder, this volume). Consequently, the scope of the databases and the recommendations are of the same order for each area. Sixth, and especially important, each area is driven by important practical organizational concerns and proffers many implications for practice. Seventh, theory and practice interpenetrate in each of these areas: In all four areas, there are examples in which the relationship is *parallel* and separate, other studies in which theory and practice *intersect*, and still others in which theory and practice are fully *integrated*.

We first examine each of these four areas of applied organizational communication research. We conclude the chapter by addressing the three relationships of theory to practice in these areas, including the emergence of a fourth form of applied organizational communication scholarship—engaged research.

Organizational Socialization

The communicative processes by which individuals acquire knowledge and adopt the attitudes and behaviors necessary to participate as organizational members is known as *organizational socialization* (Van Maanen & Schein, 1979). Organizations socialize recruits for several reasons: to (1) preview the job and organization to potential members, which aids in screening and selecting candidates (Jablin & Miller, 1990); (2) orient recruits to the organization's culture (Schein, 1992); (3) train newcomers how to perform job duties (Myers & Oetzel, 2003); and (4) develop members for advancement and leadership roles (D. Miller & Desmarais, 2007). Interest in socialization by scholars and practitioners is fueled by the increasing frequency with which workers enter and exit organizations. Premature turnover has been linked to unsuccessful assimilation (Vandenberg & Scarpello, 1990) and is an increasing concern. Approximately 4 million employees leave (quit, are laid off, or fired) each month ("Employee Tenure in 2004," 2004), and employees remain with their employers for an average of only 4 years ("Employee Tenure Summary," 2006). Each month, then, millions of people must be socialized as they enter new jobs and learn job duties, forge working relationships, and acculturate into the work environment. Although premature turnover and "job hopping" can be stressful for employees, they also are of concern to organizations, which must incur the cost of hiring and training employees, more so given that turnover rates are very high in the first few weeks of employment (Hartline & De Witt, 2004).

Organizational socialization is especially intriguing to scholars and practitioners because it is foundational in establishing relationships between newcomers and organizations and, thus, this seemingly mundane process has considerable short- and long-term implications for both parties. As newcomers are acculturated into the ways of an organization, they develop connections that influence whether they become committed to the organization and its goals (B. J. Allen, 2005; Jones, 1986). Organizational socialization practices, however, have been criticized for the potential manipulation of recruits. Although the critique is justifiable, organizations have much at stake as they integrate newcomers. Recruits bring with them assumptions and behaviors acquired from previous work and life experiences (Beyer & Hannah, 2002) that can positively affect an organization, but newcomers may not easily mesh with current members who have experience working in the environment. Newcomers can interfere with existing work practices by questioning established rules and procedures that have been honed by previous and current members (Ashford & Black, 1996; Kramer & Noland, 1999; V. D. Miller, Johnson, Hart, & Peterson, 1999). They also can bring negative attitudes or poor work behaviors that can inhibit good working relationships and productivity.

Many aspects of socialization have been explored by organizational scholars, including newcomer adaptation strategies (B. J. Allen, 2005; Ashford & Taylor, 1990) and the content and consequences of socialization (Chao, O'Leary-Kelly, Wolf, Klein, & Gardner, 1994), as well as tests of general models of socialization (Van Maanen & Schein, 1979). Much of the research on organizational socialization has been driven by practical concerns: the type of communication that characterizes the pre-entry, entry, and settling-in phases (Jablin, 1987, 2001); anticipatory socialization and assimilation (Gibson & Papa, 2000); how context affects socialization (Ashforth, Saks, & Lee, 1998; DiSanza, 1995; Hess, 1993; Myers, 2005); the role of memorable messages in newcomer socialization (Barge & Schlueter, 2004; Bullis & Bach, 1989; Stohl, 1986); the influence of organizational insiders, work groups, and friendships on socialization (Moreland & Levine, 2001; Myers & McPhee, 2006; Zorn & Gregory, 2005); the role of mentoring in newcomer adjustment (Bullis & Bach, 1989b); and the effects of technology use on newcomer socialization (Flanagin & Waldeck, 2004).

Much of the early research on socialization investigated the means and effects of organizational efforts to socialize newcomers. Socialization typologies were created (e.g., Van Maanen, 1978; Van Maanen & Schein, 1979) and subsequent studies examined the impact of socialization tactics on newcomer integration. For example, in a study of MBA graduates, Jones (1986) found that certain socialization tactics, which he labeled "institutional strategies" (collective, formal, sequential, fixed, serial, and investiture), caused newcomers to adopt custodial orientations to their roles, whereas "individualized strategies" (individual, informal, random, variable, disjunctive, and divestiture) were related to newcomers' attempts to question the status quo and personalize their roles. More recent studies have examined the effects of socialization tactics on several theorized socialization outcomes. For instance, individualized tactics are positively related to role innovation and role conflict, but negatively related to job satisfaction and commitment (Ashforth & Saks, 1996), and newcomers' proactive behaviors mediate the effects of institutional tactics on newcomers' belief that they are well suited for the organization (Kim, Cable, & Kim, 2005). Although these studies are theoretically significant, they also are practically relevant to human resources practitioners because they demonstrate how variance in a common practice—training and orienting newcomers—affects newcomer adjustment and organizational needs.

In contrast to organizations' socialization tactics, new members' proactive efforts at socialization, especially viewing newcomers as "active message senders and receivers" (Kramer & Miller, 1999, p. 360) who join organizations, has received much less attention. This perspective is especially appealing to those who are interested in reciprocal interaction that enables members to become acquainted, involved in the social system, and acquire information about how to perform duties to become assets to their organizations (Myers, 2006). Although training can introduce newcomers to much of what they need to know to perform their duties and succeed in an organization, new members also must actively seek information to acquire job competency, alleviate their uncertainty, and obtain feedback on their behaviors (Gruman, Saks, & Zweig, 2006). Thus, among the many foci of organizational socialization scholarship, communication researchers have offered greatest insights into *how* socialization actually happens, research that is useful for developing or enhancing organizational training of newcomers.

V. D. Miller and Jablin's (1991) exemplar research introduced a model of information seeking that outlined the influences and tactics used by organizational newcomers that has been the basis for a number of communication studies. V. D. Miller and Jablin proposed that newcomers seek information to answer three questions: (1) What must I do to succeed? (2) Am I succeeding? (3) Am I accepted by others? Their model depicts seven methods of information seeking: overt, indirect, third parties, testing, disguising conversations, observing, and surveillance. Several factors influence these tactics, including the amount of uncertainty faced by a newcomer, perceived social costs associated with information seeking, availability of information sources, types of information sought, individual member characteristics, and the organizational context. This theoretical information-seeking model has many practical implications and has provided a base for applied communication research, as we highlight next.

Much of the research on information seeking has focused on how it reduces newcomers' uncertainty (e.g., Kramer, 1993; Kramer, Callister, & Turban, 1995; V. D. Miller & Jablin, 1991; V. D. Miller et al., 1999; Morrison, 1995; Saks & Ashforth, 1996). Studies also have explored information seeking to reduce uncertainty concerning membership in newly formed expansion organizations (Sias & Wyers, 2001), working in an organization following a workforce reduction (Casey, Miller, & Johnson, 1997), entering the clergy (Forward, 1999), special concerns of minorities entering mostly White organizations (Teboul, 1999), and women's entry into nontraditional blue-collar jobs (Holder, 1996).

In their quest to reduce uncertainty, members must weigh social costs involved in seeking information (V. D. Miller, 1996). In line with social exchange theory (e.g., Blau,

1964; Thibaut & Kelley, 1959), social costs are pertinent in information seeking because, as Morrison and Bies (1991) argued, the seemingly benign act of asking for appraisal can affect others' perceptions of newcomers. Social costs are related to a person's public image, including the fear that coworkers will see the newcomer as ignorant or incompetent (Morrison, 1993; Teboul, 1995). Similarly, newcomers may fear negative feedback that could damage their self-esteem and indicate a need for behavioral change (Morrison & Cummings, 1992). When newcomers predict negative, as opposed to positive, consequences, they are more likely to use less direct tactics of information seeking (Teboul, 1995). However, members may actively seek feedback when they believe that it will be mostly positive and, thereby, boost their self-esteem and enhance their public image (Morrison & Bies, 1991). Other intriguing areas of research include how information-seeking tactics vary according to the type of information sought (V. D. Miller, 1996; Morrison, 1993; Waldeck, Seibold, & Flanagin, 2004), differences in information seeking between newcomers and job transferees (Kramer et al., 1995), sources of information seeking using technology (Waldeck et al., 2004), effects of information seeking on socialization and adjustment (Ashford, 1986; Ashford & Tsui, 1991), and changes in information seeking over time (Levy, Albright, Cawley, & Williams, 1995). These studies have offered numerous insights into circumstances that facilitate or inhibit newcomers' information seeking and socialization into organizations.

Future research should continue to investigate organizational socialization as a dynamic process of negotiation, answering questions such as: How do reciprocal exchanges influence and alter socialization? How do members communicate resistance to socialization, and to what effect? How do organizational culture and occupation influence information seeking, and what effects do these have on socialization?

Organizational Culture

Organizational culture has been a central focus of both theoretical (Riley, 1993) and applied scholarship (Frost, Moore, Louis, Lundberg, & Martin, 1991). Drawing from a metaphor of organizations as cultures—with rites and ceremonies, stories and myths, and taken-for-granted assumptions and values—researchers have explored the relationship between communication and organizational goals using a variety of epistemological and methodological tools consonant with postpositivist, interpretive, and critical approaches (see Eisenberg & Riley, 2001). From R. C. Smith and Eisenberg's (1987) study of root metaphors for organizational conflict at Disneyland and Pacanowsky's (1988) exploration of empowerment at W. L. Gore to Cheney's (1995) examination of democracy and globalism at a workers' cooperative in Spain and Rosenfeld, Richman, and May's (2004) study of information adequacy in a dispersed network organization, communication scholarship in this tradition integrates practically relevant and theoretically rigorous inquiry.

Eisenberg and Riley (2001) offered a thematic typology that underscores the role of communication in investigations of organizational culture. They arrayed extant research within six overarching themes: culture as symbolism and performance, text, critique, identity, cognition, and as climate and effectiveness. Although they characterized the last category as "practical," the applied findings of work across all the themes are apparent. For instance, Hylmö and Buzzanell's (2002) exploration of the organizational subcultures surrounding telecommuting practices in a hybrid federal agency is an excellent example of research within the "culture-as-text" tradition that has important practical relevance. The study drew on Martin's (1992) three cultural lenses of *integration* (which focuses on consistency across members' accounts and shared experiences), *differentiation* (which focuses on inconsistencies across members' accounts and the subcultures that represent areas of consensus among them), and *fragmentation* (which acknowledges the ambiguity that persists in both the integration and differentiation perspectives, and focuses on the lack of any consensus among organizational members). Using these lenses, Hylmö and Buzzanell demonstrated that even as scholars maintain an ironic stance and highlight the multivocal nature of cultural texts, they still can explore ways in which organizational actors might benefit from conversations about the contested spaces, ambiguity, and flux that characterize their work. In fact, because Martin's work has had such enormous heuristic value for organizational culture research, the topical relevance and theoretical rigor of Hylmö and Buzzanell's study make it an illuminating exemplar of how this important metatheoretical perspective might be used to understand both communication processes and organizational goals. Hence, we describe the study in some detail below and underscore its applied findings.

Whereas most telecommuting research views communication primarily as an outcome—the impact of time–space distantiation on organizational members' communication patterns—Hylmö and Buzzanell (2002) explored the social construction of this contemporary organizational practice through both in-house and telecommuting members' discourse. Set in a private-sector federal agency, where 11% of employees were full-time telecommuters, the researchers interviewed 37 members, 13 of whom were full-time telecommuters. Participants were asked general questions about the agency, its culture and subcultures, their work-related tasks, and their experiences with telework.

Using Martin's (1992) integration perspective, Hylmö and Buzzanell (2002) looked for coherence in interviewees' recurring themes, symbols, and practices. A utopian narrative emerged, with telecommuting policies described as evidence of the "greatness" and "uniqueness" of the agency's innovative culture, ideal working conditions, and transformational leadership. Telecommuting primarily was seen as an innovation that allowed employees to service client needs better and, secondarily, as a practice that enabled them to manage their family and other personal needs. Most important, members viewed telecommuting as one manifestation of the "employee centrism" that characterized the culture of this organization, where members chose the work context best suited for their individual needs. This utopian narrative also revealed how organizational leaders' use of strategic ambiguity, rhetorical framing, and various cultural indicators helped members to identify with this organization despite their differences.

To develop the differentiation perspective, points of disagreement across groups that lead to the formation of subcultures were examined. Instead of finding two groups clustered around spatial working conditions, the researchers observed four subcultures among employees demarcated by their own and others' assessments of their advancement potential, as well as their experiences with on-site or teleworking arrangements. They also found that employees' perceptions of promotability were related to the fluidity or fixity of their working hours, as well as to their spatial orientations. Paradoxically, in-house members who desired promotion constructed more fluid, event-based temporal boundaries and saw face-to-face interaction as critical to advancement. Telecommuting members attempted to create more fixed temporal boundaries by keeping to schedules and compartmentalizing their time, and they felt that face time was not a factor in career advancement. In contrast, teleworkers who believed they had reached a plateau in their career enacted a fluid time between work and home activities, and purposely withdrew from workplace interactions to loosen their ties to the organization, whereas similar in-house members kept rigid working hours but maintained close working relationships with others on-site. An important finding was that neither group of in-house employees saw themselves as colleagues with the telecommuters and, consequently, their discourse reflected an "us–them" mentality.

The findings from the integration and differentiation perspectives raise two practical concerns for people contemplating a telework arrangement. Despite the intent of telecommuting to offer flexibility, the findings support Steward's (2000) conclusions that teleworkers have increased workloads and fewer leisure hours than other workers due to their willingness to accommodate others' schedules. Given that individuals often select this arrangement because of challenges they face in balancing work–life concerns, it seems imperative that these findings be considered alongside the increased flexibility of such work. In addition, the need for alternative ways to develop peer relationships, mentoring, and fairness for all employees must be addressed.

Finally, using a fragmentation lens, the investigators focused on the ambiguity, paradox, tension, and contradiction reflected in in-house and telecommuting members' discourse. Telecommuting was shrouded in mystery for in-house employees, who wondered what their teleworking colleagues really did and whether relationships with them could be maintained during a time of change, given their physical absence. Their language reflected a sense of loss, which went unacknowledged by themselves and management. Hylmö and Buzzanell (2002) explained that "although many employees recognized the loss of informal interaction at one level, at a deeper level the losses went unnoted or were swept aside. The losses and feelings of disconnectedness amounted to grief because of lost or transitioning relationships" (p. 345).

As Hylmö and Buzzanell (2002) described, findings within the fragmentation lens point to promising interventions that communication and human resource professionals might consider. The perceived mystery of telecommuting by in-house employees stresses the need for open communication with all organizational members concerning telecommuting policies and practices. Hylmö and Buzzanell suggested that electronic exchanges, meetings, newsletter columns, or even videos (e.g., *A Day in the Life of a Telecommuter*) might address these issues, as well as conversations that strengthen the perceived legitimacy of different work arrangements. In addition, members should have opportunities to address feelings of loss associated with colleagues moving off-site to perform their jobs.

Studies of organizational culture, such as Hylmö and Buzzanell's (2002) study, offer practicable findings for organizational members in a range of contexts (e.g., Hecht & Parrott, 2002; Scheibel, 1994; Schrodt, 2002; Shockley-Zalabak & Morley, 1994; Trujillo, 1992; Witmer, 1997). Such research offers idiographic rather than universal, generalizable findings; consequently, these studies allow us to consider an array of communication goals and processes within diverse approaches. The unity within this diversity, however, is reflected in the commitment of cultural scholars to respond to organizational members' everyday concerns. For instance, similar to Hylmö and Buzzanell's (2002) discussion of potential interventions, F. L. Smith and Keyton (2001) articulated ways in which communitarian contracts between employers and employees can attract and retain an engaged, committed workforce. Rosenfeld et al.'s (2004, p. 50) findings about a dispersed network organization also reflected the differentiation discourse that characterized Hylmö and Buzzanell's in-house and telecommuting subcultures, and they offered guidelines for a "unified diversity" among spatio–temporally distinct organizational members. Future studies should investigate cross-context similarities in these processes and effects, and simultaneously continue to explore organization-specific dynamics.

Diffusion of Organizational Innovations

Diffusion is the process by which an innovation is communicated through channels over time among members of a social system (Rogers, 2003). Research on the diffusion of innovations focuses on communication processes that shape how, why, and when members of a social network adopt ideas, practices, or objects that they perceive as new. Such research examines how knowledge of an innovation moves from one source to another, explains why some issues and not others are taken up and talked about, and accounts for the speed of this transmission. Practitioners are concerned with these matters because it is vital for organizations to stay current with regard to procedures, practices, and technologies.

The concept of "diffusion" originated with sociologists and anthropologists in Europe early in the 20th century. However, Rogers (1962) first offered a grounded perspective of diffusion, beginning with his research on how farmers learned from one another (and from nonnative experts) about new agricultural methods and how such knowledge changed their farming views and practices. His pioneering research is responsible for the applied focus that has made this tradition a significant part of communication scholarship, in general, and organizational communication scholarship, in particular. That tradition spans a range of contexts and topics—from durable goods to industrial innovations to social movements (see, e.g., Strang & Soule, 1998; Sultan, Farley, & Lehmann, 1990; for its tradition in development communication, see Kincaid & Figueroa, this volume)—and is of concern both to theoreticians and practitioners in research and development laboratories, marketing departments, and the federal government.

The four main elements within the process of diffusion are the innovation, communication channel, time, and social system. An *innovation* is an idea, practice, or object perceived as new by an individual, group, organization, or other entity. The *communication channel* is the medium through which messages concerning an innovation are exchanged. The relevance of *time* concerns (1) the lapse between knowledge of an innovation and an adoption or rejection decision about it—the period known as the *innovation-decision process*; (2) the time lag between early and late adopters; and (3) the adoption rate, or number of new adopters within a given time period. Finally, the *social system* is the group of interrelated units or nodes (individuals, groups, organizations, etc.) involved in the larger diffusion process.

The diffusion of an innovation is facilitated by its salience within a given social system. For example, when organizational members deem an innovation to be salient, they discuss it among their social networks—extending from departmental colleagues to members of other organizations—and these discussions shape their attitudes about it. Such discussion reflects the first two stages of the innovation-decision process, which consists of (1) knowledge (which most individuals do not proceed past), (2) persuasion, (3) decision, (4) implementation, and (5) confirmation (Rogers, 2000). For illustrative purposes, consider a new communication technology. According to the diffusion model, many organizational decision makers will gain *knowledge* of the technology. Whether they are *persuaded* about its merits is a function of discussions about it in their social network—both inside and outside the organization. Hence, if no one talks about it, they are not likely to be persuaded one way or another. If they discuss it, however, those conversations shape their attitudes toward the technology, which then shape their *decision* about whether to adopt it. If they adopt it, the next step is to *implement* the technology in the company. Finally, decision makers will seek *confirmation* that they made the proper decision, based on outcomes associated with and reactions to the innovation.

Communication researchers have focused primarily on the diffusion of news events, technological innovations, and new communication technologies, exploring the diffusion process among individuals, groups, and organizations (Rogers, 2003). Central questions in this line of research concern how earlier adopters differ from later adopters, how perceived attributes of an innovation (e.g., relative advantage, compatibility, complexity, trialability, and observability) affect its rate of adoption, why the rate of diffusion increases after the development of a critical mass, and how to develop a critical mass to diffuse an innovation rapidly (Rogers, 2003).

Among recent studies, Flanagin's (2000) research concerning the social pressures facilitating adoption of an organizational Web site is an exemplar of classic diffusion research, as it considers each of these questions and highlights the applied nature of this tradition. Flanagin explored the relative impact of three factors on Web-site diffusion processes: (1) interorganizational social pressures (i.e., what an organization's competitors were doing, the organization's self-perceived visibility and status as a leader in the field, and the perceived faddishness of Web sites), (2) organizational features (i.e., size, age, and reliance on advanced technologies), and (3) perceived benefits of and impediments to establishing a Web site (i.e., enhanced profit and reputation, improved communication and information flow, and technical complexity involved in adoption). Flanagin assessed the relationship among these factors with respect to whether an organization had a Web site, were early or late adopters, and the likelihood of adoption (for those without a Web site).

Through surveying members of the regional chamber of commerce in a medium-sized West-coast U.S. city, Flanagin (2000) obtained data on 288 organizations of varying size and age, and closely representing U.S. organizational demographics in sector type (including service, retail, finance, and transportation). Fifty-six percent reported having a company Web site, whereas 44% did not. Consistent with other research, Flanagin found that organizational characteristics (Damanpour, 1987; Swanson, 1994) and perceived benefits of an innovation (Tornatzky & Klein, 1982) predicted adoption decisions. However, Flanagin found new evidence that interorganizational social pressures are key predictors as well, explaining unique variance beyond that accounted for by these other factors. Judgment about what competitors were doing (called *institutional pressure*) was the single-best predictor of Web-site adoption: If an organization believed that similar businesses owned a Web site, they were likely to have one. Other important social pressure factors were organizations' perceptions of their visibility and leadership in the field.

Among those organizations that already had a Web site, the stage at which they adopted (early or late) was positively related to how much they relied on advanced technologies (a structural feature) or whether they perceived Web sites as faddish or avant-garde (not an impediment). In addition, for current nonadopters, the likelihood of future adoption was predicted by two perceived benefits (increased communication and organizational advantage for enhanced profit and reputation), two structural features (larger size and greater reliance on advanced technologies), and, to a lesser extent, one social pressure (institutional pressure). Thus, although social pressures were critical in distinguishing adopters from nonadopters, they were not as useful in predicting the stage of adoption and the likelihood of future adoption.

Flanagin's (2000) work demonstrates the importance of social pressures at the interorganizational level in diffusion processes and adds to other research about the importance of intraorganizational communication networks in facilitating discussion about innovations, including interpersonal relationships and team membership (e.g., Albrecht & Hall, 1991; Barker, Melville, & Pacanowsky, 1993). Furthermore, this research draws attention to the importance of considering phasic influences on diffusion processes, in that early adopters may be most influenced by their organization's structural features and perceived benefits, and social pressures may explain what causes the rate of diffusion to increase after the development of the critical mass.

Research on the diffusion of innovations in organizational contexts can benefit from continued investigation of a range of different types of innovations within various types of organizational structures. For instance, the increase in "boundaryless" or network organizations provides an opportunity to explore the communication processes that underlie diffusion at a macro-organizational level. In addition, given that the majority of diffusion studies by organizational communication researchers focuses on technological innovations (Rogers, 2003), it is important to consider whether the same factors bear equal weight in the diffusion of nontechnological innovations. For instance, what leads organizations independently and voluntarily to adopt sustainable practices? In another vein, what leads some popular management books to take on a cultlike status in certain organizational circles? This second question leads to a related critique of diffusion research, in general: a proinnovation bias in which innovations implicitly are assumed to be constructive, with the intraorganizational and interorganizational diffusion of potentially damaging innovations less often considered a topic of study (G. W. Downs & Mohr, 1976). Similarly, studying "failed" innovations may yield important findings about the diffusion process. Finally, the appropriate methods necessary to study unsuccessful innovations point to the greatest challenge for diffusion research on organizational innovations: the need to conduct longitudinal research. As Flanagin (2000) noted, most diffusion studies represent variance, rather than process, research. Gathering data at several points in time is needed to overcome the limitations associated with retrospective accounts of behaviors and feelings, as well as to investigate unsuccessful innovations that do not make it to the adoption stage. Longitudinal research also can explore time ordering among factors and their phasic influences within the diffusion cycle.

Planned Organizational Change

Changes affecting organizations are pervasive and increasing (Cheney, Christensen, Zorn, & Ganesh, 2004). Organizing for continuous change, therefore, is necessary to remain open to environmental shifts (Zorn, Page, & Cheney, 2000), especially globalization forces (see Parrish-Sprowl, this volume). Planned change allows organizations to control their adaptability, become self-reflexive, envision their future, determine a strategic plan, and communicate with organizational members to embrace the necessary changes to achieve that future (Goodstein, Nolan, & Pfeiffer, 1993).

Planned organizational change can be defined as "change that is brought about through the purposeful efforts of organizational members as opposed to change that is due to environmental or uncontrollable forces" (Lewis, Hamel, & Richardson, 2001, p. 9). Daft (1989) identified four categories that apply to planned organizational change: technology, administration, products and/or services, and human resources. These categories range from simple minor efforts, such as altering physical space or introducing a new procedure, to complex major efforts, such as introducing an organization-wide new communication technology or merging with another organization.

Planned organizational change is an umbrella term encompassing intervention, and intervention includes implementation. Planned change assumes that organizations decide to alter current processes, operations, and outcomes to become more efficient, profitable, competitive, and so forth. Interventions into current practices are planned to solve targeted problems or to foster improvement by implementing progressive change (see Frey & SunWolf, this volume).

Numerous theoretical perspectives seek to explain the processes and outcomes of planned organizational change (Beer & Nohria, 2000; Edmondson, 1996), but they cohere within four approaches. First, *open systems* perspectives (Schein, 1987; Senge, 1990) view change in organizations as influencing a system of inputs, throughputs, and outputs, with change in internal components causing changes in other (interdependent) components (e.g., people, structures, and tasks). Second, *process* approaches to change advance the systems perspective by investigating causal relationships between interdependent components of an organization and by focusing on throughputs as processes that mediate inputs and outcomes over time. Third, *cognitive* models of change processes capture how organizational members acquire, organize, and make sense of change

(Bartunek, Lacey, & Wood, 1992), suggesting that members' interpretations of change influence the overall environment of change in an organization through processes such as feedback, resistance, and concern for others. Finally, *organizational development* theories (e.g., French & Bell, 1999: Worren, Ruddle, & Moore, 1999) view change from organizational members' perspectives; involve a process of discarding old and learning new information; and focus on culture, leadership, and communication through changes in individual members' skills and attitudes.

Typically, organizations employ individual-based or team-based "change agents" to design and implement planned organizational changes. *Change agents* are the primary implementers of change, regardless of whether they are internal to an organization (e.g., members from different levels and functions of the organization) or external constituents or implementers (e.g., consultants). Lewis and Seibold (1998) proposed that planned change entails managing communication among those involved with and affected by organizational change (leaders, change agents, employees, and stakeholders), managing information communicated in favor of the plan and responses to it, and preparing organizational members to conduct work in a manner consistent with the plan. Here, we consider research on the role of communication processes in the design, implementation, and foci of planned organizational change.

Design of Planned Organizational Change

Numerous areas of research and practice are associated with the design of planned organizational change. Organizational development programs are types of planned changes that seek to improve undesirable situations by imcreasing the functioning of individuals, work groups, and organizations, and by aiding organizational members to sustain efforts of continuous improvement (French & Bell, 1999). In contrast to organizational development, change management (e.g., Worren et al., 1999) instills behavioral change prior to attitudinal change or even instead of organizational learning. Through *experiencing* new change, organizational members begin to understand and embrace change efforts.

Zorn et al. (2000) investigated the logics managers invoke that, in turn, shape the way they communicate about, manage, and evaluate change in organizations. Utilizing a functional–romantic–critical framework and collecting data at a local government agency, Zorn et al. found that from a *functional* perspective, change is communicated as a necessity for improvement, managed via messages encouraging staff to enact a learning organization, and is evaluated for its effectiveness in furthering an organization's interests. From a *romantic* perspective, change is communicated as necessary for strengthening core organizational values and is managed and evaluated through inspiration and the sense of bonding it promotes among organizational members. From a *critical* perspective, change is communicated as manipulation and oppression of workers, managed through domination and re-creation of a system of concertive control, and is evaluated based on the transparent acceptance of top-down decisions. Their work on the different logics underlying change management activities, thus, illuminates communicative practices associated with the *design* of planned organizational change.

Implementation of Planned Organizational Change

Scholars in communication (Larkin & Larkin, 1994; Lewis, 1997, 1999), training and development (DeWine, 2001), organizational psychology (King & Anderson, 1995), and organizational behavior (Worren et al., 1999) share at least three assumptions concerning organizational change implementation. First, given that organizations constantly are changing, change programs must promote advances that are enduring and resilient (Ill-back & Zins, 1995). Of course, change is not perceived the same way by all organiza-tional members; managers, implementers, users, and stakeholders often have different needs, perspectives, and reactions (Lewis, 1997). Such differences are evident in research on power dynamics, conflicts of interest, and resistance surrounding organizational change (Frost & Egri, 1991).

The second assumption is that organizational changes differ widely in terms of causes and effects. External pressures typically trigger organizational change, but change can be a function of internal pressures, such as employee dissatisfaction. Lewis et al. (2001) used a systems view to suggest that numerous situational, psychological, structural, environmental, and cultural factors influence the design and implementation of planned organizational changes. In particular, Lewis and Seibold (1993) noted that implementa-tion activities tend to be influenced by the scope, novelty, and complexity of the planned change, and Lewis and Seibold (1998) indicated that the political context surrounding a change effort, timing and nature of the change, employees' participation throughout the implementation, and managers' expectations, interpretations, and influence all have sig-nificant effects on the results of an implementation process. In terms of its effects, Lewis (1999) found that planned change typically disrupts organizational work and relation-ships by introducing new structures, values, roles, and operations, as well as by imple-menting the change itself (e.g., new procedures, equipment, or personnel).

Change is not always welcome by organizational members (V. D. Miller, Johnson, & Grau, 1994); consequently, planned change efforts often are met with resistance and failure (King & Anderson, 1995; Lewis, 2000). Research has revealed many bases of such resistance and failure. Fullan, Miles, and Taylor (1980), for instance, suggested that inad-equate systematic organizational assessments and poor problem clarification, inattention to organizational readiness for change, simplistic intervention packages, and the lack of follow-up procedures are some reasons why change efforts fail. Medved et al. (2001) asserted that ownership tension, or the conflict that key players face in accepting respon-sibility for the problem and ownership of the change process, is inherent and critical to the success of change implementation efforts. Among the causes and effects of failure and resistance to change is the high degree of uncertainty experienced by organizational members (Markus, 1983). Illback and Zins (1995) also noted that focusing on only one group of people in an organization undermines the systemic nature of organizations and explains why organizational change efforts fail 50 to 90% of the time, especially with mergers and business unit reengineering (Lewis, 2000), downsizing (Appelbaum, Close, & Klasa, 1999), and quality improvement programs (Beer, 2003).

The third assumption is that communication is an integral factor in the success of planned organizational change efforts (Covin & Kilmann, 1990). Some view communi-cation merely as a tool (e.g., Hersey, Blanchard, & Johnson, 2008), whereas others view it as the process by which change occurs (Poole, Van de Ven, Dooley, & Holmes, 2000), and still others view it as part of the outcomes of change (Timmerman, 2003). In gen-eral, as Lewis and Seibold (1998) concluded, communication predicts the formation of people's attitudes regarding planned changes, resistance to change programs, behavioral coping responses to innovation, and the outcomes of organizational change programs.

Communication Foci of Planned Organizational Change

Researchers have focused on a wide variety of communicative practices related to planned organizational change, such as framing a change-related vision (Fairhurst, 1993a), influ-ence of information and social interaction on employees' participation in and anxiety toward change (K. I. Miller & Monge, 1985; V. D. Miller et al., 1994), communication channels employed by organizational members and implementers during change (Fidler & Johnson, 1984; Lewis, 1997), and use of feedback to shape proposed changes (Johnson & Rice, 1987). In particular, research on communication and planned change has focused on information related to flow (e.g., feedback loops, valence, and directionality), channels (e.g., mediated vs. face-to-face), effects (e.g., employee participation, anxiety, and resistance), and the positioning of communication as an outcome or byproduct (e.g., feedback usefulness, increased social interaction, and communication as a challenge for change agents).

Although scholars agree that involving *employees* in the change process by providing them with relevant information is an important strategy (Fulk, 1993; Rice & Aydin, 1991), K. I. Miller and Monge (1985) pointed out that the matter is much more complex than just assuming that because employees have certain needs, any opportunity they have to fulfill them will likely lead to acceptance of change efforts. Indeed, ample research shows that employees often experience anxiety and uncertainty during change; thus, they experience other needs. Openness to change is related to employees' ability to fulfill their need for achievement, have access to high-quality information, and reduce ambiguity regarding their roles (V. D. Miller et al., 1994). Hence, participating in change efforts means providing employees with information necessary to fulfill these needs and having them feel a sense of control over the consequences of changing (Lewis, 2000).

V. D. Miller et al. (1994) concluded that employees' willingness to participate in planned organizational change indicates their intention to accept change and perform their duties in a manner consistent with that change. However, one major challenge that organizations continue to face in implementing change is getting employees to accept new ways of working (Cheney et al., 2004). Lewis and Seibold (1993) proposed that employees' communicative and other behavioral responses are triggered by their concerns regarding uncertainty and differential information access, acquisition and regulation of norms, and their performance in light of the changes. Lewis (1997) found that in addition to understanding resistance and receptivity, employees' responses—such as valence (positivity vs. negativity), the decidedness or firmness of the response, and the focus of the response (self vs. others)—went beyond the typical negativity toward change reported in the literature. Furthermore, Lewis and Seibold (1993, 1996) found that organizational members search for information, consider possible alternatives to a change, persuade others to support or not support the change, and formally resist the change altogether.

Change agents' assumptions concerning the change process, their view of communication during change, and their communication-related strategies for promoting change also are important to understanding planned organizational change. First, despite possible initial resistance, change agents assume that organizational members eventually will accept a change and take on the role of change agents themselves by spreading it to coworkers (Bartunek et al., 1992) with positive effects. However, research indicates that change agents overemphasize and overanticipate problems related to change resistance, despite a high likelihood that a particular change might be *welcome* by organizational members (Lewis, 2000). Second, J. D. Ford and Ford (1995) argued that the challenges change agents confront inherently are communicative. Indeed, Lewis (2000) found that implementers rank communication among the most problematic challenges, especially because they view it as related to employee resistance and conflict as predictors of failed change efforts. Third, change agents play a central role in influencing organizational members through their interactions with them. For instance, Lewis and Seibold (1998) found a pattern of characteristics—openness and responsiveness, comfort and ambiguity, and high self-concept—related to *how* change agents promote success during implementation.

In addition, change agents use multiple communication channels to convey information to, and receive it from, different organizational groups, with Lewis (1999) reporting that the amount of information conveyed and solicited differed significantly between employees and volunteers. Change agents also distinguish between information dissemination and solicitation. They tend to use small, informal discussions and general informational meetings to promote change, and they rely on word-of-mouth to disseminate information about planned change, but resort to informal, direct channels to solicit input.

A fundamental perception that management shares with professional change agents is that planned change is necessary (Zorn et al., 2000), employee resistance will happen (Deetz, 1992), and that such resistance must be overcome, although views concerning the pervasiveness of resistance and the need to counter it have been challenged (Dent & Goldberg, 1999). Hence, managers begin to conceive of change prior to understanding its implications and take it on as an "internal campaign." To maintain the perception of stability, managers are faced with the need to implement change and develop a discourse of flexibility and openness about it, a notion that Cheney et al. (2004) termed the "dialectic of change-constancy." Fairhurst (1993a) described management's primary role during implementation as an internal marketing campaign, in which managers simultaneously disseminate and "sell" change information to mold an organization's image and values and prevent employee resistance. In focusing on communicating change to employees to influence them, V. D. Miller et al. (1994) indicated that managers often overlook the influential role that workers' needs and their social interactions with peers have on shaping upward expectations of a planed organizational change.

Organizational communication scholars, however, largely have ignored the role of internal and external stakeholders (e.g., investors, board members, and affiliates) and their interaction with change agents and other organizational members during planned organizational change. In a notable exception, Lewis et al. (2001) found that the perceived need for communication efficiency, and for consensus building, distinguished how implementers communicated change to stakeholders in six ways: (1) disseminating information equally, (2) accepting the participation of all stakeholders equally, (3) providing access to communication based only on the exchange of a valuable stakeholder resource (quid pro quo), (4) providing information on a need-to-know basis, (5) constructing messages targeted at specific stakeholders (marketing), and (6) communicating as events unfolded (reactionary).

Key questions for future research on planned organizational change include: During the stages of organizational change implementation, how are members connected via their communicative behavior? How does interdependence among organizational members influence their involvement, participation, and social interaction during the stages of planned change? What influences organizational members' perceptions of change (e.g., uncertainty, information, and involvement) and how do these perceptions influence their communicative behavior with other members? How does communication as a process influence change outcomes? How are the various dualities that are inherent in change (Seo, Putnam, & Bartunek, 2003) communicatively *managed* during planned change initiatives?

Trends in Applied Organizational Communication Research

Applied communication scholarship, in general, has taken at least three forms, each differentiated by how the relationship between theory and practice is viewed (Seibold, 2008). First, and particularly in its earliest form, applied research has been viewed as a *parallel* type of scholarship to basic research (G. R. Miller & Sunnafrank, 1984). Bifurcated as "practice *and* theory," they are seen as different research avenues and frequently of different status. Second, especially during the past 2 decades, applied communication research has been seen as the *intersection* of theory and practice (Petronio, 1999). Discussed in terms such as "theory *into* practice/theory *from* practice," they are viewed as reciprocal when the foci and paths of each intersect. Third, and increasingly of late, there are calls for and efforts at the *integration* of theory and research (Barge, 2001). Conjoined as "theory *with* practice/practice *with* theory," their recursive and mutually transformative potential has been underscored (Seibold, 2005; regarding the role of theory in applied communication research, see Barge & Craig, this volume; Frey & SunWolf, this volume).

Applied organizational communication scholarship reflects these forms and trends, as can be demonstrated in the four longstanding areas of research that we reviewed: organizational socialization, organizational culture, diffusion of organizational innovations, and planned organizational change. We first examine these areas of applied organizational communication scholarship in terms of the parallels, intersections, and integration of theory and practice, and then focus on the contributions of an emerging fourth form of applied organizational communication research—engaged scholarship.

Parallel, Intersecting, and Integrated Applied Organizational Communication Research

A number of the studies reviewed in the four areas represent applied organizational communication research that takes only a *parallel* view of the relationship between theory and practice. For an example from each area, see Jones's (1986) study of organizational socialization tactics and their relevance for newcomer training, Schrodt's (2002) report of employee identification and organizational culture, findings by Albrecht and Hall (1991) concerning the importance of intraorganizational communication networks in facilitating discussion about innovations, and research by J. D. Ford and Ford (1995) on the role of conversations in organizational change.

However, there also is applied scholarship in the four areas in which theory and practice intersect or are integrated. The *intersection* of theory and practice, again to note but one example from each area, is most apparent in Jablin and Miller's (1990) analysis of newcomer–supervisor role negotiation processes, Hylmö and Buzzanell's (2002) exploration of the organizational (sub)cultures surrounding telecommuting practices in a federal agency, Flanagin's (2000) research on the social pressures facilitating organizational Web-site adoption, and Lewis's (2000) findings concerning implementers' reports of communication problems associated with organizational change initiatives.

Scholarship in which theory and practice are *integrated* is evident in Ashforth et al.'s (1998) research on specific organizational contexts and newcomer adjustment, Pacanowsky's (1988) examination of empowerment as part of the organizational culture at W. L. Gore, the role of work-team membership and communication dynamics on organizational innovation described in a larger study by Barker et al. (1993), and the approach to communicating organizational change proffered by Larkin and Larkin (1994) as the intersection of their reading of longstanding theoretical findings and their successes as practitioners in ongoing organizational change initiatives.

Engaged Scholarship: Contributions to Integrating Theory and Practice

The field of communication recently has witnessed calls for (Applegate, 2002), and efforts at (Simpson & Shockley-Zalaback, 2005), an extension to the integration of theory and practice in applied communication scholarship that moves far beyond "application" of communication theory and research (C. Downs, 1999) and past the "translation" of scholarship into practice (Petronio, 1999). This fourth form of applied communication scholarship is a more "engaged" type (e.g., Barge, Simpson, & Shockley-Zalabak, 2008; Cheney, Wilhelmsson, & Zorn, 2002), in which theory and practice are mutually transformative and so enmeshed as to be separable mainly for reflexive and analytical purposes. *Engaged scholarship* demonstrates a dynamic, oscillating interplay between situated practices and theoretical constructs (as though they simply are the same main transportation artery). As Seibold (2005) noted, such work is characterized by

> much more involvement (even immersion) by engaged scholars [that includes] close work and learning *with* stakeholders, appropriation and application of theoretical work but *eclectically so* (and not simply as a theory-testing means to researchers' scholarship ends), and *theory shaping and (re)formulation* throughout the process. (p. 15)

Many examples of engaged scholarship exist across the field of communication (e.g., the studies in Frey & Carragee, 2007), and this form of scholarship is discussed in other chapters in this volume (e.g., Frey & SunWolf). There also are noteworthy examples of *engaged organizational communication research*, and they are becoming more prevalent. For example, in the four areas examined in this chapter, Scott and Myers (2005) studied how municipal firefighters are socialized to manage their emotions, Cheney (1995) analyzed democracy at a workers' cooperative in Spain, Rogers (1962) described how farmers learned about new agricultural methods and changed their farming practices, and Seibold (1995) detailed the creation of team management in a new design plant. We also cited engaged research in the introduction to the chapter, such as that conducted by Fairhurst (1993a), Kirby and Krone (2002), and Pearce and Pearce (2001; see also Pearce, Spano, & Pearce, this volume).

Other compelling, engaged organizational communication scholarship includes McPherson and Deetz's (2005) reflexive account of the "jagged evolution" of their action research with participants engaged in merged high-tech cultures in a state university system, Thackaberry-Ziegler's ongoing work with wildland firefighters (e.g., Thackaberry, 2004), and Eisenberg's (2005) reflexive approach to service and consulting engagements (and the importance of conscious and reflexive communication for all parties). Not only is the level of scholar immersion in all of these studies quite deep (sometimes for years) and the theory–practice relationship fluid and evolving but, at times, the research also is cocreated by scholars, practitioners, and stakeholders (Simpson & Seibold, 2008). These works and others like them (cf. Harter, Scott, Novak, Leeman, & Morris, 2006; Lucas, 2007) represent a key addition to applied organizational communication scholarship.

Conclusion

In this chapter, we framed applied organizational communication research as investigations of communication in organizational life that answer theoretically important questions *and* illuminate significant social issues, improve practices, or redress societal problems. Noting numerous areas of such scholarship in the introduction, and representative examples in each area, we focused on four areas in which communication is especially significant: organizational socialization/assimilation, organizational culture, diffusion of organizational innovations, and communication and planned organizational change. These four areas have long histories, multimethodological foundations, programmatic and replicated findings, breadth of theoretical perspectives, analyses that cross micro and macro levels, and many implications for practice. Especially important, as shown in the last section of the chapter, theory and practice interpenetrate in each of these areas: There are examples in which the relationship is parallel and separate, other studies in which theory and practice intersect, and still others in which theory and practice are full integrated. We concluded with reference to the emergence of a fourth form of applied organizational communication scholarship—engaged research. If the studies in this fourth area are emulated, and if they develop a critical mass of subsequent inquiry focused on the particular theoretical puzzles and practical challenges they raise, engaged scholarship will become a mainstay of organizational communication research in the future. When that process occurs, the term *applied* organizational communication research will be redundant.

References

Albrecht, T. L., & Hall, B. J. (1991). Facilitating talk about new ideas: The role of personal relationships in organizational innovation. *Communication Monographs, 58*, 273–288.

Allen, B. J. (2005). Social constructionism. In S. May & D. K. Mumby (Eds.), *Engaging organizational communication: Theory and research* (pp. 35–54). Thousand Oaks, CA: Sage.

Allen, M. W., Walker, K. L., Coopman, S. J., & Hart, J. (2007). Workplace surveillance and managing privacy boundaries. *Management Communication Quarterly, 21*, 172–200.

Appelbaum, S. H., Close, T. G., & Klasa, S. (1999). Downsizing: An examination of some successes and more failures. *Management Decision, 37*, 424–436.

Applegate, J. L. (2002, January). Communication as an engaged discipline: Seeing with new eyes and skating to where the puck will be. *Spectra, 38*, pp. 7–15.

Ashcraft, K. L. (2005). Feminist organizational communication studies: Engaging gender in public and private. In S. May & D. K. Mumby (Eds.), *Engaging organizational communication: Theory and research* (pp. 141–170). Thousand Oaks, CA: Sage.

Ashcraft, K. L., & Trethewey, A. (2004). Developing tension: An agenda for applied research on the organization of irrationality. *Journal of Applied Communication Research, 32*, 171–181.

Ashford, S. J. (1986). Feedback-seeking in individual adaptation: A resource perspective. *Academy of Management Journal, 29*, 465–487.

Ashford, S. J., & Black, J. S. (1996). Proactivity during organizational entry: The role of desire for control. *Journal of Applied Psychology, 81*, 199–214.

Ashford, S. J., & Taylor, M. (1990). Adaptation to work transitions: An integrative approach. In G. R. Ferris & K. M. Rowland (Eds.), *Research in personnel and human resource management* (Vol. 8, pp. 1–39). Greenwich, CT: JAI Press.

Ashford, S. J., & Tsui, A. S. (1991). Self-regulation for managerial effectiveness: The role of active feedback seeking. *Academy of Management Journal, 34*, 251–280.

Ashforth, B. E., & Saks, A. M. (1996). Socialization tactics: Longitudinal effects on newcomer adjustment. *Academy of Management Journal, 39*, 149–178.

Ashforth, B. E., Saks, A. M., & Lee, R. T. (1998). Socialization and newcomer adjustment: The role of organizational context. *Human Relations, 51*, 897–926.

Barge, J. K. (1994a). *Leadership: Communication skills for organizations and groups.* New York: St. Martin's Press.

Barge, J. K. (1994b). Putting leadership back to work. *Management Communication Quarterly, 8*, 95–109.

Barge, J. K. (2001). Practical theory as mapping, engaged reflection, and transformative practice. *Communication Theory, 11*, 5–13.

Barge, J. K. (2004). Reflexivity and managerial practice. *Communication Monographs, 71*, 70–96.

Barge, J. K., & Schlueter, D. W. (2004). Memorable messages and newcomer socialization. *Western Journal of Communication, 68*, 233–256.

Barge, J. K., Simpson, J. L., & Shockley-Zalabak, P. (Eds.). (2008). Toward purposeful and practical models of engaged scholarship [Special forum]. *Journal of Applied Communication Research, 36,* 243–297.

Barker, J. R., Melville, C. W., & Pacanowsky, M. E. (1993). Self-directed teams at XEL: Changes in communication practices during a program of cultural transformation. *Journal of Applied Communication Research, 21,* 297–312.

Bartunek, J. M., Lacey, C. A., & Wood, D. R. (1992). Social cognition in organizational change: An insider-outsider approach. *Journal of Applied Behavioral Science, 28,* 204–223.

Becker, J. A. H., & O'Hair, H. D. (2007). Machiavellians' motives in organizational citizenship behavior. *Journal of Applied Communication Research, 35,* 246–267.

Beer, M. (2003). Why total quality management programs do not persist: The role of management quality and implications for leading a TQM transformation. *Decision Sciences, 34,* 623–642.

Beer, M., & Nohria, N. (Eds.). (2000). *Breaking the code of change.* Boston: Harvard Business School Press.

Beyer, J. M., & Hannah, D. R. (2002). Building on the past: Enacting established personal identities in a new work setting. *Organization Science, 13,* 636–652.

Blau, P. M. (1964). *Exchange and power in social life.* New York: Wiley.

Bridges, W. (1995). *Jobshift: How to prosper in a workplace without jobs.* Reading, MA: Addison-Wesley.

Broome, B. J. (1995). The role of facilitated group process in community-based planning and design: Promoting greater participation in Comanche tribal governance. In L. R. Frey (Ed.), *Innovations in group facilitation: Applications in natural settings* (pp. 27–52). Cresskill, NJ: Hampton Press.

Bullis, C., & Bach, B. W. (1989). Socialization turning points: An examination of change in organizational identification. *Western Journal of Speech Communication, 53,* 273–293.

Buzzanell, P. M., & Meina, L. (2005). Struggling with maternity leave policies and practices: A poststructuralist feminist analysis of gendered organizing. *Journal of Applied Communication Research, 33,* 1–25.

Casey, M. K., Miller, V. D., & Johnson, J. R. (1997). Survivors' information seeking following a reduction in workforce. *Communication Research, 24,* 755–781.

Chao, G., O'Leary-Kelly, A. M., Wolf, S., Klein, H. J., & Gardner, P. D. (1994). Organizational socialization: Its content and consequences. *Journal of Applied Psychology, 79,* 730–743.

Cheney, G. (1995). Democracy in the workplace: Theory and practice from the perspective of communication. *Journal of Applied Communication Research, 23,* 167–200.

Cheney, G., Christensen, L. T., Zorn, T. E., Jr., & Ganesh, S. (2004). *Organizational communication in an age of globalization: Issues, reflections, practices.* Prospect Heights, IL: Waveland Press.

Cheney, G., Wilhelmsson, M., & Zorn, T. E., Jr. (2002). 10 strategies for engaged scholarship. *Management Communication Quarterly, 16,* 92–101.

Clampitt, P. G. (2009). *Communicating for managerial effectiveness* (4th ed.). Thousand Oaks, CA: Sage.

Covin, T. J., & Kilmann, R. H. (1990). Participant perceptions of positive and negative influences on large-scale change. *Group & Organization Management, 15,* 233–248.

Daft, R. L. (1989). *Organization theory and design* (3rd ed.). St Paul, MN: West.

Damanpour, F. (1987). The adoption of technological, administrative, and ancillary innovations: Impact of organizational factors. *Journal of Management, 13,* 675–688.

Deetz, S. A. (1992). *Democracy in an age of corporate colonization: Developments in communication and the politics of everyday life.* Albany: State University of New York Press.

Dent, E. B., & Goldberg, S. G. (1999). Challenging "resistance to change." *Journal of Applied Behavioral Science, 35,* 25–41.

DeWine, S. (2001). *The consultant's craft: Improving organizational communication* (2nd ed.). Boston: Bedford/St. Martin's Press.

DiSanza, J. R. (1995). Bank teller organizational assimilation in a system of contradictory practices. *Management Communication Quarterly, 9,* 191–218.

Downing, J. R. (2007). No greater sacrifice: American Airlines employee crisis response to the September 11 attack. *Journal of Applied Communication Research, 35,* 350–375.

Downs, C. (1999). Challenges for the application of organizational communication. In P. J. Salem (Ed.), *Organizational communication and change* (pp. 243–258). Cresskill, NJ: Hampton Press.

Downs, G. W., Jr., & Mohr, L. B. (1976). Conceptual issues in the study of innovation. *Administrative Science Quarterly, 21,* 700–714.

Edmondson, A. C. (1996). Three faces of Eden: The persistence of competing theories and multiple diagnoses in organizational intervention research. *Human Relations, 49,* 571–595.

Eisenberg, E. M. (2005). Creating clearings for communication. In J. L. Simpson & P. Shockley-Zalabak (Eds.), *Engaging communication, transforming organizations: Scholarship of engagement in action* (pp. 113–125). Cresskill, NJ: Hampton Press.

Eisenberg, E. M., & Riley, P. (2001). Organizational culture. In F. M. Jablin & L. L. Putnam (Eds.), *The new handbook of organizational communication* (pp. 291–322). Thousand Oaks, CA: Sage.

Employee Tenure in 2004. (2004, September 21). Washington, DC: U.S. Bureau of Labor Statistics. Retrieved July 29, 2007, from http://www.bls.gov/news.release/archives/tenure_09212004.pdf

Employee Tenure Summary. (2006, September 8). Washington, DC: U.S. Bureau of Labor Statistics. Retrieved December 12, 2006, from http://www.bls.gov/news.release/tenure.nr0.htm

Fairhurst, G. T. (1993a). Echoes of the vision: When the rest of the organization talks total quality. *Management Communication Quarterly, 6,* 331–371.

Fairhurst, G. T. (1993b). The leader–member exchange patterns of women leaders in industry: A discourse analysis. *Communication Monographs, 60,* 321–351.

Fairhurst, G. T. (2007). *Discursive leadership: In conversation with leadership psychology.* Thousand Oaks, CA: Sage.

Fairhurst, G. T., Rogers, L. E., & Sarr, R. A. (1987). Manager–subordinate control patterns and judgments about the relationship. In M. McLaughlin (Ed.), *Communication yearbook* (Vol. 10, pp. 395–415). Newbury Park, CA: Sage.

Fairhurst, G. T., & Sarr, R. A. (1996). *The art of framing: Managing the language of leadership.* San Francisco: Jossey-Bass.

Fidler, L. A., & Johnson, J. D. (1984). Communication and innovation implementation. *Academy of Management Review, 9,* 704–711.

Flanagin, A. J. (2000). Social pressures on organizational Website adoption. *Human Communication Research, 26,* 618–646.

Flanagin, A. J., & Waldeck, J. H. (2004). Technology use and organizational newcomer socialization. *Journal of Business Communication, 41,* 137–165.

Ford, J. D., & Ford, L. W. (1995). The role of conversations in producing intentional change in organizations. *Academy of Management Review, 20,* 541–570.

Ford, W. S. Z., & Etienne, C. N. (1994). Can I help you? A framework for the interdisciplinary research on customer service encounters. *Management Communication Quarterly, 7,* 413–441.

Forward, G. L. (1999). Encountering the nonprofit organization: Clergy uncertainty and information-seeking during organizational entry. *Journal of Communication and Religion, 22,* 190–213.

French, W. L., & Bell, C. H., Jr. (1999). *Organization development: Behavioral science interventions for organization improvement* (6th ed.). Upper Saddle River, NJ: Prentice-Hall.

Frey, L. R., & Carragee, K. M. (Eds.). (2007). *Communication activism* (2 Vols.). Cresskill, NJ: Hampton Press.

Frost, P. J., & Egri, C. P. (1991). The political process of innovation. In B. M. Staw & L. L. Cummings (Eds.), *Research in organizational behavior* (Vol. 2, pp. 229–295). Greenwich, CT: JAI Press.

Frost, P. J., Moore, L. F., Louis, M. R., Lundberg, C. C., & Martin, J. (Eds.). (1991). *Reframing organizational culture.* Newbury Park, CA: Sage.

Fulk, J. (1993). Social construction of communication technology. *Academy of Management Journal, 36,* 921–950.

Fullan, M., Miles, M. B., & Taylor, G. (1980). Organization development in schools: The state of the art. *Review of Educational Research, 50*, 121–183.

Gibson, M. K., & Papa, M. J. (2000). The mud, the blood, and the beer guys: Organizational osmosis in blue-collar work groups. *Journal of Applied Communication Research, 28*, 68–88.

Goodstein, L. D., Nolan, T. M., & Pfeiffer, J. W. (1993). *Applied strategic planning: A comprehensive guide.* New York: McGraw-Hill.

Gruman, J. A., Saks, A. M., & Zweig, D. I. (2006). Organizational socialization tactics and newcomer proactive behaviors: An integrative study. *Journal of Vocational Behavior, 69*, 90–104.

Harris, T. E., & Nelson, D. E. (2008). *Applied organizational communication: Theory and practice in a global environment* (3rd ed.). Mahwah, NJ: Erlbaum.

Harter, L. M., Scott, J. A., Novak, D. R., Leeman, M., & Morris, J. F. (2006). Freedom through flight: Performing a counter-narrative of disability. *Journal of Applied Communication Research, 34*, 3–29.

Hartline, M. D., & De Witt, T. (2004). Individual differences among service employees: The conundrum of employee recruitment, selection, and retention. *Journal of Relationship Marketing, 3*(2–3), 25–32.

Hecht, M. L., & Parrott, R. (2002). Creating a departmental culture for communication grants. *Journal of Applied Communication Research, 30*, 382–392.

Hersey, P., Blanchard, K. H., & Johnson, D. E. (2008). *Management of organizational behavior: Leading human resources* (8th ed.). Upper Saddle River, NJ: Pearson Prentice Hall.

Hess, J. A. (1993). Assimilating newcomers into an organization: A cultural perspective. *Journal of Applied Communication Research, 21*, 189–210.

Holder, T. (1996). Women in nontraditional organizations: Information-seeking during organizational entry. *Journal of Business Communication, 33*, 9–26.

Hylmö, A., & Buzzanell, P. M. (2002). Telecommuting as viewed through cultural lenses: An empirical investigation of the discourses of utopia, identity, and mystery. *Communication Monographs, 69*, 329–356.

Illback, R. J., & Zins, J. E. (1995). Organizational interventions in educational settings. *Journal of Educational and Psychological Consultation, 6*, 217–236.

Jablin, F. M. (1987). Organizational entry, assimilation, and exit. In F. M. Jablin, L. L. Putnam, K. H. Roberts, & L. W. Porter (Eds.), *Handbook of organizational communication: An interdisciplinary perspective* (pp. 679–740). Newbury Park, CA: Sage.

Jablin, F. M. (2001). Organizational entry, assimilation, and exit. In F. M. Jablin & L. L. Putnam (Eds.), *The new handbook of organizational communication* (pp. 732–818). Thousand Oaks, CA: Sage.

Jablin, F. M., & Miller, V. D. (1990). Interviewer and applicant questioning behavior in employment interviews. *Management Communication Quarterly, 4*, 51–86.

Johnson, B. M., & Rice, R. E. (1987). *Managing organizational innovation: The evolution from word processing to office information systems.* New York: Columbia University Press.

Jones, G. R. (1986). Socialization tactics, self-efficacy, and newcomers' adjustments to organizations. *Academy of Management Journal, 29*, 262–279.

Kim, T.-Y., Cable, D. M., & Kim, S.-P. (2005). Socialization tactics, employee proactivity, and person–organization fit. *Journal of Applied Psychology, 90*, 232–241.

King, N., & Anderson, N. (1995). *Innovation and change in organizations.* London: Routledge.

Kirby, E. L., & Krone, K. J. (2002). "The policy exists but you can't really use it": Communication and the structuration of work–family policies. *Journal of Applied Communication Research, 30*, 50–77.

Kramer, M. W. (1993). Communication and uncertainty reduction during job transfers: Leaving and joining processes. *Communication Monographs, 60*, 178–198.

Kramer, M. W., Callister, R. R., & Turban, D. B. (1995). Information-receiving and information-giving during job transitions. *Western Journal of Communication, 59*, 151–170.

Kramer, M. W., & Miller, V. D. (1999). A response to criticisms of organizational socialization research: In support of contemporary conceptualizations of organizational assimilation. *Communication Monographs, 66*, 358–367.

Kramer, M. W., & Noland, T. L. (1999). Communication during job promotions: A case of ongoing assimilation. *Journal of Applied Communication Research, 27,* 335–355.

Larkin, T. J., & Larkin, S. (1994). *Communicating change: How to win employee support for new business directions.* New York: McGraw-Hill.

Levy, P. E., Albright, M. D., Cawley, B. D., & Williams, J. R. (1995). Situational and individual determinants of feedback seeking: A closer look at the process. *Organizational Behavior and Human Decision Processes, 62,* 23–37.

Lewis, L. K. (1997). Users' individual communicative responses to intraorganizationally implemented innovations and other planned changes. *Management Communication Quarterly, 10,* 455–490.

Lewis, L. K. (1999). Disseminating information and soliciting input during planned organizational change: Implementers' targets, sources, and channels for communicating. *Management Communication Quarterly, 13,* 43–75.

Lewis, L. K. (2000). "Blindsided by that one" and "I saw that one coming": The relative anticipation and occurrence of communication problems and other problems in implementers' hindsight. *Journal of Applied Communication Research, 28,* 44–67.

Lewis, L. K., Hamel, S. A., & Richardson, B. K. (2001). Communicating change to nonprofit stakeholders: Models and predictors of implementers' approaches. *Management Communication Quarterly, 15,* 5–41.

Lewis, L. K., & Seibold, D. R. (1993). Innovation modification during intraorganizational adoption. *Academy of Management Review, 18,* 322–354.

Lewis, L. K., & Seibold, D. R. (1996). Communication during intraorganizational innovation adoption: Predicting users' behavioral coping responses to innovations in organizations. *Communication Monographs, 63,* 130–157.

Lewis, L. K., & Seibold, D. R. (1998). Reconceptualizing organizational change implementation as a communication problem: A review of literature and research agenda. In M. E. Roloff (Ed.), *Communication yearbook* (Vol. 21, pp. 93–151). Thousand Oaks, CA: Sage.

Lucas, K. (2007). Problematized providing and protecting: The occupational narrative of the working class. In W. DeGenaro (Ed.), *Who says? Working-class rhetoric, class consciousness, and community* (pp. 180–199). Pittsburg: University of Pittsburg Press.

Markus, M. L. (1983). Power, politics, and MIS implementation. *Communications of the ACM, 26,* 430–444.

Martin, J. (1992). *Cultures in organizations: Three perspectives.* New York: Oxford University Press.

McPherson, J., & Deetz, S. (2005). A high-tech organizational change initiative in the public sector: Theory engaged in practice. In J. L. Simpson & P. Shockley-Zalabak (Eds.), *Engaging communication, transforming organizations: Scholarship of engagement in action* (pp. 79–98). Cresskill, NJ: Hampton Press.

Medved, C. E., Morrison, K., Dearing, J. W., Larson, R. S., Cline, G., & Brummans, B. H. J. M. (2001). Tensions in community health improvement initiatives: Communication and collaboration in a managed care environment. *Journal of Applied Communication Research, 29,* 137–152.

Miller, D., & Desmarais, S. (2007). Developing your talent to the next level: Five best practices for leadership development. *Organization Development Journal, 25,* 37–43.

Miller, G. R., & Sunnafrank, M. J. (1984). Theoretical dimensions of applied communication research. *Quarterly Journal of Speech, 70,* 255–263.

Miller, K. I. (2007). Compassionate communication in the workplace: Exploring processes of noticing, connecting, and responding. *Journal of Applied Communication Research, 35,* 223–245.

Miller, K. I., & Monge, P. R. (1985). Social information and employee anxiety about organizational change. *Human Communication Research, 11,* 365–386.

Miller, K. I., & Monge, P. R. (1987). The development and test of a system of organizational participation and allocation. In M. L. McLauglin (Ed.), *Communication yearbook* (Vol. 10, pp. 431–455). Newbury Park, CA: Sage.

Miller, V. D. (1996). An experimental study of newcomers' information seeking behaviors during organizational entry. *Communication Studies, 47,* 1–24.

Miller, V. D., & Jablin, F. M. (1991). Information seeking during organizational entry: Influences, tactics, and a model of the process. *Academy of Management Review, 16*, 92–120.

Miller, V. D., Johnson, J. R., & Grau, J. (1994). Antecedents to willingness to participate in a planned organizational change. *Journal of Applied Communication Research, 22*, 59–80.

Miller, V. D., Johnson, J. R., Hart, Z., & Peterson, D. L. (1999). A test of antecedents and outcomes of employee role negotiation ability. *Journal of Applied Communication Research, 27*, 24–48.

Moreland, R. L., & Levine, J. M. (2001). Socialization in organizations and work groups. In M. E. Turner (Ed.), *Groups at work: Theory and research* (pp. 69–112). Mahwah, NJ: Erlbaum.

Morrison, E. W. (1993). Newcomer information seeking: Exploring types, modes, sources, and outcomes. *Academy of Management Journal, 36*, 557–589.

Morrison, E. W. (1995). Information usefulness and acquisition during organizational encounter. *Management Communication Quarterly, 9*, 131–155.

Morrison, E. W., & Bies, R. J. (1991). Impression management in the feedback-seeking process: A literature review and research agenda. *Academy of Management Review, 16*, 522–541.

Morrison, E. W., & Cummings, L. L. (1992). The impact of diagnosticity and performance expectations on feedback seeking behavior. *Human Performance, 5*, 251–264.

Murphy, B. O. (1995). Promoting dialogue in culturally diverse workplace environments. In L. R. Frey (Ed.), *Innovations in group facilitation: Applications in natural settings* (pp. 77–93). Cresskill, NJ: Hampton Press.

Myers, K. K. (2005). A burning desire: Assimilation into a fire department. *Management Communication Quarterly, 18*, 344–384.

Myers, K. K. (2006). Assimilation and mutual acceptance. In J. H. Greenhaus & G. A. Callanan (Eds.), *Encyclopedia of career development* (pp. 31–32). Thousand Oaks, CA: Sage.

Myers, K. K., & McPhee, R. D. (2006). Influences on member assimilation in workgroups in high-reliability organizations: A multilevel analysis. *Human Communication Research, 32*, 440–468.

Myers, K. K., & Oetzel, J. G. (2003). Exploring the dimensions of organizational assimilation: Creating and validating a measure. *Communication Quarterly, 51*, 438–457.

Pacanowsky, M. E. (1988). Communication and the empowering organization. In J. A. Anderson (Ed.), *Communication yearbook* (Vol. 11, pp. 356–379). Newbury Park, CA: Sage.

Parker, P. S. (2001). African American women executives' leadership communication within dominant-culture organizations: (Re)conceptualizing notions of collaboration and instrumentality. *Management Communication Quarterly, 15*, 42–82.

Pearce, K. A., & Pearce, W. B. (2001). The Public Dialogue Consortium's school-wide dialogue process: A communication approach to develop citizenship skills and enhance school climate. *Communication Theory, 11*, 105–123.

Petronio, S. (1999). "Translating scholarship into practice": An alternative metaphor. *Journal of Applied Communication Research, 27*, 87–91.

Poole, M. S., Van de Ven, A. H., Dooley, K., & Holmes, M. E. (2000). *Organizational change and innovation processes: Theory and methods for research.* New York: Oxford University Press.

Rice, R. E., & Aydin, C. (1991). Attitudes toward new organizational technology: Network proximity as a mechanism for social information processing. *Administrative Science Quarterly, 36*, 219–244.

Riley, P. (1993). Arguing for "ritualistic" pluralism: The tension between privilege and the mundane. In S. A. Deetz (Ed.), *Communication yearbook* (Vol. 16, pp. 112–121). Newbury Park, CA: Sage.

Rogers, E. M. (1962). *Diffusion of innovations.* New York: Free Press of Glencoe.

Rogers, E. M. (2000). Reflections on news event diffusion research. *Journalism and Mass Communication Quarterly, 77*, 561–576.

Rogers, E. M. (2003). *Diffusion of innovations* (5th ed.). New York: Free Press.

Rosenfeld, L. B., Richman, J. M., & May, S. K. (2004). Information adequacy, job satisfaction and organizational culture in a dispersed-network organization. *Journal of Applied Communication Research, 32*, 28–54.

Saks, A. M., & Ashforth, B. E. (1996). Proactive socialization and behavioral self-management. *Journal of Vocational Behavior, 48*, 301–323.

Scheibel, D. (1994). Graffiti and "film school" culture: Displaying alienation. *Communication Monographs, 61*, 1–18.

Schein, E. H. (1984). Coming to a new awareness of organizational culture. *Sloan Management Review, 12*, 3–16.

Schein, E. H. (1987). *Process consultation: Vol. 2. Lessons for managers and consultants.* Reading, MA: Addison-Wesley.

Schein, E. H. (1992). *Organizational culture and leadership* (3rd ed.). San Francisco: Jossey-Bass.

Schrodt, P. (2002). The relationship between organizational identification and organizational culture: Employee perceptions of culture and identification in a retail sales organization. *Communication Studies, 53*, 189–202.

Scott, C., & Myers, K. K. (2005). The socialization of emotion: Learning emotion management at the fire station. *Journal of Applied Communication Research, 33*, 67–92.

Seibold, D. R. (1995). Developing the "team" in a team-managed organization: Group facilitation in a new plant design. In L. R. Frey (Ed.), *Innovations in group facilitation: Applications in natural settings* (pp. 282–298). Cresskill, NJ: Hampton Press.

Seibold, D. R. (2005). Bridging theory and practice in organizational communication. In J. L. Simpson & P. Shockley-Zalabak (Eds.), *Engaging communication, transforming organizations: Scholarship of engagement in action* (pp. 13–44). Cresskill, NJ: Hampton Press.

Seibold, D. R. (2008). Applied communication research. In W. Donsbach (Ed.), *The international encyclopedia of communication* (Vol. 1., pp. 189–194). Malden, MA: Wiley-Blackwell.

Seibold, D. R., Kudsi, S., & Rude, M. (1993). Does communication training make a difference? Evidence for the effectiveness of a presentation skills program. *Journal of Applied Communication Research, 21*, 111–131.

Seibold, D. R., & Shea, C. (2001). Participation and decision making. In F. M. Jablin & L. L. Putnam (Eds.), *The new handbook of organizational communication: Advances in theory, research, and methods* (pp. 664–703). Thousand Oaks, CA: Sage.

Senge, P. M. (1990). *The fifth discipline: The art and practice of the learning organization.* New York: Doubleday/Currency.

Seo, M., Putnam, L. L., & Bartunek, J. (2003). Dualities and tensions of planned organizational change. In M. S. Poole & A. Van de Ven (Eds.), *Handbook of organizational change* (pp. 73–107). New York: Oxford University Press

Shockley-Zalabak, P., & Morley, D. D. (1994). Creating a culture: A longitudinal examination of the influence of management and employee values on communication rule stability and emergence. *Human Communication Research, 20*, 334–355.

Sias, P. M., & Wyers, T. D. (2001). Employee uncertainty and information-seeking in newly formed expansion organizations. *Management Communication Quarterly, 14*, 549–573.

Simpson, J. L., & Seibold, D. R. (2008). Practical engagements and co-created research. *Journal of Applied Communication Research, 36*, 265–279.

Simpson, J. L., & Shockley-Zalabak, P. (Eds.). (2005). *Engaging communication, transforming organizations: Scholarship of engagement in action.* Cresskill, NJ: Hampton Press.

Smith, F. L., & Keyton, J. (2001). Organizational storytelling: Metaphors for relational power and identity struggles. *Management Communication Quarterly, 15*, 149–182.

Smith, R. C., & Eisenberg, E. (1987). Conflict at Disneyland: A root-metaphor analysis. *Communication Monographs, 54*, 367–380.

Steward, B. (2000). Changing times: The meaning, measurement and use of time in teleworking. *Time and Society, 9*, 57–74.

Stohl, C. (1986). The role of memorable messages in the process of organizational socialization. *Communication Quarterly, 34*, 231-249.

Stohl, C., & Cheney, G. (2001). Participatory processes/paradoxical practices: Communication and dilemmas of organizational democracy. *Management Communication Quarterly, 14*, 349–407.

Strang, D., & Soule, S. A. (1998). Diffusion organizations and social movements: From hybrid corn to poison pills. *Annual Review of Sociology, 24*, 265–290.

Sultan, F., & Farley, J. U., & Lehmann, D. R. (1990). A meta-analysis of applications of diffusion models. *Journal of Marketing Research, 27*, 70–77.

Swanson, E. B. (1994). Information systems innovation among organizations. *Management Science, 40*, 1069–1090.

Teboul, JC. B. (1995). Determinants of new hire information-seeking during organizational encounter. *Western Journal of Communication, 59*, 305–325.

Teboul, JC. B. (1999). Racial/ethnic "encounter" in the workplace: Uncertainty, information-seeking, and learning patterns among racial/ethnic majority and minority new hires. *Howard Journal of Communications, 10*, 97–121.

Thackaberry, J. A. (2004). "Discursive opening" and closing in organizational self-study: Culture as trap and tool in wildland firefighting safety. *Management Communication Quarterly, 17*, 319–359.

Thibaut. J. W., & Kelley, H. H. (1959). *The social psychology of groups.* New York: Wiley.

Timmerman, C. E. (2003). Media selection during the implementation of planned organizational change: A predictive framework based on implementation approach and phase. *Management Communication Quarterly, 16*, 301–340.

Tornatzky, L. G., & Klein, K. J. (1982). Innovation characteristics and innovation adoption implementation: A meta-analysis of findings. *IEEE Transactions on Engineering Management, 29*, 28–45.

Tracy, S. J., Lutgen-Sandvik, P., & Alberts, J. K. (2006). Nightmares, demons, and slaves: Exploring the painful metaphors of workplace bullying. *Management Communication Quarterly, 20*, 148–185.

Trujillo, N. (1992). Interpreting (the work and talk of) baseball: Perspectives on ballpark culture. *Western Journal of Communication, 56*, 350–371.

Vandenberg, R. J., & Scarpello, V. (1990). The matching model: An examination of the processes underlying realistic job previews. *Journal of Applied Psychology, 75*, 60–67.

Van Maanen, J. (1978). People processing: Strategies of organizational socialization. *Organizational Dynamics, 7*, 19–36.

Van Maanen, J., & Schein, E. H. (1979). Toward a theory of organizational socialization. In B. M. Staw (Ed.), *Research in organizational behavior* (Vol. 1., pp. 209–264). Greenwich, CT: JAI Press.

Volkema, R. J., Bergmann, T. J., & Farquhar, K. (1997). Use and impact of informal third-party discussions in interpersonal conflicts at work. *Management Communication Quarterly, 11*, 185–216.

Wagoner, R., & Waldron, V. R. (1999). How supervisors convey routine bad news: Facework at UPS. *Southern Communication Journal, 64*, 193–210.

Waldeck, J. H., Seibold, D. R., & Flanagin, A. J. (2004). Organizational assimilation and communication technology use. *Communication Monographs, 71*, 161–183.

Waldron, V. R. (2000). Relational experiences and emotion at work. In S. Fineman (Ed.), *Emotion in organizations* (2nd ed., pp. 64–82). Newbury Park, CA: Sage.

Witmer, D. F. (1997). Communication and recovery: Structuration as an ontological approach to organizational culture. *Communication Monographs, 64*, 324–349.

Worren, N. A. M., Ruddle, K., & Moore, K. (1999). From organizational development to change management: The emergence of a new profession. *Journal of Applied Behavioral Science, 35*, 273–286.

Zorn, T. E., & Gregory, K. W. (2005). Learning the ropes together: Assimilation and friendship development among first-year medical students. *Health Communication, 17*, 211–231.

Zorn, T. E., Page, D. J., & Cheney, G. (2000). Nuts about change: Multiple perspectives on change-oriented communication in a public sector organization. *Management Communication Quarterly, 14*, 515–566.

15 In the Public Interest

Communication in Nonprofit Organizations

Eric M. Eisenberg
University of South Florida

Beth Eschenfelder
The University of Tampa

In his comprehensive review of the history of organizational communication, Redding (1985) traced the field's expansion in the United States to an unprecedented "triple alliance" that emerged among industry, academia, and the military. Throughout the second half of the 20th century, the U.S. government supported extensive communication research aimed at helping organizations (especially military organizations) do a better job of identifying and developing potential leaders. Although support for this type of work ebbed over time, the idea that communication scholarship should directly impact organizational effectiveness did not. For this reason, early studies of organizational communication often have been criticized for their apparent managerial bias. Moreover, despite the roots of this research in the military, the organizations studied almost always were for-profit corporations in the private sector. As a result, nearly all of the initial organizational communication theories and concepts were informed exclusively by the for-profit experience (see the review of applied organizational research by Seibold, Lemus, Ballard, & Myers, this volume).

Scholarship conducted in the 1960s began taking a broader view of organizations. The application of general systems theory (Bertalanffy, 1973), in texts such as Katz and Kahn's (1966) *The Sociology of Organizations*, Weick's (1969) *The Social Psychology of Organizing*, and Farace, Monge, and Russell's (1977) *Communicating and Organizing*, provided a generic vocabulary for human organizing, one that reached well beyond the private sector. The emerging conviction that communication was *constitutive* of organizations—and the accompanying shift in focus from reified corporations (think: IBM) to more fluid and emergent forms (think: MoveOn.org)—set the stage for a broadening of the organizational communication research agenda to include nonprofit organizations, governments, nongovernmental organizations (NGOs), and communities.

A related trend also contributed to this broadening of organizational communication research interests. Beginning in the United States in the 1980s (but with roots in Europe), critical organizational scholarship became increasingly influential in the communication field (cf., Deetz, 1992; Deetz & Kersten, 1983). Critical approaches exposed and problematized the managerial bias characteristic of past research and revealed the political interests behind seemingly objective organizational decision making. Conceptualizing communication as constituting organizations created a significant point of entry for the critical analysis of power, voice, and participation in all types of collectivities (Deetz, 1994).

A review of organizational communication scholarship in the 1990s by Mumby and Stohl (1996) identified four central problematics that scholars have consistently addressed:

(1) voice, (2) rationality, (3) organization, and (4) the organization–society relationship. This last problematic is especially salient for nonprofits, which are characterized by their explicit commitment to promoting social good and the large number and type of stakeholders who are invested in their success.

Many writers have addressed these unique characteristics by exploring how the origins and operations of nonprofit organizations align with the core dimensions of social capital, such as establishing networks, relationships, and trust, and creating shared visions and norms (e.g., Bellah, Madsen, Sullivan, Swidler, & Tipton, 1996; Chaskin, Brown, Venkatesh, & Vidal, 2001; King, 2004; Smith & Lipsky, 1993). Social capital is created when members of a community come together to form a nonprofit organization to focus on a social need not addressed by existing organizations (Chambre & Fatt, 2002). Thus, nonprofit organizations exist both to serve society and create change in it. Increased attention in organizational communication research now is being paid to this organizational–societal relationship (Mumby & Stohl, 1996). In this chapter, we focus mainly on research that explicitly addresses this relationship. What is *not* reviewed here is research that focuses solely on the service-delivery aspect of nonprofit work, such as social worker–client relationships (see Miller & Considine, this volume), or the vast amount of nonprofit management literature that addresses board development and fund-raising.

As a prelude to this review, we first provide background on the complex environment in which most nonprofit institutions exist. We begin by reviewing the history of the nonprofit sector, followed by a discussion of the major challenges facing nonprofits today. We then identify three specific communication challenges that are key to the successful management of nonprofit organizations: (1) partnering, (2) clarifying mission and identity, and (3) fostering employee involvement and identification.

Recent History of the Nonprofit Sector in the United States

Nonprofit is a legal term used by the Internal Revenue Service (IRS) to refer to organizations that may use revenues only to further their charitable or educational mission rather than distribute profits to owners or shareholders. Nonprofit organizations are ubiquitous, with the majority of them concentrated in three areas: health, education, and social services. As Salamon (2002) explained:

> The nonprofit sector is a vast and diverse assortment of organizations. It includes most of the nation's premier hospitals and universities, almost all of its orchestras and opera companies, a significant share of its theaters, all of its religious congregations, the bulk of its environmental advocacy and civil rights organizations, and huge numbers of its family services, neighborhood development, antipoverty, and community health facilities. It also includes the numerous support organizations, such as foundations and community chests that help to generate financial assistance for these organizations, as well as the traditions of giving, volunteering, and services they help to foster. (pp. 6–7)

Given this impressive list, it is surprising how little research attention has been paid to examining the role of communication in these organizations.

From the mid-1930s to the late 1970s, this sector experienced unprecedented expansion, due to the U.S government's increasing reliance on nonprofit organizations to "stimulate scientific advances and overcome poverty and ill health" (Salamon, 2002, p. 12). Especially between 1960 and the mid-1970s, "big infusions of cash were poured into social services" (Bernstein, 1991, p. vii), with thousands of new nonprofit agencies created to receive and administer the spending of these funds.

Nonprofit organizations were further propelled into the U.S. public consciousness during President Ronald Reagan's budget cutbacks aimed at dismantling inefficient and ineffective government social programs. As Boris (1998) explained, "Charities were promoted as the nongovernmental saviors of the poor and of children, the elderly, and the disabled" (¶ 2). The Republican-led U.S. Congress's "Contract with America" in 1994 also attempted to scale back the size of the federal government and its involvement in citizens' lives (Pynes, 1997), which resulted in the distribution of funds to states and local communities that were expected, in turn, to prioritize needed services and determine eligibility criteria for their areas. This "devolution" of federal government responsibilities to the state and local level created significant opportunities for nonprofit organizations to play larger roles in community planning and decision making. Nonprofit organizations were awarded government contracts because they were seen as "reputable, committed, like-minded community institutions" that could help governments to come closer to achieving their mandates (Ryan 1999, pp. 128–129).

The passage of the 1996 Personal Responsibility and Work Opportunity Reconciliation Act (PRWORA) to reform welfare added yet another wrinkle to local communities' responses to the devolution process. The most dramatic provision of the PRWORA was a 5-year lifetime limit on public assistance and a 2-year deadline for most welfare recipients to secure employment. Because the implementation of this law was passed on to the states, welfare reform legislation and policies first led to the shifting of authority and responsibility from the federal to local governments and then to NGOs, including nonprofit and for-profit organizations. Requiring swift implementation and the mandate to integrate various services, the PRWORA gave an extraordinary boost to social service organizations of all types (M. J. Austin, 2003; Poole, 2003; Skloot, 2000).

Effective devolution of social services, however, is easier said than done. A smaller federal government is appealing in principle, but nonprofit organizations rarely are prepared to accept the added responsibility. Early on, political leaders promoted the idea that the charitable sector could be sustained almost exclusively through increased volunteerism and private donations. President George H. Bush spoke often about the "backbone of America" being a "thousand points of light," a metaphor for willing "constellations" of caring volunteers. The notion of an independent charitable social safety net that could offset decreasing government support for social services persisted through the 1990s, but the porous and inadequate nature of this net ultimately became clear. An estimated two-fifths of public charities suffered a decline in inflation-adjusted dollars between 1989 and 1995, and a similar number operated on a very slim margin, with cash on hand less than or equal to 3 months of expenses (Boris, 1998). This dire economic situation has not improved over the past decade.

Put another way, the macroeconomic and political forces shaping the development of nonprofit organizations extend beyond any consideration of what best meets the needs of their clients, citizens, or communities. In this sense, nonprofit organizations face challenges that are practically identical to those encountered by private-sector, for-profit businesses, such as the need to cope with increased complexity, shrinking resources, increased competition, and nearly constant change.

One area where the for-profit, government, and nonprofit sectors are similar is that they all must deal with changing environments. There are, in fact, many ways in which nonprofits are both similar to and different from their for-profit and government counterparts. An overview of these differences is shown in Table 15.1.

As communication scholars, our main concern should be with how those associated

Table 15.1 Comparison of For-profit, Government, and Nonprofit Sectors

	For-Profit Businesses	*Government Entities*	*Nonprofit Organizations*
Purposes and Interests	• Maximize profits • Satisfy human needs by creating wealth (Steiner & Steiner 2000) • Balance interests of stockholders and customers • Free to act in own interests, even when it clashes with the public interest (Bland & Rubin, 1997)	• Provide public goods generally not profitable enough to be supplied by the private sector in efficient levels (Gordon, 1992) or perceived by the community as being more trustworthy when provided by government (Boris & Steuerle, 1999), such as indigent health-care or mental health services	• Maximize social missions (Saxon-Harrold & Heffron, 2000) • Set own goals (Gordon, 1992) • Satisfy the client, customer, or associate needs • Preferred providers for certain services to treat all citizens fairly (Boris & Steuerle, 1999)
Stereotypes	• Perceived to allocate resources most effectively and to provide least-cost solutions most responsively • Seen as hard-edged and uncaring, favoring private over societal interests (Brinkerhoff & Brinkerhoff, 2002)	• Seen as monolithic, intrusive, clumsy, and bloated; critics call for downsizing, contracting out, and business-like practices (Brinkerhoff & Brinkerhoff, 2002)	• Considered softer and kindhearted, able to mobilize voluntary effort, linked to communities, and driven by enduring prosocial values (Brinkerhoff & Brinkerhoff, 2002)
Key Relationships	• Key relationships include employees, customers, and owners, but success demands developing relationships with all sectors and publics	• Must work with outside interest groups (e.g., political, business, and/or citizens) and people whose careers and actions are outside government control (Gordon, 1992)	• Must establish relationships with a multitude of constituencies (Drucker, 1990): clients, employees, governments, business competitors, neighborhoods, and other nonprofits
Fiscal Resources	• Rely on consumer purchasing of products and services • Provide products and services to individuals based on their needs or wants, in exchange for a direct payment (Gordon, 1992)	• Generate income through mandatory taxation • Through taxation and regulation, they assure that everyone is paying their share	• Services are supported through government and private grants and donations • Although an operating budget must be maintained, profit is irrelevant because of the organization's nature • May subsidize charitable work by providing services to populations more willing or able to pay (Saxon-Harrold & Heffron, 2000)

Table 15.1 Continued

	For-Profit Businesses	Government Entities	Nonprofit Organizations
Influences and Decision-Making Structures	• Fixed and clearly delineated hierarchical structure for authority, setting goals, and making decisions • Business planning and work effort take place in private (Bland & Rubin, 1997)	• Set within political environments • Government administrators often hired by and report to elected officials and may have to adhere to bipartisan politics to maintain their job • Work and planning take place in the public forum (Bland & Rubin, 1997)	• Political forces influence human services policies and practices through intergovernmental dynamics (Cohen & Cohen, 2000) • Because of complex nonprofit partnerships, executives and board members must apply a range of relationship management skills and practices (Drucker, 1990)
Organizational Concerns	• Vulnerable to societal changes, such as science and technology, dominant ideologies, population changes, and inequality of human circumstances (Steiner & Steiner, 2000) • Must be concerned with business competition, both national and international; conducting business globally through the use of technology; and an increasing wave of mergers, acquisitions, and downsizing (G. Shaw & Weber, 1990)	• Need to maximize efficiency and effectiveness by balancing citizens' short- and long-term goals (Bland & Rubin, 1997) • Requires public administrators to meet infinite needs with finite resources (Steuerle & Hodgkinson, 1999) • Burdened with greater systems of controls, mandates, checks, and balances to prevent mismanagement (Bland & Rubin, 1997) • Due to the extra levels of involvement required in much of public managers' work, time lines often are prolonged	• Deal with concerns similar to both for-profit businesses and governments; vulnerable to societal changes and levels of controls and mandates imposed by funders

with nonprofits employ communication to respond to these external pressures. Through a comprehensive review of the literature, we identify three communication challenges that face nonprofit leaders: (1) partnering, (2) clarifying mission and identity, and (3) fostering employee involvement and identification. *Partnering* is the ability of nonprofit leaders to cultivate multiple interorganizational linkages and, thereby, achieve synergy with other nonprofit organizations, for-profit businesses, and governments. *Clarifying mission and identity* refers to the ability of these leaders to stay true to their founding missions and, at the same time, adapt to external pressures, all the while sustaining their organization's unique sense of identity. *Fostering employee involvement and identification* refers to leaders' ability to use communication to encourage employees' participation in decision making and to create a sense of loyalty and value commitment by them to the organization.

Partnering

Partnering effectively with stakeholders is the single-most significant communication challenge facing leaders of nonprofit organizations. Historically, the number and importance of stakeholder relations has been the key difference between nonprofit organizations and for-profit businesses (Drucker, 1990). Although the private sector lately has looked beyond its stockholders to other publics (e.g., Deetz, 1992), nonprofit leaders and board members *always* have known that they cannot fulfill their mission by "going it alone"; to succeed, they must "build alliances, networks, partnerships, and other types of collaborative relationships" (Waide, 1999, p. 244).

"Beyond the walls" is a phrase that the Peter F. Drucker Foundation (a charitable organization named after the late management consultant) adopted to describe the communication imperative facing all three sectors—nonprofit, government, and business—in moving toward strengthened partnership and community-building efforts (Hesselbein, 1999). As Somerville and Quinn (1999) concluded, to achieve their missions, these organizations must learn to "improvise collectively" (p. 233). These types of partnerships are a further example of the unique positioning of nonprofits described by Ott (2001): "The nonprofit sector has always been positioned rather delicately between the business sector's profit motive and the government sector's drive to meet social needs" (p. 355). Nonprofit organizations both depend on and, at times, compete with the other sectors (government and for-profit); as a result, the potential payoff is a significant impact on the quality of public life. Here, we explore the research literature on the variety of partnerships with and among nonprofit organizations, including those with for-profit businesses, governments, and other nonprofits. We also review the challenges those partnerships create and the role of communication in developing and managing those challenges.

Partnering with Business

In Tampa, Florida, the nonprofit Museum of Science and Industry (MOSI) recently partnered with State Farm Insurance to increase the impact of their efforts to educate the public about how to prepare for devastating hurricanes. Further south, an environmental organization protecting tropical rainforests partnered with a logging company to create a collaborative program that defined best practices for cultivating and harvesting tropical agricultural products. These exemplar types of partnerships have become more common among businesses and nonprofits, and are being studied more often in applied communication research.

Skloot (2000) studied collaboration between Lockheed-Martin and the Urban League in Baltimore that centered on child support enforcement and family unification. Through this partnership, the Urban League upgraded its staff's technical skills and got improved access to the community and to local politicians. This case provides a model for collaboration between nonprofit organizations and for-profit businesses, as it shows that when these organizations enter into formal partnerships, nonprofits can focus on what they do best: offer skilled, one-on-one personal involvement, assistance, and steady care. They also can build capacities of the communities they serve and better represent local needs. As Skloot concluded, "If nonprofits can work out joint ventures with richer, bigger for-profits or other nonprofits, they could specialize. They could extend their reach and serve their clients better. Each could build off its core competencies" (p. 322).

Generally speaking, nonprofits enter into symbiotic, mutually advantageous relationships with for-profit firms for financial reasons. In the process of doing so, they often discover valuable new opportunities and sources of expertise. For example, for-profit businesses bring a wealth of experience to nonprofit organizations that helps to meet bidding, payroll, printing, and technology needs (Skloot, 2000; Werther & Berman, 2001). In return, nonprofit organizations can help businesses with cause-related marketing to promote their products and build consumer brand loyalty (Werther & Berman, 2001). J. E. Austin (1998) identified other benefits of such partnerships for businesses, such as nonprofit organizations serving as places where business executives practice new skills, build leadership capabilities, and contribute more directly to their community through involvement in nonprofit boards and committees.

Collaborating on commercial ventures also helps to soften long-standing skepticism about the motivations of corporations and opens the way "for nonprofit acceptance of the business community, not simply as a source of charitable support, but as a legitimate partner for a wide range of nonprofit endeavors" (Salamon, 2003, pp. 64–65). Moreover, cause-related marketing relationships can evolve into broader relationships that mobilize corporate personnel, finances, and know-how in support of nonprofit activities. This increased interest in commercial partnerships on the part of nonprofits "has meshed nicely with the growing readiness of businesses to forge strategic alliances with nonprofits in order to generate 'reputational capital'" (Salamon, 2003, p. 65). This mutual interest, as Salamon (2003) explained, has led to a notable upsurge in these strategic partnerships.

Occasionally, nonprofits compete with for-profit businesses for consumer dollars. One reason such competition occurs is because government funders have changed to fee-based, consumer-side subsidies that more closely resemble for-profit practices. When clients can shop for services using government money, the onus is on nonprofit organizations to distinguish the services they provide as superior to the available alternatives. One instance of this dynamic, again, involves defense contractor Lockheed-Martin, which was attracted to the social welfare field after the implementation of welfare reform legislation designed to move large numbers of recipients from welfare dependence to employment (Salamon, 2003). As Salamon (2003) explained:

> What these firms offer is less knowledge of human services than information-processing technology and contract management skills gained from serving as master contractors on huge military system projects, precisely the skills needed to manage the subcontracting systems required to prepare welfare recipients for work. (p. 23)

Nonprofit providers, consequently, can find themselves working as subcontractors to for-profit entities, such as Lockheed-Martin, thereby increasing the number and salience of relationships between for-profit businesses and nonprofit organizations.

Partnering with Governments

Nonprofit organizational partnerships with government agencies yield many of the same benefits as partnerships with businesses, but the relationships are more varied and complex (Werther & Berman, 2001). Collaboration between government and nonprofit organizations is not new but has gained momentum as a result of changing attitudes and growing expectations about private-sector social responsibility (Snavely & Tracy, 2000). Nonprofit organizations often participate in government program planning and policy development, and serve as contractors to provide services desired by government agencies. As Werther and Berman (2001) claimed, "Nonprofits offer government a cost-effective and innovative way of implementing public programs" (p. 176).

The relationship between government and the nonprofit sector increasingly has been characterized more by cooperation than conflict, as governments depend now more than ever on the nonprofit sector to assist in meeting human needs (Salamon, 1994). At the same time, scholars and practitioners have mixed views about the impact of government involvement in nonprofit governance and management. Researchers who study these relationships (e.g., Akingbola, 2004; Chambre & Fatt, 2002; Grønbgerg & Salamon, 2002; Smith, 1994; Werther & Berman, 2001) cite persuasive challenges that include increasing demands by government agencies for accountability by nonprofits and funding uncertainties and constraints. Along with the demands that governments place on nonprofits comes a host of rules, policies, and decisions that may be frustrating, and, in some cases, even impair the ability of nonprofits to function effectively.

At times, the ongoing negotiation between elected government officials and nonprofit leaders can lead to much bigger problems, such as when agencies feel that government pressures them to dilute or even abandon their founding missions. Although the proliferation of government–nonprofit partnerships seems inevitable, observers are concerned about the potentially negative effects of this shift on the ability of nonprofits to stay independent and focused on fulfilling their core mission. The source of this concern is the observation that, as nonprofit organizations enter into relationships with governments, they increasingly organize themselves to mirror and imitate their government counterparts (Brinkerhoff & Brinkerhoff, 2002). These pressures pose threats to the continued pursuit of the mission of nonprofit organizations, leaving many, if not most, nonprofits to confront an "identity crisis" (Salamon, 2003, pp. 46) at some point in their history.

Challenges related to the blurring of sectors are revealed in research conducted by Alexander (1999, 2000) on nonprofit social service organizations serving children and youth in Cuyahoga County, Ohio. These studies assessed the impact of devolution and related contracting issues, and sought to identify effective nonprofit organizational coping strategies. In focus group discussions, nonprofit representatives indicated that difficulty in adapting to financial challenges posed by government agencies negatively affected their capacity to fulfill traditional public service responsibilities, such as advocacy, serving the most needy, research, and teaching. Moreover, they reported that their tactical choices increasingly were shaped by government reimbursement rates and the capacity to generate revenue. Findings from Alexander's (1999) study supported the common perception that because of partnerships with governments, most nonprofit organizations are cutting programs, charging new and higher fees, and, in extreme cases, even rationing services.

The impact of government funding on the advocacy function performed by many nonprofit organizations is one primary way their ability to fulfill their service mission may be jeopardized. Historically, nonprofits have provided an independent voice and an important linkage between governments, communities, and citizens in need, not only through the provision of services but also through their political capacity as advocates for (sometimes unpopular) social causes (Alexander, 1999). Among other things, nonprofits organize communities, respond to community needs, and articulate these needs through advocacy (e.g., via public service announcements, press releases, and even community demonstrations). As nonprofits are pushed to become more business oriented, their political character often is imperiled.

One example of the loss of political agency by nonprofit organizations is captured in research by Lune (2002) on nonprofits operating syringe exchange programs (SEPs) in New York City, where the political environment increasingly ran contrary to their missions. Like most nonprofits today, nonprofits operating SEPs depend on ongoing government support for their survival, but the controversial nature of their services can cause them to be isolated from much of the public health services and the drug treatment field. To become an "authorized" part of the health-care delivery system, the relationship between SEPs and governments seemingly had to shift; increased access to government support, thus, has come at the cost of abandoning direct political challenges to government policies in this arena.

Ensuring organizational survival has required nonprofits operating SEPs to move from "challenger" practices that contest government policy "toward conciliatory practices that implicitly or explicitly legitimate the interests of political elites, even at the cost of delegitimating their own constituency" (Lune, 2002, p. 471). Several informants in Lune's (2002) study stated that although SEPs were once "a kind of social movement," they now rarely advocate for social change. Instead, SEPs have turned toward a more subdued style of advocacy aimed at reducing the atmosphere of hostility and distrust as they try to forge lasting, undemanding relationships with other health and human service agencies. The principal survival-oriented strategy utilized by nonprofits operating SEPs has been to minimize their public visibility. A far cry from their earlier incarnation as issue advocates, today, they avoid political entanglements by trying not to be seen and by encouraging communities to forget that they even exist (Lune).

In addition to curbing advocacy efforts and influencing the types of services delivered by nonprofit organizations, governments also control service delivery by regulating the structure and qualifications of nonprofit personnel. New forms of government funding have significantly affected the staffing practices of nonprofit organizations, mainly by mandating the "professional" delivery of services an agency provides (Akingbola, 2004; Salamon, 1995). Such professionalism includes implementing minimum standards of care to ensure quality service delivery (e.g., acceptable client–provider ratios), which contribute to existing tendencies among nonprofit organizations toward professionalization and specialization (Smith & Lipsky, 1993).

Services funded through government contracts require nonprofits to hire full-time professional staff as a means of complying with stringent reporting and accountability requirements. According to Salamon (1995), "Poverty and distress have come to be seen as requiring more than amateur approaches and volunteer activity" (p. 138). Although volunteers remain an integral part of service delivery, agencies increasingly are replacing volunteers with professional staff, especially in front-line service delivery (Akingbola, 2004).

This movement toward professionalization of staff presents unique challenges for nonprofit organizations. In Lune's (2002) research on SEPs, nonprofit organizations that once were managed by recovering addicts now often are run by professional managers with no prior experience working on drug issues. As Lune explained, "The conditions for aboveground work require a degree of professionalism and accountability in accordance with the interests of those outside of the affected communities rather than those within" (p. 470).

Related trends are visible in research conducted by Akingbola (2004) within the Canadian Red Cross—Toronto Region (CRC-TR). Interviewees agreed that government funding affects staffing, explaining that (contrary to the agency's previous practices) external financial pressures led the CRC-TR to hire more staff on contract (on a temporary basis without benefits) for the delivery of services. The increased use of temporary staffing is a direct result of the uncertainty surrounding continued government funding. According to interviewees, the impact of government funding on staffing has multiple ramifications for the quality of services the agency provides, including stagnated or diminished quality of services, the inability to retain acquired program competencies, program instability, inevitable employee turnover, employee distraction, and low employee morale.

Funding restrictions and other government requirements not only significantly reduce the activities of nonprofit organizations but also simultaneously *require* other activities that may not be part of the mission of these organizations. For example, the financial requirements for operating in a contract environment discourage nonprofit organizations from serving populations with the greatest needs and providing services to their communities when outcomes are difficult to measure. The result can be a double whammy: both greater uncertainty and loss of the guiding vision. As Alexander (1999) claimed, "Government contracting may undermine a nonprofit's financial stability, while at the same time encouraging nonprofit organizations to move away from their own distinctive mission and reflect more closely the priorities of government administrators" (p. 328).

Agency leaders have little choice but to adjust their vision to obtain continued funding, but in so doing, they risk losing the heart of the enterprise—their founding mission. Strategic management in the nonprofit arena involves maintaining "a distinctive sense of organizational mission" that binds diverse stakeholders together (M. J. Austin, 2003, p. 107). Internal and external tensions must be successfully managed to ensure that new government resources and contracts do not distort the historical values and priorities of a nonprofit organization. Partnerships will not attain their desired efficiency and effectiveness if the identities of all the partners are not maintained (Brinkerhoff & Brinkerhoff, 2002).

Partnering with Other Nonprofits

Given their overlapping missions, it is common for nonprofit organizations to partner with each other. A typical example is the close relationships between United Way and many public schools, hospitals, and universities. Partnerships among nonprofits provide excellent opportunities to bring more attention and leverage to pervasive social challenges.

However, not every partnership of this type is successful. Histories of competition for resources, political maneuvering, and suspicion of one another's past motives do not engender the type of open exchange required for robust collaborative relationships (Gray, 1989). One reason for increased competitive behavior among nonprofit organizations is they often must battle for their share of limited resources that include clients, board members, volunteers, employees, donations, contracts, grants, and political power (Brody, as cited in Tuckman, 1998; Garner, 1989). Nonprofits also may compete for plum alliances with for-profit and government entities (Tuckman, 1998; Weisbrod, 1997).

For most nonprofit organizations, cooperation and competition must coexist. Oster (1995) cited Greenpeace and The Nature Conservancy as examples of nonprofit organizations that act as partners in program and advocacy efforts, and simultaneously compete for donations. Oster described the competitive–cooperative position of nonprofit organizations as being similar to that of a tennis player "engaged in a somewhat quirky tournament," stating, "at times, in this tournament, individuals face each other as single opponents. At other times, they are doubles partners, and, at still other times they switch partners and become doubles opponents" (p. 48). Furthermore, "just as in the tennis game, anticipating what the other players are likely to do is important whether they are your partners or your rivals" (Oster, p. 48). For an interesting parallel in the private sector, see Browning and Shetler's (2000) description of collaboration among competitors in the U.S. semiconductor industry.

Ideally, nonprofit organizations partner "not because collective effort necessarily helps each individual operation, but because collective action serves a greater good" (Oster, 1995, p. 57). In reality, motivations for such partnerships often are more personal and pedestrian. These relationships sometimes are sought primarily for the gain of individual nonprofits, which inevitably causes conflict in the collaboration process (Rein, 1983; Snavely & Tracy, 2000). Obstacles to collaboration uncovered in the research literature include behaviors such as turf protection, partners "hogging the glory" when collaboration succeeds, violating trust, adopting an "I" instead of a "we" attitude, and not living up to their communicative obligations (Snavely & Tracy, 2000, p. 161). Collaboration also can become a tool in power struggles over control, priorities, or resources within the social service system.

Snavely and Tracy (2000) studied collaborative practices among nonprofit organizations in rural southern Illinois and the Mississippi Delta. They interviewed mostly female leaders in the nonprofit sector who were either long-time agency employees or had played a long-term leadership role in community development and social services in their communities. Snavely and Tracy found that these leaders believed that collaboration is an effective way to deliver services and that it benefits nonprofit organizations in several ways. The directors clearly understood that their organization could never operate in isolation and that collaboration was the key to getting things done and the most effective means for extending services into the community, establishing credibility, obtaining needed community resources, and enhancing service delivery. These leaders established personal connections with one another, built bonds of trust, and committed organizational resources to working together (Snavely & Tracy).

Snavely and Tracy's (2000) research also suggested that collaboration can be difficult to accomplish due to environmental factors characteristic of rural areas, where clients are scattered over a large geographic area and community financial resources are limited. Despite these challenges, nonprofit organizations in rural regions do engage in significant collaborations. Results from this study revealed that leaders of nonprofit organizations were more actively engaged in certain types of collaboration—such as case management and community-wide planning and issue assessment—but had limited involvement in others—namely, organizational integration and major interorganizational planning.

Researchers have identified several reasons for the prevalence of partnerships among nonprofits (see Alexander, 2000; Rein, 1983; Snavely & Tracy, 2000; Werther & Berman, 2001). One comprehensive study by Kohm and La Piana (2003) that surveyed 192 "strategic restructuring partnerships" between nonprofits, staff members, board members, and funders identified four motivations for collaboration: (1) maintaining funding support, (2) saving money, (3) capitalizing on a partner organization's leadership, and (4) preserving or enhancing their organization's reputation. Some alliances, therefore, grow out of concern for administrative efficiency and the avoidance of redundant effort, whereas others are formed to prevent costly competition for resources or clients and may be used to pursue collaborative funding applications, joint fund-raising, or the sharing of human and financial resources with other organizations. A related trend is toward more joint planning among partners to develop approaches to fill service gaps, better meet client needs, and provide a fuller range of services. Collaboration also may be entered into to increase the impact of advocacy efforts and bring about social and political reform.

This section has highlighted the need for and variety of partnerships with and among nonprofit organizations, challenges those partnerships create, and the role of communication in developing and managing them. One of the more significant challenges resulting from these partnerships is the impact on a nonprofit organization's mission, such as the challenge of balancing conflict between an organization's service-oriented mission and the necessity to operate more like a business (Chambre & Fatt, 2002; Salamon, 2003). In the next section, we review research that looks more closely at the importance of nonprofit missions and further examine the role of communication in fostering stakeholder commitment.

Clarifying Mission and Identity

As discussed in the previous sections, funding pressures and government requirements can significantly impede the activities of nonprofit organizations and simultaneously require other activities that may not be central to these organizations' historical mission. For example, the financial requirements for operating in a contract environment discourage nonprofit organizations from serving populations with the greatest needs or from providing services to these communities when outcomes often are difficult to measure. This result can cause for nonprofits both greater uncertainty and loss of the guiding mission. From a communication perspective, these pressures can result in an even greater problem: the steady pressure on agencies to dilute or abandon their founding missions.

Research on leadership within nonprofit organizations, consequently, focuses on the challenge of achieving an organization's service-oriented mission in a way that is economically sustainable (Chambre & Fatt, 2002; Salamon, 2003). These two sets of criteria are not easily reconciled, inasmuch as they historically are associated with highly divergent expectations for both management and employee communication. Effective nonprofit leaders, therefore, must alleviate identify confusion and secure member buy-in to ensure successful goal attainment and loyalty among organizational stakeholders. Here, we review research that explores these challenges and the use of communication within and among nonprofit partners to mitigate them.

Mission and Identity Confusion

A contested or confused nonprofit agency identity leads to conflicts in determining or sustaining organizational strategy and structure, and too often results in management decisions that either are driven by environmental pressures or stumbled on without a clear rationale. As Young (2001a) claimed, "Nonprofit organizations must know who they are to make successful strategic and structural choices" (p. 155). Of course, there is no "one right" strategy for effectively addressing a social issue, as alternative organizational niches and identities always are available. However, selecting an identity is tantamount to an organization defining a "'north star' by which to navigate its course of action and shape strategy for the future" (Young, 2001a, p. 155). Flexibility of form allows nonprofit organizations to choose who they are, often from among several possible "organizational identities" that imply differences in strategy and structure, although good decisions about staffing, governance, and grant-making policies flow best from a sense of clarity with regard to institutional identity.

Young (2001b) provided an analysis of two instances of nonprofit umbrella associations—Girls Incorporated and CIVICUS—struggling with alternative identities that strongly influenced their choice of structure. Both nonprofits experienced changes over time that resulted in organizational stress, in the formative stage for CIVICUS and at a later critical juncture for Girls Incorporated. Through these challenging times, both organizations nurtured new, emerging identities and allowed old ones to slowly die off. As Young (2001b) explained, "They did not choose either to tolerate the pain of competing identities indefinitely—to forcefully replace one identity with another or to create some 'meta-identity' that integrates competing identities—or to create an entirely new identity" (p. 302). Allowing new identities to evolve naturally permitted these organizations to retain stakeholder support and provided time for them to comfortably adapt to what was best for the future. As Young (2001a) concluded, "The identity resolution for any given organization is critically important for achieving its social goals" (p. 155).

Member Buy-in

Securing buy-in from staff and other stakeholders associated with nonprofits can be difficult. Success in nonprofit organizations is measured largely in relation to the achievement of their mission or the effective provision of services, but consensus about the *quality* of nonprofit services is more difficult to obtain. As a result, *responsiveness* of nonprofit organizations to the needs of their stakeholders perhaps is the most important indicator of success (Lewis, Hamel, & Richardson, 2001). Herman and Renz (1999), clarifying the role of stakeholders in measuring the effectiveness of nonprofit organizations, argued that evaluations of effectiveness most often come down to stakeholder judgments, which are formed and changed in an ongoing process of sense making and negotiation. Perceptions of nonprofit organizational effectiveness are neither stable nor fixed; instead, effectiveness is socially constructed through stakeholder interaction. As Herman and Renz explained, in nonprofit organizations:

> There are activities, but there is no effectiveness until someone calls it.... All stakeholders are permitted to determine effectiveness, although some stakeholders may be considered more credible than others, and there is no regular procedure for determining effectiveness. (p. 118)

The priorities of constituent groups, thus, affect goal setting and attainment in nonprofit organizations (DiMaggio, cited in Lewis et al., 2001). Effective leadership involves understanding the criteria of effectiveness that various stakeholders apply and managing those expectations.

Leadership and Stakeholder Communication

Due to the increased emphasis on stakeholders' involvement and the critical role they play in nonprofit organizations, strong communication with stakeholders is essential to those organizations' success. Here, we explore research on the role of leaders in nonprofit organizations in building and maintaining essential stakeholder relationships, which involves environmental scanning and stakeholder analysis, developing personal relationships with community partners, and establishing bonds of trust with stakeholders.

It is essential for leaders of nonprofit organizations to participate in and have access to key social networks both within their respective organizations and in the communities they serve. Moreover, leaders must maintain a high level of trust among their various constituents, including donors, board members, employees, clients, and the public, and they must communicate and gain support for a common mission and vision (King, 2004).

Stakeholders also can provide an impetus for change and serve an important role in implementing management or change strategies (Eadie, 1997); consequently, nonprofit–stakeholder alliances are an important resource when planning agency strategy. As Garner (1989) explained, "A wise leader will recognize such alliances at the outset of planning, consider how to use them for future advantage, and avoid damaging them" (p. 119).

Identifying stakeholders and building relationships with them is a primary role of nonprofit organizational leadership that has been studied by several researchers (e.g., Eadie, 1997; Garner, 1989; M. Shaw, 2003). Eadie (1997, p. 154) recommended that nonprofit leaders perform an environmental scan to "identify external conditions and trends that are pertinent to a nonprofit organization's vision and mission," followed by an analysis that identifies potential stakeholders with related interests.

M. Shaw's (2003) research highlighted the importance of organizational leaders developing personal relationships with stakeholders. The successful partnerships studied were not built on negotiated agreements but on years of experience with partner agencies on the part of the individuals who worked together and had developed genuine affection for one another. In fact, partner agencies often implemented large-scale collaborative projects with no memorandum of understanding or contract, only a handshake and trust. M. Shaw's research included a case study of relationships between land trusts (nonprofit organizations that protect a natural resource or preserve historically or archeologically important sites) and local governments to identify conditions that foster successful collaboration. He concluded that social factors, such as experience on the part of key personnel in working with the other entity and sincere affection for each other, were more key to successful collaboration than perceived economic benefits. This finding suggests that a nonprofit agency interested in creating a viable partnership to improve a project should give careful consideration to assigning staff members, making sure that those assigned either already have or are well positioned to forge meaningful relationships.

Another implication of M. Shaw's (2003) study is that because leaders of nonprofit organizations must cultivate good working relationships with representatives of government agencies, hiring staff with prior government experience can be a wise strategy. Potential government partners likely have goals and values quite similar to those of a nonprofit partner. Establishing trust and developing a deep understanding of how various agencies operate cannot be negotiated in the course of one or two meetings before embarking on a joint venture; hence, when a history of trust and understanding are present, the collaborative effort can focus mainly on achieving project goals and not as much on developing the details of the partnership.

In addition to personal relationships, the importance of establishing open communication and dialogue in nonprofit partnerships has been studied. For instance, Medved et al. (2001) explored how communication may be used to reveal, frame, and ameliorate tensions in one community health change effort: the Comprehensive Community Health Models Initiative. Among those participating in the study, Medved et al. found that the counties that included the greatest diversity of participants in their change process produced the greatest benefit, due to fuller involvement of institutions that serve disadvantaged populations.

Leading a heterogeneous group always is a challenge, but when the potential of such a group is realized, great and innovative things can happen. Medved et al. (2001) concluded that assembling people who typically do not work together creates the potential to share important new information with mutual benefit. Leaders and group facilitators who keep the need for recruitment, inclusion, and parity in dialogue foremost in mind can heighten the odds of creative problem solving and system change.

This section described theory and research on the challenges of leading nonprofit organizations. The core tension to be managed is between a nonprofit's social mission, on the one hand, and economic and political pressures, on the other hand. In the third and final section, we examine the role of communication in promoting employee involvement and identification with nonprofit organizations, which presents special challenges due to the unique nature of the nonprofit workforce.

Fostering Employee Involvement and Identification

In nonprofit organizations, gaining employees' involvement and identification is both important and challenging. Although members of any organization need to identify with its goals and link themselves to some essential elements of the organization, this need is prominent in nonprofit organizations. In this section, we examine research addressing the unique characteristics of the nonprofit workforce that influence issues of organizational involvement and identification, explore how changes in the nonprofit sector challenge employee and stakeholder commitment, and suggest communication strategies for strengthening nonprofit members' involvement and identification.

For the most part, those who work for nonprofit organizations are motivated by strongly held values and have chosen to work in this sector for this reason. They typically have strong professional loyalties and well-articulated opinions about the right way to serve consumers (Arsenault, 1998). This behavior is more significant in the nonprofit than in the for-profit sector, because nonprofit workers likely "self-select occupations that require particular types of emotional labor" (Shuler & Davenport Sypher, 2000, p. 75). As Pines noted, human service workers tend to be unique in that their career choices are motivated by concerns such as "working with people, helping to meet people's needs, and making the world a better place to live" (cited in Shuler & Davenport Sypher, 2000, p. 73). Very often, such workers regularly go above and beyond the call of duty, even if it means increasing their emotional labor.

Human service organizations, such as community mental health centers (CMHCs), depend heavily on interpersonal relationships to function smoothly and deliver high-quality services to consumers. Contextual factors within organizations are critical in facilitating or constraining ways in which services are delivered by clinicians and case managers to consumers with serious mental illness. Morris and Bloom (2002) examined the relationship between contextual factors (such as an organization's structure, culture, and climate) and job satisfaction and organizational commitment among administrators and staff in CMHCs undergoing system changes in the financing of mental health care. Their research revealed that aggregate measures of organizational culture and climate were associated with employees' levels of job satisfaction over and above those individuals' perceptions of culture and climate, suggesting the importance of the work environment within CMHCs in promoting job satisfaction among administrators and staff on the front lines of mental health service delivery. Without an organizational environment that sustains and supports staff efforts to meet the often complex and demanding individual needs of diverse consumers, staff burnout and turnover are inevitable, and quality of care and service may be compromised (see Miller & Considine, this volume).

A shared belief in a nonprofit agency's mission is one reason employees remain committed to their job and organization. Brown and Yoshioka (2003) found that employees' positive attitudes toward the mission of a youth and recreation service organization were closely related to their satisfaction and intent to remain with the organization. They identified three broad reasons why individuals stay with a nonprofit organization: (1) belief in the mission and desire to help people, (2) satisfaction with the organization and coworkers, and (3) satisfaction with their job and opportunities for personal and professional growth. Given that nonprofit organizations rely on their mission to attract resources and guide decision making, mission statements are an important type of management communication for motivating employees and keeping them aligned with a nonprofit organization's vision, principles, and practices.

Brown and Yoshioka (2003) further clarified three basic principles that influence nonprofit employees' attitudes toward their organization's mission: awareness, agreement, and alignment. Ideally, employees must know the mission, agree with what it says, and see consistency between it and their daily work activities. Intrinsic motivations, such as attachment to mission, however, may run thin, as full-time employees earn salaries that are not competitive with other organizations. Dissatisfaction with pay tends to override employees' attachment to the mission as an explanation of why they may leave nonprofit organizations.

Challenges to Employee Involvement

Although commitment to the mission is important, it is not enough to keep employees motivated and identifying with their nonprofit organization. Several challenges facing nonprofit organizations today directly influence employment practices and employee satisfaction. For example, as explained previously, employees of many nonprofits are at the mercy of government funders (Andrus, 2000), and despite government requirements for professional staff, funding may limit salaries. Restrictions on professional practice in nonprofit organizations receiving government funds, combined with low wages, job insecurity, and intractable social problems, have made nonprofit agencies less attractive work environments for human service professionals. Focusing on the mission, therefore, may attract employees but is less effective in retaining them.

Goulet and Frank (2002) interviewed employees from government, nonprofit, and for-profit organizations to examine workers' commitment in each of these sectors. Their research supported the notion that the nonprofit sector is unique, given the organizational commitment differences between nonprofit employees and those in the other two sectors. Intrinsic motivators are important to both nonprofit and government workers, but extrinsic motivators, such as pay and benefits, remain critical. Because compensation packages in for-profit firms are far more attractive, workers in nonprofit and government organizations may be lured away from their intrinsic commitment to a "cause" (Goulet & Frank, p. 207). In a robust economy, with low levels of unemployment and frequent job shifts, employees of nonprofit and government organizations experience decreased commitment when compensation packages and other extrinsic rewards simply are not competitive with those in the private sector.

In addition to focusing on factors contributing to employees' organizational commitment, Brown and Yoshioka's (2003) research identified three primary reasons why employees leave a company: other career plans, insufficient pay and opportunities, and frustration with management. Frustration with management was expressed as the organization "is not run well" or that it "doesn't reflect the mission," both of which result in perceived inconsistencies between management's rhetoric and actions (Brown & Yoshioka, p. 13).

Another challenge to maintaining nonprofit employees' commitment is organizations' shrinking level of commitment to their workforce, as evidenced in their inability to provide health care, pensions, and related benefits (Skloot, 2000). Research has shown that such benefits have a negative impact on employees' satisfaction and commitment.

One explanation for why nonprofit organizations pay lower wages than other organizations is nonprofits supposedly are nicer places to work. Indeed, some authors have proposed that nonprofit organizations *should* make an effort to promote a work environment that reflects the beliefs of the organization (e.g., being a caring organization, family friendly, culturally diverse, and fostering supportive communication; cf., Arsenault, 1998; Fineman, 2000 Lewis et al., 2001). Emanuele and Higgins (2000), however, showed that, in many instances, nonprofit organizations are *not* more likely than other organizations to offer pleasant working conditions. Nonprofits also often are significantly less likely than other organizations to offer health-related insurance benefits, life insurance and pension benefits, and leave time. One benefit that is provided more readily by nonprofit organizations, however, is on-site daycare (Emanuele & Higgins, 2000).

As benefits decrease, policies and restrictions tighten, and wages remain low, employees' loyalty to nonprofit organizations fades (Smith & Lipsky, 1993) and executives are more easily recruited away by for-profit businesses. Those who leave are eager to break free from stifling work rules and inadequate rewards for performance; consequently, "the brain drain from the nonprofit sector threatens its leadership" (Skloot, 2000, p. 320).

In addition to decreasing benefits, nonprofit employees are affected by emotional labor, burnout, and stressors imposed by government regulations, as discussed previously. Several studies have explored factors of burnout and emotional labor in human service delivery work, and communication strategies that can mitigate their negative effects on employees and the organization as a whole (see Miller & Considine, this volume). Miller, Stiff, and Ellis's (1988) research with a large psychiatric hospital on relationships among empathy, communication, and burnout in human service professionals, for instance, found that caregivers' ability to respond through communication had a strong impact on the likelihood of burnout. Leiter (1988) proposed a predictive model of burnout in human service workers, relating burnout to social involvement with coworkers and job satisfaction, and found that burnout was greatest for workers who communicated extensively about work but had few informal supportive relationships with coworkers.

Miller, Zook, and Ellis (1989) conducted related research with employees of a retirement center in the Midwestern United States, utilizing various inventories to measure workplace burnout, work stressors and workload, role stress, and social support from supervisors, coworkers, friends, and family. They also explored the type of communication that was most effective for dealing with burnout among the various employee groups. Their findings confirmed the existence of distinct job characteristics and subcultures among administrative, nursing, housekeeping, maintenance, and food service employees, and showed that helpful communication strategies varied for the different employee groups. For example, administrative employees most valued participation in decision making, whereas nursing, housekeeping and food service employees valued social support from coworkers and supervisors.

Employee Involvement Strategies

Many authors suggest that enhancing the social support aspects of coworker communication is one key to leading human service organizations. As Leiter (1988) claimed, "The challenge for health service administration is to create work settings that utilize those aspects of work-oriented communication which enhance feelings of accomplishment, while minimizing the demands and drudgery that aggravate exhaustion" (p. 115).

Harris, Mainelli, and O'Callaghan (2002) conducted research with leaders of nonprofit organizations in the United Kingdom to determine the extent to which such organizations provide employees with "evidence of worth" (p. 399). Organizational leaders consistently stated that staff and volunteers/members were the key audiences for their communication, and that staff commitment was a prerequisite for measuring evidence of worth. Care and attention to the nonprofit workforce also is important because employees' feelings, emotions, values, and interactions contribute to an organization's culture and identity (Domagalski, 1999; Fineman, 2000; Rafaeli & Worline, 2001; Shuler & Davenport Sypher, 2000).

McAdoo and Pynes (1995) also discussed the measurement of employee job satisfaction, as well as effective communication strategies that foster employee involvement and identification in one nonprofit organization. As McAdoo and Pynes argued:

> Nowhere is the task more difficult in determining employee satisfaction than in the
> human service field where people's roles are often blurred, where the parameters

between jobs are not clearly defined, and where executives often have trouble setting clear and consistent policy across all levels of agency structure. (p. 369)

McAdoo and Pynes's (1995) research was conducted with Places for People, Inc. (PFP), a nonprofit organization providing residential, vocational, recreational, and psychosocial services for adults with severe and persistent mental illness who reside in St. Louis, Missouri. As part of PFP's public relations planning process, a questionnaire was administered to staff members to measure their attitudes toward and satisfaction with their jobs, benefits, and physical environment. Employees expressed dissatisfaction in several areas, including not feeling involved in the agency and not having a sense of ownership in its success. Employees felt that they did not have a "voice" in agency decisions that affected them personally and that information was not communicated effectively throughout the organization. They said that they did not have authority to do their job and were not recognized as responsible or accountable for work performed. Employees also reported that policies were not administered equitably across program lines, management was disinterested in the success of line staff, and that there was a distinct absence of mutual trust and respect among coworkers and between management and line staff.

McAdoo and Pynes (1995) further showed that effective team coordination is essential to securing employees' involvement and identification in nonprofit organizations. In response to the workplace quality-of-life issues uncovered as part of their research with PFP, the company implemented a series of organizational development and team-building exercises, and restructured how it staffed its core services. Program components were combined such that all services were provided by three newly established, integrated teams of professionals. The agency extended its hours of operations and team members were responsible for planning their flexible work schedules and setting goals and objectives, and they were involved in developing policy. PFP also increased staff collaboration at all staff and management levels, including direct and meaningful staff interaction with the board of directors. PFP's experience confirms the findings by Lawler and Mohrman (as cited in McAdoo & Pynes) that given the right mix of information, knowledge, power, and rewards, employees will be both more satisfied and productive.

A Feminist Perspective

Some scholars have used feminist theory to explore the struggles that nonprofit organizations face in dealing with the challenge (from governments and elsewhere) to become "more professional." Mumby's (1996) exploration of organizations as gendered sites of communication, control, and resistance reviewed studies of "women's alternative organizations," several of which were nonprofits. Mumby (p. 277) examined "the process through which women workers attempt to develop autonomous spheres of culture and identity within existing organization settings," and focused on the development of alternative organizational forms devoted specifically to women's issues (see also Buzzanell, Meisenbach, Remke, Sterk & Turner, this volume). Mumby concluded that the successful construction of alternative organizational forms in this context always is accomplished with one eye on the ideal and the other on pragmatic realities; as we discussed elsewhere, successful nonprofit organizing inevitably requires compromises and the accommodation of diverse and, at times, conflicting interests.

Ashcraft's (2000) study of a feminist nonprofit organization (SAFE) devoted to the support of survivors of domestic violence illustrates well the struggle within nonprofits to develop more "professional" relationships within their workforce. Staff members and volunteers described SAFE as an holistic community that weaves together the professional and personal lives of its members in various ways, considers personal and family needs as organizational obligations, and exhibits a "unique union of emotion and work" (Ashcraft, p. 361). Ashcraft, however, described SAFE's dilemma of remaining open to emotional expression but also setting clear limits, explaining that "despite SAFE's careful efforts to blend private and public lives, mounting tension between formal hierarchy, quasi-egalitarianism, copious emotional expression, and fear of power abuse erupted into the intense and painful drama of ethical relationship boundaries" (p. 378). The drama associated with this dilemma resulted in the development of a policy that banned all sexual relationships and urged only *professional* relations among coworkers; that policy discouraged socializing, mandated that "iffy" relationships "required immediate debriefing with a supervisor," and advised employees to pursue even friendships "with extreme caution" (Ashcraft, 2000, p. 371).

Similar to the struggles within SAFE, the study by Rodriguez of a battered women's shelter "demonstrated conflict between the establishment of an egalitarian and participatory organizational structure and the various bureaucratic, ideological, and economic exigencies that impinge on this structure" (cited in Mumby, 1996, p. 281). Mumby (1996) also reviewed Maguire and Mohtar's study of the counterdiscourses of a women's center, explaining that:

> Although the center experienced the usual tensions between the need for hierarchical structure and the development of egalitarian relationships, the members also defined themselves in terms of three discursive moves that functioned to situate them in an oppositional relationship to the mainstream culture: a) identifying state-run agencies as incompetent; b) re-educating members of these dominant publics regarding domestic violence; and c) reinforcing their outsider status by identifying false assumptions and stereotypes about them perpetuated by the dominant publics. (p. 282)

Storytelling and Identification

One way in which organizational members sustain a supportive work environment and foster identification with the organization is through storytelling. Bradshaw (2002), in his study of board–staff relations and governance of nonprofit organizations, suggested that nonprofits can be understood as socially constructed entities through storytelling. As Bradshaw explained:

> Stories serve to create both a vision of the future and a coherent sense of the past for organizational members.... Organizations rely on stories as cultural artifacts to give people a sense of direction, shared memories, and a definition of community. (p. 474)

Bradshaw suggested that the leadership function involves the creation of an organization's story and that the management function is the implementation and enactment of that story such that it shapes organizational reality.

Research conducted by Wilensky and Hansen (2001) on the stories of executives of nonprofit organizations supports the notion that it is important for nonprofit leaders to motivate employees, foster a supportive environment, and establish a connection to the organizational mission. Executives considered the organization's people (both staff and volunteers) to be its essential strength, and most executives believed that their power came from their ability to motivate and align employees with the organization's mission. One way they accomplished these goals was by creating and sharing stories within the organization that fostered employees' understanding of the mission and their association with the organization.

This review has focused on communication strategies used by leaders, volunteers, and employees of nonprofit organizations to identify and respond to significant threats and challenges facing them today. We identified three communication challenges most relevant to this process: partnering, clarifying mission and identity, and fostering employee involvement and identification. Such research still is emerging, and our understanding of the communication issues facing nonprofit organizations is improving as this sector continues to grow and transform. As the nonprofit landscape continues to change, more focused study is necessary. Toward this end, in the next and last section, we identify specific issues that warrant further research.

Future Applied Communication Research on Nonprofit Organizations

As nonprofit organizations continue to face government funding cutbacks and increased competition, new management strategies are emerging that warrant further study, including the use of mergers, consolidations, and administrative and management service organizations. According to McLaughlin (1998), the bulk of innovation in nonprofit organizations today is taking place not in services but in management. Organizations that want to survive and prosper must respond to environmental change; that response might be continuing to provide the same services but in a manner that is better and more competitive than previous ways of operating, or it may involve planning for important shifts in organizational focus and structure to better ensure long-term stability. In addition to diversifying funding sources and implementing strong management practices to streamline nonprofit agencies, the thrust of "innovation will be toward greater collaboration between nonprofit organizations and others carrying out similar missions" (McLaughlin, 1998, p. xxii).

Although still a relatively new trend in management practice and scholarly research, mergers between and among nonprofit organizations are becoming more common. Consistent with the study of for-profit business mergers, however, most attention has focused on the mechanical aspects of how to make a merger happen. As explained below, areas that have received less attention in the literature are the organizational culture of nonprofit organizations, emotional characteristics of the nonprofit workforce, and the impact that these new partnerships have on organizational effectiveness.

The first area for continued and expanded research is organizational culture (see Seibold et al., this volume), which is especially important because culture within the nonprofit sector surpasses structure as the primary means of organizing, motivating, and assessing workers' (both paid and volunteer) attitudes and behaviors. Organizational culture also is important because it commonly is cited as the reason why mergers fail—in particular, because of clashing organizational cultures and the lack of attention paid to this issue when planning and executing a merger (Bramson, 2000; DeVoge & Spreier, 1999; Feldman & Spratt, 1999; Marks & Mirvis, 1998). Although there has been ample research on organizational culture over the past 2 decades, the vast majority has focused on organizations in the private sector.

A second direction for further research is the emotional characteristics of the nonprofit human service workforce. As previously shown, care and attention to the nonprofit workforce is important because employees constitute an organization's culture and identity (Fineman, cited in Domagalski, 1999; Rafaeli & Worline, 2001; Shuler & Davenport Sypher, 2000). Unique to nonprofit human service work, the major transformation caused by mergers presents some significant challenges related to employees' emotions and the need to support, engage, and assist them in moving through such a transition. Expressing care for employees' emotions during a major change not only keeps employees content but (also) contributes to the success of the merger effort.

Third, research should look into the pragmatics of nonprofits engaging in a wider variety of strategic partnerships as a means of responding to environmental change. As nonprofit organizations explore new coping strategies and partnerships, such as reorganization, consolidation, and mergers, there is an increased need for applied communication research and practice. These trends create the need to expand researchers' and practitioners' knowledge of organizational change (see Seibold et al., this volume) in nonprofit settings, thus setting the stage for important applied communication research agendas within these organizations.

In addition to topics for further research, there are possibilities for new and expanded types of research. One strategy recommended by Lindenberg (2001) is to inject an under-represented viewpoint into the research on nonprofit organizations—specifically, the voices of managers. Managers' "often-unheard" voices can provide unique feedback to academics about how useful their frameworks turn out to be when applied within the complex world of nonprofit organizational practice. Scholars can gain new insights by taking managers' experiences into account and refining their frameworks to make them even more useful.

The voices of managers and others within nonprofit organizations perhaps can best be heard through methods such as narrative inquiry (see Ellingson, this volume), which has proven useful in researching organizational issues, such as emotion in the workplace (e.g., Miller, Considine, & Garner, 2007), which is especially relevant in the nonprofit sector. Sandelands and Boudens (2000) recommended stories as a research method that captures people's feelings and emotion in the workplace, claiming that "narratives can be used to discover universal human truths about feelings and forms of life" (p. 56; see also Fineman, 2000).

Conclusion

We began this chapter with the observation that most research on organizational communication has focused on for-profit businesses. This tendency has become problematic because of the significant growth in size and importance of the nonprofit sector. Through a review of existing research, we showed how communication is essential to meeting three challenges associated with the effectiveness of nonprofit organizations: partnering, clarifying mission and identity, and fostering employee involvement and identification. We concluded with a call for further study of the emotional aspects of communication during nonprofit organizational change, utilizing research methodologies that capture the voices and stories of nonprofit employees and leaders. Applied communication research that takes into account the unique qualities of nonprofit organizing will produce important findings that have the potential to improve quality of life for everyone.

References

Akingbola, K. (2004). Staffing, retention, and government funding: A case study. *Nonprofit Management & Leadership, 14*, 453–465.

Alexander, J. (1999). The impact of devolution on nonprofits: A multiphase study of social service organizations. *Nonprofit Management & Leadership, 10*, 57–70.

Alexander, J. (2000). Adaptive strategies of nonprofit human service organizations in an era of devolution and new public management. *Nonprofit Management & Leadership, 10*, 287–303.

Andrus, P. (2000). Mandated charity. *Celebrating Voices: A Journal of Feminist Expression, 2*(2), 18.

Arsenault, J. (1998). *Forging nonprofit alliances: A comprehensive guide to enhancing your mission through joint ventures and partnerships, management service organizations, parent corporations, mergers.* San Francisco: Jossey-Bass.

Ashcraft, K. L. (2000). Empowering "professional" relationships: Organizational communication meets feminist practice. *Management Communication Quarterly, 13,* 347–392.

Austin, J. E. (1998). The invisible side of leadership. *Leader to Leader, 8.* Retrieved September 14, 2006, from http://www.leadertoleader.org/knowledgecenter/L2L/spring98/austin.html

Austin, M. J. (2003). The changing relationship between nonprofit organizations and public social service agencies in the era of welfare reform. *Nonprofit and Voluntary Sector Quarterly, 32,* 97–114.

Bellah, R., Madsen, R., Sullivan, W. M., Swidler, A., & Tipton, S. M. (1996). *Habits of the heart: Individualism and commitment in American life* (Rev. ed.). Berkeley: University of California Press.

Bernstein, S. R. (1991). *Managing contracted services in the nonprofit agency: Administrative, ethical, and political issues.* Philadelphia: Temple University Press.

Bertalanffy, L. von. (1973). *General system theory: Foundations, developments, applications.* Harmondsworth, UK: Penguin.

Bland, R. L., & Rubin, I. S. (1997). *Budgeting: A guide for local governments.* Washington, DC: International City/County Management Association.

Boris, E. T. (1998, July 1). *Myths about the nonprofit sector.* Urban Institute. Retrieved June 5, 2002, from http://www.urban.org/publications/307554.html

Boris, E. T., & Steuerle, C. E. (1999). *Nonprofit and government collaboration and conflict.* Washington, DC: Urban Institute.

Bradshaw, P. (2002). Reframing board–staff relations: Exploring the governance function using a storytelling metaphor. *Nonprofit Management & Leadership, 12,* 471–484.

Bramson, R. N. (2000). HR's role in mergers and acquisitions. *Training & Development, 54*(10), 59–66.

Brinkerhoff, J. M., & Brinkerhoff, D. W. (2002). Government–nonprofit relations in comparative perspective: Evolution, themes, and new directions. *Public Administration and Development, 22,* 3–18.

Brown, W. A., & Yoshioka, C. F. (2003). Mission attachment and satisfaction as factors in employee retention. *Nonprofit Management & Leadership, 14,* 5–18.

Browning, L. D., & Shetler, J. C. (2000). *Sematech: Saving the U.S. semiconductor industry.* College Station: Texas A&M University Press.

Chambre, S. M., & Fatt, N. (2002). Beyond the liability of newness: Nonprofit organizations in an emerging policy domain. *Nonprofit and Voluntary Sector Quarterly, 31,* 502–524.

Chaskin, R. J., Brown, P., Venkatesh, S., & Vidal, A. (2001). *Building community capacity.* New York: Aldine De Gruyter.

Cohen, R., & Cohen, J. (2000). *Chiseled in sand: Perspectives on change in human service organizations.* Belmont, CA: Brooks/Cole, Thomson Learning.

Deetz, S. A. (1992). *Democracy in an age of corporate colonization: Developments in communication and the politics of everyday life.* Albany: State University of New York Press.

Deetz, S. A. (1994). Future of the discipline: The challenges, the research, and the social contribution. In S. A. Deetz (Ed.), *Communication yearbook* (Vol. 17, pp. 565–600). Thousand Oaks, CA: Sage.

Deetz, S. A., & Kersten, A. (1983). Critical models of interpretive research. In L. L. Putnam & M. E. Pacanowsky (Eds.), *Communication and organizations: An interpretive approach* (pp. 147–171). Beverly Hills: Sage.

DeVoge, S., & Spreier, S. (1999). The soft realities of mergers. *Across the Board, 36*(10), 27–32.

Domagalski, T. A. (1999). Emotion in organizations: Main currents. *Human Relations, 52,* 833–852.

Drucker, P. F. (1990). *Managing the non-profit organization: Practices and principles.* New York: HarperCollins.

Eadie, D. C. (1997). *Changing by design: A practical approach to leading innovation in nonprofit organizations.* San Francisco: Jossey-Bass.

Emanuele, R., & Higgins, S. H. (2000). Corporate culture in the nonprofit sector: A comparison of fringe benefits with the for-profit sector. *Journal of Business Ethics, 24,* 87–93.

Farace, R. V., Monge, P. R., & Russell, H. M. (1977). *Communicating and organizing.* Reading, MA: Addison-Wesley.

Feldman, M. L., & Spratt, M. F. (1999). *Five frogs on a log: A CEO's field guide to accelerating the transition in mergers, acquisitions, and gut wrenching change.* New York: HarperBusiness.

Fineman, S. (2000). *Emotion in organizations* (2nd ed.). Thousand Oaks, CA: Sage.

Garner, L. H., Jr. (1989). *Leadership in human services: How to articulate and implement a vision to achieve results.* San Francisco: Jossey-Bass.

Gordon, G. J. (1992). *Pubic administration in America* (4th ed.). New York: St. Martin's Press.

Goulet, L. R., & Frank, M. L. (2002). Organizational commitment across three sectors: Public, non-profit, and for-profit. *Public Personnel Management, 31,* 201–210.

Gray, B. (1989). *Collaborating: Finding common ground for multiparty problems.* San Francisco: Jossey-Bass.

Grønbgerg, K. A., & Salamon, L. M. (2002). Devolution, marketization, and the changing shape of government–nonprofit relations. In L. M. Salamon (Ed.), *The state of nonprofit America* (pp. 447–470). Washington, DC: Brookings Institution Press.

Harris, I., Mainelli, M., & O'Callaghan, M. (2002). Evidence of worth in not-for-profit sector organizations. *Strategic Change, 11,* 399–410.

Herman, R. D., & Renz, D. O. (1999). Theses on nonprofit organizational effectiveness. *Nonprofit and Voluntary Sector Quarterly, 28,* 107–126.

Hesselbein, F. (1999). Introduction: The community beyond the walls. In F. Hesselbein, M. Goldsmith, & I. Somerville (Eds.), *Leading beyond the walls* (pp. 1–6). San Francisco: Jossey-Bass.

Katz, D., & Kahn, R. L. (1966). *The social psychology of organizations.* New York: Wiley.

King, N. K. (2004). Social capital and nonprofit leaders. *Nonprofit Management & Leadership, 14,* 471–486.

Kohm, A., & La Piana, D. (2003). *Strategic restructuring for nonprofit organizations: Mergers, integrations, and alliance.* Westport, CT: Praeger.

Leiter, M. P. (1988). Burnout as a function of communication patterns: A study of a multidisciplinary mental health team. *Group & Organization Studies, 13,* 111–128.

Lewis, L. K., Hamel, S. A., & Richardson, B. K. (2001). Communicating change to nonprofit stakeholders: Models and predictors of implementers' approaches. *Management Communication Quarterly, 15,* 5–41.

Lindenberg, M. (2001). Are we at the cutting edge or the blunt edge? Improving NGO organizational performance with private and public sector strategic management frameworks. *Nonprofit Management & Leadership, 11,* 247–270.

Lune, H. (2002). Weathering the storm: Nonprofit organization survival strategies in a hostile climate. *Nonprofit and Voluntary Sector Quarterly, 31,* 463–483.

Marks, M. L., & Mirvis, P. H. (1998). *Joining forces: Making one plus one equal three in mergers, acquisitions, and alliances.* San Francisco: Jossey-Bass.

McAdoo, S., & Pynes, J. (1995). Reinventing mental health service delivery: One nonprofit's experience. *Public Administration Quarterly, 19,* 367–374.

McLaughlin, T. A. (1998). *Nonprofit mergers and alliances: A strategic planning guide.* New York: John Wiley.

Medved, C. E., Morrison, K., Dearing, J. W., Larson, R. S., Cline, G., & Brummans, B. H. J. M. (2001). Tensions in community health improvement initiatives: Communication and collaboration in a managed care environment. *Journal of Applied Communication Research, 29,* 137–152.

Miller, K. I., Considine, J., & Garner, J. (2007). "Let me tell you about my job": Exploring the terrain of emotion in the workplace. *Management Communication Quarterly, 20,* 231–260.

Miller, K. I., Stiff, J. B., & Ellis, B. H. (1988). Communication and empathy as precursors to burnout among human service workers. *Communication Monographs, 55,* 250–265.

Miller, K. I., Zook, E. G., & Ellis, B. H. (1989). Occupational differences in the influence of communication on stress and burnout in the workplace. *Management Communication Quarterly*, 3, 166–190.

Morris, A., & Bloom, J. R. (2002). Contextual factors affecting job satisfaction and organizational commitment in community mental health centers undergoing system changes in the financing of care. *Mental Health Services Research*, 4, 71–83.

Mumby, D. K. (1996). Feminism, postmodernism, and organizational communication: A critical reading. *Management Communication Quarterly*, 9, 259–295.

Mumby, D. K., & Stohl, C. (1996). Disciplining organizational communication studies. *Management Communication Quarterly*, 10, 50–72.

Oster, S. M. (1995). *Strategic management for nonprofit organizations: Theory and cases*. New York: Oxford University Press.

Ott, J. S. (2001). Part 10: The blending and blurring of the sectors. In J. S. Ott (Ed.), *The nature of the nonprofit sector* (pp. 355–364). Boulder, CO: Westview Press.

Poole, D. L. (2003). Scaling up CBOs for second-order devolution in welfare reform. *Nonprofit Management & Leadership*, 13, 325–341.

Pynes, J. E. (1997). *Human resources management for public and nonprofit organizations*. San Francisco: Jossey-Bass.

Rafaeli, A., & Worline, M. (2001). Individual emotion in work organizations. *Social Science Information*, 40, 95–123.

Redding, W. C. (1985). Stumbling toward identity: The emergence of organizational communication as a field of study. In R. D. McPhee & P. K. Tompkins (Eds.), *Organizational communication: Traditional themes and new directions* (pp. 5–33). Beverly Hills, CA: Sage.

Rein, M. (1983). *From policy to practice*. Armonk, NY: M. E. Sharpe.

Ryan, W. P. (1999). The new landscape for nonprofits. *Harvard Business Review*, 77(1), 127–136.

Salamon, L. M. (1994) The rise of the nonprofit sector. *Foreign Affairs*, 73(4), 109–122.

Salamon, L. M. (1995). *Partners in public service: Government–nonprofit relations in the modern welfare state*. Baltimore: Johns Hopkins University Press.

Salamon, L. M. (2002). *The state of nonprofit America*. Washington, DC: Brookings Institution Press.

Salamon, L. M. (2003). *The resilient sector: The state of nonprofit America*. Washington, DC: Brookings Institution Press.

Sandelands, L. E., & Boudens, C. J. (2000). Feelings at work. In S. Fineman (Ed.), *Emotion in organizations* (2nd ed., pp. 46–63). Thousand Oaks, CA: Sage.

Shaw, G., & Weber, J. (1990). *Managerial literacy: What today's managers must know to succeed*. Homewood, IL: Dow Jones-Irwin.

Shaw, M. (2003). Successful collaboration between the nonprofit and public sectors. *Nonprofit Management & Leadership*, 14, 107–120.

Shuler, S., & Davenport Sypher, B. D. (2000.). Seeking emotional labor: When managing the heart enhances the work experience. *Management Communication Quarterly*, 14, 50–89.

Skloot, E. (2000). Evolution or extinction: A strategy for nonprofits in the marketplace. *Nonprofit and Voluntary Sector Quarterly*, 29, 315–324.

Smith, S. R. (1994). Managing the challenges of government contracts. In R. D. Herman & Associates (Eds.), *The Jossey-Bass handbook of nonprofit leadership and management* (pp. 325–341). San Francisco: Jossey-Bass.

Smith, S. R., & Lipsky, M. (1993). *Nonprofits for hire: The welfare state in the age of contracting*. Cambridge, MA: Harvard University Press.

Snavely, K., & Tracy, M. B. (2000). Collaboration among rural nonprofit organizations. *Nonprofit Management & Leadership*, 11, 145–165.

Somerville, I., & Quinn, M. D. (1999). Leading in a leaderless world. In F. Hesselbein, M. Goldsmith, & I. Somerville (Eds.), *Leading beyond the walls* (pp. 227–241). San Francisco: Jossey-Bass.

Steiner, G. A., & Steiner, J. F. (2000). *Business, government, and society: A managerial perspective.* Boston: Irwin McGraw-Hill.

Steuerle, C. E., & Hodgkinson, V. A. (1999). Meeting social needs: Comparing the resources of the independent sector and government. In E. T. Boris & C. E. Stererle (Eds.), *Nonprofit and government collaboration and conflict* (pp. 71–98). Washington, DC: Urban Institute.

Tuckman, H. P. (1998). Competition, commercialization, and the evolution of nonprofit organizational structures. *Journal of Policy Analysis and Management, 17,* 175–194.

Waide, P. J., Jr. (1999). Principles of effective collaboration. In F. Hesselbein, M. Goldsmith, & I. Somerville (Eds.), *Leading beyond the walls* (pp. 243–250). San Francisco: Jossey-Bass.

Weick, K. E. (1969). *The social psychology of organizing.* Reading, MA: Addison-Wesley.

Weisbrod, B. A. (1997). The future of the nonprofit sector: Its entwining with private enterprise and government. *Journal of Policy Analysis and Management, 16,* 541–555.

Werther, W. B., Jr., & Berman, E. M. (2001). *Third sector management: The art of managing nonprofit organizations.* Washington, DC: Georgetown University Press.

Wilensky, A. S., & Hansen, C. D. (2001). Understanding the work beliefs of nonprofit executives through organizational stories. *Human Resource Development Quarterly, 12,* 223–239.

Young, D. R. (2001a). Organizational identity and the structure of nonprofit umbrella associations. *Nonprofit Management and Leadership, 11,* 289–304.

Young, D. R. (2001b). Organizational identity in nonprofit organizations: Strategic and structural implications. *Nonprofit Management & Leadership, 12,* 139–157.

16 Health Communication as Applied Communication Inquiry

Gary L. Kreps
George Mason University

Ellen W. Bonaguro
Western Kentucky University

The status of individual and collective health and well-being powerfully influences the quality of people's lives. Illness, disease, and infirmity can cause significant pain, suffering, and expense for those afflicted, as well as for their loved ones (who often provide needed care and support), interfering with people's work and home life. In response, health-care and health-promotion activities have arisen as important social processes for helping people respond to and prevent illness, enabling them to reduce the problems associated with poor health and to participate as fully as possible in life. Indeed, the modern health-care system—which includes physicians, nurses, other immediate health care providers, public health agencies, health profession educational programs, hospitals, clinics, health maintenance organizations (HMOs), pharmacies, nursing homes, hospices, medical equipment and supply companies, and health insurance companies—is a massive interorganizational infrastructure designed to promote health and well-being (Starr, 1982). Promoting health, however, is a complex process, with the health-care system often proving difficult for people to access and negotiate. Effective communication, consequently, is essential for enabling health-care providers and consumers to access and navigate the system, share relevant information, combat significant health risks, influence health behaviors, and deliver the best possible health-care. Communication, thus, is important to all aspects of health prevention, maintenance, illness, treatment, and recovery.

Applied health communication research is conducted to understand and influence the best ways to utilize communication to promote health care and illness treatment. This chapter provides a broad overview of this form of scholarship, explaining the development of health communication as an important and vibrant area of applied communication study, examining recent advancements in such inquiry, and offering suggested directions for future health communication inquiry.

Health Communication Inquiry

Health communication as an applied field of study had many starting points, triggered by scholars in sociology, psychology, and medicine (see, e.g., Kreps, 2001; Kreps, Bonaguro, & Query, 1998; Kreps, Query, & Bonaguro, 2007). Their research spurred communication scholars to examine the role of communication in promoting health, establishing health-care relationships, and other important health-related processes and practices. By 1975, a Health Communication Division had formed in the International Communication Association, followed in 1985 by one in the National Communication Association. In 1985, the *Journal of Applied Communication Research*, which already had included a dozen or more broadly defined health communication articles, published a special issue on "Doctor–Patient Communication" (Smith & Cissna, 1985), and in 1989, the journal

Health Communication began publishing articles, followed, in 1996, by the *Journal of Health Communication*.

Health communication inquiry, today, is concerned with the important influences on people's health of both face-to-face communication (in activities such as health-care interviews, counseling sessions, health-education efforts, care coordination, and the provision of social support) and mediated communication (including the many uses of print media, television, film, radio, computers, and other technologies; see Lievrouw, this volume). In broad terms, two areas of health communication inquiry can be identified: *Health-care-focused communication research* typically examines issues associated with the influence of communication on enhancing the quality, accuracy, and effectiveness of diagnoses, treatment decision making, treatment follow-up care, support, and end-of-life care; *health-promotion-focused communication research* most often focuses on the design and evaluation of health-education and promotion campaigns through analysis of message design, communication channels, and other campaign strategies and practices.

Given its relevance to preserving life and reducing suffering, health communication research tends to be problem based, concerned with identifying and proposing strategies to manage significant health-care and health-promotion problems. Although not all health communication research is applied, as some studies focus only on developing or refining theoretical constructs or are solely descriptive without proposing practical suggestions, as required in recent years for publication in the *Journal of Applied Communication Research* (see Frey & SunWolf, this volume), most of this research is problem–solution oriented and offers recommendations for practice (or studies interventions), and, hence, constitutes applied communication scholarship. For example, scholars have examined such important communication problems or issues as, and offered practical recommendations about, managing interactional difficulties and promoting high-quality communication between health-care providers and patients/consumers (e.g., S. M. Allen, Petrisek, & Laliberte, 2001; Bertakis & Azari, 2007; Cegala, 1997; Cegala et al. 2008; Edwards & Elwyn, 2001; Gittell et al., 2000; Larson & Yao, 2005; Lloyd, 2001; Mirivel, 2008; Roter, Larson, Sands, Ford, & Houston, 2008; Saultz & Albedaiwi, 2004; Scholl, 2007; Sparks, Villagram, Parker-Raley, & Cunningham, 2007; Stewart, 1995; Vanderford, Stein, Sheeler, & Skochelak, 2001; Walker, Arnold, Miller-Day, & Webb, 2002; see also Miller & Considine, this volume; Nussbaum & Ohs, this volume); meeting people's health social support needs (e.g., Albrecht & Goldsmith, 2003; Baus, Dysart-Gale, & Haven, 2005; Braithwaite & Eckstein, 2003; Brashers, Neidig, & Goldsmith, 2004; Egbert, Koch, Coeling, & Ayers, 2006; Frey, Query, Flint, & Adelman, 1998; Miczo, 2004; Oetzel, Duran, Jiang, & Lucero, 2007; Query & Wright, 2003; Robinson & Turner, 2003; Wright & Frey, 2008); decreasing gaps and disparities in access to health facilities, personnel, and information (e.g., Campo & Frazer, 2007; Case, Johnson, Andrews, Allard, & Kelly, 2004; Chang et al., 2004; Davis, 2002; Dunleavy, Crandall, & Metsch, 2005; Johnson, Andrews, & Allard, 2001; Moore & Thurston, 2008; Ray, 1996a, 1996b); preventing information errors by and within health-care entities/systems (e.g., Bates et al., 2001; Donchin et al., 2003; Eisenberg et al., 2005; Kohn, Corrigan, & Donaldson, 2000; Lyon, 2007; McKnight, Stetson, Bakken, Curran, & Cimino, 2002); assessing the nature and accuracy of health information presented by the media (e.g., Berry, Wharf-Higgins, & Naylor, 2007; Gibson, 2007; Gill & Babrow, 2007; Goodyear-Smith, Petousis-Harris, Vanlaar, Turner, & Ram, 2007; Vanderford & Smith, 1996); and conducting health communication campaigns (e.g., Backer, Rogers, & Sopory, 1993; Beaudoin & Thorson, 2007; Campo, Cameron, Brossard, & Frazer, 2004; Cho & Salmon, 2006, 2007; Cohen, Shumate, & Gold, 2007; Dutta-Bergman, 2005; Fishbein, Hall-Jamieson, Zimmer, von Haeften, & Nabi, 2002; Gagné, 2008; Hornik, 2002;

Lindsey et al., 2007; Maibach, Kreps, & Bonaguro, 1993; Maibach & Parrott, 1995; S. E. Morgan & Miller, 2002; Noar, 2006b; Randolph & Viswanath, 2004; Rimal, 2000; Salmon & Atkin, 2003; Slater, 2006; Slater, Karan, Rouner, & Walters, 2001; see also Hecht & Miller-Day, this volume; Witte & Roberto, this volume).

Within health communication inquiry, scholars view communication as *the* central social process influencing people's conceptualization of health and well-being, the provision of health-care services (both formal and informal delivery), and the promotion of personal and public health. This centrality is based on the pervasive role that communication performs in creating, gathering, and sharing health information (e.g., Brashers, Goldsmith, & Hsieh, 2002; Kreps, 2003), which is among the most important resources that guide strategic health-promoting and preserving behaviors, treatments, and decisions, both in personal and professional health-care settings (Kreps, 1988). Health information includes the critical knowledge gleaned from health-care providers' interviews with patients and from laboratory tests used to diagnose health problems; findings from clinical research and practice (as well as from long-standing culturally based traditions) conducted about the best available treatment strategies for specific health threats; analysis of data gathered in check-ups to assess the efficacy of health-care treatments and to guide the introduction of new treatment strategies to manage difficult bioethical issues and weigh the consequences involved in making complex health-care decisions; and the recognition of critical warning signs that detect imminent health risks and direct responsive behaviors designed to minimize these risks. *Health-care providers*—a term that includes the wide range of formal and informal caregivers who deliver health care and those who promote health through education efforts and information dissemination—and *health-care consumers*—a term that includes both active seekers of health care services (patients and members of their personal support systems) who interface with the health-care system and those who seek information to guide their health decisions and behaviors—communicate to generate, access, and exchange such information for making important health-promotion and treatment decisions, adjusting to changing health conditions, and coordinating health-preserving activities. Communication also enables health-promotion specialists (such as health educators, providers, public officials, and advocacy group representatives) to develop and disseminate messages to influence key audiences' health beliefs, attitudes, values, and behaviors.

Health communication inquiry, thus, is conducted to understand the powerful role of communication in health care, with applied health communication inquiry designed to help people to use communication strategically to achieve health and health care. As explained below, the breadth and depth of applied health communication scholarship is reflected in the multiple levels of interaction investigated, the numerous and diverse communication channels covered, the many health-care settings studied, and the variety of methodologies that scholars employ to understand the complex role that communication plays in health care and promotion.

The Breadth and Depth of Health Communication Inquiry

To understand the breadth and depth of health communication scholarship, we examine below the level of interaction at which such research is directed, the communication channels that are studied, the settings investigated, and the research methods employed.

Levels of Health Communication Inquiry

The primary levels of interaction often studied include intrapersonal, interpersonal, group, organizational, and societal health communication.

Intrapersonal health communication inquiry examines the symbolic processes that people use to conceptualize health and health care, such as the development of people's beliefs, attitudes, and values that predispose their health-care behaviors and decisions. Given that symbols shape people's perspectives on health, health care, and health promotion (e.g., Brown, 1995; Frey, Adelman, & Query, 1996; Sharf & Vanderford, 2003), the intrapersonal level has become critical for examining how communication influences people's cognitive, emotional, and attitudinal interpretations of health and health behaviors. For example, Gibbs and Franks (2002) showed how metaphors used by women in stories told about their experiences with cancer (e.g., "life is a journey" and "cancer is war") helped them to make sense of and cope with their illness.

Interpersonal health communication inquiry focuses on the role of communication—such as information exchange, education, and social support—in dyadic relationships—such as in the provider–consumer relationship. Interpersonal communication between health-care providers and consumers has become a central area of inquiry because of the profound influence of such interaction on the delivery of health care and the promotion of health. Indeed, Arora's (2003) review of the literature showed that physicians' communicative behavior (specifically, establishing interpersonal relationships, facilitating information exchange, and promoting patient involvement in decision making) had a positive impact on patient health outcomes, although Thorne (2006) warned that "we know that communication between chronically ill patients and their healthcare providers has tremendous potential to be instrumental in facilitating coping, self-care management, and optimal quality of life, or conversely, in being toxic and damaging those ideals" (p. 58). Thorne emphasized the need for health-care providers to advance a different approach to care from one in which patients depend on providers to one of self-care management that creates a patient–provider relationship "within which attitudes are conveyed, information exchanged, and problems articulated" (p. 108). Such an approach, however, may not be easy to enact, as physicians and patients do not always engage in the most effective communicative behaviors. J. M. Morgan and Krone (2001), for example, examined difficulties that health-care providers have in expressing their emotions with patients and encouraging patients to express their emotions, difficulties that limited the effectiveness of their communication with patients and that suggested the need for communication education to help providers better express and manage emotions when delivering health care.

Patients, of course, also demonstrate difficulties interacting with health-care providers, but research conducted by Greenfield, Kaplan, and Ware (1985) showed that patients can be trained to interact more effectively with their physicians. In a 20-minute session immediately preceding an office visit, a clinic assistant reviewed the patient's most recent visit and talked with him or her about care and management issues that warranted discussion with the physician. The findings demonstrated the positive influences of increased patient–provider communication involvement in achieving more positive health outcomes (e.g., fewer role and physical limitations, such as pain) compared to patients not taught to interact with their physician (see also the study of health communication training by Harrington, Norling, Witte, Taylor, & Andrews, 2007).

Another focus of interpersonal health communication inquiry is on how other relationships affect health outcomes for those who are ill. Brashers et al. (2004), for instance, conducted focus groups with adults with HIV or AIDS to determine their viewpoints of social support and uncertainty management, finding that peer support was particularly useful for "managing personal, social, and medical forms of uncertainty for individuals living with HIV" (p. 234). Recognizing the role that interpersonal relationships play in helping people to cope with illness becomes even more important as significant others take on the role of health-care provider. Polk's (2005) research showed how caregivers rely on both verbal and nonverbal communication to reduce their ambiguity and gain perceived control in providing care, and Beach and Good's (2004, p. 8) investigation of dyadic family members' phone calls revealed how family cancer journeys are "interactionally-organized events" comprised of communicative practices designed to manage the dilemmas associated with the disease.

Group health communication inquiry examines health communication in small group settings, such as families (see Socha, this volume), health care teams, and support groups, with a particular emphasis on identifying effective and ineffective communication among group members and the factors affecting that communication. Ellingson's (2003) long-term ethnography of an interdisciplinary geriatric oncology team at a cancer center, for instance, revealed how communication that occurred in the "backstage," outside of team meetings—specifically, informal impression and information sharing, checking clinic progress, relationship building, space management, training students, handling interruptions, and formal reporting—affected "both internal team functioning and communication with patients and companions in the front stage of health care delivery" (p. 114). Apker, Propp, and Ford's (2005) study of nurses' role contradictions in health-care teams found three factors that affected nurses' communication in those teams—hierarchy, status, and professional identity—that were related to health-care professionals not being trained to understand the work or importance of other members on the health-care team.

Other group health communication studies focus on the instrumental role of communication in social support groups in enhancing the quality of people's life and assisting them and their significant other, family members, and friends to cope with illness and death. B. R. Shaw, McTavish, Hawkins, Gustafson, and Pingree (2000), for example, studied how a computer-mediated support group empowered women with breast cancer to communicate freely with and to gain support from the other participants, which helped them to make decisions, and Toller (2005) examined how caregivers—parents in a support group for those who had experienced the death of a child—took control of their interactions, often by engaging in selective communication, to negotiate the dialectical tensions they experienced.

Organizational health communication inquiry examines how people communicate as they negotiate the health-care system, coordinate interdependent health-care groups, mobilize various health specialists, and share information to enable effective multidisciplinary provision of health care and the prevention of health risks. Because clinics, hospitals, and medical centers have evolved as central sites for health-care delivery, scholars examine how organizational communication in those sites supports or impedes achieving key health-care and promotion goals. For instance, in a revealing study, Gillespie (2001) examined how routine administrative and treatment procedures required of asthmatic Medicaid patients in a managed care system routinely disenfranchised those patients, and suggested system-wide communication policy changes to empower patients with asthma. Work by Thorne (2006) and Von Koroff, Gruman, Schafer, Curry, and Wagner (1997) also points to the importance of studying communication in health-care organizations to change these systems to better meet patients' needs, for as people live longer and have to manage chronic illnesses, they need to be served by a health-care system that teaches them how to maneuver through that system to manage their care. As Von Koroff et al. (p. 1099) stated, "As yet, no grand strategies exist for reorganizing health care systems to improve collaborative management...[but] health care leaders, providers, and consumers have roles to play" in creating such change.

Different organizational delivery systems slowly are emerging to meet consumers' health-care needs. Anderson (2004), for instance, studied the delivery of health care in a faith-based organization, showing how parish nurses provide health care that includes both emotional and spiritual dimensions, and Schuster's (2006) study showed how an alternative medical organization, a birthing center, created a climate that provides a safe and private experience that helps women to resist thinking of birth as a medical experience.

Societal health communication inquiry examines the generation, dissemination, and utilization of information communicated via diverse media to a broad range of professional and lay audiences to educate them about health care practices and policies. Dutta-Bergman (2004), for instance, found that broadcast outlets with an entertainment orientation are better suited for health communication campaigns, whereas print media, interpersonal networks, and the Internet are best for communicating health information to health-active consumers.

Societal health communication inquiry also examines how cultural communication systems influence people's health, health-care, and health-promotion perspectives and practices. Basu and Dutta (2007), for instance, showed how the context in which tribal people in India lived, particularly their marginalization and exploitation, influenced their understandings of health and their desire for structural changes in the resources that were available to them.

Societal health communication inquiry also examines how communication can be employed to affect public health policies and practices. Conrad and Millay (2001), for example, studied how political and rhetorical communication strategies were used by the members of the Texas legislature, particularly the communication of involving narratives (regarding the role of narrative in health, see, e.g., Charon, 2006; Eisenberg, Baglia, & Pynes, 2006; Frank, 1995; the essays in Harter, Japp, & Beck, 2005; Mehl-Madrona, 2007; Petraglia, 2007; Sunwolf, Frey, & Lesko, 2008), to enact the first Patient's Bill of Rights, and they discussed implications for the effective use of communication strategies to introduce new public health policies elsewhere.

Communication Channels in Health Communication Inquiry

As much of the extant research shows, face-to-face communication between providers and consumers, family members, health-care team members, and support group members is the focus of many health communication studies. Face-to-face communication is encouraged in accessing the health-care system, even for primary health-care concerns. Indeed, Rimer (2000) concluded that "one-to-one, in-person communication…is important" and that research on breast cancer shows "that a simple physician recommendation to a woman is the single most important motivator of mammography" (p. 2). This channel of communication undoubtedly will remain important as long as access to health care primarily is controlled by providers and third-party payers, with providers reimbursed based on face-to-face patient visits, although reimbursement strategies might change as a result of increased demand by consumers to use new communication technologies to provide care.

The telephone also continues to be an important channel studied by health communication scholars. For example, R. Shaw and Kitzinger (2007) examined 80 calls to a home birth helpline, focusing on the role of memory in the interactions, and Beach and Good's (2004) study was based on the analysis of telephone calls between family members coping with cancer.

New communication technologies, however, are being employed increasingly in health communication (e.g., Eng & Gustafson, 1999; Harris, Kreps, & Dresser, 2007; Neuhauser & Kreps, 2003; Wright, 2008; Zoller, 2003; see also Lievrouw, this volume).

Neville, Greene, and Lewis (2006) reported that patients now expect general practitioners (GPs) to adopt new technologies that will put "less pressure on and demand on traditional means of contacting GPs: telephone and face-to-face contact" (p. 14). For instance, many patients prefer providers to use e-mail as an additional means of communication, especially for routine matters, although Masters's (2008) review suggested that few physicians do. Neville et al. also warned that new technologies should be used to "supplement, not supplant, face-to-face consultations between doctors and patients" (p. 11).

One place where new communication technologies have had a significant impact on health communication is in online support groups. As Wright's (1999, 2000a, 2000b, 2000c, 2002, 2004) research program and many other studies clearly have shown, a significant number of people have joined online support groups and report receiving many benefits from them.

A broad range of media undoubtedly will continue to be explored in health communication research, with new communication technologies examined as they emerge. As Rimer (2000) concluded, however, there is no need to encourage one channel over another, for "as the communications menu grows, we need not view the options as dichotomous choices but instead pick and choose among them to meet the needs of different people at different times for different topics" (p. 113).

Settings for Health Communication Inquiry

The settings for health communication inquiry are quite diverse and include all of the places where health information is generated and exchanged, such as homes, offices, schools, clinics, and hospitals. Not surprisingly, many studies have been conducted in hospitals or health-care clinics. Apker et al. (2005), for instance, conducted interviews at a 348-bed tertiary hospital with 2,848 employees, and Ellingson (2007) studied the communication performances enacted by dialysis staff members—including registered nurses, patient care technicians, technical aids, a social worker, and a dietician—in a dialysis unit of a treatment center. Others have studied long-term care facilities, such as Adelman and Frey's (1994, 1997) studies of how people living with AIDS in a residential facility create and sustain healthy community (see also Carpiac-Claver & Levy-Storm, 2007; studies cited in Nussbaum & Ohs, this volume). Other scholars interview people in their home, such as Baxter, Braithwaite, Golish, and Olson's (2002) study of wives whose elderly husbands experience Alzheimer's disease and related disorders (see also Polk, 2005).

Although applied health communication researchers "who conduct their work in an academic setting…generally have the freedom to pursue their interests with relatively little interference" (Edgar, Freimuth, & Hammond, 2003, p. 626), the diversity of health-care settings creates significant challenges for field-based researchers. Legal, bureaucratic, and privacy issues often are paramount when researchers try to negotiate entry to health-care settings. Communication researchers often have opportunities, and resultant responsibilities, to enter private health-care settings and gain access to confidential information. The organizational challenges of studying health-care delivery without impeding the quality of care or intruding on people's privacy must be carefully negotiated (Committee on Quality Health Care in America, Institute of Medicine, 2001; Kreps, 1989). General regulations have been developed to protect research participants (such as the research guidelines established by Institutional Review Boards; see Seeger, Sellnow, Ulmer, & Novak, this volume) and there are additional specific guidelines to protect the privacy of health-care consumers (such as the rules covered by the Health Insurance Portability and Accountability Act; HIPPA); these regulations guide health communication research so that it does not unfairly impinge on the rights of individuals (Guttman, 2003). It is imperative that health-care consumers and providers be treated with respect and dignity, given that researchers often intrude on very sensitive, private, and emotional aspects of life and death.

Research Methods In Health Communication Inquiry

Health communication inquiry employs a broad range of research methods (including all those covered in this handbook). Although the standard for biomedical research has long been the use of randomized clinical trial experiments to promote precision, control, and prediction (see Query et al., this volume), a number of other research methods are used in health communication scholarship. For instance, scholars often use the survey method (see Query et al., this volume) to understand people's health communication beliefs and behaviors, such as the recently established Health Information National Trends (HINTS) survey administered by the Health Communication and Informatics Research Branch at the National Cancer Institute (NCI), which provides representative national data every 2 years about the U.S. public's access to, preference for, and use of information to promote health (e.g., Nelson et al., 2004). There also is a growing tradition of studying health communication using ethnography (see Ellingson, this volume), employing participant observation and in-depth interviews to enrich understanding of the lived health communication experience. Textual analysis of language use in medical encounters also has a long history in health communication inquiry (e.g., Roter & Larson, 2002; see also Condit & Bates, this volume; Tracy & Mirivel, this volume). Recent research has expanded on language analysis to study the interdependent use of both verbal and nonverbal messages in health provider–consumer interactions (e.g., Albrecht, Penner, & Ruchdeschel, 2003). In addition, as more health communication research is conducted on the same topic, meta-analysis (see Query et al., this volume) is being used to synthesize research findings (M. Allen et al., 2008; Noar, 2006a; O'Keefe & Jensen, 2007, 2008; Snyder et al., 2004).

Multimethodological designs, which are becoming increasingly popular, have helped researchers to capture many of the complexities of health communication through triangulation of data (e.g., Davenport Sypher, McKinley, Ventsam, & Valdeavellano, 2002; Kutner, Steiner, Corbett, Jahnigen, & Barton, 1999; Waitzkin et al., 2002). Such designs often are employed because health communication inquiry has become a multidisciplinary enterprise, with scholars from many disciplines, besides communication—such as allied health, dentistry, economics, health anthropology, health education, health informatics, health psychology, medical sociology, medicine, nursing, pharmacy, public health, and social work—contributing to the growing health communication research literature. Moreover, courses and programs in health communication have been included recently in many schools of medicine, nursing, pharmacy, and public health. The National Institutes of Health (NIH) and other federal agencies now bring together leading experts from numerous disciplines to evaluate the status of proposed health communication inquiry and to chart the course for future work. For example, recent interdisciplinary meetings on health communication inquiry sponsored by the NCI include the 2002 Consumer-Provider Communication Research Symposium (see http://dccps.nci.nih.gov/hcirb/consumer.html), 2007 HINTS data users conference (see http://hints.cancer.gov/presentations.jsp), and the Critical Issues in e-Health Research Conferences. Furthermore, contemporary federal funding initiatives strongly encourage multidisciplinary collaborations in health communication research, such as the recently funded Centers for Excellence in Cancer Communication Research (see http://dccps.nci.nih.gov/hcirb/ceccr/) and the new Understanding and Promoting Health Literacy research program announcement (see http://grants.nih.gov/grants/guide/pa-files/PAR-04-116.html). Scholars from a variety of disciplinary perspectives now are working together to understand and improve health communication.

Parallel Perspectives in Health Communication Inquiry

As previously mentioned, two major interdependent and parallel branches of inquiry have developed in the field of health communication. The first branch focuses on health-care delivery, both the formal delivery of health care by physicians, nurses, and other providers, as well as the informal delivery of health care and social support by people's significant other, family members, and friends. Scholars working from this perspective primarily examine how communication influences the delivery and outcomes of health care. The second branch focuses on the role of communication in health promotion, which includes both formal public health-education programs and the informal diffusion of folk-health wisdom and practices. Health-promotion scholars primarily study the persuasive use of messages and media to promote public health and influence people's health behaviors.

These two branches of the health communication field seem to parallel a long-standing, but artificial division found within the communication discipline between interpersonal and mediated communication (Reardon & Rogers, 1988). Accordingly, the health-care delivery branch has attracted scholars with a primary interest in how interpersonal and group communication influence health-care delivery, focusing on issues such as the provider–consumer relationship, therapeutic communication, social support, health-care teams, and health-care decision making. The health-promotion branch, in contrast, has attracted media scholars concerned with the development, implementation, and evaluation of communication campaigns to prevent major health risks and promote public health. For example, scholars have been involved with campaigns to prevent public risks for contracting HIV, heart disease, and cancer. Many health-promotion scholars also evaluate the use of media to disseminate health information, as well as examine how health and health care are portrayed by popular media.

Although these two major approaches to health communication inquiry have taken parallel paths, there are many areas where their paths intersect. For example, the provider–patient interaction is a prime setting for studying health promotion, as some of the most influential health-education activities occur during clinical visits between providers and consumers; consequently, health-care providers now are being trained to provide risk-prevention and health-promotion advice to patients during office visits and clinical interviews (e.g., Anis et al., 2004; Glasgow, Eakin, Fisher, Bacak, & Brownson, 2001). In addition, many multichannel health-promotion campaigns employ interpersonal communication interventions, sometimes between health-care providers and consumers, to connect these aspects of health communication (e.g., Maibach et al., 1993; Maibach & Parrott, 1995). Given that health communication operates across multiple communication channels, the separation of interpersonal and mediated aspects is limiting and artificial; consequently, many scholars have begun to study the differential and combined effects of interpersonal and mediated communication on people's health practices (e.g., Jones, Denham, & Springston, 2006, 2007). More collaboration between the health-care delivery and health-promotion branches will significantly enhance the quality of health communication inquiry.

Contributions of Health Communication Research to Public Health

Communication scholarship has made major contributions to promoting public health over the last 50 years. A large and developing body of scholarship powerfully illustrates the centrality of communication processes in achieving important health-care and health-promotion goals. For example, Kreps and O'Hair (1995) reported a series of studies showing the influences of communication strategies and programs (introduced at individual, dyadic, group, organizational, and societal levels) on people's health knowledge, behaviors, and outcomes. Dearing et al. (1996) illustrated the positive influences of social marketing and diffusion-based communication campaign strategies in encouraging at-risk populations to adopt important health risk-prevention behaviors. Large-scale, longitudinal communication intervention programs, such as the Stanford Five City Heart Health Program (Flora, Maccoby, & Farquhar, 1989), one of the first studies to integrate interpersonal and media communication in the health context, and the Minnesota Heart Health Program (Pavlik et al., 1993), also have promoted adoption of lifestyle changes to prevent cardiovascular disease and reduce gaps in public health knowledge. Thus, there is great potential in using strategic communication programs to provide health-care consumers and providers with needed information to address important public health needs.

Perhaps the greatest positive impact that health communication research has had on society is in the development and implementation of health-promotion campaigns. Promoting public health and preventing the spread of dangerous health risks is a significant goal of applied health communication scholarship. Whether focused on the prevention and control of HIV and AIDS (see Witte & Roberto, this volume), cancer, or heart disease, a combination of communication theory, research, and practice has guided health-promotion campaign efforts. These campaigns involve a broad set of communication strategies and activities that health-promotion specialists engage in to disseminate needed information to help people resist health threats.

Typically, health communication campaigns have been designed to educate target audiences about important health threats and risky behaviors that might harm them, and, thereby, to raise their consciousness about such issues. Health campaigns also are designed to move target audiences to action in support of public health. For example, communication campaigns often encourage target audiences to engage in healthy behaviors to resist serious health threats, such as adopting healthy lifestyles (e.g., exercise, nutrition, and stress reduction), avoiding dangerous situations and substances (e.g., poisons, carcinogens, or other toxic substances), engaging in early screening and diagnosis for serious health problems, and availing themselves of health-care services, when appropriate, to minimize harm.

Health communication campaigns have been instrumental in promoting public health in several important domains. Four examples illustrate the successes of such campaigns in the United States:

1. *Helping to curtail the use of tobacco products.* Tobacco use has been identified as the single-most preventable cause of morbidity and mortality within society. Health communication campaigns have educated the public about the dangers of tobacco use and how to break the tobacco habit, as well as affected many public policies, such as no-smoking laws (e.g., Pinkleton, Austin, Cohen, Miller, & Fitzgerald, 2007). As a result of the many concerted tobacco-control communication efforts, tobacco use has declined across the United States, extending many lives (e.g., Shopland, 1993).
2. *Encouraging the use of safer sexual practices to decrease sexually transmitted diseases (STDs).* In response to serious STDs, such as HIV, communication campaigns have encouraged the use of condoms to reduce their transmission. Similar campaigns have discouraged the sharing of intravenous needles by drug users. These communication efforts have prevented the spread of HIV within high-risk populations, again, undoubtedly saving many lives (e.g., Dearing et al., 1996).

3. *Promoting healthy dietary and exercise behaviors.* Many campaigns have encouraged the consumption of a low-fat, high-fiber diet that is rich in fruits and vegetables. For example, the 5-A-Day Program has been very successful at increasing people's awareness of the importance, and consumption, of fruits and vegetables in daily diets (Potter et al., 2000). Similarly, campaigns to increase physical activity have improved public health and increased resistance to a host of diseases, including heart disease, diabetes, and many cancers (e.g., Flora et al., 1989; Pavlik et al., 1993).
4. *Promoting child immunization.* Very effective campaigns have encouraged public support for vaccination of children, which now is supported by federal, state, and local health departments across the United States. These campaign efforts have protected children from a host of diseases, and virtually eliminated widespread incidences of serious health threats, such as diphtheria, tetanus, measles, polio, and smallpox, in the United States (e.g., Evans, Bostrom, Johnston, Fisher, & Stoto, 1997).

Advances in Health Communication Inquiry

Because health communication scholarship is a relatively new area of inquiry, many fruitful directions are available for future research to improve health-care policies and practices. As explained below, one exciting new direction for such research involves the study of new communication technologies for disseminating health information. Research also is needed to design and evaluate sophisticated health communication campaigns to influence people's health beliefs, attitudes, values, and behaviors.

New Communication Technologies and Health Communication Inquiry

Many scholars have called for concerted study of the ways in which new media and information technologies can advance health-care delivery and public health-promotion goals (e.g., Cassell, Jackson, & Cheuvront, 1998; Chamberlain, 1996; Clark, 1992; Eng & Gustafson, 1999; Eng et al., 1998; Neuhauser & Kreps, 2003; Wright, 2008; see also Lievrouw, this volume). *Health informatics* (sometimes referred to as *eHealth* or *e-Health*), which involves using computer-based communication technologies to process and disseminate health information, has emerged as an important and quickly growing new area of inquiry; its growth has mirrored that of the Internet as a primary source for health information and the rapid adoption of computerized tools and information systems within the modern health-care system (Atkinson & Gold, 2002; Eng & Gustafson, 1999; National Telecommunications and Information Administration, 1999).

The use of new information technologies appears to be particularly relevant to health consumers and providers confronting serious life-threatening diseases, such as cancer, heart disease, and AIDS, where the demand for accurate and up-to-date health information is especially crucial (Ahern, Phalen, & Mockenhaupt, 2003; Bernhardt & Hubley, 2001; Freimuth, Stein, & Kean, 1989; Johnson, 1997). As mentioned previously, research has shown that online support groups and communities provide individuals confronting serious health problems with relevant and timely information for managing their condition (e.g., Eysenbach, Powell, Englesakis, Rizo, & Stern, 2004; Ferguson & Frydman, 2004; Ginossar, 2008). Online information systems, thus, have great potential to provide people with quick and easy access to relevant health information.

Researchers, however, still have many questions that need to be answered about the best ways to use e-Health applications. For instance, a question has been raised regarding the accuracy and currency of the health information available via the Internet. Eysenbach, Powell, Kuss, and Sa (2002) argued that existing research on this topic is questionable due to the various methodological frameworks used by researchers to determine the accuracy and quality of health information. As Eysenbach et al. (2002) concluded, "Studies are urgently needed to help in the organizing process to develop methods and instruments to guide consumers to quality information and to identify factors that can be accessed to predict favorable patient outcomes" (p. 2698). Another question concerns who has access to this health information and who is left out. A report by the National Telecommunications and Information Administration (1995) showed that socioeconomic background, race, age, and level of education are predictors of telephone, computer, and computer-household modem penetration. Another question concerns what strategies can be used to provide health information to those who do not have such access. Moreover, it is unclear what impact this information has on health outcomes, although Stoddard et al. (2005) provided evidence that e-Health communication can improve behavioral outcomes; specifically, participants in their online smoking cessation program reported making serious attempts to quit smoking based on the program. A final question is how the positive influences of health information available via the Internet and other new communication technologies can be maximized. Programmatic health communication research certainly is needed to answer these and other important questions.

Sophisticated Health Communication Campaign Designs

The effectiveness of health communication campaigns has been shown to be influenced by numerous variables, beginning with audience members' perceptions of targeted health behaviors, the design of campaign communication messages and strategies, the employment of appropriate communication channels, the acquisition of data from formative and summative evaluation research, and the use of guiding theories of communication and social influence (e.g., Hornik, 2002; Kiwanuka-Tondo & Snyder, 2002; Maibach et al., 1993; Myhre & Flora, 2000). Planners often are guided by exemplars of effective health communication campaigns that suggest the value of employing particular message strategies (e.g., Flora, 2001; Greenberg & Gantz, 2001, Mittlemark et al., 1986). However, too many campaigns have not had strong and lasting health-promotion influences on target audiences (see the meta-analysis by Snyder et al., 2004). The most sophisticated campaigns are guided by powerful explanatory theories that identify key factors for campaign design and implementation (Pechmann, 2001; Slater, 1999; for exemplary applied communication research programs, see Hecht & Miller-Day, this volume; Witte & Roberto, this volume). For example, the stages-of-change model (Prochaska & DiClemente, 1984) has long been used by health communication campaign planners to incorporate the readiness of audience members to accept campaign messages (e.g., Parvanta & Freimuth, 2000; Slater, 1999). The health belief model (regarding its historical origins, see Rosenstock, 1974) also has been successfully employed by campaign researchers to identify health beliefs to design the best message strategies for encouraging health behavior change (e.g., Agha, 2003; King, 1985; Roberto, Meyer, Johnson, Atkin, & Smith, 2002; Witte & Roberto, this volume). The social cognitive model (Bandura, 1998) has been widely used by health communication campaign planners to analyze the social diffusion of new health behaviors in terms of the psychosocial factors governing their acquisition and adoption and the social networks through which they spread and are supported (e.g., Parrott, Steiner, & Goldenhar, 1996; Rinderknecht & Smith, 2004). The PRECEDE Model (predisposing, reinforcing, and enabling causes in educational diagnosis and evaluation; Green, Kreuter, Deeds, & Partridge, 1980) continues to offer valuable information for researchers and practitioners in designing, implementing, and evaluating health communication campaigns (e.g., Farley, Laflamme, & Vaez, 2003;

Morris, Linnan, & Meador, 2003). Relevant theoretical frameworks, thus, help researchers working with health communication campaigns to identify salient individual and community characteristics that motivate or support positive or negative health behaviors. Consequently, campaigns have begun to integrate multiple theoretical perspectives to guide health communication efforts (e.g., Murphy, 2004; Randolph & Viswanath, 2004; Rhodes & Hergenrather, 2003).

Advances in health communication campaign research have resulted in a greater understanding of the importance of audience segmentation, pilot-testing messages and strategies with target audience focus groups, and the strategic placement of messages to reach intended audiences (Maibach et al., 1993; Slater, 1996). Health communication interventions increasingly have become more refined in the development of messages to influence target audiences, narrowing the scope of audiences from broad populations to highly segmented and homogenous audiences (Slater, 1999). Early health communication interventions were developed with general message strategies that appealed to a broad audience, whereas more sophisticated studies now first carefully segment target audiences based on shared demographics, personality predispositions, beliefs and attitudes (e.g., Silk, Weiner, & Parrott, 2005), media use (Rodgers, Chen, Duffy, & Fleming, 2007), and other factors, and then create effective messages to appeal to those segmented audiences (Maibach et al., 1993). Tailored message strategies now even identify key individual factors to design specific health-promotion messages. As Kreuter, Farrell, Olevitch, and Brennan (2000) noted, "For example, if a participant expressed doubt about her ability to get regular physical activity (i.e., low self-efficacy for exercise), and the materials included information designed to enhance self-efficacy, that would be a match" (p. S230).

Growing evidence suggests the efficacy of tailoring communication to promote behavior changes, especially cancer-prevention and control behaviors (Kreps & Chapelsky Massimilla, 2002; Lipkus, Lyna, & Rimer, 1999; Rakowski et al., 1998; Rimer et al., 1999; Rimer & Glassman, 1998; Skinner, Strecher, & Hospers, 1994). In fact, Krishna, Balas, Spencer, Griffin, and Boren (1997) found that tailored, interactive, computer-based educational programs about various clinical conditions produced a significant positive effect in improved health status in several major areas of care, including diabetes mellitus, asthma, rheumatoid arthritis, and hypertension. Rimer and Glassman (1998) described the process of creating tailored print communication and found that such messages facilitated positive patient–provider interactions, fostered behavioral changes conducive to health, enhanced health-evaluation processes (by requiring collection of patient-specific information), and offered opportunities to expand the reach of health professionals, especially by sending personalized, individualized messages to patients. Advances in the use of tailored messages for health promotion, however, have raised issues about the gathering or accessing of information that identifies the specific health behaviors of an individual, leading to questions about the appropriate level of analysis for audience segmentation in health communication campaigns (Abrams, Mills, & Bulger, 1999; Kreuter & Wray, 2003). Future research can help to indicate when it is best to target campaign messages to individuals or to well-segmented target audiences.

Salmon and Atkin (2003) pointed out that health communication campaigns vary according to the dose of health information given, duration of message exposure, degree of media richness, vertical integration of communication channels, and the horizontal integration of approaches to social change. Health communication campaigns also can be viewed in terms of various stages. For instance, the four health communication campaign phases (precampaign, campaign/message development, postcampaign, and ongoing/ad hoc) that guided the "America Responds to AIDS" campaign remain an important planning tool for future campaigns (Nowak & Siska, 1995). Included in these phases are strategic planning, needs assessment, target-audience analysis, formative and summative evaluation, and message efficacy. Moreover, new planning strategies have been identified by several researchers to improve the design, implementation, and evaluation of health communication campaigns. For example, Parrott and Steiner (2003) recommended that campaigns be planned jointly with health communication researchers and public health practitioners, as "more linkages between academic health communicators and public health professionals, as well as other health professionals, afford one means of increasing the validity associated with efforts to identify, understand, and replicate these successful endeavors" (p. 647).

The Future of Health Communication Inquiry

The extant research reviewed in this chapter clearly documents the powerful influence of communication on health practices and outcomes. Moreover, health communication inquiry increasingly has become more sophisticated as it has addressed more complex issues. Given the sophistication of recent scholarship, there is growing interdisciplinary and institutional credibility for health communication researchers. As one sign of that increased credibility, health communication scholars now, more than ever, attract federal research funding. Federal agencies—such as the Centers for Disease Control (CDC); National Cancer Institute; National Heart, Lung, and Blood Institute (NHLBI); and the National Institute for Drug Abuse (NIDA)—increasingly have become more familiar with and receptive to the field of health communication. The CDC, for example, has established an Office of Communications, with a Division of Health Communication that develops message-based interventions across the many important health risk-prevention initiatives it sponsors. Similarly, the federal agency for Health Care Research and Quality (AHRQ) now emphasizes the importance of health communication research and interventions in its many publications, conferences, and outreach programs. Health communication scholars need to continue to take advantage of the growing research opportunities offered by the federal government, learning how to compete successfully for federal research grants and contracts, maintaining contacts with key members of federal agencies, and participating actively in federal research activities.

There also is a growing emphasis on public advocacy, consumerism, and empowerment in health communication research that will revolutionize health-care systems by equalizing (as much as possible) power between providers and consumers, and by relieving a great deal of strain on the system through disease prevention, self-care, and making consumers partners in the health-care enterprise (Arntson, 1989; Kreps, 1993, 1996a, 1996b). Consequently, communication research increasingly is being conducted to identify consumers' information needs and to suggest strategies for encouraging them to take control of their health and health care. Ideally, health communication research should identify appropriate sources of information available to consumers and gather data from them about the challenges and constraints they face within health-care systems, as well as develop and conduct field tests with educational media programs for enhancing consumers' medical literacy (Nielsen-Bohlman, Panzer, & Kindig, 2004; Parker & Kreps, 2005). Such research will help people to negotiate their ways through health-care bureaucracies and to develop communication skills for interacting effectively with health-care providers.

Health communication research, of course, will continue to focus on the effective dissemination of information to promote public health. However, health-promotion efforts must recognize the multidimensional nature of health communication, identify communication strategies that incorporate multiple levels and channels of human communication, and implement a wide range of prevention messages and campaign strategies targeted or tailored to specific (well-segmented) audiences. Health communication campaigns, however, must become even more sophisticated, drawing on relevant theories, methods, and communication technologies and integrating multiple communication channels—including interpersonal, group, organizational, and societal communication—to effectively target well-segmented, at-risk, and marginalized populations. Such campaigns will be even more successful in delivering messages that encourage health risk prevention and promote better health. The need to measure accurately the effectiveness of health communication campaigns also will continue to be an important area of study. New areas should include creating campaigns with community partners, as well as understanding how campaigns can influence public policy.

Health communication inquiry also increasingly is becoming concerned with the role of culture on health and health care (Kreps, 2006a). For instance, significant disparities exist in health outcomes between majority and minority populations in the United States that have been linked to the quality of health communication experienced and to access to health information (Kreps, 2005, 2006b; Kreps, Gustafson, et al., 2004; Saha, Arbelaez, & Cooper, 2003). Future research, therefore, needs to examine the health communication needs of marginalized cultural groups and to identify strategies for enhancing their health communication.

Conclusion

The field of health communication has moved toward a sophisticated, multidimensional agenda for applied research that integrates face-to-face and mediated communication in the delivery of health care and the promotion of public health. Scholars have examined the multifaceted influence of communication on health at multiple levels (intrapersonal, interpersonal, group, organizational, and societal) and across a wide range of health-care contexts. They also have evaluated the use of a broad and evolving range of communication strategies and channels, and assessed the influence of communication on important health outcomes. Such inquiry has provided important information about the development of cooperative relationships between interdependent participants in the modern health-care system, encouraged the use of sensitive and appropriate communication in health care and health promotion, empowered those affected by illness to work collaboratively with caregivers to make the best health decisions, enhanced the dissemination of relevant health information and the use of strategic communication campaigns to promote public health, facilitated the development of sensitive multicultural relations in health care, and suggested adaptive strategies for using communication to accomplish desired health outcomes. Health communication, thus, is and will continue to be a highly relevant and significant area of applied communication inquiry.

References

Abrams, D. B., Mills, S., & Bulger, D. (1999). Challenges and future directions for tailored communication research. *Annals of Behavioral Medicine, 21,* 299–306.

Adelman, M. B., & Frey, L. R. (1994). The pilgrim must embark: Creating and sustaining community in a residential facility for people with AIDS. In L. R. Frey (Ed.), *Group communication in context: Studies of natural groups* (pp. 3–22). Hillsdale, NJ: Erlbaum.

Adelman, M. B., & Frey, L. R. (1997). *The fragile community: Living together with AIDS.* Mahwah, NJ: Erlbaum.

Agha, S. (2003). The impact of a mass media campaign on personal risk perception, perceived self-efficacy and on other behavioural predictors. *AIDS Care, 15,* 749–762.

Ahern, D. K., Phalen, J. M., & Mockenhaupt, R. E. (2003). Science and the advancement of eHealth: A call to action. *American Journal of Preventive Medicine, 24,* 108–109.

Albrecht, T. L., & Goldsmith, D. J. (2003). Social support, social networks, and health. In T. L. Thompson, A. M. Dorsey, K. I. Miller, & R. Parrott (Eds.), *Handbook of health communication* (pp. 263–284). Mahwah, NJ: Erlbaum.

Albrecht, T. L., Penner, L. A., & Ruckdeschel, J. C. (2003). Understanding patient decisions about clinical trials and the associated communication process: A preliminary report. *Journal of Cancer Education, 18,* 210–214.

Allen, M., Timmerman, L., Ksobiech, K., Valde, K., Gallagher, E. B., Hookham, L., et al. (2008). Persons living with HIV: Disclosure to sexual partners. *Communication Research Reports, 25,* 192–199.

Allen, S. M., Petrisek, A. C., & Laliberte, L. L. (2001). Problems in doctor–patient communication: The case of younger women with breast cancer. *Critical Public Health, 11,* 39–58.

Anderson, C. M. (2004). The delivery of health care in faith-based organizations: Parish nurses as promoters of health. *Health Communication, 16,* 117–128.

Anis, N. A., Lee, R. E., Ellerbeck, E. F., Nazir, N., Greiner, K. A., & Ahluwalia, J. S. (2004). Direct observation of physician counseling on dietary habits and exercise: Patient, physician, and office correlates. *Preventive Medicine, 38,* 198–202.

Apker, J., Propp, K. M., & Ford, W. S. Z. (2005). Negotiating status and identity tensions in healthcare team interactions: An exploration of nurse role dialectics. *Journal of Applied Communication Research, 33,* 93–115.

Arntson, P. (1989). Improving citizens' health competencies. *Health Communication, 1,* 29–34.

Arora, N. K. (2003). Interacting with cancer patients: The significance of physicians' communication behavior. *Social Science and Medicine, 57,* 791–806.

Atkinson, N. L., & Gold, R. S. (2002). The promise and challenge of eHealth interventions. *American Journal of Health Behavior, 26,* 494–503.

Backer, T. E., Rogers, E. M., & Sopory, P. (1993). *Designing health communication campaigns: What works?* Newbury Park, CA: Sage.

Bandura, A. (1998). Health promotion from the perspective of social cognitive theory. *Psychology and Health, 13,* 623–649.

Basu, A., & Dutta, M. J. (2007). Centralizing context and culture in the co-construction of health: Localizing and vocalizing health meanings in rural India. *Health Communication, 21,* 187–196.

Bates, D. W., Cohen M., Leape L. L., Overhage J. M., Shabot M. M., & Sheridan, T. (2001). Reducing the frequency of errors in medicine using information technology. *Journal of the American Medical Informatics Association, 8,* 299–308.

Baus, R., Dysart-Gale, D., & Haven, P. (2005). Caregiving and social support: A twenty-first century challenge for college students. *Communication Quarterly, 53,* 125–142.

Baxter, L. A., Braithwaite, D. O., Golish, T. D., & Olson, L. N. (2002). Contradictions of interaction for wives of elderly husbands with adult dementia. *Journal of Applied Communication Research, 30,* 1–26.

Beach, W. A., & Good, J. S. (2004). Uncertain family trajectories: Interactional consequences of cancer diagnosis, treatment, and prognosis. *Journal of Social and Personal Relationships, 21,* 8–32.

Beaudoin, C. B., & Thorson, E. (2007). Evaluating the effects of a youth health media campaign. *Journal of Health Communication, 12,* 439–454.

Bernhardt, J. M., & Hubley, J. (2001). Health education and the Internet: The beginning of a revolution. *Health Education Research, 16,* 643–645.

Berry, T. R., Wharf-Higgins, J., & Naylor, P. J. (2007). SARS wars: An examination of the quantity and construction of health information in the news media. *Health Communication, 21,* 35–44.

Bertakis, K. D., & Azari, R. (2007). Determinants of physician discussion regarding tobacco and alcohol abuse. *Journal of Health Communication, 12,* 513–526.

Braithwaite, D. O., & Eckstein, N. J. (2003). How people with disabilities communicatively manage assistance: Helping as instrumental social support. *Journal of Applied Communication Research, 31*, 1–26.

Brashers, D. E., Goldsmith, D. J., & Hsieh, E. (2002). Information seeking and avoiding in health contexts. *Human Communication Research, 28*, 258–271.

Brashers D. E., Neidig J. L., & Goldsmith D. J. (2004). Social support and the management of uncertainty for people living with HIV or AIDS. *Health Communication, 16*, 305–331.

Brown, P. (1995). Naming and framing: The social construction of diagnosis and illness. *Journal of Health and Social Behavior, 35*(Extra issue), 34–52.

Campo, S., Cameron, K. A., Brossard, D., & Frazer, M. S. (2004). Social norms and expectancy violation theories: Assessing the effectiveness of health communication campaigns. *Communication Monographs, 71*, 448–470.

Campo, S., & Frazer, M. S. (2007). "I'm glad you feel comfortable enough to tell me that": Participatory action research for better healthcare for women who partner with women. In L. R. Frey & K. N. Carragee (Eds.), *Communication activism: Vol. 1. Communication for social change* (pp. 355–384). Cresskill, NJ: Hampton Press.

Carpiac-Claver, M. L., & Levy-Storms, L. (2007). In a manner of speaking: Communication between nurse aides and older adults in long-term care settings. *Health Communication, 22*, 59–68.

Case, D. O., Johnson, J. D., Andrews, J. E., Allard, S. L., & Kelly, K. M. (2004). From two-step flow to the Internet: The changing array of sources for genetics information seeking. *Journal of the American Society for Information Science and Technology, 55*, 660–669.

Cassell, M. M., Jackson, C., & Cheuvront, B. (1998). Health communication on the Internet: An effective channel for health behavior change? *Journal of Health Communication, 3*, 71–79.

Cegala, D. J. (1997). A study of doctors' and patients' communication during a primary care consultation: Implications for communication training. *Journal of Health Communication, 2*, 169–194.

Cegala, D. J., Bahnson, R. R., Clinton, S. K., David, P., Gong, M. C., Monk, J. P., III et al. (2008). Information seeking and satisfaction with physician–patient communication among prostate cancer survivors. *Health Communication, 23*, 62–79.

Chamberlain, M. (1996). Health communication: Making the most of new media technologies—An international perspective. *Journal of Health Communication, 1*, 43–50.

Chang, B. L., Bakken, S., Brown, S. S., Houston, T. K., Kreps, G. L., Kukafka, R., et al. (2004). Bridging the digital divide: Reaching vulnerable populations. *Journal of the American Medical Informatics Association, 11*, 448–457.

Charon, R. (2006). *Narrative medicine: Honoring the stories of illness.* New York: Oxford University Press.

Cho, H., & Salmon, C. T. (2006). Fear appeals for individuals in different stages of change: Intended and unintended effects and implications on public health campaigns. *Health Communication, 20*, 91–100.

Cho, H., & Salmon, C. T. (2007). Unintended effects of health communication campaigns. *Journal of Communication, 57*, 295–317.

Clark, F. (1992). The need for a national information infrastructure. *Journal of Biocommunication, 19*, 8–9.

Cohen, E. L., Shumate, M. D., & Gold, A. (2007). Anti-smoking media campaign messages: Theory and practice. *Health Communication, 22*, 91–102.

Committee on Quality Health Care in America, Institute of Medicine. (2001). *Crossing the quality chasm: A new health system for the 21st century.* Washington, DC: National Academy Press.

Conrad, C., & Millay, B. (2001). Confronting free market romanticism: Health care reform in the least likely place. *Journal of Applied Communication Research, 29*, 153–170.

Davenport Sypher, B., McKinley, M., Ventsam, S., & Valdeavellano, E. E. (2002). Fostering reproductive health through entertainment–education in the Peruvian Amazon: The social construction of *Bienvenida Salud! Communication Theory, 12*, 192–205.

Davis, J. J. (2002). Disenfranchising the disabled: The inaccessibility of Internet-based health information. *Journal of Health Communication, 7*, 355–367.

Dearing, J. W., Rogers, E. M., Meyer, G., Casey, M. K., Rao, N., Campo, S., et al. (1996). Social marketing and diffusion-based strategies for communicating with unique populations: HIV prevention in San Francisco. *Journal of Health Communication, 1,* 343–363.

Donchin, Y., Gopher, D., Olin, M., Badihi, Y., Biesky, M., Sprung, C. L., et al. (2003). A look into the nature and causes of human errors in the intensive care unit. *Quality and Safety in Health Care, 12,* 143–147.

Dunleavy, V. O., Crandall, L., & Metsch, L. R. (2005). A comparative study of sources of health information and access to preventive care among low income chronic drug users. *Communication Research Reports, 22,* 119–130.

Dutta-Bergman, M. J. (2004). Primary sources of health information: Comparisons in the domain of health attitudes, health cognitions, and health behaviors. *Health Communication, 16,* 273–288.

Dutta-Bergman, M. J. (2005). Theory and practice in health communication campaigns: A critical interrogation. *Health Communication, 18,* 103–122.

Edgar, T., Freimuth, V., & Hammond, S. L. (2003). Lessons learned from the field on prevention and health campaigns. In T. L. Thompson, A. M. Dorsey, K. I. Miller, & R. Parrott (Eds.), *Handbook of health communication* (pp. 625–626). Mahwah, NJ: Erlbaum.

Edwards, A., & Elwyn, G. (2001). Understanding risk and lessons for clinical risk communication about treatment preferences. *Quality in Health Care, 10*(Suppl. 1), 9–13.

Egbert, N., Koch, L., Coeling, H., & Ayers, D. (2006). The role of social support in the family and community integration of right-hemisphere stroke survivors. *Health Communication, 20,* 45–56.

Eisenberg, E., Baglia, J., & Pynes, J. (2006). Transforming emergency medicine through narrative: Qualitative action research at a community hospital. *Health Communication, 19,* 197–208.

Eisenberg, E., Murphy, A., Sutcliffe, K., Wears, R., Schenkel, S., Perry, S., et al. (2005). Communication in emergency medicine: Implications for patient safety. *Communication Monographs, 72,* 390–413.

Ellingson, L. L. (2003). Interdisciplinary health care teamwork in the clinic backstage. *Journal of Applied Communication Research, 31,* 93–117.

Ellingson, L. L. (2007). The performance of dialysis care: Routinization and adaptation on the floor. *Health Communication, 22,* 103–114.

Eng, T. R., & Gustafson, D. H. (Eds.). (1999). *Wired for health and well-being: The emergence of interactive health communication.* Washington, DC: Office of Disease Prevention and Health Promotion, U.S. Department of Health and Human Services.

Eng, T. R., Maxfield, A., Patrick, K., Deering, M. J., Ratzan, S. C., & Gustafson, D. H. (1998) Access to health information and support: A public highway or a private road? *Journal of the American Medical Association, 280,* 1371–1375.

Evans, G., Bostrom, A., Johnston, R. B., Fisher, B. L., & Stoto, M. A. (Eds.). (1997). *Risk communication and vaccination: Summary of a workshop.* Washington, DC: National Academy Press.

Eysenbach, G., Powell, J., Englesakis, M., Rizo, C., & Stern, A. (2004). Health related virtual communities and electronic support groups: Systematic review of the effects of online peer to peer interactions. *British Medical Journal, 328,* 1166–1170.

Eysenbach, G., Powell, J., Kuss, O., & Sa, E. R. (2002). Empirical studies assessing the quality of health information for consumers on the World Wide Web: A systematic review. *Journal of the American Medical Association, 287,* 2691–2700.

Farley, C., Laflamme, L., & Vaez, M. (2003). Bicycle helmet campaigns and head injuries among children. Does poverty matter? *Journal of Epidemiology and Community Health, 57,* 668–672.

Ferguson, T., & Frydman, G. (2004). The first generation of e-patients. *British Medical Journal, 328,* 1148–1149.

Fishbein, M., Hall-Jamieson, K., Zimmer, E., von Haeften, I., & Nabi, R. (2002). Avoiding the boomerang: Testing the relative effectiveness of antidrug public service announcements before a national campaign. *American Journal of Public Health, 92,* 238–245.

Flora, J. (2001). The Stanford community studies: Campaigns to reduce cardiovascular disease. In R. E. Rice & C. K. Atkin (Eds.), *Public communication campaigns* (3rd ed., pp. 193–213). Thousand Oaks, CA: Sage.

Flora, J. A., Maccoby, N., & Farquhar, J. W. (1989). Communication campaigns to prevent cardiovascular disease: The Stanford community studies. In R. E. Rice & C. K. Atkin (Eds.), *Public communication campaigns* (2nd ed., pp. 233–252). Newbury Park, CA: Sage.

Frank, A. W. (1995). *The wounded storyteller: Body, illness, and ethics.* Chicago: University of Chicago Press.

Freimuth, V. S., Stein, J. A., & Kean, T. J. (1989). *Searching for health information: The Cancer Information Service model.* Philadelphia: University of Pennsylvania Press.

Frey, L. R., Adelman, M. B., & Query, J. L., Jr. (1996). Communication practices in the social construction of health in an AIDS residence. *Journal of Health Psychology, 1,* 383–397.

Frey, L. R., Query, J. L., Jr., Flint, L. J., & Adelman, M. B. (1998). Living together with AIDS: Social support processes in a residential facility. In V. J. Derlega & A. P. Barbee (Eds.), *HIV and social interaction* (pp. 129–146). Thousand Oaks, CA: Sage.

Gagné, L. (2008). The 2005 British Columbia smoking cessation mass media campaign and short-term changes in smokers' attitudes. *Journal of Health Communication, 13,* 125–148.

Gibbs, R. W., Jr., & Franks, H. (2002). Embodied metaphor in women's narratives about their experiences with cancer. *Health Communication, 14,* 139–165.

Gibson, T. A. (2007). WARNING—The existing media system may be toxic to your health: Health communication and the politics of media reform. *Journal of Applied Communication Research, 35,* 125–132.

Gill, E. A., & Babrow, A. (2007). To hope and know: Coping with uncertainty and ambivalence in women's magazine breast cancer articles. *Journal of Applied Communication Research, 35,* 133–155.

Gillespie, S. R. (2001). The politics of breathing: Asthmatic Medicaid patients under managed care. *Journal of Applied Communication Research, 29,* 97–116.

Ginossar, T. (2008). Online participation: A content analysis of differences in utilization of two online cancer communities by men and women, patients and family members. *Health Communication, 23,* 1–12.

Gittell, J. H., Fairfield K. M., Bierbaum B., Head, W., Jackson, R., Kelly, M., et al. (2000). Impact of relational coordination on quality of care, postoperative pain and functioning, and length of stay: A nine-hospital study of surgical patients. *Medical Care, 38,* 807–819.

Glasgow, R. E., Eakin, E. G., Fisher, E. B., Bacak, S. J., & Brownson, R. C. (2001). Physician advice and support for physical activity: Results from a national survey. *American Journal of Preventive Medicine, 21,* 189–196.

Goodyear-Smith, F., Petousis-Harris, H., Vanlaar, C., Turner, N., & Ram, S. (2007). Immunization in the print media—Perspectives presented by the press. *Journal of Health Communication, 12,* 759–786.

Green, L. W., Kreuter, M. W., Deeds, S. G., & Partridge, K. B. (1980). *Health education planning: A diagnostic approach.* Palo Alto, CA: Mayfield.

Greenberg, B., & Gantz, W. (2001). Singing the (VD) blues. In R. E. Rice & C. K. Atkin (Eds.), *Public communication campaigns* (3rd ed., pp. 269–272). Thousand Oaks, CA: Sage.

Greenfield, S., Kaplan, S., & Ware, J. E., Jr. (1985). Expanding patient involvement in care: Effects on patient outcomes. *Annals of Internal Medicine, 102,* 520–528.

Guttman, N. (2003). Ethics in health communication interventions. In T. L. Thompson, A. M. Dorsey, K. I. Miller, & R. Parrott (Eds.), *The handbook of health communication* (pp. 651–679). Mahwah, NJ: Erlbaum.

Harrington, N. G., Norling, G. R., Witte, F. M., Taylor, J., & Andrews, J. E. (2007). The effects of communication skills training on pediatricians' and parents' communication during "sick child" visits. *Health Communication, 21,* 105–114.

Harris, L. M., Kreps, G. L., & Dresser, C. (2007). Health communication technology and quality cancer care. In H. D. O'Hair, G. L. Kreps, & L. Sparks (Eds.), *The handbook of communication and cancer care* (pp. 55–67). Cresskill, NJ: Hampton Press.

Harter, L. M., Japp, P. M., & Beck, C. S. (Eds.). (2005). *Narratives, health, and healing: Communication theory, research, and practice*. Mahwah, NJ: Erlbaum.

Hornik, R. C. (2002). *Public health communication: Evidence for behavior change*. Mahwah, NJ: Erlbaum.

Johnson, J. D. (1997). *Cancer-related information seeking*. Cresskill, NJ: Hampton Press.

Johnson, J. D., Andrews, J. E., & Allard, S. (2001). A model of understanding and affecting cancer genetics information seeking. *Library & Information Science Research, 23*, 335–349.

Jones, K. O., Denham, B. E., & Springston, J. K. (2006). Effects of mass and interpersonal communication on breast cancer screening: Advancing agenda-setting theory in health contexts. *Journal of Applied Communication Research, 34*, 94–113.

Jones, K. O., Denham, B. E., & Springston, J. K. (2007). Differing effects of mass and interpersonal communication on breast cancer risk estimates: An exploratory study of college students and their mothers. *Health Communication, 21*, 165–176.

King, J. (1985). Health beliefs and patient health behavior. *Journal of Applied Communication Research, 13*, 85–95.

Kiwanuka-Tondo, J., & Snyder, L. B. (2002). The influence of organizational characteristics and campaign design elements on communication campaign quality: Evidence from 91 Ugandan AIDS campaigns. *Journal of Health Communication, 7*, 59–77.

Kohn, L. T., Corrigan, J. M., & Donaldson, M. S. (Eds.). (2000). *To err is human: Building a safer health system*. Washington, DC: National Academy Press.

Kreps, G. L. (1988). The pervasive role of information in health care: Implications for health communication policy. In J. A. Anderson (Ed.), *Communication yearbook* (Vol. 11, pp. 238–276). Newbury Park, CA: Sage.

Kreps, G. L. (1989). Setting the agenda for health communication research and development: Scholarship that can make a difference. *Health Communication, 1*, 11–15.

Kreps, G. L. (1993). Refusing to be a victim: Rhetorical strategies for confronting cancer. In B. C. Thornton & G. L. Kreps (Eds.), *Perspectives on health communication* (pp. 42–47). Prospect Heights, IL: Waveland Press.

Kreps, G. L. (1996a). Communicating to promote justice in the modern health care system. *Journal of Health Communication, 1*, 99–109.

Kreps, G. L. (1996b). Promoting a consumer orientation to health care and health promotion. *Journal of Health Psychology, 1*, 41–48.

Kreps, G. L. (2001). The evolution and advancement of health communication inquiry. In W. B. Gudykunst (Ed.), *Communication yearbook* (Vol. 2, pp. 232–254). Newbury Park, CA: Sage.

Kreps, G. L. (2003). Opportunities for health communication scholarship to shape public health policy and practice: Examples from the National Cancer Institute. In T. L. Thompson, A. M. Dorsey, K. I. Miller, & R. Parrott (Eds.), *The handbook of health communication* (pp. 609–624). Mahwah, NJ: Erlbaum.

Kreps, G. L. (2005). Narrowing the digital divide to overcome disparities in care. In E. B. Ray (Ed.), *Health communication in practice: A case study approach* (pp. 357–364). Mahwah, NJ: Erlbaum.

Kreps, G. L. (2006a). Communication and racial inequities in health care. *American Behavioral Scientist, 49*, 760–774.

Kreps, G. L. (2006b, June 7). One size does not fit all: Adapting communication to the needs and literacy levels of individuals [Electronic letter]. *Annals of Family Medicine*. Retrieved July 8, 2007, from http://www.annfammed.org/cgi/eletters/4/3/205

Kreps, G. L., Bonaguro, E. W., & Query, J. L., Jr. (1998). The history and development of the field of health communication. In L. D. Jackson & B. K. Duffy (Eds.), *Health communication research: A guide to developments and directions* (pp. 1–15). Westport, CT: Greenwood Press.

Kreps, G. L., & Chapelsky Massimilla, D. (2002). Cancer communications research and health outcomes: Review and challenge. *Communication Studies, 53*, 318–336.

Kreps, G. L., Gustafson, D., Salovey, P., Perocchia, R., Wilbright, W., Bright, M., et al. (2004). Using computer technologies to provide relevant cancer information to vulnerable populations:

The NCI Digital Divide Pilot Projects. In P. Whitten & D. Cook (Eds.), *Understanding health communication technologies* (pp. 328–336). San Francisco: Jossey-Bass.

Kreps, G. L., & O'Hair, H. D. (Eds.). (1995). *Communication and health outcomes.* Cresskill, NJ: Hampton Press.

Kreps, G. L, Query, J. L., Jr., & Bonaguro, E. W. (2007). The interdisciplinary study of health communication and its relationship to communication science. In L. C. Lederman (Ed), *Beyond these walls: Readings in health communication,* (pp. 2–13). Los Angeles: Roxbury Press.

Kreuter, M., Farrell, D., Olevitch, L., & Brennan, L. (2000). *Tailoring health messages: Customizing communication with computer technology.* Mahwah, NJ: Erlbaum.

Kreuter, M. W., & Wray, R. J. (2003). Tailored and targeted health communication: Strategies for enhancing information relevance. *American Journal of Health Behavior, 27*(Suppl. 3), S227–S232.

Krishna, S., Balas A., Spencer D. C., Griffin J. Z., & Boren, S. A. (1997). Clinical trials of interactive computerized patient education: Implications for family practice. *Journal of Family Practice, 45,* 25–33.

Kutner, J. S., Steiner, J. F., Corbett, K. K., Jahnigen, D. W., & Barton, P. L. (1999). Information needs in terminal illness. *Social Science and Medicine, 48,* 1341–1352.

Larson, E. B., & Yao, X. (2005). Clinical empathy as emotional labor in the patient–physician relationship. *Journal of the American Medical Association, 293,* 1100–1106.

Lindsey, L. L. M., Hamner, H. C., Prue, C. E., Flores, A. L., Valencia, D., Correa-Sierra, E., et al. (2007). Understanding optimal nutrition among women of childbearing age in the United States and Puerto Rico: Employing formative research to lay the foundation for national birth defects prevention campaigns. *Journal of Health Communication, 12,* 733–758.

Lipkus, I. M., Lyna, P. R., & Rimer, B. K. (1999). Using tailored interventions to enhance smoking cessation among African Americans at a community health center. *Nicotine & Tobacco Research, 1,* 77–85.

Lloyd, A. J. (2001). The extent of patients' understanding of the risk of treatments. *Quality and Safety in Health Care, 10*(Suppl. 1), i14–i18.

Lyon, A. (2007). "Putting patients first": Systematically distorted communication and Merck's marketing of Vioxx. *Journal of Applied Communication Research, 35,* 376–298.

Maibach, E. W., Kreps, G. L., & Bonaguro, E. W. (1993). Developing strategic communication campaigns for HIV/AIDS prevention. In S. Ratzan (Ed.), *AIDS: Effective health communication for the 90s* (pp. 15–35). Washington, DC: Taylor & Francis.

Maibach, E. W., & Parrott, R. L. (1995). *Designing health messages: Approaches from communication theory and public health practice.* Thousand Oaks, CA: Sage.

Masters, K. (2008). For what purpose and reasons do doctors use the Internet: A systematic review. *International Journal of Medical Informatics, 77,* 4–16.

McKnight, L. K., Stetson, P. D., Bakken, S., Curran, C., & Cimino, J. J. (2002). Perceived information needs and communication difficulties of inpatient physicians and nurses. *Journal of the American Medical Informatics Association, 9*(Suppl. 1), S64–S69.

Mehl-Madrona, L. (2007). *Narrative medicine: The use and history of history and story in the healing process.* Rochester, VT: Bear.

Miczo, N. (2004). Stressors and social support perceptions predict illness attitudes and care-seeking intentions: Re-examining the sick role. *Health Communication, 16,* 347–362.

Mirivel, J. C. (2008). The physical examination in cosmetic surgery: Communication strategies to promote the desirability of surgery. *Health Communication, 23,* 153–170.

Mittlemark, M. B., Luepker, R. V., Jacobs, D. R., Bracht, N. F., Carlaw, R. W., Crow, R. S., et al. (1986). Community-wide prevention of cardiovascular disease: Education strategies of the Minnesota Heart Health Program. *Preventive Medicine, 15,* 1–17.

Moore, S. D., & Thurston, J. (2008). Cultural competence and barriers to the delivery of health care. In K. B. Wright & S. D. Moore (Eds.), *Applied health communication* (pp. 105–124). Cresskill, NJ: Hampton Press.

Morgan, J. M., & Krone, K. J. (2001). Bending the rules of "professional" display: Emotional improvisation in caregiver performances. *Journal of Applied Communication Research, 29,* 317–340.

Morgan, S. E., & Miller, J. K. (2002). Communicating about gifts of life: The effect of knowledge, attitudes, and altruism on behavior and behavioral intentions regarding organ donation. *Journal of Applied Communication Research, 30,* 163–178.

Morris, I. H., Linnan, L. A., & Meador, M. E. (2003). Applying the PRECEDE model to plan a menopause counseling programme in a managed care setting. *Evidence-Based Preventive Medicine, 1,* 53–66.

Murphy, S. (2004). Health psychology and public health: Theoretical possibilities. *Journal of Health Psychology, 9,* 13–27.

Myhre, S. L., & Flora, J. A. (2000). HIV/AIDS communication campaigns: Progress and prospects. *Journal of Health Communication, 5*(Suppl.), 29–45.

National Telecommunications and Information Administration. (1995). *Falling through the net: A survey of the "have nots" in rural and urban America.* Washington, DC: U.S. Department of Commerce.

Nelson, D. E., Kreps, G. L., Hesse, B. W., Croyle, R. T., Willis, G., Arora, N. K., et al. (2004). The Health Information National Trends Survey (HINTS): Development, design, and dissemination. *Journal of Health Communication, 9,* 443–460.

Neuhauser, L., & Kreps, G. L. (2003). Rethinking communication in the e-health era. *Journal of Health Psychology, 8,* 7–23.

Neville, R. G., Greene, A. C., & Lewis, S. (2006). Patient and health care professional views and experiences of computer agent-supported health care. *Informatics in Primary Care, 14,* 11–15.

Nielsen-Bohlman, L., Panzer, A. M., & Kindig, D. A. (Eds.). (2004). *Health literacy: A prescription to end confusion.* Washington, DC: National Academies Press.

Noar, S. M. (2006a). In pursuit of cumulative knowledge in health communication: The role of meta-analysis. *Health Communication, 20,* 169–176.

Noar, S. M. (2006b). A 10-year retrospective of research in health mass media campaigns: Where do we go from here? *Journal of Health Communication, 11,* 21–42.

Nowak, G. J., & Siska, M. J. (1995). Using research to inform campaign development and message design. In E. W. Maibach & R. L. Parrott (Eds.), *Designing health messages: Approaches from communication theory and public health practice* (pp. 169–246). Thousand Oaks, CA: Sage.

Oetzel, J., Duran, B., Jiang, Y., & Lucero, J. (2007). Social support and social undermining as correlates for alcohol, drug, and mental disorders in American Indian women presenting for primary care at an Indian health service hospital. *Journal of Health Communication, 12,* 187–206.

O'Keefe, D. J., & Jensen, J. D. (2007). The relative persuasiveness of gain-framed and loss-framed messages for encouraging disease prevention behaviors: A meta-analytic review. *Journal of Health Communication, 12,* 623–644.

O'Keefe, D. J., & Jensen, J. D. (2008). Do loss-framed persuasive messages engender greater message processing that do gain-framed messages? A meta-analytic review. *Communication Studies, 59,* 51–67.

Parker, R., & Kreps, G. L. (2005). Library outreach: Overcoming health literacy challenges. *Journal of the Medical Library Association, 93*(Suppl.), S81–S85.

Parrott, R., & Steiner, C. (2003). Lessons learned about academic and public health collaborations in the conduct of community-based research. In T. L. Thompson, A. M. Dorsey, K. I. Miller, & R. Parrot (Eds.), *Handbook of health communication* (pp. 637–649). Mahwah, NJ: Erlbaum.

Parrott, R., Steiner, C., & Goldenhar, L. (1996). Georgia's harvesting healthy habits: A formative evaluation. *Journal of Rural Health, 12*(Suppl.), 291–300.

Parvanta, C. F., & Freimuth, V. (2000). Health communication at the Centers for Disease Control and Prevention. *American Journal of Health Behavior, 24,* 18–25.

Pavlik, J. V., Finnegan, J. R., Jr., Strickland, D., Salman, C. T., Viswanath, K., & Wackman, D. B. (1993). Increasing public understanding of heart disease: An analysis of data from the Minnesota Heart Health Program. *Health Communication, 5,* 1–20.

Pechmann, C. (2001). A comparison of health communication models: Risk learning versus stereotype priming. *Media Psychology, 3,* 189–210.

Petraglia, J. (2007). Narrative intervention in behavior and public health. *Journal of Health Communication, 12*, 493–505.

Pinkleton, B. E., Austin, E. W., Cohen, C., Miller, A., & Fitzgerald, E. (2007). A statewide evaluation of the effectiveness of media literacy training to prevent tobacco use among adolescents. *Health Communication, 21*, 23–34.

Polk, D. M. (2005). Communication and family caregiving for Alzheimer's dementia: Linking attributions and problematic integration. *Health Communication, 18, 257*–273.

Potter, J. D., Finnegan, J. R., Guinard, J.-X., Huerta, E. E., Kelder, S. H., Kristal, A. R., et al. (2000). *5 A Day for Better Health Program evaluation report* (NIH Publication No. 01-4904). Bethesda, MD: National Institutes of Health, National Cancer Institute.

Prochaska, J. O., & DiClemente, C. C. (1984). *The transtheoretical approach: Crossing traditional boundaries of therapy.* Homewood, IL: Dow Jones/Irwin.

Query, J. L., Jr., & Wright, K. B. (2003). Assessing communication competence in an online study: Toward informing subsequent interventions among older adults with cancer, their lay caregivers, and peers. *Health Communication, 15*, 203–218.

Rakowski, W., Ehrich, B., Goldstein, M. G., Rimer, B. K., Pearlman, D. N., Clark, M. A., et al. (1998). Increasing mammography among women aged 40–74 by use of a stage-matched, tailored intervention. *Preventive Medicine, 27*, 748–756.

Randolph, W., & Viswanath, K. (2004). Lessons learned from public health mass media campaigns: Marketing health in a crowded media world. *Annual Review of Public Health, 25*, 419–437.

Ray, E. B. (Ed.). (1996a). Case studies *in communication and is enfranchisement: Applications to social health issues.* Hillsdale, NJ: Erlbaum.

Ray, E. B. (Ed.). (1996b). *Communication and disenfranchisement: Social health issues and implications.* Hillsdale, NJ: Erlbaum.

Reardon, K. K., & Rogers, E. M. (1988). Interpersonal versus mass communication: A false dichotomy. *Human Communication Research, 15*, 284–303.

Rhodes, S. D., & Hergenrather, K. C. (2003). Using an integrated approach to understand vaccination behavior among young men who have sex with men: Stages of change, the health belief model, and self-efficacy. *Journal of Community Health, 28*, 347–362.

Rimal, R. N. (2000). Closing the knowledge–behavior gap in health promotion: The mediating role of self-efficacy. *Health Communication, 12*, 219–237.

Rimer, B. K. (2000). Use of multiple media and breast cancer screening: An introduction. *Journal of Health Communication, 5*, 113–116.

Rimer, B. K., Conaway, M., Lyna, P., Glassman, B., Yarnall, K. S., Lipkus, I., et al. (1999). The impact of tailored interventions on a community health center population. *Patient Education and Counseling, 37*, 125–140.

Rimer, B. K., & Glassman, B. (1998). Tailoring communication for primary care settings. *Methods of Information in Medicine, 37*, 171–177.

Rinderknecht, K., & Smith, C. (2004). Social cognitive theory in an after-school nutrition intervention for urban Native American youth. *Journal of Nutrition Education and Behavior, 36*, 298–304.

Roberto, A. J., Meyer, G., Johnson, A. J., Atkin, C. K., & Smith, P. K. (2002). Promoting gun trigger-lock use: Insights and implications from a radio-based health communication intervention. *Journal of Applied Communication Research, 30*, 210–230.

Robinson, J. D., & Turner J. (2003). Impersonal, interpersonal, and hyperpersonal social support: Cancer and older adults. *Health Communication, 2*, 227–234.

Rodgers, S., Chen, Q., Duffy, M., & Fleming, K. (2007). Media usage as health segmentation variables. *Journal of Health Communication, 12*, 105–119.

Rosenstock, I. M. (1974). Historical origins of the health belief model. *Health Education Monographs, 2*, 328–335.

Roter, D., & Larson, S. (2002). The Roter interaction analysis system (RIAS): Utility and flexibility for analysis of medical interactions. *Patient Education and Counseling, 46*, 243–251.

Roter, D. L., Larson, S., Sands, D. Z., Ford, D. E., & Houston, T. (2008). Can e-mail messages between patients and physicians be patient-centered? *Health Communication, 23*, 80–86.

Saha, S., Arbelaez, J. J., & Cooper, L. A. (2003). Patient–physician relationships and racial disparities in the quality of health care. *American Journal of Public Health, 93*, 1713–1719.

Salmon, C. T., & Atkin, C. (2003). Using media campaigns for health promotion. In T. L. Thompson, A. M. Dorsey, K. I. Miller, & R. Parrot (Eds.), *Handbook of health communication* (pp. 449–472). Mahwah, NJ: Erlbaum.

Saultz, J. W., & Albedaiwi, W. (2004). Interpersonal continuity of care and patient satisfaction: A critical review. *Annals of Family Medicine, 2*, 445–451.

Scholl. J. C. (2007). The use of humor to promote patient-centered care. *Journal of Applied Communication Research, 35*, 156–176.

Schuster, M. L. (2006). A different place to birth: A material rhetoric analysis of Baby Haven, a free-standing birth center. *Women's Studies in Communication, 29*, 1–38.

Sharf, B. F., & Vanderford, M. L. (2003). Illness narratives and the social construction of health. In T. L. Thompson, A. M. Dorsey, K. I. Miller, & R. Parrott (Eds.), *Handbook of health communication* (pp. 9–34). Mahwah, NJ: Erlbaum.

Shaw, B. R., McTavish, F., Hawkins, R., Gustafson, D. H., & Pingree, S. (2000). Experiences of women with breast cancer: Exchanging social support over the CHESS computer network. *Journal of Health Communication, 5*, 135–159.

Shaw, R., & Kitzinger, C. (2007). Memory in interaction: An analysis of repeat calls to a home birth helpline. *Research on Language and Social Interaction, 40*, 117–144.

Shopland, D. R. (1993). Smoking control in the 1990's: A National Cancer Institute model for change. *American Journal of Public Health, 83*, 1208–1210.

Silk, K. I., Weiner, J., & Parrott, R. L. (2005). Gene cuisine or frankenfood? The theory of reasoned action as an audience segmentation strategy for messages about genetically modified foods. *Journal of Health Communication, 10*, 751–767.

Skinner, C. S., Strecher, V. J., & Hospers, H. (1994). Physicians' recommendations for mammography: Do tailored messages make a difference? *American Journal of Public Health, 84*, 43–49.

Slater, M. D. (1996). Theory and method in health audience segmentation. *Journal of Health Communication, 1*, 267–284.

Slater, M. D. (1999). Integrating application of media effects, persuasion, and behavior change theories to communication campaigns: A stages-of-change framework. *Health Communication, 11*, 335–354.

Slater, M. D. (2006). Specification and misspecification of theoretical foundations and logic models for health communication campaigns. *Health Communication, 20*, 149–158.

Slater, M. D., Karan, D. N., Rouner, D., & Walters, D. (2001). Effects of threatening and announcer differences on responses to televised alcohol warnings. *Journal of Applied Communication Research, 30*, 27–49.

Smith, D. H., & Cissna, K. N. (Eds.). (1985). Doctor–patient interaction [Special issue]. *Journal of Applied Communication Research, 13*(2).

Snyder, L. B., Hamilton, M. A., Mitchell, E. W., Kiwanuka-Tondo, J., Fleming-Milici, F., & Proctor, D. (2004). A meta-analysis of the effect of mediated health communication campaigns on behavior change in the United States. *Journal of Health Communication, 9*, 71–96.

Sparks, L., Villagram, M. M., Parker-Raley, J., & Cunningham, C. B. (2007). A patient-centered approach to breaking bad news: Communication guidelines for health care providers. *Journal of Applied Communication Research, 35*, 177–196.

Starr, P. (1982). *The social transformation of American medicine*. New York: Basic Books.

Stewart, M. A. (1995). Effective physician–patient communication and health outcomes: A review. *Canadian Medical Association Journal, 152*, 1423–1433.

Stoddard, J. L., Delucchi, K. L., Muñoz, R. F., Collins, N. M., Stable, E. J. P., Augustson, E., et al. (2005). Smoking cessation research via the Internet: A feasibility study. *Journal of Health Communication, 10*, 27–41.

Sunwolf, Frey, L. R., & Lesko, J. (2008). Story as medicine: Empirical research on the healing effects of health narratives. In K. B. Wright & S. D. Moore (Eds.), *Health communication: An applied sourcebook* (pp. 35–61). Cresskill, NJ: Hampton Press.

Thorne, S. (2006). Patient–provider communication in chronic illness: A health promotion window of opportunity. *Family and Community Health, 29*(Suppl. 1), 4S–11S.

Toller, P. W. (2005). Negotiation of dialectical contradictions by parents who have experienced the death of a child. *Journal of Applied Communication Research, 33*, 46–66.

Vanderford, M. L., & Smith, D. H. (1996). *The silicone breast implant story: Communication and uncertainty.* Mahwah, NJ: Erlbaum.

Vanderford, M. L., Stein T., Sheeler, R., & Skochelak S. (2001). Communication challenges for experienced clinicians: Topics for an advanced communication curriculum. *Health Communication, 13*, 261–284.

Von Korff, M., Gruman, J., Schaefer, J., Curry, S. J., & Wagner, E. H. (1997). Collaborative management of chronic illness. *Annals of Internal Medicine, 127*, 1097–1102.

Waitzkin, H., Williams, R. L., Bock, J. A., McCloskey, J., Willging, C., & Wagner, W. (2002). Safety-net institutions buffer the impact of Medicaid managed care: A multi-method assessment in a rural state. *American Journal of Public Health, 92*, 598–610.

Walker, K. L., Arnold, C. L., Miller-Day, M., & Webb, L. M. (2002). Investigating the physician–patient relationship: Examining emerging themes. *Health Communication, 14*, 45–68.

Wright, K. B. (1999). Computer-mediated support groups: An examination of relationships among social support, perceived stress, and coping strategies. *Communication Quarterly, 47*, 402–414.

Wright, K. B. (2000a). The communication of social support within an on-line community for older adults: A qualitative analysis of the SeniorNet community. *Qualitative Research in Communication, 1*, 33–43.

Wright, K. B. (2000b). Perceptions of on-line support providers: An examination of perceived homophily, source credibility, communication and social support within on-line support groups. *Communication Quarterly, 48*, 44–59.

Wright, K. B. (2000c). Social support satisfaction, on-line communication apprehension, and perceived life stress within computer-mediated support groups. *Communication Research Reports, 17*, 139–147.

Wright, K. (2002). Motives for communication within on-line support groups and antecedents for interpersonal use. *Communication Research Reports, 19*, 89–98.

Wright, K. B. (2004). On-line relational maintenance strategies and perceptions of partners within exclusively Internet-based and primarily Internet-based relationships. *Communication Studies, 55*, 239–253.

Wright, K. B. (2008). New technologies and health communication. In K. B. Wright & S. D. Moore (Eds.), *Applied health communication* (pp. 63–84). Cresskill, NJ: Hampton Press.

Wright, K. B., & Frey, L. R. (2008). Communication and support groups for people living with cancer. In D. O'Hair & G. L. Kreps (Eds.), *Handbook of communication and cancer care* (pp. 191–210). Cresskill, NJ: Hampton Press.

Zoller, H. M. (2003). Health on the line: Identity and disciplinary control in employee occupational health and safety discourse. *Journal of Applied Communication Research, 31*, 118–139.

17 Communication in the Helping Professions

Katherine I. Miller
Texas A&M University

Jennifer R. Considine
The University of Wisconsin Oshkosh

We now live in a society driven by a service economy. Following the Industrial Revolution, most workers toiled at creating "things" through manufacturing, but today, the service sector drives the economy, particularly in the United States and other Western nations. As Meyer and DeTore (1999) reported, "The service-producing sector continues to lead projected employment growth and…the 10 leading industries, accounting for 60 percent of all projected job growth over the coming decade, are all service producers" (p. 64). Moreover, much of the "service" provided involves more than selling a cheeseburger, entering data, or making flight arrangements; instead, it requires intensive physical and emotional involvement between service providers and their clients. Workers involved in the provision of *human* and *social* services are employed in what are called the *helping professions*.

Individuals with these types of jobs provide many kinds of assistance to others that fulfill a variety of physical, mental, social, and economic needs. However, across all of these professions, the provision of help requires an interpersonal relationship between the provider and client, and, consequently, to a large extent, this work—at its heart—is communicative. More than 2 decades ago, Thompson (1984) introduced the communication discipline to the "invisible helping hand" of the health and social service professions. Thompson pointed to the paradox that the helping professions were centrally about communication but had been all but ignored by communication scholars. Since Thompson's critique, substantial research—both within the communication discipline and other disciplines—has examined the role of communication processes in the helping professions. This work about the ways in which communication processes give aid to those with physical, social, mental, and emotional needs is representative of applied communication in a very fundamental way. Thus, in this chapter, we review and synthesize that research, and argue for an understanding of the "compassion work" performed by individuals in helping professions that is grounded in the constitutive and instrumental functions of communication.

In the literature we consider in this chapter, we do not hew to a strict occupational definition of the helping professions. There are, of course, some jobs that clearly fall into this category, including social workers, nurses, nursing aides, physicians, counselors, and ministers. Occasionally, we consider literature on teachers, but given the huge scope of the education literature, the wide variety of educational roles, and the coverage of this topic by Darling and Leckie in this volume, our emphasis is on other careers. Our selection of literature to review, however, stems not from specific job categories but from an understanding of "what is done" on the job. Furthermore, we use the term *profession* in a very loose sense; although it is possible to consider specific factors that demarcate professionalization (e.g., self-governance, advanced training, and organized associations), we look more generally at anyone who engages in "helping" as a living.

We divide this chapter into three major sections. First, we consider the foundations of the helping professions by examining their historical development, their basis in theories of morality, and the motivations of individuals entering them. The second major section—the heart of the chapter—considers the communicative relationship between providers and clients in the helping professions, looking at models of the helping relationship and specific communication choices made by those performing human and social service jobs. The final section explores issues of context in the helping professions by considering ways in which service-provision groups and teams, organizational structure and culture, and institutional and systemic processes can influence the work of helping professionals.

The Foundations of the Helping Professions

The foundations of the helping professions can be considered both chronologically and in terms of the values that undergird work within these professions. In this section, we first consider the historical development of the helping professions and then discuss issues of moral development that serve as a basis for this type of work.

Historical Development of the Helping Professions

Some of the helping professions we consider in this chapter have a long history, both in terms of the provision of help in relationships and in society's acknowledgment of the work as "professional." These are the professions of medicine (see Kreps & Bonaguro, this volume) and ministry, which, along with law, are widely regarded as the original and classic professions (Haber, 1991). These professions involve significant postgraduate training and certification of both technical skills and understanding of professional standards through licensure or ordination.

Historically, these professions have been dominated by men. For example, Steward, Steward, and Dary (1983) noted that "until recently, when women chose a career in one of the helping professions, they worked primarily in the 'number two' spot, such as the role of nurse in medicine" (p. 166). Although some barriers still limit women from working in these original helping professions (e.g., ordination rules in some religious denominations), increasingly, women are assuming the primary roles in both medicine and ministry.

The other helping professions we consider have more recent histories. For instance, although many of the functions of nursing have been performed throughout human history, the profession of nursing came into existence in the 19th century. In the United States, professional nursing often is dated to the Civil War and the work of Clara Barton, with Florence Nightingale seen as the founder of nursing in Europe. Professional social work began in the early 20th century as societal attitudes toward the poor and indigent began to shift. As Csikai and Rozensky (1997) explained, "Instead of viewing pauperism as a flaw of moral character, fledgling social workers came to believe that many environmental factors were involved that led people to be poor" (p. 529). Thus, the social work profession began with an interest in social justice and improving environmental conditions for the poor (Bogo, Raphael, & Roberts, 1993), although social work has grown to include advocacy for a wide range of population groups. Many of the other helping professions have developed even more recently. The prevalence of nursing aides, for instance, has increased as nurses became more "professionalized" and shifted some responsibility for hands-on care to those with less training. Furthermore, some helping professions developed as specialized arms of traditional professions; for example, Woodruff (2002) discussed the specialized role of pastoral counselors, mental health professionals with extensive religious and/or theological training.

Several historical trends have contributed to the growth of the helping professions in the last 100 years. The most important of these trends is the shift in "caring" from the private sector to the public sector. Before the 20th century, care was provided almost exclusively in the home, even for the very sick and dying. Indeed, early hospitals were little more than places where the indigent sick (and sailors passing through) could be warehoused, with little care provided there. However, in the early years of the 20th century—with the urbanization of U.S. society and the rapid development of medical treatment and technology—hospitals became locations for the treatment of acute illnesses and injuries rather than mere holding pens for the sick and poor. This medical shift (Rosenberg, 1987) increased the need for professional caregivers and coincided with an increased number of women receiving higher education in fields such as nursing and social work. As Austin (1988) noted, "An expanding labor force of women with advanced education… made the development of new kinds of human service organizations possible" (p. 551). In addition to these general societal shifts, U.S. government policies and programs also increased the prevalence of human service organizations and individuals working in the helping professions. For example, New Deal legislation in the 1930s and 1940s (e.g., the Social Security Act of 1935) and Great Society legislation in the 1960s (e.g., the introduction of Medicare and Medicaid) increased the prevalence of public assistance and, hence, the number of individuals working in this type of career.

Finally, ongoing shifts in demographics (e.g., the aging of the Baby Boom generation), medicine (e.g., the increasing prevalence of chronic diseases as opposed to acute diseases), and family structure (e.g., fewer children, dispersion of families, and decreased reliance on family members as the sole providers of care) continue to increase the importance of care provided in institutional settings. The increasing importance of caregiving organizations and institutions and the helping professions is borne out in the patterns of employment statistics. For example, the U.S. Bureau of Labor (2005) estimates that jobs in all sectors of the economy will increase by 14.8% by 2012, but jobs in community and social services will increase by 26.2%, jobs for health-care practitioners will increase by 26.0%, and jobs for health-care support occupations will increase by 34.5%. In short, the helping professions are a critical feature of U.S. society today and tomorrow. The next two sections of this chapter, then, consider questions of why care is provided at a societal level and why individuals are motivated to enter the helping professions.

The Moral Basis of the Helping Professions

The question of why people—as a society and as individuals—choose to help others and provide care has been of interest to moral philosophers, sociologists, and psychologists for many years. Although the scope of these issues is far beyond consideration within this chapter, several areas of research are worth a brief look. For example, McGaghie, Mytko, Brown, and Cameron (2002) examined the related concepts of compassion and altruism as moral bases for the health professions. These scholars viewed *compassion* as the inner psychological motivation for the performance of altruistic acts. Compassion, with its basis in a variety of religions and moral traditions, including Buddhism, Christianity, Hinduism, Islam, and Judaism, typically is related to the concept of *empathy*—feeling a cognitive or emotional connection to another person and wanting to act on that connection. Indeed, Kanov et al. (2004) recently developed a model that conceptualized "compassionate motivation" as involving noticing, feeling, and responding. Compassion is seen as a central psychological motivator for those in the helping professions; McGaghie et al. (2002) speculated that "compassion not only leads one to a career in the health professions but also maintains career enthusiasm" (p. 375).

In a similar conceptual domain, the notion of *altruism*, typically defined as acting on behalf of others rather than for one's self, has engendered a great deal of debate in the philosophical, sociological, and psychological literatures. Some scholars point to the many ways in which individuals perform acts that could be regarded as altruistic. For example, Oliner (2003) considered the motivations and behavior of rescue workers during the Holocaust, individuals who had won the "Carnegie Hero" award, and a host of others who acted altruistically, concluding that these individuals were motivated by factors such as behavioral norms inculcated through their parents and the wider community in which they were raised, social responsibility, empathy, and religious belief. Other scholars, however, have argued that all apparently altruistic acts ultimately are performed because they are pleasurable, reduce empathic distress for the helper, or because of an egoistic desire to help others (e.g., Cialdini, 1991; Kenrick, 1991; Wakefield, 1993). Undoubtedly, most people who do good acts have a mix of altruistic and egoistic motives, motives that are developed throughout socialization. As Wilson (1993) noted:

> Almost all of us encourage our children to acquire other-regarding motives. We do so in part because it is useful: generous people attract more friends and better opportunities. But most of us also do so because we think such motives are good in themselves. We want our children not only to be praised but to be praiseworthy. (p. 31)

A consideration of the moral basis of the caregiving professions also must consider the ongoing debate regarding the ethics of caring. This debate began in earnest when Gilligan (1982) published her well-known book, *In a Different Voice: Psychological Theory and Women's Development*, in which she argued that conventional moral theory (e.g., Kohlberg, 1984) neglects the perspective that women typically use in their moral reasoning, decision making, and other behavior (see Buzzanell, Meisenbach, Remke, Sterk, and Turner, this volume). Conventional moral theory, Gilligan contended, is based on a hierarchical system that lays out moral development in terms of increasing attention to fairness, rights, and rules, and involves the application of attributes such as impartiality and universality. In contrast, scholars expanding on Gilligan's work (e.g., O'Brien & Hallstein, 1999; Puka, 1990; Tronto, 1987, 1993; Wood, 1994) have developed an alternative model of morality. Tronto (1987) identified the essentials of this "ethic of care":

> First, the ethic of care revolves around…responsibility and relationships rather than rights and rules. Second, this morality is tied to concrete circumstances rather than being formal and abstract. Third, this morality is best expressed not as a set of principles but as an activity, the "activity of care." (p. 648)

In sum, the moral basis of the helping professions can be found in the psychology of compassion, the altruistic (or possibly egoistic) motivation to care for others, and a morality that highlights responsibility in relationships. These ideas provide the basis for moving care from the private realm of the home into the public sphere of organizations and institutions, and for providing care across a wide spectrum of societal groups. Questions remain, however, about what motivates individuals to become caregivers in the helping professions and how individuals who choose these careers are socialized into them. The next section considers these questions.

Individual Motivations and Socialization into the Helping Professions

To a large extent, the moral basis of the helping professions discussed above also explains the motivations of individuals entering the helping professions. For example, a study of motivations for entering medical school by Vaglum, Wiers-Jenssen, and Ekeberg (1999) found that the most prevalent motivation was being "people oriented" rather than being motivated by status, economic security, or interest in the natural sciences. Similar findings have been noted for other helping professions, such as social work (Csikai & Rozensky, 1997; Hanson & McCullagh, 1995; Leichtentritt, Davidson-Arad, & Wozner, 2002; Perry, 2003), ministry (Steward et al., 1983; Ventimiglia, 1978), and teaching (Scott, Cox, & Dinham, 1999). These and other studies support the general contention that a large part (although certainly not all) of individuals' motivations to enter a helping profession rests on idealistic visions of altruism and providing skilled service to others. Hanson and McCullagh (1995) concluded with regard to social work that "altruism, social idealism, and a commitment to social change are major factors in opting for social work as a career" (p. 28).

In some cases, however, the experience of socialization into the helping professions may deal a serious blow to people's altruistic motivations. A number of scholars have talked about the "fate of idealism" in both medicine and social work (e.g., Wagner, 1989), arguing that the training process itself or early experiences on the job can undermine people's original ideals of compassion and altruism. Wagner (1989) found that, for social workers, the drop in idealism came in the early years on the job, when new professionals found that their desire to promote social change often was thwarted by bureaucratic structures and economic conditions. For medical students, idealistic visions may be obscured even earlier in training, with Woloshuck, Harasym, and Temple (2004) finding a significant drop in attitudes during the course of medical school about the importance of physicians' communication and relationships with patients.

What is the nature of socialization into the helping professions that could engender such changes? The majority of research on this question has focused on medical school rather than other helping professions, and many of the accounts of the medical school experience are anecdotal in nature (e.g., Jauher, 2008; Klass, 1987; Konner, 1987; Rothman, 1999; Shem, 1978; the essays in Takakuwa, Rubashkin, & Herzig, 2004). These memoirs, along with other, more systematic accounts (e.g., Becker, Geer, Strauss, & Hughes, 1961; Haas & Shaffir, 1987; Harter & Krone, 2001; Light, 1983; Scheibel, 1996; Smith & Kleinmann, 1989), however, provide rich data that allow several generalizations about the socialization of physicians. First, medical training is an arduous process spanning preclinical training in the first 2 years, clinical rotations in the second 2 years, and postgraduate internships and residencies that can encompass several years or even a decade. Second, a great deal of the learning that occurs in medical school involves not the formal curriculum but an implicit curriculum of values and ideology (Hafferty & Franks, 1994) communicated through role modeling (e.g., Harter & Krone, 2001), an ideology of excellence (Scheibel, 1996), and the informal interaction and stories told by other medical students (e.g., Hafferty, 1988). Third, this informal curriculum often involves learning strategies for managing the emotional strains of a helping career through intellectualization, objectification, and the cultivation of "detached concern" (Lief & Fox, 1963).

Although it is impossible to generalize these results regarding medical school to training in careers such as nursing, social work, and counseling, similar concerns have been raised about these other helping professions. For example, Wyatt (1978) noted the "perennial" problems in nursing education of the dichotomy between theory and practice, and the tension between empathic caring for patients and the reality of professional life. Socialization processes also extend beyond formal time in school to the jobsite and, in some professions, involves continuing education regarding a wide range of communication issues (for a review, see Cegala & Broz, 2003; for a specific example, see Goodridge, Johnston, & Thomson, 1997).

This brief consideration of the motivations and socialization of individuals into the helping professions points to the importance of compassion, altruism, and relationships as factors that motivate individuals to enter helping professions and demonstrates the extent to which these impulses can be altered through socialization processes and initial experiences on the job. In the next section, we look at how individuals working in helping professions enact these principles—tempered or not—in their communication with patients and clients.

Communication in Helping Relationships

Helping professionals often enter the lives of their clients just when these clients are facing some of life's greatest struggles, including diagnosis of an illness, death of a loved one, job loss, or intense poverty. Because of the significance of these issues, practitioners in the helping professions need to develop relationships with their clients. These relationships often become central to task accomplishment—indeed, in many cases, the relationship itself *is* the primary task. For both the helping professional and the client, successful navigation of the helping relationship requires careful attention to the processes of communication. In this section, we consider the nature of communication in helping relationships and the consequences of various therapeutic interactions. We begin by considering two models of care within helping relationships, then examine both the content and processes of communication within these relationships, and conclude by considering ways in which communication in the helping professions may be both highly satisfying and highly stressful for care providers.

Models of Care

An analysis of the research on communication in the helping professions reveals two predominant models for the caregiver–client relationship. The dominant model has been termed both the "professional agency model" (Adelman & Frey, 1997) and the "medical model" (Meyerson, 1994, 1998; Walker, Arnold, Miller-Day, & Webb, 2001). In contrast, an alternative model for the helping relationship is termed the "ministry model" (Adelman & Frey, 1997), "social work model" (Meyerson 1994, 1998), "reflective practitioner model" (Moroney et al., 1998; Schön, 1983), and the "patient-centered" approach (Levenstein, McCracken, McWhinney, Stewart, & Brown, 1986). Although some of these models are associated with a particular human service occupation, with, for instance, both the professional agency model and social work model based on the social work profession, these models provide a conceptual scheme that is critical for understanding different approaches to the care relationship. Specifically, these models differ along two major dimensions: (1) the distribution and exercise of control in the care-provider and care-recipient relationship, and (2) the amount of emotional connection and emotional expression between the care provider and care recipient.

The distribution and exercise of control are central communicative concerns in the helping relationship. Within the professional agency model, care providers take the expert and assertive role, whereas care recipients act in the dependent and passive role (Morgan & Krone, 2001; Moroney et al., 1998; Thompson & Parrott, 2002; Walker et al., 2001). Organizational and institutional discourse where this type of relationship dominates tends to define clients and care recipients as "passive recipients of pre-defined services" (Tretheway, 1997, p. 28). Particularly in the medical arena, clients may come to expect this type of asymmetrical care relationship and may be upset when the dominant role is not enacted by care providers (Morgan & Krone, 2001). In contrast, the reflective practitioner model calls for a more symmetrical relationship in which care providers and recipients share control and work together to make decisions. In this model, both participants are expected to take an active role in determining the appropriate provision of care.

The second major difference between the professional agency model and the reflective practitioner model concerns the role of emotions on the part of care providers. Within the professional agency model, care providers are expected to remain emotionally detached, privileging rational decision making over emotional expression. Proponents of this model argue that such detachment protects care providers from stress and burnout (Lief & Fox, 1963). Historically, care providers have been socialized to exhibit this type of professional demeanor in the workplace, leading recipients to expect that demeanor. For example, Morgan and Krone's (2001) examination of emotional expression within a cardiac care center found that patients reacted negatively when physicians strayed from strict rationality and certainty when offering a diagnosis. As Morgan and Krone concluded, "Patients may expect doctors to exhibit certainty to quiet their own emotional turmoil stirring below the surface. To do this, patients unwittingly guide physician performances of emotion toward the rationality norms they have come to expect from medical personnel" (p. 331). Such expectations on the part of some care recipients reinforce the professional agency model by ensuring the maintenance of strict, professional boundaries (Adelman & Frey, 1997).

The reflective practitioner model, in contrast, questions the lack of emotional connection between care providers and recipients that characterizes the professional agency model. In therapeutic communication, one of the earliest proponents of this type of care relationship was Carl Rogers, who developed the concept of "person-centered therapy" (see Rogers, 1977). Within this alternative model, care providers are encouraged to emphasize love, support, and close relationships with recipients (Adelman & Frey, 1997; Karabanow, 1999; Tuominen, 2000). Tim McCormick, Chief Executive Officer of a residential facility for persons with AIDS, described his commitment to the reflective practitioner model:

> Are we in this mode of boundaries of social service delivery, which is good for a social service agency, or are we in a ministerial mode that says...love is unconditional and really knows no boundaries? Our mission statement is compassion and hope. (Adelman & Frey, 1997, p. 68)

Although care providers operating from this model connect emotionally with recipients because it fits better with their ideology of care, they also report boundary struggles within their caring relationships (Hullett, McMillan, & Rogan, 2000; Stone, 2000; Ungerson, 2000). Consequently, caregivers can become emotionally connected with clients or patients in ways that can lead to emotional distress and burnout (Miller, Stiff, & Ellis, 1988).

The juxtaposition of these two models problematizes several primary issues regarding communication and care in helping relationships. Rarely do helping relationships exist purely within one of these models; more commonly, providers and recipients must negotiate control, manage boundaries, create rules for emotional expression, and exchange information. In doing so, care providers and recipients make choices about the helping relationship created, and each choice entails a set of consequences for both parties. In the next section, we consider research that explores the variety of communication choices encountered in the helping relationship and the subsequent impact of those choices on care providers and recipients.

Communication Choices

Research has examined choices regarding both the content and processes of communication. We first examine the content of communication in the helping professions and then discuss the processes through which this content might be most "helpfully" communicated.

Content of Communication

One of the most fundamental content areas of communication in helping relationships is the exchange of information between care recipients and providers (Hullett et al., 2000). Often, care providers have specialized expert information that helps care recipients to understand their situation and make choices. For example, patients expect their physicians to give them information about diagnosis and treatment (Thompson & Parrott, 2002; see also Kreps & Bonaguro, this volume). Care providers also offer information about negotiating the complex bureaucratic systems within which care recipients function. Tretheway (1997) found that participants in a welfare program cited their social workers' provision of information about services and advice on ways to navigate the "system" to be among the social workers' most valuable and caring skills. In their study of compassionate communication, Miller (2007) argued that

> information itself constituted compassion in many instances. A priest...said that, often, compassion consisted of "providing someone with correct information"; a child abuse counselor...talked about compassion as involving the education of parents; and a prison chaplain...described the bittersweet experience of providing information about the location of a body to a victim's family as compassionate. (p. 234)

Although care providers may deliver positive information to care recipients, often, like prison chaplains, they are compelled to communicate negative information. The delivery of *bad news*, an "intervention that produces a negative alteration to a person's expectations about their [sic] present and future" (Fallowfield & Jenkins, 2004, p. 312), has been a focus of considerable communication research (for extensive reviews of this literature, see Fallowfield & Jenkins, 2004; Gillotti, Thomspon, & McNeilis, 2002). When delivering bad news, it is especially important that care providers express care and concern rather than convey the negative information in a cold and detached manner (Fallowfield & Jenkins, 2004).

In addition to providing informational support, care providers also offer emotional support to recipients. The communication of emotional support by care providers consistently is related to positive care-recipient outcomes, such as satisfaction and improved social or physical condition (Fallowfield & Jenkins, 2004; Karabanow, 1999; Sass, 2000; Sass & Mattson, 1999). Emotional support may take the form of coaching, providing encouragement, calming fears, or simply listening to care recipients (Karabanow, 1999; Nunnally & Moy, 1989). In a study of nursing home caregivers, Sass (2000) found that care providers regularly engaged in "courtesies" that involved complimenting, congratulating, encouraging, and comforting residents. As the following story illustrates, these courtesies provide positive emotional support for recipients:

> Upon reaching the Medicare wing, I saw Edna sitting in her wheelchair in the hallway near the nurses' station. Often uneasy and vocal, today she was much more quiet than usual. Bruce, a lay chaplain who was visiting residents on this wing, noticed her and approached her. He bent over from the side, put his hands on the arm of

her wheelchair and began to inquire about how she was. She told him that she was very nervous today. He began a conversation of quiet questioning and reassurance. Although I chose not to hear the content of the conversation, I could see that she was responding positively. I can't recall another time when Edna appeared so peaceful. (Sass, 2000, p. 341)

The content of caring communication may involve establishing boundaries that protect the interests of both care providers and recipients (Hepworth, 1993; Sass & Mattson, 1999; Tretheway, 1997; Tuominen, 2000; Ungerson, 2000). These boundaries might be established by specifying rules for interaction or by redirecting conversation when it is straying into areas that might make either the care provider or recipient feel vulnerable (Ungerson, 2000). Thus, as argued by the professional agency model, providers need to take care to keep their relationship with recipients professional and be wary of blurring the line between professional relationship and friendship. Tuominen (2000) found a similar need for boundary maintenance in her study of relationships between daycare providers and parents. As Julie, a family child-care provider of 15 years, stated, "It's rough. But you do learn that at some point, even though you feel bad, parents still have to be responsible for those kids. And you have to learn to turn it off. But it's hard sometimes" (Tuominen, p. 123).

Establishing boundaries may be especially important with care recipients who exhibit manipulative behavior in the helping relationship. Hepworth (1993) suggested that clients may try to manipulate care providers to control treatment options that are offered, gratify needs and desires that are not sufficiently obtained from other relationships, or avoid aversive consequences of irresponsible behavior. Because clients may engage in such strategies, which, in many cases, can subvert their healing, it is important that care providers establish and maintain some control over the communication that occurs in the helping relationship.

To accomplish this task, care providers may engage in supportive communication that holds care recipients accountable and works to gain their compliance with organizational and institutional rules or treatment plans. Sass and Mattson (1999) examined such uncomfortable social support in their ethnographic study of an at-risk youth shelter, and found that confrontational communication often was a valuable form of support. Sass and Mattson noted how this type of support was enacted in an interchange between a youth and a counselor at a retreat:

Under the direction of a loud and forceful adult, each youth had to answer the questions, "What is your act? And how is that act destroying your life?" The "act" of one youth involved a strong affinity for marijuana. This was met by a tirade from the course leader. "You've sold your life to get high. That's what you are. You're a pothead." ... Through this episode of confrontation, the leader supported the youth in his commitment to making a difference in his own life. (p. 530)

In sum, the content of care providers' communication in helping relationships is both informational and emotionally supportive, and may be both positively and negatively valenced. Challenges arise for care providers when making choices about how to balance these various types of communication content.

Process of Communication

In addition to considering communication content, researchers also have focused on communication processes in helping relationships. Two main themes emerge for care providers from this literature: the importance of perspective taking and the management of nonverbal elements of communication.

To communicate support appropriately, it is vital that care providers engage in perspective taking to understand the needs and concerns of care recipients (Bailey & Wilkinson, 1998; Nunnally & Moy, 1989; Sparks, Villagran, Parker-Raley, & Cunningham, 2007; Walker et al., 2001; Wiman & Wikblad, 2004). Care recipients report that effective provider communication encompasses the basic communication skills that allow for perspective taking, including listening, asking simple questions, being clear and articulate, speaking loudly, and maintaining eye contact (Bailey & Wilkinson, 1998; Nunnally & Moy, 1989). In their study of provider–patient relationships in a family practice clinic, Walker et al. (2001) found that perspective taking by providers was particularly important in the early stages of a caring relationship when care recipients test the trustworthiness of care providers. They suggested that care providers can exhibit trustworthiness by being sensitive to care recipients' nonverbal cues, appreciating recipients' uniqueness, engaging in verbal expressions of positive regard, and being active listeners.

As the relationship between care providers and recipients develops, providers must continue to engage in perspective taking. In their study of occupational therapy interactions, Mattsson and den Haring (1999) found that care providers often responded initially to clients' negative statements with positive motivating statements. In subsequent client interviews, however, they found that moving directly to motivational statements without determining why clients have a negative reaction in the first place can have a negative impact on both the therapist–client relationship and treatment outcomes. These studies underscore the importance of perspective taking by providers for engaging in caring communication in helping relationships.

Care recipients also expect care providers to pay careful attention to nonverbal factors in interaction. Touch, for instance, is one of the most common expressions of nonverbal care in the helping relationship (Miller, 2007; Morgan & Krone, 2001; Sass, 2000). Because care providers' work with recipients may involve touch, the manner in which touch is used can be particularly expressive. Caring touch might include holding a hand during surgery (Morgan & Krone, 2001) or the exchange of a hug on a care recipient's birthday (Sass, 2000).

The therapeutic environment also is a central nonverbal element of helping relationships, and, consequently, care providers often structure the care environment to meet the needs of their clients. This structuring of the environment may be something as simple as finding a private room when giving clients bad news (Walker et al., 2001) or providing a separate waiting area for patients with fertility issues in an obstetrician's office (Miller, 2007). Care recipients' environments also may be a source of information for care providers. Family pictures and mementos, for example, might provide valuable information about a care recipient's social system or values. As a hospital chaplain explained:

> It's amazing what you can see when you walk into a patient's room…. What I hope some of us who are in this business have done is to train our natural eye that sees those things anyway to be more acute and to see them more purposefully. (Miller, 2007, p. 231)

The third major nonverbal element of providers' caring communication is simply spending time with care recipients. Walker et al. (2001) found that recipients often equate time spent with care. Although care recipients equated quality care with extended time spent in interaction, care providers believed that quality care could be given in a shorter amount of time. The importance of time spent with care recipients may vary depending on the type of care provider. For example, nurses report wanting more time to communicate with patients, but physicians tend to overestimate the amount of time they spend with patients and believe that quality of time is more important than quantity of time (Thompson & Parrott, 2002). Spending time becomes especially important for care recipients when the content of the communication involves bad news, as recipients often want time to process the bad news before being immediately overloaded with more specific information, such as treatment options (Gillotti et al., 2002).

As evidenced by this review, communication processes in helping relationships are complicated and difficult, requiring intense awareness, skill, and dexterity on the part of care providers. In short, care providers engage in strenuous emotional, and sometimes physical, labor as they help their clients. In the next section, we examine the outcomes of this emotional labor for care providers and explore both the positive and negative consequences of helping.

Care-Provider Outcomes

Hochschild (1983) introduced the concept of *emotional labor* to refer to occupations in which employees are expected to display certain emotions to satisfy occupational goals, and the helping professions certainly fall into this category. In addition, helping professionals may encounter particularly demanding performance expectations as they strive to live up to their personal emotional expectations in addition to professional and organizational expectations (Meyerson, 1994; Mumby & Putnam, 1992).

In care settings, implicit and explicit rules dictate how care providers should manage and display their emotions. The most frequent emotion rule, particularly within the medical model, demands that care providers carefully manage their emotions and remain emotionally detached from care recipients (Adelman & Frey, 1997; Hafferty, 1988; Morgan & Krone, 2001). Although caregivers, according to this model, are expected to remain inwardly detached, outwardly, they are expected, by themselves, supervisors, and clients, to express care, sympathy, and empathy (Hullett et al., 2000; Karabanow, 1999; Stone, 2000; S. J. Tracy & Tracy, 1998).

Helping professionals often experience these emotions spontaneously as a natural result of performing organizational tasks (Mumby & Putnam, 1992). In other cases, employees may "force" an outward emotional expression in accordance with emotion rules without actually feeling that emotion at a deep level (Hochschild, 1983). In both situations, helping professionals can experience stress, as the display of unfelt emotion can produce emotional dissonance and the spontaneous expression of emotion can lead to attachments to clients that could create emotional distress.

Both types of emotional expression (spontaneous and manufactured) may be positively or negatively valenced, and providers may experience positive and negative emotions simultaneously as they interact with care recipients, coworkers, and supervisors. As noted earlier, many people enter caring careers because they feel called to do so or because caring is an important part of their personality; hence, caring interactions make them feel a sense of joy, fulfillment, and personal accomplishment (Ebenstein, 1998; Hullett et al., 2000; Tuominen, 2000). Some care providers, particularly those outside of traditional organizational and institutional settings, cite creativity, flexibility, and autonomy as further benefits (Tuominen, 2000). However, the caring professions also can be a site of negative emotions as care providers share the sadness of care recipients' situations or experience anger at structural constraints or at requirements of their organization that seem to compromise their provision of care (Copp, 1998; Karabanow, 1999). Furthermore, care providers sometimes need to cope with recipients' negative emotions, such as anger and associated aggression. For example, Goodridge et al. (1996) reported on the stress experienced by nursing assistants in a long-term care facility when their elderly patients were aggressive and abusive.

A large body of research literature has considered the negative effects of working in caring professions, with particular focus on the problems of vicarious traumatization (Beaton & Murphy, 1995; Sexton, 1999) and burnout (Albrecht, Irey, & Mundy, 1982; Coady, Kent, & Davis, 1990; Copp, 1998; Ellis & Miller, 1993; Evers & Tomic, 2003; Holm, 2002; Leiter & Maslach, 1988; Maslach, 1982; Meyerson, 1994; Miller, Birkholt, Scott, & Stage, 1995; Miller, Stiff, & Ellis, 1988; Miller, Zook, & Ellis, 1989; Pines & Kafry, 1978; Ray & Miller, 1991; Starnaman & Miller, 1992; Um & Harrison, 1998; Zhang & Zhu, 2008). *Vicarious traumatization* occurs when care providers begin to take on their clients' emotions, particularly after the client has a traumatic experience (Sexton, 1999). Doing so may make care providers more susceptible to *burnout*, characterized by emotional exhaustion, depersonalization, and decreased feelings of personal accomplishment (Maslach, 1982). Emotional exhaustion leads to feeling fatigued and an inability to deal with the emotional stress at work; depersonalization is recognized by a change in perspective in which care providers begin to detach from and see their clients as deserving of their problems. Helping professionals also may experience decreased feelings of personal accomplishment and start to feel as if they are incapable of making a difference.

Burnout has been attributed to a variety of organizational and personal stressors. Most commonly, burnout is attributed to job factors, such as workload, role conflict, and role ambiguity (e.g., Evers & Tomic, 2003; Lloyd, King, & Chenoweth, 2002; Miller, Ellis, Zook, & Lyles, 1990). Lloyd et al. (2002) also suggested that personal predispositions may increase burnout, as individuals who select human service careers may have higher predilections toward stress and anxiety than other people (see also Avtgis & Rancer, 2008; Teven, 2007).

The high emotional demands of most caring careers also contribute to burnout. For instance, E. Tracy and Bean's (1992) survey of 36 child welfare caseworkers showed that job stress and subsequent burnout were caused by the emotional impact of seeing clients' difficult living conditions, working with severely abused children, recommending removal of a child from the home, and working in high crime areas and bad weather conditions. In addition, dealing intensely with clients over limited time periods proved exhausting emotionally. A similar relationship between emotional demand and burnout was found in a study of oncology care providers, which showed that confrontation with death and dying led to significant emotional exhaustion, particularly in care providers who were more susceptible to emotional contagion (LeBlanc, Bakker, Peeters, van Heesch, & Schaufeli, 2001).

The manner in which caregivers manage their emotional connection with clients plays a central role in their propensity for burnout. Miller et al. (1988) explored the relationship between communication, emotions, and burnout, developing a model that has been verified and tested in research with human service workers (Miller et al., 1995). Miller and colleagues proposed that care providers may experience two types of empathy in caring interactions, each of which has an impact on how providers respond to clients and, ultimately, on providers' burnout: (1) *Emotional contagion* is an affective response in which care providers experience emotions parallel to that of care recipients and (2) *empathic concern* is an affective response in which providers care for clients but do not experience emotions parallel to clients. Whereas empathic concern increases care providers' abilities to communicate effectively with recipients, emotional contagion increases providers' emotional exhaustion, impairs their ability to communicatively respond to clients' needs, and subsequently increases burnout for providers (Miller, Birkholt et al., 1995; Miller et al., 1988).

The management of emotions becomes particularly important given the serious consequences that burnout carries for care providers. In a study of the impact of providers' burnout on their family relationships, Jayaratne, Chess, and Kunkel (1986) found that social workers experiencing burnout also experienced increased depression, anxiety, and irritableness, along with lower marital satisfaction. In addition to these psychological problems, burnout can lead to physical problems for providers, including coronary heart disease (House & Cottington, 1986) and high blood pressure (Fox, Dwyer, & Ganster, 1993). Provider burnout also has serious consequences for organizations; for example, Mor Barak, Nissly, and Levin (2001) reported that turnover rates among social service professionals may be as high as 60% in a typical year, with burnout being a leading cause. Burnout also can lead to decreased morale, increased absenteeism, and impaired performance (Maslach, 1982).

The Context of the Helping Professions

To this point, we have looked at the helping relationship at an interpersonal level by considering key aspects of interaction between care providers and care recipients. In the final section of this chapter, we put this interpersonal relationship into the context in which helping professionals work and communicate. Our consideration of contextual issues takes a "levels" approach, beginning with a look at communication in group and team contexts and then moving to an examination of the organizational and health-care systems level. In each of these areas, our discussion is illustrative rather than comprehensive. We consider some of the key issues that are critical for understanding the context in which helping professionals do their jobs, and we point readers to more comprehensive reviews of relevant literature. We close the chapter with a discussion of several overarching questions that could guide future applied communication research regarding communication and the helping professions.

Helping Professionals in the Group/Team Context

Especially in today's society, in which needs for help often are complex and multifaceted, a great deal of the work of those in the helping professionals takes place in groups or teams. Although some helping professions still involve a fair amount of individual work (e.g., ministry and some counseling professions), for many other helping professionals—especially those in health-care settings—the work typically involves interaction with a wide array of other professionals. In a recent review of communication in health care groups and teams, Poole and Real (2003) provided a useful framework for consideration of the team context, noting that health-care professionals work in team settings involving single or multiple disciplines, and varying levels of interdependency among team members. These teams also vary in their permanence, structure, and openness to the larger organizational and institutional context. For example, a group of nurses and nurse assistants working on a hospital's medical surgical floor represents a relatively homogeneous professional group that can remain relatively steady over time; in contrast, a team in a geriatric rehabilitation unit likely consists of a wide array of helping professions, including physicians, nurses, physical and occupational therapists, social workers, and dieticians.

Poole and Real (2003) pointed out a number of weaknesses in research on groups and teams in the health-care setting. For example, a great deal of the research is anecdotal, and there is little definitive evidence regarding outcomes—especially outcomes for patients or clients. Furthermore, much of the research in this area shortchanges a consideration of communication processes and, over time, of group development. However, from the perspective of individuals within the helping professions, it is possible to identify several conclusions regarding ways in which the group/team context influences work and communication.

First, it is clear from the extant research that the values of various helping professions present both important opportunities and critical challenges for care delivery. Obviously, as the needs of clients become more complex, it is important to pull together interdisciplinary teams to address the multiple issues involved. Interdisciplinary teams especially are prevalent—and can be particularly effective—in complex client systems, such as geriatric care (e.g., Hogan & Fox, 1990), mental health (e.g., Alexander, Lichtenstein, Jinnett, D'Aunno, & Ullman, 1996), and social work (e.g., Abramson & Mizrahi, 1996). For example, Mohr, Curran, Coutts, and Dennis (2002) pointed to the need for interdisciplinary collaboration when providing services for clients who suffer from both mental illness and intellectual disability, and Okamoto (2001), in a study of treating high-risk gang youth, argued that "interagency collaboration is considered an essential component toward effectively serving difficult, multi-problem adolescents" (p. 6). However, as representatives of various helping professions come together on these teams, they bring with them very different values that can lead to conflict and require negotiation among team members. Abramson (1993), for instance, pointed to the very different perspectives often taken by social workers and medical professionals, as social workers' training in a systemic and community-based view of working with clients can clash with the clinical perspective adopted more often by medical professionals.

These differences in professional orientation become particularly pronounced when the issue of professional power is considered. In a classic study of interdisciplinary teamwork, Banta and Fox (1972) examined the work of a health-care team in a poverty community. Members of the interdisciplinary team—physicians, public heath nurses, and social workers—brought with them very different philosophies about the cycle of poverty and how it could be broken and about how best to interact with clients. Furthermore, differences in members' education and specialized training imbued these contrasting philosophies and orientations toward care. In this case, and in many other examples of interdisciplinary care teams, there is the presumption that physicians ultimately are in control, although other members of the team (e.g., social workers or nurses) may better understand the complex needs of clients or patients. However, even when efforts are made to equalize power in interdisciplinary helping groups, the power of professional status often reasserts itself over time (Feiger & Schmitt, 1979).

Finally, the group context in which helping professionals work involves more than just interactions between members of the care group and clients. Putnam and Stohl (1990, 1996) highlighted the importance of considering "bona fide groups" that demonstrate permeable boundaries and are interdependent with their relevant contexts. This call is particularly apropos for a consideration of groups in helping contexts, as these teams are especially fluid in their membership and are highly interdependent with the organizational and institutional context. Several studies of communication in the helping professions have taken the notion of bona fide groups to heart. For example, Berteotti and Seibold (1994) demonstrated the importance of negotiating shifting boundaries, goals, and membership within hospice teams, and Lammers and Krikorian (1997) argued that a bona fide group perspective is necessary to understand the fluid, active, and goal-directed activities of surgical teams. Ellingson (2003) also extended the bona fide group perspective in her study of communication among members of a geriatric oncology team, contending that some of the most critical communication among team members occurs "backstage" as helping professionals on these teams share information, check on the clinical progress of clients, handle the formal and informal needs of the team, and build relationships among team members.

Helping Professionals in the Organizational Context

In addition to the group context in which helping professionals interact, it is critical to consider the organizational contexts in which human service workers are embedded. Scholars in organizational communication and related fields have long considered the nature and effects of organizational "culture" (for a review, see Eisenberg & Riley, 2001), arguing that organizations can be characterized in terms of values, beliefs, norms, stories, and ongoing patterns of interaction (see also Seibold, Lemus, Ballard, and Myers, this volume). Organizational culture is not a static entity but emerges through organizational interaction in ways that might be fragmented, contradictory, and contested. Clearly, the organizational cultures and subcultures in which human service professionals interact can vary greatly, and these various cultures can have important effects on how individuals feel about their jobs and how they interact with clients.

At the most basic level, the "relational" distinctions we made in the last section of this chapter regarding communication with clients can be expanded to the organizational level. We previously considered two models of care: the professional agency model and the reflective practitioner model. At the relational level, these models define the roles of practitioner and client, and the role of emotion in caregiving interaction. The distinctions made here at the relational level can be usefully raised to the organizational level, as demonstrated in Meyerson's (1994, 1998) studies of social work professionals based in hospitals with very different cultures. In one hospital (which she labeled as following the medical model), the problems of patients largely were seen in terms of individual pathology; in the other hospital (which she labeled as following the social work model), the problems of patients were considered in a more systemic way that focused on a wider range of psychosocial issues (e.g., family structure, relationships, and community resources). Most interesting was Meyerson's discussion of ways in which these models for treating patients were reflected in relationships among organizational members. Specifically, helping professionals in the social work culture were much more likely than those in the medical model culture to accept the inevitability of stress in the ambiguous context of care provision and to work effectively in the midst of this ambiguity and stress. As Meyerson (1994) summarized, "Although these social workers joked openly about the level of chaos and lack of control, they spoke enthusiastically about the unit's effectiveness" (p. 646). In contrast, stress and ambiguity were seen as pathologies in the other hospital; as Meyerson (1994) noted, "social workers in [this hospital]...tended to interpret burnout as a disease of the individual" (p. 643).

Other scholars also have noted the importance of the organization, both in defining stress and in providing support for workers in the helping professions. For example, Miller (1998) considered ways in which leaders in a nursing department created tension through an emphasis on the importance of constant change and chaos in the hospital environment. These nurses lived "on the edge of chaos," which fostered both innovation (the desired outcome) and intense stress (the unintended consequence). Karabanow (1999) considered ways in which organizational leadership and culture defined appropriate relationships with clients for social workers in a street kid agency, and Kahn (1993) looked at the ongoing stresses of human service work and ways in which coworkers were both successful and unsuccessful in "caring for the caregivers." More generally, Apker and Ray (2003) provided a comprehensive review of stress and social support processes in health-care organizations that are applicable to a wide range of human service organizations. Their review identified a variety of organizational sources of stress for human service workers (e.g., load, role stress, and emotional labor) and that the most potent forms of support often come from others within the organizational context (see, e.g., Ellis & Miller, 1993; Ray & Miller, 1990, 1994), as organizational "insiders" often are most knowledgeable both about the sources of stress and the most efficacious ways to deal with stress. This organizational support can come through formal programs (e.g., Thomas & Ganster, 1995), but is more likely to involve emotional, informational, and instrumental support from coworkers, supervisors, and subordinates.

Helping Professionals in Systems Contexts

Finally, we consider the larger institutional contexts in which human service professionals work. We could consider a number of issues with regard to the systems context of health and helping institutions, including issues of government and legislative control, media influence, interorganizational relationships, or the influence of national and ethnic culture. A consideration of these myriad issues that influence the practice of human service work is beyond the scope of this chapter; consequently, we concentrate on raising issues with regard to what many human service workers see as a critical defining feature of their work at the beginning of the 21st century: the challenges of working within a managed care environment.

Although there often is a great deal of conceptual disagreement regarding the meaning of "managed care" (Hacker & Marmor, 1999), most scholars agree that *managed care* is a philosophy and system of health and human service delivery in which care delivery and cost control explicitly are intertwined through the interaction of insurers, providers, and patients. Managed care systems attempt to balance the often contradictory goals of access, quality care, and cost containment (Miller & Ryan, 2001). Although managed care systems—and related organizational forms, such as health maintenance organizations (HMOs) and preferred provider organizations (PPOs)—have existed since the early part of the 20th century, these systems have become much more prevalent in the last 30 years and now are intimately tied to larger systems of funding in health and human services, such as Medicaid and Medicare. In emphasizing the simultaneous goals of care quality and cost containment, managed care systems often introduce specific organizational and communication processes, such as gate keeping through primary care providers, clinical effectiveness research, risk adjustment, utilization review before the approval of particular therapies or procedures, case management, interdisciplinary teams, and an emphasis on preventive therapies.

There has been a great deal of speculation regarding the effects of managed care on members of the helping profession, but limited empirical research. For example, O'Neil and Finocchio (1997) painted a rosy future for physicians, nurses, and allied health workers if members of these professions just embraced the challenges and opportunities presented by managed care. However, such rosy prognostications have been the exception (e.g., Waitzkin & Fishman, 1997). In the communication discipline, Lammers and Geist (1997) pointed to the possible negative impact of managed care on caring in helping organizations, arguing that managed care transforms patients from sufferers into consumers, turning organizations into factories, patients and clients from individuals deserving of care into members of populations requiring cost control, and providers into bureaucrats. In short, managed care is seen as a system in which the humanity of both clients and professionals are stripped away as the needs of corporate payors take precedence in the helping relationship.

In the years since these predictions regarding both the light and shadow of managed care (Lammers & Geist, 1997), some research has been conducted that provides insight into how members of the helping professions work in the context of these institutional systems. For example, Lammers and Duggan (2002) reported that physicians felt dissatisfied with their managed care experiences, although it appeared that managed care was only one of many factors contributing to their concerns about communication with clients (Miller, 2002) and that physicians' institutional beliefs may moderate the negative relationship between managed care medical practice and satisfaction (Barbour & Lammers, 2007). For the nursing profession, Miller, Apker, and colleagues (Apker, 2001; Miller & Apker, 2002; Miller, Joseph, & Apker, 2000) have conducted research about ways in which roles sometimes must be reconfigured as managed care systems take precedence in health care. For example, Miller and Apker (2002) argued that nurses often must move from their traditional role sets of offering "empathy and education" into areas such as collaboration, change management, and conflict resolution. The social work profession also is grappling with changes in practice in the managed care context. Keigher (2000) pointed to the heightened importance of "case management" in recent years, noting that social workers can be central members of case management systems in managed care because of the profession's traditional emphasis on the interdependence of care professionals and the importance of helping within the community system. However, others have noted that the enhanced interdependence required by managed care systems (and made possible through advanced computer and communication technologies; see Kreps & Bonaguro, this volume; Lievrouw, this volume) raises important concerns about patient and client confidentiality. As Rock and Congress (1999) explained, "When a managed care company is involved, as many as 17 people may know about the client's treatment" (p. 256).

This research points to some of the challenges faced by helping professionals in the "age of managed care." As payment becomes more intimately connected to care, helping professionals find themselves in uncomfortable roles involving business management and the allocation of care in an environment of limited resources. The helping relationship is less buffered from the larger environment than previously, which influences both the provision of care and the way that care providers feel about the work they do. However, managed care also offers opportunities for helping professionals, such as enhanced attention to continuity of care, increased interdependence with care providers in a variety of disciplines, and a renewed emphasis on systems of prevention rather than just systems of treatment. The future will reveal the extent to which it is possible to maintain quality relationships between care providers and recipients—and enhance outcomes for both—and cope with increased pressure for efficiency and economic viability.

Conclusion

This chapter has pointed to the complexity of communication processes for those working in the helping professions. Care providers—motivated by compassion, altruism, and a desire for interaction with others—are socialized into professions, organizations, and institutions that emphasize technical skills but often shortchange communication competencies. In relationships with clients, members of the helping professions engage in interaction that requires attention to both the instrumental and emotional needs of clients. This interaction often is intense and can lead to stress and burnout, but also immense personal satisfaction. Moreover, interactions between clients and professionals are embedded within care teams, organizational cultures, and institutional systems. These contexts add complexity to the experience of helping professionals, including concerns with interdisciplinary cooperation, social support for coworkers, role development, and confidentiality.

This review of the relevant literature regarding communication in the helping professions demonstrates both what we know and areas in which applied communication researchers can contribute in the future. Clearly, applied communication researchers can contribute most directly to understanding interactions between care providers and care recipients, such as how care can be provided in ways that offer both instrumental and emotional care for the client and that buffer the care provider from the insidious problem of burnout, how helping professionals can use verbal and nonverbal channels to balance clients' need for both information and emotional support, and, perhaps most important, how training programs can be structured to enhance the quality of communication in the helping professions and preserve the empathy and altruism that motivate many people to enter the helping professions in the first place.

Applied communication scholars, however, also can take a leading role in investigating the role of context in the communication of helping professionals. This focus is especially significant given contemporary societal changes—including the aging of the U.S. population, increasing chronicity of disease, and decreasing role of the extended family in care provision—that point to the increasing importance of helping professionals. Applied communication scholars are well positioned to investigate not just interactions between care providers and clients but to consider the complex patterns of communication among teams of helping professionals. Furthermore, researchers can apply an understanding of communication culture to human service workplaces. Finally, applied communication scholars can consider the nuances of the now-dominant managed care environment and explore ways in which human service professionals can effectively cope with—or perhaps challenge—managed care systems.

Taking advantage of these research opportunities will continue to reinforce the value of applied communication scholarship in today's complex and shifting society. Applied communication scholarship should make a difference to people in need, and there is no area in which our scholarly resources can be better deployed than that of assisting practitioners engaged in helping others to do their work in ways that are more professionally productive and personally rewarding.

References

Abramson, J. S. (1993). Orienting social work employees in interdisciplinary settings: Shaping professional and organizational perspectives. *Social Work, 38*, 152–157.

Abramson, J. S., & Mizrahi, T. (1996). When social workers and physicians collaborate: Positive and negative interdisciplinary experiences. *Social Work, 41*, 270–281.

Adelman, M. B., & Frey, L. R. (1997). *The fragile community: Living together with AIDS.* Mahwah, NJ: Erlbaum.

Albrecht, T. L., Irey, K. V., & Mundy, A. K. (1982). Integration in a communication network as a mediator of stress. *Social Work, 27*, 229–234.

Alexander, J. A., Lichtenstein, R., Jinnett, K., D'Aunno, T. A., & Ullman, E. (1996). The effects of treatment team diversity and size on assessments of team functioning. *Hospital and Health Services Administration, 41*, 37–53.

Apker, J. (2001). Role development in the managed care era: A case of hospital-based nursing. *Journal of Applied Communication Research, 29*, 117–136.

Apker, J., & Ray, E. B. (2003). Stress and social support in health care organizations. In T. L. Thompson, A. M. Dorsey, K. I. Miller, & R. Parrott (Eds.), *Handbook of health communication* (pp. 347–368). Mahwah, NJ: Erlbaum.

Austin, D. M. (1988). Women's career choices and human service organizations. *Social Work, 33,* 551–552.

Avtgis, T., & Rancer, A. S. (2008). The relationship between trait verbal aggressiveness and teacher burnout syndrome in K-12 teachers. *Communication Research Reports, 25,* 86–89.

Bailey, K., & Wilkinson, S. (1998). Patients' views on nurses' communication skills: A pilot study. *International Journal of Palliative Nursing, 4,* 300–305.

Banta, H. D., & Fox, R. C. (1972). Role strains of a health care team in a poverty community: The Columbia Point experience. *Social Science and Medicine, 6,* 697–722.

Barbour, J. B., & Lammers, J. C. (2007). Health care institutions, communication, and physicians' experienced of managed care: A multilevel analysis. *Management Communication Quarterly, 21,* 201–231.

Beaton, R. D., & Murphy, S. A. (1995). Working with people in crisis: Research implications. In C. R. Figley (Ed.), *Compassion fatigue: Coping with secondary traumatic stress disorder in those who treat the traumatized* (pp. 51–81). New York: Brunner/Mazel.

Becker, H. S., Geer, B., Hughes, E. C., & Strauss, A. L. (1961). *Boys in white: Student culture in medical school.* Chicago: University of Chicago Press.

Berteotti, C. R., & Seibold, D. R. (1994). Coordination and role definition problems in health-care teams: A hospice case study. In L. R. Frey (Ed.), *Group communication in context: Studies of natural groups* (pp. 107–131). Hillsdale, NJ: Erlbaum.

Bogo, M., Raphael, D., & Roberts, R. (1993). Interests, activities, and self-identification among social work students: Toward a definition of social work identity. *Journal of Social Work Education, 29,* 279–292.

Cegala, D. J., & Broz, S. L. (2003). Provider and patient communication skills training. In T. L. Thompson, A. M. Dorsey, K. I. Miller, & R. Parrott (Eds.), *Handbook of health communication* (pp. 95–119). Mahwah, NJ: Erlbaum.

Cialdini, R. B. (1991). Altruism or egoism? That is (still) the question. *Psychological Inquiry, 2,* 124–126.

Coady, C. A., Kent, V. D., & Davis, P. W. (1990). Burnout among social workers working with patients with cystic fibrosis. *Health and Social Work, 15,* 116–124.

Copp, M. (1998). When emotion work is doomed to fail: Ideological and structural constraints on emotion management. *Symbolic Interaction, 21,* 299–328.

Csikai, E. L., & Rozensky, C. (1997). "Social work idealism" and students' perceived reasons for entering social work. *Journal of Social Work Education, 33,* 529–539.

Ebenstein, H. (1998). They were once like us: Learning from home care workers who care for the elderly. *Journal of Gerontological Social Work, 30,* 191–201.

Eisenberg, E. M., & Riley, P. (2001). Organizational culture. In F. M. Jablin & L. L. Putnam (Eds.), *The new handbook of organizational communication: Advances in theory, research, and methods* (pp. 291–322). Thousand Oaks, CA: Sage.

Ellingson, L. L. (2003). Interdisciplinary health care teamwork in the clinic backstage. *Journal of Applied Communication Research, 31,* 93–117.

Ellis, B. H., & Miller, K. I. (1993). The role of assertiveness, personal control, and participation in the prediction of nurse burnout. *Journal of Applied Communication Research, 21,* 327–342.

Evers, W., & Tomic, W. (2003). Burnout among Dutch reformed pastors. *Journal of Psychology and Theology, 31,* 329–338.

Fallowfield, L., & Jenkins, V. (2004). Communicating sad, bad, and difficult news in medicine. *Lancet, 363,* 312–319.

Feiger, S. M., & Schmitt, M. H. (1979). Collegiality in interdisciplinary health teams: Its measurement and its effects. *Social Science & Medicine, 13A,* 217–229.

Fox, M. L., Dwyer, D. J., & Ganster, D. C. (1993). Effects of stressful job demands and control on physiological outcomes in a hospital setting. *Academy of Management Journal, 36,* 289–318.

Gilligan, C. (1982). *In a different voice: Psychological theory and women's development.* Cambridge, MA: Harvard University Press.

Gillotti, C., Thompson, T., & McNeilis, K. (2002). Communicative competence in the delivery of bad news. *Social Science & Medicine, 54,* 1011–1023.

Goodridge, D. M., Johnston, P., & Thomas, M. (1996). Conflict and aggression as stressors in the work environment of nursing assistants: Implications for institutional elder abuse. *Journal of Elder Abuse and Neglect, 8*, 49–67.

Goodridge, D., Johnston, P., & Thomas, M. (1997). Impact of a nursing assistant training program on job performance, attitudes, and relationships with residents. *Educational Gerontology, 23*, 37–51.

Haas, J., & Shaffir, W. (1987). *Becoming doctors: The adoption of a cloak of competence.* Greenwich, CT: JAI Press.

Haber, S. (1991). *The quest for authority and honor in the American professions, 1750–1900.* Chicago: University of Chicago Press.

Hacker, J. S., & Marmor, T. R. (1999). The misleading language of managed care. *Journal of Health Politics, Policy and Law, 3*, 1033–1043.

Hafferty, F. W. (1988). Cadaver stories and the emotional socialization of medical students. *Journal of Health and Social Behavior, 29*, 344–356.

Hafferty, F. W., & Franks, R. (1994). The hidden curriculum, ethics teaching, and the structure of medical education. *Academic Medicine, 69*, 861–871.

Hanson, J. G., & McCullagh, J. G. (1995). Career choice factors for BSW students: A 10-year perspective. *Journal of Social Work Education, 31*, 28–37.

Harter, L. M., & Krone, K. J. (2001). Exploring the emergent identities of future physicians: Toward an understanding of the ideological socialization of osteopathic medical students. *Southern Communication Journal, 67*, 66–83.

Hepworth, D. H. (1993). Managing manipulative behavior in the helping relationship. *Social Work, 38*, 674–682.

Hochschild, A. R. (1983). *The managed heart: Commercialization of human feeling.* Berkeley: University of California Press.

Hogan, D. B., & Fox, R. A. (1990). A prospective controlled trial of a geriatric consultation team in an acute-care hospital. *Age and Ageing, 19*, 107–113.

Holm, U. (2002). Empathy and professional attitude in social workers and non-trained aides. *International Journal of Social Welfare, 11*, 66–75.

House, J. S., & Cottington, E. M. (986). Health and the workplace. In L. H. Aiken & D. Mechanic (Eds.), *Applications of social science to clinical medicine and health policy* (pp. 392–416). New Brunswick, NJ: Rutgers University Press.

Hullett, C. R., McMillan, J. J., & Rogan, R. G. (2000). Caregivers' predispositions and perceived organizational expectations for the provision of social support to nursing home residents. *Health Communication, 12*, 277–299.

Jauhar, S. (2008). *Intern: A doctor's initiation.* New York: Farrar, Straus & Giroux.

Jayaratne, S., Chess, W., & Kunkel, D. (1986). Burnout: Its impact on child welfare workers and their spouses. *Social Work, 31*, 53–58.

Kahn, W. A. (1993). Caring for the caregivers: Patterns of organizational caregiving. *Administrative Science Quarterly, 38*, 539–563.

Kanov, J. M., Maitlis, S., Worline, M. C., Dutton, J. E., Frost, P. J., & Lilius, J. M. (2004). Compassion in organizational life. *American Behavioral Scientist, 47*, 808–827.

Karabanow, J. (1999). When caring is not enough: Emotional labor and youth shelter workers. *Social Service Review, 73*, 340–357.

Keigher, S. M. (2000). Communication in the evolving world of case management. *Health and Social Work, 25*, 227–231.

Kenrick, D. T. (1991). Proximate altruism and ultimate selfishness. *Psychological Inquiry, 2*, 135–137.

Klass, P. (1987). *A not entirely benign procedure: Four years as a medical student.* New York: Putnam.

Kohlberg, L. (1984). *The psychology of moral development: The nature and validity of moral stages.* San Francisco: Harper & Row.

Konner, M. (1987). *Becoming a doctor: A journey of initiation in medical school.* New York: Viking Press.

Lammers, J. C., & Duggan, A. (2002). Bringing the physician back in: Communication predictors of physicians' satisfaction with managed care. *Health Communication, 14*, 493–513.

Lammers, J. C., & Geist, P. (1997). The transformation of caring in the light and shadow of managed care. *Health Communication, 9*, 45–60.

Lammers, J. C., & Krikorian, D. H. (1997). Theoretical extension and operationalization of the bona fide group construct with an application to surgical teams. *Journal of Applied Communication Research, 25*, 17–38.

LeBlanc, P. M., Bakker, A. B., Peeters, M. C. W., van Heesch, N. C. A., & Schaufeli, W. B. (2001). Emotional job demands and burnout among oncology care providers. *Anxiety, Stress, and Coping, 14*, 243–263.

Leichtentritt, R. D., Davidson-Arad, B., & Wozner, Y. (2002). The social work mission and its implementation in the socialization process: First- and second-year students' perspectives. *Social Work Education, 21*, 671–683.

Leiter, M. P., & Maslach, C. (1988). The impact of interpersonal environment on burnout and organizational commitment. *Journal of Organizational Behavior, 9*, 297–308.

Levenstein, J. H., McCracken, E. C., McWhinney, I. R., Stewart, M. A., & Brown, J. B. (1986). The patient-centered clinical method: A model for the doctor–patient interaction in family medicine. *Journal of Family Practice, 3*, 24–30.

Lief, H. I., & Fox, R. C. (1963). Training for "detached concern" in medical students. In H. I. Lief, V. F. Lief, & N. R. Lief (Eds.), *The psychological base of medical practice* (pp. 12–35). New York: Harper & Row.

Light, D. (1983). Medical and nursing education: Surface behavior and deep structure. In D. Mechanic (Ed.), *Handbook of health, health care, and the health professions* (pp. 455–478). New York: Free Press.

Lloyd, C., King, R., & Chenoweth, L. (2002). Social work, stress and burnout: A review. *Journal of Mental Health, 11*, 255–265.

Maslach, C. (1982). *Burnout: The cost of caring*. Englewood Cliffs, NJ: Prentice-Hall.

Mattsson, J., & den Haring, M. J. (1999). Communication dynamics in therapy: A linguistic study from a nursing home for the elderly. *International Journal of Social Welfare, 8*, 121–130.

McGaghie, W. C., Mytko, J. J., Brown, W. N., & Cameron, J. R. (2002). Altruism and compassion in the health professions: A search for clarity and precision. *Medical Teacher, 24*, 374–378.

Meyer, M. H., & DeTore, A. (1999). Product development for services. *Academy of Management Executive, 13*(3), 64–76.

Meyerson, D. E. (1994). Interpretations of stress in institutions: The cultural production of ambiguity and burnout. *Administrative Science Quarterly, 39*, 628–653.

Meyerson, D. E. (1998). Feeling stressed and burned out: A feminist reading and re-visioning of stress-based emotions within medicine and organization science. *Organization Science, 9*, 103–118.

Miller, K. I. (1998). Nurses at the edge of chaos: The application of "new science" concepts to organizational systems. *Management Communication Quarterly, 12*, 112–127.

Miller, K. I. (2002). Complicating the diagnosis: A response to Lammers and Duggan. *Health Communication, 14*, 515–518.

Miller, K. I. (2007). Compassionate communication in the workplace: Exploring processes of noticing, connecting, and responding. *Journal of Applied Communication Research, 35*, 223–245.

Miller, K. I., & Apker, J. (2002). On the front lines of managed care: Professional changes and communicative dilemmas of hospital nurses. *Nursing Outlook, 50*, 154–158.

Miller, K. I., Birkholt, M., Scott, C., & Stage, C. (1995). Empathy and burnout in human service work: An extension of a communication model. *Communication Research, 22*, 123–147.

Miller, K. I., Ellis, B. H., Zook, E. G., & Lyles, J. S. (1990). An integrated model of communication, stress, and burnout in the workplace. *Communication Research, 17*, 300–326.

Miller, K. I., Joseph, L., & Apker, J. (2000). Strategic ambiguity in the role development process. *Journal of Applied Communication Research, 28*, 193–214.

Miller, K. I., & Ryan, D. J. (2001). Communication in the age of managed care: Introduction to the special issue. *Journal of Applied Communication Research, 29*, 91–96.

Miller, K. I., Stiff, J. B., & Ellis, B. H. (1988). Communication and empathy as precursors to burnout among human service workers. *Communication Monographs, 55,* 250–265.

Miller, K. I., Zook, E. G., & Ellis, B. H. (1989). Occupational differences in the influence of communication on stress in the workplace. *Management Communication Quarterly, 3,* 166–190.

Mohr, C., Curran, J., Coutts, A., & Dennis, S. (2002). Collaboration—Together we can find the way in dual diagnosis. *Issues in Mental Health Nursing, 23,* 171–180.

Mor Barak, M. E., Nissly, J. A., & Levin, A. (2001). Antecedents to retention and turnover among child welfare, social work, and other human service employees: What can we learn from past research? A review and metanalysis [sic]. *Social Service Review, 75,* 625–661.

Morgan, J. M., & Krone, K. J. (2001). Bending the rules of "professional" display: Emotional improvisation in caregiver performances. *Journal of Applied Communication Research, 29,* 317–340.

Moroney, R. M., Dokecki, P. R., Gates, J. J., Haynes, K. N., Newbrough, J. R., Nottingham, J. A., et al. (1998). *Caring & competent caregivers.* Athens: University of Georgia Press.

Mumby, D. K., & Putnam, L. L. (1992). The politics of emotion: A feminist reading of bounded rationality. *Academy of Management Review, 17,* 465–486.

Nunnally, E., & Moy, C. (1989). *Communication basics for human service professionals.* Newbury Park, CA: Sage.

O'Brien, D., & Hallstein, L. (1999). A postmodern caring: Feminist standpoint theories, revisioned caring, and communication ethics. *Western Journal of Communication, 63,* 32–56.

Okamoto, S. K. (2001). Interagency collaboration with high-risk gang youth. *Child and Adolescent Social Work Journal, 18,* 5–19.

Oliner, S. P. (2003). *Do unto others: Extraordinary acts of ordinary people.* Cambridge, MA: Westview Press.

O'Neil, E., & Finocchio, L. J. (1997). The future of the health professions under managed care. In J. D. Wilkerson, K. J. Devers, & R. S. Given (Eds.), *Competitive managed care: The emerging health care system* (pp. 113–133). San Francisco: Jossey-Bass.

Perry, R. (2003). Who wants to work with the poor and homeless? *Journal of Social Work Education, 39,* 321–341.

Pines, A., & Kafry, D. (1978). Occupational tedium in the social services. *Social Work, 23,* 499–507.

Poole, M. S., & Real, K. (2003). Groups and teams in health care: Communication and effectiveness. In T. L. Thompson, A. M. Dorsey, K. I. Miller, & R. Parrott (Eds.), *Handbook of health communication* (pp. 369–402). Mahwah, NJ: Erlbaum.

Puka, B. (1990). The liberation of caring: A different voice for Gilligan's "different voice." *Hypatia, 5,* 58–82.

Putnam, L. L., & Stohl, C. (1990). Bona fide groups: A reconceptualization of groups in context. *Communication Studies, 41,* 248–265.

Putnam, L. L., & Stohl, C. (1996). Bona fide groups: An alternative perspective for communication and small group decision making. In R. Y. Hirokawa & M. S. Poole (Eds.), *Communication and group decision making* (2nd ed., pp. 147–176). Thousand Oaks, CA: Sage.

Ray, E. B., & Miller, K. I. (1990). Communication in healthcare organizations. In E. B. Ray & L. Donohew (Eds.), *Communication and health: Systems and applications* (pp. 92–107). Hillsdale, NJ: Erlbaum.

Ray, E. B., & Miller, K. I. (1991). The influence of communication structure and social support on job stress and burnout. *Management Communication Quarterly, 4,* 506–527.

Ray, E. B., & Miller, K. I. (1994). Social support, home/work stress, and burnout: Who can help? *Journal of Applied Behavioral Science, 30,* 357–373.

Rock, B., & Congress, E. (1999). The new confidentiality for the 21st century in a managed care environment. *Social Work, 44,* 253–262.

Rogers, C. (1977). *Carl Rogers on personal power.* New York: Delacorte Press.

Rosenberg, C. E. (1987). *The care of strangers: The rise of America's hospital system.* New York: Basic Books.

Rothman, E. L. (1999). *White coat: Becoming a doctor at Harvard Medical School.* New York: William Morrow.

Sass, J. S. (2000). Emotional labor as cultural performance: The communication of caregiving in a nonprofit nursing home. *Western Journal of Communication, 64,* 330–358.

Sass, J. S., & Mattson, M. (1999). When social support is uncomfortable: The communicative accomplishment of support as a cultural term in a youth intervention program. *Management Communication Quarterly, 12,* 511–543.

Scheibel, D. (1996). Appropriating bodies: Organ(izing) ideology and cultural practice in medical school. *Journal of Applied Communication Research, 24,* 310–331.

Schön, D. A. (1983). *The reflective practitioner: How professionals think in action.* New York: Basic Books.

Scott, C., Cox, S., & Dinham, S. (1999). The occupational motivation, satisfaction, and health of English school teachers. *Educational Psychology: An International Journal of Experimental Educational Psychology, 19,* 287–308.

Sexton, L. (1999). Vicarious traumatisation of counselors and effects on their workplaces. *British Journal of Guidance & Counselling, 27,* 393–403.

Shem, S. (1978). *House of God: A novel.* New York: Richard Marek.

Smith, A. C., III, & Kleinmann, S. (1989). Managing emotions in medical school: Students' contact with the living and the dead. *Social Psychology Quarterly, 52,* 56–69.

Sparks, L., Villagran, M. M., Parker-Raley, J., & Cunningham, C. B. (2007). A patient-centered approach to breaking bad news: Communication guidelines for health care providers. *Journal of Applied Communication Research, 35,* 177–196.

Starnaman, S. M., & Miller, K. I. (1992). A test of a causal model of communication and burnout in the teaching profession. *Communication Education, 41,* 40–53.

Steward, M. S., Steward, D. S., & Dary, J. A. (1983). Women who choose a man's career: A study of women in ministry. *Psychology of Women Quarterly, 8,* 166–173.

Stone, D. (2000). Caring by the book. In M. H. Meyer (Ed.), *Care work: Gender, class, and the welfare state* (pp. 89–111). New York: Routledge.

Takakuwa, K. M., Rubashkin, N., & Herzig, K. E. (Eds.). (2004). *What I learned in medical school: Personal stories of young doctors.* Berkeley: University of California Press.

Teven, J. J. (2007). Teacher temperament: Correlates with teacher caring, burnout, and organizational outcomes. *Communication Education, 56,* 382–400.

Thomas, L. T., & Ganster, D. C. (1995). Impact of family-supportive work variables on work–family conflict and strain: A control perspective. *Journal of Applied Psychology, 80,* 6–15.

Thompson, T. L. (1984). The invisible helping hand: The role of communication in the health and social service professions. *Communication Quarterly, 32,* 148–163.

Thompson, T. L., & Parrott, R. (2002). Interpersonal communication and health care. In M. L. Knapp & J. A. Daly (Eds.), *Handbook of interpersonal communication* (3rd ed., pp. 680–725). Thousand Oaks, CA: Sage.

Tracy, E., & Bean, N. (1992). Family preservation workers: Sources of job satisfaction and job stress. *Research on Social Work Practice, 2,* 465–478.

Tracy, S. J., & Tracy, K. (1998). Emotion labor at 911: A case study and theoretical critique. *Journal of Applied Communication Research, 26,* 390–411.

Tretheway, A. (1997). Resistance, identity, and empowerment: A postmodern feminist analysis of clients in a human service organization. *Communication Monographs, 64,* 281–301.

Tronto, J. C. (1987). Beyond gender differences to a theory of care. *Signs: Journal of Women in Culture and Society, 12,* 644–663.

Tronto, J. C. (1993). *Moral boundaries: A political argument for an ethic of care.* New York: Routledge.

Tuominen, M. (2000). The conflicts of caring: Gender, race, ethnicity, and individualism in family child-care work. In M. H. Meyer (Ed.), *Care work: Gender, class, and the welfare state* (pp. 112–135). New York: Routledge.

Um, M.-Y., & Harrison, D. F. (1998). Role stressors, burnout, mediators, and job satisfaction: A stress–strain–outcome model and an empirical test. *Social Work Research, 22,* 100–115.

Ungerson, C. (2000). Cash in care. In M. H. Meyer (Ed.), *Care work: Gender, class, and the welfare state* (pp. 68–88). New York: Routledge.

U.S. Department of Labor, Bureau of Labor Statistics. (2005). *Employment by occupation, 2002 and projected 2012*. Retrieved October 31, 2005, from http://www.bls.gov/emp/emptab21.htm

Vaglum, P., Wiers-Jenssen, J., & Ekeberg, O. (1999). Motivation for medical school: The relationship to gender and specialty preferences in a nationwide sample. *Medical Education, 33,* 236–242.

Ventimiglia, J. C. (1978). Significant others in the professional socialization of Catholic seminarians. *Journal for the Scientific Study of Religion, 17,* 43–52.

Wagner, D. (1989). Fate of idealism in social work: Alternative experiences of professional careers. *Social Work, 34,* 389–395.

Waitzkin, H., & Fishman, J. (1997). Inside the system: The patient–physician relationship in the era of managed care. In J. D. Wilkerson, K. J. Devers, & R. S. Given (Eds.), *Competitive managed care: The emerging health care system* (pp. 136–161). San Francisco: Jossey-Bass.

Wakefield, J. C. (1993). Is altruism part of human nature? Toward a theoretical foundation for the helping professions. *Social Service Review, 67,* 406–458.

Walker, K. L., Arnold, C. L., Miller-Day, M., & Webb, L. M. (2001). Investigating the physician–patient relationship: Examining emerging themes. *Health Communication, 14,* 45–68.

Wilson, J. Q. (1993). *The moral sense.* New York: Free Press.

Wiman, E., & Wikblad, K. (2004). Caring and uncaring encounters in nursing in an emergency department. *Journal of Clinical Nursing, 13,* 422–429.

Woloschuk, W., Harasym, P. H., & Temple, W. (2004). Attitude change during medical school: A cohort study. *Medical Education, 38,* 522–534.

Wood, J. T. (1994). *Who cares? Women, care, and culture.* Carbondale: Southern Illinois University Press.

Woodruff, C. R. (2002). Pastoral counselling: An American perspective. *British Journal of Guidance & Counselling, 30,* 93–101.

Wyatt, J. F. (1978). Sociological perspectives on socialization into a profession: A study of student nurses and their definition of learning. *British Journal of Educational Studies, 26,* 263–276.

Zhang, Q., & Zhu, W. (2008). Exploring emotion in teaching: Emotional labor, burnout, and satisfaction in Chinese higher education. *Communication Education, 57,* 105–132.

18 Aging and Applied Communication Research

Jon F. Nussbaum
The Pennsylvania State University

Jennifer E. Ohs
Saint Louis University

Aging is a complex and ever-changing process from life's birth until its close. In the year 2000, males in the United States living until the age of 65 had an average of 15.8 years of life ahead and females 19.3 years (Olshansky & Carnes, 2001). As life expectancy continues to grow, improving the quality of life in the later years has become a central research agenda in numerous disciplines. Applied communication research is no exception and has been instrumental in connecting three life facets—the physical, psychological, and social—identified as vital components of successful aging (Rowe & Kahn, 1998). Applied communication research is exceptionally well situated to examine the aging process of older adults in light of these complex facets. Not only is communication central in life at all ages but it also plays a fundamental role in maintaining the good health and quality social support needed to enhance the well-being of older individuals. An applied communication perspective allows theory and research to be linked with practice, which has the potential to improve the aging process at the later end of the life span.

Applied communication research in the context of aging has concentrated primarily on addressing environments in which older individuals manage problematic health matters associated with growing older (e.g., Beisecker, 1989; Charles, Goldsmith, Chambers, Haynes, & Gauld, 1996; Greene, Adelman, & Majerovitz, 1996; Ryan & Butler, 1996). Dominant avenues of research in the framework of aging have explored the communicative experience of living in long-term care facilities/communities (e.g., Carpiac-Claver & Levy-Storms, 2007; DiBerardinis, Barwind, & Wilmot, 1981; Hullett, McMillan, & Rogan, 2000; Sigman, 1986; Williams & Guendouzi, 2000) and the challenges of communicating with family members who have Alzheimer's disease and related dementia (e.g., Baxter, Braithwaite, Golish, & Olson, 2002; Orange, 2001; Orange, VanGennep, Miller, & Johnson, 1998; Ory et al., 1985; Polk, 2005). Other related lines of inquiry have focused on managing the stigmas and stereotypes of older age (e.g., Harwood, Giles, Fox, Ryan, & Williams, 1993; Hummert, 1998; Sachweh, 1998; Williams, Kemper, & Hummert, 2003) and dealing with the complexities and obstacles associated with intergenerational exchanges (Anderson, Harwood, & Hummert, 2005; Giles, Dailey, Sarkar, & Makoni, 2007; Harwood, 1998; Lin, Harwood, & Hummert, 2008; Mesch, 2006; Ota, Giles, & Somera, 2007; Williams & Giles, 1996; Williams & Nussbaum, 2001).

These research areas address critical experiences that punctuate the course of aging for older persons. The focus on such problematic experiences, however, often overshadows work that aims to describe, explain, and enhance the normal or usual aging experience—the more mundane aspects of the aging process that make up day-by-day living for older adults. *Older adulthood*, as typically defined as the period of life after age 65, often is stereotyped as a single stage of life wrought with poor physical and mental health (Schaie & Willis, 2002). A more accurate view of aging stems from a life-span developmental approach that emphasizes aging, even at the latter end of the life span, as a process. After all, "the physical and mental changes in the 30 years prior to the end of life are, in most respects, far greater than changes over a similar time span at other ages" (Schaie & Willis, 2002, p. 79). Age 65 can be viewed simply as a chronological number marking a natural part of life with unique concerns and rewards that can provide a very gratifying existence from that point through the entirety of a life span.

Thus, to challenge the notion that the pathological course of aging is typical, a central part of this chapter concentrates on the issues associated with the normal course of aging. In addition to reviewing what applied communication research has uncovered about understanding and improving communication competencies associated with the problems of aging, we also examine what scholarship has revealed about enhancing communication in the normal, everyday experience of aging. To link applied communication research on aging to practice, an understanding of the basic, biological considerations of aging should be part of any context of inquiry. As such, we first review normal changes in communication faculties that occur as being individuals age. We then consider two avenues of applied communication research identified as being of most concern for aging adults: health communication (see Kreps & Bonaguro, this volume) and interpersonal communication. We review not only research that has been conducted to solve pathological problems associated with aging but also research that focuses on pragmatic questions facing older adults in everyday life. We close by offering recommendations for future applied communication research on aging.

Changes in Communicative Faculties in Older Age

"Usual aging," as described by Rowe and Kahn (1998), refers to well-functioning individuals at the later end of the life span who are at a substantial risk for disease or disability. Although aging persons do not necessarily fall prey to disease and disability, a gradual decline in functioning is "usual" for most individuals. "Optimal aging," in contrast, occurs when old age is characterized by health, energy, and fitness that is better than that found in the average population of that age (O'Hanlon & Coleman, 2004). Although optimal aging may not be typical, a "normal" course of aging for older adults is not a "pathological" one in which there is clear evidence of physical or mental deterioration. Understanding the usual/normal changes for individuals as they age, thus, is important in applied communication research, as these changes can help to explain and then correct some of the communication dilemmas that individuals encounter as they age.

A number of physiological and psychological changes that influence communication occur as adults age. The most widely recognized and researched physiological issue influencing communication in older age is *prescubysis*—the aging of the auditory system (e.g., Nerbonne, 1988). Prescubysis affects elderly persons' relationships due to its effects on the ability to process the content of speech (e.g., Carmichael, 1988; T. L. Thompson & Nussbaum, 1988). A typical feature of prescubysis is that listeners have trouble discriminating, listening, and comprehending words, phrases, and sentences, yet can detect that talk is occurring (e.g., Harford & Dodds, 1982; Pichora-Fuller & Carson, 2001; Villaume, Brown, & Darling, 1994; Villaume & Reid, 1990). Prescubysic listeners usually find that their difficulties with listening are amplified when environmental factors, such as background noise, disrupt the situation (Villaume et al., 1994). To compensate for their hearing and listening difficulties, prescubysic listeners often adjust their verbal interaction styles in conversations. For example, Ragan (1983) noted that prescubysis listeners use a variety of aligning actions or explicit verbal forms of metacommunication (e.g., "I didn't hear what you just said") to adapt to problematic conversation. Villaume

(1987) found that certain aligning actions, such as metatalk, remediators, clarifiers, confirmations, modifiers of utterance force, and backchannels, increase in middle age and decrease around ages 60 to 71. The use of aligning actions, however, decreases considerably when people are in their late 70s and 80s. Villaume concluded that as middle-aged adults begin to experience the onset of prescubysis, they may deal with the associated problems strategically, thus using aligning actions, in hopes of not appearing to be less powerful in speech. Specifically, Villaume et al. (1994) found that as older adults experience prescubysis, they have a tendency to rely more on people's nonverbal cues, particularly paralanguage (e.g., pitch, rhythm, volume, and intonation) to comprehend missed speech. Research also has shown that in response to age-related declines in hearing and working memory, elderly persons increase reliance on paralinguistic, prosodic (Cutler, Dahan, & van Donselaar, 1997), and other nonverbal types of cues offered by conversation partners to comprehend and recall speech (e g., G. Cohen & Faulkner, 1986; Fredrickson & Cartensen, 1990; Stine & Wingfield, 1987; Wingfield, Lahar, & Stine, 1989; Wingfield, Wayland, & Stine, 1992).

Ironically, as older adults rely more on nonverbal than verbal communication, they also exhibit a decreased ability to process these nonverbal behaviors in others (e.g., Hooyman & Kiyak, 1988; Lieberman, Rigo, & Campain, 1988; Neils, Newman, Hill, & Weiler, 1991). For example, older adults, in comparison to younger adults, who serve as the comparison group in research, tend to make more errors in judging facial expressions (McDowell, Harrison, & Demaree, 1994), are less skilled at perceiving and identifying body cues (Montepare, Koff, Zaitchik, & Albert, 1999), and have a decreased ability to differentiate levels of emotional intensity (T. L. Thompson et al., 2001). The reasons for such declining abilities in nonverbal interpretation are unclear. More research needs to address changes in the perception of nonverbal and emotional messages as individuals age, because it could have important implications for providing older adults with social support (T. L. Thompson, Aidinjad, & Ponte, 2001) and delivering emotionally laden messages to them, such as negative news in health-care settings.

Research on other physiological changes that accompany aging may provide insight to the causes of decline in nonverbal perceptions in older age. For example, Rousseau, Lamson, and Rogers (1998) synthesized a host of age-related changes in perceptual abilities that affect older adults' discernment of warnings. Relevant abilities that are affected as one ages include color vision, contrast sensitivity, glare sensitivity, temporal resolution, visual acuity, and visual search. Just as a decline in ability to perceive small details or to track stimulus changes affect people's capability to process warnings; such changes in perceptual abilities also may be relevant in other communication situations. Perceptual changes also may account for a myriad of environmental distractions that affect communication for older adults.

Various aspects of cognitive change also can affect the communication performance of older adults (Nussbaum, Hummert, Williams, & Harwood, 1996). Working memory, language comprehension, prospective memory, and symbol comprehension (Rousseau et al., 1998) tend to decline as one ages, as well as processing speed and name retrieval (Kemper, Kynette, Rash, O'Brien, & Sprott, 1989). These declines in cognitive functioning can have significant effects for older communicators (which we address in subsequent sections).

Another area of cognitive change associated with aging is Alzheimer's disease and related dementia (ADRD). Although sometimes stereotyped as part of the normal aging process, ADRD is not part of the usual aging process. The incidence of Alzheimer's disease is about 5% of individuals over 65, 20% above the age of 85, and 40% after the age of 90 (Lavretsky & Jarvik, 1994). Nonetheless, the number of elderly persons with ADRD is estimated to double or triple in the next 25 years, making it a public health concern (Kawas, 1999). ADRD has numerous effects of varying severity on communication and language (Kemper & Lyons, 1994). It impairs the semantic memory network (Kempler, 1991) and, as a result, communication is affected due to memory deficits, leading to a gradual curtailment of conversation and perhaps even a withdrawal to mutism (Kemper & Lyons, 1994). The impairments of language and communication can result in empty speech, discourse incoherence, and uninformative content in communication (Kemper & Lyons, 1994), leading to the failure to sustain everyday conversations (Rau, 1991) and to social isolation (Orange, 1991). ADRD poses serious concerns for older adults afflicted by the disease and their family members. However, although a significant portion of the population suffers from a pathological course of cognitive change, as in the case of ADRD, the vast majority of older adults will not be afflicted. Normal cognitive change as a result of aging does not result in ADRD or even a decline in intellect (O'Hanlon & Coleman, 2004). Thus, stereotypes associated with such dementia are not appropriate foundations for interactions with older adults.

The changes, whether normal or pathological, that individuals experience due to physical or psychological declines in later life have important consequences for their communication. These communicative challenges manifest in various important contexts in older adults' everyday lives. Of specific concern in applied communication research are health-care settings and interpersonal interactions. Therefore, in the following sections, we review literature examining how the challenges of aging manifest in these particular settings.

Health Communication and Aging

Changes in physiological and psychological functioning as a result of the normal aging process are at the forefront of health-care interactions with older patients. As a result, medical professionals must demonstrate sensitivity to the individual needs of each older person without falling prey to stereotypes associated with older age that may taint a medical diagnosis. The communication predicament of aging model (e.g., Nussbaum, Pecchioni, Grant, & Folwell, 2000; Ryan, Giles, Bartolucci, & Henwood, 1986; Ryan & Norris, 2001) provides a framework for understanding how health providers' expectations for interactions with older patients can affect the medical encounter. The model contends that younger individuals, such as younger physicians, notice physical cues of aging when approaching an interaction with an older individual, triggering negative stereotypical expectations of aging and, thereby, causing physicians to modify their speech behavior in their interactions and provide reinforcement for stereotyped behaviors. For example, physicians not familiar with the medical history of an older patient may apply old-age stereotypes to make the visit more time efficient (e.g., "We expect people in your age group to be lonely and depressed."). Applying old-age stereotypes may be inaccurate and can result in negative consequences for an elderly person, such as reduced self-esteem, reduced activity, less social interaction, and loss of a sense of personal control.

A host of applied health communication research supports the communication predicament of aging model (Hummert, Garstka, Ryan, & Bonnesen, 2004). Our review focuses on provider–older patient interactions, with specific emphasis on third-party companions during medical encounters and socialization in long-term care settings (for a review of applied health communication with patients who are aging, see Fowler & Nussbaum, 2008).

Provider–Older Patient Interactions

The first point to consider about physician–older patient interactions is the undeniable importance of this relationship. Physician–older patient relationships are more common than physician–younger patient relationships (U.S. Census Bureau, 1999), in part, because older adults are more likely than younger individuals to have more multiple, chronic, and acute medical problems (e.g., Greene & Adelman, 2001). Older adults' interactions with physicians have critical outcomes for their health and quality of life (T. L. Thompson, Robinson, & Beisecker, 2004). The onset of managed care in the United States precipitated the emergence of a primary care physician who serves as a "gatekeeper" for other medical services (Nussbaum, Pecchioni, & Crowell, 2001), making a primary care physician even more of a focal point in medical care for older persons. Thus, the relational component of physician–older patient interaction is particularly important (e.g., Coupland & Coupland, 2001).

Having an effective, mutually satisfying, and meaningful physician–patient relationship can have consequences for patient adherence to therapeutic regimens, health status, and reduced anxiety (Greene & Adelman, 2001). Applied communication research on the content and interactional processes of physician–older patient medical encounters reveals behaviors that create a high-quality physician–older patient relationship. From their synthesis of research on this issue, Greene and Adelman (2001) concluded that physicians need to actively develop the relationship by acknowledging the personhood and uniqueness of an older patient and supporting that person's presentation of self or view of his or her health. Research has found, however, that physicians frequently do not give older patients a chance to initiate discussion of concerns (Marvel, Epstein, Flowers, & Beckman, 1999). In light of such findings, Greene and Adelman recommended that physicians take a more "patient-centered" approach that encourages older patients to direct the flow of the interaction. Greene and Adelman also encouraged physicians to create an environment in which older patients feel free to discuss difficult-to-talk-about issues, such as depression, fear of death, advanced directives, memory loss, incontinence, and sexual dysfunction. Older patients often are hesitant to discuss such intimate issues with their physicians, which, obviously, can have severe, negative consequences for effective health care (Greene, Adelman, Rizzo, & Friedman, 1994). Physicians may encourage discussion of more delicate topics by asking questions about the physical, psychological, and social aspects of life that may be relevant factors in the health and well-being of older patients.

Greene and Adelman (2001) also noted the importance of coordinating the various facets of geriatric care. As mentioned previously, older patients frequently have multiple health-care concerns that need to be addressed by various health-care providers. To best provide health care to and develop an effective and satisfying relationship with an older patient, a primary care physician may need to collaborate with other professionals caring for that patient. Nussbaum et al. (2001) suggested that health-care teams are gaining credibility as a necessary unit for geriatric care to manage the multifaceted health problems experienced by older adults. Although research on health-care teams has demonstrated both positive and negative effects (Poole & Real, 2003), such teams potentially can result in high-quality care decisions, particularly for older individuals with diverse medical needs, as well as improve the physician–older patient relationship by helping physicians to treat more effectively the "whole" older person. The current state of medical care, however, may not be conducive to improving communication within the physician–patient visit in these ways, as the managed care culture tends to place limits on the time allotted to each visit and may not support "extra" services, such as the coordination of professionals in the form of health-care teams.

Issues of Dependency and Control: Physicians and Third Parties in the Medical Encounter

Dependency and control are additional concerns for older adults in health-care settings. Especially in comparison to younger counterparts, older patients often encounter issues of dependency and loss of perceived control from the transmittal of information to assistance in making medical decisions. As a general rule, the more physicians try to dominate the conversation, the less patients are satisfied with the interaction (Bertakis, Roter, & Putnam, 1991). In fact, Adelman, Greene, Charon, and Friedman (1992) concluded that older patients may experience difficulty getting their concerns addressed because physicians dominate conversation by not responding with as much information as such patients desire. Agee and Blanton (2000) reported that health-care providers are more likely to assume "educator" roles than to function as listeners in caregiving decision making by frail elders and their families. Research has shown that, overall, there is less concordance on major health-care goals and topics of conversation between physicians and older patients (Greene, Adelman, Charon, & Friedman, 1989), and that there is less joint decision making in interactions between physicians and older patients. Physicians also are less egalitarian, patient, engaged, respectful, and optimistic with older patients than with younger ones, which further exacerbates the problem that older patients are less assertive than younger patients (Greene, cited in Greene & Adelman, 2001).

A caveat to much of the applied communication research regarding control and decision making in medical encounters is that although older patients desire medical information, they do not always want as much involvement in medical decision making as do younger patients (Adelman, Greene, & Charon, 1991; Beisecker, 1989; Haug & Ory, 1987), perhaps due to life experiences in health care before patient-centered care was a norm. Although no clear-cut directives exist for how to deal with some older patients wanting more control than others, the personhood of older patients is an essential component of overall geriatric care, as suggested previously by Greene and Adelman (2001). Greene and Adelman consequently recommended that physicians take a "values history" or "life review" to understand an older person's life expectations and to develop an intimate understanding about the patient and his or her preferences. After all, as Greene et al. (1994) concluded, "The better physicians know geriatric patients, the less likely they are to use ageist or other stereotypes to guide communication, diagnosis, treatment, and care" (pp. 248–249). In taking a value history, the physician is likely to detect whether the older patient, in fact, wants more involvement during the medical encounter. The presence of a third party during the medical encounter also can affect the dependence and control that older adults perceive over their health and health-care decisions. Coupland and Coupland (2001) found that a third-party presence in medical consultations between physicians and older patients is relatively common. When third parties are present, they also tend to be active in the consultation proceedings, which, as Coupland and Coupland explained, complicates the medical encounter:

> When older patients are accompanied to clinics by a friend or another family member, and when the consultation then becomes, at least in a literal sense, triadic, many relational configurations become possible. For example, the accompanying person and the doctor can enter into various sorts of confederation, perhaps with persuasive intentions, trying to gain the elderly patient's compliance with a course of treatment or an advised lifestyle change. (p. 122)

Feeling a lack of control easily can arise in an older adult when a third party is involved in a medical encounter. Coupland and Coupland (2001) noted that when third parties form confederations with physicians to persuade older patients to engage in a particular medical regimen or course of action, older persons feel and become more dependent on those companions. Dependency-inducing communication during the medical consultation also may affect dependency beyond the consultation. For example, if a physician and a third party exclude an older patient from conversation during the medical encounter, the helplessness felt by the patient may transfer to interactions between the older person and the third party at home.

Although third-party companions can complicate a medical encounter, their presence should not be viewed as wholly negative. In fact, Coupland and Coupland (2001) suggested that providing health care for older persons often needs to be a collaborative and multiparty process:

> Alternatively, family members may share in voicing the experiences of their co-present elderly relatives, validating their accounts of symptoms or troubles. Third parties may collaborate with patients in telling troubles of describing health and social changes, or they may act as, in a sense, surrogate patients. (p. 122)

Although physicians cannot entirely control the appropriateness and effectiveness of third-party participants, physicians can work with older persons' companions during a medical encounter to make third-party contributions more positive. Greene and Adelman (2001), therefore, encouraged geriatricians to discuss medical concerns with family members and other caregivers who accompany older individuals, as working with those caregivers can help to provide optimal care for such patients.

Socialization of Elderly Residents in Long-Term Care Settings

Interactions with physicians comprise many of the encounters that older individuals have in medical settings. For older individuals residing in a long-term care (LTC) facility, however, a substantial amount of their daily interactions are health-related encounters that do not occur with physicians. About 20% of those over the age of 85 are likely to need LTC in some form (M. Henwood, 1990), although the quality of care in LTC institutions, which depends largely on the caregiver–resident relationship (e.g., Caris-Verhallen, Kerkstra, & Bensing, 1997), increasingly is a concern (Grainger, 2004). Nussbaum (1990) suggested that studying message exchange in nursing homes could improve their quality of care. Although the value of applied communication research in gerontological settings through discourse analysis (DA) has been advocated (e.g., Bryan & Maxim, 1998; Erber, 1994), most studies do not provide more than a cursory description of communication in nursing homes (Grainger, 2004; for an exception, see Dijkstra, Bougeois, Petrie, Burgio, & Allen-Burge, 2002; for a review of DA in applied communication scholarship, including health communication, see Tracy & Mirivel, this volume).

What applied research has found thus far is that communication in LTC settings is far from ideal. Institutionalized adults tend to have a communicatively impoverished life if only because of the absence of talk (Grainger, 2004). Moreover, the talk that does occur between caregivers and residents in LTC institutions leaves much to be desired. For example, Sigman (1986) conducted observations in nursing homes and found that staff–patient interactions often negatively affected patients' adjustment. In sum, Sigman found that patient adjustment to a nursing home is a social interaction accomplishment rather than an objective fact or trait. The staff in the nursing home studied contributed to the socialization process by selecting a ward for residents and imposing labels on them (e.g., typical veterans). Staff members also expected residents' adjustment to be a traumatic experience and, therefore, offered residents medication to ease their transition. As a result, residents' gradual adjustment to the home was "controlled by the explanatory labels and expectation frameworks held by institutional members" (Sigman, p. 47). When residents rejected a certain label assigned to them, it resulted in more negative labels being applied by the staff to those "recalcitrant" residents. The results of such socialization can have consequences on residents' psychological and medical conditions.

Grainger's (1993) study found that communication between institutionalized older people and their caregivers was disjointed due to conflicting institutional and personal goals. Nurses, for example, had many task-oriented goals, whereas residents expressed more relational needs, and, at times, nurses stayed on task-oriented communication and ignored or deflected other issues that residents communicated. Grainger (2004) attributed this tendency to nurse training, which, until recently, typically has lacked a grounding in communication and counseling. Although responding to the troubles of older patients can be frustrating, evading or deflecting difficult talk can result in many negative consequences for residents. If their troubles consistently are avoided or dismissed, residents' physical and mental health likely will be compromised (Grainger, 2004).

Furthermore, as in physician–older people interactions, dependency-inducing talk also occurs in LTC settings. Although mission statements and institutional policies may indicate that a residence or facility is meant to enable residents to become independently functioning members of society, many of the practices and characteristics of institutionalized living actually induce dependency (Goffman, 1961). Research by Grainger (2004) showed that caregivers' expectations of dependency in institutionalized older adults is apparent in their speech to older adults, just as the communication predicament of aging model suggests. Studies have found that caregivers often speak to older adults in the same manner that people talk to younger children (e.g., using shorter utterances, more redundancy, and more interrogatives) or they use baby talk, both of which create dependency (e.g., Ashburn & Gordon, 1981; Caporael, Lukaszewski, & Culbertson, 1983). Caporael (1981) also discovered that caregivers promoted dependency in those for whom they were caring by using a form of nonbaby talk that tends to have the same content as baby talk but does not exhibit the same prosody, making it less affectionate.

Patronizing communication and negative stereotypes are rampant in interactions not only with the institutionalized elderly but also with older populations as a whole (Hummert et al., 2004) and can have negative consequences for elders. In fact, elderly individuals point to stereotypes as the reason for patronizing speech being used with them (Giles, Fox, & Smith, 1993) and, as a result, they often come to believe that the stereotypes are true (Hummert et al., 2004).

Stereotypes often are activated and acted on as a response to the physical cues of aging, as mentioned previously. Health-care settings, however, are not the only context in which patronizing communication and ageist stereotypes produce significant repercussions; older adults also encounter stereotypes in everyday social settings that can significantly complicate their communicative encounters.

Interpersonal Interactions

Maintaining physical and psychological health is a common goal for the great majority of older adults (Rowe & Kahn, 1998) and having an appropriately broad social support network is key in maintaining health in older age (O'Hanlon & Coleman, 2004). Research has established that social support has positive effects on physical and mental health throughout the entirety of the life span. In particular, studies have found a positive relationship between social support and physical well-being in elderly populations (e.g., Dickson-Markman & Shern, 1990; Ryff, 1991), as well as between that population's social relationships and psychological well-being (e.g., Nussbaum, 1985; Rook, 1990). Social support also significantly enhances general well-being and provides buffering effects for various stressors, such as serious illness (Albrecht, Burleson, & Goldsmith, 1994; Burleson & Goldsmith, 1998; S. Cohen & Wills, 1985; Coyne & Smith, 1994). Other studies have found that the lack of competent social support is a risk factor for physical and mental health problems (e.g., Bertera, 2005; Kiecolt-Glaser, 1999; Segrin, 2001). As people age, however, they often become more socially isolated due to the death of friends and family members, decreased mobility, illness, and disability (Ade-Ridder & Kaplan, 1993). Decreases in social contacts as individuals age are not necessarily detrimental to the well-being of older individuals, as proposed in earlier gerontological research. Instead, socioemotional selectivity theory (e.g., Baltes & Carstensen, 2003; Carstensen, Isaacowitz, & Charles, 1999; Keyes, 2002) proposes that the importance of the practical aspects of available social interactions, such as information acquisition, identity maintenance, and emotion regulation, change as a function of perceived time. Accordingly, as people age and perceive their time to be more limited, they pay greater attention to the emotional quality of relationships. Hence, although the number of social network members may decline as people grow older, those relationships, depending how well they meet emotional needs, may be more satisfying (Keyes, 2002). Indeed, research repeatedly has demonstrated that older persons' psychological well-being and morale are significantly associated with the quality of interaction characterizing their stable relationships, but not with the overall quantity of their social encounters (e.g., Conner, Powers, & Bultena, 1979; Lowenthal & Haven, 1968; Strain & Chappell, 1982). Below, we explore research related to the importance of two types of interpersonal relationships—with friends and family members—for older persons.

Friendships

Although not plentiful, research has shown that friendships in older age are valuable to successful aging and can have a tremendous positive impact on older adults (Nussbaum, 1994). Engaging in a relationship with even one close friend may be enough to inhibit older persons' demoralization and maintain good mental health (Blau, 1973; Lowenthal & Haven, 1968). Talking with close friends helps older individuals to see each other as valued persons despite changes in physical appearance or capabilities. Friends acknowledge each other as whole persons by recognizing and admiring one another across time and in a variety of social roles and predicaments (Lemon, Bengston, & Peterson, 1972). Friends call on each other for help and support in later life, but they usually do so sporadically or only in emergencies (Cantor, 1979), which can prolong individuals' sense of autonomy (Rawlins, 2004). Carefully managed requests and aid for help between friends in older age enhances people's self-esteem; cultivates the voluntary, equal, mutual, and affective qualities of friendships; and helps friends to show caring, competence, and the ability to assist (Bamford et al., 1998). Friendships are voluntary, of equivalent status, and fairly mutual. For these reasons, friends are more closely related to psychological well-being (e.g., Phillipson, 1997) and life satisfaction for older adults (e.g., Chappell, 1983) than are family interactions. Friends relieve loneliness, meet incidental needs, connect individuals to larger communities, and foster ongoing enjoyment of life (Rawlins, 2004). Friendships, thus, play a vital role in sustaining older persons' well-being and satisfaction.

Family Relationships

Whereas friendships in older age are valued for companionship, familial relationships tend to be valued more for instrumental help (e.g., Bowling & Browne, 1991; Felton & Berry, 1992; Rook & Ituarte, 1999; Stoller & Earl, 1983; Walen & Lachman, 2000). Interactions with kin, as compared to those with friends, have been found to be more preferable for older adults (e.g., Adams & Blieszner, 1995; Reinhardt, 2001). The older one becomes, the greater the tendency to rely on family to accomplish the daily activities of life (e.g., Connidis & Davies, 1992). Unavailability or absence of family members, especially adult children, to assume caregiving responsibilities likely is the strongest predictor of nursing home placement (High, 1990).

Specific family interactions and relationships produce various outcomes for the health and well-being of older individuals. An important, if not the most important, form of social support for older adults is a spouse. The study of communication in marital relationships at the end of the life span, however, has been neglected (e.g., Braithwaite & Baxter, 1995). What research does exist has found that older marital couples are characterized by commitment, mutual dependence, sharing, stability, and high satisfaction (e.g., Huyck, 1996; Nussbaum, Pecchioni, Robinson, & Thompson, 2000; Sillars & Wilmot, 1989). Older marital partners also demonstrate lower rates of institutionalized care than those who are single (e.g., Hyuck, 1996). However, very little research has investigated marital relationships that experience critical threats due to serious illness of a marital partner in older age (Braithwaite, 2002). Marital relationships increasingly become important for older adults as couples depend on each other for companionship and physical assistance (Braithwaite, 2002). In fact, when older adults become seriously ill, spouses often serve as the primary caregiver (Huyck, 1996); indeed, Stone, Cafferata, and Sangl (1987) found that close to 36% of primary informal caregivers of adults over the age of 65 were spouses. Husbands and wives, thus, provide a considerable amount of care for their ailing spouse and, over time, adjust very well to their roles (Mares & Fitzpatrick, 2004). Nonetheless, social support for spousal caregivers, especially caregivers of those with ADRD, is critical to the health of the caregiver and can alleviate strains on the marital relationship that are associated with long-term spousal caregiving (Long & Mancini, 1990).

At times, a spousal caregiver, usually the wife, as a woman's life expectancy is longer than that of a man (Olshansky & Carnes, 2001), no longer is able to care for a partner at home. When a woman's husband moves into a nursing home, she may experience significant stress, a diminished emotional state, depression, social isolation, and physical illness (Ade-Ridder & Kaplan, 1993). Braithwaite (2002) investigated this state of "married widowhood," where a wife lives at home and the husband dwells in a long-term care community. Many of the women who experience married widowhood are hesitant to seek out and use formal services available to help them cope with adjustments and transitions that accompany having a spouse enter an LTC facility (Ade-Ridder & Kaplan, 1993; Long & Mancini, 1990). The nursing staff, however, does not usually have the time, training, or motivation to effectively manage the resident's interactions with the spouse successfully (Nussbaum, Pecchioni, Robinson, & Thompson, 2000). Braithwaite (2002) suggested that more research is needed on helping marital partners to better maintain and enact their marital relationships after a partner moves into a nursing home.

For older adults with children, the adult–child relationship becomes increasingly important as individuals age. Golish (2000) noted that the parent–child relationship is one of the most enduring and dynamic relationships that individuals have over the course of their life span. Mutual helping between parents and their children is characteristic across the life span (Cicirelli, 1981, 1983; Troll, 1986). Parents often provide support to their children well into their adult years (Bankoff, 1983; Ward, 1996), but after a parent reaches the age of 75, children begin to provide caregiving services for parents (Nussbaum, Pecchioni, Robinson, & Thompson, 2000; Ward, 1996). Despite the fact that adult children typically are called on to provide care for their parents at some point (Miller, Shoemaker, Willyard, & Addison, 2008), parents and their adult children rarely discuss parents' caregiving preferences, especially before the onset of dependency (Pecchioni & Nussbaum, 2000). This lack of discussion may be due to elderly parents remaining independent from their adult children to maintain autonomy and personhood (Nussbaum, Pecchioni, Robinson, & Thompson, 2000). If caregiving decisions fail to maintain the autonomy of a parent, the parent is at risk for potentially negative health consequences (Pecchioni & Nussbaum, 2000).

Research has identified several important considerations for mother–daughter relationships when a mother enters older age. The mother–daughter dyad is the closest parent–adult child relationship (Cicirelli, 1983; Troll, 1986), but is particularly complex, consisting of a mixture of strong positive and negative feelings (Fingerman, 2001). For example, mothers and daughters are very invested in their relationship but sometimes feel tension in balancing their simultaneous needs for intimacy and autonomy.

Understanding such tensions can have significant implications for applied communication research. Research has demonstrated that the struggle for autonomy and independence is a significant consideration in parent–adult child relationships. For example, K. L. Henwood (2004) noted that older women sometimes see very close mother–daughter relationships as a face threat due to the power associated with the daughter as the mother ages. Although research has found that older mother–daughter relationships usually are characterized by love (Fingerman, 2001), the complexities associated with control, dominance, and dependence often can taint the positive affect associated with these relationships. Mothers and daughters are invested in their relationship, but when a mother communicates a need to maintain a position as matriarch in a family, a daughter's ambivalent or resentful communication in response can certainly complicate that relationship (Fingerman, 2001).

Many questions remain regarding the older mother–daughter relationship, and the consequences of the control-related tensions characterizing that relationship still are unclear (Fingerman, 2001; Morgan & Hummert, 2000). In terms of applied consequences, research findings about parent shifts from independence to dependence on an adult child may be amplified in mother–daughter relationships, where power complexities are rampant. Given that females typically assume the caregiver role for both the young and the aged (Moen, Harris-Abbott, Lee, & Roehling, 1999), more research needs to investigate positive adjustment strategies for mothers and daughters.

Sibling relationships also can have important consequences social support in older individuals. About 80% of older people have siblings and remain in contact with them throughout their life (McKay & Caverly, 2004). Siblings provide each other with one of the longest, if not *the* longest, relationship experienced. As a result, sibling relationships can have some of the most meaningful effects on older adult life. Cicirelli (1985) found that brother–sister and sister–sister relationships usually are very close, provide a sense of security in the life of older people, and that older people feel comfortable asking their sibling(s) for assistance. Scott (1983) found that siblings were helpful for older persons making major decisions and meeting their transportation needs. Borland (1987) found that cohabitation among older adult siblings is considered to be a reasonable and comfortable alternative to institutionalization. Siblings depend on each other for companionship activities, such as recreation, regular visits, organizing family reunions, and, sometimes, even business ventures (Scott). Sibling commitment also remains stable across the life span (Rittenour, Myers, & Brann, 2007). The sibling relationship certainly can have a large and significant effect on the provision of social support in older age. Sibling relationships, like friendships, are one of the only forms of social support for an elderly individual that occurs on a relatively egalitarian level. Moreover, siblings' use of verbally aggressive messages decreases across the life span (Myers & Goodboy, 2006). Because sibling relationships can be much longer term and more solidly bonded than friendships, their implications on the health and well-being of older adults is a particularly fruitful area of inquiry for applied communication scholarship.

A final family relationship that scholars increasingly have studied is the grandparent–grandchild relationship (Nussbaum, Pecchioni, Robinson, & Thompson, 2000). Grandparents provide grandchildren with a source of learning and emotional support (Hartshorne & Manaster, 1982), and grandchildren who interact with grandparents have better attitudes toward aging and older adults (Becker & Taylor, 1996). Grandparents glean valuable benefits from their relationship with their grandchildren as well, getting satisfaction from contributing to their grandchildren's lives (McKay & Caverly, 2004; L. Thompson, Clark, & Gunn, 1985) and experiencing a sense of continuity with their own lives by sharing personal and family history (Atchley, 1991).

Although grandparent–grandchild relationships are characterized mainly by positive affect, those relationships exhibit complexities and disparaging aspects as well. For example, Harwood and Lin (2000) reported that grandparents describe not only affiliation, pride, and exchange as typifying the grandparent–grandchild relationship but also distance. In some cases, that distance is physical, with grandparents and grandchildren geographically separated, which makes the relationship harder to maintain (Holladay & Seipke, 2007). Pecchioni and Croghan (2002) found that although young adults are less likely to apply stereotypes to their closest grandparents than to other older adults, they still may not overcome negative stereotypes of older adults when interacting with their grandparents (see also Anderson et al., 2005). As a result, interactions with their grandparents still may utilize ageist stereotypes that could diminish the quality of those interactions and lower the self-esteem of grandparents (Pecchioni & Croghan, 2002). Ageist stereotypes also might explain why there are only moderate levels of agreement in the topics discussed between grandparents and college-age grandchildren (Lin, Harwood, & Bonnesen, 2002).

Stereotyping and ageism, thus, have consequences not only in health-care settings but also even in close relationships. Relationships with spouse, friends, and siblings tend to be very satisfying overall, perhaps because these relationships are less likely than other relationships to be fraught with the negative effects of ageism. However, parents' relationships with children and grandchildren seem to be constrained by factors associated with ageist expectations. Future applied communication research can help to manage people's expectations of usual aging and minimize the use of stereotypic and ageist behaviors. As such, we offer the following recommendations for future directions in applied communication research on aging.

Future Directions for Applied Communication Research on Aging

Before considering specific recommendations for future applied communication research on aging, an important point to make is that just as aging is a diverse and complex process, research seeking to understand and enrich the aging process must necessarily be a multifaceted endeavor. Applied communication scholars, therefore, have a daunting task of bridging the various aspects of aging in specific, age-relevant contexts to improve the aging experience. To simplify directions for future research, we begin by offering an overarching theoretical framework for applied communication research on aging, a framework that could benefit all aspects of the discipline. We conclude this chapter with more specific courses of action for applied communication and aging research.

The communication enhancement model (e.g., Baltes, Neumann, & Zank, 1994; Ryan, Meredith, MacLean, & Orange, 1995; Ryan & Norris, 2001) provides an excellent theoretical framework for communication research on interventions to transpose the cycle of negative communication during the aging process that often results from old-age stereotypes. The model suggests that interactions with older adults are influenced by multiple environmental factors, such as background noise that can interfere with hearing a message. Consequently, changing or modifying environmental factors upfront can improve the communication environment for older individuals. Recognizing older adults' communicative needs and cues on an individual basis can influence people to modify their behavior to accommodate an older person's personal needs and can aid in the contextual assessment and planning for an older person. Such modifications can lead to feelings of empowerment on the part of an older adult rather than dependency, as well as increased communication effectiveness and satisfaction rather than feeling stereotyped and patronized. Recognizing older adults on an individualized level as communicators and making accommodations based on older adults' personal needs (as opposed to applying blanket accommodations on the basis of stereotypes) also optimizes older adults' competence, health, and well-being, and maximizes their communication effectiveness (Ryan et al., 1995; Ryan & Norris, 2001).

Using the communication enhancement model to guide research has been thoroughly discussed elsewhere (Hummert et al., 2004); here, we emphasize the importance of applying it in applied communication contexts to develop interventions (see Frey & SunWolf, this volume) that manage specific communication situations faced by the elderly. Using this model specifically to direct applied scholarship on communication and aging facilitates a research agenda that is not chiefly concerned with the adversities of old age. Focusing primarily on the problems associated with communication and aging can reemphasize the notion that old age is a negative phase of life and reinforce the stereotypes associated with older age. Applying the communication enhancement model emphasizes the recognition of cues on a more individualized basis as a first step to optimal compensation for normal aging and to maximize effective communication with and by older adults. As a result, interventions developed from the model will encourage attention to the usual or normal process of aging as opposed to the stereotypical or pathological course of aging. For example, in health communication, instead of developing interventions that assume physical cues of aging, such as wrinkled skin or graying hair, accompany a natural psychological decline and lowered communicative competence, interventions should focus on individual communication cues, such as modifying utterance force to signal difficulties hearing, that often indicate only slight modification in interactive behavior, such as speaking with more clarity and volume so that an older conversational partner can hear one better. Although applied research has been conducted from this perspective (particularly the work by Greene, Adelman, and their colleagues), continuing this line of inquiry is critical to address the ever-changing and ever-problematic health-care delivery system (see Kreps & Bonaguro, this volume) experienced by older adults in the United States.

With the communication enhancement model as a foundation for future work, we turn to more specific applied research agendas on communication and aging that can add much knowledge to the field and enhance the experience of aging. Although there are a multitude of important research agendas that are possible, we focus on specific directions in the areas of health, group, family, and communication technology.

As discussed previously, much of the extant research on communication and aging concentrates on health communication concerns. We need to apply what we have learned from the contexts of nursing homes and physician–patient interactions to other health-care settings. Health-care provision for older adults occurs as much outside as it does inside the physician–patient interactional context. Issues of concern revolve around understanding and delivery of health insurance/Medicare/Medicaid, distribution of medication and information about medications, various therapies, and family decision-making encounters. Another important consideration is the numerous options of independent and assisted living now available for older adults. What holds true for a nursing home may not hold true for assisted-living facilities or other types of retirement communities, as the populations of individuals residing in the diverse types of available living arrangements are not homogeneous. Different forms of living could offer varied communication processes and consequences for older adults. For instance, friendship formation possibilities and intergenerational communication opportunities may be enhanced in certain living situations. Researchers, thus, should seek to understand the communicative consequences and benefits of residing in these different settings.

Another health communication issue related to aging of which we have little understanding is communication involving sexual issues. As a result of the rise in HIV and AIDS in older populations (National Commission on AIDS, 1993) and increased negative discourse surrounding sexuality and sexual dysfunction as individuals age (Kleinplatz, 2004), communicating about sexual health issues with older adults deserves increased attention in medical settings. These issues also have become more of a concern for older couples in romantic relationships, as well as throughout the entirety of the life span, yet few studies have examined how couples negotiate them (Mares & Fitzpatrick, 2004). Discourse surrounding sexual issues in health-care settings and in romantic relationships is especially important and timely, given that a continuation in sexual relationships is part of the normal/usual course of aging.

Health-care contexts also may offer valuable opportunities to study groups in older age. In 1987, Klinger-Vartabedian called for studying formal group communication of older adults as a research imperative; however, very little research regarding groups and older adults has been conducted since that time. Like individuals of all age groups, older individuals frequently find that interaction in formal groups, such as support groups or activity groups fulfills important needs (Garstka, McCallion, & Toseland, 2001). Groups of older individuals often form to enhance a healthy lifestyle, remain socially active, entertain, stay informed, take care of those who need help, or just to reminisce. The study of the formal and informal groups in which older adults participate has been neglected and should be considered a research imperative for applied communication scholars interested in aging.

Another important area of consideration for older adults is the family. As discussed previously, different familial relationships hold different meanings for older adults, but each relationship potentially plays a meaningful role in the life of older individuals. Much still needs to be understood about the mother–daughter relationship to decrease the toxic emotional stress often experienced in that relationship. The son's role in parent–adult child relationships also may be particularly important in making decisions in later life, given that the type of help that sons offer often involves financial advice (Moen et al., 1999). In addition, of course, the spouse of an adult child may be particularly significant. Moreover, as a result of finding that marital satisfaction decreased when an older adult parent lived with a couple, Bethea (2002) encouraged further examination of caregiver and care-recipient roles in family caregiving situations. Given that the trend of family caregiving likely will increase as the Baby Boom cohort moves beyond middle age, understanding how family members manage their new roles has important implications for the health and well-being of the family (Bethea, 2002).

An additional consideration within family communication concerns the role of older adults in the life of their grandchildren. An increasing number of grandparents have assumed the role of a primary caregiver to a grandchild (Bryson & Casper, 1999). When grandparents raise their grandchildren, grandparents are more likely to have stress-related illnesses and social isolation than when children are raised by a parent (Minkler & Roe, 1996). Many factors likely contribute to this stress, but few studies have addressed family communication where grandparents are the primary caregivers. Given the implications for both grandparents and grandchildren, this family structure certainly deserves consideration from applied communication researchers. An applicable line of research could utilize Harwood's (1998) work regarding intergenerational communication schemas (ICSs). Harwood suggested that younger individuals tend to apply particular cognitive schemas or maps to guide their conversations with older adults. ICSs constitute a formalized repertoire for intergenerational communication that may be useful not only in developing interventions for grandparent–grandchild interactions, for example, but also for other important intergenerational conversations that may occur in medical or educational settings, for instance (Harwood, McKee, & Lin, 2000).

A final area for applied communication research with older adults involves communication technology. Older adults who use the Internet, as opposed to those who do not, have more positive attitudes toward aging, higher levels of perceived social support, and higher levels of connectivity (Cody, Dunn, Hoppin, & Wendt, 1999). The Internet has provided older adults with new ways to express their identities (see Harwood's, 2004, study of grandparents' personal Web sites), a means to stay in touch with grandchildren who are located far away (Holladay & Seipke, 2007), and a large network for social support that helps to lower their perceived life stress (Wright, 2000), as well as a way for older adults to participate more in society (Furlong, 1989).

However, a large digital divide between the young and old is well documented (Loges & Jung, 2001). Furthermore, older adults who use the Internet may find it lacking in resources for mature issues, as seen in the lack of online resources for older adults with sexual concerns (Harris, Dersch, Kimball, Marshall, & Negretti, 1999). Given the constantly changing form of the Internet, further understanding of its role in the life of older adults, especially with regard to its implications for support, is a valuable line of applied communication research.

The potential for communication technology to enhance life for older adults certainly is not limited to Internet use. Other communication technology aimed at improving the life of older individuals include telemedicine (e.g., Greenberger & Puffer, 1989) and the use of "smart" homes equipped with blood-pressure monitors and teleconferencing equipment for residents to communicate with their health-care providers (Walters, 2002; see also Lievrouw, this volume).

Conclusion

Valuable applied research on aging with respect to health communication and interpersonal interactions has been accomplished, as demonstrated throughout this chapter. Nonetheless, applied communication and aging research can be advanced by using what is known about the normal changes in communicative faculties to augment and link current research to practice. Such work is aided by using the communication enhancement model to guide the study of communication and aging in applied contexts. There are many potential lines of applied communication research on aging that can utilize this model; they certainly are not limited to the recommendations noted here. Researchers should keep in mind that some of the most significant studies concerning aging in communication do not need to address the trendy issues in aging but simply aid in understanding everyday issues that are relevant to older adults and developing interventions to manage the day-to-day experiences of growing older. Given that later age potentially is an active and rewarding time of life, applied communication and aging scholarship should seek to describe, explain, and enhance the normal/usual living experience of older adults, in addition to improving the more problematic and pathological courses of aging. Such efforts undoubtedly will aid in understanding how physical, psychological, and social factors intertwine to affect the aging experience, providing knowledge that can be used to improve the quality of life for those at the later end of the life span.

References

Adams, R. G., & Blieszner, R. (1995). Aging well with friends and family. *American Behavioral Scientist, 39*, 209–224.

Adelman, R. D., Greene, M. G., & Charon, R. (1991). Issues in physician–elderly patient interaction. *Aging and Society, 11*, 127–148.

Adelman, R. D., Greene, M. G., Charon, R., & Friedman, E. (1992). The content of physician and elderly patient interaction in the medical primary care encounter. *Communication Research, 19*, 310–380.

Ade-Ridder, L., & Kaplan, L. (1993). Marriage, spousal caregiving, and a husband's move to a nursing home: A changing role for the wife? *Journal of Gerontological Nursing, 19*, 13–23.

Agee, A., & Blanton, P. W. (2000). Service providers' modes of interacting with frail elders and their families: Understanding the context of caregiving decisions. *Journal of Aging Studies, 14*, 331–333.

Albrecht, T. L., Burleson, B. R., & Goldsmith, D. (1994). Supportive communication. In M. L. Knapp & G. R. Miller (Eds.), *Handbook of interpersonal communication* (2nd ed., pp. 419–449). Thousand Oaks, CA: Sage.

Anderson, K., Harwood, J., & Hummert, M. L. (2005). The grandparent–grandchild relationship: Implications for models of intergenerational communication. *Human Communication Research, 31*, 268–294.

Ashburn, G., & Gordon, A. (1981). Features of a simplified register in speech to elderly conversationalist. *International Journal of Psycholinguistics, 8*, 7–31.

Atchely, R. C. (1991). Family, friends, and social support. In R. C. Atchley (Ed.), *Social forces and aging: An introduction to social gerontology* (6th ed., pp. 150–152). Belmont, CA: Wadsworth.

Baltes, M. M., & Carstensen, L. L. (2003). The process of successful aging: Selection, optimization and compensation. In U. M. Staudinger & U. Lindenberger (Eds.), *Understanding human development: Dialogues with lifespan psychology* (pp. 81–104). Boston: Kluwer Academic.

Baltes, M. M., Neumann, E. M., & Zank, S. (1994). Maintenance and rehabilitis of independence in old age: An intervention program for staff. *Psychology of Aging, 9*, 179–188.

Bamford, C., Gregson, B., Farrow, G., Buck, D., Dowshell, T., McNamee, P., et al. (1998). Mental and physical frailty in older people: The costs and benefits of informal care. *Ageing and Society, 18*, 317–354.

Bankoff, E. A. (1983). Aged parents and their widowed daughters: A support relationship. *Journal of Gerontology, 38*, 226–230.

Baxter, L. A., Braithwaite, D. O., Golish, T. D., & Olson, L. N. (2002). Contradictions of interaction for wives of elderly husbands with adult dementia. *Journal of Applied Communication Research, 30*, 1–26.

Becker, L. D., & Taylor, C. (1996). Attitudes toward the aged in a multigenerational sample. *Journal of Gerontology, 21*, 115–118.

Beisecker, A. (1989). The influence of a companion on the doctor–elderly patient interaction. *Health Communication, 1,* 55–70.

Bertakis, K. D., Roter, D., & Putnam, S. M. (1991). The relationship of physician medical interview style to patient satisfaction. *Journal of Family Practice, 32,* 175–181.

Bertera, E. M. (2005). Mental health in U.S. adults: The role of positive social support and social negativity in personal relationships. *Journal of Social and Personal Relationships, 22,* 33–48.

Bethea, L. S. (2002). The impact of an older adult parent on communicative satisfaction and dyadic adjustment in the long-term marital relationship: Adult-children and spouses' retrospective accounts. *Journal of Applied Communication Research, 30,* 107–125.

Blau, Z. S. (1973). *Old age in a changing society.* New York: New Viewpoints.

Borland, D. C. (1989). The sibling relationship as a housing alternative to institutionalization in later life. In L. Ade-Ridder & C. B. Hennon (Eds.), *Lifestyles of the elderly: Diversity in relationships, health, and caregiving* (pp. 205–219). New York: Human Services Press.

Bowling A., & Browne, P. D. (1991). Social networks, health, and emotional well-being among the older old in London. *Journal of Gerontology, 46,* S20–S32.

Braithwaite, D. O. (2002). "Married widowhood": Maintaining couplehood when one spouse is living in a nursing home. *Southern Communication Journal, 67,* 160–179.

Braithwaite, D. O., & Baxter, L. A. (1995). The relational dialectics of renewing marriage vows. *Journal of Social and Personal Relationships, 12,* 177–198.

Bryan, K., & Maxim, J. (1998). Enabling care staff to relate to older communication disabled people. *Language and Communication Disorders, 33,* 121–125.

Bryson, K., & Casper, L. M. (1999). *Co-resident grandparents and grandchildren* (U. S. Census Bureau Publication No. P23–198; 1997 March Current Population Survey.) Washington, DC: Government Printing Office.

Burleson, B. R., & Goldsmith, D. J. (1998). How the comforting process works: Alleviating emotional distress through conversationally induced reappraisals. In P. A. Anderson & L. K. Guerrero (Eds.), *Handbook of communication and emotion: Research, theory, applications, and contexts* (pp. 245–280). San Diego, CA: Academic Press.

Cantor, M. H. (1979). Neighbors and friends: An overlooked resource in the informal support system. *Research on Aging, 1,* 434–463.

Caporael, L. R. (1981). The paralanguage of caregiving: Baby talk to the institutionalized aged. *Journal of Personality and Social Psychology, 40,* 876–884.

Caporael, L. R., Lukaszewski, M. P., & Culbertson, G. H. (1983). Secondary babytalk: Judgments by institutionalized elderly and their caregivers. *Journal of Personality and Social Psychology, 44,* 746–754.

Caris-Verhallen, W., Kerkstra, A., & Bensing, J. (1997). The role of communication in nursing care for elderly people: A review of literature. *Journal of Advanced Nursing, 35,* 915–933.

Carmichael, C. W. (1988). Intrapersonal communication and aging. In C. W. Carmichael, C. H. Botan, & R. Hawkins (Eds.), *Human communication and the aging process* (pp. 31–55). Prospect Heights, IL: Waveland Press.

Carpiac-Claver, M. L., & Levy-Storms, L. (2007). In a manner of speaking: Communication between nurse aides and older adults in long-term care settings. *Health Communication, 22,* 59–67.

Carstensen, L. L., Isaacowitz, D. M., & Charles, S. T. (1999). Taking time seriously: A theory of socioemotional selectivity. *American Psychologist, 54,* 165–181.

Chappell, N. L. (1983). Informal support networks among the elderly. *Research on Aging, 5,* 77–99.

Charles, C., Goldsmith, L. J., Chambers, L., Haynes, R. B., & Gauld, M. (1996). Provider–patient communication among elderly and nonelderly patients in Canadian hospitals: A national survey. *Health Communication, 8,* 281–302.

Cicirelli, V. G. (1981). *Helping elderly parents: The role of adult children.* Boston: Auburn House.

Cicirelli, V. G. (1983). Adult children and their elderly parents. In T. H. Brubaker (Ed.), *Family relationships in later life* (pp. 47–62). Beverly Hills, CA: Sage.

Cicirelli, V. G. (1985). Sibling relationships throughout the life cycle. In L. L'Abate (Ed.), *The handbook of family psychology and therapy* (Vol. 1, pp. 177–214). Homewood, IL: Dorsey Press.

Cody, M. J., Dunn, D., Hoppin, S., & Wendt, P. (1999). Silver surfers: Training and evaluating Internet use among older adult learners. *Communication Education, 48,* 269–286.

Cohen, G., & Faulkner, D. (1986). Memory for proper names: Age difference in retrieval. *British Journal of Developmental Psychology, 4,* 197–197.

Cohen, S., & Wills, T. A. (1985). Stress, social support, and the buffering hypothesis. *Psychological Bulletin, 98,* 310–357.

Conner, K. A., Powers, E. A., & Bultena, G. L. (1979). Social interpretation and life satisfaction: An empirical assessment of late-life patterns. *Journal of Gerontology, 34,* 116–121.

Connidis, I. A., & Davies, L. (1992). Confidants and companions: Choices in later life. *Journal of Gerontology, 45,* S115–S122.

Coupland, J., & Coupland, N. (2001). Roles, responsibilities, and alignments: Multiparty talk in geriatric care. In M. L. Hummert & J. F. Nussbaum (Eds.), *Aging, communication, and health: Linking research and practice for successful aging* (pp. 121–155). Mahwah, NJ: Erlbaum.

Coyne, J. C., & Smith, D. A. F. (1994). Couples coping with a myocardial infarction: Contextual perspective on patient self-efficacy. *Journal of Family Psychology, 8,* 43–54.

Cutler, A., Dahan, D., & van Donselaar, W. (1997). Prosody in the comprehension of spoken language: A literature review. *Language and Speech, 40,* 141–201.

DiBenardinis, J., Barwind, J. A., & Wilmot, W. W. (1981). Interpersonal networks and quality of life in nursing home residents. *Journal of Applied Communication Research, 9,* 120–130.

Dickson-Markman, F., & Shern, D. L. (1990). Social support and health in the elderly. *Journal of Applied Communication Research, 18,* 49–63.

Dijkstra, K., Bougeois, M., Petrie, G., Burgio, L., & Allen-Burge, R. (2002). My recaller is on vacation: Discourse analysis of nursing-home residents with dementia. *Discourse Processes, 33,* 53–76.

Erber, N. (1994). Conversation as therapy for older adults in residential care: The case for intervention. *European Journal of Disorders of Communication, 29,* 269–278.

Felton, B. J., & Berry, C. (1992). Do the sources of the urban elderly's social support determine its psychological consequences? *Psychology and Aging, 7,* 89–97.

Fingerman, K. L. (2001). *Aging mothers and their adult daughters: A study in mixed emotions.* New York: Springer.

Fowler, C., & Nussbaum, J. F. (2008). Communication with the aging patient. In K. B. Wright & S. D. Moore (Eds.), *Applied health communication* (pp. 159–178). Cresskill, NJ: Hampton Press.

Fredrickson, B. L., & Carstensen, L. (1990). Choosing social partners: How old age and anticipated endings make people more selective. *Psychology and Aging, 5,* 335–347.

Furlong, M. S. (1989). An electronic community for older adults: The SeniorNet network. *Journal of Communication, 39*(3), 145–153.

Garstka, T. A., McCallion, P., & Toseland, R. W. (2001). Using support groups to improve caregiver health. In M. L. Hummert & J. F. Nussbaum (Eds.), *Aging, communication, and health: Linking research and practice for successful aging* (pp. 75–98). Mahwah, NJ: Erlbaum.

Giles, H., Dailey, R. M., Sarkar, J. M., & Makoni, S. (2007). Intergenerational communication beliefs across the lifespan. Comparative data from India. *Communication Reports, 20,* 75–89.

Giles, H. F., Fox, S., & Smith, E. (1993). Patronizing the elderly: Intergenerational evaluations. *Research on Language and Social Interaction, 26,* 129–149.

Goffman, E. (1961). *Asylums: Essays on the social situation of mental patients and other inmates.* Garden City, NY: Anchor Books.

Golish, T. D. (2000). Changes in closeness between adult children and their parents: A turning point analysis. *Communication Reports, 13,* 79–97.

Grainger, K. (1993). "That's a lovely bath dear": Reality construction in the discourse of elderly care. *Journal of Aging Studies, 7,* 247–263.

Grainger, K. (2004). Communication and the institutionalized elderly. In J. F. Nussbaum & J. Coupland (Eds.), *Handbook of communication and aging research* (2nd ed., pp. 479–497). Mahwah, NJ: Erlbaum.

Greenberger, M., & Puffer, J. C. (1989). Telemedicine: Toward a better health care for the elderly. *Journal of Communication, 39*(3), 137–144.

Greene, M. G., & Adelman, R. D. (2001). Building the physician–older patient relationship. In M. L. Hummert & J. F. Nussbaum (Eds.), *Aging, communication, and health: Linking research and practice for successful aging* (pp. 101–120). Mahwah, NJ: Erlbaum.

Greene, M. G., Adelman, R. D., Charon, R., & Friedman, E. (1989). Concordance between physicians and their older and younger patients in the primary care medical encounter. *Gerontologist, 29*, 808–813.

Greene, M. G., Adelman, R. D., & Majerovitz, S. D. (1996). Physician and older patient support in the medical encounter. *Health Communication, 8*, 263–280.

Greene, M. G., Adelman, R. D., Rizzo, C., & Friedman, E. (1994). The patient's presentation of self in an initial medical encounter. In M. L. Hummert, J. M. Wiemann, & J. F. Nussbaum (Eds.), *Interpersonal communication in older adulthood: Interdisciplinary theory and research* (pp. 226–250). Thousand Oaks, CA: Sage.

Harford, E. R., & Dodds, E. (1982). Hearing status of ambulatory senior citizens. *Ear and Hearing, 3*, 105–109.

Harris, S. M., Dersch, C. A., Kimball, T. G., Marshall, J. P., & Negretti, M. A. (1999). Internet resources for older adults with sexual concerns. *Journal of Sex Education and Therapy, 24*, 183–188.

Hartshorne, T. S., & Manaster, G. J. (1982). The relationship with grandparents: Contact, importance, and role conception. *International Journal of Aging and Human Development, 15*, 233–255.

Harwood, J. (1998). Young adults' cognitive representations of intergenerational conversations. *Journal of Applied Communication Research, 26*, 13–31.

Harwood, J. (2004). Relational, role, and social identity as expressed in grandparents' personal Web sites. *Communication Studies, 55*, 300–318.

Harwood, J., Giles, H., Fox, S., Ryan, E. B., & Williams, A. (1993). Patronizing young and elderly adults: Response strategies in a community setting. *Journal of Applied Communication Research, 21*, 211–226.

Harwood, J., & Lin, M.-C. (2000). Affiliation, pride, exchange, and distance in grandparents' accounts of relationships with their college-aged grandchildren. *Journal of Communication, 50*(3), 31–47.

Harwood, J., McKee, J., & Lin, M.-C. (2000). Younger and older adults' schematic representations of intergenerational conversations. *Communication Monographs, 67*, 20–41.

Haug, M. G., & Ory, M. G. (1987). Issues in elderly patient–provider interactions. *Research on Aging, 9*, 3–44.

Henwood, K. L. (2004). Adult parent–child relationships: A view from feminist and discursive social psychology. In J. F. Nussbaum & J. Coupland (Eds.), *Handbook of communication and aging research* (pp. 215–229) Mahwah, NJ: Erlbaum.

Henwood, M. (1990). No sense of urgency. In E. McEwan (Ed.), *Age: The unrecognized discrimination* (pp. 43–57). London: Age Concern.

High, D. M. (1990). Old and alone: Surrogate health care decision-making for the elderly without families. *Journal of Aging Studies, 4*, 277–288.

Holladay, S. J., & Seipke, H. L. (2007). Communication between grandparents and grandchildren in geographically separated relationships. *Communication Studies, 58*, 281–297.

Hooyman, N. R., & Kiyak, H. A. (1988). *Social gerontology: A multidisciplinary perspective*. Boston: Allyn & Bacon.

Hullett, C. R., McMillan, J. J., & Rogen, R. G. (2000). Caregivers' predispositions and perceived organizational expectations for the provision of social support to nursing home residents. *Health Communication, 12*, 277–299.

Hummert, M. L. (1998). Communication with older adults: The influence of age stereotypes, context, and communicator age. *Human Communication Research, 25*, 124–151.

Hummert, M. L, Garstka, T. A., Ryan, E. B., & Bonnesen, J. L. (2004). The role of age stereotypes in interpersonal communication. In J. F. Nussbaum & J. Coupland (Eds.), *Handbook of communication and aging research* (pp. 91–114). Mahwah, NJ: Erlbaum.

Huyck, M. H. (1996). Marriage and close relationships of the marital kind. In R. Blieszner & V. H. Bedford (Eds.), *Handbook of aging and the family* (pp. 181–200). Westport, CT: Greenwood Press.

Kawas, C. H. (1999). Alzheimer's disease. In W. R. Hazzard, J. P. Blass, W. H. Ettinger, Jr., J. B. Halter, & J. G. Ouslander (Eds.), *Principles of geriatric medicine and gerontology* (4th ed., pp. 1257–1269). New York: McGraw-Hill.

Kemper, S., Kynette, D., Rash, S., O'Brien, K., & Sprott, R. (1989). Life-span changes to adults' language: Effects of memory and genre. *Applied Psycholinguistics, 10*, 49–66.

Kemper, S., & Lyons, K. (1994). The effects of Alzheimer's dementia on language and communication. In M. L. Hummert, J. M. Wiemann, & J. F. Nussbaum (Eds.), *Interpersonal communication in older adulthood: Interdisciplinary theory and research* (pp. 58–82). Thousand Oaks, CA: Sage.

Kempler, D. (1991). Language changes in dementia of the Alzheimer type. In R. Lubinski (Ed.), J. B. Orange, D. Henderson, & N. Stecker (Assoc. Eds.), *Dementia and communication* (pp. 98–113). Philadelphia: B. C. Decker.

Keyes, C. L. (2002). The exchange of emotional support with age and its relationship with emotional well-being by age. *Journal of Gerontology, Series B: Psychological Sciences and Social Sciences, 57B*, 518–525.

Kiecolt-Glaser, J. K. (1999). Stress, personal relationships, and immune function: Health implications. *Brain, Behavior, and Immunity, 13*, 61–72.

Kleinplatz, P. J. (2004). Beyond sexual mechanics and hydraulics: Humanizing the discourse surrounding erectile dysfunction. *Journal of Humanistic Psychology, 44*, 215–242.

Klinger-Vartabedian, L. C. (1987). Formal group communication with older adults: A research imperative. *Journal of Applied Communication Research, 15*, 67–76.

Lavretsky, E. P., & Jarvik, L. F. (1994). Etiology and pathogenesis of Alzheimer's disease: Current concepts. In R. C. Hamby, J. M. Trumbull, W. Clark, & M. Lancaster (Eds.), *Alzheimer's disease: A handbook for caregivers* (2nd ed., pp. 80–92). St. Louis, MO: Mosby-Year Book.

Lemon, B. W., Bengston, V. L., & Peterson, J. A. (1972). An exploration of the activity theory of aging: Activity types and life satisfaction among in-movers to a retirement community. *Journal of Gerontology, 27*, 511–523.

Lieberman, D. A., Rigo, T. G., & Campain, R. F. (1988). Age-related differences in nonverbal decoding ability. *Communication Quarterly, 36*, 290–297.

Lin, M.-C., Harwood, J., & Bonnesen, J. L. (2002). Conversation topics and communication satisfaction in grandparent–grandchild relationships. *Journal of Language and Social Psychology, 21*, 302–323.

Lin, M.-C., Harwood, J., & Hummert, M. J. (2008). Young adults' intergenerational communication schemas in Taiwan and the USA. *Journal of Language & Social Psychology, 27*, 28–50.

Loges, W. E., & Jung, J. (2001). Exploring the digital divide: Internet connectedness and age. *Communication Research, 28*, 536–562.

Long, J. K., & Mancini, J. A. (1990). Aging couples in the family system. In T. H. Brubaker (Ed.), *Family relationships in later life* (2nd ed., pp. 29–47). Newbury Park, CA: Sage.

Lowenthal, M. F., & Haven, C. (1968). Interaction and adaptation: Intimacy as a crucial variable. In B. L. Neugarten (Ed.), *Middle age and aging: A reader in social psychology* (pp. 390–400). Chicago: University of Chicago Press.

Mares, M.-L., & Fitzpatrick, M. A. (2004). Communication in close relationships of older people. In J. F. Nussbaum & J. Coupland (Eds.), *Handbook of communication and aging research* (pp. 231–250) Mahwah, NJ: Erlbaum.

Marvel, M. K., Epstein, R. M., Flowers, K., & Beckman, H. B. (1999). Soliciting the patient's agenda: Have we improved? *JAMA: The Journal of the American Medical Association, 281,* 283–287.

McDowell, C. L., Harrison, D. W., & Demaree, H. A. (1994). Is right hemisphere decline in the perception of emotion a function of aging? *International Journal of Neuroscience, 79,* 1–11.

McKay, V. C., & Caverly, R. S. (2004). The nature of family relationships between and within generations: Relations between grandparents, grandchildren, and siblings in later life. In J. F. Nussbaum & J. Coupland (Eds.), *Handbook of communication and aging research* (pp. 251–271). Mahwah, NJ: Erlbaum.

Mesch, G. S. (2006). Family characteristics and intergenerational conflicts over the Internet. *Information Communication & Society, 9,* 473–495.

Miller, K. I., Shoemaker, M. M., Willyard, J., & Addison, P. (2008). Providing care for elderly parents: A structurational approach to family caregiver identity. *Journal of Family Communication, 8,* 19–43.

Minkler, M., & Roe, K. M. (1996). Grandparents as surrogate parents. *Generations, 20,* 34–38.

Moen, P., Harris-Abbott, D., Lee, S., & Roehling, P. (1999). *The Cornell couples and careers study.* Ithaca, NY: Cornell Employment and Family Careers Institute.

Montpare, J., Koff, E., Zaitchik, D., & Albert, M. (1999). The use of body movements and gestures as cues to emotion in younger and older adults. *Journal of Nonverbal Behavior, 23,* 133–152.

Morgan, M., & Hummert, M. L. (2000). Perceptions of communicative control strategies in the mother–daughter dyads across the life span. *Journal of Communication, 50*(3), 48–64.

Myers, S. A., & Goodboy, A. K. (2006). Perceived sibling use of verbally aggressive messages across the lifespan. *Communication Research Reports, 23,* 1–11.

National Commission on Acquired Immune Deficiency Syndrome. (1993). *Behavioral and social sciences and the HIV/AIDS epidemic.* Washington, DC: U.S. Government Printing Office.

Neils, J., Newman, C. W., Hill, M., & Weiler, E. (1991). The effects of rate, sequencing, and memory on auditory processing in the elderly. *Journal of Gerontology: Physiological Sciences, 46,* P71–P75.

Nerbonne, M. A. (1988). The effects of aging on auditory structures and functions. In B. B. Sheldon (Ed.), *Communication behavior and aging: A sourcebook for clinicians* (pp. 137–161). Baltimore: Williams & Wilkins.

Nussbaum, J. F. (1985). Successful aging: A communication model. *Communication Quarterly, 33,* 262–269.

Nussbaum, J. F. (1990). Communication within the nursing home: Survivability as a function of resident–staff affinity. In H. Giles, N. Coupland, & J. M. Wiemann (Eds.), *Communication, health, and the elderly* (pp. 155–171). Manchester, UK: Manchester University Press.

Nussbaum, J. F. (1994). Friendship in older adulthood. In M. L. Hummert, J. M., Wiemann, & J. F. Nussbaum (Eds.), *Interpersonal communication in older adulthood: Interdisciplinary theory and research* (pp. 209–225). Thousand Oaks, CA: Sage.

Nussbaum, J. F., Hummert, M. L., Williams, A., & Harwood, J. (1996). Communication and older adults. In B. R. Burelson (Ed.), *Communication yearbook* (Vol. 19, pp. 1–48). Newbury Park, CA: Sage.

Nussbaum, J. F., Pecchioni, L., & Crowell, T. (2001). The older patient–health care provider relationship in a managed care environment. In M. L. Hummert & J. F. Nussbaum (Eds.), *Aging, communication, and health: Linking research and practice for successful aging* (pp. 23–42). Mahwah, NJ: Erlbaum.

Nussbaum, J. F., Pecchioni, L., Grant, J., & Folwell, A. (2000). Explaining illness to older adults: The complexities of the provider–patient interaction as we age. In B. B. Whaley (Ed.), *Explaining illness: Research, theory, and strategies* (pp. 171–194). Mahwah, NJ: Erlbaum.

Nussbaum, J. F., Pecchioni, L. L. Robinson, J. D., & Thompson, T. L. (2000). *Communication and aging* (2nd ed.). Mahwah, NJ: Erlbaum.

O'Hanlon, A., & Coleman, P. (2004). Attitudes towards aging: Adaptation, development, and growth into later years. In J. F. Nussbaum & J. Coupland (Eds.), *Handbook of communication and aging research* (2nd ed., pp. 31–63). Mahwah, NJ: Erlbaum.

Olshansky, S. J., & Carnes, B. A. (2001). *The quest for immortality: Science at the frontiers of aging.* New York: Norton.

Orange, J. B. (1991). Perspectives of family members regarding communication changes. In R. Lubinski (Ed.), J. B. Orange, D. Henderson, & N. Stecker (Assoc. Eds.), *Dementia and communication* (pp. 168–187). Philadelphia: Decker.

Orange, J. B. (2001). Family caregiving, communication, and Alzheimer's disease. In M. L. Hummert & J. F. Nussbaum (Eds.), *Aging, communication, and health: Linking research and practice for successful aging* (pp. 225–248). Mahwah, NJ: Erlbaum.

Orange, J. B., VanGennep, K. M., Miller, L., & Johnson, A. M. (1998). Resolution of communication breakdown in dementia of the Alzheimer's type: A longitudinal study. *Journal of Applied Communication Research, 26,* 120–138.

Ory, M. G., Williams, T. F., Emr, M., Lebowitz, B., Rabins, P., Salloway, J., et al. (1985). Families, informal supports, and Alzheimer's disease. *Research in Aging, 7,* 623–644.

Ota, H., Giles, H., & Somera, L. P. (2007). Beliefs about intra- and intergenerational communication in Japan, the Philippines, and the United States: Implication for older adults' subjective well-being. *Communication Studies, 58,* 173–188.

Pecchioni, L. L., & Croghan, J. M. (2002). Young adults' stereotypes of older adults with their grandparents as the targets. *Journal of Communication, 52,* 715–731.

Pecchioni, L. L., & Nussbaum, J. F. (2000). The influence of autonomy and paternalism on communicative behaviors in mother–daughter relationships prior to dependency. *Health Communication, 12,* 317–338.

Phillipson, C. (1997). Social relationships in later life: A review of the research literature. *International Journal of Geriatric Psychiatry, 12,* 505–512.

Pichora-Fuller, M. K., & Carson, A. J. (2001). Hearing health and the listening experience for older communicators. In M. L. Hummert & J. F. Nussbaum (Eds.), *Aging, communication, and health: Linking research and practice for successful aging* (pp. 43–75). Mahwah, NJ: Erlbaum.

Polk, D. M. (2005). Communication and family caregiving for Alzheimer's dementia: Linking attributions and problematic integration. *Health Communication, 18,* 257–273.

Poole, M. S., & Real, K. (2003). Groups and teams in health care: Communication and effectiveness. In T. L. Thompson, A. M. Dorsey, K. I. Miller, & R. Parrott (Eds.), *Handbook of health communication* (pp. 369–402). Mahwah, NJ: Erlbaum.

Ragan, S. (1983). Alignment and conversational coherence. In R. T. Craig & K. Tracy (Eds.), *Conversational coherence: Form, structure, and strategy* (pp. 157–171). Beverly Hills, CA: Sage.

Rau, M. T. (1991). Impact on families. In R. Lubinski (Ed.)., J. B. Orange, D Henderson, & N. Stecker (Assoc. Eds.), *Dementia and communication* (pp. 152–167). Philadelphia: B. C. Decker.

Rawlins, W. K. (2004). Friendships in later life. In J. F. Nussbaum & J. Coupland (Eds.), *Handbook of communication and aging research* (pp. 273–299). Mahwah, NJ: Erlbaum.

Reinhardt, J. P. (2001). Effects of positive and negative support received and provided on adaptation to chronic visual impairment. *Applied Developmental Science, 5*(2), 76–85.

Rittenour, C. E., Myers, S. A., & Brann, M. (2007). Commitment and emotional closeness in the sibling relations. *Southern Communication Journal, 72,* 169–183.

Rook, K. S. (1990). Social relationships as a source of companionship: Implications for older adults' psychological well-being. In B. R. Sarason, I. G. Sarason, & G. R. Pierce (Eds.), *Social support: An interactional view* (pp. 219–250). New York: Wiley.

Rook, K. S., & Ituarte, P. H. G. (1999). Social control, social support, and companionship in older adults' family relationships and friendships. *Personal Relationships, 6,* 199–211.

Rousseau, G. K., Lamson, N., & Rogers, W. A. (1998). Designing warnings to compensate for age-related changes in perceptual and cognitive abilities. *Psychology & Marketing, 15,* 643–662.

Rowe, J. W., & Kahn, R. L. (1998). *Successful aging.* New York: Pantheon Books.

Ryan, E. B., & Butler, R. N. (1996). Communication, aging, and health: Toward understanding health provider relationships with older clients. *Health Communication, 8,* 191–197.

Ryan, E. B., Giles, H., Bartolucci, G., & Henwood, K. (1986). Psycholinguistic and social psychological components of communication by and with the elderly. *Language and Communication*, 6, 1–24.

Ryan, E. B., Meredith, S. D., MacLean, M. J., & Orange, J. B. (1995). Changing the way we talk with elders: Promoting health using the communication enhancement model. *International Journal of Aging and Human Development*, 41, 87–105.

Ryan, E. B., & Norris, J. E. (2001). Communication, aging, and health: The interface between research and practice. In M. L. Hummert & J. F. Nussbaum (Eds.), *Aging, communication, and health: Linking research and practice for successful aging* (pp. 279–297). Mahwah, NJ: Erlbaum.

Ryff, C. (1991). Possible selves in adulthood and old age: A tale of shifting horizons. *Psychology and Aging*, 6, 286–295.

Sachweh, S. (1998). Granny darling's nappies: Secondary babytalk in German nursing homes for the aged. *Journal of Applied Communication Research*, 26, 52–65.

Schaie, K. W., & Willis, S. L. (2002). *Adult development and aging* (5th ed.). Upper Saddle River, NJ: Prentice-Hall.

Scott, J. P. (1983). Siblings and other kin. In T. H. Brubaker (Ed.), *Family relationships in later life* (pp. 47–62). Beverly Hills, CA: Sage.

Segrin, C. (2001). *Interpersonal processes in psychological problems*. New York: Guildford Press.

Sigman, S. J. (1986). Adjustment to the nursing home as a social interactional accomplishment. *Journal of Applied Communication*, 14, 37–58.

Sillars, A. L., & Wilmot, W. W. (1989). Marital communication across the life span. In J. F. Nussbaum (Ed.), *Life-span communication: Normative processes* (pp. 225–253). Hillsdale, NJ: Erlbaum.

Stine, E. L., & Wingfield, A. (1987). Process and strategy in memory for speech among younger and older adults. *Psychology and Aging*, 4, 18–25.

Stoller, E. P., & Earl, L. L. (1983). Help with activities of every day life: Sources of support for noninstitutionalized elderly. *Gerontologist*, 23, 64–70.

Stone, R., Cafferata, G. L., & Sangl, J. (1987). Caregivers of the frail elderly: A national profile. *Gerontologist*, 27, 616–626.

Strain, L. A., & Chappell, N. L. (1982). Confidants: Do they make a difference in quality of life? *Research on Aging*, 4, 479–502.

Thompson, L., Clark, K., & Gunn, W. (1985). Developmental stages and perceptions of intergenerational continuity. *Journal of Marriage and the Family*, 47, 913–920.

Thompson, T. L., Aidinjad, M. R., & Ponte, J. (2001). Aging and the effects of facial and prosodic cues on emotional intensity ratings and memory reconstructions. *Journal of Nonverbal Behavior*, 25, 101–126.

Thompson, T. L., & Nussbaum, J. F. (1988). Interpersonal communication: Intimate relationships and aging. In C. W. Carmichael, C. H. Botan, & R. Hawkins (Eds.), *Human communication and the aging process* (pp. 95–109). Prospect Heights, IL: Waveland Press.

Thompson, T. L., Robinson, J. D., & Beisecker, A. E. (2004). The older patient–physician interaction. In J. F. Nussbaum & J. Coupland (Eds.), *Handbook of communication and aging research* (pp. 451–477) Mahwah, NJ: Erlbaum.

Troll, L. E. (1986). Parents and children in later life. *Generations*, 10, 23–25.

U.S. Census Bureau. (1999). *Statistical abstract of the United States: The national data book* (119th ed.). Washington, DC: U.S. Government Printing Office.

Villaume, W. A. (1987, April). *Aligning actions and controversial coherence: Toward a cross-classified taxonomy of how aligning actions are used in conversation.* Paper presented at the joint meeting of the Southern Speech Communication Association and Central States Speech Association, St. Louis, MO.

Villaume, W. A., Brown, M. H., & Darling, R. (1994). Presbycusis, communication, and older adults. In M. L. Hummert, J. M. Wiemann, & J. F. Nussbaum (Eds.), *Interpersonal communication in older adulthood: Interdisciplinary theory and research* (pp. 83–106). Thousand Oaks, CA: Sage.

Villaume, W. A., & Reid, T. (1990). An initial investigation of aging, aligning actions, and presbycusis. *Journal of Applied Communication Research, 18,* 8–31.

Walen, H. R., & Lachman, M. E. (2000). Social support and strain from partner, family, and friends: Costs and benefits for men and women in adulthood. *Journal of Social and Personal Relationships, 17,* 5–30.

Walters, R. A. (2002, October). *McKeesport, PA: Focus on the independence of its senior citizens.* Speech presented at the Colloquium Series of The Gerontology Center, The Pennsylvania State University, State College, PA.

Ward, R. A. (1996). Which is the dependent generation? In J. R. Logan & G. D. Spitze (Eds.), *Family ties: Enduring relationships between parents and their grown children* (pp. 28–55). Philadelphia: Temple University Press.

Williams, A., & Giles, H. (1996). Intergenerational conversation: Young adults' retrospective accounts. *Human Communication Research, 23,* 220–250.

Williams, A., & Guendouzi, J. (2000). Adjusting to "the home": Dialectical dilemmas and personal relationships in a retirement community. *Journal of Communication, 50*(3), 65–82.

Williams, A., Kemper, S., & Hummert, M. L. (2003). Improving nursing home communication: An intervention to reduce elderspeak. *Gerontologist, 43,* 242–247.

Williams, A., & Nussbaum, J. F. (2001). *Intergenerational communication across the life span.* Mahwah, NJ: Erlbaum.

Wingfield, A., Lahar, C. J., & Stine, E. A. (1989). Age and decision strategies in running memory for speech: Effects of prosody and linguistic structures. *Journal of Gerontology, 44*(4), 106–113.

Wingfield, A., Wayland, S., & Stine, E. (1992). Adult age difference in the use of prosofy for syntactic parsing and recall of spoken sentences. *Journal of Gerontology, 47,* 350–356.

Wright, K. (2000). Computer mediated social support, older adults, and coping. *Journal of Communication, 50*(3), 100–118.

19 Applied Political Communication Research

Lynda Lee Kaid
University of Florida

Mitchell S. McKinney
University of Missouri

John C. Tedesco
Virginia Tech University

Political communication traces its roots to the earliest attempts by classical scholars to describe democratic functions, with Aristotle, Plato, Quintilian, Cicero, and others concerned about rhetorical devices and uses of language and oratory that affected public life in the early days of Greek and Roman societies (e.g., Newall, 2005). From these early roots, political communication has evolved into a multidisciplinary field that draws from research in, among other disciplines, communication, political science, psychology, sociology, and marketing. Although many definitions have been offered for this field of study, Chaffee's (1975) simple, straightforward description sufficiently captures its essence: "the role of communication in political processes" (p. 15).

We focus this chapter on applied political communication research that provides knowledge about political processes that sometimes explicitly, yet more often implicitly, informs the communicative practices of a democracy. As political communication scholars, we view democracy as a civic dialogue, an ongoing conversation between and among elected leaders or candidates and the citizens they lead or wish to lead. The interaction between those who govern and those who are governed largely is conducted through mediated communication, and, thus, the media play a large role in this civic dialogue. Although most of the scholarship reviewed here was designed and conducted to test hypotheses or answer research questions grounded in specific political communication theories, the results of such studies, although not explicitly designed for application to, or intervention in, democratic processes, provide useful knowledge that may well be translated for such uses. We focus in this chapter on five areas of research where such applications and interventions occur most frequently: political speaking, political campaign debates, political advertising, political news, and political uses of new technologies.

Political Speaking

A long-standing area of applied political communication is the study of political speaking, which concentrates on source and message aspects of the communication process. From Aristotle's recommendations for successful persuasion in the Greek poli-state to modern-day political speechwriters, communication analysts have identified themes in political messages, political speakers' motives, rhetorical strategies employed, and the effectiveness of political speakers and speeches. Early research on political speaking relied almost exclusively on critical/interpretive/rhetorical analysis (see Condit & Bates, this volume), applying various perspectives to study great orators, such as William Jennings Bryant,

Winston Churchill, John F. Kennedy, Martin Luther King, and the "great communicator" Ronald Reagan. Moreover, because applied communication scholarship on political speaking focuses on particular messages or speakers (Jamieson, 1988), researchers often analyzed the effectiveness of techniques used in various genres of speechmaking, such as apologia (e.g., Ware & Linkugel, 1973) and presidential inaugural speeches (e.g., Hart, 1987) and State of the Union addresses (e.g., D. R. Hoffman & Howard, 2006).

Researchers also have analyzed techniques of political speechwriting (e.g., Ritter & Medhurst, 2003). One of the most comprehensive discussions and applications of general communication research and persuasion principles to political speaking is provided by Trent and Friedenberg (2007) in their classic text on campaign communication. Although most communication research on political speaking uses rhetorical/critical methodologies, contributions have been made by the application of quantitative methodologies (see Query et al., this volume). For instance, Hart (1984) developed and applied a computerized content analysis system (DICTION) to identify the "verbal style" of presidential speeches. Quantitative research methods, including opinion polls, also have been used to measure the effectiveness of specific political speeches, and field experiments have been conducted to measure changes in candidate images attributable to particular political speeches (e.g., Sanders & Kaid, 1981).

Research on political speaking has allowed applied political communication scholars and practitioners to craft speeches that assist political leaders in making their cases to the U.S. public. Many communication scholars, for instance, have written speeches for and advised candidates running for political office and helped officeholders to explain or persuade constituents about policy issues. Political speechwriters use research on the effectiveness of rhetorical devices, such as repetition and thematic focus, humor, and use of symbols such as metaphors, and research on various aspects of delivery, such as tonal variation, cadence, gestures, and other nonverbal communicative behaviors. For instance, Craig R. Smith, now at California State University, Long Beach, applied his scholarly knowledge of political communication as a speechwriter for President Gerald Ford. Political communication researchers also have served as analysts and commentators of political speech, sometimes in a public forum and often via the media. Political communication scholars who frequently appear in the news media to apply their knowledge include Kathleen Hall Jamieson (University of Pennsylvania), Robert Denton (Virginia Tech University), Kurt Ritter (Texas A&M University), and Bruce Gronbeck (The University of Iowa). In this way, political scholars use information acquired from applied research studies to help audiences better understand and evaluate the speech of political leaders and policy makers.

Political Campaign Debates

Political campaign debates involve candidates meeting face-to-face in a formal debate exchange. In fact, the debate stage or forum often is the only campaign event where candidates appear side by side, allowing viewers of these frequently televised events to compare candidates and their messages. The debate encounter typically is structured by varying rules of engagement and interaction with opponents, with the most common debate rule affording equal time to all candidates. The primary audience for the debate exchange is the voting public, with the principal purpose of this form of campaign communication to produce a more informed electorate.

Perhaps the justification cited most often for televised campaign debates, particularly presidential debates, is that they reach large audiences. Since the inception of televised presidential debates in 1960, such debates have continued to generate the largest viewing audience of any single televised campaign event (McKinney, 2007). Pfau (2003) also pointed out that debates, with their attendant media hype, may be the only televised political event capable of attracting the attention of the "marginally attentive" citizen who may tune out other forms of campaign communication.

Much can be learned from existing research on political campaign debates that is useful for campaigns and candidates preparing for debate participation. The following sections provide an overview of major research findings regarding debate effects, with specific attention to the limited research on lower level or nonpresidential debates, media coverage of debates, and how candidates' messages and viewer learning from debates are affected by debate formats.

Effects of Political Debates

For most people, the usefulness of political debates hinges on whether viewing debates influences citizens' vote choice. The empirical evidence on this matter is quite clear: Very little change in voting intentions follows exposure to political debates. Most citizens who watch debates do so to cheer on the candidate they already support. However, although debates may not alter the voting preferences of previously committed viewers, ample evidence has found that debates help undecided, conflicted, or weakly committed viewers to form or change their voting preference. Although undecided and uncommitted citizens may constitute a small segment of the debate-viewing audience, it is exactly this slice of the electorate to which most general-election campaign messages are targeted and, in close contests, these voters ultimately may decide the election outcome. At the presidential level, for example, postdebate Gallup polling data from the nine presidential campaigns that featured general-election debates suggest that televised debates played a decisive role in the outcome of more than half of those elections, including the 1960, 1976, 1980, 2000, and 2004 elections (McKinney, 2007; McKinney & Carlin, 2004).

Beyond the behavioral effects of debate viewing, numerous studies have shown that debates facilitate citizens' acquisition of issue information and influence their perceptions of candidates' character or image traits (for a review of this research, see McKinney & Carlin, 2004). Debate viewing also may activate a number of latent civic and democratic tendencies, including decreasing viewers' reported political cynicism; enhancing citizens' sense of political efficacy, interest in the ongoing campaign, and likelihood of voting; and encouraging citizens to seek additional campaign information following debate viewing and greater participation in a campaign through activities such as talking to others about preferred candidates (for a review of this research, see McKinney & Chattopadhyay, 2007).

Learning from Nonpresidential Debates

Although overwhelming attention has focused on the quadrennial U.S. presidential debates, campaign debates occur even more frequently among candidates seeking local, state, and other federal offices. The scant evidence available suggests that state and local televised debates differ in both content and viewer effects from their presidential counterparts. Studies conducted by Lichtenstein (1982) and Pfau (1983), for instance, found that citizens who watched both local and presidential debates reported learning more from local candidates than they did from presidential candidates. Local-level debates also had a greater effect on viewers' vote choice, as many viewers knew little about local candidates and had not selected a candidate before watching those debates.

Nonpresidential debates also afford scholars opportunities to answer research questions not easily examined in the context of presidential debates. For example, given that female political candidates are seeking—and achieving—public office in greater numbers than ever before, many of these candidates engage in campaign debates. Edelsky and Adams (1990) studied six mixed-gender state and local debates, finding clear differences between male and female candidates' communication patterns, such as "men got better treatment (safer turn spaces, extra turns, more follow-ups on their topics) and they took control of more resources (more time for their positions, and engaged in more of the 'aggressive' speaking)" (p. 186). Banwart and McKinney's (2005) examination of gubernatorial and U.S. Senate candidates' debate styles in mixed-gender races, however, found more similarities than differences between female and male candidates' communication patterns, which resulted from a pattern of "gendered adaptiveness," whereby male candidates debating a female opponent adopted a greater number of "feminine" communication strategies and female candidates debating a male opponent adopted a greater number of "masculine" communication strategies.

It also is more common today for independent and minor-party candidates to be included in state and local debates. With the exception of limited research surrounding Ross Perot's inclusion in the 1992 presidential debates, however, scholars know very little about the impact of minor-party or independent candidates in debates. Beiler's (2000) analysis of Jesse Ventura's successful bid for Minnesota Governor in 1998 showed how the election of this former professional wrestler and bodybuilder actually may have turned on his inclusion in the three gubernatorial debates that were broadcast statewide. Ventura gained steadily in credibility with voters throughout the debate series, aided by his antiestablishment appeals to independents and those who previously had not voted. Prentice's (2005) examination of congressional (U.S. House and Senate) and gubernatorial debates identified communication obstacles experienced by third-party candidates engaged in campaign debates with major-party opponents. Specifically, ways in which a debate dialogue is framed, guided by journalists' questioning, typically ignores or negates third-party worldviews and ideologies; moreover, major-party candidates regularly ignore or communicatively demean third-party opponents and frequently co-opt or diminish the issue positions championed by third-party candidates.

Media Coverage of Debates

In addition to attracting scholarly interest, debates attract a high level of media attention. At the presidential level, for example, analysis of major network news broadcasts during the fall campaign, from Labor Day to Election Day, reveals that debate-related news segments are among the most frequent campaign stories (Kaid, McKinney, & Tedesco, 2000). McKinney and Lamoureux (1999) suggested that the debate news narrative is best viewed as an ongoing media drama performed in three acts. First, the typical news story begins with the requisite "debate over the debates," focusing on one candidate challenging his or her opponent to debate. This stage of the narrative also deals with uncertainties such as how many debates will take place, what formats will be adopted, and who will be allowed to participate, particularly when "legitimate" third-party or independent candidates are involved. The second phase of the drama sets expectations for each candidate, with people learning from the media who is considered the stronger or more experienced debater, who is expected to attack whom and how, and possible debate strategies that candidates will likely pursue. Finally, after the actual debate takes place, the news narrative reveals who won or lost, or performed better than or not as well as expected, highlighting candidate attacks, stumbles, or gaffes.

Research conducted on the news media's coverage of debates has examined both the content and effects of that reporting. In characterizing the content of debate coverage, although issue discussion constitutes the major element of debates, issues are not the main focus of debate reporting (Kaid et al., 2000); instead, media coverage focuses largely on candidates' performance and highlights the "horse-race" aspects of the campaign, with heavy reporting of "snap" postdebate polls showing who won the debate and much speculative analysis regarding the likely impact of the debate on the election outcome.

A number of experimental studies have tested the effects of exposure to postdebate media commentary. Lowry, Bridges, and Barefield (1990) found that viewers exposed to postdebate analysis featuring an instant poll showing that a particular candidate had won the debate were significantly more likely to identify that candidate as the debate winner than were viewers not exposed to the postdebate commentary. Experimental studies by McKinnon, Tedesco, and Kaid (1993) and McKinnon and Tedesco (1999) also found media commentary effects, with exposure to postdebate "spin" significantly increasing respondents' evaluations of candidates. In analyzing the influence of postdebate media commentary, Chaffee and Dennis (1979) concluded that "it may well be that the press's interpretation of the debate…is more important in determining the impact on the electorate than is the debate itself" (p. 85).

Debate Format and Candidates' Messages

A limited amount of empirical work has tested relationships between debate format and candidates' message content. Because debates remained virtually unchanged at the presidential level until the 1990s, until then sticking largely to the standard "joint press-conference" design, the scant systematic analysis of debate formats is somewhat understandable. However, the limited findings that now are available make it increasingly clear that debate format matters in several important ways.

In analyzing possible format effects in general-election presidential debates, perhaps the most systematic analysis is the research program by Diana Carlin and colleagues examining the influence of debate format on candidate clash (e.g., Carlin, Howard, Stanfield, & Reynolds, 1991; Carlin, Morris, & Smith, 2001). Their analyses address the contention that televised debates are devoid of actual candidate clash (when candidates offer analysis of their issue positions versus opponents' positions, and through direct attack of opponents' positions) and direct comparison of issue positions, finding that particular format features influence candidates to engage in such clash. Specifically, Carlin et al. (1991) found in their comparative content analysis of the presidential debates in 1960, 1976, 1980, 1984, and 1988 that candidate clash is limited when format design limits rebuttal times or when the same or similar questions are not posed to both candidates. More recently, Carlin et al. (2001) found that the type of questions asked influences candidate clash, such that "comparative" questions (asking candidates to contrast their positions to those of their opponent) generate significantly more clash than do less comparative questions, often put to candidates by citizen questioners in town-hall debates. Finally, when comparing the amount of clash that occurred across three debate formats—the formal-podium debate, the less formal candidate-"chat" debate, and the town-hall debate—the formal-podium debate demonstrated the greatest overall level of candidate clash and the more conversational chat debate featured the least amount of clash.

Kaid et al.'s (2000) analysis of the two most common debate formats now used at the presidential level—the formal-podium debate with journalist questioners and the town-hall debate with citizen questioners—found three significant content differences: Town-hall debates (1) contain significantly less candidate attack; (2) lead candidates to develop significantly more issue (rather than image) appeals; and (3) feature significantly more candidate-positive (rather than opponent-negative) discourse. Kaid et al.'s (2000) study confirmed Benoit and Wells's (1996) finding that town-hall debates contain the least amount of candidate attack, leading to the conclusion that "the format of the debates—and in particular when audience members are able to clearly express their desires to the candidates—can affect the nature of persuasive attack produced by the rhetors" (p. 59).

To test the relationship between debate format and issues discussed, Kaid et al. (2000) conducted an experimental study that examined the degree to which issues discussed by candidates in a journalist-controlled podium debate versus a citizen-controlled town-hall debate corresponded to issues that voters thought were most important. Their study found a debate-format effect relating to issue agendas, such that in the journalist-led podium debate, the public's predebate issue agenda was unrelated to the agenda of issues that respondents thought were discussed during the debate, whereas in the town-hall debate, viewers' predebate issue agenda was significantly correlated with the rank order of issues stressed in the debate itself. This difference in issue-agenda agreement supports the notion that a town-hall format, in which citizens ask candidates questions, taps more directly into the issue priorities of ordinary voters than does a podium debate.

Finally, McKinney, Dudash, and Hodgkinson (2003) tested viewer learning from exposure to debates, examining both issue and image learning across three debate formats: the more formal journalist-led podium debate, a more informal conversational debate with candidates seated at a table with a single journalist moderator, and a citizen-led town-hall debate. Comparing respondents' overall issue and image learning from the three debates combined, approximately two-thirds of all claims of learning were about candidate image and one-third was about issue learning. However, the debate format had an effect on the type of learning that occurred, such that chat debates led viewers to focus less on candidates' performance and image considerations, and more on issue appeals. Moreover, whereas chat debates resulted in an almost equal amount of issue and image learning, the podium and town-hall debates resulted in almost three times as many candidate-image observations than claims of issue learning.

In summary, the limited research available suggests that the structure of a political debate can have significant effects on candidates' communication and viewers' learning. Specifically, content-analytic research suggests that the more formal podium debates conducted by a professional moderator encourage greater candidate clash and more aggressive and attack-oriented candidate discourse, but when the public is included in the debate dialogue, candidates reduce their level of clash and attack, adopt a more personable or "humanizing" style, focus more on issue than image discussion, and address issues that are of greatest concern to the public. Finally, limited evidence suggests that the debate structure may influence the type of learning—issue versus image—resulting from debate exposure.

The decades of research about political debates provides useful information for candidates preparing for debate participation, as well as those planning debate encounters that are most useful to citizens. The foundation of a participatory democracy is an informed and engaged citizenry, perhaps best demonstrated in campaign debates in which those desiring to be leaders stand before the public and argue why they should be granted one of the greatest expressions of power that citizens have—their vote. To aid that process, communication scholars often have applied research about debates to actual campaigns. For instance, communication scholar, and now consultant, Myles Martel (1983) served as the chief debate advisor to Ronald Reagan during his 1980 presidential campaign. Diana Carlin (The University of Kansas) has served as a consultant to the Commission on Presidential Debates, advising on format and production of presidential debates. Carlin also coordinates the DebateWatch program that involves college and university faculty organizing groups of citizens and students in their local communities to engage in postdebate discussions (Carlin, 2005; Carlin & Anderson, 2003), and Carlin and Mitchell McKinney (University of Missouri) have worked with international colleagues to organize Debate-Watch groups throughout the world and to advise on the organization of political debates in other countries (see Beom, Carlin, & Silver, 2005). The media also often turn to communication scholars, such as Carlin, Robert Friedenberg (Miami University), McKinney, Sidney Kraus (Cleveland State University), Judith Trent (The University of Cincinnati), and David Zarefsky (Northwestern University), for commentary on political debates.

Political Advertising

Political advertising occupies a central role in the electoral process of most democratic systems, whether represented by the paid advertising system that characterizes the United States or by unpaid political programming provided by broadcast outlets in many other democracies (see Kaid & Holtz-Bacha, 2006). Political advertising also represents one of the clearest, most direct applications of communication research. As a result, researchers have investigated the content of political television advertising, identifying the "video-style" of candidates by analyzing the verbal, nonverbal, and television production content of political ads (Kaid & Johnston, 2001). More important to political practitioners are findings about the effectiveness of various strategies and components of political advertising, with researchers establishing that political advertising can have identifiable effects on people's knowledge and attitudes about political candidates and issues, as well as their voting decisions (e.g., Kaid, 2004, 2006).

Early research on political advertising effects suggested that televised political advertising was especially valuable because of its ability to overcome partisan selective exposure, meaning that television spots help candidates to get their messages to a large number of voters who might not ordinarily seek out those messages but are exposed to them as part of routine television programming (Atkin, Bowen, Nayman, & Sheinkopf, 1973). Televised political advertising also has proven particularly effective at persuading undecided voters (Bowen, 1994) and those who are not highly involved in politics (Rothschild & Ray, 1974). The following sections examine (1) how political advertising affects people's knowledge about candidates and issues, attitudes toward candidates, and their voting; (2) negative political advertising; (3) communication channels employed in political advertising; and (4) issue advocacy in political advertising.

Effects of Political Advertising on Knowledge about Candidates and Issues

Among the most important findings about the effectiveness of political advertising has been the establishment of learning effects from exposure. For instance, voters exposed to televised political ads, compared to those who are not, are more likely to recall a candidate's name (Kaid, 1982; West, 1994), an important factor in candidates' success at the polls. Voters' knowledge about campaign issues and candidate positions on those issues is increased by exposure to political advertising (Franz, Freedman, Goldstein, & Ridout, 2008; Pfau, Holbert, Szabo, & Kaminski, 2002; Ridout, Shaw, Goldstein, & Franz, 2004).

The content of a political ad may affect voters' recall of information; for instance, ads focused on the image and character qualities of candidates appear to be particularly successful at increasing voters' knowledge about those candidates (Kaid & Sanders, 1978). Advertising exposure also can affect voters' judgments about issue salience and, thereby, have an agenda-setting effect for both issues (Golan, Kiousis, & McDaniel, 2007; Roberts, 1992; West, 1993) and candidates' perceived attributes (Sulfaro, 2001).

Political advertising is so effective that researchers have found it to be more valuable in eliciting voters' knowledge gain than exposure to television news (Brians & Wattenberg, 1996; Holbert, Benoit, Hansen, & Wen, 2002; Patterson & McClure, 1976). Even political debates, a much longer and presumably information-rich communication format, appear to be less successful at transferring issue knowledge to voters than is political advertising (Just, Crigler, & Wallach, 1990).

Effects of Political Advertising on Attitudes toward Candidates

Political communication research also has considered how exposure to political advertising affects voters' evaluations of candidates, which may be more important than information gained from political advertising. Consequently, numerous experimental and survey studies have investigated effects of political advertising on people's evaluations of candidates (e.g., Fridkin & Kenney, 2004; Kahn & Geer, 1994; Kaid, 1991, 1994, 1997, 1998, 2001; Kaid & Chanslor, 2004; Kaid, Leland, & Whitney, 1992; Pfau, Kendall et al., 1997; Tedesco & Kaid, 2003; West, 1993).

In contrast to knowledge and information gain, where image ads appear to be successful, political ads that emphasize issue content are most effective at increasing people's positive attitudes toward candidates (Kaid, Chanslor, & Hovind, 1992; Kaid & Sanders, 1978; Thorson, Christ, & Caywood, 1991). The emotional content in ads also generates emotional responses related to the evaluation of candidates (Chang, 2001; Kaid, 1994; Kaid, Leland, & Whitney, 1992; Tedesco, 2002).

Effects of Political Advertising on Voting Behavior

In the political arena, the behavioral effect of most concern to practitioners is the decision to vote for or against a candidate, and political communication scholars have demonstrated that political advertising affects directly such electoral decisions. Direct voting effects have been shown by research that identifies the vote impact of exposure to specific advertising messages (Goldstein & Freedman, 2000; Kaid & Sanders, 1978; West, 1994).

Effects of Negative Political Advertising

Over the past several decades, the tenor of political advertising has become more negative, giving rise to a considerable amount of political communication research to determine conditions under which such advertising is and is not effective. However, the definition of *negative advertising* is not as obvious as it may seem; in fact, it is the subject of great debate. In their work on videostyle, Kaid and Johnston (2001) defined negative advertising as that which focuses on or targets opponents rather than the candidate who sponsors the ad. Benoit (1999) described the function of such advertising as "attacking" and Franz et al. (2008) used the term *attack advertising*. Some advertising, labeled *comparative advertising*, provides both negative advertising about an opponent and positive information about the sponsor (Meirick, 2002; Sorescu & Gelb, 2000). Whatever the label or definition, negative advertising seems to create a knee-jerk negative reaction from citizens who proclaim loudly and often that they dislike and disapprove of it (Franz et al., 2008; Kaid, 2004; Kaid, McKinney, & Tedesco, 2000).

Despite widespread dislike of negative advertising, one reason for its increased use has been political practitioners' belief that it works. Indeed, there is considerable evidence that this conclusion is more than just a presumption or "gut reaction" by practitioners, as research shows that negative advertising exposure, compared to positive ads, can lead to higher levels of voters' knowledge about candidates and issues (Basil, Schooler, & Reeves, 1991; Brians & Wattenberg, 1996; Chang, 2001; Johnson-Cartee & Copeland, 1989; Kahn & Kenney, 2000; A. Lang, 1991).

Although positive ads appear to be more successful than negative or comparative ads at producing more favorable attitudes toward candidates (Kahn & Geer, 1994; Shen & Wu, 2002), negative advertising can deflate the image evaluation of opponents or targeted candidates (Kaid & Boydston, 1987; Tinkham & Weaver-Lariscy, 1993; West, 1994). In fact, Jasperson and Fan (2002) found that the effects of negative information were four times greater than that of positive information with respect to people's favorability toward candidates.

Backlash from negative advertising, however, sometimes causes declining evaluation of sponsoring candidates, even as it decreases positivity toward targeted candidates (Garramone, 1984; Jasperson & Fan, 2002; Merritt, 1984). The conditions under which negative advertising is used, however, can diminish this problem. For instance, research confirms that the old adage "the best defense is a good offense" applies to political advertising; hence, inoculation, or getting one's message out first, on a vulnerable issue can greatly reduce the likelihood that voters will be persuaded by opponents' subsequent negative attacks on that issue (Pfau & Burgoon, 1988; Pfau & Kenski, 1990).

Independent or third-party sponsorship also makes negative ads more credible and believable (Garramone, 1984, 1985; Garramone & Smith, 1984; Groenedyk & Valentino, 2002; Kaid & Boydston, 1987; Shen & Wu, 2002). However, the widely accepted view of the effectiveness of negative advertising has been questioned recently by new research findings suggesting that independent sponsorship does not necessarily outperform but exerts the same impact as candidate sponsorship (Kaid, Fernandes et al., 2008; Pfau, Holbert et al., 2002).

The content of negative ads can be decisive in determining their effects, with negative ads attacking opponents' issue positions being more effective than negative ads attacking opponents' personal qualities (Fridkin & Kenney, 2004; Johnson-Cartee & Copeland, 1989; Kahn & Geer, 1994; Pfau & Burgoon, 1989; Roddy & Garramone, 1988). The success of intertwining personal and issues attacks may explain the success of the 2004 ads against the Democratic presidential candidate John Kerry, sponsored by the Swift Boat Veterans for Truth, that related primarily to Kerry's Vietnam War experience and competence to be "Commander-in-Chief," and made direct and implied criticisms of his character and leadership potential, but related the attacks to military or terrorism issues. The use of contrast/comparative ads also sometimes can offset potential backlash effects (Meirick, 2002).

Research has made clear that negative political advertising demands a response from targeted candidates. Rebuttal ads by candidates have been shown to diminish the effectiveness of such attacks (Garramone, 1985; Kahn & Geer, 1994; Roddy & Garramone, 1988; Sonner, 1998).

Communication Channels Employed in Political Advertising

Most of the previous discussion focused on source, message, and receiver variables that relate to the effectiveness of political advertising. Very little research has addressed whether the channel or medium through which political ads are transmitted makes a difference in their effects. Research has suggested the presence of consistent interaction effects between channels and sources of political advertising, such that some candidates are more successful on television, whereas others are more successful using radio or print media (e.g., Andreoli & Worchel, 1978; Cohen, 1976). The emergence of the Internet as a vehicle for political advertising has restimulated research on the communication channel question. Kaid (2002, 2003), for instance, identified some differences in evaluations of the 2000 presidential candidates presented in television advertising versus the same advertising on the Web. In the 2004 presidential campaign, John Kerry was evaluated more positively by those who saw his advertising on the Web, whereas George Bush fared better when his ads were viewed on television (Kaid & Postelnicu, 2005).

Other political advertising topics that have been important to those making applications to real-world concerns have included research on political advertising for female candidates (Bystrom, Banwart, Kaid, & Robertson, 2004; Kahn, 1996) and the spread of U.S. political advertising to international venues (Kaid & Holtz-Bacha, 2006). Communication researchers also have been leaders in applying research on advertising to issue-advocacy situations where such advertising is designed to affect public policy outcomes rather than people's vote in a specific election (Kaid, Tedesco, & Spiker, 1996; West, Heith, & Goodwin, 1996).

Communication scholars also have applied their research expertise on political advertising when they have been called on to write, produce, research, and evaluate advertising spots for political campaigns and issue advocacy groups. Kaid and Tedesco, for instance, have applied their research on political advertising to campaigns at several levels, as have Mary Banwart (The University of Kansas), Dianne Bystrom (Director of the Carrie Chapman Catt Center for Women and Politics at Iowa State University), Kathy Kendall (The University of Maryland), Karen Johnson-Cartee (The University of Alabama), and Ruth Ann Weaver Lariscy (The University of Georgia).

Political communication research also has been applied to news media commentary about political advertising. Often labeled "adwatches," both newspaper and television news reporters have developed systems for analyzing the accuracy of claims made by political candidates in their ads (Kaid, McKinney, Tedesco, & Gaddie, 1999; McKinnon & Kaid, 1999; Tedesco, Kaid, & McKinnon, 2000). Scholars at the Annenberg School for Communication at the University of Pennsylvania now are involved directly in checking and verifying political advertising claims through their Web site, FactCheck.org, which offers the media and the public detailed analyses of political advertisements.

Political News

Many political communication researchers investigate journalistic, stylistic, and technological aspects of news media. As explained below, media gatekeeping, news bias, and news media content; agenda-setting and agenda-building; and news framing are robust research traditions addressing journalistic practices and their effects.

Media Gatekeeping, News Bias, and News Media Content Research

Media gatekeeping, initially articulated by social psychologist Kurt Lewin (1947), first was applied to newsrooms in White's (1964) landmark observations of editorial decision making during the 1960s. White investigated how editors functioned as gatekeepers through their ability to select, filter, shape or withhold information appearing in their newspapers. More recent analyses have revealed that newsworthiness of information and space constraints (column inches and broadcast time) are the leading editorial considerations predicting what appears in the news (Shoemaker & Reese, 1996). Ironically, a common theme in recent research is whether anyone actually is monitoring the gate. Media sensationalism and tabloidization, coupled with the increased blending of information and entertainment, have led researchers to question editorial decision making (Delli Carpini & Williams 2001; Shaw, 1994; B. A. Williams & Delli Carpini, 2000). Researchers also have begun studying gatekeeping on media Web sites, where space constraints are not as restrictive as in print and broadcast media (Singer, 2001).

Media bias is one of the more contentious issues in research about news content. There is much debate about how to operationalize bias, but more important, about the sources used by scholars to assert their claims of media bias. For example, studies focusing only on ABC, NBC, and CBS television networks fail to capture the widely reported politically right- and left-leaning tendencies of Fox and CNN, respectively. Furthermore, the word *media* is far more complex than network news or major daily newspapers (see Lievrouw, this volume). For example, few researchers have focused on talk radio, which sometimes is perceived to have a conservative bias. Although bias is a fertile concept, allegations of it must be made on strong methodological footing or the research loses credibility.

Media bias research often focuses on conservative and liberal bias (e.g., Domke, Watts, Shah, & Fan, 1999; Eisinger, Veenstra, & Koehn, 2007; Niven, 2002), corporate bias (e.g., Alterman, 2004), and negative bias (e.g., Farnsworth & Lichter, 2008; Lichter, Noyes, & Kaid, 1999). Researchers also study bias related to coverage of particular events, such as journalistic practices during times of war (e.g., Hallin, 1992; Kaid, Myrick et al., 1994). Although researchers draw different conclusions regarding whether there is conservative and liberal media bias during election campaigns in the United States, research on international events supports a pro-American bias by U.S. media. The changing reporting styles through embedded journalism during the U.S. war in Iraq also drew scholarly attention to the tone of media coverage, trust in the military, and framing of military and war between embedded and nonembedded journalists (Haigh et al., 2006).

An important consideration of news media content is the "horse-race" style of media reporting, which focuses on candidates leading in the polls to the detriment of more detailed political information (e.g., Farnsworth & Lichter, 2009; Kaid & Strömbäck, 2008; Trent & Friedenberg, 2007). Researchers also have explored the transformation of news in the Internet era, strategies that newspapers employ on their Web sites to improve coverage of public affairs (Rosenberry, 2005), how Internet and traditional news compare with regard to media agendas and information processing by audiences (Ku, Kaid, & Pfau, 2003), and how the new media environment is shifting away from traditional media sources and toward cable and Internet sources that are available all the time (Benoit & Hansen, 2004).

A very practical area of news coverage research highlights the restrictions imposed on news that reaches the public as a result of the tendency to shorten the amount of coverage given to political candidates' statements. Researchers have verified repeatedly that the time given to direct statements by candidates in presidential campaigns has shrunk in recent years to 7 to 8 seconds (Farnsworth & Lichter, 2008; Hallin, 1992; Lichter et al., 1999). Such research provides candidates and officeholders alike with important lessons about how to structure and limit their public statements to fit the short "sound-bite" mentality of journalistic reporting.

Agenda-Setting and Agenda-Building

Agenda-setting, as first articulated by McCombs and Shaw (1972), is the process by which media influence the salience of issues on the public agenda. Subsequently, scholars have pursued five directions of research: (1) basic agenda-setting; (2) attribute agenda-setting; (3) contingent conditions for agenda-setting effects; (4) agenda-building, or the process by which sources influence the media agenda; and (5) agenda-setting consequences (McCombs, 2004).

Agenda-setting research extends through many contexts and directions of influence (Weaver, McCombs, & Shaw, 2004), including campaign agenda-building for media (Tedesco, 2001, 2005a, 2005b), intermedia agenda-setting effects (Dearing & Rogers, 1996; Reese & Danielian, 1989), political advertising and agenda-setting (e.g., Lopez-Escobar, Llamas, McCombs, & Lennon, 1998; Ridout & Mellen, 2007; Roberts & McCombs, 1994), and the agenda-setting power of the U.S. president (Wanta & Foote, 1994; Wanta, Stephenson, Turk, & McCombs, 1989). Research also explores agenda-setting and polling (Son & Weaver, 2006); agenda-setting and civic awareness and involvement (Kiousis, McDevitt, & Wu, 2005; Weaver, 1994); Web influence on media agendas (Ku et al., 2003), second-level or attribute agenda-setting (Kiousis, 2005); and relationships between candidates, media, and public agendas (McCombs, Shaw, & Weaver, 1997; R. E. Miller & Wanta, 1996). Research exploring various media, campaigns, and sources offers mixed results on the power of agenda-setting; consequently, Reese's (1991) metaphor of a "revolving door" of mutual influence appears fitting.

Agenda-building research investigates source influences on the media agenda (see, e.g., Gandy, 1982). Investigation of newsroom sources during the Watergate scandal pioneered agenda-building research (G. E. Lang & Lang, 1981). Tedesco (2002) asserted that the 24-hour news cycle, convergent technologies that allow media transfer, and the speed of modern political campaigns have contributed to the likelihood that sources influence the media agenda. Individuals and organizations with information resources have the power to create information subsidies, such as advertisements, press releases, blogs, speeches, and Web sites, where information may be distributed in print and broadcast formats, and disseminated across a network of news media (Gandy, 1982; Turk, 1986, Turk & Franklin, 1987). Information subsidies from campaigns are shaped in multiple message forms, including political advertisements, direct mail, press conferences, speeches, press releases, and Web-page content.

News Media Framing

Debate continues in the scholarly community about whether attribute agenda-setting and framing are mutually exclusive conceptualizations of media interpretation and presentation of news (Golan & Wanta, 2001; McCombs & Ghanem, 2001; McCombs et al., 1997). However, framing research has a clear and distinct research tradition complete with broad approaches and definitions of framing (e.g., Edelman, 1993; Entman, 1993; Gamson & Modigliani, 1987; Gitlin, 1980; Iyengar, 1991). In fact, framing may be viewed as a news function (a predictor variable) and as a criterion variable in effects research (Price, Tewksbury, & Powers, 1997; Scheufele, 1999). Researchers have identified a wide range of dominant framing strategies, including episodic and thematic framing (Iyengar & Simon, 1993); issue-specific or generic frames of conflict, human interest, economy, morality, and responsibility (DeVreese, Peter, & Semetko, 2001; Semetko & Valkenburg, 2000); substantive and ambiguous framing (A. P. Williams et al., 2008); and macroframes of cynicism, metacommunication, and speculation (Constantinescu & Tedesco, 2007).

Social norms and values, interest group pressures, journalistic routines, political bias of journalists, and newsroom ownership constraints are among the significant influences that affect framing (Shoemaker & Reese, 1996). Researchers have addressed framing of political and health policies (Callaghan & Schnell, 2001; Hoffman & Slater, 2007), framing of media during elections (D'Angelo, Calderone, & Territola, 2005), framing and news discourse (Pan & Kosicki, 1993), and framing of politically oriented television dramas, such as *West Wing* (Holbert et al., 2005). Another emerging area of research focuses on media framing during reporting of war, with research about journalistic framing in the post-Cold War era (Norris, 1995), framing by the press during the Abu Ghraib scandal (Bennett, Lawrence, & Livingston, 2006), and framing of the war in Iraq (Dimitrova, Kaid, Williams, & Trammell, 2005).

New Technologies in Political Communication

The emergence of the Internet and its quick adoption and implementation by political campaigns, political advocacy and activist groups, and governmental and nongovernmental organizations offer researchers countless opportunities to study new applications of political communication content and effects. Selnow's (1998) prediction that the Internet would become as essential to political communication as traditional media appears realized only a decade removed from his forecast, as political candidates and groups now rely heavily on the Internet for functions such as fund-raising, voter mobilization, media relations, and voter information campaigns (e.g., consider the Obama presidential campaign). The Internet, thus, has emerged—and is expanding—as a primary source of political communication.

Scholarly attention to the Internet's role in political communication demonstrates a variety of established and developing research applications. Here, we address five research applications of the Internet in political communication settings: (1) the Internet and campaign communication content and effects, (2) e-Government initiatives, (3) political activism, (4) the public sphere, and (5) voter uses and gratifications (see also the essays in Chadwick & Howard, 2008; Lievrouw, this volume).

The Internet and Campaign Communication Content and Effects

Although the 1992 presidential campaign conducted by Bill Clinton pioneered application of the Internet for dissemination of speech text (Whillock, 1997), political candidates realized quickly the promotional possibilities of even a basic, glossy, e-brochure-style Web site. Consequently, by the 1996 election cycle, most major party candidates for national office had established a Web presence (Browning, 2002; D'Alessio, 1997; Davis, 1999; Tedesco, Miller, & Spiker, 1999). The Internet's emergence coincided with discussion of declining civic engagement, increasing political cynicism, and declining social capital (connections within and between social networks; e.g., Cappella & Jamieson, 1997; Kaid, McKinney, & Tedesco, 2000; Putnam, 1995). The Internet, however, had a polarizing effect on the research community. Some scholars were optimistic that the Internet could offer citizens new political uses and rewards (e.g., Budge, 1996; Rheingold, 2002), primarily because of the Internet's structural opportunities, such as inherent interactivity, generally low cost, freedom from boundaries, high speed, and lateral, horizontal, and nonhierarchical modes of communication, that could enhance democracy (Barber, Mattson, & Peterson, 1997; Sparks, 2001). Other scholars were skeptical of the Internet's ability to reinvigorate civic engagement because they said it would have little effect on politics or support, and that it would strengthen established political organizations (e.g., Bimber, 1998, 2000; Davis, 1999; Margolis, Resnick, & Tu, 1997).

Despite rapid adoption of the Internet by political candidates and campaigns, most researchers concluded that candidates and elected officials failed to utilize the Internet to its potential (e.g., Congress Online Project, 2002; D'Alessio, 2000; Foot & Schneider, 2002; Owen, Davis, & Strickler, 1999; Stromer-Galley, 2000). Much of the criticism was directed at the lack of interactivity, absence of lateral means of communication, and overwhelming reliance on self-promotional material apparent in the political use of the Internet. For instance, there is only slight evidence that candidates are engaging voters through interactive applications, with English and Tedesco's (2007) analysis of the 2006 U.S. Senate candidates' official blogs revealing that only 3 of the 67 major-party candidates allowed visitors to interact with the campaign by posting to their blogs, although the content of the posts suggests limited, if any, filtering by the campaigns. Stromer-Galley's (2000) argument that candidates avoid interactivity mostly due to dangers associated with loss of message control remains valid. Perhaps even the slight move toward interactive tools, such as an open-post blog, forecast the possibility that citizens will come to expect interactive opportunities with candidates and campaigns. Schneider and Foot's (2006) comparison of 2000 and 2004 campaign Web sites also suggested increases in connecting and mobilizing features. Foot and Schneider (2002) were critical of scholars who assert that online politics offers little more than a resemblance of off-line politics because those scholars overlook the enormous Web sphere of political campaign sites and their ability to shift information consumers to information producers via coproduction, transcend class and race boundaries, and persuasively mobilize people. Furthermore, candidates are including more hyperlinking as a form of interaction on their campaign Web sites and blogs (Trammell, Williams, Postelnicu, & Landreville, 2006). Such interactivity is important because political Web-site visitors view it favorably (Stromer-Galley & Foot, 2002).

A significant focus of new technology and political communication research concerns the effects of the Internet on civic engagement, political efficacy, and trust of politicians. Underlying much of that research is an assessment of whether the Internet promotes social capital. Although Putnam (2000) implicated television as the primary cause for a decline in social capital, other researchers have challenged Putnam's claims by freeing television (Norris, 1996, 2000) and the Internet (Norris, 2001) from blame. In fact, Shah, Kwak, and Holbert (2001) argued that information-seeking and information-exchanging users of the Internet are more engaged in their communities and more trusting of their fellow citizens. More recent experimental research on the interactive features of political Web sites demonstrates a strong relationship between interactivity and young adults' political efficacy and political information efficacy (Tedesco, 2006, 2007). In addition, Min's (2007) evaluation of online and face-to-face deliberation showed that both forms can increase political participation, political efficacy, and issue knowledge. Interesting results from the American National Election Survey also have revealed direct Internet effects on information acquisition but contingent effects on actual civic engagement and participation (Xenos & Moy, 2007). Similar research conducted by Xenos and Foot (2005), based on a sample of 200 races from the 2002 U.S. elections, challenged the "politics-as-usual" argument by demonstrating that third-party and challenger candidates are not significantly different in their employment of issue content, and that biographical, archived information on Web sites offers a significant alternative to dynamic media, such as paid political advertising and news stories.

The Internet and E-Government Initiatives

Much of the application of Internet research to e-Government initiatives essentially asks whether the Web can reform democracy in positive ways by encouraging greater public participation. Analysis of 270 municipal Web sites in California revealed that the vast majority did not contain participatory features and rarely included mechanisms to enhance deliberative opportunities (Musso, Weare, & Hale, 2000). Contrary to some fears that the Internet would "rob us of our political commons, and isolate us from each other" (Neuman, 2001, p. 203), findings from the experimental community of Netville— a cutting-edge, wired community in the Toronto suburbs, with homes provided access to the latest in high-speed Internet, desktop videophones, discussion forums, and other Web-based entertainment applications—revealed that computer-mediated communication actually strengthened community bonds and supported new relationships among community members (Hampton & Wellman, 2001). Specifically, Netville residents who made use of the technology, compared to those who did not, were better at sustaining established community ties and establishing new community networks. A subsequent analysis by Hampton (2007) of four Boston neighborhoods to test the generalizability of the results about Netville found that individuals with a predisposition for local interaction were more likely to use the Internet for local engagement, whereas residents without preexisting local network ties were less likely to adopt it for community engagement. Additional research exploring community-level social capital reveals a strong relationship between community members' length of Internet use and their social capital-building behavior. Social capital also serves as a predictor of effective computer-mediated communication for civic involvement (Kavanaugh & Patterson, 2001).

Stromer-Galley (2002) observed that the comfort and security of participating from private space (e.g., via the Internet) heighten the prospect of citizens' communication in the political process. In addition, online interactive features lead to increased opportunities for public engagement and deliberation (Coleman, 2004). More specifically, interactive structures online promote public deliberation, provide valuable feedback to political representatives, and engage citizens to participate in the transformation from transmission politics to dialogical, direct representation (Coleman, 2005). In fact, analysis of whether the Internet promotes different political activities and invites varied political users also is an important applied consideration for e-Government, with responses from more than 1,200 Americans showing that the Internet fosters different political activities than does offline political engagement (Jensen, Danziger, & Venkatesh, 2007). Although research regarding online and offline political engagement usually reports a correlation between these two forms of political activities, Jensen et al. (2007) reported that "online practices of community involvement are empirically distinguishable from offline practices" and that there were "notable differences in the predictors of online and offline political participation" (p. 47). More specifically, democratization of the political process online—or a broader public sphere—decreased the strength of traditional socioeconomic status variables (e.g., income, age, and length of residence) as predictors of political engagement online.

The Internet and Political Activism

Explorations into the Internet's role in the mobilization and effectiveness of activism generally conclude that the Internet provides activist groups with critical tools to collect and mobilize around social issues (Bennett 2003; Dartnell, 2006; Herman & Ettema, 2007; Mann, 1995; Rheingold, 2002; Van Aelst & Walgrave, 2004; see also Lievrouw, this volume). Mann (1995) was among the first to recognize that social activists were developing coalitions and networks through Internet user groups. Scammell (2000) noted the likely transformation to an age of a "citizen–consumer" who wields power through politically conscious choices based on platforms ranging from the environment to fair trade and from animal rights to human rights. Although evidence of the Internet "changing everything" is not apparent in politics—at least not yet—Scammell asserted that the Internet greatly transforms activist politics. In addition, a formal content analysis of activist organizations' Web sites revealed evidence of the Internet's facilitation of a transnational activist network (Van Aelst & Walgrave, 2004). Bennett's (2003) exploration of activist networks, particularly those labeled as "resource poor" in comparison to conventional political party organizations, showed that communication patterns among these networked groups are shifting the political game. Through case study analyses of political strategies applied by activist hubs, such as NetAction and Global Exchange, Bennett demonstrated that activist groups are using the Internet successfully to sustain campaigns; create broad, accessible, and transportable communication networks; control their identity and transform it based on issue demand; and create information subsidies that influence traditional media agendas. Media convergence and software developments allow activists to enter hyperlinked communication networks in a variety of ways, which Bennett argued enables the shift from information consumers to information producers of news, thus providing tools to influence traditional media agendas. Bennett cautioned, however, that the very features that enable activist groups in the networked environment—control, decision making, and collective identity—also threaten those groups that cannot manage control across network hubs.

The Internet and the Public Sphere

Perhaps one of the most vibrant areas of applied political communication research and new technologies focuses on whether the Internet is fostering an online public sphere (Bennett & Entman, 2001; Dahlberg, 2001, 2007; Streck, 1998). Such research generally explores whether the Internet enhances deliberative democracy, invites broader participation from people disengaged from the political process, and promotes rational political decision making. There are mixed reviews on the Internet's ability to promote a more representative public sphere, with some scholars arguing that the Internet will reinforce politics as usual (Davis, 1999; Margolis & Resnick, 2000), but the research on activism presented previously demonstrates that the Internet is engaging marginalized groups and enabling them to create and sustain communication networks. In addition, Dahlgren (2005) suggested that the public sphere includes participatory opportunities beyond the activist domain, including e-Government initiatives, civic forums, and journalistic feedback domains and blogs. Case study analysis from Hamburg, Germany indicates that the Internet has the ability to strengthen democratic practices; in fact, Albrecht (2006) found that online deliberation was close to the rational–critical model expressed in deliberative theories.

Future Applied Political Communication Research

Future research in applied political communication faces many challenges. One important direction is the renewed interest in the role of interpersonal communication. Although Katz and Lazarsfeld (1955) identified an early role for interpersonal communication in politics, subsequent research has focused more often on the influence of the media. Recently, however, there has been a resurgence of interest in the importance of interpersonal communication—particularly political discussion—in political knowledge and participation. Research has confirmed that political knowledge and participation can be traced directly to the amount and frequency of political discussion in which individuals engage (Eveland & Thompson, 2006; Kwak, Williams, Wang, & Lee, 2005; McClung, 2006). In a study that involved direct intervention through use of interpersonal communication in schools, McDevitt and Chaffee (2000) showed that introducing children in low-income households to political information can positively affect their political socialization and activate their parents' interest and participation in politics, thereby reducing the knowledge gap through personal discussions. However, enhanced knowledge levels only occur when political discussions take place among those with similar viewpoints; discussion with third parties who disagree does not lead to greater knowledge about political issues (Feldman & Price, 2008). Feldman and Price (2008) also found relationships and interactions between interpersonal discussions, disagreement, and debate viewing, suggesting more complex interactions among interpersonal and media information sources as antecedents of political knowledge and learning. Future applied political communication research must address these interactions more fully.

Another important direction for future research is the increasingly important role played by alternative media in the formation of people's political knowledge and attitudes. Young citizens, in particular, no longer get their information about politics from traditional news exposure but, instead, increasingly turn to alternative formats, including entertainment venues, such as *The Daily Show*, *Colbert Report*, *Saturday Night Live*, and YouTube; social networking sites, such as Facebook and MySpace; and virtual environments, such as Second Life. Researchers have begun to investigate the effects of some of these alternative sources (e.g., Holbert, Lambe, Dudo, & Carlton, 2007; Sweetser & Kaid, 2008), but much more needs to be done to understand the motivations and political participation patterns of young citizens.

Young citizens also seem less interested and involved in politics than their older peers, and they exhibit lower levels of political information efficacy, meaning that they do not have much confidence in their knowledge about politics, which leads them to be less likely to vote and participate in politics (Kaid, McKinney, & Tedesco, 2007). Promising new research (Kenski & Stroud, 2006) suggests that Internet use is positively related to enhanced levels of internal and external political efficacy. Future research needs to search out ways to use new communication technologies and venues to engage the youngest citizens in politics.

The 2008 presidential campaign also has raised the salience of several other important factors in political communication. Future research undoubtedly will place more importance on the study of race (see Nicotera, Clinkscales, Dorsey, & Niles, this volume), gender (see Buzzanell, Meisenbach, Remke, Sterk, & Turner, this volume), and even age (see Nussbaum & Ohs, this volume) as factors in the formation of political opinions and behaviors.

Space constraints also limited the ability to cover adequately the robust and growing applications of political communication in international contexts. The expansion of the global economy and the importance of the government in citizens' lives will make these applications of communication even more important in the future (see Parrish-Sprowl, this volume).

Conclusion

The scholarship reviewed in this chapter represents only a portion of the many venues and contexts in which political communication researchers have applied theory and research to understand and manage ongoing, real-world political problems, issues, and situations. The research areas we considered (political speaking, political debating, political advertising, political news, and political uses of new technologies) showcase the centrality of political campaign communication within the political communication field, making it important to remember that applied political communication encompasses an even wider net of communicative practices and interactions between political actors and citizens in democratic systems. Furthermore, although we focused on political processes in the

United States, the study of political communication and its application throughout the world is an expanding field. Hence, if democracy is to survive and flourish, political communication scholars must continue to explore and apply their knowledge in ways that make an important difference.

References

Albrecht, S. (2006). Whose voice is heard in online deliberation? A study of participation and representation in political debates on the Internet. *Information, Communication & Society, 9*, 62–82.

Alterman, E. (2004). *What liberal media? The truth about bias in the news.* New York: Basic Books.

Andreoli, V., & Worchel, S. (1978). Effects of media, communicator, and message position on attitude change. *Public Opinion Quarterly, 42*, 59–70.

Atkin, C. K., Bowen, L., Nayman, O. B., & Sheinkopf, K. G. (1973). Quality versus quantity in televised political ads. *Public Opinion Quarterly, 37*, 209–224.

Banwart, M. C., & McKinney, M. S. (2005). A gendered influence in campaign debates? Analysis of mixed-gender United States Senate and gubernatorial debates. *Communication Studies, 56*, 353–373.

Barber, B. R., Mattson, K., & Peterson, J. (1997). *The state of "electronically enhanced democracy:" A survey of the Internet.* New Brunswick, NJ: Walt Whitman Center for the Culture and Politics of Democracy.

Basil, M., Schooler, C., & Reeves, B. (1991). Positive and negative political advertising: Effectiveness of ads and perceptions of candidates. In F. Biocca (Ed.), *Television and political advertising: Vol. 1. Psychological processes* (pp. 245–262). Hillsdale, NJ: Erlbaum.

Beiler, D. (2000). The body politic registers a protest. In M. A. Bailey, R. A. Faucheux, P. S. Herrnson, & C. Wilcox (Eds.), *Campaigns & elections: Contemporary case studies* (pp. 121–136). Washington, DC: CQ Press.

Bennett, W. L. (2003). Communicating global activism: Strengths and vulnerabilities of networked politics. *Information, Communication & Society, 6*, 143–168.

Bennett, W. L., & Entman, R. M. (2001). Mediated politics: An introduction. In W. L. Bennett & R. M. Entman (Eds.), *Mediated politics: Communication in the future of democracy* (pp. 1–32). New York: Cambridge University Press.

Bennett, W. L., Lawrence, R. G., & Livingston, S. (2006). None dare call it torture: Indexing and the limits of press independence in the Abu Ghraib scandal. *Journal of Communication, 56*, 467–485.

Benoit, W. L. (1999). *Seeing spots: A functional analysis of presidential television advertisements, 1952–1996.* New York: Praeger.

Benoit, W. L., & Hansen, G. J. (2004). The changing media environment of presidential campaigns. *Communication Research Reports, 21*, 164–173.

Benoit, W. L., & Wells, W. T. (1996). *Candidates in conflict: Persuasive attack and defense in the 1992 presidential debates.* Tuscaloosa: University of Alabama Press.

Beom, K., Carlin, D. B., & Silver, M. D. (2005). The world was watching—And talking: International perspectives on the 2004 presidential debates. *American Behavioral Scientist, 49*, 243–264.

Bimber, B. (1998). The Internet and political transformation: Populism, community, and accelerated pluralism. *Polity, 31*, 133–160.

Bimber, B. (2000). The study of information technology and civic engagement. *Political Communication, 17*, 329–333.

Bowen, L. (1994). Time of voting decision and use of political advertising: The Slade Gorton–Brock Adams senatorial campaign. *Journalism Quarterly, 71*, 665–675.

Brians, C. L., & Wattenberg, M. P. (1996). Campaign issue knowledge and salience: Comparing reception from TV commercials, TV news, and newspapers. *American Journal of Political Science, 40*, 172–193.

Browning, G. (2002). *Electronic democracy: Using the Internet to transform American politics* (2nd ed.). Medford, NJ: CyberAge Books.

Budge, I. (1996). *The new challenge of direct democracy.* Cambridge, MA: Polity Press.

Bystrom, D., Banwart, M., Kaid, L. L., & Robertson, T. (2004). *Gender and candidate communication: VideoStyle, WebStyle, and newsStyle.* New York: Routledge.

Callaghan, K., & Schnell, F. (2001). Assessing the democratic debate: How the news media frame elite policy discourse. *Political Communication, 18,* 183–213.

Cappella, J. N., & Jamieson, K. K. (1997). *The spiral of cynicism: The press and the public good.* New York: Oxford University Press.

Carlin, D. B. (2005). DebateWatch: Creating a public sphere for the unheard voices. In M. S. McKinney, L. L. Kaid, D. G. Bystrom, & D. B. Carlin (Eds.), *Communicating politics: Engaging the public in democratic life* (pp. 223–234). New York: Peter Lang.

Carlin, D. B., & Anderson, K. (2003). Across the ages: Views of the 2000 debates from college freshmen to senior citizens. In L. L. Kaid, J. C. Tedesco, D. G. Bystrom, & M. S. McKinney (Eds.), *The Millennium election: Communication in the 2000 campaigns* (pp. 229–242). Lanham, MD: Rowman & Littlefield.

Carlin, D. P., Howard, C., Stanfield, S., & Reynolds, L. (1991). The effects of presidential debate formats on clash: A comparative analysis. *Argumentation and Advocacy, 27,* 126–136.

Carlin, D. P., Morris, E., & Smith, S. (2001). The influence of format and questions on candidates' argument choices in the 2000 presidential debates. *American Behavioral Scientist, 44,* 2196–2218.

Chadwick, A., & Howard, P. N. (Eds.). (2008). *Routledge handbook of Internet politics.* New York: Routledge.

Chaffee, S. H. (1975). Foreword: Asking new questions about communication and politics. In S. H. Chaffee (Ed.), *Political communication: Issues and strategies for research* (pp. 13–20). Beverly Hills, CA: Sage.

Chaffee, S. H., & Dennis, J. (1979). Presidential debates: An empirical assessment. In A. Ranney (Ed.), *The past and future of presidential debates* (pp. 75–106). Washington, DC: American Enterprise Institute for Public Policy Research.

Chang, C. (2001). The impacts of emotion elicited by print political advertising on candidate evaluation. *Media Psychology, 3,* 91–118.

Cohen, A. (1976). Radio vs. TV: The effects of the medium. *Journal of Communication, 26*(2), 29–35.

Coleman, S. (2004). Connecting Parliament to the public via the Internet: Two case studies of online consultations. *Information, Communication & Society, 7,* 1–22.

Coleman, S. (2005). The lonely citizen: Indirect representation in an age of networks. *Political Communication, 22,* 197–214.

Congress Online Project. (2002). *Assessing and improving Capitol Hill Web sites.* Washington, DC: Author. Retrieved March 30, 2008, from http://www.cmfweb.org/storage/cmfweb/documents/CMF_Pubs/congressonline2002.pdf

Constantinescu, A., & Tedesco, J. C. (2007). Framing a kidnapping: Frame convergence between online newspaper coverage and reader discussion posts about three kidnapped Romanian journalists. *Journalism Studies, 8,* 444–464.

Dahlberg, L. (2001). The Internet and democratic discourse: Exploring the prospects of online deliberative focus extending the public sphere. *Information, Communication & Society, 4,* 615–633.

Dahlberg, L. (2007). The Internet, deliberative democracy, and power: Radicalizing the public sphere. *International Journal of Media and Cultural Politics, 3,* 47–64.

Dahlgren, P. (2005). The Internet, public spheres, and political communication: Dispersion and deliberation. *Political Communication, 22,* 147–162.

D'Allesio, D. (1997). Use of the World Wide Web in the 1996 US election. *Electoral Studies, 16,* 489–500.

D'Alessio, D. (2000). Adoption of the World Wide Web by American political candidates, 1996–1998. *Journal of Broadcasting & Electronic Media, 44,* 556–568.

D'Angelo, P., Calderone, M., & Territola, A. (2005). Strategy and issue framing: An exploratory analysis of topics and frames in campaign 2004 print news. *Atlantic Journal of Communication, 13*, 199–219.

Dartnell, M. Y. (2006). *Insurgency online: Web activism and global conflict.* Toronto, Canada: University of Toronto Press.

Davis, R. (1999). *The web of politics: The Internet's impact on the American political system.* New York: Oxford University Press.

Dearing, J. W., & Rogers, E. M. (1996). *Communication concepts: Vol. 6. Agenda-setting.* Thousand Oaks, CA: Sage.

Delli Carpini, M. X., & Williams, B. A. (2001). Let us infotain you: Politics in the new media environment. In W. L. Bennett & R. M. Entman (Eds.), *Mediated politics: Communication in the future of democracy* (pp. 160–181). New York: Cambridge University Press.

De Vreese, C. H., Peter, J., & Semetko, H. A. (2001). Framing politics at the launch of the Euro: A cross-national comparative study of frames in the news. *Political Communication, 18*, 107–122.

Dimitrova, D. V., Kaid, L. L., Williams, A. P., & Trammell, K. D. (2005). War on the Web: The immediate news framing of Gulf War II. *Harvard International Journal of Press/Politics, 10*(1), 22–44.

Domke, D., Watts, M. D., Shah, D. V., & Fan, D. P. (1999). The politics of conservative elites and the "liberal media" argument. *Journal of Communication, 49*(4), 35–58.

Edelman, M. J. (1993). Contestable categories and public opinion. *Political Communication, 10*, 231–242.

Edelsky, C., & Adams, K. (1990). Creating inequality: Breaking the rules in debates. *Journal of Language and Social Psychology, 9*, 171–190.

Eisinger, R. M., Veenstra, L. R., & Koehn, J. P. (2007). What media bias? Conservative and liberal labeling in major U.S. newspapers. *Harvard International Journal of Press/Politics, 12*(1), 17–36.

English, K., & Tedesco, J. C. (2007). 2006 U.S. Senate candidate blogs: An analysis of dialogical opportunities. In M. G. Adams & A. F. Alkhafaji (Eds.), *Business research yearbook* (Vol. 14, pp. 182–188). Beltsville, MD: International Graphics.

Entman, R. M. (1993). Framing: Toward clarification of a fractured paradigm. *Journal of Communication, 43*(4), 51–58.

Eveland, W. P., Jr., & Thomson, T. (2006). Is it talking, thinking, or both? A lagged dependent variable model of discussion effects on political knowledge. *Journal of Communication, 56*, 523–542.

Farnsworth, S. J., & Lichter, S. R. (2008). Trends in network television news coverage of U.S. elections. In J. Strömbäck & L. L. Kaid (Eds.), *The handbook of election news coverage around the world* (pp. 41–57). New York: Routledge.

Feldman, L., & Price, V. (2008). Confusion or enlightenment? How exposure to disagreement moderates the effects of political discussion and media use on candidate knowledge. *Communication Research, 35*, 61–87.

Foot, K. A., & Schneider, S. M. (2002). Online action in campaign 2000: An exploratory analysis of the U.S. political Web sphere. *Journal of Broadcasting & Electronic Media, 46*, 222–244.

Franz, M. M., Freedman, P. F., Goldstein, K. M., & Ridout, T. M. (2008). *Campaign advertising and American democracy.* Philadelphia: Temple University Press.

Fridkin, K. L., & Kenney, P. J. (2004). Do negative messages work? The impact of negativity on citizens' evaluations of candidates. *American Politics Research, 32*, 570–605.

Gamson, W. A., & Modigliani, A. (1987). The changing culture of affirmative action. In R. A. Braumgart (Ed.), *Research in political sociology* (Vol. 3, pp. 137–178). Greenwich, CT: JAI Press.

Gandy, O. H., Jr. (1982). *Beyond agenda setting: Information subsidies and public policy.* Norwood, NJ: Ablex.

Garramone, G. M. (1984). Voter responses to negative political ads. *Journalism Quarterly, 61*, 250–259.

Garramone, G. M. (1985). Effects of negative political advertising: The roles of sponsor and rebuttal. *Journal of Broadcasting & Electronic Media, 29,* 147–159.

Garramone, G. M., & Smith, S. J. (1984). Reactions to political advertising: Clarifying sponsor effects. *Journalism Quarterly, 61,* 771–775.

Gitlin, T. (1980). *The whole world is watching: Mass media in the making and unmaking of the new left.* Berkeley: University of California Press.

Golan, G. J., Kiousis, S. K., & McDaniel, M. L. (2007). Second-level agenda setting and political advertising. *Journalism Studies, 8,* 432–443.

Golan, G. J., & Wanta, W. (2001). Second-level agenda setting in the New Hampshire primary: A comparison of coverage in three newspapers and public perceptions of candidates. *Journalism & Mass Communication Quarterly, 78,* 247–259.

Goldstein, K., & Freedman, P. (2000). New evidence for new arguments: Money and advertising in the 1996 Senate elections. *Journal of Politics, 62,* 1087–1108.

Groenedyk, E. W., & Valentino, N. A. (2002). Of dark clouds and silver linings: Effects of exposure to issue versus candidate advertising on persuasion, information retention, and issue salience. *Communication Research, 29,* 295–319.

Haigh, M. H., Pfau, M., Danesi, J., Tallmon, R., Bunko, T., Nyberg, S., et al. (2006). A comparison of embedded and nonembedded print coverage of the U.S. invasion and occupation of Iraq. *Harvard International Journal of Press/Politics, 11*(2), 139–153.

Hallin, D. C. (1992). Sound bite news: Television coverage of elections, 1968–1988. *Journal of Communication, 42*(2), 5–24.

Hampton, K. (2007). Neighborhoods in the network society: The e-neighbors study. *Information, Communication & Society, 10,* 714–748.

Hampton, K., & Wellman, B. (2001). Long distance community in the network society: Contact and support beyond Netville. *American Behavioral Scientist, 45,* 476–495.

Hart, R. P. (1984). *Verbal style and the presidency: A computer-based analysis.* Orlando, FL: Academic Press.

Hart, R. P. (1987). *The sound of leadership: Presidential communication in the modern age.* Chicago: University of Chicago Press.

Herman, A. P., & Ettema, J. S. (2007). A community confronts the digital divide: A case study of social capital formation through communication activism. In L. R. Frey & K. M. Carragee (Eds.), *Communication activism: Vol. 2. Media and performance activism* (pp. 255–281). Cresskill, NJ: Hampton Press.

Hoffman, D. R., & Howard, A. D. (2006). *Addressing the state of the union: The evolution and impact of the president's big speech.* Boulder, CO: Lynne Rienner.

Hoffman, L. H., & Slater, M. D. (2007). Evaluating public discourse in newspaper opinion articles: Values-framing and integrative complexity in substance and health policy issues. *Journalism & Mass Communication Quarterly, 84,* 58–74.

Holbert, R. L., Benoit, W. L., Hansen, G. J., & Wen, W.-C. (2002). The role of communication in the formation of an issue-based citizenry. *Communication Monographs, 69,* 296–310.

Holbert, R. L., Lambe, J. L., Dudo, A. D., & Carlton, K. A. (2007). Primacy effects of *The Daily Show* and national TV news viewing: Young viewers, political gratifications, and internal political self-efficacy. *Journal of Broadcasting & Electronic Media, 51,* 20–38.

Holbert, R. L., Tschida, D., Dixon, M., Cherry, K., Steuber, K., & Airne, D. (2005). The *West Wing* and depictions of the American presidency: Expanding the domains of framing in political communication. *Communication Quarterly, 53,* 505–522.

Iyengar, S. (1991). *Is anyone responsible? How television frames political issues.* Chicago: University of Chicago Press.

Iyengar, S., & Simon, A. (1993). News coverage of the Gulf crisis and public opinion: A study of agenda-setting, priming, and framing. *Communication Research, 20,* 365–383.

Jamieson, K. H. (1988). *Eloquence in an electronic age: The transformation of political speechmaking.* New York: Oxford University Press.

Jamieson, K. H. (1996). *Packaging the presidency: A history and criticism of presidential campaign advertising* (3rd ed.). New York: Oxford University Press.

Jasperson, A. E., & Fan, D. P. (2002). An aggregate examination of the backlash effect in political advertising: The case of the 1996 U.S. Senate race in Minnesota. *Journal of Advertising, 31*(1), 1–12.

Jensen, M. J., Danziger, J. N., & Venkatesh, A. (2007). Civil society and cyber society: The role of the Internet in community associations and democratic politics. *Information Society, 23,* 39–50.

Johnson-Cartee, K. S., & Copeland, G. A. (1989). Southern voters' reaction to negative political ads in 1986 election. *Journalism Quarterly, 66,* 888–893, 986.

Just, M., Crigler, A., & Wallach, L. (1990). Thirty seconds or thirty minutes: What viewers learn from spot advertisements and candidate debates. *Journal of Communication, 40*(3), 120–133.

Kahn, K. F. (1996). *The political consequences of being a woman: How stereotypes influence the conduct and consequences of political campaigns.* New York: Columbia University Press.

Kahn, K. F., & Geer, J. G. (1994). Creating impressions: An experimental investigation of political advertising on television. *Political Behavior, 16,* 93–116.

Kahn, K. F., & Kenney, P. J. (2000). How negative campaign enhances knowledge of Senate elections. In J. A. Thurber, C. J. Nelson, & D. A. Dullo (Eds.), *Crowded airwaves: Campaign advertising in elections* (pp. 65–95). Washington, DC: Brookings Institution Press.

Kaid, L. L. (1982). Paid television advertising and candidate name identification. *Campaigns and Elections, 3,* 34–36.

Kaid, L. L. (1991). The effects of television broadcasts on perceptions of political candidates in the United States and France. In L. L. Kaid, J. Gerstlé, & K. R. Sanders (Eds.), *Mediated politics in two cultures: Presidential campaigning in the United States and France* (pp. 247–260). New York: Praeger.

Kaid, L. L. (1994). Political advertising in the 1992 campaign. In R. E. Denton, Jr. (Ed.), *The 1992 presidential campaign: A communication perspective* (pp. 111–127). Westport, CT: Praeger.

Kaid, L. L. (1997). Effects of the television spots on images of Dole and Clinton. *American Behavioral Scientist, 40,* 1085–1094.

Kaid, L. L. (1998). Videostyle and the effects of the 1996 presidential campaign advertising. In R. E. Denton, Jr. (Ed.), *The 1996 presidential campaign: A communication perspective* (pp. 143–159). Westport, CT: Praeger.

Kaid, L. L. (2001). TechnoDistortions and effects of the 2000 political advertising. *American Behavioral Scientist, 44,* 2370–2378.

Kaid, L. L. (2002). Political advertising and information seeking: Comparing the exposure via traditional and Internet media channels. *Journal of Advertising, 31*(1), 27–35.

Kaid, L. L. (2003). Effects of political information in the 2000 presidential campaign: Comparing traditional television and Internet exposure. *American Behavioral Scientist, 46,* 677–691.

Kaid, L. L. (2004). Political advertising. In L. L. Kaid (Ed.), *Handbook of political communication research* (pp. 155–202). Mahwah, NJ: Erlbaum.

Kaid, L. L. (2006). Political advertising in the United States. In L. L. Kaid & C. Holtz-Bacha (Eds.), *The Sage handbook of political advertising* (pp. 37–61). Thousand Oaks, CA: Sage.

Kaid, L. L., & Boydston, J. (1987). An experimental study of the effectiveness of negative political advertisements. *Communication Quarterly, 35,* 193–201.

Kaid, L. L., & Chanslor, M. (2004). The effects of political advertising on candidate images. In K. L. Hacker (Ed.), *Presidential candidate images* (pp. 133–150). Lanham, MD: Rowman & Littlefield.

Kaid, L. L., Chanslor, M., & Hovind, M. (1992). The influence of program and commercial type on political advertising effectiveness. *Journal of Broadcasting & Electronic Media, 36,* 303–320.

Kaid, L. L., Fernandes, F., Shen, F., Yun, H., Kim, Y., & LeGrange, A. G. (2008). *Effects of message content and sponsorship on political advertising.* Unpublished manuscript, University of Florida, Gainesville.

Kaid, L. L., & Holtz-Bacha, C. (Eds.). (2006). *The Sage handbook of political advertising.* Thousand Oaks, CA: Sage.

Kaid, L. L., & Johnston, A. (2001). *Videostyle in presidential campaigns: Style and content of televised political advertising.* Westport, CT: Praeger.

Kaid, L. L., Leland, C. M., & Whitney, S. (1992). The impact of televised political ads: Evoking viewer responses in the 1988 presidential campaign. *Southern Communication Journal, 57,* 285–295.

Kaid, L. L., McKinney, M. S., & Tedesco, J. C. (2000). *Civic dialogue in the 1996 presidential campaign: Candidate, media, and public voices.* Cresskill, NJ: Hampton Press.

Kaid, L. L., McKinney, M. S., & Tedesco, J. C. (2007). Political information efficacy theory and younger voters. *American Behavioral Scientist, 50,* 1093–1111.

Kaid, L. L., McKinney, M. S., Tedesco, J. C., & Gaddie, K. (1999). Journalistic responsibility and political advertising: A content analysis of coverage by state and local media. *Communication Studies, 50,* 279–293.

Kaid, L. L., Myrick, M., Chanslor, M., Roper, C., Hoviland, M., & Trivoulidis, N. (1994). CNN's Americanization of the Gulf War: An analysis of media, technology, and storytelling. In T. A. McCain & L. Shyles (Eds.), *The 1,000 hour war: Communication in the Gulf* (pp. 147–160). Westport, CT: Greenwood Press.

Kaid, L. L., & Postelnicu, M. (2005). Political advertising in the 2004 election: Comparison of traditional television and Internet messages. *American Behavioral Scientist, 49,* 265–278.

Kaid, L. L., & Sanders, K. R. (1978). Political television commercials: An experimental study of the type and length. *Communication Research, 5,* 57–70.

Kaid, L. L., & Strömbäck, J. (2008). Election news coverage around the world: A comparative perspective. In J. Strömbäck & L. L. Kaid (Eds.), *The handbook of election news coverage around the world* (pp. 419–429). New York: Routledge.

Kaid, L. L., Tedesco, J., & Spiker, J. A. (1996). Media conflicts over Clinton policies: Political advertising and the battle for public opinion. In R. E. Denton, Jr. & R. L. Holloway (Eds.), *The Clinton presidency: Images, issues, and communication strategies* (pp. 103–121). Westport, CT: Praeger.

Katz, E., & Lazarsfeld, P. F. (1955). *Personal influence: The part played by people in the flow of mass communications.* Glencoe, IL: Free Press.

Kavanaugh, A. L., & Patterson, S. J. (2001). The impact of community computer networks on social capital and community involvement. *American Behavioral Scientist, 45,* 496–509.

Kenski, K., & Stroud, N. J. (2006). Connections between Internet use and political efficacy, knowledge, and participation. *Journal of Broadcasting & Electronic Media, 50,* 173–192.

Kiousis, S. (2005). Compelling arguments and attitude strength: Exploring the impact of second-level agenda setting on public opinion of presidential candidate images. *Harvard International Journal of Press/Politics, 10*(2), 3–27.

Kiousis, S., McDevitt, M., & Wu, X. (2005). The genesis of civic awareness: Agenda setting in political socialization. *Journal of Communication, 55,* 756–774.

Ku, G., Kaid, L. L., & Pfau, M. (2003). The impact of Web site campaigning on traditional news media and public information processing. *Journalism & Mass Communication Quarterly, 80,* 528–547.

Kwak, N., Williams, A. E., Wang, X., & Lee, H. (2005). Talking politics and engaging politics: An examination of the interactive relationships between structural features of political talk and discussion engagement. *Communication Research, 32,* 87–111.

Lang, A. (1991). Emotion, formal features, and memory for televised political advertisements. In F. Biocca (Ed.), *Television and political advertising: Vol. 1. Political processes* (pp. 221–243). Hillsdale, NJ: Erlbaum.

Lang, G. E., & Lang, K. (1981). Watergate: An exploration of the agenda-building process. In G. C. Wilhoit & H. DeBock (Eds.), *Mass communication review yearbook* (Vol. 2, pp. 447–468). Beverly Hills, CA: Sage.

Lewin, K. (1947). Frontiers in group dynamics: II. Channels of group life; social planning and action research. *Human Relations, 1,* 143–153.

Lichtenstein, A. (1982). Differences in impact between local and national televised political candidates' debates. *Western Journal of Speech Communication, 46,* 291–298.

Lichter, S. R., Noyes, R. E., & Kaid, L. L. (1999). No news or negative news: How the networks nixed the '96 campaign. In L. L. Kaid & D. G. Bystrom (Eds.), *The electronic election: Perspectives on the 1996 campaign communication* (pp. 3–13). Mahwah, NJ: Erlbaum.

Lopez-Escobar, E., Llamas, J. P., McCombs, M., & Lennon, F. R. (1998). Two levels of agenda setting among advertising and news in the 1995 Spanish elections. *Political Communication, 15,* 225–238.

Lowry, D. T., Bridges, J. A., & Barefield, P. A. (1990). The effects of network TV "instant analysis and querulous criticism": Following the first Bush–Dukakis debate. *Journalism Quarterly, 67,* 814–825.

Mann, B. (1995). *Politics on the Net.* Indianapolis, IN: Que.

Margolis, M., & Resnick, D. (2000). *Politics as usual: The cyberspace "revolution."* Thousand Oaks, CA: Sage.

Margolis, M., Resnick, D., & Tu, C.-C. (1997). Campaigning on the Internet: Parties and candidates on the World Wide Web in the 1996 primary season. *Harvard International Journal of Press/Politics, 2*(1), 59–78.

Martel, M. (1983). *Political campaign debates: Images, strategies, and tactics.* New York: Longman.

McClung, S. D. (2006). The electoral relevance of political talk: Examining disagreement and expertise effects in social networks on political participation. *American Journal of Political Science, 50,* 737–754.

McCombs, M. E. (2004, November). *The evolution of agenda-setting theory.* Paper presented at the meeting of the National Communication Association, Chicago, IL.

McCombs, M., & Ghanem, S. I. (2001). Agenda setting and framing. In S. D. Reese, O. H. Gandy, Jr., & A. E. Grant (Eds.), *Framing public life: Perspectives on media and our understanding of the social world* (pp. 67–81). Mahwah, NJ: Erlbaum.

McCombs, M. E., & Shaw, D. L. (1972). The agenda-setting function of the mass media. *Public Opinion Quarterly, 36,* 176–187.

McCombs, M. E., Shaw, D. L., & Weaver, D. (1997). *Communication and democracy: Exploring the intellectual frontiers in agenda-setting theory.* Mahwah, NJ: Erlbaum.

McDevitt, M., & Chafee, S. (2000). Closing gaps in political communication and knowledge: Effects of a school intervention. *Communication Research, 27,* 259–292.

McKinney, M. S. (2007). Presidential debates. In T. M. Schaefer & T. A. Birkland (Eds.), *Encyclopedia of media and politics* (pp. 898–892). Washington, DC: CQ Press.

McKinney, M. S., & Carlin, D. B. (2004). Political campaign debates. In L. L. Kaid (Ed.), *Handbook of political communication research* (pp. 203–234). Mahwah, NJ: Erlbaum.

McKinney, M. S., & Chattopadhyay, S. (2007). Political engagement through debates: Young citizens' reactions to the 2004 presidential debates. *American Behavioral Scientist, 50,* 1169–1182.

McKinney, M. S., Dudash, E. A., & Hodgkinson, G. (2003). Viewer reactions to the 2000 presidential debates: Learning issue and image information. In L. L. Kaid, J. C. Tedesco, D. G. Bystrom, & M. M. McKinney (Eds.), *The millennium election: Communication in the 2000 campaign* (pp. 43–58). Lanham, MD: Rowman & Littlefield.

McKinney, M. S., & Lamoureux, E. R. (1999). Citizen response to the 1996 presidential debates: Focusing on the focus groups. In L. L. Kaid & D. G. Bystrom (Eds.), *The electronic election: Perspectives on the 1996 campaign communication* (pp. 163–177). Mahwah, NJ: Erlbaum.

McKinnon, L. M., & Kaid, L. L. (1999). Exposing negative campaigning or enhancing advertising effects: An experimental study of adwatch effects on voter evaluations of candidates and their ads. *Journal of Applied Communication Research, 27,* 217–236.

McKinnon, L. M., & Tedesco, J. C. (1999). The influence of medium and media commentary on presidential debate effects. In L. L. Kaid & D. G. Bystrom (Eds.), *The electronic election: Perspectives on the 1996 campaign communication* (pp. 191–206). Mahwah, NJ: Erlbaum.

McKinnon, L. M., Tedesco, J. C., & Kaid, L. L. (1993). The third 1992 presidential debate: Channel and commentary effects. *Argumentation and Advocacy, 30,* 106–118.

Meirick, P. (2002). Cognitive responses to negative and comparative political advertising. *Journal of Advertising, 31*(1), 49–62.

Merritt, S. (1984). Negative political advertising: Some empirical findings. *Journal of Advertising, 13*(3), 27–38.

Miller, R. E., & Wanta, W. (1996). Sources of the public agenda: The president–press–public relationship. *International Journal of Public Opinion Research, 8,* 390–402.

Min, S.-J. (2007). Online vs. face-to-face deliberation: Effects on civic engagement. *Journal of Computer-Mediated Communication, 12*(4), Article 11. Retrieved March 22, 2008, from http://jcmc.indiana.edu/vol12/issue4/min.html

Musso, J., Weare, C., & Hale, M. (2000). Designing Web technologies for local governance reform: Good management or good democracy? *Political Communication, 17,* 1–19.

Neuman, W. R. (2001). The impact of new media. In W. L. Bennett & R. M. Entman (Eds.), *Mediated politics: Communication in the future of democracy* (pp. 299–320). New York: Cambridge University Press.

Newall, P. (2005). *Rhetoric.* Retrieved November 23, 2007, from http://www.galilean-library.org/int21.html

Niven, D. (2002). *Tilt? The search for media bias.* Westport, CT: Praeger.

Norris, P. (1995). The restless searchlight: Network news framing of the post-Cold War world. *Political Communication, 12,* 357–370.

Norris, P. (1996). Does television erode social capital? A reply to Putnam. *PS: Political Science & Politics, 29,* 474–480.

Norris, P. (2000). *A virtuous circle: Political communications in postindustrial societies.* New York: Cambridge University Press.

Norris, P. (2001). *Digital divide: Civic engagement, information poverty, and the Internet worldwide.* New York: Cambridge University Press.

Owen, D., Davis, R., & Strickler, V. J. (1999). Congress and the Internet. *Harvard International Journal of Press/Politics, 4*(2), 10–29.

Pan, Z., & Kosicki, G. M. (1993). Framing analysis: An approach to new discourse. *Political Communication, 10,* 55–75.

Patterson, T. E., & McClure, R. D. (1976). *The unseeing eye: The myth of television power in politics.* New York: Putnam.

Pfau, M. (1983). Criteria and format to optimize political debates: An analysis of South Dakota's "Election '80" series. *Journal of the American Forensic Association, 19,* 205–214.

Pfau, M. (2003, March). *The changing nature of presidential debate influence in the new age of mass media communication.* Paper presented at the Conference on Presidential Rhetoric, Texas A&M University, College Station, TX.

Pfau, M., & Burgoon, M. (1988). Inoculation in political campaign communication. *Human Communication Research, 15,* 91–111.

Pfau, M., & Burgoon, M. (1989). The efficacy of issue and character attack message strategies in political campaign communication. *Communication Reports, 2,* 52–61.

Pfau, M., Holbert, R. L., Szabo, A., & Kaminski, K. (2002). Issue-advocacy versus candidate advertising: Effects on candidate preferences and democratic process. *Journal of Communication, 52,* 301–315.

Pfau, M., Kendall, K. E., Reichert, T., Hellweg, S. A., Lee, W., Tusing, K. J., et al. (1997). Influence of communication during the distant phase of the 1996 Republican presidential primary campaign. *Journal of Communication, 47*(4), 6–26.

Pfau, M., & Kenski, H. C. (1990). *Attack politics: Strategy and defense.* New York: Praeger.

Prentice, C. (2005). Third party candidates in political debates: Muted groups struggling to express themselves. *Speaker and Gavel, 42,* 1–12.

Price, V., Tewksbury, D., & Powers, E. (1997). Switching trains of thought. The impact of news frames on readers' cognitive responses. *Communication Research, 24,* 481–506.

Putnam, R. D. (1995). Bowling alone: America's declining social capital. *Journal of Democracy, 6,* 65–78.

Putnam, R. D. (2000). *Bowling alone: The collapse and revival of American community.* New York: Simon and Schuster.

Reese, S. D. (1991). Setting the media's agenda: A power balance perspective. In J. A. Anderson (Ed.), *Communication yearbook* (Vol. 14, pp. 309–340). Newbury Park, CA: Sage.

Reese, S. D., & Danielian, L. H. (1989). Intermedia influence and the drug issue: Converging on cocaine. In P. J. Shoemaker (Ed.), *Communication campaigns about drugs: Government, media, and the public* (pp. 47–66). Hillsdale, NJ: Erlbaum.

Rheingold, H. (2002). *Smart mobs: The next social revolution.* Cambridge, MA: Perseus.

Ridout, T. N., & Mellen, R., Jr. (2007). Does the media agenda reflect the candidates' agenda? *Harvard International Journal of Press/Politics, 12*(2), 44–62.

Ridout, T. N., Shaw, D. V., Goldstein, K. M., & Franz, M. M. (2004). Evaluating measures of campaign advertising exposure on political learning. *Political Behavior, 26,* 201–225.

Ritter, K., & Medhurst, M. J. (2003). *Presidential speechwriting: From the New Deal to the Reagan revolution and beyond.* College Station: Texas A&M University Press.

Roberts, M. S. (1992). Predicting voting behavior via the agenda-setting tradition. *Journalism Quarterly, 69,* 878–892.

Roberts, M., & McCombs, M. (1994). Agenda-setting and political advertising: Origins of the news agenda. *Political Communication, 11,* 249–262.

Roddy, B. L., & Garramone, G. M. (1988). Appeals and strategies of negative political advertising. *Journal of Broadcasting & Electronic Media, 32,* 415–427.

Rosenberry, J. (2005). Few papers use online techniques to improve public communication. *Newspaper Research Journal, 26*(4), 61–73.

Rothschild, M. L., & Ray, M. L. (1974). Involvement and political advertising effect: An exploratory experiment. *Communication Research, 1,* 264–285.

Sanders, K. R., & Kaid, L. L. (1981). Political rallies: Their uses and effects. *Central States Speech Journal, 32,* 1–11.

Scammell, M. (2000). The Internet and civic engagement: The age of the consumer–citizen. *Political Communication, 17,* 351–355.

Scheufele, D. A. (1999). Framing as a theory of media effects. *Journal of Communication, 49*(1), 103–122.

Schneider, S. M., & Foot, K. A. (2006). Web campaigning by U.S. presidential primary candidates in 2000 and 2004. In A. P. Williams & J. C. Tedesco (Eds.), *The Internet election: Perspectives on the Web in campaign 2004* (pp. 21–36). Lanham, MD: Rowman & Littlefield.

Selnow, G. W. (1998). *Electronic whistle-stops: The impact of the Internet on American politics.* Westport, CT: Praeger.

Semetko, H. A., & Valkenburg, P. M. (2000). Framing European politics: A content analysis of press and television news. *Journal of Communication, 50*(2), 93–109.

Shah, D. V., Kwak, N., & Holbert, R. L. (2001). "Connecting" and "disconnecting" with civic life: Patterns of Internet use and the production of social capital. *Political Communication, 18,* 141–162.

Shaw, D. (1994). Surrender of the gatekeepers. *Nieman Reports, 48*(1), 3–5.

Shen, F., & Wu, H. D. (2002). Effects of soft-money issue advertisements on candidate evaluations and voting preference: An exploration. *Mass Communication & Society, 5,* 295–410.

Shoemaker P. J., & Reese, S. D. (1996). *Mediating the message: Theories of influence on mass media content* (2nd ed.). White Plains, NY: Longman.

Singer, J. (2001). The metro wide Web: Changes in newspapers' gatekeeeping role online. *Journalism & Mass Communication Quarterly, 78,* 65–80.

Son, Y. J., & Weaver, D. H. (2006). Another look at what moves public opinion: Media agenda setting and polls in the 2000 U.S. election. *International Journal of Public Opinion Research, 18,* 174–197.

Sonner, B. S. (1998). The effectiveness of negative political advertising: A case study. *Journal of Advertising Research, 38*(6), 37–42.

Sorescu, A. B., & Gelb, B. D. (2000). Negative comparative advertising: Evidence favoring fine-tuning. *Journal of Advertising, 29*(4), 25–40.

Sparks, C. (2001). The Internet and the global public sphere. In W. L. Bennett & R. M. Entman (Eds.), *Mediated politics: Communication in the future of democracy* (pp. 75–98). New York: Cambridge University Press.

Streck, J. (1998). Pulling the plug on electronic town meetings: Participatory democracy and the reality of the Usenet. In C. Toulouse & T. W. Luke (Eds.), *The politics of cyberspace: A new political science reader* (pp. 18–47). New York: Routledge.

Stromer-Galley, J. (2000). On-line interaction and why candidates avoid it. *Journal of Communication, 50*(4), 111–132.

Stromer-Galley, J. (2002). New voices in the public sphere: A comparative analysis of interpersonal and online political talk. *Javnost/The Public, 9*(2), 23–42.

Stromer-Galley, J., & Foot, K. A. (2002). Citizen perceptions of online interactivity and implications for political campaign communication. *Journal of Computer-Mediated Communication, 8*(1). Retrieved March 17, 2008, from http://jcmc.indiana.edu/vol8/issue1/stromerandfoot.html

Sulfaro, V. A. (2001). Political advertisements and decision-making shortcuts in the 2000 election. *Contemporary Argumentation and Debate, 22*, 80–99.

Sweetser, K. D., & Kaid, L. L. (2008). Stealth soapboxes: Political information efficacy, cynicism, and uses of celebrity Weblogs among readers. *New Media & Society, 10*, 67–91.

Tedesco, J. C. (2001). Issue and strategy agenda-setting in the 2000 presidential primaries. *American Behavioral Scientist, 44*, 2048–2067.

Tedesco, J. C. (2002). Televised political advertising effects: Evaluating responses during the 2000 Robb–Allen Senatorial election. *Journal of Advertising, 31*(1), 37–48.

Tedesco, J. C. (2005a). Intercandidate agenda setting in the 2004 Democratic primary. *American Behavioral Scientist, 49*, 92–113.

Tedesco, J. C. (2005b). Issue and strategy agenda setting in the 2004 presidential election: Exploring the candidate–journalist relationship. *Journalism Studies, 6*, 187–201.

Tedesco, J. C. (2006). Web interactivity and young adult political efficacy. In A. P. Williams & J. C. Tedesco (Eds.), *The Internet election: Perspectives of the Web in campaign 2004* (pp. 187–202). Lanham, MD: Rowman & Littlefield.

Tedesco, J. C. (2007). Examining Internet interactivity effects on young adult political information efficacy. *American Behavioral Scientist, 50*, 1183–1194.

Tedesco, J. C., & Kaid, L. L. (2003). Style and effects of the Bush and Gore spots. In L. L. Kaid, J. C. Tedesco, D. Bystrom, & M. S. McKinney (Eds.), *The millennium election: Communication in the 2000 campaign* (pp. 5–16). Lanham, MD: Rowman & Littlefield.

Tedesco, J. C., Kaid, L. L., & McKinnon, L. M. (2000). Network adwatches: Policing the 1996 primary and general election presidential ads. *Journal of Broadcasting & Electronic Media, 44*, 541–555.

Tedesco, J. C., Miller, J. L., & Spiker, J. A. (1999). Presidential campaigning on the information superhighway: An exploration of content and form. In L. L. Kaid & D. G. Bystrom (Eds.), *The electronic election: Perspectives on the 1996 campaign communication* (pp. 51–63). Mahwah, NJ: Erlbaum.

Thorson, E., Christ, W. G., & Caywood, C. (1991). Effects of issue–image strategies, attack and support appeals, music, and visual content in political commercials. *Journal of Broadcasting & Electronic Media, 35*, 465–486.

Tinkham, S. F., & Weaver-Lariscy, R. A. (1993). A diagnostic approach to assessing the impact of negative political television commercials. *Journal of Broadcasting & Electronic Media, 37*, 377–399.

Trammell, K. D., Williams, A. P., Postelnicu, M., & Landreville, K. D. (2006). Evolution of online campaigning: Increasing interactivity in candidate Web site and blogs through text and technical features. *Mass Communication & Society, 9*, 21–44.

Trent, J. S., & Friedenberg, R. V. (2007). *Political campaign communication: Principles and practices* (6th ed.). Lanham, MD: Rowman & Littlefield.

Turk, J. V. (1986). Information subsidies and media content: A study of public relations influence on the news. *Journalism Monographs, 100*, 1–29.

Turk, J. V., & Franklin, B. (1987). Information subsidies: Agenda-setting traditions. *Public Relations Review, 13*(4), 29–41.

Van Aelst, P., & Walgrave, S. (2004). New media, new movements? The role of the Internet in shaping the "anti-globalization" movement. In W. van de Donk, B. D. Loader, P. G. Nixon,

& D. Rucht (Eds.), *Cyberprotest: New media, citizens, and social movements* (pp. 197–122). New York: Routledge.

Wanta, W., & Foote, J. (1994). The president–news media relationship: A time series analysis of agenda-setting. *Journal of Broadcasting & Electronic Media, 38,* 437–448.

Wanta, W., Stephenson, M. A., Turk, J. V., & McCombs, M. E. (1989). How the president's State of the Union talk influenced news media agendas. *Journalism Quarterly, 66,* 537–541.

Ware, B. L., & Linkugel, W. A. (1973). They spoke in defense of themselves: On the generic criticism of apologia. *Quarterly Journal of Speech, 59,* 273–283.

Weaver, D. (1994). Media agenda setting and elections: Voter involvement or alienation? *Political Communication, 11,* 347–356.

Weaver, D. H., McCombs, M., & Shaw, D. (2004). Agenda-setting research: Issues, attributes, and influences. In L. L. Kaid (Ed.), *Handbook of political communication research* (pp. 257–282). Mahwah, NJ: Erlbaum.

West, D. M. (1993). *Air wars: Television advertising in election campaigns, 1952–1992.* Washington, DC: CQ Press.

West, D. M. (1994). Political advertising and news coverage in the 1992 California U.S. Senate campaigns. *Journal of Politics, 56,* 1053–1075.

West, D. M., Heith, D., & Goodwin, C. (1996). Harry and Louis go to Washington: Political advertising and health care reform. *Journal of Health Politics, Policy and Law, 21,* 35–68.

Whillock, R. K. (1997). Cyber-politics. *American Behavioral Scientist, 40,* 1208–1225.

White, D. M. (1964). The gatekeeper: A cast study in the selection of news. In L. A. Dexter & D M. White (Eds.), *People, society, and mass communications* (pp. 160–172). New York: Free Press of Glencoe.

Williams, A. P., Kaid, L. L., Landreville, K., Fernandes, J., Yun, H. J., Bagley, A., et al. (2008). The representation of European Union elections in news media coverage around the world. In L. L. Kaid (Ed.), *The EU expansion: Communicating shared sovereignty in the parliamentary elections* (pp. 153–173). New York: Peter Lang.

Williams, B. A., & Delli Carpini, M. X. (2000). Unchained reaction: The collapse of media gatekeeping and the Clinton–Lewinsky scandal. *Journalism, 1,* 61–85.

Xenos, M. A., & Foot, K. A. (2005). Politics as usual, or politics unusual? Position taking and dialogue on campaign Websites in the 2002 U.S. elections. *Journal of Communication, 55,* 169–185.

Xenos, M. A., & Moy, P. (2007). Direct and differential effects of the Internet on political and civic engagement. *Journal of Communication, 57,* 704–718.

20 Applied Communication Research in Educational Contexts

Ann L. Darling and Liz Leckie
The University of Utah

> Education is the point at which we decide whether we love the world enough to assume responsibility for it. (Arendt, 1968, p. 196)

> There is no real teacher who in practice does not believe in the existence of the soul, or in a magic that acts on it through speech. (Bloom, 1987, p. 20)

We open with these two quotations, from very different thinkers, because they capture the essence of why it is important to have a chapter on educational contexts in a handbook on applied communication research. On a pragmatic level, schools are one of the few social institutions in which all people participate on some level. Some form of K-12 schooling is compulsory in the United States today, with anyone from age 5 to 16 required, by law, to attend school. Many individuals do not terminate their education in high school but go on to pursue an undergraduate, graduate, or professional degree. The system of employment that supports these educational experiences is vast; there are networks of teachers, administrators, and other staff who, although not students, are actively engaged in the social institution of education. Educational contexts, thus, are pervasive and implicate almost everyone. However, a pragmatic view alone is insufficient to capture the importance that education plays in society. Like many scholars, we believe that education is the basic tool of democracy (which, as we know, is not perfect) and that without access to and resources for education, access to good health, safety, and ideas about a better life is seriously compromised. Thus, we agree with Arendt (1968) that to be educated means to love and take responsibility for the world.

As Bloom (1987) posited, participation in educational contexts is a communicative accomplishment. At this point, it is almost a cliché to say that the difference between knowing and teaching is communication. We add that the difference between accessing information and learning also is communication. Because communication is vital to an educational enterprise and because education is a pervasive and essential component of U.S. culture, it is important to explore how communication functions in educational contexts. We need to know more about how teachers do and might use communication to better facilitate student learning, and we need to know more about how students use communication to engage or resist learning opportunities. We need to know more about how communication in educational contexts acts as a catalyst for social change or as a guardian for the status quo. This chapter explores how applied research has enhanced, and can better enhance, our understanding of communication in educational contexts.

We begin with some discussion of the parameters of this chapter. In particular, we first discuss three types of communication research that explore educational contexts and then describe our understanding of the characteristics of applied research. The bulk of this chapter then is devoted to a review of published applied communication research designed to explore significant problems that occur in educational contexts. That review is presented with respect to three significant issues: teaching as applied communication, classrooms as an applied communication context, and schools as communities created through applied communication. At the end of the chapter, we discuss the type of applied communication research in educational contexts that we hope to see more of in the future and the problems that we foresee in conducting that research.

Identifying Communication Research in Educational Contexts

Communication research that takes place in or examines questions about educational contexts traditionally has fallen into two categories or types: communication education research and instructional communication research. The first type of research has the longer history; in fact, some have argued that the modern version of our disciplinary work began with the set of curiosities that led to this type of research (Friedrich, 2002). *Communication education research* begins with questions about how to teach and learn communication as a subject matter, with a focus on better understanding ways in which instruction (teaching) can facilitate (or harm) the process of teaching or learning about communication. This research poses questions regarding, for instance, what types of model or sample speeches are best used when teaching introductory public speaking, how to conduct effective mock interviews in an organizational communication class, and what are the best ways to use videotape in that instruction (for an excellent review of such research, see Staton-Spicer & Wulff, 1984).

The second type of research about communication in educational contexts, *instructional communication*, begins with the observation that teaching is a communicative practice and focuses on questions about how communication facilitates or inhibits teaching and learning, regardless of subject matter. Sprague (1992a) traced this type of research to a 1972 conference where scholars shared their insights regarding how communication theory and research might be useful for understanding how people teach and learn together, mostly in classrooms. Research on interpersonal communication was among the first to be "imported" in this manner to discover, describe, predict, and control patterns of behavior in classrooms. Broadly, instructional communication research asks questions about types of communicative practices that teachers can use to promote better learning for students and what communicative behaviors teachers can use to keep students on task (for an excellent recent review of this research, see Waldeck, Kearney, & Plax, 2001a).

Research endeavors in both communication education and instructional communication seek to articulate generalizable claims that can be used to test, extend, or build theory. A third and more recent type of research that is relevant to our chapter has been referred to as the *scholarship of teaching and learning* (SoTL). Initiated by Boyer's (1987b) landmark monograph on types of scholarship characterizing the work of the professoriate, this research initially was promoted by the Carnegie Foundation and has evolved into a national movement. SoTL is not grounded in research about teaching and learning communication to develop generalizable propositions, as is communication education research, nor is it grounded in research about how teaching and learning are influenced by communication principles and practices, in general, as in instructional communication research. Instead, SoTL research is guided by a curiosity about one's own teaching and learning—in our case, about communication—and explores those questions using well-defined and appropriate tools of inquiry with the commitment to share whatever is learned in public, peer-reviewed venues (Darling, 2002). SoTL work is quite personal in that it explores teaching and learning in an individual classroom, but it also is social in that the research is shared in public venues, such as in certain journals and at conferences. Because this type of research is so new, published reviews are not yet available, although the volumes of *Communication Education* published after 2003 include examples of this work in the communication discipline.

Defining Applied Communication Research

Our task in this chapter is not to provide a comprehensive review of research that falls into each of the three categories described above but, instead, to review *applied* research from each of these areas. Making distinctions about what research is applied in a discipline that some have argued is practical by nature is not an easy task (e.g., Craig, 1989; see also Barge & Craig, this volume). That task becomes more complicated in the case of research about educational contexts, because, in a broad sense, all communication education, instructional communication, and SoTL research is driven by a specific concern about teaching, learning, and communicating in a particular context (such as classrooms or schools). Still, an important distinction can be made between basic research that is designed to develop generalizable propositions and research that addresses a particular problem using such generalizable propositions.

Most definitions of applied communication research incorporate language about the importance of a specific context. Keyton (2000), for example, suggested that applied communication research "addresses or identifies a significant and practical communication issue or problem" and that "applied problems are those that exist naturally in context for interactants...[in that] the problem must be legitimate for the interactants" (pp. 166, 168).

Many, but not all, definitions assert that applied communication research should do more than continue an academic dialogue; it should be driven by a motivation to investigate systemic inequalities and, ultimately, to make a difference in people's lives. Cissna (2000) made this point when he stated that "applied communication researchers are motivated not only to understand the world but also to change it in some respect" (pp. 169–170). Cissna advocated, in particular, that "the discipline should encourage its members to engage in research that (a) illuminates specific communication contexts or situations, (b) provides insight into the solution of social problems, or (c) leads to interventions that make a difference in people's lives" (p. 196). This mandate to conduct research that makes a difference has continued to shape the development of applied communication scholarship (see Frey & SunWolf, this volume). Once communication education problems have been identified, applied communication research should seek to ameliorate those problems through the application of communication theories and principles.

Over the course of the last decade or so, some scholars have suggested a specific agenda for applied communication research that uses communication theories and principles to ameliorate problems of social justice. Frey, Pearce, Pollock, Artz, and Murphy (1996) articulated this *communication approach to social justice* as "engagement with and advocacy for those in our society who are economically, socially, politically, and/or culturally underresourced" (p. 110; see also Frey, 1998; Frey & SunWolf, this volume; Seeger, Sellnow, Ulmer, & Novak, this volume). According to Frey et al., research commitments that inform a "sensibility" to social justice include foregrounding ethical concerns, performing structural analysis of ethical problems, adopting an activist orientation, and identifying with others. Taken together, these statements about applied communication research concerned with a social justice agenda require that such research be situated in an actual context, explore the nature of a pressing problem of social injustice, and seek to resolve that problem in a just way.

In preparing to write this chapter, we were interested in finding research that fit the parameters of applied research in educational contexts generally, as well as projects that examined an educational setting through the lens of social justice. Thus, the research reviewed in this chapter addresses a specific communication problem, as it is experienced by interactants in a particular educational context (i.e., classroom or school), using theories generated from basic research about communication with a clear goal to resolve that problem. In addition, we were especially interested in locating any contribution to a social justice agenda emerging from scholarship in communication education, instructional communication, and SoTL.

Our reading and discussion of the applied communication research in educational contexts led us to organize this review in support of three general propositions: (1) teaching is an applied communication process, (2) classrooms are an applied communication context, and (3) schools are communities created by and through communication. In the next section, we review research supporting each of these propositions. Within each discussion, we describe research that has a social justice agenda; however, as we assert in the conclusion to this chapter, more research in educational contexts with a social justice agenda needs to be conducted.

Teaching as Applied Communication

Much of the basic research in communication education, instructional communication, and SoTL examines relationships between teachers' communicative behaviors and learning outcomes. We were surprised, therefore, that our search for *applied* communication research that focused on teachers as communicators was not more fruitful. It seems that despite the abundant programs of research—such as those on teacher power, teacher immediacy, and teacher socialization—very little, in our estimation, has been done to *use* that research to manage or resolve specific problems experienced in particular educational settings. In this section, we first describe an applied communication project that revealed important information about the role of power in one particular educational research program. We then review five studies that explore types of teacher messages as related to either student learning or student engagement with the learning process.

Power Matters

Despite the importance of teacher communicative behavior to student engagement with learning tasks and to manage student behavior in classrooms, little communication research responds to applied problems of learning engagement and behavior management in particular classrooms. This finding is especially surprising given the well-established program of communication research on teacher power (e.g., McCroskey & Richmond, 1983; Richmond & McCroskey, 1992; Schrodt et al., 2008; Schrodt, Witt, & Turman, 2007; Turman & Schrodt, 2006). Because this is such an important potential area for applied communication research in educational contexts, we review the one published applied study that was conducted.

Weber, Martin, and Patterson (2001) conducted research within the context of a successful intervention program, Project Adapt (PA), for at-risk middle school students. Students were referred to this program because of rather serious behavior problems in school settings (e.g., pulling a knife on another student, being caught with drugs, or threatening to kill a teacher). Despite those dramatic and dysfunctional experiences, once in this program, students demonstrated significant and consistent gains on cognitive outcome measures (i.e., test scores and grades). Seeking to understand these significant gains in this context, Weber et al. used a classic process–product design to explore relationships among teacher communicative behavior (specifically, teachers' use of power, as conceptualized within the teacher power research program), student interest in learning (defined along the three dimensions of meaningfulness, impact, and competence), and affective learning.

Forty-six PA students completed a battery of questionnaires early and late in the semester designed to measure teacher power, student interest, and affective learning. The results demonstrated strong relationships among these variables. In general, PA teachers tended to use more prosocial behavioral alteration techniques (BATs) than did teachers the students studied with the previous year. Furthermore, particular prosocial BATs (e.g., immediate reward, deferred reward, and reward from teacher) were related to both student interest and affective learning. As subsequent focus group interviews conducted with a smaller group of these students about their experiences with the teachers in this special program showed:

> When probed for reasons why they liked these teachers and administrators better than the previous ones, two main themes emerged. Student responses reflected either (a) a respect for the discipline that the PA staff was able to implement or (b) a perception that the PA staff cared for each of the students. (Weber et al., 2001, p. 84)

This study, thus, provided not only insight into how specific teacher communicative behaviors might influence students who have not had success in a school setting but also the meanings that these particular students ascribed to those experiences. One possible reason for the effectiveness that prosocial BATS had in this setting is that they were interpreted by students as positive discipline—discipline enacted in the context of caring.

Weber et al.'s (2001) study demonstrates the important contributions that basic instructional communication research can make to an applied research project. We hope that more of this type of work is conducted and published, but we also urge scholars pursuing applied communication research about how teacher power is exerted in classrooms in response to particular problems to embrace contextualized and dynamic conceptualizations of power as enacted through communicative behavior. We join Sprague (1992b) in observing that postmodern notions of power reveal the fluid ways that authority and subordination get negotiated in individual relationships, groups, and organizations. Furthermore, given the rich collectivities that comprise most classrooms today, issues of power as understood through intersections of race, class, ethnicity (see Nicotera, Clinkscales, Dorsey, & Niles, this volume), gender (see Buzzanell, Meisenbach, Remke, Sterk, & Turner, this volume), and sexual orientation are important to elaborate. Postmodern notions of power in the classroom, thus, are important for instructional communication research driven by a social justice sensibility.

Message Forms Matter

The five studies included in this section focus on forms of messages that matter to student learning in particular contexts. Four studies explore traditional teacher message forms (e.g., lectures, instructions, and discussion strategies); the other study looks at message forms inspired by new technology. Taken together, these explorations provide grounded, contextualized evidence about the importance of teachers' communicative behavior in relation to targeted learning outcomes and students' experiences of learning in classrooms.

Baus (1995) experimentally tested the relationship between teachers' mode of presentation and students' retention of complex material. Put in the language of applied communication research, the problem investigated was how knowledge about message types can inform teachers' use of communication to help students retain complex material. Specifically, this study explored whether messages that are seen and heard (via lecture and role-play) were more effective in terms of student retention than messages that were only seen or heard.

Undergraduate students who participated in this experiment were exposed to one of three conditions: (1) lecture only, (2) lecture plus student role-plays, or (3) lecture plus videotaped role-plays plus student role-plays. Despite the fact that Baus (1995) reported no significant findings, this project provides an example of applied communication research that needs to be conducted. Given the importance of message and channel redundancy to effective communication, this research needs to be replicated to clarify the nature of any relationships among teacher messages, channel redundancy, and student learning.

Henricksen (1996) also explored how message forms influence student behavior, focusing on much younger students (ages 6 to 9) and their comprehension of the concepts of "buying" and "selling" rather than retention of complex information, as did Baus (1995). The applied communication question that inspired Henricksen's research was not an educational one, strictly speaking; she wanted to extend research claims about young children's critical-viewing skills. In particular, she sought to identify the interpretation skills that young children use when viewing advertisements. Because she focused on types of instruction given to children (by her as the researcher) and children's responses to those instructions, it is relevant to this chapter.

Using an experimental design, Henricksen (1996) tested relationships among forms of instruction (direct or indirect) and types of transactions (buy or sell). One hundred twelve children ages 6 to 9 sat at tables with Bert and Ernie dolls (from the popular television show, *Sesame Street*) and were given either a direct instruction, such as "You buy a train from Ernie," or an indirect instruction, such as "Make Bert sell a train to Ernie" (p. 99). The findings are especially important for applied communication research in educational contexts, as children were more successful in performing tasks when given direct rather than indirect instructions. In explaining these findings, Henricksen surmised that indirect instructions require perspective taking and that perspective-taking skills tend to occur later developmentally and are supported by proactive forms of instruction, such as role-playing, rather than lecturing about television form and content.

Two studies used SoTL as an approach to understand how teacher communicative behaviors (message forms) influence student learning. Wulff and Wulff (2004) described the evolution of the first author's teaching style from relying on lecture to using more active approaches to teaching and learning, such as class discussion. Quantitative and qualitative perceptual data were gathered to ascertain the degree to which students learned, to determine whether teachers' communicative behaviors made a difference in that learning, and to document specific types of teacher behaviors that made a difference. The quantitative standardized data took the form of course-evaluation information and formal assessments of student learning, and the qualitative data (used to understand and interpret the quantitative data more fully) were acquired via interviews conducted with and questionnaires completed by students (several times during the course). The analysis revealed four teacher communicative behaviors that students reported as important to their learning in the course: encouraging open communication, demonstrating examples interactively, structuring opportunities for application through problem solving, and engaging students in reflection about their learning.

Also using the structure of SoTL, Dallimore, Hertenstein, and Platt (2004) were interested in how teachers use communication to inspire more vibrant classroom discussions.

In the context of graduate courses in an MBA program, Dallimore et al. specifically focused on strategies that teachers might use to elicit participation from students less inclined to volunteer their observations and comments. Questions about the perceived effectiveness of a strategy known as *cold calling* (calling on students whose hands are not raised) were at the center of this investigation. Students in two MBA courses, one that was required and the other an elective, completed questionnaires about the quality and effectiveness of the discussions held in class. The teacher of these two classes (also one of the authors) engaged in cold calling in both classes. The results confirmed Dallimore et al.'s suspicion that cold calling enhances the quality and effectiveness of classroom discussion. Students reported six categories of teacher behaviors that were helpful to the quality and effectiveness of discussion: (1) required and graded participation, (2) incorporating instructors' and students' ideas and experiences, (3) active facilitation, (4) asking effective questions, (5) creating a supportive classroom environment, and (6) affirming student contributions and providing constructive feedback.

Each of the studies reviewed in this section dealt with questions about communicative behavior in traditional face-to-face settings, whereas a study by Waldeck, Kearney, and Plax (2001b) focused on electronic communication. Specifically, these researchers focused on whether students preferred to use e-mail rather than face-to-face meetings to engage their teachers. Thus, the applied communication problem at the center of this project was how teachers and students can use e-mail effectively to accomplish instructional goals. The researchers employed two well-established constructs from instructional communication research—extra-class communication and willingness to communicate—to understand how e-mail messages might influence the teaching and learning process.

Two hundred eighty-nine undergraduate students completed a battery of questionnaires, with questions about computer access and savviness included. The findings revealed three types of reasons for why students used e-mail: (1) personal or social reasons (to self-disclose, discuss personal feelings and ideas, learn more about the teacher, and impress the teacher), (2) procedural or clarification reasons (to ask for course or task direction, guidance, information, and feedback), and (3) efficiency reasons (to avoid wasting time and minimize face-to-face or phone contact). Of these reasons, students identified procedural or clarification reasons as the most important, with efficiency as an important second reason (see also the recent study of characteristics of parent–teacher e-mail by Thompson, 2008)

The researchers also examined whether teacher message behaviors influenced students' willingness to use e-mail to communicate for instructional purposes. Waldeck et al. (2001b) found that when teachers used immediacy in their e-mail messages (e.g., began their messages with the student's first name and inserted smiley faces and other emoticons to help students understand the meaning of those messages), students were more willing to communicate with their teachers online.

To conclude this section, first, surprisingly, little *applied* communication research exists about how teacher communicative behavior can help or harm student learning. Scholars, thus, need to explore more fully how concepts from the robust instructional communication literature might generate understandings of specific learning or engagement problems in classrooms and schools. Second, the research that does exist demonstrates ways in which applied research can enrich our understandings of teaching and communication by providing evidence of how certain message types and forms appear to be more effective than others in terms of student learning and student willingness to engage in the learning process.

Classrooms as an Applied Communication Context

The previous section reviewed applied communication research on the act of teaching, with scholars trying to better understand how teacher power and teacher messages work in the classroom. This section highlights applied communication research that focuses on teaching methods employed in classrooms and how those methods may contribute to student learning. Here, we review 11 studies about how various teaching methods used in certain contexts may invite student learning to occur in ways not previously considered. Scholarship examining teaching methods was the most abundant type of applied research in educational contexts, and we describe this body of work with respect to four categories: college classrooms, classrooms redefined, service-learning education, and deliberative education.

College Classrooms

Researchers have explored the use of communicative practices in the service of pedagogical objectives within specific classrooms. Two studies were situated within composition classes, with both of those classes bringing students and their community together, although they did so using very different techniques.

In the first study, Swan (2002) considered how graduate students in a public policy program engaged with members of the Community Literacy Center in Pittsburg, Pennsylvania. Using a communication tool called the "community problem-solving dialogue" (CPSD), students and community members created and developed a community-centered project that focused on how to write collaboratively about urban issues. Specifically, students used tools of discourse analysis (see Tracy & Mirivel, this volume) to examine how students and community members use strategies to write and talk about complex social problems. Specifically, students analyzed the rhetorical strategies and decision-making moves made during the development of the project. Using the CPDS tool, students learned how strategies were employed by the multiple parties and determined which decisions were privileged in this community–university collaboration.

Swan's (2002) exploration demonstrated how educational experiences can enhance the use of communicative practices—rhetorical strategies—in community–university collaborations to uncover the type of situated, specific knowledge that is important for working toward solutions to social problems. Swan asserted that teaching students skills of rhetorical practice and the CPSD—in particular, skills of seeking the story behind the story, rival hypotheses, and options and outcomes—opened an important space for community representation in the classroom. Using this tool as a map for how to talk and write about problems, students and community members together identified pressing problems in a specific context, and students learned about the possible multiple dimensions of social problems and the possibilities for change in that context. However, Swan observed several roadblocks to the inclusion of community expertise in academic research. In particular, the disciplinary focus on the outcomes of academic work tended to neglect local data received from community members and erased many community members' concerns.

Garcia (2002) also focused on classroom strategies to promote communication across communities. She developed a pedagogy in a first-year composition classroom that used poetry to access the diverse cultural and linguistic skills, experiences, and knowledge that students at California State University, Monterey Bay (CSUMB) bring to the classroom. This program was created in response to CSUMB's vision statement, which promises to serve the diverse people of California (especially working-class, historically undereducated, and low-income populations), and to create a multilingual, multicultural intellectual community. Garcia's objectives for the course were to create a space where all students felt that their voice was valued and recognized, their multiple knowledges validated, and where various literacy practices were employed.

In reflecting on these students and on the program, Garcia (2002) described how, in some instances, integration of nonmajority students' cultural practices and diverse literacies triggered and reinforced negative stereotypes rather than promoted transformative relationships across racial and ethnic groups. She realized that when this occurred in the classroom, Chicana/o students used silence to cope with these comments, which served a number of purposes, including avoiding bitter outbursts and potential backlash, and signaling their disagreement with the statements made. This important recognition highlights silence as a form of literacy in the multiracial classroom.

Several studies have explored communication instruction in classrooms focused on a different disciplinary subject matter, commonly referred to as "communication across the curriculum." This work applies communication pedagogy within noncommunication classrooms, such as in engineering courses, with the central question being how to import communication instruction effectively into these classrooms. An entire special issue of *Communication Education* on "Communication Genres in Disciplinary Discourse Communities: Theoretical and Pedagogical Explorations of Communication across the Curriculum and in the Disciplines" (Dannels, 2005) was devoted to this scholarship, which built on an impressive corpus of previous research (for comprehensive reviews of this literature, see Cronin & Glen, 1991; Dannels, 2002).

Although some of this scholarship is more clearly identified as basic research (e.g., Darling & Dannels, 2003), other studies are more applied in structure and purpose. Two studies, in particular, seem especially salient, as both adopted SoTL as their framework. In the first study, Dannels, Anson, Bullard, and Peretti (2003), all members of a National Science Foundation grant team that was awarded funds to explore effective ways to implement communication instruction in chemical engineering classrooms, used qualitative methods to focus on students' responses to the communication instruction. They identified four learning issues: (1) integrating multidisciplinary information, (2) managing varied audiences and feedback, (3) aligning content and communication tasks, and (4) addressing interpersonal team issues. Consistent with the SoTL framework, Dannels et al. reflected on how these learning issues need to be integrated in future communication instruction in chemical engineering classrooms.

Chanock (2005) also used the SoTL framework to explore student learning about oral presentations in an honors archeology course. Using theories of functional grammar to guide the analysis of her ethnographic observations of the classroom, Chanock described five features that, according to participants in the honors seminar, distinguished more effective disciplinary speakers from those perceived to be less effective: mode of presentation, structure of presentation, use of visual aids, speakers' "presence," and oral grammar.

Classrooms Redefined

The second set of studies differs from the first set in that the projects extend beyond traditional college classrooms, taking communication education to the workplace and to even more unconventional settings. In perhaps the most provocative study, Hartnett (1998) called attention to a context quite distinct from the traditional higher education classroom—a prison classroom. Hartnett described a communication pedagogical activity—a reenactment of the Lincoln–Douglas debate (with a slight historically inaccurate modification of adding the Black abolitionist David Walker to the event)—conducted as a final assignment in a speech communication course on "Historical Forms of Public Address," a course that might be taught in any classroom on any campus in the United States. Students first were given time and resources to research the original Lincoln–Douglas debates and then, after being given time to practice, reenacted the debate, framing their arguments using actual discourse from the original debate. Members of the prisoners' families, as well as prisoners not enrolled in the course and guards and prison officials, attended the debate, meaning that the final performance had a distinctly public audience.

Elegantly described in Hartnett's (1998) essay, this debate was an unqualified success, both with regard to oral performance skills that students/prisoners mastered and in terms of demonstrating how they had internalized racist discourse of the past. Specifically, Hartnett pointed out that the internalization of racism by the students/prisoners demonstrated how the tropes of racism of a previous historical time still exist today. Hartnett, however, did not view this classroom success as the only, or even primary, contribution made by this event; instead, he described ways in which the debates, and talk about them, reached beyond the classroom to the general prison population and prison administration, guards, and family members who were drawn into discussions of slavery, race, and current developments in U.S. prison culture.

Service-Learning Classrooms

A number of studies have focused on the *service-learning course*, an approach to learning that integrates academic instruction with public service and individual reflection. Because this approach encourages students to take the knowledge that they are learning and use it in a specific community context, classrooms implementing service-learning practices are an important focus for applied communication research in educational contexts. Consequently, the following literature applies the concept of service learning to a number of communication curricula and courses (e.g., intercultural communication, organizational communication, teaching communication, and research methods).

In the context of an intercultural communication course with a service-learning dimension, Crabtree (1998) explored ways to use intercultural communication as a subject matter and as a skill set to encourage college students to create a two-way process of empowerment when working with people who are visibly, culturally, and economically different from them—in this instance, with people in "developing" countries (see Kincaid & Figueroa, this volume). This course was part of the Center for Civic Education and Leadership at Crabtree's university, and was designed with a required service-learning component, typically conducted in a Third-World nation (e.g., Peru, Mexico, and Guatemala had been visited in the past). Crabtree's case study described students' transformative experiences in the two sites of El Salvador and Nicaragua.

Student journals provided the corpus of the data, with Crabtree's analysis focusing on participants' cognitive, affective, and behavioral transformations. Journal entries revealed how students' learning and confidence in their understanding of the subject matter—intercultural communication—encouraged and structured a transformational learning experience. Specifically, students' work illustrated their growth in cultural knowledge, strong levels of communication motivation, and the development of relational network integration. Crabtree asserted that students' writing demonstrated an approach to intercultural communication that "depicts a concern for participatory collaboration, global awareness, and action for social justice" (p. 195).

In the studies conducted by Braun (2001) and O'Hara (2001), students employed communication audits as part of their service-learning project in an upper division organizational communication course. In Braun's project, students worked with a program, titled "Communities for Education/Education for Communities," created to foster better communication between the local school district and its constituencies—in particular, with families of students in grades 7 through 12. In that communication course, students worked together in teams to study the organizational communication that occurred and to offer suggestions for improved practices, becoming student consultants to the organization. Braun concluded that this service-learning approach to an organizational communication course allowed students to influence a community partner—in this case, the local school district. Students, in turn, reported an increased understanding of course content, felt personally connected to the curriculum, and experienced powerful and memorable learning opportunities. Braun articulated a number of practical suggestions to improve the course, including starting fieldwork earlier and better preparing students for the uncertainty they are likely to face as they conduct community-based research.

O'Hara (2001) described a service-learning organizational communication course she designed using principles of democratic education and what 12 students learned from that course about communication, democratic practice, and social justice. As an applied communication research project, O'Hara described student learning as a process rather than as a set of outcomes, and she attached that process to a specific set of experiences that students had in this course.

Similar to Crabtree's (1998) study, O'Hara (2001) asked students to keep a journal and to produce several papers. Analysis of these writings revealed that students were confronted with the need to develop team relationships that were productive and to negotiate relationships with clients who were difficult. The course also appeared to achieve its goals of enhancing students' capacities for civic engagement and sensitivities to social justice. In short, students learned that the content of their communication instruction was dependent on the relational contexts in which they were assigned to work. This was an important learning for these students, who reported feeling more confident in their ability to use their education to make a difference.

Two case studies employed service learning to encourage students to teach oral communication to two populations. Students who took a communication training and development course offered by Gibson, Kostecki, and Lucas (2001) worked with the Work First and School to Work programs, which assist people with career counseling and job skill training as they transition into the labor force. Students in this course took on the role of student–trainer and offered instruction to improve program participants' job-related communication skills, such as interviewing, resume writing, conflict management, listening feedback, and team building.

Using a framework much like those found in SoTL projects, Gibson et al. (2001) drew on 11 best-practice principles identified by the National Society for Experiential Education to design and implement this service-learning course. They found through guided classroom dialogue and review of students' work that these principles served as an important foundation for improving students' performance in the course. Furthermore, they asserted that the principles provided an effective framework for dialogue with other teachers. The authors concluded that four principles emerged as core elements of the service-learning project: intent, authenticity, mentoring, and reflection.

Staton and Tomlison (2001) utilized a service-learning approach in their course on "Communication Education Outreach" to provide students with opportunities to integrate theory and practice, develop critical-reflection skills, and gain practical experience. Drawing on calls by Boyer (1987a), the *Goals 2000: Educate America Act* (1994), and the Speech Communication Association (1996) concerning the need to educate elementary school-age children to be more proficient orators, Staton and Tomlison developed a course where college students teach oral communication skills to children in grades K-12. Using students' in-class participation, quality of their written work, evaluation of their teaching performance, and final course grades as the corpus of their data, the authors asserted that this class allowed communication education students to expand and refine their cognitive understanding of communication concepts and principles, and to integrate theory and practice aids to prepare for actual classroom teaching.

Finally, two articles analyzed service learning in undergraduate communication research methods courses. Although both Keyton (2001) and Artz (2001) employed service-learning pedagogy, they took drastically different approaches to teaching research methods. Keyton focused on the practical issues associated with using service learning to teach research methods, suggesting that applied methods courses with a service-learning orientation need to consider how research can be designed and conducted to answer specific questions asked by the agencies with which students work. Framing research in this way leads students to gain new awareness of underserved populations about significant social and policy issues. Moreover, students conducting such applied research frequently interact with people from backgrounds different from themselves and, in the process, students learn more deeply about their capacity to conduct research and to utilize their communication skills with diverse people.

Keyton (2001) described three term-length service-learning projects that students engaged in over her numerous years of teaching a research methods course. She examined how students in these projects used their skills to offer suggestions to the nonprofit organizations and agencies with which they worked. Because the work in which students were engaged was tied to problems in the context, research methods, and, specifically, statistics, were employed as meaningful tools to solve real-world problems rather than studied as abstract concepts. In her most general conclusion, Keyton asserted that when utilized effectively, the goal of service learning is to encourage students to assess social problems and, thereby, to become active participants in solving the problems and concerns of underserved agencies and organizations.

Artz (2001) also argued for using a service-learning orientation to teach communication research methods, but his course taught students a very different orientation to communication research than did Keyton's course. Specifically, his course, entitled "Critical Ethnography for Communication Studies," taught students to use critical ethnographic research skills in their service-learning projects. Using this qualitative, social justice-oriented research methodology, students' attention was attuned to how communication theory and practice might address social justice problems, raise social awareness of those problems, and promote civic activity to solve them by offering more socially and economically just opportunities.

In his essay, Artz (2001) was critical of how service-learning approaches usually are implemented. He argued that the focus too often is on students' individual acts of altruism and is motivated by charity rather than the collective need to change fundamental systemic practices that give rise to social injustice. Artz's course, in contrast, encouraged students to examine the symbolic, cultural, and social practices that undergird social problems, and to articulate how communication is central to both systemic oppression and liberating activities.

Using students' written responses to and quantitative evaluations of the course, Artz (2001) described how this approach to teaching communication research methods moved students from seeing service as charity to viewing service as advocacy (see also Frey et al., 1996). He argued that this orientation to service learning and communication research methods directed students' attention to, as Thomas (1993) put it, "symbols of oppression by shifting and contrasting cultural images in ways that reveal subtle qualities of social control" (p. 20). However, Artz also warned that teaching a critical ethnographic methods course with a service-learning advocacy orientation does not guarantee certain outcomes. Despite the focus of the course, some students did not conduct a critical ethnography. Moreover, students who already were advocates for particular social issues were better able to engage in research activities and advocacy, whereas students who chose projects only for the class frequently were frustrated and demonstrated difficulty establishing relationships with community partners. Most students in the course, however, became more aware of inequality and some gained further insights into the power of communicative practices to promote equality. Furthermore, by offering students opportunities to use their understandings and skills, the course led them to connect the relationships among communication, institutional structures, and political and cultural practices. In doing so, students joined or recommitted to the struggle for social justice and democratic communication.

Deliberative Education

Instruction in the arts of deliberation has been one significant heritage of an education in communication (see, e.g., McDevitt & Kiousis, 2006; Murphy, 2004). Several recent studies focus attention on how the application of deliberation skills might enhance students' tendencies toward civic engagement and democratic participation.

McMillan and Harriger's (2002) case study reported on their experiences of teaching deliberation in three courses. Based on literature suggesting that college-age people today feel politically alienated and demonstrate apathy toward political participation, the researchers hypothesized that teaching students deliberation skills should act as an antidote to these troubling trends. Based on their observations and reflections as teachers, McMillan and Harriger described six lessons about how larger societal struggles with deliberation manifest themselves in the classroom. These lessons are discussed here at some length and include recommendations for pedagogy implicated by each lesson.

The first lesson that McMillan and Harriger (2002) reported concerns how undergraduate students appear to approach group process. They noted that students do not come to college with positive or sophisticated views about group process, and that these negative feelings underlie their antipathy toward deliberative processes. Thus, among the first steps in a curriculum seeking to engage students in deliberative processes is attention to their initial and implicitly held assumptions about those processes. Second, they noted that students do not come to college well skilled in deliberative processes but, instead, come prepared to be individual orators of some skill; hence, they do not arrive ready to listen, question, probe, and decide in collaborative settings. Third, they reported that merely giving students opportunities to engage in deliberation increases their knowledge and curiosity about a particular issue; in other words, deliberation can trigger a more expansive understanding and appreciation of focal issues. Fourth, topics that are intrinsically interesting to students proved to be more potent in stimulating energetic deliberation. The issue of relevance, of course, is not new to educational scholars but these first four lessons, taken together, provide the interesting observation that although the act of deliberation matters per se, it matters *more* if students deliberate on issues that are important to them. Fifth, much of the theorizing on democratic practice identifies context as an essential aspect of the process, and McMillan and Harriger noted that context also is significant in classroom deliberations. Specifically, their students reported that for deliberative pedagogy to be effective, the classroom climate must be a safe one (where individuals do not fear humiliation or reprisal) that has a high degree of "internal efficacy" (a sense that any individual student has the capacity to alter the system in some meaningful way). Finally, McMillan and Harriger reported that the greatest challenge to deliberative pedagogy was diversity, which meant "providing a space that accommodates all players" (p. 249). For both teachers and students, the most imposing challenge to successful deliberation was developing ways to accommodate different points of view and varying interests created during discussions.

Two additional studies on deliberative education support McMillan and Harriger's (2002) work. Gravel (2001), also concerned about students' civic apathy and cynicism, drew on the idea that issues that were local and relevant successfully engaged students in deliberative practices and, consequently, would be more likely to increase their willingness to become civically involved. Modeling his course using the theories and practices of a local agency, the Industrial Areas Foundation (IAF), Gravel focused instruction on getting students to become more active and willing participants in discussions about how power operated in their community through dialogues about real-life and real-time issues related to church, family, and neighborhood associations. Gravel incorporated assignments in his course that encouraged students to see institutional power relations and that increased their skills of deliberation and persuasion by engaging in the process of building relationships among individuals and local community groups.

Gayle (2004) explored the notion that effective deliberation requires skills not commonly developed prior to college. Extending McMillan and Harriger's (2002, p. 174) observations about the need for skill development, Gayle focused on the degree to which students were willing and able to engage in attitude change, referred to as "subjective reframing," as a result of their participation in deliberations about controversial topics. Using SoTL as an empirical framework, Gayle's 34 honors public-speaking students participated in this project. Students gave three presentations on the same topic, with at least two presentations including viewpoints in opposition to one another. Students also reflected on their listening practices, reflections that were recorded on videotape and in student journals. Gayle's analysis of the data focused on the types of listening behaviors of which students were self-reflectively aware. The findings showed that students demonstrated attitude change and could be self-reflectively aware of the types of listening behaviors that might motivate such change. In this case, students who listened to the evidence presented were likely to experience subjective reframing.

In concluding this section, we note, first, that applied communication research that examines teaching methods has focused on communication classrooms in the context of higher education and that more studies need to be conducted on communication teaching methods in the K-12 environment. Even more exciting are studies that followed Hartnett's (1998) lead, for given the rapid growth of the prison industry and the alarming large number of men and growing number of women getting their education in prison (see, e.g., Novek & Sanford, 2007), we need to better understand the power of various pedagogies in that setting. Second, there is a great deal of applied research that examines communication pedagogy, with service learning and deliberative education appearing to be practices that a number of teachers are using with some success. Studies of service learning and deliberative education show that these pedagogical tools can help students to become more deeply engaged in their learning experiences. However, more research with a social justice sensibility needs to be done to understand the relative power of these pedagogies to be socially, as well as individually, transformative.

Schools as Communities Created through Applied Communication

The previous two sections highlighted research that focused on teachers and classrooms. This section reviews applied communication scholarship that examines schools. This research explores ways in which schools are embedded within communities (e.g., ways in which parents, families, friends, and neighbors, and neighborhoods participate in educational processes) and how schools function as communities (e.g., students, faculty, and staff from across a campus or several campuses working together on projects), revealing the rich relationships between education and community.

Community Provides Support through Communication

Any educator who has worked in the K-12 setting recognizes that successful schools are embedded in caring communities. Principals, teachers, and counselors all agree that parental involvement, neighborhood engagement, and support from friends and family all matter a great deal to individual student learning, as well as to school success. Despite this widely held conviction among educational practitioners and scholars, until very recently, little research has explored specific ways in which communication influences community support and student success in educational contexts.

Rosenfeld and his colleagues have engaged in programmatic research to understand the types of social support that are available and important to students and schools identified as being "at-risk." This research program has explored relationships between supportive communication and school outcomes for both at-risk students and students not identified as being at-risk in middle schools (Rosenfeld, Richman, & Bowen, 1998) and high schools (Rosenfeld & Richman, 1999). Reasoning that supportive communication, if present from the right people and in the right ways, ought to lessen the degree to which students identified as being at-risk because of their social or economic status experience negative school outcomes (e.g., poor attendance, behavioral problems, and negative affect for school), these scholars sought to identify the sources and types of support that might be most helpful. Thus, these studies explore ways in which communicative behavior—specifically, supportive communication—distinguishes between individuals who, given their social and economic standing, have a likelihood of having successful school experiences from those who do not.

For both the Rosenfeld and Richmond (1999) and Rosenfeld et al. (1998) studies, the data were obtained from a national database, the School Success Profile, a comprehensive instrument used to measure a wide range of school success indicators. Analyses of those data indicated that, in general, parents are a primary source of support for both at-risk students and not at-risk students in both middle and high school, results, which by themselves, happily, are unsurprising. The results also showed, however, that for at-risk students, parents were identified as *the only* source of communicative support, as these students did not report receiving support for positive school outcomes from teachers, administrators, friends, or other family members. Parents' and adult caretakers' supportive communicative behavior, however, did help at-risk students to achieve higher school engagement and satisfaction, as well as fewer behavior problems.

Barge and Loges (2003), in another study of parental involvement, focused on differing perceptions and meanings of parental involvement among parents, students, and teachers in a middle school context. Meanings of parental involvement were explored because of the particularly powerful role that parents can play in helping middle school students to have successful educational experiences. Parents and students engaged in focus group conversations about the meanings of parental involvement, and data from teachers were acquired through the completion of a questionnaire.

Barge and Loges (2003) reported both similarities and differences in people's perceptions of parental involvement. All three groups (parents, teachers, and students) viewed parental involvement as attempting to build positive relationships with teachers and as monitoring children's academic progress. However, there also were clear differences between the groups. Specifically, ideas about discipline and encouragement varied across the groups, as did the role of extracurricular activities and community networks. Barge and Loges concluded by proposing that two discourses—information transmission and partnership—guided understanding and communication conduct in this setting. Information-transmission discourse framed effective communication as that through which "schools provide academic data on student performance to parents and parents actively soliciting this data," whereas participation discourse framed effective communication as being "about creating supportive relationships among parents, teachers, and community members to foster the academic and social development of the child" (Barge & Loges, pp. 158–159). Barge and Loges recommended that the discourse of partnership has more potential than the discourse of information transmission to create and maintain environments in which all students can have successful school experiences.

Recently, Rosenfeld, Richman, Bowen, and Wynns (2006) began exploring relationships among the communication of social support, exposure to community violence, and school outcomes for high school students. They focused on the degree to which the availability of social support mitigates the negative influences of violence on school outcomes, such as attendance, trouble avoidance, school satisfaction, and grades. Using a national probability-sampling database, 1109 high school students completed the School Success Profile, which includes items measuring perceived neighborhood danger, personal neighborhood danger, and indications of social support.

Rosenfeld et al. (2006) reported that neighborhood violence, especially when experienced personally, has clear and negative consequences on students' school behavior and outcomes. Moreover, the communication of social support appears to mitigate school satisfaction and grades, but has less impact on attendance and trouble avoidance. The authors concluded that providing social support is necessary but insufficient to address the problems experienced by at-risk youth and the effects of community violence; issues of poverty and institutionalized forms of discrimination also must be confronted if schools are to be safe places for all students and institutions that foster positive social change.

Communication across Communities Can Engage Social Justice

A final set of studies relate community involvement, communication education, and social justice. These studies have been conducted in a wide range of settings, from campuses to school boards to entire nations, but each study explores applied questions about ways in which communicative practices and/or educational practices about communication can promote the agenda of social justice. These studies, thus, go beyond questions of how communities can better serve the needs of schools and learn how communities can promote social change through communication education.

Christian (2007) and her colleagues (Christian & Lapinski, 2003; Christian & Prater, 2003) have been interested in how principles of civic journalism might be employed to promote a social justice agenda. Civic journalism counters the neutrality and objectivity commonly identified as defining features of journalism. Instead, civic journalism asserts that journalists should take responsibility for the communities in which they work and make overt attempts to improve those communities through the practice of journalism. Christian's projects, therefore, explore ways in which an education in civic journalism might have effects on communities.

Christian (2007) reported how, over the course of several years, she developed a partnership between her undergraduate journalism students and students enrolled in a school newspaper class at a local high school. The goal of the partnership, called the Student

Newspaper Diversity Project, was to coproduce an annual special edition of the school newspaper that focused on diversity in the local community. In pursuing that goal, university and high school students learned about each other through mentoring relationships, students gained journalistic skills, and everyone involved (including members of the surrounding community when one issue of the newspaper was circulated across that community) became engaged in conversations about diversity in the community.

Based on individual interviews and focus group conversations, Christian (2007) concluded that high school and university students were affected by the project in two important ways. First, students became aware of how their prejudices were challenged and changed in some instances due to their participation in the project. Second, students learned more about journalism as a craft as they engaged the project. Christian's project, therefore, appears to have been successful on many levels.

Exploring the context of higher education, Artz (1998) described how an education in communication can facilitate a social justice project. Specifically, undergraduate communication majors at Loyola University of Chicago used their understanding of communication to address the problem of low African-American enrollment at that university by launching a campaign for institutional change. Using Bitzer's (1968) concept of a "rhetorical situation" as a guide, Artz described how students worked together to gain multiple and sometimes opposing viewpoints on the situation, and to develop possible solutions to that problem. Consistent with a social justice perspective, students successfully organized and implemented a conference on "African-Americans in Higher Education" that targeted issues on their campus but also invited speakers from nearby universities.

Artz (1998) described the process of using communication to advance this particular social justice project, with the undergraduate students involved becoming applied communication practitioners as they engaged in the process of facilitating talk and promoting action. What initially was a classroom project became a campus-wide initiative spurred by dialogue, debate, and consensus building. Although Artz observed that it was too soon to tell whether socially just ends would be achieved in this situation, the students' struggles to bring the issue to the attention of the campus more broadly, as well as their personal struggle to hear and understand multiple viewpoints, created an educational experience for them that was rich with opportunities for transformational learning.

Because boardrooms are a place where school policies, which direct daily conduct in classrooms and schools, are created, they are an important site of educational practice. Despite the importance of these settings, few communication researchers have studied them. One study by Tracy and Ashcraft (2001) is a notable exception and is especially important because it explores discourse about a district-wide diversity policy, which, when put into practice, could have direct implications for social justice.

Tracy and Ashcraft (2001) analyzed discussions of the Boulder Valley School Board (BVSB) and its community as participants created a strategic plan to craft a school district-wide diversity policy. These applied communication researchers claimed that the common occurrence of disputing word choice and meaning was an effective strategy for managing interactional dilemmas and, ultimately, led to a more inclusive diversity policy. Through examining these discussions, Tracy and Ashcraft found that BVSB members used three frames to discuss the language choices in the diversity policy document: technical editing, inadvertent changing of a policy, and wordsmithing.

The researchers argued that these word battles are means by which individuals assert their importance, play out personal animosities, and avoid more important tasks. As Tracy and Ashcraft (2001) explained, "Warring over words enables groups to navigate troubled waters—to become clearer about what a valued commitment is to mean, and to build agreement among group members" (p. 311). In other words, power negotiations often occur in the context of quibbles over word choice. Awareness about the subtexts of policy discussions—in this case, discussions about a diversity policy—is important to the overall goal of communicating effectively of and about social justice, as well as the creation of more inclusive policies and products.

According to Tracy and Ashcraft (2001), struggling with hard-to-articulate problems can lead to more tolerance of controversial positions. Understanding the complexities of dilemmas increases the likelihood that group members forward innovative and effective conversational moves. This study also illustrated how mundane and apparently obstructive communication patterns can move a group toward the goals of social justice. In this instance, power was negotiated through seemingly automatic, taken-for-granted conversation about language choice.

Two studies in South Africa explored communication curriculum projects in a national context. In both studies, teams of researchers were interested in understanding how communication pedagogy or curriculum might facilitate that country's recovery from the devastation of apartheid. The study by Newfield, Andrew, Stein, and Maungedzo (2003) explored the use of multimodal communication pedagogies in the context of an outcomes-based education (OBE) model in Johannesburg. The South-African version of OBE explicitly attended to policies that addressed inequities of the apartheid past; focused on principles of redress, social justice, multilingualism, and multiculturalism; and encouraged consideration of issues of equity in teaching, learning, and assessment. Teachers across the curriculum used pedagogical strategies to provide students with learning opportunities across visual, linguistic, and performative communication modes, with students encouraged to write poetry, dance, and create quilts rather than focus on the written word as the only mode of communication. The teachers' interest in multimodal communication pedagogies focused on building a democratic culture that "privilege[d] multiperspectival knowledge and lead to new forms of deliberation, analysis, and communication" (Newfield et al., p. 63).

Newfield et al. (2003) conducted a case study of Robert Maungedzo, an English-as-a-Second-Language teacher, and how he responded to the OBE model by using a number of pedagogical approaches to encourage and motivate the disaffected Soweto youth in his course to explore their culture and identity. Maungedzo designed the class projects as a way for these youth to communicate their identities and cultures in an exchange program with students living in China. Students created cloth maps of South Africa, called a "Tebuwa cloth"; wrote *izibongo*, historical South-African praise poems; constructed three-dimensional objects representative of their "cultural groups"; and composed contemporary poems in English.

Newfield et al. (2003) claimed that the complexities of this project and other multimodal approaches to OBE required the development of new criteria for assessing the learning achieved by students. Specifically, they argued that multimodal assessment needs to move beyond assessing independent objects (e.g., individual papers or test scores) to evaluating objects in relation to their contexts, histories, creative processes, and the inherent value of students' work. They asserted that placing human agency and resourcefulness at the center of educationally produced objects stresses the importance of meaning making within a social world that relies on the transformation, design, recruitment, reflection, and interaction with others rather than seeing those objects as isolated and discrete creations. Education in this context, thus, was a means for underrepresented populations to learn how to express themselves by various methods in a complex world.

Jones and Bodtker (1998) also reported on a social justice curriculum project in South Africa that involved an international team of educators from the United States and South Africa collaborating to develop conflict resolution education for four high schools in four communities in the Gauteng province. They described the process that evolved as this group of international educators worked together in the service of this ambitious project. Using dialectical theory as applied to groups (e.g., Smith & Berg, 1987) and focusing specifically on significant turning points (e.g., Baxter & Bullis, 1986), Jones and Bodtker discussed how the paradoxes of identity (individual or representative identity and collective or shared identity), authority (balancing attempts to gain or exercise authority with needs to avoid disempowering other members of the group), and participation (engaging in appropriate levels of disclosure, trust, and intimacy) influenced the group process and, ultimately, the success of the project.

Jones and Bodtker's (1998) case analysis has much to offer those interested in systematic institutional change in the service of social justice. It reveals, in rich detail, the ways that individuals of different backgrounds (in this instance, international, as well as interdisciplinary) struggled to develop common ground. Threats to common ground, such as loyalties to identities and groups external to the project group, were carefully described. Jones and Bodtker concluded that "in our analysis, the role of community as a context for group identity, as an alternative focus for energy from which group members can reinvent themselves, becomes more apparent" (p. 370). This case study encourages further consideration of the role of conflict in social justice education. Given the natural tendency for groups to resist fundamental changes to the status quo, however inequitable, Jones and Bodtker's analysis of how this particular group navigated tensions in identity, authority, and participation provides useful information for planning similar types of educational interventions.

Directions for Future Research

The literature reviewed in this chapter focused attention on questions about communication in educational contexts and concerns about particular problems in those contexts that might be effectively addressed by communication theory, research, and practice. This review leads us to conclude that there is a great deal of exciting applied communication research in educational contexts. In this final section, we celebrate that observation and pose new questions and concerns worth exploring.

We began by exploring applied research focused on teacher communicative behavior. Given the extensive program of research on teacher power (e.g., Waldeck et al., 2001a), and given that classroom management is among the most compelling communication challenges of practicing teachers (Wang, Haertel, & Walberg, 1993), we expected to see a much more robust collection of studies exploring how teachers' use of power affects specific classroom management problems. Instead, the one relevant essay by Weber et al. (2001) reported that teachers in a program designed for students who had not been successful in school used positive forms of power and were perceived by those students as caring.

Given this very hopeful finding, more applied communication scholarship needs to explore problems of classroom management using the research on teacher power. Such applications might do much to help teachers understand the communicative dimensions of classroom management, as well as help scholars interested in how power is communicated in classrooms to understand the localized and contextualized dynamics of that application. We join Sprague (1992b) in expressing concern, along with curiosity, about the degree to which our currently decontextualized tools for measuring power will stand the test of application in actual classrooms, with complex combinations of students and talents, and in the service of widely varying notions of control and management. Still, in the spirit of good academic inquiry, we look forward to a solid, evidence-based conversation about this important issue.

A second collection of essays reviewed centered on questions about how teachers' messages facilitate students' learning. Some of this research emerged from communication education and instructional communication areas, but communication scholars increasingly are gravitating toward the SoTL framework as a way to understand better particular applications of teacher message behavior in relation to student learning outcomes. In addition, newly energized research about communication across the curriculum is making important contributions to understanding how communication skills develop and enhance learning in a variety of classrooms, such as in engineering, business, and design courses.

However, given the rising importance and ubiquity of new communication technologies (see Lievrouw, this volume), we were surprised to discover only one applied research project by Waldeck et al. (2001b) that explored how new communication technologies might help or hurt teaching and learning. In addition to understanding how and why students might use e-mail to contact their teachers, we recommend learning how teachers and their students might use communication message arenas, such as blogs and chat rooms, to clarify course content, develop skills, and collaborate. There also are many questions that emerge from a social justice perspective about issues of access to such technologies and cultural imperatives for, or prohibitions against, using technologies for particular types of relating, as well as questions of voice and inclusion.

The studies reviewed also revealed a number of projects that focus on engaged pedagogical approaches to student learning, with research on service learning and deliberative education in the communication classroom some of the most abundant. The findings from this research demonstrate how an education in communication applied to a specific context encourages stronger connections and more holistic understanding of the role of communication in these settings than similar courses without a service-learning or deliberative education component. For example, some of the service-learning projects invite us to consider how to create better connections between communication subject matter and skill development (such as intercultural communication, organizational communication, research methods, and teaching communication). This work also is particularly important because it demonstrates how, through engaged pedagogical approaches, students report stronger personal connections to the curriculum (e.g., Artz, 2001; Braun, 2001; Gravel, 2001; Keyton, 2000; McMillan & Harriger, 2002) and increased confidence and deeper understanding of the subject matter of communication (e.g., Artz, 2001; Braun, 2001; Crabtree, 1998; Keyton, 2000; O'Hara, 2001; Staton & Tomlison, 2001). Furthermore, much of this work suggests that service learning and deliberative education are promising pedagogical tools for increasing students' social awareness and willingness to become civically involved (e.g., Artz, 2001; Crabtree, 1998; Gayle, 2004; Gibson et al., 2001; Gravel, 2001; Keyton, 2000; McMillan & Harriger, 2002; O'Hara, 2001). Many scholars reported that students in these settings saw new ways to integrate theory with practice, and how to use their education to make a difference in their lives and in the lives of others (e.g., Artz, 2001; Crabtree, 1998; Gravel, 2001; O'Hara, 2001; Staton & Tomlison, 2001).

Given these findings, we are intrigued by the possibilities of this work, as it invites educators and scholars to consider how communication education might create possible solutions to some of society's most vexing problems. However, this hope does not come without worry. We also heed the cautions expressed about seeing engaged pedagogy as a panacea for solving all of society's ills. Specifically, Artz (2001) warned that engaging in service with the intent to better society must be viewed critically, and he cautioned that the view of service as charity, which dominates pedagogy and research, leads to temporary solutions that reinforce the status quo and keep dominant systems in place and people who have been historically disenfranchised on the margins. Artz's warning encourages us to consider that engaged pedagogical approaches, such as service learning, can be extensions of implicit social contracts of dominance and inequity. We, thus, cannot assume that pedagogies, in and of themselves, can do the work of social justice. Teachers and scholars need to move beyond taken-for-granted assumptions about how individuals engage in the social act of teaching or learning to focus on the social functions that are produced and reproduced in schools. Given that service learning and deliberative education are social and applied pedagogical approaches, the question becomes how we might construct more critical understandings of the role of communication and communicators in specific, applied educational settings.

In addition to the pedagogical approaches that encourage and facilitate community engagement, we are optimistic about the number of studies that extend the work of civic engagement and social justice outside of the individual classroom. A number of studies explored applied questions about how communicative practices in educational settings can serve a social justice agenda (e.g., Artz, 1998; Barge & Loges, 2003; Jones & Bodkter, 1998; Newfield et al., 2003; Rosenfeld & Richman, 1999; Rosenfeld et al., 1998; Tracy & Ashcraft, 2001). These studies move beyond questions of how communication can better serve the needs of schools and learning to how communities also may be engaged in social change through communication education. Given that schools are located in neighborhoods and communities, and impacted by local, state, and national decisions, scholars need to understand more fully the embedded nature of communication in educational contexts and its implications for promoting social justice.

Specifically, the studies reviewed in this chapter teach us about how schools and communities—broadly defined—may work together to create more inclusive practices (e.g., Artz, 1998; Barges & Logues, 2003; Jones & Bodtker, 1998; Rosenfeld et al., 1998) and policies (e.g., Newfield et al., 2003; Tracy & Ashcraft, 2001). However, as Hartnett (1998) cautioned, the work of social justice is not only about agenda setting or creating "blueprints for change, but rather to an open-ended and literally infinite process of articulating needs and aspirations within a democratically organized social space" (p. 233). This view means that education and scholarship focused on communication in educational contexts that is socially just must remain constantly diligent and critical of how access, representation, resources, and equity in schooling affect those who have been historically marginalized and disenfranchised in society and, therefore, in schools and classrooms.

The research reviewed in this chapter also introduces new questions, as well as highlights responsibilities, for those who study communication in educational contexts. Specifically, it is the responsibility of communication scholars who are interested in education to critically examine how issues of power, access, equity, and equality are negotiated through and in day-to-day practice. As the applied communication research that has been conducted shows, one way that scholars can focus on the creation of social justice in educational contexts is through examinations of daily conversations that occur in classrooms, hallways, boardrooms, and staff lounges. The work of Jones and Bodkter (1998) and Tracy and Ashcraft (2001) teach us that issues of power and inclusiveness, related to educational contexts, are negotiated in policy-making and curricular conversations, and the research conducted by Artz (2001) and Barges and Loges (2003) illustrates how we need to provide opportunities for people to talk about important educational issues in more skillful and inclusive ways.

Conclusion

As this chapter clearly demonstrates, the tradition of applied communication in educational contexts is alive and well. Scholarship from the perspectives of communication education and instructional communication has continued to make contributions to

understanding how teachers can communicate more effectively and how particular pedagogies can be employed skillfully. Increasingly, the Scholarship of Teaching and Learning
framework is being adopted to conduct applied research about communication teaching
and learning. However, as we argued in the opening section of this chapter, a commitment to applied communication research for and about social justice in educational contexts means a commitment to systemic social and cultural transformation. Fulfilling our
obligation to social change, thus, is an imperative charge to scholars in communication
education and instructional communication. In fact, it is difficult to imagine how social
justice will ever advance without attention to classrooms, schools, and the process of education in the United States today. Furthermore, it is not sufficient for that commitment to
take the form of academic dialogue; it must be expressed on social, political, economic,
organizational, and personal levels. A commitment to social justice in research, teaching,
and other practices requires adopting an activist orientation and connecting with those
who are different from us, inventing ways to share resources equitably, and devoting
ourselves to creating a society that embraces and cherishes all of its members. Thus, we
end this chapter by imploring our colleagues who are interested in communication in
educational contexts to join us in this work. Simply put, we must do more.

References

Arendt, H. (1968). *Between past and future: Eight exercises in political thought.* New York:
Viking Press.

Artz, L. (1998). African-Americans and higher education: An exigence in need of applied communication. *Journal of Applied Communication Research, 26,* 210–231.

Artz, L. (2001). Critical ethnography for communication studies: Dialogue and social justice in
service-learning. *Southern Communication Journal, 66,* 239–250.

Barge, J. K., & Loges, W. E. (2003). Parent, student, and teacher perceptions of parental involvement. *Journal of Applied Communication Research, 31,* 140–163.

Baus, R. D. (1995). Using performance to increase retention of dialectic tension management strategies. *Journal of Applied Communication Research, 23,* 230–238.

Baxter, L. A., & Bullis, C. (1986). Turning points in developing romantic relationships. *Human
Communication Research, 12,* 469–493.

Bitzer, L. F. (1968). The rhetorical situation. *Philosophy in Rhetoric, 1,* 1–14.

Bloom, A. (1987). *The closing of the American mind: How higher education has failed democracy
and impoverished the souls of today's students.* New York: Simon & Schuster

Boyer, E. L. (1987a). *College: The undergraduate experience in America.* New York: Harper &
Row.

Boyer, E. L. (1987b). *Scholarship reconsidered: Priorities of the professorate.* Princeton, NJ: Carnegie Foundation for the Advancement of Teaching.

Braun, M. J. (2001). Using self-directed teams to integrate service-learning into an organizational
communication course. *Southern Communication Journal, 66,* 226–238.

Chanock, K. (2005). Investigating patterns and possibilities in an academic oral genre. *Communication Education, 54,* 92–99.

Christian, S. E. (2007). A marriage of like minds and collective action: Civic journalism in a
service-learning framework. In L. R. Frey & K. M. Carragee (Eds.), *Communication activism:
Vol. 2. Media and performance in activism* (pp. 97–128). Cresskill, NJ: Hampton Press.

Christian, S. E., & Lapinski, M. (2003). Support for the contract hypothesis: High school students' attitudes toward Muslims post 9-11. *Journal of Intercultural Communication Research,
32,* 247–263.

Christian, S. E., & Prater, A. (2003). Publishing the n-word in a student newspaper: A dialogue on
the racial, ethical, and educational issues. *Journal of Intergroup Relations, 3,* 20–38.

Cissna, K. N. (2000). Applied communication research in the 21st century. *Journal of Applied
Communication Research, 28,* 169–173.

Crabtree, R. D. (1998). Mutual empowerment in cross-cultural participatory development and service learning: Lessons in communication and social justice from projects in El Salvador and Nicaragua. *Journal of Applied Communication Research, 26*, 182–209.

Craig, R. T. (1989). Communication as a practical discipline. In B. Dervin, L. Grossberg, B. O'Keefe, & E. Wartella (Eds.), *Rethinking communication: Vol. 1. Paradigm issues* (pp. 97–122). Newbury Park, CA: Sage.

Cronin, M. W., & Glen, P. (1991). Oral communication across the curriculum in higher education: The state of the art. *Communication Education, 40*, 356–367.

Dallimore, E. J., Hertenstein, J. H., & Platt, M. B. (2004). Classroom participation and discussion effectiveness: Student-generated strategies. *Communication Education, 53*, 103–115.

Dannels, D. P. (2002). Communication across the curriculum and in the disciplines: Speaking in engineering. *Communication Education, 51*, 254–268.

Dannels, D. P. (Ed.). (2005). Communication genres in disciplinary discourse communities: Theoretical and pedagogical explorations of communication across the curriculum and in the disciplines [Special issue]. *Communication Education, 54*(1).

Dannels, D. P., Anson, C. M., Bullard, L., & Peretti, S. (2003). Challenges in learning communication skills in chemical engineering. *Communication Education, 52*, 50–56.

Darling, A. L. (2002). Scholarship of teaching and learning in communication: New connections, new directions, new possibilities. *Communication Education, 51*, 47–49.

Darling, A. L., & Dannels, D. P. (2003). Practicing engineers talk about the importance of talk: A report on the role of oral communication in the workplace. *Communication Education, 52*, 1–16.

Frey, L. R. (1998). Communication and social justice research: Truth, justice, and the applied communication way. *Journal of Applied Communication Research, 26*, 155–164.

Frey, L. R., Pearce, W. B., Pollock, M. A., Artz, L., & Murphy, B. A. O. (1996). Looking for justice in all the wrong placed: On a communication approach to social justice. *Communication Studies, 47*, 110–127.

Friedrich, G. W. (2002). The communication education research agenda. *Communication Education, 51*, 372–375.

Garcia, D. (2002). Making multiple literacies visible in the writing classroom: From Cupareo, Guanajuato, to Cal State, Monterey Bay. *Social Justice, 29*(4), 122–136.

Gayle, B. M. (2004). Transformations in a civil discourse public speaking class: Speakers' and listeners' attitude change. *Communication Education, 53*, 174–184.

Gibson, M. K., Kostecki, E. M., & Lucas, M. K. (2001). Instituting principles of best practice for service-learning in the communication curriculum. *Southern Communication Journal, 66*, 187–200.

Goals 2000: Educate America Act. Public Law No. 103–227. (1994).

Gravel, A. (2001). Power and change in the 21st century: An exploration of the Industrial Areas Foundation as a model of theory and pedagogy in the persuasion course. *Communication Education, 50*, 177–186.

Hartnett, S. (1998). Lincoln and Douglas meet the abolitionist David Walker as prisoners debate slavery: Empowering education, applied communication, and social justice. *Journal of Applied Communication Research, 26*, 232–253.

Henricksen, L. (1996). Naïve theories of buying and selling: Implications for teaching critical-viewing skills. *Journal of Applied Communication Research, 24*, 93–109.

Jones, T. S., & Bodtker, A. (1998). A dialectical analysis of a social justice process: International collaboration in South Africa. *Journal of Applied Communication Research, 25*, 357–373.

Keyton, J. (2000). Applied communication research should be practical. *Journal of Applied Communication Research, 28*, 166–168.

Keyton, J. (2001). Integrating service-learning in the research methods course. *Southern Communication Journal, 66*, 201–210.

McCroskey, J. C., & Richmond, V. P. (1983). Power in the classroom I: Teacher and student perceptions. *Communication Education, 32*, 175–184.

McDevitt, M., & Kiousis, S. (2006). Deliberative learning: An evaluative approach to interactive civic education. *Communication Education, 55*, 247–264.

McMillan, J. J., & Harriger, K. J. (2002). College students and deliberation: A benchmark study. *Communication Education, 51*, 237–253.

Murphy, T. A. (2004). Deliberative civic education and civil society: A consideration of ideals and actualities in democracy and communication education. *Communication Education, 53*, 74–91.

Newfield, D., Andrew, D., Stein, P., & Maungedzo, R. (2003). "No number can describe how good it was": Assessment issues in the multimodal classroom. *Assessment in Education: Principles, Policy & Practice, 10*, 61–82.

Novek, E., & Sanford, R. (2007). At the checkpoint: Journalistic practices, researcher reflexivity, and dialectical dilemmas in a women's prison. In L. R. Frey & K. M. Carragee (Eds.), *Communication activism: Vol. 2. Media and performance activism* (pp. 67–95). Cresskill, NJ: Hampton Press.

O'Hara, L. S. (2001). Service-learning: Students' transformative journey from communication student to civic-minded professional. *Southern Communication Journal, 66*, 251–266.

Richmond, V. P., & McCroskey, J. C. (Eds.). (1992). *Power in the classroom: Communication, control, and concern.* Hillsdale, NJ: Erlbaum.

Rosenfeld, L. B., & Richman, J. M. (1999). Supportive communication and school outcomes, Part II: Academically "at-risk" and other low income high school students. *Communication Education, 48*, 294–307.

Rosenfeld, L. B., Richman, J. M., & Bowen, G. L. (1998). Supportive communication and school outcomes for academically "at-risk" and other low income middle school students. *Communication Education, 47*, 309–325.

Rosenfeld, L. B., Richman, J. M., Bowen, G. L., & Wynns, S. L. (2006). In the face of a dangerous community: The effects of social support and neighborhood danger on high school students' school outcomes. *Southern Communication Journal, 71*, 273–289.

Schrodt, P. Witt, P. L., Myers, S. A., Turman, P. D., Barton, M. H., & Jernberg, K. A. (2008). Learner empowerment and teaching evaluations as functions of teach power use in the college classroom. *Communication Education, 57*, 180–200.

Schrodt, P., Witt, P. L., & Turman, P. D. (2007). Reconsidering the measurement of teacher power use in the college classroom. *Communication Education, 56*, 308–332.

Smith, K. K., & Berg, D. N. (1987). *Paradoxes of group life: Understanding conflict, paralysis, and movement in group dynamics.* San Francisco: Jossey-Bass.

Speech Communication Association. (1996). *Speaking, listening, and media literacy standards for K through 12 education.* Annandale, VA: Author.

Sprague, J. (1992a). Expanding the research agenda for instructional communication: Raising some unasked questions. *Communication Education, 41*, 1–25.

Sprague, J. (1992b). Critical perspectives on teacher empowerment. *Communication Education, 41*, 181–203.

Staton, A. Q., & Tomlison, S. D. (2001). Communication education outreach in elementary school classrooms. *Southern Communication Journal, 66*, 211–225.

Staton-Spicer, A. Q., & Wulff, D. H. (1984). Research in communication and instruction: Categorization and synthesis. *Communication Education, 38*, 377–391.

Swan, S. (2002). Rhetoric, service, and social justice. *Written Communication, 19*, 76–108.

Thomas, J. (1993). *Doing critical ethnography.* Newbury Park, CA: Sage.

Thompson, B. (2008). Characteristics of parent–teacher e-mail communication. *Communication Education, 57*, 201–223.

Tracy, K., & Ashcraft, C. (2001). Crafting policies about controversial values: How wording disputes manage a group dilemma. *Journal of Applied Communication, 29*, 297–316.

Turman, P. D., & Schrodt, P. (2006). Student perceptions of teacher power as a function of perceived teacher confirmation. *Communication Education, 55*, 265–279.

Waldeck, J. H., Kearney, P., & Plax, T. G. (2001a). Instructional and developmental communication theory and research in the 1990s: Extending the agenda for the 21st century. In W. B. Gudykunst (Ed.), *Communication yearbook* (Vol. 24, pp. 207–229). Thousand Oaks, CA: Sage.

Waldeck, J. H., Kearney, P., & Plax, T. G. (2001b). Teacher e-mail message strategies and students' willingness to communicate online. *Journal of Applied Communication Research, 29*, 54–70.

Wang, M. D., Haertel, G. D., & Walbergh, H. J. (1993). Toward a knowledge base for school learning. *Review of Educational Research, 63*, 249–294.

Weber, K., Martin, M. M., & Patterson, B. R. (2001). Teacher behavior, student interest, and affective learning: Putting theory to practice. *Journal of Applied Communication Research, 29*, 71–90.

Wulff, S. S., & Wulff, D. H. (2004). "Of course I'm communicating; I lecture every day": Enhancing teaching and learning in introductory statistics. *Communication Education, 53*, 92–102.

21 Communication for Participatory Development
Dialogue, Action, and Change

D. Lawrence Kincaid and María Elena Figueroa
Johns Hopkins University

More than halfway to the 2015 deadline, measurable progress has been achieved on some of the eight millennium development goals established in 2000 by leaders of 189 countries (United Nations, 2007). For instance, according to the United Nations (UN; 2007), from 1990 to 2004, the proportion of people living in extreme poverty (living on a dollar or less a day) dropped from 1.25 billion (32%) to 980 million (19%), and child mortality declined worldwide. However, severe problems remain, as half a million women die annually from preventable and treatable complications from pregnancy and childbirth, and there has been little progress in halving the proportion of underweight children. Moreover, in Sub-Saharan Africa, only 5% of children under age 5 sleep under insecticide-treated bed nets, an effective tool for preventing malaria, far short of the 60% target that was set for 2005. Deaths from AIDS increased to an estimated 2.1 million in 2007, with more than 15 million children having lost one or both parents to the disease. Half the population of the developing world still lives without basic sanitation and over a billion people lack access to safe water. Meanwhile, many of the benefits of global economic growth are not being equally shared.

Development communication examines communication issues related to efforts to solve the types of problems just identified, especially in less developed countries. As a distinct field of study, development communication was established in the 1950s and 1960s when the developed world began providing economic aid to increase food production, reduce poverty, slow population growth, and improve health and education in less developed and newly emerging countries. The emphasis of this aid was on improving national infrastructure and transferring modern (scientific) technology to these countries. Lerner's (1958) classic study of the modernization of traditional societies theorized development as a process in which urbanization leads to increased literacy, which increases exposure to media. These changes are followed by wider economic participation (e.g., higher per capita income) and increased political participation (e.g., voting). Literacy and media exposure, thus, were considered crucial mediating variables (steps) between urbanization and economic or political participation. The rapid diffusion of the transistor radio, followed by television, also made the study of media and development a compelling area for communication scholarship.

In the United States, the field of development communication can be traced to the disciplines of rural sociology, journalism and mass communication, and education. To a great extent, the field was launched by the adaptation of the diffusion of innovation model from rural U.S. agricultural settings to a wide range of development problems around the world (E. M. Rogers, 1962, 1969, 1973), studies of the role of media in national development (e.g., Schramm, 1964), and the development of participatory approaches to the education of people living in poor, marginalized sectors of society (e.g., Freire, 1970).

Research on the diffusion of innovations has a long history in the United States, but in the context of national development programs, this type of communication research mainly has been applied in developing countries, which may account for its underrepresentation in the applied communication research literature. Jacobson (1993, 2003) used the context of national development to argue that the value of pragmatism justifies the acceptance of participatory communication research by academic disciplines. Justification is further enhanced by improving the theory of participatory communication in development programs.

It is beyond the scope of this chapter to review the entire field and all of the relevant points of controversy regarding development communication (for this history, see Casmir, 1991; Dube, 1988; Fraser & Restrepo-Estrada, 1998; Kim, 2005; Mayo & Servaes, 1994; Melkote, 1991; Nair & White, 1993; E. M. Rogers, 1999; Servaes, 1999, 2004). Hornik's (1988) review identified an important trend in development communication that continues today: the split of practitioners and scholars alike into two related approaches. One approach focuses on media campaigns designed to change individual behavior (e.g., Andreasen, 1995; Fishbein et al., 2001; Hornik, 2002; Piotrow, Kincaid, Rimon, & Rinehart, 1997; Rice & Atkin, 2001); the other approach focuses on communication for participatory development within local communities with an emphasis on dialogue, group communication, and social networks (e.g., Beltrán, 1976; Beltrán & Gonzalez, 1998; Berrigan, 1981; Bessette & Rajasunderam, 1996; Calvelo Rios, 1998; Chambers, 1997; Coldevin & FAO, 2001; Díaz Bordenave, 1976, 1998; Dudley, 1993; Gumucio Dagrón, 2001; McKee, Manoncourt, Yoon, & Carnegie, 2000; Portales, 1986; Prieto Castillo, 1998; E. M. Rogers & Kincaid, 1981; Servaes, Jacobson, & White, 1996; Simpson, 1986; White, 1995).

This chapter focuses on the second trend of communication—participatory development. Rather than review the extant literature, highlight the main approaches and trends, and then identify the controversies, strengths, and shortcomings of this approach, we reverse the order. Our review of the literature revealed that what is missing is a comprehensive, coherent model of communication for participatory development that synthesizes the literature and addresses the main controversies and shortcomings in the field. Therefore, we offer such a model, one that can be used by practitioners to design and implement effective development programs, and by applied communication scholars to conduct research on those programs. As we explicate the model, relevant literature is reviewed in a manner that follows and supports the model. Thus, in this chapter, we present a model that synthesizes the literature and demonstrates how applied communication research can be theory based as well as pragmatic, focusing on real problems and practical situations across a variety of social, cultural, global, and professional areas of society.

Our review of relevant literature identified the following eight issues related to communication for participatory development:

1. The concept of development needs to be reformulated in a manner that applies to human development in local communities, as well as the traditional focus on national development.
2. Participatory development requires dialogue—a symmetrical, two-way process of communication, but many prevailing approaches to development communication use an asymmetrical, one-way process of communication.
3. No model of the development process reconciles the demand for social change at the community level and the need for requisite changes at the individual level.
4. Scholars and practitioners agree that community members should determine the goals of development themselves, but the problem-specific nature of funding often means

that external change agents impose development goals on communities. External change agents can play the valuable role of catalyst and facilitate the process, but motivation and leadership needs to come from within a community itself.

5. The role of conflict in communication generally is ignored in participatory development, even though it is common feature of most communities. Therefore, a model of the process needs to recognize conflict and suggest methods to manage it.

6. Ownership, self-determination, and social change are considered necessary to build community capacity and to sustain the process of development without further outside stimuli.

7. Communities should have access to local media, such as community radio, posters/billboards, traveling theater groups, and even cell phones, to produce content for their development objectives rather than rely on content originating from external sources that primarily serve the purposes of those sources.

8. Self-assessment needs to guide the process and motivate sustained, collective action.

A model of participatory development, thus, needs to be theoretically sound and useful to communication scholars but also useful to community leaders and communication practitioners. The model of communication for participatory development that we use to organize and synthesize the literature addresses these eight key issues, and it provides a tool useful for both research and practice. Specifically, because development is assumed to be "people oriented," communication for participatory development needs to be based on dialogue, conflict management, and mutual understanding and agreement. The model also resolves other controversial issues that hinder progress in the field—problems subsumed under the general notion of "local culture," such as community factions, entrenched power structures, equitable participation, sharing of benefits, and styles of leadership that may discourage, as well as facilitate, participation and collective action.

The Concept of Development

Dissatisfaction with the pace of development, the discovery of unforeseen obstacles, and an increase in the inequitable distribution of income throughout the world has led to considerable controversy regarding the concept of development itself, the constraints of national political economies, and the proper role of communication for development. Since the 1950s, *development* has been defined as the increase in gross national product (GNP) or national per-capita income that is due to changes in the structure of a country's economy, such as the growth of industry, a decline in agriculture, and an increased percentage of people living in cities rather than the countryside (Gillis, Perkins, Roemer, & Snodgrass 1992). Thus, the dominant development paradigm of the 20th century focused on modernization and wealth accumulation as keys to economic growth.

The economic side of development clearly was reflected in the priority placed on economic growth in the first, second, and third UN development decades (1960s, 1970s, and 1980s). Criticism of this narrow perspective, however, eventually led to a much broader conceptualization of development (Goulet, 1985). Even the United Nations Development Programme (2002) recognized that "preoccupation with economic growth and the creation of wealth and material opulence has obscured the fact that development is ultimately about people" (p. 15).

The increase in poverty and disease burden worldwide in the 1990s created the need for a people-centered paradigm of development. Consequently, at the 2000 UN Millennium Summit, human well-being and poverty reduction were at the center of global development objectives (United Nations Development Programme, 2003). *Human devel-*

opment was interpreted as a process of "expanding [people's] choices to live full, creative lives with freedom and dignity.... Fundamental to expanding human choices is building human capabilities" (United National Development Programme, 2003, p. 28). The goal of human development was viewed as increasing the prospects for living a long and healthy life, being educated, having a decent standard of living, and enjoying political and civil freedoms to participate in the life of one's community. Thus, the concept of development has evolved into the process of capacity building and human improvement, in general, with eight specific development goals established to guide development in the 21st century: (1) eradicate extreme poverty and hunger; (2) achieve universal primary education; (3) achieve gender equality and empower women; (4) reduce child mortality; (5) improve maternal health; (6) combat HIV, AIDS, malaria, and other diseases; (7) ensure environmental sustainability; and (8) create a global partnership for development.

The active participation of community members in their development makes it possible to accomplish higher level needs, such as self-esteem and belonging, as well as basic physical and safety needs (Maslow, 1998). In Korea and Bangladesh, for example, women acknowledged an increase in their prestige and status after becoming leaders in women's village development groups (Kincaid, 2000b; Kincaid & Yum, 1976; E. M. Rogers & Kincaid, 1981). Participatory development, thus, "places substantial value on local initiative and diversity [and] on self-organizing systems developed around human-scale organizational units and self-reliant communities" (Korten, 1984, p. 300). Such development involves a process of change in which people gain greater control over their environment to bring about social, as well as material, advancement for the majority of the people (E. M. Rogers, 1976).

Participatory development scholars usually emphasize Freire's (1970) principle of the central role of the community in its development. This principle means that external change agents should (1) function as facilitators or catalysts who help community members to discuss and decide how to improve their lives, and (2) recognize that people have the ability to identify their needs and conduct self-assessments, make decisions about courses of action, and participate in the political processes that affect their lives (Bracht, 1999; Green & Kreuter, 1991).

Communication for Participatory Development

Communication for participatory development (CFPD) is a planned activity, using local media and dialogue among various stakeholders about a common problem or shared goal to develop and implement activities that contribute to its solution or accomplishment (Bessette, 2004). Stakeholders usually are individual members of the community itself, but they also may be organized groups within a community, local or regional authorities, nongovernmental organizations (NGOs), government institutions providing services at the community level, and policy-makers. The guiding philosophy of CFPD, as mentioned previously, can be traced to the work of Freire (1970), the Brazilian educator who conceived of communication as dialogue and participation for the purpose of creating cultural identity, trust, commitment, ownership, and (in today's term) empowerment. CFPD builds on this philosophy and the broad literature on development communication created by practitioners, activists, and scholars.

The call for a model of development communication based on *dialogue* rather than monologue, *horizontal* rather than vertical information sharing, *social* rather than individual change, and equitable *participation*, local *ownership*, and *empowerment* (Gray-Felder & Dean, 1999; Gumucio Dragón, 2001; United Nations Population Fund, 2001) has grown stronger with the decentralization of authority and access to new communication technologies that occurred during the 1990s (Beltrán, 1993a, 1993b; Díaz Bordenave, 1994, 1998; see also Lievrouw, this volume). An appropriate model of CFPD, therefore, should be based on dialogue, information sharing, mutual understanding and agreement, and collective action. Such a model needs to account for conflict and its management, as well as for cooperation. Finally, it also needs to identify social, as well as individual, outcomes. The convergence theory of communication (E. M. Rogers & Kincaid, 1981), grounded in dialogue and extended to account for divergence (Kincaid, 2002), meets the first two requirements; the CFPD model presented here satisfies the third requirement.

Communication as Convergence and Divergence

Convergence theory represents communication as a horizontal process of sharing information between two or more participants within social networks that leads to social outcomes—such as mutual understanding, mutual agreement, and collective action—as well as psychological outcomes—such as perception, interpretation, understanding, belief, and action (Kincaid, 1988, 1993; E. M. Rogers & Kincaid, 1981). *Dialogue* is a conversation between two or more people in which participants seek to clarify what each one thinks and believes. Dialogue itself constitutes a minimal form of cooperative, collective action. The underlying assumption of dialogue is that convergence is desirable and possible, and that all participants, not just one of the parties, are willing to listen and change.

Convergence does not mean consensus; it specifies only the direction of movement when dialogue is effective. Sometimes, however, this symmetrical process of dialogue breaks down. In that case, one or both parties quit listening, impose a point of view on the other, and feedback becomes ineffective. Convergence, therefore, slows and may reverse into divergence, with differences being exaggerated, turning harmony into polarization and cooperation into conflict. Hammond, Anderson, and Cissna (2003) referred to these two aspects of dialogue as "convergence" and "emergence."

The inherent properties of dialogue suggest that, over time, most groups converge toward a state of greater internal uniformity, sometimes referred to as "local culture" (Kincaid, 1988, 1993), with the term *local* implying a bounded group of individuals. Convergence theory is valid, in part, because of the important role played by boundaries and bounded normative influence (Kincaid, 2002, 2004). Within the boundaries created by dialogue itself, convergence occurs because those who do not agree or see an issue the same way as other participants tend to stop participating and "drop out" of the group, perhaps forming a competing faction within the community. Simply leaving a group (moving outside the network boundaries created by dialogue) automatically creates greater uniformity among those who remain within the group compared to those outside of it. This convergence process is enhanced by *bounded normative influence*—"the tendency of social norms to influence behavior within relatively bounded, local subgroups of a social system rather than in the system as a whole" (Kincaid, 2004, p. 38). This social network principle resolves the paradox of how a new minority position can avoid becoming extinguished by majority pressure and eventually can grow and become the new majority. Within its local boundaries, its members *are* the majority and, thus, are able to sustain their new position and then grow by gradually recruiting new members outside of their boundaries from the larger community.

The existence of divergent subgroups or factions within a community implies two simultaneous processes: (1) convergence among members *within* each bounded subgroup and (2) divergence *between* subgroups over time. A boundary, determined by observation, interviews with key informants, self-reports, and social network analysis within a community, defines who is included and excluded from dialogue. Splitting communities into factions with different points of view increases cohesion within each faction but reduces the overall social cohesion of the larger community. Factionalism of this type reduces the capacity of community members to solve mutual problems through collective action. If the lack of cohesion is severe, cooperative action can come to a complete halt or force one community faction to continue by itself.

By clarifying the meanings, values, and real interests of each party, however, dialogue also may lead to divergence and conflict. In the extended convergence–divergence model of communication, conflict is included as a possible outcome of dialogue (Howard, 1999; Kincaid, 2002). The extended model has six phases: (1) scene-setting, (2) build-up, and (3) resolution; or (4) climax and (5) conflict; and ending in (6) implementation (see Figure 21.1).

Four of the six phases correspond to the original convergence theory. In the first phase, *scene-setting*, the fixed parameters of the problem or goal are established. In the *build-up* phase, dialogue leads to convergence and, hence, a common frame of reference (mutual understanding). If each party agrees on a common position that it can trust the other to implement (*resolution* phase), the parties cooperate in some form of collective action (*implementation* phase). Mutual understanding ensures each party's trustworthiness, but if flaws are revealed in the *resolution* stage, mistrust may arise, throwing the parties back into a new *build-up* phase with an increased possibility of conflict. Once *resolution* is reached, an atmosphere of mutual goodwill and trust makes the possibility of a successful *implementation* more likely.

The common frame of reference may or may not represent each party's actual point of view. One or both parties may deceive the other by leaving something out or the parties

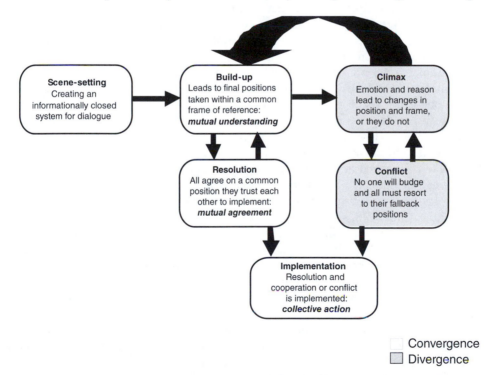

Figure 21.1 Communication as a process of convergence and divergence. *Note.* From "Drama, Emotion, and Cultural Convergence" by D. L. Kincaid, 2002, *Communication Theory, 12,* p. 142. Copyright 2000 by Blackwell Publishing. Reprinted with permission.

may create a mutual understanding that does not reflect their true preferences. A common framework built on deceit, however, ultimately may undermine implementation and damage future attempts at dialogue and collective action.

In the case of divergence, the build-up phase ends without agreement (resolution) and the process enters into a *climax* phase. The action shifts to confrontation and threats of taking fallback positions, which could range, for example, from refusing to provide labor and other resources for a community development project to physical violence in a more serious conflict. Power comes into play when one or both parties adopt the threat-taking fallback position. During confrontation, the parties disagree on the terms of the resolution or openly distrust one another to implement them. Fear and anger, thus, may interfere with reason. If these feelings can be overcome, the action still can shift back into a new *build-up* phase where dialogue can be tried again to manage the differences; if not, a decisive moment is reached, and one or both parties begin to implement fallback positions. If one or both parties prefer this latter outcome, the threatened fallback positions will be implemented and an open *conflict* phase follows. If one or both parties fear this outcome sufficiently, there may be enough pressure to get them to change their positions to avoid conflict and return to another *build-up* phase.

In situations where mutual understanding and agreement cannot be reached, to avoid conflict, something must give within this fixed framework or the framework must change. For example, one or the other party's objectives may change, the threat of taking fallback positions may be withdrawn if not yet implemented, or beliefs about the fixed boundaries (preferences and courses of action) of the confrontation may change, including the goals themselves.

According to this approach to conflict (Howard, 1999), it is the rigidity of the final positions taken in the climax phase that creates a high level of emotion, both positive and negative. Without this emotion—fear of conflict, a threatened future, or a desire for a mutually beneficial solution—there is no motivation to change and very little pressure to avoid conflict. Emotion alone, however, is insufficient unless it is supported by rational arguments, sound logic, and evidence. Rational arguments can increase mutual understanding and produce a common frame of reference, and evidence builds credibility. Emotion alone is not taken seriously because it is transitory, but if it is accompanied by sound logic and evidence, a new position may be found that is credible and can produce a mutual agreement (Howard, 1999). Together, logic and emotion make it possible to reopen dialogue and move participants back into a new build-up phase. If a satisfactory resolution can be reached at that time, the process results in collective action.

Conflict can be managed by a variety of decision-making processes: by leaders alone; discussion until no objections are expressed and consensus is apparent; forwarding a proposal and a voice vote, show of hands, or secret ballot; or by the issue simply being postponed and left unresolved. All of these practices rely on some form of communication; even leaders acting unilaterally need to tell their followers what they have decided. If communication cannot create a sufficient level of agreement on a course of action, then compromise, mediation, or arbitration is necessary. If these approaches fail, the parties in conflict may resort to threats, violence, or avoidance, all of which undermine the participatory development process.

Ultimately, dialogue is one of the primary means of managing community conflict, as long as people still are willing to talk with one another. Convergence can be resumed when (1) participants with differing points of view listen to one another, as indicated by paraphrasing each other's point of view to the other's satisfaction (effective listening); (2) each party acknowledges conditions under which the other's point of view can be accepted as valid (empathy); and (3) each party acknowledges the overlap or similarity of the points of view (agreement; Rapoport, 1967, as derived from C. R. Rogers's, 1951, client-centered therapy).

Community Dialogue and Collective Action

CFPD begins with community dialogue and leads to collective action that can result in individual and social changes that improve the welfare and capacity of all members of a community. CFPD draws on a broad literature on development communication that was initiated in the early 1960s. In particular, the work of Latin-American theorists and communication activists is used because of its clarity and emphasis on a people-inclusive, integrated approach to communication for development. In addition, theories of group/ organizational dynamics (e.g., Schein, 1992; Zander, 1971/1996), conflict management (e.g., Carpenter & Kennedy, 1988; Yankelovich, 1999), leadership (e.g., Scholtes, 1998), quality improvement (e.g., Tenner & DeToro, 1992; Walton, 1986), future search (Weisbord, 1992; Weisbord & Janoff, 1995), and, as previously explained, the convergence theory of communication (Kincaid, 1988; E. M. Rogers & Kincaid, 1981) all are incorporated into the CFPD model (see Figure 21.2).

How change begins is not very clear in most of the literature on development communication. It usually is assumed or hoped that communities spontaneously initiate dialogue about an issue and take action. Díaz Bordenave (1998), for example, described a community process that begins with "identification of the problem." It is unclear, however, how a particular issue ever becomes "a problem" if a community sees it as something that is a normal part of life, such as a particular level of maternal mortality or girls not going to school. In contrast, the CFPD model makes explicit the role of catalysts in this process. A variety of catalysts can stimulate a community to discuss a problem, leading to a greater sense of dissatisfaction, lack of cooperation, or community conflict, or perhaps denial that the problem is serious enough to warrant any community response at all.

The community dialogue and collective action components describe a sequence of steps that take place within a community, sometimes simultaneously, that leads to solving a common problem (for a detailed description of each step in the process, see Figueroa, Kincaid, Rani, & Lewis, 2002). The literature and practical experience indicate that if these steps are completed successfully, community action is more likely to be successful (Howard-Grabman & Snetro, 2003). In this sense, CFPD is a descriptive model that explains why community projects are successful or unsuccessful. It also is a prescriptive model that can be used by external change agents and local leaders to increase the likelihood that development projects succeed. Finally, it is a predictive model that can be used to pose hypotheses about what happens during a community development project.

Dialogue alone can produce considerable individual change in terms of knowledge, emotional involvement, and aspiration, as well as social change in terms of shared ownership, collective efficacy, and the emergence of new leaders, for instance, In Gwalior, India, for example, dialogue created a "serious engagement of the [community] in issues of concept, cause and cure of leprosy" (Krishnatray & Melkote, 1998, p. 340); it also produced emotional bonds between the community and people with this disease, leading to lower stigma compared to communities that lacked such dialogue. Women's clubs (*Mahila Mandals*) in India provided a space for dialogue to identify problems and solutions that benefited women diary farmers by giving them higher control over their resources and market sales (Shefner-Rogers, Rao, Rogers, & Wayangankar, 1998). It also is possible, however, that opposition to change may arise in the dialogue phase due to divergent individual and group interests based on tradition, economic self-interest, control and power,

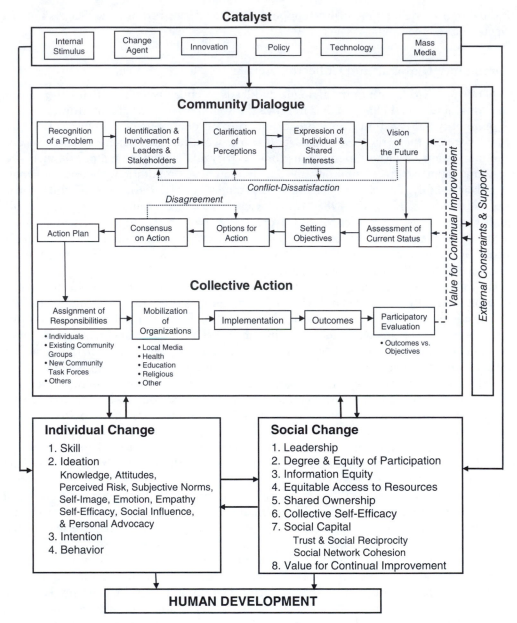

Figure 21.2 A model of communication for participatory development. *Note.* From *Communication for Social Change: An Integrated Model for Measuring the Process and Its Outcomes* (Working Paper No. 1) by M. E. Figueroa, D. L. Kincaid, M. Rani, and G. Lewis, 2002, New York: Rockefeller Foundation. Adapted with permission.

ethnicity, threat to self or communal identity, competition, or simply fear of change itself. Leaders play a crucial role in minimizing and managing these threats.

The nature of the problem may lend itself to a particular type of leadership, generated from within the group that initiates the process, appointed externally, or from the pre-existing leadership structure of the community. The style of leadership may be formal or informal, stable or unstable, based on general competence or specialized knowledge, and autocratic and hierarchical or participatory and democratic, depending on local cultural tradition. The style of leadership that is adopted is contingent on the situation in which a group operates, such as level of group acceptance and support, task structure and clarity of goals, and degree of leaders' power to control followers by reward and punishment (Fiedler, 1965; see also Chemers, 2001). However, some leadership styles are more participatory and lead to greater sharing of information and other resources, whereas other styles may reinforce an existing inequitable power structure in the community. An equitable form of leadership is more likely to happen when a wide, as opposed to small, range of members and groups in the community participate and endorse a particular leadership structure. The participation of those who are most affected by the problem (stakeholders and beneficiaries) is such an important characteristic of participatory development that it often is an implicit goal of external change agents who are committed to this form of development (Beltrán, 1993b; Bessette, 2004; Bessette & Rajasunderam, 1996; Breton, 1997; Ghai, 2003; Gray-Felder & Dean, 1999; Gumucio Dagrón, 2001; Howard-Grabman & Snetro, 2003; Korten, 1984; McKee et al., 2000; Putnam, 1993; Servaes et al., 1996; White, 1995).

Once community members' perceptions are clarified, they can begin to set objectives and take appropriate action. Setting objectives tends to make everyone's individual and shared needs explicit. A strong attitude of "What's in it for me?" may undermine the whole process and have to be replaced by one of "What's in it for all of us?" Self-interest and other sources of conflict often are glossed over in applied programs and, consequently, in the literature as well. A blindly optimistic, or Pollyanna, stance when it comes to human conflict and other obstacles, however, is not uncommon in development programs.

A community project to improve newborn care in Pakistan (Shafique, 2005) illustrates just how pervasive conflict is and how important its management is for program success. In the beginning, it was very difficult to get any men to participate because village elders disapproved of women's discussion of maternal and newborn care in public meetings. Due to social class, three subgroups in one village wanted to exclude a fourth subgroup. There also were numerous attempts to undermine new leaders, and some community activists demanded a financial incentive to participate. Finally, many people complained that they did not have enough time to participate. Via community dialogue, however, these obstacles eventually were overcome enough for the project to succeed. After almost a year of effort, the participating communities attributed the survival of nearly all newborns (no deaths and only three stillbirths) to adopting new life-saving practices.

Effective leadership is required to overcome these obstacles to participatory development. Further clarification may be needed (see the arrow back to the clarification of perceptions box in Figure 21.2) or new leaders and stakeholders may have to get involved (see the arrow back to the box for identification and involvement of leaders and stakeholders). The majority may have to convince a reluctant minority to go along, or conversely, a minority may have to recruit new members to become a new majority. These issues sometimes are easier to resolve if a community creates a clear "ideal picture" of the future that it wants to achieve. Such a common vision expresses the changes and benefits that community members expect to achieve, helping individuals and subgroups to see how their interests fit into the larger picture. Once such a shared vision is clear, it also is easier for a community to decide how to get there (Weisbord, 1992; Weisbord & Janoff, 1995). For instance, by using video to stimulate dialogue, group meetings, and other participatory methods, the "Building Bridges for Quality" project in rural Peru helped community and district health providers to identify priorities, create a shared vision and set goals, and develop strategies together to improve health services and practices in the home (Howard-Grabman, 2000).

The assessment of the current situation tells a community where it is now and how far it has to go to realize its vision of the future. Assessment can be quantitative or qualitative. Quantification of the problem (see Query et al., this volume) gives a clear idea of its size, such as the number of children who had diarrhea in the last month, mothers who died during childbirth in the last year, or new orphans due to AIDS. A quantitative estimate of the problem makes it easier to set measurable objectives and to evaluate progress later. Unclear and ambiguous goals may make it impossible for a community to ever know what it may have accomplished. The act of comparing one's current status with one's desired status and then setting realistic goals also is a major source of group motivation (Zander, 1996). Research has shown, however, that if a goal is set too high, it seems unrealistic and, consequently, reduces group motivation, confidence, and self-efficacy. On the other hand, if a goal is set too low, it can be accomplished with very little effort and motivation will be low. Moderate, achievable goal setting creates the high level of group motivation that is required for people to take sufficient action to solve their problems (Zander, 1996).

Community consensus for a chosen course of action is important later for obtaining resources and for getting people to volunteer or accept various assignments to implement a plan of action. In Nicaragua, uneven community involvement in the planning of a hygiene project resulted in fragmented and unclear information about the project's goals and implementation process, undermining members' interest (Tapia, 2002). The more that community members participate and see the proposed action as "their own," the more likely they will take action. A dialogue process that leaves people feeling that they share ownership of a project is expected to increase their commitment, involvement, and sense of collective self-efficacy if the project succeeds. Finally, a specific timetable for each activity that has to be accomplished creates realistic deadlines for moving effectively toward the solution of the problem. The action plan also specifies who does what activity and when and, thereby, helps a community to organize and coordinate its efforts to accomplish the project's goals.

During the collective action phase, it may not be necessary for community members to take responsibility for all of the tasks that need to be accomplished, especially if there are organizations that can help. Thus, one of the assigned tasks may be to obtain support and assistance from preexisting community resources, such as schools, local health centers, and local media organizations.

Díaz Bordenave (1998) identified several ways in which the media can facilitate community dialogue and mobilization. In the dialogue phase, media can (1) support the diagnosis of problem situations and the presentation of a problem to a community (e.g., there are many examples of how radio has assisted in getting the "voices" of most community groups involved in dialogue processes; see the *Journey of Life* radio serial drama in Ethiopia described by Witte & Roberto, this volume), (2) stimulate community deliberation and prioritization of problems, (3) support the exchange of ideas and experiences between distant communities, and (4) help community organizations to find solutions to problems. In the action phase, communication and local media can contribute by (5) informing a community about available services and how to access them; (6) training community members to use the media to inform the public about their needs; (7) helping communities to obtain legitimization and support from authorities; (8) providing feedback to the community about the progress and achievements of community projects; and (9) praising/rewarding communities for their achievements and, thereby, enhancing members' self-esteem and collective self-efficacy. The degree of participation by organizations in the community also should positively influence the sense of ownership of the program and promote social cohesion among community members.

Without an adequate assessment of what a community accomplishes and fails to accomplish, motivation for continual improvement will decline and members will lose confidence in their leaders. The self-reports of community members regarding how a project has affected their lives may be the most important form of feedback. Such reports spread by means of informal social networks without the need for public meetings. If the objectives of the community are quantitative, a formal evaluation of the amount of change can be undertaken. If, for instance, the problem is an unacceptable level of diarrhea among children under the age of 5, the action taken by the community should be followed by a reduction in the number of children who have diarrhea, which community members easily can track. To know the results of community projects, some observation or counting of events/incidents needs to be done to measure the level of achievement. Self-evaluation occurs when a community compares the observed outcomes of its project to both the status assessed when the objectives were set and to its members' shared vision for the project. When community members do the evaluation themselves, it also contributes to the community's reinforcement of, motivation for, and capacity for further development (Fetterman, Kaftarian, & Wandersman, 1996; Feurestein, 1986; Wallerstein, 2002). For instance, a community-based health-information system in rural Bolivian villages helped those communities to monitor their health and to plan and act as partners in the local health system. As a result, children's health practices were higher in those communities compared to ones without that system (Willis, Schroeder, Howard-Grabman, Marsh, & Gonzalez, 2001).

After the implementation of a community project, self-evaluation amounts to a reassessment of the "new" status of the community with respect to the problem. This process is shown in the CFPD diagram by the broken arrow moving from participatory evaluation back to the steps for vision of the future and the assessment of current status. At this point, the community is ready to renew the process, moving forward to a new round of objective setting and collective action, either for the same problem or for a new one. By engaging in this reassessment process, a community reinforces its sense of collective efficacy, which creates or increases the community's shared belief in and value of continual improvement.

Dialogue and collective action also are affected by contextual factors in the environment that constrain or support the progress of a community toward its envisioned goals. Although the CFPD model emphasizes the expansion of people's choices, those choices never are totally free and unconstrained by forces outside of their control. Relevant external factors include physical resources (e.g., land and water); local, regional, national, and international governing bodies and the sociopolitical systems underlying them (e.g., executive, legislative, and juridical institutions and organizations); provision of and access to services (e.g., schools, health care, electricity, roads, and media); socioeconomic factors (e.g., access to credit, jobs, markets, and trade); religious institutions; and culture, in general (e.g., local beliefs and norms).

For instance, elements in the sociopolitical system determine whose voice will be heard and, therefore, who benefits from policy and legislative change. As Carnegie et al. (2000) contended, "Without adequate, positive change in the socio-political system the poor will remain poor and the voiceless will remain without a voice" (p. 191). There are many examples of projects that do not evolve beyond the initial pilot phase due to a lack of political support or corruption. Community members of Camicachi in Puno, Peru, for instance, saw their plans for better quality of care vanish after they reported corrupt behavior engaged in by one of the health providers in their health post (Tapia, 2003). Before any mutual plans could be developed, all the providers from the health center stopped participating in the dialogue, bringing the entire process to an end.

Socioeconomic and political constraints have received the most attention from development scholars in the last few decades. Overcoming those constraints often is cited as a crucial step for sustainable development and the eradication of poverty. Economic growth alone, however, is not enough if people do not have fair access to the opportunities it creates; hence, some degree of power sharing is necessary. The World Bank (2004) took an optimistic perspective regarding participatory development, stating that "empowerment strengthens the capacity of poor people to have a say in decisions that affect their lives...and can also improve how politics and institutions respond to the needs of the poor" (p. 36). The CFPD model suggests that local communities may have to do more than just empower themselves: The two-way arrows between dialogue/collective action and environmental constraints/support indicate that for some problems, a community may have to change the external environment before it can take effective action to achieve its objectives. Doing so means advocating, as a cohesive group, for resources to support the implementation of a community plan (e.g., strengthening services and access to technology), or advocating for new laws or policies to enhance community access to resources (e.g., credit and health services).

Identifying and getting the involvement of leaders and stakeholders within and outside the community is one of the initial phases in the CFPD model and may determine the ultimate success of CFPD. Accomplishing this goal hardly is ever easy, especially in the context of entrenched local power, political factions, social norms, and strong vested interests outside the community. In Bangladesh, for example, it is not possible for women to meet in small discussion groups because strong norms of *purdah* (modesty) and husbands' opposition do not allow it (Kincaid, 2000b). However, if those who oppose a project become part of the community dialogue from the beginning, they also may gain a "stake" in the project and see how their political and material interests can be advanced (e.g., Jovanovic, Steger, Symonds, & Nelson, 2007).

Communication and Social Change

As a result of dialogue and collective action, change is expected to occur at both the individual and community levels. The lower left-hand side of the CFPD model lists many types of individual change that can occur, based on stage models of behavior change (e.g., Piotrow et al., 1997; Prochaska, DiClemente, & Norcross, 1992; E. M. Rogers, 1995) and ideational models of behavior (e.g., Bandura, 2004; Fishbein et al., 2001; Kincaid 2000a). The model also indicates that individual changes can occur as a result of direct influence of some of the catalysts identified in the model, such as media messages that promote specific health practices or the construction of a health clinic near a community. However, because social change at the community level is not as well understood as individual change and sometimes merely is implied, the remainder of this chapter focuses first on social change and then examines individual change.

The lower right-hand side of the CFPD model lists eight community outcomes of participatory development that enable human development and social change. The sociological literature defines *social change* as a transformation in the organization of a society and its overall structure as represented by changes in the distribution of resources, whether educational, economic, power based, or discursive (Farley, 1990; Underwood 2002). Human development is more likely to happen with these structural changes than without them. The CFPD model assumes that through participatory development, conditions for social change are enabled by means of dialogue and collective action. Participatory development leads to an increased pool of ideas and a new worldview, articulation of goals and a vision of the future, cohesive communication networks that allow access to resources previously unavailable, enhanced collective consciousness of community status, collective capacities for change, and enhanced self-confidence to act (Sztompka, 1993). This context for social change is represented in the model by eight social outcomes. The last one, *value for continual improvement*, is understood as the transformation of a community into a "learning organization" that continuously seeks ways to advance (Deming, 1986). If a community effectively completes the steps outlined in the model and accomplishes one or more of its objectives, we expect the following potentially profound social outcomes for the community, above and beyond the benefits to individual members who participate:

1. *Leadership, an improvement in the capacity or ability to guide, direct, or influence a group's course of action toward a desired goal.* A leader's traits, style, and behavior influence community participation (Goodman et al., 1998; Trimizi, 2002). Leadership that is encouraging and supportive motivates members' ideas and efforts, guiding and inspiring them to higher levels of involvement and a stronger sense of accomplishment (Storey & Kenney, 2004). Thus, one main consequence of successful participatory development is effective, transformational leadership that broadens and elevates the interests of the community to accomplish a common vision (Bass, 1985).

The cultural context of leadership is a particularly important component of development (Bebbington, Dharmawan, Fahmi, & Guggenheim, 2004). In Indonesia, for example, the presence of a leader whose characteristics resonated with the community's social conventions and cultural values produced a strong response from the community to participate in collective health efforts and to contribute resources (Storey & Kenney, 2004). Although no single style of leadership applies in all situations (Lord & Brown, 2004), some societies and ethnic subcultures expect a directive type of leadership. Nevertheless, the CFPD model assumes that engaging and inclusive leadership is more likely than other forms of leadership to enhance other social change outcomes, such as information equity, shared ownership of the project, and social cohesion.

2. *The degree and equity of participation, an increase in the number and diversity of community members who participate in a development process.* Diversity includes the extent to which traditionally disenfranchised or marginalized community members (e.g., economically disadvantaged, minority ethic groups, women, and youth) participate, as well as the range of members' activities (number of steps in the CFPD process; Ghai, 2003). Dialogue at the community level, as described in the CFPD model, requires a space for previously unheard or dissenting voices (Howard-Grabman & Snetro, 2003). Development projects that fail to include those with the highest need or those more hesitant to change run the risk of addressing the wrong issues or accomplishing short-lived improvements. Inclusion of these groups in the dialogue and action phases guarantees that conflicting or restrictive issues get to be known and negotiated, if not resolved, so that a legitimate shared vision can emerge for the community. In Bangladesh, for example, an arsenic mitigation water project allowed open participation and was flexible enough to respond to people's preference for a community-piped water system rather than household-based options (Hoque et al., 2004). However, because of their design or funding source, many projects tend to compartmentalize health problems, such that even if community participation is sought, people "are often asked to participate based on pre-decided low-cost options" (Hoque et al., 2004, p. 76).

Addressing the participation of women and ethnic minorities in the dialogue phase may create problems of power distribution within communities, giving space to conflicts of interest between various community groups. In these situations, change agents should seek the support of additional formal or informal leaders or groups, skillfully manage these conflicts, and encourage all voices to be heard, but still make the conflict of interest explicit (Institute of Development Studies, 2001). Leadership and participation are different sides of the same coin: Leaders need a strong base of actively involved members (followers) and members need strong, inspirational leadership. A mix of formal and informal leaders, such as reputational leaders, opinion leaders, and others who set community norms (Goodman et al., 1998), may assist in managing these conflicts and, thereby, enhance the degree and equity of community members' participation. Although no universal formula can be applied to secure participation, "appropriate solutions have to be found from within…rather than being imposed from the outside" (Lattimer, 2003, p. 2). Among the *barrios* of the Solingalpa, Nicaragua, for instance, existing political divisions created misconceptions about whether a new community center was being built for the entire community or not, but these misunderstandings and divisions were resolved through community dialogue with representatives from the barrios and the project organizations (Crabtree, 1998).

Social norms are the collectively agreed-on standards and rules that are adhered to and accepted by the majority of the members of a particular society or group, whereas *norms of participation* refer to a community's beliefs and rules about how and who should or should not attend meetings, speak up, and share in making decisions. Norms of participation also include what is considered "fair" regarding individual contributions and the sharing of benefits. Social norms also determine how leaders are chosen and how they are expected to behave.

Participation is influenced by, and affects, other social outcomes of CFPD, such as network cohesion, trust, and collective efficacy. Similarly, social networks and the history of community action can facilitate or delay participation (Howard-Grabman & Snetro, 2003).

3. Information equity, an increase in the distribution of knowledge about a problem—how well knowledge is shared among individuals within a group and between community groups. High levels of information equity likely positively affect participation in the implementation of a program, shared ownership of it, and distribution of benefits. Conversely, a successful participatory project is expected to reduce information inequity in a community.

Two dimensions of information equity have been identified: (a) sufficient and accurate knowledge about a problem, and (b) the free flow of information within a community. In communities where income and education inequality are high, there is a greater likelihood that information inequality also is high (Kawachi, Kennedy, Lochner, & Prothrow-Stith 1997). This principle amounts to an application of the *knowledge gap hypothesis*—that people with higher education have a better ability to acquire information than those with lower education (Tichenor, Donohue, & Olien, 1970; Viswanath & Finnegan, 1996)—within locally bounded communities (Rucinski, 2004; Viswanath, Kosicki, Fredin, & Park, 2000).

4. Equitable access to resources, an increase in the distribution of tangible resources— how much they are shared among individuals within a group or between groups within a community. Of all the community outcomes specified by the CFPD model, equitable access to resources may be the hardest to accomplish. There is a consensus that development programs should make an effort to avoid reinforcing existing socioeconomic structures if they impede community members' equitable access to available resources, especially resources generated by their efforts. Obviously, equitable access to resources requires that there be resources to share. Many development problems are related to the scarcity of resources, sometimes as basic as food and water.

Strictly speaking, the social changes specified by the CFPD model are changes *in* the system, whereas far-reaching social–structural changes are changes *of* the system. There always is hope, as Sztompka (1993, p. 6) noted, that system changes "accumulate and finally touch the core of the system, turning into changes *of*" the system. For example, the communication program for women dairy farmers in India increased their involvement in dairy cooperatives, but it also increased their access to market resources and their control over production and earnings (Shefner-Rogers et al., 1998). Increasing access to resources, such as education, employment, and income, which often are beyond the reach of certain societal groups or classes, not only changes the dynamics of social interaction but also leads to improvements in the quality of life, in general. Meaningful social change simply does not occur as long as there has been no impact on the socially unjust conditions that affect so many people's lives (Breton, 1997).

5. *Perceived shared ownership, an increase in community members' belief that a joint project belongs to them rather than to outsiders or a small subgroup within the community.* As Kraemer (1993) explained:

> Ownership develops when partners play a key role in formulating and implementing a project and understand the benefits of participation. The recognition by each partner that he will be better able to achieve his own goals by collaborating and helping his partners reach their respective goals is the best way to ensure partners are committed for the long haul. (p. 23)

There are at least six dimensions to shared ownership: (a) importance of an issue or program to participants, (b) sense of responsibility for the program, (c) contribution to the program, (d) extent to which benefits from the project are shared, (e) personal identification with the program, and (f) personal accountability. *Ownership*, one of the keys to sustained change, means that "local people must have a sense of responsibility for and control over programs promoting change so that they will continue to support them after the initial organizing effort" (Thompson & Kinne, 1999, p. 30). To achieve a sense of responsibility and control, external change agents need to accept different views from the community and not anticipate community decisions and plans in advance (Howard-Grabman & Snetro, 2003). Ownership also makes it possible to address issues of accountability when plans do not move forward as agreed.

6. *Collective efficacy, an increase in a community's shared belief in its collective capability to attain its goals and accomplish desired tasks* (Bandura, 1986). Such efficacy involves the belief that effective collective action is possible and can succeed. Collective efficacy is distinct from individual self-efficacy. For example, if individual members are capable and their self-efficacy beliefs are high, low confidence in their group's capacity for collective action still may inhibit dialogue and collective action. Collective efficacy is not a monolithic group attribute; instead, individuals who occupy different roles or positions in the same group may differ in their perceptions of the group's collective efficacy (Bandura, 1995). It is expected that a community's collective efficacy influences the group's goal setting, dialogue, collective effort, and, especially, its persistence when barriers arise.

Collective efficacy is not general; it applies to specific contexts or tasks (Bandura, 1986, 1997). There are three main dimension of collective efficacy. First, *perceived efficacy to take action as a group* refers to the confidence of community members to work together as a group to solve a common problem. This dimension may be affected by contextual factors in the form of a community's past experiences, such as a history of factionalism or other conflicts in the community. Second, *perceived capability of other community members* refers to community members' perceptions of other members' talents and abilities to accomplish their work. Third, *perceived efficacy to solve problems as a group* refers to members' perceived confidence to solve a specific problem or address a particular issue at the community level by working together. In Ghana, for example, community members' high sense of collective efficacy to fight HIV and AIDS was positively associated with providing support to people living with the disease (Bazant & Boulay, 2007).

7. *Social capital, an increase in a community's capacity to cooperate for mutual benefit* (Collier, 1998; Krishna & Shrader, 1999). Social capital is a relatively new addition to development theory (Edmondson, 2003; Lyson, 2000; Mayer & Rankin, 2002; Navarro, 2002; Trigilla, 2001). Putnam (1993) described social capital as features of social organization, such as social networks, norms, and trust, which facilitate coordination and cooperation for mutual benefit. The concept can be traced back to Coleman (1988), who emphasized aspects of social structure that facilitate the actions of actors within the structure. Like economic and human capital, social capital contributes to participatory development by making possible the achievement of certain ends that are not attainable in its absence. Social capital is inherent in the structure of relations among persons; as Coleman (1990) explained, "it is lodged neither in individuals nor in physical implements of production" (p. 302). Social capital is derived from the "investment in social relations by individuals through which they gain access to embedded resources to enhance expected returns of instrumental or expressive actions" (Lin, 1999, p. 9). Social capital can be measured by the level of social trust or social reciprocity, and by the cohesiveness of the social networks within a community.

Social trust is the general confidence that one has in the integrity, ability, and good character of other people in a community. Trust is the glue that holds a group or community together, making cooperative action possible. The central question is whether members trust others to have any influence over important issues.

Social reciprocity refers to the mutual interchange of favors, privileges, and benefits in a relationship. For example, if someone helps another person to build a well or harvest the crops, the person who receives the favor is expected to return the favor at a later date. Hence, the central question is whether others in the community are perceived as opportunistic, disregarding their obligations to others, or whether there is a sense that others will voluntarily fulfill their obligations or will only do so if they think that they will be punished for failing to help.

Social network cohesion has two dimensions: (a) the density and interconnectedness of the social ties and communication links within a bounded community (Kincaid, 1993), and (b) the forces that act on members of a group or community to remain in it and actively contribute to it. Communities with low network cohesion are characterized by separated factions with few interconnecting ties that serve as "bridges" among them. The lack of such bridges is an obstacle to participatory development, but if successful, the CFPD process can reduce differences and increase the number of interconnecting ties. As network cohesion increases, members will be more likely to want to belong to the group, get along well with one another, share group goals, and remain loyal and united in the pursuit of those goals.

To qualify as a form of "surplus value," the social capital of a community must have the potential to be transformed into "work." Furthermore, the social capital of a community must be capable of being increased by some type of investment in human or other resources. The dialogue and collective action process described by the CFPD model is a learning process by which community members' participation increases their motivation for cooperative action and creates structures—such as networks, teams, and leader–follower relationships—which increase the social capital of a community—its capacity for future collective action.

8. *Value for continual improvement, an increase in community members' regard for improvement of their status as they resolve problems by means of dialogue and collective action, and accomplish one or more of their shared goals.* Deming (1986) used the

term *continual improvement* to refer to general processes of improvement that transform organizations and their members. This value is an inherent part of learning organizations where "people continually expand their capacity to create the results they truly desire, where new and expansive patterns of thinking are nurtured, where collective aspiration is set free, and where people are continually learning to see the whole together" (Senge, 1990, p. 3). For instance, as they progressed from small-scale to large-scale village development projects, the women who participated in mothers' clubs in Korea during the 1970s gained a sense of individual and collective self-efficacy, which, in turn, increased their capacity and desire for continual improvement (E. M. Rogers & Kincaid, 1981). Collective improvement, thus, enhances community members' desire to find solutions to other problems.

Individual behavior change often is the expected outcome of health-promotion campaigns (see Kreps & Bonaguro, this volume), especially those dedicated to single health problems, such as childhood diarrhea, malaria, contraception, immunization, and HIV prevention (see Witte & Roberto, this volume). The urgency of the problem, concentration of resources, and narrow focus increase the efficiency and likelihood of success. In some situations, however, without social support and changes in social norms, individual change may be self-sustaining. Conversely, when only social change occurs, the capacity for development may increase, but without the individual change necessary for development. This complementary relationship is indicated in the CFPD model by the two-way arrows between individual and social change outcomes. Success is expected to reinforce both collective and individual change, as well as increase a community's value for continual improvement.

A good example of this complementary relationship is the prevention of malaria by removing stagnant water sources in the area around homes. If only a few individuals in a community practice this behavior, there will be little impact on the mosquito population and, consequently, no incentive to continue the practice. However, if a collective decision is made and everyone within a certain radius takes *joint action* at the same time, an effective, long-term solution to the problem of mosquito-born diseases can result. If the incidence of malaria becomes noticeably lower and, hence, observable to the community, the new behavior and collective decision will be reinforced, and the community's value for continual improvement will increase.

Implications for Applied Communication Research

Our comprehensive, theoretical model of CFPD was created to synthesize the wide-ranging and diverse literature on development communication and social change. In practice, participatory development ranges from community events, such as demonstrations and local fairs, through community meetings and the comprehensive application of the CFPD process of dialogue and collective action. As one progresses along this participation continuum, the requirement to apply concrete criteria of effectiveness increases substantially. The CFPD model specifies the critical steps that should be undertaken, as well as individual and social outcomes that should result when participatory development is effective. In the future, applied communication researchers need to examine several important, unanswered questions.

Many of the separate components of CFPD have been tested across a variety of social and cultural settings, but the model as a whole only now is beginning to be applied and evaluated. Applied communication research needs to be conducted on all components of the model at the same time under a variety of social and cultural conditions. Over time, with replication and research, the model can be refined and some of the "best practices" can be documented and then applied by others in their programs. At some point, the application and testing of CFPD also needs to be taken to scale, applied in a systematic way to an entire region or country for a particular development objective, because much of the existing literature and practice is limited to a small number of pilot programs and promising case studies.

It is especially important to investigate the nature, importance, interrelationships, and cumulative effects of the social outcomes specified by the model (e.g., leadership, cohesion, ownership, information equity, goal setting and self-assessment, and participation) and to determine which ones are most related to effective CFPD. The measurement of social outcomes lags behind the measurement of individual outcomes; consequently, measurement of all of the social outcomes needs improvement. In the literature and in practice, participation usually is treated in a simplistic manner by ascertaining how many people attended various meetings, perhaps with some indication of their gender, age, socioeconomic status, and other characteristics. To understand participation more fully, researchers need to observe the interaction among participants and between leaders and followers to determine how many and to what degree they are engaged in each step of the CFPD process: proposing new problems, sharing power in the decision-making process, recommending solutions, assuming responsibility for implementation and assessment of outcomes, and so forth. Measurement of these dimensions of participation then can be correlated with participants' perceived level of ownership and motivation to continue using the CFPD process with new problems.

The extant literature also revealed a split between the emphasis on individual change and social change. Further applied communication research is needed to clarify the nature of the relationship between these two types of change. Longitudinal research also is required to test the hypothesis that the combination of individual change and social change leads to higher levels of self-sustained development. Intensive case study research needs to examine how the steps specified in the CFPD process unfold and the extent to which the actual sequence of events is related to development outcomes. Can some steps be skipped altogether? Are there critical paths that cannot be skipped for the process to be effective? What level of intensity and completion of each step is required for the process to be effective and to achieve the desired individual and social outcomes?

One of the key elements found in practice and identified by the model is conflict and its management during the CFPD process. There are, however, many unanswered questions: How is conflict managed in different cultural and socioeconomic settings, and for different types of development problems? Can a minority or even a majority faction within a community continue the process alone? Does it make a difference if the "door is left open" (or not) for dissenting community members or groups to join later in the process and perhaps share in the benefits of a successful project? How do the methods used to manage conflict affect future CFPD efforts?

Unless the CFPD process is initiated spontaneously from within a community, the methods and amount of involvement by outside change agents may determine how effective the process is and, more important, whether the process continues in their absence. Applied research is needed to determine the proper balance between the type and amount of external initiative and leadership versus internal leadership and responsibility. What level of imbalance may lead to dependency and stagnation? Is there an ideal exit strategy for external change agents? We do know that improvement in local capacity that external agents leave behind determines how self-sustaining the CFPD process will be without external assistance.

The other division encountered in the literature is between local community action and mediated communication, such as radio and television. One question concerns the role that media can play to support, reinforce, and legitimize the CFPD process in local communities and perhaps improve the effectiveness of the process. Because these two approaches usually are treated as mutually exclusive, if not in competition for resources, the possibility of featuring community action projects on television and radio typically is overlooked. Applying the principles of social learning theory and social comparison theory, it makes sense to select the best community action projects and let members tell stories about their projects on radio and television. Audiences in the surrounding area or throughout the entire country then could participate vicariously and perhaps learn enough to emulate what they see and hear, or at least initiate a dialogue in their communities. In this sense, media could not only reinforce local efforts but also multiply the impacts of successful programs on a larger scale.

Conclusion

If development ultimately is about people, communication for development needs to be based on some element of human involvement and active participation. Participatory communication is the core component of the communication for participatory development model, as it is in most approaches to communication for development and social change. By focusing on people's active participation in the process, the model provides a framework to guide and improve applied communication research on development.

The communication for participatory development model, however, goes beyond dialogue per se by not assuming idealistically that once people begin discussing their problems, positive change automatically occurs. Full implementation of the communication for participatory development process is required, with active goal setting, assignment of responsibilities for action, and self-assessment of progress. Without well-organized collective action, participatory communication programs for development may result only in discouragement, heightened levels of dissatisfaction, and a lower sense of collective efficacy in a community. Dialogue *and* collective action are the participatory processes by which people can develop themselves, increase their collective efficacy, and continue to improve the communities in which they live.

Authors' Note

We acknowledge the Rockefeller Foundation for partnering with the Center for Communication Programs, Johns Hopkins University Bloomberg School of Public Health, on the development of the integrated model of Communication for Social Change (CFSC). Much of the material in this chapter is based on the working paper by Figueroa et al. (2002), done with the support of the Foundation and members of the new CFSC Consortium, a nonprofit organization dedicated to advancing the field of communication for social change globally (http://www.communicationforsocialchange.org). Special thanks to Brian Byrd, James Deane, Warren Feek, Denise Gray-Felder, Alfonso Gumucio-Dagrón, and Jim Hunt.

References

Andreasen, A. R. (1995). *Marketing social change: Changing behavior to promote health, social development, and the environment.* San Francisco: Jossey-Bass.

Bandura, A. (1986). *Social foundations of thought and action: A social cognitive theory.* Englewood Cliffs, NJ: Prentice-Hall.

Bandura, A. (Ed.). (1995). *Self-efficacy in changing societies*. New York: Cambridge University Press.

Bandura, A. (1997). *Self-efficacy: The exercise of control*. New York: Freeman.

Bandura, A. (2004). Health promotion by social cognitive means. *Health Education and Behavior, 31*, 143–164.

Bass, B. M. (1985). Leadership: Good, better, best. *Organizational Dynamics, 13*, 26–40.

Bazant, E. S., & Boulay, M. (2007). Factors associated with religious congregation members' support to people living with HIV/AIDS in Kumasi, Ghana. *AIDS and Behavior, 11*, 936–945.

Bebbington, A., Dharmawan, E. F., Fahmi, E., & Guggenheim, S. (2004). Village politics, culture and community-driven development: Insights from Indonesia. *Progress in Development Studies, 4*, 187–205.

Beltrán, S. L. R. (1976). Alien premises, objectives, and methods in Latin American communication research: A critical perspective in light of U.S. influences. *Communication Research, 3*, 107–134.

Beltrán, S. L. R. (1993a). Communication for development in Latin America: A forty-year appraisal. In D. Nostbakken & C. Morrow (Eds.), *Cultural expression in the global village* (pp. 9–31). Penang, Malaysia: Southbound/International Development Research Centre.

Beltrán, S. L. R. (1993b). The quest for democracy in communication: Outstanding Latin American experience. *Development, 3*, 45–47.

Beltrán, S. L. R., & Gonzalez, F. S. (Eds.). (1998). *Movilización comunitaria para la salud: dialogo multidisciplinario* [Community mobilization for health: Multidisciplinary dialogue]. Baltimore: Johns Hopkins University Center for Communication Programs.

Berrigan, F. J. (1981). *Community media and development*. Paris: United Nations Educational, Scientific and Cultural Organization.

Bessette, G. (2004). *Involving the community: A guide to participatory development communication*. Ottawa, Canada: Southbound/International Development Research Centre.

Bessette, G., & Rajasunderam, C. V. (1996). *Participatory communication for development: A West African agenda*. Ottawa, Canada: Southbound/International Development Research Centre.

Bracht, N. (Ed.). (1999). *Health promotion at the community level: New advances* (2nd ed.) Thousand Oaks, CA: Sage.

Breton, M. (1997). Les étapes de l'empowerment en régime démocratique: Vers un modèle de pratique [The empowerment stages in democratic regimes: Towards a model of practice]. *Intervention, 109*, 43–53.

Calvelo Rios, J. M. (1998). *El modelo de interlocución: Un nuevo paradigma de comunicación* [The interpersonal communication model: A new communication paradigm]. Retrieved January 28, 2005, from http://www.iicd-runa.org/frame1.html

Carnegie, R., Mckee, N., Dick, B., Reitemeier, P., Weiss, E., & Yoon, C. S. (2000). Making change possible: Creating an enabling environment. In N. Mckee, E. Manoncourt, Y. C. Saik, & R. Carnegie (Eds.) *Involving people, evolving behaviour* (pp. 157–211). New York: United Nations Children's Fund.

Carpenter, S. L., & Kennedy, W. J. D. (1988). *Managing public disputes: A practical guide to handling conflict and reaching agreements*. San Francisco: Jossey-Bass.

Casmir, F. L. (Ed.). (1991). *Communication in development*. Norwood, NJ: Ablex.

Chambers, R. (1997). *Whose reality counts? Putting the first last*. London: Intermediate Technology.

Chemers, M. M. (2001). Leadership effectiveness: An integrative review. In M. A. Hogg & R. S. Tindale (Eds.), *Blackwell handbook of social psychology: Group processes* (pp. 376–399). Malden, MA: Blackwell.

Coldevin, G., & FAO. (2001). Participatory communication and adult learning for rural development. *Journal of International Communication, 7*(2), 51–69.

Coleman, J. S. (1988). Social capital in the creation of human capital. *American Journal of Sociology, 94*(Suppl.), S95–S120.

Coleman, J. S. (1990). *Foundations of social theory*. Cambridge, MA: Belknap Press.

Collier, P. (1998). *Social capital and poverty* (The World Bank Social Capital Initiative Working Papers, No. 4). Washington, DC: World Bank.

Crabtree, R. D. (1998). Mutual empowerment in cross-cultural participatory development and service learning: Lessons in communication and social justice from projects in El Salvador and Nicaragua. *Journal of Applied Communication Research, 26*, 182–209.

Deming, W. E. (1986). *Out of the crisis*. Cambridge: Massachusetts Institute of Technology, Center for Advanced Engineering Study.

Díaz Bordenave, J. (1976). Communication of agricultural innovations in Latin America: The need for new models. *Communication Research, 3*, 135–154.

Díaz Bordenave, J. (1994). Participative communication as a part of building the participative society. In S. A. White (Ed.; with K. Sadanandan Nair & J. Ascroft), *Participatory communication: Working for change and development* (pp. 35–48). Thousand Oaks, CA: Sage.

Díaz Bordenave, J. (1998). Relación de la comunicación con los procesos de movilización comunitaria para la salud [Relationship between communication and community mobilization process for health]. In S. L. R. Beltrán & F. S. Gonzalez (Eds.), *Movilización comunitaria para la salud: dialogo multidisciplinario* (pp. 78–103). Baltimore: Johns Hopkins University Center for Communication Programs.

Dube, S. C. (1988). *Modernization and development: The search for alternative paradigms*. Atlantic Highlands, NJ: Zed Books.

Dudley, E. (1993). *The critical villager: Beyond community participation*. New York: Routledge.

Edmondson, R. (2003). Social capital: A strategy for enhancing health? *Social Science and Medicine, 57*, 1723–1733.

Farley, J. E. (1990). *Sociology*. Englewood Cliffs, NJ: Prentice-Hall.

Fetterman, D., Kaftarian, S. J., & Wandersman, A. (Eds.). (1996). *Empowerment evaluation: Knowledge and tools for self-assessment & accountability*. Thousand Oaks, CA: Sage.

Feurestein, M. (1986). *Partners in evaluation: Evaluating development and community programmes with participants*. London: Macmillan.

Fiedler, F. E. (1965). A contingency model of leadership effectiveness. In L. Berkowitz (Ed.), *Advances in experimental social psychology* (Vol. 1, pp. 149–190). New York: Academic Press.

Figueroa, M. E., Kincaid, D. L., Rani, M., & Lewis, G. (2002). *Communication for social change: An integrated model for measuring the process and its outcomes* (Working Paper No. 1). New York: Rockefeller Foundation.

Fishbein, M., Triandis, H. C., Kanfer, F. H., Becker, M., Middlestadt, S. E., & Eichler, A. (2001). Factors influencing behavior and behavior change. In A. Baum, T. A. Revenson, & J. E. Singer (Eds.), *Handbook of health psychology* (pp. 3–16). Mahwah, NJ: Erlbaum.

Fraser, C., & Restrepo-Estrada, S. (1998). *Communicating for development: Human change for survival*. New York: I. B. Tauris.

Freire, P. (1970). *Pedagogy of the oppressed* (M. B. Ramos, Trans.). New York: Herder & Herder.

Ghai, Y. (2003). *Participation and minorities, a report*. London: Minority Rights Group International.

Gillis, M., Perkins, D. H., Roemer, M., & Snodgrass, D. R. (1992). *Economics of development* (3rd ed.). New York: Norton.

Goodman, R. M., Speers, M. A., Mcleroy, K., Fawcett, S., Kegler, M., Parker, E., et al. (1998). Identifying and defining the dimensions of community capacity to provide a basis for measurement. *Health Education and Behavior, 25*, 258–278.

Goulet, D. (1985). *The cruel choice: A new concept in the theory of development*. Lanham, MD: University Press of America.

Gray-Felder, D., & Dean, J. (1999). *Communication for social change: A position paper and conference report*. New York: Rockefeller Foundation.

Green, L. W., & Kreuter, M. W. (1991). *Health promotion planning: An educational and environment approach* (2nd ed.). Mountain View, CA: Mayfield.

Gumucio Dagrón, A. (2001). *Making waves: Stories of participatory communication for social change*. New York: Rockefeller Foundation.

Hammond, S. C., Anderson, R., & Cissna, K. N. (2003). The problematics of dialogue and power. In P. J. Kalbfleisch (Ed.), *Communication yearbook* (Vol. 27, pp. 125–157). Mahwah, NJ: Erlbaum.

Hoque, B. A., Hoque, M. M., Ahmed, T., Islam, S., Azad, A. K., Ali, N., et al. (2004). Demand-based water options for arsenic mitigation: An experience from rural Bangladesh. *Public Health, 118,* 70–77.

Hornik, R. C. (1988). *Development communication: Information, agriculture, and nutrition in the Third World.* New York: Longman.

Hornik, R. C. (Ed.). (2002). *Public health communication: Evidence for behavior change.* Mahwah, NJ: Erlbaum.

Howard, N. (1999). *Confrontation analysis: How to win operations other than war.* Vienna, VA: Evidence Based Research.

Howard-Grabman, L. (2000). Bridging the gap between communities and service providers: Developing accountability through community mobilisation approaches. *Institute of Development Studies Bulletin, 31*(1), 88–96.

Howard-Grabman, L., & Snetro, G. (2003). *How to mobilize communities for social change.* Baltimore: Johns Hopkins University Center for Communication Programs.

Institute of Development Studies. (2001, November). *Cutting edge pack report summary: Gender and participation.* Retrieved January 28, 2005, from http://www.bridge.ids.ac.uk/reports/CEP-part-sum.pdf

Jacobson, T. L. (1993). A pragmatist account of participatory communication research for national development. *Communication Theory, 3,* 214–230.

Jacobson, T. L. (2003). Participatory communication for social change: The relevance of the theory of communicative action. In P. L. Kalbfleisch (Ed.), *Communication yearbook* (Vol. 27, pp. 87–123). Thousand Oaks, CA; Sage.

Jovanovic, S., Steger, C., Symonds, S., & Nelson, D. (2007). Promoting deliberative democracy through dialogue: Communication contribution to a grassroots movement for truth, justice, and reconciliation. In L. R. Frey & K. M. Carragee (Eds.), *Communication activism: Vol 1. Communication for social change* (pp. 67–108). Cresskill, NJ: Hampton Press.

Kawachi, I., Kennedy, B. P., Lochner, K., & Prothrow-Stith, D. (1997). Social capital, income inequality, and mortality. *American Journal of Public Health, 87,* 1491–1498.

Kim, Y. Y. (2005). Inquiry in intercultural and development communication. *Journal of Communication, 55,* 554–577.

Kincaid, D. L. (1988). The convergence theory and intercultural communication. In Y. Y. Kim & W. B. Gudykunst (Eds.), *Theories in intercultural communication* (pp. 280–298). Beverly Hills, CA: Sage.

Kincaid, D. L. (1993). Communication network dynamics, cohesion, centrality, and cultural evolution. In W. Richards & G. A. Barnett (Eds.), *Progress in communication science* (Vol. 12, pp. 111–132). New York: Ablex.

Kincaid, D. L. (2000a). Mass media, ideation, and contraceptive behavior: A longitudinal analysis of contraceptive change in the Philippines. *Communication Research, 27,* 723–763.

Kincaid, D. L. (2000b). Social networks, ideation, and contraceptive behavior in Bangladesh: Longitudinal analysis. *Social Science & Medicine, 50,* 215–231.

Kincaid, D. L. (2002). Drama, emotion, and cultural convergence. *Communication Theory, 12,* 136–152.

Kincaid, D. L. (2004). From innovation to social norm: Bounded normative influence. *Journal of Health Communication, 9*(Suppl. 1), 37–57.

Kincaid, D. L., & Yum, J. O. (1976). The needle and the ax: Communication and development in a Korean village. In W. Schramm & D. Lerner (Eds.), *Communication and change: The last ten years—and the next* (pp. 83–97). Honolulu: University Press of Hawaii.

Korten, D. C. (1984). People-centered development: Toward a framework. In D. C. Korten & R. Klauss (Eds.), *People-centered development: Contributions toward theory and planning frameworks* (pp. 299–309). West Hartford, CT: Kumarian Press.

Kraemer, J. (1993). *Building villages to raise our children: Collaboration.* Cambridge, MA: Harvard Family Research Project.

Krishna, A., & Shrader, E. (1999). *Social capital assessment tool.* Washington, DC: World Bank's Conference on Social Capital and Poverty Reduction.

Krishnatray, P. K., & Melkote, S. R. (1998). Public communication campaigns in the destigmatization of leprosy: A comparative analysis of diffusion and participatory approaches. A case study in Gwalior, India. *Journal of Health Communication, 3,* 327–344.

Lattimer, M. (2003). Preface. In Y. Ghai, *Public participation and minorities* (p. 2). London: Minority Rights Group International.

Lerner, D. (with Pevsner, L. W.). (1958). *The passing of traditional society: Modernizing the Middle East.* Glencoe, IL: Free Press.

Lin, N. (1999). Building a network theory of social capital. *Connections, 22*(1), 28–51.

Lord, R. G., & Brown, D. J. (2004). *Leadership processes and follower self-identity.* Mahwah, NJ: Erlbaum.

Lyson, T. A. (2000). Review of [*Community organizing: Building social capital as a development strategy*]. *Contemporary Sociology, 29,* 400–401.

Maslow, A. H. (1998). *Toward a psychology of being* (3rd ed.). New York: Wiley.

Mayer, M., & Rankin, K. N. (2002). Social capital and (community) development: A north/south perspective. *Antipode, 34,* 804–808.

Mayo, J., & Servaes, J. (1994). *Approaches to development communication: An orientation and resource kit.* Paris: United Nations Educational, Scientific and Cultural Organization.

McKee, N., Manoncourt, E., Yoon, C. S., & Carnegie, R. (Eds.). (2000). *Involving people, evolving behaviour.* New York: United Nations Children's Fund.

Melkote, S. R. (1991). *Communication for development in the Third World: Theory and practice.* Newbury Park, CA: Sage.

Nair, K. S., & White, S. A. (Eds.). (1993). *Perspectives on development communication.* Thousand Oaks, CA: Sage.

Navarro, V. (2002). A critique of social capital. *International Journal of Health Services, 32,* 423–432.

Piotrow, P. T., Kincaid, D. L., Rimon, J. G., & Rinehart, W. (1997). *Health communication: Lessons from family planning and reproductive health.* Westport, CT: Praeger.

Portales, D. (1986). Perspectivas de la comunicación alternativa en América Latina [Perspectives of alternative communication in Latin America]. In M. C. Simpson Grinberg (Ed.), *Comunicación alternativa y cambio social en América Latina* (pp. 89–103). Tlahuapan, Puebla, Mexico: Premiá editora de libros.

Prieto Castillo, D. (1998). En torno a comunicación y la movilización comunitaria [On communication and community mobilization]. In S. L. R. Beltrán & F. S. Gonzalez (Eds.), *Movilización comunitaria para la salud: dialogo multidisciplinario* (pp. 51–75). Baltimore: Johns Hopkins University Center for Communication Programs.

Prochaska, J. O., DiClemente, C. C., & Norcross, J. C. (1992). In search of how people change: Applications to addictive behaviors. *American Psychologist, 47,* 1102–1114.

Putnam, R. D. (1993). The prospective community: Social capital and public life. *American Prospect, 13,* 1–8.

Rapoport, A. (1967). *Fights, games, and debates.* Ann Arbor: University of Michigan Press.

Rice, R. E., & Atkin, C. K. (Eds.). (2001). *Public communication campaigns* (3rd ed.). Thousand Oaks, CA: Sage.

Rogers, C. R. (1951). *Client-centered therapy, its current practice, implications, and theory.* Boston: Houghton Mifflin.

Rogers, E. M. (1962*). Diffusion of innovations.* New York: Free Press.

Rogers, E. M. (with Svenning, L.). (1969). *Modernization among peasants: The impact of communication.* New York: Holt, Rinehart & Winston.

Rogers, E. M. (1973). *Communication strategies for family planning.* New York: Free Press.

Rogers, E. M. (1976). Communication and development: The passing of the dominant paradigm.

In E. M. Rogers (Ed.). *Communication and development: Critical perspectives* (pp. 121–148). Beverly Hills, CA: Sage.

Rogers, E. M. (1995). *Diffusion of innovations* (4th ed.). New York: Free Press.

Rogers, E. M. (1999). New perspectives on communication and development: Overview. *Communication Research, 3,* 99–107.

Rogers, E. M., & Kincaid, D. L. (1981). *Communication networks: Toward a new paradigm for research.* New York: Free Press.

Rucinski, D. (2004). Community boundedness, personal relevance, and the knowledge gap. *Communication Research, 31,* 472–495.

Schein, E. H. (1992). *Organizational culture and leadership* (2nd ed.). San Francisco: Jossey-Bass.

Scholtes, P. (1998). *The leader's handbook: Making things happen, getting things done.* New York: McGraw-Hill.

Schramm, W. (1964). *Mass media and national development: The role of information in the developing countries.* Stanford, CA: Stanford University Press.

Senge, P. M. (1990). *The fifth discipline: The art and practice of the learning organization.* New York: Doubleday/Currency.

Servaes, J. (1999). *Communication for development: One world, multiple cultures.* Cresskill, NJ: Hampton Press.

Servaes, J. (2004). *Toward a new perspective for communication and development.* Nijmegen, The Netherlands: Institute of Mass Communication, Catholic University of Nijmegen.

Servaes, J., Jacobson, T. L., & White, S. A. (Eds.). (1996). *Participatory communication for social change.* Thousand Oaks, CA: Sage.

Shafique, M. (2005). *Qualitative evaluation report of the positive deviance maternal and new-born care project in Haripur district.* Unpublished manuscript.

Shefner-Rogers, C. L., Rao, N., Rogers, E. M., & Wayangankar, A. (1998). The empowerment of women dairy farmers in India. *Journal of Applied Communication Research, 26,* 319–337.

Simpson, G. M. (1986). Comunicación alternativa: Dimensiones, límites, posibilidades [Alternative communication: Dimensions, limits, possibilities]. In G. M. Simpson (Ed.), *Comunicación alternativa y cambio Social en América Latina* (pp. 89–103). Tlahuapan, Puebla, Mexico: Premiá editora de libros, S.A.

Storey, J. D., & Kenney, L. C. (2004, May). *Effects of culturally appropriate community leadership on participation in local health improvement efforts in Indonesia.* Paper presented at the meeting of the International Communication Association, New Orleans, LA.

Sztompka, P. (1993). *The sociology of social change.* Cambridge, MA: Blackwell.

Tapia, M. (2002). *Community mobilization, dialogue and collective action around hygiene and environmental sanitation: The experience of the Mitch project in Nicaragua.* Unpublished manuscript, Johns Hopkins Bloomberg School of Public Health, Center for Communication Programs.

Tapia, M. (2003). *Building bridges for quality: An intercultural experience in the Peruvian Andes seen through the lenses of the social change framework.* Unpublished manuscript, Johns Hopkins Bloomberg School of Public Health, Center for Communication Programs.

Tenner, A. R., & DeToro, I. J. (1992). *Total quality management: Three steps to continuous improvement.* Reading, MA: Addison-Wesley.

Thompson, B., & Kinne, S. (1999). Social change theory: Applications to community health. In N. Bracht (Ed.), *Health promotion at the community level: New advances* (2nd ed., pp. 29–46). Thousand Oaks, CA: Sage.

Tichenor, P. J., Donohue, G. A., & Olien, C. N. (1970). Mass media flow and differential growth in knowledge. *Public Opinion Quarterly, 34,* 159–170.

Trigilla, C. (2001). Social capital and local development. *European Journal of Social Theory, 4,* 427–442.

Trimizi, S. A. (2002). The 6-L framework: A model for leadership research and development. *Leadership and Organization Development Journal, 23,* 269–279.

Underwood, C. (2002). Belief and attitude change in the context of human development. In I.

Sirageldin (Ed.), *Sustainable human development in the twenty-first century: An evolutionary perspective*. Oxford, UK: United Nations Educational, Scientific and Cultural Organization, Encyclopedia of Life Support Systems. Retrieved March 22, 2007, from http://www.eolss.net/E6-60-toc.aspx

United Nations. (2007). *The millennium development goals report*. New York: Author. Retrieved August 7, 2007, from http://www.un.org/millenniumgoals/pdf/mdg2007.pdf

United Nations Development Programme. (2002). *Arab human development report 2002: Creating opportunities for future generations*. New York: Author. Retrieved February 20, 2009, from http://www.naxaoline.org/download/UNDP/EnglishVersion/Ar-Human-Dev-2002.pdf

United Nations Development Programme. (2003). *Human development report 2003: Millennium development goals: A compact among nations to end human poverty*. New York: Author. Retrieved February 20, 2009, from http://hdr.undp.org/media/hdro3_complete.pdf

United Nations Population Fund. (2001). *Focus on HIV/AIDS communication and evaluation*. Managua, Nicaragua: Author.

Viswanath, K., & Finnegan, J. R., Jr. (1996). The knowledge gap hypothesis. In B. R. Burleson (Ed.), *Communication yearbook* (Vol. 19, pp 187–227). Thousand Oaks, CA: Sage.

Viswanath, K., Kosicki, G. M., Fredin, E. S., & Park, E. (2000). Local community ties, community boundedness, and local public affairs knowledge gaps. *Communication Research, 27*, 27–50.

Wallerstein, N. (2002). Participatory evaluation model for coalitions: The development of systems indicators. *Health Promotion Practice, 3*, 361–373.

Walton, M. (1986). *The Deming management method*. New York: Dodd, Mead.

Weisbord, M. R. (1992). *Discovering common ground: How future search conferences bring people together to achieve breakthrough innovation, empowerment, shared vision, and collaborative action*. San Francisco: Berrett-Koehler.

Weisbord, M. R., & Janoff, S. (1995). *Future search: An action guide to finding common ground in organizations and communities*. San Francisco: Berrett-Koehler.

White, S. A. (Ed., with Sadanandan, K. N., & Ascroft, J.). (1995). *Participatory communication: Working for change and development*. Thousand Oaks, CA: Sage.

Willis, C. P., Schroeder, D. G., Howard-Grabman, L., Marsh, D., & Gonzalez F. (2001). *Strengthening local health partnerships in Bolivia with community-based health information*. Unpublished manuscript.

World Bank. (2004). *Partnerships in development: Progress in the fight against poverty*. Washington, DC: Author. Retrieved July 17, 2006, from http://www.worldbank.org/progress/progress_in_development.pdf

Yankelovich, D. (1999). *The magic of dialogue: Transforming conflict into cooperation*. New York: Simon & Schuster.

Zander, A. F. (1996). *Motives and goals in groups*. New Brunswick, NJ: Transaction.

Part V

Exemplary Programs of Applied Communication Research

22 Drug Resistance Strategies Project

Using Narrative Theory to Enhance Adolescents' Communication Competence

Michael L. Hecht and Michelle Miller-Day

The Pennsylvania State University

According to the 2002 National Survey on Drug Use and Health[1] (Substance Abuse and Mental Health Services Administration [SAMHSA], 2003), an estimated 22 million people aged 12 and older were categorized as abusers of alcohol or drugs and required treatment. Data from the 2003 Monitoring the Future study indicated that although the adolescent drug problem in the United States has improved over the past decade, youth alcohol and other drug use still is a significant public health issue (Johnston, O'Malley, Bachman, & Schulenberg, 2004). Use rates, however, have fluctuated up and down since the time that tracking began; the more troubling issue is the harm experienced from substance use and abuse. This harm has been and continues to be a significant social issue at all recorded levels of use.[2]

Thus, substance use and abuse in the United States is a significant social problem with implications for individual, community, and societal functioning. The goal of prevention is to ultimately minimize the impact of this problem by deterring and decreasing alcohol and other drug usage across all age, gender, racial, and ethnic groups. Although prevention efforts have existed for over a century, federal support for drug prevention efforts was placed on the front of the world stage in the 1980s with the "Just Say No" campaign championed by Nancy Reagan.

The Drug Resistance Strategies (DRS) project is an interdisciplinary, multimethod, funded program of research that we began in 1989 as a response to this problem and currently is funded through 2013. This program includes both action research and intervention research. The action research involves a series of studies describing narrative accounts of adolescent drug offer processes (e.g., who offers, how offers are made, and how they are resisted) with particular emphasis on understanding the role of ethnicity and gender in those processes. This work spanned middle school, high school, and college-aged populations, and involved narrative interviews, as well as survey research with large data sets. Our intervention research involved the development and implementation of drug prevention curriculum for high school and middle school students that was based on this action research. The curriculum, called *keepin' it REAL*, is culturally grounded and derived from narrative theory and communication competence theory. In our longitudinal evaluation study, the curriculum has demonstrated positive effects on reducing substance use and changing norms and attitudes.

The DRS project constitutes applied research because it utilizes extant theory and research to understand and intervene into practical, socially relevant problems (i.e., drug use and abuse). Moreover, the project has refined theory and uncovered generalizable knowledge (e.g., the role of ethnicity and ethnic identity in drug offers and refusals), adding to the science of drug prevention as part of "the new social research" or "action inquiry" paradigm (Torbert, 1991) that tests theories *through* their application. For example, a new theory of social norms was applied to drug norms and was supported by the findings of our work (Elek, Miller-Day, & Hecht, 2006). In addition, although much has been written about the need for integrating multiculturalism within intervention programming (Green, 1998), little empirical evidence of its efficacy existed prior to the implementation of the DRS curriculum (Hecht, Marsiglia et al. 2003).

In this chapter, we provide an account of the program's history, including an overview of the research design, methods, and findings, and we discuss the theoretical, methodological, and practical significance of this research program. We start by discussing the theories that guided this project. We then tell the story of this project, giving an account of its history as we describe our research. The third section examines the significance of this applied communication research program, followed by concluding remarks.

Guiding Theories of the Drug Resistance Strategies Project

The DRS project always has had a strong theoretical basis. Although different aspects of the project have utilized different theories, as explained below, the overall project has been guided by two overarching theoretical approaches: narrative theory and communication competence theory.

Narrative Theory

Narrative theory conceptualizes human thought and behavior as based in *narratives* or *stories*, a pervasive, transcultural mode of discourse through which people organize information and experiences of the world (White, 1981). Narratives are not only one of the primary means for making sense of experience (Cook-Gumperz, 1993; Fisher, 1987) and moral choices (Botvin, Schinke, Epstein, & Diaz, 1994) but they also serve as an organizing principle for behavior (Botvin et al., 1994; Howard, 1991). Howard (1991) argued that human thought, itself, may be conceptualized as narrative or storytelling. As McAdams (1993) noted, "We each seek to provide our scattered and often confused experiences with a sense of coherence by arranging the episodes of our lives into stories" (p. 11). More than thoughts, narratives are a meaningful form of communicative behavior through which people express themselves as they form self-images, as well as plan and understand their actions. As McAdams asserted, "Much of what passes for everyday conversation among people is storytelling of one form or another" (p. 28).

Narrative also has a cultural element because it is intimately tied to membership in speech communities. Storytelling draws on socially shared symbol systems that express membership and make stories meaningful to listeners. These narratives provide "good reasons" that justify actions based on the dominant stories within a group (Fisher, 1987). There is ample evidence to suggest that narratives are structured differently in different ethnic groups (Holland & Kirkpatrick, 1993; Howard, 1991), including the narratives in African-American and Mexican-American communities (Botvin et al., 1994; Hecht, Jackson, & Ribeau, 2003).

Narratives are highly salient in adolescents' lives. Adolescents increasingly understand narratives as their cognitive capabilities mature (Johnson & Ettema, 1982), which allows them to think about the world and themselves in abstract terms, expanding from what *is* to what *ought* to be (Inhelder & Piaget, 1958). Even young school children recognize story characters and use them as motivation, as well as the basis for their narratives (McAdams, 1993). The fundamental challenge of adolescence and young adulthood is to create meaningful answers to questions that form the basis for identity (McAdams, 1993). Adolescents often construct personal narratives to affirm their uniqueness, providing them with both a means to understand themselves and the world, as well as a vehicle for expressing that understanding.

Narratives also can provide models for adolescents' behavior. Social learning theory (Bandura, 1982) suggests that models derived from adolescents' experiences can transfer identification and learning into behavior change. It is important to model resistance and life skills for situations in which adolescents commonly find themselves (Polich, Ellickson, Reuter, & Kahan, 1984) and include both participatory modeling and observational learning (Bandura, 1982). The overall social learning model, then, is to provide modeling, guided performance, and reinforcement. From a narrative perspective, this means *viewing* the narratives of others (observational modeling and learning), *participating* in narratives (participatory modeling), and *accepting* the new narratives.

Research indicates that people see narrative messages as more realistic (Greene & Brinn, 2003), easier to relate to, and more memorable than statistical evidence (Kopfman, Smith, Ah Yun, & Hodges, 1998), and that narrative messages are evaluated more positively, seen as more causally relevant, and rated as more credible than a real news story (Feeley, Marshall, & Reinhart, 2006), with messages that combine narrative and statistical evidence being more persuasive than those presenting either type of evidence alone (Allen et al., 2000). This research also suggests an alternative to traditional approaches to drug knowledge—*narrative knowledge*. Narrative knowledge, which supplements other types of information, in this case, means awareness of stories of drugs, drug use, and drug users. Research suggests that the perceived "story" of drug use among adolescents presents a positive picture of drugs with images of users as mature and unconventional, and drug use seen as a way of "killing time" (Alberts, Miller-Rassulo, & Hecht, 1991; Jessor, Chase, & Donovan, 1980; Krizek, Hecht, & Miller, 1993). Krizek et al. (1993) found that those who are at less risk and do not use drugs believe that drug use is a way of losing control of one's life (i.e., if they use drugs, they will not be able to control how they behave), whereas those at higher risk or who already use drugs talk about using drugs to take control of one's life (i.e., by using drugs, they escape adult and societal controls). Thus, the narratives about drugs, drug users, and drug use need to be modified to prevent drug use. Pilot tests of narrative-based prevention programs have proven successful in reducing substance use (Hecht, Corman, & Miller-Rassulo, 1993), particularly in minority schools (Botvin et al., 1994; Constantino, Malgady, & Rogler, 1988).

Narrative theory has guided our work from the beginning. Initially, we focused on drug offer narratives (i.e., stories about times when adolescents were offered drugs) to describe the social processes of adolescent substance use. Narrative research then was conducted to explicate adolescents' experience of drugs, drug use, and drug offers. Narrative also guided our prevention efforts, as our curriculum utilized narratives in which peer models of adolescents refuse drug offers to redefine the story of drug use norms and risk, as well as to develop communication competence and life skills.

Drug Resistance as Communication Competence

It should be clear from the discussion of narrative theory that one of the key elements to understanding adolescent drug use and developing effective prevention programs are the social processes through which drugs come to be offered and either refused or accepted and used. Although narratives can describe those processes, we utilized communication competence theory to better understand drug offer–resistance interactions.

Responding to drug offers involves a type of communicative competence in which messages are constructed to resist social influence. If peer pressure is one of the keys to adolescent drug use, as many believe, understanding this pressure and developing communication skills for resisting it involves social competencies. For example, it certainly is difficult for drug prevention programs to invoke a norm of resistance if teens lack the requisite communication skills to manifest normative behavior.

A theoretical model of communication competence argues that competence is a relational phenomenon and identifies four necessary components: knowledge, motivation, skills, and outcomes (Spitzberg & Cupach, 1984). When applied to drug resistance, *knowledge* includes understanding the effects of drugs, the context, and the other person(s) offering them; *motivation* entails perceptions of peer drug norms, attitudes toward drugs, perceptions of consequences of drug use, and desire to engage in resistance to offers; *skills* are the messages used in refusal; and *outcomes* are the consequences of these messages for self, others, and relationships.

This model conceptualizes competence as a relational phenomenon, which stresses the fact that any conversation has outcomes for both parties and that communication that optimizes these mutual outcomes is maximally effective. When cast into a drug-resistance framework, this means that if Jose offers cocaine to his friend Jim, and Jim's reply both resists the offer and does not offend Jose, continued pressure from Jose is less likely to occur than if the refusal offended Jim, Jim's resistance is successful, and the relationship between Jose and Jim is maintained. Thus, to resist competently offers of drugs, teens need adequate knowledge, appropriate motivation, and skills necessary to produce desirable relational outcomes.

The identification of resistance competencies falls under the general area of research in social influence communication (McLaughlin, Cody, & Robey, 1980), a normative process in which messages are evaluated along a social acceptability dimension (Boster, 1988). Thomas and Seibold (1995), for instance, found that college students utilized a variety of tactics that varied in the degree of assertiveness and invasiveness when attempting to intervene in peers' alcohol use.

Although a great deal of research attention has focused on how people gain the compliance of others, little is known about how people resist influence attempts. What little research on resistance exists applies to general social situations (e.g., buying a new suit or cutting down a tree) and public policy issues (e.g., legalization of heroin) rather than more significant personal and interpersonal issues, such as drug and alcohol use, leaving these more personal and interpersonal issues vulnerable to social influence (McGuire, 1964). We do know that refusal, in general, requires the knowledge component of perspective taking (understanding the view of the person or persons making the offer) and a large and complex repertoire of refusal skills (Kline & Floyd, 1990). Other aspects of cognitive development, such as egocentrism, await investigation (Greene, Kremar, Rubin, Walters, & Hale, 2002). Studies of tobacco smoking reveal three general strategies of resistance: (1) appropriateness (fear of disapproval), (2) consistency (personal convictions), and (3) effectiveness (fear of effects; Reardon, Sussman, & Flay, 1989). Moreover, Harrington (1995) discovered that alcohol-resistance strategies that saved the face of the persuader maintained a favorable interpersonal relationship between persuader and resister, whereas those interactions where "negative face support" was employed by the resister cultivated a less favorable relationship by decreasing satisfaction and attraction between the interactants. Women also appeared more able than men to employ resistance behavior that did not negatively affect the relationship of persuader and resister. In addition, direct refusals prompted more "simple offer" follow-up strategies and a refusal to a simple offer of alcohol received more follow-up attempts than a refusal to a complex offer (Harrington, 1997).

Communication competence is not only a relational and skills-based phenomenon but it also is a culturally based one as well (Hammer & Vaglum, 1989; Hecht, Jackson, & Ribeau, 2003; LaFromboise, Coleman-Hardin, & Gerton, 1995). Culture shapes worldviews, norms, rules, attitudes, values, and beliefs, and, thereby, influences the perceptual processes by which messages are sent and received (Baldwin, Faulkner, Hecht, & Lindsley, 2006). As a result, communication that adjusts to and accommodates a person's culture is likely to be more effective than communication that does not (Hecht, Jackson, & Ribeau, 2003; Shepard, Giles, & Le Poire, 2001), and cultural sensitivity is essential to general communication effectiveness (Hammer & Vaglum, 1989). In a sense, culture provides not only criteria for judging competence (i.e., telling cultural members when something is effective and appropriate) but it also defines knowledge, motivation, and skills, as well as relational dimensions (Spitzberg, 1997). Research has demonstrated that members of various ethnic groups differ in their general communication competencies and norms (Collier, Ribeau, & Hecht, 1986; Hecht & Ribeau, 1984; Hecht, Ribeau, & Alberts, 1989; Hecht, Ribeau, & Sedano, 1990). Cultural competence, thus, introduces a new way of thinking about adolescent substance use and prevention curricula (Cross, Bazron, Dennis, & Isaacs, 1989), leading to a consideration of the role of ethnicity and ethnic identity in drug offers, and to developing culturally grounded interventions from the perspective of group members.

The communication competence model provided a framework for both our research and prevention efforts. We first attempted to describe the competencies involved in the social processes of adolescent drug use and then used this model to develop an intervention designed to decrease adolescent substance use. The following description is the story of our research efforts.

The Story: An Account of the Program's History

This section reviews the history of our project, by describing the three major studies that we have conducted and a fourth study that currently is in progress.

DRS1: In Reaction to "Just Say No"

In 1980, Nancy Reagan, spouse of U.S. President Ronald Reagan, traveled to 65 cities in 33 states to raise awareness about the dangers of drugs and alcohol, coining the catch-phrase heard everywhere, "Just say no." A plethora of "just say no" prevention messages subsequently surfaced in the media during the 1980s, most containing fear appeals (e.g., the public service announcement sponsored by the Partnership for a Drug-Free America: "This is your brain"—*showing an egg*—"This is your brain on drugs"—*showing the egg frying in a smoldering skillet*) or simplistic appeals to adolescents indicating that just a simple "no" should suffice when resisting offers of alcohol or other drugs.

Although this simplistic message proved inadequate (Tobler et al., 2000), it did resonate with a prevention research community that was moving from education, self-esteem, and fear-based campaigns to those focused on social skills. Operating from a peer-pressure model that conceptualized adolescent substance use and abuse as arising largely (perhaps even primarily) from peer influence, this new approach focused on teaching adolescents skills for resisting peer pressure to use drugs. These resistance or refusal skills were seen as central to enabling and empowering adolescents to "say no" to drug offers. Although this model later was expanded to include social norms and a broader range of life skills (e.g., decision making), the central element continued to be resistance skills. It was in this environment that the DRS project was born.

As communication scholars interested in health issues, we believed that drug prevention messages generated by adult educators were neither grounded in the actual experiences of youth nor guided by theory and, thus, were not maximally effective in teaching youth how to communicatively resist offers of drugs or deter their actual drug use. We believed that prevention messages should reflect aspects of adolescents' experience and culture. Thus, the first step in our initial endeavor was to adequately identify the communication strategies that youth reported that they *actually used* when resisting offers of alcohol or other drugs.[3] We used this information to assess different ways of presenting prevention messages to youth to enhance their communication competence in refusing drug offers. By listening to the narratives of youth about their drug offer–resistance episodes, we hoped to identify how they understood the resistance strategies they employed and to learn more about how they perceived issues of substance use. Through this process, we learned that resistance, indeed, is not as simple as "just say no."

Our first project (DRS1, 1989–1992) was a pilot study, formative in nature. Narrative and communication competence theories suggested that we start by understanding the social processes of drug offers from adolescents' perspective (i.e., who, where, and how offered, and how refused) and that narratives could be used not only to understand these processes but also to alter substance use and abuse. Thus, this first project was conducted with a sample of high school students from Mesa, Arizona to (1) identify drug-resistance strategies youth report using in drug-offer scenarios, and (2) develop and assess the effectiveness of teaching the identified resistance strategies.

Intensive interviews were conducted with high school and college students to gather and analyze their narrative descriptions of drug offer–resistance episodes (Alberts, Hecht, Miller-Rassulo, & Krizek, 1992; Alberts et al., 1991; Hecht, Alberts, & Miller-Rassulo, 1992; Miller, Alberts, Hecht, Trost, & Krizek, 2000). This research resulted in a series of typologies describing the "who, what, where, and how" of drug offers—the narrative knowledge about drugs, drug use, and drug users.

People offering substances ranged from strangers, acquaintances, and coworkers to friends and family. In the older (high school) samples, the most frequent offerers were friends and family members (including siblings, parents, and other relatives), with strangers, the stereotypic offerer in many adult narratives about drugs, the least frequent.

This research also revealed that drugs are offered in a variety of places. We were surprised at the detailed descriptions of the locations that youth provided, including homes (their own, as well as those of friends), social situations, and public places (e.g., parks). By far, most offers to high school students were made in social situations, such as parties, whereas college students were more likely to receive offers in homes (Miller et al., 2000).

Drug offers varied from mere availability to more complex persuasive interpersonal appeals involving a rationale. The range of offers included *mere availability* (e.g., substances were just present and it was implied that the person could use them), *simple verbal* (e.g., "Want some?") or *nonverbal* (e.g., handing someone a marijuana joint) *offers*, *minimizing the effects of use* (e.g., "Come on, have a drink, it's no big deal"), *appealing to group norms* (e.g., "Have a smoke, everyone is doing it"), and *stating benefits of use* (e.g., "It's fun" or "Getting high is cool") or *costs of nonuse* (e.g., "Don't be a nerd").

We next distinguished between simple offers and those involving pressure. We also found the existence of sequential offers, with an initial offer made, followed by a response, and then a second or follow-up offer. The majority of the offers were simple ones (mere availability and simple offer), although when offers were sequential, the follow-up offers were more likely than the original offer to include pressure to use drugs, a finding that has important implications for prevention implementations, most of which focus only on responding to initial offers.

Central to this work was the identification of four drug-resistance strategies that now have been validated from early adolescents (11-year-olds) to young adults of various ethnicities and regions of the United States. These strategies were identified by the acronym, REAL, which stood for the four resistance strategies: *refuse* (e.g., direct refusal by saying "no"), *explain* (e.g., offering an explanation or giving an excuse), *avoid* (e.g., avoiding the environment where drugs are present or avoiding the offer), and *leave* (e.g., leaving the scene). We also identified a variety of explanation strategies (e.g., stating a lack of desire or a fear of consequences, or explaining that the resistor was "not that type of person"). Overall, refusal was the most frequent strategy, with avoidance being the most sophisticated or complex because it required anticipating or planning for the presence of drugs, perspective taking, and other higher order cognitive skills. Avoidance also was more likely to be used by older adolescents than younger ones (Miller et al., 2000).

These studies suggested certain patterns in drug offers. First, resistance is a problematic situation for which there are no easy or clear solutions that must be solved as a puzzle or problem (Hecht, Jackson, & Ribeau, 2003). Adolescents often want to refuse a drug offer but do not wish to alienate the offerer. Drug offer–resistance episodes may involve both implicit and explicit pressure to comply, although, in general, there is less explicit pressure than previous literature suggests, and even implicit pressure tends to decrease with age (Miller et al., 2000). Where pressure exists, it is exerted after an initial offer is refused or when offers are made in larger groups (Miller, 1999). Second, in general, simple, nonverbal offers are the strategy that is most likely to gain compliance, whereas simple refusals or leaving the situation are the most effective overall resistance strategies. Third, we found that a control metaphor emerged in adolescents' talk about drugs, with this talk differentiating those at risk for use from those who are not (Krizek et al., 1993). Those using substances or at high risk for doing so tended to say that drug use allowed them to take control of their life because they escaped adult influence and asserted independence, whereas nonusers who were at lower risk said they avoided drugs so as not to lose control through the psychological effects of consumption. This control metaphor was built into later prevention campaigns. The groups also differed in their expectations about use, with people in the high-risk/use group having positive expectations about use (e.g., drugs make a party more enjoyable) and those in the low-risk/nonuse group having negative expectations (e.g., they will get sick if they drink).

In the second phase of DRS1, we used the narratives gathered in the first phase to create performance scripts providing active models for adolescent behavior. The narratives were scripted into both live and videotaped performances by a professional writer using transcripts of our narrative interviews and performed by professional actors who were of college age. The videotapes received awards at the New York Film and TV Festival, as well as at the Questar Competition. The impacts of both live and videotaped performance were compared with a control group (i.e., youth who did not receive either performance but, instead, participated in whatever prevention programs were in use at their school at the time), testing for effectiveness in reducing drug use. Both video and live performance interventions reduced self-reported substance use at a posttest 30 days after the intervention (Hecht et al., 1993). The successful completion of this pilot research study led directly to the second DRS study, which was designed to extend our research on communication competence in drug offer–resistance episodes by considering the role of ethnicity and gender among a middle school population.

DRS2: Ethnicity and Gender in Adolescent Drug Use

The initial project (DRS1) provided a descriptive base for understanding the social processes of drugs offers, as well as a pilot test of our narrative approach to intervention. However, we were unable to examine ethnic variation due to the homogeneous nature of the student bodies where our work was conducted. Increasingly, it was becoming clear to communication researchers that culture played an important role in communication competence (Hecht, Jackson, & Ribeau, 2003; Spitzberg, 1997), and that in the drug arena, there were important ethnic differences in use rates (Grunbaum et al., 1999) and, especially, in the efficacy of prevention programs (Castro, Proescholdbell, Abeita, & Rodriguez, 1999).

Culture is important for interventions because, as we documented in DRS1, the norms, attitudes, and behavioral repertoires that adolescents use to make and enact decisions about substance use are derived, at least in part, from cultural background and identity. As a result, cultural sensitivity is essential to the efficacy of interventions (Vargas & Koss-Chioino, 1992). In the most general sense, interventions are communicative events, and research shows that communication that adjusts to and accommodates culture is more effective than that which does not (Hecht, Marsiglia et al., 2003; Shepard et al., 2001). Communication that fails to adjust to culture risks the disaster that befell General Motors when trying to market its car "Nova" in Spanish-speaking countries only to find out that "No Va" in Spanish means "doesn't go." Effective messages, therefore, must be based on the underlying worldviews that develop through enculturation, and this is particularly true of interventions that seek to promote change (Vargas & Koss-Chioino, 1992).

DRS2 (1993–1997) contributed conceptually to our program of research on adolescent drug use by focusing on younger, middle school youth rather than high school and college youth, and also by examining the roles of ethnic and gender identities. Our goal was to replicate and extend our previous research to this younger population and to see if we could describe ethnic and gender similarities and differences. Doing so helps to understand the role of culture (ethnicity and gender) in the social processes surrounding drug use (e.g., decision making, offers, and refusals) and provides the basis for culturally grounding the implementation we planned on developing in the next phase (DRS3). As we did in the first project (DRS1), we began with narrative interviews and then conducted a large-scale questionnaire survey.

Drug-Offer Processes

Initially, narrative interviews (30 to 45 minutes) were conducted with 158 middle school students from five schools (Hecht, Trost, Bator, & MacKinnon, 1997), who were recruited from their classes and relatively evenly distributed across three major ethnic groups (i.e., Mexican American, European American, and African American). The interviews were conducted in small, private rooms at the schools by trained college students and were tape-recorded with participants' permission. After a short, warm-up period, the interviewer asked participants to recall a time when they were offered drugs and to describe what happened. Prompts were designed to elicit the "who, what, where, and how" of the situation. Interviews were transcribed verbatim and the narrative accounts were open coded using inductive processes of constant comparison suggested by Strauss and Corbin (1990). The analysis of the interviews were followed up by analyzing questionnaire responses collected from 3,080 seventh-grade students (Moon, Hecht, Jackson, & Spellers, 1999). Recent (last 30 days) and lifetime use of alcohol, tobacco, and marijuana were measured, as was ethnic group membership, ethnic identity, sex, and other demographic variables. The questionnaires also asked respondents to recall a time when they have been offered drugs and to indicate which drug was offered, where the offer was made, their relationship to the offerer, how the offer was made, and how they responded.

Eighty-eight participants (56%) reported that they had been offered drugs, including 51 (53%) males and 37 (47%) females. Marijuana was the most commonly offered drug (60% of the offers), followed by alcohol (16%), inhalants (11%), and tobacco (8%). The results indicated that middle school youth were most likely to receive offers from acquaintances, which differed from findings for high school (Alberts et al., 1992) and college (Hecht et al., 1992) students, where most offers were from family members or friends. As with the older sample, simple offers were described most frequently (97% in the interview study), with about a quarter of these offers repeated. Although only 4% of those interviewed reported accepting the initial offers of drugs, 9% of the repeated offers were accepted. These different acceptance rates illustrate the impact of implicit and explicit peer pressure, as well as developmental differences, with less explicit pressure in the middle school sample than in the high school and college samples.

The four resistance strategies of refuse, avoid, explain, and leave, again, emerged as the primary strategies. In this age group, avoidance tended to be operationalized through indirect refusals. Two explanations, nonuse identity (e.g., "I'm not that kind of person") and fear of consequences (e.g., "I'll get a headache if I drink"), were found, which was in contrast to the four explanations used by older students (stating a lack of desire, claiming the substance is illness inducing, suggesting an alternative activity, and labeling the activity immoral). Thus, there was some overlap between the samples (fear of consequences and illness inducing are similar, and immorality is part of nonuse identity), but younger respondents reported a more restricted range and smaller repertoire, with an average of only 1.5 strategies per youth. The most common response to an initial offer was a simple "no" (90% in the interviews), which included both direct and indirect refusals. The next most-common responses were to leave, followed by some type of explanation, and then avoidance. Of those receiving offers, 26% experienced a repeat or follow-up offer. A simple no also was the most likely response to a repeated offer (70%), followed by leaving (43%), and some type of explanation (30%). Repeated offers provoked threats of turning the offerer in to authority figures (13%). The most common reasons for refusal were the substance's negative effects on mind or body, and personal preference. The small repertoire of resistance strategies and the lack of more complex strategies, such as avoidance, by this younger group suggest the importance of skills training for this age group. More work is needed, however, on a wider range of developmental issues.

Ethnicity and Gender in Drug-Offer Processes

Ethnic and gender effects then were examined through a separate analysis of the interviews and questionnaires. Although the patterns described previously were common to all groups, reflecting the most common scenario in each group, some ethnic and gender differences did emerge in both studies. Thus, the differences must be interpreted keeping the overarching similarities in mind. Overall, Latino/as were significantly more likely than the other groups to be offered drugs, especially alcohol, marijuana, hard drugs, and inhalants. Latino/as also were more likely than the other groups to receive offers from a peer family member, such as a sibling or cousin, but were least likely to receive offers from a parent, and those offers tended to be extended at parties and in other situations where other people were around. In addition, compared to the other groups, Latino/as were more likely to respond with a simple no than to use the other strategies in the REAL system. European Americans were more likely than Africa Americans to be offered drugs. Compared to both Latino/as and African Americans, European Americans were more likely to be offered cigarettes by a male or female acquaintance through simple offers at friends' homes or on the street. Finally, compared to the other two groups, African Americans were more likely to receive offers in the park that were extended by dating partners or by their parents, and they were more likely to refuse using the explain strategy.

Although the general pattern described here tended to hold for both males and females, some gender differences also were observed. Males were more likely than females to be offered all types of drugs in public (i.e., at the park or on the street) and to be offered them by a parent, male acquaintance, brother, male cousin, or male stranger through offers that stated the benefits of use, and they resisted using explanations, especially those involving humor. It perhaps was most significant that males were more likely than females to experience repeat offers. In contrast, compared to males, offers to females were more likely to be simple offers or offers that minimized the effects of use made by a female acquaintance, boyfriend, sister, or female cousin in private locations (i.e., friends' homes). Females also perceived drug offers as negatively affecting their relationship with offerers (Miller-Day, 2002).

The studies suggested that female Latinas probably were the most unique group. Not only did they receive the greatest number of offers than the other groups but they also differed from other females with respect to which substance was offered (more likely to be offered marijuana), where the offers were made (more likely at school and with a friend present), and to resist with a simple "no."

We also examined ethnic and gender differences in risk and resiliency factors (Moon, Jackson, & Hecht, 2000). *Risk factors* are those that increase chances of drug use, such as poverty and single families; *resiliency factors* are those that protect people from risks, such as family and school bonding. We found that a linear model of these factors (variables are either risk or resiliency factors) was superior to a curvilinear model (e.g., high scores on a factor indicate risk, whereas low scores indicate resiliency). For males, risk had a direct effect on use and an indirect effect through age of first use, but male resiliency affected use only through age of first use. For females, resiliency had a stronger and independent effect, as well as an indirect effect through age of first use, whereas risk had only an indirect effect through first use. These findings suggest that males should be exposed to resiliency factors at a very early age, prior to experimentation, but that early exposure is less important for females because resiliency has an independent effect for this group.

Ethnicity played a similar role as did gender.[4] Among Mexican Americans, both risk and resiliency had independent effects; in addition, their effects were mediated by age of first use. However, among European-American youth, risk had an independent effect that was not mediated by age for first use, whereas the influence of resiliency was only through age of first youth. These results mean that, as with males, in general, European Americans need to be exposed to resiliency factors prior to experimentation.

We also discovered gender differences in heterosexual relational processes (Barnett & Miller, 2001; Trost, Langan, & Kellar-Guenter, 1999), such as males' susceptibility to a dating partner's drug offer being influenced by the intimacy of the relationship but not by males' self-esteem, whereas for females, both factors were important. Although junior high boys typically are not as interested in girls as girls are in them (Peterson, 1988), we found that boys who wanted a partner felt vulnerable to the perceived pressure they received from drug offerers of the opposite sex (Trost et al., 1999). Females also tended to perceive that drug offers negatively affected their relationship with the offerer. When offered a drug by a friend, there was likely to be no explicit pressure but there was an implicit pressure to respond politely to a friendly offer. When the goal was to resist the offer, there was a heightened awareness of self-presentation, especially when the offer was made in groups larger than five, with the refuser rather than the offerer placed in the role of the "bad guy" for being impolite (Miller, 1999).

This work addresses the need for increased understanding of the identity goals of those involved in drug offer–resistance episodes. The next step was to put this research to work in an intervention targeted at middle school students, embarking on a path of *action inquiry* that was increasingly more participatory.

DRS3: Interdisciplinary, Multimethod Intervention through Participatory Action Research

Botvin (1986) argued that feelings of ownership of programs are crucial to drug prevention effectiveness, because direct involvement with developing a program heightens identification with the content and investment in the success of the program. Therefore, three objectives directed the second level of funding for this program of research: (1) to involve youth in the development of their own prevention programming; (2) to identify culturally grounded, age-appropriate prevention messages in their narratives; and (3) to develop prevention media that reflected these culturally grounded prevention messages.

Our third project (DRS3; 1997–2002) developed, implemented, and evaluated a culturally grounded, middle school *keepin' it REAL* curriculum. Expanding to include scholars from other disciplines, such as social work and education, and emphasizing cultural sensitivity in prevention programming, DRS3 emerged as a cross-disciplinary project that employed a "*from* kids *through* kids *to* kids design" using a participatory action approach to create the curriculum, which consisted of 10 lessons promoting antidrug norms and teaching resistance and other social skills, reinforced by booster activities and a media campaign (Gosin, Marsiglia, & Hecht, 2003). This approach was designed to maximize participants' identification, realism, and interest (Miller, Hecht, & Stiff, 1998).

Most drug prevention programs are created by and for European Americans and tested on this ethnic group. It has been suggested that the failure of some prevention programs can be traced to their lack of cultural sensitivity (Palinkas, Atkins, Jerreira, & Miller, 1995). Minority youth tend to prefer performers of their ethnicity in media portrayals (Dorr, 1982), and African Americans and Latino/as responded more favorably to messages from members of their ethnic group in a federally sponsored billboard campaign (Eigen & Siegel, 1991). These results are not surprising, as ethnic group members tend to differ in how they process media information (Korzenny, McClure, & Rzyttki, 1990) and many minorities experience racial isolation from media portrayals (Johnson & Ettema, 1982).

It is not surprising, then, that prevention specialists have called for a shift to ethnically sensitive content in drug prevention programming (Botvin et al., 1994; Schinke et al., 1985). DRS3 was developed, in part, to heed that call. Culture can be utilized in drug prevention in many ways; the examples above include people's involvement in their culture and use of indigenous images. However, we believe that culturally grounding drug prevention messages goes beyond mere utilization of cultural imagery and practices to develop interventions from the perspective of the targeted group. Our interventions, therefore, are developed from the narratives or stories that group members tell about their experiences, infused with the cultural values central to their group norms (Gosin, Marsiglia, & Hecht, 2003), and developed through a participatory action research method in which group members collaborate in developing the intervention (Gosin, Dustman, Drapeau, & Harthun, 2003).

In addition to cultural values informing the development of the DRS3 curriculum, communication competence theory also guided its development by focusing on teaching the three components of competence: knowledge, motivation, and skills (see Figure 22.1). Utilizing narrative theory, narrative knowledge was the first component—teaching adolescents stories about drug resistance. Motivation was defined by social norms, as literature suggests that norms motivate people to avoid drugs (Beauvais & Oetting, 1999) by creating standards against which their behaviors are judged, as well as criteria for determining how to behave. We utilized norm focus theory, which expanded the prevailing conceptualization of norms from perceptions of peer drug use prevalence (labeled *descriptive norms* by the theory) to include *injunctive norms*, or what ought to be done (e.g., whether adolescents believe that their peers believe drug use is right or wrong), and *personal norms*, or how an individual believes that he or she should act (e.g., whether the person believes that drug use is a positive experience; Cialdini, Reno, & Kallgren, 1990). Finally, skills were defined as resistance skills (REAL), decision making, and risk assessment.

Five videotapes taught the resistance skills and formed the core of the program (Holleran, Dustman, Reeves, & Marsiglia, 2002). The videos were created from the narratives that adolescents provided in DRS2 and from additional formative research. The first video provided an overview of the program and the others taught the four resistance skills. Radio and television public service announcements (PSAs) were created from these classroom videos to reinforce the program's content. Students at a local performing arts high school produced the videos with guidance from project personnel and were awarded regional Emmys for their efforts. The other lessons contained discussions and role-playing scenarios based on other DRS3 narratives, and all of the content reflected the formative research framed in narrative form. Thus, the content came from adolescents ("from kids"), much of it was created by adolescents ("through kids"), and it was presented to adolescents ("to kids").

Three versions of the curriculum were developed. One was developed to reflect Mexican-American culture, the numerically largest group in the targeted schools. The second version, labeled the European-American/African-American curriculum, targeted the next two largest groups. These three groups constituted over 95% of the target population. These versions were developed by utilizing the DRS2 and DRS3 ethnicity findings to shape the materials, using the DRS3 and formative research narratives of each group separately. Cultural values were identified for each group based on previous research and

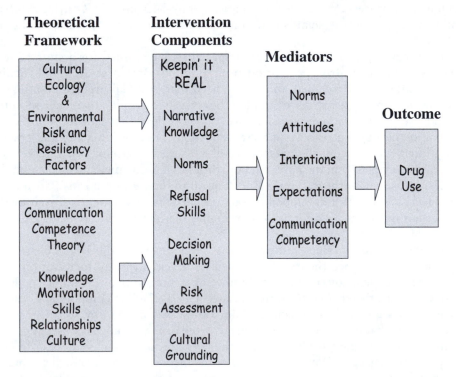

Figure 22.1 Conceptual model for prevention curriculum.

infused into each version (Gosin, Marsiglia, & Hecht, 2003). The third version, called the "multicultural curriculum," was developed by using lessons from each of the other two versions.

The three versions of the curriculum and a control condition were randomly assigned to 35 middle schools that volunteered for the study; control schools continued to implement their preexisting prevention program. Students completed baseline questionnaires and follow-up posttest questionnaires 1 month, 8 months, and 14 months after the intervention (6,035 total respondents). In addition, ethnographic data collection occurred in 12 schools to describe the school cultures (e.g., practices, values, and norms unique to individual schools) and to document the implementation of and youth reactions to the intervention.

Data analyses were conducted to compare the three versions to each other and to the control condition. The results demonstrated significant effects for both the Mexican-American curriculum and the multicultural curriculum. The multicultural intervention influenced a wider range of outcomes at the last follow-up, which occurred 14 months after the end of the intervention. The curriculum had not only a positive influence on norms (i.e., encouraging antidrug norms), drug expectancies (i.e., decreasing expectations of positive effects from drugs), and resistance skills but also, more important, reduced adolescent substance use (Hecht, Marsiglia et al., 2003; see Figure 22.2). This research is one of the earliest empirical assessments of a multicultural approach, and the curriculum was identified in 2004 as a "Model Program" by the Substance Abuse and Mental Health Service Administration's National Registry of Effective Programs.

Culture and Adolescent Drug Use

At the same time, other analyses of the data were conducted to further explore basic questions about culture and adolescents' drug use. Ethnicity was one focus of these analyses. Previous research had been critiqued for "ethnic glossing"—an overly simplistic,

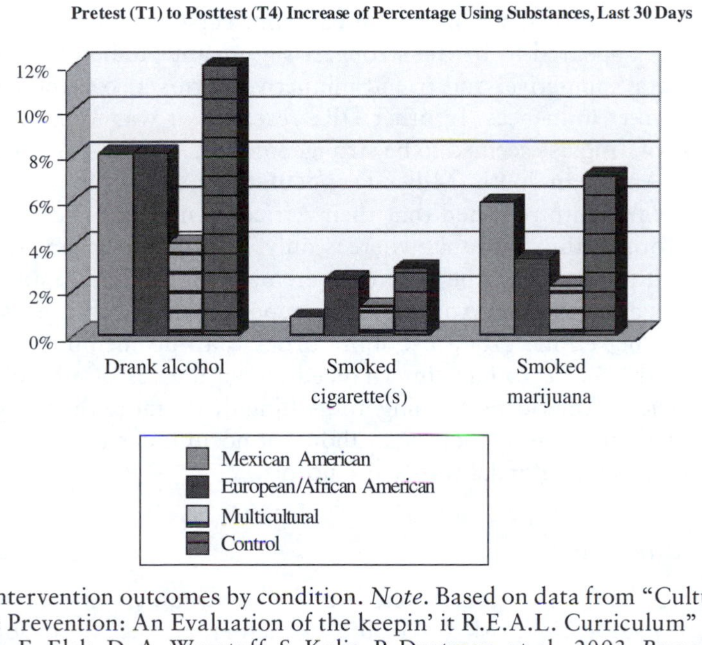

Pretest (T1) to Posttest (T4) Increase of Percentage Using Substances, Last 30 Days

Figure 22.2 Intervention outcomes by condition. *Note.* Based on data from "Culturally Grounded Substance Use Prevention: An Evaluation of the keepin' it R.E.A.L. Curriculum" by M. L. Hecht, F. F. Marsiglia, E. Elek, D. A. Wagstaff, S. Kulis, P. Dustman, et al., 2003, *Prevention Science, 4,* 233–248.

homogenizing approach to ethnicity in which differences or within-group heterogeneity is ignored and all members of a certain group are considered to be alike (Collins, 1995; Hecht, Marsiglia, & Hecht, 2003). Marsiglia, Kulis, and Hecht (2001) found that ethnic labels (e.g., African American or European American) and ethnic identity (i.e., extent to which individuals identify with attitudes and values of a particular ethnic group) interacted, with the joint effects being more significant that either one alone. Mirroring research on adult samples (Larkey & Hecht, 1995), ethnic identity did not function the same way for all the groups studied. Among Mexican Americans and African Americans, ethnic pride was negatively related to drug use, whereas ethnic typicality (feeling that one's behavior was typical of one's ethnic group) was positively related. Among European Americans, the associations were reversed, with pride positively associated with use and typicality negatively associated.

Other work examined the effects of *acculturation*, the process of adjusting to a new culture, on substance use. Acculturation level was associated with drug use among Mexican and Mexican-American adolescents, with the less acculturated, Spanish-speaking adolescents the least likely to use substances (Marsiglia, Kulis, Wagstaff, Elek, & Dran, 2005; Marsiglia & Waller, 2002). These analyses suggest a complicated approach to identity and culture reflected in the communication theory of identity (Hecht, Jackson, & Ribeau, 2003).

Norms and Adolescent Drug Use

This research also focused on the role of norms in drug use (Elek et al., 2006). Previous research had shown that descriptive norms, youth's beliefs in the prevalence of drug use among their peers, were a significant factor in adolescents' substance use (Hansen & Graham, 1991). Although other types of norms have been examined, no consistent conceptual framework had been applied in such research. The use of the norm focus theory provided such a framework and enabled us to predict that all three norm types—descriptive, injunctive, and personal norms—play a role in adolescent substance use, and our findings were consistent with this prediction. Personal norms, rarely studied in the drug literature, appeared to be the strongest significant predictor of substance use. Descriptive, parental injunctive, and friend injunctive norms also demonstrated significant, although weaker influences. In other DRS research, it was found that descriptive norms supportive of drug use seemed to be stronger among African-American youth than among European-American youth (Miller-Day & Barnett, 2004). In that study, 59% of all African-American youth reported that their African-American peers, in general, use more drugs than other ethnic groups, whereas only 16% of European-American youth reported this about their group. The findings were even more extreme among the youth who used drugs, as every African American who reported using substances believed that members of his or her ethnic group use more drugs than do members of other ethnic groups. These youth seemed to have internalized media images of ethnicity and drugs, which portray African Americans as using and selling drugs more than any other ethnic group. Overall, these findings support the validity of norm focus theory, expanding and enriching our understanding of substance use norms.

DRS4: Bigger, Faster, and Longer

Currently, the project is in its fourth phase and focuses on developmental processes, examining age of intervention, risk and resiliency factors, and acculturation using a longitudinal design over 5 years. The curriculum will be enhanced to deal with acculturation factors and then modified for implementation in the fifth grade. The enhanced multicultural curriculum will be implemented again when these students reach seventh grade, and all students will be tracked through ninth grade. This procedure will allow us to compare control students to students who receive the implementation in fifth grade only, seventh grade only, and both fifth and seventh grades.

The developmental nature of communication competence suggests the importance of examining these processes longitudinally. Early adolescence marks the beginning of a critical period for the development of risky behaviors due to changes in youth characteristics and contextual influences affecting youth adjustment (e.g., Botvin et al., 1994; Greene & Brinn, 2003). Along with the biological changes of puberty, changes in orientation toward adult authority, relative influence of peers, structure of schooling, and goals and values all help to shape a sense of personal identity. Contextually, youth move from self-contained, single-teacher elementary classrooms to large, fluid middle schools or junior high schools. This shift leads to increased levels of stress and distress, as well as to reductions in parent and teacher support and monitoring. As a result, adolescents find themselves with increasing unsupervised time and exposure to peers, factors related to higher levels of drug use and delinquent behavior (Flannery, Williams, & Vazsonyi, 1999). The shift from parental influence to peer influence, which occurs gradually between the sixth and ninth grades, is a critical developmental change that has strong implications for adolescents' risk for drug initiation (Bailey & Hubbard, 1990). Once this shift occurs, peer influence appears to be the single-most influential risk factor related to adolescents' drug use (Kandel, 1995). Intervening before children experience an expansion in their peer networks, therefore, may increase the effectiveness of drug prevention efforts. Previous DRS research suggests that due to the developmental nature of risk and resiliency factors, it is important to enhance resiliency factors prior to boys' experimentation with drugs (Moon et al., 2000). Thus, a substantial body of research supports the view that early adolescence and the transition from elementary to middle/junior high school are critical periods for interventions to prevent initiation and later misuse of drugs. Little, however, is known about the most efficacious age for implementation (Gottfredson & Wilson, 2003).

Developmental issues are important when acculturation is salient. Acculturation has been identified as a risk factor for Mexican immigrant children and for U.S.-born Mexican-American children, in that more acculturation is associated with higher levels of delinquency and substance use, and with lower educational aspirations (Vega & Gil, 1999). Our previous work is consistent with these findings, suggesting that Spanish-speaking Latino/as are less at risk for drug use, implying protective factors from the traditional culture (Marsiglia et al., 2005; Marsiglia & Waller, 2002). This finding may suggest that the shift from primary identification with traditional culture to identification with U.S. culture may either increase risk or reduce resiliencies. Acculturation may introduce and reinforce behaviors of the mainstream culture that may be at odds with the culture of origin (Vega, Zimmerman, Warheit, Apospori, & Gil, 1997) or it may induce stress as individuals attempt to resolve conflicting cultural differences, leading to attempts to reduce stress through a variety of destructive behaviors, such as drug use (Beauvais, 1998). In addition, the resources of the traditional culture that operate as resiliency factors may no longer be accessed as youth become more acculturated.

Based on these findings, we are conducting a longitudinal study of acculturation, ethnic identity, and drug use. We measure level of acculturation by assessing identification with both the U.S. and Mexican cultures, language transition and choice, and acculturation stress, and we will examine how these and ethnic identity develop and transition over time. In addition, we utilize the ecological risk and resiliency approach (Bogenschneider, 1996) to track other risk and resiliency factors (e.g., family-centeredness/familism and positive cultural integration) as they relate to adolescents' drug use. It may be, for example, that adolescents are less at risk if they have higher levels of identification with either or both cultures, but are most at risk when they do not identify with either and, as a result, do not have access to either set of cultural protective factors. One might assume that higher levels of identification, particularly the pride dimension, operates in a similar fashion and enhances acculturation effects. Our longitudinal design will allow us to examine these processes.

We started this longitudinal analysis by examining the relationship between communication skills and substance use in young children. This study revealed that youth who make more active decisions, a key component of the curriculum, are less likely than other youth to initiate substance use prior to fifth grade (Hecht, Warren, Wagstaff, & Elek, 2008)

Our other research has continued to examine the role of culture in making decisions about substance use. These studies indicate that ethnic identity is a protective factor for Mexican-heritage youth, with stronger identification associated with more antidrug norms, less positive drug expectations, stronger refusal efficacy, and less intent to use substances (Ndiaye, Hecht, Wagstaff, & Elek, in press). These findings hold for both boys and girls, but play a bigger role in influencing norms for Mexican-born youth. Ongoing analyses are examining the role of biculturalism and show it to be a protective factor (Ndiaye, Hecht, Matsunaga, & Elek, 2008).

Initial evaluation results are less promising, suggesting that the fifth-grade intervention was not particularly effective (Hecht, Elek et al., 2008). Immediate and short-term effects were observed on resistance skills (i.e., students learned them) and norms. However, the effects on norms were iatrogenic (e.g., boomerang), with students believing that *more* of their peers were using substances as a result of the intervention. Although further analyses are forthcoming, it appears that the fifth grade may be too early for this type of targeted intervention focused on a particular health challenge. We also speculate that a narrative intervention of this type may not be the most efficacious, because it exposes students, the vast majority of whom have never received a drug offer, to situations they have not yet experienced.

Significance of this Applied Communication Research Program

The DRS project (1989–2013) is one of the few programs of its type, reaching out across disciplines and utilizing multiple theories and methods, including both cross-sectional and longitudinal designs. With its roots in the communication discipline, the project has involved academics in psychology, biobehavioral health, social work, sociology, and education, as well as youth in middle schools and high schools of Phoenix, Arizona, and others in these communities. With the Arizona project concluding in 2008 and a new rural version of the project being implemented and examined in Pennsylvania and Ohio through 2013, it has grown and expanded into one of the longest-running applied communication research projects, providing a disciplinary model for a funded line of research and demonstrating the utility of applied communication research to the National Institutes of Health.

Theoretical Contributions

The DRS project also has made a number of theoretical contributions. Although traditional methods of theory development involve tests that allow for falsification, the DRS project provides theoretical support through its successful application of communication competence theory, narrative theory, and norm focus theory, as well as the principles of cultural grounding, multiculturalism, and performance-based interventions. For example, communication competence theory led us to employ a design that included knowledge, motivation, and skills as components of competently navigating offer–refusal episodes as we considered relational outcomes and cultural issues. Narrative theory guided our approach to the knowledge component, as well as the form of the intervention. We had difficulty locating empirical tests of cultural grounding and multiculturalism within the context of intervention programming and, thus, our studies are among the first to provide support for this approach to education and prevention. Finally, although other research had examined various norm types, this research was largely scattered and atheoretical, with descriptive norms the overriding influence. Our work, thus, expanded the scope of drug norms in prevention interventions.

Second, the DRS project contributes to our understanding of gender difference and ethnic identity. We have demonstrated that identity, indeed, is a layered construct as described by the communication theory of identity. Our work shows the importance of a complex conceptualization that encompasses both labels and identity, and demonstrates that identity does not function the same way for all groups.

Third, the DRS project describes a socially and personally important social influence process—how drugs get offered and refused, and the importance of norms and interpersonal relationships in offer–resistance episodes. It is rare for communication research to demonstrate impact on socially significant behaviors (although, admittedly, self-reported behavior).

Methodological Contributions

These theoretical contributions were achieved by a line of research that has combined qualitative methods, including focus groups, in-depth interviews, and in situ observation, with quantitative methods, including survey questionnaires and experimental research, in isolation and in combination. Across all four research projects, we have used qualitative methods exclusively (i.e., in-depth interviews and focus groups), quantitative methods exclusively (i.e., survey questionnaires and experimental research), qualitative methods to inform quantitative findings (e.g., interviews and postexperiment observations), and, finally, quantitative methods to flesh out qualitative findings (e.g., survey development to discover broader patterns of strategy use and systematic gender and ethnic differences hinted at in earlier qualitative data). In addition, unique analyses were used in this ongoing project, such as longitudinal data collection, missing data analysis called "planned missingness" (Graham, Cumsille, & Elek-Fisk, 2003; Schafer & Graham, 2002), and hierarchical linear modeling (Hecht, Marsiglia et al., 2003). These methodological issues have made this a complex project, but also one that has contributed significantly to the field of applied communication by demonstrating the use of multiple-method designs (see Query et al., this volume).

Practical Importance

On the local level, many of the youth of Phoenix have been exposed to a customized and effective prevention program that not only reduces drug use but also develops risk-assessment, decision-making, and communication skills. With the recent federal mandate for evidence-based prevention (i.e., programs found to have effects on drug use using randomized, controlled designs), *keepin' it REAL* provides these schools with a program that not only fulfills this requirement but also is aligned to their statewide educational standards.

On a larger level, this is one of only a few culturally grounded, effective programs and may be the only evidence-supported multicultural drug prevention program. The program already has been adopted in Monterrey, Mexico and Laredo, Texas, with applications planned for Austin, Texas; northern Delaware; Flint, Michigan; Erie, Pennsylvania; and Tuscaloosa, Alabama. The Substance Abuse Services and Mental Health Administration established the National Registry of Effective Programs to provide guidance to communities and schools seeking evidence-based programs (http://www.modelprograms.samhsa. gov). The *keepin' it REAL* curriculum not only meets these standards but, in 2004, also attained model program status. In addition, this applied communication research program demonstrates the significance of action inquiry in the discipline of communication by seeking to advance theoretical knowledge at the same time that it addresses significant social problems in communities.

Conclusion

In this chapter, we described research conducted as part of the Drug Resistance Strategies project. This project exists due to the support of the National Institute on Drug Abuse (National Institutes of Health) and has spanned faculty at three universities and many academic disciplines. The project provides an example of a new direction in applied communication research, one in which theories are tested through multiple methods to solve important social problems. This is a project in which people inside and outside of the academy work together to achieve significant social change, bringing many different theoretical and methodological tools to show how communication principles and practices can transcend disciplinary boundaries and help to solve the problem of drug use and abuse.

Authors' Note

The research reported in this chapter was supported by a series of five grants from the National Institute on Drug Abuse (Michael Hecht, Principal Investigator for 1 R01 DA05629-10A1, 2 R01 DA05629-03A4, 3 R01 DA05629-05A1, 5R01 DA005629-10; Flavio Marsiglia, Principal Investigator for 1 R01 DA14825). We are grateful to this institute for its continued support.

Notes

1. This national survey (formerly called the National Household Survey on Drug Abuse) obtains drug use data from approximately 70,000 persons per year and serves as the primary source of information on the prevalence, patterns, and consequences of drug and alcohol use and abuse in the general U.S. civilian non-institutionalized population, age 12 and older.
2. More controversial are "harm reduction" programs that aim not at drug use reduction but, instead, seek to ameliorate the harm that accrues when substances are used. Also controversial are programs that aim at abuse rather than use in the belief that most harm is associated when substances are used frequently and at high levels. These issues are beyond the scope of this chapter, but our position is one of harm reduction through social skills enhancement.
3. Self-reports were used throughout this phase of the project. Although a recall bias potentially was a problem, it is almost impossible to observe resistance naturalistically because illegal behaviors are being performed when adolescents are offered drugs. Thus, however desirable, direct observation of resistance, especially in an era of increased scrutiny about research conducted with human participants (see Seeger, Sellnow, Ulmer, & Novak, this volume), is

highly problematic. We were forced, therefore, to rely on narratives and other accounts as our data sources.

4. There were too few African Americans for inclusion in these analyses.

References

Alberts, J. K., Hecht, M. L., Miller-Rassulo, M., & Krizek, R. L. (1992). The communicative process of drug resistance among high school students. *Adolescence, 27,* 203–226.

Alberts, J. K., Miller-Rassulo, M., & Hecht, M. L. (1991). A typology of drug resistance strategies. *Journal of Applied Communication Research, 19,* 129–151.

Allen, M., Bruflat, R., Fucilla, R., Kramer, M., McKellips, S., Ryan, D. J., et al. (2000). Testing the persuasiveness of evidence: Combining narrative and statistical forms. *Communication Research Reports, 17,* 331–336.

Bailey, S. L., & Hubbard, R. L. (1990). Developmental variations in the context of marijuana initiation among adolescents. *Journal of Health and Social Behavior, 31,* 58–70.

Baldwin, J. R., Faulkner, S. L., Hecht, M. L. & Lindsley, S. L. (2006). *Redefining culture: Perspectives across the disciplines.* Mahwah, NJ: Erlbaum.

Bandura, A. (1982). Self-efficacy mechanism in human agency. *American Psychologist, 37,* 122–147.

Barnett, J., & Miller, M. (2001). Adolescents' reported motivations to use or not to use alcohol and other drugs. *Social Studies, 92,* 209–212.

Beauvais, F. (1998). Cultural identification and substance use in North America: An annotated bibliography. *Substance Use and Misuse, 33,* 1315–1336.

Beauvais, F., & Oetting, E. R. (1999). Drug use, resilience, and the myth of the golden child. In M. D. Glantz & J. L. Johnson (Eds.), *Resilience and development: Positive life adaptations* (pp. 101–107). New York: Kluwer Academic/Plenum Press.

Bogenschneider, K. (1996). An ecological risk protective theory for building prevention programs, policies, and community capacity to support youth. *Family Relations, 45,* 127–138.

Boster, F. J. (1988). Comments on the utility of compliance-gaining message selection tasks. *Human Communication Research, 15,* 169–177.

Botvin, G. J. (1986). Substance abuse prevention research: Recent developments and future directions. *Journal of School Health, 56,* 369–374.

Botvin, G. J., Schinke, S. P., Epstein, J. A., & Diaz, T. (1994). Effectiveness of culturally focused and generic skills training approaches to alcohol and drug abuse prevention among minority youths. *Psychology of Addictive Behaviors, 8,* 116–127.

Castro, F. G., Proescholdbell, R. J., Abeita, L., & Rodriguez, D. (1999). Ethnic and cultural minority groups. In B. S. McCrady & E. E. Epstein (Eds.), *Addictions: A comprehensive guidebook* (pp. 499–526). New York: Oxford University Press.

Cialdini, R. B., Reno, R. R., & Kallgren, C. A. (1990). A focus theory of normative conduct: Recycling the concept of norms to reduce littering in public places. *Journal of Personality and Social Psychology, 58,* 1015–1026.

Collier, M. J., Ribeau, S. A., & Hecht, M. L. (1986). Intracultural communication rules and outcomes within three domestic cultural groups. *International Journal of Intercultural Relations, 10,* 439–457.

Collins, R. L. (1995). Issues of ethnicity in research on prevention of substance abuse. In G. J. Botvin, S. Schinke, & M. A. Orlandi (Eds.), *Drug abuse prevention with multiethnic youth* (pp. 28–45). Thousand Oaks, CA: Sage.

Cook-Gumperz, J. (1993). The relevant text: Narrative, storytelling, and children's understanding of genre: Response to Egan. *Linguistics and Education, 5,* 149–156.

Costantino, G., Malgady, R. G., & Rogler, L. H. (1988). Folk hero modeling therapy for Puerto Rican adolescents. *Journal of Adolescence, 11,* 155–165.

Cross, T., Barzon, B. J., Dennis, K. W., & Isaacs, M. R. (1989). *Towards a culturally competent system of care: A monograph on effective services for minority children who are severely emotionally disturbed.* Washington, DC: CASSP Technical Assistance Center, Georgetown University Child Development Center.

Dorr, A. (1982). Television and the socialization of the minority child. In G. L. Berry & C. Mitchell-Kernan (Eds.), *Television and the socialization of the minority child* (pp. 15–36), New York: Academic Press.

Eigen, Z. D., & Siegel, J. D. (1991, May). *Communicating health messages to high-risk youth: OSAP's "Don't do drugs, call a friend" billboard campaign.* Paper presented at the meeting of the International Communication Association, Chicago, IL.

Elek, E., Miller-Day, M., & Hecht, M. L. (2006). Influences of personal, injunctive, and descriptive norms on early adolescent substance use. *Journal of Drug Issues, 36,* 147–172.

Feeley, T. H., Marshall, H. M., & Reinhart, A. M. (2006). Reactions to narrative and statistical written messages promoting organ donation. *Communication Reports, 19,* 89–100.

Fisher, W. R. (1987). *Human communication as narration: Toward a philosophy of reason, value, and action.* Columbia: University of South Carolina Press.

Flannery, D. J., Williams, L. L., & Vazsonyi, A. T. (1999). Who are they with and what are they doing? Delinquent behavior, substance use, and early adolescents' after-school time. *American Journal of Orthopsychiatry, 69,* 247–253.

Gosin, M. N., Dustman, P. A., Drapeau, A. E., & Harthun, M. L. (2003). Participatory action research: Creating an effective prevention curriculum for adolescents in the Southwest. *Health Education Research: Theory & Practice, 18,* 363–379.

Gosin, M., Marsiglia, F. F., & Hecht, M. L. (2003). keepin' it R.E.A.L.: A drug resistance curriculum tailored to the strengths and needs of pre-adolescents of the Southwest. *Journal of Drug Education, 33,* 119–142.

Gottfredson, D. C., & Wilson, D. B. (2003). Characteristics of effective school-based substance abuse prevention. *Prevention Science, 4,* 27–38.

Graham, J. W., Cumsille, P. E., & Elek-Fisk, E. (2003). Methods for handling missing data. In J. A. Schinka & W. F. Velicer (Eds.), *Comprehensive handbook of psychology: Vol. 2. Research methods in psychology* (pp. 87–114). New York: Wiley.

Green, J. W. (1998). *Cultural awareness in the human services: A multi-ethnic approach* (3rd ed.). Boston: Allyn & Bacon.

Greene, K., & Brinn, L. S. (2003). Messages influencing college women's tanning bed use: Statistical versus narrative evidence format and a self-assessment to increase perceived susceptibility. *Journal of Health Communication, 8,* 443–461.

Greene, K., Krcmar, M., Rubin, D. L., Walters, L. H., & Hale, J. L. (2002). Elaboration in processing adolescent health messages: The impact of egocentrism and sensation seeking on message processing. *Journal of Communication, 52,* 812–831.

Grunbaum, J. A., Kann, L., Kinchen, S. A., Ross, J. G., Gowda, V. R., Collins, J. L., et al. (1999), October 29). Youth risk behavior survey, United States, 1998. *Morbidity and Mortality Weekly Report, 48*(7), 1–41.

Hammer, T., & Vaglum, P. (1989). The increase in alcohol-consumption among women: A phenomenon related to accessibility or stress? A general population study. *British Journal of Addiction, 84,* 767–775.

Hansen, W. B., & Graham, J. W. (1991). Preventing alcohol, marijuana, and cigarette use among adolescents: Peer pressure resistance training versus establishing conservative norms. *Preventive Medicine, 20,* 414–430.

Harrington, N. G. (1995). The effects of college students' alcohol resistance strategies. *Health Communication, 7,* 371–391.

Harrington, N. G. (1997). Strategies used by college students to persuade peers to drink. *Southern Communication Journal, 62,* 229–242.

Hecht, M. L., Alberts, J. K., & Miller-Rassulo, M. (1992). Resistance to drug offers among college students. *International Journal of the Addictions, 27,* 995–1017.

Hecht, M. L., Corman, S. R., & Miller-Rassulo, M. (1993). An evaluation of the drug resistance project: A comparison of film versus live performance media. *Health Communication, 5,* 75–88.

Hecht, M. L., Elek, E., Wagstaff, D. A., Kam, J. A., Marsiglia, F. F., Dustman, P., et al. (2008). Immediate and short-term effects of the 5th grade version of the *keepin' it REAL* substance use prevention intervention. *Journal of Drug Education, 38,* 225-251.

Hecht, M. L., Jackson, R. L., II, & Ribeau, S. A. (2003). *African American communication: Exploring identity and culture* (2nd ed.). Mahwah, NJ: Erlbaum.

Hecht, M. L., Marsiglia, F. F., Elek-Fisk, E., Wagstaff, D. A., Kulis, S., Dustman, P., et al. (2003). Culturally-grounded substance use prevention: An evaluation of the *keepin' it R.E.A.L.* curriculum. *Prevention Science, 4,* 233–248.

Hecht, M. L, & Ribeau, S. (1984). Ethnic communication: A comparative analysis of satisfying communication. *International Journal of Intercultural Relations, 8,* 135–151.

Hecht, M. L., Ribeau, S., & Alberts, J. K. (1989). An Afro-American perspective on interethnic communication. *Communication Monographs, 54,* 385–410.

Hecht, M. L., Ribeau, S., & Sedano, M. V. (1990). A Mexican-American perspective on interethnic communication. *International Journal of Intercultural Relations, 14,* 31–55.

Hecht, M. L., Trost, M., Bator, R., & MacKinnon, D. (1997). Ethnicity and gender similarities and differences in drug resistance. *Journal of Applied Communication Research, 25,* 1–23.

Hecht, M. L., Warren, J. R., Wagstaff, D. A., & Elek, E. (2008). Substance use, resistance skills, decision making, and refusal efficacy among Mexican and Mexican American preadolescents. *Health Communication, 23,* 349-357.

Holland, T. P., & Kilpatrick, A. C. (1993). Using narrative techniques to enhance multicultural practice. *Journal of Social Work Education, 29,* 302–308.

Holleran, L., Dustman, P., Reeves, L., & Marsiglia, F. F. (2002). Creating culturally grounded videos for substance abuse prevention: A dual perspective on process. *Journal of Social Work Practice in the Addictions, 2,* 55–78.

Howard, G. S. (1991). Culture tales: A narrative approach to thinking, cross-cultural psychology, and psychotherapy. *American Psychologist, 46,* 187–197.

Inhelder, B., & Piaget, J. (1958). *The growth of logical thinking from childhood to adolescence: An essay on the construction of formal operational structures* (A. Parsons & S. Milgram, Trans.). New York: Basic Books.

Jessor, R., Chase, J. A., & Donovan, J. E. (1980). Psychosocial correlates of marijuana use and problem drinking in a national sample of adolescents. *American Journal of Public Health, 70,* 604–613.

Johnson, J., & Ettema, J. S. (1982). *Positive images: Breaking stereotypes with children's television.* Beverly Hills, CA: Sage.

Johnston, L. D., O'Malley, P. M., Bachman, J. G., & Schulenberg, J. E. (2004). *Monitoring the Future national results on adolescent drug use: Overview of key findings, 2003* (NIH Publication No. 04-5506). Bethesda, MD: National Institute on Drug Abuse.

Kandel, D. B. (1995). Ethnic differences in drug use: Patterns and paradoxes. In G. J. Botvin, S. Schinke, & M. A. Orlandi (Eds.), *Drug abuse prevention with multiethnic youth* (pp. 81–104). Thousand Oaks, CA: Sage.

Kline, S. L., & Floyd, C. H. (1990). On the art of saying no: The influence of social cognitive development on messages of refusal. *Western Journal of Speech Communication, 54,* 454–472.

Kopfman, J. E., Smith, S. K., Ah Yun, J. K., & Hodges, A. (1998). Affective and cognitive reactions to narrative versus statistical organ donation messages. *Journal of Applied Communication Research, 26,* 279–300.

Korzenny, F., McClure, J., & Rzyttki, B. (1990). Ethnicity, communication, and drugs. *Journal of Drug Issues, 20,* 87–98.

Krizek, R. L., Hecht, M. L., & Miller, M. (1993). Language as an indicator of risk in the prevention of drug use. *Journal of Applied Communication Research, 21,* 245–262.

LaFromboise, T., Coleman-Hardin, L. K., & Gerton, J. (1995). Psychological impact of biculturalism: Evidence and theory. In N. R. Goldberger & J. Veroff (Eds.), *The culture and psychology reader* (pp. 489–535). New York: New York University Press.

Larkey, L. K., & Hecht, M. L. (1995). A comparative study of African American and European American ethnic identity. *International Journal of Intercultural Relations, 19,* 483–504.

Marsiglia, F. F., Kulis, S., & Hecht, M. L. (2001). Ethnic labels and ethnic identity as predictors of drug exposure and use among middle school students in the Southwest. *Journal of Research on Adolescence, 11,* 21–48.

Marsiglia, F. F., Kulis, S., Wagstaff, D., Elek, E., & Dran, D. (2005). Acculturation status and substance use prevention with Mexican and Mexican-American youth. *Journal of Social Work Practice in the Addictions*, 5, 85–112.

Marsiglia, F. F., & Waller, M. (2002). Language preference and drug use among Southwestern Mexican American middle school students. *Children & Schools*, 25, 145–158.

McAdams, D. P. (1993). *Stories we live by: Personal myths and the making of the self.* New York: Morrow.

McGuire, W. J. (1964). Inducing resistance to persuasion: Some contemporary approaches. In L. Berkowitz (Ed.), *Advances in experimental social psychology* (Vol. 1, pp. 191–229). New York: Academic Press.

McLaughlin, M. L., Cody, M. J., & Robey, C. S. (1980). Situational influences on the selection of strategies to resist compliance-gaining attempts. *Human Communication Research*, 7, 14–36.

Miller, M. A. (1999). The social process of drug resistance in a relational context. *Communication Studies*, 49, 349–375.

Miller, M. A., Alberts, J. K., Hecht, M. L., Trost, M., & Krizek, R. L. (2000). *Adolescent relationships and drug use.* Mahwah, NJ: Erlbaum.

Miller, M. A., Hecht, M., & Stiff, J. (1998). An exploratory measurement of engagement with live and film media. *Journal of the Illinois Speech and Theatre Association*, 49, 69–83.

Miller-Day, M. (2002). Parent–adolescent communication about alcohol, tobacco, and other drug use. *Journal of Adolescent Research*, 17, 604–616.

Miller-Day, M., & Barnett, J. (2004). "I'm not a druggie": Adolescents' ethnicity and (erroneous) beliefs about drug use norms. *Health Communication*, 16, 207–231.

Moon, D. G., Hecht, M. L., Jackson, K. M., & Spellers, R. (1999). Ethnic and gender differences and similarities in adolescent drug use and the drug resistance process. *Substance Use and Misuse*, 34, 1059–1083.

Moon, D. G., Jackson, K. M., & Hecht, M. L. (2000). Family risk and resiliency factors, substance use, and the drug resistance process in adolescence. *Journal of Drug Education*, 30, 373–398.

Ndiaye, K., Hecht, M. L., Matsunaga, M., & Elek, E. (2008, May). *Ethnic identity and risk behaviors.* Poster session presented at the meeting of the Society for Prevention Research, San Francisco, CA.

Ndiaye, K., Hecht, M. L., Wagstaff, D. A., & Elek, E. (in press). Mexican-heritage preadolescents' ethnic identification and perceptions of substance use. *Substance Use and Misuse.*

Palinkas, L. A., Atkins, C. J., Jerreira, D., & Miller, C. (1995, May). *Effectiveness of social skills training for primary and secondary prevention of drug use in high-risk female adolescents.* Paper presented at the meeting of the Society for Prevention Research, Scottsdale, AZ.

Peterson, A. C. (1988). Adolescent development. *Annual Review of Psychology*, 39, 583–608.

Polich, J. M., Ellickson, P. L., Reuter, P., & Kahan, J. P. (1984). *Strategies for controlling adolescent drug use.* Santa Monica, CA: Rand.

Reardon, K. K., Sussman, S., & Flay, B. R. (1989). Are we marketing the right message? Can kids "just say 'no'" to smoking? *Communication Monographs*, 56, 306–324.

Schafer, J. L., & Graham, J. W. (2002). Missing data: Our view of the state of the art. *Psychological Methods*, 7, 147–177.

Schinke, S. P., Schilling, R. F., Gilchrist, L. D., Bobo, J. K., Trimble, J. E., & Cvetkovich, G. T. (1985). Preventing substance abuse with American Indian youth. *Social Casework*, 66, 213–217.

Shepard, C., Giles, H., & Le Poire, B. A. (2001). Communication accommodation theory. In W. P. Robinson & H. Giles (Eds.), *The new handbook of language and social psychology* (pp. 33–56). New York: Wiley.

Spitzberg, B. H. (1997). Intercultural effectiveness. In L. A. Samovar & R. E. Porter (Eds.), *Intercultural communication: A reader* (8th ed., pp. 379–3391). Belmont, CA: Wadsworth.

Spitzberg, B. H., & Cupach, W. R. (1984). *Interpersonal communication competence.* Beverly Hills, CA: Sage.

Strauss, A., & Corbin, J. (1990). *Basics of qualitative research: Grounded theory procedures and techniques.* Newbury Park, CA: Sage.

Substance Abuse and Mental Health Services Administration. (2003). *Results from the 2002 National Survey on Drug Use and Health: National findings* (Office of Applied Studies, NHSDA Series H-22, DHHS Publication No. SMA 03–3836). Rockville, MD: Author.

Thomas, R. W., & Seibold, D. R. (1995). Interpersonal influence and alcohol-related interventions in the college environment. *Health Communication, 7,* 93–123.

Tobler, N. S., Roona, M. R., Ochshorn, P., Marshall, D. G., Streke, A. V., & Stackpole, K. M. (2000). School-based adolescent drug prevention programs: 1998 meta-analysis. *Journal of Primary Prevention, 20,* 275–336.

Torbert, W. R. (1991). *The power of balance: Transforming self, society, and scientific inquiry.* Newbury Park, CA: Sage.

Trost, M. R., Langan, E. J., & Kellar-Guenter, Y. (1999). Not everyone listens when you "just say no": Drug resistance in relational context. *Journal of Applied Communication Research, 27,* 120–138.

Vargas, L. A., & Koss-Chioino, J. D. (1992). *Working with culture: Psychotherapeutic interventions with ethnic minority children and adolescents.* San Francisco: Jossey-Bass.

Vega, W. A., & Gil, A. G. (1999). A model for explaining drug use behavior among Hispanic adolescents. *Drugs and Society, 14,* 57–74.

Vega, W. A., Zimmerman, R. S., Warheit, G. J., Apospori, E., & Gil, A. G. (1997). Acculturation strain theory: Its application in explaining drug use behavior among Cuban and other Hispanic youth. *Substance Use & Misuse, 32,* 1943–1948.

White, H. (1981). The value of narrativity in the presentation of reality. In W. J. T. Mitchell (Ed.), *On narrative* (pp. 1–23). Chicago: University of Chicago Press.

23 Applied Research on Group Decision Support Systems
The Minnesota GDSS Project

Marshall Scott Poole
University of Illinois at Urbana-Champaign

Gerardine DeSanctis[1]
Duke University

In the 1980s, computing and information technology underwent a fundamental transformation from centralized systems inaccessible to most users to personal computers and networks that put computing within reach of everyone. That era witnessed widespread adoption of personal computers by businesses and in the home, the initiation and growth of the Internet, the spread of e-mail, and growth in teleconferencing and videoconferencing—in short, a spread of advanced communication and information technologies into everyday life.

Groups and teams are a critical lynchpin of organizations and, naturally, there was in interest in supporting them with the rapidly advancing communication and information technologies. Computer conferencing developed as one promising technology to enable distributed groups to communicate and coordinate their work. Another new technology, the group decision support system, also was emerging.

A *group decision support system* (GDSS) is a computer-based technology designed to help committees, project teams, or other small task groups to identify and analyze problems, make decisions, manage conflict, and plan, among other things. GDSSs offered the promise to help overcome well-known weaknesses in group decision processes (e.g., groupthink) and, at the same time, to capitalize on the many benefits of having multiple parties participate in the decision process. Our research program on this system began in 1985, a time when GDSSs were under development in university and corporate laboratories. A race was on to experiment with different GDSS forms, determine which technology designs were most effective, and understand how these systems might change the nature of group and organizational communication processes.

We were both young assistant professors at the University of Minnesota in 1985, Poole in the Department of Speech-Communication (in the College of Liberal Arts) and DeSanctis in the Department of Information and Decision Sciences (in the Business School). Our complementary interests in group communication and decision support systems formed the base for an interdisciplinary research project that, over the course of 20 years, produced 11 doctoral dissertations and more than 60 published articles, book chapters, and proceedings contributions.[2] More important, this research program spawned an extensive line of scholarship in the fields of communication and information systems that built on adaptive structuration theory, the theoretical model we developed—far more research than we ever could have imagined when we first began our studies.

In this chapter, we chart the development of our applied communication research program, describing opportunities and challenges we confronted in the course of our work, highlighting major findings, and reflecting on important factors that facilitated this research program and on lessons learned about applied communication research. We first explain the foundations of this research program, followed by some of the laboratory and field studies we conducted. We conclude the chapter with a discussion of the contributions of this applied communication research program to practice.

Foundations of the Research Program

Several elements provided a strong foundation for our research program, including interesting and pressing research questions, a theoretical framework to guide the research, and a strong group of colleagues and collaborators. As explained below, these elements led to a systematic plan to explore GDSS processes and impacts, and to develop a technological platform necessary to conduct our studies.

Core Research Questions

Our research questions originally evolved from our previous interests and respective fields, but we soon found that the questions and orientations of our fields complemented each other very well. The research took on a life of its own, leading us to questions we never would have posed individually.

On the communication side, a key question was how we might explain variations in group decision processes and resultant outcomes, even when groups start with similar resources and attempt to utilize the same decision techniques. Poole and other communication scholars looked to communication processes to explain these variations. They had shown that the then-dominant "stage theories" of group decision making, in which task groups were said to pass through a set series of stages in making decisions—for example, orientation, problem definition, solution generation, and choice—generally did not apply, even in controlled laboratory settings. More complex and dynamic theoretical approaches, therefore, were needed to advance understanding of basic group communication processes. Structuration theory, which had been developed in sociology to explain the evolution of large-scale social phenomena, was being developed and refined by Poole, Seibold, and McPhee (1985, 1996), and their colleagues to illuminate small group phenomena, such as the development of decisions, as well as argumentation and influence, in groups.

On the information systems side, management scientists were trying to develop decision support systems to structure group problem solving, with the goal of improving decision efficiency and effectiveness. Classical behavioral decision theory posited that if decision makers were given tools and techniques to overcome known biases and dysfunctions in human decision processes—such as the tendency to make decisions on the basis of anecdotal examples rather than thorough analysis—decision making might be improved. In the group context, this leap was proving extraordinarily difficult due to (1) the challenge of developing technology that could accommodate multiparty participation in the decision process and (2) the inadequacy of existing theory to predict or explain technology effects. In many arenas, information technology (IT) was not providing the advantages for which technologists hoped. For example, word-processing technology originally was supposed to revolutionize office work, but often it was reduced to a fancy typewriter and did little to improve the productivity of clerical workers (Johnson & Rice, 1987). Computer conferencing, originally predicted to promote understanding among geographically separated individuals, had uneven effects, sometimes actually worsening their communication (Johansen, Vallee, & Spangler, 1979; Rice, 1984).

DeSanctis and colleagues (e.g., DeSanctis & Gallupe, 1987) had been developing a theoretical basis for understanding group decision support. A key issue they faced was that early on in the study of group decision support, researchers realized that GDSS technology did not necessarily bring about the advantages intended by designers. Fresh theoretical perspectives were needed to spur innovative technology design, as well to understand the technology implementation process.

Effective group decision support was a significant issue in contemporary society in the mid-1980s: Driven by advances in computer and telecommunications technology (see Lievrouw, this volume), there was an explosion of interest in "groupware," ranging from presentation software to computer conferencing to group support systems (Johansen, 1988). The growth of the team-based quality movement and interest in team-oriented management practices led academics and organizational leaders alike to search for novel tools that could make these processes more effective. The emergence of local and wide-area network technologies and the Internet, and the need for integration of information within and across organizational boundaries as joint ventures and alliances proliferated, also made it possible and necessary for distributed groups to work over networks, and emphasized the need for tools to help these groups to work effectively. Organizations, thus, had a significant interest in implementing advanced IT and making it successful.

Mingling these two lines of interests, our project pointed us toward examination of a fundamental research problem—"Why does technology often fail to bring anticipated benefits?"—in a context of contemporary organizational interest—groupware. Pursuing this question soon bred a theoretical framework and additional questions, as discussed below.

Theoretical Framework

As we discussed this convergence of interests to work out a plan of action, we placed great emphasis on developing a theoretical framework that could illuminate the questions posed for consideration. We evolved an integration of structuration theory (Poole et al., 1985) with the early theory of group decision support (DeSanctis & Gallupe, 1987; Huber, 1984).

DeSanctis and Gallupe (1987) had just published a framework for research on GDSSs that specified key variables and effects. They distinguished three levels of support provided by GDSSs. *Level-1* features provide support for enhanced communication among group members, including idea listing, evaluation techniques (e.g., voting or rating), and minute taking. *Level-2* features offer advanced decision support tools, such as multicriteria decision making, stakeholder analysis, and problem formulation, that members could not execute on their own in a reasonable amount of time. A major barrier to the use of these level-2 procedures, however, is group members' lack of knowledge and skills, as members often are reluctant to spend precious time and energy researching available procedures and preparing required information and materials. Even with adequate preparation, these level-2 procedures will not work very well if members (and facilitators) do not have the necessary group process skills, which require special training and considerable experience. By "automating" procedures, GDSSs can reduce the work involved. *Level-3* features provide guidance for groups by advising members on strategies and approaches for using level-1 and level-2 tools and, thereby, reduce the need for members to acquire specialized knowledge about decision tools and how to adapt and operate a GDSS. Some level-3 features are passive, such as text boxes that automatically pop up between steps of a GDSS procedure and tell members what the next step involves and the actions they need to take to carry out this step (Limayem & DeSanctis, 2000); other level-3 features are more active, such as an agent-based system that monitors the inputs members are making and gives advice suited to the particular problems they are having.

At about the same time, Poole et al. (1985) had worked out a view of group decision making based on structuration theory (for a general introduction to structuration theory in group and organizational communication studies, see Poole & McPhee, 2005; Poole et al., 1996). They posited that groups could best be understood in terms of how members actively structured practices, such as decision making. Structuration occurs in group interaction as members draw on rules and resources (structures) that are both the medium and outcome of interaction. This perspective on groups (explained further below) views the group system and its components—such as tasks, roles, norms, procedures, and relationships—as processes in which members draw on these components in their activities and, thereby, simultaneously produce and reproduce them.

The appeal of integrating the GDSS framework and structuration theory was that it combined a focus on structuring the potential of technology with the processes by which structures are created, used, and modified over time by group members. This integration promised an explanation of the uneven results obtained from implementation of various IT and groupware, in particular. The focus on IT also enabled us to tackle a key problem confronting structurational views of groups: the difficulty of identifying structures as they are used by group members. The GDSS made structures quite apparent because many were built into the technology, and by centering our analysis on them, additional, less obvious structural features in play, such as implicit group norms, could be identified. The GDSS also was a great "lab rat" for structuration research, because it enabled straightforward identification of how structural features were used and also manipulation of the structures they embodied.

The basic model of structuration that guided our research is portrayed in Figure 23.1. We had the main components of the model, represented by the boxes, in mind at the outset. The

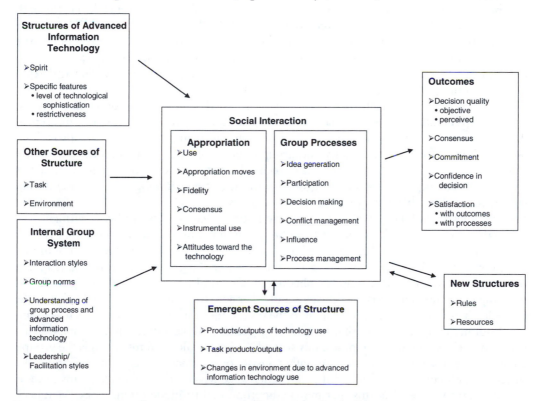

Figure 23.1 Summary of major constructs and propositions of adaptive structuration theory.

specific dimensions and factors, listed within each box, were general suggestions when we commenced our research and were specified over the course of the project.

The model represents a specific instantiation of structuration theory to the context of technology use in groups and organizations, which we termed *adaptive structuration theory* (AST; DeSanctis & Poole, 1994; Poole & DeSanctis, 1990). AST argues that the effects of a GDSS on group processes and outcomes depends on the design of structures embodied in the technology (structural potential) and on the emergent (adaptive) structures that form in a group as members interact with a technology over time. Procedures and GDSS features embody what Giddens (1979) termed *structures*—rules and resources that actors use to generate, organize, and sustain social systems, such as groups and organizations. A GDSS presents a group with an array of potential structures to draw on (see the top-left box in Figure 23.1). We (DeSanctis & Poole, 1994; Poole & DeSanctis, 1990, 1992) distinguished two aspects of technological structures: (1) their *spirit*, the general values and attitudes a technology is designed to promote (such as democratic decision making); and (2) the specific *features* built into a system (e.g., anonymous input of ideas or one vote per group member). The spirit is the principle of coherence that holds a set of rules and resources together, the general values that the system is designed to encourage the group to enact. As such, the spirit is the "official line" that a technology presents to groups regarding how to act when using it, how to interpret its features, and how to fill in gaps in procedure that are not explicitly specified. In a well-designed GDSS, the features are designed to promote the spirit of the technology, but they are functionally independent and may be used in ways contrary to that spirit.

Structuration is a process through which groups select, adapt, and develop their working structures from among those provided by a GDSS. In general terms, *structuration* can be defined as the process by which systems are produced and reproduced through members' use of rules and resources (Giddens, 1979; Poole et al., 1985). The theory assumes that structures are dualities in that they are used to produce and reproduce the group system, and to do a group's work, but the structures themselves are produced and reproduced through a group's activities. Hence, for example, when a group utilizes a GDSS's voting procedure, it is employing the rules that constitute the procedure to act, but it also is reminding itself that these rules exist, working out a way of using the rules, and perhaps creating a special version of them—in short, a group is producing and reproducing its own version of the procedure for present and future use. AST, thus, provides a dynamic view of GDSS technology and group interaction that focuses on the emergence of new social orders through active use of technology structures. Consequently, AST has the potential to explain how similar groups with the same technology, tasks, and internal structures achieve different processes and outcomes.

Outcomes from GDSS use, such as decision quality, consensus, and commitment (the top-right box in Figure 23.1), result from how structures implicit in a GDSS are brought into interaction and how they are combined with other available structures in the immediate context, such as those related to a group's task or the group's environment (e.g., the organization in which the group is embedded; the second box on the left of Figure 23.1). Existing procedures for making decisions and other activities often must be melded with the procedures built into a GDSS to adapt it to the task. Other aspects of the task, such as looming deadlines or specific types of information required to make a decision, also shape structuration of the group decision process. A second source of rules and resources is the group's environment; for task groups, this usually consists of the encompassing organization. An organization's culture (see Seibold, Lemus, Ballard, & Myers, this volume), for instance, is an important source of norms that may be appropriated to guide group work. Members' previous experience with the task and general social norms, such as reciprocity or equity, also can be imported into a group's interaction. Another general category of influences on structuration are the structures underlying a group's internal system, which include interaction styles (e.g., group conflict management styles), group norms, members' level of understanding of advanced IT, and leadership/facilitation styles (the bottom-left box).

As a group appropriates a GDSS, it creates a set of structuring processes that guides its interaction—in this case, decision-making interaction (the top-middle box). Some of these structuring processes assimilate the GDSS to the group's existing practices, but other sources of structure emerge during use of the GDSS, including GDSS outputs (e.g., tallies of ideas and ratings of options), task products (e.g., problem analyses and plans), and responses from the organizational environment (e.g., reactions of clients to the group's decision; the bottom-middle box). These emergent sources exert an independent influence on group interaction, often moving it in directions quite different from those normally enacted by the group. New structures also may result that influence subsequent interaction (bottom-right box). For example, following use of a GDSS brainstorming tool, a group might decide to add a rule that it should generate multiple options before making any decision, thereby changing its prior procedures.

Central to the structuration of group processes through GDSSs is the interplay between the spirit of a technology and the specific features that members use (the top-left box). A group's reading of the spirit of a GDSS determines its mode of appropriation of GDSS features. For example, if group members perceive that a GDSS is intended to speed up its decision-making processes, they might apply voting procedures in such a way that they rush to their next agenda item after taking a vote. In some cases, a group's reading of the spirit may not be consistent with how the designers and implementers present a GDSS. For example, the designers and implementers may have stressed a GDSS as a vehicle for rational and careful decision making, but some group members may want the GDSS to be a tool to cut down on meeting time and, therefore, they add an emphasis on speed. This new emphasis may be inconsistent with the structure of the system that is set up to support careful, rational decision making, creating tensions between system capacities and the uses to which they are put. Such cases are called *ironic appropriations* of a GDSS, because they turn its structures in ways contradictory to its intended spirit. Some ironic appropriations, such as those discussed in this paragraph, are deleterious, but others may represent novel and improved ways of using the GDSS.

As we developed this theoretical framework, we defined specific characteristics of a GDSS that could influence the structuration process. The most important characteristic is a GDSS's *level of technological sophistication*—that is, whether a system provides level-1, 2, or 3 support. A second variable is *restrictiveness*—the degree to which a system limits users' freedom in applying a technology. A very restrictive system must be used in a formulaic manner, which tends to result in faithful use of a GDSS but may be inflexible and difficult to adapt to a particular situation, whereas a less restrictive system leaves more room for users to improvise and adapt but it also leaves open the possibility of ironic use.

We also identified six general constructs that characterize structuration. The first is the degree of *use* of a GDSS in terms of how many features are employed and how often they are used by a group. The second is *appropriation moves*, the particular ways in which a GDSS is used, how it is combined with other structures, and how it is interpreted in group interaction (including the interpretation of the spirit of a GDSS). These appropriation moves represent the operations group members are engaging in when they use a GDSS, which take the form of bids to use or interpret the GDSS in certain ways, or to combine it with other structures, and other members' responses to these bids. The third is *fidelity*, the degree to which a GDSS is appropriated faithfully as opposed to ironically. The fourth is the degree of *consensus* on how a GDSS should be appropriated, which influences the ease with which the system is used, consistency of use, and its effectiveness in promoting desirable outcomes, as conflicts over use of a system likely detract from group effectiveness and, if not managed constructively, could lead to power struggles in using the technology or even to refusal of part of the group to use a GDSS. The fifth is the particular uses to which a group puts a GDSS, including task, process, power, social, individualistic, and exploratory uses (we termed this last the *instrumental use* of a GDSS). The sixth construct is *attitudes toward the technology*, members' comfort with a GDSS, respect for it as useful, and the challenge members believe a system poses for a group to work hard and excel.

The theoretical model just described began as a looser framework that had all the major components in Figure 23.1, but much less detail on specific constructs. As we applied for grants and conducted successive studies, the model was modified and made more specific until it assumed its (more or less) final form, although its development continues, as additional studies and secondary analysis of the original data proceed.

The Research Team

This project was a collective effort that would have been impossible without talented, committed collaborators and colleagues. Senior faculty who worked with the project included Gary Dickson, one of the founders of the management information systems discipline; John Bryson of the Hubert Humphrey School of Public Affairs at the University of Minnesota; Les Wanniger of the Information and Decision Sciences Department at the University of Minnesota; Marianne D'Onofrio, Central Connecticut State University; and Richard Heath and Lora Robinson of St. Cloud State University. Other senior faculty researchers who collaborated during various phases of the project included Starr Roxanne Hiltz, New Jersey Institute of Technology; Kate Kaiser, Marquette University; Colin Eden and Fran Ackerman, Strathclyde University, Scotland; and K. S. Raman and colleagues at the University of Singapore.

A major source of innovation and energy came from dissertation projects conducted by doctoral students. In chronological order, these dissertators included Brent Gallupe, Richard Watson, Ilze Zigurs, V. Sambamurthy, Fred Niederman, Dale Shannon, Joo-Eng Lee-Partridge, Moez Limayem, Chelley Vician, and Michele Jackson. Timothy Kuhn and Laurie Prior wrote master's theses based on data collected by the project. Other research assistants included Sarah Belknap, Julie Billingsley, Derek Bolt, Carol Broullette, Michael E. Holmes, Janet Kelly, Laurie Kirsch, Rebecca Lind, Russ Littlefield, Dan Luitjens, D. J. McBride, Randy Snyder, Jonathan Trower, and V. Venkatraj. We could not have built or maintained our GDSS, the Software Aided Meeting Management (SAMM; described later) system, without our system developers and programmers, who included Mike Beck, David Chang, Aditya Gupta, Aditya Gurajada, Surya Prasad-Koneru, and Usha Rani.

Research Plan

As we were working out the theoretical basis of the study, DeSanctis, Watson, Gallupe, and others were developing GDSS prototypes that enabled us to conduct a series of experiments to compare the effects of level-1, 2, and 3 systems in various task contexts. We developed a research plan to systematically implement this series of experiments and used that plan as the basis of a grant application submitted to the Office of Naval Research (which was turned down) and, subsequently, to the National Science Foundation (NSF; which was awarded after substantial revision). The reviews of both applications were very detailed and gave us guidance that substantially improved our plan. With a substantial funding base, we were able to proceed with our research and eventually branch out in some unexpected directions.

Our original plan proposed a series of research questions. The first question revolved around whether there was any net improvement due to GDSS use in group decision outcomes, such as decision quality, member satisfaction with the decision-making process, and member commitment to the group's decision. In addressing this question, we compared three conditions: (1) groups with no support, (2) groups with a manual version of the procedures built into a GDSS, and (3) groups with a GDSS. By comparing conditions (1) and (2) with condition (3), we could determine the effects due to computerization, whereas comparing condition (1) with conditions (2) and (3) determined the effects due to structured procedures, whether automated or not. These were important questions to investigate at the outset because they would establish the potential and efficacy of the technology. Too often, advocates of new technologies presume or overstate their value, and technological skeptics are well aware of this tendency. Thus, it was important to establish whether there was a net gain from adopting GDSSs and the conditions that best promoted any such gain. It also was important to sort out whether computerization or procedures (or both) were responsible for any benefits. Our initial judgment was that if GDSS groups performed better than unsupported groups and as well as groups using manual procedures, there a justification for implementing GDSSs. In this case, computerization adds efficiency to effective procedures, and, over time, as technology improved and groups became used to GDSSs, we expected GDSS groups to outperform groups using manual procedures.

The second question focused on assessing the impact of different levels of GDSS features on group processes and outcomes. As noted previously, a level-2 GDSS provides more structure for groups than does a level-1 system, and a level-3 system provides guidance in addition to structured procedures and, thereby, offers more (or at least a different type of) support for groups. Information technologists are oriented to building ever more elaborate systems; consequently, they tend to favor higher level systems over "plain vanilla" level-1 systems. However, group members often feel that their work is sufficiently difficult that they do not want to change how they operate (Poole, 1991). A level-1 system, which imposes less structure and is not as complex as the other levels, therefore, may be preferable in some cases for group members. In addition, there often is resistance to any type of change in many organizations. We, thus, needed evidence of clear benefits of higher level GDSSs to warrant their adoption and use. If such evidence was not forthcoming, it was best to stick with simple communication support.

In addressing these two questions, we considered how the nature of the task affected GDSS impacts, as it seems intuitively obvious that GDSSs might be better suited for some tasks than for others. Hence, we conducted experiments using several different tasks: (1) a college admissions task with a verifiable correct answer, (2) a budget allocation task with no definite right-or-wrong answer (degree of consensus a group achieved on the allocations was one effectiveness criterion employed for this task), (3) a planning task with solutions that could be assessed by experts in the area, and (4) a creativity task with outcomes that could be assessed by area experts.

To study structuration, we needed to observe group interaction in addition to analyzing outcomes of the sessions. Hence, for each experiment, we left the groups free to appropriate the procedure or GDSS features as they wished (resulting in variation in structuration) and we videotaped their interaction for future analysis, which is described below.

The Group Decision Support System Laboratory

The GDSS system and laboratory evolved gradually over a number of years (for a more detailed summary, see Dickson, Poole, & DeSanctis, 1992). Gallupe programmed our first GDSS prototype on a VAX computer. It had three user terminals and a monitor serving as a public screen, and incorporated three simple features: idea input and display, ranking, and voting.

Watson used some of the lessons from Gallupe's design to develop a prototype GDSS, CAM (Computer-Aided Meeting), for his dissertation. This system was implemented on an IBM PC/AT using the Xenix operating system (a version of UNIX). CAM accommodated four users seated at personal computers (PCs), who could see their group's work displayed on a 24-inch monitor. The system was housed in long narrow room used for classes and storage in the Carlson School of Management. This room served as the laboratory for the first few experiments we conducted.

In 1988, we obtained sufficient resources from grants and university sources to build a more ambitious system. We obtained space in the Humphrey School of Public Affairs at the University of Minnesota for a GDSS laboratory that was designed to simulate the most advanced types of decision rooms that might be installed by organizations interested in using a GDSS.

Development of the GDSS was supported by the NSF grant and by donations from several private corporations, including the NCR Corporation, International Business Machines (IBM) Corporation, and Texaco. The NCR Corporation donated a Tower 32 minicomputer and six workstations for the system. Groups met around a rectangular table—and later around a specially built horseshoe-shaped conference table—with a terminal and keyboard for each group member. Because the chairs swiveled and had rolling feet, users could move about comfortably to face one another. A large monitor—later a projector and screen—at the front of the room displayed group information (e.g., vote tallies or idea lists generated during the meeting). Two video cameras recorded group interaction during GDSS sessions on a split-screen setup, backed up by a stereo audio-recording system in case the cameras malfunctioned. Figure 23.2 shows the final configuration of the SAMM laboratory for an 11-person group.

SAMM was designed for groups of 3 to 16 persons meeting synchronously in a decision room (Dickson et al., 1992). As a menu-driven system, using the UNIX operating system,

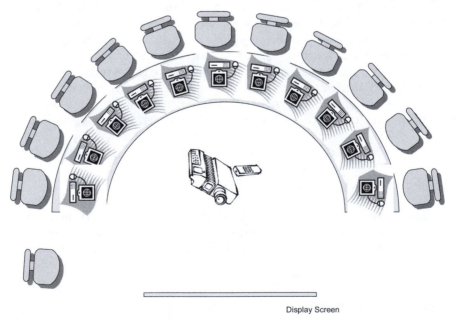

Display Screen

Figure 23.2 An 11-seat group decision support room.

SAMM provided groups with a range of procedural control options: Members could control the system themselves or a facilitator or technician could help. Throughout its development, SAMM was designed around a specific spirit embodying several values: (1) participatory decision making guided by rational discussion; (2) democratic, shared leadership; (3) efficient use of group resources; (4) constructive conflict management that confronted key disagreements and issues (confrontive conflict management); and (5) an informal, safe group climate.

The original SAMM system incorporated four features that constituted a level-1 system: (1) an agenda; (2) brainstorming of a list of ideas; (3) evaluation of those ideas through rating, ranking, and voting; and (4) a screen for entering a group's final decision. Over the next 3 years, several level-2 decision tools were added, including stakeholder analysis (a strategic planning tool), multicriteria decision analysis (which evaluates options against relevant criteria), and problem formulation (which helps to define and explore problems to be solved). Also added were public and private messaging, options to send several preformatted messages to the main screen (e.g., "Let's move on!"), a computerized scratchpad for making notes, and facilities for storing records and minutes. The system was built in a series of modules, some of which were reused in later features. For example, all three level-2 tools had idea listing as one of the steps, and the basic brainstorming module was reused in this step. The final set of features is diagrammed in Figure 23.3.

As computer technology advanced, minicomputers and terminals were replaced by client–server applications. In 1990, IBM donated an RS6000 server and several client PCs, and the system was rewritten to allow use of X-windows color displays in UNIX. This system update took a considerable amount of time and effort, but was necessary to

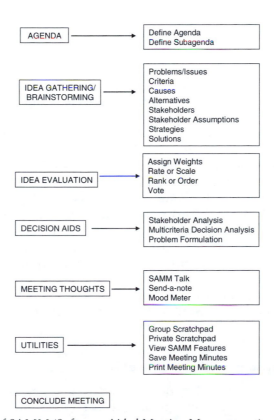

Figure 23.3 Features of SAMM (Software Aided Meeting Management) system.

keep the technology fresh and credible to information systems scholars and to practitioners interested in applying GDSSs.

It may seem unusual to conduct applied research in the laboratory, but the group decision support room was very similar to those being installed at the time in many organizations, and bringing decision makers into university decision rooms also was a common practice at the time. Groups of managers and employees from both private and public organizations used SAMM in our decision room to define requirements for computer systems and for strategic planning. Hence, there was continuity between our GDSS lab and the applied settings in which GDSSs were being used.

Other universities and organizations inquired about SAMM, and we licensed it for use at several universities, including Marquette University, University of North Carolina Wilmington, Stanford University, Claremont Graduate School, Washington University, and Lavalle University. Private organizations that acquired it included IBM, Bellcore, the NCR Corporation, and Texaco. A version of SAMM that ran on Apple computers (SAGE) was created at the National University of Singapore and used at University of Georgia, University of Illinois at Urbana-Champaign, Queen's University (Canada), University of Oulu (Finland), University of Jyväskylä (Finland), and Edith Cowan University (Australia). This diffusion led to additional research projects based on SAMM.

The GDSS lab was the site for a series of studies that explored the theoretical model according to the research plan described previously. Eventually, this laboratory was our key to a series of applied studies in field settings. The next two sections, necessarily abbreviated in this history of the project, detail the laboratory and field studies that made up our program of research (for a more extensive summary of findings, see DeSanctis et al., 2008).

Laboratory Studies

Commencing in 1986, our research team conducted a series of experiments to investigate the effects of GDSSs on decision making, conflict management, and negotiation. As noted previously, we conducted experiments in which properties of our GDSS were manipulated and their effects measured on relevant outcomes, including objective and perceived group decision quality, consensus, members' satisfaction with the decision process, and members' commitment to the decision. We used groups of 3 to 7 individuals to assess the effects of group size, which generally were negligible. Unlike many laboratory experiments, we did not exercise high degrees of control over or tightly script group members' behavior but purposely allowed them a measure of freedom to use (or not use) the GDSS as they saw best. Our theory predicted differences in appropriation of the technology and procedures across groups, and we gave the experimental groups some room to allow any differences to emerge so that we could study the appropriation process. We videotaped all sessions and subsequently analyzed the group processes and appropriations that mediated the experimental effects. The results of these studies, thus, can be differentiated into those related to GDSS effects on outcomes and those focused on group processes during use of the GDSS. We review the results related to effects first and then turn to the processes that produce those effects.

Studies of Group Decision Support System Effects

The first set of studies conducted by our research team, as mentioned previously, compared unsupported groups (baseline groups), level-1 GDSS groups, and groups using a manual version of the level-1 procedures (manual groups) to test for the impact of procedures and computerization separately. Studies focused on problem identification (Gallupe, DeSanctis, & Dickson, 1988), decision making with a task having a verifiable answer (Zigurs, Poole, & DeSanctis, 1988), and decision making with a task having no verifiable answer (Watson, DeSanctis, & Poole, 1988).

This first set of studies indicated that groups using a level-1 GDSS performed as well as or better than groups using manual procedures, which suggested that the computerized management of procedures was workable and could be valuable to groups. Moreover, GDSSs improved performance more for difficult tasks than for relatively easy ones. However, these studies also indicated that group members did not particularly like using a GDSS. We wondered if this feeling was due to the fact that the GDSS required them to learn procedures, such as idea listing and voting—which are quite easy to do in a face-to-face group—via a computer, making those procedures seem awkward and imposing a learning curve on participants. There also was more conflict in GDSS groups than in manual groups, which we thought might be the result of the shared display of ratings, which tends to highlight any differences among members and, thereby, steer the discussions toward points on which members disagree.

We speculated that GDSSs might not evoke such a negative reaction for procedures that were difficult for groups to do manually. For example, multicriteria decision analysis requires groups to rate a list of options on a number of dimensions (e.g., feasibility, cost, benefit, and acceptability), weight those dimensions in terms of importance, multiply ratings by weights, and average those ratings to yield a final score for each option. The effort involved is considerable and if a group wanted to get an idea of what individual members thought of the various options, listing the original ratings and weights on a handwritten chart for all to see took a considerable amount of time. When members conduct multicriteria decision analysis with a GDSS, however, they simply enter their ratings and weights, and the computer calculates several different types of scores, lists individual ratings and weights, and conducts additional analyses almost instantly. What might take group members an hour and a half to do by hand, the GDSS does in 15 minutes; members can then spend the remaining 75 minutes discussing the options, making a decision, and planning its implementation. We reasoned that for this type of level-2 procedure, a GDSS might outperform manual procedures.

A second set of studies, therefore, compared level-1 and level-2 GDSSs across several types of tasks. These studies used level-2 techniques, including stakeholder analysis (Sambamurthy & DeSanctis, 1990), multicriteria decision analysis (Dickson, DeSanctis, Poole, & Limayem, 1991), and problem formulation (Niederman & DeSanctis, 1995). The results were mixed, with the Sambamurthy and DeSanctis (1990) and Niederman and DeSanctis (1995) studies indicating that level-2 GDSSs led to better results than did level-1 support. However, no differences in outcomes were found by Dickson et al. (1991), who observed that the groups seemed to have trouble using the level-2 features. In the Sambamurthy and Niederman studies, a good deal of guidance and support had been built into the experimental instructions that Dickson et al.'s study had not supplied. This difference led us to conclude that facilitation and support for users through activities such as training were important to the effectiveness of GDSSs (Dickson, Lee-Partridge, Limayem, & DeSanctis, 1996).

We conducted studies on training in decision procedures (DeSanctis, D'Onofrio, Sambamurthy, & Poole, 1989), member roles in using a GDSS (Vician & DeSanctis, 2000), and facilitation styles for GDSS sessions (Dickson et al., 1996; Dickson, Lee-Partridge, & Robinson, 1993). These studies showed that if training and guidance are provided, groups use a GDSS more effectively, members understand it better, and their attitudes toward the system and their satisfaction with the decision process are more positive. The studies also showed that flexible facilitation, which gives members some control over how the GDSS is used, is more effective than firm facilitation, which compels members to use a GDSS as the facilitator specifies, but that both types of facilitation yield better results than no facilitation with level-2 GDSS features.

The next question concerned whether we could build guidance and facilitation into the technology in a level-3 GDSS that incorporated rules for guiding groups through complex procedures. Limayem's dissertation studied a prototype level-3 GDSS that guided groups through multicriteria decision analysis (Limayem & DeSanctis, 2000). Specifically, an add-on to SAMM was constructed that displayed screens explaining each step of the procedure and how to interpret system results. The system informed group members about uncompleted steps so that they could rectify omissions. It also displayed summary discussions after the group had rated or weighted ideas, and it indicated items on which there were wide differences in individual judgments or evaluations, so that members could discuss reasons for the differences and attempt to come to consensus. All guidance was provided through text messages that, in effect, automated facilitation. The system was not as flexible as a human facilitator but it was quite consistent and perhaps more thorough than were many facilitators. The results indicated that adding level-3 guidance significantly improved the ability of groups to benefit from level-2 decision aids. This finding has been replicated by Limayem (2006) and Limayem, Banarjee, and Ba (2006).

These findings, of course, do not simply materialize out of thin air; they are enacted and constituted in group interaction during GDSS use. A second major component of our research, therefore, was analysis of group processes that mediated the effects of GDSSs.

Group Process Studies

Group process is the vehicle through which members identify problems, enact decisions, engage in conflict, and plan how to implement those decisions, among other things. By observing how members used a GDSS versus manual procedures, we got some idea of how this technology influenced how groups carried out these activities.

Our studies of group process took both functional and constitutive approaches. Some analyses focused on the functions of group interaction, such as task functions involved in making decisions (e.g., defining the decision problem and analyzing the problem). As explained below, the results of these studies were in line with mainstream studies of group decision-making, problem-solving, and conflict management processes. A second set of analyses focused on adaptive structuration in the constitution of decisions, plans, and other group activities. These studies required us to develop methods for studying structuration processes in interaction at the microlevel (act-to-act), mesolevel (interaction episodes and phases), and global level (entire meetings and series of meetings).

Functions of Group Decision Support Systems in Group Processes

Due to the intensive work involved in interaction analysis, we sampled a subset of the groups from the experimental studies conducted with large numbers of groups, generally 10 to 15 groups per condition. Groups were sampled to reflect the mean and range of outcomes in the original samples for each condition in the experimental design. We prepared transcripts of the meetings and coded them in multiple passes using various coding systems. What we coded was determined by expectations regarding the impacts of GDSSs on group processes; for example, GDSSs were expected to foster more organized group decision processes, greater equality of member influence, and consideration of more ideas by members. We developed a list of more than 15 possible effects and worked out ways to identify them through interaction analysis. In some cases, we used established coding systems, such as Poole's (1981) decision functions coding system. In other cases, we developed procedures for coding indicators of possible GDSS effects; for example, to assess whether GDSSs helped groups to generate and consider a greater number of ideas than manual systems, we developed rules for counting ideas expressed during interaction.

The first set of analyses focused on interaction processes that could illuminate the results of the effects studies (Poole & Holmes, 1995; Poole, Holmes, Watson, & DeSanctis, 1993; Sambamurthy, Poole, & Kelly, 1993). These studies indicated that groups using a GDSS devoted a large proportion of time to procedural messages, suggesting that understanding the system, deciding how to use it, addressing problems with it, and coordinating GDSS use occupy a good deal of members' time. Such time represents "friction" that detracts from an immediate focus on the task. However, this effort generates a higher level of understanding of the procedures than is attained in baseline or manual groups. Groups using a GDSS had more organized and less complex decision processes than did manual groups, but groups using manual procedures devoted less time to discussing and organizing procedures, and a greater proportion of time to goal emphasis and substantive and critical discussion of ideas, and they also followed more complex phase sequences in making decisions, than did GDSS groups.

Several previous research findings suggested that using a GDSS had important effects on conflict management in groups; consequently, we conducted studies of conflict management processes in the laboratory groups (Poole, Holmes, & DeSanctis, 1991; Sambamurthy & Poole, 1992). The process analyses indicated that groups using a GDSS engaged in more open conflict—both substantive and affective—than groups using manual procedures (consistent with members' perceptions of group process reported in the previous section). Groups using a level-2 GDSS were found to manage conflict more effectively than did groups using a level-1 GDSS, because the level-2 GDSS gives groups structured procedures for managing conflict in constructive ways. For example, level-2 procedures, such as stakeholder analysis, enable group members to explore alternative weightings of stakeholders and assumptions, which enable them to identify more easily integrative solutions and "middle grounds" than can groups using simple rating procedures provided by a level-1 system. Groups using manual procedures tend to avoid open conflict; members use low-key critical discussion to work out disagreements and make a final decision. Manual groups confront conflict less openly than do groups using a level-2 GDSS and, therefore, are less likely to reap the benefits of well-managed conflict, such as increased diversity of ideas (e.g., Folger, Poole, & Stutman, 2009).

Structuration of Group Decision Support Systems

We expected the impacts of GDSSs (and of manual procedures) on group outcomes to be mediated by their structuration during the group discussion. We expected groups to vary in how they appropriated a GDSS and that these variations were related to outcomes. We, thus, tested for within-cell variation in effects due to different appropriations.

To study structuration, it was necessary to devise methods for identifying how it occurred. We focused primarily on group interaction, because structuration is a collective process in which members work out appropriations as they interact. We investigated structuration at two levels. First, we studied it at the microlevel by tracking interaction moves that appropriate, produce, and reproduce structures (Poole & DeSanctis, 1992; for a detailed description of the appropriation move coding system, see DeSanctis & Poole, 1994). Second, we identified global patterns of structuration across an entire group decision or series of decisions, focusing on phases or general patterns of structuration (e.g.,

Poole, DeSanctis, Kirsch, & Jackson, 1995). From these two analyses, we were able to characterize structuration in terms of: (1) general types of appropriations made by groups, as well as which members made and controlled them; (2) phases of appropriation that occurred in the groups; (3) critical junctures at which appropriation of a GDSS changed; (4) conflicts in the structuring process; (5) ironic uses of a GDSS; (6) attitudes guiding structuration process (e.g., respect, challenge, and comfort); and (7) instrumental uses of a GDSS. Various sets of these indicators were used in studies by Armstrong, Perez, and Sambamurthy (1993), Poole and DeSanctis (1992), Poole, Lind, Watson, and DeSanctis (1992), and Sambamurthy, DeSanctis, and Poole (1995).

These studies showed that faithful appropriation of a GDSS was positively related to consensus change (an increase in the level of consensus at the end of discussion compared to the level at the beginning) and that the relationship between faithful GDSS appropriation and consensus is mediated by group interaction. Hence, to the extent that appropriation fosters interaction consistent with task requirements, it has a positive effect on consensus change. Interestingly, we found a negative relationship between faithfulness and members' confidence in the decision. It was likely that engaging in a complex procedure made members believe they had done a thorough job, which increased their confidence. The results also showed that a restrictive GDSS increases appropriations of the GDSS related to substantive discussion of the issues involved in the decision, whereas groups using GDSSs low in restrictiveness focus more on organizing their decision process and use of the GDSS.

A group that effectively appropriates a GDSS organizes ill-defined tasks around the GDSS structures and does not "force fit" the task to the GDSS. Effective appropriation also is promoted by having only one or two members who guide the use of GDSS features and procedures. Positive attitudes (e.g., comfort, respect, and challenge) toward a GDSS promote effective appropriation, but effective groups also encourage members to take a critical approach to using a GDSS. Key junctures, such as problems with a GDSS, conflicts, and transitions between tasks or steps within tasks, are particularly important occasions for structuration.

These results complemented and enlarged on our studies of group process functions. In particular, they suggested that how groups appropriate a GDSS influences outcomes. These group interactions have a strong direct influence on outcomes, but appropriation influences the nature of group interactions and has modest direct effects on outcomes. The results of the laboratory studies remained "test-tube" results, however, until we were able to conduct our research in the field.

Field Studies

In the third and fourth years of our program of laboratory studies, we had opportunities to conduct two extended field studies to observe GDSSs in action. Throughout the life of the project, we regularly invited practitioners into the GDSS laboratory in Minneapolis to demonstrate the system, and some university and business groups had utilized the lab for meetings. We learned much from these encounters with natural groups and tried to put these insights into the ongoing design and development of SAMM.

Both of the extended field studies came about as a result of our laboratory research and development. Our partners in the field studies were interested in applying GDSSs in their organizations. When they learned of our studies and that we had designed a GDSS they could use, they contacted us and the field studies were set up. We agreed that if they provided the computers, we would provide SAMM and support it for free, as long as we could study groups using it in their organizations. What followed were two of our most exciting projects: the Internal Revenue Service-Minnesota Project and the Texaco GDSS Studies.

Group Decision Support Systems and Quality Improvement in the Internal Revenue Service

The Internal Revenue Service (IRS) field study was a matter of chance. Howard Lewis, one of two supervisors of a quality improvement program in the IRS's Manhattan District Office, heard Sambamurthy presenting results from our GDSS laboratory studies at a conference in 1988. Lewis had been interested in finding software to support quality improvement teams, and the procedures built into SAMM—such as brainstorming, evaluation, and multicriteria decision making—fit the IRS quality team program well. Lewis and George Desharnais, the other IRS supervisor, contacted us and came to visit our lab, and we planned a field experiment to evaluate SAMM's effectiveness and determine how it might be used to enhance quality improvement.

Lewis and Desharnais obtained IRS funding to purchase an NCR Tower computer similar to the one that we had in Minnesota. They installed it in a decision room (initially a separate small room; later, the back half of a large room they used as an office) in the Manhattan District Office, a few blocks from the World Trade Center. We purchased two cameras and video-recording equipment to capture the interaction of the groups as they used the GDSS.

The research design called for a natural experiment in which we videotaped all meetings of 10 quality teams that met in the room, with GDSS use varying naturally. Hence, in some meetings, SAMM was not used at all; in others, level-1 features were used; and in still others, level-2 features were used. By comparing the same group as it used the various level features in some meetings but not in others, we assessed the impacts of salient structural variables in the field. These studies also gave us an opportunity to study group learning and implementation of the GDSS over an extended period. Groups varied in size from 5 to 10 members, typically worked for 1 to 1.5 years on their projects, and were assisted in the application of the quality process and use of the GDSS by a facilitator.

DeSanctis, Poole, Desharnais, and Lewis (1992) reported some initial experiences with SAMM in the IRS. Interviews with members and facilitators suggested that SAMM could lead to notable improvements in quality team processes. One facilitator described the following incident in an interview that we conducted with him:

> A group had been engaged in back-and-forth exchanges over a difficult issue— whether to include some of a list of "novel" ideas in an action plan—for an hour. I entered a question on Quickpoll (a SAMM feature): "Who could live with including one novel item in our plan?" (This was projected on the common display screen). All five members entered their answers into the poll and the total was five "yes" responses. SAMM helped them see that they were arguing over nothing.

In another interview, a facilitator commented:

> A team was floundering for direction and decided to do a stakeholder analysis. There was no facilitator who knew how to use the system. The members followed instructions from the user's guide and had no problems employing the procedure. The facilitator, who had been tacitly anti-SAMM up to that point, told us that SAMM had turned the meeting around.

These initial experiences with the IRS quality teams also suggested some possible improvements in the GDSS—notably, enabling it to be used by distributed groups (which were not particularly successful) and facilities to support emotional aspects of quality team work, such as group integration and the expression of negative feelings and conflict (which increased effectiveness). The design of SAMM tended to over-rationalize a group and focus its attention on work to the exclusion of emotion. We subsequently tried to develop training and modules of the system (such as short message exchange) to deal with this other side of groups.

DeSanctis, Poole, Lewis, and Desharnais (1992) focused on structuration of SAMM in the 10 quality improvement teams and 12 additional staff teams that used SAMM for one or two meetings. A third study followed the use of SAMM by four quality improvement teams over an extended time (Poole et al., 1995). Jackson and Poole (2003) studied 37 brainstorming sessions conducted by IRS quality teams and a few teams from Texaco (see below), comparing sessions where teams used SAMM to brainstorm to teams that recorded their brainstorming on flipcharts or paper.

Working with our collaborators at the IRS also helped us to develop SAMM. Using complex software, such as SAMM, is different in the field than in the laboratory. In our GDSS lab, one of the research team members set up SAMM, was available to fix problems, and kept users from doing things outside the "normal" limits of typical SAMM use. In the field, in contrast, SAMM was exposed to a much wider array of users who did many interesting things and made lots of "errors." This field use exposed weaknesses in the system that our programmers worked to correct. Desharnais and Lewis also had many creative ideas about how the system could be improved; new ideas, problems, and solutions came almost weekly. Due to resource limitations, we were not always able to respond to these issues as rapidly as we liked but the back-and-forth discussions resulted in significant improvements in SAMM.

Group Decision Support Systems and Continuous Improvement Teams in Texaco

Our connection with Texaco was the result of our published articles. Brad Jackson, a new technology manager at Texaco, had read several of our articles and called DeSanctis in 1991 to inquire about the potential of using SAMM at Texaco. At that time, Texaco had undertaken a major initiative to develop self-directed teams with a strong emphasis on quality improvement, and groupware, such as SAMM, promised to help these teams work more effectively.

Brad Jackson and his manager, Ed McDonald, Vice President for Technology Development, found resources to acquire an NCR Tower system to install the original version of SAMM and, subsequently, an IBM system to support the UNIX version of SAMM. SAMM was installed in a conference room at Texaco and later in an elaborate decision room that included videoconferencing and other groupware. Texaco gave us a substantial grant and we won funding from NSF to support this project, as well as a larger study of implementation of groupware and other advanced IT in Texaco.

We made arrangements with Texaco similar to those that had worked well with the IRS. We installed video cameras and recorded naturally occurring meetings of a set of teams that had access to SAMM. In some team meetings, SAMM was used; in other meetings, teams worked without it. Comparison across supported and unsupported meetings enabled us to assess the effects of SAMM, and studying the development of system appropriation and use over time allowed us to understand structuration of SAMM in these teams.

DeSanctis, Poole, Dickson, and Jackson (1993) studied structuration in three teams using SAMM over a period of 8 months. Teams varied widely in composition, organizational level, and task. Team 1 consisted of 14 high-level managers charged with technology planning, Team 2 had eight medium-level personnel who provided support for computer users, and Team 3 had seven lower level personnel who were designing a procedure for automating database operations at night, a very complex task. We analyzed between 6 and 10 video-recorded meetings of each team, chosen such that they spanned the observational period, supplemented by questionnaires completed by team members after most meetings and interviews conducted with them. Vician, DeSanctis, Poole, and Jackson (1992) conducted an in-depth case study of Team 3 that extended 6 months longer than the DeSanctis et al. observations and underscored the importance of the team leader in managing appropriation of the GDSS.

Poole et al. (1995) analyzed the appropriation of SAMM in five IRS teams and three Texaco teams. Based on in-depth analysis of multiple meetings of these teams, they identified five global appropriation types—holistic patterns of GDSS appropriations, ranging from autonomous groups, which achieved independent mastery of the GDSS and felt free to adapt it and improvise, to rejectors who abandoned the system altogether.

As in the IRS case, working with Texaco stimulated further development and refinement of SAMM. We developed training and support materials to help the IRS and Texaco teams in its use. For example, we developed a flowchart to guide leaders through the process of planning a SAMM meeting and a decision tree to help them choose tools for specific tasks. These developments met with varying levels of success, and we refined them based on user feedback.

Summary

Our field studies suggested several important conclusions. First, there is more and better use of a GDSS when it is introduced in a newly formed group than in an already-established one. Second, existing problems or conflicts in a group tend to carry over into its use of a GDSS, lessening the benefits that groups can derive from it. Third, consistent with our laboratory studies, use of level-2 GDSS tools increased group effectiveness when natural groups face complex tasks and disagreements among members. Fourth, effective appropriation of a GDSS depends on a continuous learning process on the part of all (or most) members, with the leader playing an important role in guiding the GDSS and encouraging members to use the system during the learning process.

However, inconsistent with the results of our laboratory studies, the field studies showed that using a GDSS, in comparison to not using it, facilitates more balanced participation by members, especially by quiet or low-power members. This difference probably stems from the fact that students who participated in the laboratory studies did not have meaningful power differences, whereas such differences are common in natural organizations. A second inconsistent finding in the field studies was that conflict over the use of a GDSS does not necessarily reduce team effectiveness or limit the positive impacts of the GDSS on group processes and outcomes.

Contributions of the Applied Communication Research Program to Practice

Several practical lessons can be drawn from these applied communication studies. First, groups will change and adapt a GDSS—and any system, for that matter—as they use it. It is important to accept this phenomenon rather than assume that a system will be used as implementers intend. Implementers should monitor how a GDSS is being employed to determine if it is being used in productive ways and—just as important—whether dysfunctional ironic uses develop. Dysfunctional ironic uses can be avoided proactively through training and guidance, and reactively through intervention by the implementer. Not all ironic uses, however, are dysfunctional. Implementers of advanced IT, such as a GDSS, should expect to find novel and interesting applications, and take advantage of them.

Second, the process of appropriation does not involve just using a GDSS; equally significant is how group members make sense of the system and develop an interpretation of a GDSS and its spirit. Implementers should attempt to discover how group members understand a system and become actively involved in shaping the meaning of that system for users.

The field studies, in particular, suggested that groups learn to use a GDSS gradually. This learning is a spiraling process in which members learn to use some features and then work with them until they achieve a comfort level and are ready to move up to the next set of features and become comfortable with them. A key part of learning is adapting GDSS features to specific tasks facing a group, which often involves some translation and adaptation of the task to fit the GDSS features and reinterpretation of GDSS features, such that they match the task. An effective facilitator can be a very important part of this process, suggesting new tools and how to rethink the task at hand to fit the technology.

Junctures in a group's development—periods when it faces a problem in its work or with a technology, when an external "shock" impinges on the group and causes a setback or redefinition of goals, or when members are in conflict—are especially important in the process of learning and interpreting a GDSS. For facilitators, it is important to recognize when these junctures occur, so that special effort can be taken to ensure that a GDSS "delivers" for a group. At these times, members' beliefs and attitudes often are more fluid than they are during regular GDSS use, and a bad experience with a GDSS can undermine user acceptance, whereas a good experience can enhance acceptance and facilitate learning new applications of the system.

As noted, facilitation is an important factor in effective use of a GDSS. A facilitator can suggest uses of a GDSS and encourage (or even press) members to try them. It also is important, however, to give groups sufficient leeway to experiment with a GDSS and make it their own. An overcontrolling leader or facilitator encourages members to remain dependent on guidance to use a GDSS and distances them from it. The most effective teams in our field studies exhibited a willingness to experiment with a system and ingenuity in applying it. Ideally, teams should attain functional autonomy with a system to take control of it and adapt it to meet their needs.

A facilitator should be equally knowledgeable in and comfortable with the technology and the procedures. In many groups that we studied, facilitators were focused either on the technology or on process, and this restricted focus made the facilitators less effective. Ideally, facilitators should be able to match the technology and process. Most facilitators in our field studies had previous experience on the quality improvement and continuous improvement teams. They had enjoyed the experience and volunteered to facilitate because they wanted to help other teams.

One of the barriers to the adoption of GDSSs, however, is the overhead expenses connected with their facilitation. Organizations often do not have—or are not willing to commit—resources to employ specially trained facilitators. Even when facilitators are available, team leaders must spend time working with them to select procedures and to plan meetings, as well as building "social capital" by convincing reluctant members to learn and use a GDSS. This overhead cost, when combined with lower levels of satisfaction that GDSS users typically display until they get accustomed to a system and have some successes with it, is a disincentive to the use of GDSSs. To successfully implement GDSSs, organizations must commit the necessary resources and encourage employees to take the time to master the technology and its application. Level-3 GDSSs, which build guidance into the system, potentially can reduce the overhead involved in implementing GDSSs. The growth in sophistication of agent-based advisory systems promises the development of level-3 systems that can learn and adapt to the particular requirements of groups and teams.

The results of our laboratory and field studies also point to the benefits of higher order level-2 features, such as stakeholder analysis or problem formulation procedures, which may be substantially greater than those resulting from level-1 tools. However, the same studies also show that level-2 features often are difficult for groups to understand and use properly, and may take time to master. Facilitation, training, and other support, thus, are necessary for groups to capitalize on level-2 features. Learning to use and interpret the results of level-2 features requires an investment of time and resources, but over the long term, it can reduce the time and effort required for a group to conduct a sound analysis, come to consensus, and make high-quality decisions.

The benefits of level-2 GDSSs, however, underscore an irony: Most systems currently being offered to support groups and teams, especially virtual teams, provide only level-1 features, such as threaded messaging, videoconferencing, file sharing, and shared applications of drawing or word-processing tools, but our laboratory studies clearly show that groups using level-1 tools tend to underperform or, at best, equal groups using manual versions of the same tools; have higher levels of conflict than manual groups; and have difficulty managing these conflicts. Only through use of level-2 features can GDSS groups engage in more constructive conflict management and produce better outcomes than groups using manual procedures. A key challenge to those wishing to benefit from GDSSs, therefore, is to find systems that incorporate level-2 tools and motivating groups to use those tools.

Retrospective

Reflections on the Project

Some of the factors that contributed to the success of this project are obvious. People, first and foremost, are the key to effective research. We have been fortunate to work with fine doctoral students, colleagues, research assistants, and collaborators. Especially important are the complementary skills and interests that members of the project team from information systems, communication, and computer science brought to the endeavor. Our colleagues from industry brought knowledge and skills in how to use GDSSs in pressing projects, and a vision of the potential of this technology that went beyond our academic imaginations.

The timing of the project was a second factor that contributed to its success. The questions we asked were exigent to both scholars and practitioners. GDSSs and other types of groupware had caught the attention of academics and practitioners in the late 1980s and early 1990s, and we rode that current as the project unfolded. In addition, in both the communication and management disciplines, there was an interest in social constructionist theory and research and, consequently, the opportunity to rigorously develop a theory of the structuration of information systems and group decisions was a great motivator for the project.

Funding was a third key to this project. In part due to the timeliness of the project, we were able to garner considerable resources in terms of money to support the project, research assistants, and material resources, such as computers, video-recording equipment (not cheap in those days), and facilities to house the project. Resources smoothed the way for the project and attracted talented colleagues.

Other success factors are more subtle but equally critical. The interplay of theory and research was a vital dynamic. This project was more theory driven than many applied communication research projects. We believe that developing a detailed theoretical framework at the outset gave us a reference point for our research, enabling us to see the larger implications of individual studies and to plan a systematic research program. The theory-driven nature of the research also helped to win funding for our project from a scientific establishment that, frankly, was skeptical of research in communication and information systems, fields that, at the time, were not prolific sources of grant applications.

The interplay of laboratory and field research also shaped the evolution of this project. GDSS research was more academically driven than much of the research on IT and telecommunications, which tends to pick its subjects from current practice and often lags behind industry in technology applications. GDSSs, in contrast, largely were designed in university settings and, consequently, were idealized versions built around what academics believed was useful for practitioners. In turn, practitioners interested in groupware looked to universities for ideas, and extrapolated the results of laboratory research to the field. However, because GDSSs were designed to further practice, results from the field were essential tests of concepts and ideas developed in the laboratory bell jar. Moreover, in our case, quantitative laboratory experiments led to opportunities to conduct field experiments and qualitative observations of users' experiences with our system in actual situations, as practitioners sought us out because of our laboratory experiment results. The results of the field research fueled further development of the SAMM system and suggested additional laboratory experiments.

Finally, the interplay of theory and practice greatly enriched the project. The impetus to develop and test theories that explained how the GDSS could help groups to improve their functioning was an important normative influence on this project. Such theories could guide design of GDSSs and other groupware, and, thus, were eminently practical. Like many academic researchers, our theories often were developed "for theory's sake" (see Frey & SunWolf, this volume), and initially failed to inform practice (although they were gratifying to academics!). Practitioners' questions often "brought us up short" and encouraged us to work through our theories more carefully to give them traction for organizational groups. Although we cannot claim to have responded to these challenges fully, they did channel us toward more practical theory (see Barge & Craig, this volume).

As we carried out this project, several other research groups were studying groupware as well, and the controversies (and competition) that arose among these groups proved to be very useful. Led by Nunamaker, an impressive group of scholars at The University of Arizona developed a sophisticated GDSS that eventually evolved into the commercially successful GroupSystems group support system. The Arizona and Minnesota groups developed a friendly competition that raised the intellectual bar in GDSS research and applications.

The successive layers of studies grew, in part, by plan and, in part, by trying to push beyond what we currently knew. Each study surprised us to some degree and we responded by adding new research directions. Some paths we were certain we would take never were followed, whereas others we had not foreseen became major tracks.

This last comment highlights the role that chance played in our project. Our account emphasizes the systematic aspects of the research program and the structure of the findings. That is not to say, however, that everything was planned, or unfolded as planned. We owe much to serendipity. First, there was the coincidence that we both moved to Minnesota and found each other at a time when our interests converged. We also had exceptionally good fortune to attract talented graduate students to this research. Both field studies resulted from coincidences of a sort as well. In these cases, chance led in more productive directions than planning, and we were fortunate to have the resources and flexibility to follow the opportunities presented to us.

Challenges

We confronted several challenges in conducting this project. The need to develop and manage complex technology was a persistent demand throughout. Communication and information technologies are moving targets; the speed with which they develop and their rate of change is breathtaking. An experimental GDSS system, such as SAMM, always was under development, requiring resources to develop, maintain, and document the technology. The field research, especially, required us to find and correct "bugs" in SAMM so that it could be used effectively in those sites. In some cases, emergency repairs or direct consultation were needed to get the system to work, which required our developers to drop everything else until they solved those immediate problems. Other requests from our field collaborators for additional features or "tweaks" to SAMM to meet their needs better were handled as time and resources became available. Although challenging, management of system development was interesting, and it often suggested additional research ideas.

Maintaining the laboratory facilities also required time and resources. We had to bring in grants to cover the cost of equipment, programmers, and lab assistants. Grants, publications, publicity, and letting university committees use the facility gratis all helped to build a reservoir of goodwill and to justify the use of scarce university facilities for our project in the face of requests from other researchers for those facilities. The field labs also posed special challenges. We made many trips to the field sites to make sure that the equipment operated properly; repair and upgrade the software; consult with our field collaborators; and bring videotapes, questionnaires, and other data back to Minnesota. All of this work took a lot of effort independent of the research itself.

It was difficult to obtain funding from the federal programs for this project. As noted earlier, although this research concerned a hot topic, both of us were from fields that had not then typically received NSF funding. Moreover, much of the social-scientific establishment was not ready for the particular type of theory we employed—structuration theory—which did not fit the then-common cause–effect mold for funded projects. We had to do a lot of translation of this theory into traditional formats, such as laboratory experimentation, to convince funders to support the project. We did, however, have the good fortune to have sponsors who put their trust in us.

Finally, there is something of a paradox in research on experimental information and communication technologies in the field: For the purposes of research, it is important to observe unsuccessful as well as successful uses of a system. No communication or information technology works perfectly when it first is installed, and we learn as much from problems with it as when the system works perfectly. This is particularly true for research informed by AST, because testing that theory requires observations of ironic, as well as faithful, uses of GDSSs. Helping groups to use a system perfectly reduces the type of variation needed to study its impacts on group processes and outcomes. However, on the practical side, it was critical that SAMM work well and generate clear benefits for adopters. If the system had too many problems and bugs, or if using it proved counterproductive, there was no incentive for organizations to continue using it. Our field collaborators obtained resources to support the study by promising that our GDSS enhanced team performance, and cases when it did not work well had the potential to make them look bad. Hence, in some cases, there was a potential conflict between what we needed to observe as researchers and what fostered a good, long-term collaboration with the people and organizations involved in this research. We walked a fine line around these issues throughout the project. It is to our field collaborators' credit that they understood our need to study failures and problems, as well as successes, and that they never complained or sought to limit our studies.

All of these challenges were less problems than opportunities for learning and growth. Addressing them helped us to develop valuable knowledge and skills that we would not otherwise have learned. These challenges also led to a more balanced project that had stronger practical implications than might have been the case if we had not had to grapple with "real-world" concerns.

Conclusion

This applied communication research project took on a life of its own and has continuing influence. A number of other scholars have employed and elaborated the adaptive structuration theory framework. Some have used it in studies of information systems; others have extended it into areas such as geography, technology standards, and strategic change in organizations.

Our subsequent research also has reverberations of this project. We received a grant to develop a prototype level-3 GDSS, and research conducted on this project currently is in process. DeSanctis went on to study how new organizational forms were shaped by information technologies and Poole studied quality improvement in health-care teams. Many research team members have gone on to study communication and information technology—initially, group support systems, but later branching out widely into other information systems topics.

SAMM is now decommissioned, but the level-3 design developed in the subsequent grant was used as the basis for team software developed by Brad Jackson and colleagues in two private companies, and he currently is developing more advanced designs for groupware. Lewis has become a technology advocate in the Internal Revenue Service and continues to work to introduce innovative technology.

We could never in our wildest dreams have envisioned how this applied communication project would grow and where it would take us as scholars and as practitioners. We feel fortunate to have had a chance to work with cutting-edge technology in a number of rich environments. We hope that others will pick up where we left off and conduct applied studies in a concentrated and long-term fashion on communication and information technologies that have the potential to help groups function more effectively.

Authors' Note

The authors gratefully acknowledge support for this project by the National Science Foundation; NCR Corporation; IBM; General Electric Corporation; Texaco Inc.; the Internal Revenue Service; the Hewlitt Foundation; and the MIS Research Center, the Department of Information and Decision Sciences, and the Department of Speech-Communication of the University of Minnesota.

Notes

1. Sadly, Gerardine DeSanctis passed in August 2005. She will be missed. Gerry participated in writing the first draft, but any errors or omissions in the final version are solely attributable to the first author.
2. A complete list of the publications of the Minnesota GDSS Project can be obtained at http://hdl.handle.net/2142/5350.

References

Armstrong, C., Perez, J., & Sambamurthy, V. (1993). *Micro-level structuration behaviors in decision-making groups: The effects of alternative GDSS structures.* Unpublished manuscript, Department of Information and Management Sciences, Florida State University, Tallahassee.

DeSanctis, G., D'Onofrio, M., Sambamurthy, V., & Poole, M. S. (1989). Comprehensiveness and restrictiveness in group decision heuristics: Effects of computer support on consensus decision-making. In J. I. DeGross, J. C. Henderson, & B. R. Konsynski (Eds.), *Proceedings of the Tenth Annual International Conference on Information Systems* (pp. 131–140). New York: ACM Press.

DeSanctis, G., & Gallupe, R. B. (1987). A foundation for the study of group decision support systems. *Management Science, 33,* 589–609.

DeSanctis, G., & Poole, M. S. (1994). Capturing the complexity in advanced technology use: Adaptive structuration theory. *Organization Science, 5,* 121–147.

DeSanctis, G., Poole, M. S., Desharnais, G., & Lewis, H. (1992). Using computing to facilitate the quality improvement process: The IRS-Minnesota project. *Interfaces, 21*(6), 23–36.

DeSanctis, G., Poole, M. S., Dickson, G. W., & Jackson, B. M. (1993). An interpretive analysis of team use of group technologies. *Journal of Organizational Computing, 3,* 1–29.

DeSanctis, G., Poole, M. S., Lewis, H., & Desharnais, G. (1992). Using computing in quality team meetings: Some initial observations from the IRS-Minnesota project. *Journal of Management Information Systems, 8*(3), 7–26.

DeSanctis, G., Zigurs, I., Poole, M. S., Desharnais, G., D'Onofrio, M., Gallupe, B., et al. (2008). The Minnesota GDSS projects: Group support systems, group processes, and outcomes. *Journal of the Association for Information Systems, 9,* 551–608.

Dickson, G. W., DeSanctis, G., Poole, M. S., & Limayem, M. (1991). Multicriteria modeling and "what if" analysis as conflict management tools for group decision making. In I. Zigurs (Ed.), *DSS-91: Eleventh International Conference on Decision Support Systems* (pp. 133–141). Providence, RI: Institute of Management Sciences.

Dickson, G. W., Lee-Partridge, J. E., Limayem, M., & DeSanctis, G. (1996). Facilitating computer-supported meetings: A cumulative analysis in a multiple-criteria task environment. *Group Decision and Negotiation, 5,* 51–72.

Dickson, G. W., Lee-Partridge, J. E., & Robinson, L. H. (1993). Exploring modes of facilitative support for GDSS technology. *MIS Quarterly, 17,* 173–194.

Dickson, G., Poole, M. S., & DeSanctis, G. (1992). An overview of the Minnesota GDSS research project and the SAMM system. In R. P. Bostrom, R. T. Watson, & S. T. Kinney (Eds.), *Computer augmented teamwork: A guided tour* (pp. 163–179). New York: Van Nostrand Reinhold.

Folger, J. P., Poole, M. S., & Stutman, R. K. (2009). *Working through conflict: Strategies for relationships, groups, and organizations* (6th ed.). Boston: Pearson Education.

Gallupe, R. B., DeSanctis, G., & Dickson, G. W. (1988). Computer-based support for group problem-finding: An experimental investigation. *MIS Quarterly, 12,* 277–296.

Giddens, A. (1979). *Central problems in social theory: Action, structure, and contradiction in social analysis.* Berkeley: University of California Press.

Huber, G. P. (1984). Issues in the design of group decision support systems. *MIS Quarterly, 8,* 195–204.

Jackson, M. H., & Poole, M. S. (2003). Idea generation in naturally occurring contexts: Complex appropriation of a simple procedure. *Human Communication Research, 29,* 560–591.

Johansen, R. (with Charles, J., Mittman, R., & Saffo, P.). (1988). *Groupware: Computer support for business teams.* New York: Free Press.

Johansen, R., Vallee, J., & Spangler, K. (1979). *Electronic meetings: Technical alternatives and social choices.* Reading, MA: Addison-Wesley.

Johnson, B. M., & Rice, R. E. (1987). *Managing organizational innovation: The evolution from word processing to office information systems.* New York: Columbia University Press.

Limayem, M. (2006). Human versus automated facilitation in the GSS context. *DATA BASE for Advances in Information Systems, 37,* 156–166.

Limayem, M., Banerjee, P., & Ma, L. (2006). Impact of GDSS: Opening the black box. *Decision Support Systems, 42,* 945–957.

Limayem, M., & DeSanctis, G. (2000). Providing decisional guidance for multicriteria decision making in groups. *Information Systems Research, 11,* 386–401.

Niederman, F., & DeSanctis, G. (1995). The impact of a structured-argument approach on group problem formulation. *Decision Sciences, 26,* 451–474.

Poole, M. S. (1981). Decision development in small groups I: A comparison of two models. *Communication Monographs, 48,* l–23.

Poole, M. S. (1991). Procedures for managing meetings: Social and technological innovation. In R. A Swanson & B. O. Knapp (Eds.), *Innovative meeting management* (pp. 53–110). Austin, TX: 3M Meeting Management Institute.

Poole, M. S., & DeSanctis, G. (1990). Understanding the use of group decision support systems. In J. Fulk & C. Steinfield (Eds.), *Organizations and communication technology* (pp. 175–195). Newbury Park, CA: Sage.

Poole, M. S., & DeSanctis, G. (1992). Microlevel structuration in computer-supported group decision-making. *Human Communication Research, 19,* 5–49.

Poole, M. S., DeSanctis, G., Kirsch, L., & Jackson, M. (1995). Group decision support systems as facilitators of quality team efforts. In L. R. Frey (Ed.), *Innovations in group facilitation: Applications in natural settings* (pp. 299–322). Cresskill, NJ: Hampton Press.

Poole, M. S., & Holmes, M. E. (1995). Decision development in computer-assisted group decision making. *Human Communication Research, 22,* 90–127.

Poole, M. S., Holmes, M., & DeSanctis, G. (1991). Conflict management in a computer-supported meeting environment. *Management Science, 37,* 926–953.

Poole, M. S., Holmes, M., Watson, R. T., & DeSanctis, G. (1993). Group decision support systems and group communication: A comparison of decision making in computer-supported and non-supported groups. *Communication Research, 10,* 176–213.

Poole, M. S., Lind, R., Watson, R., & DeSanctis, G. (1992). *The process of using group decision support systems as a key influence on communication processes and outcomes.* Unpublished manuscript, Department of Speech-Communication, University of Minnesota, Minneapolis.

Poole, M. S., & McPhee, R. D. (2005). Structuration theory. In S. May & D. K. Mumby (Eds.), *Engaging organizational communication theory & research: Multiple perspectives* (pp. 171–195). Thousand Oaks, CA: Sage.

Poole, M. S., Seibold, D. R., & McPhee, R. D. (l985). Group decision-making as a structurational process. *Quarterly Journal of Speech, 71,* 74–l02.

Poole, M. S., Siebold, D. R., & McPhee, R. D. (1996). The structuration of group decisions. In R. Y. Hirokawa & M. S. Poole (Eds.), *Communication and group decision making* (2nd ed., pp. 114–146). Thousand Oaks, CA: Sage.

Rice, R. E. (1984). *New media: Communication, research, and technology.* Beverly Hills, CA: Sage.

Sambamurthy, V., & DeSanctis, G. (1990). An experimental evaluation of GDSS effects on group performance during stakeholder analysis. In J. F. Nunamaker (Ed.), *Proceedings of the Twenty-Third Annual Hawaii International Conference on System Sciences* (Vol. 3, pp. 79–89). Los Alamitos, CA: IEEE Computer Society Press.

Sambamurthy, V., DeSanctis, G., & Poole, M. S. (1995). *The effects of GSS structures on group decision-making on cognitive-conflict tasks.* Unpublished manuscript, Information and Management Sciences Department, Florida State University, Tallahassee.

Sambamurthy, V., & Poole, M. S. (1992). The effects of variations in capabilities of GDSS designs on management of cognitive conflict in groups. *Information Systems Research, 3,* 224–251.

Sambamurthy, V., Poole, M. S., & Kelly, J. (1993). Effects of level of sophistication of a group decision support system on group decision-making processes. *Small Group Research, 24,* 523–546.

Vician, C., & DeSanctis, G. (2000). The impact of role training in a user-driven group support system environment. *Group Decision and Negotiation, 9,* 275–296.

Vician, C., DeSanctis, G., Poole, M. S., & Jackson, B. (1992). Using group technologies to support the design of "lights out" computing systems: A case study. In K. E. Kendall, K. Lyytinen, & J. I. DeGross (Eds.), *The Impact of Computer Technologies on Information Systems Development: Proceedings of the IFIP WG 8.2 Working Conference, Minneapolis, MN, USA* (pp. 151–178). Amsterdam: North Holland.

Watson, R. T., DeSanctis, G., & Poole, M. S. (1988). Using GDSS to facilitate group consensus: Some intended and unintended consequences, *MIS Quarterly, 12,* 463–478.

Zigurs, I., Poole, M. S., & DeSanctis, G. L. (1988). A study of influence in computer-mediated group decision making. *MIS Quarterly, 12,* 625–644.

24 Fear Appeals and Public Health
Managing Fear and Creating Hope

Kim Witte
Michigan State University

Anthony J. Roberto
Arizona State University

Suppose that one wanted to convince young adults in Africa to abstain from sexual activity or to use condoms to avoid contracting HIV, or to convince gun owners to store their guns locked and unloaded to reduce the number of unintentional firearm injuries and deaths. Applied communication researchers and practitioners face these situations every day, wanting to shape, change, or reinforce people's behaviors in a wide variety of contexts for their intended purposes. The question, however, is, "What is the best way to change behavior?"

A review of the persuasion and health communication literatures, and the other chapters in this handbook, reveal a plethora of options. This chapter discusses one approach that capitalizes on a naturally existing response to many health issues—fear. As we explain, by using a theory that specifies how to employ fear to promote adaptive responses, communication scholars and practitioners can develop campaigns that result in significant and sustained behavior change.

Over the past decade and a half, the extended parallel process model (EPPM; Witte, 1992, 1998) has become a popular tool for applied communication researchers interested in the design, implementation, and evaluation of fear-arousing messages. Prior to the development of the EPPM, the effectiveness of fear-arousing messages, or "fear appeals," appeared inconsistent at best, largely because early research focused almost exclusively on how and when fear-arousing messages worked, and ignored how and when they failed. Based on prior theories, Witte developed the EPPM to explain both the successes and failures of fear-arousing messages. As such, the EPPM provides important guidance and insight regarding how and when such messages influence behavior.

We begin this chapter with an overview of the EPPM, including an explanation of the model and a brief history of the research guided by it. We then focus on the design, implementation, and evaluation of two applied communication programs that we conducted that were explicitly guided by the EPPM. We conclude with several lessons learned and recommendations about the use of fear appeals that emerged from these applied communication programs.

The Extended Parallel Process Model

The EPPM is concerned with the effects of four variables on behavior change: perceived susceptibility, perceived severity, response-efficacy, and self-efficacy (see Table 24.1 for a definition and examples of each term). The first two variables constitute *perceived threat*; the last two variables constitute *perceived efficacy*. Three outcomes are possible depending on one's levels of perceived threat and efficacy: (1) no response, (2) a response that controls or limit one's degree of fear (i.e., fear control), and (3) a response that controls or

Table 24.1 Message Examples for Threat and Efficacy Variables from Two Applied Communication Research Programs

Variable	Ethiopia HIV and AIDS Prevention Program	Michigan Gun-Safety Program
Perceived susceptibility How likely is it that the threat will occur?	"Listen, HIV/AIDS does not differentiate between people on any grounds. It can affect anyone who is not cautious." "A person who has got the virus is not aware of it for some time, and because of this, there are many … so many people who have got infected by the virus."	"You never expect something like this to happen to you. You expect it to happen to the guy down the street or across town. But it can happen to you." The dramatic portrayal of children finding and playing with a gun (e.g., "Look what I found," "Hey, I want to see it," and "Let's pretend that you're the bad guy").
Perceived severity How serious are the short- or long-term physical or mental consequences of the threat?	"As far as Desta is concerned, she was ill for 2 years [before she died of AIDS]." "You must be aware that HIV/AIDS has no cure; it is fatal. So you must be cautious." "Both of them died of HIV/AIDS one after another and their children were forced to live with their relatives at different places."	"You can see the path of the bullet dragging bone fragments from the skull across the brain. This girl died of her injuries." (Voice-over accompanying the image of an X-ray of a cross section of a skull.) Telling listeners that guns can seriously injure or kill their children or their children's friends.
Response-efficacy Is the recommended behavior safe and effective?	"You can be certain to protect oneself against HIV/AIDS by abstaining from sexual intercourse before marriage." "Be faithful to your one partner after marriage." "I'm saying that a condom is essential for protection against unwanted pregnancy and HIV/AIDS."	"If I just had a trigger-lock on the gun, none of this would have happened." The dramatic portrayal of children *not* being able to fire the gun they found because it is protected by a gun trigger-lock (e.g., "Something's over the trigger…. I can't pull it.").
Self-efficacy Do I have the necessary skills (e.g., knowledge and ability) and resources (e.g., time and money) to engage in the recommended behavior?	"If it is used correctly and properly, a condom is a reliable means of protection against pregnancy and HIV/AIDS." "It's amazing! It's killing two birds with one stone…. Condoms can protect against unwanted pregnancy and AIDS."	"Trigger-locks are inexpensive and easy to use. The two pieces fit over the trigger-guard so the trigger cannot be pulled." (Voice over accompanying the image of a trigger-lock.) Providing gun owners with toll-free number they could call to get a free gun trigger-lock (i.e., "If you are a gun owner, and want to help ensure the safety of your family, call toll-free 1-###-###-LOCK for a free gun trigger-lock. That's toll-free 1-###-###-L.O.C.K. for a free gun trigger-lock.").

limits the degree of danger (i.e., danger control). As long as perceived efficacy is greater than perceived threat, individuals engage in danger control, thinking carefully about the recommended response and adopting their behavior to reduce the danger. However, when perceived threat is greater than perceived efficacy, individuals engage in fear control, focusing on managing their fear rather than reducing the danger. In short, perceived threat motivates action; perceived efficacy determines the nature of that action—specifically, whether people attempt to control the danger or control their fear. This critical point, when perceived efficacy exceeds perceived threat, is an important concept in the development of effective applied communication messages.

Figure 24.1 provides a visual representation of the EPPM. When utilizing the EPPM for intervention design, one must first specify the goal (the recommended response) and the threat (what motivates the recommended response). To illustrate the three possible outcomes mentioned previously, assume that the effects of a hypothetical intervention are being evaluated. The goal (the recommended response) of the intervention is to get an individual who does not currently exercise to engage in 20 minutes of cardiovascular activity four times a week to reduce the risk of heart disease (the threat). The following section illustrates the three paths an individual might take depending on his or her levels of perceived threat and efficacy.]

Fear Control and Danger Control Paths

Low-Threat Path

If perceived threat is low, *no response* will occur (see Figure 24.2). That is, if an individual does not believe that she or he is susceptible to heart disease (e.g., "Heart disease does not run in my family"), or if she or he does not believe that heart disease has severe consequences (e.g., "Many people with heart disease lead a normal life"), the person will not be motivated to pay attention to the message and, therefore, will not respond to it. In this instance, the hypothetical intervention has failed to promote a perception of threat. It is important, therefore, for both perceived susceptibility and perceived severity to be high for one's appraisal of threat to be high.

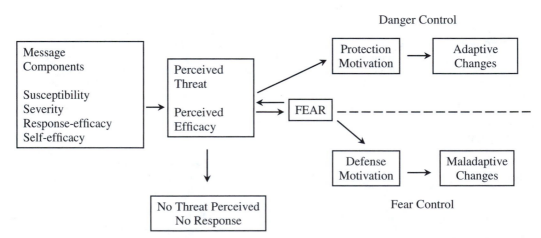

Figure 24.1 The extended parallel process model. *Note.* From "Putting the Fear Back into Fear Appeals: The Extended Parallel Process Model" by K. Witte, 1992, *Communication Monographs, 59,* p. 338. Copyright 1992 by Taylor & Francis, Ltd. Reprinted with permission.

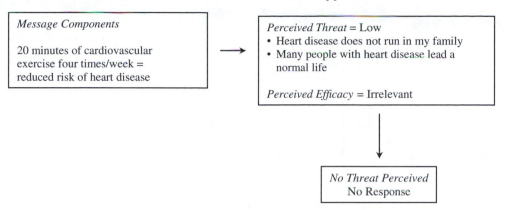

Figure 24.2 The extended parallel process model—Low-threat example.

High-Threat/Low-Efficacy Path

If perceived threat is high and perceived efficacy is low, an individual will engage in *fear control* (see Figure 24.3). That is, if an individual believes that she or he is susceptible to heart disease (e.g., "Heart disease runs in my family") and believes that heart disease has severe consequences (e.g., "Heart disease can be fatal"), the individual's level of perceived threat will be high. Because the person is motivated to act (because perceived threat is high), she or he will engage in the second appraisal of efficacy. If, during the appraisal of efficacy, the person does not believe the recommended response is effective (low response-efficacy, such as "Exercise alone is not enough"), or does not believe that she or he has the ability to engage in the recommended response (low self-efficacy, such as "I do not have time to exercise"), the person's level of perceived efficacy will be low. In this case, the intervention has not promoted high-efficacy perceptions (i.e., although the person perceives a threat, she or he does not perceive a viable option to reduce it) and, consequently, the intervention fails or backfires (Stephenson & Witte, 2001). In this instance, because being afraid is an uncomfortable state, the person will take steps to reduce the fear that do not necessarily decrease the actual danger. Three common strategies for controlling fear are *defensive avoidance* (e.g., ignoring information about the health threat), *denial*

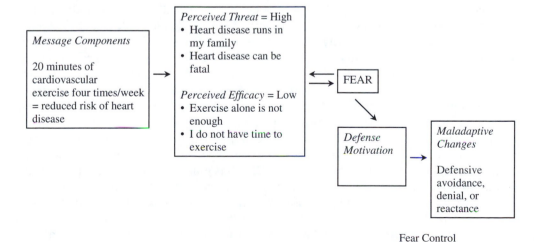

Fear Control

Figure 24.3 The extended parallel process model—High-threat/low-efficacy example.

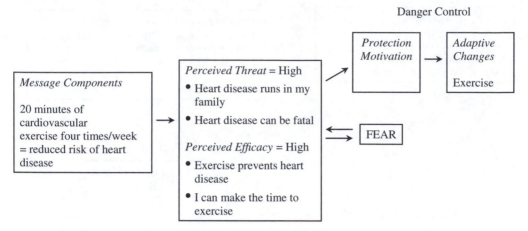

Figure 24.4 The extended parallel process model—High-threat/high-efficacy example.

(e.g., refusing to believe that there is a health threat), or *reactance* (e.g., rejecting the intervention message as manipulative). Both response-efficacy and self-efficacy must be high for one's appraisal of efficacy to be high.

High-Threat/High-Efficacy Path

When both perceived threat and perceived efficacy are high, an individual will engage in *danger control* (see Figure 24.4). In this instance, the hypothetical intervention has accomplished all of its goals by convincing the person that both a personally relevant and serious threat exists, and by providing an effective means to reduce the threat that she or he is able to perform. It is only when both perceived threat and perceived efficacy are high that a person will focus on potential solutions to the problem, which will likely lead to attitude or behavior change in the advocated direction.

A Brief History of the EPPM

The EPPM is an integration and extension of three previous theoretical perspectives on fear appeals: (1) the fear-as-acquired drive model, (2) the parallel process model, and (3) protection motivation theory (reviewed in Witte, Meyer, & Martell, 2001). The most notable difference between the EPPM and these other fear appeal theories is that previous theories focused largely on individuals who adopted the recommended response (i.e., danger control) after being exposed to a fear appeal message, lumping everyone else into the no-response category. In reality, however, the no-response category was comprised of two groups: those who truly had no response to the campaign and those who engaged in fear control, which masks as no behavior change. The EPPM was the first fear appeal theory to specify how interactions between perceived threat and efficacy lead to danger or fear control, and to explain when one process is expected to dominate over the other.

Since the EPPM first was published in 1992, it has guided dozens of studies focusing on numerous target populations and health-related topics around the world. Sample topics and target audiences include promoting radon awareness and reduction among African Americans (Witte, Berkowitz, Lillie et al., 1998); preventing HIV or AIDS among youth in juvenile detention centers (Witte & Morrison, 1995); a computer-based pregnancy, sexually transmitted disease, and HIV prevention intervention for rural Appalachian high school students (Roberto, Zimmerman, Carlyle, & Abner, 2007; Roberto, Zimmerman, Carlyle, Abner, Cupp, & Hanson, 2007); preventing bulimia (Smalec & Klingle, 2000); preventing hepatitis B in high-risk adolescents (Roberto, 2004; Slonim et al., 2005); preventing smoking in Canada (Thesenvitz, 2000); communicating occupational risks to workers (Tan-Wilhelm et al., 1999); and preventing genital warts (Witte, Berkowitz, Cameron, & Lillie, 1998) and skin cancer (Stephenson & Witte, 1998). Most recently, the EPPM has been applied in several international family planning and HIV or AIDS prevention projects in Ethiopia (Belete, Girgre, & Witte, 2003; Witte, Girma, & Girgre, 2001, 2002–2003), Kenya (Witte, Cameron, Lapinski, & Nzyuko, 1998), Namibia (Smith, Downs, & Witte, 2007), Uganda (Mulogo et al., 2006), and India (Witte, Singhal, Muthuswamy, & Duff, 2003).

A review of the literature, through the first quarter of 2007, revealed 44 peer-reviewed research publications that were explicitly guided by or significantly related to the EPPM (see Table 24.2). Notably, this table does not include publications that were conceptual or only tangentially related to the EPPM; formative and qualitative in nature; based on content analyses; appeared in manuscripts published in journals or books not covered by Social Science Citation Index or PsychInfo; or the numerous unpublished presentations, conference papers, theses, and dissertations that also have been guided by the EPPM.

A review of these studies reveals several interesting patterns regarding EPPM-related research. First, fear appeals are pervasive. Not only have such appeals been applied to a vast array of topics and target audiences but they also have been adapted to a variety of communication channels, including television, video, radio, pamphlets, and other print materials. Second, fear appeal messages containing strong efficacy and threat components appear to work better than messages focusing on other combinations of these variables. Third, sometimes favorable conditions already exist for fear appeals; that is, perceived threat or efficacy already may be at desired levels and the task of applied communication researchers and practitioners becomes one of increasing perceptions of just those variables that are not already high. Fourth, increasing perceived threat may differentially influence disease-detection (e.g., skin cancer self-examinations) and disease-prevention (e.g., wearing sunscreen) behaviors. Millar and Millar (1996a, 1996b, 1998, 2000) argued that this effect may occur because disease-prevention messages, by definition, provide ways to cope with and reduce health threats, whereas disease-detection behaviors merely provide means of identifying or confirming health problems and do not offer any immediate plans of action to cope with the threats. Thus, it may be particularly important to include an efficacy component when promoting disease detection. Fifth, applied communication scholars and practitioners need to determine and emphasize what may be threatening (or efficacious) for target audience members (e.g., social threats for youth or economic threats for poor women). Finally, fear appeals may have to be adapted based on cultural differences (e.g., individualistic versus collectivist cultures).

Given this overview of the EPPM, the next section of this chapter focuses on the design, implementation, and evaluation of two applied communication programs that were explicitly guided by this model: (1) a large-scale international program, called "*Journey of Life*," that focused on family planning and HIV or AIDS prevention in Ethiopia, and was overseen by Witte; and (2) a smaller scale statewide program designed to reduce unintentional firearm injuries and death in Michigan, overseen by Roberto. These two applied communication programs were selected because they clearly illustrate the flexibility and ease with which the EPPM can be incorporated into both larger and smaller programs dealing with a variety of topics that may be implemented at an international or local (e.g., statewide or county) level.

Table 24.2 A Brief Chronological Overview of Studies Guided by the Extended Parallel Process Model

Study	Topic	Target Audience/ Sample	Results/Conclusions
Witte, Stokols, Ituarte, & Schneider (1993)	Bicycle safety helmet use	Parents of children between ages of 5 and 18	Cues to action increased perceived threat and perceived threat led to more positive attitudes, intentions, and behaviors
Witte (1994)	HIV and/or AIDS prevention	Sexually active undergraduates not in a long-term relationship	Fear was associated with fear control but not danger control; perceived efficacy was related to danger control but not fear control; when efficacy was high, perceived threat mediated the relationship between fear and behavior
Anderson & McMillion (1995)	Breast cancer self-examinations	African-American undergraduate women	Racially similar models increased efficacy and behavioral intent
Dillard, Plotnick, Godbold, Freimuth, & Edgar (1996)	HIV and/or AIDS prevention PSAs	Undergraduate students	Fear appeal messages often affected a variety of emotions; fear was positively related to message acceptance
Millar & Millar (1996a)	Six health-promotion or disease-detection behaviors	Individuals from a large urban community and undergraduate students	Low-threat messages led to more positive attitudes and intentions for disease-detection behaviors; high-threat messages led to more positive attitudes and intentions for health-promotion behaviors
Millar & Millar (1996b)	Six health-promotion or disease-detection behaviors	Individuals from a large urban community and undergraduate students	Low-threat messages decreased message processing for disease-detection behaviors and increased message processing for health-promotion behaviors; the opposite pattern was found for high-threat messages
McMahan, Witte, & Meyer (1998)	Electromagnetic fields	Undergraduate students	Interaction effect between threat and efficacy on attitudes; main effects for efficacy on intentions, behavior, and fear control
Witte, Berkowitz, Cameron, & Lillie (1998)	Preventing spread of genital warts	Sexually active undergraduate women	Fear appeals with high-threat/high-efficacy components increased positive attitudes, intentions, and behavior more than fear appeals with high-threat/low-efficacy components
Dorsey, Miller, & Scherer (1999)	Alcohol use and abuse on college campuses	Undergraduate students	Both interactions with friends and self-efficacy contributed to students engaging in excessive drinking

Table 24.2 Continued

Study	Topic	Target Audience/ Sample	Results/Conclusions
Tan-Wilhelm et al. (2000)	Occupational risks	Workers at a beryllium plant	Workers receiving high-threat/ high-efficacy notification reported greater perceived threat and efficacy, more positive attitudes toward safety practices, and engaged in more protective behaviors
Witte & Morrison (2000)	Condom usage to prevent HIV and/ or AIDS	Sexually active undergraduates not in a long-term relationship	Trait anxiety increased perceived threat and decreased perceived efficacy, but was unrelated to danger-control and most fear-control responses
Morman (2000)	Testicular cancer self-examination	College men under the age of 32	Magazine advertisements that were high threat/high efficacy led to greater behavioral intent to perform self-exams than similar high-threat/low-efficacy materials, regardless of the type of message (fact versus narrative)
Millar & Millar (2000)	Six health-promotion or disease-detection behaviors	Individuals from a large urban community and undergraduate students	Including an efficacy prime led to a more positive attitude, cognitive response, and message processing for disease-detection but not for health-promotion behaviors
Witte & Allen (2000)	Fear appeal effects	Meta-analysis of 98 fear appeal studies	Fear appeals with high-threat/ high-efficacy components produced the greatest behavior change, whereas fear appeals with high-threat/low-efficacy components produced defensive responses
Roberto et al. (2000)	Gun-safety video	Adolescents and young adults taking hunter-safety classes	Gun-safety video increased knowledge, susceptibility, and severity, but ceiling effects occurred for both self- and response-efficacy
Moscato et al. (2001)	Alcohol consumption	Undergraduates in 38 national fraternal organizations	Perceived severity, response-efficacy, and self-efficacy were negatively related to drinking behavior; perceived susceptibility was not related to drinking behavior; and drinkers who heard the fear appeal message drank less than those who did not hear it
Egbert & Parrott (2001)	Breast and cervical cancer detection	Southeastern U.S. farm women	Women's actual knowledge, perceived knowledge, and perceived social norms were positively related with self-efficacy; perceived barriers were negatively related with self-efficacy

(*continued*)

Table 24.2 Continued

Study	Topic	Target Audience/ Sample	Results/Conclusions
Treise & Weigold (2001)	HIV and/or AIDS prevention and condom use	Undergraduate students	Repetition and fear increased positive attitude toward and intention to use condoms, even after accounting for inputs specified by the theory of reasoned action
Hullett & Witte (2001)	International communication	International college students	The EPPM predicted adaptive and maladaptive behaviors in cross-cultural encounters
Murray-Johnson et al. (2001)	AIDS prevention	African-American and Mexican immigrant junior high school students and U.S. and Taiwanese college undergraduates	Interaction effect between target of the threat and cultural orientation on fear; a main effect for cultural orientation on intentions
Lee & Ferguson (2002)	Effects of anti-tobacco ads	College students	Fear ads were rated as more interesting by all participants; there was a strong negative relationship between rebelliousness and intent to quit smoking after watching fear ads
Tay & Watson (2002)	Driver fatigue	University staff and students	Those exposed to high-threat/ high-efficacy messages outperformed those exposed to high-threat/no-efficacy messages with regard to both intentions and behavior
Block & Williams (2002)	Consequences of caffeine and olestra	Undergraduate students	Decreased elaboration by high-relevance receivers led to increased freezing (defensive avoidance) and decreased severity, response-efficacy, and self-efficacy
Roberto et al. (2002)	Gun safety	Gun owners in the general population	Gun-safety radio PSA increased knowledge, susceptibility and severity increased but not significantly, and there was a ceiling effect for self- and response-efficacy; individuals who called for a free trigger-lock rated it effective and easy to use
Slater, Karan, Johnson, & Walters (2002)	Effects of televised alcohol warnings	A random sample that closely approximated national averages for many demographic variables	All warnings increased posttest knowledge, especially when accompanied by the threatening visual; effects of announcer gender and vocal quality were significant but trivial

Table 24.2 Continued

Study	Topic	Target Audience/ Sample	Results/Conclusions
Henley & Donovan (2003)	Emphysema	Western Australian smokers between 16–25 and 40–50 years old	Young people did not feel immortal; there were no differences between responses of 16–25 year olds to death threats and non-death threats; younger people responded more to all threats than did older people
Ruiter, Verplanken, Kok, & Werrij (2003)	Breast cancer self-examinations	College females	No interaction effect between threat and efficacy; instead, threat contributed positively to fear control but not to danger control, and efficacy contributed positively to danger control and negatively to fear control
Rimal & Real (2003)	Skin cancer	Undergraduate students (study 1) and general population (study 2)	When risk and efficacy were made salient, risk guided action, but when risk and efficacy were not salient, both variables jointly guided action
Ruiter, Verplanken, DeCremer, & Kok (2004)	Breast cancer self-examinations	First-year undergraduate women	Fear appeals resulted in danger control only among respondents high in need for cognition
McKay, Berkowitz, Blumberg, & Goldberg (2004)	Cardiovascular disease	Adults aged 50 and older	Pamphlets increased both self- and response-efficacy about the ability of both foods and vitamins to lower homocysteine level
Roskos-Ewoldsen, Yu, & Rhodes (2004)	Breast cancer self-examinations	Undergraduate females	Efficacy increased and threat decreased positive attitudes and attitude accessibility toward adaptive behavior
Block (2005)	Drinking and driving	Undergraduate students	Individuals high in independent self-construal had more favorable attitudes toward other-referenced fear appeals than toward self-referenced fear appeals
Fry & Prentice-Dunn (2005)	Breast cancer	Undergraduate females	Coping information reduced defensive actions to health threats; previous exposure increased both adaptive and defensive responses
Gore & Bracken (2005)	Symptoms and dangers of meningitis	Undergraduate students	A high-efficacy message with a very low-threat component moved individuals from a fear-control response to a danger-control response
de Hoog, Stroebe, & de Wit (2005)	Repetitive strain injury	Undergraduate students	Perceived susceptibility, but not perceived severity, influenced perceived threat, fear, intentions, and behavior

(continued)

Table 24.2 Continued

Study	Topic	Target Audience/ Sample	Results/Conclusions
Lindsey (2005)	Bone-marrow donation	Undergraduate students	Anticipated guilt mediated the relationship between message and outcome variables for unknown-other threat appeals
McMath & Prentice-Dunn (2005)	Skin cancer	Undergraduate students	High-threat-appraisal information was the most powerful predictor of intentions to take precautionary measures against skin cancer
Morrison (2005)	Protective action against rape	Undergraduate students	Fear appeals targeted only toward women influenced both women's and men's intentions and behaviors
Shehryar & Hunt (2005)	Drinking and driving	Undergraduate students	Nature of the threatening consequences (death versus arrest or serious injury) influenced responses to such messages
Keller, Siegrist, & Gutscher (2006)	Flooding risks	Undergraduate students	Individuals presented with information concerning a longer time period and with personal experience of flooding had greater perceptions of risk
Brewer, Chapman, Gibbons, Gerrard, & McCaul (2007)	Effects of risk perceptions on vaccination behavior	Meta-analysis of 34 risk perception and health behavior studies	Susceptibility and severity predicted vaccination behavior; relationship between risk perceptions and behavior was larger than suggested by prior meta-analyses
Roberto, Zimmerman, Carlyle, & Abner (2007)	Pregnancy, STD, and HIV prevention	Sophomores at two rural high schools	High-threat/high-efficacy tailored messages decreased initiation of sexual activity and increased knowledge, attitudes toward waiting to have sex, condom negotiation self-efficacy, and situational self-efficacy
Roberto, Zimmerman, Carlyle, Abner, Cupp, & Hanson (2007)	Pregnancy, STD, and HIV prevention	Sophomores at nine rural high schools	High-threat/high-efficacy-tailored messages increased adolescents' knowledge, attitudes toward waiting to have sex, susceptibility, and condom self-efficacy
Smith, Ferrara, & Witte (2007)	AIDS-related illness	Namibian adults	Social threat and collective efficacy motivated intentions to adopt recommended actions

Two Applied Communication Programs Guided by the Extended Parallel Process Model

Journey of Life

Background and Need

Ethiopia is located in the Horn of Africa and has among the largest population and fastest growth rates of any country in Africa, with nearly 75 million people in 2006 and the population expected to reach 145 million by 2050 (Population Reference Bureau, 2006). To contain the rapid population growth, a family planning program has been implemented in Ethiopia since the late 1960s. Although awareness of family planning methods is high (86% for all 15- to 49-year-old women and 91% for all 15- to 49-year-old men), the use rate is low (only 18% of all 15- to 49-year-old women and 15% for all 15- to 49-year-old men; Central Statistical Authority [Ethiopia] and ORC Macro, 2006). Ethiopia also is facing a soaring epidemic of HIV infection, with about 1,000 persons a day in Ethiopia contracting HIV (Kaiser Daily HIV/AIDS Report, 2004). Although estimates vary and precise figures are difficult to obtain, the Central Statistical Authority [Ethiopia] and ORC Macro (2006) estimated that 1.4%% of all 15- to 49-year-old Ethiopians are HIV positive. According to that source, women are more than twice as likely as men to have HIV (1.9% and .9%, respectively), and those living in urban areas are over six times more likely to have HIV than those living in rural areas (6% and .7%, respectively). Adults are not the only ones affected by the AIDS epidemic in Ethiopia; over 1 million children have been orphaned by the disease (U.S. Agency for International Development, 2003).

The Ethiopia Reproductive Health Communication Project (ERHCP) was a 4-year initiative that focused on information, education, and communication (IEC) capacity-building and behavior change communication materials for family planning use and HIV or AIDS prevention. The National Office of Population in Ethiopia initiated ERHCP under the umbrella of a 7-year agreement of the Essential Services for Health in Ethiopia program funded by the U.S. Agency for International Development (USAID). The project was implemented under the guidance of an IEC committee comprised of various stakeholders, with technical assistance from the Johns Hopkins University Population Communication Services. The primary goals of this project were to provide (1) education about and stress the importance of modern family planning methods, and (2) information about the dangers of, and how to avoid, HIV or AIDS. Witte was the researcher and evaluator for this project.

One important aspect of this project was the *Journey of Life* (*JOL*) radio serial. Although similar radio formats had been used in several developing countries with some positive effects, those messages generally were not theory based. *JOL*, in contrast, was explicitly guided by the EPPM and designed to increase perceptions of threat and efficacy. A discussion of the design, implementation, and evaluation of this applied communication intervention follows.

Formative Evaluation

Formative evaluation is conducted either before (preproduction) or after (postproduction) program materials have been created for the purposes of gaining insight into and input from target audience members before a program is completed and implemented on a large scale. Both quantitative and qualitative preproduction formative evaluations were conducted for this project to understand better the motivations, barriers, and benefits perceived by the Ethiopian public with respect to family planning use and HIV or AIDS prevention (Witte, Girma, & Girge, 2001). Quantitative formative evaluation consisted of a baseline questionnaire completed by 792 individuals randomly selected (working with a research firm in Ethiopia) from 10 of Ethiopia's most densely populated towns in five major regions; qualitative formative evaluation consisted of 20 focus groups conducted in those same 10 towns. The following formative evaluation results regarding communication channels, family planning, and HIV or AIDS prevention served as a basis for developing the *JOL* radio serial.

COMMUNICATION CHANNELS

Formative evaluation results indicated that radio was very popular in Ethiopia and that it was the news media source used most frequently by both men and women. Almost 91% of those questioned had radios, with drama (73.3%) and news (67.1%) cited as the types of radio programs listened to most frequently. Radio also was one of the most frequently cited sources of information about HIV or AIDS, and "family planning information is largely received through the radio with limited exposure through the television and print media" (Central Statistic Authority [Ethiopia] and ORC Macro, 2006, p. xxiv), with only 33% of Ethiopians questioned owning televisions, and the adult literacy rate being only 39.1% (The World Bank, 2002). Thus, using radio to disseminate information about family planning and HIV or AIDS prevention seemed the best media choice.

FAMILY PLANNING

Both susceptibility and severity were high with respect to family planning in that individuals perceived a definite risk of having more children than they wanted, and the negative consequences of having more children than desired were significant (e.g., maternal death, poverty, and unmet family plans). Response-efficacy was high for abstinence, condoms, and other modern birth-control methods, but self-efficacy was low for using condoms, and only moderate for abstinence and other birth-control methods. Put somewhat differently, respondents believed that most birth-control methods prevented pregnancy, but they doubted their ability to use the pill or condoms correctly or consistently, or believed that they were unable to practice family planning methods due to lack of knowledge, poor spousal interaction, limited access to family planning services, or fear of contraceptive side effects. According to the EPPM, this finding of high threat and low efficacy leads people to engage in fear control. To lead people to engage in danger control, any intervention needed to increase perceived efficacy toward family planning and, at the same time, reinforce the already high levels of perceived threat.

HIV OR AIDS PREVENTION

Perceived susceptibility to HIV or AIDS was very low, with over three-quarters of respondents believing that they were not vulnerable to HIV infection, even if they were sexually active. However, the perceived severity of HIV or AIDS was very high, with a significant majority labeling it as "the worst thing that could happen" (91%) or "a sure death sentence" (86%). In most cases, response-efficacy and self-efficacy levels regarding the various prevention methods mirrored those for family planning (e.g., respondents believed that abstinence prevented HIV or AIDS, but they had some doubts about their ability to remain abstinent). There was, however, one very notable exception: Condoms were thought to be ineffective or potentially dangerous with regard to contracting HIV or AIDS. Furthermore, 12% of respondents did not know about condoms at all, 40% did not believe they were able to use condoms correctly or consistently, and a number of negative perceptions existed about condoms, including embarrassment about using them, concerns about breakage and spillage during intercourse, and the beliefs that condoms reduce sexual pleasure and actually spread HIV. These findings suggested that the intervention needed to increase perceived susceptibility among audience members (i.e., to motivate them to act) and, at the same time, lower perceptions of severity because they were so high and potentially could lead to hopelessness, which is characteristic of fear control. In addition, perceived efficacy needed to be increased to create a high-threat/high-efficacy perceptual environment to promote individuals to engage in danger control.

Applied Communication Materials

JOL was an entertainment–education (Singhal & Rogers, 2003) radio serial designed to deliver prosocial educational messages in an entertaining format to 15- to 30-year-old Ethiopian adolescents and young adults. *JOL* provided education about the use of modern family planning methods, the dangers of HIV and AIDS, and how to prevent HIV and AIDS. Characters were created to serve as positive role models, negative role models, or transitional models (individuals who start out as negative role models but turn into positive role models by the end). Previous theory and research suggested that role modeling by the characters should affect listeners' perceptions of self-efficacy (Bandura, 1986).

 JOL was developed by Ethiopian scriptwriters and production staff with technical assistance from Johns Hopkins Bloomberg School of Public Health's Center for Communication Programs, and support from the USAID. The radio serial contained twenty-six 20-minute episodes, which aired one per week for 6 months. The main message of *JOL* was *yichalal* ("it is possible"), meaning that it was possible for Ethiopians to improve their quality of life by planning their families, and that it was possible to control the HIV and AIDS epidemics by taking appropriate measures to control the spread of these diseases. The series sought to generate feelings of hope and confidence that determining one's family size and protecting oneself from HIV and AIDS can be achieved by all.

 Information about family planning and HIV and AIDS prevention were intermingled throughout the various plots of the radio serial. Example episodes focusing on family planning included "Overpopulation and its Consequences" and "Benefits of Family Planning." Example episodes focusing on HIV and AIDS prevention included "Transmission of HIV/AIDS" and "Preventing HIV/AIDS." There also were seven episodes dealing with various other contraceptives. At the conclusion of each episode, listeners were invited to submit a written response to a weekly quiz. For example, at the end of the episode focusing on condoms, listeners were asked, "Which birth-control method can protect us against unwanted pregnancy and HIV/AIDS if we use it correctly and properly?" Each week, a male and a female participant were randomly selected from among those who submitted the correct answer to receive a prize and to have their names announced during the following week's show. Examples of how each EPPM variable was addressed in the *JOL* radio serial are included in Table 24.1.

Process Evaluation

A *process evaluation* typically is conducted during an intervention to determine whether the intervention is being implemented as intended. However, it is not uncommon to gather process evaluation data shortly after an intervention concludes to assess people's exposure to and opinions of the intervention materials. Both qualitative and quantitative process evaluation data were collected to assess *JOL*. Qualitative data consisted of 6-month case studies of two unmarried females, two unmarried males, and one married couple. All case study participants completed biweekly individual interviews, kept daily diaries, and were subjects of field observations of their dwelling, behaviors, community, and environment (Ferrara, Witte, & Jerato, 2002). Quantitative process evaluation data consisted of exposure and opinion items on two general population questionnaires administered at the conclusion of *JOL* (Belete et al., 2003; Farr, Witte, Jarato [sic; Jerato], & Menard, 2005; Witte, 2003).

Five major themes emerged from the qualitative case studies that were conducted as the intervention was being implemented to see whether the messages were being interpreted as intended: (1) *show feedback—JOL* was entertaining, popular, viewed as valuable by the community, and contained characters with whom listeners identified; (2) *influence on life*—listeners learned a lot about HIV and AIDS prevention, and family planning, and changed their behaviors; (3) *advocacy behaviors*—listeners were motivated to share facts, engage in discussion, and correct mistaken perceptions with others about issues featured in *JOL*; (4) *information-seeking behaviors*—listeners were motivated to seek further information about condoms and AIDS from a variety of additional interpersonal and mediated sources; and (5) *beliefs*—listeners developed or changed their beliefs about child spacing and a variety of contraceptives, and had greater knowledge about the causes (susceptibility) and consequences (severity) of HIV and AIDS.

Posttest process evaluation questionnaire items indicated that 17.1% of the target population had heard of *JOL* and 15.7% listened to it on a regular basis ($M = 15$ episodes). This figure is typical of radio programs such as this, both domestically and abroad (for a discussion of exposure rates to radio-based interventions, see Roberto, Meyer, Johnson, Atkin, & Smith, 2002). Participants who listened to *JOL* on a regular basis were asked a variety of questionnaire items designed to determine both their opinions of the show and how the show affected them. The results indicated that *JOL* was perceived very positively, with both the story and production quality rated very highly by over 93% of respondents. Furthermore, a great majority found *JOL* to be both educational (99%) and entertaining (85%).

Outcome Evaluation

An *outcome evaluation* typically is conducted after an intervention has concluded to determine its effects. The outcome evaluation assessed the effects of *JOL* on the focal audience via three ways: (1) posttest interview questionnaires, (2) a pre–post panel interview questionnaire, and (3) dose-response analysis (where, presumably, the greater the dosage—in this case, episodes—the greater the effects; Belete et al., 2003; Witte, 2003). A brief overview of the outcome evaluation results follows.

FAMILY PLANNING

Results from the posttest interview questionnaire indicated that participants agreed or strongly agreed that *JOL* influenced them to use family planning (93%), increased their perceived susceptibility (46%) and severity (97%) of unwanted pregnancy, and increased their perceived response-efficacy (90%) and self-efficacy (97%) of using modern family planning methods.

HIV AND AIDS PREVENTION

Results from the posttest interview questionnaire also indicated that a vast majority of participants agreed or strongly agreed that *JOL* influenced them to protect themselves against HIV infection (96%), increased their perceived susceptibility (66%) and severity (98%) regarding HIV and AIDS, and increased their response-efficacy (95%) and self-efficacy (96%) for HIV and AIDS prevention. Results from the pre–post panel interview questionnaire indicated that *JOL* increased listeners' perceived susceptibility, response-efficacy, and self-efficacy, and significantly decreased both their reactance and defensive avoidance. Furthermore, perceived severity, which was high in the baseline, decreased slightly. Finally, dose-response analysis revealed significant correlations between the number of *JOL* episodes listened to and numerous *JOL* target variables (e.g., threat and efficacy). The preponderance of evidence from this set of results suggested that the EPPM-guided *JOL* had positive and desired behavioral and perceptual effects on audience members.

The Firearm Injury Reduction Education Program

Background and Need

In 2001, over 29,000 deaths in the United States were attributed to firearm-related injury, including 11,348 homicides, 802 unintentional deaths, and 16,896 suicides (Centers for Disease Control and Prevention, National Center for Injury Prevention and Control, 2004). Although fewer individuals die from unintentional injuries compared to homicides and suicides, for every unintentional gun-related death, there are at least 13 accidental gun-related injuries (Annest, Mercy, Gibson, & Ryan, 1995). The availability of a gun in a home is cited as a major contributing factor in most of these cases, especially when the gun is stored loaded but not locked. In response to statistics such as these, the U.S. Department of Health and Human Services (2000) funded *Healthy People 2010*, a program designed to prevent gunshot injuries and deaths in the United States. The objectives of this program included: (1) reducing the proportion of people who possess weapons that are inappropriately stored and, therefore, dangerously available; and (2) enacting laws requiring that firearms be properly stored to minimize access to them and the likelihood of discharge by minors. Mercy (1993) emphasized the need for actions designed to reduce gun violence to be guided by scientific research methods. Furthermore, the Committee on Injury and Poison Prevention (1992) emphasized that no gun injury program whose goal is prevention has been thoroughly and systematically evaluated.

The goal of the Firearm Injury Reduction Education (FIRE) Program, sponsored by the Michigan Department of Community Health, was to "increase the number of gun owners who engage in safe storage and handling practices to reduce the number of unintentional firearm injuries and deaths in Michigan" (Roberto & Meyer, 1999, p. 9). The objectives designed to reach this goal involved increasing gun owners' (1) knowledge of six gun-safety practices, (2) perceived susceptibility to and severity of firearm injury, and (3) response-efficacy and self-efficacy toward the six gun-safety practices. To meet these objectives, a variety of applied communication materials were developed; all materials were EPPM based, guided by formative evaluation, and evaluated using sound social-scientific techniques. Roberto was the principal investigator for this project and oversaw the design, implementation, and evaluation of all components discussed below.

Formative Evaluation

The FIRE Program incorporated both preproduction and postproduction formative evaluation research (see Roberto, Johnson, Meyer, Robbins, & Smith, 1998). Preproduction formative evaluation was conducted to refine existing ideas and to generate new ideas, and included: (1) six focus groups conducted with adults and adolescents who owned or used firearms on a regular basis, (2) 11 in-depth individual interviews conducted with law enforcement officers and gun shop owners who had considerable knowledge about firearms and the people who purchase them, and (3) telephone interview questionnaire data obtained from a representative sample of over 500 adults in the general population in the one Michigan county that served as the treatment group for one of the interventions described below.

Preproduction formative evaluation revealed several important findings. First, people's susceptibility to accidental firearm injuries was low, as individuals did not believe that they, their children, or individuals who might visit their household (including their children's friends) were likely to gain access to their guns or be involved in a gun accident. Second, comments from adolescents, in particular, suggested that severity should be highlighted via realistic portrayals of the short- and long-term effects of a gunshot wound. Third, many individuals were unaware of trigger-locks, which suggested that self-efficacy could be increased by demonstrating how such locks work. Fourth, virtually everyone perceived trigger-locks with a key mechanism to be a more effective deterrent (i.e., greater response-efficacy) than trigger-locks with a combination mechanism, which were perceived to be opened more easily by persistent individuals. In addition, we learned a variety of other important information not directly related to the EPPM, including important source characteristics, vocabulary, and radio stations listened to most commonly by gun owners. Because perceived threat was low, it was not surprising to find that many people were not engaging in the recommended gun-safety practices. The task of the FIRE Program, thus, became one of increasing perceived threat and simultaneously maintaining high levels of efficacy.

Based on preproduction formative evaluation results, a variety of materials were developed, including a gun-safety video, two radio public service announcements (PSAs), a direct-mail coupon, a poster, and two pamphlets. Postproduction formative evaluation was conducted to obtain feedback once draft materials were created but before they were finalized and fully implemented, and consisted of additional focus groups and individual interviews conducted with adults and adolescents who owned or used firearms on a regular basis (Roberto, Meyer, Johnson, & Atkin, 2000). For example, focus groups conducted with adolescents suggested that the first draft of the gun-safety video was not graphic enough to increase the perceived severity of firearm injuries. Focus group participants made several suggestions for improvement, which led to the inclusion of testimony from a trauma surgeon, graphic photographs and X-rays of preoperative and postoperative accidental gunshot wounds, and a graphic police photograph from the scene of one of the accidents presented in the video. An additional round of postproduction focus groups conducted with adolescents suggested that the inclusion of such information was more likely to have the intended effect on perceived severity, which was necessary if the target audience was going to be swayed from no response to a danger-control response.

Applied Communication Materials

The FIRE Program consisted of three main interventions: (1) a coordinated radio PSA and direct-mail campaign designed to increase knowledge of six important gun-safety practices (Meyer, Roberto, & Atkin, 2003), (2) a radio PSA campaign designed to promote gun trigger-lock use (Roberto et al., 2002), and (3) a gun-safety video designed to increase perceived threat of accidental gunshot injury and knowledge and perceived efficacy of the six important gun-safety practices (Roberto et al., 2000). Other support materials (e.g., two pamphlets and a poster) also were developed and used at various points throughout the larger project. Although all materials were guided, at least in part, by the EPPM, the trigger-lock PSA and gun-safety video relied almost exclusively on it. Consequently, these two aspects of this applied communication campaign are discussed in more detail below.

GUN-SAFETY VIDEO

Bullet "Proof"—The Case for Gun Safety (Bancroft, Roberto, & Bishop, 1998) is a Telly Award®-winning video designed for 12- to 18-year-old adolescents (mostly males) attending the Michigan Department of Natural Resources' (DNR) Hunter-Safety Class (which everyone in Michigan must take before they can get a hunting license). This 20-minute video contains segments from five videotaped interviews conducted with individuals whose lives have been, and continue to be, affected by accidental gunshot injuries (for a detailed summary of each case, see Roberto et al., 2000).

All interview protocols were created using variables from the EPPM. For example, each interviewee was asked to discuss the circumstances surrounding the injury, the short- and long-term physical and emotional consequences of the injury, and how the injury might have been prevented. The three main sections of the video were explicitly designed to increase viewers' perceptions of threat and efficacy. For instance, the section designed to increase perceived severity contained the most graphic images, statements, and statistics about accidental gun injuries and death, along with discussions of short- and long-term mental and physical consequences of such injuries. The section highlighting perceived susceptibility had interviewees share how they never thought they could or would be involved in an accidental shooting. They also noted how their general experiences with firearms were similar to those of the target audience, and that if they could be involved in such an incident, it could happen to anyone. The section dealing with response-efficacy and self-efficacy had each interviewee discuss how various relevant gun-safety practices could have prevented his or her accident. One of the interviewees also demonstrated how to use a trigger-lock in this section. Example statements and images are included in Table 24.1.

TRIGGER-LOCK RADIO PUBLIC SERVICE ANNOUNCEMENT

A radio PSA focusing on the danger to children from an unlocked and loaded gun also was created using the EPPM as a guide (Roberto et al., 2002). At the end of the message, a toll-free phone number was provided that individuals could call to receive a free gun trigger-lock. The PSA aired on three radio stations in one mid-Michigan county; these stations were specifically selected because formative evaluation indicated that these were the stations listened to most frequently by adult gun owners. The intervention lasted 3 weeks, during which time the PSAs ran on each station at least six times a day Monday through Friday, and at least two times each weekend day. Approximately 75% of the airtime was purchased to insure that the PSA played during peak morning and afternoon drive times. Example statements from the PSA are included in Table 24.1.

Process Evaluation

Because the gun-safety video intervention implementation and evaluation only took about an hour per class, the need for process evaluation was minimal. In this instance, process evaluation simply consisted of making sure that the video was shown in a manner that could easily be heard and seen by all participants, and using a questionnaire that asked viewers to rate the video on a variety of positive and negative dimensions.

Process evaluation for the trigger-lock PSA was considerably more extensive than for the gun-safety video, and consisted of telephone questionnaires conducted with the general population to assess exposure levels to the radio PSAs, an automated telephone questionnaire administered to individuals who called to receive the free gun trigger-lock, and archival data in the form of radio station invoices indicating exactly when and how many times the PSAs aired (Roberto et al., 2002). The general population interviews revealed that nearly one-fifth (19%) of those questioned in the experimental county (which included approximately 70,000 households) recalled hearing the PSA. The automated telephone questionnaire revealed that males who used guns primarily for hunting purposes and who planned to use the trigger-lock themselves were most likely to call for the free trigger-lock; notably, this was one very important subgroup in this campaign. Finally, the radio station invoices indicated that the PSA ran 340 times during the 3-week intervention, including 87 times on the classic rock station, 110 times on the country western station, and 143 times on the urban contemporary station. Although seemingly simple, these were important steps because they ensured that the interventions were implemented as intended and, therefore, provided greater confidence in the outcome evaluation results obtained.

Outcome Evaluation

Each component of the FIRE Program was evaluated using a quasi-experimental design, with the primary dependent variables being gun-safety knowledge, perceived threat, perceived efficacy, behavioral intent, and behavior. The following sections discuss the outcome evaluation of the gun-safety video and the trigger-lock radio PSA.

GUN-SAFETY VIDEO

The gun-safety video was evaluated using a posttest-only control-group design with random assignment during seven DNR hunter-safety classes (Roberto et al., 2000). The experimental group (exposed to the video) listed nearly twice as many gun-safety practices compared to the control group. This finding is particularly impressive because many of these individuals already knew a fair amount about guns and gun safety prior to taking the class. The experimental group also perceived significantly more susceptibility and severity than did the control group. However, both groups displayed very high levels of response-efficacy and self-efficacy for the six recommended gun-safety practices. This ceiling effect left little room for movement; consequently, no differences were observed for either variable. However, given that threat was increased, and efficacy was high already, the EPPM suggests that these individuals were ready to enact the danger-control process by engaging in the recommended gun-safety practices.

TRIGGER-LOCK RADIO PUBLIC SERVICE ANNOUNCEMENT

The outcome evaluation of the trigger-lock radio PSA consisted of three main types of data collection: (1) a general population telephone interview questionnaire conducted in one experimental and one control county; (2) an automated telephone interview questionnaire completed by individuals who called to receive the free gun trigger-lock; and (3) a follow-up questionnaire mailed to individuals who were sent a free gun trigger-lock (Roberto et al., 2002). The general population telephone questionnaire revealed that individuals exposed to the message in the experimental county where the radio PSA aired had greater gun-safety knowledge than did individuals in the control county. None of the differences regarding perceived threat were statistically significant, although the experimental county tended to have higher perceived susceptibility and severity than did the control county. Regarding perceived efficacy, as with the gun-safety video, a ceiling effect left little room for upward movement; consequently, no differences in self-efficacy or response-efficacy were found. Outcome evaluation results from the automated telephone questionnaire revealed that 799 individuals called the toll-free number for a free gun trigger-lock (or approximately one out of six gun-owning households exposed to the message). The follow-up mail questionnaire sent to these individuals revealed that 95% of respondents had tried the trigger-lock, and 87% reported that the trigger-lock currently was on one of their guns at the time they filled out the questionnaire (i.e., approximately 6 weeks after the trigger-locks were sent out). Seventy-eight percent said that they had not previously owned a trigger-lock but, nonetheless, rated it as high in response-efficacy and self-efficacy after having an opportunity to try it. Allowing gun-owners to try a trigger-lock free of charge increased perceived efficacy in a variety of ways, such as overcoming the cost barrier and allowing them to see for themselves that a trigger-lock was effective and easy to use. With perceived efficacy exceeding perceived threat, it is not surprising that so many gun-owners both tried and continued to use the trigger-lock.

Discussion and Recommendations

This chapter examined two applied communication programs that were explicitly guided by the EPPM: the *Journey of Life* radio serial, which focused on family planning and HIV and AIDS prevention in Ethiopia, and the Firearm Injury Reduction Education Program, which was designed to reduce the number of unintentional firearm injuries and deaths in Michigan. A number of important insights and lessons were learned as a result of these programs. This final section of the chapter provides several recommendations that might be helpful to applied communication researchers and practitioners, in general, and particularly to those interested in using the EPPM to guide their work.

The Importance of Previous Theory and Research for Applied Communication Programs

Using existing theory and research to guide applied communication programs not only saves a considerable amount of time and money but also allows for a more systematic and efficient advancement of science and practice by not continually having to reinvent the wheel. For example, without previous theory and research, how will one know what variables are most likely to change the desired behavior, or how will one determine what questions to ask (and how to ask them) during focus groups or on questionnaires? For all of these reasons, agencies that fund applied communication programs now typically require that such programs be informed by previous theory and research.

If there is any fear felt by people about the issue to be addressed, researchers and practitioners may be able to harness the power of that fear by following the steps outlined in the EPPM. However, if after reading this chapter a person does not believe that a fear appeal approach is right for his or her program, there are a number of alternative theories that may be considered instead. Examples include, but are not limited to, the theory of reasoned action, theory of planned behavior, the health belief model, or social cognitive theory (for a review and comparison of these theories, see Murray-Johnson & Witte, 2003). In fact, it is not uncommon to ask questions about variables from multiple theoretical perspectives during the formative evaluation phase of an applied communication program and then select the theory that seems best suited to the topic and target audience. Regardless of which theory ultimately is selected, the design, implementation, and evaluation of an applied communication program will be considerably easier and stronger if guided by previous theory and research.

The Importance of Targeted Messages

One of the more useful aspects of the EPPM is that messages can be designed based on the target audience's appraisals of susceptibility, severity, response-efficacy, and self-efficacy. For example, most Ethiopians already are aware of the negative personal and societal consequences of overpopulation and HIV and AIDS (i.e., perceived severity is already high), but many Ethiopians do not believe that they have the knowledge or ability to prevent these negative consequences. Under such circumstances, an applied communication program is advised to focus existing resources on increasing self-efficacy and response-efficacy to move people from fear control to danger control.

The exact opposite pattern was observed during the formative and outcome evaluations of the gun-safety program. For that program, perceived susceptibility and severity were very low; consequently, gun owners were not motivated to engage in, or often to even remember, the recommended gun-safety practices (in spite of the fact that these practices were perceived as both effective and easy to perform). Thus, to move gun owners from no response to a danger-control response, the task was one of increasing their motivation to remember and practice these very simple rules rather than convincing them that these rules are effective and easy to perform.

In sum, equipped with information about a target audience's current levels of threat and efficacy, an applied communication program can save valuable resources by focusing more on those perceptions that are not already favorable to the desired behavioral outcome. Of course, not *all* Ethiopians believed that overpopulation and HIV or AIDS had severe consequences, nor did *every* gun owner in that Michigan country think that all of the gun-safety practices were effective or easy to perform. Moreover, individuals' perceptions continually are changing, meaning that favorable circumstances that exist at one time may not exist at another. For all of these reasons, it still may be worthwhile to address all four threat and efficacy variables to some extent (especially if resources exist to do so). However, particularly when resources or access to the target audience are limited, the EPPM provides a good way to prioritize what variables should be addressed.

The Importance of Measuring Both Danger Control and Fear Control

The EPPM reminds us that just because people do not engage in a recommended response does not mean that no response occurred at all. Thus, it is important to measure both danger control and fear control when conducting an outcome evaluation of any intervention that is guided by the EPPM, because learning that "no response" occurred to a campaign calls for a very different strategy than a "fear-control" response to a campaign. The former signifies that perceived threat was not activated, which means there is no motivation even to attend to the issue; the latter means that one's campaign had an *unintended* effect, where too much threat was created, resulting in people losing hope and giving up on controlling the danger.

Outcome evaluations of most applied communication programs typically measure danger-control responses, such as changes in people's attitudes, intentions, or behaviors. However, if a more complete picture of what really happened is desired, measuring fear-control responses is equally important. For example, to measure defensive avoidance, receivers might be asked if the message made them want to avoid thinking about the issue, or to measure reactance, they might be asked if the message made them feel angry, manipulated, or exploited.

The evaluation of the *JOL* contained measures of both danger and fear control. As a result, we know that the *JOL* significantly reduced both reactance and defensive avoidance—two common ways to control one's fear. Conversely, the lack of fear-control measures was a potential flaw in the evaluation of the gun-safety program. For example, some of the images in the gun-safety video were graphic, and although teenagers seemed to find them motivating, we occasionally observed adults closing their eyes or turning their head away during parts of the video (both of which are anecdotal examples of defensive avoidance). In hindsight, including measures of fear control would have helped to determine the exact effects of the video.

The Importance of Evaluation

Both the *JOL* and FIRE programs included a variety of strong evaluation components. Formative evaluation was employed to generate ideas and obtain feedback from the target audience before the interventions were created and implemented, process evaluation was used to track program implementation, and outcome evaluation was conducted to determine the effects of these applied communication programs. Each type of evaluation provides important information. For example, it is not fair to conclude that a program did not work (assessed through outcome evaluation) if it was not implemented as intended (assessed through process evaluation). Conversely, if a program was implemented as intended and no changes occurred, something else might be tried in the future.

The Advantage of Using Multiple Research Methods

Throughout their design, implementation, and evaluation, the *JOL* and the FIRE programs each included all or most of the following research methods: focus groups, in-depth individual interviews, content analysis, secondary/archival data, self-administered and interview questionnaires, and field experiments. Each method was used in a different way—to inform the design, track the implementation, or assess the effectiveness of these programs. By doing so, the *JOL* and the FIRE programs highlight the importance and value of using both qualitative and quantitative research methods. For example, it is difficult to gain the type of rich information needed to design an applied communication program by asking target audience members to respond only to closed-ended questionnaire items. Conversely, it perhaps is even more difficult to determine the effects of an intervention without employing appropriate sampling techniques, questionnaires, and experimental research designs.

Conclusion

> If there is to be the anguish of uncertainty, there must be some lurking hope of deliverance; and that this is so would appear from the fact that fear sets [people] deliberating—but no one deliberates about things that are hopeless. (Aristotle 1932, p. 132)

The extended parallel process model is one theoretically based, empirically tested method for generating effective health risk messages in a variety of applied communication contexts. The model states that to obtain behavior change in the desired direction, messages must not only convince receivers that an outcome is both personally relevant and serious but also show them that the recommended response is effective, as well as provide them with the necessary skills and resources to perform the recommended response. Fear-arousing messages that do not fully consider even one of these four variables—susceptibility, severity, response-efficacy, or self-efficacy—will not be effective. In sum, what these applied communication research programs show is that if researchers and practitioners want to influence people's behavior, increasing fear is only part of the process; it is just as important to provide hope for overcoming the threat causing the fear.

Authors' Note

Both authors contributed equally to this chapter. The *Journey of Life* radio serial was created by Johns Hopkins Bloomberg School of Public Health/Center for Communication Programs and funded by the U.S. Agency for International Development and the National Office of Population of Ethiopia. The Firearm Injury Reduction Education Program was funded by the Michigan Department of Community Health. Figures 24.2 to 24.4 were adapted from a presentation by Michael Titus in Roberto's graduate seminar on Communication and Persuasion. Sample applied communication materials for both programs discussed in this chapter may be downloaded free of charge at http://www. anthonyroberto.com/eppm/hacr /.

References

Anderson, R. B., & McMillion, P. Y. (1995). Effects of similar and diversified modeling on African-American women's efficacy expectations and intentions to perform breast self-examinations. *Health Communication, 7*, 327–343.

Annest, J. L., Mercy, J. A., Gibson, D. R., & Ryan, G. W. (1995). National estimates of nonfatal firearm-related injuries. *Journal of the American Medical Association, 273*, 1749–1754.

Aristotle. (1932). *The rhetoric of Aristotle* (L. Cooper, Trans.). Englewood Cliffs, NJ: Prentice-Hall.

Bancroft, J., Roberto, A. J. (Producers), & Bishop, B. (Director). (1998). *Bullet "proof"—The case for gun safety* [Motion picture]. Lansing: Michigan Department of Community Health.

Bandura, A. (1986). *Social foundations of thought and action: A social cognitive theory*. Englewood Cliffs, NJ: Prentice-Hall.

Belete, S., Girgre, A., & Witte, K. (2003, March). *Summative evaluation of "Journey of Life": The Ethiopia Reproductive Health Communication Project*. Addis Ababa: Johns Hopkins Bloomberg School of Public Health/Center for Communication Programs and Ethiopia National Office of Population. Retrieved July 31, 2008, from http://db.jhuccp.org/mmc/media/treth4.pdf

Block, L. G. (2005). Self-referenced fear and guilt appeals: The moderating role of self-construal. *Journal of Applied Social Psychology, 35*, 2290–2309.

Block, L. G., & Williams, P. (2002). Undoing the effects of seizing and freezing: Decreasing defensive processing of personally relevant messages. *Journal of Applied Social Psychology, 32*, 803–833.

Brewer, N. T., Chapman, G. B., Gibbons, F. X., Gerrard, M., McCaul, K. D., & Weinstein, N. D. (2007). Meta-analysis of the relationship between risk perception and health behavior: The example of vaccination. *Health Psychology, 26*, 136–145.

Centers for Disease Control and Prevention, National Center for Injury Prevention and Control. (2004). *WISQARS injury mortality reports, 1999–2002*. Retrieved September 18, 2004, from http://webapp.cdc.gov/sasweb/ncipc/mortrate10_fy.html

Central Statistical Authority [Ethiopia] and ORC Macro. (2006, September). *Ethiopia demographic and health survey 2005*. Addis Ababa, Ethiopia and Calverton, MD: Central Statistical Authority and ORC Macro. Retrieved July 30, 2008, from http://www.measuredhs.com/pubs/pdf/FR179/FR179.pdf

Committee on Injury and Poison Prevention. (1992). Firearm injuries affecting the pediatric population. *Pediatrics, 89,* 788–790.

de Hoog, N., Stroebe, W., & de Wit, J. B. F. (2005). The impact of fear appeals on processing
and acceptance of action recommendations. *Personality and Social Psychology Bulletin, 31,*
24–33.

Dillard, J. P., Plotnick, C. A., & Godbold, L. C., Freimuth, V. S., & Edgar, T. (1996). The multiple
affective outcomes of AIDS PSAs: Fear appeals do more than scare people. *Communication
Research, 23,* 44–72.

Dorsey, A. M., Miller, K. I., & Scherer, C. W. (1999). Communication, risk behavior, and perceptions of threat and efficacy: A test of a reciprocal model. *Journal of Applied Communication
Research, 27,* 377–395.

Egbert, N., & Parrott, R. (2001). Self-efficacy and rural women's performance of breast and cervical cancer detection practices. *Journal of Health Communication, 6,* 219–233.

Farr, A. C., Witte, K., Jarato [sic; Jerato], K., & Menard, T. (2005). The effectiveness of media use
in health education: Evaluation of an HIV/AIDS television campaign in Ethiopia. *Journal of
Health Communication, 10,* 225–235.

Ferrara, M., Witte, K., & Jerato, K. (2002). *A case study of "Journey of Life": A process evaluation of a radio serial drama.* Addis Ababa: Johns Hopkins Bloomberg School of Public Health/
Center for Communication Programs and Ethiopia National Office of Population.

Fry, R. B., & Prentice-Dunn, S. (2005). Effects of coping information and value affirmation on
responses to a perceived health threat. *Health Communication, 17,* 133–147.

Gore, T. D., & Bracken, C. C. (2005). Testing the theoretical design of health risk messages:
Reexamining the major tenets of the extended parallel process model. *Health Education and
Behavior, 32,* 27–41.

Henley, N., & Donovan, R. J. (2003). Young people's response to death threat appeals: Do they
really feel immortal? *Health Education Research, 18,* 1–14.

Hullett, C. R., & Witte, K. (2001). Predicting intercultural adaptation and isolation: Using the
extended parallel process model to test anxiety/uncertainty management theory. *International
Journal of Intercultural Relations, 25,* 125–139.

Kaiser Daily HIV/AIDS Report. (2004, May 24). *Global challenges: 1,000 people contract HIV
daily in Ethiopia; epidemic affecting economy, official says.* Retrieved August 5, 2008, from
http://www.kaisernetwork.org/daily_reports/rep_index.cfm?hint=1&DR_ID=23863

Keller, C., Siegrist, M., & Gutscher, H. (2006). The role of affect and availability heuristics in risk
communication. *Risk Analysis, 26,* 631–639.

Lee, M. J., & Ferguson, M. A. (2002). Effects of anti-tobacco advertisements based on risk-taking
tendencies: Realistic fear vs. vulgar humor. *Journalism & Mass Communication Quarterly,
79,* 945–963.

Lindsey, L. L. M. (2005). Anticipated guilt as behavioral motivation: An examination of appeals
to help unknown others through bone marrow donation. *Human Communication Research,
31,* 453–481.

McKay, D. L., Berkowitz, J. M., Blumberg, J. B., & Goldberg, J. P. (2004). Communicating cardiovascular disease risk due to elevated homocysteine levels: Using the EPPM to develop print
materials. *Health Education Behavior, 31,* 355–371.

McMahan, S., Witte, K., & Meyer, J. (1998). The perception of risk messages regarding electro-
magnetic fields: Extending the extended parallel process model to an unknown risk. *Health
Communication, 10,* 247–259.

McMath, B. F., & Prentice-Dunn, S. (2005). Protection motivation theory and skin cancer risk:
The role of individual differences in response to persuasive appeals. *Journal of Applied Social
Psychology, 35,* 621–643.

Mercy, J. A. (1993). The public health impact of firearm injuries. *American Journal of Preventive
Medicine, 9*(Suppl. 1), 8–11.

Meyer, G., Roberto, A. J., & Atkin, C. K. (2003). A radio-based approach to promoting gun
safety: Process and outcome evaluation implications and insights. *Health Communication, 15,*
299–318.

Millar, M. G., & Millar, K. (1996a). Effects of anxiety on disease detection and health promotion behaviors. *Basic and Applied Social Psychology, 18,* 61–74.

Millar, M. G., & Millar, K. (1996b). The effects of message anxiety on response times to disease detection and health promotion behaviors. *Journal of Behavioral Medicine, 19,* 401–413.

Millar, M. G., & Millar, K. (1998). Processing messages about disease detection and health promotion behaviors: The effects of anxiety. *Health Communication, 10,* 211–226.

Millar, M. G., & Millar, K. (2000). The effects of coping primes on responses to messages about disease detection behaviors. *Psychology and Health, 15,* 271–281.

Morman, M. T. (2000). The influence of fear appeals, message design, and masculinity on men's motivation to perform testicular self-exam. *Journal of Applied Communication Research, 28,* 91–116.

Morrison, K. (2005). Motivating women and men to take protective action against rape: Examining direct and indirect persuasive fear appeals. *Health Communication, 18,* 237–256.

Moscato, S., Black, D. R., Blue, C. L., Mattson, M., Galer-Unti, R. A., & Coster, D. C. (2001). Evaluating a fear appeal message to reduce alcohol use among "Greeks." *American Journal of Health Behavior, 25,* 481–491.

Mulogo, E. M., Witte, K., Bajunirwe, F., Nabukera, S. K., Muchunguzi, C., Batwala, V. K., et al. (2006). Birth plans: Influence on decisions about seeking assisted deliveries among rural communities in Uganda. *East African Medical Journal, 83*(3), 74–83.

Murray-Johnson, L., & Witte, K. (2003). Looking toward the future: Health message design strategies. In T. L. Thompson, A. M. Dorsey, K. I. Miller, & R. Parrott (Eds.), *Handbook of health communication* (pp. 473–495). Mahwah, NJ: Erlbaum.

Murray-Johnson, L., Witte, K., Liu, W. Y., Hubble, A. P., Sampson, J., & Morrison, K. (2001). Addressing cultural orientations in fear appeals: Promoting AIDS-protective behaviors among Mexican immigrant and African American adolescents and American and Taiwanese college students. *Journal of Health Communication, 6,* 335–358.

Population Reference Bureau. (2006). *2006 world population data sheet.* Washington, DC: Author. Retrieved August 5, 2008, from http://www.kaisernetwork.org/daily_reports/rep_index.cfm?hint=1&DR_ID=23863

Rimal, R. N., & Real, K. (2003). Perceived risk and efficacy beliefs as motivators of change: Use of the risk perception attitude (RPA) framework to understand health behaviors. *Human Communication Research, 29,* 370–399.

Roberto, A. J. (2004). Putting communication theory into practice: The extended parallel process model. *Communication Teacher, 18,* 38–43.

Roberto, A. J., Johnson, A. J., Meyer, G., Robbins, S. L., & Smith, P. K. (1998). The Firearm Injury Reduction Education (FIRE) Program: Formative evaluation insights and implications. *Social Marketing Quarterly, 4*(2), 25–35.

Roberto, A. J., & Meyer, G. (1999). *A resource guide for the Firearm Injury Reduction Education Program.* Lansing: Michigan Department of Community Health.

Roberto, A. J., Meyer, G., Johnson, A. J., & Atkin, C. K. (2000). Using the extended parallel process model to prevent firearm injury and death: Field experiment results of a video-based intervention. *Journal of Communication, 50*(4), 157–175.

Roberto, A. J., Meyer, G., Johnson, A. J., Atkin, C. K., & Smith, P. K. (2002). Promoting gun trigger-lock use: Insights and implications from a radio-based health communication intervention. *Journal of Applied Communication Research, 30,* 210–230.

Roberto, A. J., Zimmerman, R. S., Carlyle, K. E., & Abner, E. L. (2007). A computer-based approach to preventing pregnancy, STD, and HIV in rural adolescents. *Journal of Health Communication, 12,* 53–76.

Roberto, A. J., Zimmerman, R. S., Carlyle, K. E., Abner, E. L., Cupp, P. K., & Hansen, G. L. (2007). The effects of a computer-based pregnancy, STD, and HIV prevention intervention: A nine-school trial. *Health Communication, 21,* 115–124.

Roskos-Ewoldsen, D. R., Yu, H. J., & Rhodes, N. (2004). Fear appeal messages affect accessibility of attitudes toward the threat and adaptive behaviors. *Communication Monographs, 71,* 51–71.

Ruiter R. A. C., Verplanken, B., DeCremer, D., & Kok, G. (2004). Danger and fear control in response to fear appeals: The role of need for cognition. *Basic and Applied Social Psychology*, 26, 13–24.

Ruiter, R. A. C., Verplanken, B., Kok, G., & Werrij, M. Q. (2003). The role of coping appraisal in reactions to fear appeals: Do we need threat information? *Journal of Health Psychology*, 8, 465–474.

Shehryar, O., & Hunt, D. M. (2005). A terror management perspective on the persuasiveness of fear appeals. *Journal of Consumer Psychology*, 15, 275–287.

Singhal, A., & Rogers, E. M. (2003). *Combating AIDS: Communication strategies in action.* Thousand Oaks, CA: Sage.

Slater, M. D., Karan, D. N., Johnson, A. J., & Walters, D. (2002). Effects of threatening visuals and announcer differences on responses to televised alcohol warnings. *Journal of Applied Communication Research*, 30, 210–230.

Slonim, A. B., Roberto A. J., Downing, C. R., Adams, I. F., Fasano, N. J., Davis-Satterla, L., et al. (2005). Adolescents' knowledge, beliefs, and behaviors regarding hepatitis B: Insights and implications for programs targeting hepatitis B and other vaccine-preventable diseases. *Journal of Adolescent Health*, 36, 178–186.

Smalec, J., & Klingle, R. S. (2000). Bulimia interventions via interpersonal influence: The role of threat and efficacy in persuading bulimics to seek help. *Journal of Behavioral Medicine*, 23, 37–57.

Smith, R. A., Downs, E., & Witte, K. (2007). Drama theory and entertainment education: Exploring the effects of a radio drama on behavioral intentions to limit HIV transmission in Ethiopia. *Communication Monographs*, 74, 133–153.

Smith, R. A., Ferrara, M., & Witte, K. (2007). Social sides of health risks: Stigma and collective efficacy. *Health Communication*, 21, 55–64.

Stephenson, M. T., & Witte, K. (1998). Fear, threat, and perceptions of efficacy from frightening skin cancer messages. *Public Health Reviews*, 26, 147–174.

Stephenson, M. T., & Witte, K. (2001). Creating fear in a risky world: Generating effective health risk messages. In R. E. Rice & C. K. Atkin (Eds.), *Public communication campaigns* (3rd ed., pp. 88–102). Thousand Oaks, CA: Sage.

Tan-Wilhelm, D., Witte, K., Liu, W. Y., Newman, L. S., Janssen, A., Ellison, C., et al. (1999). Impact of a worker notification program: Assessment of attitudinal and behavioral outcomes. *American Journal of Industrial Medicine*, 36, 1–9.

Tay, R., & Watson, B. (2002). Changing drivers' intentions and behaviours using fear-based driver fatigue advertisements. *Health Marketing Quarterly*, 19, 55–68.

Thesenvitz, J. (2000, February). *Understanding and using fear appeals for tobacco control.* Toronto, Canada: Council for a Tobacco-Free Ontario, Program Training and Consultation Centre, and The Health Communication Unit (University of Toronto). Retrieved July 31, 2008, from http://www.ptcc-cfc.on.ca/pubs/fa-web.pdf

Treise, D., & Weigold, M. F. (2001). AIDS public service announcements: Effects of fear and repetition on predictors of condom use. *Health Marketing Quarterly*, 18, 39–61.

U.S. Agency for International Development. (2003, December). *Country profile Ethiopia: HIV/AIDS.* Washington, DC: Author. Retrieved July 31, 2008, from http://www.usaid.gov/our_work/global_health/aids/Countries/africa/ethiopiabrief.pdf

U.S. Department of Health and Human Services. (2000, November). *Healthy People 2010: Understanding and improving health* (2nd ed., 2 Vols.). Washington, DC: U.S. Government Printing Office. Retrieved July 31, 2008, from http://www.healthypeople.gov/document/tableofcontents.htm

The United States President's Emergency Plan for AIDS Relief. (2008). *2008 country profile: Ethiopia.* Retrieved July 30, 2008, from http://www.pepfar.gov/press/81577.htm

Witte, K. (1992). Putting the fear back into fear appeals: The extended parallel process model. *Communication Monographs*, 59, 329–349.

Witte, K. (1994). Fear control and danger control: A test of the extended parallel process model (EPPM). *Communication Monographs*, 61, 113–134.

Witte, K. (1998). Fear as motivator, fear as inhibitor: Using the extended parallel process model to explain fear appeal successes and failures. In P. A. Andersen & L. K. Guerrero (Eds.), *The handbook of communication and emotion: Research, theory, applications, and contexts* (pp. 423–450). San Diego, CA: Academic Press.

Witte, K. (2003, September). *Preventing HIV/AIDS through entertainment education in Ethiopia*. Speech presented to the Africa Studies Center, Michigan State University, East Lansing.

Witte, K., & Allen, M. (2000). A meta-analysis of fear appeals: Implications for effective public health campaigns. *Heath Education Behavior, 27,* 591–614.

Witte, K., Berkowitz, J., Cameron, K., & Lillie, J. (1998). Preventing the spread of genital warts: Using fear appeals to promote self-protective behaviors. *Health Education & Behavior, 25,* 571–585.

Witte, K., Berkowitz, J., Lillie, J., Cameron, K., Lapinski, M. K., & Liu, W. Y. (1998). Radon awareness and reduction campaigns for African-Americans: A theoretically-based formative and summative evaluation. *Health Education & Behavior, 25,* 284–303.

Witte, K., Cameron, K. A., Lapinski, M. K., & Nzyuko, S. (1998). Evaluating HIV/AIDS prevention programs according to theory: A field project along the Trans-Africa highway in Kenya. *Journal of Health Communication, 4,* 345–363.

Witte, K., Girma, B., & Girgre, A. (2001). *Ethiopia reproductive health communication project: Family planning HIV/AIDS prevention formative and baseline study.* Addis Ababa: Johns Hopkins Bloomberg School of Public Health/Center for Communication Programs and Ethiopia National Office of Population.

Witte, K., Girma, B., & Girgre, A. (2002–2003). Addressing the underlying mechanisms to HIV/AIDS preventive behaviors in Ethiopia. *International Quarterly of Community Health Education, 21,* 163–176.

Witte, K., Meyer, G., & Martell, D. (2001). *Effective health risk messages: A step-by-step guide.* Thousand Oaks, CA: Sage.

Witte, K., & Morrison, K. (1995). The use of scare tactics in AIDS prevention: The case of juvenile detention and high school youth. *Journal of Applied Communication Research, 23,* 128–142.

Witte, K., & Morrison, K. (2000). Examining the influence of trait anxiety/repression-sensitization on individuals' reactions to fear appeals. *Western Journal of Communication, 64,* 1–27.

Witte, K., Singhal, A., Muthuswamy, N., & Duff, D. (2003). *Compilation of three quantitative reports assessing effects of Taru* [Report]. Athens: Ohio University.

Witte, K., Stokols, D., Ituarte, P., & Schneider, M. (1993). Testing the health belief model in a field study to promote bicycle safety helmets. *Communication Research, 20,* 564–586.

World Bank. (2002). *World Bank development indicators 2002* [CD-Rom]. Washington, DC: Author.

25 The Multiple Faces of the Public Dialogue Consortium
Scholars, Practitioners, and Dreamers of Better Social Worlds

Kimberly Pearce

De Anza College, Public Dialogue Consortium

Shawn Spano

San José State University, Public Dialogue Consortium

W. Barnett Pearce

Fielding Graduate University, Public Dialogue Consortium

A journey of a thousand miles begins with a single step. (Confucius)

It is easy to resonate with this quotation attributed to Confucius, because our most significant personal and collective stories are about journeys of one sort or another. We all know that a journey, any journey, starts somewhere with a step or an action. We also know that how we punctuate the first step always is arbitrary because it is possible to designate any number of places as the beginning. We have mused and amused ourselves about where to begin the story of the Public Dialogue Consortium (PDC) and the program of applied communication research that emerged from that collaboration. We initially thought to begin with the day a small group of us met for the first time in 1995 to work together, but then we wondered about starting a bit later when, in 1997, the Internal Revenue Service (IRS) recognized the PDC as a not-for-profit organization. Ultimately, we decided to begin the story long before the PDC was a gleam in anyone's eye by describing the personal journeys of four academicians in the field of communication, whose passions to improve the quality of communication and to help make the world a better place were very much a part of the road on which they already were traveling.

Barnett Pearce began developing the theory of the coordinated management of meaning (CMM) as a young professor in the 1970s. That theory, and his subsequent career, has been devoted to understanding ways in which our social worlds are made in patterns of communication and how best to co-construct patterns that enable people with incommensurate social worlds to live together in peace.

His colleague and friend, Stephen Littlejohn, also was interested in conflict resolution and mediation. In the 1980s, Pearce and Littlejohn worked together on the Kaleidoscope Project at the University of Massachusetts (more about this shortly). Their work together on this project was the beginning of a series of convention presentations, coauthored articles, and a book about moral conflicts and the quality of public discourse (W. B. Pearce & Littlejohn, 1997).

Shawn Spano and Kim Pearce were graduate students during the early 1980s. They, too, were professionally and personally interested in CMM, moral conflicts, and the quality of public communication. They met in the early 1990s when Shawn was hired at San José State University (SJSU) and Kim was teaching just up the road at De Anza College.

Our common interests inspired the four of us to work together on a number of projects beginning in 1995. During that year, we partnered with other scholars and communication students, played with ideas, utilized CMM in the public domain, experimented with the Kaleidoscope model, and began developing models of our own. It was out of these ideals and commitments, and our sheer joy of working together, that the PDC eventually came to be.

Without naming it at the time, we also were embarking on a new journey of doing applied communication research. Cissna (2000, p. 170) described applied research as "intended for someone other than a community of scholars and includes in its conversation people who are not within the scholarly community," and Frey (2000) said that applied communication research is, among other things, about scholars bringing their communication expertise and resources to bear to make a difference in people's life (see also Frey & SunWolf, this volume). These descriptions easily could appear in a "PDC manifesto." Our story is a convergence of intellectual and social passions, and of rigor and artistry; it is about creating an organization for the purpose of, among other things, doing applied communication research. What follows is an "insider's view" of our work.

Overview of the Public Dialogue Consortium and Its Relationship to Applied Communication Research

Without initially knowing it, what was to become the PDC began in 1995 when the four of us invited a group of communication professors, students, and practitioners to develop a Kaleidoscope project modeled on work done during the 1980s at the University of Massachusetts. Kaleidoscope originally was designed as an experiment in public discourse and an innovative attempt to create new patterns of communication for discussing difficult and controversial issues (see Carbaugh, Chen, Cobb, & Shailor, 1986; Leppington, 1995; Littlejohn, 1986; W. B. Pearce & Littlejohn, 1997). A Kaleidoscope event consists of two or more disputants known to have opposing views on an issue, a moderator, a reflecting team, and a live audience. The role of the moderator and reflecting team is to prompt discussion through questions and observations that allow the disputants, and the audience, to examine the issue at hand from multiple points of view. The desired outcomes of a Kaleidoscope session include improved relationships among people who disagree passionately with each other, better understanding of how intelligent and thoughtful people can hold diametrically opposed views, and the opening of spaces for new understandings of the positions to which people are committed. The means to achieve these goals is a transformation of the pattern of communication to something more akin to dialogic communication rather than the more usual forms of debate and polarized conflict (see, e.g., Barge, 2002).

The first events that our newly formed group conducted were two campus Kaleidoscope sessions in Northern California, one at De Anza College on the topic of affirmative action and the other at SJSU on the topic of intercollegiate athletics. After extensive analysis of these events (Spano & Calcagno, 1996), we were sufficiently encouraged by our efforts to continue working together, but critical of the one-session, college-campus-only Kaleidoscope format. We set out to expand our repertoire and ways of working by attending training sessions sponsored by other practitioner groups, and by using what we learned to create a unique framework for connecting theory (CMM) to a range of communicative practices that we call "public dialogue."

At this point, we decided to become a "bona fide" organization. We experimented with a number of names and eventually decided to call ourselves the "Public Dialogue Consortium." One of our student members volunteered to prepare and file the paperwork to become a 501(c)(3), not-for-profit organization; 6 months later, we were recognized by the IRS as an official organization. Simply put, our primary mission is to improve the quality and patterns of communication about the issues that matter to participants in organizations and communities.

A number of activities stand out as crucial to the early development of the PDC methodology. One was a 2-day international conference for dialogue practitioners that was sponsored, and largely funded, by the PDC. Participants included individuals and groups from Colombia, Argentina, Australia, and England, as well as from several places in the United States. The format consisted of a series of demonstrations by each of the participating practitioner groups, with ample time for reflection and critical analysis. It was a remarkable event that surfaced a rich variety of goals, methods, and approaches. Perhaps most important, the conference served as a source of comparison and inspiration for the PDC. We were able to draw from the methods we observed, adapting and integrating them into our approach, which, at the time, still was in its formative stages.

Another activity, really a series of activities, consisted of countless training sessions and simulations among members of the PDC. Typically, these sessions were framed around a particular skill, event design, or process design. For example, a few members of the PDC attended a National Issues Forum (NIF) training session (for information about the NIF, see its Web site: http://www.nifi.org/; for communication research about NIF forums, see Gastil & Dillard, 1999a, 1999b; Harringer & McMillan, 2007, 2008; McMahan, 1985; Ryfe, 2006) and reported back to the group what they learned, and together, we discussed the assumptions, strengths, and limitations of that approach to deliberation and "choice work." We then crafted an event design and role-play scenario in which we practiced deliberation skills and then carefully and critically analyzed our performance.

Our signature project, beginning in 1996 in the city of Cupertino, California, was a multiyear public dialogue process (Spano, 2001). We worked closely with the city manager, city council, local high schools and the schools' superintendent, De Anza College (located in Cupertino), sheriff's department, chamber of commerce, and local newspapers, among others, to create events that involved major stakeholders. We spent considerable time together mapping out different strategic processes, designing events, practicing facilitation skills, and reflecting on what we learned from working in the community. Prior to each public meeting, the PDC provided 2-day trainings for select high school students, college students from De Anza College and SJSU majoring in communication, and adults in the community to provide specific facilitation skills for the chosen event. (Our goal was to have a strong intergenerational presence in each public meeting.) We also invited city officials from other communities and communication colleagues from around the country to observe and critique various events; immediately after the public meeting, we met to listen to their observations. In addition, we regularly solicited feedback from participants, community leaders, and the facilitators. It was a highly productive learning environment, something akin to a postdoctoral research seminar with a strong applied focus.

The work in Cupertino launched us into several communities in the United States and beyond. Since our inception, we have been involved in over 30 projects with wide-ranging foci. We provide a sampling of the types of projects we have done by offering four brief examples and a more extended description of one. (For more information about PDC projects, methodologies, and ways of working, visit our Web site: www.publicdialogue.org.)

The Anne Frank Dialogue Project occurred in Albuquerque, New Mexico from January to June in 2000. The PDC designed a dialogue process for citizens interested in discussing historical and contemporary implications of the Holocaust. We developed a dialogue guide, which was mailed to 50 community members interested in hosting dialogue groups in their homes, schools, churches, and workplaces. A culminating event occurred in May 2000 for community members interested in organizing action groups in their community.

Gear Up Waco was part of a 5-year program in which the PDC partnered with Baylor University and other educational institutions in McClennon County, Texas, to identify at-risk middle school students and track them toward higher education. Using Department of Education's Gear Up funding, the PDC collaborated with other agencies to produce video projects; engage in parent, student, and teacher dialogues; start a parental leadership program; and mobilize community resources. We provided a pilot training program in conflict management for teachers in Brazos Middle School and designed and facilitated a daylong conference for agencies, titled "Creating Parent–Student Communities of Hope and Imagination."

The town of Los Gatos, California, is a charming and sought-after bedroom community just northwest of San José. For the past 5 years, the PDC has worked with the town council, staff members, whole departments, and local residents who serve on town commissions and boards to enhance the way that members of the town government and the public communicate and work together. To date, over 30 events consisting of off-site meetings, retreats, and trainings with a range of participants have been conducted.

The PDC was involved in an international project that occurred in 2003 in Central Maluku, Indonesia, in collaboration with the International Catholic Migration Commission (ICMC), the Institute for Social Transformation (INSIST), and an Indonesian nongovernmental organization (NGO). The Interfaith Peacebuilding Institute was designed to foster a shared vision of community recovery through dialogue. In the aftermath of a devastating conflict between Christian and Muslim communities in the district, 40 participants assembled for a 4-day dialogue. Participants found this to be a new and empowering form of communication, and they expressed a clear desire to continue dialogue within and between their communities. The conversations explored many topics of mutual concern, including traditional and religious resources for recovery and community approaches to peace and reconstruction. In addition, the project included a research component that provided funding for an Institute monograph published by the ICMC and a journal article by Lowry and Littlejohn (2006), entitled "Dialogue and the Discourse of Peacebuilding in Maluku, Indonesia," that appeared in *Conflict Resolution Quarterly*.

The work we did in San Carlos, California, between 1999 and 2002, provides a more comprehensive example of a PDC project (K. A. Pearce, 2002). The City Manager, Mike Garvey, had spent most of his energies and resources solving and repairing the infrastructure problems common to most metropolitan cities. When Sylvia Nelson became mayor in 1999, her goal was to move beyond the "fix-it" framework and focus on the dreams of San Carlos residents. Garvey enthusiastically endorsed her ideas, also believing that the city was ready for future visioning. Under Nelson's leadership, the Quality of Life Steering Group was formed, consisting of 15 residents representing a cross-section of the community. Shortly after the formation of the group, the PDC received a Request for Proposal (RFP) asking us to design a half-day event similar to a "Future Search Conference" (e.g., Weisbord & Janoff, 2000) in which residents could focus on the quality of life in their community. Instead, we proposed a 4-month process with two community-wide bookend events, with additional means of gathering information from residents interspersed between the events. We were one of three organizations invited to provide a 1-hour presentation for the Quality of Life Steering Committee; the day after our presentation, we were awarded the contract. The committee told us that they liked our focus on process (several activities instead of one) and our emphasis on intergenerational facilitation. We noted that young people were conspicuously absent from the committee and we said that we wanted the committee to recruit high school students to help us facilitate the first event; unfortunately, this was the only aspect of our work with that committee that did not go as expected, as the person who volunteered to recruit students was unable to do so.

Our first event was designed to elicit the dreams of residents; specifically, we asked them to identify what "quality of life" meant to them and to "blue sky" what this looked like in the manifestation of city projects, events, and activities. The Steering Committee did the recruiting for the event, keeping in mind the goal of including all segments of the community. We also trained the committee members to facilitate small group discussions using the Technology of Participation (ToP) workshop model of participation (see http://www.ica-usa.org/). The question that became the centerpiece for discussion was the following: "If the quality of life in San Carlos was as good as it could be, what would be happening?" The first meeting with approximately 120 residents was spirited, good-natured, and lively. The PDC summarized the ideas generated from the meeting and, together with the Steering Committee, we developed four broad scenarios of what would be happening in San Carlos to enhance the quality of life: emphases on (1) recreation, culture, and community programs; (2) traffic, public safety, and transportation; (3) economic development, economic vitality, and the environment; and (4) education.

The following meeting with the Steering Committee was designed to plan the second public meeting, which would occur in 3 months. During that second meeting, we decided collectively to mail a thank-you letter from the mayor to those who participated in the first public meeting, along with the four scenarios and visions developed from the meeting, and a one-page questionnaire to help structure a consistent set of conversations about what residents liked best and least, and the resources needed to implement each scenario. We asked each participant to interview the members of five households before the next public meeting to deepen and broaden the conversations occurring in the community. The city also posted this information on its Web site and in other public places. Our hope was that if most of the 120 residents did this activity and a handful of residents responded through the Internet, over 600 conversations would occur during the 3-month interval between meetings.

The second meeting enjoyed remarkable attendance, with 100 of the initial 120 residents participating (with many who were not able to attend mailing their interview results to the mayor), along with residents showing up for the first time. During that meeting, members of the PDC facilitated an NIF type of conversation deliberating the advantages and disadvantages of each scenario, and exploring the underlying values that were most important to the residents as the city made decisions about the next steps. Like the first meeting, residents were spirited and engaged as they heard various perspectives from those in their group, as well as the voices of household members who were interviewed and summarized by the residents who interviewed them.

During our follow-up meeting with the Steering Committee, the PDC presented a 40-page summary of the second public meeting. The report included three sections: a summary of each group, a summary of each scenario, and, overall recommendations. The Steering Committee handed this report to the city council, along with a recommendation that the committee work with the appropriate staff offices and personnel to implement the suggestions. The city council approved the recommendation, and the Steering Committee spent the next 2 years working with the staff (and with the PDC—we were rehired to work with the committee on this new phase) to make residents' visions reality. Mayor Nelson sent a letter to participants thanking them for their participation and describing the next phase of the project. She also held a press conference to discuss the city's vision and future plans for the Quality of Life project. The project has changed and expanded over the years, despite the retirement of Nelson and Garvey, and without further help from the PDC.

Contributions to Applied Communication Scholarship

The methodology that has evolved from the PDC's early activities and events counts as applied communication scholarship in several ways. The methodology is focused on the achievement of practical outcomes within contexts that inform and are informed by theory. This characteristic, of course, is consistent with most definitions of applied communication scholarship and the increasingly widespread view that theory and practice are reflexively connected (see Barge & Craig, this volume; Frey & SunWolf, this volume). Keyton (2000), for example, argued that applied communication research should be practical, arising in response to social problems and providing solutions for them; as she explained, it is the researcher's task to "build triangulated relationships between problem, theory, and method" (p. 167). Wood (2000) has been the most explicit on this account, stating that the defining feature of applied communication research "is its insistence on putting theory and research into the service of practice and, equally, of studying practices to refine theory in order to gain new understandings of how communication functions and how it might function differently, or better" (p. 189).

By sometimes situating ourselves in a first-person position with the participants in our work, we align ourselves with some, but not all, applied communication researchers. We make this choice because we intend to go beyond descriptive and analytical research (i.e., studying others' communication from a third-person position) to an interventionist research orientation (i.e., joining with others in communication, from a first-person position). In this regard, we concur with Frey's (2000) statement that applied communication researchers should go "beyond the descriptive task of studying 'an other'... [by] involving themselves in the life of 'another'" (p. 181; see also Frey & SunWolf, this volume). However, our work includes research from the third-person perspective as well, as we find such research useful when it meets three conditions: (1) the research is informed by theory that is sufficiently reflexive, (2) the researcher engages directly with local participants, and (3) the purposes of the research are tied to the achievement of practical outcomes. Ultimately, it is our goal to use descriptive and analytical-based research as a resource for intervening into the communication of others and, we hope, for creating positive change in that communication.

We conceptualize our applied communication research program as comprising three levels, each of which operates in a hierarchical relationship to the others. We call one level "service delivery," which consists of working with local participants to improve the quality of public communication in their communities, broadly defined. Not surprisingly, service delivery is focused on practical issues that arise from problem-oriented situations. More specifically, it consists of consultations, facilitations, and trainings that are designed to encourage and promote the use of dialogue, primarily as it operates in public contexts.

Theory development is a second level of our applied communication research program. In our projects, we focus on the continued development of CMM and related principles of social constructionism. Within the CMM framework, and consistent with Wood's (2000) description of applied communication research, we base our approach to theory development on the always-shifting foundation of reflexivity. Thus, CMM evolves and develops as theoretical concepts are applied to concrete practices and, conversely, as the results of those practices are used to refine and gain insight into the theory.

Research and evaluation constitute the third level. We have used both qualitative research methods, such as thematic textual analysis (W. B. Pearce & Pearce, 2000a;

Spano & Calcagno, 1996), and quantitative research methods, such as closed-ended survey questionnaires (Spano, 2001), to investigate and evaluate our attempts at promoting public dialogue. Along with other scholars, we believe that applied scholarship should embrace the full array of investigatory approaches and traditions that characterize the methodological terrain of the communication field (Frey, 2000; Frey & SunWolf, this volume; Query et al., this volume; Wood, 2000).

Community-based action research figures more prominently in our work than in the standard list of methods used in communication; in fact, it is our preferred method. As Stringer (2007) explained, action research is a form of inquiry that favors collaborative and participatory procedures in which researchers assist local participants in defining, understanding, and developing action-oriented solutions to the problems that confront them.

The three contexts of service delivery, theory development, and research and evaluation have shifting hierarchical relationships among one another, meaning that any one of them can serve as a context for the others, depending on the contingencies of the situation and the goals and purposes we are trying to achieve. For example, when PDC members engage local participants in defining problems, we are likely to privilege service delivery as the highest context. Among other things, this stance obligates us to assume a practitioner role and adopt the grammar of the local community. Given a conflict between, for instance, collecting research data or helping the client, we unswervingly help the client. Conversely, as we engage colleagues in discussions of theory development, we are likely to assume an academic role within a more scholarly or philosophical form of discourse. It is important to note that the PDC methodology involves enacting all three levels, in differing relationships at different times, in response to a particular applied communication research project.

The choice of what context assumes the highest position is vitally important because it determines how a particular project is framed, including the sequence of actions that we and others take as the project develops and unfolds. It is fair to say that in the beginning, the PDC positioned theory development as the highest context, followed closely by service delivery as the middle context. Hence, service delivery was seen primarily as an experiment leading to improvements in the theory. Perhaps distinguishing us from other applied communication researchers, the research level was the lowest context, and was conducted to assess the effectiveness of our practice fully, as much as to test or extend our theory. Later in this chapter, we examine some of the implications for how we organized and balanced these three levels.

The Way We Work: The PDC Approach

As we said at the beginning of this chapter, the history of the PDC started long before the organization became official. We drew not only on the theory of CMM as it might be written in a communication textbook but also on a grammar of practice in which the theory and certain forms of practice already were productively intermingled (see, e.g., Littlejohn & Domenici, 2001; W. B. Pearce, 2001; W. B. Pearce & Pearce, 2000b). In what follows, we describe some of the key concepts that guide our approach and link these concepts to specific practices, actions, and techniques to illustrate how our approach to public dialogue works.

Taking a Communication Perspective

We take the position that the social world is polysemic—that every event and object is capable of being described, equally satisfactorily, in many different vocabularies, many of which preclude the others. In this polysemic world, we act on the basis of a preferential option for a communication perspective, choosing to see events and objects of the social world as made and remade in processes of communication. This perspective generates the following primary questions:

- In description, what are people doing to and with each other? Out of what context are they acting? Into what context are they acting?
- In analysis, how is this social world being made?
- In critique and intervention, what are people making together? How can they make better social worlds?
- In action, how can people go forward together?

These questions give a distinctive flavor to our work, both in our research and practice. For example, our decision to privilege dialogue as a form of communication, and our understanding of what that entails, is shaped by a communication perspective (W. B. Pearce & Pearce, 2004). In the corporate world, there also is a major emphasis on dialogue, but most of this work is grounded on a particular concept of physics (specifically, the work of David Bohm; e.g., 2004) and a view of persons that reflects a cognitive individualism that stands in contrast to the social constructionism with which CMM has affinities. W. B. Pearce and Pearce (2000a) teased out some of these distinctions in their comparative analysis of what various practitioners call "dialogue." A communication perspective also gives our work a distinctive flavor in comparison to other approaches to civic engagement, such as the 16 "discourse organizations" reviewed by Ryfe (2003), the "emerging field of public deliberation" surveyed by Williamson and Fung (2004, p. 3), and most of the projects featured in Gastil and Levine's (2005) edited handbook on deliberative democracy or Gastil's (2008) recent text.

How does our theoretical commitment to a communication perspective translate into practical action? Most immediately, it obligates us to foreground communication in all of the projects and events we design and facilitate. Consider, for example, a typical PDC event: a large community forum designed to give local residents, elected officials, and professional staff in a community the opportunity to identify and discuss the most pressing issues in their city (Spano, 2006). The communicative groundwork for this forum was established in news releases and invitation letters, all of which emphasized the interactive nature of the event and the opportunity for forum participants to talk and listen to each other about community issues. This message was reiterated by a member of the PDC at the beginning of the event as part of opening remarks. Note that these context-setting descriptions focus on the process and structure of the event rather than on the content. In line with a communication perspective, we seek to call forth the constitutive nature of the conversations that take place in public dialogue projects. We are successful to the extent that participants come to recognize that community issues and community events—indeed, the very nature of the "community" itself—are created and recreated through processes of communication.

Focusing on the Form of Communication

Simply put, the grammar of practice of the PDC assumes that if one gets the form of communication right, good things will happen. As a result, we pay less attention to things that others treat as important, such as the attitudes and beliefs of the participants in our projects, or their knowledge about certain policies or issues. We see ourselves as the curators of the process of communication, nurturing and supporting particular forms of communication. Rather than experts on the topic, we aspire to be "virtuosos" (W. B.

Pearce & Pearce, 2000a) in the arts of calling into being forms of communication that have certain characteristics.

Focusing on the form of communication, of course, is translated into practice in all aspects of the PDC approach, perhaps most noticeably in our insistence on structuring projects and events in such a way that they create conditions and opportunities for people to participate in dialogic forms of communication. Our conceptualization of dialogue draws from the work of Martin Buber (e.g., 1970), who focused on the relational properties of dialogue as a process for navigating the tensions between self and other. From this conceptualization, we derived a number of working principles and integrated these into our grammar of practice. For example, when facilitating events, we place an equal or greater emphasis on listening as speaking, adopt an inclusive language that welcomes as many different voices into the process as possible, try to ensure that all participants have the experience of being heard and understood, approach difference and conflict as sites for exploration and growth, take a systemic or relational view that focuses on the co-construction of meaning and action, and embrace an appreciative orientation that emphasizes the positive resources of a community or group rather than its problems and deficits. We seek to incorporate these principles into our facilitation practices to foster forms of communication that have the qualities and characteristics of dialogue.

Using CMM Concepts to Understand the Communication Process

CMM views communication systemically, but from a very specific systemic perspective. It has much more affinity with second-order cybernetics, chaos theory, and complex adaptive systems than with information theory or general systems theory. That is, it does not so much look at wholes as at patterns of iterative processes. In this way of thinking, communication always is a matter of doing something, in specific contexts, and in a give-and-take, turn-taking relationship with other people that produces interactive sequences that have an order. One of the key models in CMM is the "serpentine" process, in which the management of meaning undulates as the string of actions extends into the future.

Taking this idea on board, in our practice, we always look at what is happening *now* as being *after* something else and *before* something else again. One of our criticisms of some other practitioner groups is that they think of doing "events" rather than facilitating "processes," or, in systemic language, we do not share their belief in the efficacy of "one-shot interventions." To the contrary, in our work, we regularly start each meeting with a sometimes lengthy reminder of what has gone before and how that has shaped what we will do in the present meeting, and we end with a very clear and credible statement of what will happen next. From a purely practitioner's perspective, we know that people will drop out or develop a cynical apathy if their hard work disappears, but from a communication perspective, we understand such actions as a failure to achieve the quality of communication that permits good things to happen.

Strings of communicative actions are not undifferentiated, of course. We have borrowed from Watzlawick, Beavin, and Jackson (1967) the idea of *punctuation* (in which perceived causality stems from what is perceived as the first act in a sequence), and from Harré and Secord (1972) the idea of *episodes* (in which a narrative depends on the events designated as the beginning and ending of the story). The idea of episodes was used to good effect in two research studies: Spano and Calcagno (1996) analyzed the episodic structure of one of the PDC's Kaleidoscope sessions, and Spano (2001) described the Cupertino Community Project as a series of phases. We utilize the concepts of punctuation and episodic structure most directly in the development of strategic process designs and event designs. For example, when mapping out the phases of a project or event with local participants, we purposefully draw attention to the sequence of communicative actions and the various possibilities for how a given project or event can be punctuated.

Each action is meaningful, of course, but it also has multiple meanings. CMM excels in illuminating the complexity of communication. In this instance, the theory unfolds the meanings of each act within a cluster of reciprocally contextualized stories having to do with what episode is being performed, what relationship exists (or is desired or feared) among participants, and what identities various participants have in this situation or in the organizational or ethnic culture in which the event occurs. This conceptualization is CMM's hierarchy model.

With the hierarchy model in mind, as we design and facilitate public dialogue processes, we are very careful to analyze the ordinal relationship among embedded stories and to act strategically to emphasize those stories that best serve as contexts for forms of communication that enable participants to go forward together productively. Consider, for example, the following exchange in which a PDC facilitator responds to a comment from a group participant with a question designed to produce a different hierarchical order in the participant's cultural and relational contexts:

> **Participant:** What I see happening here is that our community is being taken over by these new immigrants, and this is creating conflict with the old-timers, the people who have lived here for a long time. [This comment locates culture as the highest level of the hierarchy.]

> **Facilitator:** How would you characterize your relationships with the new immigrants? In what ways are they different, if at all, from your relationships with the old-timers? [This question is designed to place relationships as the highest context.]

CMM's daisy model provides another way of illuminating the complexity of events. We assume that each act is part of multiple conversations, each with its own hierarchy of reciprocally embedded contexts. When we work, hundreds of people often are in the room, many of whom have passionate commitments to one side or another of the topics on the table, and most of whom either do not know the others there or perceive them as "enemies." The daisy model depicts any action as surrounded by numerous petals, each representing a different conversation in which the meaning of an act might vary. In situations such as the ones in which we work, every statement or action immediately becomes a "turn" in multiple conversations, given meaning by the stories that contextualize it in those conversations, and calling forth specific responses.

As practitioners, we take the complexity of communication on board as a caution against trying to overmanage the meanings of things or the actions that people take. Rather, our attention is on the form of communication. Like chaos theorists, we believe that communication is unpredictable and that it is strongly affected by various "attractors," initial conditions, and other relevant concepts. We set ourselves to be, as good facilitators, sufficiently involved with the communication processes that we facilitate so that we are aligned with their ebbs and flows, and sufficiently detached so that we can make strategic decisions about whether and in what manner to intervene.

Using Coordinated Management of Meaning Concepts to Develop a Public Dialogue Model

We developed a three-level model for thinking about the flow or patterns of public dialogue as they unfold over time (K. A. Pearce, 2002). The "top" level is called "strategic process design" and looks at patterns over a sequence of meetings or specific events. Unlike conventional, top-down methods of public communication (see Yankelovich, 1991), public dialogue strategic designs engage community members at the beginning of the process, before issues are identified and actions for resolution are formulated. Moreover, the process unfolds organically; meetings or events build off each other as they move toward emergent rather then pre-established outcomes. K. A. Pearce (2002), for example, outlined a strategic process design that consists of five phases, labeled according to the acronym SHEDD: (1) *S*etting started, (2) *h*earing all the voices, (3) *e*nriching the conversation, (4) *d*eliberating the options, and (5) *d*eciding and moving forward together (see also K. A. Pearce & Pearce, 2001). Spano (2006) outlined a comparable process design consisting of six phases: (1) issue identification, (2) eliciting different views, (3) framing the issue, (4) generating options for action, (5) deliberating and deciding, and (6) implementing public agreements.

The "middle" level is called "event design" and focuses on specific meetings. Among other things, we design a meeting differently if it occurs at the beginning or at the end of a process, indicating that the goals and structures of a particular event depend on how and where the event fits into the overall strategic design. For example, an event that occurs in the context of "hearing all the voices" or "eliciting different views" will have a less structured format than an event that is designed to produce a specific decision. Indeed, part of the trick to designing successful public dialogue meetings and events involves balancing the tension between openness and structure (Spano, 2006).

Typically, PDC meetings and events take the form of small groups (e.g., discussion groups, deliberation groups, and study circles), large public forums (50–150 attendees), one-on-one interviews, and facilitation training workshops. Although there are a number of stand-alone event designs available to public dialogue practitioners, such as open space technology (Owen, 2008) and future search (Weisbord & Janoff, 2000), we almost always design meetings and events that are customized to the unique contingencies of the situation in which we work.

The "lowest" level is called "in-the-moment intervention and facilitation skills" and refers to those things that can be said at a specific moment during a meeting that changes the meeting from one form of communication to another. For example, a pause followed by a question seeking understanding might function as an attractor (to use the language of chaos theory) of dialogue, whereas immediately responding with a rebuttal of what was just said might initiate a debate, and responding with an insult might initiate a fight. In addition to enacting skills that foster dialogue as the preferred form of communication, it also is important to recognize that the use of a particular facilitation technique is made in response to the particular event in which the technique is used. For example, a facilitator who is leading a group to identify the full range of issues facing its community will employ facilitation skills differently than the facilitator who is asking community members to choose from among a list of issues that has been generated already.

The PDC has taken on a number of facilitation techniques and practices used by other practitioner groups, and, in some cases, we have modified them to fit our approach to public dialogue. In addition to standard facilitation practices, such as time management, active listening, and ensuring that everyone participates, we also seek to use and develop what might be called "advanced" techniques. Two techniques are central to our approach; the first was adapted for use in public contexts from our work with systemic family therapists (McNamee, Lannamann & Tomm, 1983; W. B. Pearce & Pearce, 1999) and the second from our work with the "appreciative inquiry" community (e.g., Barrett & Fry, 2005; Cooperrider & Whitney, 1999, 2005; Lewis, Passmore, & Cantore, 2008; Preskill & Catsambas, 2006; Reed, 2007; Thatchenkery & Chowdhry, 2007). *Systemic questioning* is a technique used to draw out relationships and connections within communities, groups, and organizations, and *appreciative questioning* is used to inquire into the positive resources that exist within communities, groups, and organizations. Both of these facilitation techniques are used, of course, to initiate discussion and conversation; at the same time, they also serve as a basis for reflecting and reframing what others say.

These concepts and models have furthered our thinking and development of communication theory, particularly CMM and public dialogue, and their uses in community settings have sensitized us to the challenges and demands of the scholar–practitioner model of applied communication research. We next describe some of the challenges that we have faced and the lessons learned from them.

Paradoxes, Tensions, and Lessons Learned

Working skillfully in communities as applied communication researchers requires abilities that transcend the domains of scholarship and praxis. In our work, we have talked among ourselves about the need to be "artisans" or "code-switchers" as we tack back and forth between conversations with communication scholars, community leaders, and city residents. In this section, we reflect on the paradoxes and tensions of doing applied communication research in an organizational context and the lessons we have learned about public dialogue processes.

In the spirit of deepening our learning, as we prepared this chapter and in keeping with the reiterative cycle of "doing" applied communication research, we conducted interviews with some of the key people involved in a variety of PDC projects as a way to enrich our stories of what has worked well and what we could have done differently. Among the people we interviewed were city managers, city staff, project participants, and members of the PDC's board of directors. Quotations and excerpts from these interviews are included in this section.

Paradoxes and Tensions of Doing Applied Communication Research within an Organizational Framework

As a number of communication scholars recently have observed, paradoxes and tensions are normal conditions of modern organizational life and, as such, they should be embraced as potential resources for theory development and practical action (e.g., Harter & Krone, 2001; Pepper & Larson, 2006; Stohl & Cheney, 2001; Tretheway & Ashcraft, 2004). Moreover, alternative organizations, such as the PDC, which are modeled on a dialogic sensibility rather than a technical or rational one, are well positioned to investigate and benefit from the paradoxical situations that inevitably result from being an "organization."

Since the time that members of the PDC made the decision to organize, we have encountered and sometimes struggled with three pragmatic paradoxes, each of which has wide-ranging implications for our theoretical and methodological approaches and for our organizational structure. Each of these paradoxes are described below.

Academic and Practical Orientations

By far, the most challenging aspect of our work is managing the paradox and tension that often comes from pursuing both academic and practical goals. On the one hand, as we interact with our academic colleagues, we are pressed to articulate the theoretical and methodological basis of our approach. However, as we leave these conversations and join with public officials, residents, and other people in applied settings, we are obliged to adopt the grammar of the local community. The PDC functions as both a scholarly group and a practitioner group, each of which requires a distinct kind of knowledge, grammar, and sensibility. The paradox occurs when our commitments to one group undermine our commitments to the other, recognizing, of course, that we are committed to both.

Given that the PDC was built on the foundation of the scholar–practitioner model, it is not surprising that we have fully embraced this paradox. Indeed, we find the challenges inherent in working with different communities to be enriching and invigorating. Such work has led us, for example, to grapple with questions about whether to introduce local participants to our theoretical framework of CMM and social constructionism, and how to do so. Our work also has forced us to consider the nature of academic research and how best to report the findings from applied communication projects to the scholarly community.

How successful have we been in navigating this paradox? One way to answer this question is to listen to how people from different discourse communities evaluate the PDC. An academic colleague praised the theoretical focus of the PDC, claiming that our scholarly approach distinguishes us from other practitioner groups and is a major contributor to our success. Another person, a city manager with whom we have worked for a number of years, claimed just the opposite. He singled out the PDC's applied orientation as our most distinctive and effective quality. He cautioned us not to become too theoretical or academic because "it might take away from the main value to what you do, which is producing practical outcomes."

We have learned that the ability to manage the tensions of what we are doing in any given moment (e.g., Who is the client? In what discourse are we operating? What is the highest context in this moment?) comes from working with a scholarly team rather than working individually. The "collective group perspective" enables us most effectively to name, act into, and manage the inevitable tensions experienced as we conduct applied communication research.

Formal and Informal Structures

When the PDC officially incorporated as a nonprofit organization, the move imposed a number of constraints on the organization, as prescribed by law, such as electing officers to manage day-to-day operations and selecting a board of directors to oversee finances. Moving from a loosely affiliated collection of individuals to a formal organizational structure required us to be much more explicit in setting out rules, procedures, and guidelines. Here lies the paradox of organizational structure and formalization (Stohl & Cheney, 2001): how to develop a creative, spontaneous, and nontraditional organization within a context that requires formal roles and decision-making procedures.

For a variety of reasons, we have not been very successful in managing this paradox. Indeed, it has become something of an Achilles heel, the one point that threatens to undermine the entire organization. After trying a number of different organizational models, ranging from highly centralized to highly decentralized, the PDC currently is organized with a minimum level of formal structure and decision making. One unintended (even paradoxical) consequence of our ongoing struggle with organizational structure is that the PDC actually has developed into a more disorganized organization and, conversely, our methodological approach has become more diffuse and varied. Regrettably, this change makes it more difficult for us, in a systematic way, to reflect, test, and build on our theoretical perspective and ways of working.

Primary and Secondary Commitments

One of the reasons for incorporating as a nonprofit organization was to enable the PDC to seek grants and donations, thus providing the financial resources necessary for large-scale research and development efforts. As it turned out, we have had limited success securing these types of funding (we received two grants from the Packard Foundation to help fund our early work in Cupertino), and have relied, instead, on individual contracts tied to specific projects and activities. Although these contracts have provided us with sufficient resources to engage in a respectable amount of service-delivery activity, they have not provided the level of funding that allows us to do PDC work on or even near a full-time basis. Almost all of the PDC project managers hold full-time academic appointments, or what we sometimes fondly refer to as "our day jobs." This situation creates another paradox: The secondary commitment to PDC among its members makes it difficult to secure the time and resources necessary to establish a foundation that might enable the members to make PDC their primary commitment.

Responding to this situation has not been nearly as difficult as the paradox of formalization. Indeed, although there certainly are benefits to making PDC our primary commitment, there also are advantages to maintaining a secondary commitment to the organization. Having full-time jobs enables us to be selective about the types of applied projects that we choose. There have been several cases, for example, where we decided to walk away from potentially lucrative projects because the leadership (e.g., city manager, city council members, city staff, or public officials) had a hidden agenda or pre-established outcome in mind that prohibited us from developing a genuine and authentic public dialogue process. As a corollary to this point, a city manager with whom we work said that she appreciates that the business of the PDC is not to create business for ourselves. "If you don't think you can add value," she said, "you'll suggest other options and arrangements." The ability to choose our projects based on principle rather than money helps us to stay grounded in a scholar–practitioner approach to the work.

Lessons Learned about Civic Engagement, Public Dialogue, and Applied Communication Research

Although the PDC uses CMM in all levels of our work, most of our clients know very little, if anything, of the theory and, as discussed previously, that is one of the tensions of using a scholar–practitioner model in community settings. When it comes to working with our clients on a public dialogue process, we realize that the highest context for city officials is the effect that a project has on the city rather than its contribution to the theory to which we subscribe. From our perspective, however, we always are balancing contexts of theory, practice, and research, which makes doing applied communication research (rather than working, for example, solely as practitioners) possible.

We divide this section into three subcategories: what we have learned about civic engagement, community dialogue, and doing applied communication research. The articulation of these lessons takes us to the edge of our learning and provides the frame for the next iterative cycle of research and theory development.

Lessons Learned About Civic Engagement

Civic engagement refers to the direct involvement of residents in community issues and decision-making processes. We have learned over the years that people, even very busy people working in fast-paced urban areas, such as Silicon Valley, have stakes in their communities and are willing to volunteer their time if they believe they can affect change. This learning stands in stark contrast to the popular notion that the public is apathetic, disengaged, and too preoccupied with its self-interests to participate in civic engagement activities. To the contrary, it is our experience that as participants experience ownership of a public participation process and, thereby, have a meaningful say in the outcomes, they become more invested in their communities. This leads to our first lesson: *Ordinary residents will participate in the civic life of their communities if the process in which they are asked to participate has integrity.* By "integrity," we mean that the outcomes are shapeable in important ways by participants themselves and not predetermined by government officials, community leaders, technical experts, or others who assume positions of privilege and power. However, how do residents know whether a process truly is characterized by meaningful participation with results that are participant driven?

One answer we give to this question is that civic engagement requires support from the "top" for initiatives from the "bottom." It requires, elicits, and supports a different type of leadership by elected officials and city staff than what traditionally has been perceived as leadership. A story from San Carlos, California, illustrates how unusual is this model of leadership. The local press learned about the Quality of Life project that the PDC designed and facilitated, and called Mayor Sylvia Nelson to ask what would be the result. As Sylvia recounted the story, the ensuing conversation left the reporter scratching his head. The reporter expected a list of the mayor's pet projects but, instead, Sylvia replied by saying that she did not know what the outcome would be; in fact, it was important for her not to know, because the process itself was designed to determine those outcomes. This answer was as incomprehensible as if she suddenly had started speaking in a foreign language! "What do you mean you don't know the outcome?" she was asked, incredulously. We are sure that the reporter left wondering what in the world was going on in San Carlos.

The all-too-familiar DAD ("Decide–Advocate–Defend") model of public communication (K. A. Pearce, 2002) is initiated when people or groups commit themselves to bringing about some predetermined policy. Leadership in this model is expressed by analyzing the situation, selecting an appropriate response to it, and championing the "right policy" in a way that garners sufficient support to get it enacted. In a public dialogue process, leadership is expressed by championing the "right process," such that the energies, creativity, and wisdom of the whole community are brought to bear. The leader becomes the custodian or curator of the process, not the standard-bearer of one of the many ideas for what the outcome of the process might be. The second lesson, then, might be stated: *Civic engagement requires leaders who champion an inclusive, genuine dialogic process rather than promote a set of predetermined ideas or outcomes.*

This model of leadership is not easy. In his book on cognitive complexity and the challenges of modern life, Kegan (1994) described leaders who take charge of a process rather than of a particular outcome as operating at the more demanding "systemic" level. For this to happen, such leaders have to unlearn, resist, or somehow avoid falling into the stereotype of the public held by many public officials and administrators. There is much anecdotal evidence supporting the conclusion that the public is ignorant of the technical facts associated with many public policies, shallow and self-serving in its attention to these issues, and fickle in its support. Many leaders think that involving the public in any meaningful process is like opening Pandora's Box; it is better for the functioning of government to "keep the lid on" by keeping the public happy and at a distance. However, as Yankelovich (1991) noted, the public is not always ignorant, shallow, and fickle; these characteristics, at least sometimes, are caused by their experiences of being distanced through the DAD pattern of public discourse, with processes that claim to invite their participation but result in predetermined conclusions and are conducted using public event designs that limit their voices to, for instance, a series of disjointed 3-minute statements. Hence, the characteristics of the public that some leaders cite as *reasons* for politics-as-usual may be a *result* of politics-as-usual. If the public is invited into a genuine civic-engagement process, can it—will it—prove to be a valuable collaborator? Leaders of successful civic-engagement processes need to believe that it can, and actions based on that belief just might prove to be a self-fulfilling prophecy.

Although there are many reasons why leaders are reluctant to initiate genuine civic-engagement processes, one particularly significant reason is the polarized and adversarial nature of public communication today (e.g., W. B. Pearce & Littlejohn, 1997; Tannen, 2001). One of our interview participants, a city manager, put it this way:

> The problems that the public encounters today are as significant as they've ever been, yet there is less trust. This has led many government officials to use consultants and facilitators as a defense mechanism, as a way to control difficult people or to keep a lid on things so they don't get out of hand.

Of course, this approach only perpetuates the negative spiral and self-fulfilling prophecy described above. In the case of this particular city manager, he realized the need and value of genuine public participation, and recognized it as an integral feature of our methodology. As he explained, "The PDC is the only association I know of in my 41 years in local government that tries to promote a genuine dialogue, a really and truly balanced approach that creates opportunities for everyone to talk and listen."

This type of leadership requires a leader to support a process even though it might not lead to the outcome that she or he favors. There is a kind of emotional maturity involved in staying with a process because one knows that the process is important, even though it does not necessarily go the way one wants. Some of us in the PDC learned this lesson when we were training to be mediators. Our instructor said that intelligence and good problem-solving skills can keep a person from being a good mediator! This statement surprised us, because we thought these were desirable attributes. How could these attributes prevent us from being good mediators? He explained that intelligent people who are good problem solvers often are able to see a solution to the dispute being mediated, but it is not the solution that the disputants see, and any attempt to persuade or influence them to accept that solution changes "mediation" into something else. In the same way, a mayor or a city manager interested in collaborating with the public in the governance of his or her city must respect the public's ideas of what is the "solution" or the "vision." Notice that we said "respect"—that does not mean that the mayor or city manager cannot be a part, and a very important part, of the process but that he or she may not make categorical decisions to disregard the voice of the public.

Sometimes when we are beginning a new project, we do a song-and-dance routine with the "leaders"—those who have the ability to veto the decisions reached during a civic-engagement process, or to call off the process before it is finished. We tell them that they will hear things that they did not expect to hear and do not want to hear; that the process will reach a point where it seems that it is about to explode or stall, and that they will be tempted to end it. However, we explain that these are the "golden moments" for which we are waiting! These are the moments in which whatever happens shakes things loose and shapes the rest of the project. It is precisely during these times that the leaders must recommit themselves to support the project. As another city manager we interviewed said:

It is critical for communication consultants like the PDC to prepare leaders so they know what they are in for in terms of time and outcomes. This is especially important if they are looking for a quick fix. If the leader is not prepared, then pre-work is necessary to ensure realistic expectations. You have to at least try to take them down a path they may not be prepared to go.

Once city officials experience the benefits of a productive public dialogue process, they are more inclined to involve citizens meaningfully in future processes.

However, the advantages of this shift in decision making also has its downsides. The most significant challenge to this work is time. Our third lesson, therefore, is: *Civic engagement requires a significant commitment of time.* As more people are involved in a process, the time it takes, for instance, to coordinate events, hear all voices, follow up effectively, and keep all relevant participants "in the loop" grows exponentially. This issue of time was one of the frustrations voiced by some of the interviewees. One of them put it like this:

> If you are coming together for such important work, make sure there is enough time for the work to be done—time during the meeting and reflective time between meetings. It also is important not to schedule meetings during the summer vacation period.

Balancing the time needed for participants in a public participation process to do their best work against all the other time-consuming obligations they face is a tension point that is not easily resolved.

Several of the people we interviewed recognized time as a limitation or challenge of the PDC approach. This was especially evident in terms of training and skill building, as one of the interviewees indicated:

> Perhaps the greatest weakness of the PDC's approach is the cost in time, particularly the need for trained and sophisticated facilitators or practitioners to get the process started and to serve as resource people. It seems that the skills taught, or the awareness required, are not intuitive, given the dominant communication practices in our culture. It's not the kind of skill one can teach with low-cost, low-energy handouts or one-way instruction. It seems best to teach and learn it through modeling, with plenty of time for reflection. This works against quick solutions.

Although the time-consuming nature of public dialogue is a challenge, it is important to point out that there are benefits as well: Participants come to a deeper understanding of important issues in their community than they otherwise would, and they are more thoroughly invested and committed to the outcomes and decisions that are made about those issues.

A fourth learning about civic engagement also involves time: We learned that initial goals give way to new ones as the process unfolds (Spano, 2006). We did not realize this until the 2-year project with the city of San Carlos had ended and we reflected on our interviews with participants. One of the questions we asked participants was, "Was the goal of the process achieved?" Interestingly enough, as we probed, we discovered that just about everyone had a different story of what was the "goal" of the process. We found the diverse stories very curious, as the project goals were clearly stated in the city's RFPs. Participants' various stories revealed that a public dialogue process is a "moving target" and without realizing or naming it, those involved in the process co-constructed new objectives and goals as the process unfolded. Thus, for example, the initial goal of involving a broad constituency in identifying future goals to improve the quality of life in San Carlos metamorphosed into the implementation of action steps. Once learned, it seems obvious that goals will change, and, as well, expectations, because the process changes what we know and how we know it. Our fourth lesson, then, is: *By definition, a process invites initially stated goals to shift as new relationships form, new ideas are generated, and perspectives are enlarged.* If participants can be aware of these shifting goals and name them, the new goals they co-construct will be shared goals.

We suggest that this fourth lesson be interpreted as part of our commitment to praxis and practical theory (see Barge & Craig, this volume). In his assessment of some of our earlier Cupertino Project work, for example, Stewart (2001) noted that this orientation was demonstrated when PDC members

> changed plans and activities in response to feedback,...consistently approached the project as a fluid, complex, and emergent system of interdependent people and processes,...[and] encouraged all participants to join them in the serious and focused process of making-it-up-as-they-go-along. (p. 239)

Lessons Learned About Public Dialogue

In the preceding paragraphs, we talked about the extraordinary leadership required to shift from the DAD model to the public deliberation and dialogue model of decision making. One reason this shift is so difficult is the lack of perspicacious distinctions our society makes with respect to communication. Making various patterns of communication visible is a goal of our work, and it is why we privilege the underutilized patterns of public dialogue over the well-trod patterns of public debate and adversarial one-upmanship. Our experience with a variety of public processes reinforced that communication is invisible and that foregrounding patterns of communication is a foreign idea. However, when people are invited into dialogic patterns of relating, they want more. We found this claim to be true at all levels (e.g., working one-on-one with city staff or committees and observing small group discussions at public meetings), and we consistently observed that participants worked better, responded more favorably, were more receptive to ideas contrary to theirs, and arrived at better decisions when the communication was characterized by respect, deep listening, openness, and curiosity.

Although things will go better when people feel that their ideas are valued and conversations are respectful and open, this is easier said than done. It is very difficult to remain open in a conversation with someone with whom we disagree and about an issue in which we have a stake. Until our society acknowledges the importance of foregrounding patterns of communication, engaging in public dialogue has the best chance of flourishing in discussions facilitated by skilled practitioners. This idea was echoed earlier by the interviewee who emphasized the need for dialogue training, skill, and awareness as a counterweight to more conventional forms of public communication. Our work over the years, thus, has reinforced lesson five: *Dialogue does not occur naturally; it is a rare form of communication that must be carefully nurtured and facilitated to be enacted successfully.* Such success can happen in communities when skilled practitioners train, model, and invite participants into dialogic patterns of relating. Left to their own devices, most communities resort to more common, and adversarial, patterns of communication.

The current city manager of Cupertino surely would agree with this fifth lesson, having come to recognize the need for trained practitioners to bring about dialogue. When asked to identify particular events or examples that effectively demonstrated the PDC approach, he pointed to one of the potentially controversial public forums that the city sponsored to address racial and cultural issues. The topic was "a real difficult one," he said, "and yet participants were able to have a really good conversation." From his perspective, this was made possible because the PDC design team and facilitators "set parameters for dialogue so that people could say what was really bothering them, even if it sounded harsh." He was especially impressed when an older White woman told the other participants at her table that she did not really like Chinese people, and when the other participants, including two Chinese Americans, responded by asking her about her experiences and why she felt the way she did. He went on to say, "Without the parameters for dialogue, I don't think the woman would have made that statement and I don't think the others would have been able to hear and respond to her like they did."

Lessons Learned About Applied Communication Research

As noted previously, the scholar–practitioner model underlying the work of the PDC requires a reciprocal engagement between academic and local communities; that is, it requires the agility and ability to move back and forth between scholarly discourse and the discourse of local participants. This feature of our applied communication research program is demonstrated most clearly in the multiple commitments we make to service delivery, theory development, and research and evaluation. Indeed, the inclusion of service delivery—a form of communication intervention—within the context of theory and research is one of the features that distinguishes our approach from other applied research methods. The fluid and ever-shifting position of the researcher within our methodology requires the development of skills, sensibilities, and judgments that include yet extend beyond the traditional parameters of quantitative and qualitative communication research. Lesson six, therefore, is: *Communication scholarship that fully embraces the reflexive relationship between theory and practice opens the door to creative and unconventional approaches to applied research.*

We strive as much as possible to engage dialogically with the different discourse communities we encounter in our work. This feature of our applied communication approach is marked by a number of principles and practices that transcend the boundaries of most quantitative and qualitative research methods. First, this view situates dialogue as both the object of our scholarly investigations and as the means through which we inquire into the results of our practices. Among other things, this perspective places a premium on what Kvale (1995, p. 26) called the "quality of craftsmanship," or the ability to inquire and assess in an ongoing fashion the nature of a public dialogue project as it unfolds and evolves.

Second, it involves engaging in dialogic conversations with a variety of stakeholders about the meanings of various actions and outcomes associated with a research project. In this way, research claims and conclusions themselves are polysemic, open to the multiple interpretations of stakeholders who are located both inside and outside the local community setting. One of the tasks of the researcher, then, is to facilitate these different interpretations.

A third way that our applied research approach enlarges the domain of traditional quantitative and qualitative inquiry is by assessing the consequences of the dialogic actions and interventions that are taken in collaboration with local participants. These are not static judgments, of course, given that public dialogue projects evolve organically as goals and outcomes shift and change (see lesson four). This view implies that judgments related to consequences, or what Kvale (1995, p. 32) called "pragmatic validity," also must be assessed in an ongoing manner and through ongoing dialogue with relevant stakeholders. Moreover, it follows that judgments about the effectiveness of dialogic actions will be based in different sources of evidence and experience, including both quantitative and qualitative methods of data collection. Ultimately, however, judgments about consequences and outcomes rest on whether the relevant stakeholders experience those outcomes as desirable and worthwhile. We see our research task as initiating dialogic actions in collaboration with others and assessing the consequences of those actions in dialogic conversation with others.

Concluding Thoughts

For those of us involved in the PDC, the journey to improve the quality of communication started long before the organization was a gleam in anyone's eye. The formalization of the PDC provided a scaffold for us to do applied communication research in ways that otherwise never would have been possible. The organization legitimates our work in the world, as there is something about being affiliated with a bona fide organization to which city managers, city councils, and community residents can relate. However, unbeknownst to them, the organization and the very work itself are grounded in communication theory and applied communication research. Before we ventured into our work with the PDC, we could not have appreciated the potential and power of doing the type of applied communication research that we now do. Our understanding of the dance between research and practice has grown, shifted, and deepened. We have seen firsthand the contribution that our discipline can make and the good things that can happen when, as Frey (2000) said, we bring our communication expertise and resources to bear to make a difference in people's lives.

References

Barge, J. K. (2002). Enlarging the meaning of group deliberation: From discussion to dialogue. In L. R. Frey (Ed.), *New directions in group communication* (pp. 159–177). Thousand Oaks, CA: Sage.

Barrett, F. J., & Fry, R. E. (2005). *Appreciative inquiry: A positive approach to building cooperative capacity.* Chagrin Falls, OH: Taos Institute.

Bohm, D. (2004). *On dialogue* (Rev. ed.; L. Nichol, Ed.). New York: Routledge.

Buber, M. (1970). *I and thou* (W. Kaufman, Trans.). New York: Scribner. (Original work published 1923)

Carbaugh, D., Chen, V., Cobb, S., & Shailor, J. (1986). *Ceremonial discourse: From debate to dialogue* (Report to the Kaleidoscope Committee). Amherst: University of Massachusetts.

Cissna, K. N. (2000). Applied communication research in the 21st century. *Journal of Applied Communication, 28,* 169–173.

Cooperrider, D. L., & Whitney, D. (1999). *Appreciative inquiry.* Williston, VT: Berrett-Koehler.

Cooperrider, D. L., & Whitney, D. (2005). *Appreciative inquiry: A positive revolution for change.* San Francisco: Berrett-Koehler.

Frey, L. R. (2000). To be applied or not to be applied, that isn't even the question: But wherefore art thou, applied communication researcher? Reclaiming applied communication research and redefining the role of the researcher. *Journal of Applied Communication Research, 28,* 178–182.

Gastil, J. (2008). *Political communication and deliberation.* Los Angeles: Sage.

Gastil, J., & Dillard, J. P. (1999a). The aims, methods, and effects of deliberative civic education through the National Issues Forums. *Communication Education, 48,* 179–192.

Gastil, J., & Dillard, J. P. (1999b). Increasing political sophistication through public deliberation. *Political Communication, 16,* 3–23.

Gastil, J., & Levine, P. (Eds.). (2005). *The deliberative democracy handbook: Strategies for effective civic engagement in the twenty-first century.* San Francisco: Jossey-Bass.

Harré, R., & Secord, P. F. (1972). *The explanation of social behaviour.* Totowa, NJ: Rowman & Littlefield.

Harriger, K. J., & McMillan, J. J. (2007). *Speaking of politics: Preparing college students for democratic citizenship through deliberative dialogue.* Dayton, OH: Kettering Foundation Press.

Harriger, K. J., & McMillan, J. J. (2008). Contexts for deliberation: Experimenting with democracy in the classroom, on campus, and in the community. In J. R. Dedrick, L. Grattan, & H. Dienstfrey (Eds.), *Deliberation & the work of higher education: Innovations for the classroom, the campus, and the community* (pp. 235–265). Dayton, OH: Kettering Foundation Press.

Harter, L. M., & Krone, K. J. (2001). The boundary-spanning role of a cooperative support organization: Managing the paradox of stability and change in non-traditional organizations. *Journal of Applied Communication Research, 29,* 248–277.

Kegan, R. (1994). *In over our heads: The mental demands of modern life.* Cambridge, MA: Harvard University Press.

Keyton, J. (2000). Applied communication should be applied. *Journal of Applied Communication Research, 28,* 166–168.

Kvale, S. (1995). The social construction of validity. *Qualitative Inquiry, 1,* 19–40.

Leppington, R. (1995, November). *Transforming the "undiscussable": A case study in "civil" discourse.* Paper presented at the meeting of the Speech Communication Association, San Antonio, TX.

Lewis, S., Passmore, J., & Cantore, S. (2008). *Appreciative inquiry for change management: Using AI to facilitate organizational development.* Philadelphia: Kogan Page.

Littlejohn, S. W. (1986). *Looking through the other end: Kaleidoscope from the inside* (Report to the Kaleidoscope Committee). Amherst: University of Massachusetts.

Littlejohn, S. W., & Domenici, K. (2001). *Engaging communication in conflict: Systemic practice.* Thousand Oaks, CA: Sage.

Lowry, C., & Littlejohn, S. (2006). Dialogue and the discourse of peacemaking in Maluku, Indonesia. *Conflict Resolution Quarterly, 23,* 409–426.

McMahan, E. M. (1985). The National Issues Forum: Bridging the human gap through innovative learning. *Journal of the Association for Communication Administration, 51,* 83–85.

McNamee, S., Lannamann, J., & Tomm, K. (1983). Milan clinicians and CMM theoreticians meet: Was it a fertile connection? *Journal of Strategic and Systemic Therapies, 2,* 57–62.

Owen, H. (2008). *Open space technology: A user's guide* (3rd ed.). San Francisco: Berrett-Koehler.

Pearce, K. A. (2002). *Making better social worlds: Engaging in and facilitating dialogic communication.* Redwood City, CA: Pearce Associates.

Pearce, K. A., & Pearce, W. B. (2001). The Public Dialogue Consortium's school-wide dialogue process: A communication approach to develop citizenship skills and enhance school climate. *Communication Theory, 11,* 105–123.

Pearce, W. B. (2001, February). *CMM: Reports from users.* Paper presented at the meeting of the Western States Communication Association, Coeur d'Alene, ID. Retrieved September 27, 2005, from http://www.pearceassociates.com/essays/reports_from_users.pdf

Pearce, W. B., & Littlejohn, S. W. (1997). *Moral conflict: When social worlds collide.* Thousand Oaks, CA: Sage.

Pearce, W. B., & Pearce, K. A. (1999). "Tornando-se público": Trabalhando sistemicamente em contextos publicos [Going public: Working systemically in public contexts]. In D. Fried Schnitman & S. W. Littlejohn (Eds.), *Novos paradigmas em mediaçâo* (pp. 275–296; J. Haubert Rodrigues & M. A. G. Domingues, Trans.). Porto Alegre, Brazil: Artmed.

Pearce, W. B., & Pearce, K. A. (2000a). Combining passions and abilities: Toward dialogic virtuosity. *Southern Communication Journal, 65,* 161–175.

Pearce, W. B., & Pearce, K. A. (2000b). Extending the theory of coordinated management of meaning (CMM) through a community dialogue process. *Communication Theory, 10,* 405–423.

Pearce, W. B., & Pearce, K. A. (2004). Taking a communication approach to dialogue. In R.

Anderson, L. A. Baxter, & K. N. Cissna (Eds.), *Dialogue: Theorizing difference in communication* (pp. 39–56). Thousand Oaks, CA: Sage.

Pepper, G. L., & Larson, G. S. (2006). Cultural identity tensions in a post-acquisition organization. *Journal of Applied Communication Research, 34*, 49–71.

Preskill, H., & Catsambas, T. (2006). *Reframing evaluation through appreciative inquiry*. Thousand Oaks, CA: Sage.

Reed, J. (2007). *Appreciative inquiry: Research for change*. Thousand Oaks, CA: Sage.

Ryfe, D. M. (2003). The practice of public discourse: A study of sixteen discourse organizations. In J. Rodin & S. P. Steinberg (Eds.), *Public discourse in America: Conversation and community in the twenty-first century* (pp. 184–200). Philadelphia: University of Pennsylvania Press.

Ryfe, D. M. (2006). Narrative and deliberation in small group forums. *Journal of Applied Communication Research, 34*, 72–93.

Spano, S. (2001). *Public dialogue and participatory democracy: The Cupertino community project*. Cresskill, NJ: Hampton Press.

Spano, S. (2006). Theory, practice, and public dialogue: A case study in facilitating community transformation. In L. R. Frey (Ed.), *Facilitating group communication in context: Innovations and applications with natural groups: Vol. 1. Facilitating group creation, conflict, and conversation* (pp. 271–298). Cresskill, NJ: Hampton Press.

Spano, S., & Calcagno, C. (1996). Adapting systemic consultation practices to public discourse: An analysis of a public conflict episode. *Human Systems: The Journal of Systemic Consultation and Management, 7*, 17–43.

Stewart, J. (2001). Dialogue in the Cupertino community project. In S. Spano (Ed.), *Public dialogue and participatory democracy: The Cupertino community project* (pp. 237–243). Cresskill, NJ: Hampton Press.

Stohl, C., & Cheney, G. (2001). Participatory processes/paradoxical practices: Communication and the dilemmas of organizational democracy. *Management Communication Quarterly, 14*, 349–407.

Stringer, E. T. (2007). *Action research* (3rd ed.). Thousand Oaks, CA: Sage.

Tannen, D. (2001). *The argument culture: Moving from debate to dialogue*. New York: Random House.

Thatchenkery, T., & Chowdhry, D. (2007). *Appreciative inquiry and knowledge management: A social constructionist perspective*. Northampton, MA: Edward Elgar.

Tretheway, A., & Ashcraft, K. L. (Eds.). (2004) Organized irrationality? Coping with paradox, contradiction, and irony in organizational communication [Special issue]. *Journal of Applied Communication Research, 32*(2).

Watzlawick, P., Beavin, J. H., & Jackson, D. D. (1967). *Pragmatics of human communication: A study of interactional patterns, pathologies, and paradoxes*. New York: Norton.

Weisbord, M. R., & Janoff, S. (2000). *Future search: An action guide to finding common ground in organizations and communities* (2nd ed.). San Francisco: Berrett-Koehler.

Williamson, A., & Fung, A. (2004). Public deliberation: Where we are and where can we go? *National Civic Review, 93*(4), 3–15.

Wood, J. T. (2000). Applied communication research: Unbounded and for good reason. *Journal of Applied Communication Research, 28*, 188–191.

Yankelovich, D. (1991). *Coming to public judgment: Making democracy work in a complex world*. Syracuse, NY: Syracuse University Press.

Author Index

Subject Index

Page numbers in italics refer to Figures or Tables.

eBooks – at www.eBookstore.tandf.co.uk

A library at your fingertips!

eBooks are electronic versions of printed books. You can store them on your PC/laptop or browse them online.

They have advantages for anyone needing rapid access to a wide variety of published, copyright information.

eBooks can help your research by enabling you to bookmark chapters, annotate text and use instant searches to find specific words or phrases. Several eBook files would fit on even a small laptop or PDA.

NEW: Save money by eSubscribing: cheap, online access to any eBook for as long as you need it.

Annual subscription packages

We now offer special low-cost bulk subscriptions to packages of eBooks in certain subject areas. These are available to libraries or to individuals.

For more information please contact webmaster.ebooks@tandf.co.uk

We're continually developing the eBook concept, so keep up to date by visiting the website.

www.eBookstore.tandf.co.uk